ISRAELITE AND JUDAEAN HISTORY

old
Test
ament
lib
Rary

ISRAELITE AND JUDAEAN HISTORY

Edited by
JOHN H. HAYES
and
J. MAXWELL MILLER

SCM PRESS LTD
BLOOMSBURY STREET LONDON

334 00742 9

First published 1977
by SCM Press Ltd
56 Bloomsbury Street, London WC1

© 1977 John H. Hayes and J. Maxwell Miller

Printed in Great Britain by
Richard Clay (The Chaucer Press) Ltd
Bungay, Suffolk

CONTENTS

MAPS

CONTRIBUTORS

W. MALCOLM CLARK, PhD (Yale University), Associate Professor of Religion and Chairman of the Department of Religion, Butler University, Indianapolis, Indiana.

WILLIAM G. DEVER, PhD (Harvard University), Professor of Near Eastern Archaeology, University of Arizona, Tucson, Arizona.

HERBERT DONNER, Dr Theol, Dr Phil (Leipzig University), Ordentlicher Professor of Old Testament, Tübingen University, Tübingen, Germany.

JOHN H. HAYES, PhD (Princeton Theological Seminary), Associate Professor of Old Testament, Candler School of Theology, Emory University, Atlanta, Georgia.

DOROTHY IRVIN, Dr Theol (Tübingen University), Book Review Editor for *Journal of Ecumenical Studies*, at present without academic position.

A. R. C. LEANEY, DD (Oxford University), Professor of Christian Theology and Head of Department of Theology (retired), University of Nottingham, Nottingham, England.

A. D. H. MAYES, PhD (Edinburgh University), Fellow of Trinity College and Lecturer in Hebrew and Semitic Languages, University of Dublin, Dublin, Ireland.

J. MAXWELL MILLER, PhD (Emory University), Associate Professor of Old Testament, Candler School of Theology, Emory University, Atlanta, Georgia.

JACOB NEUSNER, PhD (Columbia University), Professor of Religious Studies and Ungerleider Distinguished Scholar of Judaic Studies, Brown University, Providence, Rhode Island.

BUSTENAY ODED, PhD (Hebrew University), Professor of Biblical History and Chairman of the Jewish History Department, University of Haifa, Haifa, Israel.

PETER SCHÄFER, Dr Phil (Freiburg University), Ausserplanmässiger Professor of Jewish Studies, Martin-Buber-Institut für Judaistik, Köln University, Köln, Germany.

J. ALBERTO SOGGIN, PhD (University of Rome), STD (University of Basel), Professor of Old Testament, Waldensian Theological Seminary, Professor of Hebrew Language and Literature, Institute of Near Eastern Studies, University of Rome, Visiting Professor, Pontifical Biblical Institute, Rome, Italy.

THOMAS L. THOMPSON, PhD (Temple University), Visiting Lecturer in Old Testament, University of North Carolina, Chapel Hill, North Carolina.

GEO WIDENGREN, Theo Dr (University of Uppsala), Emeritus Professor of the History and Psychology of Religions, University of Uppsala, Uppsala, Sweden.

PREFACE

In recent years, due to revaluations of the written sources and ever-increasing archaeological data, many of the views widely accepted among modern biblical scholars regarding Israelite and Judaean history have been called into question. This is especially true for the period before David and Solomon. The purposes of this volume are to review the currently available sources of information for Israelite and Judaean history, to assess the present status of scholarly discussion, and to present a reconstruction of the history of Israel and Judah as understood by some of today's leading biblical scholars.

This is a composite work. Following a chapter which gives a brief survey of the history of the study of Israelite and Judaean history, the different periods are treated in turn by scholars selected on the basis of the focus of their scholarly interest and research. Each contributor was asked (1) to survey and evaluate the written and archaeological evidence pertinent to the period, (2) to indicate the historical issues which have emerged during the past scholarly discussion of this evidence, and (3) to reconstruct as much of the historical outline of the period as possible. Not every chapter follows a similar outline nor gives equal stress to these three factors. For some periods, the problems of the source material and the history of research are more difficult and significant than in others. For other periods, a full reconstruction of the history can be made with reasonable confidence and thus in some chapters the problems of proposed reconstructions and the nature of the source materials are of less magnitude and consequence. Chapters II to V are almost exclusively concerned with the nature of the source material and the problems of scholarly research, whereas chapters VI to XI are primarily oriented to the reconstruction of the history.

This volume is not intended as simply another proposed reconstruction of Israelite and Judaean history. It is a handbook for the study of that history and one in which the reader can see different leading historians at work. One might expect that a composite handbook produced by a number of leading specialists with various scholarly backgrounds would be rather disjointed. This has not turned out to be the case although the careful reader will discover that the contributors are not always in agreement. The writers granted the editors rather extensive freedom to revise and correlate the contributions and this has made possible a more homogeneous volume than otherwise would have been the case.

Bibliographical information has been provided throughout the book although no attempt has been made to produce comprehensive bibliographies. Efforts were made to note, in addition to writings supporting the point under discussion, those works which have been highly influential in the history of scholarship, comprehensive in treatment, and/or helpful in pointing the reader to additional viewpoints and bibliography. The first part of the General Bibliography contains a list of the major histories of Israel and Judah. In the text, an author's name marked with an asterisk denotes a work listed there. Excellent bibliographical data on the archaeological sites can be found in the four-volume *Encyclopedia of Archaeological Excavations in the Holy Land* edited by Michael Avi-Yonah.

No attempt has been made to follow a single chronological system. The chronological problems associated with the period from the death of Solomon to the fall of Jerusalem are notoriously difficult. An Appendix provides a discussion of some of these problems, a bibliography, and a chart outlining several chronological schemes.

The editors express their appreciation to the various contributors for their willingness to participate in this project. In addition, thanks are extended to our colleague Frederick C. Prussner who translated chapters VII and X from German, to Yehoshua Gitay who translated chapter VIII from Hebrew, to Charles E. Zimmerman, Jr. who drew the maps for the volume, and to several graduate students at Emory, especially Rebecca Youngblood, Lynne Deming, and Phillip Callaway, for assistance in checking bibliographical references, proof-reading, and preparing the indices. Jean Cunningham of SCM Press provided careful and thorough editorial assistance above and beyond the call of duty. A special word of commendation is extended to Joyce Ann Baird who worked so conscientiously and diligently in typing the manuscript.

Emory University   J.H.H.
Candler School of Theology   J.M.M.

ABBREVIATIONS

ÄA	Ägyptologische Abhandlungen, Wiesbaden
AASOR	Annual of the American Schools of Oriental Research, New Haven/Cambridge, Mass./Missoula
AB	Anchor Bible, Garden City
ABL	*Assyrian and Babylonian Letters belonging to the Kouyunjik Collections of the British Museum* I–XIV, ed. R. F. Harper, Chicago: University of Chicago Press 1892–1914
ABR	*Australian Biblical Review*, Melbourne
AC	*L'antiquité classique*, Brussels
AcOr	*Acta Orientalia*, Leiden
ADAJ	*Annual of the Department of Antiquities of Jordan*, Amman
ADATS	Alter Orient und Altes Testament Sonderreihe, Kevelaer et al.
ADPV	Abhandlungen des Deutschen Palästina-Vereins, Wiesbaden
AES	Atiqot English Series, Jerusalem
ÄF	Ägyptologische Forschungen, Glückstadt
AFLNW	Arbeitsgemeinschaft für Forschung des Landes Nordrhein-Westfalen, Cologne
AfO	*Archiv für Orientforschung*, Graz et al.
AGAJU	Arbeiten zur Geschichte des antiken Judentums und des Urchristentums, Leiden
AGSU	Arbeiten zur Geschichte des Spätjudentums und Urchristentums, Leiden
AHGHIR	Abhandlungen der Herder-Gesellschaft und des Herder-Instituts zu Riga
AJA	*American Journal of Archaeology*, Princeton
AJBA	*Australian Journal of Biblical Archaeology*, Sydney
AK	*Archiv für Kulturgeschichte*, Berlin
ALUOS	*Annual of the Leeds University Oriental Society*, Leiden
AmSc	*American Scholar*, New York
AnBib	Analecta Biblica, Rome
ANEP	*The Ancient Near East in Pictures*, ed. J. B. Pritchard, Princeton: Princeton University Press 1954

ANET	*Ancient Near Eastern Texts*, ed. J. B. Pritchard, Princeton: Princeton University Press ³1969
AnSc	*Annals of Science*, London
AO	Der Alte Orient, Leipzig
AOAT	Alter Orient und Altes Testament, Neukirchen-Vluyn
AOr	*Archiv Orientálni*, Prague
AOS	American Oriental Series, New Haven
AOTS	*Archaeology and Old Testament Study* (see Bibliography 2)
AP	*Aramaic Papyri of the Fifth Century BC*, ed. A. Cowley, London: Oxford University Press 1923
APEF	*Annual of the Palestine Exploration Fund*, London
AR	*Ancient Records of Assyria and Babylonia*, ed. D. D. Luckenbill, Chicago: University of Chicago Press 1926–7
ARE	*Ancient Records of Egypt*, ed. J. H. Breasted, Chicago: University of Chicago Press 1906–7
ARM(T)	*Archives royales de Mari. Transcriptions et traductions*, Paris
AS	*Anatolian Studies*, London
ASNP	*Annali della Reala Scuola Normale Superiore di Pisa*, Florence et al.
ASTI	*Annual of the Swedish Theological Institute in Jerusalem*, Leiden
AT	Arbeiten zur Theologie, Stuttgart
ATANT	Abhandlungen zur Theologie des Alten und Neuen Testaments, Zürich
ATD	Das Alte Testament Deutsch, Göttingen
AThD	Acta Theologica Danica, Copenhagen
AUSS	*Andrews University Seminary Studies*, Berrien Springs, Michigan
BA	*Biblical Archaeologist*, New Haven
BAH	Bibliothèque archéologique et historique, Paris
BAR	*Biblical Archaeology Reader*, New Haven
BARev	*Biblical Archaeology Review*, Washington
BASOR	*Bulletin of the American Schools of Oriental Research*, New Haven
BBB	Bonner Biblische Beiträge, Bonn
BBLA	Beiträge zur biblischen Landes- und Altertumskunde, Stuttgart
BCE	Before the Common Era
BCSR	Bibliothèque catholique des sciences religieuses, Paris
BeO	*Bibbia e Oriente*, Milan
BEUP	Babylonian Expedition of the University of Pennsylvania, Philadelphia
BFPLUL	Bibliothèque de la Faculté de Philosophie et Lettres de l'Université de Liège, Paris
BGBE	Beiträge zur Geschichte der biblischen Exegese, Tübingen
BGBH	Beiträge zur Geschichte des biblischen Hermeneutik, Tübingen
BHT	Beiträge zur historischen Theologie, Tübingen
BIA	*Bulletin of the Institute of Archaeology*, London
Bib	*Biblica*, Rome

BibOr	Biblica et Orientalia, Rome
BIES	*Bulletin of the Israel Exploration Society*, Jerusalem
BJRL	*Bulletin of the John Rylands Library*, Manchester
BKAT	Biblischer Kommentar. Altes Testament, Neukirchen
BKP	Beiträge zur klassischen Philologie, Meisenheim an Glau
BL	*Bibel und Leben*, Düsseldorf
BO	*Bibliotheca Orientalis*, Rome
BR	*Biblical Research*, Amsterdam
BS	*Bibliotheca Sacra*, London
BSt	Biblische Studien, Neukirchen-Vluyn
BTAVO	Beihefte zum Tübinger Atlas der Vorderen Orients, Wiesbaden
BTB	*Bulletin de théologie biblique/Biblical Theology Bulletin*, Rome
BVSAWL	Berichte über die Verhandlungen der Sächsischen Akademie der Wissenschaft zu Leipzig
BWANT	Beiträge zur Wissenschaft vom Alten und Neuen Testament, Stuttgart
BZ	*Biblische Zeitschrift*, Paderborn
BZAW	Beihefte zur *Zeitschrift für die Alttestamentliche Wissenschaft*, Giessen/Berlin
CAH	*Cambridge Ancient History* I–II, London: Cambridge University Press ³1972–5
CBOTS	Coniectanea Biblica: Old Testament Series, Lund
CBQ	*Catholic Biblical Quarterly*, Washington
CBQMS	*Catholic Biblical Quarterly* Monograph Series, Washington
CE	Common Era
CHB	*Cambridge History of the Bible* I–III, Cambridge: Cambridge University Press 1963–70
CHM	*Cahiers d'histoire mondiale*, Paris
CMD	*Classica et Mediaevalia*. Dissertationes, Copenhagen
CNI	*Christian News from Israel*, Jerusalem
CP	*Classical Philology*, Chicago
CPJ	*Corpus Papyrorum Judaicarum*, Cambridge: Harvard University Press 1957
CRINT	*Compendia Rerum Iudaicarum ad Novum Testamentum*, Assen: Van Gorcum 1974 ff.
CSA	Cahiers de la Société Asiatique, Paris
CTA	*Corpus des tablettes en cunéiformes alphabétiques*, ed. A. Herdner, Paris: Imprimerie Nationale 1963
CTM	*Concordia Theological Monthly*, St Louis
CV	*Communio Viatorum*, Prague
DAWB	Deutsche Akademie der Wissenschaften zu Berlin
DBS	*Dictionnaire de la Bible*. Supplément, Paris
DEO	Documents d'études orientales, Damascus
DMOA	Documenta et Monumenta Orientis Antiqui, Leiden
DZGW	*Deutsche Zeitschrift für Geschichtswissenschaft*, Freiburg et al.

EB	Études bibliques, Paris
EF	Erträge der Forschung, Darmstadt
EHFLS	*Études historiques de la Faculté des Lettres de Strasbourg*
EI	*Eretz-Israel,* Jerusalem
EJ	*Encyclopedia Judaica,* Jerusalem
EJY	*Encyclopedia Judaica Yearbook,* Jerusalem
EnBr	*Encyclopaedia Britannica,* London/Chicago
ET	*Expository Times,* Edinburgh
EvTh	*Evangelische Theologie,* Munich
FF	*Forschungen und Fortschritte,* Berlin
FFC	Folklore Fellows Communications, Helsinki
FGLP	Forschungen zur Geschichte und Lehre des Protestantismus, Munich
FRLANT	Forschungen zur Religion und Literatur des Alten und Neuen Testaments, Göttingen
FSTRP	Forschungen zur systematischen Theologie und Religionsphilosophie, Göttingen
FWG	Fischer Weltgeschichte, Frankfurt
GS	*Gesammelte Studien*
HAT	Handbuch zum Alten Testament, Tübingen
HAW	Handbuch der Altertumswissenschaft, Munich
HES	Historia Einzelschriften, Wiesbaden
HiRel	*History of Religions,* Chicago
HKAT	Handkommentar zum Alten Testament, Göttingen
HMES	Harvard Middle Eastern Studies, Cambridge, Mass.
HR	*Historia Religionum* I, ed. C. J. Bleeker and G. Widengren, Leiden: E. J. Brill 1969
HSAT	Die Heilige Schrift des Alten Testaments, Bonn
HSDU	Die Heilige Schrift in deutscher Übersetzung, Würzburg
HSM	Harvard Semitic Monographs, Cambridge, Mass./Missoula
HTR	*Harvard Theological Review,* Cambridge, Mass.
HUCA	*Hebrew Union College Annual,* Cincinnati
HZ	*Historische Zeitschrift,* Munich
IASHP	*Israel Academy of Sciences and Humanities,* Jerusalem
IB	Interpreter's Bible, Nashville
ICC	International Critical Commentary, Edinburgh
IDB	*Interpreter's Dictionary of the Bible,* Nashville
IEJ	*Israel Exploration Journal,* Jerusalem
Int	*Interpretation,* Richmond, Va.
ISLL	Illinois Studies in Language and Literature, Urbana
ISSSA	International Studies in Sociology and Social Anthropology, Leiden
JANES	*Journal of the Ancient Near Eastern Society of Columbia University,* New York
JAOS	*Journal of the American Oriental Society,* Baltimore
JBL	*Journal of Biblical Literature,* Missoula

JCS	*Journal of Cuneiform Studies*, New Haven
JDT	*Jahrbücher für deutsche Theologie*, Stuttgart et al.
JEA	*Journal of Egyptian Archaeology*, London
JEH	*Journal of Ecclesiastical History*, London
JEOL	*Jaarbericht van het Vooraziatisch–Egyptisch Gezelschap 'Ex Oriente Lux'*, Leiden
JESHO	*Journal of the Economic and Social History of the Orient*, Leiden
JHI	*Journal of the History of Ideas*, New York
JHNES	Johns Hopkins Near Eastern Studies, Baltimore
JITLW	Jahresbericht der israelitisch-theologischen Lehranstalt in Wien
JJS	*Journal of Jewish Studies*, London
JNES	*Journal of Near Eastern Studies*, Chicago
JNGG	*Jahrbuch für Numismatik und Geldgeschichte*, Munich
JPOS	*Journal of the Palestine Oriental Society*, Jerusalem et al.
JQR	*Jewish Quarterly Review*, London
JR	*Journal of Religion*, Chicago
JRS	*Journal of Roman Studies*, London
JSJ	*Journal of the Study of Judaism in the Persian, Hellenistic and Roman Period*, Leiden
JSS	*Journal of Semitic Studies*, Manchester
JTC	*Journal for Theology and the Church*, New York
JTS	*Journal of Theological Studies*, Oxford
JWCI	*Journal of the Warburg and Courtauld Institutes*, London
KAI	H. Donner and W. Röllig, *Kanaanäische und Aramäische Inschriften*, I–III, Wiesbaden: Otto Harrassowitz 1962–4
KAT	Kommentar zum Alten Testament, Gütersloh
KHAT	Kurzgefasstes exegetisches Handbuch zum Alten Testament, Leipzig
KHC	Kurzer Hand-Commentar zum Alten Testament, Tübingen
KS	*Kleine Schriften*
LAPO	Littératures anciennes du Proche-Orient, Paris
LASBF	*Liber Annuus. Studii biblici franciscani*, Jerusalem
LB	Lire la Bible, Paris
LCL	Loeb Classical Library, London/Cambridge, Mass.
MANE	Monographs on the Ancient Near East, Leiden
MH	*Museum Helveticum*, Basle
MHUC	Monographs of the Hebrew Union College, Cincinnati/Jerusalem
MS	*Mediaeval Studies*, Toronto
MT	Massoretic text
MTS	Marburger Theologische Studien, Marburg
MVÄG	*Mitteilungen der Vorderasiatisch-Ägyptischen Gesellschaft*, Leipzig
MWL	Märchen der Weltliteratur, Düsseldorf–Cologne
ND	Tablets from Nimrud
NEB	New English Bible, London

NF	Neue Folge
NKZ	*Neue kirchliche Zeitschrift*, Erlangen
NS	New Series
NTS	*New Testament Studies*, Cambridge
NTT	*Nederlands Theologisch Tidsskrift*, Wageningen
OA	*Oriens Antiquus*, Rome
OAC	Oriens Antiqui Collectio, Rome
OBL	Orientalia et Biblica Lovaniensia, Louvain
OLZ	*Orientalistische Literaturzeitung*, Berlin
OPBIAA	Occasional Publications of the British Institute of Archaeology in Ankara
OS	*Oudtestamentische Studiën*, Leiden
OT	Old Testament
OTL	Old Testament Library, London/Philadelphia
OTMS	*The Old Testament and Modern Study* (see Bibliography 2)
OTS	Old Testament Studies, Edinburgh
OTWSA	Die Ou Testamentiese Werkgemeenskap in Suid-Afrika, Pretoria
PEFQS	*Palestine Exploration Fund Quarterly Statement*, London
PEQ	*Palestine Exploration Quarterly*, London
PJ	*Preussische Jahrbücher*, Berlin
PJB	*Palästina Jahrbuch*, Berlin
PL	Patrologia Latina (Migne), Paris
PLONS	Porta linguarum orientalium, neue Serie, Wiesbaden
PMLA	*Proceedings of the Modern Language Association of America*, New York
PMS	Publications in Mediaeval Studies, Notre Dame
PTMS	Pittsburgh Theological Monograph Series, Pittsburgh
QMIA	Qedem: Monographs of the Institute of Archaeology, Jerusalem
RA	*Revue d'assyriologie et d'archéologie orientale*, Paris
RAI	*Rencontre assyriologique internationale*, Paris
RB	*Revue biblique*, Paris
REJ	*Revue des études juives*, Paris
RGG	*Die Religion in Geschichte und Gegenwart*, Tübingen
RHA	*Révue hittite et asianique*, Paris
RHR	*Revue de l'histoire des religions*, Paris
RIL	*Rendiconti dell'Istituto Lombardo*, Milan
RR	*Radical Religion*, Berkeley
RSO	*Rivista degli Studi Orientali*, Rome
SAB	Sitzungsberichte der Deutschen Akademie der Wissenschaften zu Berlin
SANT	Studien zum Alten und Neuen Testament, Munich
SAOC	Studies in Ancient Oriental Civilization, Chicago
SAT	Die Schriften des Alten Testaments, Göttingen
SBASOR	Supplements to *BASOR*, Missoula

SBLDS	Society of Biblical Literature Dissertation Series, Missoula
SBLMS	Society of Biblical Literature Monograph Series, Missoula
SBL TT/PS	Society of Biblical Literature Text and Translations/Pseudepigrapha Series, Missoula
SBM	Stuttgarter biblische Monographien, Stuttgart
SBS	Stuttgarter Bibelstudien, Stuttgart
SBT	Studies in Biblical Theology, London/Naperville
SH	*Scripta Hierosolymitana*, Jerusalem
SJ	Studia Judaica, Berlin
SJLA	Studies in Judaism in Late Antiquity, Leiden
SKGG	Schriften der Königsberger Gelehrten Gesellschaft, Halle
SNT	Supplements to *Novum Testamentum*, Leiden
SNTSMS	Society for New Testament Studies Monograph Series, London
SNVAO	Skrifter utgitt av Det Norske Videnskaps-Akademi i Oslo
SOTMS	Society for Old Testament Study Monograph Series, London
SPB	Studia Post-Biblica, Leiden
SR	*Studies in the Renaissance*, New York
SSAWL	Sitzungsberichte der Sächsischen Akademie der Wissenschaften zu Leipzig, Berlin
SSEA	Schriften der Studiengemeinschaft der Evangelischen Akademien, Tübingen
SSN	Studia semitica Neerlandica, Assen
ST	*Studia Theologica*, Lund
StSem	Studi Semitici, Rome
STU	*Schweizerische Theologische Umschau*, Bern
SVT	Supplements to *Vetus Testamentum*, Leiden
TA	Theologische Arbeiten, Berlin
TB	Theologische Bücherei, Munich
TD	*Theology Digest*, St Mary, Kansas
TH	Théologie historique, Paris
TLZ	*Theologische Literaturzeitung*, Leipzig
TR	*Theologische Rundschau*, Tübingen
TRHS	Transactions of the Royal Historical Society, London
TS	Theologische Studien, Zürich
TSJTS	Texts and Studies of the Jewish Theological Seminary, New York
TSTS	Toronto Semitic Texts and Studies, Toronto
TU	Texte und Untersuchungen zur Geschichte der altchristlichen Literatur, Berlin
TUMSR	Trinity University Monograph Series in Religion, San Antonio
TynBul	*Tyndale Bulletin*, London
TZ	*Theologische Zeitschrift*, Basle
UCPH	University of California Publications in History, Berkeley/London

UF	*Ugarit-Forschungen*, Neukirchen-Vluyn
UMBS	University of Pennsylvania Museum Publications of the Babylonian Section, Philadelphia
UMSSS	University of Missouri Studies in the Social Sciences, Columbia
UNHAII	Uitgaven van het Nederlands Historisch-Archaeologisch Instituut te Istanbul
UUA	Uppsala Universitets Årsskrift, Uppsala
VB	Vorderasiatische Bibliothek, Leipzig
VF	*Verkündigung und Forschung*, Munich
VT	*Vetus Testamentum*, Leiden
VW	Verständliche Wissenschaft, Berlin
WD	*Wort und Dienst*, Bielefeld
WF	Wege der Forschung, Darmstadt
WHJP	*World History of the Jewish People, First Series: Ancient Times*, ed. B. Mazar, Jerusalem 1970
WMANT	Wissenschaftliche Monographien zum Alten und Neuen Testament, Neukirchen-Vluyn
WO	*Welt des Orients*, Göttingen
WTJ	*Westminster Theological Journal*, Philadelphia
WUNT	Wissenschaftliche Untersuchungen zum Neuen Testament, Tübingen
WZKMUL	*Wissenschaftliche Zeitschrift der Karl-Marx-Universität Leipzig* (Gesellschafts- und Sprachwissenschaftliche Reihe), Leipzig
WZUL	*Wissenschaftliche Zeitschrift Universitäts Leipzig*
ZA	*Zeitschrift für Assyriologie*, Leipzig/Berlin
ZÄS	*Zeitschrift für Ägyptische Sprache und Altertumskunde*, Berlin
ZAW	*Zeitschrift für die alttestamentliche Wissenschaft*, Berlin
ZDMG	*Zeitschrift der Deutschen Morgenländischen Gesellschaft*, Wiesbaden
ZDPV	*Zeitschrift des Deutschen Palästina-Vereins*, Wiesbaden
ZKG	*Zeitschrift für Kirchengeschichte*, Stuttgart
ZNW	*Zeitschrift für die neutestamentliche Wissenschaft*, Berlin
ZTK	*Zeitschrift für Theologie und Kirche*, Tübingen

GENERAL BIBLIOGRAPHY

1. MAJOR HISTORIES OF ISRAEL AND JUDAH

*(Authors' names marked in the text with an asterisk
refer to the works cited below)*

Albright, W. F., 'The Biblical Period', in *The Jews: Their History, Culture and Religion* I, ed. L. Finkelstein, New York: Harper & Brothers 1949, 3–69 = *The Biblical Period From Abraham to Ezra*, revised and expanded, New York: Harper Torchbooks 1963

Ben-Sasson, H. H., ed., *History of the Jewish People: Volume I, Ancient Times*, Tel Aviv: Dvir 1969 (Hebrew) = *History of the Jewish People*, London/Cambridge: Weidenfeld & Nicolson/Harvard University Press 1976

Bright, J., *A History of Israel*, Philadelphia/London: Westminster Press/SCM Press 1959, ^{2}1972

Beek, M. A., *Geschiedenis van Israël van Abraham tot Bar Kochba*, Zeist: W. De Haan 1957 = *A Short History of Israel from Abraham to the Bar Cochba Rebellion*, London: Hodder & Stoughton 1963 = *Concise History of Israel; from Abraham to the Bar Cochba Rebellion*, New York: Harper & Row 1964

Bendixon, S., *Israels Historia. Fran aldsta tider till Herodes' tronbestigning* I–II, Stockholm: Sohlmans 1948

Benzinger, I., *Geschichte Israels bis auf die griechische Zeit*, Berlin/Leipzig: Göschen 1904

Bruce, F. F., *Israel and the Nations: From the Exodus to the Fall of the Second Temple*, London/Grand Rapids: Paternoster Press/Eerdmans 1963

Cornill, C. H., *Geschichte des Volkes Israel von den ältesten Zeiten bis zur Zerstörung Jerusalems durch die Römer* = *History of the People of Israel from the Earliest Times to the Destruction of Jerusalem by the Romans*, Chicago: Open Court Publishing Company 1898

Daniel-Rops, H., *Histoire sainte: Volume I: Le peuple de la Bible*, Paris: Fayard 1947 = *Israel and the Ancient World: A History of the Israelites from the Time of Abraham to the Birth of Christ*, London: Eyre & Spottiswoode 1949

Dennefeld, L., *Histoire d'Israel et de l'ancient Orient*, BCSR 4, 1935

Edersheim, A., *Bible History*, I–VII: *The World before the Flood and the History of the Patriarchs*, New York: F. H. Revell n.d.; *The Exodus and the Wanderings in the Wilderness*, New York: F. H. Revell 1876; *Israel in Canaan under Joshua and the Judges*, New York: F. H. Revell 1887; *Israel under Samuel, Saul, and David, to the Birth of Solomon*, London: The Religious Tract Society 1887; *History of Judah and Israel from the Birth of Solomon to the Reign of Ahab*, London: Religious Tract Society 1880; *The History of Israel and Judah from the Reign of Ahab to the Decline of the Two Kingdoms*, New York: James Pott & Co. 1885; *The History of Israel and Judah from the Decline of the Two Kingdoms to the Assyrian and Babylonian Captivity*, New York: James Pott & Co. 1887

Ehrlich, E., *Geschichte Israels von den Anfängen bis zur Zerstörung des Tempels (70 n. Chr.)*, Berlin: Walter de Gruyter 1958 = *A Concise History of Israel from the Earliest Times to the Destruction of the Temple in AD 70*, London/New York: Darton, Longman & Todd/Harper Torchbooks 1962/5

Ewald, H. G. A., *Geschichte des Volkes Israel bis Christus* I–V, Göttingen: Dieterichschen Buchhandlung, 1843–55, ²1851–9, ³1864–8 (seven volumes) = *The History of Israel* I–VI, London: Longmans, Green, and Co. 1869–83

Foakes-Jackson, F. J., *The Biblical History of the Hebrews to the Christian Era*, Cambridge/New York: W. Heffer and Sons/George H. Doran 1903, ⁴1921

Graetz, H. H., *Geschichte der Juden von den ältesten Zeiten bis auf die Gegenwart* I–XI, Leipzig: O. Leiner 1861–75 = *History of The Jews* (abridged) I–VI, Philadelphia: The Jewish Publication Society of America 1891–8

Gunneweg, A. H. J., *Geschichte Israels bis Bar Kochba*, Stuttgart: W. Kohlhammer 1972

Guthe, H., *Geschichte des Volkes Israel*, Freiburg: J. C. B. Mohr 1899; Tübingen/Leipzig: J. C. B. Mohr, ²1904, ³1914

Heinisch, P., *Geschichte des Alten Testaments*, Bonn: Hanstein, 1950 = *History of the Old Testament*, Collegeville: Liturgical Press 1952

Hengstenberg, E. W., *Geschichte des Reiches Gottes under dem alten Bunde* I–II, Berlin: Gustav Schlawitz 1869–71

Herrmann, S., *Geschichte Israels in alttestamentlicher Zeit*, Munich: Chr Kaiser 1973 = *A History of Israel in Old Testament Times*, London/Philadelphia: SCM Press/Fortress Press 1975

Hitzig, F., *Geschichte des Volkes Israel*, Leipzig: S. Hirzel 1869

Jirku, A., *Geschichte des Volkes Israel*, Leipzig: Quelle & Meyer 1931

Johnston, L., *A History of Israel*, New York: Sheed and Ward 1964

Kapelrud, A. S., *Israel. Fra de eldste tider till Jesu fødsel*, Oslo/Bergen: Universitetsforlaget 1960, ²1963 = *Israel: From the Earliest Times to the Birth of Christ*, Oxford: Basil Blackwell 1966

Kaufmann, Y., *History of the Religion of Israel* I–VIII, Tel-Aviv: Bialik Institute-Dvir 1937–56 (Hebrew) = *The Religion of Israel: From the Beginnings to the Babylonian Exile* (abridged), Chicago/London: University of Chicago Press/George Allen & Unwin 1960

Kent, C. F., *A History of the Hebrew People* I–II, London/New York: Smith,

Elder & Co/Charles Scribner's Sons 1896–7; *A History of the Jewish People during the Babylonian, Persian, and Greek Periods*, London/New York: Smith, Elder & Co/Charles Scribner's Sons 1899

Kittel, R., *Geschichte der Hebräer*, Gotha: Friedrich Andreas Perthes 1888–92, I–II = *A History of the Hebrews* (London–Edinburgh/New York: Williams and Norgate/G. P. Putnam's Sons 1895–6). Revised as *Geschichte des Volkes Israel* I–II, Gotha: Friedrich Andreas Perther 1909–16; Stuttgart: W. Kohlhammer: I, ⁷1932; II, ⁷1925; III/1–2, ²1929

Klostermann, A., *Geschichte des Volkes Israel bis zur Restauration unter Esra und Nehemia*, Munich: C. H. Beck 1896

Köhler, A., *Lehrbuch der biblischen Geschichte*, Erlangen: Andreas Deichert 1875–93

König, E., *Geschichte des Reichs Gottes bis auf Jesus Christus*, Braunschweig/Leipzig: Hellmuth Wollermann 1908

Lehmann-Haupt, C. F., *Israel. Seine Entwicklung im Rahmen der Weltgeschichte*, Tübingen: J. C. B. Mohr 1911

Lods, A., *Israel, des Origines au Milieu du VIIIᵉ Siècle*, Paris: La Renaissance du Livre 1930 = *Israel, from Its Beginnings to the Middle of the Eighth Century*, London/New York: Routledge & Kegan Paul/Alfred A. Knopf 1932

Metzger, M., *Grundriss der Geschichte Israels*, Neukirchen-Vluyn: Neukirchener Verlag 1963

Meyer, E., *Geschichte des Alterthums* I–V, Stuttgart: J. G. Cotta 1884–1902; Basle: Benno Schwabe 1953 (5 volumes in 8)

Milman, H. H., *The History of the Jews, from the Earliest Period down to Modern Times*, London: John Murray 1829; quoted from Harper's Family Library edition, New York 1834

Mowinckel, S., *Israels opphav og eldste historie*, Oslo: Universitetsforlaget 1967

Neher, A. and R., *Histoire biblique du Peuple d'Israël* I–II, Paris: Adrien-Maisonneuve 1962

Niebuhr, C. (= C. Krug) *Geschichte des ebräischen Zeitalters*, Leipzig: E. Pfeiffer, 1894

Nielsen, E., *Grundriss af Israels historie*, Copenhagen: G. E. C. Gads 1959, ²1961

Noth, M., *Geschichte Israels*, Göttingen: Vandenhoeck & Ruprecht, 1950, ²1954 = *The History of Israel*, London/New York: A. & C. Black/Harper & Row (1958) ²1960

Oesterley, W. O. E. and Robinson, T. H., *A History of Israel* I–II, London: Oxford University Press 1932

Oettli, S., *Geschichte Israels bis auf Alexander den Grossen*, Calw-Stuttgart: Calwer Vereinsbuchhandlung 1905

Olmstead, A. T. E., *History of Palestine and Syria to the Macedonian Conquest*, New York: Charles Scribner's Sons 1931

Orlinsky, H. M., *Ancient Israel*, Ithaca: Cornell University Press 1954, ²1960

Ottley, R. L., *A Short History of the Hebrews to the Roman Period*, New York/London: Macmillan/Cambridge University Press 1901

Paton, L. B., *The Early History of Syria and Palestine*, New York: Charles Scribner's Sons 1901

Piepenbring, C., *Histoire du peuple d'Israël*, Paris: Librairie Grassart 1898

Prideaux, H., *The Old and New Testament Connected in the History of the Jews and Neighbouring Nations, from the Declension of the Kingdoms of Israel and Judah to the Time of Christ* I–II, London: R. Knaplock 1717–18; quoted from edition of 1823–4

Renan, E., *Histoire du peuple d'Israël* I–V, Paris: Calmann Lévy 1887–93 = *History of the People of Israel* I–V, Boston: Roberts Brothers 1888–96

Ricciotti, G., *Storia d'Israele* I–II, Torino: Societa Editrice Internationale 1932, ²1934 = *The History of Israel* I–II, Milwaukee: Bruce Publishing Co. 1955

Sayce, A. H., *The Early History of the Hebrews*, London: Rivingtons, 1897

Schedl, C., *Geschichte des Alten Testaments* I–V, Innsbruck: Tyrolia-Verlag 1956–64 = *History of the Old Testament* I–V, Staten Island: Alba House 1973

Schlatter, A., *Geschichte Israels von Alexander dem Grossen bis Hadrian*, Calw-Stuttgart: Calwer Vereinsbuchhandlung 1901, ²1906, ³1925

Schürer, E., *Lehrbuch der neutestamentlichen Zeitgeschichte*, Leipzig: J. C. Hinrichs 1874 = *Geschichte des judischen Volkes im Zeitalter Jesu Christi* I–III, 1886–9 = *A History of the Jewish People in the Time of Jesus Christ* I–V, Edinburgh/New York: T. & T. Clark/Charles Scribner's Sons 1885–98/1897–8. Revised edition, *The History of the Jewish People in the Age of Jesus Christ (175 BC–AD 135)* I, revised and edited by G. Vermes and F. Millar, Edinburgh: T. & T. Clark 1973

Seinecke, L., *Geschichte des Volkes Israel*, Göttingen: Vandenhoeck & Ruprecht 1876

Sellin, E., *Geschichte des Israelitisch-Jüdischen Volkes* I–II, Leipzig: Quelle & Meyer 1924–32

Shuckford, S., *The Sacred and Profane History of the World Connected, From the Creation of the World to the Dissolution of the Assyrian Empire at the Death of Sardanapalus, and to the Declension of the Kingdom of Judah and Israel under the Reigns of Ahaz and Pekah* I–II, London: R. Knaplock & J. Tonson 1728–30; quoted from edition of 1810

Smith, H. P., *Old Testament History*, New York: Charles Scribner's Sons 1903

Stade, B., *Geschichte des Volkes Israel* I–II, Berlin: G. Grote 1888–95

Stanley, A. P., *Lectures on the History of the Jewish Church* I–III, New York: Charles Scribner's Sons 1863–76

de Vaux, R., *Histoire ancienne d'Israël: Des Origines à l'Installation en Canaan*, Paris: J. Gabalda, 1971; *La Periode des Juges*, Paris: J. Gabalda 1973 = *The Early History of Israel: To the Period of the Judges*, London/Philadelphia: Darton, Longman & Todd/Westminster Press 1976

Weber, G. and Holtzmann, H., *Geschichte des Volkes Israel und der Entstehung des Christentums* I–II, Leipzig: Wilhelm Engelmann 1867

Wellhausen, J., *Israelitische und jüdische Geschichte*, Berlin: Georg Reimer 1894, ²1895, ³1897; reprinted, Berlin: Walter de Gruyter 1958
Winckler, H., *Geschichte Israels in Einzeldarstellungen* I–II, Leipzig: Pfeiffer 1895–1900
Wood, L. T., *Survey of Israel's History*, Grand Rapids: Zondervan 1970

2. FESTSCHRIFTEN AND OTHER COLLECTIONS

cited by (short) title as indicated by bold type

Freedman, D. N. and Greenfield, J. C. (eds.), **New Directions** in *Biblical Archaeology*, Garden City: Doubleday 1969 (Anchor Books ed. 1971)
Goedicke, H. (ed.), **Near Eastern Studies** in *Honor of W. F. Albright*, Baltimore: Johns Hopkins Press 1971
Goedicke, H. and Roberts, J. J. M. (eds.), **Unity & Diversity**. *Essays in the History, Literature and Religion of the Ancient Near East*, Baltimore: Johns Hopkins Press 1975
Hayes, J. H. (ed.), **Old Testament Form Criticism**, TUMSR 2, 1974
Hempel, J. and Rost, L. (eds.), **Von Ugarit nach Qumran** (Festschrift Otto Eissfeldt), BZAW 77, 1958
Hyatt, J. P. (ed.), **The Bible in Modern Scholarship**, Nashville: Abingdon Press 1965
Maass, F. (ed.), **Das ferne und nahe Wort** (Festschrift Leonhard Rost), BZAW 105, 1967
Rowley, H. H. (ed.), *The Old Testament and Modern Study* (cited as OTMS), London: Oxford University Press 1951
Sanders, J. A. (ed.), **Near Eastern Archaeology** in *the Twentieth Century* (Festschrift Nelson Glueck), Garden City: Doubleday 1970
Thomas, D. Winton (ed.), *Archaeology and Old Testament Study* (cited as **AOTS**), London: Oxford University Press 1967
Wiseman, D. J. (ed.), *Peoples of Old Testament Times* (cited as **Peoples of OT Times**), London: Oxford University Press 1973
Wolff, H. W. (ed.), **Probleme biblischer Theologie** (Festschrift G. von Rad), Munich: Chr. Kaiser Verlag 1971
Wright, G. E. (ed.), **The Bible and the Ancient Near East** (Festschrift W. F. Albright), Garden City: Doubleday 1961

3. SOME OTHER BOOKS FREQUENTLY CITED

Aharoni, Y., *The Land of the Bible; A Historical Geography*, London/Philadelphia: Burns & Oates/Westminster 1967
Albright, W. F., *The Archaeology of Palestine*, Harmondsworth/Baltimore: Penguin Books 1949

Albright, W. F., *From the Stone Age to Christianity: Monotheism and the Historical Process*, Baltimore: Johns Hopkins Press 1940; 2nd ed., Garden City: Doubleday 1957

Alt, A., *Kleine Schriften zur Geschichte des Volkes Israel* (cited as *KS*) I–II, Munich: C. H. Beck 1953; III, ibid. 1959

Alt, A., *Essays on Old Testament History and Religion* (cited as *Essays*), Oxford/Garden City: Blackwell/Doubleday 1966

Eissfeldt, O., *Kleine Schriften* (cited as *KS*), ed. R. Sellheim and F. Maass, Tübingen: J. C. B. Mohr, I, 1962; II, 1963; III, 1966; IV, 1968; V, 1973

Eissfeldt, O., *The Old Testament: An Introduction*, Oxford/New York: Blackwell/Harper & Row 1965

Fohrer, G., *Einleitung in das Alte Testament*, Heidelberg: Quelle & Meyer 1965 = *Introduction to the Old Testament*, Nashville/London: Abingdon Press/SPCK 1968/70

Fohrer, G., *Studien zur alttestamentlichen Theologie und Geschichte (1949–1966)* (cited as *Studien*), BZAW 115, 1969

Hengel, M., *Judentum und Hellenismus*, WUNT 10, 1969, ²1973 = *Judaism and Hellenism: Studies in their Encounter in Palestine during the Early Hellenistic Period*, I (text) and II (notes), London/Philadelphia: SCM Press/Fortress Press 1974

Kenyon, K., *Digging up Jerusalem*, London/New York: Ernest Benn/Praeger 1974

Noth, M., *Überlieferungsgeschichtliche Studien. Die sammelnden und bearbeitenden Geschichtswerke im Alten Testament*, SKGG 18/2, 1943, 43–266; reissued separately, Tübingen: Max Niemeyer 1957

Noth, M., *Überlieferungsgeschichte des Pentateuchs*, Stuttgart: W. Kohlhammer 1948 = *A History of the Pentateuchal Traditions*, Englewood Cliffs: Prentice Hall 1972

Noth, M., *Gesammelte Studien zum Alten Testament* (cited as *GS*) I–II, TB 6 and 39, 1951 and 1969

Noth, M., *The Laws in the Pentateuch and Other Essays*, Edinburgh/Philadelphia: Oliver & Boyd/Fortress Press 1966

Noth, M., *Aufsätze zur biblischen Landes- und Altertumskunde* I–II, ed. H. W. Wolff, Neukirchen-Vluyn: Neukirchener Verlag 1971

Rad, G. von, *Gesammelte Studien zum Alten Testament* (cited as *GS*) I, TB 8, 1958

Rad, G. von, *The Problem of the Hexateuch and Other Essays*, Edinburgh/New York: Oliver & Boyd/McGraw-Hill 1966

Rad, G. von, *Gesammelte Studien zum Alten Testament* II, ed. R. Smend, TB 48, 1973

Rost, L., *Das kleine Credo und andere Studien zum Alten Testament*, Heidelberg: Quelle & Meyer 1965

Rowley, H. H., *From Joseph to Joshua: Biblical Traditions in the Light of Archaeology*, London: Oxford University Press 1950

Rowley, H. H., *The Servant of the Lord and Other Essays*, London: Lutterworth Press 1952; rev. ed. Oxford: Blackwell 1965

Rowley, H. H., *Men of God: Studies in Old Testament History and Prophecy*, London: Thomas Nelson & Sons 1963

Soggin, J. A., *Old Testament and Oriental Studies* (cited as *OT Studies*), BibOr 29, 1975

Weippert, M., *Die Landnahme der israelitischen Stämme in der neueren wissenschaftlichen Diskussion*, FRLANT 92, 1967 = *The Settlement of the Israelite Tribes in Palestine: A Critical Survey of Recent Scholarly Debate*, SBT II/21, 1971

Wright, G. E., *Shechem: the Biography of a Biblical City*, New York/London: McGraw-Hill/Duckworth 1965

In the bibliographies at the beginning of each section, cross-references are to other bibliographies, not to the text.

I

THE HISTORY OF THE STUDY OF ISRAELITE AND JUDAEAN HISTORY

§1. THE EARLIEST TREATMENTS OF ISRAELITE AND JUDAEAN HISTORY

U. **Cassuto**, 'The Beginning of Historiography Among the Israelites', *EI* I, 1951, 85–8 (Hebrew) = his *Biblical and Oriental Studies* I, Jerusalem/London: Magnes Press/Oxford University Press 1973, 7–16; R. G. **Collingwood**, *The Idea of History*, London: Oxford University Press 1946; P. **Collomp**, 'La place de Josèphe dans la technique de l'historiographie hellénistique', *EHFLS* CVI, 1947, 81–92 = *Zur Josephus-Forschung*, ed. A. Schalit, WF 84, 1973, 278–93; R. C. **Dentan**, ed., *The Idea of History in the Ancient Near East*, AOS 38, 1955; J. **Finegan**, *Handbook of Biblical Chronology*, Princeton: Princeton University Press 1964; J. G. **Gager**, *Moses in Greco-Roman Paganism*, SBLMS 16, 1972; H. **Gelzer**, *Sextus Julius Africanus und die byzantinische Chronographie* I–II, Leipzig: B. G. Teubner, 1880–98; H. **Gese**, 'Geschichtliches Denken im alten Orient und im Alten Testament', *ZTK* LV, 1958, 127–45 = 'The Idea of History in the Ancient Near East and the Old Testament', *JTC* I, 1965, 49–64; N. N. **Glatzer**, *Untersuchungen zur Geschichtslehre der Tannaiten*, Berlin: Schocken Verlag 1933; R. M. **Grant**, *The Letter and the Spirit*, London: SPCK 1957; D. J. **Harrington**, *The Hebrew Fragments of Pseudo-Philo's Liber Antiquitatum Biblicarum Preserved in the* Chronicles of Jeraḥmeel, SBL TT/PS 3, 1974; G. **Kisch**, *Pseudo-Philo's Liber Antiquitatum Biblicarum*, PMS 10, 1949; K. **Koch**, 'Spätisraelitisches Geschichtsdenken am Beispiel des Buches Daniel', *HZ* CXCIII, 1961, 1–32; S. N. **Kramer**, 'Sumerian Historiography', *IEJ* III, 1953, 217–32; H. **Lindner**, *Die Geschichtsauffassung des Flavius Josephus im Bellum Judaicum*, AGAJU 12, 1972; M. A. **Meyer**, *Ideas of Jewish History*, New York: Behrman House 1974; R. L. P. **Milburn**, *Early Christian Interpretations of History*, London/New York: A. & C. Black/Harper & Brothers 1954; A. **Momigliano**, 'Pagan and Christian Historiography in the Fourth Century AD', *The Conflict between Paganism and Christianity in the Fourth Century*, ed. A. Momigliano, London: Oxford University Press 1963, 79–99; idem, 'The Second Book of Maccabees', *CP* LXX, 1975, 81–91; S.

Moscati, *Historical Art in the Ancient Near East*, StSem 8, 1963; S. **Mowinckel**, 'Israelite Historiography', *ASTI* II, 1963, 4–26; A. T. **Olmstead**, *Assyrian Historiography: A Source Study*, UMSSS III/1, 1916; E. **Otto**, 'Geschichtsbild und Geschichtsschreibung in Ägypten', *WO* III/3, 1964/6, 161–76; R. H. **Pfeiffer**, *Introduction to the Old Testament*, New York: Harper & Brothers 1941; G. **von Rad**, 'Der Anfang der Geschichtsschreibung im alten Israel', *AK* XXXII, 1944, 1–42 = 'The Beginnings of Historical Writing in Ancient Israel', *The Problem of the Hexateuch*, 1966, 166–204; H. **Schulte**, *Die Entstehung der Geschichtsschreibung im alten Israel*, BZAW 128, 1972; J. N. **Sevenster**, *The Roots of Pagan Anti-Semitism in the Ancient World*, SNT 41, 1975; M. **Stern**, *Greek and Latin Authors on Jews and Judaism: Volume I: From Herodotus to Plutarch*, Jerusalem: Israel Academy of Sciences and Humanities 1974; J. W. **Swain**, 'The Theory of Four Monarchies', *CP* XXXV, 1940, 1–21; V. **Tcherikover**, 'Jewish Apologetic Literature Reconsidered', *Eos* XLVIII, 1956, 169–93; H. St J. **Thackeray**, *Josephus: The Man and the Historian*, New York: Jewish Institute of Religion Press, 1929; C. **Trieber**, 'Die Idee der vier Weltreiche', *Hermes* XXVII, 1892, 321–44; B. Z. **Wacholder**, *Nicolaus of Damascus*, UCPH 75, 1962; idem, ' "Pseudo-Eupolemus": Two Greek Fragments on the Life of Abraham', *HUCA* XXXIV, 1963, 83–113; idem, 'Biblical Chronology in the Hellenistic World Chronicles', *HTR* LXI, 1968, 451–81; idem, *Eupolemus: A Study of Judaeo–Greek Literature*, MHUC 3, 1974; N. **Walter**, *Der Thoraausleger Aristobulos*, TU 86, 1964; idem, 'Zu Pseudo-Eupolemus', *Klio* XLIII–XLV, 1965, 282–90; F. V. **Winnett**, 'Re-examining the Foundations', *JBL* LXXXIV, 1965, 1–19; J. **Yoyotte**, 'L'Egypte ancienne et les origines de l'antijudaïsme', *RHR* CLXIII, 1963, 133–43.

The writing of history as a narrative about past events is a very ancient undertaking. Its roots, so far as Western historiography is concerned, are anchored in the cultures of Israel and Greece.

History, as a genre or literary type, is found in much of the Hebrew scriptures where events are understood in a theological or, to use Collingwood's terminology (14), 'theocratic' perspective. In spite of this perspective, much of the narrative material in these scriptures is historiographical in intent in so far as it attempts a narrative account of past events. To suggest, as is frequently done, that Israel was the creator of historical writing (see Pfeiffer, 357) probably goes beyond the evidence. Egyptian, Mesopotamian, and Hittite inscriptions, annals, chronicles, narratives, and art in many ways approach genuine historical thought and writing (see Dentan, Otto, Kramer, Olmstead, Gese, and Moscati) and tend to moderate extravagant claims about the originality and priority of Israelite historical writing. In addition, the origins and character of historical writing in Israel, especially with regard to the materials in the pentateuch, remain a much debated and unsettled issue (see von Rad, Cassuto, Winnett, Mowinckel, and Schulte). Since the Hebrew scriptures have been and remain the primary sources for reconstructing the history of Israel and Judah, questions regarding the nature, character, and antiquity of these traditions will be discussed in various places in the following chapters.

The first discussions of Israelite and Judaean history, apart from the biblical traditions, stem from the Hellenistic Age and were the products of both Jewish and non-Jewish authors. In the early Graeco-Roman period, Jewish–Roman relations and Jewish apologetic concerns engendered several treatments of Jewish history and life. From the second to the fifth century CE, with the emergence and dominance of rabbinic Judaism and the growth and state recognition of Christianity, concern with and interpretation of earlier Israelite and Judaean history passed into the hands of Christian historians and theologians whose assumptions and descriptions set a pattern that remained basically unchallenged throughout the Middle Ages. These three phases of the discussion are the concern of this section.

Much of the literature dealing with Israelite and Judaean history from the Hellenistic Age either did not discuss the subject in any great detail or, more probably, has been irretrievably lost. Except for the biblical book of Daniel and the apocryphal books of I and II Maccabees, only the fragments of this Hellenistic literature preserved in the works of Josephus, in Eusebius' *Praeparatio Evangelica*, and in a few other Graeco-Roman writers survive (see Stern for non-Jewish writers). None the less, it is highly probable that most Hellenistic universal historians included a section on the history of the Jews in their works.

Among pagan authors, discussions of the origin of the Jews and the figures of Abraham and Moses dominate. Both favourable and slanderous treatments appear. Hecataeus of Abdera (about 300 BCE), in his work on the culture, history, politics, and religion of ancient Egypt, discussed the origins of the Jews in terms of their expulsion from Egypt at divine urging and their subsequent colonization of Judaea. Josephus (*Contra Apionem*, I 183–204) quotes from a work by Hecataeus which was wholly concerned with the Jews, although Josephus' passage only contains miscellaneous material about Jewish matters during the early Hellenistic Age. Hecataeus' treatment of the Jews and their history was generally favourable and, while praising Moses as a cult founder and lawgiver, he shows little, if any, direct knowledge of the Jews and their sacred writings. Hecataeus' description of Moses and subsequent Jewish history which tended to telescope everything around Moses was highly influential upon practically all Hellenistic and even Graeco-Jewish writers (see Wacholder, 1974, 85–96).

Over against the material in Hecataeus (and Theophrastus, Megasthenes, and Clearchus) which took a favourable attitude towards the Jews, one finds widespread use of a version of the exodus and the career of Moses which heaps calumny upon the Jews. Utilizing an old story form (see Yoyotte) which told of a foreign invasion of Egypt, a reign of terror by outsiders, and a triumph over this dominance by a hero-king (see *ANET*, 231–4, 260), these descriptions of Jewish history depicted the Hebrews as an impure people, Moses as a polluted Egyptian priest, and portrayed Jewish life and practices as hostile to everything non-Jewish (Gager, 113–33). This hostile propaganda was basically centred in Alexandria and reflects the tension between Jews of the Egyptian diaspora and the native, especially priestly, Egyptian population. The roots of this anti-Jewish polemic were no doubt multiple (see Sevenster) and the tension is already reflected in Aramaic papyri of the fifth century BCE from Egypt. Variations on this theme of Jewish origins are reflected in Egyptian literature for over six centuries (Gager, 113) and no doubt formed a vital part of the arsenal of anti-Jewish propaganda offering a supportive rationale for repressive measures.

Perhaps the most significant example of this anti-Jewish version of Moses and the origins of the Jews is that attributed to Manetho (third century BCE) by Josephus (*Contra Apionem*, I 73–91, 93–105, 228–52), who claims to be quoting from Manetho's *Aegyptiaca*, although Josephus seems to retell Manetho's treatment in two different versions (see Stern, 62–5). Manetho's phil-Egyptian version or Josephus' interpretation of it identified or associated the expulsion of the Hyksos with the biblical account of the Hebrew departure from Egypt, an interpretation sometimes found in modern histories of ancient Israel.

Among the materials preserved by Eusebius from the collective work of Alexander Polyhistor (*Concerning the Jews*) are fragments of a historical work by the so-called Pseudo-Eupolemus (*Praeparatio Evangelica*, IX 17–39). This writer was apparently a Samaritan and one of the first to present biblical history under the form of Hellenistic historical writing (see Wacholder, 1963 and Walter, 1965). Some time near the beginning of the second century BCE, he combined biblical materials with traditions from non-Jewish writers such as Berossus and Hesiod in order to show Abraham as the source of the culture of the Phoenicians and Egyptians, and thus indirectly the source of Greek culture, since Herodotus, Plato, and Hecataeus had argued that the Greeks had acquired much wisdom from the Egyptians. Such a position carried the assertion that the biblical tradition represented the oldest wisdom of mankind. Abraham was the teacher of a multitude of nations (see Gen. 17.5)! Pseudo-Eupolemus utilized various elements of Babylonian and Greek mythology, perhaps the pseudepigraphal Enoch tradition, and haggadic traditions about Abraham. His work depicts Abraham in universalistic categories and is clearly concerned with apologetic interests.

Shortly after Pseudo-Eupolemus, and perhaps partially dependent upon him, the Alexandrian Jewish philosopher Aristobulus (see II Macc. 1.10) expounded Judaism as a philosophy and sought to show that the Mosaic law was a true philosophy and in no way contradictory to philosophical wisdom (see Walter, 1964). His work was apparently addressed to the young King Ptolemy VI Philometor (181–145 BCE) but may have been intended for a larger, even predominantly Jewish audience. Such apologetic works – both historical and philosophical – must have been addressed, at least in a limited way, to non-Jewish pagans (so Gager, 78–9) and not just to renegade Jews who had forsaken Judaism or were strongly tempted by the option of apostasy (so Tcherikover). The work of Pseudo-Eupolemus suggests that historical writing as an apologetic concern addressed to non-Jews developed in Palestine in Hellenistic circles before the Maccabaean revolt and probably not just in Samaria (see Wacholder, 1963, 112–13).

The Maccabaean struggles against the Seleucids triggered extensive Jewish historical writing. Eupolemus (see Wacholder, 1974), probably shortly after the Maccabaean Revolt (see I Macc. 8.17; II Macc. 4.11), wrote a work on Jewish history which discussed, among other matters, the date of the exodus and the figure of Moses (dated chronologically much earlier than in the MT), the Solomonic temple, and the Davidic–Solomonic state where the discussion reflects the influence of the expansion of the Hasmonaeans and their international political relations. Eupolemus, as a Hellenized, priestly supporter of the Maccabees, demonstrates a strong patriotic and nationalistic interpretation of Jewish history and less of the universalistic spirit which characterized Pseudo-Eupolemus. According to Clement of Alexandria (*Stromata*, I 141), Eupolemus calculated the time between Adam and the fifth year of Demetrius I Soter (162–150 BCE) as 5,149 years. In his chronological concerns, Eupolemus expressed the widespread interest in world chronology which was characteristic of many Hellenistic writers (see Wacholder, 1968). Jason of Cyrene, about whom nothing is certainly known, produced a five-volume history of the early Maccabaean struggles (see II Macc. 2.23) probably covering the years 176–160 BCE. His work has been summarized as II Maccabees (see Momigliano, 1975, and below, ch. X §1 A ii) by an unknown epitomizer who probably not only condensed the massive work but added some popular haggadic legends (II Macc. 1.11–18), supernaturalistic touches, and martyrological stories (II Macc. 6–7). II Maccabees is more akin to Hellenistic than biblical historiography – in its direct address to the reader, its edifying quality, its conscious literary strivings, and its concern to entertain and enhance the reader's enjoyment (see especially II Macc. 1.1–6; 15.38f.).

I Maccabees, like II Maccabees, may be classified as contemporary history since its focus of concern is the Maccabaean struggles down to 134 BCE, probably near the book's date of composition. This work is more similar to the narrative style of Kings and Chronicles, that is to biblical historiography, than II Maccabees although the work is in some regards more pro-Hasmonaean than the latter.

One further work engendered by the Maccabaean struggles should be noted, namely the book of Daniel. While apocalyptic rather than purely historical in form, the book of Daniel does however reflect a concern widespread in Hellenistic historiography – the concern with universal history which has already been noted in the work of the Samaritan Pseudo-Eupolemus. Daniel utilized the concept of four world monarchies in discussing universal history, a concept widely and earlier employed by Greek and Hellenistic writers as well as later Roman authors (see Trieber and Swain). In Daniel one can discern a tripartite division in the author's treatment of world history (so Koch, 28): (1) the time before the capture of Jerusalem, known from the biblical historical works (more assumed than discussed by the author); (2) the era of the four world empires manifesting a great decline in civilization; and (3) the futuristic eternal kingdom about to dawn. This understanding and schema of history, later adopted and adapted by Christian historians, were to dominate historical treatments of Israelite and Judaean history until the post-Reformation period.

Four writers of Jewish history from the Graeco-Roman period deserve attention: Alexander Polyhistor (first century BCE), Nicolaus of Damascus (born about 64 BCE), Justus of Tiberias (first century CE), and Flavius Josephus (about 37–100 CE). Alexander was from

Miletus although he wrote in Rome where he had been taken by Lentulus during Sulla's eastern campaign. The latter manumitted and appointed him a pedagogue. Among Alexander's more than twenty-five works, one was entitled *Concerning the Jews*, fragments of which have been preserved in Eusebius' *Praeparatio Evangelica*. Much of his writings apparently consisted of compilations. His writing on the Jews probably belongs to the period shortly after Pompey's conquest of the Seleucid empire and reflects the Roman fascination with and curiosity about things Eastern. In the preserved fragments, Alexander, who was not Jewish, quotes Jewish and pro-Jewish as well as non-Jewish and anti-Jewish authors, seemingly adhering faithfully and undiscriminatingly to his sources. His account of Jewish history began with the pre-patriarchal ancestors and may have extended down to his own day. The order of the events narrated follows the sequence of the biblical books, beginning with Genesis and extending through Kings and Chronicles, which might suggest that he was familiar with the biblical books in translation. His quotations from some rather obscure writers would indicate his utilization of a significant Roman library. An important feature of Alexander's work is its reflection of the extensive chronological synchronization of Egyptian, Babylonian, Greek, and biblical history and data. For example, Alexander associated the biblical flood and Noah with Berossus' Babylonian flood story and Xisuthrus. Already in the second and first centuries BCE, numerous attempts had been made to produce a world chronology and an Alexandrian biblical chronological 'school' can perhaps be traced back to the Hellenistic Jewish writer Demetrius who wrote during the reign of Ptolemy IV Philopator (221–204 BCE) (Wacholder, 1974, 98–104). The Greek version of the pentateuch certainly reflects the activity of such a chronological school.

Nicolaus of Damascus, who had served as tutor to Cleopatra's children and written a biography of Augustus, became a court official and counsellor to Herod the Great some time before 14 BCE, probably as part of the latter's desire to turn Jerusalem into a major literary centre. Among his works were an autobiography and a world history composed in 144 books. Nicolaus' history, written in Jerusalem and under the patronage of Herod, to whose reign about one-fifth of the work was devoted, was a true universal history which integrated Jewish history into the larger context of world history which was traced back to the times of mythical origins. With the exception of Josephus, Jewish and Christian historians seem to have made little use of Nicolaus' work, although extensive portions were available to Photius, the ninth-century anthologist and patriarch of Constantinople.

Justus of Tiberias, a contemporary and antagonist of Josephus and like him apparently an unenthusiastic supporter of the revolt against Rome, produced not only a history of the Jewish war but also a chronicle of the Jewish kings extending from Moses to the time of Agrippa II. Justus seems to have made extensive use of Hellenistic universal chronicles, synchronizing the date of the exodus with the assumed contemporary Attic and Egyptian rulers. Justus' extensive chronological synchronization, through the work of Julius Africanus, exercised a significant influence upon Christian biblical chronography.

Pride of place among Graeco-Roman Jewish historians must be assigned to Flavius Josephus although this may be as much due to the accident of historical preservation as to the excellence of historical presentation in his works. In the last quarter of the first century BCE, Josephus produced four major writings: *Bellum Judaicum*, a history of the Jewish war in seven books; *Antiquitates Judaicae*, a history of the Jewish people from earliest times down to the outbreak of the Jewish–Roman war in 66 BCE in twenty books; *Vita*, an autobiographical work primarily describing Josephus' role in the war; and *Contra Apionem*, a treatise on the antiquity of the Jewish people in two books. All of Josephus' works were written for apologetic or polemical purposes, a factor which exercised significant influence and perhaps frequently produced distortions in his presentations. Whether Josephus was a traitor to his own people or a nationalist with loyalties that transcended the passion of Zealotism has been much debated, but that he was a sagacious opportunist has seldom been doubted.

In spite of Josephus' argument that 'the industrious writer is not one who merely remodels the scheme and arrangement of another's work, but one who uses fresh materials and makes the framework of the history his own' (*War*, I 15), much of his historical work relied heavily upon previous authors, a factor sometimes acknowledged, sometimes not (see *Schürer, 43–63, on his sources). Josephus was consciously aware of his interest, apologetic concerns, and the need to justify his presentations, and he commented briefly on his historiographic method. The account of the Jewish war, his finest work, was written to demonstrate that the Jewish revolutionary party was the dominant factor in the Jewish–Roman strife and the cause of the destruction of the temple and to correct previously published non-Jewish versions of the conflict (*War*, I 1–18). As to the first purpose,

Josephus informed his Greek and Roman readers that, in spite of his desire to 'recount faithfully the actions of both combatants' (*War*, I 9), his own reflections and private sentiments held that his country 'owed its ruin to civil strife, and that it was the Jewish tyrants who drew down upon the holy temple the unwilling hands of the Romans' (*War*, I 10). As to the second purpose, Josephus felt that he had to correct the view that the Romans were 'the conquerors of a puny people' (*War*, I 8) and to combat ill-informed historians: 'As for the native Greeks, where personal profit or a lawsuit is concerned, their mouths are at once agape and their tongues loosed; but in the matter of history, where veracity and laborious collection of the facts are essential, they are mute, leaving to inferior and ill-informed writers the task of describing the exploits of their rulers. Let us at least hold historical truth in honour, since by the Greeks it is disregarded' (*War*, I 16).

In the *War*, Josephus' interpretation of the events of his day is presented, in Thucydidean fashion, in three speeches attributed to Agrippa (II 345–401), Josephus himself (V 362–419), and Eleazar, the leader of the Masada rebels (VII 323–36, 341–88) (see Lindner). The central elements in Josephus' interpretations were twofold. (1) As in Polybius, Roman dominance was understood as the work of providence or God. Josephus has Agrippa declare: 'Divine assistance . . . is ranged on the side of the Romans, for, without God's aid, so vast an empire could never have been built up' (II 391). Josephus reports that in his speech to the defenders of Jerusalem, he, after surveying the history of Israel's suffering, sought to convince the Jews that 'the Deity has fled from the holy places and taken His stand on the side of those with whom you are now at war' (V 412). Thus, like the prophets of old, Josephus applied a theological rationalization to explain the conditions of history. (2) The decimation of the nation and the trauma of the temple's destruction were interpreted by Josephus as divine recompense (V 413–19). Josephus has Eleazar declare: 'We have been deprived, manifestly by God Himself, of all hope of deliverance', for God was expressing his 'wrath at the many wrongs which we madly dared to inflict upon our countrymen'. He even has Eleazar interpret the rebels' suicidal death as a form of payment to God: 'The penalty for those crimes let us pay not to our bitterest foes, the Romans, but to God through the act of our own hands' (VII 331–3). With good Deuteronomistic theology, Josephus explained the calamity which befell the Jews as divine punishment for the sins of the people, though as the sins of a minor element in the population.

Josephus' other major historical work, his *magnum opus*, was entitled *Jewish Antiquities* or, literally translated, *Jewish Archaeologies*. Involved in Josephus' presentation of the 'ancient history and political constitution' of the Jews to the Greek-speaking world (*Ant.* I 5) were two subsidiary influences, one clearly expressed and the second clearly deducible. In the first place, the translation of the pentateuch into Greek in Alexandria, as reported in the letter of Aristeas, and the assumed Graeco-Roman interest in this work on Jewish history led Josephus to hope that a widespread interest in Jewish history in its entirety existed among non-Jews (*Ant.* I 10–14). The curiosity and encouragement of his patron, Epaphroditus, reinforced his hope. Josephus' model led him to approach the topic in terms of translating the Hebrew records (*Ant.* I 5) although his work can in no way be classified as a translation and even to designate it a paraphrase is misleading.

Secondly, in 7 BCE, Dionysius of Halicarnassus had published in twenty books a work on Roman archaeologies (*Antiquitates Romanae*), written in Greek, in which he utilized various types of source material in order to demonstrate the great antiquity of Rome in line with the general interest in antiquity reflected in Hellenistic writers who however stressed Babylonian, Greek, Egyptian, or Jewish antiquity rather than Roman. Josephus seems to have adopted consciously the pattern and interest of Dionysius in the general structure of his work in order to demonstrate that Jewish history was able to stand on an equal footing with that of any other culture in terms of both antiquity and intrinsic interest.

In the present discussions, only a few general characteristics of Josephus' history can be noted:

1. Although Josephus declares that his aim is to set forth 'the precise details of our Scripture records . . . neither adding nor omitting anything' (*Ant.* I 17), he did deliberately omit some traditions as well as supplement the biblical materials. Some of his conscious omissions were clearly calculated to avoid providing anti-Jewish protagonists with any material that might be used to support the scurrilous claims that the Jews worshipped God in animal form, specifically the ass. One of the prominent concerns in his *Contra Apionem* is the refutation of this accusation. Noteworthy in this regard is his omission of any reference to the story of the Israelite worship of the golden calf (Ex. 32) in his history. Numerous non-biblical legends, many with parallels in rabbinic and Hellenistic haggadah, were added to his presentation. Among these are the stories of Moses' command of the Egyptian army in expelling the Ethiopians

(*Ant.* II 238–53; a similar but not identical version appears in the second century BCE writings of the Alexandrian Artapanus), the worship of Alexander the Great in the Jerusalem temple and his special favours to the Jews (*Ant.* XI 329–45; a very popular theme in later rabbinic tradition), and numerous less significant stories. Josephus does not explicitly differentiate between the biblical and the haggadic non-biblical traditions; the two seem to stand on an equal footing in his work.

2. In his discussion of Abraham and Moses, Josephus glorifies both characters, but at the same time he stops short of portraying them as immortals. Abraham is depicted as the first monotheist whose monotheism was derived from his speculation on the irregularity of natural and astronomical phenomena and was responsible for his persecution in Mesopotamia and subsequent settlement in Canaan (*Ant.* I 154–7). In Egypt, Abraham taught astronomy (already discovered by the antediluvian ancients; *Ant.* I 69–71) and arithmetic to the ignorant Egyptians, who subsequently passed along this learning to the Greeks (*Ant.* I 166–8; somewhat similarly Artapanus, see Eusebius, *Praeparatio Evangelica*, IX 18). Josephus presents Moses, whose birth and significance were revealed to Pharaoh and Amram (*Ant.* II 205–16), as a philosopher, lawgiver, statesman, and military hero (see especially *Ant.* I 18–26; II 238–53; III 179–87; IV 176–95). Josephus stresses not only Moses' death but Moses' authorship of the account of his death so that none could claim that, like Enoch (*Ant.* I 84), 'by reason of his surpassing virtue he had gone back to the Deity' (*Ant.* IV 326; see III 96; and compare Philo *De Vita Mosis*, II 288–91) and thus been granted special immortality, as seems to have been claimed in certain circles (see Origen, *Contra Celsum*, I 21).

3. Although Josephus declares that 'some things the lawgiver Moses shrewdly veils in enigmas, others he sets forth in solemn allegory' (*Ant.* I 24), his work is surprisingly free of allegorical interpretation, in strong contrast to the work of Philo (see, for example, Philo's *De Migratione Abrahami*). Josephus however sought to show the correlation between Moses' writing and natural philosophy, for example, in the depiction of the tabernacle and priestly garments as 'an imitation of universal nature' (*Ant.* III 123, 179–87).

4. A further noteworthy characteristic in Josephus' history is his recognition of many of the critical problems and difficulties in the biblical text, a characteristic shared by many of his Jewish contemporary and later rabbinic interpreters of the scriptures. His work demonstrates that the ancients perceived many of the issues which were to occupy scholarly investigations centuries later. Working

within a framework which accepted the inspiration and veracity of the scriptures and gave no thought to the possibility of diversity and development in the literary text, Josephus handled these problems through supplementation and harmonization. A few examples will suffice as illustrations. In discussing Cain, for example, Josephus is careful to point out that Adam and Eve had not only sons but daughters as well (*Ant.* I 52; cf. Jubilees 4.1–8) and that Cain feared that he would be a prey to wild beasts in his wanderings and thus needed a protective marking (*Ant.* I 59). In the discussion of the tribal allotments in the book of Joshua, one should logically conclude that since the distribution was an *ad hoc* operation by lot, then equality in tribal territories should be expected. Josephus knew that this had not been the case and this he explained in terms of land valuation and tribal population (*Ant.* V 76–80). In discussing the capture of Jerusalem, Josephus was aware of the contradictions in Joshua 15.63; Judges 1.8, 21; and II Samuel 5.1–10 and the need to harmonize such contradictions. Josephus accomplished this task by having two Jerusalems – a lower city captured as noted in Judges 1.8 and an upper city not taken until the time of David (*Ant.* V 124; VII 61–4). In the stories of David's first association with Saul, the biblical text has David entering Saul's service as a musician and armour bearer (I Sam. 16) whereas the subsequent story of David's combat with Goliath depicts Saul as unaware of David's identity. Josephus harmonizes the traditions by playing down the identity problem, omitting any reference to I Samuel 17.55–8 (perhaps due to his dependence upon the Greek text where these verses do not appear), and by suggesting that David had previously been placed on furlough by Saul (*Ant.* VI 175). II Samuel 21.19, where Elhanan is said to have killed Goliath, is harmonized with I Samuel 17 by Josephus' omission of the name of Goliath in the former.

5. Another notable feature of Josephus' historical treatment is his rationalization of miraculous and extraordinary events. Josephus was somewhat troubled by Old Testament miracles (as was apparently the author of Wisdom of Solomon 19.6–21), or at least wondered about the incredulity of Gentile readers. Josephus dealt with the miraculous by carefully guarding himself and his own opinion and/or by explaining the miraculous through rationalization. When speaking of accounts in which miracle played a significant role, Josephus frequently pointed out that he was merely recounting the story as he 'found it in the sacred books' (see *Ant.* II 347). At other times, he used a rather set formula suggesting that on these matters 'everyone should decide according to his fancy' or 'everyone is wel-

come to his own opinion' (see *Ant.* I 108, II 348 and frequently elsewhere). This tendency to point the reader to his own opinion was
already used by Dionysius of Halicarnassus (*Roman Antiquities*, I 48),
from whom Josephus may have borrowed it, and was later stated as
a rule for historians by Lucian in his third-century CE work, *How to
Write History*:

> Should any myth come into question, it should be related but not wholly
> credited: rather it should be left open for readers to conjecture about it as
> they will, but do you take no risks and incline neither to one opinion nor to
> the other (60).

On several occasions, Josephus offers a rationalistic or naturalistic
explanation for the unusual. The great longevity of the antediluvians
was due not only to their being 'beloved of God' but also to their use
of astronomy and geometry and a diet 'conducive to longevity' (*Ant.*
I 104–8). The Hebrew passage through the sea is paralleled by the
retirement of the Pamphylian Sea before Alexander (*Ant.* II 347f.).
The purification of the bitter waters of Marah was due to the drain-
ing off of the contaminated part (*Ant.* III 8). Josephus pointed out
that quail were abundant around the Arabian gulf and that manna
was still a phenomenon in that region (*Ant.* III 25, 31). Even natural
causes are offered as one solution to the plagues which beset the
Philistines after their capture of the ark (*Ant.* VI 9). In explaining
the rescue of Jerusalem and the slaughter of 185,000 Assyrians in a
single night, Josephus drew upon the story of Herodotus which told
of an invasion by mice of the Assyrian military camps (*Ant.* X 18–
22). Josephus, however, was no thoroughgoing rationalist who shied
away from references to the miraculous. In his description of the fall
of Jerusalem (*War*, VI 288–300), he refers to numerous miraculous
portents which heralded the fall of the holy city. Whether he
believed these to be actual occurrences or was merely seeking to
emphasize for his audience the gravity of the occasion with rhetorical exaggeration is, of course, beyond the realm of solution.

6. A final characteristic of Josephus' account of Israelite and
Judaean history is his lack of any sense of development in the
people's institutions and religion. The orthodox practices, beliefs,
and institutions of his day were assumed to have existed from the
time of Moses (see the book of Jubilees where the patriarchs are
depicted as exemplary practitioners of the Mosaic law). That the
whole of Jewish law and the institutional structure of Judaism had
been given on Mount Sinai was a firmly anchored concept in later
rabbinic Judaism. Josephus certainly operated with a very similar
assumption.

After Josephus, ancient Judaism produced no historian in any way comparable. Very few Jewish writings from the rabbinic and Talmudic periods can be called historical works. Three perhaps should be noted. The *Megillat Taanit* ('The Scroll of Fasts') is an Aramaic document probably written near the beginning of the second century CE (see below, ch. X §1 A vi). Containing a list of thirty-six days on which Jews were not to fast because of the joyous events which occurred on those days, the work provides some narrative material on events during the period of the second temple. However, in no way can it really be designated a real history. The *Seder Olam Rabbah* ('The Order of the World'), probably from the second century CE, is a chronological work generally ascribed to Rabbi Yose ben Ḥalafta (for the chronological scheme, see Finegan, 123–30). The work established a chronology based on the calculation of dates from the creation of the world (*libriath haʿolam* or *anno mundi*). While it is primarily concerned with the dating of biblical events, a final chapter surveys the period from Alexander the Great to the revolt of Bar Kokhba in 132–5 CE. Meyer has summarized the value of this work in the following terms: The author's

endeavour to establish a single consistent chronology, reconciling apparent variations in the biblical text, would place his work very much in the rabbinic tradition of seeking to resolve scriptural contradictions which might otherwise create some doubt about the accuracy of the text. Though he confined himself almost entirely to biblical history, mixed chronicle with midrash, and sometimes departed from chronological sequence, the author of *Seder Olam* did evince a desire to establish a sequential framework for Jewish history. His concern was unusual for that time (14).

Pseudo-Philo's *Liber antiquitatum biblicarum* was apparently produced in the first century CE as a Jewish handbook on biblical history (on the text, see Kisch and Harrington). The work is primarily a midrashic chronicle of biblical history from Adam to David characterized by extensive omissions, modifications, and additions to the biblical texts. Its exact purpose is unknown. Many of its additions have parallels in other Jewish haggadah. The work was translated into Greek and subsequently into Latin, perhaps in the process being turned into a Christian handbook.

The sudden cessation of the writing of historical works by the Jews has been explained in various ways. The causes of this phenomenon were probably multiple; among them were the Jewish loss of a national and cultic centre, the sense of a demise of sacred history with the destruction of the temple, the further scattering of the Jews in the diaspora which intensified the dissipation of any concept of continuing political history, the canonization of scripture which presented the Jews with a closed sacred past, the general disillusionment with historical processes attendant upon the failure of two major Jewish revolts against Rome, and the rabbinical orientation towards the law and its application and the rabbinical demands for total purity of life and separation from the world. Jewish historians in the Hellenistic and Graeco-Roman world had borrowed the forms and interests of Hellenistic historiography and ethnography and utilized these for apologetic, propaganda, and polemical purposes. Josephus was a primary example. After the Bar Kokhba war, these purposes seem to have lost their appeal. Jewish apocalyptic, with its special historical concerns, was reduced to only a glowing ember in the Hadrianic fires.

The early Christian church inherited from Judaism a collection of scriptures strongly oriented to history. This combined with the belief that God had finally and fully revealed himself in the historical person, Jesus of Nazareth, meant that Christians could not ignore past history; in fact it had to claim the history of the old covenant as its own. The apologetic desire to present Christianity as the true heir of Old Testament faith and the evangelistic-confessional proclamation of the church as the special object of God's providence led to the attempt to view 'theocratic' history in systematic form. This systematization of history took both chronological and philosophical forms, although even the chronological perspectives were undergirded with major theological claims. The earliest specimens of Christian interpretation and systematic treatments of history were more chronological than historiographic in form.

The Christian chronographers had to summarize the history which the converts were now supposed to consider their own; they had also to show the antiquity of the Jewish–Christian doctrine, and they had to present a model of providential history. The result was that, unlike pagan chronology, Christian chronology was also a philosophy of history. Unlike pagan elementary teaching, Christian elementary teaching of history could not avoid touching upon the essentials of the destiny of man (Momigliano, 1963, 83).

Little is known of the Christian chronographers and their works prior to the establishment of Christianity as the state religion in the fourth century CE. Among the most important of these pre-Constantinian Christian 'historians' were Clement of Alexandria, Julius Africanus, and Hippolytus of Rome. Their concerns were primarily apologetic – to counter the contempt of Christianity as a novelty – and their methods were primarily those of their precursors, the Graeco-Jewish historians and Hellenistic chronographers.

The work of Julius Africanus (about 170–245 CE), of which only fragments have survived, will illustrate the approach of these Christian chronographers (see Gelzer). Africanus' work, which was still available to Jerome (*De viris illustribus*, 63), consisted of five volumes. He treated the history of the world from creation until his own day and like practically all patristic writers saw chronology in eschatological perspectives. He allotted 6,000 years for the world's duration and dated the birth of Jesus to 5500 *anno mundi*. Such time schemes or world ages were common in Jewish apocalyptic writings and are even found in rabbinic sources. (Rabbi Katina, in b. Sanhedrin 97a, spoke of a 6,000-year scheme – 2,000 years of *tohu*, 2,000 years of torah, and 2,000 years in the messianic age.) Africanus did not share the view of his North African contemporary Tertullian, who claimed that 'to be ignorant of everything outside the rule of faith is to possess all knowledge'. He worked out an elaborate synopsis of sacred and profane history, using as a fixed point the accession of Cyrus, and sought to collaborate his synchronisms with quotations from secular sources. He dated the flood to 2262 after creation and apparently placed the exodus in the year 3707. The first of these reckonings differs from the LXX, which places the flood 2,242 years after creation, and the date of the exodus was correlated with a Greek version of the flood assigned to the time of Ogygos, the legendary first king of Thebes. The date of Cyrus' accession was derived from Diodorus of Sicily, who had stated that Cyrus became king of the Persians in the opening year of the fifty-fifth Olympiad. The Olympiad system was based on the quadrennial celebration of the Olympic games, with the first of these supposedly held in what would be our 776/775 BCE. (For Africanus' chronological system, see Finegan, 140–6.)

In Africanus, one sees a flicker of textual criticism, so essential to scientific historiography. In a letter to Origen, he outlined seven reasons for considering the story of Susanna as late and fictitious and thus as no original part of the book of Daniel. He also noted and discussed the differences in the Matthean and Lukan genealogies of Jesus. Africanus' textual criticism and scepticism of sources however nowhere approached that of the non-Christians Celsus and Porphyry. In their attacks on Christianity, the former criticized the miraculous and absurd in the Bible and the latter denied the Mosaic authorship of the pentateuch, pointed out inconsistencies in Genesis, understood the book of Daniel against the times of Antiochus Epiphanes, and called attention to major disagreements in the Gospels.

Eusebius of Caesarea, who died about 340 CE, utilized the works of his Christian and pagan predecessors in the study of chronography and produced an extensive chronology of world history. Although especially indebted to the work of Africanus, Eusebius frequently deviated from him and developed a new system for synchronistic tabulation. Unfortunately, Eusebius' chronographic work has survived only in Jerome's Latin translation and adaptation and in an anonymous Armenian translation. In his so-called *Chronographia*, he produced an outline of the history of five major nations – the Assyrians, Hebrews, Egyptians, Greeks, and Romans. In calculating the reigns of these nations' rulers, he engaged in some critical discussions of the systems used for dating. The chronological differences among the Greek, Hebrew, and Samaritan texts were discussed with Eusebius generally opting for the LXX calculations. In his so-called *Chronicon*, Eusebius utilized a series of parallel columns for presenting the synchronism of the various empires. He took the birth of Abraham as his fixed point for reckoning and placed this in 3184 *anno mundi*. The flood was dated to 2242 and the exodus 505 years after the birth of Abraham. By choosing Abraham as the beginning point in his calculations, Eusebius thus partially sidestepped the LXX-Hebrew chronological problems, since the major differences are found in the early chapters of Genesis (for Eusebius' chronological reckonings, see Finegan, 147–87).

Eusebius did not produce his chronology in any hope of detailing the coming of the eschatological end-time, nor did he, like Africanus, work with any world-age scheme. Uncertainty about the times and seasons, he wrote, applies 'not merely to the final cataclysm but to all times'. For him, 'chronology was something between an exact science and an instrument of propaganda' (Momigliano, 1963, 85). Eusebius' career spanned the time that saw the church move from a persecuted sect to a state institution. His days were times of triumph for Christianity and Eusebius' writings affirm this as the providential purpose of God whose action in human affairs was the real nucleus of the historical process.

Eusebius was not only the ablest of the ancient Christian chronographers, he was also the father of ecclesiastical history. Eusebius was the first to produce a history of the church – which for him extended from the incarnation until his own day, in which the saviour had wrought a great and final deliverance and destroyed the enemies of true religion. In approaching his subject, Eusebius confessed, in the first chapter of his *Ecclesiastical History*, that 'as the first of those that have entered upon the subject, we are attempting a kind of trackless and unbeaten path'. In executing his narration of church history, Eusebius spoke of the fragmentary knowledge of the past and the evidence available:

> We are totally unable to find even the bare vestiges of those who may have travelled the way before us; unless, perhaps, what is only presented in the slight intimations, which some in different ways have transmitted to us in certain partial narratives of the times in which they lived; who, raising their voices before us, like torches at a distance, and as looking down from some commanding height, call out and exhort us where we should walk, and whither direct our course with certainty and safety. Whatsoever, therefore, we deem likely to be advantageous to the proposed subject, we shall endeavour to reduce to a compact body by historical narration. For this purpose we have collected the materials that have been scattered by our predecessors, and culled, as from some intellectual meadows, the appropriate extracts from ancient authors (I 1).

In carrying out this procedure, Eusebius made a lasting contribution to Western historiography.

> A new chapter of historiography begins with Eusebius not only because he invented ecclesiastical history, but because he wrote it with a documentation which is utterly different from that of pagan historians (Momigliano, 1963, 92).

Over one hundred works are cited directly or referred to as read by Eusebius. It is true, as Eusebius' critics have frequently noted, that his intellectual qualifications were somewhat defective, that he sometimes suppressed that which might disgrace religion, that he occasionally misquoted sources, and that he sometimes failed to note that his quoted documents were contradictory. None the less, Eusebius realized that the writing of history is dependent upon the reading and discriminating study of the documents of the past. Considering the number of spurious documents he chose not to utilize, one must judge Eusebius an outstanding source critic for his age.

Eusebius wrote his works in the glow of Christianity's newly acquired status. In the glare of the conflagration kindled by the barbarian invasion of the Roman empire, Augustine (354–430 CE), the converted ex-teacher of rhetoric, sought to gather the whole of human history into a theological–eschatological framework. Christianity, like the empire, found itself on the defensive in the days of Augustine and he launched a counter-offensive against paganism's attempts to lay the blame for the empire's troubles on the steps of the church. For the later Augustine, any attempt to present the Roman empire in messianic terms would have constituted a heresy of the first order.

Augustine took the six-day scheme of creation and transposed these into a sixfold periodization of sacred history, the history of *De civitate dei* versus *De civitate terrena*: Just as there were six days of creation, so there were six ages of history: the first from Adam to the flood, the second from the flood to Abraham, the next three (as outlined in St Matthew's gospel) from Abraham to David, from David to the Babylonian captivity, and from the Babylonian captivity to the birth of Christ. Then came the sixth age, in which the human mind was recreated in the image of God, just as on the sixth day of creation man was created in the image of God. In this age men now lived (*De civitate dei*, XXII 30). The time from Adam to Noah constituted the first day and saw the light of a promised redeemer given to the fallen parents of the human race. The second day – the period of childhood – extended from Noah to Abraham with the ark as the symbol of the promise of salvation. From Abraham to David was the third day of youthful adolescence, and, as God has separated the waters on the third day, so he in this age separated the chosen people from the heathen masses. From David to the exile was the day of early manhood. The period of full manhood – the fifth day – extended from the scattering of the chosen people until the coming of the Messiah. The period of old age – the sixth day – was the age of Christian salvation with its new Adam (Jesus) and its new Eve (the church). The seventh day, corresponding to the divine sabbath, would dawn with the return of Christ in glory to establish a peace that would know no end. Augustine thus placed his own time within the waning period of the sixth day. That day had dawned with John the Baptist, with Christ's incarnation the sun had risen, and with the spread of Christianity noonday had arrived. The sun had now begun its descent and senility set in but Augustine warned against precise speculation on the arrival of sunset.

In Augustine's schematization, a number of factors are of significance. (1) He is not so much concerned with history as with the philosophy of history. (2) It is sacred history, the history of *De civitate dei* that is important, not the outer events or occurrences nor human actions and causality. (3) The past of mankind and of Israel and Judah are of importance only as the prelude to the age of redemption which itself is only a prelude to that final timeless period of total salvation and damnation. (4) Augustine's vision embodies a penultimate pessimism about his own day which was the age of senility, the time before the end. (5) Augustine sought 'to direct man's gaze from the contemplation of himself and the achievements of his reason upwards to the majesty of God' (Milburn, 85).

In *The City of God*, Augustine had attempted to prove that the calamities which had befallen the Romans were not limited to the period of the church and, whenever they had occurred, were the result of the corruption of manners and the vices of the soul. The expansion of this thesis he bequeathed to his contemporary and admirer, Orosius. The latter's *Historiarum adversus paganos libri septem*, completed in 418 CE, was an attempt 'to trace the beginning and man's wretchedness from the beginning of man's sin' (I 1). Orosius prefaced his main discussion with a description of Asia, Europe, and Africa, thus manifesting a recognition of the importance of geography for history (as had Caesar, Cicero, and Sallust). Orosius' work is important for subsequent historiography not because he 'set forth . . . the desires and punishments of sinful men, the struggles of the world and the judgments of God, from the beginning of the world down to the present day, that is, during five thousand six hundred and eighteen years' (VII 43) but because of his particular periodization of world history. According to Orosius, there had existed four world empires – Babylon, Macedon, Carthage, and Rome. His thesis is no doubt based on a particular interpretation of the four empires in Daniel (Babylonian, Persian, Median, and Greek) which identified the fourth empire with Rome. However, Orosius took a far more favourable attitude towards the Roman empire than his idol Augustine. For him, the iron teeth and claws of the fourth beast were a deterrent to the barbarians and the antichrist.

Before summarizing the early church's historiographic legacy to the Middle Ages, three additional factors should be noted. In the first place, the theory of the plenary inspiration of scripture had become widespread by the fifth century CE. Such a view of the origin and nature of the Bible stifles any drastic critical approach to the biblical materials. Since the Bible was and remains the basic source material for the history of Israel and Judah, such a position almost by necessity means that the historian retells, expands, elucidates, and harmonizes the biblical source material but does not deal with it critically. Secondly, the hermeneutical principles widely employed in the church allowed the interpreter to find several meanings in any given text: the historical and various mystical, analogical, figurative, and allegorical senses. This multiple layer method of interpretation was indebted not only to Greek allegorical treatments of epic and mythical materials and to rabbinic exegesis but also to the philosophical–allegorical interpretation of Aristobulus and Philo of Alexandria (see Grant). The allegorical approach to biblical interpretation meant that interpreters did not have to confront directly the problems and difficulties within the biblical text. When in doubt, appeal could be made to the rule of faith and the established tradition: *Quod ubique, quod semper, quod ab omnibus creditum est.*

Thirdly, hagiography, the writing of accounts of the lives and sufferings of saints, had become widespread in the fourth and fifth centuries, perhaps influenced to a degree by the Hellenistic conception of the divine man. Athanasius' *Life of St Anthony* and Sulpicius Severus' *Life of St Martin of Tours* are good examples. These hagiographies were eulogistic and rhetorical biographies which offered a sort of dateless and timeless semi-historical work. They actually functioned to draw men away from the matter-of-fact world and pointed to that transcendental realm which impinged upon historical reality. Eusebeius, in his life of Constantine, demonstrated how difficult it was to write a Christian biography of a person involved in affairs military, political, and economic. Hagiography was concerned with different matters. Yet hagiography was to be standard fare in medieval times and in its own way an impediment to the development of serious historiography.

What the early church transmitted to the Middle Ages did not encourage the development of serious historiography. No developed Christian historiography comparable to the work of Herodotus, Thucydides, or even Livy, Tacitus, and Josephus, was passed on unless Eusebius' *Ecclesiastical History* be the exception. Augustine, Orosius, and their contemporaries had not dialogued with the secular historians of the pagan revival in the late fourth and early fifth centuries, such as Ammianus Marcellinus. These were left 'to die from natural causes' (Momigliano, 1963, 99). The works of the Greek and Hellenistic historians belonged to the pagan past and in the West could quickly sink into a long dormant eclipse. Source and textual criticism were suffocated by the weight of a totally inspired collection of scriptures and allegorical interpretation was at hand to provide any needed escape valve. Concern with the transcendental, with the sacred side of the historical process, with the philosophical–eschatological dimensions oriented man towards the other world and away from the questions of human causality and action.

§2. THE MEDIEVAL PERIOD

S. W. **Baron**, *History and Jewish Historians*, Philadelphia: Jewish Publication Society of America 1964; A. D. von den **Brincken**, *Studien zur lateinischen Weltchronistik bis in das Zeitalter Otto von Freisings*, Düsseldorf: M. Triltsch 1957; C. **Brooke**, *The Twelfth Century Renaissance*, London: Thames and Hudson 1969; H. **Farmer**, 'William of Malmesbury's Life and Works', *JEH* XIII, 1962, 39–54; D. **Flusser**, 'Josippon', *EJ* X, 1971, 296–8; E. B. **Fryde**, 'Historiography and Historical Methodology', *EnBr* VII, 1974, 945–61; D. **Knowles**, *The Evolution of Medieval Thought*, London: Longmans, Green and Co. 1962; idem, *The Historian and Character and Other Essays*, London: Cambridge University Press 1963; U. **Köpf**, *Die Anfänge der theologischen Wissenschaftstheorie im 13. Jahrhundert*, BHT 49, 1974; B. M. **Lacroix**, 'The Notion of History in Early Medieval Historians', *MS* X, 1948, 219–23; idem, *L'Historien au moyen age*, Montréal/Paris: Institut d'études médiévales, 1971; A. **Luneau**, *L'historie du salut chez les Pères de l'Eglise. La doctrine des âges du monde*, TH 2, 1964; R. A. **Markus**, *Saeculum: History and Society in the Theology of St Augustine*, London: Cambridge University Press 1970; M. A. **Meyer**, *Ideas of Jewish History*, New York: Behrman House 1974; C. **Morris**, *The Discovery of the Individual, 1050–1200*, London: SPCK 1972; M. E. **Reeves**, *The Influence of Prophecy in the Later Middle Ages*, London: Oxford University Press 1969; F. **Rosenthal**, *A History of Muslim Historiography*, Leiden: E. J. Brill 1952, ²1968; R. **Schmidt**, 'Aetates Mundi. Die Weltalter als Gliederungsprinzip der Geschichte', *ZKG* LXVII, 1955/6, 288–317; B. **Smalley**, *The Study of the Bible in the Middle Ages*, Oxford: Basil Blackwell 1952; idem, *Historians in the Middle Ages*, London: Thames and Hudson 1974; R. W. **Southern**, 'Aspects of the European Tradition of Historical Writing: 1. The Classical Tradition from Einhard to Geoffrey of Monmouth', *TRHS*, fifth series, XX, 1970, 173–96; '2. Hugh of St Victor and the Idea of Historical Development', XXI, 1971, 159–79; '3. History as Prophecy', XXII, 1972, 159–80; '4. The Sense of the Past', XXIII, 1973, 243–63.

Three major types of historical tradition during the medieval period have been distinguished by Southern: classical, early scientific, and prophetic.

The aim of the classical imitators was to exemplify virtues and vices for moral instruction, and to extract from the confusion of the past a clear picture of the destinies of peoples. The aim of the scientific students of universal history was to exhibit the divine plan for mankind throughout history, and to demonstrate the congruity between the facts of history revealed in the Bible and the facts provided by secular sources. As for the prophetic historians, their aim was first to identify the historical landmarks referred to in prophetic utterances, then to discover the point at which

history had arrived, and finally to predict the future from the still
unfulfilled portions of prophecy (1973, 242).

Much of medieval historiography can be analysed in these
categories.
A characteristic of practically all historical works during the
Middle Ages is what has been called 'history without historical perspective' (Smalley, 1974, 50).

The student of medieval historiography must learn to do without perspective in historical presentation. A medieval writer could distinguish
stages in the history of salvation, but they were religious stages. He did not
discern change or development in temporal history. He saw continuity in
customs and institutions. . . . Roman emperors are made to talk and behave
like medieval rulers. Alternatively, a writer learned in the Latin classics
tended to make medieval rulers talk and behave like the Caesars. The
historian did not only look back to the Old and New Testaments for parallels and precedents; he lived in an expanding Bible. The writer of a saint's
Life felt that he was adding a new page to the Gospel story; the recorder of
a warrior's deeds was continuing the tale of ancient and Old Testament
heroes. Past and present interlock: ancient precedents imposed themselves
on the present; the past resembled the present as the historian saw it. He
had no sense of anachronism (Smalley, 1974, 63).

This lack of any sense of the past as past is vividly reflected in
medieval art which portrayed ancient kings, prophets, and saints in
the dress, armament, and physical setting of medieval times.
Before examining some of the historical works of this period
related to the history of the study of Israelite and Judaean history
and to historiography in general, some particular comments should
be made. First of all, distinction must be made between the
European West and the Byzantine East. In the West, Greek literature fell into temporary oblivion; in addition to the basic patristic
literature, the primary classical sources used and imitated were
Roman. The most widely used of Roman writers were Suetonius,
Sallust, Cicero, Virgil, Ovid, and Livy. This meant, of course, a
strong emphasis on rhetoric to which history was a sub-genre. In the
East, the Byzantine scholars were heirs to the classical Greek traditions, Hellenistic historiography, and early Christian historical writings due to the survival of the Greek language. In the East, however,
the writings of Polybius and Plutarch had a significant impact which
influenced historical writing towards contemporary history and biography. In the West, the lower level of literacy prejudiced much
historiography towards the miraculous and mythical. The rise of

territorial states in the West produced a desire to relate 'national' and contemporary history to the general sweep of sacred history.

Secondly, medieval historical works as a rule dealt with pedestrian matters such as city and monastic records and annals, with propagandistic concerns as in the case of royal biographies, or with pietistic orientations exemplified in the lives of saints and other writings of a hagiographic character as well as in the devotional use made of the biblical traditions. Most of these works contribute little or nothing to either the development of historiographic methodology or to the study of Israelite and Judaean history.

Thirdly, the medieval period was no cultural and educational monolith. The concept of the Middle Ages as a barbarian period of constant decline is a legacy from Renaissance historiography. Two periods, the Carolingian in the late eighth and early ninth centuries, and the twelfth century have rightly been described as periods of true renaissance.

In the early medieval period, four historians are pre-eminent: Gregory of Tours (about 540–94), Isidore of Seville (about 560–636), the Venerable Bede (about 673–735), and Paul the Deacon (about 720–800). Each of these produced histories which, to a lesser or greater degree, filled out the shadowy past of their people by drawing up a historical pedigree which traced its origins to some great but misty figure or people of the past. (Virgil had done this for the Romans in his account of Aeneas and the Trojans who settled in Latium and Jordanes, who died about 554, had traced the Goths back to the biblical Magog and the Scythians in his rewriting of Cassiodorius' *De Origine Actibusque Getarum*.) Of these, Isidore and Bede are of interest for the history of the biblical period.

In his *Chronica Majora*, Isidore borrowed from several earlier Christian chronographers and produced a chronology extending from creation to 615 CE. In his universal scheme, Isidore devised the practice of dating everything backward and forward from the birth of Jesus. In his *Etymologiae*, an encyclopaedia summarizing the known information on topics as diverse as grammar, mathematics, and medicine, Isidore discussed the topic of history writing.

Predictably, history is seen as a subsection of grammar, which itself is part of rhetoric. Grammar Isidore defines as 'the art of writing', and history as 'a written narrative of a certain kind'. He distinguishes history from fable and myth: fable expresses truth by means of fiction . . . while poetic myth expresses truth by means of fictions about the gods. . . . History differs from these kinds of narrative in being true in itself. It is 'the narration of deeds done, by means of which the past is made known' (Smalley, 1974, 22).

Isidore went on to argue that history must depend upon the account of eyewitnesses. He writes: 'None of the ancients would write
history unless he had been present and had seen what he narrated;
we grasp what we see better than what we gather from hearsay.
Things seen are not represented falsely' (quoted, ibid., 24). A historian writing about the past is thus basically forced to be a compiler
dependent upon his sources which hopefully are or rely upon
eyewitness accounts.

By all standards, Bede was the most outstanding historian of the
early Middle Ages. In his *Ecclesiastical History of the English People*
(*Historia ecclesiastica gentis Anglorum*), he adopted a Eusebian approach to church history, listing and quoting from his sources 'in
order to remove all occasions of doubt about those things I have
written, either in your mind or in the minds of any others who listen
to or read this history', as he wrote in his dedication to King
Ceolwulf of Northumbria. In his treatment of the biblical period,
Bede stood within what Southern has called the scientific tradition of
medieval historiography (1971, 161). Bede adopted the six-age
scheme of Augustine (on this scheme, see Schmidt and Luneau) and
popularized Isidore's BC–AD dating. Within the six-age pattern, Bede
incorporated a genuine concept of autonomous development in history. Southern has described Bede's originality in the following manner:

Just as the first Day began with the separation of light from darkness, and
ended with the fall of Night, so the first Age began with the creation of
man, continued with the separation of the good from the bad, and ended
with the destruction of the universal Flood. Bede applied this form of
exegesis to each of the six ages. As a result, each age acquired a distinct
momentum, similar in pattern but distinct in its results: at the beginning of
each there was an act of restoration, succeeded by a period of divergent
development, leading to a general disaster which set the scene for a new act
of restoration. I think that Bede is quite original in giving to each Age this
rhythm of dawn, growth, and destruction, containing the promise of a new
dawn. It is a rhythm which has some faint similarity to the Hegelian
dialectic of history, and this similarity is strengthened by the way in which
Bede ties his ages of history together in a movement analogous to the seven
ages in the life of man. The first age, Infancy, is the time beyond the reach
of memory before the Flood; the second, Childhood, is the time before
Abraham when human language was first formed; the third, Adolescence,
is the time of potency, when the generation of the Patriarchs began; the
fourth, Maturity, is the time when mankind became capable of kingly rule;
the fifth, Old Age, is the time of growing afflictions; the sixth, Senility, is
the time in which the human race moves into the decrepitude which

precedes the age of eternal rest. . . . Bede brought history to the point at which it could be looked on not only as a succession of distinct ages with a development of their own, but also as a kind of biological process preceding from age to age (ibid., 162f.).

Although Southern has here probably overstated the originality of Bede (see Markus, 17–28, where Augustine's scheme is discussed in both creation-week and biological terms), this medieval historian certainly grasped something of the developmental process in human affairs and pondered deeply over the shape of universal history. However, in most of his works, Bede manifests the medieval fascination with the miraculous and the visionary, but it must be remembered that he, especially in the ecclesiastical history, was writing for the edification of his audience and was stressing the role of divine providence in Anglo-Saxon conversion to Christianity.

In the Carolingian period, under the Frankish rulers Charlemagne (768–814) and his son Louis the Pious (814–40), significant intellectual and educational developments occurred. Royal prescription decreed that monasteries and bishops' houses should be centres of education. At Charlemagne's palace school, the seven liberal arts – the Trivium (grammar, rhetoric, and dialectic) and the Quadrivium (music, arithmetic, geometry, and astronomy) – were cultivated. Latin was restored to the position of a literary language, and there was a revival of interest in classical texts, both Christian and pagan. The works of Sallust and Suetonius were especially influential. Einhard drew upon Suetonius' *Lives of the Caesars* for his life of Charlemagne and thus chose to imitate a style that differed radically from general medieval hagiography and biography and allowed for a rather secular and critical interpretation. Einhard's treatment of Charlemagne gave impetus to numerous royal biographies, but biography as a form became an instrument of the church and rulers tended to be treated from clerical perspectives. Thus they hardly advanced the general cause of historiography. The classical eulogy and the Christian tradition of saints' *Lives* combined to reduce the amount of factual information required in biography.

The Suetonian model permitted more precision, but it proved to be too bare for medieval taste. The rhetorical tradition defeated it. We cannot expect to find objectivity either; biographers wanted to praise or excuse. Their saving grace is that they remember the traditional advice to the historian to tell the truth and to report events as an eyewitness wherever possible. . . . Sudden flashes of realism light up their most conventional stories. If we judge them as propagandists, we have to admire their ingenuity. All do their best for rulers who fell short of what was expected of a Christian hero' (Smalley, 1974, 78).

Historians who quoted and imitated Sallust's *Catiline Conspiracy* and *Jugurthan War* failed to make use of a significant factor in his works: 'there is no sign of any interest in Sallust's theory of historical causation ... none of them so much as noticed that he had an overall theory of the development and decline of political societies' (Southern, 1970, 179f.).

The Carolingian revival of learning was oriented towards preparation for Bible study. During the reign of Charlemagne, several attempts were made to revise the Latin text of the Bible (see Loewe, in *CHB* II 133–40). The most important was that of Alcuin, presented to the king at his coronation as emperor on Christmas Day, 800. Alcuin was certainly familiar with the Greek text and used this occasionally to correct the Latin. Some evidence exists to suggest that at least some Christian scholars were acquainted with Jewish interpretations of the Old Testament – with their emphasis on a literal reading of the text – if not with Hebrew itself (see Smalley, 1952, 37–46). During this period 'there begins a veneration for the Fathers that invests their views on the meaning of Scripture with dogmatic authority' (Loewe, *CHB* II, 140). Commentaries produced by piecing together excerpts from the fathers were common in the ninth century. Such commentaries not only served the devotion of the faithful but also brought to attention 'the inconsistencies and gaps in the patristic tradition' (Smalley, 1952, 38). Differences among the patristic authorities meant that attempts had to be made at reconciliation or harmonization or as in the case of Paschasius and John the Scot – who was familiar with Greek theology – one might be led to compare, criticize, and even discuss the differences and the meaning of the text.

The primary concern of historians during the Carolingian period was contemporary history. Royal historiography possessed a commanding subject in Charlemagne and his family. During the period, 'a new form of historical writing is evolved in the *Annales*, which develop gradually from entries in a liturgical calendar to an increasingly fuller narration' (Lacroix, 1948, 222) but this too was oriented towards contemporary events. Nothing comparable to the works of Augustine, Orosius, or Bede were produced during this time.

What might be called national history continued as a major concern of the post-Carolingian period as it had been in the early medieval period. 'The lesson that destiny of nations is the noblest of all historical themes' (Southern, 1970, 188) was not lost. Most of these works were similar in intent to the earlier histories of Jordanes, Gregory of Tours, Bede, and Paul the Deacon. 'A whole series of

attempts was made to apply to other races the theme in Virgil's
Aeneid of a noble group of people guided by the gods towards a
splendid destiny' (Fryde, 949). Widukind produced his work on
Saxon history, Dudo wrote about the Normans, and Richer about
the Franks. This form of writing reached its apogee in the romantic
and fantastic *Historia regum Britanniae* by Geoffrey of Monmouth
(about 1100–54). He attempted to establish for the Celts a more
illustrious and detailed past and a more glorious and consequential
destiny than was the case of any other national historian. Trojan
origins, visions and heavenly visitations, and Arthur and his Knights
of the Round Table are described in imaginary and graphic contours.

Although some, even contemporary, readers were not deceived by the
work, and William of Newburgh, one of the best English historians of the
12th century, denounced it as a tissue of absurdities, many seriously accepted it as history (Fryde, 949).

Scholars are accustomed to speak of the late eleventh and twelfth
centuries as a proto-Renaissance, as a time of great progress in learning and culture. Knowles has summarized the humanism of this
period by outlining its three dominant characteristics: 'first, a wide
literary culture', which demonstrated itself in a 'capability of self-
expression based on a sound training in grammar and a long and
often loving study of the foremost Latin authors'; 'next, a great and
what in the realm of religious sentiment could be called a personal
devotion to certain figures of the ancient world; and, finally, a high
value set upon the individual, personal emotions, and upon the
sharing of experiences and opinions within a small circle of friends'
(Knowles, 1963, 19f.). During this period, the universities at Paris,
Bologna, and Oxford were founded. The Crusades to recover the
holy land from the Seljukian Turks reached their culmination in the
establishment of the Latin kingdom of Jerusalem. Contacts between
the East and West, in spite of the church split in 1054, produced
cross-fertilization between Byzantium and Latin Europe. Aristotelian logic and philosophy, partially through the mediation of the
Arabs, began to dominate Western thought through translations and
the greater availability of his works.

The introduction of the whole canon of Aristotle to the West was a
process continuing over a hundred years. The first wave, that of the logical
works, was absorbed easily and avidly. . . . The second wave, that of the
difficult and profound philosophical works, gave more trouble and was less
easily absorbed, though its effects were epoch-making. Finally, the ethical

and political and literary treatises presented Europe with a philosopher who regarded human life from a purely naturalistic, this-world point of view ... the atmosphere, the presuppositions of this great body of thought were not medieval and Christian, but ancient Greek, not to say rationalistic in character (Knowles, 1962, 193).

Aristotelian thought made possible the birth of 'theology' in the systematic and scholastic sense that was to dominate religious studies in the thirteenth to fifteenth centuries (see Köpf).

Aristotle's thought, it should be recalled, did not encourage historiographic studies. For Aristotle, history was too chaotic:

The historian has to expound not one action, but one period of time and all that happens within this period to one or more persons however disconnected the several events may be (*Poetics*, 1459a).

History also lacked the element of universality:

The historian describes the thing that has been; the poet the kind of thing that might be. Hence poetry is more important and philosophic than history, for its statements have universal validity, while those of the historian are valid only for one time and one place (*Poetics*, 1451b).

The urge to systematization is basically anti-historical in perspective.

This period of the proto-Renaissance, in its earliest phase, also witnessed some significant developments in historiography. In England, after the Norman Conquest of 1066, radical changes characterized society and the old cultural systems were challenged. In response to the threat of change, English monastics saw themselves as the custodians of the past and to preserve that past monasteries became the centres of antiquarian concerns (see Southern, 1973). Monastic charters were collected, documents transcribed, historical and annalistic texts assembled, buildings and inscriptions studied, and the remains of saints gathered.

The post-Conquest monks were sure that they had a great past, but they were uncertain of their present and future. ... The monastic antiquaries searched the records to give detail and lucidity to their inherited conviction of greatness ... (Southern, 1973, 262).

William of Malmesbury (about 1080–1143), in his ecclesiastical and secular histories of England, demonstrated how such antiquarian material could be used to reconstruct a realistic view of the past. No parallel to such antiquarianism exists before the sixteenth and seventeenth centuries, but the latter was to lack both the passion and purpose of the former.

At least two major theologians and canonists of the twelfth century worked with a concept of development and change in history (see Southern, 1971). These were Hugh of St Victor (about 1096–1141), and Otto of Freising (about 1115–58). Hugh was not strictly a historian, although he wrote a chronicle of world history for use as a student's handbook in which he stressed the importance of time, place, people, and events for the understanding of history. In his theological works, a dynamic view of history pervades his discussions. His arguments rest on the presupposition that man moved in history from the primitive and simple to the more sophisticated and developed. He sought to outline the various stages, for example, in the history of the sacrament of penance showing that its final form was the product of the needs of the early church. Thus doctrine goes through developmental stages and the needs of human institutions play a role. In his description of the world ages, Hugh's thought has a certain evolutionary ring. The first age of man, from the fall to Abraham, was 'the age of natural law when men groped around for remedies for their ills by the light of reason and experience'. Primitive man developed various sacraments, sacrifices, and offerings to present to their gods. The second age, which began embryonically with Abraham and fully with Moses, was 'the age of written law when God intervened actively in human history' and provided mankind with the means of education and sacramental union. In the third age, which began with Christ, grace replaced law and the inspirations of the spirit supplanted the commandments (see Southern, 1971, 166f.). In these ages, man co-operated with God in a forward movement towards higher forms of human existence. Hugh, in his writings on the liberal arts, argued again for stages in human development from the primitive to the advanced. He declared:

Men wrote and talked before there was grammar; they distinguished truth from falsehood before there was dialectic; they had laws before there was rhetoric; they had numbers before there was arithmetic; they sang before there was music; they measured fields before there was geometry; they observed the stars and seasons before there was astronomy (quoted in Southern, 1971, 171).

In technology, it was the operation of human reason which functioned to meet the needs of man. Physical necessity prompted man towards achievement. 'There arose the theoretical sciences to illuminate ignorance, ethics to strengthen virtue, and the mechanical arts to temper man's infirmity' (quoted in Southern, 1971, 170).

Hugh's sense of historical development in all categories of life presented a rather optimistic view of the historical process, a view in which novelty was not only accepted but also declared good.

Otto, the bishop of Freising in Bavaria and a member of the imperial family, produced a universal history from creation to his own day relying on the schemes of six ages and four world monarchies. The work is basically Orosian in orientation. In a number of ways, Otto differed from or extended the thought of Augustine and Orosius. He identified the city of God with the church and in Henry IV's submission to Pope Gregory VII at Canossa in 1077 he saw the triumph of the 'heavenly' over the 'earthly' city. Although Otto shared the Orosian view of the decline of human rule, he was none the less able to affirm, especially in his work on Frederick I, that history was not a tragedy and that empire could be an instrument of peace. Otto gave detailed treatment to the so-called 'transfer thesis', the idea that civilization and empire moved from East to West. The idea was implicit already in Eusebius and perhaps already used at the Frankish court before Otto. He, however, worked out analogies between the ancient empires and those in Europe. The empire of his day was understood as the continuation of the fourth empire – the Roman – which had simply moved westward. Otto applied the transfer theory not only to political power but to religion and education as well: 'Note well that all human power and knowledge began in the East and end in the West, so that in this way the variability and weaknesses of all things may be made clear' (quoted in Southern, 1971, 177).

The Middle Ages witnessed the blossoming of what might be called 'prophetic or apocalyptic' historiography. The six-age scheme and the four monarchies theory of world history were, of course, derived from biblical texts which were either taken as prefigurations or as predictions. Biblical commentators had solved to their own and their contemporaries' satisfaction most of the assumed predictions in the biblical texts. However, numerous attempts were made to define more closely some of the loose ends, especially the interpretation of Daniel 7, Revelation 6 and the appearance of the antichrist. The general ambiguity of apocalyptic texts tends to allow for their constant reinterpretation by those disposed to see themselves living in the last days and to see their enemies as the antichrists. The ambiguity of the biblical texts had even been heightened in some cases by patristic exegesis. Jerome, for example, had suggested that the ten horns in Daniel 7 might refer to the ten kings who would be the instruments of the Roman empire's destruction and would be followed by the antichrist. If the Bible were the inspired truth, then these prophecies must have some concrete historical referent, or so reasoned medieval lovers of prophecy.

In addition to biblical prophecies, various other elements contributed to medieval prophetical historiographic interests: numerous Sibylline documents, developing astrological investigations stimulated by Islamic science and the introduction of the astrolabe and the improved ability to calculate astronomical phenomena, and the prophecies of such figures as Merlin and Hildegard of Bingen (see Reeves and Southern, 1972). The most famous apocalyptic historian of the time was Joachim of Fiore (about 1132–1202) whose fame and thought endured long after his passing. Joachim advanced a trinitarian conception of history. The time of ancient Israel and Judah was the age of God the Father, the second age of God the Son began with Jesus, and the age of the Holy Spirit was soon to dawn. The world of the new age was to be the time of the monks and was to be inaugurated by the appearance of a new Elijah and twelve holy men. (Many saw in the mendicant friars of the following decades a fulfilment of his prophecies.) The antichrist was to appear for the first time before the dawn of the final age and the reign of the Spirit. Needless to say, many were later seen as the embodiment of the antichrist; the most frequent candidate being the Muslims, a view already expounded by ninth-century Spanish theologians. The views of 'Joachimism' and prophetic historiography scarcely advanced the cause of Israelite and Judaean historiography. They did, however, tend to dispose men towards the future and hope and for several generations occupied the thoughts of many, not the least of whom was Sir Isaac Newton.

Before leaving this section, a few comments should be made about Jewish historiography in the Middle Ages. The surprising factor is that nothing comparable to Christian and Muslim historiography existed in Judaism during this period (for the latter, which had no influence on Western historiography, see Rosenthal). The primary concerns of medieval Judaism centred upon either halakhic or philosophical–ethical matters. When they appear, historical matters in the Talmud are anecdotal. When the Jewish authorities 'discussed the past, particular incidents, rather than its totality, caught their attention' (Meyer, 71). It is possible to take the various writings of a Jewish scholar like Maimonides (1135–1204) and distil from these his comments on and interpretations of various historical events reported in the Bible (see Baron, 109–63). These are basically retelling, with commentary, of the biblical narratives supplemented by haggadah and chronological notations. From these it is possible to reconstruct Maimonides' historical world-view, but this is hardly historiography.

One special work deserves mention. This is the Hebrew writing called *Josippon*, so named because of its association with Josephus. Written in southern Italy in the mid-tenth century, *Josippon* begins with the table of nations in Genesis 10, contains a discussion of the founding of Rome, and provides a history of the Jews, primarily of the second temple period down to the fall of Masada. The unknown author made use of the Latin version of most of the books in Josephus' *Antiquities* and a Latin adaptation of Josephus' *War*. The book was widely used in the Middle Ages, was even translated into Arabic in the eleventh, and apparently was supplemented in the twelfth century (on Josippon, see Flusser).

§3.   FROM THE RENAISSANCE TO THE ENLIGHTENMENT

D. C. **Allen**, *The Legend of Noah: Renaissance Rationalism in Art, Science, and Letters*, ISLL 33/3–4, 1949, ²1963; K. W. **Appelgate**, *Voltaire on Religion: Selected Writings*, New York: Frederick Ungar 1974; K. **Barth**, *Die Protestantische Theologie im 19. Jahrhundert*, Zollikon/Zürich: Evangelischer Verlag 1947 = *Protestant Theology in the Nineteenth Century: Its Background and History*, London/Valley Forge: SCM Press/Judson Press 1972; I. **Berlin**, 'Herder and the Enlightenment', *Aspects of the Eighteenth Century*, ed. E. R. Wasserman, Baltimore: Johns Hopkins Press 1965, 47–104; P. **Burke**, *The Renaissance Sense of the Past*, London: Edward Arnold 1969; H. **Butterfield**, *The Origins of Modern Science 1300–1800*, London/New York: G. Bell & Sons/Macmillan 1949, ²1957; G. R. **Cragg**, *Reason and Authority in the Eighteenth Century*, London: Cambridge University Press 1964; L. **Diestel**, *Geschichte des Alten Testamentes in der christlichen Kirche*, Jena: Mauke's Verlag 1869; H. W. **Frei**, *The Eclipse of Biblical Narrative: A Study in Eighteenth and Nineteenth Century Hermeneutics*, New Haven: Yale University Press 1974; E. B. **Fryde**, 'Historiography and Historical Methodology', *EnBr* VIII, 1974, 945–61; P. **Gay**, *Deism: An Anthology*, Princeton: Van Nostrand 1968; E. **Grant**, 'Late Medieval Thought, Copernicus, and the Scientific Revolution', *JHI* XXIII, 1962, 197–220; E. M. **Gray**, *Old Testament Criticism: Its Rise and Progress from the Second Century to the End of the Eighteenth*, New York: Harper & Brothers 1923; C. **Hartlich** and W. **Sachs**, *Der Ursprung des Mythosbegriffes in der modernen Bibelwissenschaft*, SSEA 2, 1952; P. **Hazard**, *La Crise de la Conscience Européene*, Paris: Boivin 1935 = *The European Mind (1680–1715)*, London: Hollis & Carter 1953; J. M. **Headley**, *Luther's View of Church History*, New Haven: Yale University Press 1963; R. **Hooykaas**, 'Science and Reformation', *CHM* III/I, 1956, 109–39; G.

Hornig, *Die Anfänge der historisch-kritischen Theologie. Johann Salomo Semlers Schriftverständnis und seine Stellung zu Luther*, FSTRP 8, 1961; D. R. **Kelley**, *Foundations of Modern Historical Scholarship: Language, Law, and History in the French Renaissance*, New York: Columbia University 1970; D. A. **Knight**, *Rediscovering the Traditions of Israel*, SBLDS 9, 1973, ²1975; H.-J. **Kraus**, *Geschichte der historisch-kritischen Erforschung des Alten Testaments*, Neukirchen-Vluyn: Neukirchener Verlag 1956, ²1969; W. G. **Kümmel**, *Das Neue Testament: Geschichte der Erforschung seiner Probleme*, Freiburg: K. Alber 1958 = *The New Testament: The History of the Investigation of its Problems*, Nashville/London: Abingdon Press/SCM Press 1972/3; S. F. **Mason**, 'The Scientific Revolution and the Protestant Reformation', *AnSc* VIII, 1952, 64–87, 154–75; D. R. **McKee**, 'Isaac de la Peyrère, A Precursor of Eighteenth-Century Critical Deists', *PMLA* LIX, 1944, 456–85; A. **Momigliano**, 'Ancient History and the Antiquarian', *JWCI* XII, 1950, 285–315 = his *Studies in Historiography*, London: Weidenfeld and Nicolson 1966, 1–39; C. K. **Pullapilly**, *Caesar Baronius: Counter-Reformation Historian*, Notre Dame: University of Notre Dame Press 1975; A. **Rabil**, *Erasmus and the New Testament: The Mind of a Christian Humanist*, TUMSR 1, 1972; H. **Reventlow**, 'Die Auffassung vom Alten Testament bei Hermann Samuel Reimarus und Gotthold Ephraim Lessing', *EvTh* XXV, 1965, 429–48; B. R. **Reynolds**, 'Latin Historiography: A Survey 1400–1600', *SR* II, 1955, 7–66; J. W. **Rogerson**, *Myth in Old Testament Interpretation*, BZAW 134, 1974; K. **Scholder**, 'Herder und die Anfänge der historischen Theologie', *EvTh* XXII, 1962, 425–40; idem, *Ursprünge und Probleme die Bibelkritik im 17. Jahrhundert. Ein Beitrag zur Entstehung der historisch-kritischen Theologie*, FGLP X/33, 1966; L. **Stephen**, *History of English Thought in the Eighteenth Century* I–II, London/New York: Smith, Elder & Co./G. P. Putnam's Sons 1876, ²1881; E. G. **Waring**, *Deism and Natural Religion: A Source Book*, New York: Frederick Ungar 1967; R. **Weiss**, *The Renaissance Discovery of Classical Antiquity*, Oxford: Basil Blackwell 1969; T. **Willi**, *Herders Beitrag zum Verstehen des Alten Testaments*, BGBH 8, 1971.

The foundations of modern historiography were laid in the Renaissance which began in Italy in the fourteenth century and spread northward. The militant humanism of this period certainly had its roots in medievalism, in spite of its scorn for the Middle Ages; but its intellectual and technological accomplishments were revolutionary both in themselves and in their implications. One of the products of the Renaissance was history as an independent discipline. A second result was a critical approach to many of the problems and issues of life. The radical consequences of these two developments for the study of Israelite and Judaean history, however, were not to be developed fully until the nineteenth century.

During the Renaissance, four elements which pervaded much of the intellectual activity were generative of momentous consequences for future historiography. These were a true sense of anachronism, a renewed interest in antiquarianism, a critical stance towards the literary evidence from the past, and the attempt to understand the causation of historical events through reason (see Burke). One must not, of course, assume that a majority of the educated and scholarly figures of the Renaissance period shared these perspectives, any more than one should assume that after the publication of Darwin's *Origin of Species* everyone gave up the idea that God created man in a paradise state.

As was noted earlier, medieval writers as a rule lacked a historical perspective on the past as past, as different in space and time from the contemporary. In the fourteenth century, a historical sensibility began to develop. This appears, for example, in Giotto's fresco painting in the Arena Chapel at Padua (about 1305) which depicts Pontius Pilate clean-shaven, with garlanded head, and wearing a Roman robe embossed with a golden, imperial eagle. He appears as a figure from the past, not as a contemporary. Petrarch (1304–74) was well aware of the differences between his own day and those of his beloved Rome before the conversion of Constantine. So much so, that he described his own times as barbarian and wrote 'nostalgic' letters to the classical authors expressing his longing to escape from the present and to find solace in those happier bygone days of old. Renaissance authors slowly recognized that everything had changed over time – laws, words, clothes, customs, arts, and buildings (see Burke, 39–49). There was, in other words, a historical relativity to all things.

Antiquarianism was a natural accompaniment to the revived interest in the past (see Momigliano and Weiss). In the Renaissance, men like Petrarch were not only interested in ancient literary works but in what would be called archaeological remains. Coins, inscriptions, and ancient ruins were of interest not just as relics from the past but as means to reconstruct the past. Petrarch used coins to discover what Roman emperors looked like and in his epic poem *Africa* drew upon the ruins of Rome, which he had visited, in describing the city at the time of the Carthaginians' visit. In 1446, Flavio Biondo produced a topographical description of Rome dependent upon both the literary sources and his personal visits to the ruined sites. The fact that Renaissance scholars frequently misinterpreted antiquities or distorted their antiquarian knowledge is beside the point, for the issue is not their correctness in detail but their methodological procedure.

The discipline of documentary criticism was a speciality of many

Renaissance scholars. The most outstanding and influential early Renaissance literary critic was Lorenzo Valla (about 1406–57). Petrarch, however, had already (in 1355) used internal and external evidence to prove that a document exempting Austria from the jurisdiction of the Emperor Charles IV was a forgery (see Burke, 50–54). In 1439, Valla disproved the authenticity of the Donation of Constantine in which Constantine had supposedly assigned temporal power over Italy to Pope Sylvester I and his successors. (Otto of Freising and other medieval authors had suspected that the document was a forgery, as did Valla's contemporaries Nicholas of Cusa and Reginald Pecock, independently.)

> The significance of Valla's declamation was neither in applying philological criteria, for Petrarch and others, including canonists, had taken this step, nor in denying the authenticity of the document, which had already been placed in doubt; rather it was in exhibiting the whole array of humanist weapons – polemic and personal vituperation as well as criticism stemming from grammar, logic, geography, chronology, history, and law (Kelley, 38).

Valla and others applied their literary criticism to numerous documents, both classical and Christian, to prove their inauthenticity or to elucidate their origin and history.

In 1460, Nicholas of Cusa wrote the *Sieving of the Koran* (cribratio Alcoran) which treated the Koran as Nicholas had already treated the *Donation.* He identified three elements in its composition: Nestorian Christianity, a Jewish adviser of Muhammad, and the corruptions introduced by Jewish 'correctors' after Muhammad's death. This was to treat the Koran as a historical document, and to write the history of its leading ideas (Burke, 59).

The status of the Bible as the word of God exempted it from such treatment for the moment.

The literary legends about national origins and hagiographic legends about the saints were open to criticism by the humanists. Two examples will suffice. The Italian historian, Polydore Vergil, published a history of England in 1534 in which he took up the older attack on Geoffrey of Monmouth's depiction of the Trojan Brutus as the founder of Britain. His basic argument rested on an appeal to the ancient sources: none of the ancient Roman authors and sources make any reference to this Brutus. (Similar attacks were made on other national and foundational legends; see Burke, 71–5.) In a short biography prefaced to his edition of Jerome's works, Erasmus (in 1516) argued that many of the legendary traditions 'contaminate the saints with their old wives' tales, which are childish, ignorant, and absurd' and that the best source for knowledge about Jerome was the man himself.

For who knew Jerome better than Jerome himself? Who expressed his ideas more faithfully? If Julius Caesar is the most reliable source for the events of his own career, is it not all the more reasonable to trust Jerome on his? And so, having gone through all his works, we made a few annotations and presented the results in the form of a narrative, not concealing the fact that we consider it a great enough miracle to have Jerome himself explaining his life to us in all his famous books. If there is anyone who must have miracles and omens, let him read the books about Jerome which contain almost as many miracles as they do sentences (text in Burke, 70).

The literary study of the early Renaissance humanists was not oriented merely to the detection of forgery and the exposure of many venerated traditions as non-historical legends. There was a very positive side to the focus on documentary evidence. 'The mere problem of gaining access to the past began to supersede the problem of how to make use of it' (Kelley, 24). The humanists stressed that the recovery of the past through documentary sources had to depend upon philology and grammar. This meant a literal and realistic reading of the sources and at times textual criticism to restore the sources. Valla, in his *Annotations on the New Testament* published by Erasmus in 1505, came close to placing the biblical sources on the same footing with other ancient documents. Valla had also concluded that 'none of the words of Christ have come to us, for Christ spoke in Hebrew and never wrote down anything' (quoted in Fryde, 952). Erasmus, who argued for a 'return to the sources' (*versetur in fontibus*), defended Valla's position on the need for textual criticism to restore the sources of theology (see Rabil, 58–61). This meant that the reliability of the Old Testament versions must be established on the basis of Hebrew and the New Testament on the basis of Greek. (Pope Clement V at the Council of Vienne in 1311–12 had called for the training of teachers in three languages – Greek and Hebrew in addition to Latin.) In interpreting the Bible, Erasmus argued that the role of the grammarian was more important than that of theologian.

Nor do I assume that theology, the very queen of all disciplines, will think it beneath her dignity if her handmaiden, grammar, offers her help and the required service. For even if grammar is somewhat lower in dignity than other disciplines, there is no other more necessary. She busies herself with very small questions, without which no one progresses to the large. She argues about trifles which lead to serious matters. If they answer that theology is too important to be limited by grammatical rules and that this whole affair of exegeting depends on the inspiration of the Holy Spirit, then this is indeed a new honor for the theologian that he alone is allowed to speak like a barbarian (quoted in Rabil, 59).

In spite of Erasmus' emphasis on grammar in the understanding of the biblical text, he refused to disavow allegorical interpretation, although he warned that it should not be overdone, should apply everything to Christ, and requires a pious mind (see Rabil, 109–13). Here he shows himself closer kin to Augustine than to Valla.

The trivial concerns of the grammarian or the 'very small questions' grammar asks – to use Erasmus' terminology – were part of a major revolution in thought. The difference between the medieval interpretative gloss on a text and the grammatical analysis of a text is enormous; they belong to two different worlds of thought. The humanists of the Renaissance openly broke with the scholastic method, caustically opposed it, and asserted the superiority of their new methods. Valla declared:

> The discourse of historians exhibits more substance, more practical knowledge, more political wisdom . . . , more customs, and more learning of every sort than the precepts of any philosophers. Thus we show that historians have been superior to philosophers (quoted in Kelley, 19).

The difference between scholasticism and humanism in the Renaissance period has been described in the following terms:

> By proliferating abstractions and superfluous distinctions, scholastic philosophy had lost contact with concrete reality. It had cut men off from meaning, hence from their own humanity. Valla's philosophy, on the other hand, emphasized precisely these standards – concreteness, utility, and humanity. . . . Indeed, a return to reality may be taken as the slogan of Valla's entire philosophy (Kelley, 29).

The quest or return to reality was not only the source of the humanistic or historical revolution of the Renaissance but also the basis for the scientific revolution which has its roots in the same period (see Grant). Science had to overcome the legacy of Aristotelian scholasticism. It is difficult to overstate the importance of the scientific revolution, which reached a climax in the sixteenth and seventeenth centuries, for all aspects of life including biblical studies, although Butterfield seems to have been successful in this regard:

> Since that revolution overturned the authority in science not only of the middle ages but of the ancient world – since it ended not only in the eclipse

of scholastic philosophy but in the destruction of Aristotelian physics – it outshines everything since the rise of Christianity and reduces the Renaissance and Reformation to the rank of mere episodes, mere internal displacements, within the system of medieval Christendom (Butterfield, vii).

Mechanics and astronomy were the first scientific disciplines to develop.

These new approaches to reality were concerned with questions of explanation and causation in both natural and human orders. The way was opened for a view of the world which operated according to 'natural law' even if that law be understood as the will of God. The historical implication of such a view is enormous: man can understand past events as analogous to present events. Human, climatic, geographical, and other factors could be viewed as causal elements in historical events both past and present. This rise of explanation in historical studies marked a significant development in historiography.

In medieval historical writing there are explanations of an extremely specific kind, in terms of the motives of individuals; there are also explanations of an extremely general kind, in terms of the hand of God in history, or the decay of the world; but middle-range explanations are lacking (Burke, 77).

These 'middle-range explanations' – what today we would call sociological, economical, geographical, climatic considerations – have their beginnings in the Renaissance (see the collection of texts in Burke, 77–104).

The Protestant Reformation of the sixteenth century, which in many ways represents merely a radical and religious application of Renaissance principles and aims, made at least four significant contributions that were ultimately of great importance in the history of Hebrew historiography.

First of all, the reformers placed the Bible at the centre of the theological enterprise. *Sola scriptura* was the keynote of the Reformation (see Kraus, 6–9). In emphasizing the Bible as the rule and norm of faith, the reformers stressed a literal interpretation of the scriptures. Luther wrote:

The Holy Spirit is the plainest writer and speaker in heaven and earth, and therefore His words cannot have more than one, and that the very simplest, sense, which we call the literal, ordinary, natural sense.
All heresies and error in Scripture have not arisen out of the simple words of Scripture. . . . All error arises out of paying no regard to the plain words

and, by fabricated inferences and figures of speech, concocting arbitrary interpretations in one's own brain.

In the literal sense there is life, comfort, strength, learning, and art. Other interpretations, however appealing, are the work of fools.

In addition to an emphasis on the literal reading of scripture, the reformers argued that scripture is its own interpreter. Luther declared:

Scripture itself by itself is the most unequivocal, the most accessible, the most comprehensible authority, itself its own interpreter, attesting, judging, illuminating all things.

(For the above texts, see Kümmel, 20–3.) This emphasis upon a literal reading of the scriptures, which had earlier been stressed in Judaism over against a christocentric reading of the Old Testament, did not immediately produce any critical-historical approach to the Bible. Even Luther retained a prophetic-christocentric attitude towards the Old Testament. The idea of the divine inspiration of scripture or the Bible as the word of God halted the reformers short of any really critical approach, although Luther relegated Hebrews, James, Jude, and Revelation to an appendix in his New Testament translation primarily because of theological reasons which he buttressed with an appeal to the dispute over these documents in the early church (see Kümmel, 24–6). Matthias Flacius Illyricus' *Clavis scripturae sacrae* (1567), one of the first handbooks on biblical hermeneutics, is representative of Protestantism's stress on the importance of the literal or grammatical sense, but warns that there are no contradictions in scripture and that exegesis must be in agreement with faith (for excerpts from his work, see Kümmel, 27–30). This emphasis on the literal reading of the biblical materials was ultimately to make literary-critical analysis not only possible but also necessary.

A second contribution of the reformers was an iconoclastic attitude towards tradition. This phenomenon was widely current in many circles during the times as previous examples have shown. The reformers sought to restore the purity of the church and return to the origins; components and traditions which appeared to have intervened extraneously could be repudiated. Such attitudes, however, fostered a sense of criticism although it was much easier to be critical of post-biblical than biblical traditions. An example of a significant critique of an ancient and venerated tradition is represented by Carolus Sigonius who challenged the traditional Jewish view of the origin of the synagogue. An expert on Greek and Roman institutions, Sigonius, in his *De republica Hebraeorum libri VII* (1583), argued as follows regarding the antiquity of the synagogue:

The origin of the synagogue is by no means an old one. We find, indeed, no mention of it [in scripture] either in the history of the Judges or in the history of the Kings. If it is at all admissible to venture a conjecture in this kind of antiquity, I would surmise that synagogues were first erected in the Babylonian exile for the purpose that those who have been deprived of the temple of Jerusalem, where they used to pray and teach, would have a certain place similar to the temple, in which they could assemble and perform the same kind of service (quoted by I. Sonne, *IDB* I 478).

Many concepts, positions, and traditions, however, were taken over uncritically by the reformers. Both Luther and Melanchthon accepted the four monarchies approach to world history. The Frenchman Jean Bodin, in his *Method for the Easy Understanding of Histories* (1566), thus sensed he was breaking new ground when he included an essay on the 'refutation of those who postulate four monarchies and the golden age'.

A third contribution of the Reformation and the Catholic Counter-Reformation can be seen in the fact that the history of the church became a dominant issue in the struggles within the church in the sixteenth and seventeenth centuries. Historiography was a major weapon in both arsenals. Protestants argued that the teachings of Jesus and the faith of the primitive church had become distorted by the hierarchy of the church. (They differed among themselves as to the precise date at which the apostasy occurred.) Catholics sought to prove that the church at the time was the true successor of primitive Christianity and that the church was basically the same as it had always been. Luther and Calvin's writings reflect the general Protestant view of church history (on Luther, see Headley) although Luther wrote in the introduction to Robert Barnes' *Vitae Romanorum pontificum* (1535) that it was a wonderful delight and the greatest joy to see that history, as well as scripture, could be used to attack the papacy. In Eusebian fashion, historians on both sides turned again to the extensive study and employment of documents, to even a greater extent than many humanist historians, who, especially in Italy, were more interested in literary form than documentation, being strongly influenced by the rhetorical tradition (see Reynolds). The greatest monuments to this historical controversy are the thirteen-volume *Historia ecclesiae Christi* (1559–74) produced by the Magdeburg Centuriators, under the leadership of Matthias Flacius, and the twelve-volume rejoinder, *Annales ecclesiastici*, by Caesar Baronius. (On the historical controversy, see Pullapilly, especially 144–77.) As a result of this use of historiography as a battlefield, ecclesiastical history in the sixteenth and seventeenth centuries displayed a greater erudition, a more minute analysis of sources, and a more historiographic sophistication than secular history. Unfortunately none of this energy and insight was applied to the study of Israelite and Judaean history, although the issue established history as an important element in religious controversy.

The fourth significant development which grew out of the Reformation was religious freedom which allowed for enormous theological diversity. The rejection of authoritarianism in tradition, priesthood, and religious practice permitted an increased appeal to private judgment, often, of course, uncompromisingly certain that it reflected the true biblical and Christian point of view. Thus theological positions were capable of absorbing modernity while claiming to be founded upon true antiquity. This permitted significant shifts on the questions of authority and revelation which made biblical criticism not only possible but sometimes desirable. 'The exercise of private judgment permitted the Protestant not so much to avoid as to conclude compromises: he could come to terms with the new ideas around him' (Gay, 1968, 19). Protestantism thus had a built-in flexibility which made accommodation possible.

> It is to Calvin's great credit that he recognized the discrepancy between the scientific world system of his days and the biblical text, and secondly, that he did not repudiate the results of scientific research on that account (Hooykaas, 136).

The Italians, Lelio (1525–62) and Faustus Socinus (1539–1604), with their moderate unitarian theology and their assumption that the veracity of scripture should be subjected to rational judgment, were among the first to formulate a view of religion whose modernity even antagonized the reformers (see Scholder, 1966, 34–55; Kraus, 41–3).

Following the Council of Trent (1545–63), which reaffirmed the Vulgate canon and text of the Bible but recommended the latter's revision, a long debate ensued between Catholics and Protestants and among Protestants themselves over which Old Testament text – Latin, Greek, or Hebrew – was authoritative. Even the inspiration of the Hebrew vowel points became involved (see Diestel, 253 f., 326–8; Allen, 39–65). The attempts to decide such issues led to heated controversy and, though perhaps not widely recognized, to humans sitting in judgment over the text.

The reformers had argued that a person could interpret the scriptures aided by divine light or *fides divina*. Luther, at the Diet of

Worms (1521), had spoken of being 'convinced by the testimony of the scriptures or by clear reason' (text in Kümmel, 20). Gradually the *fides divina* had to give more and more to 'clear reason' and the divine or inward light tended to become 'really the *Lumen naturale* under a mask' (Allen, 45). The seventeenth century witnessed the dethronement of the Bible as the authoritative source of knowledge and understanding and saw biblical interpreters and historians utilizing the products of the *lumen naturale* (see Scholder for seventeenth-century developments and biblical studies).

The heliocentric theory in astronomy, expounded in Copernicus' *De revolutionibus orbium coelestium* and opposed by Luther and Melanchthon, was undergirded by Kepler's mathematical work and Galileo's theory of dynamics and his invention of the telescope. Kepler suggested that science should be used in understanding the Bible and proposed (in 1606) that the Bethlehem star was due to the unusual conjunction of Mars, Saturn, and Jupiter in the sign of Taurus in 6 BCE. The discovery and exploration of new lands brought to attention the existence of peoples beyond the purview of the biblical texts. Travel accounts reported on the life and customs of distant lands. For the first time – in the writings of figures like Pietro della Valle and Michael Nau – reports on monuments, sites, and life in Palestine became known. The scientific revolution possessed its philosophical counterpart in the thought of Francis Bacon and René Descartes. Based on an empirical and critical approach to all knowledge, the new philosophy sought, as Bacon stated, 'a total reconstruction of sciences, arts, and all human knowledge, raised upon proper foundations'. The establishment of history as an independent discipline in the major universities necessitated the self-consciousness of the field as a 'science'. The earliest professors of history were primarily commentators on the writings of ancient historians. The first professor of history at Cambridge University was dismissed in 1627 because his comments on Tacitus were considered politically dangerous. (Hobbes in *Leviathan*, written in 1651, commented: 'As to rebellion in particular against monarchy, one of the most frequent causes of it, is the reading of the books of policy, and histories of the ancient Greeks, and Romans. . . . From the reading, I say, of such books, men have undertaken to kill their kings' [ch. 29].) Historians produced manuals on the art of history writing and the use and criticism of documents. The most important of the latter was Jean Mabillon's *De re diplomatica* (1681). Generally, in the seventeenth century, antiquarian or archaeological and historical concerns were pursued separately. The former was undertaken, with some exceptions, by dilettantes possessed by an abundance of leisure and some interest in the arts and travel. Much energy and money were expended to secure artifacts for the adornment of museums and living rooms. Near the end of the century efforts were made to combine historical and antiquarian interests; some scholars went so far as to claim the superiority of archaeological over literary evidence in reconstructing history (see Momigliano, 14). The seventeenth century was also a time of general questioning of authority, both political and religious, as the Puritan movement and the Cromwellian revolution in England demonstrate.

The impact of the intellectual climate of the seventeenth century upon the study of biblical history can be illustrated through the selection of three examples: the desire to produce a definitive biblical chronology, the attempt to defend a literal interpretation of biblical events through the use of the new sciences, and the growing literary-critical approach to Old Testament documents.

In 1583, Scaliger (1540–1609), the most outstanding philologist of his day, published his *De emendatione temporum*, which provided a synchronized world chronology incorporating Greek, Roman, and Jewish calculations and utilizing recent astronomical discoveries. In 1606, he published his *Thesaurus temporum*, a collection of every chronological relic extant in Greek and Latin. The most influential biblical chronology in the English-speaking world was published in 1650–54 by the Irish bishop James Ussher (1581–1656). In the preface to his *Annales Veteris et Novi Testamenti*, Ussher confidently assured the reader:

If anyone well seen in the knowledge not only of sacred and exotic history, but of astronomical calculation, and the old Hebrew calendar, should apply himself to these studies, I judge it indeed difficult, but not impossible, for such a one to attain, not only the number of years, but even of days from the creation of the world.

Of the date of creation, he wrote:

In the beginning, God created Heaven and Earth, Genesis 1, verse 1, which beginning of time, according to our chronologers, fell upon the entrance of the night preceding the 23rd day of October in the year of the Julian Calendar, 710 ... Marginal note: the year before Christ, 4004 (texts in Burke, 47 f.).

Subsequently, Ussher's chronological calculations were placed in the margin of the King James Version of the scriptures. Chronographers, of course, differed in their calculations, but many of the scientific minds of the seventeenth century sought to establish scientifically the biblical chronological data. Even so great a mathematical mind as that of Isaac Newton, in a work published posthumously in 1733, sought to demonstrate the accuracy of the predictions in Daniel when applied to papal power. He also sought to make biblical chronology agree with the course of nature, astronomy, sacred history, and the classical histories, especially Herodotus.

One of the most debated topics in the seventeenth century was Noah's flood – its historicity, nature, and extent. In a classical study, Allen has shown how all the sciences of the time were drawn upon to expound the flood in a literal sense and to explain it in rational terms. Scholars discussed the chronology of the flood, the size of the ark, the number and names of the animals, the amount of food needed to feed the ark's passengers, and so on. The most vexing problem was, of course, the question of the origin of sufficient water to flood the entire earth to a depth of fifteen cubits. With the discovery of new lands and new animals, living quarters on the ark became more crowded. Even astronomical phenomena, such as comets, were brought into the picture as explanations. A local flood theory developed when reasonable arguments for a universal flood wore thin. Such an enormous superstructure of arguments was developed to support a literal flood until the whole thing was doomed to topple from its own weight. What resulted from such attempts to support the literal historicity of biblical narratives was a 'rational exegesis, a form of pious explanation that innocently damned the text that it expounded'. 'Theologians now required the Bible to conform to the reason of men' (Allen, 65, 89f.).

A third seventeenth-century development was the application of literary and documentary criticism to the Old Testament, especially the pentateuch. Documentary criticism meant that questions about the origin, nature, and historical reliability were to be asked of the biblical materials. Earlier scholars, such as Isaac ben Suleiman in the tenth century, Ibn Ezra in the twelfth century, Carlstadt and others in the sixteenth century, had raised questions about the Mosaic authorship of the pentateuch. The significant biblical critics of the seventeenth century were Thomas Hobbes (1588–1679), an English philosopher, Benedict de Spinoza (1632–77), a Dutch–Jewish philosopher, Hugh Grotius (1583–1645), a Dutch jurist and theologian, and Richard Simon (1638–1712), a French Catholic priest (see Gray, 75–115; Knight, 39–54, and bibliography given there).

Spinoza outlined the programme of biblical criticism.

The history of the scriptures should . . . teach us to understand the various vicissitudes that may have befallen the books of the prophets whose tradition has been handed down to us; the life, character and aim of the author of each book; the part which he played; at what period, on what occasion, for whom and in what language he composed his writings. Nor is that enough; we must know the fortune of each book in particular, the circumstances in which it was originally composed, into what hands it subsequently fell, the various lessons it has been held to convey, by whom it was included in the sacred canon, and, finally, how all these books came to be embodied in a single collection (Spinoza, *Tractatus theologica-politicus*, VII).

Several assumptions can be discerned in this newly budding biblical criticism. (1) The Bible is to be subjected to critical study just as any other book. (2) The biblical material has a history of transmission which can be elucidated by determining the various circumstances through which it passed. (3) Internal statements, styles, and repetitions make it possible to deny single and Mosaic authorship of the pentateuch. It should be noted that Grotius, Hobbes, and Spinoza had moved away from the typical Jewish and Protestant view of religious authority and revelation and that their criticism was probably the result rather than the cause of such a move.

The most important and influential seventeenth-century biblical critic was Simon (see Hazard, 180–97, for a perceptive essay on him). As a Catholic, Simon sought to show that Protestantism's reliance upon the Bible was not as sound a principle as the Catholic reliance upon Bible, tradition, and the church. He stressed the importance of a thorough knowledge of Hebrew for Old Testament study as well as textual criticism and philology. Simon emphasized the process by which the biblical materials were transmitted, pointing to their supplementation and alteration. Claiming inspiration for the revisers of the materials, on the analogy of church tradition, Simon argued that those who had the power to write the sacred books also had the power to revise them. Simon deliberately stressed the word 'critic' and 'criticism' in his writing, using it in the title of practically all his works. He explained the usage this way:

My readers must not be surprised if I have sometimes availed myself of expressions that may sound a little strangely in their ears. Every art has its own peculiar terminology, which is regarded more or less as its inviolable property. It is in this specialized sense that I have employed the words *critic* and *criticism* . . . together with some others of the same nature, to which I was obliged to have recourse in order to express myself in the terms proper to the art of which I was treating. These terms will come as no novelty to scholars, who have for some time been accustomed to their use in our language (quoted from Hazard, 182).

Simon addressed his writings to the general educated audience, and wrote in French, not Latin, and his *Histoire critique du Vieux Testament*, published in 1678, had, by 1700, gone through four Latin, two English, and seven French editions. The object of multiple attacks for its questioning of venerated traditions and positions, the book was condemned by the Congregation of the Index in 1683.

The humanists' and reformers' insistence on a 'return to the sources' and a literal reading of the text had been based on the conviction that there one could find the pristine faith, piety, and history. This confidence was to be shattered on the rocks of biblical criticism. What literary criticism found in the Bible was to produce a quagmire that was increasingly to absorb scholarly attention.

In the eighteenth century, and for the first time in Western history, a diversity of philosophical–theological systems with scholarly respectability competed in the intellectual market-place. These included a variety of approaches to Christian theism ranging from scholasticism to experiential pietism, Pyrrhonic agnosticism, atheism, and pragmatic rationalism (see Hazard for the general background and Barth, 33–173, for a descriptive analysis). The sanctity of tradition, the customs of culture, and the regulations of the market-place all favoured the theistic option; however, Christianity and the Bible were subjected to an unprecedented and trenchant examination and critique. The agent of this activity was deism.

Deism's roots can be traced to various earlier influences and anticipatory figures. McKee has done this in the case of Isaac de la Peyrère, who in 1655 published a work advancing such hypotheses as the existence of men before the creation of Adam and the non-Mosaic authorship of the pentateuch. Gay provides a good description of the exponents of the movement:

All deists were … both critical and constructive. … All sought to destroy in order to build, and reasoned either from the absurdity of Christianity to the need for a new philosophy or from their desire for a new philosophy to the absurdity of Christianity. … Deism … is the product of the confluence of three strong emotions: hate, love, and hope. The deists hated priests and priestcraft, mystery-mongering, and assaults on common sense. They loved the ethical teachings of the classical philosophers, the grand unalterable regularity of nature, the sense of freedom granted the man liberated from superstition. They hoped that the problems of life – of private conduct and public policy – could be solved by the application of unaided human reason, and that the mysteries of the universe could be, if not solved, at least defined and circumscribed by man's scientific inquiry (13).

Various stances towards the Bible were taken by the deists, but as a rule, they sought to distil the biblical traditions, to siphon off the supernatural, the miraculous, and the unbelievable, and to leave behind the pure essence of a reasonable faith. (On deism, see the readings in Waring and Gay; for descriptive discussions, see Stephen and Cragg.)

During the height of the deistic controversy in England (1700–50), two major studies of Israelite and Judaean history were published. *Prideaux's work, which covers the period from the reign of Tiglath-pileser III to the lifetime of Jesus, comprises three volumes which totalled almost 1,400 pages. The work went through over a score of editions and was translated into German and French. Prideaux relied primarily upon the biblical traditions and Josephus, but made use of practically every known literary document from antiquity. Only occasionally did Prideaux take a critical attitude towards his sources. He challenged the authenticity of the letter of Aristeas and its account of the origin of the LXX and provided the reader with a history and description of the study of the LXX (II, 264–98). Prideaux disagreed with Josephus on Alexander's route to Jerusalem (II, 132) and argued that the synagogue had its origin in the days of Ezra (II, 12f.).

*Shuckford wrote his volumes to present the history from creation to the point where Prideaux had begun. Like his predecessors, from the fourth century on, Shuckford presented universal history in a biblical perspective, beginning with Adam and Eve. This was still the classical model. Sir Walter Raleigh had started at this point in his widely used *History of the World*, published in 1614, and although unfinished it covered history down to the Roman period. Basically the same model was employed in the multi-volume *An Universal History from the Earliest Time to the Present*, written by a consortium of scholars, mostly from Oxford and Cambridge, and published in 1736–50 (see Southern, 1971, 178f.). Shuckford, like Prideaux, was thoroughly familiar with all the ancient sources as well as the history of research. Both, for example, used, quoted, and opposed Spinoza and Simon. Shuckford's work, which was never completed beyond the time of Joshua, was, perhaps because of the biblical material covered, more influenced by the deistic controversy than that of Prideaux. In describing the magicians at the court of Pharaoh, Shuckford presents them as deistic philosophers:

In Moses's time, the rulers of the Egyptian nation, ... were then the most learned body in the world, *beguiled by the deceit of vain philosophy*. ... The Pagan divinations, arts of prophecy, and all their sorceries and enchantments, as well as their idolatry and worship of false gods, were founded, not upon superstition, but upon learning and philosophical study; not upon too great a belief of, and adherence to revelation, but upon a pretended knowledge of the powers of nature. Their great and learned men erred in these points, not for want of freethinking, such as they called so; but their opinions upon these subjects were in direct opposition to the true revelations which had been made to the world, and might be called the deism of these ages; for such certainly was the religion of the governing and learned part of the Heathen world in these times (I, 565–6).

Like his predecessors, Shuckford stretched his intellectual powers in defence of the biblical chronology, arguing that the antediluvians enjoyed longevity because before the flood the earth was situated so as to have a perpetual equinox, thus sparing its inhabitants the rigours of seasonal change (I, 20f.). He argued that 'at the flood, the heavens underwent some change: the motion of the sun was altered, and a year, or annual revolution of it, became, as it now is, five days and almost six hours longer than it was before' (I, iii). However, Shuckford, who was thoroughly familiar with the problems of textual criticism, was occasionally willing to amend the Hebrew text on the basis of the Greek (for example, Deuteronomy 34.6 should read 'they buried him', II, 229; thus Moses did not write the account of his death). He sensed the problem of the divine names in Genesis and Exodus, and devoted an extended discussion to the use of the names Jehovah, El Shaddai, and Elohim (I, 517–30). His solution to the problem was not to postulate a multiplicity of documents but to theorize about the diversity of persons in the godhead.

Outside England, the deist impulse led to some very scathing attacks on Christianity and the Bible. The Frenchman Voltaire (1694–1778) never tired of pointing out what he called the absurdities, inconsistencies, and low morality found in the Bible. To claim that God was its author was to make 'of God a bad geographer, a bad chronologist, a bad physicist; it makes him no better a naturalist' (quoted in Appelgate, 26). To claim that Moses wrote the pentateuch was to claim Moses to be a fool. Voltaire suggested that much of the Old Testament was borrowed by the Jews from other peoples, and proposed that Moses may have never lived: 'If there only were some honest and natural deeds in the myth of Moses, one could believe fully that such a personage did exist' (quoted in Appelgate, 102). The significance of Voltaire was his popularization, in caustic language, of many of the issues which had previously been the concerns of erudite scholars. Voltaire, however, approached the Bible and its historical materials not so much as a critic but as an assassin.

In Germany, the impact of deism can be seen in the work of H. S. Reimarus (1694–1768) who, at his death, left behind what the philosopher Lessing published as the *Wolfenbüttel Fragments*. One of these fragments was an essay on 'the passage of the Israelites through the Red Sea' (for a selection, see Gay, 158–63; for a study of Reimarus and the Old Testament, see Reventlow). Reimarus sought to show the impossibilities in a literal interpretation of the biblical description of the crossing of the sea. According to Exodus 12.37f., about six hundred thousand Hebrew men left Egypt not counting the women, children, and mixed multitude and animals which accompanied them. Reimarus says this would give a figure of about three million people, three hundred thousand oxen and cows, and six hundred thousand sheep and goats. Approximately five thousand wagons would have been needed to carry provisions and three hundred thousand tents would have been required to house the people at ten per tent. Had the multitude marched ten abreast, the three million would have formed a column one hundred and eighty miles long. It would have required nine days as a minimum for such a group to march through the parted sea. Reimarus' arguments, and there were others who made similar points, hit at the very heart of those who took the Bible as literally inspired and as factually infallible.

Among the founding fathers of the United States were many with deistic leanings. Jefferson edited a version of the New Testament devoid of any miracles and concluding with the death of Jesus. Thomas Paine, an Englishman who spent several years in the US supporting the Revolutionary War and some time in France in exile, was a brutal controversialist in his attack upon the Bible. 'Paine's peculiarity consists in the freshness with which he comes upon very old discoveries, and the vehemence with which he announces them' (Stephen, I, 461). In his book *The Age of Reason*, Paine wrote:

Whenever we read the obscene stories, the voluptuous debaucheries, the cruel and torturous executions, the unrelenting vindictiveness, with which more than half the Bible is filled, it would be more consistent that we called it the word of a demon than the word of God. It is a history of wickedness that has served to corrupt and brutalize mankind; and, for my part, I sincerely detest it, as I detest everything that is cruel. ... Speaking for myself, if I had no other evidence that the Bible is fabulous than the sacrifice I must make to believe it to be true, that alone would be sufficient to determine my choice (see the selection from Paine in Gay, 164–76).

The significance of the deistic movement and the enlightenment of the eighteenth century was not in the area of historiography *per se*. The deists, in their discussions of the Bible and the history portrayed in the Bible, presented the issues of biblical criticism to the general public. In addition, their scathing attacks on the defences supporting a factual, literal reading of the text were devastating. It would never again be easy to present Israelite and Judaean history by simply retelling and amplifying the biblical narratives.

Several developments, in addition to the deistic controversy, occurred in the eighteenth century which should be noted since they were greatly to affect the study of Israelite and Judaean history. The use of ancient literature in comparative studies of the Old Testament became more common and less apologetic. In 1685, John Spencer, of Corpus Christi College in Cambridge, published his *De legibus Hebraeorum ritualibus et earum rationibus* in which he compared the ritual laws of the Old Testament with relevant material from Egypt, Greece, and Rome. Comparative study, as the deists demonstrated, could cut in two directions; it could be used to support either the uniqueness or the dependency of the biblical materials. The study of Palestinian geography was advanced by Hadrian Reland's *Palaestina ex monumentis veteribus illustrata* (1714) and the pioneer work in Palestinian antiquities, *Compendium antiquitatum Hebraeorum*, by Johann David Michaelis, appeared in 1753.

The basic elements in the documentary criticism of the Old Testament were established during this time. The German pastor Henning Bernhard Witter (1683–1715) and the French physician Jean Astruc (1684–1766) laid down some of the criteria for source criticism of the pentateuch. The classic four-source theory of the pentateuch was to be worked out in the nineteenth century but the five pillars of documentary criticism were established in the eighteenth. These pillars are (1) the use of different names for the deity, (2) varieties of language and style, (3) contradictions and divergences, (4) repetitions and duplications, and (5) indications of composite structure.

A third phenomenon to be noted is the maturation of the science of Old Testament introduction. Pioneers in this area were Michaelis and Johann Salomo Semler (see Kraus, 97–113; Kümmel, 62–73; and on Semler, see Hornig). Both of these men were influenced by English deism (see Kümmel, 415 nn. 59, 63). With Johann Gottfried

Eichhorn's *Einleitung in das Alte Testament* (1780–3), the basic problems of Old Testament introduction – growth of the canon, history of the text, and origin and nature of the individual books – were discussed in handbook form. With Eichhorn, the humanistic argument that the literature of the Old Testament should be investigated like any other literature was integrated into the mainstream of Protestant biblical study.

A fourth factor in the eighteenth century was the poetic or 'romantic' reaction to the classicism and rationalism of the enlightenment. In Old Testament studies, this movement is most closely associated with the work and thought of Johann Gottfried Herder (1744–1803) who was influenced by such figures as Jean-Jacques Rousseau (1712–78), Johann Georg Hamann (1730–88), and Robert Lowth (1710–87). The latter's *De sacra poesi Hebraeorum* (1753) studied Hebrew poetry along the lines of research applied to Greek and Latin poetry, arguing that poetry represented man's earliest form of speech and was as expressive of truth as philosophy. The pietist Hamann had also expressed an emphasis on poetry as the mother-tongue of the human race and, like most pietists, stressed the reader's immediacy to the biblical materials. Rousseau glorified primitive man as a free and happy being living in accordance with nature and instinct, and for whom language was his basic expression of the natural and communal spirit. (On Herder's broad concerns and their relationship to enlightenment thought, see Berlin; on his hermeneutics, see Frei, 183–201.) Herder emphasized the necessity of entering empathically into the human world out of which the Bible had come, rather than seeking understanding merely through critical and technical analysis. He was more interested in the group than the individual and in the manner in which the group gave expression to its distinctive culture, not necessarily according to any universal laws. Cultures are like plants which grow in unique ways dependent upon the situation of the place, the circumstances of the times and the generative character of the people. Whatever can take place among mankind does take place; life does not operate along rationalistic lines. Herder's approach to the human past stressed an appreciative and imaginative relationship to the 'spirit' and not a rational, judgmental relationship. (See Scholder, 1962, and Willi on Herder's general contributions to Old Testament study.)

A final development in eighteenth-century Old Testament research was the introduction of mythological study. The systematic study of classical mythology originated with the German classicist Christian Gottlob Heyne (1729–1812) who argued that myth was one of primitive man's basic modes of expressing his experiences and understanding of life and nature. The first application of mythological studies to the Old Testament was made by Eichhorn, a student of Heyne at Göttingen, who published a work on Genesis 1–3 entitled *Die Urgeschichte* (1779). Eichhorn's work, which was greatly influenced by Lowth, was taken up by Johann Philipp Gabler (1753–1826). The concept of myth, when applied to parts of the Old Testament, greatly affected the manner in which scholars examined these materials and naturally led directly to the question of the historical factuality of their content. Later, what could be labelled as mythical was removed from the arena of the historical. (On the early stages of mythological research on the Old Testament see Hartlich-Sachs, 1–53, and Rogerson, 1–15.)

§4. THE NINETEENTH CENTURY

S. W. **Baron**, *History and Jewish Historians*, 1964; F. J. **Bliss**, *The Development of Palestine Exploration*, New York: Charles Scribner's Sons 1906; F. G. **Bratton**, *A History of Egyptian Archaeology*, New York: Thomas Y. Crowell 1968; C. A. **Briggs**, *The Higher Criticism of the Hexateuch*, New York: Charles Scribner's Sons 1893, ²1897; J. E. **Carpenter**, *The Bible in the Nineteenth Century*, London: Longmans, Green and Co. 1903; T. K. **Cheyne**, *Founders of Old Testament Criticism*, London: Methuen & Co. 1893; G. P. **Gooch**, *History and Historians in the Nineteenth Century*, London: Longmans, Green & Co. 1913, ²1952; H. V. **Hilprecht**, *Explorations in Bible Lands during the Nineteenth Century*, Philadelphia/Edinburgh: A. J. Holman & Co./T. & T. Clark 1903; E. G. **Kraeling**, *The Old Testament since the Reformation*, London/New York: Lutterworth Press/Harper & Brothers 1955; New York: Schocken Books 1969; H.-J. **Kraus**, *Geschichte der historisch-kritischen Erforschung des Alten Testaments*, Neukirchen-Vluyn: Neukirchener Verlag, 1956, ²1969; S. **Lloyd**, *Foundations in the Dust: A Story of Mesopotamian Exploration*, London: Oxford University Press 1947; Harmondsworth/Baltimore: Penguin Books 1955; R. A. S. **Macalister**, *A Century of Excavation in Palestine*, London: Religious Tract Society 1925; L. **Perlitt**, *Vatke und Wellhausen*, BZAW 94, 1965; R. J. **Thompson**, *Moses and the Law in a Century of Criticism since Graf*, SVT 19, 1970; J. **Wellhausen**, *Geschichte Israels* I, Berlin: Georg Reimer 1878 = *Prolegomena zur Geschichte Israels*, Berlin: Georg Reimer 1883 = *Prolegomena to the History of Israel*, Edinburgh: A. & C. Black 1885; idem, 'Die Composition des Hexateuchs', *JDT* XXI, 1876, 392–450, 531–602, XXII, 1877, 407–79 = *Die Composition des Hexateuchs und die historischen Bücher des Alten Testaments*, Berlin: Georg Reimer 1899; idem, 'Israel', *EnBr* XIII, ⁹1880, 396–420 = *Prolegomena to the History of Israel*, 427–548; idem, 'Heinrich Ewald',

Festschrift zur Feier der 150jährigen Bestehens der Königlichen Gesellschaft der Wissenschaften zu Göttingen, Berlin: Weidmannsche Verlagsbuchhandlung 1901, 61–81 = idem, *Grundrisse zum Alten Testament*, ed. R. Smend, TB 27, 1965, 120–38; J. A. **Wilson**, *Signs and Wonders upon Pharaoh: A History of American Egyptology*, Chicago: University of Chicago Press 1964.

Major developments in the nineteenth century which form the background for Israelite historiography may simply be noted since they have been so frequently discussed. In the first place, more liberal stances in theology came to characterize many segments of the religious communities. This liberalism was less dogmatic in its theological orientation, more progressive in its relationship to contemporary culture and thought, and more humanistic in its perspectives than previous generations. This gradual shift can be seen, for example, in the rise of the so-called *Wissenschaft des Judentums* movement which sought 'to see in Jewish history the gradual progression of Jewish religious or national spirit in its various vicissitudes and adjustments to the changing environments' (Baron, 76). This liberal spirit, which was now located within the life of the religious communities themselves, was willing to break with traditional beliefs and approaches and to take a more critical attitude towards the biblical materials.

Secondly, major advances were made in general historiography. The nineteenth was the century of history. Of special importance was the development of what has been called a positivistic approach to history, which not only attempted but also believed it possible to reconstruct past history 'as it had actually happened' (*wie es eigentlich gewesen*). The most prominent of these outstanding positivistic historians were Barthold Georg Niebuhr (1776–1831), Leopold Ranke (1795–1885), and Theodor Mommsen (1817–1903). Practically every aspect of human life was subjected to historical exploration in the nineteenth century (for the major developments and historians, see Gooch).

Thirdly, the decipherment of ancient Near Eastern languages – especially Egyptian hieroglyphics and Akkadian cuneiform – opened the long-closed literary remains of Israel's neighbours to study and interpretation (see Lloyd, Bratton, and Wilson). The full impact of these new fields of learning was not to be felt fully until the last years of the nineteenth and the first decades of the twentieth century. None the less, for the first time scholars could examine the literary products of these cultures at first hand and thus were no longer dependent upon the ancient, secondary sources.

Fourthly, the exploration of the Near East and Palestine raised historical geography to a level of real competence. Explorers like the Swiss Johann Ludwig Burckhardt (1784–1817) and the American Edward Robinson (1794–1863) whose three-volume work, *Biblical Researches in Palestine, Mount Sinai and Arabia Petraea* (1841), based on his travels in 1838, reported on sites, place-names, and customs and used modern names to identify many places mentioned in the Bible. In 1865, the Palestine Exploration Fund was established and, in 1872–8, it sponsored a geographical survey of western Palestine (the Conder–Kitchener expedition). Other national societies were begun to encourage and finance exploration. Archaeological excavations at several sites in Palestine were undertaken (see Bliss, Hilprecht, and Macalister).

Fifthly, the isolation and dating of the 'documents' which went to make up the pentateuch continued apace. The so-called four-source hypothesis which argued that four major documents (J, E, P, D) were redactionally combined to produce the pentateuch gradually came to dominate discussions after mid-century. The character, content, and date of the individual documents were considered of great significance in understanding the religious development of Israelite and Judaean life and in evaluating the historical reliability of the documentary materials. (On the development of critical research, see Briggs; Carpenter; Kraus, 152–308, 242–74; Thompson.)

A survey of Israelite and Judaean history in the nineteenth century can best be made by examining some innovative works from the period. The first work to be noted, and perhaps the first really critical history of Israel ever written, is that by Henry Hart *Milman (1791–1868). Milman, a graduate of Oxford University, was ordained in 1816. During his early days, he wrote poetry and plays and from 1821 to 1831 held a professorship of poetry at Oxford. In 1849, he was appointed dean of St Paul's. Most of Milman's rather extensive literary output were works in church history. His *History of the Jews* was first published in 1829 and met with significant opposition. The work, however, was issued in a number of editions by various publishers until the first decade of the present century. Of the twenty-eight books in his three-volume history, the final ten are concerned with the history of the Jews following the Bar-Kochba war.

Milman's history was addressed to the general reading public and tends to be rather sketchy and to avoid any detailed discussion of controversial points or of methodology. The extent of his familiarity with Old Testament studies cannot be really determined. Only a few isolated references are made to significant figures, although Milman was acquainted with travel reports on the Near East and Palestine and makes rather frequent reference to these. Milman adopted a developmental approach to Jewish history:

Nothing is more curious, or more calculated to confirm the veracity of the Old Testament history, than the remarkable picture which it presents of the gradual development of human society: the ancestors of the Jews, and the Jews themselves, pass through every stage of comparative civilization (I, v).

Excepting only their knowledge of God and their custodianship of the promises, 'the chosen people appear to have been left to themselves to pass through the ordinary stages of the social state' (I, vi; see III, 346). Milman approached the Bible with a very limited view of inspiration and noted that 'much allowance must . . . be made for the essentially poetic spirit, and for the Oriental forms of speech, which pervade so large a portion of the Old Testament' (I, viii) and that God 'addressed a more carnal and superstitious people chiefly through their imagination and senses' (I, vi). He warned his readers that miracle would play little role in his interpretation of history, noting that those who have criticized the belief in revelation are 'embarrassing to those who take up a narrow system of interpreting the Hebrew writings; to those who adopt a more rational latitude of exposition, none' (I, xi). Whereas *Prideaux and *Shuckford were unwilling to accommodate their historical discussions to the views of the biblical critics, for Milman, there was no other option.

Milman began his history with the patriarchs and made no reference to the materials in Genesis 1–10. Abraham is described as an 'independent Sheik or Emir' (I, 10) or 'the stranger sheik' who is allowed 'to pitch his tent, and pasture his flocks and herds' in Canaan (I, 20). Milman considered the different stories of the endangering of the wife to be 'traditional variations of the same transaction' (I, 20). 'Abraham is the Emir of a pastoral tribe, migrating from place to place. . . . He is in no respect superior to his age or country, excepting in the sublime purity of his religion' (I, 22f.). In describing patriarchal society, Milman wrote:

Mankind appears in its infancy, gradually extending its occupancy over regions, either entirely unappropriated, or as yet so recently and thinly peopled, as to admit, without resistance, the new swarms of settlers which seem to spread from the birthplace of the human race, the plains of central Asia. They are peaceful pastoral nomads, travelling on their camels, the ass the only other beast of burthen. . . . The unenterprising shepherds, from whom the Hebrews descended, move onward as their convenience or necessity requires, or as richer pastures attract their notice (I, 29f.).

The description of the patriarchs as 'the hunter, the migratory herdsman, and the incipient husbandman', suggests that the record draws upon 'contemporary traditions' (I, 32). The Israelite ancestors are thus a *Volk* who differ from their contemporaries only in their theological view of God.

.In discussing the stay in Egypt, Milman argued against identifying the period with the Hyksos era but dated it later, refusing however to hypothesize a specific time (I, 40–2). He noted that biblical tradition assigns either 430 (MT) or 215 (LXX) years to the stay, but that both of these are irreconcilable with the mere two generations which separated Moses from Levi, a factor which also raised uncertainty about the number of Israelites leaving Egypt (I, 48f., 119). Milman described the plagues and the crossing of the Red Sea, but spoke of the 'plain leading facts of the Mosaic narrative, the residence of the Hebrews in Egypt, their departure under the guidance of Moses, and the connexion of that departure with some signal calamity, at least for a time, fatal to the power and humiliating to the pride of Egypt' (I, 73). In describing the crossing of the sea, he refers to a report by Diodorus Siculus concerning the erratic behaviour of the water in the area (I, 72; see *Herrmann, 63). The quails and manna in the desert are explained in naturalistic terms and the changing of bitter water to sweet is explained chemically. In footnotes in the second edition, Milman reports on the chemical analysis of water especially secured from a Palestinian spring called Marah which suggested high concentrations of 'selenite or sulphate of lime' which could be precipitated by 'any vegetable substance containing oxalic acid . . . and rendered agreeable and wholesome'. He also reports that a traveller had brought him a sample of manna produced by the tamarisk tree (I, 117).

The pentateuchal legislation – 'the Hebrew constitution' (I, 79) – is attributed to Moses, 'the legislator constantly, yet discreetly, mitigating the savage usages of a barbarous people' (I, 113).

The laws of a settled and civilized community were enacted among a wandering and homeless horde who were traversing the wilderness, and more likely, under their existing circumstances, to sink below the pastoral life of their forefathers, than advance to the rank of an industrious agricultural community. Yet, at this time, judging solely from its internal evidence, the law must have been enacted. Who but Moses ever possessed such authority as to enforce submission to statutes so severe and uncompromising? Yet, as Moses incontestably died before the conquest of Canaan, his legislature must have taken place in the desert. To what other period can the Hebrew constitution be assigned? To that of the judges? a time of anarchy, warfare, or servitude! To that of the kings? when the republic had undergone a total change! To any time after Jerusalem became the metropolis? when the holy city, the pride and glory of the nation, is not even alluded to in the whole law! After the building of the temple? when it is equally silent as to any settled or durable edifice! After the separation of the kingdoms? when the close bond of brotherhood had given place to implacable hostility! Under Hilkiah? under Ezra? when a great number of the statutes had become a dead letter! The law depended on a strict and equitable partition of the land. At a later period it could not have been put into practice without the forcible resumption of every individual property by the state; the difficulty, or rather impossibility, of such a measure, may be estimated by any reader who is not entirely unacquainted with the history of the ancient republics. In other respects the law breathes the air of the desert. Enactments intended for a people with settled habitations, and dwelling in walled cities, are mingled up with temporary regulations, only suited to the Bedouin encampment of a nomad tribe (I, 78f.).

Milman certainly realized that the dating of the law was the central issue in Old Testament interpretation and that when one dates the law is highly determinative for how one writes the history. Also, he raised practically all the possible options for dating the law.

Milman follows the basic biblical account of the conquest and division of the land. The judges of early Israel, whose title is associated with 'the Suffetes of the Carthaginians', are described as 'military dictators' operating in emergencies within the 'boundaries of their own tribe'. Their qualifications were their 'personal activity, daring, and craft', and they appear 'as gallant insurgents or guerilla leaders'. In the case of Deborah, several tribes came together in 'an organized warlike confederacy'. The tribes were disunited because of their disobedience to the Mosaic law and were compelled to arms in furthering the incomplete conquest in 'war of the separate tribes against immediate enemies' (I, 155f.). Although the Bible speaks of the judges being raised up by the Lord, 'their particular actions are nowhere attributed to divine action' (I, 158f.). The absence of Judah and Simeon from the song of Deborah (Judg. 5) suggests that perhaps they 'had seceded from the confederacy, or were occupied by enemies of their own' (I, 160).

Enough has been said of Milman's work to suggest his approach since many of the basic issues arise in treating the period prior to David. Although Milman was probably the first to treat Israelite and Judaean history from a secular orientation and in the same terms one would write a history of Greece or Rome, his name and an exposition of his position are seldom mentioned in surveys of Old Testament studies.

A second innovative work was the lengthy, multi-volume history by Heinrich Georg August *Ewald (1803–75), one of the most outstanding Oriental and Semitic scholars of the nineteenth century (on Ewald, see Wellhausen, 1901; Cheyne, 66–118; Kraus, 199–205). He was a student and successor of Eichhorn at Göttingen. Ewald's history is as verbose and dull as Milman's is crisp and entertaining.

Almost one half of the first volume of Ewald's history is devoted to the problem of the sources for Israelite history (I, 11–203). Ewald says his 'ultimate aim is the knowledge of what really happened – not what was only related and handed down by tradition, but what was actual fact' (I, 13). Tradition thus preserves an image of what happened but it is also formed by imagination, which may blur the details or form of the event it remembers, and is shaped by the memory, which tends to obliterate details and contract the overall content (I, 14–16). Chronological distance from the events reduces the extent and trustworthiness of the tradition:

> The Hebrew tradition about the earliest times – the main features of which, as we have it, were fixed in the interval from the fourth to the sixth century after Moses – still has a great deal to tell about Moses and his contemporaries; much less about the long sojourn in Egypt, and the three Patriarchs; and almost nothing special about the primitive times which preceded these Patriarchs, when neither the nation, nor even its 'fathers', were yet in Canaan. So, too, the Books of Samuel relate many particulars of David's later life passed in the splendour of royalty, but less about his youth before he was king (I, 17).

Tradition has supports in songs, proverbs, and personal names, and in visible monuments such as altars, temples, and memorials (I, 17–21). The strongest support of tradition, however, is the institution such as annually recurring festivals which recall the incidents (I, 21 f.). Foreign elements also enter traditions: names are added, numbers lose exactness, events shift their chronological moorings, and similar traditions become associated (I, 22–6). Tradition rests in imagination and feeling more than understanding and thus is closely associated with nationalistic sentiments (I, 26–31). Different events are remembered in different styles of traditions and since tradition is very plastic it may be moulded by religious interests, aetiological concerns, and mythological perspectives (I, 31–41).

The earliest Israelite historians found the tradition that they used as 'a fluctuating and plastic material, but also a mass of unlimited extent' (I, 41). At the writing-down stage, tradition went through further change. The modern historian must 'distinguish between the story and its foundation, and exclusively . . . seek the latter with all diligence' (I, 45).

Tradition has its roots in actual facts; yet it is not absolutely history, but has a peculiar character and a value of its own. . . . It is our duty to take the tradition just as it expects to be taken – to use it only as a means for discovering what the real facts once were (I, 44).

Thus, Ewald has a high regard for tradition's relationship to historical facts and for the historian's ability to use the tradition to discover the facts. By the Mosaic era, writing was known in Israel and a historiography possible (I, 49–51).

Ewald divides the historical books into three groups: the Great Book of Origins (the hexateuch), the Great Book of Kings (Judges–Kings + Ruth), and the Great Book of Universal History down to the Greek Times (Chronicles–Ezra–Nehemiah + Esther). Ewald then analyses these great books as to their sources. The basic source of the hexateuch was what Ewald called the 'Book of Origins' (what is today called P) which he dated to the period of the early monarchy (I, 74–8). This book incorporated older fragments and materials and was subjected to various modifications, prophetic and Deuteronomistic, before it attained its final form at the end of the seventh or the beginning of the sixth century (I, 131). In similar manner, Ewald proceeds to analyse the other two historical complexes, their origin, components, modifications, and history.

Before beginning his reconstruction of the history, Ewald discussed some problems of chronology (I, 204–13) and general geographical matters (I, 214–55). Ewald follows the four-age theory of P and speaks of the three ages of the preliminary history of Israel: creation to Noah, Noah to Abraham, and Abraham to Moses. In discussing the first two ages, Ewald compares the traditions with those of other peoples, discusses the ages of the characters, and avoids any real straightforward statements about the factuality of the materials. Behind the patriarchal figures are to be seen tribal groups. The oldest extant tradition about Abraham is Genesis 14 (I, 307). The patriarchal ancestors spoke and thought monotheistically but not quite in the Mosaic form (I, 320f.). The Hebrews are pictured entering Egypt at different times in various migrations, beginning in the Hyksos period, but the exodus is not to be associated with the expulsion of the Hyksos (I, 388–407).

The Hebrew nation as a theocracy came into being under Moses in the wilderness. The event of the exodus, which inaugurated this period, cannot be fully reconstructed:

Whatever may have been the exact course of this event, whose historical certainty is well established; its momentous results, the nearer as well as the more remote, were sure to be experienced, and are even to us most distinctly visible (II, 75).

Under Moses, the golden theocratic age of Israel began, the law was given, and the age reached maturity under his leadership and that of Joshua. From Joshua to the monarchy was a time of the decay of the pure theocracy and the relaxation of the national bond.

Enough has been said of Ewald's work to suggest its general approach. His work was innovative in that it sought to base the discussion of the history on a systematic study of the biblical traditions and sources. Ewald, however, basically adhered to the theological perspective of the biblical text while modifying the miraculous element. As in the Bible, the golden age of Israelite history is the age of Moses. After wading through Ewald's presentation, one possesses the impression of having read a historical commentary on the historical books, but not of having read a history of Israel.

A third innovative history of the nineteenth century was the work by Heinrich *Graetz (1817–91). His work is not of major significance *per se* but because it represents the first modern history of ancient Israel and Judah written by a Jew. Graetz had been preceded by his younger Jewish contemporary, Isaac Marcus Jost (1793–1860), whose nine-volume history of the Jews from Maccabaean times until the nineteenth century was the first major Jewish history in modern times (on Jost, see Baron, 240–75). The first volume of Graetz's work covered the period from Moses to the death of Simon in 135 BCE (on Graetz and his history, see Baron, 263–75). The work is primarily a rather free – at times rather romanticized – narration built upon the biblical materials. Very few of the problems are given any detailed treatment. The real importance of Graetz's work is the fact that it depicts the history free from any overriding theological stance or biblical orthodoxy.

A final nineteenth-century historian to be noted was Julius Wellhausen (1844–1918), who was the most influential and significant Old Testament scholar of the time. Before producing a reconstruction of Israelite history, Wellhausen carried out a detailed examination of the literary traditions in the hexateuch. He accepted and supported the documentary criticism which argued that there were four sources in the pentateuch which originated in the order J, E, D, P. In his *Prolegomena*, Wellhausen supported this theory with an incisive analysis of the history of worship and religion, which sought to demonstrate that Israelite religious life had gone through various states which are reflected in the documents of the pentateuch. Some of Wellhausen's major conclusions on the literary and religious history were the following. (1) The theocratic organization of Israel and the priestly laws of the pentateuch were the basis not for life in the age of Moses but for post-exilic Judaism. (2) The eighth century was the age of real literary activity in Israel: 'The question why it was that Elijah and Elisha committed nothing to writing, while Amos a hundred years later is an author, hardly admits of any other answer than that in the interval a non-literary had developed into a literary age' (1885, 465). (3) The Yahwistic (J) and Elohistic (E) sources came into being during the early days of classical prophetism and reflect the pre-prophetic religion of Israel (1885, 360f.). (4) Under the influence of the prophets, Deuteronomy was produced in the seventh century (1885, 487–8). (5) Deuteronomy was strictly a law-book and J was a history-book; the combination of these two was the beginning of the combination of law and narrative which was the pattern followed by P (1885, 345). (6) The priestly work derives from post-exilic times and reflects the atmosphere of theocratic Judaism. (7) The presentations of the earliest phase of Israelite history, the patriarchal period, in the various sources were coloured by the times in which the sources were written and thus cannot be used for historical purposes:

> We attain to no historical knowledge of the patriarchs, but only of the time when the stories about them arose in the Israelite people; this later age is here unconsciously projected, in its inner and outward features, into hoar antiquity, and is reflected there like a glorified mirage (1885, 318f.).

It should be noted that Wellhausen makes such a statement only for the patriarchal period, and not for the following ones. (8) Wellhausen saw Israelite religion developing through three phases: (*a*) the stage of primitive religion characterized by popular sentiments, a spontaneous and simple faith, and a nature orientation; (*b*) the stage of ethical concerns and consciousness initiated by the prophets; and (*c*) the stage of ceremonial and ritual religion influenced by the priestly legislation and further separated from the orientation to nature. Wellhausen seems to have sympathized most with the religion of the earliest phase, although he shared in the general nineteenth-century excitement over the 'rediscovery' of the prophets as creative individuals and exponents of personal and ethical religion (1885, 464–70; *1958, 78–103).

Various attempts were, and still are, made to counter Wellhausen's position by arguing that he imposed Hegelian philosophy or evolutionary thought on the Old Testament (see Thompson, 35–49, and bibliography there). This attempt to condemn by association has really no foundation in fact (see Perlitt). The basic influences upon Wellhausen were the emphasis laid by Herder and by Romanticism on primitivism, with its opposition to cultic ceremonial and things priestly, the positivistic approach to history exemplified in Niebuhr, Ranke, and Mommsen, the general nineteenth-century concern with stages in the history of practically everything, which most frequently argued for progressive development (in a good sense), although this was not completely the case with Wellhausen, the Lutheran theological position *vis-à-vis* the problem of law and gospel, and the general philosophy of history inherent in Christianity. (Even *Bright, who criticizes Wellhausen for his evolutionary thought, calls the epilogue to his history 'Toward the Fullness of Time'.) The primary influence on Wellhausen's reconstruction of Israelite history was, of course, the results and consequences of his literary study of the Old Testament.

Wellhausen's article on Israel, published in the ninth edition of the *Encyclopaedia Britannica* in 1880, was his basic statement on the topic. His later publications expanded the content but made no substantive changes; thus this article in its 1885 reprint can serve to present his views. For him, the ancestors of Israel were part of a Hebrew group, which included the ancestors of the Edomites, Moabites, and Ammonites, which settled in south-eastern Palestine. Some time in the fifteenth century BCE, a part of this Hebrew group left southern Palestine and moved into Goshen in Egypt. They were later subjected to forced labour until Moses reminded them of the God of their fathers and taught them self-assertion against the Egyptians. When Egypt was scourged by a plague, the Hebrews fled secretly to return to their old home. The fleeing Hebrews were pursued by the Egyptians but were able to ford a shallow sea which had been blown back by a high wind. A struggle ensued between the Egyptians and Hebrews but the former in their chariots were at a disadvantage and were annihilated by the returning waters (429f.).

After visiting Sinai, the emigrants settled at Kadesh for many years and there had their sanctuary and judgment-seat. Some attempts to move northwards into Canaan may have been made while the Hebrews pastured their flocks over an extended area around Kadesh. They left Kadesh to aid their kinsmen against Sihon in Transjordan, being joined by kindred elements. At this stage some groups – the six Leah clans and Joseph, a Rachel clan – may have already existed as organized tribes (430–2). From the historical tradition in the pentateuch, Wellhausen argued that some picture of Moses can be seen: he was the founder of Torah, called into activity the feeling for law and justice, and was the founder of the nation, but presented the Hebrews with no new concept of God (432–40).

The first movement into Palestine was led by Judah; the second wave by Joseph. There the divisions of Israel and Judah developed. Joshua was the leader of the Joseph and Benjamin groups (441–4). After some united effort at conquest, the tribes and families fought for their own land. Much of the indigenous population was absorbed. Gradually Israel advanced from pastoralism to agriculture (441–6). Yahweh was the god of Israel and Israel the people of God in its earliest days. In origin, the name Yahweh was a special name of the god El; Yahweh was the warrior El (433 f.). For a time, Baalism and Yahwism existed side by side. Gradually Yahwism absorbed elements of Baalism including the main elements in the cult (447 f.).

This summary of Wellhausen's reconstruction of the early history of Israel sufficiently demonstrates his approach. Wellhausen refused to understand Israel's history by postulating a golden period at some point early in its history, from which subsequent generations degenerated.

§5. CURRENT APPROACHES

W. F. **Albright**, 'Archaeology Confronts Biblical Criticism', *AmSc* VII, 1938, 176–88; idem, 'The Ancient Near East and the Religion of Israel', *JBL* LIX, 1940, 85–112; D. M. **Beegle**, *The Inspiration of Scripture*, Philadelphia: Westminster Press 1963; J. **Bright**, *Early Israel in Recent History Writing: A Study in Method*, SBT 19, 1956; M. **Buss**, 'The Study of Forms', in *Old Testament Form Criticism*, 1974, 1–56; J. **Dus**, 'Mose oder Josua? (Zum Problem des Stifters der israelitischen Religion)', *AOr* XXXIX, 1971, 16–45 = 'Moses or Joshua? (On the Problem of the Founder of Israelite Religion)', *RR* II, 1975, 26–41; D. N. **Freedman**, 'Archaeology and the Future of Biblical Studies 1. The Biblical Languages', in *The Bible in Modern Scholarship*, 1965, 294–312; P. **Haupt**, 'Midian und Sinai', *ZDMG* LXIII, 1909, 506–30; W. **Keller**, *Und die Bibel hat doch recht. Forscher beweisen die historische Wahrheit*, Düsseldorf: Econ-Verlag 1956 = *The Bible as History: A Confirmation of the Book of Books*, London/New York: Hodder & Stoughton/William Morrow & Co. 1956; D. A. **Knight**, *Rediscovering the Traditions of Israel*, SBLDS 9, 1973, [2]1975; H. **Lindsell**, *The Battle for the Bible*, Grand Rapids: Zondervan 1976; G. E. **Mendenhall**, 'The Hebrew Conquest of Palestine', *BA* XXV, 1962, 66–87 = *BAR* III, 1970, 100–26; idem, *The Tenth Generation*, Baltimore: Johns Hopkins Press 1973; idem,

'The Monarchy', *Int* XXIX, 1975, 155–70; M. **Noth**, *Das System der zwölf Stämme Israels*, BWANT IV/I, 1930; idem, *Die Gesetze im Pentateuch (Ihre Voraussetzungen und ihr Sinn)*, SKGG 17/2, 1940 = his *GS* I, 1957, 9–141 = 'The Laws in the Pentateuch: Their Assumptions and Meaning', in his *Laws in the Pentateuch*, 1966, 1–107; idem, *Überlieferungsgeschichtliche Studien*, 1957; idem, *History of the Pentateuchal Traditions*, 1972; G. **von Rad**, *Das formgeschichtliche Problem des Hexateuch*, BWANT IV/26, 1938 = his *GS* I, 1958, 9–86 = *Problem of the Hexateuch*, 1966, 1–78; idem, 'The Beginnings of Historical Writing in Ancient Israel' (see ch. I §1), *Problem of the Hexateuch*, 1966, 166–204; R. J. **Thompson**, *Moses and the Law in a Century of Criticism since Graf*, SVT 19, 1970; M. **Weber**, *Gesammelte Aufsätze zur Religionssoziologie. III. Das antike Judentum*, Tübingen: J. C. B. Mohr 1921, ²1923 = *Ancient Judaism*, Glencoe: The Free Press 1952; J. A. **Wilcoxen**, 'Narrative', *Old Testament Form Criticism*, 1974, 57–98.

Subsequent chapters in this volume discuss the modern history of research on particular periods of Israelite history. At this point, a brief comment on the general methodology of the major current approaches to the history will be made to provide some background for later discussions.

One approach which is still used by conservative scholars is the orthodox or traditional approach. This position operates on the assumption that the Bible is of supernatural origin and in its autograph form (which is no longer available) was totally free of any error (on this view of the Bible, see Lindsell). Other scholars who would classify themselves as conservative would not take so rigid a view of biblical inspiration (see Beegle). The orthodox view, similar to mainline biblical studies of the seventeenth and eighteenth centuries, works primarily from the evidence of the biblical text, supplying this with illustrative and supportive material drawn from extra-biblical texts and archaeological data. At points, the biblical texts need to be harmonized where apparent contradictions seem to appear. This view of the biblical materials is sometimes extended to the seven-day creation scheme, to be dated about 4000 BCE, and to the flood. *Wood's history supplies a good representation of this approach. He is able to supply exact dates for biblical events which are all taken as historically accurate: Abraham was born in 2166 BCE, Isaac married Rebekah in 2026 BCE, Jacob was seventy-seven years old when he went to Haran and hired himself to Laban for fourteen years, the exodus occurred in 1446 BCE, and so on. Biblical figures are accurate: over two million Hebrews left Egypt. Miracles happened as described, although God normally employed natural law when this was available: the sea was opened to approximately a mile in width to allow passage of the fleeing Hebrews (132f.) and the earth 'slowed, in its speed of rotation on its axis, approximately to half that of normal' in order to provide Joshua with additional daylight in his battle near Gibeon (181). Sufficient has been noted to illustrate this approach. In the following chapters, practically no attention will be given to this view since it does not assume that one has to reconstruct the history of Israel; one has only to support and elucidate the adequate history which the Bible already provides.

A second approach to Israelite history is what might be called the archaeological approach, since it seeks to substantiate much of the biblical data by appeal to evidence external to but supportive of the biblical text. This approach to Israelite history, built on the earlier antiquarian interests, became a fully conscious approach in the late nineteenth century as a reaction to documentary criticism of the pentateuch and the historical approaches, such as that by Wellhausen, built on documentary criticism (see Thompson, 91–6, 132–9, and bibliography there). In recent years, this approach has been associated in a special way with William Foxwell Albright (1891–1971) and his students (but see the widely popular book by Keller), although there are many archaeologists who would not share his methodological approach. Albright formulated his approach to the history and religion of Israel in the 1920s and 1930s and this remained basically unchanged throughout his career. His methodology rests on two basic arguments. (1) The traditions of the Old Testament are generally quite reliable. One should assume that these traditions embody historical memory and that the tendency to preserve traditions rather than create them was a fundamental characteristic of Near Eastern life, including Israelite, where one finds 'a superstitious veneration both for the written word and for oral tradition' (1938, 183). (2) Archaeological remains – both literary and artifactual – provide a source of material external to the Bible which can be used as a control against the unnecessary dependency upon literary, philosophical, or fundamentalist hypotheses. Since archaeology 'is concrete, not speculative', it can play this role (1938, 179; see Bright, 11–33, 111–26). Albright and his students operated on the assumption that archaeology had and would support the historicity of the biblical traditions.

Archaeological and inscriptional data have established the historicity of innumerable passages and statements of the Old Testament; the number of such cases is many times greater than those where the reverse has been proved or has been made probable (Albright, 1938, 181).

Before archaeology there was no adequate alternative to the creation of hypothetical frameworks for the biblical narrative; but as the factual evidence has become available, there is less and less excuse for such exercises in ingenuity, and in due course there will be none (Freedman, 298).

Probably few, if any, of Albright's students would go as far as the following statement of Mendenhall on the role of archaeology, but an emphasis on external evidence points in this direction:

We have an abundance of documentation from excavations comprised of primary, contemporary, and datable sources that yield all kinds of information about the social, political, ethnic, and religious traits of man in the Near East. . . . Unless biblical history is to be relegated to the domain of unreality and myth, the biblical and the archaeological must be correlated. Methodologically, the archaeological documents, especially the written ones, must be given priority and considered seriously (Mendenhall, 1973, 142).

A third typological approach to Israelite history may be called the traditio-historical approach (see Knight for the history and description of this methodology). This methodology is most closely associated with Albrecht Alt (1883–1956), Martin Noth (1902–68), and Gerhard von Rad (1901–71). The impetus for this approach goes back to Hermann Gunkel (1862–1932) who was the pioneer in Old Testament form-critical studies (on Gunkel, see Buss, 39–52; Wilcoxen, 57–79). Gunkel's work was postulated upon a number of perspectives which were ultimately of significance in the traditio-historical study of the Old Testament. (1) The writing down of Old Testament traditions in the form of documents was a late stage in a long process, and the writers of the documents were more like redactors or editors than authors. (2) Old Testament traditions had a long history of usage in an oral stage before they were written down. (3) Traditions may be divided into genres according to the content and mood of the materials, their formal language of expression, and their setting in life. (4) The basic form of the tradition is the individual unit or genre. (5) In the patriarchal traditions, the primary unit is the saga. (6) The individual sagas had their particular function in the setting in which they were used and the function of many of these was aetiological; they were used to 'explain' the origin of some physical feature, custom, practice, or ethnic relationship. (7) The individual sagas could be combined to produce cycles of traditions. (8) History writing in Israel developed out of this saga tradition.

Von Rad contributed four perspectives that were to be influential in traditio-historical studies in the latter's impact on the study of

Israelite history. (1) He isolated the small summaries of Israel's pre-monarchic history and related the usage of these to cultic celebrations (1–50). (2) The Sinai tradition was not originally a part of the historical summaries but had a different setting in the cult. (3) The cultic summaries were seen as the basis of the Yahwist's (J) history of early Israel which incorporated the Sinai theme and was prefaced by the primeval history. (4) The time of David and Solomon was the period when Israelite historiography developed out of the narrative art of the saga (166–204; so *Meyer, II/2, 285f.).

A number of preliminary stages led to Noth's history of Israel along traditio-historical lines. In 1930, he used the concept of the Greek amphictyony to explain the organization of the tribes in pre-monarchical Israel (so already, in limited ways, *Ewald I, 370, and Haupt). The unity of the twelve tribes during this period was primarily religious but with some legal basis as well. In 1940, Noth published his study of pentateuchal law, whose origin he associated with the life of the tribal amphictyony. Noth's study of the Deuteronomistic history (1943) stressed the late editorial work in the book of Joshua and its account of the conquest. His study of the pentateuchal traditions (1948) argued that the major traditions in the pentateuch can be divided into five major themes: guidance out of Egypt, guidance into the land, promise to the patriarchs, guidance in the wilderness, and revelation at Sinai. Each of these themes was originally independent of the others. These themes were first combined during the time of the tribal league – the pre-monarchical source 'G' in which these were combined was the basis for the later sources such as J from the Davidic–Solomonic period.

When these concepts are applied to the history of Israel, Noth has to begin his treatment with the tribal league. Since the early themes have only been associated secondarily, their historical outline is unreliable. Nothing substantial can be known about Moses since he has been introduced secondarily into the thematic traditions. The patriarchal traditions cannot be penetrated to discover anything of real historical value. The dominant account of the conquest is Deuteronomistic, although some early, primarily aetiological, materials are found in the accounts. Since the tribes moved into Palestine separately, no united leadership of the tribes can be ascribed to Joshua. It was the amphictyonic Israel which first imposed the 'all Israel' concept upon what were originally independent traditions and independent pasts. This time of the sacral amphictyonic organization is, for Noth, something like a golden age from which the later ages deviated.

A further approach to the early history of Israel is the attempt to understand early Israelite life in socio-economical categories. The first scholar to work along these lines was the sociologist Max Weber (1864–1920) in his *Ancient Judaism* although he was not an Old Testament specialist. This approach has been taken up recently by Mendenhall, Dus, Gottwald, and others. Although there are some major differences within this approach, the following are generally shared convictions. (1) Israel as a people or tribal confederacy originated in the land of Canaan. (2) Her origin was primarily the product of an internal revolt within Canaan against the Canaanite city-states' economic and political structures. The peasants and pastoralists involved in this revolt sought liberation and freedom from their oppressive overlords. (3) Israel created a new order of society in its tribal and covenant relationships. (4) The idea of Israel's origin in nomadic culture and the concept of a general conquest from outside the land must be given up. (5) The establishment of the monarchy was in many ways a return to the pre-revolutionary state of affairs and thus represents a paganization of the life and faith of liberated Israel.

These four approaches represent the basic alternatives at present employed in reconstructing Israelite history. The crucial period is, of course, the pre-monarchic times. Obviously, different scholars utilize insights and evidence from other approaches than that which is dominant in their own methodology. Some historians, especially *Herrmann and *de Vaux, cannot be said to be dominated by any exclusive methodology but are more eclectic.

II

THE PATRIARCHAL TRADITIONS

§1. PALESTINE IN THE SECOND MILLENNIUM BCE: THE ARCHAEOLOGICAL PICTURE

Strictly speaking a discussion of the so-called 'Patriarchal Age' could cover the entire ancient Near East in the second millennium BCE, since attempts have been made to locate the patriarchal era throughout the Middle and Late Bronze Ages, and evidence to corroborate varying theories has been adduced all the way from Mesopotamia to Egypt. However, in the following brief survey we must limit our scope chiefly to Palestine and the question of archaeology and patriarchal backgrounds, referring the reader to the respective bibliographies for wider orientation as well as details on specific topics.

A. Palestine in the second millennium BCE and biblical backgrounds

W. F. **Albright**, *From the Stone Age to Christianity*, ²1957; idem, 'The Impact of Archaeology on Biblical Research – 1966', *New Directions*, 1969, 1–16; J. **Barr**, 'Story and History in Biblical Theology', *JR* LVI, 1976, 1–17; J. **Bright**, *Early Israel in Recent History Writing: A Study in Method*, SBT 19, 1956; B. S. **Childs**, *Biblical Theology in Crisis*, Philadelphia: Westminster Press 1970; F. M. **Cross**, 'W. F. Albright's View of Biblical Archaeology', *BA* XXXVI, 1973, 2–5; W. G. **Dever**, ' "Biblical Archaeology" – or "The Archaeology of Syria–Palestine",' *CNI* XXII, 1972, 21 f.; idem, *Archaeology and Biblical Studies: Retrospects and Prospects*, Evanston: Seabury–Western 1974; idem, 'Archaeology', *IDB Supplementary Volume*, 1976, 44–52; J. J. **Finkelstein**, 'The Bible, Archaeology, and History: Have the Excavations Corroborated Scripture?', *Commentary* XXVIII, 1959, 341–9; A. E. **Glock**, 'Biblical Archaeology – An Emerging Discipline?', *The Archaeology of Jordan and Other Studies*, ed. L. T. Geraty, Berrien Springs: Andrews University Press (forthcoming); J. **Huesman**, 'Archaeology and Early Israel: The Scene Today', *CBQ* XXXVII, 1975, 1–16; M. **Noth**, 'Der Beitrag der

Archäologie zur Geschichte Israels', *SVT* VII, 1960, 262–82 = his *Aufsätze* I, 1971, 34–51; J. B. **Pritchard**, 'Culture and History', *The Bible in Modern Scholarship*, 1965, 313–24; G. **von Rad**, 'History and the Patriarchs', *ET* LXXII, 1960/61, 213–16; M. S. **Smith**, 'The Present State of Old Testament Studies', *JBL* LXXXVIII, 1969, 19–35; J. A. **Soggin**, 'Ancient Biblical Traditions and Modern Archaeological Discoveries', *BA* XXIII, 1960, 95–100; T. L. **Thompson**, *The Historicity of the Patriarchal Narratives: The Quest for the Historical Abraham*, BZAW 133, 1974; J. **Van Seters**, *Abraham in History and Tradition*, New Haven: Yale University Press 1975; R. **de Vaux**, 'Method in the Study of Early Hebrew History', *The Bible in Modern Scholarship*, 1965, 15–29; idem, 'On Right and Wrong Uses of Archaeology', *Near Eastern Archaeology*, 1970, 64–80; M. **Weippert**, *The Settlement of the Israelite Tribes*, 1971; G. E. **Wright**, *God Who Acts: Biblical Theology as Recital*, SBT 8, 1952; idem, *Biblical Archaeology*, Philadelphia/London: Westminster Press/Gerald Duckworth 1957; idem, 'Archaeology and Old Testament Studies', *JBL* LXXVII, 1958, 39–51; idem, 'Modern Issues in Biblical Studies; History and the Patriarchs', *ET* LXXI, 1959/60, 292–6; idem, 'Biblical Archaeology Today', *New Directions*, 1969, 167–86; idem, 'What Archaeology Can and Cannot Do', *BA* XXXIV, 1971, 70–6.

(*i*) *The relationship of archaeology to Israelite history*

In the 'Golden Age' of Near Eastern archaeology, which began at the turn of the century, discovery after discovery promised to dispel the darkness which obscured the original world of the Bible. It seemed a propitious (indeed irresistible) time for resuming the task which nineteenth-century biblical criticism had abandoned, that of reconstructing a historical, social, and cultural milieu of the second millennium BCE in which early Israelite origins could be understood. The first generation of archaeologists and biblical scholars was naturally preoccupied with amassing the data, but by the 1930s there began to appear comprehensive syntheses of the archaeological and literary remains from the ancient Near East which attempted to paint a broad and detailed canvas against which biblical personalities and events could be portrayed in a more 'credible' manner. The most magisterial of these syntheses was Albright's *From the Stone Age to Christianity*, published in 1940. In the post-war years Near Eastern archaeology developed improved field techniques and more sophisticated conceptual tools for analysis of the data, which to some scholars promised precision approaching that of the scientific disciplines. As the 'archaeological revolution' continued and confidence in it grew, it even seemed possible to reconstruct specific events of biblical history in their original context, among them the migration of Abraham from Ur and the settlement of the ancestors of Israel in Canaan.

Today there is a growing realization that the formative period in the correlation of archaeological data with research on Israelite origins is over. Despite confident statements in the handbooks (reminiscent of similar statements on 'the assured results of biblical criticism'), the results of a generation of intensive research have been inconclusive. Consequently there is a disenchantment with theoretical reconstructions which is shared by scholars in both disciplines. Near Eastern historians and archaeologists have been forced to specialize simply to cope with the growing mass of data; many doubt whether syntheses are possible any longer, and in any case they are not concerned to provide these simply for the convenience of the biblical historian. For their part, biblical scholars have become suspicious of the positivist historical philosophy which underlay many archaeological and literary syntheses and increasingly are ignoring them or subjecting them to sustained attack. On the pivotal question of archaeology and the historical backgrounds of the patriarchs, the latest exhaustive discussion by Thompson in 1974 comes back full circle to Wellhausen's dictum: 'Surely, no historical knowledge can be attained about the patriarchs, but only of the time when the stories about them arose among the Israelite people' (Thompson, 7). Thompson's conclusion is echoed in Van Seters' work published the following year (1975). Whether this view is justified or will eventually carry the day is unimportant for the present discussion, but it is a clear indication that we have reached an impasse.

We cannot return to an earlier stage of research, attempting a new and even more ambitious synthesis of archaeology and biblical criticism – even if that were possible within the present confines. In fact, we can break out of the impasse only by separating the two lines of inquiry and by developing new models for understanding *both* the archaeological and the biblical data. Not until that has been accomplished can dialogue and perhaps a new synthesis be undertaken.

'Biblical archaeology' cannot claim independent status or authority; strictly speaking it is not a discipline at all in the academic sense, but rather an interdisciplinary inquiry in which biblical scholars and archaeologists engage in a dialogue. The difficulty with most works of biblical archaeology is simply that they are monologues, usually written by biblical scholars for other biblical scholars. At best, the archaeological and biblical data are not presented with equal balance, competence, or judgment. At worst, hidden theological presuppositions determine the outcome of the inquiry. The result is that most discussions of biblical archaeology remain inconclusive or controversial, and they tend furthermore to discredit the whole enterprise of relating archaeology to biblical studies.

A dialogue by definition can proceed only from the articulation of differing and independent points of view. The obvious solution to the frustration produced by recent treatments on biblical archaeology seems to be to distinguish two fundamental disciplines, to define each in terms of its autonomous objectives and methods, and to allow each to develop according to its own canons. This is not to isolate archaeology from biblical studies, as some fear (see Cross), but rather to clear the way for a true dialogue, one which will respect the integrity of both disciplines, and will profit from the specialized knowledge of each (see further below and Dever, 1972, 1974).

(ii) Towards the definition of a discipline: Current trends in Syro-Palestinian archaeology

Archaeology, more than any other branch of the humanities, is constantly reshaping itself by virtue of the unique data with which it works – data which are constantly new, both in terms of the unceasing flow of archaeological discoveries themselves and the changing theories which they generate. While archaeology is always 'revolutionary' by nature, there are a number of recent developments which make Syro-Palestinian archaeology particularly so. Here we can do no more than catalogue briefly the factors which are in process of transforming the discipline. Among these factors are: the British–American revolution in stratigraphic excavations, which has exponentially multiplied the amount of reliable evidence dug, recorded, and published; the borrowing of techniques from the natural sciences, which has forced field archaeologists to confront multi-disciplinary staffs, broader categories of data which must be recovered, and unfamiliar tools of analysis; the increasing 'secularization' of Palestinian archaeology as it comes of age as an independent branch of general archaeology, rather than an adjunct of biblical studies; the proliferation of rival American, European, and more recently the Israeli and other national 'schools' in the Middle East, which provides alternatives to traditional American-style 'biblical archaeology'; the influence of the 'new archaeology', with its anthropological rather than historical orientation and its 'explicitly scientific' approach to theory and method. And we may add the advent of the computer, which makes it possible to manipulate vast quantities of data and to test for variables and patterns of association which were formerly irrecoverable; the growing use of mathematical models, statistics, systems-theory, and other techniques derived from ancillary disciplines; the demands for relevance and responsibility from applied archaeology and cultural ecology. The list could easily be expanded, but the implications are clear. First, the rate of change (if not of progress) is so rapid that the *usable* archaeological evidence brought to light from ancient Syria–Palestine in the last fifteen years outweighs the discoveries of the previous century. (For a survey of approximately this period, see Dever, 1976.) Secondly, the very wealth of new information threatens to overwhelm us, not only in demanding assimilation but in challenging all previous formulations; the pace of discovery is such that a dozen new questions are raised for every old question which is answered.

In the face of the developments outlined above, Syro-Palestinian archaeology today exhibits a certain self-consciousness which is new in its history and which takes several forms.

1. The first manifestation is common to other disciplines undergoing rapid expansion, i.e., specialization. A concomitant, again familiar in most developing disciplines, is the trend towards professionalism. Since Palestinian archaeology has traditionally been an 'amateur' pursuit, carried on largely by biblical scholars (especially in America), these developments are being lamented and even resisted in some quarters. But they are probably inevitable if archaeologists are to cope with the growing mass of data and the new demands which the discipline is making.

2. The second manifestation of self-consciousness is a new stress on the limitations of archaeology. At first glance this may be surprising in view of the vistas opening before us, but it represents a sobered reaction against the over-confidence of the previous generation. Today it is clear that much of our synthetic work was premature. As Morton Smith has said, 'Palestine itself has no more impressive ruins than those that litter the history of biblical archaeology' (31).

The new caution is not due merely to the fear that syntheses may rapidly become obsolete. It is also based on a realistic appraisal of the nature of our evidence. Now that we have a more representative view of Palestine in the context of the entire ancient Near East, it is clear that the country was always a cultural backwater, impoverished artistically as well as economically. Furthermore, its stormy political history has led to frequent pillage, destruction, and rebuilding by a long succession of peoples of various cultures, which has rendered the stratification of its mounds complex and has left its material remains in a poor state of preservation. Finally, the damp climate of central Palestine and the choice of papyrus and parchment as writing materials have combined to rob us of all but a handful of epigraphic remains (the Bible being a notable exception). Even if we are fortunate enough to turn up literary remains, they are usually so fragmentary as to be enigmatic, and thus their correlation with the artifactual remains often poses severe difficulties. In short, in contrast to neighbouring cultures, much of the archaeology of Palestine before the Israelite era is really 'prehistory'.

The final factor which has brought about a more moderate stance is the recognition, even among biblical archaeologists, that archaeology at best can play only a modest role in recreating 'the world of the Bible'. This represents a definite shift of opinion in recent years as to the potential contribution of archaeology to either the historical or the theological dimension of the Bible.

3. The third manifestation of the new self-consciousness is the growing demand for an independent status for Syro-Palestinian archaeology alongside (or even replacing) biblical archaeology. The logic of such a proposal has been outlined above, in describing the impasse now reached in most works on biblical archaeology. Furthermore, the trends we have noted within the field of archaeology itself have generated the necessary momentum. The present writer seems to have been the first archaeologist to advocate a deliberate separation of Syro-Palestinian archaeology from biblical studies. The idea is not novel, of course. There is a long-established secular tradition of Palestinian archaeology in Europe, one which is now flourishing in Israel. But in America the Albright-Wright 'school' so dominated the scene that Palestinian archaeology has been considered primarily a subsidiary of biblical studies, rather than an independent discipline (on the above see Dever, 1974). Until the early 1970s this state of affairs was presumed to such a degree that a defence of it had rarely been offered, any more than a definition of what was meant by 'biblical archaeology' (but see provisionally Albright and Wright, 1969). Not all biblical scholars were reconciled. In his 1968 presidential address before the Society of Biblical Literature Morton Smith recommended that 'for a correct history of the Israelites we must have the archaeological facts determined quite objectively and independently by competent archaeologists, and the biblical facts likewise determined by competent philologians, and then we can begin to compare them' (Smith, 34). But Smith's plea was to go unheeded for several years.

Today the scene has shifted – in fact more rapidly than the writer's programmatic essay had anticipated. It is not so much a matter of this view having prevailed (for even today there has been little critical discussion of the issues) as it is of the further development of trends which were already obvious. As a consequence Syro-Palestinian archaeology is now well on the way to becoming an autonomous professional discipline, i.e., a branch of general archaeology rather than an adjunct to biblical studies. This development is not taking place in theological seminaries but in the context of the secular university, where the field is finding both recruits and financial support. The pendulum has swung so fast and so far that Glock has suggested that the question is no longer whether Syro-Palestinian archaeology can survive, but whether there is room alongside it for biblical archaeology, at least as an *academic* discipline.

(iii) An old discussion resumed: What can archaeology contribute to biblical studies

The 1950s gave birth to the well-known controversy on early Israelite origins, between the 'German school' represented by Alt, von Rad, and Noth on the one hand and the 'American school' of Albright, Wright, Bright, and their followers on the other. The controversy was precipitated by the 'biblical theology' movement which reached its peak precisely in the late 1950s. At issue were fundamental differences in theological positions; in the application of literary, form-critical, and tradition-historical analyses; and in principles of historiography. Biblical archaeology became involved as one aspect of the larger debate over methodology, particularly since it had played a pivotal role in the work of the American protagonists.

The controversy came to a head partly as a result of the appearance of Wright's *Biblical Archaeology* in 1957, following closely upon his provocative works of the same period in biblical theology, especially *God Who Acts: Biblical Theology as Recital* (1952). The notices in Germany were highly critical and precipitated a sharp exchange of views over archaeology and fundamental issues in biblical history among Wright, Noth, and von Rad. The debate as far as the writing of the history of Israel was concerned was summarized by Bright in his *Early Israel in Recent History Writing* (1956). The views of the two schools found crystallization in the major histories of *Noth and *Bright. Here one of the crucial issues was the patriarchal era and the degree to which archaeology had helped to establish its historicity (see Wright, 1958; von Rad, 1960/61), from which the discussion then naturally moved to the question of the role of archaeology in general in biblical studies (see especially Noth, 1960; and see the succinct summary of the main positions in Soggin). Although it is an oversimplification, the American position could be termed 'maximalist' and the German 'minimalist' (for discussion and references, especially qualifications on Albright's charge of 'nihilism' levelled against Noth, see Thompson, 5–7, 52–4).

It was at this point that the combination of Wright's 'biblical theology' and his 'biblical archaeology' led to confusion. Wright's thesis that God 'acting in history' is central to the proclamation of Israel's faith led him to conclude that 'in biblical faith everything depends upon whether the events actually occurred' (1952, 126). To many this came dangerously close to historicism. And when a biblical theologian of this persuasion was at the same time a well-known Palestinian archaeologist, the whole enterprise could be called into question. Though it was rarely suggested that Wright's own archaeological work suffered from theological bias, suspicions lingered about less professional archaeologists and about biblical archaeology in general.

The chief justification for reviving the old debate on the contribution of archaeology to biblical studies is that the issues were never resolved. Inasmuch as both schools produced viable approaches to the history of Israel, marked by sound scholarship and persuasive argument, the discussion was polarized early in the course of its development. Throughout the 1960s there was no significant modification of views. Noth had asserted that Syro-Palestinian archaeology should be conceived as a discipline apart from biblical studies, an independent science with methods of its own and aims evolving from its own work. His chief criticism was that 'it has still not entirely overcome the improper search for direct Biblical connections' (*Noth, 47). That the German critique of the positivist basis of American biblical archaeology has not substantially changed may be seen from the 1971 work of the young Tübingen scholar Manfred Weippert. In America the Albright–Wright school prevailed, but not all biblical scholars were reconciled to its views. Many liberal scholars regarded biblical archaeology as an unfortunate accompaniment of neo-orthodoxy, a thinly-disguised fundamentalism appealing now to archaeology for external support. In Finkelstein's scathing attack on Glueck (1959) and Morton Smith's caricature of 'pseudorthodox' archaeologists one sees both the heat (if not the light) which the argument was still capable of generating, and the fact that the patriarchal era was still at issue.

By the early 1970s the atmosphere was more conducive to a

renewed confrontation of the basic issues. For one thing, biblical scholarship had already written the obituary of the short-lived biblical theology movement of the 1950s and could begin to put the archaeological aspects of the earlier debate in perspective (see Childs, 32–50; Barr, 1–3). The adoption of newer models from sociology and other disciplines also made archaeology of less crucial importance (see below, §D/1). However, to underline the fact that historical and theological approaches were not being abandoned, major reassessments of early Israelite history have appeared within the last two years in the works of Thompson (1974) and Van Seters (1975). These treatments alone would justify resuming the old discussion on archaeology and biblical studies. And it is no coincidence that the patriarchs are once again in the forefront of the discussion. (See the anticipation of the discussion and the résumé of earlier views in Huesman.)

For their part, biblical archaeologists by the early 1970s had also moved away from earlier positions. It is significant that both de Vaux and Wright, who had strongly defended the historicity of Israel's faith on the basis of archaeology, nevertheless in their latest works seemed to modify their claims, for archaeology's contribution not only to history but also to faith. One of de Vaux's last articles, 'On Right and Wrong Uses of Archaeology', was severely critical of the apologetic use of archaeology by biblical scholars, noting that 'what the Bible records is "sacred history"; it provides a religious interpretation of history . . . Archaeology can assist us only in establishing the facts that have been so interpreted' (de Vaux, 1970, 69; see also the important statements in his 1965 article). Wright followed de Vaux with a supportive treatment of his own, also his last statement on the subject. He stressed the limitations of all archaeological 'proof' and concluded that even when available such proof 'does not extend to the validity of the religious claims the Bible would place upon us' (Wright, 1971, 73; see also Pritchard's earlier cautions, 319).

The positions of both biblical scholars and archaeologists outlined above suggest that there are now possibilities for a consensus. It would be premature to predict a consensus on the results of archaeology, as witness the present critiques of Thompson and Van Seters, as well as the discussion which is likely to ensue in the reviews. But in the area of methodology the general agreement noted above on the need for separating the two means of inquiry, as well as on the limited role of archaeology in historical and theological reconstructions, has at least produced the essential conditions for a dialogue in the future. Already the outlines of a minimal statement can be drafted. Yet because the Bible is not history in the modern critical or scientific sense, archaeology is limited in the contribution it can make. Archaeology may clarify the historical context of events described in biblical history, but it cannot confirm the interpretation of these events by the biblical writers, much less the modern theological inferences to be drawn from them. (For the most constructive recent exchange, see the symposia conducted by de Vaux, Greenberg and Mendenhall, and by Freedman and Pritchard, in *The Bible in Modern Scholarship*, ed. J. P. Hyatt, 1965, 15–43, 294–324.) With that provision in mind, we turn to an archaeological survey of Syria–Palestine in the second millennium BCE.

B.   *The Middle and Late Bronze Ages in Syria–Palestine*

Y. **Aharoni**, *Land of the Bible*, 1967; W. F. **Albright**, *From the Stone Age to Christianity*, [2]1957; idem, 'The Chronology of MB I (Early Bronze–Middle Bronze)', *BASOR* CLXVIII, 1962, 36–42; idem, 'The Eighteenth-Century Princes of Byblos and the Chronology of Middle Bronze', *BASOR* CLXXVI, 1964, 38–46; idem, 'Remarks on the Chronology of Early Bronze IV–Middle Bronze IIA in Phoenicia and Syria Palestine', *BASOR* CLXXXIV, 1966, 26–35; idem, 'The Amarna Letters From Palestine', *CAH* II/2, 1975, 98–116; R. **Amiran**, 'The Pottery of the Middle Bronze Age I in Palestine', *IEJ* X, 1960, 204–25; idem, *Ancient Pottery of the Holy Land*, Jerusalem/New Brunswick: Massada Press/Rutgers University Press 1969; J. **von Beckerath**, *Untersuchungen zur politischen Geschichte der zweiten Zwischenzeit in Ägypten*, ÄF 23, 1964; J. **Bottéro** et al., *The Near East: The Early Civilizations*, London/New York: Weidenfeld and Nicolson/Delacorte Press 1967 = *Die altorientalischen Reiche* I, FWG 3, 1967; W. G. **Dever**, 'The "Middle Bronze I" Period in Syria and Palestine', *Near Eastern Archaeology*, 1970, 132–63; idem, 'The Peoples of Palestine in the Middle Bronze I Period', *HTR* LXIV, 1971, 197–226; idem, 'The EB IV–MB I Horizon in Transjordan and Southern Palestine', *BASOR* CCX, 1973, 37–63; idem, 'The Gezer Fortifications and the "High Place": an Illustration of Stratigraphic Methods and Problems', *PEQ* CV, 1973, 61–70; idem, 'The MB II Stratification in the Northwest Gate Area at Shechem', *BASOR* CCXXVI, 1974, 31–52; idem, 'MB IIA Cemeteries at 'Ain es-Sâmiyeh and Sinjil', *BASOR* CCXVII, 1975, 23–36; idem, 'The Beginning of the Middle Bronze Age in Syria–Palestine', *Magnalia Dei: The Mighty Acts of God* (Festschrift G. E. Wright), ed. F. M. Cross, W. Lemke, and P. D. Miller, Garden City: Doubleday 1976, 3–38; M. S. **Drower**, 'Syria *c.* 1550–1400 BC', *CAH* II/1, 1973, 417–525; idem, 'Ugarit', *CAH* II/2, 1975, 130–60; H. J. **Franken**, 'Palestine in the Time of the Nineteenth Dynasty: The Archaeological Evidence', *CAH* II/2, 1975, 331–7; P. **Garelli**, *Le Proche-*

Orient asiatique des origines aux invasions des Peuples de la Mer, Paris: Presses Universitaires de France 1969; S. **Gitin**, 'Middle Bronze I "Domestic" Pottery at Jebel Qaʿaqīr', *EI* XII, 1975, 46–62; W. W. **Hallo** and W. K. **Simpson**, *The Ancient Near East: A History*, New York: Harcourt Brace Jovanovich 1971; V. **Hankey**, 'A Late Bronze Age Temple at Amman', *Levant* VI, 1974, 131–78; W. C. **Hayes**, 'Egypt: From the Death of Ammenemes III to Seqenenre II', *CAH* II/1, 1973, 42–76; W. **Helck**, *Die Beziehungen Ägyptens zu Vorderasien im 3. und 2. Jahrtausend v. Chr.*, ÄA 5, 1962, [2]1971; J. B. **Hennessy**, 'Excavation of a Late Bronze Age Temple at Amman', *PEQ* XCVIII, 1966, 155–62; T. G. H. **James**, 'Egypt: From the Expulsion of the Hyksos to Amenophis I', *CAH* II/1, 1973, 289–312; K. M. **Kenyon**, 'The Middle and Late Bronze Age Strata at Megiddo', *Levant* I, 1969, 25–60; 1971, see under Posener; idem, 'Palestine in the Middle Bronze Age', *CAH* II/1, 1973, 77–116; idem, 'Palestine in the Time of the Eighteenth Dynasty', *CAH* II/1, 1973, 526–56; M. **Kochavi**, 'The Middle Bronze Age I (the Intermediate Bronze Age) in Eretz–Israel', *Qadmoniot* II/2, 1969, 38–44 (Hebrew); J.-R. **Kupper**, 'Northern Mesopotamia and Syria', *CAH* II/1, 1973, 1–41; P. W. **Lapp**, *The Dhahr Mirzbâneh Tombs: Three Intermediate Bronze Age Cemeteries in Jordan*, New Haven: American Schools of Oriental Research 1966; idem, 'The Conquest of Palestine in the Light of Archaeology', *CTM* XXXVIII, 1967, 283–300; idem, *Biblical Archaeology and History*, Cleveland: World Publishing Company 1969; idem, 'Palestine in the Early Bronze Age', in *Near Eastern Archaeology* 1970, 101–31; P. W. and N. **Lapp**, *Discoveries in Wadi ed-Daliyeh*, AASOR 41, 1976; M. **Liverani**, ed., *La Siria nel Tardo Bronzo*, OAC 9, 1969; A. **Malamat**, 'Syrien–Palästina in der 2. Hälfte des 2. Jahrtausends', *FWG* 3/II, 1966, 177–211; idem, 'Northern Canaan and the Mari Texts', *Near Eastern Archaeology*, 1970, 164–77; B. **Mazar**, 'The Middle Bronze Age in Palestine', *IEJ* XVIII, 1968, 65–97; S. **Mittmann**, *Beiträge zur Siedlungs- und Territorialgeschichte des nördlichen Ostjordanlandes*, ADPV, 1970; E. D. **Oren**, 'A Middle Bronze Age I Warrior Tomb at Beth-Shan', *ZDPV* LXXXVII, 1971, 109–34; idem, 'The Early Bronze IV Period in Northern Palestine and its Cultural and Chronological Setting', *BASOR* CCX, 1973, 20–37; P. J. **Parr**, 'The Origin of the Rampart Fortifications of Middle Bronze Age Palestine and Syria', *ZDPV* LXXXIV, 1968, 18–45; G. **Posener**, J. **Bottéro**, K. M. **Kenyon**, 'Syria and Palestine *c.* 2160–1780 BC', *CAH* I/2, 1971, 532–94; K. W. **Prag**, 'The Intermediate Early Bronze–Middle Bronze Age: An Interpretation of the Evidence from Transjordan, Syria and Lebanon', *Levant* VI, 1974, 69–116; A. F. **Rainey**, 'The World of Sinuhe', *Israel Oriental Studies* II, 1972, 369–408; D. B. **Redford**, 'The Hyksos Invasion in History and Tradition', *Orientalia* XXXIX, 1970, 1–51; J. D. **Seger**, 'The Middle Bronze Age Fortifications at Gezer and Shechem: A Hyksos Retrospective', *EI* XII, 1975, 34–45; T. L. **Thompson**, *The Historicity of the Patriarchal Narratives*, BZAW 133, 1974; O. **Tufnell** (with W. A. **Ward**), 'Relations Between Byblos, Egypt and Mesopotamia at the End of the Third Millennium BC: A Study of the "Montet Jar"', *Syria*

XLIII, 1966, 165–214; idem, 'The Pottery from Royal Tombs I–III of Byblos', *Berytus* XVIII, 1969, 5–33; J. **Van Seters**, *The Hyksos: A New Investigation*, New Haven: Yale University Press 1969; W. A. **Ward**, *Egypt and the East Mediterranean World 2200–1900 BC*, Beirut: Khayat 1971; J. **Weinstein**, 'Egyptian Relations with Palestine in the Middle Kingdom', *BASOR* CCXVII, 1975, 1–16; G. E. **Wright**, *The Pottery of Palestine from the Earliest Times to the End of the Early Bronze Age*, New Haven: American Schools of Oriental Research 1937; idem, 'The Archaeology of Palestine', *The Bible and the Ancient Near East*, 1961, 73–112; idem, *Shechem*, 1965; idem, 'The Archaeology of Palestine from the Neolithic through the Middle Bronze Age', *JAOS* XCI, 1971, 276–93; G. R. H. **Wright**, 'Tell el-Yehūdīyah and the Glacis', *ZDPV* LXXXIV, 1968, 1–17; Y. **Yadin**, *Hazor, the Head of all Those Kingdoms*, London: Oxford University Press 1972.

The second millennium BCE in Syria–Palestine comprises the end of the Early Bronze Age and the transition to the Middle Bronze Age; the whole of the Middle and Late Bronze Ages (hereafter 'MB' and 'LB'); and the forepart of the Iron Age (on the latter, see below, ch. IV, §3).

Before beginning our survey it may be helpful to assess several general treatments which cover the period under consideration. There is no satisfactory history of the MB–LB periods in Syria–Palestine. Standard larger works on the ancient Near East include volume 3, parts I–III, of the shorter and more unified *Fischer Weltgeschichte* edited by Bottéro et al. (1965–7), the first part translated into English (see Bottéro, 1967), the first part of the very commendable two-volume history of Garelli, and the massive, superbly-documented third edition of the *Cambridge Ancient History*, volumes I–II, first issued in fascicles and now available in four volumes (1970–5). The only serviceable one-volume history of the ancient Near East is Hallo and Simpson (1971). However, with the exception of the chapters by de Vaux and Kenyon in the new *CAH*, the coverage of Syria–Palestine (particularly the archaeological evidence) is deficient in all these works, which concentrate on the literary documentation from Egypt and Mesopotamia. The second volume of the Israeli-produced *World History of the Jewish People*, on the patriarchs, contains chapters by eminent authorities but is too popular to be used for critical scholarship.

For Palestine proper the only authoritative survey which covers the archaeological evidence is still Wright's chapter in the *Bible and the Ancient Near East* (1961), but it is brief and beginning to be dated. Albright's classic *Archaeology of Palestine*, out of print, is in process of revision by the present writer. Perhaps the best recent synthesis is found in de Vaux's history, which contains a *Prologue* combining a historical sketch with a summary of the archaeological evidence (*de Vaux, 55–123). However, the pace of archaeological discovery is such that constant reference must be made to the more recent, specialized discussions cited in the bibliography above. If archaeological handbooks are lacking, we are more fortunate in other branches of Palestinology. Aharoni's *Land of the Bible* (1967) has become the standard historical geography, and Amiran's *Ancient Pottery of the Holy Land* (1970) provides for the first time a popular yet thoroughly reliable study of the pottery of Palestine.

(i) The Middle Bronze I period

The period following the end of the Early Bronze Age was something of a 'Dark Age' until recently. Albright had characterized it in the 1930s as 'Middle Bronze I', dated it about 2100–1900 BCE, and regarded it as the initial phase of the Middle Bronze period. Wright's pioneer classification of the pottery in 1937 was followed by an important treatment by Ruth Amiran (1960) which demonstrated ceramic parallels with Syria and Upper Mesopotamia.

Between the time of these two ceramic analyses, material had mounted from many sites in Syria and Palestine but came mostly from large cemeteries at sites conspicuously lacking in stratified remains. For Palestine note should be made particularly of Tell el-'Ajjûl, Lachish, Megiddo, and Jericho. More recently Gibeon, Mirzbâneh/'Ain es-Sâmiyeh, the Wâdī ed-Dâliyeh, and other sites in the central hills have given a glimpse of one of the characteristic regional assemblages of the 'families' of the period. In the Judean hills to the south, large cemeteries at Khirbet el-Kīrmil and the settlement-cemetery complex at Jebel Qa'aqīr hint at extensive occupation but suggest that it was seasonal and only semi-sedentary (for a study of the largest repertoire of domestic pottery yet analysed, from Jebel Qa'aqīr, see Gitin, 1975). Since the explorations of Glueck between 1932 and the 1950s it has been recognized that the only significant distribution of settlement sites is to be found on the fringes of the country, in Transjordan and the Negeb. Only recently have excavations been conducted at Khirbet Iskander, 'Arô'er, Ikhtanu, Bâb edh-Dhrâ' and Har Yeruḥam (south of Beersheba), but already they promise to revolutionize our understanding of the period. (On the above see the surveys of Dever, 1970, 1971.)

Several recent works review the current evidence and suggest new lines of research. Lapp's otherwise admirable summation (1966) suffered from an overriding theory of ethnic origins which has commended itself to few scholars. Kenyon's review of the evidence in the revised *Cambridge Ancient History* (1971; first published in fascicle form in 1965) resulted in an impressive presentation of the 'Amorite hypothesis', especially in conjunction with the authoritative treatments of Egypt and Syria by Posener and Bottéro in the same chapter. The present writer has provided a fully-documented summary of MB I studies up until recently (Dever, 1970) and has subsequently offered his own analysis in terms of geographic-cultural 'families' (Dever, 1971 and 'EB IV–MB I Horizon'). In dealing with the previously unpublished Beth-shan tombs Oren produced an integrated picture of northern Palestine in MB I (his 'EB IV'), and drew attention to connections with Syria and with the Early Bronze period (Oren, 1973). The latest overview by Prag (1974) sets the discussion in a wider context by presenting new material from Transjordan, Syria, and Lebanon, as well as by raising the larger question of the economic basis of the MB I (her 'EB–MB') period.

The proliferation as well as the variety of the new evidence has generated attempts at synthesis, but it has not yet produced a consensus, even on some of the most fundamental issues such as terminology. Kenyon suggested as early as the 1950s that the new data, particularly that from the Jericho tombs, characterized the period as a nomadic interlude between the great urban cultures of the third and the second millennia BCE, for which the term 'Intermediate EB–MB' was more suitable (see Kenyon in Posener et al., 1971, 567–83 and references there to earlier statements). The link with the Middle Bronze period proper had indeed been tenuous, and several scholars supported Kenyon's perception of the period by adopting variants of the 'Intermediate' terminology, among them Kochavi and Lapp (Kochavi, 1969; Lapp, 1966). The latter, however, went further in deriving the distinctively new elements in this culture from 'Kurgan' invaders from beyond the Caucasus. But by the early 1970s the elusive EB IV period immediately preceding the phase in question began to be clarified by new material, including the first homogeneous EB IV tomb group from Bâb edh-Dhrâ' (see discussion of T. Scaub's publication in Dever, 'EB IV – B I Horizon'). Consequently MB I emerged in the view of some scholars as the last phase of the Early Bronze Age in terms of its material cultures. Thus Olávarri, Oren, Dever, and others have advocated reviving Wright's earlier suggestion of EB IV for the period, stressing both its continuity with the Early Bronze Age and the fact that the culture was indigenous rather than intrusive in character (see Dever, 'EB IV – MB I Horizon', and references there). In this view new elements in ceramic, metallic and tomb types are best accounted for by postulating semi-nomadic newcomers from Syria among the survivors who fled from the urban centres at the collapse of Early Bronze Age Palestine, the result being a hybrid material culture which first emerges in Transjordan. Thus the traditional Amorite hypothesis of Albright, de Vaux, and Kenyon (though not its connection with the biblical patriarchs) has recently been defended as an alternative to the views of Lapp and Kochavi (Dever, 1971; we shall return to this question presently).

In conclusion, there has been a virtual explosion in MB I studies in the past two decades, brought about by a wealth of newly excavated material as well as by a burst of creative theorizing. Yet we must caution that archaeologists still cannot draw a comprehensive picture of the MB I culture as a whole, let alone account for its origins or identify the ethnic movements which may be connected with its appearance in Palestine. The material at our disposal is too scant and too unrepresentative. There is an agreement only on the links of MB I with the Early Bronze rather than the Middle Bronze period; the tendency to stress its semi-sedentary character more than its nomadic aspects; and the preference for dates about a century higher than Albright's dates, i.e., about 2200–2000 BCE. The remaining differences are largely determined by the particular aspect of the evidence which is selected for emphasis.

The above sketch of MB I may seem more detailed than is justified for such an ephemeral cultural phase in the archaeology of Palestine. Yet the period must loom out of proportion simply because it has often been designated by archaeologists and biblical scholars as the 'Patriarchal Age'. We shall postpone the question of the legitimacy of this usage until we complete the survey of the other archaeological phases with which the patriarchal era has been equated.

(ii) *The Middle Bronze IIA period*

This period, dated about 2000–1800 BCE, was originally distinguished as the initial phase of the Middle Bronze period proper (MB IIB–C) by Albright in the 1930s on the basis of Tell Beit Mirsim (strata G–F). At that time there was insufficient material to fill the period, but subsequent material from the 'Courtyard Cemetery' at Tell el-'Ajjûl, Megiddo XV–XIII, Shechem, Gezer, and now from the Israeli excavations at Râs el-'Ain (biblical Aphek), confirms Albright's perception of MB IIA. The evidence is still scant and widely scattered, largely because at many sites MB IIA marks the beginning of a long continuous build-up, and the stratification reveals the latest and most impressive remains far better. Nevertheless the most recent attempts at synthesis have shown the MB IIA period emerging as a distinct cultural phase. (For the history of MB IIA studies and a summary of the latest data see Dever, 1976.)

Several conclusions about MB IIA would find general support today. The urban character of the period, especially in contrast to MB I, is now beyond doubt, even though many sites were not fortified until near the end of the period. The more MB IIA remains that are unearthed, the more certain it becomes that this is the formative phase of the material culture which flourished in Syria–Palestine throughout most of the second millennium BCE and which characterizes the classic 'Canaanite/Amorite' civilization. The zenith of this long period is reached some two centuries later in MB IIC, but the basic expression of the material culture is already achieved by MB IIA, as witnessed in styles of domestic architecture, ceramic and metallic types, and the plastic arts (on the weapons, for instance, see Oren, 1971; Dever, 1975). Imports indicate Egyptian influence and perhaps trade but do not support Albright's notion of an Egyptian political empire in Asia (see Ward, 1971; Weinstein, 1975). However, MB IIA does correlate in general with the end of the First Intermediate period and the renascence beginning with the Twelfth Dynasty in Egypt (about 1991–1786 BCE). Similarly, the overall cultural situation in Palestine is part of larger developments in Mesopotamia after the Sargonic era came to an end and Amorite influence began to mount with the Ur III period (about 2060–1950 BCE). These correlations, taken together with the higher chronology now necessary for MB I, have resulted in a tendency to raise Albright's dates for MB IIA from about 1900–1750 BCE to about 2000/1950–1800 BCE. (See Albright, 1962, 1964, 1966, and Dever, 1976 and references there; on the significance of Byblos and especially the Royal Tombs, see Tufnell and Ward, 1966, and Tufnell, 1969.)

The most intriguing question about this period concerns the origin of the MB IIA material culture and the possibility of identifying its appearance with ethnic movements. The question cannot yet be resolved, but already there is agreement on the main lines of future research. Although attempts have been made to relate the pottery to the preceding period (see Amiran, 1960, 205–6; and contrast Dever, 1970, 159, n. 65; 1976), it is clear that the material culture of MB IIA as a whole cannot be derived from MB I. The striking thing about this culture is the fact that it appeared suddenly in Palestine, without local antecedents. Once established it persisted throughout several centuries, during which it was so homogeneous that its evolution in its later phases can be accounted for almost entirely by internal development.

Very little in the way of reliable stratified material has yet been published from contemporary contexts in Syria. The Hama sequence (supplemented by that of the current Italian excavations at Tell Mardikh) suggests that at least along the Orontes cultural development proceeded from the end of the third millennium through the first half of the second millennium BCE without a major break (see discussion and references in Dever, 1970, 137f.). Furthermore, although detailed comparisons are difficult due to the lack of reliable materials, it may be argued that the pottery of Palestine is more closely related to that of Syria in the MB IIA period than in any other in the country's history. These observations suggest that after the disruption of life in Palestine at the end of the third millennium BCE (EB IV–MB I) there was a fresh cultural impetus from Syria, resulting in the emergence of a homogeneous and vigorous urban culture which came to dominate the entire Syro-Palestinian area in the Middle Bronze Age. Since this period in Upper Mesopotamia and Syria is marked by the Amorite expansion, nearly all scholars today equate MB IIA in Palestine with the arrival and establishment of the Amorites (Wright, 1961; 1971, 288f.; Mazar, 1968, 69–75; Kenyon, 1973, 82–7; *de Vaux, 58–64; Dever, 1976; Rainey, 1972, 389–93).

The only objection to this theory arises when the previous period, MB I, is also connected with the Amorite expansion. Lapp and others have asked how both periods can be explained by reference to the Amorites when the material cultures of the two are so strikingly different (Lapp, 1966, 94, 114; Rainey, 388f.). The answer is deceptively simple, as has been pointed out elsewhere (Dever, 1971, 224f.). The Amorite movements so well known from the texts clearly did not constitute a single 'wave' but rather extended over several centuries. While the earlier Amorites infiltrating Palestine in the EB IV–MB I period came from a semi-nomadic culture on the fringes of Syria, succeeding groups of Amorites in MB IIA coming from the same areas had meanwhile been partially or wholly urbanized. Thus they brought with them to Palestine a material culture which appeared radically new there but had actually been flourishing for some time in Syria.

(iii) The Middle Bronze IIB–C period

This period, about 1800–1500 BCE, has proved less susceptible to revision than the preceding two periods largely because it had been better documented from the beginning. Its main characteristics having already been distinguished by Albright and his successors, research has concentrated on filling in the picture. Several recent treatments summarize the wealth of new information available. Kenyon's thorough critical analysis of the stratification of the major sites (1969, 1973) has dated some of the crucial material more precisely. Mazar (1968) has brought together both the archaeological remains and the literary sources to provide a masterful synthesis which sets the Middle Bronze Age in Syria–Palestine against its larger background in the ancient Near East. A review-article by Wright (1971) on Kenyon's contributions to the revised *Cambridge Ancient History* (Kenyon, 1973) contains valuable insights and balanced judgments on the period as a whole.

The MB IIB–C period, as we have suggested, represents a continuous development from MB IIA, the full flowering of the Canaanite (or Amorite) culture which reached its zenith in the powerful and prosperous Syro-Palestinian city-states of late MB IIC (about 1600 BCE). The Mari texts mentioning tin-trading parties journeying to Hazor and Laish/Dan (Malamat, 1970) are but one indication of the international character of this era, in which travel and trade flowed along the entire Fertile Crescent. Palestine was a province of greater Syria, as shown by the clear links in ceramic and metallic repertoires, and particularly by the occurrence in both areas of cities fortified by similar earthen embankments, formidable masonry revetments, and three entry-way gates (see the latest discussion in Seger, 1974, 43–5). The latter earthen works or *glacis* can no longer be identified exclusively with the Middle Bronze Age (Parr, 1968) nor with the 'Hyksos' (G. R. H. Wright, 1968), but the art of constructing them reached its peak in MB IIB–C, when they are found at nearly every excavated site in Syria–Palestine.

The Egyptian term 'Hyksos' for this period had been used by Engberg (and sometimes even by Albright and his followers) in an ethnic sense and was thus indiscriminately applied to fortifications, weapons, and pottery. More recently scholars have come to regard these as the typical expressions of the vigorous and prosperous material culture of the indigenous population of Syria–Palestine, for which the terms Amorite or Canaanite are more suitable (Mazar, 1968, 94–6; Van Seters). However, elements of these Western Semitic peoples did infiltrate Egypt in the time of the Fifteenth Dynasty and dominated Lower Egypt briefly from their power-base in Palestine before they were expelled at the end of the Seventeenth Dynasty (Helck, 92–173; von Beckerath, 109–203; Redford, 1–55; Hayes, 54–76; James, 289–96). The current Austrian excavations at Daba'a in the Delta, not far from the Hyksos capital at Avaris (see *de Vaux, 77–8), have brought to light an assemblage of typically Palestinian MB IIA/B material (about 1800 BCE), indicating that the Asiatic presence in Egypt began quite early and was probably a peaceful infiltration at first.

The Hurrian peoples, who were expanding in Syria–Palestine in the period from the eighteenth to the sixteenth century BCE, may have introduced some new methods of warfare, especially chariotry, but their role if any in the penetration of Egypt remains unclear. It is likely, however, that the Hurrian military aristocracy (the so-called *maryannu* warriors) provided a model for the feudal society which characterized the Syro-Palestinian city-states, as well as contributing to the extraordinary cultural dynamism of the period. (This is particularly characteristic of the last phase in MB IIC; for an appreciation of the latter see Wright, 1971, 293; and especially Mazar, 1968, 90–6; and contrast the minimalist view of Kenyon, 1973, 116.)

Detailed study of the complex stratification at several sites has produced much additional data as well as a firmer chronological basis for subdivision within the period. Kenyon's preliminary reports of her work at Jericho (Kenyon, 1973, 90–9 and references there) are of the greatest importance for the study of the fortifications as well as the rich material from tombs and domestic deposits. The same author's reworking of the Megiddo material (1969) brought a good deal of order out of chaos at this important site. The renewed excavations at Gezer from 1964 to 1974 clarified Macalister's discoveries early in this century and has made possible detailed reconstructions of the monumental fortifications, the 'High Place', and other structures of MB IIB–C (see summary and references in Dever, 1973, 65–70; Seger, 39–42). At Shechem, the similar application of modern stratigraphic methods by Wright and others disentangled various elements from the German excavations and revealed that the city began in MB II and quickly reached its height (see Wright, 1965, 57–79, 103–38; and the summary in Seger, 34–8). The last two seasons at Shechem, in 1972–3, near the North-west Gate revealed a large barracks and the earliest tripartite temple yet discovered, completing the fullest picture obtained to date of the 'agora' of an ancient Syro-Palestinian town (Dever, 1974, 31–52).

When the stratified MB II sequence from Hazor XVII–XVI is fully published it will add substantially to the overall picture (see provisionally Yadin). Finally, current Israeli excavations at Dan, Acco, Tel Poleg, Yabneh-yam, and elsewhere should provide corroborative detail.

The chronology of MB II has been progressively refined. Today the tendency is to raise the dates for the beginning of MB IIB by about fifty years to about 1800 BCE, a shift away from Albright's long-held 'Low Chronology' towards the 'Middle Chronology' of Sidney Smith and others, based partly on the Mari and Hazor-Dan synchronisms. (For Albright's last 'ultra-low' chronology and reasons for its rejection see Albright, 1962, 1964, 1966; Malamat, 1970, 170f.; and Dever, 1976, and references there.) The discernment of a break within the period about 1650 BCE and its separation into MB IIB and MB IIC phases is not followed by Kenyon and is regarded with scepticism by some Israeli excavators. American scholars, however, generally support the distinction, first advanced by Albright on the basis of Tell Beit Mirsim (strata E–D) and supported later by the detailed stratified sequences at Shechem and Gezer (contrast Kenyon, 1973, 114–16, with Mazar, 91–6, and Seger, 42–5). While both the above views stress the inner continuity of MB II, the American view sees MB IIC as an entity which is discernible both ceramically and stratigraphically, as well as in the fact that the most impressive fortifications and other developments of the material culture must have been compressed into the last century of the Middle Bronze Age, giving it a distinctive character.

The end of the period is marked by massive destruction levels at every site thus far excavated, undoubtedly to be correlated with the expulsion of the 'Hyksos' beginning under the last king of the Seventeenth Dynasty, Kamose (about 1540 BCE) and continuing under his successors of the early Eighteenth Dynasty. Recent work has shed much more light on the political and cultural processes which brought the Middle Bronze Age to an end. It can now be shown that some cities were destroyed and abandoned early; others like Shechem were destroyed several times in quick succession; and still others like Ta'anach and Gezer persisted until the MB II C/LB I horizon. (The latter phase is distinguishable in terms of relative *ceramic* chronology but still cannot be dated absolutely; it may fall as late as the destructions of Thutmose III about 1468 BCE.) Thus the transition from the Middle Bronze to the Late Bronze Age represents neither an abrupt nor a complete break in culture (for summaries of the evidence see Kenyon, 1973, 526–56; Seger, 42–5).

(iv) The Late Bronze Age

This period, about 1550/1500–1200 BCE, has not witnessed anything like the dramatic illumination which has transformed our knowledge of the Middle Bronze Age in recent years. There has been a steady increase of new data but little that alters Albright's fundamental description of the period many years ago. The most reliable evidence excavated in recent years has come from Hazor, Shechem, Ta'anach, Ashdod, Gezer, Dan, and Deir 'Alla, supplementing that from previously dug sites such as Tell Beit Mirsim, Tell el-'Ajjûl, Megiddo, and Lachish. For Syria, the few recent summary treatments (Malamat, 1966; Liverani; Drower, 1975) must still rely largely on the literary evidence, particularly the rich mythological texts from Ugarit, in the absence of trustworthy stratified sequences. In Palestine the regrettable lack of texts is partly filled by the Amarna letters, whose reflection of political, social, and economic conditions has been admirably summarized by Albright (1975). The strictly archaeological data, which are relatively more abundant, have been brought together and critically evaluated by Kenyon (1973, first published in 1971) in what is easily the best synthesis available for the time of the Eighteenth Dynasty (about 1570–1304 BCE). This treatment for the most part needs only to be augmented by reference to material published more recently from Hazor, Ashdod, and Gezer. Northern Transjordan was probably settled throughout the LB period, but published evidence is lacking to detail this occupation (Mittmann). The occupational gap in Southern Transjordan postulated by Glueck is slowly being filled (see Thompson, 1974, 193f. for convenient references), including an LB II temple at Amman (see Hennessy; Hankey).

The end of the LB period in the Nineteenth Dynasty (about 1304–1200 BCE) has recently been surveyed by Franken, but his treatment cannot be recommended. Thus there exist no satisfactory up-to-date summaries of the evidence for the LB IIB period in the thirteenth century BCE.

The following emerge as the most significant points of current attempts to characterize the period. It is difficult to discern LB IA (about 1500–1450 BCE) as a separate phase due to the fact that the period is marked by a partial or even complete gap in occupation at many sites, following the Egyptian destructions at the end of MB IIC. Furthermore, where the period is attested it is signalled chiefly by the *floruit* of imported pottery such as Cypriot Monochrome, Bichrome, and Base Ring I wares, which first appeared on the MB

IIC/LB I horizon but often cannot be placed in precise stratigraphic relationships or independently dated. The brief LB IB period (about 1450–1400 BCE) witnessed the gradual renascence of town life at many sites. The following period, LB II, is distinguished by the reoccupation of virtually every MB II site and the revival of the basic Canaanite culture of the Middle Bronze Age, now in its final stages of development.

The first phase, LB IIA (about 1400–1300 BCE), corresponds roughly to the 'Amarna Age' in Egypt, when Palestine was nominally under Egyptian court rule but was in fact at the mercy of rapacious Egyptian commissioners and petty princes of the local city-states – a condition reflected in both the Amarna letters from Palestine and the excavated levels of early LB II (Albright, 1975, 98–116). LB IIB (about 1300–1200 BCE) represents the last gasp of the long Middle Bronze–Late Bronze Age Canaanite culture of Syria–Palestine. It may be set off from LB IIA chiefly by the break at some sites, perhaps reflecting the campaigns of Sethos I and Ramesses II of the Nineteenth Dynasty at the turn of the fourteenth century BCE. In addition, at most sites the stratigraphic sequence becomes confused and the material is poorly attested, imports cease, and the local pottery (as Albright observed long ago) is the most monotonous in the history of Palestine.

The Late Bronze period in Syria–Palestine ended with the widespread upheaval in the Levant at the end of the thirteenth century BCE, with the break-up of the Mycenaean world and the displacement of the 'Sea Peoples'; the fall of the Hittite Empire; the collapse of the Mitannian (Hurrian) Kingdom; the resurgence of Assyria; the yielding of the Kassites to the Second Dynasty of Isin in Babylon (a bit later); and the expansion of the early Aramaean peoples (Hallo and Simpson, 117–20). While LB traditions in Palestine continue into the twelfth century at sites like Megiddo, Beth-shan, Shechem, and Gezer, other sites like Hazor and Bethel show a virtually complete stratigraphic and ceramic break (*contra* Franken). The evidence is complex and difficult to assess but no doubt reflects the disruptions caused by both Philistine ('Sea Peoples') and Israelite incursions, as well as the continuity of Canaanite culture at some sites. A detailed account of the Late Bronze/Iron I transition and the archaeological background for the Israelite conquest will be found in Lapp's admirable survey of all the available evidence to 1967 (Lapp, 1967, 283–300; see below, ch. IV §3).

C. The history of a specific problem –
the biblical patriarchs in the light of archaeology

W. F. **Albright**, 'Palestine in the Earliest Historical Period', *JPOS* XV, 1935, 193–234; idem, *The Archaeology of Palestine*, 1949; idem, 'Abram the Hebrew: a New Archaeological Interpretation', *BASOR* CLXIII, 1961, 36–54; idem, *Archaeology, Historical Analogy, and Early Biblical Tradition*, Baton Rouge: Louisiana State University Press 1966; idem, *Yahweh and the Gods of Canaan*, London/Garden City: Athlone Press/Doubleday 1968; J. **Bright**, *Early Israel in Recent History Writing*, SBT 19, 1956; F. M. **Cross**, *Canaanite Myth and Hebrew Epic: Essays on the History of the Religion of Israel*, Cambridge: Harvard University Press 1973; W. G. **Dever**, 'The Middle Bronze I Period in Syria and Palestine', *Near Eastern Archaeology*, 1970, 132–63; idem, 'Archaeological Methods and Results: A Review of Two Recent Publications', *Orientalia* XL, 1971, 459–471; **O. Eissfeldt**, 'Palestine in the Time of the Nineteenth Dynasty. (*a*) The Exodus and Wanderings', *CAH* II/2, 1975, 307–30; H. J. **Franken** and W. J. A. **Powers**, 'Glueck's Explorations in Eastern Palestine in the Light of Recent Evidence', *VT* XXI, 1971, 118–23; J. C. L. **Gibson**, 'Light from Mari on the Patriarchs', *JSS* VII, 1962, 44–62; N. **Glueck**, *Explorations in Eastern Palestine I–IV*, AASOR 14–15, 18–19, 25–8, 1934, 1935, 1939, 1951; idem, 'Explorations in Western Palestine', *BASOR* CXXXI, 1953, 6–15; idem, 'Further Explorations in the Negev', *BASOR* CXXXVII, 1955, 10–22; idem, 'The Age of Abraham in the Negev', *BA* XVIII, 1955, 2–9; idem, *Rivers in the Desert: A History of the Negev*, New York/London: Grove Press/Weidenfeld & Nicolson 1968; C. H. **Gordon**, 'Biblical Customs and the Nuzu Tablets', *BA* III, 1940, 1–12 = *BAR* II, 1964, 21–33; idem, *Introduction to Old Testament Times*, New York: Ventnor Publishers 1953; idem, 'Abraham and the Merchants of Ura', *JNES* XVII, 1958, 28–31; P. C. **Hammond**, 'Hebron', *RB* LXXIII, 1966, 566–9; LXXV, 1968, 253–8; J. **Huesman**, 'Archaeology and Early Israel: The Scene Today', *CBQ* XXXVII, 1975, 1–16; K. **Kenyon**, *Digging Up Jerusalem*, 1974; P. **Lapp**, 'Bâb edh-Dhrâʿ, Perizites and Emim', *Jerusalem through the Ages*, ed. Y. Aviram, Jerusalem: Israel Exploration Society 1968, 1–25; A. **Malamat**, 'Origins and the Formative Period', in *Ben-Sasson, 3–87; idem, 'Mari', *BA* XXXIV, 1971, 2–22; B. **Mazar**, 'The Historical Background of the Book of Genesis', *JNES* XXVIII, 1969, 73–83; idem, ed., *WHJP* I/2, 1970; M. **Noth**, *History of Pentateuchal Traditions*, 1972; idem, 'Mari und Israel. Eine Personennamenstudie', in *Geschichte und Altes Testament* (Festschrift Albrecht Alt), Tübingen: J. C. B. Mohr 1953, 127–52; idem, *Die Ursprünge des alten Israel im Lichte neuer Quellen*, AFLNW 94, 1961 = his *Aufsätze* II, 1973, 245–72; G. **von Rad**, *Das erste Buch Mose, Genesis*, ATD 1–4, 1959 = his *Genesis*, OTL, 1961; idem, 'History of the Patriarchs, *ET* LXXII, 1960/61, 213–16; H. H. **Rowley**, 'Recent Discovery and the Patriarchal Age', *BJRL* XXXII, 1949/50, 44–79 = his *Servant of the Lord*, 1965, 281–318; idem. *From Joseph to*

Joshua, 1950; A. **Soggin**, 'Ancient Biblical Traditions and Modern Archaeological Discoveries', *BA* XXIII, 1960, 95–100; E. A. **Speiser**, 'The Wife–Sister Motif in the Patriarchal Narratives', *Biblical and Other Studies*, ed. A. Altmann, Cambridge: Harvard University Press 1963, 15–28 = his *Oriental and Biblical Studies*, ed. J. J. Finkelstein and M. Greenberg, Philadelphia: University of Pennsylvania Press 1967, 62–82; idem, *Genesis*, AB 1, 1964, D. W. **Thomas**, ed., *AOTS* 1967; T. L. **Thompson**, *The Settlement of Sinai and the Negev in the Bronze Age*, BTAVO 8, 1975; R. **de Vaux**, 'Les Patriarches hébreux et les découvertes modernes', *RB* LIII, 1946, 321–48; LV, 1948, 321–47; LVI, 1949, 5–36 = his *Die Hebräischen Patriarchen und die modernen Entdeckungen*, Düsseldorf 1959; idem, 'Les Patriarches hébreux et l'histoire', *RB* LXXII, 1965, 5–28 = his 'The Hebrew Patriarchs and History', *TD* XII, 1964, 227–40; idem, *Les Institutions de l'Ancien Testament* I–II, Paris: Éditions du Cerf 1958 = *Ancient Israel: Its Life and Institutions*, London/New York: Darton, Longman and Todd/McGraw-Hill 1961; idem, 'Method in the Study of Early Hebrew History', *The Bible in Modern Scholarship*, 1965, 15–29; J. **Van Seters**, *Abraham in History and Tradition*, 1975; E. **Vogel**, 'Negev Survey of Nelson Glueck: Summary', *EI* XII, 1975, 1–17; H. **Weidmann**, *Die Patriarchen und ihre Religion in Licht der Forschung seit Julius Wellhausen*, FRLANT 94, 1968; M. **Weippert**, *Settlement of the Israelite Tribes*, 1971; D. J. **Wiseman**, ed., *Peoples of OT Times*, 1973; G. E. **Wright**, *Biblical Archaeology*, 1957; idem, 'Archaeology and Old Testament Studies', *JBL* LXXVII, 1958, 39–51; idem, 'Modern Issues in Biblical Studies: History and the Patriarchs', *ET* LXXI, 1960, 292–6. (See also the bibliography in B above.)

Various attempts have been made to interpret the biblical patriarchs in the light of archaeology. Several of these interpretations will be surveyed in this section and the newer evidence will then be presented so as to characterize the discussion at present and focus on the central issues.

(i) The patriarchs and the Middle Bronze I period

The attempt to relate the patriarchs to the MB I period represents what might be called the classic formulation, deriving from Albright's characterization of MB I in the 1930s as a semi-nomadic interlude marked by Caliciform pottery from Syria and Mesopotamia. Albright felt that this period provided a suitable background for the migration of the biblical patriarchs (see Albright, 1935, 193–234; and for later elaborations, see references in Thompson, 1974, 55). Confirmation for the hypothesis seemed to come from Glueck's explorations in southern Transjordan, from 1932 onwards, which revealed that the area flourished in MB I but was virtually deserted for centuries thereafter. Thus the date of Genesis 14 with its description of Abraham's war with the Kings of the East and the destruction of the 'cities of the plain' could be fixed in MB I (Glueck, 1934, 81 f.; 1935, 137 f.; 1939, 268; 1951, 423; in *AOTS*, 1967, 445; 1968, 68–74; and see Albright's adoption of Glueck's views in 1949, 82 f.). So confident of this correlation was Glueck that when he found a similar picture of MB I occupation in the Negeb in the 1950s he characterized it as 'The Age of Abraham in the Negev' (Glueck, 1955, 2–9; 1968, 68–84, 100–7).

When Albright returned to the discussion in 1961, in his well-known article 'Abram the Hebrew: A New Archaeological Interpretation', it is significant that he attributed his inspiration directly to a re-examination of Glueck's Negeb pottery (Albright, 1961, 36 f.). He collected impressive evidence for the spread of donkey caravanning in the nineteenth century BCE. In order to encompass Abraham and the MB I period within that century he lowered his end-date from 1900 to 1800 BCE. Albright portrayed Abraham as an itinerant merchant who frequented the trade routes southward through the Negeb towards Sinai. The specific sites mentioned in the Genesis accounts of the patriarchal wanderings – Shechem, Bethel, Hebron, Beersheba, and Gerar – according to Albright were settled in MB I, as attested by archaeology. Even the old association of the patriarchs and MB I with Genesis 14, abandoned after 1940, was taken up again (on the above see Albright, 1961, 36–54). This view, a nuance rather than a rejection of the Amorite hypothesis, still maintaining the MB I date, remained Albright's position in his latest works (Albright, 1966, 22–41; 1968, 47–95).

A number of archaeologists specifically challenged Albright's Amorite/Patriarchal/MB I equation, among them Aharoni (in *AOTS*, 1967, 387); Rainey (in B above, 1972, 390–1); and Kochavi (in B above, 1969, 43–4). The present writer has been the most vigorous defender of the 'Amorite hypothesis' for MB I, particularly against the alternatives proposed by Lapp and Kochavi (Dever, in B above, 1971, 220–6) while simultaneously cautioning that the problem of the biblical patriarchs was 'a separate question and one that is likely to prejudice the discussion of MB I' (Dever, in B above, 1971, 266, n. 66).

Mazar has similarly separated the discussion of archaeological phases from the problem of the biblical patriarchs and has cautioned that recent attempts to establish the date and historicity of the patriarchal era 'have gone too far' (Mazar, in B above, 1968, 66–70; 1969, 76). And, of course, Albright's MB I date, along with all other second millennium BCE dates suggested by archaeological evidence, has been ruled out by the recent treatments of Thompson (in B above, 1974) and Van Seters (1975). Other authorities who dealt with the MB I period ignored the question entirely, among them Amiran (in B above, 1960); Kenyon (in B above, 1971, 592–4 with references to earlier treatments); Oren (in B above, 1973); and Prag (in B above, 1970). Only Wright followed Albright's MB I date, and he stressed that it was 'extremely tentative' (1957, 40–52). It is significant that in later treatments Wright described the patriarchal period as part of the general ' "Amorite" age of the first half of the second millennium BC' (1960, 5) and discussed MB I without reference to this problem (Wright, in B above, 1961, 86–8; 1971, 287–90).

(ii) The patriarchs and the Middle Bronze II period

Most archaeologists and biblical scholars have not followed Albright and Glueck's MB I date but have been content to assign the patriarchal age to the early second millennium generally, i.e., MB II, about the twentieth to the sixteenth century BCE. Noteworthy among them is the late Roland de Vaux, one of the principal architects of the 'Amorite hypothesis'. While the views of Albright and Glueck were crystallizing, de Vaux had been summarizing the increasing archaeological illumination of the early second millennium BCE in a series of articles between 1946 and 1965, giving his final conclusions in his posthumous book *The Early History of Israel*. De Vaux pictured the earlier waves of Amorites of the Ur III period overrunning the country in EB IV–MB I (1946, 342–7; 1971, 62–5), without necessarily making them directly responsible for the disruption of urban life at the end of EB III (de Vaux, 1946, 338f.; *1976, 63f., 263–6). He connected the patriarchal migrations, however, with the second wave of these Amorites, whose influx in the nineteenth century BCE stimulated the urban renascence of the MB IIA period (1948, 325f., 336; *1976, 66–8, 265f.). De Vaux preferred this correlation over that of MB I largely because the social milieu in which the patriarchs were portrayed in Genesis characterized them as pastoralists moving on the fringes of an urban society, i.e., as peoples in the process of being sedentarized, like the Amorites of the Mari period in MB IIA (1948, 346, 347; 1949, 12–18; *1976, 205, 216, 221–5, 229–33, 265). While de Vaux's was the most comprehensive and best-documented defence of the Amorite hypothesis, he did not accept Albright's last attempts to connect Amorite movements with donkey caravanning (*1976, 225–9) but stressed instead the pastoral aspect of nomadism at Mari and in the Bible (see the succinct statement of his views, 1965, 12–18).

Many biblical scholars have agreed with de Vaux on placing the so-called patriarchal era *generally* in MB II, without, however, dating it precisely. Among these scholars would be Speiser (1964, XLIV–LII; in Mazar, 1970, 168); Bright in his influential history (*Bright, 81–5); Yeivin (in Mazar, 1970, 201–18); Mendenhall (in Wright in B above, 1961, 39); Cross (in A above, 1973, 3–12); Freedman (in *The Bible and Modern Scholarship*, 1965, 296–9) and Malamat (1971, 13; see also his much fuller exposition in Ben-Sasson).

(iii)   *The patriarchs and the Late Bronze Age*

The minority view among scholars which places the patriarchal era in the LB period is based largely on parallels between social and legal customs in Genesis and in the fifteenth- to thirteenth-century BCE texts from Nuzi and Ugarit. This view is espoused chiefly by Gordon (1940, 1–12; 1953, 75, 102–4; 1958, 28–31; see Speiser in Altmann, 1963, 15–28). Indirect support for an LB date has been drawn from recent interpretations of Israelite law in the light of Hittite parallels in the mid-late second millennium BCE as in the work of Mendenhall, Baltzer, Hillers, McCarthy, and others (see Hoffner in Wiseman, 1973, 213–31, for references). Rowley's 'double exodus' theory would have placed an early entry of the Hebrews under Jacob in the context of the 'Apiru movement of the Amarna Age in Palestine in the fourteenth century BCE (Rowley, 1950, 66–164), but Rowley confesses that he was 'not disposed to try to fix the age of Abraham' (1950, 114–15; see also his valuable review of the problem published in 1949/50). Eissfeldt, while relying only to a limited extent on the archaeological evidence, argued that the time of the patriarchs was most likely the two centuries prior to the final settlement of the land, that is, about the fourteenth and thirteenth centuries (1975, 312–14). He pointed to the biblical genealogies which separated Abraham from the time of the settlement by only four generations. Reckoning about forty years to a generation would place the patriarchs in the latter part of the LB age.

This summary of archaeological opinion may be brought to a close by referring the reader to Thompson's much more extensive survey (particularly on the MB I and LB dates; in B above, 1974, 1–9, 144–297) which is useful despite its polemical character.

(iv)   *Scepticism concerning archaeology and the historicity of the patriarchs*

The view that the patriarchs were never historical figures, and that the only 'history' to be extracted from the Genesis narratives is the history of the *traditions* about them, goes back at least to

Wellhausen and the early literary critics, but it has been buttressed powerfully by the more recent development of *Gattungsgeschichte* and *Redaktionsgeschichte*, especially in Germany. Here the views of Alt and Noth are fundamental to the modern discussion. It is significant, however, that neither actually denied the historicity of the patriarchs. Alt's *Der Gott der Väter* (1929) used texts brought to light by archaeology to reconstruct a much earlier context for patriarchal religion than Wellhausen's scheme would have allowed (see Cross's extension of these views in 1973, 3–75).

Noth's conclusions regarding the patriarchs rest upon his monumental *Überlieferungsgeschichte* (1948), which sought to work out the history of the literary and oral traditions behind the Genesis narratives in their present form. The best synthetic statement of his early view is to be found in the first edition of his *Geschichte Israels*, published shortly thereafter (1950, [2]1954). In Noth's view the traditions concerning the patriarchs and their cults were originally independent and circulated somewhere on the fringes of the desert; they were adopted only later by the twelve-tribe league and transferred to local Palestinian shrines, where further accretion resulted from the process of aetiology. The inclusion of the patriarchal 'theme' (*Thema*) in the pentateuch is due to the 'G' (*Grundlage*) and J sources, who incorporated this material because its portrayal of the 'promise to the fathers' made an ideal prehistory to the exodus-conquest and fulfilment themes which had by then become the central focus of Israel's national epic. Noth does not deny that the patriarchs themselves may originally have been actual historical figures, but the nature of the biblical sources precludes the writing of any history of them as such. (On the above, see Noth, 1972, 42–146, 252–9; *History*, 82–4, 121–7; see the convenient summary in Bright, 1956, 40–52.)

It must be observed that Noth did not ignore archaeological evidence, or refuse to use it, as Albright and his followers sometimes implied (for this observation, see Soggin, 1960, 98; Weippert, 1971, 127–30; Thompson, in B above, 1974, 5–7; and references in the above to Noth's published works). But Noth was sceptical when archaeologists assumed that their 'external' evidence, because it consisted of empirical data, could be utilized 'objectively', while the 'internal' evidence resulting from tradition-history and form-criticism could only be 'subjective' (see *Noth, 45–6; above, §1A iii of this chapter). Although they were not as significant as the fundamental methodological differences, there were pragmatic considerations as well; Noth remained unconvinced that Syro-Palestinian archaeology had actually attained the precision it claimed. His conclusion therefore is that 'only little light falls from external evidence, especially on the patriarchs' (Noth, in A above, 41).

Another pivotal member of the German school was von Rad. He was not concerned about whether actual historical events lay behind the Genesis narratives, but only about the traditions themselves, about their individual elaboration and especially their later cultic use in Israel's proclamation of *Heilsgeschichte*. Israel's incorporation of the traditions means that 'the historicity of the patriarchal narratives now rests essentially upon the community's experience of faith' (*Genesis*, 39). While von Rad allows that sagas and cult legends are by no means poetic fantasies, the overriding tendency of these forms is to dissolve the original events into a sort of 'higher history' which witnesses to God in a timeless way, allowing the church to appropriate the Old Testament as part of its own *kerygma* (on the above see von Rad, *Genesis*, 201–42; and especially his response to Wright in 1960/61). Without dwelling on the theological complexity and richness of von Rad's thought, it is sufficient to observe that this sort of typological, 'spiritualizing' exegesis dislocates the tradition in such a way that the quest for any historical basis is no longer relevant.

Lately there are signs that classic theories of the German school are making a belated appearance in America. Thompson's recent book belongs to this category. As he admits, he is closer to the position of Wellhausen, Gunkel, Gressmann, Galling, and others than that of the 'American school' (Thompson, 1974, 1–9). His exhaustive survey of the archaeological data is intended largely to refute the claim made by Albright and others that the historicity of the patriarchs has been established by archaeology. His own view is that 'on the basis of what we know of Palestinian history of the second millennium BC and of what we understand about the formulation of the literary traditions of Genesis, it must be concluded that any such historicity as is commonly spoken of in both scholarly and popular works about the Patriarchs of Genesis is hardly possible and totally improbable' (328). It is not surprising that Thompson concludes that although there may be an indirect contribution, 'the study of the archaeology and the history of the early Second Millennium has nothing to offer directly to the interpretations of the traditions about Abraham, Isaac, and Jacob' (195). Van Seters' recent work *Abraham in History and Tradition* independently reaches conclusions similar to those of Thompson. Unlike Thompson, it is largely a work of tradition-history, and it must be judged by biblical scholars on those merits.

(v) Recent archaeological evidence bearing on the date of the patriarchs

At this point we can assess only the recent archaeological evidence which possibly reflects on the date of the patriarchs and circumscribes their movements in Palestine. If the world of the patriarchs can be narrowed in time and place, it may then be possible to isolate and discuss the data which are relevant to the reconstruction of a social and cultural milieu into which they might be fitted. Let us take the negative evidence first.

1. *The date of the sites.* A date in MB I is ruled out for the patriarchs simply because the latest evidence shows that the main centres traditionally associated with their movements, *pace* Albright, are conspicuously lacking in MB I remains.

Of the sites Albright lists (1961, 47f.), Shechem is the parade example. Albright had cited the recent excavations of Wright and others in support of what he regarded as an MB I occupation at Shechem. Elsewhere I have shown that this is based on a misunderstanding of the excavators' preliminary report, which referred only to the chance find of an MB I tomb. In fact, the excavations showed conclusively that the history of occupation of Shechem began in the subsequent period, in the Middle Bronze IIA period. Apart from this, the only earlier remains on the mound belong to a small settlement of the Late Chalcolithic period, more than a millennium earlier. (Dever, in B above, 1970, 142–4, 159, n. 64; confirmed by Wright in B above, 1971, 289.)

At Bethel, Albright's view that the site was 'extensively peopled' in MB I (Albright, 1961, 47) is supported by a mere handful of sherds. Kelso's final publication in 1968 claims to have located various remains of MB I, including a city wall and a temple. But in a long review article I have shown how fanciful Kelso's report is; his MB I sanctuary, for instance, is nothing more than the foundation phase of the MB II city gate. The remainder of Kelso's MB I town is even more ephemeral. Bethel can hardly have been more than a camp-site in MB I. (On the above, see Dever, 1971, 464–6.)

As for Hebron, which was archaeologically unknown when Albright wrote, the excavations of Hammond at Jebel Er-Rumeide in the 1960s revealed that the town was founded and first fortified in MB II. The writer's discoveries have brought to light several isolated MB I cemeteries and even some seasonal settlements in the Hebron hills, but no trace of occupation anywhere in the immediate vicinity of Hebron (see Dever, in B above, 1970, 146–50).

Albright's long-held identification of Gerar with Tell Abū Ḥureireh

(Albright, 1961, 47 f.) is disputed; the site remains unexcavated and cannot be positively identified. In any case, MB I pottery found in the vicinity of Tell Abū Ḥureireh tells us nothing specific about the location of Gerar or its possible role in any patriarchal era. Certainly Albright's conclusion that 'the recent discovery and identification of the true site of the previously elusive Gerar have confirmed its importance as a caravan center' (Albright, 1961, 48) remains without archaeological support. The most that can be said is that scattered surface finds indicate several MB I sites along the Wadi Gaza, all of them apparently small unwalled villages similar to those of the central Negeb.

Beersheba, so prominently associated with patriarchal wanderings in the Genesis narratives, has so far produced no trace of MB I occupation. Extensive surveys and excavations by Aharoni, Kochavi, and other Israeli archaeologists in Beersheba and vicinity have in fact revealed a conspicuous lack of MB I sites throughout the northern Negeb. The work of the Israelis complements the earlier work of Glueck in showing that the only known complex of MB I settlements in the Negeb stretches from Har Yeruḥam (eighteen miles south of Beersheba) southward into the remote central Negeb and westward towards Sinai. The sites are small, well off the possible caravan routes, and were probably seasonal settlements connected with primitive dry farming. Although much more study of settlement and subsistence patterns needs to be undertaken, it is clear that the archaeological picture of the MB I period in the Negeb has nothing to do either with the Beersheba area or with Albright's donkey caravanning from central Palestine into the Sinai (*contra* Albright, 1961, 44–8; on the Negeb sites, see Dever, in B above, 1970, 151 f.; Vogel; Thompson, 1975).

The remaining sites mentioned in Genesis in connection with the patriarchs are Dothan, Ai, Jerusalem, and the cities in the Valley of Siddim and the Valley of the Kings. Dothan (Gen. 37.17) was a great urban site of the Early Bronze and Middle Bronze II periods, as shown by J. P. Free's excavations in 1953–62, but it was deserted in MB I, as were most of the sites in central Palestine. Ai (Gen. 12.8; 13.3) was destroyed before the end of the Early Bronze period, about 2400 BCE, and was not reoccupied until the twelfth century BCE, as confirmed by both the excavations of Mlle Marquet-Krause in 1933–5 and those of J. A. Callaway in 1964–73. Salem in Genesis 14.18 has been identified with Jerusalem, but this is dubious. The text may be corrupt (even Albright emends to eliminate Salem; 1961, 52), and the association suggested in Psalm 76.2 is probably a piece

of late propaganda for the Jerusalem priesthood. In any case, even if
Jerusalem were to be correctly identified in Genesis 14.18, Kenyon's
excavations have shown that the city as such originated about 1800
BCE, i.e., in MB IIB, when its first mention appears in the Brussels
Execration Texts (1974, 78–89). Of course Dothan, Ai, and
Jerusalem, whatever the archaeological evidence, may be eliminated
from consideration on the plausible ground that their mention is an
anachronism, as is demonstrable in the case of other references in the
patriarchal narratives.

Finally, of Sodom, Gomorrah, Zoar, and the other cities apparently to be located at the southern end of the Dead Sea (Gen. 14.1–
3, etc.) and the 'cities of the plain', possibly near the Lisan in
Transjordan (Gen. 19.24–8), the less said the better. Ralph Baney's
abortive Dead Sea expedition in search of Sodom and Gomorrah
(undertaken with Albright's encouragement) cannot be construed as
a serious archaeological enterprise, and in any case turned up nothing pre-Roman (if that ancient). Albright had long connected the
great site of Bâb edh–Dhrâ' on the Lisan with the 'cities of the plain',
as Paul Lapp was to do later. However, Lapp's own excavations in
1963–5 showed that the town-site was destroyed and abandoned at
the end of EB III, about 2400–2300 BCE, leaving only a squatter
occupation in EB IV and a few scattered tombs belonging to MB I
(the remains from the site are still unpublished, but see provisionally
Lapp, 1968).

2. *The nineteenth-century caravanning trade.* It is important to recall
that Albright's evidence for donkey caravanning (Assyrian texts,
Sinai inscriptions, Beni Hasan paintings, etc.) pertains to the nineteenth century BCE at earliest, which would place Abraham in the
Middle Bronze IIA period (about 2000–1800 BCE). Albright attempted to circumvent this dilemma by lowering his absolute date
for the end of MB I from about 1900 to 1800 BCE. But elsewhere I
have cited two correlations of evidence from Shechem and Megiddo
with absolute chronology in Egypt, either of which would rule out
Albright's low dates for MB I and MB IIA (Dever, in B above, 1970,
142–4 and 1971, 224). It is worth noting that no scholar has followed
Albright's latest ultra-low chronology. Today there is a consensus on
raising, not lowering, the dates for this horizon; and virtually all
Palestinian archaeologists agree that the maximum range for the
beginning of MB IIA is between 2000 and 1900 BCE. Thus if
Abraham is to be seen as a nineteenth-century BCE donkey caravaneer
(Albright, 1961, 38–42, 52) he would have to be placed not in MB I
but in MB IIA. This would indeed suit the evidence we have cited

above from Shechem, but not that from other sites associated with the patriarchs in the biblical tradition. To date, not a single MB IIA site has been found in all of southern Transjordan or the Negeb – one of the principal arenas of patriarchal activities in Genesis.

Before leaving Albright's views to turn towards a newer appreciation of the archaeological evidence, we may observe that his latest caravan hypothesis (1961, 36–54; summarized in 1968, 47–95, 232–4) has won almost no support. The negative reviews of Speiser, Emerton, and especially Weippert are cited by Thompson, along with his own objections (Thompson, 1974, 172–5; see also Rainey, 1972, 390f.; and Mazar, 1968, 76, all in B above). Albright's own students have maintained an embarrassed silence on the subject. Finally, it should be noted that few archaeologists who specialize in MB I have even alluded to Albright's view, and none has accepted it.

D.   Prolegomenon to a reconsideration of archaeology and patriarchal backgrounds

Robert McC. **Adams**, *The Evolution of Urban Society: Early Mesopotamia and Prehispanic Mexico*, Chicago: Aldine Publishing Co. 1966; A. **Alt**, *Der Gott der Väter*, BWANT III/12, 1929 = his *KS* I, 1953, 1–78 = 'The God of the Fathers', *Essays*, 1966, 1–77; D. H. K. **Amiran**, 'The Pattern of Settlement in Palestine', *IEJ* III, 1953, 65–78; 192–209; 250–60; idem and Y. **Ben-Arieh**, 'Sedentarization of Beduin in Israel', *IEJ* XIII, 1963, 161–81; T. **Ashkenazi**, *Tribus semi-nomades de la Palestine du Nord*, Paris: Paul Geuthner 1938; D. **Bahat**, 'Beth Shemesh', *IEJ* XXIII, 1973, 246f.; G. **Bucellati**, *The Amorites of the Ur III Period*, Naples: Istituto Orientale de Napoli 1966; J. A. **Callaway** and R. E. **Cooley**, 'A Salvage Excavation at Raddana', *BASOR* CCI, 1971, 9–19; H. **Charles**, *Tribus moutonnières du Moyen-Euphrate*, DEO 8, 1939; idem, *La sédentarisation entre Euphrate et Balik*, Beirut: L'Institute Français 1942; D. O. **Edzard**, *Die 'Zweite Zwischenzeit' Babyloniens*, Wiesbaden: Otto Harrassowitz 1957; C. **Epstein**, 'Beth-Shemesh', *IEJ* XXII, 1972, 157; B. A. **Fernea**, *Shaykh and Effendi: Changing Patterns of Authority Among the El Shahana of Southern Iraq*, HMES 14, 1970; J. J. **Finkelstein**, 'The Genealogy of the Hammurapi Dynasty', *JCS* XX, 1966, 95–118; idem, 'An Old Babylonian Herding Contract and Genesis 31:38ff.', *JAOS* LXXXVII, 1968, 30–6; F. **Gabrieli**, ed., *L'antica società beduina*, StSem 2, 1959; I. J. **Gelb**, 'The Early History of the West Semitic Peoples', *JCS* XV, 1961, 27–47; C. H. J. **de Geus**, 'De Amorieten in de Palestijnse archeologie: een recente theorie kritisch bezien', *NTT* XXIII, 1968/69, 1–24 = 'The Amorites in the Archaeology of Palestine', *UF* III, 1971, 41–60; R. **Giveon**, *Les bédouins Shosou des documents égyptiens*, DMOA 18, 1971; N. K. **Gottwald**, 'Were the Early Israelites Pastoral Nomads?', *Rhetorical Criticism: Essays in Honor of James Muilenburg*, ed. J. J. Jackson and

M. Kessler, PTMS 1, 1974, 223–55; idem, 'Domain Assumptions and Societal Models in the Study of Pre-Monarchic Israel', *SVT* XXVIII, 1975, 89–100; A. **Haldar**, *Who Were the Amorites?*, MANE 1, 1971; J. **Henninger**, *Über Lebensraum und Lebensformen der Frühsemiten*, AFLNW 151, 1968; idem, 'Zum frühsemitischen Nomadentum', *Viehwirtschaft und Hirtenkultur: Ethnographische Studien*, ed. L. Földes, Budapest: Akadémiai Kiadó 1969, 33–68; H. B. **Huffmon**, *Amorite Personal Names in the Mari Texts*, Baltimore: Johns Hopkins University Press 1965; W. G. **Irons** and N. **Dyson-Hudson**, eds., *Perspectives on Nomadism*, ISSSA 13, 1972; D. L. **Johnson**, *The Nature of Nomadism: A Comparative Study of Pastoral Migrations in Southwestern Asia and Northern Africa*, Department of Geography Research Papers 118, Chicago: University of Chicago Press, 1969; H. **Klengel**, 'Halbnomadischer Bodenbau im Königreich von Mari', *Das Verhältnis von Bodenbauern and Viehzüchtern in historischer Sicht*, DAWB 69, 1968, 75–81; idem, *Zwischen Zelt und Palast*, Wien: Verlag Anton Schroll, 1972; F. R. **Kraus**, *Könige, die in Zelten wohnten*, Amsterdam: N. V. Noord-Hollandsche Uitgevers Maatschappij, 1965; J.-R. **Kupper**, *Les nomades en Mésopotamie au temps des rois de Mari*, BFPLUL 142, 1957; idem, 'Le rôle des nomades dans l'histoire de la Mésopotamie ancienne', *JESHO* II, 1959, 113–27; idem, ed., *La civilisation de Mari*, XVe Rencontre Assyriologique Internationale, Paris: Société de l'Édition 'Les Belles Lettres' 1967; M. **Liverani**, 'Per una considerazione storica del problema amorreo', *OA* IX, 1970, 5–27; idem, 'The Amorites', *Peoples of OT Times*, 1973, 100–33; J. T. **Luke**, *Pastoralism and Politics in the Mari Period: A Re-Examination of the Character and Political Significance of the Major West Semitic Tribal Groups on the Middle Euphrates, c. 1828–1753 BC* (Ph.D. Dissertation, University of Michigan; Ann Arbor: University Microfilms 1965); A. **Malamat**, 'Mari and the Bible: Some Patterns of Tribal Organization and Institutions', *JAOS* LXXXII, 1962, 143–50; idem, 'Aspects of Tribal Societies in Mari and Israel', in Kupper, 1967, 129–38; idem, 'King Lists of the Old Babylonian Period and Biblical Genealogies', *JAOS* LXXXVIII, 1968, 163–73; G. E. **Mendenhall**, 'The Hebrew Conquest of Palestine', *BA* XXV, 1962, 66–87 = *BAR* III, 1970, 100–20; S. **Moscati**, *The Semites in Ancient History: An Inquiry into the Settlement of the Beduins and their Political Establishment*, Cardiff: University of Wales Press 1959; A. L. **Oppenheim**, *Ancient Mesopotamia: Portrait of a Dead Civilization*, Chicago: University of Chicago Press 1964; X. **de Planhol**, 'Nomades et pasteurs I–XI', *Revue Géographique de l'Est* I–XI, 1961–71; A. **Reifenberg**, *The Struggle Between the Desert and the Sown: Rise and Fall of Agriculture in the Levant*, Jerusalem: The Jewish Agency 1955; M. B. **Rowton**, 'The Physical Environment and the Problem of the Nomads', in Kupper, 1967, 109–21; idem, 'Autonomy and Nomadism in Western Asia', *Orientalia* XLII, 1973, 247–58; idem, 'Urban Autonomy in a Nomadic Environment', *JNES* XXXII, 1973, 201–15; idem, 'Enclosed Nomadism', *JESHO* XVII, 1974, 1–30; idem, 'Dimorphic Structure and the Problem of the 'Apirû-'Ibrîm', *JNES* XXXV, 1976, 13–20; E. A. **Speiser**, 'Census and Ritual Expiation in Mari and Israel', *BASOR* CXLIX, 1958, 17–25; F.

M. **Tocci**, *La Siria nell'età di Mari*, StSem 3, 1960; **UNESCO**, *The Problems of the Arid Zone*, Proceedings of the Paris Symposium, Arid Zone Research 18, Paris: UNESCO, 1962. (See also bibliographies in B and C above.)

In this section we shall suggest a new approach to the question of patriarchal backgrounds by focusing attention on recent discoveries and literature relating to *Siedlungsgeschichte*, i.e., the sedentarization of West Semitic semi-nomads in the early second millennium BCE.

(i)   The study of nomadism and sedentarization in the ancient Near East

The primary data for the study of nomadism and sedentarization in the ancient Near East derive largely from Mesopotamian texts from Babylonia in the Third Dynasty of Ur (about 2060–1950 BCE), the Dynasties of Isin and Larsa (about 1960 BCE onwards), and the Old Babylonian period (about 1830 BCE onwards); and texts from Upper Mesopotamia and Syria principally in the so-called Mari Age (about eighteenth-century BCE).

The major work on Western Semitic history in the earlier Babylonian texts is that of Edzard on the Isin–Larsa period (1957), complemented by Buccellati's specialized study of the earlier Amorites of the Ur III period (1966). These fundamental treatments outline the semi-nomadic background of the Western Semitic peoples who first appeared in great numbers among the Babylonian city-states of Mesopotamia in the twentieth and nineteenth centuries BCE. Of far greater importance, however, are the Mari texts, which document the crest of this wave in Upper Mesopotamia and Syria in the eighteenth century BCE.

The French excavations since 1933 at Tell el-Ḥarīrī on the middle Euphrates, the ancient city-state of Mari, have produced more than 25,000 cuneiform documents dating from about 1765–1694 BCE (according to the Low Chronology). With preliminary publication of some texts already in the late 1930s, and especially with the inauguration of the monumental series *Archives Royales de Mari* (= *ARM*, *ARMT*, 1946 onwards), an astonishing wealth of data began to illuminate the early second millennium BCE. The texts from Mari were especially significant since Mari lay on the borders of the settled zone and the steppe and thus reflected social and political relations between nomadic tribes and the urban centres. Kupper's masterful analysis and synthesis of the texts, *Les nomades en Mésopotamie au temps des rois de Mari* (1957), followed by Gelb's favourable review-article (1961), focused attention primarily on the value of the Mari documents for the early history and diffusion of the

West Semitic peoples (Amorites and/or Canaanites) and their languages. These initial studies were followed by Huffmon's philological analysis of the distinctive Amorite type of personal names in the Mari texts (1965).

A new stage in the study of the Mari texts began in the latter 1960s. The first departure came with Luke's dissertation (1965), which criticized Kupper's use of outworn 'invasion' theories of Semitic origins. These hypotheses reflected nineteenth-century anthropological theory, with its notion of unilinear evolution from primitive to advanced societies and its assumption that all Semitic peoples had passed in turn through nomadic to sedentary stages of culture. Further complicating the picture was nineteenth-century Romanticism's false analogy between ancient Near Eastern pastoralists and modern camel-mounted Arab Bedouin, whose frequent *razzias* or raids were a familiar feature of life in the Middle East. The result of these misconceptions was the assumption of an unremitting conflict between 'the Desert and the Sown'; ethnic movements and socio-political change in the ancient Near East were thus explained by succeeding 'waves' of nomads from the great Arabian desert who inundated the settled zones (see Luke, 9–35).

To be sure, Kupper had modified the original wave theory of A. Sprenger (1861, 1875) and H. Winckler (1903) on the basis of more recent ethnographic and anthropological data, substituting a process of infiltration for invasion, as Moscati (1959) was also to do. Luke argues, however, that both these scholars exaggerated the role of the nomads, largely because they assumed that nomadism always precedes village life in the cultural process, and because they underestimated the degree of peaceful interaction between the two. Luke concludes that it was not the relentless pressure of the nomads which produced the conflict between tribesmen and the central government, so vividly portrayed in the Mari texts, but rather the attempt of the urban political economy to impose itself on the village-pastoral economy, including the nomads. Previous scholars had confused cause and effect (Luke, 38). It is noteworthy that Luke's critique of Kupper amplifies theories of socio-political change first applied by his teacher Mendenhall to the period of the Israelite conquest (Mendenhall, 1962, 69–71).

In a series of programmatic essays beginning in 1967, Rowton has taken up the suggestion made by Oppenheim some years ago that Assyriology's narrow philological concerns must be broadened by the perspectives of cultural anthropology (see Oppenheim, 29f.). Rowton utilized anthropological models and ethnographic data from modern nomadic populations of the Middle East in order to understand the phenomenon of pastoral nomadism in the ancient Near East. The conclusions which are relevant for the present discussion are scattered throughout several publications but may be summarized as follows (for details see the works by Rowton in the above bibliography). Several of these conclusions, though reached independently from Luke, are in striking agreement.

In Western Asia the semi-arid steppe zone of about 100–250 mm (4–10 inches) annual rainfall, suitable only for pastoralism, is partly encircled by less arid agricultural areas (see Map 1). The unique physical geography of this region means that the nomads of the steppe are in constant contact with more permanently settled areas, forming a symbiosis which is a highly specialized adaptation to the environment. Following Lattimore's pioneer work *Inner Asian Frontiers of China* (1940), Rowton calls this 'enclosed nomadism'. This phenomenon resulted in a 'dimorphic' socio-political system in the ancient Near East, in which the basic dichotomy was not between nomadic and sedentary peoples, but rather between the 'autonomous tribal chiefdom', composed of both pastoralists and villagers, and the sovereign state dominated by powerful urban centres. Although sedentarization was part of the normal development of semi-nomadic tribes under certain conditions (following Barth's great work on the Basseri of South Persia, 1961), it was not this development, much less the invasion of barbaric nomads from the desert, which was the source of conflict. It was rather the struggle between interrelated and interdependent elements of the same society for political authority.

The role of tribal or territorial confederations in the political process has been neglected and misunderstood, even in modern Middle Eastern societies. The Mari texts are significant because they demonstrate the antiquity of the dimorphic society, and furthermore they provide our first precise documentation for the role of the nomads in the political struggle in antiquity. These enclosed nomads cannot be comprehended by the usual term 'semi-nomadic', for the 'semi' implies either that they were *partially* nomadic (a mixed tribe in the process of being sedentarized) or *part-time* nomads (a fully nomadic tribe characterized by seasonal migration or transhumance). Rowton describes Mari groups like the Yaminites and Haneans as 'integrated tribes', i.e., town-tribe confederations, of which one branch was sedentary all the year round, the other branch moving seasonally into the steppes or mountains with the flocks in search of pasturage. Thus the frequently-noted *nawûm* in the

Mari texts does not refer simply to 'pasture-land' but to the entire complex which characterized the countryside: camp-group, traditional grazing lands, herds. These migratory units are described as containing up to 2,000 men of military age. Their seasonal movements through settled areas, whether or not they practised raiding, constituted a threat which the authorities met not so much by resistance as by the attempt to integrate the tribespeople. Evidence of this is seen by Rowton in the appointment of a *merḫu*, or governmental liaison officer, to accompany the *nawûm* on trek; or in the schemes for manipulating the selection and the function of the *sugagum*, or tribal sheikh. Rowton broadens his theory to include the earlier Amorites of the Ur III and Isin–Larsa periods, concluding that the dominance of Western Semitic nomads in the Mesopotamian city-states by the eighteenth century BCE represented the evolution of dimorphic chiefdoms into dimorphic states.

Rowton's position thus falls between Kupper's emphasis on nomadic infiltration and Luke's stress on sedentary aspects, but is closer to the latter. Both Rowton and Luke agree on the symbiotic relations of nomads and townspeople; on the source of conflict in the urban attempt to impose order; and on the rejection of Bedouin nomadism and invasion hypotheses as adequate explanations for the phenomena encountered in the Mesopotamian texts dealing with tribal groups of the early second millennium BCE.

Following Kupper's seminal monograph in 1957 and paralleling the modifications by Luke and Rowton discussed above, a number of studies by other Near Eastern scholars dealt with the new texts in terms of the history and significance of nomadism. Most of these analyses were along the lines of traditional *Kulturgeschichte*. Kupper himself returned to the discussion with nuances of his earlier views (Kupper, 1959). The collection of essays edited by Gabrieli (1959) emphasized the link between ancient Near Eastern pastoralism and modern semi-nomadic societies. Kraus (1965) dealt with the 'seventeen kings who lived in tents' prefixed in the first two sections of the Assyrian King List to Shamshi-Adad I (about 1748–1716 BCE). The next year Finkelstein (1966) discovered a text parallel to the Assyrian King List, dealing with the genealogy of the Hammurabi dynasty and suggesting that there was a genre of *palû*-texts which attempted to link both the Old Assyrian and Old Babylonian kings with real or eponymous West Semitic tribal ancestors. In Germany the works of Henninger (1968, with full bibliography; 1969) and of Klengel (1968; 1969, with references to earlier works) provided comprehensive discussions of Western Semitic nomads at Mari and elsewhere in Upper Mesopotamia and Syria in the light of nomadism in general. Giveon's study of the Shasu Bedouin of Southern Transjordan mentioned in Egyptian New Kingdom texts (1971) is relevant, since these peoples may be connected with the Sutean tribes of the Mari texts.

Several recent studies by Near Eastern scholars have attempted to connect earlier tribal movements, particularly those of the Amorites of the Ur III period, with the archaeological evidence from Syria and Palestine. The writer's 1971 treatment in terms of the MB I phase (cited in B above) discusses the literature until 1970. The following year there appeared a major (though often uncritical) survey of the Amorite problem by Haldar (1971). He suggests climatic change and the abandonment of urban centres in Syria as factors in the Amorite expansion into Mesopotamia, but stresses throughout the sedentary character of these people. De Geus' survey of the Amorites in the archaeology of Palestine (1971) is largely concerned to deny the invasion hypothesis but is too nebulous to make a positive contribution.

The most recent, and archaeologically the most authoritative, treatments of the Amorites in Syria–Palestine are those of Liverani (1970, 1973), which adopt Rowton's 'dimorphic society' as a model, particularly with reference to the evidence from Tell Mardikh (forty miles south of Aleppo). We may be sure that Liverani's views will be a point of departure for future discussions, as he is preparing a major publication on the Amorites. In addition, he and other Italian excavators of Mardikh have just announced the discovery of some 15,000 tablets from the twenty-fourth century BCE, some in 'Proto-Canaanite' – a find which is likely to be even more significant than the Mari texts in future discussion, since it is much closer to Syria–Palestine both geographically and linguistically.

There is a considerable older literature on modern nomadic groups in the Middle East, some of which is attracting renewed interest as the anthropological approach continues. The fundamental works for the area under consideration are M. F. Oppenheim's four-volume *Die Beduinen* (1939–71), now somewhat dated; and especially F. Barth's *Nomads of South Persia: the Basseri Tribe of the Khamseh Confederacy* (1961). For the immediate region of north Syria the early works of Charles on the Agedat (1939, 1942) are still useful, at least in a descriptive sense, as are those of Ashkenazi (1938) on northern Palestine. C. M. Doughty's massive *Travels in Arabia Deserta* (1838) and A. Musil's *The Manners and Customs of the Rwala Bedouins* (1928) predate the Malinowskian revolution in anthropological fieldwork (see below), but nevertheless contain detailed accounts of nomadic tribes in Northern Arabia and Transjordan before their transformation by modern society. Although essentially works of cultural geography rather than social anthropology, Amiran's studies of Bedouin populations in nineteenth- and twentieth-century Palestine (1953, 1963) are exceedingly valuable for the history of settlement in this marginal region. Also, one may cite Reifenberg's contrast between 'the Desert and the Sown' (1955), though this deals primarily with the ecological consequences of the neglect of soil and water resources, rather than with the intrusion of nomads. The revival of interest in nomadic populations of Asia and Africa is no doubt due partly to the realization that the nomadic way of life is doomed in developing areas, and also due to the related problems of arid lands research in general (see, for example, UNESCO, 1962). Finally, we point to Fernea's excellent work on changing patterns in the Middle East (1970) and to de Planhol's comprehensive annotated bibliography on nomadism, now in its eleventh instalment (1961–71).

The older works we have sketched are now being complemented by up-to-date treatments in geography, ethnography, social anthropology, and sociology. Two works of special importance may be singled out. First is Johnson's paper on the nature of nomadism, drawn from case studies in South-western Asia and North Africa (1969). He focuses upon the neglected factor of ecological compulsions, concluding that nomadism is a specialized development of agriculture in marginal regions, part of a complex, changing 'dynamic equilibrium' with the environment. He further stresses the importance of charting the seasonal migrations of nomadic groups, which are not random but follow a predetermined pattern. Of particular value is Johnson's enumeration of the factors defining nomadism or, in his preference, 'pastoral nomadism' (see Johnson, 12–18).

The second volume, Irons and Dyson-Hudson's anthology on nomadism (1972), is a superb introduction to the field of nomadic studies. In the major synthetic essay, Dyson-Hudson sketches the history of nomadic studies, pointing out that the modern approach dates only from the works of Malinowski in the late 1920s and that of Lattimore in 1940. However, the emergence of a coherent theory of social anthropology, based on first-hand observation of nomadic societies, dates only from the 1950s and has not yet made its full impact. In this lucid and provocative essay, Dyson-Hudson eschews cultural history and typology, along with orientalist and geographical approaches, for the behavioural approach, stressing that until we have much more analytical description of the variables of particular nomadic societies we cannot generalize on nomadism. Among the factors to be studied are pastoral management, family-stock interdependencies, non-sedentary relationships, eco-social linkages, movement patterns, the political consequences of spatial mobility, the interconnection of value structure, and ecological response (1972, 2–26).

The only Near Eastern anthropologist to discuss this subject (albeit tangentially) in recent years in the light of current anthropological theory is Adams, whose *Evolution of Urban Society* (1966) is already a minor classic. He cites Oppenheim's observation that in ancient Mesopotamia

dramatic changes need not have been the result, necessarily, of foreign invasion but could have been brought about by a rather slow economic and political process of increasing social unrest which would not be reflected in extant documents. The most effective remedy against these potentially dangerous elements were projects of internal and frontier colonization . . . (Oppenheim, 1964, 83).

Adams elaborates by suggesting that the basic symbiosis of herdsmen and cultivators, commented upon by nearly all recent scholars, tended to produce inequalities, bitter intercommunity struggles, and a fundamental instability in Mesopotamian society. The decisive force in political change would have been internal pressure from marginal cultivators, due to even slight environmental shifts or increases in nomadic pressures. However, the contemporary texts, written from the urbanists' point of view, would naturally have characterized the changes as due to invasions of barbarians (see Adams, 1966, 55–61).

Before proceeding to the application of newer theories, it may be useful to summarize the salient points of the discussions of nomadism/sedentarization thus far. (*a*) The description of Amorites/Western Semites in the texts of the early second millennium do not suggest primarily a geographic or ethnic entity (though the various peoples are understood as deriving from the West and speaking a West Semitic dialect), much less a factual representation of invading barbarians. The designation is largely socio-economic, i.e., peoples who are 'foreigners' to the fully urbanized way of life in the Mesopotamian city-states. (*b*) The peoples so described are not true nomads, but semi-nomadic pastoralists who were partly settled in the marginal steppe zones, coming increasingly into contact with village and urban life. This explains the attribution of towns (*ālānu*) to them; it accounts for their roles as suppliers of animals, farmers, purveyors of various goods, caravaneers, mercenaries, governmental officials, and ultimately as kings of several Amorite city-states (see Buccellati, 1966, 336–46); and finally it explains the decreasing use of the appellative MAR.TU ('Amorite') and the preference for Akkadianized names. (*c*) The process of sedentarization was not one of unilinear evolution; although some tribal elements did infiltrate towns, many individuals and groups reverted to semi-nomadic ways of life in the open countryside (Mendenhall's 'withdrawal'). The result was a dimorphic society, with a large, non-nucleated population, perennially in flux and constituting a social and political challenge to the urban centres. (*d*) Rather than forcing us to dismiss the textual evidence that the Amorites had come to power throughout Upper Mesopotamia and Syria by the eighteenth or seventeenth century BCE (as Thompson does, in B above, 1974, 70–2), the new understanding of village-pastoral and urban relationships helps to account for the subtle and complex process by which the social and political change was probably accomplished. (*e*) However, the model we propose constitutes no more than a working hypothesis. The Mesopotamian texts, reflecting the narrow point of view of the urbanists, are not sufficiently representative to enable us to reconstruct the full picture.

(*ii*) *Archaeological evidence for the 'dimorphic society'*

One of the obstacles for the model we are discussing is that the archaeological record does not adequately reflect the village-pastoral aspect of the dimorphic society and can scarcely be expected to do so. This lack of documentation is especially crucial in Upper Mesopotamia and Syria, from whence our picture derives. It means that the picture is undoubtedly distorted by two factors: excavations have been confined to the impressive urban sites; and even where we do have texts describing the pastoralists, they are all written from the perspective of the city-dwellers and their overriding socio-political concerns. The steppe-regions have not been investigated archaeologically except for isolated surface surveys, and in any case semi-nomads and transitory settlers leave few traces. (For the Amorites in the archaeological record, see Dever, in B above, 1971, 213–21.)

However, there is some new archaeological evidence. Salvage operations at a construction site in Israel in 1971–3 brought to light an open, unwalled village about three-quarters of a mile south-east of the fortified Middle Bronze Age site of Beth-shemesh and contemporary with it (Epstein, 1972; Bahat, 1973). The village consists of a dozen or more simple house-courtyard complexes, built along a straggling path up the hill. The houses contained mostly domestic pottery and frequent stone implements such as sickle-flints and saddle-querns, suggesting agricultural activity. The houses exhibit only one basic building type and the pottery is homogeneous, indicating a brief period of occupation in MB IIB (about eighteenth century BCE), or precisely the Mari Age. Thereafter the village was abandoned and forgotten.

This is the first 'satellite village' of a walled Middle Bronze city that archaeology has revealed in Palestine, and that by chance. But it is certain that many other examples exist and will be discovered in time. In the Late Bronze Age numerous such villages must be presumed in the open countryside, to judge from the Ḥabiru and other scattered elements of the population described in the Amarna Letters (see Albright, in B above, 1975; and Mendenhall, 1962, 73–8). A small agricultural village of the early Iron Age (twelfth to the eleventh century BCE), almost exactly like that at Beth-shemesh, has recently been excavated near *el-Bireh* (Ramallah) and may be identified with biblical Beeroth (see Callaway and Cooley). That the earlier settlement patterns persisted into the Iron Age is confirmed by the custom of the biblical writers who, when giving the town-lists of the conquest and settlement periods, named only the main fortified city in each district together with its 'daughters' or outlying villages (*bānôt*; see Num. 21.25, 32; 32.42; Josh. 15.47; Judg. 1.27; 11.26; I Chron. 18.1). Elsewhere in similar passages *ḥaṣērîm* or 'unfortified villages' are mentioned (Gen. 25.16; Lev. 25.29, 31; Josh. 13.23; 15.20–62; 21.2), directly comparable to Mari *ḥaṣārum* (see below; and note that *bānôt* and *ḥaṣērîm* are used in parallel in Josh. 15.47; Neh. 11.25).

(iii) Nomadism and sedentarization and patriarchal backgrounds

The theoretical importance of the material from the early second millennium BCE for questions of early Israelite origins has long been recognized, especially after the Mari texts provided such abundant data. However, the initial studies were not followed up and thus the potential remains largely unexploited. The resumption of the earlier inquiry, modified in the light of current studies of pastoral nomadism, provides the most promising direction for future research on patriarchal backgrounds.

Until the 1960s the analysis of the Mari texts by Old Testament scholars was largely confined to general comparative studies, especially on Hebrew and early West Semitic names (see Noth, in C above, 1953) or single institutions such as the office of prophecy (as in A. Lods' 1946 essay in *Studies in Old Testament Prophecy*, ed. H. H. Rowley). A new departure was marked by Noth's monograph in 1961, where the Aramaean traditions associated with the patriarchs in Genesis were traced back to the 'Proto-Aramaean' peoples and dialects of Mari (see Noth, in C above, 1961, 31–2; and the critique in Thompson, in B above, 1974, 5, 75–8).

The next year saw the first emphasis on comparative sociology with Gibson's article on Mari and the patriarchs (1962), and especially in the initial study in English by Malamat (1962), who has continued the comparative study of patterns of tribal organization and institutions at Mari and in the Bible (1967, 1968). Also the same year Mendenhall developed his sociological approach to the problem of Israelite origins (1962), although the use made of the Mari data applied mostly to the period of the conquest. Among earlier treatments de Vaux's works on Mari and patriarchal parallels, beginning as early as 1948 and becoming steadily more sociological in his later studies, are of primary importance.

Despite these programmatic treatments, neither the Mari data nor nomadic theories have been fully exploited. Luke's study of tribal organization at Mari refers to the problem of the biblical patriarchs only in passing (1965, 29–30, 43), though he concludes that the patriarchs are best understood as village-pastoralists of the Mari type. The only Old Testament scholar to employ fully the sociological models of Mendenhall, Luke and Rowton is Gottwald, who has recently published a provocative critique of the older notion of a 'nomadic ideal' in early Israel (1974, 223–55). Gottwald's treatment is a sophisticated elaboration of the model advocated here but is applied largely to the period of the conquest and settlement. He deals with the patriarchal traditions and the Mari material only incidentally. Although he does not presume to date or authenticate the biblical traditions archaeologically, he does acknowledge that on the basis of survivals in Genesis 'the socio-economic data permit the interpretation that some or all of the patriarchal groups were trans-humance pastoralists' (Gottwald, 1974, 242 f.). Gottwald refers further to the unpublished dissertation of Siegfried Schwertner, '*Das Verheissene Land'. Bedeutung und Verständnis des Landes nach den frühen Zeugnissen des Alten Testaments* (Heidelberg 1966), which reaches similar conclusions on the patriarchal period.

No scholar has as yet combined *all* of the following elements, crucial in our view to any reconstruction of patriarchal backgrounds: (1) an analysis of the social milieu of the patriarchs as reflected in Genesis; (2) the evidence of the Mari texts for tribal societies and their socio-political roles; (3) the study of sedentarization in the light of current social anthropology; and (4) the cultural history of Syria–Palestine as reconstructed by archaeology. De Vaux certainly came the closest, especially in his monumental *Histoire* (1971); and his treatments can still be regarded as the most nearly satisfactory from all points of view – including his final caution that the conclusions, especially as based on archaeology, must remain tentative.

While the present discussion is intended to be no more than a prolegomenon to a fresh examination of patriarchal backgrounds, it has been suggested that Mari provides vital clues. Some of the points of contact with biblical traditions have already been recognized, but they need to be re-emphasized.

(*a*) Firstly, both societies are 'dimorphic'. The evidence from Mari, presented at length above, is so persuasive that several scholars have already adopted Rowton's dimorphic terminology and model (Liverani, 1970, 5–27; Malamat, in C above, 1971, 16; *de Vaux, 230f.; see also Buccellati, 1966, 323–53; Luke's independent adoption of Charles' original dimorphism, 1965, 29; and Haldar, 1971, 76). This model has not yet been fully employed in the analysis of the Genesis narratives, but we may suggest that it would explain, among other things, the frequent custom of camping in the vicinity of towns (Gen. 12.6–9; 13.12–18; 33.18–20; 35.16–21; 37.12–17); the occasional practice of agriculture (Gen. 26.12f.); the ease of social and economic exchange with townspeople (Gen. 21.25–34; 23.1–20; 26.17–33; 33.18–20); and the fact that Abraham, Lot, and Isaac even dwell in the towns for various periods of time as 'resident aliens' (Hebrew *gēr*, Gen. 23.4; this word and its cognates are typically used in patriarchal narratives rather than *yāšaḇ*, 'to dwell': see Gen. 12.10; 15.13; 17.8; 20.1; 21.23, 34; 26.3; 28.4; 32.4; 35.27; 36.7; 37.1; 47.4, 9). Perhaps the episodes best clarified by the notion of a dimorphic society are the separation of Abraham and Lot and Lot's taking up residence within the orbit of the Canaanite towns (Gen. 13.8–13; 19.1–4; note that Lot pitched his tent 'toward Sodom', '*ad seḏōm*, and 'was sitting in the gate', *yōšēḇ be-ša'ar*, which may mean simply that he dwelt near the gate outside the town, as the Mari tribespeople are sometimes described as doing); the contrasting yet complementary vocations of Jacob and Esau (Gen. 25.27–34); and particularly the relation of Jacob to the Shechemites (Gen. 33.18–34.31).

(*b*) Secondly, in both dimorphic societies the groups representing the village-pastoral morpheme are virtually identical. The Mari tribespeople and the tribes of Genesis are portrayed not as part of a marauding horde from the desert, like modern Bedouin; nor as ass-nomads and donkey caravaneers; nor merchant-princes. They are pastoralists, i.e., sheep-breeders who move their encampments periodically in search of water and pasturage. It is clear that at Mari the camel is unknown; that donkeys, while attested, were not the chief means of livelihood; and that subsistence systems were based on sheep-herding with some admixture of agriculture and trade with the village economy (Luke, 1965, 75–9, 113–23, 160–3). The same is true in the patriarchal narratives, where the mention of camels has long been recognized as an anachronism (for discussion and references, see *de Vaux, 222–5). The main thread of the stories concerns the semi-nomadic life of shepherds who live in tents and move with their flocks, sometimes over considerable distances, seeking traditional and sometimes disputed pastures and wells (Gen. 13.5–11; 18.1–8; 21.25–31; 24.62–7; 26.1–33; chs. 29–31; 33.12–17; 36.6–8). Since pastoral life in these narratives is interwoven with town life to some extent but is never characterized as truly urban, it exhibits, perhaps analogous to Mari, one aspect of the dimorphic society.

(*c*) Lastly, both societies in question are tribally organized. At Mari we have detailed evidence on the '(Ben) Yaminites', the 'Suteans', the 'Haneans', the 'Amorites', and others (Kupper, 1957; Luke, 1965; see also Buccellati, 1966, on the earlier Ur III Amorites). The biblical 'Benjaminites' may be nominally related to the Mari 'Yaminites', both meaning 'Sons of the South'; and possibly the 'Sons of Sheth' in Moab (Num. 24.17) are to be connected with the 'Suteans' of Transjordan, known also from New Kingdom Egyptian texts (see Giveon, 1971). The tribal structure of the society portrayed in Genesis is similarly clear, even though the late form of the written traditions has obscured some aspects. The main features are social units which are interrelated, extended families or clans (Gen. 12.1–5; 24.1–9; 28.1–5), and a system which is patriarchal if not patrilineal (see *bêṯʾāḇ*, 'paternal house, family', in Genesis 12.1 and 24.38–40, along with other 'houses' of the patriarchs in Genesis 24.2; 31.14, 43; 36.6; 46.26, 27, 31; 47.12; 50.8; and compare Mari *bīt abim*). (Here de Vaux's discussions may be highly recommended, 1961, in C above, 3–55; *1976, 221–56.)

(*d*) The initial studies of Malamat and others on tribal institutions at Mari and in Israel suggest even more detailed comparisons (although references are relatively infrequent). Note, for instance, such Mari terms as *ummatum* for a tribal unit (Hebrew *'ummāh*, 'tribe, people') and *ḫibrum* for an extended family or small clan (Hebrew *ḥeḇer*, 'association'; see the proper name 'Heber the Kenite', as the head of a breakaway nomadic clan in Judges 4.11). (On the above see Malamat, 1962, 143–6.) Note also that the details of Jacob's agreement as Laban's chief shepherd in Genesis 31.38–42 are illuminated by an Old Babylonian contract (see Finkelstein, 1968).

Another area of comparative studies would concern tribal settlements. Again, Malamat (1962, 146f.) draws attention to such Mari terms as *nawûm* for 'pastoral abode' (see also Rowton, 1974, 18–30 and references there; compare Hebrew *nāweh* 'meadow, pasture'); and *ḫaṣārum* for 'enclosure, camp' (Hebrew *ḥāṣēr*, 'unfortified village'; see especially the 'villages' of the sons of Ishmael in Genesis 25.16).

Finally, the social institutions of the two tribal societies might be compared, especially patrimony (Mari *niḫlatum*, 'to assign hereditary portion'; compare Hebrew *naḥalāh*, 'inheritance', particularly of tribal lands; see Malamat, 1962, 148–50); the custom of census-taking (Mari *ṭēbibtum*; see Luke, 1965, 248–56; Speiser, 1958, 17–25); and, finally, the prominent place given to genealogies (see Finkelstein, 1966, and Malamat, 1968, on the Mari and Old Babylonian texts; and note the biblical genealogies).

(*f*) We have deliberately by-passed the comparisons often made between Mari and certain aspects of early Israelite traditions, especially in common nomenclature (patriarchal personal names or place-names like Harran and Naḥor), religious customs (covenant-making), and the like, since these have been adequately discussed elsewhere (see *de Vaux, 186–220, 267–87 for references; secondarily, *Bright, 76–102; and the summary in Malamat, in C above, 1971, 12–21). Such comparisons are often used to confirm 'the essential historicity' of the biblical traditions concerning the patriarchs, or to fix their origins in the Mari period, i.e., in the Middle Bronze Age. Our contention is more modest and at the same time more ambitious: simply that the Mari material can serve as a helpful analogy; and that comparative studies on Mari and the Bible have scarcely begun. In this sense the recent books of Thompson and Van Seters, which tend to dismiss the parallels for want of a suitable analytical model, demonstrate the inadequacy of past approaches rather than pointing the direction for future research.

Van Seters concludes of the studies of de Vaux and Malamat on social institutions at Mari that 'what is revealing is how little these nomadic structures correspond to data in the Old Testament especially in the patriarchal stories' (in C above, 1975, 17). Van

Seters cites Henninger (1969) and Gabrieli (1959) but shows no awareness of the other literature or the sociological models we have discussed. Thus in his brief discussion of 'nomadism' (1975, 13–28) he is able to argue that 'there is very little in the patriarchal stories that reflects the nomadic life of the second millennium' (1975, 16). As proof, he cites the sedentary life of Abraham in Ur; the absence of the typical movement towards sedentarization; the use of the term *gēr*, 'resident alien', for the patriarchs; the role of patrimony (*naḥalāh*), which is 'foreign to nomadic life'; the fact that Isaac practises agriculture; the general numbers and prosperity of the patriarchs; and finally the unimportance of Harran as a centre of nomadic movements in the early second millennium BCE. The adoption of the model we have proposed would remove all these objections.

Thompson is correct in rejecting the admittedly dated models of Albright and Glueck on nomadism and socio-political change, but he substitutes no other. Regarding the newer anthropological and ethnographic studies summarized above, he cites Rowton's 1967 study with approval but does not employ the other literature. Especially damaging is the omission of Klengel (1968, 1972); Henninger (1968, 1969); Liverani (1970, 1973); and above all Luke. As a consequence, Thompson's exhaustive discussion of the early history of the West Semitic peoples, especially the pastoral nomads, is reduced to clarification of minutiae and fails to comprehend the data as a whole. He concludes that in the Ur III texts 'information about the semi-nomads is, typically, almost totally lacking'; and that the Mari evidence is not historically related to the Bible and can serve as no more than an analogue, 'useful only as a crutch in analysing historical problems such as the origin of Israel' (Thompson, in B above, 1974, 85–8).

E. Conclusion

We have argued that the Mari material provides the best available data, and that the conception of a dimorphic society provides the best analytical model, for any promising direction in future research on patriarchal backgrounds. Does that enable us to locate a 'patriarchal era' precisely? No, but it does emphasize that the more we know of the historical and cultural framework of the *Siedlungsgeschichte* of the early West Semitic peoples, as well as of the archaeological phases of Syria–Palestine in the Bronze Age, the more suitably the *nucleus* of the patriarchal traditions may fit into the second millennium BCE. It may even be possible to narrow the time-span somewhat. The MB I period is ruled out simply because the urban sites against which the Genesis narratives are set are not yet occupied: the requisite urban element of the dimorphic society is missing.

The period other than MB I in which Palestine experienced major new increments of West Semitic ('Amorite') peoples is the MB IIA–B era, precisely the late Ur III and Mari periods in Mesopotamia and Syria, when large numbers of pastoral nomads were being assimilated. If the biblical traditions are accorded any historical worth (and that is a question best left to biblical scholars), and if their original milieu was a village-pastoral/urban society basically like that reflected in the Mari texts (a question admittedly still unresolved), then the nucleus of these traditions might go back to the MB IIA–early B period, from about the twentieth to the eighteenth century BCE. In any case the problems are not all solved by advancing an MB IIA–B date, since the Negeb and Transjordan traditions cannot be reconciled with the complete lack of MB IIA–B sites in these areas.

Can the Late Bronze Age be understood, in the light of these new models, as the background for the patriarchal traditions? Several scholars have always preferred this period (see C iii above). Doubtless there were pastoral nomads in the Late Bronze Age, as in virtually every other period in Palestine. However, little textual evidence of them survives – certainly nothing like the Mari documents which enable us to portray the West Semitic pastoral nomads as a major element of the Middle Bronze Age population. The only distinct social or ethnic sub-groups of the Canaanite–Hurrian population of Late Bronze Age Palestine which are known to us at present are the 'Apiru, the Shasu, and the Aramaeans.

It would be tempting to regard 'Abram the Hebrew' in Genesis 14 as a typical 'Apiru of the Amarna Age, but this chapter is a notorious crux. Even if the identification Hebrew = 'Apiru is applied more generally to Israelite origins, as in Mendenhall's provocative model for the conquest period (1962, 71–84), there are difficulties with this view. In addition to problems of etymology and ethnic identification there is the larger question of whether the patriarchs pictured in Genesis resemble the Amarna Age 'Apiru as a socioeconomic class. The former are peaceful nomadic pastoralists (except in Genesis 14), while the latter are freebooters, usually in conflict with the urban authorities. (For orientation to the vast literature on the 'Apiru, as well as more extended criticism of Mendenhall's thesis, see Weippert, in C above, 1971, 55–106; and Cazelles, in *Peoples of OT Times*, 1973, 1–24.)

The second Late Bronze Age group available for comparison is the Shasu, mentioned alongside the ʿApiru as early as the time of Amenophis II (about 1436–1410 BCE), located primarily in southern Transjordan and considered nomadic. The first full-scale study by Giveon (1971) summarizes the meagre textual evidence, which is supplemented archaeologically only by Glueck's observation that after a long gap in occupation southern Transjordan was resettled towards the end of the Late Bronze Age. However, the Shasu are still too poorly known to be adequately characterized (as reviewers of Giveon's work have pointed out), and in any case they are largely confined to Transjordan. The most that can be said is that sociologically the Shasu may provide an analogy to the early Israelites; it has been suggested that some of them joined the Israelite tribal confederation (this is implied by Mendenhall, in D above, 1962, 81–4; see also Gottwald, in D above, 1974, 248–51; *Herrmann, 58–60).

The final subgroup known to us in the Late Bronze Age consists of the Aramaeans. These were originally nomadic or semi-nomadic peoples who emanated from the fringes of the Syro-Arabian Desert. It is clear that the Aramaeans burgeoned forth only after about 1200 BCE in the wake of Assyrian decline. The connection of the biblical patriarchs with the Aramaeans rests primarily upon the 'Aramaean tradition' in the Old Testament (see Gen. 25.20; 28.1–5; 31.20, 47; Deut. 26.5, etc.), but many modern scholars regard this as an anachronism, reflecting the Aramaean ascendancy of the period of the judges or the monarchy when the biblical narratives were being written and edited. (See, for example, Malamat, in *Peoples of OT Times*, 1973, 140, whose article provides a convenient sketch of the Aramaeans, 134–49; Mazar, in C above, 1969, 76–80; Gibson, in C above, 1962, 53f.). It may be appropriate to cite Noth's 'Proto-Aramaean' hypothesis here (see Noth, in C above, 1953; 1961; *History*, 82–4, 123–7). However, Noth's designation was more linguistic than ethnic, and it referred to the early West Semitic peoples as a whole. Noth connected the biblical patriarchs with the later Aramaean expansion in the thirteenth and twelfth centuries BCE, but very tentatively and on linguistic grounds which are now generally disputed (see Thompson, in B above, 1974, 75–8, 298–308, for a critique and references to the almost universal rejection of Noth's 'Proto-Aramaean' designation for the early West Semitic peoples and languages).

Noth's preference for a Late Bronze Age setting for the patriarchs is based partly on the conclusion that the biblical editors' separation of the patriarchal era from that of the conquest is artificial. The same is true of Eissfeldt's treatment which telescopes the biblical chronology to suggest a fourteenth-century BCE date for the patriarchal period but does not cite any archaeological or textual data from Late Bronze Age Syria–Palestine to support this date (Eissfeldt, in C above, 312–19). It is worth noting, however, that other German scholars who are also sceptical about the Albright–Wright–Bright reconstruction of the conquest era still leave open the possibility of the patriarchal age belonging to a considerably earlier period (see Alt, in D above, 1966, 45–9; and especially Weippert, in C above, 1971, 57, n. 6, where it is stated that 'the ancestors of the later Israelites were full nomads of the Middle and Late Bronze Ages').

To conclude our discussion, it is well to observe that our preference for the Middle Bronze Age for patriarchal backgrounds is due in part to the paucity of evidence at present for the Late Bronze Age. That may be largely the result of the accidents of excavation and could change overnight with new discoveries.

We shall not treat here the view of Thompson (in B above, 1974) and Van Seters (in C above, 1975) that the patriarchal traditions belong in their entirety to the Iron Age, since that rests on the *a priori* assumption that they are late literary inventions. A judgment on this matter should be left to literary and form critics. However, if Thompson and Van Seters are correct, archaeology can reconstruct no 'historical' background for the contents of the patriarchal traditions, since by definition there is none (on Thompson and Van Seters, see below, §2D iii of this chapter).

§2. THE BIBLICAL TRADITIONS

W. F. **Albright**, 'From the Patriarchs to Moses. I. From Abraham to Joseph', *BA* XXXVI, 1973, 5–33; J. M. **Holt**, *The Patriarchs of Israel*, Nashville: Vanderbilt University Press 1964; R. **Martin-Achard**, *Actualité d'Abraham*, Neuchâtel: Éditions Delachaux et Niestlé, 1969; R. **Michaud**, *Les patriarches. Histoire et theologie* LB 42, 1975; A. **Parrot**, *Abraham et son Temps*, Neuchâtel: Éditions Delachaux et Niestlé 1962 = *Abraham and His Times*, Philadelphia: Fortress Press 1968; G. **von Rad**, 'History and the Patriarchs', *ET* LXXII, 1960/61, 213–16; H. H. **Rowley**, 'Recent Discovery and the Patriarchal Age', *BJRL* XXXII, 1949/50, 44–79 = his *Servant of the Lord*, ²1965, 281–318; J. **Scharbert**, 'Patriarchentradition und Patriarchenreligion. Ein Forschungs- und Literaturbericht', *VF* XIX/2,

1974, 2–22; H. **Seebass**, *Der Erzvater Israel und die Einführung der Jahweverehrung in Kanaan*, BZAW 98, 1966; T. L. **Thompson**, *The Historicity of the Patriarchal Narratives*, BZAW 133, 1974; J. **Van Seters**, *Abraham in History and Tradition*, 1975; R. **de Vaux**, 'Method in the Study of Early Hebrew History', *The Bible in Modern Scholarship*, 1965, 15–29; idem, *Die Patriarchenerzählungen und die Geschichte*, SBS 3, 1965; C. **Westermann**, *Genesis 12–50*, EF 48, 1975; G. E. **Wright**, 'Modern Issues in Biblical Studies: History and the Patriarchs', *ET* LXXI, 1959/60, 292–6.

A. The problem of patriarchal history

W. M. **Clark**, 'The Flood and the Structure of the Pre-patriarchal History', *ZAW* LXXXIII, 1971, 184–211; R. **Culley**, 'Oral Tradition and Historicity', *Studies on the Ancient Palestinian World*, ed. J. W. **Wevers** and D. B. **Redford**, TSTS 2, 1972, 102–16; idem, 'An Approach to the Problem of Oral Tradition', *VT* XIII, 1963, 113–25; J. E. **Huesman**, 'Archeology and Early Israel: The Scene Today', *CBQ* XXXVII, 1975, 1–16; D. A. **Knight**, *Rediscovering the Traditions of Israel: The Development of the Traditio-Historical Research of the Old Testament with Special Consideration of Scandinavian Contributions*, SBLDS 9, 1973, [2]1975; A. B. **Lord**, *The Singer of Tales*, Cambridge: Harvard University Press, 1960; J. M. **Myers**, 'The Way of the Fathers', *Int* XXIX, 1975, 121–40; A. de **Pury**, 'Genèse XXXIV et l'histoire', *RB* LXXVI, 1969, 5–49; R. R. **Wilson**, *Genealogy and History in the Old Testament: A Study of the Form and Function of the Old Testament Genealogies in their Near Eastern Context* (Ph.D. dissertation, Yale University; Ann Arbor: University Microfilms 1972).

The earliest history of a people is often the most difficult time to reconstruct. When we come to the beginning of Hebrew history, even the definition of 'patriarchal history' is problematical. If we define the topic as the history of Palestine before Joshua, we have to decide how far back to extend this prehistory. If, on the other hand, we define the topic as the history of the Hebrews before the time of Moses, we find that Genesis does not give us a history of the ancestors of the Israelites but rather a history of the descendants of Abraham. Also, the existence of a distinct Hebrew cultural or ethnic entity prior to the time of the judges is debatable. To exclude the history of the Canaanites would be analogous to treating the prehistory of the United States only in terms of English history. Thus here we will be discussing what we can determine about the history and historicity of the Genesis patriarchs. Did events happen as the present narratives relate? Has the interpretation affected the narration? Is the present sequence of episodes historical and did the incidents pertain originally to the person of whom they are now told?

What can we say of the culture and the religion of the patriarchs? If we could answer these questions, we would not have written a history of the patriarchs. Rather we would have written a history of how the stories arose, were transmitted, and assumed their present form. One problem is that the patriarchal stories make no reference to known events of ancient Near Eastern history (*Bright, 74). If we could see the patriarchs as part of a larger cultural, political, or religious movement, this movement might constitute a significant stage of Israelite prehistory. Until recently there was a consensus that the patriarchs dated to the first half of the second millennium as part of a movement of semi-nomadic West Semitic peoples (Amorites) from the desert fringes into the settled areas of the ancient Near East (see Huesman, Myers, and *Bright, 76–85; for extensive critiques, see Thompson and Van Seters). But this consensus can no longer be assumed. The pentateuch does conceive of a distinct patriarchal period. But it is not clear when the traditions intend to 'date' the patriarchs. Statements about the number of years between an event mentioned in Genesis and some later event do not agree with calculations based on the number of elapsed generations (*de Vaux, 319; Thompson, 9–16; *Kaufmann, 216). Possibly a specific dating was a late development. Originally there may have been only a vague impression of 'before Moses'. It is possible that the patriarchal traditions lack any significant historical core or that they come from different times. The same tendency which created the primeval history of Genesis 1–8 and the 'universal history' of Genesis 9–11 (Clark) might have created an artificial 'patriarchal period'. Bright's defence of the accuracy of the traditions on the grounds that they fit with other known data of the patriarchal period assumes a non-existent consensus as to when the ancient Hebrews dated the patriarchs (*Bright, 70).

Other problems face the student of patriarchal history. (1) The 'all Israel' perspective of the material may have forged links between originally unconnected events and peoples. (2) If we date the patriarchal narratives some centuries before the exodus, there is a gap between the descent to Egypt and the exodus (*de Vaux, 291–2). The pentateuch recognizes a four-hundred-year hiatus (Ex. 12.40; Gen. 15.13). How is it that no information was preserved of these years? Alternatively, if only some patriarchal groups went to Egypt while others remained in Canaan, do we extend the patriarchal period to the time of the exodus? Genesis 34 has often been dated to the Amarna period because of Levi's and Simeon's role in the Shechem area which was later settled by other tribes (see de

Pury; *de Vaux, 171 f.; Eissfeldt, in *CAH*, II/2, 317). (3) Since the
traditions were put into written form no earlier than the period of
the judges, how do we account for the substantial period of oral
transmission of prose materials (but see below, p. 133)? Mere assertion of an unbroken chain of transmission is not enough (*Bright,
71). Van Seters argues that the period of accurate oral transmission
is brief (159; see Culley, 1972). Because of difficulty of transmission,
oral traditions will be passed on in illiterate societies only so long as
they remain functional (Van Seters, 162). Further, the diversity of
the patriarchal materials implies different groups for whom these
different materials were relevant and thus a variety of transmitters
(tradents) at any one time (Van Seters, 158). Some changes occur
due to random variation in the telling of the story (Lord; Culley).
Other materials will be preserved only if they are altered to remain
functionally relevant in changed circumstances (see Wilson on the
fluidity of segmented genealogies, 31–44, 114, 240–1). (4) The problem of evidence is debated. Any historian must evaluate by internal
and external means each piece of written evidence and not make *a
priori* assumptions about its historical accuracy or lack thereof.
Despite Bright's contrary assertion (70), there are a number of
episodes which many scholars regard as 'invented' (e.g., 12.1–3; 14)
and others which many regard as having arisen only during the
transmission of the material (see Knight, 205, 209). What is proof?
Are arguments based on the analysis of patriarchal traditions more
subjective than interpretations of data of archaeology, language, and
social custom from extra-biblical sources? Such a position is associated with the 'Albright–Bright' school (*Bright, 76, 96) as
against the 'Alt–Noth' school which correctly argues that literary
data are neither more nor less objective than are archaeological data
(see de Vaux, 'Method . . .').

B.   Some earlier views of the patriarchs

O. **Eissfeldt**, 'Stammessage und Novelle in den Geschichten von Jakob
und von seinen Söhnen,' *Eucharisterion, Studien zur Religion und Literatur des
Alten und Neuen Testaments* I (Festschrift Hermann Gunkel), FRLANT 36,
1923, 56–77 = his *KS* I, 1962, 84–104; N. **Habel**, *Literary Criticism of the Old
Testament*, Philadelphia: Fortress Press, 1971; A. **Jeremias**, *Das Alte
Testament im Lichte des alten Orients*, Leipzig: J. C. Hinrichs, ²1906 = *The Old
Testament in the Light of the Ancient East* I–II, London/New York: Williams &
Norgate/G. P. Putnam's Sons 1911; A. F. **Key**, 'Traces of the Worship of
the Moon God Sin among the Early Israelites', *JBL* LXXXIV, 1965, 20–6;

J. **Lewy**, 'The Late Assyro-Babylonian Cult of the Moon and its Culmination at the Time of Nabonidus', *HUCA* XIX, 1945/6, 405–89; B. **Luther**, 'Die israelitischen Stämme,' *ZAW* XXI, 1901, 1–76; A. D. H. **Mayes**, *Israel in the Period of the Judges*, SBT II/29, 1974; E. **Meyer**, 'Der Stamm Jakob und die Entstehung der israelitischen Stämme', *ZAW* VI, 1886, 1–16; J. W. **Rogerson**, *Myth in Old Testament Interpretation*, BZAW 134, 1974; A. **Spycket**, 'Le culte du dieu-lune à Tell Keisan', *RB* LXXX, 1973, 384–95; H. **Weidmann**, *Die Patriarchen und ihre Religion im Licht der Forschung seit Julius Wellhausen*, FRLANT 94, 1968; J. **Wellhausen**, *Prolegomena zur Geschichte Israels*, 1883 = *Prolegomena to the History of Ancient Israel*, 1885; G. R. H. **Wright**, 'Joseph's Grave under the Tree by the Omphalos at Shechem', *VT* XXII, 1972, 476–86.

This section will be based on Weidmann's excellent survey of the study of the patriarchs during the past century. Wellhausen's revolutionary methodological study of Israel's history first appeared in 1878. By his time, a general consensus had been reached among source critics. The D source (mainly Deuteronomy) was from the late monarchy. It formed the basis of Josiah's reformation. From the time of the exile or later came the P source. From the early and middle monarchy came the J and E sources respectively. J, E, and P ran from Genesis to Numbers, although E was somewhat fragmentary. To literary arguments used to distinguish the sources (see Habel), Wellhausen added historical correlation. For example, King Josiah's reform in the seventh century confined sacrifice to the temple at Jerusalem. Previously, there were a number of legitimate cultic sites. Thus there was a historical development from sacrifice at numerous locations to an effort to confine sacrifice to the Jerusalem temple and finally to the undisputed acceptance of sacrifice only at Jerusalem. How did this relate to the literary sources of Genesis? In J and E, the patriarchs offer sacrifice at numerous sites. In P, the patriarchs offer no sacrifices, and after Sinai there is only one sacrificial location at a time. Wellhausen (17–82) argued that the history of sacrifice confirmed the relative dating of the pentateuchal sources. For Wellhausen, the patriarchs were projections of the time of the monarchy and provided models for J's contemporaries. The stories justified Israel's possession of Palestine and legitimated cultic sites of non-Hebrew origin by linking them with these projected ancestors. Wellhausen divided Israel's history into three periods. The high point was the prophetic period. This was preceded by evolution out of a cultic stage and was followed by a decline into post-exilic Jewish legalism. Israel's religion began with Moses and the people's memory did not reach back before that time.

Wellhausen's followers – Beer, Budde, Hölscher, Marti, Meinhold, R. Smend, and especially Stade – buttressed the argument for the non-historicity of the patriarchs by pointing to the saga-like nature of the stories (Weidmann, 18–35). Both individual stories and the whole pre-exodus dwelling of Israel's ancestors in Canaan are non-historical. The religion of the patriarchs as portrayed in Genesis is not the religion of Israel's ancestors but rather the religion of pre-Israelite inhabitants of the land.

While Wellhausen stopped with Moses, his followers applied his method to the pre-Mosaic period. (1) Remnants found in later religion which are incompatible with prophetic religion come from an earlier period. (Subsequent studies, however, have emphasized the existence of folk religion contemporaneous with major 'official' religions of a culture.) (2) Remnants which fit with a nomadic life were possibly from the pre-Mosaic period, as (3) were those which fit into a pre-monotheistic but also pre-polytheistic stage of religious evolution. (4) Parallels may be drawn from pre-Islamic Arabic culture, from present bedouin Arabic cultures, and from primitive religion. Mesopotamian and Egyptian cultures, however, represented a higher stage of evolution, polytheism. (5) Tylor's theory on the origin of religion from animism as modified by Spencer who linked all religion in origin to cults of the dead was accepted. The resulting picture of pre-Mosaic religion was called 'polydaemonism'. The wilderness was a wild and dangerous place, alive with all sorts of spirits who dwelt in holy springs, trees, and stones. The term 'El' designated the attribute of might associated with these spirits. If historical, the patriarchs were tribal heroes honoured at the grave site. Later Yahwism was more discontinuous than continuous with this pre-Mosaic religion.

The views of Wellhausen and his followers quickly became dominant. Some conservative Christian and Jewish scholars rejected Wellhausen's conclusions because they believed that as divine revelation the biblical account must be literally accurate. Another group of conservative scholars – Baethgen, Dillman, *Kittel, *Klostermann, and *König – accepted source-critical theory and recognized that the time gap between the documents and the events meant that the documents could not be treated as eyewitness accounts (Weidmann, 36–43). But they regarded the conclusions of the Wellhausen school as overly negative for the following reasons (Weidmann, 41–3). (1) The saga rests on memory of some actual happening. (2) General agreement among J, E, and P supports their historical reliability. (3) Oral tradition can be extremely accurate (see *de Vaux, 181 f., for additional bibliography). (4) Writing in the ancient Near East goes back before the time of Abraham, and Abraham came from Mesopotamia which was a literate civilization (see *de Vaux, 180). The first three arguments remain points of contention in current discussion. This group affirmed the historicity of individual patriarchs and the essential personality portrait of each. The kernel of individual episodes and the overall outline were historical. They made a sharp distinction between patriarchal religion and the religion of other pre-Mosaic peoples. Prophetic religion tried to recapture the religion of the Mosaic period. The unique religious advance of Moses requires some preparation which is the patriarchal religion. Patriarchal religion included monolatry, revelation, the promises, a high ethical code, simple cult, and a personal relationship to God.

One continuing question has been to what extent the patriarchs stand for larger entities. Ishmael represents the Arabs, Esau the Edomites, and Laban the Aramaeans. Could Abraham, Isaac, and Jacob (and Israel) be personifications of groups? *Guthe (see Weidmann, 45) provided rules on how to derive tribal history from patriarchal stories. (1) The husband/father represents one group. (2) The wife/mother represents a lesser group. (3) Marriage stands for a joining of two groups. (4) Concubinage is a link between two unequal groups. (5) Death of a person means disappearance of a group. (6) Birth indicates emergence of a new group. We may add, (7) a journey is a migration of the group. Guthe's application of the rules was rigid, but the relationship between the patriarchs as individuals and the patriarchs as personifications of groups (strongly advocated by Eissfeldt) remains problematical. (*a*) Is the identification of the group with an individual secondary or primary? (*b*) The Aramaeans and the Edomites appear only in the second half of the Late Bronze Age. What implications does this have for the Laban and Esau traditions? (*c*) Does each detail of the narrative represent an experience of the group? (*d*) Since the twelve-tribe system dates no earlier than the period of the judges (see Mayes), what implications does this have for stories of Jacob and his sons which presuppose the twelve-tribe ideology (see *Kaufmann, 218 f.)? Because of the link of the twelve-tribe system with the question of Israel's structure during the period of the judges, the related stories of the birth of Jacob's twelve sons in Genesis 29–30 and the 'blessing' of Genesis 49 will not be discussed in this chapter (see Wilson, 224–7; Mayes, 27–30).

At one time, the patriarchs were interpreted in the light of Arabic parallels and primitive religion was assumed as the starting-point of Hebrew religious evolution. With the expansion of knowledge of ancient Near Eastern civilizations, Israel was now viewed as a recent arrival on the stage of history. The 'pan-Babylonianism' of Winckler and his students asserts the dominance of Babylonian culture and astral mythology over the entire ancient Near East (Weidmann, 65–88). The first of three world periods (the moon) represents a primitive monotheism. Abraham left Mesopotamia in protest against the coming of the next age when Babylonia (Jupiter = Marduk) and polytheism rise to dominance. Many allusions to moon mythology are pointed out: associations with centres of the moon cult (Ur and Haran); identification of Sarah with the moon goddess of Haran; equating of Terah with Yerah (a word for moon); Laban = white = moon; Laban's two daughters as two phases of the moon, etc. Winckler recognized the need to distinguish between the mythological form of the patriarchal stories and the historical content. Jeremias said that the mythological form did not seriously affect the historical value. But Jensen found little of historical value and interpreted the patriarchal cycles as versions of the Gilgamesh epic. The astral myth theory (see Rogerson, 45–51) does not play a major role in current discussion although a relation to the moon cult is still advocated by some (see Key, Lewy, and Spycket). This approach suffered from a failure to bring external parallels into synthesis with conclusions reached from internal analysis of the patriarchal traditions.

At about the same time as the pan-Babylonians, another mythological interpretation argued that the patriarchs were originally local Canaanite deities (Meyer; Luther; see Weidmann, 89–94). When Yahweh worship was introduced, these gods (note the divine visitors of Gen. 18) were deposed and the myths became folk sagas. This theory had little influence. A recent example of mythic interpretaton is Wright's analysis of the Joseph narrative in terms of the myth and ritual of a dying and rising god.

C. The sources and their interpretation

K. **Koch**, 'Zur Geschichte der Erwählungsvorstellung in Israel', *ZAW* LXVII, 1955, 205–26; G. E. **Mendenhall**, *The Tenth Generation: The Origins of the Biblical Tradition*, Baltimore: Johns Hopkins University Press 1973; L. **Perlitt**, *Bundestheologie im Alten Testament*, WMANT 36, 1969; D. B. **Redford**, *A Study of the Biblical Story of Joseph (Genesis 37–50)*, SVT 20, 1970.

We may divide the sources available for the study of patriarchal history into direct and indirect sources and into internal and external sources. Internal, direct evidence comes from the biblical accounts. External evidence comes from outside the Bible. No explicit external mention of any of the patriarchs has appeared. The following are the most frequently mentioned types of external (mainly indirect) evidence (see *Herrmann, 29f.; Thompson). (1) Letters found in the royal archives of the city of Mari on the upper Euphrates (eighteenth century) give us insight into the life of non-urban, North-west Semitic groups in that kingdom. (2) The Egyptian execration texts (about 1800 BCE) are directed against enemies of the Egyptian empire. The two main published groups of texts have been compared to determine if there was any social or political change in Palestine in the brief interval between the two groups (Thompson, 98–117; *Bright, 55). (3) The Sinuhe story, a historical novel, tells of the adventures of an Egyptian official who fled from Egypt to Canaan–Syria at the death of Pharaoh Amenemhet I (1962 BCE). (4) The Amarna letters contain communications between the Egyptian central administration at Amarna and rulers of Canaanite city-states in the fourteenth century. (5) Many documents, mainly from the second half of the second millennium, refer to activities of Ḥapiru/‘Apiru. Two major questions are: (*a*) Is there a linguistic or historical connection between Ḥapiru and the biblical term 'Hebrew'? (*b*) Is the primary reference of Ḥapiru to a social class or to an ethnic entity (see Mendenhall, 122–41, and below, p. 144)? (6) Legal documents contain possible parallels to the patriarchal narratives, especially Babylonian legal documents and the Nuzi texts (fifteenth century) from a city in eastern Mesopotamia with a substantial Hurrian population. The biblical Horites are in some cases identical with the Hurrians. (7) North-west Semitic personal names may be compared with names found in the patriarchal traditions. (8) Archaeological data provide information about places mentioned in the patriarchal narratives and aid in reconstructing the general history of the period (see §1B–C above).

Most biblical references to the patriarchs outside Genesis occur in fixed formulaic expressions. These include references to 'the God of (one or all three patriarchs)', the land promised to Abraham, Isaac, and Jacob; and the covenant made with Abraham, Isaac, and Jacob. Jacob and Israel often refer to the later nation or people (e.g., Num. 23.7, 10; Isa. 9.8), although sometimes there is evocation of patriarch and people together (Hos. 12.2; Obad. 10; Mal. 1.2). Isaac is mentioned only in parallel with one of the other patriarchs. Examples of references to specific incidents are Neh. 9.7; Ezek. 33.24; I Sam. 12.8; and Hos. 12.12. The mention in Joshua 24 of Terah, Nahor, and the leading out of Mesopotamia would be very important if a date in the period of the judges was certain. But many date the present formulation of Joshua 24 to the Deuteronomistic period (see Perlitt, 239–84; Mayes, 37–9). There are also the chronological data mentioned above (see p. 122). Contradictions within and between chronological and genealogical information may relate to different functional purposes and settings of the different traditions and need not imply different literary sources or different periods of origin (see Wilson, 219, 241). Redford notes that in Egypt an intense interest in genealogy arises from the Twenty-second Dynasty on. This roughly parallels chronologically the genealogical interest of P in Genesis (Redford, 5–8; Wilson, 153–8). Thus internal sources for patriarchal history are largely limited to Genesis.

(i) Source criticism

C. **Brekelmans**, 'Die sogenannten deuteronomischen Elemente in Genesis bis Numeri. Ein Beitrag zur Vorgeschichte des Deuteronomiums', *SVT* XV, 1966, 90–6; R. **Clements**, *Abraham and David: Genesis 15 and its Meaning for Israelite Tradition*, SBT II/5, 1967; G. W. **Coats**, 'Abraham's Sacrifice of Faith: A Form-Critical Study of Genesis 22', *Int* XXVII, 1973, 389–400; idem, *From Canaan to Egypt: Structural and Theological Context for the Joseph Story*, CBQMS 4, 1976; F. M. **Cross**, *Canaanite Myth and Hebrew Epic*, 1973; R. C. **Culley**, 'Structural Analysis: Is it Done with Mirrors?', *Int* XXVIII, 1974, 165–81; O. **Eissfeldt**, *Hexateuch-Synopse*, Leipzig: J. C. Hinrichs, 1922; G. **Fohrer**, *Introduction to the Old Testament*, 1968; J. **Gibson**, 'Light from Mari on the Patriarchs', *JSS* VII, 1962, 44–62; A. **Hurvitz**, 'The Evidence of Language in Dating the Priestly Code', *RB* LXXXI, 1974, 24–56; K. **Koch**, *Was ist Formgeschichte?*, Neukirchen-Vluyn: Neukirchener Verlag 1964, 1967² = *The Growth of the Biblical Tradition*, London/New York: A. & C. Black/Charles Scribner's Sons 1969; M. R. **Lehmann**, 'Abraham's Purchase of Machpelah and Hittite Law', *BASOR* CXXIX, 1953, 15–18; M. **Liverani**, 'The Amorites', in *Peoples of OT Times*, 1973, 100–33; N. **Lohfink**, *Die Landverheissung als Eid*, SBS 28, 1967; S. E. **McEvenue**, *The Narrative Style of the Priestly Writer*, AnBib 50, 1971; S. **Mowinckel**, *Tetrateuch–Pentateuch–Hexateuch*, BZAW 90, 1964; R. **North**, 'The Hivites', *Bib* LIV, 1973, 43–62; M. **Noth**, *History of Pentateuchal Traditions*, 1972; D. L. **Petersen**, 'A Thrice-Told Tale: Genre, Theme, and Motif', *BR* XVIII, 1973, 30–43; H. **Petschow**, 'Die neubabylonische Zwiegesprächsurkunde und Gen 23', *JCS* XIX, 1965, 103–20; J. G. **Plöger**, *Literarkritische, formgeschichtliche und stilkritische Untersuchungen zum Deuteronomium*, BBB 26, 1967; R. **Polzin**, '"The Ancestress of Israel in

Danger" in Danger', *Semeia III: Classical Hebrew Narrative*, ed. R. C. Culley, Missoula: Society of Biblical Literature/Scholars Press 1975, 81–98; G. **von Rad**, *Die Priesterschrift im Hexateuch*, BWANT IV/13, 1934; idem, 'The Form-Critical Problem of the Hexateuch' (see ch. I §5), *Problem of the Hexateuch*, 1966, 1–78; R. **Rendtorff**, 'Der "Jahwist" als Theologe? Zum Dilemma der Pentateuchkritik', *SVT* XXVIII, 1975, 158–66; W. **Richter**, *Die Bearbeitungen des 'Retterbuches' in der deuteronomischen Epoche*, BBB 21, 1964; W. **Rudolph** and P. **Volz**, *Der Elohist als Erzähler, ein Irrweg der Pentateuchkritik?*, BZAW 63, 1933; J. **Schreiner**, 'Segen für die Völker in der Verheissung an die Väter', *BZ* NF VI, 1962, 1–31; H. **Schulte**, *Die Entstehung der Geschichtsschreibung im Alten Israel*, BZAW 128, 1972; E. A. **Speiser**, *Genesis*, AB 1, 1964; G. M. **Tucker**, 'The Legal Background of Genesis 23', *JBL* LXXXV, 1966, 77–84; J. **Van Seters**, 'The Terms "Amorite" and "Hittite" in the Old Testament', *VT* XXII, 1972, 64–81; J. G. **Vink**, *The Date and Origin of the Priestly Code in the Old Testament*, Leiden: E. J. Brill 1969; P. **Weimar**, 'Aufbau und Struktur der priesterschriftlichen Jakobsgeschichte', *ZAW* LXXXVI, 1974, 174–203; idem, 'Die Toledot-Formel in der priesterschriftlichen Geschichtsdarstellung', *BZ* NF XVIII, 1974, 65–93; R. N. **Whybray**, 'The Joseph Story and Pentateuchal Criticism', *VT* XVIII, 1968, 522–8; F. V. **Winnett**, 'Re-Examining the Foundations', *JBL* LXXXIV, 1965, 1–19.

The basic outline of the sources presented by Wellhausen is still dominant. The D source occurs only in a few fragments in the patriarchal materials (Brekelmans). The P source provides the final framework of the pentateuch, but there is disagreement on whether P once existed as an independent account (see Cross, 293–325; Wilson, 318; Weimar; McEvenue). Von Rad's theory that P should be divided into two sources has not won any following (1934). P is commonly dated to the exilic period (Vink). However, the linguistic arguments of Hurvitz for an earlier date deserve consideration, as does Weimar's multi-stage analysis of the P tradition. P's account of the Abraham covenant (Gen. 17) and of Jacob's departure to Mesopotamia in Genesis 28 are non-independent variants of earlier traditions (see Lohfink on Gen. 15 and 17; *de Vaux, 161–3). Abraham's departure from Haran is narrated only in P (Gen. 11.31; 12.4b–5; see 24.4; 27.43; 28.10; 29.4; Josh. 24.2). The link of Abraham with Haran has been significant in various reconstructions of patriarchal history including Albright's view of Abraham as a caravaneer and the thesis of the patriarchs as part of a movement of Amorites (see above, §1C), and also the connection of the patriarchs with a moon cult (see above, p. 127). Further, Jacob dwells with Laban in Haran (see Hos. 12.12) and certain names of the

Abraham genealogy (Gen. 11.10–26 = P) have been identified with cities of the upper Euphrates region (*de Vaux, 195 f.). Gibson provides a detailed argument for the historicity of Abraham's migration from Ur to Haran to Palestine. But while Haran is mentioned in records of the early second millennium, it was much more important in the first millennium (Van Seters, 1975, 24). The stories emphasizing Jacob's links with Haran understand Laban as an Aramaean, but the Aramaeans did not settle in this area until late in the Late Bronze Age. Also, Laban's link to Haran may be secondary (see below, p. 139; Seebass, 48). Van Seters points out that there is no evidence of close links between Haran and Ur in the second millennium. Only later did both cities become centres of Aramaean and Chaldean settlement and centres of the moon cult supported by Nabonidus. Any Amorite migration would radiate from the north Syrian desert fringe towards the settled areas, contrary to Abraham's movement from Ur to Haran (Thompson, 87). While some of the names of Genesis 11.10–26 occur in Middle Bronze Age records, others are mentioned only in Iron Age texts (Van Seters, 1975, 58 f.). Wilson's study casts doubt on whether a genealogy of the sixth century can preserve accurately information from the first half of the second millennium. Thus P's account of Abraham's departure from Haran is probably not based on accurate historical information. That Abraham came from Ur is even less likely. Ur 'of the Chaldeans' would be an anachronism prior to the first millennium (Gen. 15.7; Neh. 9.7; see below, p. 143). J's introduction in 12.1–4a only indicates that Abraham departed from outside of Canaan (Josh. 24.4).

The other major independent tradition of P concerns Abraham's purchase of a burial-site from the Hittites at Hebron (Gen. 23). Many scholars accepted Lehmann's argument that Hittite legal parallels supported dating this tradition as far back as the first half of the second millennium. However, closer parallels occur in Neo-Babylonian documents of the first millennium (Petschow; Tucker; Thompson, 95 f.; Van Seters, 98–100). The reference to Hittites fits best with first millennium usage when Hatti became a general designation for Syria and Palestine (Van Seters, 1972; 1975, 45–7; see Ezek. 16.3). Similarly, Van Seters argues that the use of 'Amorite' is not supportive of a Middle Bronze Age Amorite identification of the patriarchs but is a later anachronistic ideological application to the inhabitants of Canaan (Van Seters, 1975, 43–5; 1972; see Liverani; North; on the traditional list of pre-conquest inhabitants of Canaan, see Clements, 20 f.; Lohfink, 70–2; Richter, 41–4; and Plöger, 73 f.).

Thus I conclude that the P source does not contain any independent, ancient patriarchal traditions.

J is commonly regarded today as a Judaean author from the time of the united monarchy (see Van Seters, 1975, 148–53). Fohrer and Eissfeldt advocate that J should be divided into J and a premonarchial source (see *de Vaux, 161–4; for Van Seters' exilic date of J, see below, pp. 146f. I shall proceed on the assumption of a single J source. An increasing number of scholars doubt the existence of an independent E source (see Rudolph; Mowinckel, 6–8; Whybray; Coats, 1976, 55–79; Van Seters, 1975, 125–30, 311). The beginning of E has most often been found in Genesis 15. But no agreement has been reached on what part of Genesis 15 belongs to E, and form-critical considerations argue against a division of the chapter into two sources. Genesis 22, the sacrifice of Isaac by Abraham, has been one of the classic E texts. Again the arguments in favour of allotting Genesis 22 to E are not conclusive (Speiser, 166; Coats, 1973, 396).

If both E and J sources are accepted, several questions arise. (1) Do J and E offer independent witness to the patriarchal tradition? (2) Which source more often contains the older version of the traditions? Most commonly it is assumed to be J, although Noth argued in favour of E (1972, 38). (3) If the two sources are not independent, then which is a revision of which? (4) Are J and E mere collectors or are they authors who have created a new work by imposing their perspectives on the materials? Von Rad argues that J's creativity was expressed by his arrangement of the individual stories and through introductory and transitional passages (e.g., Gen. 12.1–3; Von Rad, 1966, 70, 74–8; see Schreiner). But Rendtorff points out that while a unity of structure and theme is found within J in the patriarchal material, the same thematic and structural devices do not extend through all of J. (5) If J and E are independent, how were they combined? Bright (72) follows Albright in arguing that the basic framework is J and that all E materials which differed significantly were inserted into the J frame. (6) If independent, do J and E have a common ancestor? Noth argued for a common source in the time of the judges (1972, 38–41; Speiser, XXXVII; see below, ch. III §2D). Cross speaks of a common epic tradition of the premonarchical period (293). This would imply that traditions found in both J and E date back at least to the period of the judges. (7) How do we treat variants in parallel versions of the same tradition? These may be either transmissional (unintended) variants at the oral or written stages, or compositional (intentional) variants at the oral or written stages (see Van Seters, 1975, 161–4). Culley argues that it should be possible to recognize formal signs which would indicate origin in the oral stage (1963). It has been assumed that those features which occur in all versions of parallel traditions are the most ancient, just as in reconstructing the ancestor of a language group those features found in the largest number of daughter languages were assumed to come from the common ancestor. Diffusion theory emphasizes that some common characteristics are of recent origin. Similarly, would not new motifs which proved effective have diffused quickly throughout all variants of the story at the oral stage? The most studied example of parallel versions of the same tradition is the episode of the endangered wife (Gen. 12.10–20; 20; 26.6–16; see Koch, 1969, 111–32; Petersen; Culley, 1974; Polzin). These episodes also raise the problem of literary motif versus historical event in the patriarchal traditions.

In summary: the P source does not contain any independent, old patriarchal traditions. While J and E preserve pre-monarchical traditions, they may represent only one independent witness. Elements common to J and E do not necessarily belong to the oldest traditions.

(ii) The form-critical approach: Gunkel

W. F. **Albright**, *Yahweh and the Gods of Canaan*, 1968; B. S. **Childs**, 'A Study of the Formula, "Until this Day"', *JBL* LXXXII, 1963, 279–92; idem, 'The etiological tale re-examined', *VT* XXIV, 1974, 387–97; P. **Gibert**, 'Légende ou Saga', *VT* XXIV, 1974, 411–20; H. **Gressmann**, *Die älteste Geschichtsschreibung und Prophetie Israels*, SAT II/1, ²1921; idem, 'Sage und Geschichte in den Patriarchenerzählungen', *ZAW* XXX, 1910, 1–34; H. **Gunkel**, *Genesis*, HKAT I/1, 1901, ²1902, ³1910; idem, *The Legends of Genesis* (translation of the introduction to *Genesis*), Chicago: Open Court Publishing Co. 1901, reprinted with an introduction by W. F. Albright, New York: Schocken Books 1964; R. M. **Hals**, 'Legend: A Case Study in OT Form-Critical Terminology', *CBQ* XXXIV, 1972, 166–76; C. A. **Keller**, 'Über einige alttestamentliche Heiligtumslegenden', *ZAW* LXVIII, 1955, 141–68, LXVIII, 1956, 85–97; B. O. **Long**, *The Problem of Etiological Narrative in the Old Testament*, BZAW 108, 1968; W. **Richter**, *Exegese als Literaturwissenschaft. Entwurf einer alttestamentlichen Literaturtheorie und Methodologie*, Göttingen: Vandenhoeck & Ruprecht 1971; G. M. **Tucker**, *Form Criticism of the Old Testament*, Philadelphia: Fortress Press 1971; J. A. **Wilcoxen**, 'Narrative', *Old Testament Form Criticism*, 1974, 57–98.

Gunkel is the father of Old Testament form-criticism. His concern was to penetrate behind the written sources by studying the genres of the texts. The more we know about the various genres, their life-settings, purposes, and history, the more successful we can be at reconstructing the original form of a text. Gunkel called the Genesis accounts *Sage*, which is generally translated as saga or legend. Both translations have been criticized. It has been argued that *Sage* should refer to the cycle of stories rather than to the single episode. Technically, 'saga' denotes a particular type of Scandinavian and Icelandic literature. Legend originally designated legends of the saints (on Gen. 22 as legend, see Coats, 1973; Hals). Gibert notes that in French legend has long included both *legende* and the equivalent of German *Sage*. More narrowly, legend is also used of stories of sacred places and rituals (Keller). Saga is oral and may be rhythmic (Albright, 1968; see Lord). It was recited around the 'camp fire' and differed from historical narrative (see Wilcoxen, 74–78). Characteristics of saga included its non-tendentious nature, the direct activity of God, a vagueness as to time and place, and the priority of the self-contained account. Gunkel's belief that the oldest sagas were necessarily brief is frequently challenged (Wilcoxen, 64f.). Saga was balanced and simple in structure. The characters, limited to two or three in one scene, were often ideal types. Little description was given of external details or psychological states. Action dominated, and imagination played a large role. Sagas could be historical, ethnographic (depicting relations of tribes and races in terms of a story), and aetiological (to explain how a certain situation originated). Aetiological sagas were ethnological (the origins of relations between groups), etymological (origin of words), cultic, and geological. Usually different genres were mixed in a single saga. The Joseph story, the sacrifice of Isaac, and the marriage of Rebekah belonged to a genre which Gunkel called the romance. It was long, descriptively detailed, and complex. Romances derived from internal expansion of a saga and originated later than sagas.

Individual sagas were joined with other sagas of similar subject or localization, sometimes by a journey or a genealogical notice. Journeys, genealogies, and the sequence of incidents were without historical basis. Wilson's study supports the view that genealogies do not originate for historiographic purposes although they may contain some historical information (65, 161, 244f.). Two stories might be merged, one enframing the other (Gunkel, 1964, 80). Added materials along with alterations and omissions impaired the historical value of the traditions. Gunkel and Gressmann regarded both saga and myth as derivative of folktales. For example, a shepherd-hunter folktale underlies the Jacob–Esau story. Later scholars distinguished between historical content and narrative development. Some stories were not Israelite in origin: the story of Ishmael was an Ishmaelite ethnological saga. Such stories have been adapted by secondary attribution to an Israelite character or by changing the localization (Wilcoxen, 71). Since each saga has its own history, the sagas can go back to different ages. Scholars who have been strongly influenced by Gunkel have doubted the possibility of reconstructing a unified patriarchal history.

(iii) The religion of the patriarchs: Alt

A. **Alt**, 'The God of the Fathers', *Essays* 1966, 1–77; W. M. **Clark**, *The Land Promise Theme in the Old Testament* (Ph.D. dissertation, Yale University; Ann Arbor: University Microfilms 1964); B. **Diebner**, 'Die Götter des Vaters. Eine Kritik der "Vätergott"-Hypothese Albrecht Alts', *Dielheimer Blätter zum Alten Testament* IX, 1975, 21–51; O. **Eissfeldt**, 'El and Yahweh', *JSS* I, 1956, 25–37; idem, 'Jahwe, der Gott der Väter', *TLZ* LXXXVIII, 1963, 481–90 = his *KS* IV, 1968, 79–91; idem, 'Jakobs Begegnung mit El und Moses Begegnung mit Jahwe', *OLZ* LVIII, 1963, 325–31 = his *KS* IV, 92–8; K. **Galling**, *Die Erwählungstraditionen Israels*, BZAW 48, 1928; M. **Haran**, 'The Religion of the Patriarchs: an Attempt at a Synthesis', *ASTI* IV, 1965, 30–55; D. R. **Hillers**, 'Paḥad Yiṣḥāq', *JBL* XCI, 1972, 90–2; J. **Hoftijzer**, *Die Verheissungen an die drei Erzväter*, Leiden: Brill 1956; O. **Kaiser**, 'Traditionsgeschichtliche Untersuchung von Genesis 15', *ZAW* LXX, 1958, 107–26; J. **Lewy**, 'Les textes paléo-assyriens et l'Ancien Testament', *RHR* CX, 1934, 29–65; J. **Luke**, *Pastoralism and Politics in the Mari Period* (Dissertation, 1965); V. **Maag**, 'Der Hirte Israels. Eine Skizze von Wesen und Bedeutung der Väterreligion', *STU* XXVIII, 1958, 2–28; idem, 'Sichembund und Vätergötter', *Hebräische Wortforschung* (Festschrift Walter Baumgartner), SVT 16, 1967, 205–18; H. D. **Preuss**, *Jahweglaube und Zukunftserwartung*, BWANT 87, 1968; W. **Staerk**, *Studien zur Religions- und Sprachgeschichte des alten Testaments* I, Berlin: Georg Reimer 1899.

Alt's analysis of patriarchal religion has received a broader acceptance than any other aspect of patriarchal studies (for a recent rejection, see Diebner). Alt argued that the Old Testament makes a distinction between the cult of Yahweh and the religion of the patriarchs (see Galling) in Exodus 3 and 6.2–8. Further, personal names containing the element 'Yahweh' are lacking in the pre-Mosaic period. It was the newness of the Yahweh cult which helped unite the tribes into Israel. Alt found two religious types in Genesis. One was the localized cults of Canaan associated with El names. Originally distinct from these 'Elim' cults was the worship of the 'God of my (your, etc.) father(s)'. Since the link between the patriarchs was secondary, the 'God of my father' must be earlier than 'God of my fathers' (= God of Abraham, Isaac, and Jacob). 'God of PN' meant that PN was the first person to worship that god. The 'mighty one of Jacob' (Gen. 49.24) and the 'kinsman (or "fear") of Isaac' (Gen. 31.42, see Hillers) were ancient epithets of these nameless gods. (The 'shield of Abraham', Gen. 15.1, is of different origin, see Kaiser.) This religious type was not linked to one locale. It was based on a personal revelation and each clan had its own father-god, as is clear in the treaty between Jacob and Laban (31.53). The promises of posterity were an aspect of this religion. As the descendants of the cult founders came into contact with the settled land, there was added the promise of land (to be fulfilled in the immediate future). When a clan settled in Canaan, the 'god of the father' was identified with the local 'Elim' god of the area. The cult legends of the patriarchs were forgotten and the legends of the Canaanite sanctuaries were substituted. Only Genesis 15 (due to its archaism and lack of localization) preserved an original patriarchal revelation. After the conquest, the worship of Yahweh as the national god co-existed with the cults of the merged patriarchal/ Elim gods until they were identified with each other. As various groups came into contact with one another, the 'god of Abraham' was identified with the 'god of Jacob' and the 'god of Isaac'.

Subsequent studies modified Alt's thesis. Eissfeldt recognized that the Elim cults are local manifestations of the god El, the head of the Canaanite pantheon. The El cult had replaced the god of the father cult before the introduction of Yahwism (Eissfeldt, *OLZ*; *CAH*, II/2, 311, see Gen. 33.18–20). By contrast, Maag thought that the strength of the patriarchal god cult caused its identification with Yahweh (1967, see Josh. 24). Seebass dates the identification of Yahweh with the god of the father to the wilderness period (82). Others have argued that patriarchal religion from its inception was an El cult, and that (El) Shaddai was a major deity of the Amorites (see Cross, in Ci above, 1–75; *de Vaux, 276–8). For Cross, El is the god of the patriarchal league who leads the group in war to secure new lands (58f.). A personal god occurs in other ancient Near Eastern religions (Lewy; Cross, 9f.) although not all cited cases are similar to the patriarchal gods (*de Vaux, 268–74). The promise of land is regarded by many as the most ancient part of the patriarchal traditions with dubious assertion of nomadic desire for settled land (so *Bright, 100; Noth; von Rad; but see Luke, 25–32, 278). Clark argues (1964) on form-critical grounds that J is responsible for projecting the land promise into the patriarchal period and for post-poning the fulfilment until the conquest generation (see Staerk;

Galling). Hoftijzer dated the land promise to the exilic period on source-critical grounds. Maag (1958) overextends the evidence in his detailed picture of patriarchal religion. Preuss derives the historical emphasis of Old Testament religion from patriarchal religion.

(iv)   The history of tradition approach: Noth

A. **Alt**, 'Die Wallfahrt von Sichem nach Bethel', *In piam memoriam Alexander von Bulmerincq*, AHGHIR VI/3, 1938, 218–30 = his *KS* I, 1953, 79–88; B. W. **Anderson**, 'Martin Noth's Traditio-Historical Approach in the Context of Twentieth-Century Biblical Research', in M. Noth, *A History of the Pentateuchal Traditions*, 1972, xiii–xxxii; M. C. **Astour**, 'Political and Cosmic Symbolism in Genesis 14 and its Babylonian Sources', *Biblical Motifs: Origins and Transformations*, ed. A. Altmann, Cambridge: Harvard University Press 1966, 65–112; M. A. **Beek**, 'Das Problem des aramäischen Stammvaters (Deut. 26.5)', *OS* VIII, 1950, 193–212; B. S. **Childs**, 'Deuteronomic Formulae of the Exodus Traditions', *Hebräische Wortforschung*, SVT 16, 1967, 30–9; R. J. **Clifford**, 'The Word of God in the Ugaritic Epics and in the Patriarchal Narratives', *The Word in the World* (Festschrift F. L. Moriarty), ed. R. J. Clifford and G. W. MacRae, Cambridge: Weston College Press 1973, 7–18; G. W. **Coats**, 'The Traditio-historical Character of the Reed Sea Motif', *VT* XVII, 1967, 253–65; idem, 'Redactional Unity in Genesis 37–50', *JBL* XCIII, 1974, 15–21; A. **Jepsen**, 'Zur Überlieferungsgeschichte der Vätergestalten', *WZKMUL* III, 1953–4, 139–55; O. **Keel**, 'Das Vergraben der "fremden Götter" in Genesis XXXV 4b', *VT* XXIII, 1973, 305–36; R. **Kilian**, *Die vorpriester-lichen Abrahamsüberlieferungen. Literarkritisch und traditionsgeschichtlich untersucht*, BBB 24, 1966; idem, 'Zur Überlieferungsgeschichte Lots', *BZ* NF XIV, 1970, 23–37; E. **Lipiński**, '"Anaq-Kiryat 'arba'–Hébron et ses sanctuaires tribaux', *VT* XXIV, 1974, 41–55; S. E. **Loewenstamm**, 'Zur Traditionsgeschichte des Bundes zwischen den Stücken', *VT* XVIII, 1968, 500–6; B. O. **Long**, 'Recent field studies in oral literature and their bearing on O.T. criticism', *VT* XXVI, 1976, 187–98; R. **Polzin**, 'Martin Noth's A History of Pentateuchal Traditions', *BASOR* CCXXI, 1976, 113–20; J. R. **Porter**, 'Pre-Islamic Arabic Historical Traditions and the Early Historical Narratives of the Old Testament', *JBL* LXXXVII, 1968, 17–26; H. **Reventlow**, *Opfere deinen Sohn. Eine Auslegung von Genesis 22*, BSt 53, 1968; L. **Rost**, 'Das kleine geschichtliche Credo', *Das kleine Credo*, 1965, 11–25; H. C. **White**, 'The Initiation Legend of Ishmael', *ZAW* LXXXVII, 1975, 267–306; G. **Widengren**, 'Oral Tradition and Written Literature among the Hebrews in the Light of Arabic Evidence, with Special Regard to Prose Narratives', *AcOr* XXIII, 1958, 201–62.

In contrast to Gunkel, von Rad focused on the structure of the pentateuch which he argued was based on short, credo-like recitations of Israel's history (Deut. 26.5–10), originating in the cult of the

period of the judges. J inserted the Sinai tradition into the pentateuchal framework and prefaced it with the primeval history (Gen.
1–11). J also expanded considerably the patriarchal section. Von
Rad's 'credo' thesis gained wide acceptance, but recently it has come
under increasing attack. Rost argues that in Deuteronomy 26 only
parts of vv. 5 and 10 are original, referring to a 'wandering' ancestor
who settled in Canaan. (Similarly Seebass; on the choice between
'wandering' and 'ready to perish' as well as who the ancestor was,
see Beek, Seebass, 1–5.) Childs points out that the Reed Sea event is
omitted in Deuteronomistic versions of the credo while being central
to the pentateuchal account. Thus some argue that the 'credo' is a
late summary of the pentateuch (see *de Vaux, 165f.; Coats, 1967;
Van Seters, 1975, 143).

Building upon von Rad, Noth isolated five pentateuchal themes:
primeval history, patriarchs, exodus, Sinai, and wilderness. Anderson notes six principles which guided Noth's effort to isolate the
original kernel and to outline the expansion of each theme. Older
traditions are: (1) short; (2) cultic or religious; (3) anonymous and
typical; (4) awkward or archaic in their present context (e.g., the
Penuel incident); and (5) attached to specific places. Only one figure
is connected originally with one locale. This *Ortsgebundenheit* principle has been severely criticized (*Bright; Van Seters, 1975, 147f.).
(6) The primary unit is the independent saga. Genesis 24, for
example, is shown to be late by its discursiveness, by its function of
linking together the Jacob and Isaac traditions, and because it takes
over the motif of the Aramaean wife from the Jacob tradition.
Anderson offers valid criticisms of these six principles while recognizing that Noth does not apply them in a rigid manner. Indeed, Noth's
'inconsistency' in applying them is the basis of Polzin's critique (see
also Knight, 193–213). In addition, (7) the core of the patriarchal
traditions is the promise of land and posterity (Noth, 1972, 111, 190,
253). (8) When an individual personifies a group, the episode does
not portray historical *events* but rather a *situation*. (9) The pentateuchal tradition exhibits an 'all Israel' perspective which presupposes the tribal league of the period of the judges. (10) While any
reconstruction of the development of the tradition is hypothetical,
such reconstruction is a prerequisite to dealing with the 'history' of
the patriarchs.

Noth argued that the patriarchal theme was introduced into the
pentateuchal outline through the Jacob traditions (Deut. 26.5)
localized in Shechem and developed by the central Palestinian tribes
in the judges period. The connection of Jacob with Bethel reflects

the transfer of the cultic centre from Shechem to Bethel (see Alt, 1938). Keel's re-examination of Genesis 35.2–5 makes Alt's theory of a ritual pilgrimage between the two sites dubious. Keel argues that while the burial of sacred objects may rest on old Shechemite tradition, the link with Jacob is monarchical or later. The Isaac–Abraham traditions were introduced into the pentateuch by the southern tribes. Links with Jacob reflect interaction between central and southern tribes (through Judah). Isaac traditions have been pushed into the background by the Abraham traditions (Noth, 1972, 111f.). Since Jacob was already established as the father of the twelve tribes with Isaac as his father, Abraham was made the father of Isaac. Genuine Isaac traditions are found only in parts of Genesis 26 and are localized at Beer-Lahai-Roi (1972, 107). In contrast, de Vaux suggests that there was no original Isaac cycle and that Genesis 26 is an effort to 'fill out' the shadowy figure of Isaac (167f.). Any Abraham traditions which parallel Isaac or Jacob traditions, plus anything connected with Hebron/Mamre, are secondary. (So Noth; some scholars localize the Abraham material at Mamre, e.g., Jepsen, 70.) Noth finds an original Abraham tradition only in the land promise of Genesis 15.7–21 (see Loewenstamm; and below, p. 146). Finally, the Joseph story has no historical basis. It originates among the central Palestinian tribes to join together the patriarchal and exodus themes (Noth, 1972, 209–13; similarly, Coats, 1974, 1976). Redford points to a tradition (Gen. 49) which presupposes Jacob's death in Canaan (25).

An example of originally non-patriarchal material is the Lot/Sodom complex in Noth's view. Lot (the ancestor of pre-Edomite inhabitants of Zoar, Gen. 19.30–8) was linked with Haran (originally a survivor of Sodom's destruction who came to live at Beth-Haran at the edge of the Jordan valley) in Hebron where Abraham was secondarily introduced into the story (1972, 152–4; Lipiński). Kilian, whose reconstruction differs in some details, dates the connection of Lot with Abraham to about 1200 BCE (1966, 1970). Other non-Hebrew traditions concern the origins of the Ishmaelites (Noth, 1972, 108; White), the abolition of human sacrifice in Genesis 22 (1972, 114; see Van Seters, 1975, 227–40; Coats, 1973; Kilian, 1966, 263–78; Reventlow), and the Penuel story. Only Genesis 34 has a definable historical setting (as above, p. 122). Contrary to Albright (1968, 60f.), Noth dismisses Genesis 14 as a late scholarly creation (also *de Vaux, 216–20; Astour; and Van Seters, 1975, 305, who regards Elam as an intentional archaism for Persia). The Esau tradition arises among Leah elements in Gilead when the herdsman was replacing the hunter (Noth, 1972, 97f.). These Leah elements had earlier moved from central Palestine. The identification of Esau with Edom occurs later (also *de Vaux, 169f.) among Judaean clans who bordered Edom. The Jacob–Laban tradition originates in the post-settlement period of contacts with Aramaeans in Transjordan (Gen. 32). Jacob's stay with Laban is a later elaboration using the motif of the 'deceived deceiver' (Noth, 1972, 99). Laban's transposition to upper Mesopotamia is later still. In summary, for Noth relatively little accurate information is preserved concerning the patriarchs. Much of the material is later elaboration and secondary connective material.

Many subsequent studies apply a methodology similar to Noth's to a restricted body of material. Mention should be made of Jepsen's giving priority to the east Jacob over the west Jacob traditions (see *Gunneweg, 18; Seebass, 47–9), of Kilian's analysis of the Abraham tradition, and of Seebass' study of the relationship of Shechem (= Israel) and Bethel (= Jacob) traditions. Kilian goes far beyond the evidence in allotting almost each phrase of the text to one of five stages extending from pre-J to pre-P (1966, 284–320) although he offers many valuable insights. More study is needed of the itinerary motif and of other 'secondary' elements. Wilson's study shows that the genealogy has its own function and does not usually originate as a joining device (Wilson, in A above, 67, 166, 188, 247f.). Polzin and others accuse Noth of an unjustifiable bias in favour of the primacy of the individual saga (Cross; see Knight, in A above, 204, 210). But Noth does view the Joseph complex as an integral whole. Due to the shortness of individual episodes, Wilcoxen (in Cii above 65) suggests that we have an inventory of plots on which a narrator could elaborate. But Van Seters denies the oral origin of the material and says that its 'all Israel' perspective presupposes a centralized state (§2 above, 1975, 145). Clearly, further study of the life-setting(s) of the material is needed. Long warns (1976) against trying to impose arbitrarily either the Ugaritic epic model (Cross; Clifford) or the Yugoslavian story-telling model (Lord). Porter's sketch of pre-Islamic Arabic narrative traditions parallels Noth's results concerning the origin, content, and redaction of the patriarchal traditions (see Widengren).

(v) *Beyond Gunkel and Noth: Westermann*

N. K. **Gottwald**, 'Were the Early Israelites Pastoral Nomads?', *Rhetorical Criticism* (see §1D), 1974, 223–55; A. **Jolles**, *Einfache Formen*, Darmstadt, Wissenschaftliche Buchgesellschaft, ⁴1969; E. **Kutsch**, *Verheissung und*

Gesetz. Untersuchungen zum sogenannten 'Bund' im Alten Testament, BZAW 131, 1973; E. **Muir**, *The Structure of the Novel*, London/New York: Hogarth Press/Harcourt, Brace & World 1928/9; H. D. **Preuss**, '. . . ich will mit dir sein!', *ZAW* LXXX, 1968, 139–73; C. **Westermann**, 'Arten der Erzählung in der Genesis', *Forschung am Alten Testament. Gesammelte Studien*, TB 24, 1964, 9–91; idem, *Genesis 12–50*, EF 48, 1975.

Westermann switches the focus from geographical localization (Noth) to the primary social community behind the text (1975, 18, 28, 48, 116f.). The oldest patriarchal accounts are from a pre-tribal period and have as their social horizon the family or clan. Some narratives have tribal horizons (Gen. 29–31; 34 – both transitional, 1964, 81f.); some have state horizons (25.21–6; 1975, 49). Influenced by Jolles' analysis of Icelandic saga (but see Van Seters, 1975, 134–38), Westermann introduces a new delineation of the genres of Genesis 12–36. A narrative presents a difficult situation which leads to a climax and resolution (1964, 33). In the Abraham cycle there are three ancient 'family narratives': the endangering of Sarah, the birth of Isaac, and the birth of Ishmael (1964, 59), focusing on the relation of mother to child (1964, 59) and the preservation of the family from one generation to the next (1975, 37). The promise of a son occurs in one ancient tradition (Gen. 18; 1975, 37, 118), but no original family narratives contain a land promise. Westermann thinks that such did once exist (1964, 32; 1975, 42). Narratives with more than one promise come from the stage when independent stories are combined into larger units (1964, 32; 1975, 116). Thus develops the 'promise narrative' and the posterity promise (1964, 20). No original promise motifs are found in the Jacob family narratives (1964, 87), contrary to Seebass who argues unconvincingly that the land promise is originally connected only with the Jacob–Bethel tradition (23–5). Other genres include the genealogical materials (having a tribal or state setting, 1964, 78); the later theological narratives (e.g., Gen. 22; 1975, 44, 71); the notice, generally only a verse or two (1964, 34); the account which reformulates a family narrative in some other genre (e.g., Gen. 15); the added scene (1964, 34); and the debased narrative in which the focus has shifted from narrative tension to descriptive portrayal (1964, 69). However, to regard descriptive narrative as derivative of dynamic narrative is dubious (see Muir; Coats, 1973). A genre of wandering notices (e.g., Jacob's encounter with God at Bethel; 1964, 84) fits well the family setting once the model of a continuous movement from nomadism to settled life is changed for that of the semi-nomadic pastoralist living in a symbiotic relation with the settled agriculturalist and engaging in seasonal transhumance (Gottwald; Luke; §1D above). The Jacob stories are from a more developed stage of the tradition as is evidenced in the longer, interrelated units (1975, 36). The focus is on brother to brother relations (1964, 66, 87), and the dominant themes are 'blessing' and the 'god with you' motif (Preuss, '. . . ich will . . .'; Rendtorff, 163). Covenant is a late motif in the patriarchal traditions (Kutsch; Perlitt).

In summary: Westermann's effort to refine the classical genre designations is an advance, although further clarification is needed. To define a genre according to its primary forming community rather than according to its structure creates difficulties (Petersen; Long, 1976, 191–4). It is not clear whether the different nature of the Jacob and Abraham traditions relates to a different chronological setting, to a different cultural setting, or to a different ethnic setting. The non-Yahwistic nature and the family setting of the oldest traditions suggest their origin either in the pre-Mosaic period or later in a different cultural segment of the total society (see below, p. 148). The clan- or family-oriented, wandering pastoralist is not limited to one stage of Israel's history. Similarly, tribal structure occurs in different contexts and periods (see Gottwald).

D.   *The date and setting of the patriarchal traditions*

W. **Beltz**, *Die Kaleb-Traditionen im Alten Testament*, BWANT 98, 1974; F. M. Th. de Liagre **Böhl**, 'Das Zeitalter Abrahams', *Opera Minora*, Groningen–Djakarta: J. B. Wolters 1953, 26–49; W. M. **Clark**, 'Law', *Old Testament Form Criticism*, 1974, 99–139; W. J. **Dumbrell**, 'Midian – a land or a league?', *VT* XXV, 1975, 323–37; G. **Fohrer**, 'Die Vorgeschichte Israels im Lichte neuer Quellen', *Studien*, 1969, 297–308; R. **Giveon**, *Les bédouins Shosou des documents égyptiens*, DMOA 18, 1971; W. **Helck**, 'Die Bedrohung Palästinas durch einwandernde Gruppen am Ende der 18. und am Anfang der 19. Dynastie', *VT* XVIII, 1968, 472–80; H. **Heyde**, *Kain, der erste Jahwe-Verehrer*, AT I/23, 1965; W. Th. **In der Smitten**, 'Genesis 34 – Ausdruck der Volksmeinung?', *BO* XXX, 1973, 7–9; K. **Koch**, 'Die Hebräer vom Auszug aus Ägypten bis zum Grossreich Davids', *VT* XIX, 1969, 37–81; O. **Loretz**, 'Hebräisch ḥwṭ "bezahlen, erstatten" in Gen. 31.39', *ZAW* LXXXVII, 1975, 207f.; A. **Malamat**, 'Aspects of Tribal Societies in Mari and Israel', *RAI* XV, 1967, 129–38; B. **Mazar**, 'The Historical Background of the Book of Genesis', *JNES* XXVIII, 1969, 73–83; A. **Meinhold**, 'Die Gattung der Josephgeschichte und des Estherbuches: Diasporanovelle', *ZAW* LXXXVII, 1975, 306–24, LXXXVIII, 1976, 72–93; J. M. **Miller**, 'The Descendants of Cain: Notes on Genesis 4', *ZAW* LXXXVI, 1974, 164–74; R. **Rendtorff**, 'El, Ba'al und Jahwe', *ZAW* LXXVIII, 1966, 278–92; H. **Richardson**, 'Civil Religion in Theological Perspective', *American Civil Religion*, ed. R. E. Richey and D. G. Jones, New York: Harper & Row 1974, 161–84; W. M. W. **Roth**, 'The Wooing of Rebekah: A Tradition-Critical Study of Genesis 24', *CBQ* XXXIV, 1972, 177–87; H. **Shanks**, 'The Patriarchs' Wives as Sisters – Is the Anchor Bible Wrong?', *BARev* I/3, 1975, 22–6; G. **Wallis**, 'Die Stadt in den Überlieferungen der Genesis', *ZAW* LXXVIII, 1966, 133–48; idem, 'Die Tradition von den drei Ahnvätern', *ZAW* LXXXI, 1969, 18–40; M. **Weippert**, 'Abraham der Hebräer? Bemerkungen zu W. F. Albrights Deutung der Väter Israels', *Bib* LII, 1971, 407–32; idem, 'Semitische Nomaden des zweiten Jahrtausends, Über die *S3św* der ägyptischen Quellen', *Bib* LV, 1974, 265–80, 427–33; R. R. **Wilson**, 'The Old Testament Genealogies in Recent Research', *JBL* XCIV, 1975, 169–89.

Efforts to place the patriarchs historically and culturally have proceeded primarily by attempting to establish correlations between data from Genesis with data from ancient Near Eastern sources. (1) The ancient Near Eastern data must be correctly interpreted prior to efforts to correlate it to the biblical materials. Some legal parallels to patriarchal customs cited by Speiser, Gordon, and others prove to be invalid because the Nuzi or other text is misinterpreted (see *de Vaux, 241–56; Thompson, 196–203; Van Seters, 1975, 65–103; Clark, 1974, 137f.; recently, Loretz and Shanks). (2) The specification of the relevant ancient Near Eastern data must not be distorted by citing parallels which support one date while ignoring parallels from other periods (e.g., *Bright, 78f.). (3) The biblical data should be examined internally prior to seeking parallels which tend to short-cut this investigation. Too often a parallel exists only when on the basis of the extra-biblical source the biblical text is reconstructed to agree with the extra-biblical source. (4) Only now can appropriate comparisons be made. In the case of conflict between conclusions arrived at from internal analysis and conclusions arrived at from external correlations, an adequate resolution must show how one or the other interpretation is inadequate.

The best synthesis of external evidence with form and tradition research is de Vaux's history. De Vaux argues that the connection of Abraham with Ur and Haran is historical. He emphasizes place and personal names in the patriarchal traditions which appear in the Haran and Ur areas, some of which date to the beginning of the second millennium. The link to Ur could not have arisen in the time of J when Ur was in eclipse (de Vaux, but see above, p. 131). Links to the Aramaeans would not date to a period when the Aramaeans were the enemies of the Hebrews. However, the Aramaean link could arise in the period of the judges, and both Aramaean and Ur traditions could date after the fall of the Aramaeans (Van Seters, 1975, 24–6). De Vaux says that patriarchal names are common only in the Middle Bronze Age and are not used as Hebrew names later in the Old Testament. Thompson disagrees and says that these names are possible at any period (17–51). De Vaux argues that there are racial, cultural, and geographical continuities between the Amorites and Aramaeans so that calling the patriarchal ancestors Aramaeans is not anachronistic (similarly *Bright, 90). In contrast, Thompson disputes whether there is an Amorite migration (144–71; see Gottwald, 232 f.). De Vaux regards the ancestors of the Israelites as part of the Ḫapiru whom he regards as an ethnic entity (see *Herrmann, 54; Koch, 'Die Hebräer . . .'; Weippert, 1972; on the relation of Ḫapiru and Shosu to Edomites, Moabites, and Israelites, see Helck; Giveon; Weippert, 1974; and Gottwald, 248–51). This makes the patriarchs both ethnic Amorites and ethnic Ḫapiru. The patriarchs are semi-nomadic goat and sheep-herders in the fringe area between desert and sown. De Vaux notes that all stops on the patriarchal routes fall within this area. While noting Rowton's thesis of the dimorphic pattern of agricultural/pastoral symbiosis, de Vaux still speaks of the patriarchs as in transition from nomadic to sedentary life (229–31). The life-style of the patriarchs is distinguished from that of groups without fixed links to the settled land (Ishmael, Esau, and Cain; see Heyde and Miller). Mari words for pasturage occur as place-names in Judah and the Negeb where they retain their meaning rooted in the semi-nomadic way of life (232; Malamat). Semi-nomadism accords well with other features of patriarchal life: tent dwellers, obligation of hospitality, code of vengeance, unlimited authority of the family head, and the extended family as the social unit without indication of larger units. References to camels and anticipations of later tribes and peoples are anachronisms. Albright's view of Abraham as a merchant caravaneer following the trade routes between Haran and Egypt across the Negeb is rejected as out of harmony with what is known of semi-nomadism (as well as due to rejection of Albright's interpretation of Genesis 14 and 15, of his translation of Ḫapiru as 'caravaneer', and his interpretation of archaeological data from the Negeb; see Weippert, 1972; Huesman; Thompson, 172–86). De Vaux places the patriarchs in the nineteenth to eighteenth centuries. The three-patriarch scheme is an oversimplification. The Abraham traditions are independent of the Jacob traditions which belong to a group whose immediate origin was from the Transjordanian fringe. Israel is the ancestor of a different group which settled in the Shechem area (172–4, 648f.). These groups and others had been interconnected prior to the judges period (175–7). I have not dealt with the social organization of patriarchal groups above the extended family. Presumably, different types of relationships were entered into for different purposes. The Mari texts know of tribal federations as well as tribes and smaller units (Luke, 64–9, 142; also the Shosu as a federation, see Giveon; Gottwald, 248–51). Some have extended the amphictyonic thesis to suggest that twelve- (or six-) tribe leagues were the normal form of political supra-organization among the semi-nomads (see Dumbrell for bibliography). Recent revision or abandonment of the amphictyonic thesis for Israel makes such an application questionable. Also some tribal lists of Genesis cited in support of the twelve-tribe thesis are questionable in their interpretation or date (e.g., Edom in Genesis 36, see Wilson, 1972, 320f.). De Vaux thinks that behind the Joseph story are traditions of several descents to Egypt from the time of the Hyksos to shortly before the exodus. Some of these groups (Joseph) stayed in Egypt until the exodus while others (Judah and Levi) returned to Canaan after a shorter period. De Vaux essentially accepts Alt's view of patriarchal religion. The use of kinship names expressed the close link of the group with its god. The absence of Baal in patriarchal traditions supports a Middle Bronze Age date as this would be before Baal's rise to prominence (278f.; see Rendtorff, 1966). Patriarchal religion was typical of semi-nomadic religion (283–7).

Despite de Vaux's impressive synthesis, problems remain: (1) the time gap between patriarchs and exodus; (2) the concept of the patriarchs as in transition from nomadic to sedentary life; (3) the anachronisms; (4) the links with Aramaeans and other Late Bronze/Early Iron Age peoples. In preference to a Middle Bronze Age identification of the patriarchs with the Amorites, I suggest three viable alternatives.

(1) The patriarchs belong to the phase of Hebrew history immediately prior to the settlement reflected in Joshua (e.g., Eissfeldt, *CAH* II/2, 314). This preserves a distinct patriarchal period and overcomes the gap between patriarchal and settlement traditions. Yet the difficulty of anachronisms is overcome only if the period is extended into the Early Iron Age (*Herrmann: end of the second millennium, 45). Gordon's and Speiser's dating early in the Late Bronze Age depends on dubious parallels to the Nuzi materials, vague similarities to Ugaritic materials, and the calculation of five generations from Abraham to Moses. Weippert argues that patriar-

chal traditions represent Hebrew settlement from the nineteenth to the twelfth centuries (1972). *Gunneweg and Böhl relate the patriarchs to a peaceful settlement (Leah group; see above, pp. 139 f.; also Fohrer; *Kaufmann, 219; and Lohfink with reference to Genesis 15 and Shechem) as contrasted to a military conquest in the Joshua traditions (Rachel group). Clements argues that the oldest part of Genesis 15 concerns the settlement of an Abraham group in the Hebron area prior to the Amarna age. This tradition was taken up by later Calebites in this area. When Calebites (see Beltz) were incorporated into a Judaean league in the judges period, the Abraham tradition became part of the history of all Israel.

(II) A second alternative is espoused by Thompson and Van Seters. Thompson suggests that individual episodes were taken from the contemporary Canaanite/Israelite culture by J who created the distinctively Israelite patriarchal tradition. This eliminates most anachronisms such as the monarchical perspective of the promise of the land in Genesis 13 and 28 (Clark, 1964), the subjugation of Edom to Judah (25.23), and the concern with theological problems of monarchical times (Wallis, 1969; Roth on Genesis 24; Redford, in C above, on Joseph). According to Van Seters, the oldest (monarchical) patriarchal traditions include Abraham in Egypt (Gen. 12.10–20), Hagar's flight (16.1–12), and the birth of Isaac. This material was supplemented before the time of J in Genesis 20 and 21. But the decisive role in the formulation of the patriarchal traditions is played by J in the exilic period (see Redford for a late dating of the Joseph narrative and Coats' counterargument, in Cii above, 1976, 78 f.). Like Thompson, Van Seters gives an extensive critique of the external evidence on which a Middle Bronze Age date has been based. He also undertakes an extensive form and tradition analysis. The significance of the patriarchal themes of blessing, posterity, and especially promise of land in the exilic period are obvious. Genesis 15.7–21 parallels an exodus from Ur of the Chaldeans to the exodus from Egypt in the light of the situation of the sixth-century exile (Clark, 1964, 61–72; see Van Seters, 1975, 249–78). This explains the introduction in Genesis 15.7–21 of themes of 'exile and return' by anticipating the going to and returning from Egypt. In der Smitten sees in Genesis 33.18–34.31 a reflection of relationships of the post-exilic period (but see above, p. 122). Meinhold places the Joseph story in the diaspora. However, Van Seters goes significantly further in regarding the larger part of the tradition as a redactional creation of the exilic period. He links the movements of Jacob and Abraham from Babylon to Canaan with this period. The concern for

ethnic purity in the marriage of Isaac and Jacob relates to problems
of self-identity and preservation in the exilic period (Van Seters,
1975, 276–8).

It is impossible to offer a detailed critique of Van Seters here. In
rejecting Van Seters' and Thompson's positions, I am influenced by
the following considerations. (1) From a tradition-history viewpoint,
the application of the traditions to the monarchical situation (e.g.,
Edom = Esau, see Wilson, 1972, 319f.) seems to be an overlay
presupposing an earlier stage of the tradition. For example, the pre-
eminence of Rachel tribes in the twelve-tribe list fits best before the
dominance of Judah in the monarchy (Wilson, 1972, 233–7).
(2) The development of the traditions demands more time than is
allowed for by Thompson. Van Seters' presentation is weak in not
accounting for the ultimate origin of the patriarchs. (3) The different
perspective of the Jacob, Abraham, and Joseph materials suggests
different origins rather than a dominant J influence. (4) The concern
for relationships of groups served by segmented genealogies (Wilson,
1972, 48, 165, 230) as well as the ethnographic aspects of some
traditions fits better into a pre-state period. The different perspectives of family, tribe, and state are also difficult to explain if the
material is formed in the state period. An exilic date (Van Seters)
would, of course, mitigate this objection.

(III) The patriarchal period is a theological construct, just as is the
view that the 'conquest' begins only with the crossing of the Jordan
river, and as is the periodization of primeval and universal history
(see above, p. 122). I support this view and place the formative
period of the patriarchal traditions in the Late Bronze and Early
Iron Age. The argument for a connection of the patriarchs with the
Aramaeans is stronger than is the argument for a link of the
patriarchs to the Middle Bronze Age Amorites. Many commonly
cited anachronisms cease to be anachronisms (see Mazar) including
the relationship to the Philistines, the Aramaeans, the Ishmaelites,
and the 'Canaanites' (Gen. 38). Mazar and Herrmann emphasize
that the perspective of the genealogies of Genesis 10 should be dated
towards the end of the second millennium (*Herrmann, 42). Recent
studies have maintained that all the cities which play a significant
role in the patriarchal traditions were occupied simultaneously only
in the Early Iron Age (Mazar; Thompson, contrary to *Bright, 81).
The genealogical link between the individual patriarchs is secondary, as is the immigration from Mesopotamia. (The three-patriarch
scheme has parallels in Mesopotamian three-generation genealogies,
Wilson, 1972, 77, 163.) I would abandon the sedentarization/immi-

gration model of understanding the patriarchs (which is implicit in option 1 above). Significantly, in the pre-P exodus traditions, there is no reference to the patriarchal promises. This is surprising considering the role of the promises as a basic structuring and unifying theme in the patriarchal narratives (Rendtorff, 1975, 165f.). Only the promise of a son is an original promise within the Abraham traditions. Pre-Deuteronomistic references do not view the patriarchs in relationship to the exodus events. This suggests a self-contained transmission of the patriarchal traditions into the monarchical period, and puts in question efforts to link one of the patriarchs with the exodus/conquest group. Coextensiveness of religious ideology, statehood, and culture is a recent phenomenon (Richardson, 166–70). There may have been an element within ancient Israelite society which saw its basic identity in terms of the patriarchal traditions. These traditions might have had their setting among the pastoral-nomadic segment of the total Canaanite society, with ethnic and historical links to the Aramaean phenomenon of the end of the second millennium. Anti-city (Wallis, 1966; Luke, in Cii above, 38; Gottwald in Cv above, 240, 254f.) and anti-nomad (Gottwald, 242–4) feelings are stronger than anti-Canaanite feelings in the patriarchal traditions (Eissfeldt, in Ciii above, 1963, 88). It is the 'conquest' traditions which are focused on control of the cities. Alternatively, we might suggest that a different functional sphere of interest of the patriarchal narratives (domestic) has facilitated their crystallization as a separate period of history from the chronologically overlapping traditions of conquest/judges which have a primary functional setting in the political sphere (see Wilson, in A above, 1972, 45–7). The different sphere of interest would correspond to a difference in the size of group involved (Luke, 63). In the monarchical period, the concept of a separate patriarchal period and unified ancestry of the Israelite people developed. This helped the monarchy to legitimate itself and to bind together different elements of the population. Contrary to Van Seters, the universalistic borders in Genesis 13 and 28 reflect the empire concept of the Davidic state (Clark, in Ciii above, 1964, 108). However, the patriarchal traditions remained relatively independent at the popular level until events of exile and return brought about a far-reaching merging of the traditions.

III

THE JOSEPH AND MOSES NARRATIVES

§1. HISTORICAL RECONSTRUCTIONS OF THE NARRATIVES

W. F. **Albright**, *From the Stone Age to Christianity*, [2]1957; W. **Beyerlin**, *Herkunft und Geschichte der ältesten Sinaitraditionen*, Tübingen: J. C. B. Mohr 1961 = *Origins and History of the Oldest Sinaitic Traditions*, Oxford: Basil Blackwell 1965; G. W. **Coats**, *Rebellion in the Wilderness: The Murmuring Motif in the Wilderness Traditions of the Old Testament*, Nashville: Abingdon Press 1968; G. **Fohrer**, *Überlieferung und Geschichte des Exodus: Eine Analyse von Ex 1–15*, BZAW 91, 1964; R. **Giveon**, *Les bédouins Shosou des documents égyptiens*, DMOA 18, 1971; N. **Glueck**, *The Other Side of the Jordan*, New Haven: American Schools of Oriental Research 1940; M. **Greenberg**, *The Ḥab/piru*, AOS 39, 1955; W. **Helck**, 'Ṯkw und die Ramses-Stadt', *VT* XV, 1965, 35–48; S. **Herrmann**, *Israels Aufenthalt in Ägypten*, SBS 40, 1970 = *Israel in Egypt*, SBT II/27, 1973; D. **Irvin**, *Mytharion: The Comparison of Tales from the Old Testament and the Ancient Near East*, AOAT 32, 1976; J. W. **Jack**, *The Date of the Exodus in the Light of External Evidence*, Edinburgh: T. & T. Clark 1925; K. A. **Kitchen**, *Ancient Orient and the Old Testament*, London/Chicago: Tyndale Press/Inter-Varsity Press 1966; D. J. **McCarthy**, *Treaty and Covenant: A Study in Form in the Ancient Oriental Documents and in the Old Testament*, AnBib 21, 1963; G. E. **Mendenhall**, 'Covenant Forms in Israelite Tradition', *BA* XVII, 1954, 50–76 = *BAR* III, 1970, 25–53; P. **Montet**, *Le drame d'Avaris*, Paris: Geuthner, 1941; E. W. **Nicholson**, *Exodus and Sinai in History and Tradition*, Oxford/Richmond: Basil Blackwell/John Knox 1973; M. **Noth**, *Das zweite Buch Mose, Exodus*, ATD 5, 1959 = *Exodus: A Commentary*, OTL, 1962; idem, *A History of Pentateuchal Traditions*, 1972; H. M. **Orlinsky**, *Understanding the Bible through History and Archaeology*, New York: KTAV, 1972; S. M. **Paul**, *Studies in the Book of the Covenant in the Light of Cuneiform and Biblical Law*, SVT 18, 1970; L. **Perlitt**, *Bundestheologie im Alten Testament*, WMANT 36, 1969; G. **von Rad**, 'The Form-Critical Problem of the Hexateuch' (see I §5), *Problem of the Hexateuch*,

1966, 1–78; D. B. **Redford**, 'Exodus I 11', *VT* XIII, 1963, 401–18; idem, 'The "Land of the Hebrews" in Gen. XL 15', *VT* XV, 1965, 529–32; idem, *A Study of the Biblical Story of Joseph (Genesis 37–50)*, SVT 20, 1970; idem, 'The Hyksos Invasion in History and Tradition', *Orientalia* XXXIX, 1970, 1–51; L. **Rost**, *Das kleine Credo*, 1965; H. H. **Rowley**, *From Joseph to Joshua*, 1950; H. **Schmid**, *Mose: Überlieferung und Geschichte*, BZAW 110, 1968; T. L. **Thompson**, *The Historicity of the Patriarchal Narratives*, BZAW 133, 1974; idem, *The Settlement of Sinai and the Negev in the Bronze Age*, BTAVO B/8, 1975; J. **Van Seters**, *The Hyksos: A New Investigation*, 1966; idem, *Abraham in History and Tradition*, 1975; J. **Vergote**, *Joseph en Égypte. Genèse chap. 37–50 à la lumière des études égyptologiques récentes*, OBL 3, 1959; T. C. **Vriezen**, 'The Credo in the Old Testament', *OTWSA*, 1963, 5–17; M. **Weippert**, *The Settlement of the Israelite Tribes*, 1971; idem, ' "Heiliger Krieg" in Israel und Assyrien', *ZAW* LXXXIV, 1972, 460–93; idem, 'Semitische Nomaden des zweiten Jahrtausends. Über die *Š3św* der ägyptischen Quellen', *Bib* LV, 1974, 265–80, 427–33.

The Joseph and Moses traditions, together with the patriarchal narratives and the stories of the entry into Palestine, form the great pentateuchal aetiology of Israel held together by the framework of promise and fulfilment (see Thompson, 1974, 328f.). The immeasurable theological and ideological importance of this aetiology for an understanding of early Israelite religion has involved Old Testament scholarship in elaborate and far-reaching discussion concerning the proper context within which the individual narratives themselves, and the development of the pentateuchal tradition as a whole, are to be understood. The discussions of possible extra-biblical bases for understanding the historical background of the Joseph and Moses narratives have been bound up with similar discussions about the patriarchal narratives (see ch. II above). These discussions, dependent upon extra-biblical materials, have frequently been only marginally affected by the research on the general development of the pentateuch.

Attempted reconstructions of historical events concerning Joseph and Moses suffer from a lack of concrete historical materials related to Palestine and Sinai even more than the similar reconstructions of a 'patriarchal period'. This scarcity of historical materials has limited scholars to the construction of hypotheses which have frequently been consciously recognized as inadequate. Most such hypotheses offer only a minimal historical background for the narratives but assume that such a minimum is necessary if the literature is to be understood adequately. In formulating such hypotheses, scholars tend to ask only *how* the narratives can be understood as traditions about Israel's early history; in doing so they beg the more essential question of *whether* these narratives can be so understood.

A.   *The dating of the sojourn and the exodus*

Attempts to date the sojourn of 'Israel' in Egypt often associate it with the so-called 'Hyksos' dynasties during which foreign influence in Egypt is thought to have been greater than was normally the case (on the Hyksos, see Van Seters, 1966). It is assumed that Egypt at that time was ruled by a non-native element and that this period accordingly offered a favourable climate for Semitic migration into the Delta region. At the same time, it is assumed that a non-Egyptian such as Joseph could more likely have risen to prominence under the Hyksos than under 'native' rulers. The biblical narrative of the enslavement of Israel in Egypt (Ex. 2) is accordingly associated with the Egyptian overthrow of the Hyksos during the latter half of the sixteenth century (Albright, 150; Orlinsky, 48–50). This thesis sought support in the occurrence of the name Jacob, in what was falsely claimed to be its 'original' form (Jacob-el), on several Hyksos scarabs. However, this interpretation of the name has not been able to maintain itself. While the names Jacob–Hadad and Jacob–Baal do appear on such scarabs, the name Jacob-el does not appear in Egypt before the New Kingdom, after the so-called Hyksos expulsion (see Thompson, 1974, 43–50).

The heart of the Hyksos argument for a historical reconstruction of the sojourn in Egypt lies in the assumed analogy of the 'Hyksos movements' to those in the narratives about Israel – both stressing an entry into and subsequent departure from Egypt. Rowley, however, has pointed out several difficulties in harmonizing what we know of the Hyksos with the biblical narratives (25–9). The correspondence of the Hyksos chronology with that of Israel's sojourn in Egypt (Gen. 15.13; Ex. 12.40–1; Gal. 3.17) is no longer thought to support the association of the Hyksos movement and the Joseph–Moses narratives. This is due not so much to the obviously unhistorical character of the biblical chronologies for this period (Thompson, 1974, 9–16) but rather to the fact that these dates cannot be harmonized with the nearly universally accepted thirteenth-century date for the exodus thought to be necessary on the basis of extra-biblical evidence (Kitchen, 57–71; *Bright, 121). It is important to note, however, that most extra-biblical sources employed to support a thirteenth-century date for the exodus apply rather to the question of the date of the Israelite settlement in Palestine than to the date of the sojourn and exodus. These thirteenth-century materials can be understood to support a dating of the sojourn in Egypt and the exodus only if the general pentateuchal structure and order of events are presupposed.

The Merneptah stela (*ANET*, 376–8), which refers to a conquered group in Palestine with the name 'Israel', is commonly thought to refer to the Israelites of the Bible, and accordingly to prove that the Israelites must have already been in Palestine by 1220 BCE. This, unlike the attempt to discover the Israelite tribe of Asher in the Ras Shamra and thirteenth-century Egyptian texts (see Kitchen, 69f.), is certainly a possible interpretation of the Merneptah stela, but it is neither a necessary interpretation, nor one that – with questions of chronology aside – can easily be harmonized with the biblical narratives of the conquest (see below, pp. 267, 281). The Merneptah stela may refer to a conflict of the historical Israel with Egyptian troops, but it can hardly be used to date the events related in the Joshua narratives and can certainly not be used to date the exodus.

Similarly, archaeological excavations in Palestine which place the beginning of the transition from the Late Bronze Age to the Iron Age towards the end of the thirteenth century are used to support a thirteenth-century date for the exodus (Kitchen, 61–9; *Bright, 121, 127–30). Although the archaeological evidence for this transition period has been assumed to reflect the establishment of Israel in Palestine, one should not automatically assume that major cultural shifts – when this can be identified at all from archaeological evidence – reflect the immigration of new peoples. Even if one granted a connection between this cultural transition phase and the Israelite movement into Canaan, the difficulties involved in harmonizing the archaeological evidence and reconstructions with the conquest narratives of Joshua and Judges would still remain (Weippert, 1971; *Bright, 129f.; see further, ch. IV §3). Any relevance that this archaeological material has to the dating of the exodus and the sojourn in Egypt (which are related to the settlement of Israel through the pentateuchal structure and the Joshua conquest narratives) is dependent upon both an understanding of the settlement as conquest *and* an acceptance of the historicity of the pentateuchal framework.

The difficulty of determining the relevance of the extra-biblical materials to the pentateuchal narratives, and not merely to the issue of the history of Israel, is the most significant factor frustrating attempts to reconstruct an early biblical period. Glueck's explorations in southern Transjordan, published in 1940, do perhaps preclude a dating before the beginning of the Iron Age for the biblical tradition of Israel's attempt at passage through this territory (Num. 20–21). The biblical narrative presupposes both Edomite and Moabite settlements, but Glueck found very little archaeological evidence in this region that could be dated to the Late Bronze Age (see Rowley, 20–22; Kitchen, 61 f.). The problem is not so much archaeological, although even here the issues are considerable (Thompson, 1974, 193 f.), since Glueck's evidence is both incomplete and largely based on what he did *not* find. The real problem lies in the fact that all possible dates *later than the thirteenth century* are arbitrarily excluded in attempts to harmonize this evidence with the other biblical traditions (see Rowley, 22 n. 1). The attempt to date this tradition is seen as relevant not to the specific tradition as such but to the pentateuchal framework as a whole, in spite of the pentateuch's admittedly obvious lack of coherence and the secondary nature of its structure (see below, §2).

The failure to consider possible later dates for the traditions is particularly apparent with respect to the single element of the Joseph and Moses narratives which can be concretely related to extra-biblical historical sources, namely, the reference to Pithom and Raamses in Exodus 1.11 as the setting for the Hebrews' forced labour in Egypt. It has been widely claimed that the reference to these two cities in Exodus establishes a nearly certain thirteenth-century date for the enslavement of the Hebrews in Egypt. The biblical site Raamses is undoubtedly to be identified with the Egyptian capital of Ramesses II (Pr R'mś-św) which was founded by Sethos I (1305–1290 BCE) and completed under Ramesses II (1290–1224 BCE) (see Rowley, 32; Kitchen, 57–60; Schmid, 15; *Bright, 119–21). There is indeed no doubt that the reference to these cities in the biblical narrative must postdate the beginning of the Ramesside period. (Pithom (= Pr 3Itm) occurs in several Egyptian texts dated from the Ramesside to the Christian period, and is mentioned in connection with the city of Tkw (= biblical Succoth, Ex. 12.37), a city which also existed in the Ramesside period. Nevertheless, Redford (1963) has challenged even the use of this relatively secure identification in support of a thirteenth-century date for the biblical narrative by pointing out that the names Pithom, Raamses, and Succoth also occur in late texts. Instead he suggests a date for the biblical tradition in the late seventh or sixth centuries. This, of course, would exclude all possibility of historicity for the biblical narratives and has not gone unchallenged. Helck, in responding to

Redford, correctly reconfirms the dating of these Egyptian cities to the thirteenth century, but his arguments fail to exclude from consideration a later dating for the biblical tradition's reference to these cities. Assuredly, if the traditions do reflect an historical enslavement of the Hebrews prior to the existence of Israel, the evidence of these names would require a date in the Ramesside period, but if historicity is not presupposed of the biblical tradition, then any period in which the storyteller could have known these names is adequate to explain the tradition's reference to them.

B. *The Egyptian background of the narratives*

The arguments which have been used to date the biblical narratives about Joseph and Moses do not appear in isolation from other considerations. Support is found for an early dating of the narratives in specific aspects of the traditions which it is claimed reflect the known world of the ancient Near East and thus lend plausibility to the historical character of the narratives. The most important of these appear to demonstrate the authenticity of the Egyptian background of the Joseph and Moses narratives (see Montet and Vergote; and Redford, 1963, 1970 for a different opinion). The authenticity of the Egyptian background of the narratives is thought to support the claim that the stories do reflect an historical presence of Israel in Egypt.

The reference to the cities of Pithom and Raamses has already been mentioned. These cities did not exist exclusively during the Ramesside period, and so cannot be used directly as an argument for historicity; yet the names are authentically Egyptian. Similarly, the name Moses is authentically Egyptian. (The names Hophni, Phinehas, and Merari might also be mentioned; see *Bright, 119.) The element 'moses' is commonly known from such famous New Kingdom names as Tuthmosis and Ahmose. But the use of the name Moses in the biblical story of his birth indicates the striking ambiguity of this kind of 'evidence'. Noth (1972, 162f.) has already shown that, given the long period of Egyptian control of Palestine, the use of Egyptian names by Semitic-speaking peoples in Palestine itself was sufficiently common. We might also assume that a minimum knowledge about Egypt – but not necessarily a detailed and accurate knowledge – became part of any educated person's *Palestinian* heritage. Furthermore, many aspects of the narratives stressed by Vergote and Montet as authentically Egyptian may be seen as generally Near Eastern in character and not peculiarly

Egyptian. There are also aspects of the narratives which are not Egyptian and can hardly be reconciled with an Egyptian setting for the narratives.

It is important to realize, moreover, that the generally accurate 'Egyptian tone' or 'colouring' is more than adequately explained by the fact that the Israelite narrator has chosen after all to set his story in Egypt. Thus, Moses' name has a context in the folk-tale itself, in that he is found by Pharaoh's daughter and brought up as an Egyptian. The folk etymology of the name, however, as is appropriate to an Israelite story, is Hebrew and fails, incidentally, to understand the meaning of the Egyptian root from which the name Moses is derived. In addition, though the general motifs of the birth of Moses are found in the Egyptian tale of the hiding of Horus from Seth (see Helck, 48), similar story elements common to both of these are found in the Hittite tale of 'Brother Good and Brother Bad' and an even closer parallel is the cuneiform tale of the birth of Sargon the Great (*ANET*, 119; see Irvin, and below, section 3/E of this chapter). The basket of bulrushes and pitch in which the child is placed is a specifically Mesopotamian element which is also found in the Gilgamesh Epic. Similarly, the story of Joseph and his master's wife resembles in detail the Egyptian 'Tale of Two Brothers' (*ANET*, 23–5). Yet both the Egyptian and the biblical tales must also be compared with the early Hittite tale of Elkunirsha (*ANET*, 519; see below, §3A). The Joseph and Moses narratives have yet to be studied systematically in the context of similar ancient Near Eastern narratives, but the international ambience of such folktale motifs excludes identification of them as specifically Egyptian in origin simply on the basis of Egyptian parallels.

The laws in Exodus, on the other hand, are not Egyptian, but are concretely Palestinian in origin, belonging within the sphere of cuneiform law (Paul, 104). Their representation in the story as the words of Yahweh (for example, Ex. 20), rather than as a specifically legal form, lends divine authority to the legal tradition. This is similar, though not entirely equivalent, to the prologue of Hammurabi's code where the divine authority for lawmaking, rather than the laws themselves, is derived from the god Shamash (*ANET*, 164f.).

C.   Semites in Egypt

Efforts have been made to explore various evidence for Semitic influence in Egypt – especially during the Ramesside period – in order to illustrate and authenticate the Egyptian setting and trust-worthiness of the biblical narratives (see *Bright, 119–20; Orlinsky, 48). These attempts have not met with much success.

Historically, Semites have played a very large role in the Egyptian Delta. The Delta area is commonly assumed to have been the loca-tion of the biblical 'land of Goshen' where the Hebrews supposedly settled (Gen. 45.10; 46.28 and elsewhere) although, as pointed out by Redford (1963, 412), this name is neither Egyptian nor is it found in Egyptian texts. It is often argued that Semitic shepherds were frequently allowed to enter Egypt during times of famine, like the twelfth-century Shasu from Edom (*ANET*, 259; see *Herrmann, 61), and that Israel's historical entry into Egypt might well have occurred in this manner. Bright, in so arguing, also refers to Semitic loan-words in the Egyptian language as a further demonstration of the depth of Semitic influence in Egypt. In addition, he also refers to the 'Apiru in Egypt, to Egyptianized Canaanite deities, and to the use of Semitic slaves in the Nineteenth and Twentieth Dynasties: all with the purpose of demonstrating the likelihood that those who later became Israel had been among these Semites in the Delta (*Bright, 119). But even this much cannot be accepted without reservation (for the following, see Thompson, 1974, 118–43). Though the Egyptians themselves consistently distinguished them-selves from Semitic peoples and the Egyptian language is genuinely non-Semitic, Semites were, from as early as the third millennium, indigenous to Egypt, and West Semitic loan-words entered Egyptian at a very early stage. The eastern Delta shows extensive Semitic influence throughout the history of Egypt. Texts and archaeological finds from the Middle Kingdom demonstrate noticeably the 'Egyptianization' of Semitic gods. Already in the Admonitions of Ipuwer (twentieth to eighteenth centuries; *ANET*, 441–4), it is implied that Semitic desert dwellers were becoming 'Egyptians'. By 1742 BCE, Semitic slaves from Palestine (some of whom bear Egyptian names) were being used in Egypt (see Thompson, 1974, 91), as they were throughout the next fifteen hundred years. The 'Apiru had been in Egypt as slaves from at least the time of Amenophis II (1438–1412 BCE; see *ANET*, 247) and were still there during the reign of Ramesses IV (1151–1145 BCE; see Greenberg, 57). In this regard, it should be noted, in addition, that the 'Apiru ought not be too facilely identified as Semitic; nor is the basis for their identifica-tion with the biblical 'Hebrew' very substantial. From at least the time of Sesostris II (about 1896 BCE), West Semites had been as-similated into Egyptian culture, some of whom rose to high office.

With the New Kingdom's wars in Syria, many prisoners were brought to Egypt to work in construction. This is reflected in the many new technical terms in Egyptian which were borrowed from West Semitic, e.g., *trtt* 'wall', *šer* 'fortification', *tr* 'gate', and so on. During the Ramesside period entire towns were settled by prisoners of war. In the reign of Ramesses III (1184–1153 BCE) some of these prisoners joined the Egyptian army; others took positions in the Egyptian bureaucracy.

In his study of the biblical story of Joseph (1970, 251 f.), Redford has shown that the Semitic presence in Egypt continued at least down to the fifth century BCE. His arguments *against* a Ramesside or thirteenth-century dating for the background to the Joseph narratives are convincing, although his arguments in favour of a date of about 650–425 BCE are less than convincing. However, the real weakness of the arguments based on extra-biblical data to illustrate the background of these narratives is not found in the fact that numerous periods in Egyptian history could be seen as providing this background. Even if the thirteenth century were the only period when Semites could have entered Egyptian service, the identification of the Semitic elements there at that time with the Israelite sojourn and exile suffers from two major problems. In the first place, that there was at least a minimal coherence or sense of identity among the different Semites living in Egypt is an unwarranted assumption, although this is implied in any treatment that seeks to correlate the biblical and extra-biblical evidence. Secondly, the attempt at such a correlation requires a harmonization of the originally quite distinct movements or wanderings depicted in the biblical tradition. That is, if the 'historical events' behind the Joseph and Moses traditions are to be reconstructed in terms of extra-biblical evidence on the basis of analogous events in the Egyptian and Semitic worlds, an historical migration must be suggested which would either parallel the movements of the biblical Israel or, at the least, produce a harmonized reconstruction of the movements recounted in the biblical narratives.

D.   The Shasu and the Aramaean migration

Such a reconstruction has been suggested on the basis of the Aramaean migrations which took place towards the end of the second millennium (see *Herrmann, 56–86; 1973). Specifically, Herrmann identifies the Israelite movements of the pentateuchal narratives with the Shasu tribes which appear in Egyptian records of

the Ramesside period (on the Shasu, see Giveon; Weippert, 1974).
Herrmann claims that the Shasu people left the mountains of Edom
and the Arabian peninsula as part of an Aramaean migration in the
thirteenth century. Some groups of Shasu entered Egypt, as is mentioned in a twelfth-century report of an Egyptian frontier official
(*ANET*, 259). This is the history behind the Joseph narratives,
which he identifies as a kind of 'redactional fiction' (*Herrmann,
57–8). Other Shasu tribes went to Kadesh where they were
gradually amalgamated with disparate Shasu groups of the Sinai
region. The Shasu bearers of the patriarchal traditions he assumes to
have been already in Palestine. One of the Shasu in Egypt, Moses,
rose to a position of privilege, in the manner of other Semites bearing
Egyptian names, and then led the escape of the Egyptian Shasu
towards the end of the thirteenth century. The Kadesh Shasu
entered Palestine from the south, bringing other Shasu tribes with
them, each bearing their own traditions. The Shasu under Moses
entered Palestine from Transjordan. In such a reconstruction,
Herrmann appears simply to recite a more or less unharmonized
biblical story and to claim with remarkable confidence that those
whom the Bible called Israelites were in fact Shasu, and therefore
must have been historical, since we do find Shasu in contemporary
though unrelated historical documents.

Herrmann also claims that the origins of Yahwism are to be found
among the Shasu in Arabia. His 'evidence' for this is the only tang-
ible extra-biblical material he has for connecting the Shasu with the
Israelites and with the pentateuchal stories. This is the name from
the geographical lists of Amenophis III (1403–1364 BCE) and
Ramesses II (1290–1224 BCE): *t' sh3 s̆.w yhw3* = 'The Shasu land
Yhw3' (see *Herrmann, 76 f.). However, there is in this name no
real relation either with Yahwism or with the Israelites. Nevertheless, although Yhw3 is a *place* name, a hypocoristic form similar to
Yaḫwi-ilu, a personal name found in cuneiform texts (Weippert,
1972, 491 n. 144) and though it is only related to the Old Testament
divine name etymologically, Herrmann claims that it was the Shasu
of Yhw3 who brought Yahwism to Sinai. Admittedly, Herrmann is
only trying to suggest a hypothesis which approximates the 'probable' historical roots of the biblical tradition. Actually what he ends
up suggesting is really an alternative past for Israel to that related in
the narratives of the pentateuch. This alternative is based not so
much on the biblical traditions themselves as on the lack of a specific
coherence in these traditions. In the same manner, his alternative is
supported not by our historical knowledge of the Aramaean and

Shasu migrations, but by the gaps in our knowledge of these migrations. The historical reality of the Aramaean migrations towards the end of the second millennium is itself hypothetical and is based on the later establishment of Aramaean states in Transjordan and in northern and southern Mesopotamia. The patriarchal traditions, and especially the genealogies, understand the Israelites as neighbours of the Aramaeans, and as politically and culturally related to them, but explicitly as alien in striking contrast to the still enigmatic Deuteronomy 26.5 (see Thompson, 1974, 298–308). There is as yet no historical evidence of the Aramaeans having been in the south, or having been in any way related to the Shasu. Nor do we know that the Shasu *originated* in the Arabian peninsula or in Edom. Moreover, the Egyptian use of the term Shasu is often generic, and does not consistently refer to any specific ethnic group. This usage is comparable to the Middle Kingdom's use of such terms as *ṣt.tyw, mnṯw, ḥryw-shʿ* and *ʿ3mw* to refer, at times indiscriminately, to desert dwellers, foreigners, Asiatics, and Semites generally (see Thompson, 1974, 132–3). We do not even know that the Shasu were ever in Kadesh, nor that they played any role in Egypt comparable to the roles which other Semites played, particularly the Egyptianized Semites, let alone that they ever escaped from Egypt. What little we know archaeologically of the Bronze Age inhabitants of Sinai and the Negeb in general, and of the geographical range of shepherds living in the region at this early period, does not lend itself readily to the picture which Herrmann paints of the Shasu, moving from North Arabia to Edom to Kadesh to Palestine, and from Edom to Egypt to Kadesh back to Transjordan and into Palestine (see Thompson, 1975). Finally, Herrmann's underlying assumption that the disparateness of the biblical wilderness traditions is best explained as independent memories about the historical past held by separate Sinai groups presupposes that these traditions belong to the historiographical literary genre of *Stammessage* or 'tribal tale'. Indications, however, that they do in fact belong to this genre are lacking. The historiographical intentionality which Herrmann presupposes as the all-informing motivation of his narratives is nowhere in evidence as constitutive of the disparate traditions. Those major historiographical elements which do appear, are, as Herrmann himself readily acknowledges, primarily those redactional structures which weave the disparate independent traditions into the pentateuchal whole. It is, indeed, the recognition of this which forms the starting-point of Herrmann's analysis. The narrative elements, however, which are woven together, when they are not aetiological, appear essentially as *historically unattached*, as fundamentally ahistorical folk-narratives or heroic tales which have only incidentally attached themselves to a given heroic ancestor, wilderness locality, or developing literary theme. They may well have developed, as Herrmann presupposes, around specifically independent groups in their own localities. But what cannot be argued is that they are relating events out of the history of such a hypothetical group. In the analogous situation of the Jacob narratives, Jacob's children are born to Leah, Rachel, and their two maids, but it clearly cannot be argued that Genesis 29–31 refers to any historical division of the Israelite tribes so that Rachel tribes and Leah tribes can be spoken of, since all the details of this narrative, and especially the birth episodes and the naming motifs, refer not to the eponymic significance of Jacob's son as the tribes of Israel, but rather quite explicitly to the conflict endemic to the literary motif of a dispute between co-wives. The characteristic of this narrative – as of the wilderness narratives – as *Stammesgeschichte* (or as historiographical at all) is limited to the very superficial 'point of attraction' that many of the protagonists of the narratives are also eponymous. Nowhere, however, is this eponymous characteristic functional in the narratives themselves, nor does it inform them in such a way that we can see the activities of a group in that of the individual. The relationship between the historical group and the narrative individual is always vicarious and never equivocal. It is wholly illegitimate, without contrary indication, to see this eponymous element as indicative of a more serious historiographical intention.

E. *Hittite treaties and early Israelite covenant*

Efforts have also been made to reconstruct the historical background for individual aspects of the Moses tradition. One of the more important of these is Beyerlin and Mendenhall's attempt to understand the theophany of Exodus 20 as an early covenant based on Hittite treaty forms from the middle of the second millennium. Briefly, Beyerlin argues that the vassal covenant treaties used by the Hittites in the fourteenth and thirteenth centuries are identical in form to the Israelite decalogue of Exodus 20. His conclusion from this comparison is that in the time of Moses this Hittite treaty form was sufficiently widely known as to be available to the Israelites who used it in the original form of the decalogue (Beyerlin, 52–6). This reconstruction of the origin of the decalogue constitutes the major element of Beyerlin's attempt to counter Noth's view of the Sinai theophany (for some of the issues in the debate, see Nicholson). Noth argued that the Sinai theophany was originally a part of the later Israelite cult and was only secondarily and at a late date joined to the exodus traditions for aetiological purposes (on Noth's view, see §2D below). For Beyerlin, the importance of the parallel between Exodus 20 and the Hittite treaties is its capability of providing a pre-settlement context for the Sinai covenant. Such a context would connect the Sinai 'event' with the traditions of the deliverance from Egypt as early as the Mosaic period and thereby establish the essential historicity of the Sinaitic origins of Yahwism.

Beyerlin's attempts to demonstrate how Yahweh's people could have become aware of the Hittite treaty formulas are tenuous. McCarthy (5 f., 152–67) has argued convincingly that Exodus 20 cannot be understood as a treaty. The Hittite treaty form contained the following elements (see Beyerlin, 52–6): (1) A scribal introduction identifying the king, followed by (2) a 'historical' prologue mentioning past favours by the king which justify (3) the king's expectation of the vassal's faithfulness. The treaty was completed with (4) a prohibition by the king forbidding any change in the contract and (5) a clause specifying capital punishment for breaking the treaty. The claims of Hittite parallels to Exodus 20 cannot be maintained even in form since Exodus 20 is in every way quite different. It begins with a scribal introduction, but this does not identify Elohim, but rather identifies what follows as his declaration. The identification of Elohim as Yahweh is in the form of a self-identification, lacking in the Hittite treaty, which constitutes the beginning of what might be termed a historical prologue (Ex. 20.2–3). However, this does not form the basis of any further expectations on Yahweh's part, but is part of the further self-identification. The obligation to fulfil the succeeding series of explicit commands and prohibitions is not simply a declaration of fealty, as in the Hittite text, but is absolute and autocratic. Furthermore, Exodus 20 contains no hint of mutuality, which is implicit in covenant and treaty agreements. Elements 4 and 5 of the Hittite treaties are completely missing from Exodus 20, and verses 4, 6, and 12 may well preclude a death penalty.

The commands of Exodus 20 are neither treaties nor laws but rather are part of a narrative about Israel's God who is identified as the god Yahweh of the deliverance narratives and who commands absolutely. The form of Exodus 20 is that of a theophany. Its content presupposes not only a knowledge of the deliverance narratives but also the settlement and establishment of Israel in Palestine. Thus the

Hittite treaties of the Late Bronze Age cannot be used to provide a context for understanding the Exodus traditions, or to buttress arguments for the great antiquity of the biblical materials.

F. The 'small historical creed'

There is little doubt that many of the narratives in the exodus and wilderness traditions reflect situations and conflicts of the later Israel and that they had their original context in the religious polemics surrounding the development of the cult of the historical Israel. The narrative of the golden calf in Exodus 32, for example, had its original *Sitz im Leben*, that is, its sociological-historical context, in the cultic conflict surrounding Jeroboam's golden calves set up in Dan and Bethel (see I Kings 12; Noth, 1962, 243–7; Coats, 184–6).

The function of the exodus narrative, however, is not itself cultic. Its function is, instead, aetiological. Such an opinion differs radically from the views of von Rad and Noth, who sought the origin of the Sinai narratives in specifically cultic legends which supposedly had their *Sitz im Leben* in a festival of covenant renewal. According to von Rad and Noth, these originally cultic legends found their place in the pentateuchal narrative only secondarily (von Rad, 6–14; Noth, 1972, 59–62, 252–5). Noth extended von Rad's interpretation to maintain that 'the cultic-hymnic primary confession that "Yahweh led Israel out of Egypt" constituted the starting-point of the entire pentateuchal tradition', and that it was *cultic action* which gave expression centrally to what sustained the life of the sacral twelve-tribe federation and held it together' (1972, 253).

The implications of von Rad's, and especially Noth's, thesis are serious and far-reaching. Needless to say, subsequent scholarship has raised serious objections to this thesis and the deductions drawn from it. The difficulty of maintaining that the Sinai theophany was originally understood as a covenant has been noted in the preceding section. The existence of a 'sacral twelve-tribe federation' or amphictyony has been challenged by a number of scholars (see Fohrer, 3f. and below, ch. V, §2B). Furthermore, Noth's interpretation rests heavily on his assumption of an original source ('G') behind what he identifies as material common to both J and E. Such an assumption allowed Noth to see the development of the pentateuchal tradition in a far more schematic form than is justified and to offer a simplicity of interpretation which does not do justice to the concrete texts we now possess (see further, §2D below).

Fundamental to the reconstruction offered by von Rad and Noth are two questions: (1) Was the cultic setting of the so-called 'pentateuchal confessions' originative in such a manner that it justifies speaking of them as creeds? (2) Were the identifiably cultic creeds really primary to and causative of the pentateuchal narratives? The texts in question are Deuteronomy 6.20–5; 26.5aβ–9; and Joshua 24.2–13. Von Rad claimed that these were all composed on the same pattern and consequently were variants of a single original which he called a 'short historical credo'. Much has been made of von Rad's claim that the theme of 'revelation at Sinai' is missing from these confessions as well as from such cultic hymns as Psalms 78, 105, 135, 136 (von Rad, 8–13; Noth, 1972, 59–62). This absence of the Sinai theme from this material led von Rad and Noth to argue for a fundamental separation of this theme from the history of the development of the other pentateuchal themes (patriarchs, exodus, wilderness wanderings, and settlement in the land).

In Deuteronomy 6.20–5, a credal intention, though not necessarily a temple cult setting, is implicit in the form of the recital as a response to the child's question about why we should fulfil the statutes of Yahweh (v. 20). The response contains the following elements: *Because* (1) we were slaves in Egypt and Yahweh *brought us out* (v. 21); (2) He *worked wonders* in Egypt before our eyes (v. 22); (3) He brought us out *to give us the land* promised to our fathers (v. 23); and (4) He *commanded* us to fulfil these statutes to *preserve us to the present* (v. 24). The reasons are finally summed up with the Deuteronomistic theological assertion that the fulfilment of these laws is righteousness because *Yahweh has commanded it* (v. 25). The order of the four 'themes' of this recital does not follow an order of events because the intention of the recital – an answer to the child's question – is oriented towards, and requires, the emphasis on the final summation which forms the 'theme' of the whole: the commands of Yahweh. This demonstrates on formal grounds that the credal intention is clearly primary to the recital of 'historical events'. Moreover, the integral part which verses 20 and 25 play in the recital (see also v. 24b) mark the *whole* as an unambiguous, Deuteronomistic credal *interpretation* of the pentateuchal narratives (for similar conclusions, see Rost, 11–25, and Vriezen). Moreover, not only does this recital not *lack* the 'Sinai theme', that is, an emphasis on the commandments, but this theme is central to an understanding of the recitation as credal.

Deuteronomy 26.5aβ–9 is, in form, content, and structure, quite different from Deuteronomy 6.20–5. In its present form, it is found within the context of the agricultural festival of the presentation of the first fruits (vv. 2–5aα, 10–11). This in turn is set in the pentateuchal narrative within the larger context of Moses' instructions about the future. In form, it is a hymn of recital comparable to the 'Song of the Sea' in Exodus 15. However, unlike Exodus 15, this passage refers to Yahweh throughout in the third person. This factor indicates that the cultic setting given the text in Deuteronomy 26 derives from the redactional work which placed the hymn into the context of Moses' instructions. Verse 10a is a secondary continuation of the hymn in the I–Thou style and gives an aetiological intention to the psalm as applicable to the offerings of first fruits. The original song had its ending in verse 9, which is also aetiological in nature and identical to the aetiological intention of the pentateuchal narrative as a whole: a recital of the saving history of the acts of God and an ideological explanation of how Israel came to possess the land of Palestine. This indicates a comparatively early origin for the hymn, but it also shows that its present cultic context is indicative of neither its origin nor its primary meaning. Just as, for example, the Hittite narrative of Iluyankash (see *ANET*, 125f.) was *given* a cultic setting but did not originate in the cult, so also this originally independent biblical song. Possible indications that the song is early may be found in verse 5, with its reference to 'a wandering Aramaean', and by the lack of any reference to the land as promised. The latter probably indicates ignorance of the patriarchal and Joseph narratives as part of the pentateuchal framework. Also, the 'Sinai theme' is absent. However, such possible indications of the hymn's early character are very inconclusive, since in the final analysis no common pattern is to be found in the recitals, and the selection of 'themes' in each may well be arbitrary. In Deuteronomy 26, the following 'themes' are included in the recital: (1) the entrance into Egypt, (2) becoming a people, (3) the oppression, (4) the cry to Yahweh for help, (5) Yahweh's deliverance, and (6) the bringing of Israel into this land. Just as Deuteronomy 6 lacks the themes of the entrance into Egypt and becoming a nation, so Deuteronomy 26 does not have the theme of Yahweh's commandments, i.e., the 'Sinai theme'.

Joshua 24.2–13 fits even less into the context von Rad and Noth wish to place it. This recitation is found within the context of a prophetic speech of Joshua at Shechem. The speech reflects what might be called the 'Yahweh Alone' faction and belongs within the religious polemics against non-Yahwistic cults. There is no reason to suppose that it ever had a context independent of the narrative about the Yahweh cult place at Shechem. The passage itself is no cultic recital, nor does it show any indication of ever having been used culticly. Its original context is that of a narrative which has a concrete and explicit orientation to a specific place and to a specific historical religious conflict. There are indications that the passage is no earlier than its present context. The recital shows familiarity in Joshua 24.2 f. with at least the J editorial structure of the Abraham 'wandering' tradition (see Thompson, 1974, 308–11). Since the tradition of Abraham's wandering is, as such, a creation of the Yahwistic author (J), the Joshua 24 recital must be later than J.

Even more interestingly, the Joshua 24 recitation of the crossing of the sea (vv. 6 f.) clearly reflects the crossing narrative as told in Exodus 14. It is Exodus 14, rather than the Joshua recitation or even the song in Exodus 15, which is apparently the earliest and original narrative, of which these others are later secondary traditions. This is clear from the following observations: Exodus 14 cannot be under-stood to have been originally a unified whole. Exodus 14.1–4, 8–10 sets the original narrative in terms of a motif of the entrapping of the Egyptian army with the theological motivation of the manifestation of Yahweh to the Egyptians. As such, it is an obvious continuation of the plague narratives. Verses 5–7 and 11–14, however, expand this narrative on the basis of the 'Traditional Epiphany Episode' (see Irvin, 17 and tables, sheet 2) of a saving divinity answering a cry of distress in terms of the murmuring motif of the wilderness traditions, and in doing this construct a bridge between the narratives of the Israelites in Egypt and those of the wilderness.

An originally self-subsistent narrative bringing to final completion the contest between Yahweh and the Egyptians of the plague nar-ratives through the destruction of the Egyptian army (Exodus 14.1–4, 8–10, 15–18, 21aα, bβ, 22 f., 26, 27aα, bβ, 28–30) has been revised and expanded for theological and literary reasons (Exodus 14.5–7, 11–14, 19 f., 21aβ–ba, 24 f., 27aβ–ba, and possibly 31). This secon-dary revision does not originate in an independent narrative but develops directly from the base narrative. Thus verses 11–14 inter-pret the cry of distress of the base narratives (v. 10b) as a murmuring against Moses; so, also, verses 19 f. develop the image of the base narrative's pillar of cloud, which in Exodus 13 leads Israel, into a new synthetic symbol of conflicting opposites; fire and cloud, light and darkness which stands between Israel and the Egyptians.

This secondary, derivative character of Exodus 14's revision is significant for understanding the relative position of both Exodus 15 and Joshua 24.6 f. and the context and origin of the crossing tradi-tion as a whole. Both Exodus 15 and Joshua 24.6 f. use details of *both* the original base narrative of Exodus 14 and the secondary expansion, which decisively indicates that any relationship of dependence of the different accounts must understand the revised Exodus 14 as earlier than both Exodus 15 and Joshua 24.6f. That the details used have their coherent and originative context in Exodus 14 after that narrative had been integrated into the pentateuchal narratives as a whole adequately demonstrates the existence of just such a dependent relationship. (Compare Exodus 15.4 with 14.28; 15.8 with 14.22, as well as Exodus 15.9 with 14.8f.; 15.7b, 8a, 10a with 14.21aβ–ba and 15.6 with 14.14, 25b. Similarly Joshua 24.6 is to be compared with Exodus 14.23; Joshua 24.7aα with Exodus 14.20, 24; Joshua 24.7aβ with Exodus 14.26; and Joshua 24.7ba with Exodus 14.13, 31).

Joshua 24.2–13 is therefore neither cultic nor early. Nor indeed is it credal: the credal statement in the Joshua narrative at this point is found in Joshua 24.17f. The recital in Joshua 24.2–13 fails to mention the 'Sinai theme'. Moreover, its themes, or better, 'saving acts', have a quite different orientation from the recitations in Deuteronomy 6 and 26. Joshua 24.2–13 neither speaks of the entrance into the land nor mentions the commands of Yahweh, but rather stresses the saving activity of Yahweh who *delivered them from oppression*: from the Egyptian chariots at the sea, from the Amorites, from Balak and Balaam, from the men of Jericho, and from the peoples of Canaan. This was the basis for the people's choice to serve Yahweh alone (Joshua 24.18b).

In summing up this section, it seems clear that the only context and date which can be considered as the historical background for the Joseph and Moses narratives and for the formation of the earliest traditions related to these narratives is Israel during the period before the formation of the pentateuch as a coherent whole. This is all that can be said with any confidence. This means that there is no extra-biblical evidence nor any biblical material that allows the historian to reconstruct a historical base or context for the Joseph and Moses narratives other than that of the later Israel sometime before the formulation of the pentateuchal traditions. The question of the formation of the pentateuchal traditions with regard to the Joseph–Moses narratives must now be examined.

§2. THE JOSEPH – MOSES
TRADITIONS AND PENTATEUCHAL CRITICISM

W. **Beyerlin**, *Herkunft und Geschichte der ältesten Sinaitraditionen*, 1961 = *Origins and History of the Oldest Sinaitic Traditions*, 1965; H. **Cazelles**, et al., *Moïse, l'homme de l'alliance*, Tournai: Desclée, 1955; G. W. **Coats**, *Rebellion in the Wilderness*, 1968; idem, 'History and Theology in the Sea Tradition', *ST* XXIX, 1975, 53–62; idem, *From Canaan to Egypt: Structural and Theological Context for the Joseph Story*, CBQMS 4, 1975; O. **Eissfeldt**, *Hexateuch Synopse*, Leipzig: J. C. Hinrichs 1922; idem, 'Stammessage und Novelle in den Geschichten von Jakob und von seinen Söhnen', *Eucharisterion* I (see II §2B), 1923, 56–77 = his *KS* I, 1962, 84–104; idem, *The OT: An Introduction*, 1965; G. **Fohrer**, *Überlieferung und Geschichte des Exodus*, BZAW 91, 1964; idem, *Introduction to the OT*, 1968; V. **Fritz**, *Israel in der Wüste*, MTS 7, 1970; K. **Galling**, *Die Erwählungstradition Israels*, BZAW 48, 1928; K. H. **Graf**, *Die geschichtlichen Bücher des Alten Testaments*, Leipzig: P. O. Weigel, 1866; H. **Gressmann**, 'Sage und Geschichte in den Patriarchenerzählungen', *ZAW* XXX, 1910, 1–34; idem, *Mose und seine Zeit. Ein Kommentar zu den Mose-Sagen*, FRLANT 18, 1913; idem, 'Ursprung und Entwicklung der Joseph-Sage', *Eucharisterion* I (Festschrift H. Gunkel), FRLANT 36, 1923, 1–55; H. **Gunkel**, *Genesis, übersetzt und erklärt*, HKAT I/1, 1901; idem, 'Jakob', *PR* CLXXVI, 1919, 339–62 = 'Jacob', *What Remains of the Old Testament and Other Essays*, New York: Macmillan Co. 1928, 151–86; idem, 'Die Komposition der Joseph-Geschichte', *ZDMG* LXXVI, 1922, 55–71; idem, 'Mose', *RGG*[2] IV, 1930, 230–7; D. **Irvin**, *Mytharion*, AOAT 32, 1976; P. **Jensen**, *Das Gilgamesch-Epos in der Weltliteratur* I–II, Strassburg/Marburg: K. J. Trübner 1906/28; A. **Jeremias**, *Das Alte Testament im Lichte des alten Orients*, 1904, [2]1906 = *The Old Testament in the Light of the Ancient East* I–II, 1911; O. **Kaiser**, 'Stammesgeschichtliche Hintergründe der Josephsgeschichte', *VT* X, 1960, 1–15; A. **Kuenen**, *De Godsdienst van Israël* I–II, Haarlem: Kruseman 1869–70 = *The Religion of Israel to the Fall of the Jewish State* I–III, London: Williams & Norgate 1874–5; idem, *Historisch-kritisch onderzoeck naar het ontstaan en de verzameling van de bocken des Ouden Verbonds* I–II, Leiden: P. Engels 1861–5, [2]1885–93 = *An Historico-Critical Inquiry into the Origin and Composition of the Hexateuch*, London: Macmillan and Company 1886; E. **Meyer**, *Die Israeliten und ihre Nachbarstämme*, Halle: Max Niemeyer 1906; M. **Noth**, *Überlieferungsgeschichtliche Studien*, 1957; idem, *A History of the Pentateuchal Traditions*, 1972; E. **Osswald**, *Das Bild des Mose in der kritischen alttestamentlichen Wissenschaft seit Julius Wellhausen*, TA 18, 1962; G. **von Rad**, *The Problem of the Hexateuch*, 1966, 1–78; idem, *Die Josephsgeschichte*, BSt 5, 1954; idem, *Biblische Josepherzählung und Josephsroman*, München: Chr. Kaiser 1965; idem, *Das erste Buch Mose-Genesis*, ATD 2–4, [9]1972 = *Genesis: A Commentary*, OTL, 1972; D. B. **Redford**, *A Study of the Biblical Story of Joseph*, SVT 20, 1970; W. **Rudolph** and P. **Volz**, *Der Elohist als Erzähler: Ein Irrweg der Pentateuchkritik?*, BZAW 63, 1933; L.

Ruppert, *Die Josephserzählung der Genesis. Ein Beitrag zur Theologie der Pentateuchquellen*, SANT 11, 1965; H. **Schmid**, *Mose. Überlieferung und Geschichte*, BZAW 110, 1968; C. A. **Simpson**, *The Early Traditions of Israel*, Oxford: Basil Blackwell 1948; R. **Smend**, *Das Mosebild von Heinrich Ewald bis Martin Noth*, BGBE 3, 1959; R. J. **Thompson**, *Moses and the Law in a Century of Criticism since Graf*, SVT 19, 1970; T. L. **Thompson**, *The Historicity of the Patriarchal Narratives*, BZAW 133, 1974; J. **Wellhausen**, *Geschichte Israels* I, 1878, ²1883 = *Prolegomena to the History of Israel*, 1885; idem, *Die Composition des Hexateuchs und der historischen Bücher des Alten Testaments*, ³1899; H. **Winckler**, *Religionsgeschichtler und geschichtlicher Orient*, Leipzig: J. C. Hinrichs 1906.

A. The documentary hypothesis

Discussions concerning the historical relevance of the pentateuchal narratives have primarily centred on the work of two scholars: Julius Wellhausen and Martin Noth. The publication of a number of articles treating the literary composition of the hexateuch by Wellhausen in 1876 (which later bore the title: *Die Composition des Hexateuchs*) and the first volume on the history of Israel in 1878 acted as a catalyst in a growing crisis in Old Testament critical scholarship. As a result of this crisis, the problems of the history and the development of the pentateuch have ever since dominated the field of Old Testament exegesis. Wellhausen's work, based on earlier studies of Graf (1866) and Kuenen (1874/5; also 1886) brought together questions about the authorship of the pentateuch which had been raised with increasing persistence since the late Middle Ages (see Simpson, 19–28). The results of his work established a synthesis which has subsequently become known as the 'Graf–Wellhausen' or the 'Documentary' hypothesis. This synthesis argued that the hexateuch was a composite work, the result of a redaction of four originally independently composed, self-subsisting documents. (For later revisions of the documentary hypothesis see especially Eissfeldt, 1922; 1965; Fohrer, 1964; 1968.) According to Wellhausen, the earliest of these documents, identified as J (or the Yahwistic source), was written down in the eighth century. The second source, E (or Elohistic), was usually given a date later in the divided monarchy, or at least post-J. The two sources were combined during the later monarchy with necessary harmonization by a redactor to form a composite work. The third source observed in the pentateuch, D (or Deuteronomic), consists primarily in the book of Deuteronomy, which was written about the time of Josiah. In the process of joining D to the already combined JE work, the redactor added much

'Deuteronomistic' material to the earlier narratives, giving them a peculiarly Deuteronomistic theological perspective. The final document, P (or Priestly), was post-exilic in origin and was conflated with the JED tradition to form the basis of the present pentateuch/hexateuch.

The documentary hypothesis as presented by Wellhausen has been the point of departure for most subsequent scholarship, both favourable and antagonistic. A key element of Wellhausen's position was the assertion that the documents were fundamentally original and creative compositions, and, consequently, not relevant to the history of Israel's earliest beginnings. Although not essential to the documentary hypothesis as such, this assumption has played a major implicit role in discussions concerning the use of the pentateuchal traditions in reconstructing Israelite history. The sources were understood as more reflective of the period of their composition, at the time of the J, E, D, and P authors, than of the earlier periods of Israelite history (Wellhausen, 1885, 318f.). On the grounds of his analysis of the pentateuch, Wellhausen, therefore, rejected the possibility of knowing or reconstructing a Mosaic period, or any events which, prior to the earliest source, preceded the establishment of Israel as a people. Attacks on 'Wellhausenism' in the following decades (see R. J. Thompson, 72–101) proved ultimately ineffective against a growing domination of the views of Wellhausen and his supporters in Old Testament criticism (see R. J. Thompson, 58–71). At the same time, the attempt of Winckler, Jeremias, and especially Jensen of the so-called 'Pan-Babylonian School' to examine the literary affinities of the pentateuchal narratives with comparable literature from the ancient Near East ended disastrously as a result of a near total lack of methodological integrity.

B.   *The history of religion school*

The work of Meyer (1906) and what became known as the 'history of religion' school marked the first major departure from the documentary hypothesis (see Simpson, 29–32; Osswald, 126–50). Following Wellhausen (1885, 342–5), Meyer observed that the Sinai narratives did not form part of the original tradition of the exodus. The oldest form of the tradition depicted the Israelites as going directly from the sea to Kadesh and from there into southern Palestine. In examining the *content* of the tradition in the earliest form in which it was written, Meyer concluded that the original construction of the Moses saga understood Kadesh as a cultic centre, the base of the Israelites' wilderness life, and the scene of the most important events (see Simpson, 31 f.). Associated with the Kadesh traditions were the miracle stories of the water, the manna, and the quails. The institutions of the judges and the elders were established, and the law was given to Israel at Kadesh. Moses was not portrayed in these traditions as an historical individual, but was rather understood as a folkloric ancestor of the priests at Kadesh. The 'genuine' Sinai was identified with an alleged volcano in the Hauran and was brought only secondarily into the larger Kadesh narrative. The historical nucleus of the original Israelite tradition was the fact of their being saved and the flight from Egypt. Furthermore, Meyer was bothered by the observation that the Hebrews who fled from Egypt became Israelites in the wilderness narratives, and he suggested the possibility that the Israelites may have taken over the traditions of the Egyptian sojourn from other unrelated tribal groups.

More interesting than Meyer's often unconvincing conclusions are the new perspectives from which he examined the traditions: (1) The traditions have a history prior to the documents in which they are found. (2) An analysis of the origin of the narratives from which the pentateuchal documents have been formed may lead to a non-Israelite substratum of the saga. (3) A search for the historical nucleus (or seed) from which the saga or an element of it has developed, whether a phenomenon (Sinai as a volcano) or an event (the flight from Egypt), leads to an evaluation of the quality of the tradition's historicity. (4) To distinguish the essential literary relationship between two aspects of a tradition as primary and secondary (Kadesh/Sinai) aids in separation of the historically more relevant from the historically less relevant secondary accretions. (5) To distinguish an element of a tradition (Moses in the Kadesh saga) as lacking in a concrete or essential relationship to that tradition suggests its secondary origin.

These analytical questions have dominated most subsequent examinations into the origins of the pentateuchal traditions. In the work of Gunkel, Gressmann, and others, a major effort was made to discover possible historical events which might have given rise to the legendary pentateuchal narratives and thereby to overcome the impasse of Wellhausen's methodological programme. This new direction in the analysis of the narratives was firmly anchored by Gunkel (1901; 1930) through his systematic identification of the myths, legends, poems, genealogical tales, and other original units that make up the documents of the pentateuch, each of which had its own diverse and independent origin. In emphasizing the components out of which the documents were developed, Meyer and Gunkel, and with them Gressmann, have shown that questions about the historical background and the historicity of the pentateuch cannot be answered simply by dating the written sources as Wellhausen had attempted. J and E are rather to be understood, not as authors, but primarily as editors and collectors of yet earlier traditions (see Gressmann, 1910, 1913). The documentary hypothesis does not reflect the earliest history of the traditions. This is rather to be found in the *Sitz im Leben* and in the historical nucleus of the individual pericopes. Their presupposition that the *Sitz im Leben* and the historical nucleus could in fact be discovered by a reduction of the larger sagas to their earliest and simplest components, and that ultimately, in the content of these earliest forms, historical events and realities would be discernable, remained unanalysed and uncritical. As a result, those elements of the tradition which were irreducible were given historical weight: a sojourn at Kadesh, a covenant at a volcano, the destruction of an Egyptian army at a sea, a flight from Egypt, an alliance with the Midianites, and so on. The literary forms identified by the 'history of religion school' were ultimately understood as literary embellishments of an originally historical memory. Only Galling (1928) understood the necessity of distinguishing questions related to the history of the traditions from those related to their historicity. Subsequent critical scholarship, however, has not followed Galling, and has accepted as axiomatic that whatever in the pentateuchal tradition is secondary is either historically suspect or has some independent historical basis, and what is irreducible and original is historical. Later scholars, in speaking of these traditions as legend, generally assumed that legend refers to an imaginatively expanded folk-history.

This direction in pentateuchal scholarship was also strengthened by major revisions of the documentary hypothesis. These revisions were strongly influenced by the 'history of religion school', and were addressed primarily to the question of the pre-literary levels of the pentateuch.

C.   *Revisions of the documentary hypothesis and early historiography*

Eissfeldt reasserted the importance of source criticism, which Gunkel had considered to be an insufficient methodology. He argued that the existence of and differences found in tale variants of the written documents (L, J, E, P; see Eissfeldt, 1923, 56–9) must be explained in terms of the composition of the documents themselves rather than be understood as related to the original form of the narratives. According to Eissfeldt, the earliest form of a doublet is most likely to be found in the earliest of the respective documents. Within limits, the existence of tale variants is a cardinal indication that more than one literary document is involved. Thus Eissfeldt accepted and argued for the existence of a pentateuchal document ('L' or J^1) in addition to J, E, D, and P.

Gunkel had classified the stories of the patriarchs and Joseph found in J and E as 'pure family tales' (Gunkel, 1922, 66; see also Gressmann, 1923, 51). Any special significance which these traditions might have as historiographical legends about Israel was assumed to be secondary and was considered to reflect the sociological and political realities of the Israelite tribes (Gunkel, 1919). Eissfeldt recommended a form-critical analysis of the narratives on the basis of their historiographical intention. In the earliest document of the pentateuch (L or J^1) Eissfeldt found two independent types of narratives: historical narratives about individuals, and *Stammessage* ('tribal tales'). In the *Stammessage*, the protagonists of the narrative are representations or personifications of historical groups, rather than historical individuals. These two forms were often brought together by a third type: artificially constructed, unhistorical narrative material which joined and harmonized originally distinct pericopes. The thrust of Eissfeldt's argument against Gunkel is the conclusion that the stories about the patriarchs and Joseph were *originally* historiographic in intent, and that they have taken on a mixed and *apparently* fictional character through the intrusion of fictional elements which are identifiably redactional and therefore represent secondary developments of the tradition.

Although the identification of *Stammessage* as an original element in the formation of the pentateuchal narratives has become a methodological presupposition of much modern pentateuchal criticism (see Kaiser; Ruppert, 17 f.), the classification of these narratives on the basis of historiographical intention is much more complex, and hardly allows the confidence in their historical relevance which Eissfeldt assumes. On the basis of historiographical intention, at least five distinct classifications of these traditions are discernible: (1) The heroic tale, which has, on form-critical grounds, no observable historiographic character. (2) Elements of the *Stammessage* which are historiographic in intention, but which are not functional in the narrative plots, serving primarily as 'points of attraction'. Eissfeldt's understanding of *Stammessage* is hardly functional in the

Joseph and Moses narratives, for here the use of eponymous heroes as protagonists in the narratives does not relate to the development of plot but only identifies these heroes as ancestral. Even Jacob in the Joseph narratives does not *function* as an eponymous hero. Rather the dominant plot development has the individual hero Jacob and his family entering Egypt to become a people there (Coats, CBQMS, 1975). The eponymic function in the narratives of Joseph and Moses are not representations or personifications of historical groups in which the action of individuals contains veiled references to the actions of historical groups. Rather, the narratives are quite explicitly narratives about the ancestors of known historical groups. As such, they are not *Stammessage*, but heroic tales. The eponymous characters of these stories act as such, with all the individuality of heroes of heroic tales, but they are also heroes-for-us, or heroes for a specific group. The essential behaviour of these protagonists of the tales, nevertheless, show that these ancestors have independent lives of their own, bound only by the normal story-telling conventions of heroic tales. (3) Tales based on a historical situation or status (*Standessage*). These are similar to type 2 in that they involve symbolic representation of groups, but they are not truly historiographic, reflecting instead the historical realities or interrelationships contemporary to the narration. (4) Aetiologies, which are intermediate to types 2 and 3, relating contemporary reality in terms of an original past. (5) Redactional elements, which generally do not develop as whole independent narratives, but rather interrelate and harmonize earlier tales. Importantly, they are often essentially historiographical, but nevertheless obviously unhistorical.

Only the first of these types has any possibility of claiming historicity. However, even with this class, the possibility of its employment for historical purposes is severely limited, since the 'heroic tale' as a narrative type is markedly ahistorical both in structure and development. Historical accretions to such narratives – when they exist at all (see T. L. Thompson, 187–9) – are generally subsumed under and transformed by the needs of the ahistorical literary base. If the hero of a tale happens also to be an historical person, whether Gilgamesh, Sargon, David, or Alexander, this fact of his historicality is largely irrelevant to an analysis of the tales about him, which remain historiographically indistinguishable from comparable tales about Cain, Noah, Enkidu, and Bata. Neither their existence nor any aspect of their biographies can be reconstructed through any study of the tales in which they play such prominent roles.

D.   The 'themes' of the pentateuch's 'Grundlage'

Martin Noth, like Eissfeldt, assumed that behind the doublets and variant traditions of the written documents J and E there existed an original tradition from which divergencies developed in the process of the tradition's history. This he considered to be, not the earliest of the extant documents as Eissfeldt did, but rather a hypothetical common basis (*Grundlage*: G), from which both J and E independently drew the nucleus of their content (Noth, 1972, 38–41). Taking this hypothesis as his starting-point Noth observed that, apart from the primeval history of Genesis 1–11 which had been added at a later date, and Numbers 32, the orientation of the pentateuchal tradition as a whole was in terms of all Israel. He thus suggested that the beginning of the tradition presupposes the existence of the historical Israel after the occupation of Palestine. Noth followed von Rad in seeing the development of the pentateuch as a tradition which had begun in credal formulas related to Israel's cult (see above, §1F). These credal statements were thought to recount certain basic themes of Israel's history which God had directed. The earliest of these in the development of the pentateuch according to Noth was the 'Guidance out of Egypt' theme. At the beginning of the history of Israel, the biblical tradition, according to Noth, makes reference to this act in prophecies, in old narratives, and in hymns. In the 'short historical creed' it appears as the true major act of God (Noth, 1972, 47–51). In this 'theme' Noth saw a *primary confession of Israel* and at the same time . . . *the kernel of the whole subsequent Pentateuchal tradition*' (1972, 49). Because of its character as an irreducible original tradition, Noth assumed that this theme was based on an historical occurrence. In an attempt to identify this historical event, he suggested that the creed originally referred to the 'destruction of the Egyptians in the Sea', the oldest preserved 'testimony' of which is the so-called 'Song of Miriam' (Ex. 15.21b). He argued that the celebration of this historical event within the cult led to the expansion of this theme from hymnic celebration to a narrative form. The narratives which developed in the celebration of this event were recited at cultic gatherings throughout the territories of the Israelite tribes. This theme constituted the crystallization point of the pentateuchal narrative in its entirety, which was filled out by the narratives of the sojourn in Egypt, the enslavement, and the flight, and gradually expanded with the addition of the other confessional themes: 'Guidance into the Arable Land', then the 'Promise to the Patriarchs', the 'Guidance in the Wilderness' and the 'Revelation at Sinai'.

Some of the difficulties of Noth's reconstruction have already been discussed (see above, §1F), particularly his dependence on von Rad's identification of Deuteronomy 6, and 26 and Joshua 24 as cultic creeds. We have also seen the difficulty in identifying the 'themes' of these recitations as commonly held, since each passage develops its own specific theme: the commands of Yahweh, the entrance into the land, and Yahweh who delivers. Finally, it must be pointed out that Noth's five themes as such are not to be found in the original narratives of the pentateuch. Fohrer has noted that there are many themes in the pentateuchal narratives, and that the legitimacy of isolating five as special formative themes is questionable (1964, 3f., 119). In fact, each individual narrative has its own theme or shares in one of the many major themes of the pentateuch. But even these major themes are not those which Noth suggests. In Genesis 37–50 there is the theme of Joseph's success: the success of the unpromising. There is also the theme of Jacob going down to Egypt and becoming Israel in Egypt (see Coats, CBQMS, 1975). The former theme reflects an origin in literary motivations, and the latter is redactional *Stammesgeschichte*. In Exodus 7–10 and 14–15 there is the theme of the acts of Yahweh against the Egyptians, with Exodus 14 acting as a bridge to the murmuring theme of the wilderness collection of narratives (see Coats, 1968). Both of these themes are theologically oriented and have developed on the basis of tale motifs which simply lack historiographical orientation.

Particularly questionable is Noth's use of the 'Guidance out of Egypt' theme, which is at the heart of his reconstruction of the development of the pentateuch. The 'Song of Miriam' (Ex. 15.21b), rather than being the earliest witness to an historical event, repeats the opening lines of the 'Song of the Sea' (Ex. 15.1–18) in a grammatical form which places it into an integrated context within the narrative and should therefore be properly understood as a responsorial to that song. This song is itself, as was noted above, a secondary development of the narrative about the crossing of the sea originally related in Exodus 14. The earliest form of the narrative in Exodus 14 does not properly develop a *theme* of 'Guidance out of Egypt', but rather it shares in the theme of the manifestation of Yahweh's power before the Egyptians, found in the so-called 'plague narratives'. It might be further argued that the theme 'Guidance out of Egypt' is not to be found anywhere as a theme of the individual originative narratives of the book of Exodus. There is no story, properly speaking, of an exodus. The concept that Yahweh guided Israel out of Egypt as a thematic concept is not originative of these narratives, but is rather the cumulative effect of the combined cultic narrative of the passover (Ex. 12–13) and the story of the crossing of the sea (Ex. 14). The passover narrative, along with the final plague of the killing of the first born son, is a secondary embellishment of the narrative chain whose central theme is the power of Yahweh shown to the Egyptians. The revised story of the crossing of the sea (Ex. 14, see above) created a bridge between the Egyptian narratives about Yahweh's contest with the Pharaoh and the Egyptians and the wilderness narratives, linked together by the murmuring motif. Noth's theme of the 'Guidance out of Egypt' which recurs so often in later Old Testament literature is not the original nucleus of the narrative of the exodus. Rather, it presupposes the tradition as a whole.

Similarly the theme 'Promise to the Patriarchs' presupposes the existence of the patriarchal narratives as such, and belongs to the redaction of these narratives, rather than to their origin. The theme 'Guidance in the Wilderness' simply does not exist as a theme, though Yahweh's guidance does play a functional role in several of the wilderness narratives. That the 'Sinai theme' is introduced secondarily into the pentateuchal framework (so Galling, 26–9) perhaps does justify speaking of a Sinai tradition in the same sense that one might speak of a Horeb tradition or a Kadesh tradition, but this refers to the redaction of the narratives which make up this tradition and tells us nothing about its origin. Furthermore, Sinai functions merely as the location of this tradition, and is no more thematic in this revelation narrative than Kadesh is in its tradition. The theme of the Sinai tradition is the revelation of Yahweh and the commands of Yahweh to Israel. This theme is also shared by other revelation narratives. The theme of a narrative reflects its ideological purpose, but not its origin. That is only occasionally made apparent through implication. (For further discussion of Noth's thesis and alternatives to it, see Schmid; Fohrer, 1964; Fritz; Cazelles; *de Vaux; Beyerlin; and Smend.)

Fundamental to an evaluation of the historical relevance of the pentateuchal traditions is the effort to ascertain the earliest and irreducible elements of a given tradition. This has, unless one were to follow Noth in constructing a hypothetical original tradition which no longer exists and consequently is no longer subject to analysis (see the remarks on Speiser in T. L. Thompson, 6–8, 202), the largely *negative* function of aiding in the identification of both secondary embellishments and expansions of the tradition, as well as the editorial, often historiographical *interpretation*, which has been given to a pericope through its present pentateuchal context. As was well understood by Gunkel and Gressmann, the documentary hypothesis itself – and the relative dating given to those documents – is of little direct importance to the historical question other than as a means of identifying the larger editorial influences which have affected the earlier narratives and components from which these documents were formed. With the documentary hypothesis, a relative chronology of the major editorial structures can be established but *not* a chronology of their contents. A study of Near Eastern narratives comparable to the tales of the pentateuch (see below, §3) suggests, moreover, that an explanation of tale variants and doublets in terms of the history of the traditions (such as Noth's *Grundlage* thesis) or a revised documentary hypothesis (such as Eissfeldt's) is unnecessary. In such narrative literature, variants occur with each story-teller, with the addition or deletion of individual motifs. Or they may originate from an independent use of similar or common motifs. Parallel tales can also develop as variations on a common theme. Repetitions found within a tale may well indicate editorial activity; they may also serve an internal *function* within the narrative. (For a systematic treatment of some of these problems, see Irvin.)

An evaluation of the historicity of the primary components of the pentateuch – to the extent that they are identifiable at all – is, on the basis of the pentateuch alone, impossible. Not only is historical intention proper lacking as an obvious characteristic of these primary pericopes, but the identifiable underlying structures which influence their composition are characteristically fictitious and ahistorical. Those historiographical elements which are observable tend to be symbolic, aetiological, and mythical, and reflect *by intention* the interests of the narrator or his audience. 'Events' are not related in these stories, but rather *meaningful* events form the substance of the narration, and this meaning is in terms of the form of the literature, the development of a motif, or the expansion and elucidation of a theme.

The problem is not simply that the narratives lack historicity, but rather that the pentateuchal narratives are impervious and irrelevant to questions about the historicity of events or figures of the past. Nothing more historically concrete about the historical Moses and Yahweh can be known than about the historical Tammuz and Ishtar; nor is our knowledge about the wandering in the wilderness qualitatively different from what we know of Odysseus' journey.

E. *The pentateuch as narrative*

More promising for a basic understanding of the Joseph and Moses narratives is the renewed interest given to the literary and theological questions involved in the analysis of the pentateuchal composition, in contrast to the historical interests which have dominated critical scholarship on the pentateuch from Meyer to Noth. This interest seeks to examine how and why successive stages of the tradition perceived its past, rather than to examine the actual contours of that past (Coats, 1968, 17). This is not simply a denial of the importance of the 'original events' (though it is at times based on the conviction that that original past is irrecoverable; see Osswald, on von Rad, 240f.). It is based on a recognition that the literary question about the ideologies reflected in the various traditions is primary to a recovery of possible historiographical elements in the tradition; for history is not a 'proper category for describing the significance of Old Testament traditions' (Coats, *ST*, 1975, 57). Also, the necessity of maintaining a methodological separation between historical evaluation and an analysis of the history of the tradition must be stressed. The recovery of the earliest traditions is not a task proper to the historian, but is rather a literary task involving analysis of the traditions and their intention(s). Such an analysis is preliminary to and not at all identical with an evaluation of the historical value of the traditions.

The most important work in this direction has been involved in analysis of the Joseph stories, rather than the Moses traditions or the pentateuch as a whole. Of central importance has been von Rad's interpretation of these narratives (see 1954; 1965; 1972). Von Rad understood the Joseph tradition as essentially different from the cycles of tales evident in the patriarchal narratives, specifically in its character as a single, unified narrative with an interest in the unity and development of the personality of Joseph. That is, the Joseph tradition is specifically a novella, rather than a loosely knit collection of individually self-sufficient tales (von Rad, 1954, 5–7). Von Rad found the ideological and theological perspective of the narrative to have been derived from the context of early Israelite wisdom, offering, by means of the narrative, a portrayal of the wisdom literature's ideal of the wise young man (see especially 1972; 1954, 11–15).

Though von Rad would see this novella as ultimately derived from the two earlier documents J and E (1972), Coats, going beyond the earlier criticisms of the documentary hypothesis made by Rudolph (1933), and more recently by Redford (1970), argues convincingly for the inherent structural unity of the Joseph novella. In doing so, he supports throughout von Rad's interpretation of the tradition as a novella, and of Joseph as the ideal figure of the wisdom literature (Coats, CBQMS, 1975). Two pivotal questions, however, arise in regard to Coats' important study: (1) If, as Coats admits, the inherent unity of the Joseph tradition does not preclude earlier stages of the tradition wherein the component tales might be understood as independently existing, to what extent would this affect our understanding of the central themes? (2) If the inherent structural unity of the narrative is accepted, must it not also be asked whether von Rad's interpretation of the tradition as a novella and of Joseph as the ideal young man of the wisdom literature is justified specifically in terms of the narrative as a whole? That is, does this interpretation reflect the central motivating factors involved in the tradition? At stake in these questions is von Rad's and Coats' evaluation of the Joseph tradition as unique in the pentateuch.

In lieu of a detailed criticism, only the following observations can be made here. Genesis 37–50 does not seem to concentrate on the personality of Joseph, nor can his personality be said to 'develop'. In the tradition as a whole he is seen neither as ideal nor as good. Joseph's behaviour in Genesis 37 can hardly be understood as 'immature disdain' (so Coats, CBQMS, 1975, 82). Nor is his accusation that his brothers are spies understood *in terms of the narrative* as either cruel or despotic (so Coats, ibid., 88). If there is immaturity and cruelty to be found here, it is that of the narrator; for he is on Joseph's side entirely. The psychological distance implicit in a novella is here simply absent. Joseph's boasting in Genesis 37 is a plot motif, a necessary correlative of the eventual fulfilment of his dream. What is involved in Joseph's alleged 'psychology' is obviously a literary motif of reversal of fortune. It is the necessary balance and tension required by such a motif which is responsible for the 'cruelty', not Joseph's character. The psychological disposition of the audience, not Joseph, is involved here. Nor does Genesis 39–41 see Joseph as a 'saint, incapable of mistakes' (so Coats, ibid., 82). Rather, the dominant theme here is Joseph's rise to success, developing a recurrent motif of the success of the unpromising, a theme which requires a recurrence of misfortune to be overcome. Joseph's virtue is not central; his faithfulness to his master is a minor plot element, his means to success. Nor is his use of power in Genesis 42–4 understood thematically as ideal, but rather pragmatically as successful. The difference in Joseph's personality between Genesis 39–41 and Genesis 42–4 is simply that of Joseph as servant and Joseph as vizier! Is Joseph really seen *by the narrative* as the ideal young man of the wisdom literature? Is not the philosophically wise and proverbially just man of literature rather the old wise man, like Ahikar, Nestor, or Solomon? Is not the young man of literature rather clever: wise for his own gain? Is Joseph the ideal figure of the wisdom literature or is he rather the successful young man, akin to Aqhat, Jacob, or David?

The relationship of the Joseph narrative to Proverbs, as stressed by von Rad and Coats, is forced, and the development of the personality of Joseph as a theme of the narrative is an exegesis derived from the modern concept of the novella. What is unique in the Joseph tradition is its length (perhaps to be compared in this respect with the book of Ruth), but it does not thereby distinguish itself structurally and traditio-historically from the Jacob–Laban narrative. Necessary to an understanding of all of the pentateuchal traditions is an analysis of the tales and motifs which have gone into the formation of the tradition. Such an analysis must take place within the context of comparable ancient Near Eastern narratives.

§3. THE JOSEPH AND MOSES STORIES AS NARRATIVE IN THE LIGHT OF ANCIENT NEAR EASTERN NARRATIVE

J. **Bolte** and G. **Polivka**, *Anmerkungen zu den Kinder- und Hausmärchen der Brüder Grimm* I–V, Leipzig: Dieterich 1913–32; R. **Borger**, *Handbuch der Keilinschriftliteratur* I–III, Berlin: Walter de Gruyter 1967–75; E. **Brunner-Traut**, *Altägyptische Märchen*, MWL, 1963, ²1965; L. **Cagni**, *L'Epopea di Erra*, StSem 34, 1969; A. **Caquot**, ed., *Les religions du Proche-Orient asiatique. Textes babyloniens, ougaritiques, hittites*, Paris: Fayard/Donoël 1970; G. R. **Driver**, *Canaanite Myths and Legends*, OTS 3, 1956; A. **Erman**, *Die Literatur der Aegypter*, Leipzig: J. C. Hinrichs 1923 = *The Literature of the Ancient Egyptians*, London: Methuen 1927 = *The Ancient Egyptians: A Sourcebook of Their Writings*, New York: Harper Torchbooks 1966; J. **Friedrich**, 'Churritische Märchen und Sagen in hethitischer Sprache', *ZA* XLIX, 1949, 224–39; J. **Gray**, *The Krt Text in the Literature of Ras Shamra: A Social Myth of Ancient Canaan*, DMOA 5, 1955, ²1964; H. **Gunkel**, *The Legends of Genesis*, Chicago: Open Court Co. 1901; New York: Schocken Books 1964; H. G. **Güterbock**, 'Die historische Tradition und die literarische Gestaltung bei Babyloniern und Hethitern (bis 1200)', *ZA* XLII, 1934/5, 1–91; XLIV, 1938, 45–149; idem, *Kumarbi. Mythen vom churritischen Kronos aus den hethitischen Fragmenten zusammengestellt*, Zürich/New York: Europa-Verlag 1946; A. **Heidel**, *The Babylonian Genesis: The Story of Creation*,

Chicago: University of Chicago Press 1942, ²1951; idem, *The Gilgamesh Epic and Old Testament Parallels*, Chicago: University of Chicago Press 1946, ²1949; H. A. **Hoffner**, Jr., 'The Elkunirsa Myth Reconsidered', *RHA* XXIII, 1965, 5–16; B. **Hrozný**, 'Sumerisch-babylonische Mythen von dem Gotte Ninrag (Ninib)', *MVÄG* 8/V, 1903, 159–286; D. **Irvin**, *Mytharion*, AOAT 32, 1976; S. N. **Kramer**, 'A Blood-Plague Motif in Sumerian Mythology', *AOr* XVII, 1949, 399–405; idem, 'Inanna's Descent to the Nether World', *JCS* IV, 1950, 199–214; idem, '"Inanna's Descent to the Nether World" Continued and Revised II', *JCS* V, 1951, 1–17; idem, *The Sumerians: Their History, Culture, and Character*, Chicago: University of Chicago Press 1963; idem, 'Dumuzi's Annual Resurrection: An Important Correction to "Inanna's Descent"', *BASOR* CLXXXIII, 1966, 31; W. G. **Lambert** and A. R. **Millard**, *Atra-ḫasīs: The Babylonian Story of the Flood*, London: Oxford University Press 1969; H. **Otten**, 'Die Überlieferungen des Telepinu-Mythus', *MVÄG* XLVI/1/VII, 1941, 16–29; W. K. **Simpson**, ed., *The Literature of Ancient Egypt: An Anthology of Stories, Instruction, and Poetry*, New Haven: Yale University Press 1972; S. **Thompson**, *The Folktale*, New York: Holt, Rinehart, and Winston 1946; idem, *Narrative Motif-Analysis as a Folklore Method*, FFC 161, 1955; idem, *Motif-Index of Folk-Literature* I–VI, Bloomington: Indiana University Press 1932–6; ²1955–8.

As soon as ancient Near Eastern literature outside the Bible began to be known, people realized that it was in many ways similar to the Bible. After all, it had been written in countries near Bible lands, and the Bible itself speaks of communication throughout the centuries with Egypt to the south-west and Mesopotamia to the north-east. Early in the last century, when the trilingual Behistun inscription gave the first clues to the decipherment of cuneiform languages, Egyptian could already be read. By the last quarter of the nineteenth century, it became impossible to ignore the numerous and striking similarities to the Old Testament found in Akkadian and Egyptian literature. Scholars were divided into at least two schools of thought, as usual, on this matter. Some thought that to read this body of written material with a view to comparing it with the Old Testament and thus elucidating the scriptures was somewhat irreverent and lacking in faith. Others thought that any new information that would help understand something as interesting and important as the Bible was all to the good. Thus religious controversy on this subject raged through the latter part of the last century. This debate of a hundred years ago continues today; the two sides have scarcely changed at all in their views. However, the ground they have been fighting over has shifted to other questions. Today it is not considered inappropriate to use Near Eastern texts to shed light on the

Bible, as long as these texts are historical records and inscriptions, annals of kings, administrative documents, contracts of financial transactions, and treaties between peoples. It is still not usual to use ancient Near Eastern fiction with a view to elucidating Old Testament narrative. That, however, is what will be done in the following pages.

Today, most Old Testament scholars do not know the names or the books of the principal folktale scholars. Fifty years ago, this was not the case. Although the work of sorting and classifying the folktale material whose collection was initiated by Jakob and Wilhelm Grimm had only begun, it was followed with interest by many who, in the impetus of the comparative movements at the end of the last century, thought it would yield results of value to Old Testament study. The best known of these is Hermann Gunkel.

Parallel elements were identified and studied by Bolte and Polivka in their commentary on the Grimm collection of tales. Their attempts only made clearer the need for a larger system of classification for folktale study. Notice that the word here is folktale, not folklore. There are many different kinds of lore; some lore does not concern literary forms at all. Among all the different areas of folk knowledge, only the tale is being talked about in this essay. In response to the strongly felt need to systematize, two units were worked out, according to which stories and story parts could be ranged in order as similar and different. One is the tale type. This was already inherent in the Grimm brothers' collection of several different versions of the same tale. Krohn and Aarne are responsible for the system of classification now in use in the folktale study of tales by type. Tales in the Old Testament and the ancient Near East have not been classified by type and probably never will be (except of course when they may be seen to fall easily into already known types) because there are too few of them for thorough analysis. In the case of European and some other folk literatures, the existence of several hundred examples of each type makes it possible to see the skeletal outlines of the tale type with some accuracy. Such accuracy would not be possible within the limited material of the Old Testament and the ancient Near East. In any case, no one has worked on the idea.

There is another element used for classification which exists in tales independent of tale type. It is called the folktale motif. This may vary in size and be a tiny element within one incident in the story or it may be an entire story in itself. The definition of motif now used is 'the smallest element in a tale having power to persist in tradition' (S. Thompson, 1946, 415). Motifs were first classified into a system by Aarne and his short index was expanded into six quarto volumes by Stith Thompson (1955–8).

Old Testament folktale motifs have never been listed and classified; neither have the motifs in ancient Near Eastern or Greek literature, although all are well suited to classification in the Aarne–Thompson system. But even without the finalizing of ancient oriental motif analysis in a printed table, enough can be gained from studying Thompson's index to notice many motifs in the Old Testament previously unnoticed in one's own reading, and to see how a particular motif may be paralleled in the various literatures of the world.

However, the application of motif analysis, as done by folktale scholars, to the study of ancient Near Eastern and Old Testament tales is of dubious value, not because the motifs are not there – they are and are easy to see – but because the variety of questions asked of Old Testament narratives and the wish to draw a great deal of information from a relatively small body of material make strict method far more necessary here than in the more relaxed field of, for example, the European folktale.

In order to use motif study for the Old Testament at all, it is necessary to narrow down the Thompson definition of motif ('the smallest element in a tale having power to persist in tradition'). This is because not all elements in a tale are properly narrative elements; not all are necessarily related to plot movement. Some can occur in other literary forms which are not tales. For the sake of exactness, and without criticizing the above definition, which is quite adequate for its purposes, I will speak of a plot-motif, rather than a motif, and define it as 'a plot element which moves the story forward a step'. These too, of course, have the power to persist in tradition. (For the first formulation of this more limited definition see Irvin, 1–4.) This limitation focuses attention on elements which are characteristic of *narratives*, as distinguished from other literary forms, and inhibits the comparison of non-narrative with narrative elements, or non-narrative elements appearing in tales with non-narrative elements appearing in other forms.

A second narrative unit which can be identified in ancient tales consists of a series of events in the story. The series taken together forms a more or less set part of the tale, and examples of the same series of events occur in the Old Testament and in ancient Near Eastern tales. I have named this unit the Traditional Episode, and have previously identified the following: the Traditional Dinner

Council Episode, the Traditional Birth Episode, the Traditional Epiphany Episode, and the Traditional Messenger Episode (see Irvin, 9–13). In the stories in the book of Exodus another example, the Traditional Episode of Sending the Saviour, can be found which will be discussed with its Near Eastern parallels after the discussion of the plot-motifs in the Joseph and Moses narratives.

The purpose of using plot-motifs and traditional episodes is not to find out where tales were 'borrowed' from, and they cannot be used to trace migrations of peoples. Likewise, they cannot be used for the purposes of comparing religions in the ancient Near East, at least not until we know more about them. What they can be used for is tale study. Primarily, they assist in discovering what is happening in a story. In tales written so long ago, in cultures so different from ours, it is not easy to tell what is going on in a story, what the causality is, how one plot element influences the next or is linked to it. In addition, comparing the use of the same motif or plot-motif or traditional episode in different stories is one of the few ways of gaining insight into the values of the tale-teller and the hearers, of learning what they thought important, and of finding out *their* meaning for a tale.

It may be asked why, in bringing in literature of the ancient Near East to compare with the Old Testament, the discussion is limited to early literature, leaving the Old Testament Apocrypha and Hellenistic writings out of consideration. It is true that these later works would offer additional material for comparison and furnish many striking similarities. But only works written earlier than the Old Testament can be used to gain information about the world of ideas in which the Old Testament took shape. Another reason against using late writings is that some of them were obviously influenced by or modelled on the Old Testament; thus they do not shed light on the Old Testament – rather, the case is the other way around.

The question of whether a narrative is to be called a saga, a myth, an epic, a legend, a *Novelle*, a *Stammessage*, and so on has been left out of consideration in this article. Such distinctions were not known or adhered to in the periods from which our stories date, and modern application of these terms is apt to be somewhat arbitrary, because it is not clear which ancient characteristics deserve which modern labels. Also, the body of material available for study is so small – about one hundred ancient Near Eastern tales in addition to the Old Testament – that, as in the question of tale types, any culling of general features of groups is very unreliable. Many tablets and papyri are fragmentary, and many tales broken or unfinished. We cannot confidently classify ancient Near Eastern narratives now, although the attempt to do so makes very interesting work.

For each of the ancient Near Eastern tales referred to below there exists a vast bibliography. Place and circumstances of discovery are published; photographs of the papyrus or tablet are given. The broken pieces have been put together either physically or in the mind of the translator. Works so long that they cover several tablets pose the problem of the order of the tablets, which in antiquity were sometimes titled but never numbered. In some cases the work has been translated several times into English, in other cases not at all. There are always discussions about the reading of difficult signs, as well as about the meaning of little-used words, and the significance of the story. Since there is so much material to read behind each translation used here, there is not space to give bibliography for each. Therefore I will refer parenthetically in the text only to the most easily accessible translation, or the best, or both. Usually that translation will give some bibliography.

Bibliography for the Sumerian and Akkadian tales will be found in Borger. Bibliography for the Egyptian tales will be found in Erman and, more completely, in Brunner-Traut. For Ugaritic bibliography see Driver and Irvin (72–80) and for bibliography on Hittite tales see Irvin, 57–71.

A.   *The spurned seductress*

Marriages in ancient Near Eastern societies, biblical as well as others, were not arranged by a man proposing to a woman. Because the ownership of land and other property, in particular its division and merger through inheritance, marriage, and the appearance of the next heir, were considered paramount by the wider society, the preferences of the individuals most concerned were negligible. Marriages were arranged by parents for their children. This was true of families who owned land. In cases in which no property was in question, however, or in which the woman had a widow's status, personal preference might be allowed to play a role, and certainly this is the situation most interesting to story-tellers and hearers. The literature of the ancient Near East which speaks of romantic attraction, both in and outside of the Bible, presents the attraction as being equally likely on the part of the man or the woman. The possibility that the attraction, from whichever side, might not be mutually felt, is dealt with in ancient stories, all antedating by a good many thousand years the revival of themes of unrequited love in Europe in the

Middle Ages, and particularly in the courtly love tradition. Illicit love too was a stock-in-trade of literature in the world of the Bible. Those unwilling to deal with Old Testament narrative on the Old Testament's terms feel that incidents such as David's behaviour with Bathsheba, or the attempted seduction of Joseph, probably should not be included. But since such stories are given, let us try to consider the Old Testament's presentation of Joseph's temptation in the context of meaning given by similar stories in the ancient Near East.

The wife of Joseph's master, in Genesis 39, invites Joseph to lie with her, and when he refuses, importunes him all the more. Angered by his continued refusal, she pretends that he attempted to seduce her, and has him imprisoned. Some have thought this a particularly Egyptian story, because Egyptian papyri give a tale with this plot, 'The Story of the Two Brothers' (d'Orbiney Papyrus, about 1200 BCE; see Brunner-Traut, 28–40; Simpson, 92–107; *ANET* 23–5). In this Egyptian story, the elder brother, Anubis, owns the property and is married. The younger brother, Bata, described as strong and handsome, does most of the hard work on the farm. One day when he is sent home by the older brother to fetch seed, the brother's wife tries to seduce him, and when she is unsuccessful, pretends to her husband that the younger brother importuned her, and when she refused him, beat her. The younger brother's escape from the enraged elder, and his attempts to prove his innocence, as well as his subsequent adventures, form a long, picaresque story, but here we want to refer only to the plot element of the spurned seductress who turns the tables and reports the unwilling young man as a seducer.

By the time this story had been written in the Bible, or even on papyrus, it was already so old that the Hittites, to keep up their audience's flagging interest, had been obliged to add a new twist. The story of Elkunirsha (see *ANET*, 519; Hoffner, 1965) is not thought to be exclusively Hittite, because two of the important characters, the god Elkunirsha and his wife Ashertu, bear Semitic rather than Hittite (i.e., Indo-European) names. Elkunirsha is easily seen to be El *qônê 'āreṣ*, 'El the Creator of Earth', a title of the god El found in Ugaritic literature. Ashertu is a Semitic name for a goddess, probably the same as Astarte in Ugaritic tales.

Ashertu repeatedly sends her maids to invite the young and handsome Storm-god to visit her in her tent. He always says no. At length, angered by his persistent refusal, the goddess gives him one last chance, and tells him that if he does not come, she will tell Elkunirsha, her husband, that the Storm-god attempted to overpower her. The Storm-god has no intention of acceding, but is frightened by her threat, and with an intelligence and decisiveness rare in heroes of this tale, he sets off himself as fast as possible to see the high god Elkunirsha in his tent, tell him the story, and assure him of his innocence. We do not know what would have been the reaction of Bata's brother or of Joseph's master, had they heard the tale first from the lips of the innocent young man, but in the case of Elkunirsha, the story-teller sets a level of sophistication that shows us that an audience in 1500 BCE was not simple-minded in its literary preferences. We must keep this possible level of sophistication in mind when we read the Bible, which was written centuries later. Elkunirsha calmly tells the panting and protesting Storm-god to go ahead and lie with Ashertu, and together they work out a rather cruel plan so to irritate her that she will not again annoy the Storm-god with her invitations. Although the end of the tablet is broken off, it is likely that Ashertu worked out her own plan of retaliation for this.

Another example of this plot occurs in the Gilgamesh Epic (Tablet VI, see Heidel, 1949, 49–56), when the stalwart hero returns from slaying the frightful Humbaba and turns down the offers of the goddess Ishtar. Ishtar is of course not married, so the element of the illicit is not present in this story. Elements it has in common with stories discussed so far are the unwelcome invitation from the female, the rejection by the hero, her unwillingness to accept the rejection, and her retaliation. In the Gilgamesh story, Ishtar approaches the hero and points out to him how happy they will be together. Gilgamesh refuses her offers of love, and when she asks why, reminds her of the lamentable histories of her other lovers, and the fates she inflicted on them when she grew tired of them. This series of little tales forms a number of aetiologies about the origin of certain natural phenomena concerning the horse, certain birds, and others. Ishtar, angered when he persists in his refusal, retaliates by asking Anu and Antum, her father and mother, to loose on him the Bull of Heaven, and Gilgamesh must add to his victories by overcoming this enemy too.

It has been seen that the unwelcome solicitations, perseveringly refused, serve to build up the image of the hero as a clean young man, while the retaliation of the disappointed goddess or woman serves the plot by involving the hero in a further series of adventures. The reader feels that vindication is due to Joseph, after his virtuous behaviour and his unjust imprisonment. In the setting of the Egyptian prison, Joseph's vindication must take the form of political success, and one of his fellow prisoners, the Pharaoh's butler, provides the means through which Joseph and his talents will come to the notice of the Pharaoh. Thus, although the plot-motif of the spurned seductress is the same in all these stories, and although the plot-motif of denunciation to the husband of what the seductress *wishes* the hero had done, instead of what he did, is common to three of the examples given, the use of the stories is in each case quite different. Here the specifically Old Testament theology becomes apparent. In the Gilgamesh story, Gilgamesh refuses Ishtar and perpetuates his image as a misogynic he-man; the incident serves as an entering wedge for the Bull of Heaven adventure. In the three stories in which the spurned seductress carries false tales to her husband, the treatment of the false witness and the moral resolution of the issue is in each case very different. In the story of the Two Brothers, the elder becomes convinced of the younger's innocence, too late, and while he returns to punish his wife, he does not succeed in saving his brother, whom he has driven away to a series of adventures, mostly sad ones. The Hittite treatment appears anti-moral; for its jolting effect, however, it relies on a firm basis of conventional morality in its hearers, who, finally, can scarcely tell whether Ashertu or El is most to be reprobated; the vindication of the innocent young hero, paramount but tragic in the Egyptian story, is here forgotten as an issue. This story relies for a further jolt on a simpler version of the same story, present in the minds of the listeners, in which the husband hears and believes the wife, with sad consequences for the hero. The meaning of this plot-motif in the Joseph story is different yet again; Joseph is vindicated, if not by divine intervention (as in the Egyptian story) then at least certainly by divine purpose, and his vindication and rise to power serve, finally, only as small mosaic stones in a vast and continuing story about divine purpose. Against the background of the larger story the plot-motif of the spurned seductress, at first so thrilling because illicit, fades and is discarded unfinished, and no one ever recalls that the wife was never punished, nor that the uprightness of Joseph was never established in the eyes of the husband.

B.   *The interpreter of dreams*

Joseph's rise to power from his prison cell comes about because he can interpret dreams. He learned how to do this by starting with easy dreams that anyone could understand (Gen. 37). His brothers and father were angered by his dreams, which were transparently about his own future superiority. And yet these early dreams, for which interpretation was scarcely necessary, still serve the function of dreams in tales, which is *to come true*. A complete survey of all the dreams in ancient Near Eastern stories and in the Old Testament would take up too much space; however, their use in the story is always the same, because they always come true. They serve to let the audience (more than, ironically, the characters in the story) know what is going to happen in the future. This does not detract from the story, any more than knowing the outcome in advance detracts from the Iliad. It does not even reduce tension. But it does provide, like prophecy in tales, or instructions from gods, an iron-clad conclusion. This has the effect of raising the narrative to a higher level of sophistication, long before the highly-touted fore-knowledge of Homeric epic poems, because interest is shifted from *what* happens to *how* it happens. (But the development of ambiguity in the foregone conclusion must be left to the Greeks, I think.) Thus we know when Joseph is seventeen that he will surpass his family, and gain honour above them, although we do not see that this is likely, and in fact, his dreams, instead of pointing out a way to success, have, within the plot, the opposite effect. They cause his brothers to become jealous of him and conspire to get rid of him. From the bottom of the pit, success looks even less likely.

Some distinctions must be kept in mind when discussing dreams in the ancient Near East. In the first place, quite aside from the tales, there was a great interest in real dreams and what they portended, especially the dreams of important people and rulers. Whole books were written on how to interpret dreams; it was a science. But this has almost nothing to do with dreams in tales, because in real life, dream interpretation was chancy, and the dream books not all alike. In tales, the relationship between dreams and subsequent events was foreseeable and rigid.

Secondly, some dreams in stories do not need any interpretation. They contain straightforward instruction from a god, who tells a mortal in a dream what to do. The mortal is under compulsion to carry out the instructions to the letter, and sometimes the carrying out can be retold in the exact words of the dream, as in the Ugaritic Keret story (see Driver, 2–5, 28–47; *ANET* 142–5; Gray, 11–29).

Two parallels to dreams needing interpretation may be men-tioned. In the Assyrian version of the Gilgamesh Epic (I.v–II.i, Heidel, 23–7) the reader learns that the arrival of the companion Enkidu will be foretold to Gilgamesh in a dream. Gilgamesh dreams two dreams, and takes them to his mother, the wise Ninsun, for interpretation. In the first dream he has seen one of the stars fall from heaven, and in the second he has seen an axe lying in the walled city of Uruk. His mother interprets both dreams to predict the arrival of the strong and faithful companion Enkidu.

In the Hittite (perhaps originally Hurrian) story of the hunter Keshi, Keshi dreams seven dreams (see Friedrich, 234–9). He goes to his mother for an interpretation.

C.   *The success of the unpromising*

The story of the successful administrator Joseph meeting his brothers in the Pharaoh's court when they come to Egypt to buy wheat for their famine-stricken family is of a sort found relatively seldom in the ancient Near East but often in the Bible, which seems to show a predilection for the plot-motif 'the success of the unpromising'. The ancient Near East prefers to tell of gods and heroes who may be expected to succeed; interest in their exploits can be maintained only by making their challenges more difficult and their deeds more astonishing each time. This unrelieved machismo seems less attractive to the composers of the Old Testament than to other ancient Near Eastern scribes. Or perhaps the difference in proportion is due to accidents of preservation, or differences in methods of transmitting different forms of narrative in antiquity. In any case, although the Old Testament has its share of hero tales (in what Sir Walter Scott would call 'the big bow-wow strain') it has also a large number of tales about women and men whose success astounds all the more because it could not reasonably have been looked for at the beginning of the story. And heroic literature yields a theology less suited to dealing with the world one ordinarily encounters than does the literature of the unpromising. The Old Testament authors understood this well.

So there are few marked similarities in plot between ancient Near Eastern literature and the overall story of Joseph's and Moses' rise to success. One exception is the Sargon Saga, which will be discussed in the section dealing with the persecuted baby. However, there are similarities in detail with the Joseph story, some already presented and one to follow.

D.   *The treasure in the sack*

In Genesis 42 the money paid by the brothers for the grain is restored to them by Joseph, who orders it to be put into the mouths of their sacks. They discover it and on their second trip to Egypt they attempt to return it. Nevertheless, after their second departure, they find that their money has been put into the mouths of their sacks again, and in addition, Joseph's own silver cup is in the sack of Benjamin, the youngest brother. This causes them to go back to Egypt to return the cup, and leads to the threats against Benjamin and Joseph's revelation of himself to his brothers.

Ordinarily in comparing tales we find parallels in plot-motif and in Traditional Episode. Close parallels in detail are usually misleading, especially if made too much of, as it is seldom narrative elements which are similar in such cases, but other features which cannot be compared except by some sort of association unrelated to tale-telling as such. Here, however, we do seem to have an unusual and close parallel in narrative detail with the 'Stories at the Court of King Cheops' (Papyrus Westcar, written in the seventeenth century, but the story probably goes back as early as the Fifth Dynasty; see Brunner-Traut, 11–24; Simpson, 15–30). In one story in this collection, 'The Birth of the Three Children', Ruddedet, the wife of the priest Rawoser, is said to be pregnant with triplets, whose father is the sun-god Re. A prophecy says that these triplets will one day be Pharaohs of Egypt. Therefore several divine midwives are ordered to attend on Ruddedet, but they go disguised as travelling dancers, since Ruddedet and Rawoser do not seem to know that a remarkable fate awaits their children. When the midwives depart after the birth of the three children, Rawoser pays them with a sack of barley. As goddesses, they do not need a reward. As dancers, they say they will pick up the sack of grain on their way back from their entertainment tour. But into the sack they put three crowns, for the three children. Ruddedet and Rawoser have occasion to open the sack before the dancers return. They are astonished to find the three crowns, and rejoice over the future greatness of their sons.

E.   *The persecuted baby*

A type of 'success of the unpromising' is the child who, abandoned or persecuted as a baby, survives and grows up to become important and famous. Persecutions of young men, such as that of Joseph by his brothers, may be a variant of this plot-motif. There are striking similarities, long since noticed, between the birth story of Moses and that of Sargon the Great (see *ANET*, 119). The Sargon birth story is cast in the literary form known as *naru*-literature (see Güterbock,

1934/5; 1938). A *naru* is an inscribed stone of the sort set up by kings and rulers to commemorate their own deeds. The inscription is in the first person, 'I did such-and-such . . .' *Naru*-literature is not found chiselled into such commemorative stones. It is found written on cuneiform tablets, and is fictional, but written in the first person to give it an air of verisimilitude. To make it more interesting, the 'I' is always a famous ruler. One such story pretends to have been written by Sargon the Great of Akkad. It tells how his mother bore him in secret and put him in a basket made of rushes and covered it with a lid of rushes. She sealed it with pitch and put the basket in the river. It was drawn out by Akki, a drawer of water, who brought the child up as his own. By the favour of Ishtar, the child grew up to be a great king. Moses' mother too sent her endangered child off to an unknown fate in a basket made of rushes, and he was found by the daughter of the Pharaoh, who kept him to bring him up. He grew up to be a great leader. However, in addition to these simple but explicit parallels, the Old Testament story distinguishes itself by the use of irony, seldom found in ancient Near Eastern literature: the very Pharaoh who commanded the death of the Hebrew children brings one up in his own house; the Pharaoh's daughter sends the child back to his own mother to be nursed; the Pharaoh was quite right in thinking the Hebrew slaves would not remain silent and obedient. The Moses story also has a larger scope than the Sargon story, as will be discussed below.

Other endangered children are saved in the Old Testament (see Gen. 21–2). In the first story, Hagar is sent away by Abraham because of Sarah's jealousy. She wanders in the desert until her water supply is used up and her son is on the point of death from thirst. Then God shows her a well of water and the two are saved. Genesis 22 gives the story of the binding of Isaac, in which Yahweh, after ordering Abraham to kill and sacrifice his promised son to him like an animal, provides, at the last moment, a ram to be offered instead of the child.

There is also a Hittite story, somewhat broken, about the saving of a child (see Güterbock, 1946, 121 f.; Friedrich, 224–33). In this story, 'The Sun-god and the Cow', the cow bears a young one, whose father is the Sun-god. The cow is angry with her offspring and seeks to kill it, because it does not look like a calf; it has two legs instead of four. The Sun-god saves it from its mother's wrath and sends it to be put where it will be found by a pious fisherman who is childless. He and his wife are happy to accept the child and bring it up, and the tablet breaks off in the midst of their plot to make the neighbours think it has been born to them. We do not find out what the child grows up to be.

In the Hittite tale of Ullikummi (*ANET*, 121–5) the god Kumarbi begets a son who is to avenge him on his enemies. After the birth of the son Ullikummi, Kumarbi sends the child in the care of his friends, probably by a subterranean route, to a safe place where he is to grow up to avenge his father. Here there is no plot-motif of the persecution of the baby, properly speaking, because it is averted. The child is, however, saved, and grows up to pose a threat to all the gods.

In most of these stories, saving the child is important not so much on humanitarian grounds but because of what the child grows up to be. Sargon, favoured by the goddess Ishtar, grows up to become a ruler of legendary greatness. In the Old Testament, however, the reason why saving the child is important is usually because of his significance in the divine plan that spans a number of generations. In the case of Moses, the persecution of the baby is especially critical because Moses himself is destined to be a leader and saviour.

Of course there are also later stories with the plot-motif of the persecuted baby, but for the reasons given above, these will not be taken into consideration here.

F.   *The bloody bridegroom*

In Exodus 4.24–6 Moses with his wife and child is on his way back to Egypt, there to carry out the commands he has received from Yahweh and liberate his people. But one night while they are staying at an inn along the way, Yahweh, who should be pleased with what Moses is obediently doing, tries to kill him. The way in which he seeks to kill Moses is not given, nor is the reason, but Moses' wife Zipporah seems to know why it happened, and how to turn away the divine wrath. She seizes a stone knife (rituals generally use tools of an older form than daily life) and circumcises their son. She then touches the bloody foreskin to Moses' feet, and utters a proverb; that is to say, the origin of a current proverb is 'explained' by a folk aetiology by connecting it with this story. It is thought that the proverb refers to a custom of circumcising young men before marriage. This puzzling passage cannot be understood at all except on the basis of comparative plot-motif.

An Egyptian tale uses the same plot-motif of deceiving a blood-thirsty divinity. In the story of the 'Deliverance of Mankind from Destruction' (this text is found on the walls of the tombs of Seti I,

Ramesses II and Ramesses III at Thebes, fourteenth to twelfth centuries, but the story is undoubtedly older; *ANET*, 10f.), human beings are plotting against the god Re and Hat-hor is sent out to slay them. She kills a number on the first day, and says she is going back tomorrow to continue. Re thinks enough have been killed, but cannot prevent her, so he orders red colouring mixed with vast quantities of beer, and has it poured out at the place where she plans to continue the slaughter. When the goddess sees the beer, she thinks it is the blood of humans. Pleased, she begins to drink it. Thus it serves the dual purpose of making her think that large numbers of humans have been slaughtered and of making her drunk. The rest of humanity is saved from destruction.

The appearance of blood rather than the drawing of it assuages the deity in the Exodus story in which Zipporah, understanding that Yahweh wants Moses circumcised, manages to make him think this has taken place by applying the blood from her son's foreskin to Moses' 'feet'. It is well known that 'feet' in the Old Testament is often used as a euphemism for saying sex organs. Hittite says 'knee' with the same meaning (see A. Goetze, 'Kingship in Heaven', *ANET*, 120f., line 25). The secondary sense in which 'feet' is used in the passage is quite obscured by the NEB translation 'touched Moses with it'. However, earlier, more careful translations make it possible to see the line of the story in the original. This is a story which has always awakened dissatisfaction in its hearers, because it is thought that Yahweh is treating Moses unfairly, and because it presents Yahweh as anthropomorphic. However, its purpose is to show that the future command concerning circumcision will be a very important matter.

G.   *The inanimate animal*

Providing a special delight to hearers, a special photographic problem to movie-makers, and a particular puzzle to literal-minded zoologists is Moses' staff that turned into a serpent.

When Moses (Ex. 4.1–5) asks how he is to convince his people that Yahweh has appeared to him and that he is acting under Yahweh's instructions, Yahweh tells him to cast his staff on the ground. Moses obeys and sees it turn into a snake. Moses runs away from it but, under instructions, returns and picks it up, when it again becomes a staff. The origin of this idea will be evident to anyone who has ever stepped, or nearly stepped, on a stick and realized at the last horrified moment that the object was a snake. This passage is a rehearsal for an event that never takes place, as, when the wonder *is* worked (Ex. 7.8–12) it is done not to convince the Israelites of Moses' message, but to oblige and convince the Pharaoh, and Aaron does it, not Moses. Some of the starch is taken out of Aaron's presentation when Pharaoh's court magicians, by their magic arts, are able to do the same with their staves. This should not be surprising, as we shall see below, but triumphantly, the serpent of Moses and Aaron eats up the magicians' serpents. This further wonder certainly demonstrates that God is behind what Moses says in Pharaoh's court, although the Pharaoh himself seems unaware of the implications of what he sees going on before him. Particularly impressive is the proof the serpent offers of being a real, live serpent by eating the other ones.

The same impressive display is offered on the side of virtue against vice in the Egyptian story of 'The Wax Crocodile' (Brunner-Traut, 11–14; Simpson, 16–19). In this story the wife of a priest at the court waits until her husband has gone to accompany the Pharaoh on a pilgrimage and brings her lover in. She spends the afternoon dallying with him in the garden. Alerted by the servants, the priest returns early to find the lover taking a refreshing swim in the lily pond. The priest is of course able to do many things by his magic arts; he makes a wax crocodile seven inches long, so small he can hold it in the palm of his hand. Then he throws it into the water. It comes to life, seven feet long, and as the reader has come to expect, seizes the lover. But when the priest puts out his hand to take it, it becomes a seven-inch wax crocodile again, and he picks it up. The Pharaoh is invited to watch the display, and the wife is put to death.

The proof that the serpent in the Moses story was a real live one because it could bite is repeated in 'The God and his Unknown Name of Power' (two manuscripts exist from the Nineteenth Dynasty, 1350–1200; *ANET*, 12–14). The goddess Isis, plotting to learn the secret name of the god Re, makes a snake from Re's spittle, mixed with dust. She puts it where he will pass by and it bites him. None of the other deities can heal Re; Isis insists that she must know his real name in order to cast out the poison. Reluctantly, he finally tells her and she heals him. The story was used as a charm to heal scorpion stings.

In the Sumerian story 'The Descent of Inanna' (see Kramer, 1950, 1951, 1966; *ANET*, 52–7), the goddess Inanna has left instructions, before going down into the underworld, for her rescue if she does not return. When she is held there, the god Enki makes two creatures from the dirt under his fingernails and sends them to her rescue, one carrying the bread of life and the other the water of life. This plot-motif, however, shades off into stories about the forming of human beings from clay. There are many stories having this plot-motif in the ancient Near East, but they cannot be considered here.

The different uses of the stories of an inanimate object that comes alive and acts like an animal (more specifically, in most of the above examples, that can eat or bite) should be compared. The motivation of Isis in the story about the secret name of Re is not edifying; the use of the story, aside from its interest, was to cure scorpion bites. In the story of 'The Wax Crocodile', the magic is performed in the service of an uncompromising righteousness; the story has a moral, although the reader suspects it may be second in interest to the love triangle, adultery, ambush, murder, magic, violence, status-seeking, and other thrilling features. The use of the inanimate animal in the Moses story, however, must be considered as something much more than a moral ending tacked on to a thriller, and even above a moralizing story, because the wonder is called on to support not a prosy bit of conventional morality but a prophecy (Moses' demands of Pharaoh) which lay outside the moral codes governing the world in which it was written, and was antagonistic to them. The prophecy is, in the story, a political imperative in the service of a not-yet-formulated morality. The imperative is unrealistic, the success unlikely, the morality questionable, the Israelites hesitant. The wonder is required to bear a great deal of weight.

H.   *The obedient water*

The story of how the fleeing Hebrews were saved contains many exciting elements, among them the remarkable behaviour of the sea. The role of the sea is presented in two forms in Exodus, once in poetry (Ex. 15.1–18) and once in narrative (Ex. 14). It would be useful to study the poetry in comparison with other ancient Near Eastern poems of similar intent. Here only the narrative will be studied.

The ambiguous character of water is played upon in a number of amusing or thrilling stories in Egyptian and biblical literature. On the good side, water is necessary for humans to drink and wash in; it contains fish and provides a smooth road for boats. Even salt water boasts the latter uses. On the other hand, water is dangerous. You can drown in it; you cannot pass through on foot. Thus water serves as a barrier to those not provided with boats. If only water were a little more obedient! If it were there when you needed it (as when

Moses produces it by striking the rock with his staff in Exodus 17.5–6) and would conveniently remove itself when you wanted it out of the way! This is wishful thinking. Water does not behave this way (Gunkel, 7 f.). All the better, the teller of the 'Stories at the Court of King Cheops' would say (see Brunner-Traut, 11–24; Simpson, 19–22).

Prince Baufre tells about King Snofru's boredom. The king's scribe suggests to the bored king that he go for a cruise in a boat rowed by twenty singers. The king takes this suggestion, and his boredom is alleviated, until suddenly the boat stops and the singing comes to an end. He asks why and receives the answer that one of the singers had dropped an ornament from her hair into the water. The king offers to buy her another one but she refuses. Nothing can replace the original. In despair the Pharaoh turns to his scribe, who simply folds the lake in two, piling one half of the water on top of the other half. The ornament is easily picked up off the lake floor and the king's cruise continues.

The stunning picture of the usually fluid water standing up like gelatine is not easily forgotten, but it is used with more tension and more effect on the hearer in Exodus 14, when the Lord instructs Moses to stretch out his hand over the sea and divide it, so that the people pass through on dry land, with the waters standing up in walls on their right and on their left. Water that parts to let people pass through is found elsewhere in the Old Testament in stories which, although memorable, do not match Exodus 14. In II Kings 2.6–14 Elijah, before being taken up in his fiery chariot, rolls up his mantle and strikes the water of the Jordan with it, so that the water parts to one side and to the other, and Elijah and his disciple Elisha could go over on dry ground. Elisha, when he takes up the mantle of his teacher from where it fell, is able to use it similarly and with like effect. Thus he too crosses the Jordan dryshod. This shows that with the mantle he has inherited the double share of Elijah's spirit for which he asked. The function of this as well as of the following stories (one of which is a water-sweetening story similar to that of Moses at Marah) is to legitimate this prophet as successor to Elijah. Even more theologically significant is Joshua 3.7–4.7, in which it is the ark of the covenant, carried on poles by twelve men, which causes the Jordan to stop flowing, so that the waters from upstream stand up in a heap while all Israel passes over on dry ground. Not necessary for the two above narratives, but very important for the Exodus passage, is the question of whether the waters will be caused to return to their place. In Exodus 14.26–31 Moses is directed to stretch out his hand over the sea, so that the water comes back upon the Egyptians, their chariots, their drivers, and all the host of Pharaoh. Rather than merely forming a barrier, the water covers and destroys them.

Other examples of water which appears where wanted are the production of water from the rock in the desert by Moses (Ex. 17.5f.) and by Aaron (Num. 20.7–13) and two Egyptian stories. In the 'Tale of the Two Brothers' (*ANET*, 23–5), as innocent Bata flees from his enraged elder brother, he calls on the Sun-god Re to protect him. The Sun-god is always the god of justice and rescuer of the unjustly persecuted in ancient Near Eastern cultures because he sees everything. Re responds by causing a body of water filled with crocodiles to appear between the brothers, giving Bata a chance to shout out an explanation and convince his brother of his innocence.

When the Pharaoh, in another of the stories at the court of King Cheops, 'The Birth of the Three Children' (see Brunner-Traut, 11–24; Simpson, 22–30), plans to visit Ruddedet, he laments not being able to go by boat, as the Nile will not have overflowed its banks by that time of the year. His magician offers to provide four ells of water so that the Pharaoh can make his journey conveniently.

I. The plagues

Early societies were at the mercy of natural catastrophes to an extent which seldom occurs nowadays. Seeing large numbers of people suddenly killed or deprived of their homes and livelihood by sickness or flood or other disaster was an experience that imprinted itself in narrative and devotional literature. God's relationship to these disasters was even more of a question here than in the case of a single sickness and death, or a single drowning.

Natural disasters in the literature of the ancient Near East, or in the Old Testament, are always attributed directly to God, as in most of the Near East today. However, in comparing the narratives of disasters, it will be seen that the way in which the event is attributed to the divine will differs in the Old Testament and in ancient Near Eastern literature, and in fact, differs within the Old Testament. It is theologically very important to explore this attribution.

There is probably more comparative material for disasters than for any other plot-motif in the Old Testament. It cannot be discussed with thoroughness here.

'Once the bond between gods and humans has been broken', says the 'Erra Epic', 'it is difficult to restore' (Cagni, III c 49). The breaking of the bond is usually presented in ancient Near Eastern literature as coming from the side of the gods. Reasons are given for sending floods and other disasters upon humanity. Likewise, in the plagues in Exodus, the reason has been made clear with each of the plagues upon Pharaoh. In the Mesopotamian stories, the reason for a disaster – be it flood or sickness or something else – is usually noise. This rather odd reason is not given for any visitation from God in the Old Testament (although there is a possible echo of it in Genesis 18.20). In the Enuma Elish the great gods are presented as the parents of the minor gods, the child gods who disturb their elders by running around and making noise, so that the parents decide to kill their offspring for the sake of peace and a chance to sleep. In other stories, such as 'Erra' and 'Atrahasis', it is the humans who disturb the gods with their noise, and this is the reason given for such punishments as floods and plagues. Sometimes there are other reasons for a plague. Hat-hor was sent to kill off numbers of human beings because they had plotted against Re, in the story referred to above, 'The Saving of Mankind from Destruction' (*ANET*, 10f.). In the Sumerian story of Inanna and Shukallituda (see Kramer, 1949; 1963, 162–4), the latter, a human gardener, rapes the goddess Inanna one night while she is on a journey. Intending to punish him and unable to find him among the people in whose midst he has hidden, she sends a plague on the entire region; she turns all the water into blood, so that people going to fetch water find nothing but blood to drink. When this does not succeed, she sends more plagues; the second takes the form of storms; the third is not clear because the text is broken.

As for the type of plague, some of the Exodus plagues are paralleled in ancient Near Eastern literature and others are not. Exodus 7.14–24, in which water is turned to blood, has the Sumerian parallel just noted. A plague of flies (as in Ex. 8.20–32) is just averted in the Atrahasis story, or so it appears. After the flood which was intended to destroy all humanity, from which only Atrahasis and those with him were saved, Anu is seen approaching a gathering of the gods carrying large flies. Ishtar, who is angry with him for the destruction he has already caused, changes the flies to lapis lazuli and makes a necklace out of them (see Lambert and Millard, III, v, 46–vi, 4). The necklace is to be a reminder of the atrocity of destroying humanity by flood, a reminder not to do it again, as is her necklace after the flood in the Gilgamesh Epic (see Heidel, 1949, XI, 162–5) and the rainbow in Genesis 9.12–15.

The Old Testament shows a God disturbed by sin and the refusal to obey him, rather than by noise, and the punishments are inflicted with the purpose of dissuading people from sinning, or of punishing their sins. This is quite different from the Mesopotamian stories, where the question of reform for salvation does not arise. In the Mesopotamian stories also there is usually a division of votes within the pantheon; some gods are for plaguing the humans but others are against the idea and may protect and help the humans. Significantly, it is the gods rather than the humans who repent and reform after a plague. This is certainly not the case with the plagues of Exodus 7–11.

This redirection of divine motivation for sending a plague or causing a flood or other misfortune was a theological development of great importance. The older ancient Near Eastern stories of divine wrath over the noise that the humans (or in 'Enuma Elish' the minor gods) were making were effective in horror, but pedagogically they were wasted.

There are many more similarities in narrative elements between ancient Near Eastern literature and the stories of the pentateuch than those briefly outlined above. The same is true for the traditional episode which follows.

J.   The traditional episode of sending the saviour

A traditional episode is not simply a list of events in a story. Its importance lies in the fact that it is an organic whole whose parts are related to each other because the story-teller needs this relationship in order to tell the story. This relationship lies behind even a difficult, broken, or interrupted text. The events, if somewhat predictable and standardized, are linked by a function more ancient than the tales we have now. The traditional episode demonstrates in the technique of tale-telling the craft of the artisan, meeting the need to keep up the tale, to have elements ready to hand so that interest will not lag (see Irvin, 9–11, 105 f.). Being, so to speak, ready made, it permits creativity in its execution and in its juncture with the rest of the story. And this creativity in event often obscures the sameness of pattern, so that the ability to compare episodes not only clarifies what is happening, but gives insight into the motivation of the author.

The traditional episode of 'sending the saviour' (see the chart below) as it is used in ancient stories, contains some among the following elements: (1) The problem to be solved is described. This description may stand at the very beginning of the tale, or it may be a condition which has arisen from a previous incident in the story. In some stories, action is taken by an individual character to solve the problem. In such a case the traditional episode of sending the saviour would not be used. An example of this is the Ugaritic story of Baal and Yam (see *ANET*, 130f.; Caquot, 382–90). Here, although Baal acts to save not only himself but the entire divine assembly from the power of Prince Sea (Yam), he acts on his own, and is not sent by them. However, his outfitting with weapons by Kothar-and-Khasis exemplifies elements 14 to 17 of the episode. When the first weapon is not successful, he is outfitted anew and tries again. A second or even third attempt after failure is a not uncommon feature of this episode; it may occur at several different points, as a glance at the accompanying table will show.

(2) The element next in order in this episode is the meeting of the gods. In some stories they are presented as already having assembled ('Keret', Isa. 6, Ezek. 1). In other stories we see them being invited, or witness their arrival ('Enuma Elish', Job, 'Telepinu'). In some Old Testament stories the court is pictured, but there is usually no discussion or consultation, as monotheism prefers to attenuate the importance of the other gods. Here Job is an exception.

The problem may now be retold before the assembly (3) or perhaps they already know what it is. Usually the chief god suggests a solution (4) but, skipping this step, he may simply ask 'Who will do such-and-such?' (5) or he may name an individual for the task (6).

In some stories the hero named demurs (7). He may be afraid; he may not consider himself adequate to the problem. In any case, the literary function of this hesitation is to heighten suspense, as the hearers are afraid there will be no saviour. In some cases a reassuring remark from the deity will be enough to overcome his hesitation (8) as in 'Bel and the Labbu' (see Hrozný) but in other stories another hero must be called on (9), as in Exodus 4.14f. and 'Enuma Elish' (see Heidel, 1951, Tablet II, 53–95).

'Enuma Elish' gives an example of element 10, in which the hero stipulates a reward if he is successful. Marduk demands that he be put in charge of the Tablets of Destinies, which have hitherto been worn by his enemy, Kingu.

Wonders are an integral part of this episode, worked either by the hero, or for the hero by the summoning god. The function of the wonder varies. In some stories it is performed by the summoning god as reassurance to the hesitant hero (12) and may be instrumental in persuading him to accept the task. This is the purpose of the wonders in Exodus 4.1–9. The wonder may serve as a trial of strength (11) performed by the hero to demonstrate his fitness for the task.

This is the case with the creation and destruction of a garment by the word of Marduk, before the divine assembly ('Enuma Elish' IV, 19–26). The wonder may also be a way of outfitting the hero with weapons, or resources, as in 'Bel and the Labbu' (reverse 1–4), Exodus 4.1–9 (although here only two of the three wonders are used as weapons), and possibly in Ezekiel 2.8–3.3, where presumably the prophet would now be supplied with the words he needs for his mission.

After final instructions (14), the hero departs (15). When the story has got this far, success is assured, no matter how many obstacles the hero encounters. Sometimes the conquest goes according to plan, so that the victory may be retold in the same words as the instructions ('Bel and the Labbu', reverse 5–7). In other cases, unforeseen problems may arise, as in 'Anzu' (*ANET*, 514–17); the enemy may be better provided for than was thought, and have a defence against the hero's devices. Occasionally a second or third hero must be sent out after the failure of the first. All this increases suspense and rewards perseverance. But the form of the episode demands final success. *Stories which are not about ultimate success are not cast in this form.*

It is clear that the sending of Moses to free his people is framed in the same traditional episode as the sending of a young god to vanquish a monster. In the variety of uses to which the traditional episode of sending the saviour is put in the pentateuch and in the Old Testament prophetic passages analysed in the table, we see a theological flowering, firmly based on older heroic literature and aware of the hold of that type of tale over the minds of the hearers. This remarkable re-use of an old standardized heroic form for theological purposes is strikingly effective, and its effectiveness is not diminished by our knowing in advance how it is going to turn out. Within the form, there can be no doubt of the saviour's ultimate success, and the Moses narrative fits its traditional framework so tightly that the hearer has no choice but to follow with the response this traditional episode has always evoked. In this particular story, it means that the reader must see the worship of Yahweh and obedience to his law as a very desirable achievement, comparable to vanquishing a dangerous monster, and comparably heroic. The established forces of order, of government, of custom, of power, are presented as the villain. This was quite unusual in the ancient Near East; still, it might almost characterize Old Testament theology, with its dedication to the success of the unpromising and its hymn to upheaval (see I Sam. 2.1–10).

The following chart (pp. 204–9) analyses the appearance of the

Traditional Episode of Sending the Saviour in five ancient Near Eastern narratives, three Old Testament texts, and the Moses story. The elements of the episode (no story contains every element) are as follows:

1. The problem described.
2. The meeting of the divine assembly.
3. The problem presented.
4. The solution proposed.
5. The question 'Who will go?'
6. The hero is called.
7. The hero demurs.
8. The hero is reassured; alternatively
9. another hero is called.
10. The hero stipulates a reward.

Wonders are worked for or by the hero:

11. As a trial of strength, or
12. as part of his reassurance, or
13. as part of his instructions.
14. Instructions (and weapons) are given.
15. The hero departs.
16. The conflict.
17. The outcome.

[*Text continues on p. 210.*

Bel and the Labbu	Anzu
(1) obverse, 1–13: Description of distress and of labbu	(Text broken)
(2) 14–16: All the gods are frightened	
	(4) I, iii, 105–9: Anu says 'I will find a god and appoint him in the assembly as vanquisher of Zu.'
(5) 17–19: 'Who will go and kill labbu?' Kingship promised	
(6) 20–2: Tishpak told to kill labbu and become king	
(7) 24: Tishpak says, 'I do not know ... labbu.' (Text broken)	(Text broken)
(14) reverse 1–4: Orders given for storm wind and cloud to serve as weapons	(14) II, 1–27: Mother gives instructions for battle to hero
	(15) II, 28f.: Hero departs
	(14) After initial defeat. Adad carries additional instructions from Ea (Text broken)
(16–17) 5–7: Victory told in same words as 1–4	(16–17) II, 30ff.: Battle
	(17) Line 27 of broken text gives victory

Enuma Elish

		(2) II, 89–91: All the gods assemble, are frightened
		(6) II, 92: Anshar announces Marduk as champion
(1) I, 105 ff.: Tiamat prepares for battle. II, 4–7: Ea is frightened		
	(6) II, 72–6: Anshar sends Anu to negotiate with Tiamat.	
(6) II, 53: Anshar orders Ea to battle Tiamat (Text broken) (7?) Ea defeated or demurs		(10) II, 123–9; III, 57–9: Marduk sets conditions for reward; will determine destinies instead of Anshar
		(11) IV, 19–26: Marduk creates and destroys garment in assembly by word
	(14) II, 77 f.: Anshar tells Anu what to say	(15) IV, 33 ff.: Marduk departs for battle
	(16–17) II, 79–85: Anu returns in fear. Anshar decides to send Marduk	(16–17) IV, 97 ff.: Marduk defeats Tiamat

Telepinu

(1) 2–4: Barrenness and famine told
(2) 4–6: Sun-god invites gods to assemble
(3) 7–9: Problem again described:
Telepinu is lost

(15–17) 9–11: All gods go out to look for
Telepinu, but in vain

(15–17) 12–16: Sun-god sends Eagle to
search, but in vain

(14–16) 17–22: Goddess Hannahanna
sends Bee.
Instructions.
(Text broken but Bee probably
succeeded)

Keret	Isaiah 6	Ezekiel 1–2
(1) i, ii: Keret's sickness described and lamented		
	(2) 1–3: Description of divine assembly	(2) 1.26–8: Yahweh seated on throne
(5) v, 11f.: El asks in assembly for someone to heal Keret 'Who among the gods will . . .?' 8–30: He asks seven times in vain. El decides to create solution himself by magic. El creates Sha'taqat	(5) 8: Yahweh says 'Whom shall I send and who will go for us?' Then I said, 'Here am I! Send me.'	
		(6) 2.3: 'Son of man, I send you . . .'
		(8) 2.6: 'Do not be afraid . . .'
(14) vi, 1–2: El sends Sha'taqat to heal Keret, saying 'Death be broken . . . Sha'taqat, prevail.'	(14) 9: Yahweh says, 'Go and say to this people . . .' with full instructions	(14²) 2.8–3:3: Instructed to eat scroll with words of lamentation and woe
		(14) 3.4–11: 'Go . . . and speak. . . .'
		(15) 3.12–15: Ezekiel lifted and transported
(17) vi, 8–14: Sha'taqat heals Keret		

208

Job

(1) 1.1–5: Description of Job's goodness

(2) 1.6: Heavenly court

(3) 1.7–11: Discussion of problem

(4) 1.12: Yahweh gives Satan permission to try Job

(2) 2.1–2 Second court scene

(3) 2.3–5: Second discussion of problem

(4) 2.6: Yahweh gives Satan enlarged permission

(14) 1.12: Yahweh limits Satan's powers

(15) 1. 'So Satan went forth . . .'

(16–17) 1.22: Satan defeated

(14) 2.6: but still limited

(15) 2.7: Satan goes forth again

Moses

(3) Ex. 3.7–9a: Yahweh said 'I have seen the affliction . . .'		
(4) 3.8: 'I have come down to deliver them . . .'		
(6) 3.10: 'Come, I will send you to Pharaoh'		
(7) 3.11: Moses said, 'Who am I that I should . . .'	(7) 4.10: Moses says he cannot make speeches	(7) 4.13: Moses asks him to send someone else
(8) 3.12: 'I will be with you . . .'	(8) 4.11f.: Yahweh promises help with speeches	(9) 4.14f.: Yahweh agrees to send Aaron too
(12) 4.1–5: Yahweh works serpent wonder. 4.6–7: Leprosy wonder. 4.8–9: Instruction for turning Nile to blood if necessary		
	(14) 4.15–17 Yahweh's final instructions	(14) 4.21 Yahweh tells Moses to work wonders to persuade Pharaoh
	(15) 4.18–20 Moses sets out	
	(16–17) 4.29–31 Moses and Aaron convince their people	(16–17) Ex. 5ff.: Recounts at length the conflicts and outcome

§4. THE NARRATIVES ABOUT THE ORIGIN OF ISRAEL

The literary form of the pentateuchal narratives is significant in a discussion of the early history of Israel not only because of the ahistorical nature of the tales which make up the pentateuch, which prevents us from assuming that historical events, however veiled or hidden, lie at the source of these tales, but also because the narrative framework which links the narratives in a construct of *Heilsgeschichte* is essentially secondary and derivative from the conjunction of originally independent narratives. In fact, it may even be ventured that the book of Exodus itself lacks an exodus narrative, and that such a historiographical perspective is an accidental distortion of the intentionality which formed the narratives related in this biblical book and has resulted from the union of tales which have a quite other literary and theological motivation.

Nor can it really help the historian to refer to those narratives which in some demonstrable way irreducibly relate or refer to the origin of Israel in Egypt and to argue, however inconclusively, that some historical reality must have lain behind this consciousness which has subsequently dominated the theology and cult of Israel, for the originality of a narrative and its irreducible adherence to a given setting, or even the observable historical presuppositions of the narrator, are not truly relevant to questions about historical authenticity or historicity. This methodological impasse becomes apparent in a brief review of the more important primary and irreducible narratives and references to the origin of Israel.

In the Joseph narratives the stories relating to Joseph in the Pharaoh's court have their original setting in Egypt, but this refers only secondarily to the origins of Israel until it is taken up into the final redaction of the Joseph narratives under the overriding theme by which Jacob enters Egypt to become there the people of Israel. This, however, is an editorial bridge of the pentateuchal narratives as a whole, linking the patriarchal to the Moses narratives, to answer the question of how Israel came to Egypt. The story of Joseph and his master's wife has no essential geographical setting, but acquires an Egyptian setting by its inclusion in the Joseph cycle. On the other hand, the Moses birth narratives, the story of Israel's enslavement, the plague narratives and the related stories of the passover and the crossing of the sea in Exodus 14 (in the base narrative), all seem to have been originally set in Egypt by their narrators. Though none of these manifests an explicit historiographical intention of placing the origin of the people Israel in Egypt, the passover narrative, which is an aetiological narrative of origins, does place the causative context of one of Israel's central festivals in Egypt, and the other narratives at least presuppose that Egypt is a land of patriarchal activity. The explicit intentionality of Deuteronomy 26.5-9, on the other hand, does seem to link Egypt with the origin of Israel historiographically, though the references to patriarchal events in Egypt do seem to be secondarily derived from the pentateuchal narratives as a whole.

The pentateuch also has narratives of Israel's origins in the wilderness, both at Kadesh and at Sinai. These, like the passover narrative, are fundamentally aetiological narratives of origin, but the primary content of these aetiologies is not one aspect of Israel's existence, but that existence itself. Nevertheless, these narratives are both mutually exclusive and disjunctive from the narratives with Egyptian settings. If either of the wilderness narrative cycles were to be seen to reflect the historical origin of Israel, this would *de facto* exclude any such origin in Egypt, unless one were to follow a collective theory of Israel's origins in the manner of *Herrmann.

However, the story-tellers of ancient Israel hardly limited themselves to the wilderness and Egypt as places for Israel's ultimate origins. The Joshua narratives, the Jacob–Esau narratives, and the geneaology of Nahor (see Thompson, 1974, 300) presuppose an origin of Israel in the separation of its people from related Semitic tribes of Transjordan. Similarly, some irreducible elements in the Jacob–Laban narratives place the homeland of the patriarchs on the fringe of the Syro-Arabian desert, east of Palestine (Gen. 29.1; see Thompson, 1974, 301).

Other non-derivative pentateuchal narratives place the homeland of Israel in Mesopotamia. Both J (Gen. 11.28f.; 15.7) and P (Gen. 11.31) have irreducible sources which place Israel's origins in Ur of Chaldaean (southern) Mesopotamia. P also has a tradition which sees Israel's origins in the north Mesopotamian city of Harran (Gen. 12.4b), which corresponds to the northern Mesopotamian orientation of the genealogy of Shem (Gen. 11.10-26; see on the above, Thompson, 1974, 298-311) which places the origin of Israel's ancestors there. Independently, Genesis 2 places the origin of mankind, and by implication, Israel, in Mesopotamia.

Deuteronomy 26.5, on the other hand, refers to an unknown patriarch of Israel as an Aramaean, apparently implying an origin in the northern Transjordan or Syrian desert. Also, references to the family of Abraham from Padan Aram imply a Syrian origin of the Israelites.

From a slightly different perspective the stories of David's conflicts with the Aramaeans of Damascus and at least possibly Genesis 15.2–4 (see Thompson, 1974, 203–30) relate how Israel came to exist as an independent nation as a result of its struggles against Damascus. Similarly, the tales about the battles of Samson, Saul and David are tales about Israel's origin, how it was forged as a nation out of the wars with the Philistines. The origin of Israel spoken of in Ezekiel 16.3–22 relates undoubtedly to unknown narratives which place the origin of the southern kingdom and its people in the land of Canaan: 'Your birth and your nativity is of the land of Canaan . . .' But also in the pentateuch, we find narratives which relate the origin of Israel to Palestine itself. The stories of Abraham and Lot, and particularly the separation narrative in Genesis 13, relate the origin of Israel in the separation of the Israelite peoples from those of the Moabites and Ammonites; similarly, the Abraham/Ishmael narratives separate Israel from its southern neighbours. Granted that these narratives are essentially aetiological, with references to political or social realities of Israel of the time in which the narratives are told, are they not none the less historiographically oriented to questions about Israel's origins, and do they not show that the narrators are free to relate any account consonant with their own aetiological purpose? Must not the same be said, methodologically, of the narratives which refer Israel's origins to Egypt or the wilderness, to Mesopotamia, Syria, or Transjordan: the narrow aetiological purpose of any given narrative can be determinative of both the substance and the setting of the narrative.

Of all of the origin narratives listed above, the David narratives appear at first the most amenable to the historian, not only because they are set closer in time to the historical Israel, but also because they offer a causality for the founding of a nation that is at least in broad outlines plausible. Nevertheless they are not to be preferred, for fundamental methodological reasons: (1) Their historiographical intentionality is at least questionable and (2) not only is their historical relevance and accuracy unattested, but their literary genre is essentially ahistorical and the guiding motivations of their construction are fundamentally disruptive of historical categories. Of these narratives as well as all of the narratives of the pentateuch, the historical problem is not so much that they are historically unverifiable, and especially not that they are untrue historically, but that they are radically irrelevant as sources of Israel's early history.

IV

THE ISRAELITE OCCUPATION OF CANAAN

§1. THE BIBLICAL SOURCES

The primary source of information regarding the Israelite occupation of Palestine is the biblical account of the conquest which extends from Numbers 13 to Judges 1. Certain other biblical materials are relevant in a less direct fashion – e.g., the patriarchal genealogies and narratives, the exodus account, the stories in the book of Judges and the chronological notations scattered throughout Genesis–II Kings.

A.   The account of the conquest in Numbers 13–Judges 1

The biblical account of the conquest in Numbers 13–Judges 1 reflects certain internal inconsistencies. Moreover, critical literary analysis has revealed that this account is composite, based on various ancient traditions which represent different literary genres and which have undergone changes during the process of transmission from ancient times. Before noting some of the internal inconsistencies and exploring the literary-critical factors, it will be useful to summarize the highlights of the account.

(i)   The biblical account in summary

After their exodus from Egypt and experiences at Mount Sinai, the people of Israel arrived at Kadesh in the wilderness of Paran (Num. 10.11 f.; 13.3, 26, etc.). Moses sent men from there to spy out the land (Num. 13–14). They returned with terrifying reports which incited the congregation to rebel against the leadership of Moses and Aaron and to begin preparations for a return to Egypt. This rebellion was halted by a theophany at the tent of meeting, at which time God issued a divine decree to the effect that the entire generation would wander for forty years and die in the wilderness. Caleb and Joshua alone were excepted, because they had urged immediate invasion of Canaan, convinced that God would deliver it into Israel's hands regardless of the superior strength of the Canaanites and other inhabitants of the land. On the following day, in spite of Moses' warning that divine support for an invasion of the land was no longer available, the Israelites 'presumed to go up to the heights of the hill country'. 'Then the Amalekites and the Canaanites who dwelt in that hill country came down and defeated them and pursued them, even to Hormah' (Num. 14.44a, 45).

At some point during the years of wandering which followed, the Israelites requested permission from the king of Edom to pass through his land. This permission was denied and they chose a circuitous route which avoided conflict (Num. 20.14–21). When the Canaanite king of Arad challenged their presence in the Negeb, however, the Israelites utterly destroyed the Canaanite cities in that vicinity, 'so that the name of the place was called Hormah' (Num. 21.1–3). Sihon, king of the Amorites in the Transjordan, intended to prevent Israel from passing through his land also, and went out to meet them in battle at Jahaz. Again Israel was victorious, and thereby gained possession of the central Transjordan from the Arnon to the Jabbok and as far east as the Ammonite frontier (Num. 21.21–31). Another victory over the Amorites at Jazer increased Israel's holdings in the central Transjordan (Num. 21.32), and still another victory at Edrei over Og, the king of Bashan, brought the northern Transjordan under Israelite control (Num. 21.33–5).

The whole of Transjordan except for the lands of Edom, Moab, and Ammon now belonged to the Israelites, who established their camp in the plains of Moab across the Jordan from Jericho (Num. 22.1). Reuben, Gad, and half the tribe of Manasseh requested territorial allotments in the Transjordan. Moses granted their request, with the understanding that these two and a half tribes would give full support to the remaining tribes during the forthcoming invasion of the promised land west of the Jordan (Num. 32).

After Moses' death, and presumably forty years after the spying incident at Kadesh, Joshua mobilized the Israelite tribes and conducted a systematic conquest of the west Jordanian territory (Josh. 1–12). Gilgal near Jericho served as base camp for the operation (Josh. 4.19; 5.10; 9.6, etc.), and the conquest occurred in three phases: First, there were three crucial victories in the central hill country – i.e., the conquest of Jericho (Josh. 6); the conquest of Ai (Josh. 7–8); and the defence of Gibeon, whose inhabitants had negotiated a treaty with the Israelites, against a coalition of kings led by Adoni-zedek of Jerusalem (Josh. 9.1–10.28). Second, there was a southern campaign which involved the conquests of Libnah, Lachish, Eglon, Hebron, and Debir, and brought southern Palestine under Israelite control (Josh. 10.29–43). Third, Joshua defeated a coalition of northern kings led by Jabin of Hazor, thus gaining possession of northern Palestine (Josh. 11.1–15). Having conquered the whole land west of the Jordan except for certain outlying areas (Josh. 13.1–7) in less than five years (see Josh. 14.7, 10), Joshua divided the land among the nine and a half tribes who had not yet received territorial allotments (Josh. 13.8–19.51).

Thus Yahweh gave to Israel all the land which he swore to give to their fathers; and having taken possession of it, they settled there. And Yahweh gave them rest on every side just as he had sworn to their fathers; not one of all their enemies had withstood them, for Yahweh had given all their enemies into their hands (Josh. 21.43 f.).

(ii) Internal inconsistencies

Actually the preceding summary of the biblical account of the conquest pertains only to that portion of the account found in the books of Numbers, Deuteronomy, and Joshua. The overriding impression one receives from Numbers–Joshua is that, after an initial delay of forty years, the whole of the promised land was conquered systematically and in a relatively short period of time by a unified Israel under the leadership of Moses and Joshua. With Judges 1, however, which supposedly pertains to the period immediately following Joshua's death (see Judg. 1.1), the reader encounters a situation in which the Israelites are just beginning to gain a foothold in Canaan. Moreover, this is being accomplished neither as the result of a unified effort on the part of 'all Israel' nor entirely as the result of military conquests. We read, instead, of scattered military operations undertaken by individual tribes and tribal groups (Judg. 1.3–15, 17–20, 22–6, 35) and of peaceful settlement among the indigenous population of the land (Judg. 1.16). In striking contrast to the sweeping claims of numerous passages in the book of Joshua which insist that Joshua conquered the whole land of Canaan and virtually wiped out its indigenous population (see especially Josh. 10.40–2; 11.16–20, 23; 12.7–24; 21.43–5), Judges 1 concludes with a long list of cities (twenty in all) whose inhabitants we are told the various tribes either did not or could not drive out (Judg. 1.21, 27–33). These turn out to be some of the most important and most strategically located cities of the land.

The same situation is reflected in the narratives which follow in the book of Judges. These narratives depict Israelite tribes associated with each other only loosely. Their occupation of the land is confined mainly to the mountainous regions of Palestine, and they must struggle to maintain their existence even there. Few if any of the major cities of the land appear to be in their control. Even Shiloh and Shechem, where important tribal assemblies supposedly had been held during Joshua's day (see Josh. 18.1; 24.1), are mentioned only rarely in these narratives, and in contexts which lead one to suspect that they were still essentially non-Israelite cities (see Judg. 9; 21.16–23). A similar situation exists with regard to the Transjordanian territory which Moses had supposedly wrested from Sihon and Og. The most one could conclude from the book of Judges is that there were some enclaves of Israelite settlers in the Transjordan (see especially Judg. 3.12–30; 8.4–17; 10.17–12.6).

There is noticeable tension, therefore, between the sweeping claims of the Numbers–Joshua account of the conquest on the one hand and the traditions preserved in the book of Judges on the other. But it is not simply a matter of apparent conflict between the Numbers–Joshua account and the stories in Judges. Also within the Numbers–Joshua account one finds scattered passages which suggest that such statements as Joshua 21.43f. (quoted above) overestimate the thoroughness and success of Israel's initial conquests under Moses and Joshua. Thus, while Numbers 21.21–35 (see also Deut. 2.24–3.13; Josh. 13.8–12; Judg. 11.12–28) implies that the whole Transjordan excluding Edom, Moab, and Ammon fell into Israel's hands as a result of the victories at Jahaz, Jazer, and Edrei, one reads further on in Numbers of conquests in the Transjordan by individual tribal groups: 'And the sons of Machir the son of Manasseh went to Gilead and took it, and dispossessed the Amorites who were in it' (Num. 32.39). 'And Jair the son of Manasseh went and took their villages, and called them Havvoth-jair' (Num. 32.41). 'And Nobah went and took Kenath and its villages, and called it Nobah, after his own name' (Num. 32.42). Still further, in Joshua 13.13, we read, 'Yet the people of Israel did not drive out the Geshurites or the Maacathites; but Geshur and Maacath dwell in the midst of Israel to this day.'

The account in Joshua 10.29–43 of Joshua's southern campaign concludes as follows:

So Joshua defeated the whole land, the hill country and the Negeb and the lowland and the slopes, and all their kings; he left none remaining, but utterly destroyed all that breathed, as Yahweh God of Israel commanded.

And Joshua defeated them from Kadesh-barnea to Gaza, and all the country of Goshen, as far as Gibeon. And Joshua took all these kings and their land at one time, because Yahweh God of Israel fought for Israel (Josh. 10.40–42).

Among the cities specifically mentioned as having been defeated by Joshua at that time are Hebron and Debir. But further on in Joshua the conquests of Hebron and Debir are attributed to Caleb and Othniel respectively (Josh. 15.13–19; see Judg. 1.9–15). Also in Joshua one finds the following note: 'But the Jebusites, the inhabitants of Jerusalem, the people of Judah could not drive out; so the Jebusites dwell with the people of Judah at Jerusalem to this day' (Josh. 15.63; see Judg. 1.21; II Sam. 5.6–9).

Joshua 11.12–16, taken as a whole, suggests that Joshua also 'utterly destroyed' and 'smote with the edge of the sword' a large number of the cities and inhabitants of northern Palestine. Yet this is qualified considerably by verse 13: 'But none of the cities that stood on mounds did Israel burn, except Hazor only; that Joshua burned.' Joshua 13.1–7 describes extensive outlying territories which 'remained to be possessed' after Joshua had completed the conquest. Likewise, in Joshua 17.14–18, the 'tribe of Joseph' is heard complaining to Joshua: 'The hill country is not enough for us; yet all the Canaanites who dwell in the plain have chariots of iron, both those in Beth-shean and its villages and those in the Valley of Jezreel' (Josh. 17.16).

In summary, there is tension throughout the Numbers 13–Judges 1 account of the Israelite conquest which only becomes more obvious in Judges 1. One receives the overriding impression in Numbers 13–Joshua of an initial, systematic, and complete conquest of the promised land by a unified Israel under the leadership of Moses and Joshua. But there are scattered passages throughout which suggest that this is really an oversimplification of how Israel gained possession of the land, and the traditions preserved in the book of Judges clearly presuppose a more gradual process during which the various tribes tended to act individually and were not always initially successful.

(iii) 'Hexateuch' or 'Deuteronomistic History'?

W. **Beyerlin**, 'Gattung und Herkunft des Rahmens im Richterbuch', *Tradition und Situation. Studien zur alttestamentlichen Prophetie* (Festschrift A. Weiser), ed. E. Würthwein and O. Kaiser, Göttingen: Vandenhoeck & Ruprecht 1963, 1–29; E. **Jenni**, 'Zwei Jahrzehnte Forschung an den Büchern Joshua bis Könige', *TR* XXVII, 1961, 1–32, 97–146; S. **Mitt-**

mann, *Deuteronomium 1, 1–6, 3 literarkritisch und traditionsgeschichtlich untersucht*, BZAW 139, 1975; S. **Mowinckel**, 'Israelite Historiography', *ASTI* II, 1963, 4–26; idem, *Tetrateuch–Pentateuch–Hexateuch. Die Berichte über die Landnahme in den drei altisraelitischen Geschichtswerken*, BZAW 90, 1964; C. R. **North**, 'Pentateuchal Criticism', *OTMS*, 1951, 48–83; M. **Noth**, *Überlieferungsgeschichtliche Studien*, 1957; G. **von Rad**, 'Hexateuch oder Pentateuch?', *VF* 1947/8 1/2, 1949, 52–6; A. N. **Radjawane**, 'Das deuteronomistische Geschichtswerk', *TR* XXXVIII, 1973/4, 177–216; R. **Schmid**, 'Meerwunder- und Landnahme-Traditionen', *TZ* XXI, 1965, 260–8; H. **Schulte**, *Die Entstehung der Geschichtsschreibung im Alten Israel*, BZAW 128, 1972; R. **Smend**, 'Das Gesetz und die Völker. Ein Beitrag zur deuteronomistischen Redaktionsgeschichte', *Probleme biblischer Theologie*, 1971, 494–509; N. H. **Snaith**, 'The Historical Books', *OTMS*, 1951, 84–114; M. **Weinfeld**, 'The Period of the Conquest and of the Judges as seen by the Earlier and Later Sources', *VT* XVII, 1967, 93–113; H. **Weippert**, 'Die "deuteronomistischen" Beurteilungen der Könige von Israel und Juda und das Problem der Redaktion der Königsbucher', *Bib* LIII, 1972, 301–39.

That Genesis–Numbers is a composite work based on older sources or cycles of tradition is well known. It is altogether reasonable to suspect, moreover, that there is some connection between the sources which lie behind Genesis–Numbers and the conquest traditions in the book of Joshua. On the one hand, these sources anticipate and presuppose Israel's possession of the land of Canaan. On the other hand, the book of Joshua, which describes Israel's taking of the land, includes passages which may be said to reflect literary characteristics similar to those of the Genesis–Numbers sources and to represent their logical continuation. By the turn of the century, therefore, and until the 1940s, most critical biblical scholars were inclined to treat Genesis to Joshua (actually to Judges 1) as a compositional unit – i.e., the 'hexateuch'. Those who have followed this approach have not always agreed in their identification and/or delineation of the hexateuchal sources (see the review articles with bibliography by North, Snaith, and Jenni). Typically they have identified them as 'J', 'E', 'D', and 'P'; assigned to 'J' a series of passages which suggest that the Israelite effort to gain possession of Canaan was neither unified nor very successful at first (Num. 21.1–3; 32.39, 41–2; Josh. 11.13; 13.13; 17.14–18; and Judg. 1); attributed to 'E' much of the 'pre-Deuteronomic' core of the conquest narratives in Joshua 2–11; and credited 'P' with the detailed description of the tribal allotments in Joshua 13.1–21.43. In accordance with this approach it is presumed that 'J' and 'E' were combined to produce an account of Israel's origins which extended in coverage from creation through the conquest, and possibly further. Later this composite 'JE' account was combined with 'P' and expanded at least twice within Deuteronomistic circles who introduced the book of Deuteronomy as Moses' farewell address and extended the coverage into the exile – i.e., through II Kings.

Noth advanced a different hypothesis in 1943, however, which identifies Deuteronomy to II Kings as a basic compositional unit, a 'Deuteronomistic History'. According to Noth, this theological interpretation of Israel's history from Moses to the exile is essentially the work of a single author-compiler who probably lived in Palestine during the exile and who had access to a wide variety of oral and written traditions. Generally the Deuteronomistic compiler made only minor changes in the wording of the traditions which he used. But he was selective, he carefully arranged these traditions into a coherent account; and he introduced his own ideas by means of summary passages, speeches, and prayers which he composed himself. He also used the summaries, speeches, and prayers to divide Israel's history into four major periods:

The period of Moses – summarized in Deut. 1.1–3.29.

The period of the conquest – delimited by Yahweh's speech in Josh. 1 and Joshua's farewell address in Josh. 23.

The period of the judges – concluded with Samuel's speech in I Sam. 12.

The period of the kings – each king's reign is summarized and evaluated. See also II Kings 17.

Although Noth emphasized the careful organization and continuity of theological perspective throughout the Deuteronomistic history, he conceded that some fairly extensive passages must have been introduced secondarily to the original Deuteronomistic compiler's account. Following is a summary of Noth's literary critical analysis of that portion of the Deuteronomistic history which has to do with the conquest:

Josh. 2.1–11.20a: A collection of narratives compiled by an anonymous collector probably about 900 BCE.

Deut. 1.1–3.29 (–4.40?); Josh. 1; 8.30–5; 11.20b–23 + 14.6aβ–15; 12: Summary passages, etc., composed by the original Deuteronomistic writer. He also made occasional editorial additions in Josh. 2.1–11.20a.

Josh. 13.1–20.9; 21.43–22.6; 24.1–28: Secondary additions to the Deuteronomistic history, but deriving also from circles which were Deuteronomistically influenced (see especially the

literary style in 21.43–22.6 and 24.1–28). The addition of 13.1–
20.9, which pertains to the tribal allotments, called for the transfer of 14.6aβ–13 from the original Deuteronomistic compiler's
summary in Josh. 11.20b–23 to its present position.

Josh. 21.1–42; 22.7–34; Judg. 1: Still later additions to the
Deuteronomistic history. Josh. 15.13–19 is introduced and other
glosses added to Joshua on the basis of Judg. 1 (see, for
example, Josh. 15.63; 16.10; 17.11–13 and 19.29b–30).

Noth recognized that the earliest Genesis–Numbers sources probably
treated the period of the conquest. But he denied any literary connection between these sources and the pre-Deuteronomistic collection of conquest narratives in Joshua 2.1–11.20a. Nor did he find
any traces of the Genesis–Numbers sources in the several fairly extensive blocks of material which, according to his analysis, were
introduced into the Deuteronomistic history secondarily.

Noth's hypothesis soon gained wide acceptance, to the extent that
the designation 'Deuteronomistic history' has tended to displace
'hexateuch' in recent scholarly discussion. Yet a significant number
of leading scholars found it unconvincing from the beginning, or
accepted it only with major modifications (see Radjawane for a
summary of positions and bibliography). The chief objection has
always been that it seems to make an artificial break between
Genesis–Numbers, whose sources anticipate the Israelite taking of
Canaan, and the book of Joshua which describes the conquest. Thus
for example von Rad and Mowinckel protested vigorously that the
'hexateuch' must be considered a basic compositional unit. And a
number of younger scholars who may be less confident than
Mowinckel that the Genesis–Numbers sources can be traced verse by
verse in Joshua and Judges 1, suspect that they are there nevertheless
(for example, Schmid; Weinfeld; Schulte, 77–105). Moreover, it
becomes increasingly apparent that the so-called 'Deuteronomistic
history' exhibits a less coherent overall structure than Noth admitted
(see Radjawane, 204–11), and close examination of its individual
sections suggest that the process by which it was compiled and
redacted was far more complex than Noth envisaged (see, for
example, Smend; Beyerlin; Weippert; and Mittmann).

Obviously the final word is yet to be said on the matter, but two
conclusions hold regardless of whether one thinks in terms of a 'hexateuch' or a 'Deuteronomistic history'. First, it is clear that the
biblical account of the conquest in Numbers 13–Judges 1 is a highly
composite construction. Second, when one attempts to disentangle

the various literary strata which compose this account, it becomes
increasingly apparent that older traditions which seem unaware of
an initial conquest of the whole land of Canaan by a unified Israel
have been incorporated into later materials which do. In fact, the
concept of an initial conquest by all Israel appears to be largely
Deuteronomistic – again whether one thinks in terms of a secondary
Deuteronomistic redaction and expansion of a 'hexateuch' or of an
original Deuteronomistic compilation of a 'Deuteronomistic history'.
Several passages on conquest traditions require individual attention.

(*iv*) *Numbers 13–14; 20.14–21; 21.1–3, 21–35; 32*

Y. **Aharoni**, 'Forerunners of the Limes: Iron Age Fortresses in the Negev',
IEJ XVII, 1967, 1–17; B. **Baentsch**, *Exodus–Leviticus–Numeri*, HKAT I/2,
1903; J. R. **Bartlett**, 'The Historical Reference of Numbers xxi 27–30',
PEQ CI, 1969, 94–100; idem, 'Sihon and Og, Kings of the Amorites', *VT*
XX, 1970, 257–77; A. **Bergman** (Biran), 'The Israelite Tribe of Half-
Manasseh', *JPOS* XVI, 1936, 224–54; K. **Budde**, *Die Bücher Richter und
Samuel. Ihre Quellen und ihr Aufbau*, Giessen: Ricker 1890; C. F. **Burney**,
Israel's Settlement in Canaan, London: Oxford University Press 1918; A. **Dill-
mann**, *Numeri, Deuteronomium und Josua*, KHAT, ²1886; V. **Fritz**, *Israel in
der Wüste*, MTS 7, 1970; G. B. **Gray**, *Numbers*, ICC, 1903; H. **Gressmann**,
Mose und seine Zeit. Ein Kommentar zu den Mose-Sagen, FRLANT 18, 1913; H.
Holzinger, *Numeri*, KHC 4, 1903; B. **Mazar**, 'The Sanctuary of Arad and
the Family of Hobab the Kenite', *JNES* XXIV, 1965, 297–303; E. **Meyer**,
'Kritik der Berichte über die Eroberung Palaestinas (Num. 20, 14 bis Jud.
2, 5)', *ZAW* I, 1881, 117–46; S. **Mittmann**, 'Num 20, 14–21 – eine redak-
tionelle Kompilation', *Wort und Geschichte* (Festschrift Karl Elliger), ed. H.
Gese and H. P. Rüger, AOAT 18, 1973, 143–9; idem, *Deuteronomium 1, 1–6,
3 literarkritisch und traditionsgeschichtlich untersucht*, BZAW 139, 1975; S. **Mowinckel**, *Tetrateuch–Pentateuch–Hexateuch. Die Berichte über die Landnahme in
den drei altisraelitischen Geschichtswerken*, BZAW 90, 1964; idem, *Erwägungen
zur Pentateuch-Quellenfrage*, Oslo: Universitetsforlaget 1964; M. **Noth**, 'Num
21 als Glied der "Hexateuch"-Erzählung', *ZAW* LVIII, 1940/41, 161–89
= his *Aufsätze* I, 1971, 75–101; idem, 'Das Land Gilead als Siedlungsgebiet
israelitischer Sippen', *PJB* XXXVII, 1941, 50–101 = his *Aufsätze* I, 347–
90; idem, 'Israelitische Stämme zwischen Ammon und Moab', ZAW LX,
1944, 11–57 = his *Aufsätze* I, 391–433; idem, *History of Pentateuchal
Traditions*, 1972; idem, *Das vierte Buch Mose. Numeri*, ATD 7, 1966 =
Numbers, OTL, 1968; M. **Ottosson**, *Gilead, Tradition and History*, CBOTS 3,
1969; W. **Richter**, 'Die Überlieferungen um Jephtah, Ri 10, 17–12, 6', *Bib*
XLVII, 1966, 485–556; M. H. **Segal**, 'The Settlement of Manasseh East of
the Jordan', *PEFQS* L, 1918, 124–31; J. **Simons**, 'Two Connected
Problems Relating to the Israelite Settlement in Transjordan', *PEQ*

LXXIX, 1947, 27–39, 87–101; C. **Steuernagel**, *Die Einwanderung des israelitischen Stämme in Kanaan. Historisch-kritische Untersuchungen*, Berlin: Schwetschke 1901; W. A. **Sumner**, 'Israel's Encounters with Edom, Moab, Ammon, Sihon and Og', *VT* XVIII, 1968, 216–28; J. **Van Seters**, 'The Conquest of Sihon's Kingdom: a Literary Examination', *JBL* XCI, 1972, 182–97; R. **de Vaux**, 'Notes d'histoire et de topographie transjordaniennes', *RB* L, 1941, 16–47 = his *Bible et Orient*, Paris: Éditions du Cerf, 1967, 115–49; S. **Wagner**, 'Die Kundschaftergeschichten im Alten Testament', *ZAW* LXXVI, 1964, 255–69; M. **Wüst**, *Untersuchungen zu den siedlungsgeographischen Texten des Alten Testaments, I. Ostjordanland*, BTAVO B/9, 1975.

Numbers 13–14: This narrative regarding Israel's spying out of the land and subsequent defeat at Hormah consists of an old tradition (probably 'J') which has been expanded by 'P'. Not every verse can be assigned with certainty, but the break-down is essentially as follows:

J: 13.17b–20, 22–4, 26b–31; 14.4, 23bβ–24, 39–45 (14.11b–24a is a Deuteronomistic digression within this core tradition).

P: 13.1–17a, 21, 25–6, 32–3; 14.1–3, 5–10, 26–38.

According to the expanded 'P' version, the spies were sent to explore the whole of the promised land, from the wilderness of Zin to the entrance of Hamath; Caleb and Joshua both are said to have urged invasion; and the divine decree is taken to mean that none of the congregation who were of age at the time of the incident, except for Caleb and Joshua, would be allowed to enter any portion of Canaan. When the 'P' elements are stripped away, however, we find that the older tradition has the spies exploring specifically the vicinity of Hebron; Caleb alone among the spies is said to have called for invasion; and the divine decree is less sweeping:

... none of those who despised me shall see it. But my servant Caleb, because he has a different spirit and has followed me fully, I will bring into the land into which he went, and his descendants shall possess it' (14.23 f.).

The territory spied out – i.e., the exceedingly fruitful vicinity of Hebron (see 13.23) – is to be reserved now for Caleb and his descendants. It will not be available as a possession for the remainder of Israel. This does not necessarily mean, as is implied in the expanded 'P' version, that the remainder of the congregation will be denied entrance to any portion of the promised land.

According to the expanded 'P' version, the divine decree finds its fulfilment with the forty years of wandering. During the forty years the whole congregation who were of age at the time of the spying incident will die out and thus never set foot in Canaan. But the older core tradition knows nothing of the forty-year delay, and has the decree fulfilled in part by an incident which occurred the next day (see 14.39–45). We are told, namely, that early the next morning, in spite of the divine decree which limited the availability of Hebron and associated hill country to Caleb and his descendants, the people presumed to go up and proceeded as far as 'the heights of the hill country'. 'Then the Amalekites and the Canaanites who dwelt in that hill country came down, and defeated them, and pursued them even to Hormah' (14.45).

This incident represents the fulfilment of the negative side of the decree. That Hebron and the associated hill country was forbidden to all but Caleb and his descendants was confirmed. But what of the positive side? One expects to be told that Caleb did go up then and take possession of the area. A tradition regarding Caleb's taking possession of Hebron and vicinity does in fact occur in three different versions further on in the biblical account of the conquest (Josh. 14.6–15; 15.13–19; Judg. 1.9–15). All three versions have been edited for integration into their present literary contexts. But in no case was the integration entirely successful.

In Joshua 14.6–15 Caleb reminds Joshua that the Hebronite hill country (see especially vv. 9, 12) had been promised to him and his descendants and requests permission to enter and take possession of it. This pericope seems intrusive in its present context, and Noth was probably correct in contending that it has been transferred from Joshua 11.21–3 (Noth, 1957, 24, n.2; 44–7). Both Joshua 11.21–3 and 14.6–15 are cast in the typical Deuteronomistic style and are designed to accommodate the concept of a conquest of the whole land of Canaan by all Israel forty years later than the spying incident. For example, Joshua 11.21–3 says that Joshua wiped out the Anakim from the southern Palestinian hill country, 'from Hebron, from Debir, from Anab, and from all the country of Judah', and Caleb states in Joshua 14.10, 'Yahweh has kept me alive . . . these forty-five years . . . while Israel walked in the wilderness.' But one gets the impression that this accommodation is forced. Tension is especially apparent in Joshua 14.11f., which seems to presume that the Anakim remain to be driven out of Hebron. This tension may be due in part to secondary glosses derived from Joshua 15.13–19 (e.g., 14.12aβ–b may be such a gloss). But there is also the possibility that Joshua 11.21–3 + 14.6–15 is based ultimately on an old tradition similar to Joshua 15.13–19.

Joshua 15.13–19 and Judges 1.9–15 are parallel versions of a single account. Note that Joshua 14.6aα . . . 15.13 are redactional verses, intended to subsume the Calebites under the tribal division of Judah. Caleb is artificially subsumed under Judah in Judges 1.9–15 also, even to the extent that verses 9f. now attribute the conquest of Hebron to Judah. Originally this account described a specifically Calebite conquest, however, and one which seems to be a logical sequel to the older core tradition in Numbers 13–14. That is, it relates how Caleb and his relatives entered and took possession of precisely that territory which was spied out from Kadesh, granted to Caleb and his descendants because he exhibited 'a different spirit' at that time, and denied to the remainder of Israel. Literary critics who have sought to trace the Genesis–Numbers sources into Joshua and Judges often have associated Joshua 15.13–19/Judges 1.9–15 with 'J' and seen this account as the Yahwistic sequel to Numbers 14.39–45 (see Meyer, 134f.; Steuernagel, 74f.; Burney, 30f.; Mowinckel, 1964, 32).

Numbers 21.1–3. This pericope (see also the derived statement in Num. 33.40) usually is assigned to 'J' or 'JE'. However, the geographical setting and sequential context which the incident would have had in 'J' is unclear. One should not presume from the 'P' materials which precede and follow (Num. 20.22–9 and 21.4–9) that the incident was associated with Mount Hor. Commentators generally agree that the reference to 'the king of Arad' is a scribal gloss. 'The way of Atharim' is mentioned nowhere else in the Old Testament; although Aharoni made a strong case for identifying it as a route from the vicinity of Kadesh-barnea through the Negeb to the vicinity of Hormah. Finally, if both the older core tradition of Numbers 13–14 and this pericope in Numbers 21.1–3 belong to 'J', as seems likely, it is somewhat surprising that the name 'Hormah', which this pericope explains, already is presupposed in 14.45. Possibly the original Yahwistic sequence is now reversed.

If that be the case, and if Joshua 15.13–19/Judges 1.9–15 does represent a continuation of 'J' tradition, the following picture emerges: Israel approached the southern hill country from Kadesh through the Negeb along 'the way of Atharim' (Num. 21.1). The Canaanites who dwelt in the Negeb fought against Israel, but Israel defeated them and destroyed their cities so that the name of the place came to be called 'Hormah' (21.2–3). Spies were then sent into the southern Palestinian hill country, particularly into the vicinity of Hebron (Num. 13.17b–20, 22–4). They returned with fantastic reports regarding the fruitfulness of the area, but also of its defensive strength (Num. 13.26b–29). Caleb called for invasion, but the

remainder of the people were afraid and began to make plans to
return to Egypt (Num. 13.30f.; 14.4). Yahweh promised that he
would bring Caleb into the land which had been spied out and that
his descendants would possess it, but that the remainder of the congregation would not see it (Num. 14.23b–24). Israel presumed to
invade the southern hill country anyhow, but the Amalekites and
Canaanites who lived in the hill country defeated them and pursued
them as far as Hormah (Num. 14.39–45). Caleb and his relatives
entered and took possession (Josh. 15.13–19; Judg. 1.9–15). This
literary-critical reconstruction is hypothetical, of course; and even if
it is essentially correct, the question of the historicity of the events
narrated remains open. The explanation offered for the name
'Hormah' is in any case a folk aetiology. Note that Judges 1.17
repeats the same aetiology in a slightly different historical setting:
'And Judah went with Simeon his brother, and they defeated the
Canaanites who inhabited Zephath, and utterly destroyed it. So the
name of the city was called Hormah.' Actually there is some reason
to believe that Hormah, which is identified in Joshua 15.30 and 19.4
as a city on Judah's (Simeon's) southern frontier, was already called
by that name as early as the beginning of the Middle Bronze Age
(see Mazar).

Numbers 20.14–21; 21.21–35. These two passages record Israel's
encounter with Edom (20.14–21) and the conquest of the kingdoms
of Sihon and Og (21.21–35). Earlier commentators were inclined to
assign both passages to 'J', 'E', or 'JE', recognizing some minor
inconsistencies within the former (compare Num. 20.17 with Num.
20.19) and redactional additions to the latter. But there is nothing
specific in either of these passages to indicate a connection with the
older Genesis–Numbers sources, and the results of recent studies
suggest that they are almost entirely Deuteronomistic and redactional in origin (Fritz, 28f.; Van Seters; Mittmann, 143–9; Wüst, 9–
59).
   Numbers 20.14–21 states that the king of Edom denied Israel's
request to pass through his territory and came out against them with
a strong force. Other clearly Deuteronomistic passages in
Deuteronomy–Judges allude to similar inhospitable treatment which
Israel received from the Ammonites and Moabites. Jephthah's message to the king of Ammon in Judges 11.12–28 indicates that the
Moabites denied Israel thoroughfare through their land, and
Deuteronomy 23.3–4 states:

No Ammonite or Moabite shall enter the assembly of Yahweh; ...

because they did not meet you with bread and with water on the way, when you came forth out of Egypt, and because they hired against you Balaam . . . to curse you.

Moses' speech in the opening chapters of Deuteronomy presents a slightly different perspective. There one reads that God specifically excluded the territorial possessions of Edom, Moab, and Ammon from the land promised to Israel; that he commanded the Israelites to avoid any conflict with these three nations as they passed around (or across?) their boundaries, and that the Edomites and Moabites did sell the Israelites food and drink along the way (Deut. 2.4–29).

Regarding Numbers 21.21–35, commentators have long since recognized that the report of Og's defeat in verses 33–5 is a secondary note derived from Deuteronomy 3.1f., 3b (see Dillmann; Holzinger; Baentsch). The preceding verse regarding Israel's conquest of Jazer and the corresponding gloss in verse 24b also have the appearance of redactional notes, in anticipation of Numbers 32.1, where the land of Jazer is singled out for the settlement of Reuben and Gad (see below). Numbers 21.26, 31 are designed to incorporate the old song of verses 27–30 into its present context. That leaves the report of Israel's conquest of Sihon's kingdom (vv. 21–4a, 25) which, in spite of Noth's attempt to establish it as 'E' (Noth, 1971, 75–101), appears to be a typically Deuteronomistic composition.

The song in Numbers 21.27–30 clearly has an independent origin (see the slightly different version in Jer. 48.45–7), and has been used in Numbers 21 to justify Israel's possession of former Moabite territory. The implication is that Israel actually did not take the territory from Moab, but from the Amorites who themselves had taken it from Moab earlier. This concern to justify Israel's possession of Moabite territory is further indication of the Deuteronomistic orientation of the passage. Both the idea that the lands of Edom, Moab, and Ammon were forbidden to the Israelites for a possession and the explanation that Israel received the Moabite territory in question from Sihon and the Ammonites, find their clearest expression in two clearly Deuteronomistic passages already mentioned above – i.e., Moses' farewell address (see especially Deut. 2.4f., 9, 19) and Jephthah's message to the king of Ammon (Judg. 11.12–28). Commentators have often observed, incidentally, that Jephthah's message would make more sense if addressed to a king of Moab. Perhaps it was at an earlier stage of the narrative's literary history (for a full discussion of the views involved and bibliography see Richter).

In short, these, the biblical descriptions and allusions to Israel's

encounters with Edom, Ammon, and Moab at the time of the
exodus, as well as the accounts of her victories over Sihon and Og,
belong essentially to the Deuteronomistic stratum of the Old
Testament. Moreover, the diversity and inconsistencies of the
relevant passages suggest that more than one stage of
Deuteronomistic compilation and/or redaction was involved. It is
difficult to assess the historicity of the reports regarding the treatment Israel received from Edom, Ammon, and Moab, since these
reports are clearly influenced by Deuteronomistic ideology and in
conflict with each other. The claim that Israel gained immediate
and full possession of the central and northern Transjordan by
defeating Sihon and Og is probably an exaggeration or entirely
fanciful. Regarding the traditionally Moabite territory north of the
Arnon, for example, which Sihon supposedly had taken from Moab,
certain non-Deuteronomistic passages testify to the fact that this
territory was in Moabite hands during the period of the Judges (see
Judg. 3.12–13 and further evidence collected by Noth, 1971, 396–
408). Also, comparison of the song in Numbers 21.27–30 with the
alternate version in Jeremiah 48.45–7 reveals that it originally had
nothing to do with a victory of Sihon over Moab. No doubt the song
does commemorate an ancient victory over Moab, and Numbers
21.27 does indeed call Heshbon 'the city of Sihon'. But aside from
the redactional verses which incorporate the Numbers version into
its present context (Num. 21.26 and 31) and the secondary phrase in
verse 19c, there is nothing in the song to suggest that it commemorates a victory by Sihon over Moab. Note that this phrase, 'to an
Amorite king, Sihon', disrupts the metre of the song and does not
appear in the Jeremiah version. More likely this old song commemorates an Israelite victory over Moab, possibly during David's
reign (see Bartlett, 1969; Mowinckel, 1964, 54; as well as Van Seters,
194 n. 30, who argues that the song could be late post-exilic in
origin).

Numbers 32. Early materials embedded in Numbers 32 stand as further warning that the Deuteronomistic presentation of the conquest
of the Transjordan is somewhat fanciful. Commentators generally
recognize that material from one or more of the older Genesis–
Numbers sources has been incorporated into this chapter, and
usually point to verses 39 and 41–2 as the most obvious traces of 'J'
or 'E'. Recently the chapter has been subjected to an exceedingly
detailed and penetrating analysis by Mittmann, who identifies as its
oldest literary core verses 1, 16–17b, 34–9, 41–2.

Now the sons of Reuben and the sons of Gad had a very great multitude of cattle; and they saw the land of Jazer ... and behold the place was a place for cattle ... and said, 'We will build sheepfolds here for our flocks, and cities for our little ones, but we will take up arms, ready to go before the people of Israel, until we have brought them to their place.' ... And the sons of Gad built Dibon, Ataroth, Aroer, Atroth-shophan ... And the sons of Reuben built Heshbon, Elealeh, Kiriathaim, Nebo, Baal-meon ..., and Sibmah; and they gave names to the cities which they built. And the sons of Machir the son of Manasseh went to Gilead and took it, and dispossessed the Amorites who were in it ... And Jair the son of Manasseh went and took their villages, and called them Havvoth-jair. And Nobah went and took Kenath and its villages, and called it Nobah, after his own name.

This core account is to be assigned to 'J' or 'E', in Mittmann's opinion; and he suspects that even this core represents an expanded tradition which originally had to do only with Reuben's settlement of the land of Jazer (Mittmann, 1975, 95–107).

Whether or not one accepts Mittmann's conclusions in every detail, it is obvious that the chapter incorporates old traditions which do not presume that Israel gained possession of the Transjordan as a result of an initial and complete conquest by a unified Israel under Joshua. On the contrary, these traditions reflect the same situation as Judges 1. There seems to be a pan-Israelite consciousness (see Num. 32.17b; Judges 1.1b–2), but Israel's taking possession of the land is viewed as having been primarily a matter of individual tribal actions. Note also that, according to Mittmann's reconstruction, Reuben's (and Gad's?) occupation of the land of Jazer would have been a process of peaceful settlement involving the building of sheepfolds and cities rather than warfare.

One would assume from the present literary context of these traditions that they pertain to tribal movements which occurred during Moses' career and before the main body of Israel had crossed the Jordan westward. However, Judges 10.3–4 must be taken into account, which states that Havvoth-jair was named after a Gileadite judge who supposedly lived during the period of the judges. Also certain other passages may be taken to suggest that the Israelite settlement of the Transjordan occurred after Israel had already gained a foothold west of the Jordan and was largely a movement from west to east. Joshua 15.6 and 18.17 refer to 'the stone of Bohan, the son of Reuben' which was located not far from Jericho on the west side of the Jordan. This may suggest that Reubenites were settled in that vicinity at one time. The Song of Deborah in Judges

5, which commemorates an early Israelite victory west of the Jordan, mentions both Reuben and Machir.

Judges 12.1–6 describes a tribal conflict in connection with which Ephraimites crossed over the Jordan and fought against Gileadites. Verse 4 is obscure: 'Then Jephthah gathered all the men of Gilead and fought with Ephraim; and the men of Gilead smote Ephraim, because they said, "You are fugitives of Ephraim, you Gileadites, in the midst of Ephraim and Manasseh."' One naturally presumes that it was the Gileadites who called the Ephraimites 'fugitives' (or perhaps better translated 'survivors'), since the narrative goes on to report the tactics used by the Gileadites to capture and kill the Ephraimite survivors of the battle. But an alternate interpretation of the verse has the Ephraimites referring to the Gileadites as 'fugitives of Ephraim', their point being that the Gileadites did not deserve to be considered an autonomous tribe since they were but fugitives or renegades from Ephraim and Manasseh (e.g., *Ewald, II, 299–303). This second interpretation implies, of course, that Gilead had been settled by Ephraimites and Manassites from the west. (Note in this regard that 'the forest of Ephraim' mentioned in II Sam. 18.6 apparently was located in Transjordan.)

Joshua 17.14–18 is an equally obscure passage also open to more than one interpretation. K. Budde advanced the ingenious hypothesis that this passage, along with Numbers 32.39, 41 f. and Joshua 13.13, belongs to a single literary source which was fragmented during the process of the compilation of the hexateuch. Reconstructed according to his hypothesis, the following sequence emerges:

Joshua 17.14–18: The house of Joseph complained that their inheritance in the west-Jordanian hill country was not large enough. Joshua agreed and instructed them to expand into the forest. The reference here would not be to the forests of the hill country west of the Jordan, since the Josephites already were settled there, but to the forests east of the Jordan.

Numbers 32.39, 41–2: Then Machir, Jair, and Nobah, all of them Manassite clans, crossed the Jordan into Gilead, took villages, built others, and named them after themselves. This would have occurred after the Mosaic period, which reduces the apparent chronological conflict between Numbers 32.41 and Judges 10.3 f.

Joshua 13.13: Yet the people of Israel (i.e., represented by these three Manassite clans) did not drive out the Geshurites or the Maacathites, who continued to dwell among them.

Budde's hypothesis, widely accepted by earlier critics, has been dropped from more recent discussion due largely to the influence of Noth's Deuteronomistic History hypothesis which denied any source connection between Genesis–Numbers and Deuteronomy–II Kings. Yet the idea that Joshua 17.14–18 anticipates colonization of the Transjordan from the west has lingered on, sometimes supported by the rather forced argument that 'the land of the Perizzites and the Rephaim' must have been situated east of the Jordan (e.g., Noth, 1937, 107; Soggin, 1972 (see A v below), 183).

(*v*) *Joshua 1–12*

A. **Alt**, 'Josua', *Werden und Wesen des Alten Testaments*, ed. P. Volz et al., BZAW 66, 1936, 13–29 = his *KS* I, 1953, 176–92; A. G. **Auld**, 'Judges I and History: a Reconsideration', *VT* XXV, 1975, 261–85; M. A. **Beek**, 'Josua und Retterideal', *Near Eastern Studies*, 1971, 35–42; J. **Blenkinsopp**, 'Are There Traces of the Gibeonite Covenant in Deuteronomy?', *CBQ* XXVIII, 1966, 207–19; idem, *Gibeon and Israel: The Role of Gibeon and the Gibeonites in the Political and Religious History of Early Israel*, SOTMS 2, 1972; B. S. **Childs**, 'The Etiological Tale Re-examined', *VT* XXIV, 1974, 387–97; J. **Dus**, 'Gibeon – eine Kultstätte des Šmš und die Stadt des benjaminitischen Schicksals', *VT* X, 1960, 353–74; idem, 'Die Analyse zweier Ladeerzählungen des Josuabuches (Jos 3–4 und 6)', *ZAW* LXXII, 1960, 107–34; K. **Elliger**, 'Josua in Judäa', *PJB* XXX, 1934, 47–71; F. C. **Fensham**, 'The Treaty between Israel and the Gibeonites', *BA* XXVII, 1964, 96–100; V. **Fritz**, 'Die sogenannte Liste der besiegten Könige in Josua 12', *ZDPV* LXXXV, 1969, 136–61; idem, 'Das Ende der spätbronzezeitlichen Stadt Hazor Stratum XIII und die biblische Überlieferung in Josua 11 und Richter 4', *UF* V, 1973, 123–39; J. **Halbe**, 'Gibeon und Israel', *VT* XXV, 1975, 613–41; M. **Haran**, 'The Gibeonites, the Nethinim and the Sons of Solomon's Servants', *VT* XI, 1961, 159–69; H. W. **Hertzberg**, 'Adonibezek', *JPOS* VI, 1926, 213–21 = his *Beiträge zur Traditionsgeschichte und Theologie des Alten Testaments*, Göttingen: Vandenhoeck & Ruprecht 1962, 28–35; G. H. **Jones**, '"Holy War" or "Yahweh War"?', *VT* XXV, 1975, 642–58; C. A. **Keller**, 'Über einige alttestamentliche Heiligtumslegenden', *ZAW* LXVII, 1955, 141–68; LXVIII 1956, 85–97; J. **Liver**, 'The Literary History of Joshua IX', *JSS* VIII, 1963, 227–43; N. **Lohfink**, 'Die deuteronomistische Darstellung des Übergangs der Führung Israels von Moses auf Josue', *Scholastik* XXXVII, 1962, 32–44; B. O. **Long**, 'Etymological Etiology and the Dt. Historian', *CBQ* XXXI, 1969, 35–41; D. J. **McCarthy**, 'The Theology of Leadership in Joshua 1–9', *Bib* LII, 1971, 165–75; idem, 'Some Holy War Vocabulary in Joshua 2', *CBQ* XXXIII, 1971, 228–30; F. **Maass**, 'Hazor und das Problem der Landnahme', *Von Ugarit nach Qumran*, 1958, 105–17; B. **Maisler** (Mazar), 'Beth She'arim, Gaba, and Harosheth of the Peoples', *HUCA* XXIV, 1952–3, 75–84; K. **Möhlenbrink**, 'Die Landnahmesagen des

Buches Josua', *ZAW* XV, 1938, 238–68; M. **Noth**, 'Bethel und Ai', *PJB*
XXXI, 1935, 7–29 = his *Aufsätze* I, 1971, 210–28; idem, 'Die fünf Könige
in des Höhle von Makkeda', *PJB* XXXIII, 1937, 22–36 = his *Aufsätze* I,
281–93; idem, *Das Buch Josua*, HAT 7, 1938, ³1971; W. M. **Roth**,
'Hinterhalt und Scheinflucht (Der stammespolemische Hintergrund von Jos
8)', *ZAW* LXXV, 1963, 296–304; P. P. **Saydon**, 'The Crossing of the
Jordan, Jos. chaps. 3 and 4', *CBQ* XII, 1950, 194–207; K.-D. **Schunck**,
*Benjamin. Untersuchungen zur Entstehung und Geschichte eines israelitischen
Stammes*, BZAW 86, 1963; J. A. **Soggin**, 'Kultätiologische Sagen und
Katechese im Hexateuch', *VT* X, 1960, 341–7 = 'Cultic–Aetiological
Legends and Catechesis in the Hexateuch', in his *OT Studies*, 1975, 72–7;
idem, 'Gilgal, Passah und Landnahme. Eine neue Untersuchung des kulti-
schen Zusammenhangs der Kap. III–VI des Josuabuches', *SVT* XV, 1966,
263–77; idem, *Joshua: A Commentary*, OTL, 1972; G. M. **Tucker**, 'The
Rahab Saga (Joshua 2): Some Form-Critical and Traditio-Historical
Observations', *The Use of the Old Testament in the New and Other Essays*
(Festschrift W. F. Stinespring), ed. J. M. Efrid, Durham: Duke University
Press 1972, 66–86; E. **Vogt**, 'Die Erzählung vom Jordanübergang, Josue 3–
4', *Bib* XLVI, 1965, 125–48; M. **Weippert**, '"Heiliger Krieg" in Israel und
Assyrien. Kritische Anmerkungen zu Gerhard von Rads Konzept des
"Heiligen Krieges im alten Israel"', *ZAW* LXXXIV, 1972, 460–93; G. J.
Wenham, 'The Deuteronomic Theology of the Book of Joshua', *JBL* XC,
1971, 140–8; J. A. **Wilcoxen**, 'Narrative Structure and Cult Legend: A
Study of Joshua 1–6', *Transitions in Biblical Scholarship*, ed. J. C. Rylaars-
dam, Chicago: University of Chicago Press 1968, 43–70; Y. **Yadin**, *Hazor:
The Head of All Those Kingdoms*, 1972.

Three major stages are discernible in the transmission history of
Joshua 1–12. The individual narratives which represent the core of
these chapters appear to have originated and circulated for a time
independently. Later, perhaps gradually, they were combined to
form a narrative cycle pertaining to the conquest. Finally the narrative cycle was edited and incorporated into the Deuteronomistic
survey of Israel's history (see, e.g., Möhlenbrink, Noth, 1971, 11–13,
Tucker). Scholars are widely divided in their opinion regarding
whether (or to what extent) these narratives preserve memories of
actual Israelite conquests. Certainly as the narratives stand now they
reflect strong aetiological, liturgical, and theological interests which
tend to detract from their historical reliability (see, e.g., Noth, 1935;
Soggin, 1960, 1966; McCarthy). Also, since they focus largely on the
small tribal territory of Benjamin, one must suspect that the concept
of a pan-Israelite conquest under the leadership of Joshua (an
Ephraimite) has been superimposed artificially.

The accounts of the conquests of Jericho (Joshua 6.1–21) and Ai

(7.2–5; 8) are similar in a number of ways. For example, each has been intertwined redactionally with another story: the Jericho account with a Rahab story (2.1–24; 6.17, 22–6) and the Ai account with the story of Achan's sin (7.1, 6–26). Both accounts reflect the 'Holy War' motif – i.e., the account of the conquest of Jericho emphasizes that Israel's victories were to be granted by Yahweh and were in no way dependent upon human might, while the description of the initial defeat at Ai illustrates Israel's helplessness when the 'Holy War' regulations were not maintained and Yahweh refused to act in Israel's behalf. Also the two accounts provide related aetiological explanations for two prominent ruins which stand in close proximity to each other (present-day *Tell es-Sulṭân* and *et-Tell*). The accounts claim that both ruins are the remains of Canaanite cities destroyed by Joshua. Archaeological evidence to be discussed below casts considerable doubt upon the validity of this claim.

Certain noticeable tensions in Joshua 9, the account of the establishment of a covenant with the Gibeonite league (Gibeon, Chephirah, Beeroth, and Kiriath-jearim), suggest that this account has been modified and expanded during the process of transmission. Note, for example, the lack of clarity as to whether it was Joshua or 'the men of Israel' in charge of the negotiations. Also to be taken into account are other Old Testament passages which indicate that, in spite of an attempt by Saul to destroy the Gibeonites (II Sam. 4.1–3; 21.1–14), Gibeon served as an important cultic centre during Solomon's reign (I Kings 3.3–15; I Chron. 21.29; II Chron. 1.3–5). Thus it is reasonable to suppose that the narrative in Joshua 9 harks back to an actual covenant which existed between early Israel and the Gibeonites. But possibly it depicted the Gibeonite covenant in a more positive light at first. Later this covenant would have become increasingly problematic for Israel, in the light of Saul's pogrom and especially of the Deuteronomistic insistence upon non-pagan centralized worship in Jerusalem. Correspondingly, the narrative would have been modified during the process of retelling so as to lay blame for the covenant upon Gibeonite trickery and thus to justify Israel's ill-treatment of the Gibeonites (see Liver; Blenkinsopp, 1966; Soggin, 1972, 106–15).

At least three separate traditions have been combined in Joshua 10: an account of the defeat of a coalition of kings led by Adoni-zedek of Jerusalem (vv. 1–15); an account of the execution of five kings at Makkedah (vv. 16–27); and an account of a military campaign into the Shephelah and southern hill country (vv. 28–43). The Adoni-zedek tradition is clearly related traditio-historically to the

account of Judah's defeat of Adoni-bezek in Judges 1.4–8. Both kings
are associated with Jerusalem; and their names are strikingly similar,
which raises the possibility that we are dealing with a textual corruption rather than with two different names. Perhaps both accounts
represent variant versions of a single tradition which originally
involved either an Adoni-zedek of Jerusalem or an Adoni-bezek of
Bezek (e.g., Auld). Another possibility is that they represent two
originally independent traditions which have fallen under the literary influence of each other (e.g., Hertzberg). The list of Adoni-
zedek's allies corresponds roughly to the list of cities conquered during the southern campaign, which suggests that one of the lists may
be largely dependent upon the other. But there are some significant
differences.

Adoni-zedek's allies (v. 3)	*Cities conquered (vv. 28–43)*
	Makkedah
Piram king of Jarmuth	Libnah
Japhia king of Lachish	Lachish (supported by Horam
	king of Gezer)
Debir king of Eglon	Eglon
Hoharm king of Hebron	Hebron
	Debir

Although the description of the southern campaign clearly is
influenced by the 'Holy War' concept and makes sweeping claims
regarding Joshua's conquests which are not very convincing, commentaries generally have concluded that it is based on an authentic
military itinerary (e.g., Elliger; Soggin, 1972, 129–32). But not all
concede the authenticity of the itinerary (e.g., Noth, 1937; Fritz,
1969), and those who do often doubt that the itinerary originally
had anything to do with Joshua. One of the obvious problems is the
appearance of Hebron and Debir in the list. In other passages, as
observed above, the conquest of these two cities is credited to
Caleb/Judah (Josh. 15.13–19; Judg. 9.1–15). K. Elliger argued that
the itinerary originally pertained to a series of Calebite conquests.
Actually it is not impossible that the itinerary pertains to an even
later period of Israel's history – e.g., Saul is credited with conquests
in the vicinity of Philistia and the Negeb (see I Sam. 14.47f., 52;
15.1–9).

Essentially the same is to be said of the account of Joshua's victory
over the northern kings (Josh. 11.1–15). The victory is credited to
Yahweh and described in the most general and sweeping terms.
Nevertheless, specific details do emerge which suggest that the account recalls an actual historical event. Specifically, we are told that

the coalition of northern kings was led by Jabin king of Hazor and included the kings of Madon, Shimron, and Achshaph. These kings encamped at the waters of Merom, where they were defeated by Israel and chased 'as far as Great Sidon and Misrephoth-maim, and eastward as far as the valley of Mizpeh'. Finally, in a rather generalized account (vv. 10–15), we are told that Joshua turned back and took Hazor, smote its king and all its inhabitants, and burned the city. A question as to whether the battle remembered in this narrative should be associated with Joshua is raised by the fact that Judges 4 identifies Jabin as the ruler of Hazor during Deborah's day. 'And Yahweh sold them into the hand of Jabin king of Canaan, who reigned in Hazor; the commander of his army was Sisera . . .' (Judg. 4.2). How could this be if Joshua already had killed Jabin and burned Hazor? Two observations should be made. First, with regard to the account of Joshua's victory over the northern coalition, the concluding verses which describe his taking and burning of Hazor (Josh. 11.10–15) are especially general, sweeping, and even somewhat anti-climactic. One is surprised, moreover, in view of the fact that Jabin is introduced by name already in verse 1, to find the king of Hazor referred to anonymously in verse 10. Possibly the report of the taking and burning of Hazor does not belong to the historical core of the account. Secondly, it is noteworthy that Jabin plays no specific role in the account of Deborah's battle and that the scene of the battle was some distance from Hazor. A number of scholars have concluded, accordingly, that the reference to Jabin in Judges 4.2 is a secondary gloss (e.g., Fritz, 1973; Yadin, 131f.).

The summary of Israel's initial conquests west of the Jordan (Josh. 12.7–24) is recorded in a formulary style which actually refers to the king of each city rather than to the city itself. Literally it reads: 'The king of Jericho, one; the king of Ai which is beside Bethel, one; the king of Jerusalem, one; etc.' Almost half of the cities whose kings are listed here appear for the first time in connection with the conquest (Geder, Adullam, Tappuah, etc.). The conquests of three of the cities are recorded in later contexts and not credited to Joshua (Jerusalem, see Judg. 1.8; II Sam. 5.6–10; I Chron. 11.4–9; Bethel, see Judg. 1.22–6; Gezer, see I Kings 9.16f.). Four of the cities are listed in Judges 1 among those whose inhabitants the Israelites were unable or unwilling to drive out (Jerusalem, Taanach, Megiddo, Dor). Probably this summary is based on an independent list of some sort, and a fairly strong case can be made for associating it with the period of king Solomon (Fritz, 1969).

(*vi*) *Joshua 13–22*

Y. **Aharoni**, 'The Province-list of Judah', *VT* IX, 1959, 225–46; idem,
Land of the Bible, 1967; W. F. **Albright**, 'The List of Levitic Cities', *Louis
Ginzberg Jubilee Volume*, New York 1945, 49–73; A. **Alt**, 'Judas Gaue unter
Josia', *PJB* XXI, 1925, 100–16 = his *KS* II, 1953, 276–88; idem, 'Das
System der Stammesgrenzen im Buche Josua', *Beiträge zur Religionsgeschichte
und Archäologie Palästinas* (Festschrift Ernst Sellin), Leipzig: A. Deichert
1927, 13–24 = his *KS* I, 1953, 193–202; idem, 'Festungen und Levitenorte
im Lande Juda', *KS* II, 1953, 306–15; A. G. **Auld**, 'Judges I and History: a
Reconsideration', *VT* XXV, 1975, 261–85; F. M. **Cross** and G. E.
Wright, 'The Boundary and Province Lists of the Kingdom of Judah', *JBL*
LXXV, 1956, 202–26; G. **Fohrer**, 'Altes Testament – "Amphiktyonie"
und "Bund"?', *TLZ* XCI, 1966, 801–16, 893–904 = his *Studien*, 1969, 84–
119; A. H. J. **Gunneweg**, *Leviten und Priester*, FRLANT 89, 1965; Z. **Kallai
(-Kleinmann)**, 'The Town Lists of Judah, Simeon, Benjamin and Dan',
VT VIII, 1958, 134–60; B. **Mazar**, 'The Cities of the Priests and Levites',
SVT VII, 1960, 193–205; S. **Mowinckel**, *Zur Frage nach dokumentarischen
Quellen in Joshua 13–19*, Oslo 1946; M. **Noth**, *Das System der zwölf Stämme
Israels*, BWANT IV/1, 1930; idem, 'Studien zu den historisch-
geographischen Dokumenten des Josuabuches', *ZDPV* LVIII, 1935, 185–
255 = his *Aufsätze* I, 1971, 229–80; K.-D. **Schunck**, *Benjamin*, BZAW 86,
1963; M. **Weippert**, 'Das geographische System der Stämme Israels', *VT*
XXIII, 1973, 76–89.

The statement in Joshua 13.1a, 'Now Joshua was old and advanced
in years . . . ,' is repeated almost word for word in Joshua 23.1b,
which anticipates Joshua's farewell address in 23.2–16. Between
13.1a and 23.1b is a lengthy excursus which calls attention to certain
outlying territories which 'remained to be possessed' (13.1b–14),
reviews the tribal allotments assigned by Moses in Transjordan
(13.15–33), describes the allotments assigned by Joshua to the tribes
west of Jordan (chs. 14–21), and reports a misunderstanding which
occurred between them and the Transjordanian tribes soon after the
latter had returned to their homes (ch. 22; see Num. 32). Earlier
commentators were inclined to see these chapters as an essentially
Priestly excursus (note especially the 'P' elements in ch. 18; e.g., the
reference to the 'tent of meeting') with remnants of the older 'hexateuchal' sources (e.g., 13.13; 17.14–18). The more recent tendency
(see however Mowinckel) has been to agree with Noth that these
chapters represent a secondary appendix to the Deuteronomistic
history, yet one which also derives from Deuteronomistic circles
(note the Deuteronomistic character of the interim summary in
21.43–22.6).

In either case it is clear that the excursus is a patchwork of various sorts of materials, most of which cannot be considered pre-monarchical in origin. The city list in 15.20–61 + 18.21–8 almost certainly dates from the period of the divided kingdoms (Alt, 1925; Cross and Wright; Kallai; Aharoni, 1959). The levitical city arrangement described in chapter 21 may be entirely idealistic, and those scholars who do attribute some historicity to the account generally associate it with the united monarchy (Albright, Mazar) or with Josiah's reign and following (Alt, 1925; Gunneweg, 64). Alt's hypothesis that the boundary descriptions for Judah (15.1–12), Ephraim (16.1–8), Manasseh (17.7–10), Benjamin (18.12–20), Zebulun (19.10–14), Asher (19.24–9), and Naphtali (19.33 f.) are derived ultimately from a source which represented tribal claims during the late pre-monarchical period has been widely accepted with occasional modifications (Noth, 1935; Cross and Wright; Aharoni, 1967, 227–39). But this hypothesis is not without problems. Alt himself recognized that the boundary descriptions for even these seven tribes differ considerably both in character and in the extent of detail, and close examination has led more than one scholar to conclude that these descriptions are based on a plurality of sources from different periods (Kallai; Schunck, 149–53).

The idea that Israel was divided into twelve well-defined tribes during pre-monarchical times is itself probably artificial (see Fohrer in contrast to Noth, 1930), and some of the materials incorporated into Joshua 13–22 do not presuppose such an arrangement. We have seen already that 15.13–19 (= Judg. 1.9–15) is a specifically Calebite tradition which has been subsumed under Judah. Joshua 13.31 (especially when read with LXXA; see Num. 32.39 f.) suggests that Machir has been subsumed under Manasseh in similar fashion. The curious and probably very old tradition preserved in 17.14–18 refers to 'the tribe of Joseph', which the compiler(s) of the Joshua 13–22 excursus took to mean Ephraim and Manasseh (see 16.1; 17.1; also Gen. 48.5–22). Note, however, that the similar designation 'house of Joseph' appears to have been given broader application by the compiler(s) of Judges 1 (see Auld and below).

(vii) Judges 1

A. G. **Auld**, 'Judges 1 and History: a Reconsideration', *VT* XXV, 1975, 261–85; E. **Bertheau**, *Das Buch der Richter und Ruth*, KHAT, ²1883; K. **Budde**, *Die Bücher Richter und Samuel. Ihre Quellen und ihr Aufbau*, 1890; idem, 'Richter und Josua', *ZAW* VII, 1887, 93–166; C. F. **Burney**, *The Book of Judges: With Introduction and Notes*, London: Rivingtons 1918; G. **Dalman**,

'Die Stammeszugehörigkeit der Stadt Jerusalem und des Tempels', *Abhandlungen zur semitischen Religionskunde und Sprachwissenschaft* (Festschrift W. W. G. von Baudissin), ed. W. Frankenberg and F. Küchler, BZAW 33, 1918, 107–20; C. H. J. **de Geus**, 'Richteren 1:1–2:5', *VT* XXXVI, 1966, 32–53; H. **Haag**, 'Von Jahwe geführt. Auslegung von Richter 1. 1–20', *BL* IV, 1963, 103–15; B. **Mazar**, 'The Sanctuary of Arad and the Family of Hobab the Kenite', *JNES* XXIV, 1965, 297–303; E. **Meyer**, 'Kritik der Berichte über die Eroberung Palaestinas (Num. 20, 14 bis Jud. 2, 5)', *ZAW* I, 1881, 117–46; J. M. **Miller**, 'Jebus and Jerusalem: A Case of Mistaken Identity', *ZDPV* XC, 1974, 115–27; G. F. **Moore**, *A Critical and Exegetical Commentary on Judges*, ICC, 1895; E. **O'Doherty**, 'The Literary Problem of Judges 1, 1–3, 6', *CBQ* XXVIII, 1956, 1–7; K.-D. **Schunck**, 'Juda und Jerusalem in vor- und frühisraelitischer Zeit', *Schalom* (Festschrift Alfred Jepsen), ed. K.-H. Bernhardt, AT I/46, 1971, 50–7; R. **Smend**, 'Das Gesetz und die Völker. Ein Beitrag zur deuteronomistischen Redaktionsgeschichte', *Probleme biblischer Theologie*, 1971, 494–509; M. **Weinfeld**, 'The Period of the Conquest and of the Judges as Seen by the Earlier and the Later Sources', *VT* XVII, 1967, 93–113; J. **Wellhausen**, *Die Composition des Hexateuchs und der historischen Bücher des Alten Testaments*, ³1899.

Judges 1 is surely one of the most tantalizing chapters in the Old Testament, at least from the perspective of literary critics and historians. Earlier literary critics were inclined to see it as an essentially unified piece and to assign it to 'J' or 'JE' (e.g., Meyer, Wellhausen). More recent scholars, due largely to the implications and popularity of Noth's hypothesis regarding the Deuteronomistic history, have had less to say regarding its possible connection with the Genesis–Numbers sources; and one recent study seeks to demonstrate that Judges 1 is a highly composite chapter designed to supplement, correct, and explain the Deuteronomistic presentation of the conquest and period of the Judges (Auld).

In any case, the chapter (with Judg. 2.1–5) disrupts the continuity of the Deuteronomistic presentation of Israel's early history and seems to deny the concept of an initial conquest of the whole land of Canaan by a unified Israel under the leadership of Joshua. Also, much of the material in the chapter is introduced piecemeal in the books of Numbers and Joshua in more or less different versions. We have noted already the double accounts of the naming of Hormah (see Num. 21.1–3; Judg. 1.16f.) and of the taking of Hebron and Debir (Josh. 15.13–19; Judg. 1.10–15), and observed that the Adonizedek and Adoni-bezek pericopes are somehow related (see Josh. 10.1–15; Judg. 1.4–8). Also the book of Joshua incorporates a slightly different version of the list of cities whose inhabitants the people of Israel 'did not drive out' (compare Josh. 15.63; 16.10; 17.11–13; 19.29b–30 with Judg. 1.27–29, 31). On the two occasions where materials presented in Joshua and Judges 1 are most nearly identical – i.e., the parallel accounts regarding the taking of Hebron and Debir, and the corresponding notations regarding the Jebusite remnant in Jerusalem – the Joshua version seems to have the strongest claim to authenticity. Joshua 15.13–19 correctly associates the taking of Hebron and Debir specifically with the Calebites and Othnielites (see above), whereas in Judges 1 this has been subsumed under the activities of Judah and Simeon and the report revised accordingly. It appears that Judges 1.21 has been revised intentionally to indicate that the men of Judah/Benjamin 'did not' (as opposed to 'could not', see Josh. 16.63) drive the Jebusites out of Jerusalem (Weinfeld). The same type of revision probably occurred in Judges 27–33. Also it seems certain on historical and geographical grounds that it was the people of Judah rather than of Benjamin who had to contend with the Jebusite inhabitants of Jerusalem (Miller).

The redactional change in Judges 1.21 from 'the people of Judah' to 'the people of Benjamin' may have occurred after the initial formulation of Judges 1, since the very position of the verse within the chapter also seems to presuppose that it pertains to the tribe of Judah. Note that the various materials introduced in the chapter are organized into two parts: first the matters pertaining to the conquest and settlement activities of Judah and Simeon (vv. 1–21), and then matters pertaining to the corresponding activities of the house of Joseph (vv. 22–36). In both parts materials which indicate successful conquest/settlement are introduced first, followed by qualifying and explanatory remarks.

vv. 1–17 The tribes of Judah (under which are subsumed the Calebites and Othnielites) and Simeon defeated Adoni-bezek, destroyed Jerusalem, took Hebron and Debir, settled in the Negeb near Arad, and destroyed Zephath which they renamed Hormah.

vv. 18–21 But Judah did *not* (read with the LXX) take any of the land of the Philistines or drive out the inhabitants of the plain or drive out the Jebusites from Jerusalem. Hebron was given to Caleb in accordance with Moses' command, and in fact it was Caleb rather than Judah at large who expelled the three sons of Anak.

vv. 22–6 The house of Joseph took Bethel.

vv. 27–36   But the Manassites, Ephraimites, Zebulunites, Asherites, Naphtalites, and Danites (all theoretically subsumed under the category 'house of Joseph') did not drive out the inhabitants of Beth-shean, Taanach, Dor, Ibleam, Megiddo, Gezer, Kitron, Nahalol, etc. Furthermore, the Amorites pressed the Danites back into the hill country and persisted in dwelling in Harheres, Aijalon, and Shaalbim; but the house of Joseph subjected them to forced labour.

Certainly this chapter contains very old and historically valuable material, but material which has undergone certain redactional modifications and is now organized artificially. This warns against any attempt to reconstruct an itinerary for a Judahite invasion on the basis of the chapter.

The Adoni-zedek/Adoni-bezek episode remains a mystery. The claim in Judges 1.8 that the men of Judah took Jerusalem is rendered unlikely by verse 21 and the testimony of II Samuel 5.6–10 (see I Chron. 11.4–9) which indicates that Jerusalem remained a non-Israelite stronghold until David's day. The conquest of Hebron and Debir seems to have been specifically a matter for the Calebites and Othnielites, who, as observed above, may have entered from the south. A similar situation exists with regard to the settlement of the Negeb near Arad and Hormah. The Kenites are said to have gone up with Judah 'from the city of palms into the wilderness of Judah'. Elsewhere Jericho is referred to as the city of palms (see Deut. 34.3; Judg. 3.13; II Chron. 28.15). Yet the related account in Numbers 21.1–3 presumes an invasion from the south, and there is some indication that there was an ancient site south of the Dead Sea which was known also as the 'city of palm trees' (i.e., from the *Mishnah*, Yebamoth 16.7, cited by Mazar, 300 n. 17). The single conquest credited to the house of Joseph in this chapter, the conquest of Bethel, is said to have been accomplished by subterfuge. The cities whose inhabitants the various northern tribes did not (or could not) drive out represent some of the oldest and most strategically located ones in the land.

B.   Other biblical materials

A. **Alt**, 'Erwägungen über die Landnahme der Israeliten in Palästina', *PJB* XXXV, 1939, 8–63 = his *KS* I, 1953, 126–75; C. F. **Burney**, *Notes on the Hebrew Text of the Books of Kings*, London: Oxford University Press 1903;

idem, *The Book of Judges*, 1918; P. C. **Craigie**, 'The Conquest and Early Hebrew Poetry', *Tyn Bul* XX, 1969, 76–94; O. **Eissfeldt**, 'Der geschichtliche Hintergrund der Erzählung von Gibeas Schandtat (Richter 19–21)', *Festschrift Georg Beer*, Stuttgart: W. Kohlhammer 1935, 19–40 = his *KS* II, 1963, 64–80; D. N. **Freedman**, 'Early Israelite History in the Light of Early Hebrew Poetry', *Unity & Diversity*, 1975, 3–35; H. **Gunkel**, *Genesis*, HAT, 1901, ⁵1964; M. D. **Johnson**, *The Purpose of the Biblical Genealogies*, SNTSMS 8, 1969; A. H. **Jones**, *Bronze Age Civilization: The Philistines and the Danites*, Washington: Public Affairs Press 1975; O. **Kaiser**, 'Stammesgeschichtliche Hintergründe der Josephsgeschichte', *VT* X, 1960, 1–15; S. **Lehming**, 'Zur Überlieferungsgeschichte von Gen. 34', *ZAW* LXX, 1958, 228–50; B. **MacDonald**, *The Biblical Tribe of Benjamin: Its Origin and Its History during the Period of the Judges*, Ph.D. diss., Catholic University of America 1974; A. **Malamat**, 'The Danite Migration and the Pan-Israelite Exodus-Conquest: A Biblical Narrative Pattern', *Bib* LI, 1970, 1–16; idem, 'The Aramaeans', *Peoples of OT Times*, 1973, 134–55; J. M. **Miller**, *The Old Testament and the Historian*, Philadelphia/London: Fortress Press/SPCK 1976; S. **Mowinckel**, '"Rahelstämme" und "Leastämme",' *Von Ugarit nach Qumran*, 1958, 129–50; J. **Muilenburg**, 'The Birth of Benjamin', *JBL* LXXV, 1956, 194–201; E. **Nielsen**, *Shechem: A Traditio-Historical Investigation*, Copenhagen, G. E. C. Gad 1955, ²1959; M. **Noth**, *Das System der zwölf Stämme Israels*, BWANT IV/1, 1930; L. B. **Paton**, 'Israel's Conquest of Canaan', *JBL* XXXII, 1913, 1–53; A. **de Pury**, 'Genèse XXXIV et l'histoire', *RB* LXXVI, 1969, 5–49; H. H. **Rowley**, *From Joseph to Joshua*, 1950; R. **Schmid**, 'Meerwunder- und Landnahme-Traditionen', *TZ* XXI, 1965, 260–8; K.-D. **Schunck**, *Benjamin*, BZAW 86, 1963; E. P. **Uphill**, 'Pithom and Raamses: Their Location and Significance', *JNES* XXVII, 1968, 291–316; XXVIII, 1969, 15–39; J. **Wellhausen**, *Prolegomena to the History of Ancient Israel*, 1885; Y. **Yadin**, 'And Dan, Why Did He Remain in Ships?', *AJBA* I, 1968, 9–23; H.-J. **Zobel**, *Stammesspruch und Geschichte. Die Angaben der Stammessprüche von Gen 49, Dtn 33 und Jdc 5 über die politischen und kultischen Zustände im damaligen 'Israel'*, BZAW 95, 1965.

The basic sources relevant to the Israelite conquest of Canaan are the narratives in Numbers 13–Judges 1. But certain other biblical materials also are relevant, or at least appear to be. For example, the numerous chronological notations scattered throughout Genesis–II Kings combine to form a chronological framework for Israel's early history which, if valid, would date the exodus from Egypt and the conquest of Canaan in about 1496 BCE and 1456–1451 BCE respectively. These dates are arrived at by beginning with the fall of Jerusalem in 597 BCE as a fixed point in the Julian calendar (this date fixed by the Babylonian Chronicle), figuring back with the regnal periods recorded for the kings of Judah (II Kings 24.18, 8;

23.36, etc.) to Solomon's founding of the temple (I Kings 6.1), and from there back to Exodus. Numbers 14.33 calls for forty years of wandering in the wilderness between the exodus and the conquest, and Joshua 14.7, 10 allows five years for the conquest.

This chronological framework is problematic, however, for several reasons: (1) The various manuscript traditions provide some significantly different readings for the crucial chronological notations (see the tables compiled by Burney, 1903, xlii–xliii and Johnson, 262–5). The dates given above were calculated on the basis of the Massoretic tradition. (2) There are internal inconsistencies within the biblical chronological data. For example, I Kings 6.1 (Massoretic tradition) indicates that 480 years elapsed from the exodus to Solomon's founding of the temple. But this is not enough time to allow for the forty years of wandering (Num. 14.33) plus five years for the conquest (Josh. 14.7, 10) plus the chronological requirements of the book of Judges (see the table compiled by Burney, 1918, l–li) plus the careers of Samuel, Saul, and David. (3) Early and mid-fifteenth-century dates for the exodus and conquest are too late to accommodate the traditional view that the Israelite exodus is to be associated with the expulsion of the Hyksos from Egypt (see Josephus, *Contra Apionem*, I 84–105) yet too early to square with Exodus 1.11, which identifies Pithom and Raamses as the cities of Israelite bondage in Egypt. Almost certainly any building project associated with these two cities would have occurred during the reign of Ramesses II (ca. 1304–1237) or one of his immediate successors (see most recently Uphill). (4) The chronological framework is highly schematic and reflects the influence of historical speculation during the Maccabaean period. This is especially obvious when one considers the figures supplied by the Massoretic tradition. These figures appear to have been calculated in order to emphasize four pivotal points in Israel's cultic history: the exodus which according to the scheme would have occurred at the end of two-thirds of a Great Year of 4,000 years, Solomon's founding of the first temple 480 years later, the end of the exile and dedication of an altar in Jerusalem after another 480 years, and finally the Maccabaean rededication of the second temple which would have ended the 4,000 years (Wellhausen, 308f.; Johnson, 32–6; Miller, 75–7).

Actually the whole arrangement of the materials in Genesis–II Kings appears somewhat artificial. This arrangement presumes that all Israel descended from Abraham the father of Isaac the father of Jacob and that the ancestors of all participated in essentially the same pre-monarchical history. Accordingly, this history is divided into quite distinct periods: the patriarchal sojournings in Palestine, the Egyptian bondage and exodus, the desert wanderings and conquest of Canaan, and finally the period of the judges. Close examination, however, reveals that the patriarchal narratives, if historical in any sense, are probably reflections of ethnic and tribal history rather than biography, and that the combination of the Abraham, Isaac, and Jacob traditions to form a continuous family story is a redactional device (see above, ch. II §2). The biblical account of the Egyptian bondage and exodus is equally problematic. Several scholars have concluded from their analyses of the exodus traditions that there were at least two different exoduses (see Rowley, 6 n. 1 for earlier positions along these lines; more recently Schmid and *de Vaux, 374–6), and it is generally held that no more than a small portion of the ancestry of later Israel actually participated in the Egyptian experiences in any case. We have observed that the concept of an initial conquest of the whole land of Canaan is an idealistic view confined to the later strata of Numbers–Joshua. The older materials in these books reflect individual tribal movements and occasional military confrontations primarily in the central hill country and indicate that much of the land remained 'unconquered' until Israel grew strong. That being the case, it would appear that the process of conquest and settlement actually continued into the 'period of the judges' and was not completed until the days of Saul and David.

These observations have significant implications for our study. On the one hand, it follows that any attempt to date the conquest which assumes that it occurred in direct sequence with the exodus is methodologically problematic. In fact the character of the Israelite occupation of Canaan may have been such as to preclude the assignment of an absolute date. On the other hand, some of the materials in the books of Genesis and Judges may have more direct relevance for the study of the conquest than their present literary contexts imply.

It is significant, for example, that the patriarchal genealogies and narratives presume a close connection between Israel's ancestors and the Aramaeans (see especially Gen. 25.20; 31.20 and also Deut. 26.5). This suggests that the origin and settlement of the Israelite tribes are to be understood within the broader context of the Aramaean movements (*Herrmann, 69–85; but see above, ch. III §1D). The origin of the Aramaeans remains obscure, but the written records as now available indicate their appearance near the end of the Late Bronze Age on the fringes of the Syro-Arabian desert where they established kingdoms which were to flourish contemporary with Israel and Judah during the Iron Age (Malamat, 1973).

One suspects that the distinction made between the Leah, Rachel, and concubine tribes (see especially Gen. 29.31–30.34; 35.16–21) also has something to say about their various origins and the process of their settlement in Canaan, although it is difficult to know just what. A number of earlier scholars were convinced that it was the Rachel tribes who participated in the Egyptian experience, in contrast to the Leah group; yet some contended that it probably was the other way around (see the various opinions summarized by Paton and Kaiser). The fact that Benjamin's birth is said to have occurred in Palestine, in contrast to those of the other brothers, has been taken as evidence either that the Benjaminites were an older Palestinian tribe which already had settled in the land before the Josephites arrived (so Muilenburg) or that they were but a southern offshoot of the Josephites (specifically of Ephraim) which achieved independent tribal status only secondarily (so Eissfeldt, MacDonald, and similarly Schunck). The tribal sayings in Genesis 49 and Deuteronomy 33 may shed some light on the early patterns of tribal settlement. Note that these sayings associate Zebulun and Issachar with the sea (Gen. 49.13; Deut. 33.18f.), and that the same is true of Dan and Asher in the song of Deborah (Judg. 5.17). Perhaps these tribes were once settled along the Mediterranean coast. Indeed, a fairly strong case can be made for viewing the Danites as a branch of the Sea Peoples in origin, specifically the Danuna (see Yadin, Jones, and below).

The negotiations between Jacob and the king of Shechem described in Genesis 34 have been taken as indicative of the kinds of peaceful arrangements worked out between the Canaanite city-states and the Israelite tribes during the latter's settlement of the land, even though in this particular case the outcome was not so peaceful (Alt, 146f.). This narrative along with the saying in Genesis 49.5–7 has also been taken as evidence that Simeon and Levi were once autonomous tribes settled in the vicinity of Shechem (see Gunkel, 371f., and works cited there; *Noth, 70f.; Nielsen, 259–83). Note that the saying characterizes Simeon and Levi as violent brothers (tribes) who, apparently because of certain violent and wanton acts, are (to be) scattered in Israel. It is tempting to see this characterization as reminiscent of the deed described in Genesis 34, where Simeon and Levi are said to have massacred treacherously all the males of Shechem. Also it corresponds to the tribal allotments in the book of Judges, where Simeon and Levi are allotted possessions within the bounds of those of the other tribes. However considerable caution is in order with regard to this line of thought. Genesis 34 is a composite account and there is reason to suspect that its references to Simeon and Levi are secondary glosses added in the light of Genesis 49.5–7 (Lehming, de Pury). The two other passages occasionally cited and indicative of early Simeonite and Levite settlement in the northern hill country, Judges 1.3–17 and 17.7–13, are not at all convincing.

The Samson stories in Judges 13–16 reflect a situation in which the Danites are dominated by the Philistines; and these stories are followed by an account of a Danite migration to northern Palestine in search of a new home (Judg. 17–18). We are told that the Danites fell upon the city of Laish; massacred its inhabitants and burned the city; and then rebuilt it, dwelt there and renamed it 'Dan' after their ancestor. This must be considered a 'conquest story' regardless of the fact that the biblical compilers associated it with the period of the judges (Malamat, 1970). Moreover, these stories in Judges 13–18 reaffirm the testimony of several passages already discussed, which suggest that the earliest Israelite settlement west of the Jordan was confined to the mountainous regions, and that even the Israelite foothold there was divided by non-Israelite enclaves which extended from the coastal plain into the hill country near Jerusalem. II Samuel 5.6–10 (see Josh. 15.63; Judg. 1.21) indicates that Jerusalem itself remained a non-Israelite stronghold until David's day. The narrative in Joshua 9 recalls an early treaty which allowed Gibeon and three nearby cities to remain autonomous. Judges 1.18 (LXX), 34–6 concede that Judah did not take the major cities of the Philistine plain, while the Amorites 'pressed the Danites back into the hill country' and 'persisted in dwelling in Har-heres, in Aijalon, and in Shaalbim'. Joshua's command to the tribe of Joseph related in Joshua 17.15 may be relevant here also: 'If you are a numerous people, go up to the forest and there clear the ground for yourselves in the land of the Perizzites and the Rephaim, since the hill country of Ephraim is too narrow for you.' The reference to the Rephaim may be intrusive to this verse and, as we have seen, some scholars insist that the land of the Perizzites and the Rephaim must have been in Transjordan. But the geographical proximity of the Perizzites and the Rephaim seems to be confirmed by II Samuel 5.18–20, which places Baal Perazim in the valley of Rephaim; and the valley of Rephaim clearly was located near Jerusalem in the general direction of the Philistine coast (see Josh. 15.8; 18.16).

The story in Judges 4 of the battle initiated by Deborah and fought in the vicinity of Megiddo and Taanach reaffirms the implication of Joshua 17.16b and Judges 1.27 that the valley of Jezreel remained in non-Israelite hands until fairly late in the period of the judges (see below, ch. V, pp. 314, 323). This means that the story of Deborah's victory also belongs to the conquest traditions. Moreover, some scholars have contended that the song of Deborah in Judges 5 is one of the earliest examples of Hebrew poetry and thus is an especially valuable source for the historian (Craigie, Freedmann). Note that the poem mentions only ten tribes: including Ephraim and Machir (but with no specific reference to Manasseh) and excluding Judah, Simeon, and Levi. However, the date of the battle depicted in Judges 4–5 cannot be determined exactly and perhaps should be placed late in the pre-monarchical period (see below, ch. V, pp. 313–14).

§2. EGYPTIAN SOURCES

W. F. **Albright**, 'A Prince of Taanach in the Fifteenth Century BC', *BASOR* XCIV, 1944, 12–27; idem, 'Northwest-Semitic Names in a List of Egyptian Slaves from the Eighteenth Century BC', *JAOS* LXXIV, 1954, 222–33; R. D. **Barnett**, 'The Sea Peoples', *CAH* II/2, 359–78; J. R. **Bartlett**, 'The Land of Seir and the Brotherhood of Edom', *JTS* XX, 1969, 1–20; idem, 'The Rise and Fall of the Kingdom of Edom', *PEQ* CIV, 1972, 26–37; idem, 'The Moabites and Edomites', *Peoples of OT Times*, 1973, 229–58; J. **Bottéro**, *Le problème des Habiru à la 4ᵉ Rencontre Assyriologique Internationale*, CSA 12, Paris: Imprimerie Nationale, 1954; J. **Černy**, 'Report on Inscriptions', *Lachish IV: The Bronze Age*, ed. O. Tufnell, London: Oxford University Press 1958, 133; E. **Edel**, 'Die Stelen Amenophis' II. aus Karnak und Memphis mit dem Bericht über die asiatischen Feldzüge des Königs', *ZDPV* LXIX, 1953, 97–176; W. F. **Edgerton** and J. A. **Wilson**, *Historical Records of Ramses III*, SAOC 12, 1936; R. **Giveon**, *Les bédouins Shosou des documents égyptiens*, DMOA 18, 1971; A. **Goetze**, *Kleinasien*, HAW III/1, 1933, ²1957; M. **Greenberg**, *The Hab/piru*, AOS 39, 1955; W. **Helck**, 'Die Bedrohung Palästinas durch einwandernde Gruppen am Ende der 18. und am Anfang der 19. Dynastie', *VT* XVIII, 1968, 472–80; idem, *Die Beziehungen Ägyptens zu Vorderasien im 3. und 2. Jahrtausend vor Christus*, ÄA 5, 1962, ²1971; F. W. **James**, *The Iron Age of Beth Shan*, Philadelphia: University of Pennsylvania Museum 1966; J. J. **Janssen**, 'Eine Beuteliste von Amenophis II. und das Problem der Sklaverei im alten Ägypten', *JEOL* XVII, 1963, 141–7; K. A. **Kitchen**, 'Some New Light on the Asiatic Wars of Rameses II', *JEA* L, 1964, 47–50; idem, 'The Philistines', *Peoples of OT Times*, 1973, 53–78; J. A. **Knudtzon**, *Die El-Amarna-Tafeln*, VB 2, 1907–15; E. **Macdonald**, J. L. **Starkey**, and L. **Harding**, *Beth-Pelet II*, London: British School of Archaeology in Egypt

1932; A. **Malamat**, 'Campaigns of Amenhotep II and Thutmose IV to Canaan', *SH* VIII, 1961, 218–31; idem, 'The Egyptian Decline in Canaan and the Sea-Peoples', *WHJP* I/3, 1971, 23–8, 294–301; B. **Mazar**, 'The Historical Development', *WHJP* I/3, 1971, 3–22, 291–3; C. F. **Nims**, *Thebes of the Pharaohs: Pattern for Every City*, London: Paul Elek 1965; M. **Noth**, 'Thebes', *AOTS*, 1967, 21–35; A. F. **Rainey**, *El Amarna Tablets 359–379. Supplements to J. A. Knudtzon, Die El-Amarna-Tafeln*, AOAT 8, 1970; B. **Rothenberg**, 'Notes and News', *PEQ* CI, 1969, 57–9; J. **Simons**, *Handbook for the Study of Egyptian Topographical Lists Relating to Western Asia*, Leiden: E. J. Brill 1937; S. **Smith**, *The Statue of Idri-mi*, OPBIAA 1, 1949; M. **Weippert**, *The Settlement of the Israelite Tribes*, 1971; idem, 'Semitische Nomaden des zweiten Jahrtausends. Über die *S3św* der ägyptischen Quellen', *Bib* LV, 1974, 265–80, 427–33; S. **Yeivin**, *The Israelite Conquest of Canaan*, UNHAII 17, 1971.

The Israelite occupation of the land of Canaan belongs to the Late Bronze Age and/or the beginning of Iron I, regardless of whether one favours an earlier date as suggested by the chronological framework of Genesis–II Kings or a later date based on such factors as the reference to Pithom and Raamses in Exodus 1.11, and whether one thinks in terms of a unified military entry or a gradual process of settlement and consolidation. An ever-increasing number of non-biblical written documents have become available during the past century which shed light on the political and sociological circumstances of the Near East during LB and Iron I – e.g., the Hittite texts from Boğazköy, the Ugaritic texts from Ras Shamra, and the various Egyptian documents from the Eighteenth to Twentieth Dynasties. The Egyptian documents shed the most direct light on circumstances in Palestine at the time, since Palestine was within the realm of strong Egyptian influence. The pertinent Egyptian documents fall roughly into four categories:

1. The scenes depicted and texts inscribed in hieroglyphs on the buildings and monuments left by the Pharaohs of the Eighteenth to Twentieth Dynasties. The most important of these are to be found at the site of ancient Thebes, which was the chief royal city of the Pharaohs of the Eighteenth Dynasty, except for Amenophis IV (Akhenaten), and remained an important official and religious centre throughout the Nineteenth and Twentieth Dynasties. Especially important for our purposes are the reports of the military campaigns of these Pharaohs into Syria–Palestine (*ANET*, 232–64), and the lists of peoples and cities conquered there (Simons). Noteworthy among the Egyptian inscriptions discovered elsewhere than Thebes are three stelae uncovered during the archaeological excava-

tions at Beth-shan: two from the reign of Sethos I and one from the reign
of Ramesses II (*ANET*, 255).

2. Letters written in Akkadian on clay tablets representing correspondence between the Egyptian court and vassal rulers of Palestine,
Phoenicia, and Syria. Almost all of the letters of this sort discovered
thus far derive from the reigns of Amenophis III–IV and were found
in the el-Amarna district of Egypt, the site of the royal residence of
Amenophis IV (Knudtzon; Rainey; *ANET*, 483–90). A much
smaller archive of letters, possibly from the reign of Amenophis II, was
discovered at Taanach (Albright; Malamat, 1969).

3. Miscellaneous papyrus texts from the Nineteenth Dynasty
which provide slight glimpses of the traffic between Egypt and
Palestine. Papyrus Anastasi III contains the notes of an official
situated on Egypt's north-eastern frontier, for example, and Anastasi
VI is a report from another frontier official regarding the passage of
Bedouin (*shasu*) tribes from Edom into the Nile Delta in search of
pasturage (*ANET*, 258f.). Anastasi I is a satirical letter from an
Egyptian official to a scribe in which he attempts to demonstrate the
scribe's incompetency by proposing various hypothetical situations.
Some of the situations described pertain to and shed light on circumstances in Syria–Palestine at the time (*ANET*, 475–9).

4. Miscellaneous inscribed objects from archaeological sites in
Palestine which testify to Egyptian presence there during the Late
Bronze Age: scarabs, finds bearing cartouches of the various
Pharaohs, etc. (see summary by Malamat, 1971). Numerous finds of
this sort associated with an Egyptian temple and pertaining to the
Pharaohs of the Nineteenth and Twentieth Dynasties have been
recovered at the ancient mining centre at Timna (Rothenberg). A
bowl found at Lachish bears a hieratic inscription which records the
deliverance of tribute in the form of produce to an Egyptian official
(Černý, 133). A jar found at Tell el-Far'ah (south) is inscribed with
the name of Sethos II (MacDonald et al., 28f.).

It will not be possible here to treat these Egyptian sources
individually, even though each has its own particular contribution to
make to a knowledge of the circumstances in Syria–Palestine during
the Late Bronze and Iron I Ages, as well as its own particular
interpretational problems. The following factors summarize the
evidence of these materials in so far as their contents are of importance to the history of Syria–Palestine.

The Canaanite city-states. These were fortified cities with surrounding
territories and smaller villages ruled over by hereditary kings. It

becomes apparent from the Egyptian texts, and is confirmed by archaeology, that these city-states were concentrated in the more fertile areas and along the important communication routes. This means that they were located primarily in northern Transjordan and in the lowlands west of the Jordan, in contrast to central and southern Transjordan and the central Palestinian hill country. There were a few notable city-states in the central hill country (e.g., Shechem and Jerusalem), but these appear to have been located at some distance from one another. Generally the Egyptians exercised their authority through the rulers of these city-states, occasionally replacing a local ruler with someone considered more reliable and loyal. Also garrisons of Egyptian and mercenary soldiers were placed in certain strategic cities (e.g., Gaza and Beth-shan). Tuthmosis III (1504–1450 BCE) was the first Pharaoh of the New Kingdom to succeed in gaining control of most of Syria–Palestine. During the latter part of the reign of Amenophis III (1417–1379 BCE) and during the reign of Amenophis IV (1379–1362 BCE) Egyptian authority in the area deteriorated. This is especially obvious from the Amarna letters. The rulers of the Nineteenth Dynasty, especially Sethos I (1316–1304 BCE) and Ramesses II (1304–1237 BCE), attempted with some success to reassert Egyptian authority. Merneptah (1237– (?) BCE) claims in the so-called 'Israel Stela' to have pacified all the lands of Syria–Palestine even as far as the realm of the Hittites. But this is clearly an exaggeration, and the Pharaohs which followed in the Nineteenth and Twentieth Dynasties played an ever-decreasing role in Syro-Palestinian affairs (Malamat, 1971).

The ethnic and social composition of the population of LB Palestine. The population of LB Palestine was ethnically heterogeneous and socially divided. This is illustrated by the lists of booty which Amenophis II claims to have derived from two military campaigns into Syria–Palestine (*ANET*, 245–7). He claims from the first campaign: '... *maryannu*: 550; their wives: 240; Canaanites: 640; princes' children: 232; princes' children, female: 323; ...' etc. Claimed for the second campaign (but see Edel and Janssen) are: '... princes of Retenu: 127; brothers of princes: 179; *'Apiru*: 3,600; living *Shasu*: 15,200; *Kharu*: 36,300; ...' etc. The princes and *maryanu* were the rulers and aristocracy of the city-states, while the *Kharu* (= *Huru* or Horites?) represent the general population. The Canaanites in this instance appear to be a specific group of some sort. This is suggested by the relatively small number of Canaanite captives indicated, and the fact that they were listed between the *maryannu* and the princes' children. Possibly they were wealthy citizens or merchants (Aharoni, 61 f., 156). The designation 'land of Canaan (*mât Kinaḫḫi*)' first appears in the inscription on the statue of Idrimi, king of Alalakh, in the mid-fifteenth century BCE, where it is understood to include a city on the Phoenician coast (Smith, 14 f., 72–4).

The *'Apiru* have received much attention from biblical scholars because of the possible etymological connection between the names ''*Apiru*' and 'Hebrew', and because the *'Apiru* first became known in modern times from the Amarna letters (discovered in 1887 and following) where they appear as disruptive elements among the Palestinian city-states. It seemed altogether reasonable at first to equate the *'Apiru* with the Hebrews and to see the Amarna letters as an extra-biblical witness to the Israelite invasion of Palestine. This would mean that the conquest occurred during the first half of the fourteenth century BCE, and for a while it appeared that a fourteenth-century date also was in accord with archaeological evidence from Jericho, Ai, and Hazor (see below). However it soon became apparent from other recovered texts that the *'Apiru* were not an ethnic group confined to fourteenth-century Palestine, but a social class which was present throughout the second millennium BCE and throughout the ancient Near East. Generally speaking, *'Apiru* seems to have been a designation for individuals or groups who stood outside the acknowledged social system for one reason or another, and thus were not afforded the legal protection which the system normally guaranteed its members (Weippert, 1971, 65). There were of course some variations in the use of the term (and the corresponding ideogram, SA.GAZ). Occasionally in the Amarna letters, for example, *'Apiru* seems to apply to anyone who challenged Egyptian authority. There is nothing to suggest that any of the *'Apiru* of the Amarna period were recent intruders into Palestine.

While present-day scholars generally agree that the *'Apiru* of the Egyptian texts and the Hebrews of the Old Testament cannot be simply equated, the possibility remains under consideration that there is some etymological and perhaps historical connection between the terms ''*Apiru*' and 'Hebrew'. The Old Testament depicts the patriarchs as 'sojourners' in lands inhabited by peoples with whom they did not identify and as tent dwellers who camped near cities to which they did not belong. In other words, with regard to their social status, it might be fair to say that the Old Testament depicts the patriarchs as *'Apiru*. On the other hand, there are passages in the Old Testament where the term 'Hebrew' may designate one's social or legal status rather than ethnic origin (for a discussion of these passages, see Weippert, 1971, 83–102).

Shasu seems to have been a general designation for the non-sedentary folk, whom the Egyptians encountered throughout Syria–Palestine and Transjordan (see Giveon; Weippert, 1974; and above, ch. III §1D).

The earliest references to Edom, Moab, and Israel. The lands of Seir are mentioned as early as the Amarna letters (*ANET*, 488) and there are references to *Shasu* from Seir in texts from the reigns of Ramesses II and III (Kitchen, 1964, 66; *ANET*, 262). Papyrus Anastasi VI from the late Nineteenth Dynasty (end of the thirteenth century BCE) provides a reference to *Shasu* tribes from Edom (see above and *ANET*, 259). Seir and Edom are closely associated in the Old Testament, but one need not assume that they were identical (Bartlett, 1969). Whatever their connection, the Egyptian texts seem to know Seir and Edom as the homeland(s) primarily of *Shasu* tribes rather than of sedentary peoples. This fact is not altered by the stela from Tell er-Raṭâba in the eastern Delta which describes Ramesses II as

> Making great slaughter in the land of (the) Shasu,
> He plunders their tells,
> Slaying their (people) and building with towns bearing
>   his name.
>   (Translation from Kitchen, 1964)

Moab appears in a brief topographical list from the reign of Ramesses II; and Kitchen (1964) has identified at Thebes (on a wall of the Luxor temple) what he believes to be the report of a military campaign undertaken by this Pharaoh into Transjordan. He translates the relevant lines of the inscription as follows:

Town which the mighty arm of Pharaoh, L.P.H., plundered in (the) land of Moab: B(w)trt. (Scene A.I)
Town which the mighty arm of Pharaoh, L.P.H., plundered: Yn(?)d . . . , in the mountain of Mrrn. (Scene B.III)
The t[own which] the mighty arm of Pharaoh, L.P.H., [plundere]d, of Tbniw (= Dibon). (Scene B.IV)

If Kitchen is correct, it would appear that already by the beginning of the thirteenth century Moab possessed a sedentary population with towns, one of which was Dibon. However Kitchen's reading is open to question. The first and third lines quoted above are original lines of a palimpsest, and Kitchen himself indicates that the names 'Moab' and 'Dibon' could be read only after prolonged study which involved some reconstruction of the text. Extensive archaeological excavations at the site of Moabite Dibon (there was also a Judaean Dibon; see Neh. 11.25) produced no evidence that the place was occupied before about the middle of the ninth century BCE, and this seems to be characteristic of other Moabite sites as well (see below). *B(w)trt, Yn(?)d,* and 'the mountain of *Mrrn*' are otherwise unknown.

Mention has been made above of the so-called 'Israel stela', in which Merneptah claims to have pacified all the lands of Syria–Palestine. Actually the inscription in this stela is a victory hymn which celebrates Merneptah's defeat of the Libyans. But the hymn concludes with a brief section pertaining to Syria–Palestine, which provides the first and only mention of Israel in early Egyptian documents (*ANET,* 376–8). The reference is to Israel as a people and the context places them in Palestine. Merneptah's victory over the Libyans occurred during the early 1230s BCE. Papyrus Anastasi I, the satirical letter, is probably to be dated near the end of the same century (*ANET,* 475–9). The letter refers in passing to one 'Qazardi the chief of Aser'. Again the context may suggest a Syro-Palestinian setting, which opens the possibility of a connection between this Aser and the Old Testament tribe of Asher (see Yeivin in response to Albright, 1954).

Note that the names 'Moab', 'Edom', and 'Israel' all make their first appearance in the Egyptian texts during the course of the thirteenth century. One should perhaps not make too much of this, especially since these references are isolated (Edom and Israel are mentioned once each; Moab possibly twice), and since the Egyptians may have used their terminology rather loosely. That is, the Egyptians may have subsumed for a long time under the loose terms ''*Apiru*' and '*Shasu*' various peoples whose descendants later were to be identified more specifically as Edomites, Moabites, or Israelites (Helck, 1968).

The Sea Peoples. We learn from the Egyptian documents of a movement of people which affected the lands bordering the eastern Mediterranean (Anatolia, Syria–Palestine, Egypt, Libya) beginning at least as early as the period of the Amarna letters and reaching a climax during the reigns of Merneptah and Ramesses III (i.e., from the first half of the fourteenth century to approximately 1200 BCE). The peoples involved seem to have originated in the area of the Aegean and Anatolia. As the movement reached a climax at the end of the thirteenth century, probably in more than one wave, these peoples brought to an end the Hittite empire (Goetze, 184–6), over-ran Cyprus (or part of it), and seized and destroyed numerous cities in Syria–Palestine (Carchemish, Alalakh, Ugarit, Tell Abu-Hawam, etc.). Finally, having regrouped in Syria, a confederation of these peoples pushed towards Egypt during the reign of Ramesses III. The confederation was composed of Philistines (Peleset), Tjekker, Sheklesh, Danuna, and Weshesh. Ramesses III claims to have defeated them during his eighth year (*ANET*, 262 f.) and to have 'settled them in strongholds, bound by his name' (*ARE*, 201).

This evidence is in keeping with what we know about the Philistines from the Old Testament – i.e., we find them settled in the southern coastal region of Palestine, where effective Egyptian rule probably continued for some years after Ramesses' victory, expanding from there into the central hill country, and associated with Beth-shan, which probably remained an Egyptian stronghold well into the Iron I period (James, 149–54). The Tjekker settled further north along the Palestinian coast in the vicinity of Dor, where they were encountered by Wen-Amun in approximately 1100 BCE (*ANET*, 25–9). Also, as we have already indicated, it is tempting to associate the tribe of Dan with the Danuna. This would presuppose that the Danuna also settled along the Palestinian coast, between the Philistines and the Tjekker. The Old Testament writers may have used the name 'Philistine' rather loosely on occasion, including within this category other elements of the Sea Peoples. It may be, for example, that the Philistines who fastened Saul's body to the wall of Beth-shan were actually Tjekker or some other group of the Sea People rather than the Philistines of the pentapolis (I Sam. 31.8–13; James, 136–8).

§3. ARCHAEOLOGICAL EVIDENCE

Y. **Aharoni**, 'Problems of the Israelite Conquest in the Light of Archaeological Discoveries', *Antiquity and Survival* II, 1957, 131–50; W. F. **Albright**, 'Further Light on the History of Israel from Lachish and Megiddo', *BASOR* LXVIII, 1937, 22–6; idem, *The Archaeology of Palestine*, 1949, ⁴1960; A. **Alt**, 'Megiddo im Übergang vom kanaanäischen zum israelitischen Zeitalter', *ZAW* LX, 1944, 67–85 = his *KS* I, 1953, 256–73; J. R. **Bartlett**, 'The Rise and Fall of the Kingdom of Edom', *PEQ* CIV, 1972, 26–37; C. **Bennett**, 'Umm el-Biyara-Pétra', *RB* LXXI, 1964, 250–3; LXXIII, 1966, 372–403; idem, 'Tawilân (Jordanie)', *RB* LXXVI, 1969,

386–90; LXXVII, 1970, 371–4; idem, 'Excavations at Buseirah, Southern Jordan', *Levant* V, 1973, 1–11; VI, 1974, 1–24; A. **Ben-Tor**, 'The First Season of Excavations at Tell-Yarmuth, 1970', *Qedem* I, Jerusalem: The Institute of Archaeology, The Hebrew University of Jerusalem 1975, 54– 87; J. A. **Callaway**, 'The 1964 'Ai (Et-Tell) Excavations', *BASOR* CLXXVIII, 1965, 13–40; idem, 'The 1966 'Ai (Et-Tell) Excavations', *BASOR* CXCVI, 1969, 2–16; idem, 'The 1968–1969 'Ai (Et-Tell) Excavations', *BASOR* CXCVIII, 1970, 7–31; idem, 'New Evidence on the Conquest of 'Ai', *JBL* LXXXVII, 1968, 312–20; W. G. **Dever** et al., *Gezer I: Preliminary Report of the 1964–66 Seasons*, Jerusalem: Hebrew Union College Biblical and Archaeological School in Jerusalem, 1970; idem, *Gezer II: Report of the 1967–70 Seasons in Fields I and II*, Jerusalem: Hebrew Union College/Nelson Glueck School of Biblical Archaeology 1974; T. **Dothan**, 'Archaeological Reflections on the Philistine Problem', *Antiquity and Survival* II, 1957, 151–64; idem, 'Review of O. Tufnell, *Lachish IV (Tell ed-Duweir): The Bronze Age*', *IEJ* X, 1960, 58–64; J. A. **Emerton**, 'Beth-shemesh', *AOTS*, 1967, 197–206; H. J. **Franken**, 'The Excavations at Deir 'Allā', *VT* X, 1960, 386–93; XI, 1961, 361–72; XII, 1962, 378–82; XIV, 1964, 377– 9; idem, *Excavations at Deir 'Allā*, I, Leiden: Brill 1969; idem, 'Tell es-Sultan and Old Testament Jericho', *OS* XIV, 1965, 189–200; idem, 'Palestine in the Time of the Nineteenth Dynasty. (b) Archaeological Evidence', *CAH* II/2, 331–7; V. **Fritz**, 'Erwägungen zu dem spätbronzezeitlichen Quadratbau bei Amman', *ZDPV* LXXXVII, 1971, 140–52; idem, 'Das Ende der spätbronzezeitlichen Stadt Hazor Stratum XIII und die biblische Überlieferung in Josua 11 und Richter 4', *UF* V, 1973, 123–39; idem, 'Erwägungen zur Siedlungsgeschichte des Negeb in der Eisen I–Zeit (1200– 1000 v. Chr.) im Lichte der Ausgrabungen auf der Ḥirbet el-Mšāš', *ZDPV* XCI, 1975, 30–45; N. **Glueck**, *Explorations in Eastern Palestine I–III*, AASOR 14, 1934, 1–113; 15, 1935; 18–19, 1939; idem, 'Transjordan', *AOTS*, 1967, 429–53; P. C. **Hammond**, 'Hebron', *RB* LXXII, 1965, 267–70; LXXIII, 1966, 566–9; LXXV, 1968, 253–8; G. L. **Harding** et al., *Four Tomb Groups from Jordan*, APEF VI, 1953, 27–41; S. **Horn**, 'The Excavations at Tell Hesban, 1973', *ADAJ* XVIII, 1973, 87–8; J. L. **Kelso**, *The Excavation of Bethel 1934–1960*, AASOR 39, 1968; K. M. **Kenyon**, *Digging up Jericho*, London/New York: Ernest Benn/Praeger 1957; idem, 'Jericho', *AOTS*, 1967, 264–75; K. A. **Kitchen**, 'The Philistines', *Peoples of OT Times*, 1973, 53–78; idem, *Ancient Orient and Old Testament*, London/Chicago: Tyndale Press/Inter-Varsity Press, 1966; M. **Kochavi**, 'Khirbet Rabûd = Debir', *Tel Aviv* I, 1974, 2–33; P. W. **Lapp**, 'The Conquest of Palestine in the Light of Archaeology', *CTM* XXXVIII, 1967, 283–300; F. **Maass**, 'Hazor und das Problem der Landnahme', *Von Ugarit nach Qumran*, 1958, 105–17; A. **Malamat**, 'The Egyptian Decline in Canaan and the Sea-Peoples', *WHJP* III, 1971, 23–38; J. **Marquet-Krause**, *Les fouilles de 'Ay(et-Tell) 1933–35*, Paris: Geuthner, 1949; S. **Mittmann**, *Beiträge zur Siedlungs- und Territorialgeschichte des nördlichen Ostjordanlandes*, ADPV, 1970; E. **Olávarri**, 'Sondages à 'Arô'er sur l'Arnon', *RB* LXXII, 1965, 77–94; LXXVI, 1969,

230–59; J. B. **Pritchard**, 'Excavations at el-Jib', *ADAJ* VI–VII, 1962, 121f.; VIII–IX, 1964, 86f.; idem, *The Bronze Age Cemetery at Gibeon*, Museum Monographs, Philadelphia: University of Pennsylvania 1963; idem, 'Excavations at Tell es-Sa'idiyeh', *ADAJ* VIII, 1964, 95–8; *Archaeology* XVIII, 1965, 292–4; XIX, 1966, 289–90; idem, 'Archaeology and the Future of Biblical Studies: Culture and History', *The Bible and Modern Scholarship*, 1965, 313–24; W. L. **Reed**, 'Gibeon', *AOTS*, 1967, 231–43; J. A. **Soggin**, 'La conquista israelitica della Palestina nei sec. XIII e XII e le scoperte archeologiche', *Protestantesimo* XVII, 1962, 193–208 = 'Archaeological Discoveries and the Israelite Conquest of Palestine in the Thirteenth and Twelfth Centuries', in his *OT Studies*, 1975, 11–30; O. **Tufnell**, 'Lachish', *AOTS*, 1967, 296–308; A. D. **Tushingham**, *The Excavations at Dibon (Dhībân) in Moab, the Third Campaign 1952–53*, AASOR 40, 1972; R. **de Vaux**, 'On Right and Wrong Uses of Archaeology', *Near Eastern Archaeology*, 1970, 64–80; M. **Weippert**, *The Settlement of the Israelite Tribes*, 1971; idem, 'The Israelite "Conquest" and the Evidence from Transjordan', forthcoming in the *The Era of Israelite Origins: Investigations in the Archaeology and Chronology of the End of the Late Bronze Age and the Beginning of the Early Iron Age*, ed. F. M. Cross (to be published by the American Schools of Oriental Research); G. E. **Wright**, 'Fresh Evidence for the Philistine Story', *BA* XXIX, 1966, 70–86; G. R. H. **Wright**, 'The Bronze Age Temple at Amman', *ZAW* LXXVIII, 1966, 350–6; Y. **Yadin**, 'Hazor', *AOTS*, 1967, 244–63.

The general archaeological features of Palestine during the Late Bronze Age were treated in ch. II. Some further comments are in order here regarding the end of LB and the transition to Iron I, since this is an especially crucial time for any reconstruction of Israel's origins. The name 'Israel' first appears in non-biblical documents at the very end of LB (Merneptah's 'Israel Stela') and by the middle of the Iron I period Israelite tribes had gained a footing in Palestine, as is evidenced by the narratives in the books of Judges and I–II Samuel.

Extensive socio-political disruption and turmoil throughout the Levant are characteristic of this period. The Sea Peoples were on the move during the latter part of LB. Egyptian authority declined rapidly in Palestine in the wake of their movements and was all but non-existent by the beginning of Iron I. The most significant artifactual features which mark the transition between LB and Iron I in Palestine are: (1) A number of the cities which had flourished throughout the Middle and/or Late Bronze Ages met with violent destructions at the end of LB (roughly the thirteenth century BCE). Notable among these are: Megiddo, Beth-shan, Hazor, Tell Abu Hawam, Aphek, Bethel, Gezer, Beth-shemesh, Tell Beit Mirsim,

Ashdod, Tell deir 'Alla (actually an undefended temple mound), and
possibly Tell el-Ḥesi. (2) Numerous villages sprang up in those areas
which show little or no evidence of earlier sedentary population
during LB, or where the LB cities were rather widely scattered – i.e.,
in the central Palestinian hill country, the lower Galilee, the north-
eastern Negeb, and central and southern Transjordan. Typical of
the villages which sprang up during Iron I and came to play an
important role in Israel's early history are Ramah, Shiloh, Geba
(Jeba'), and Mizpah (Tell en-Nasbeh). Small settlements also
emerged, sometimes after a brief occupational gap, on the ruins of
many of the destroyed Bronze Age cities. (3) Iron tended to replace
bronze for tools and weapons and the use of cisterns with non-porous
plaster linings rendered settlements less dependent upon a permanent water supply. Otherwise the material remains of the Iron I
settlements reflect a noticeable decline in technique and sophistication compared with those of the LB period.

Nevertheless, with one outstanding exception, the techniques and
styles of Iron I suggest more of a cultural continuum from LB than a
cultural break. This exception is the appearance of so-called
'Philistine pottery' at the beginning of Iron I (early twelfth century
BCE). Otherwise one would not conclude from the material remains
themselves that newcomers entered Palestine from the outside at any
particular time during LB or Iron I. Since Philistine pottery reflects
the influence of Aegean styles and emerges in Palestine at roughly
the same time and in the same area that the Philistines are known
from the Old Testament to have settled, it seems reasonable to
associate the one with the other. One must keep in mind, of course,
that the designation 'Philistine' may be used rather loosely in some
Old Testament passages. Thus I Samuel 31, which associates
Philistines with Beth-shan at the time of Saul's death, may actually
pertain to other elements of the Sea Peoples than the Philistines of
the pentapolis. This would explain the rather limited appearance of
Philistine pottery at Beth-shan (Kitchen, 1973, 61). On the other
hand, some allowance must be made for peaceful interaction
through ordinary trade and commerce between the Philistines and
their neighbours which would affect the ceramic distribution. Thus
the presence of Philistine pottery at Tell deir 'Alla does not necessarily mean that the Philistines expanded their political authority
east of the Jordan (Weippert, 1967, 132; against G. E. Wright,
1966).

Largely under the influence of Albright, whose work will be
discussed below, it has become commonplace among present-day

biblical scholars to state or imply that the wave of city destructions which occurred at the end of LB is attributable to the Israelite invasion under Joshua and to presume that the Iron I settlements which sprang up contemporary with or shortly after these destructions were by and large Israelite villages. This may not be entirely misleading. Obviously the turbulent times which marked the end of LB and the beginning of Iron I would have presented ideal circumstances for the Israelite tribes to enter Palestine and gain a foothold there. Nevertheless any attempt simply to equate the LB disturbances and rise of Iron I settlements on the one hand with the Israelite conquest and settlement on the other encounters serious difficulties.

1. As seen above, critical analysis of the biblical conquest traditions raises a prior question as to whether there was a unified Israelite invasion of such a magnitude as to have left archaeological traces. If one concludes that there was a forced Israelite entry into Palestine, the question still remains as to whether this entry involved the destructions of the major Bronze Age cities. Joshua 11.13 states that, with the exception of Hazor (this exception itself being somewhat doubtful from a literary-critical standpoint; see above), the Israelites did not destroy any of those cities which were situated on 'tells'. Judges 1.21, 27–36 lists a number of the major cities of the land (including Megiddo, Beth-shan, Gezer, and Beth-shemesh) whose inhabitants the Israelites did not or could not drive out. The Bible specifically identifies only four cities as actually having been destroyed and burned by the Israelites: Zephath/Hormah, Jericho, Ai, and Hazor.

2. The cities which do present archaeological evidence of having been destroyed at the end of LB are, for the most part, not the ones which figure prominently in the biblical conquest traditions. Hazor, Lachish, and Bethel are the only certain exceptions; Tell el-Ḥesi may or may not be biblical Eglon. On the other hand, archaeological evidence from the cities which do figure prominently in the conquest traditions indicates that most of them either made the transition from LB to Iron I without experiencing any major disturbance (Hebron, Debir = Khirbet Rabud; admittedly the archaeological evidence at both of these sites is meagre) or apparently were not even occupied to speak of during LB (Hormah, Arad, Heshbon, Jericho, Ai, Gibeon, Jarmuth).

3. Some of the LB destructions may have been due to localized causes. For example, the excavators of Tell deir ʿAlla (possibly biblical Succoth) traced the destruction of its LB phase to an earth-

quake soon after 1200 BCE (Franken, 1960–4). To the extent that there was a pattern of LB destructions which can be attributed to a common cause, it must be kept in mind that these destructions were not confined to Palestine, but occurred throughout the Levant and almost certainly are to be associated with the Sea Peoples. As seen above, these movements reached a climax during the latter part of the thirteenth century. The destructions at this time of the cities along the Palestinian coast are undoubtedly to be attributed to the Sea Peoples (e.g., Tell Abu Hawam, Jaffa, Tel Mor, Ashdod, Ashkelon; see Malamat, 1971, 29), but possibly also the destruction of such inland sites as Aphek, Lachish (Tufnell, 302), Beth-shemesh IV (Emerton, 199), Megiddo VII (Alt, Soggin), Beth-shan VII (Fritz, 1973, against James, 149), and Hazor XIII (Fritz, 1973). Also to be taken into account is Egypt's desperate attempt to maintain authority in Palestine in the wake of the Sea People disturbances. Merneptah in particular claims to have 'plundered Canaan with every evil' and implies successful military actions against Ashkelon and Gezer (see Dever, II, 50).

4. The biblical traditions which depict the Israelite tribes in the earliest stages of their occupation of those areas which are known archaeologically to have undergone a surge of sedentary population during Iron I reflect throughout an awareness that other peoples also were settled there and in some cases had established villages before the arrival of the Israelites (see, for example, Josh. 9; 11.2f.; 17.15, etc.). Thus the rise of the Iron I villages cannot be attributed simply to the Israelites; except, of course, in so far as one counts among the Israelites at this stage all the various groups which may eventually have been absorbed into Israel (Hittites, Hivites, Perizzites, Jebusites, Japhletites, etc.). Neither is it necessary to explain the rise of villages in those areas sparsely settled earlier in terms of an influx of population from outside Palestine. The appearance of these villages may have been due largely to socio-political and/or technological developments from within – e.g., the increased use of iron tools and the invention of plastered cisterns would have rendered it more feasible to clear the forests of the hill country and establish permanent settlements there. In fact, it has been argued recently that the archaeological evidence actually suggests a cultural expansion from the coastal plain eastward into the central hill country, rather than from Transjordan to the west (J. A. Callaway and L. E. Stager in unpublished papers).

In light of the above general archaeological considerations, it is now possible to re-examine the successive stages of the conquest as presented in the biblical account with specific attention to the available archaeological data relevant for each stage.

The attempted invasion of the Judaean hill country from the south (see especially Num. 14.24, 39–45; 21.1–3; Josh. 12.14; as well as Judg. 1.16f.). These passages presuppose the existence of Canaanite cities in the vicinity of Arad and Hormah at the time of the conquest, and Hormah is said to have been destroyed. The archaeological evidence currently available from the southern Judaean hill country and the north-eastern Negeb (i.e., south of Hebron with the exception of Khirbet Rabud) suggests a gap in sedentary occupation from MB II until Iron I. Arad was not reoccupied until the eleventh century BCE, although one or more of the sites which are possible candidates for Hormah may have been settled as much as a century earlier. (For a discussion and bibliography regarding the current status of archaeological research in this area and the various proposals regarding the location of Hormah, see Fritz, 1973, 1975).

The problem of passage through Edomite territory (Num. 20.14–29; 21.4–20; see also Num. 33.1–49; Deut. 2.1–8; Judg. 11.6–18). Glueck conducted extensive surface surveys in Transjordan during the 1930s and concluded that the area south of the Jabbok witnessed a gap, or at least a decisive dip, in sedentary occupation which extended throughout the Middle Bronze Age until soon before the end of LB. This was followed by a surge in sedentary occupation which began during the thirteenth century BCE, in Glueck's opinion, and which he believed corresponded to the rise of the kingdoms of Edom and Moab. More recent archaeological investigations in the territory of ancient Edom suggest a considerably later date for the surge in sedentary occupation. Three sites in central Edom (Umm el-Biyara, Tawilan, and Buseirah) have now been excavated by Bennett, none of which produced any clear evidence of sedentary occupation before the ninth century BCE. The results of her excavations at Buseirah are especially crucial for reconstructing Edomite history, since this is the site of Bozrah, the chief royal city of the Edomites (Gen. 36.33; Isa. 34.6; 63.1; Jer. 49.13, 22; Amos 1.12). Already before Bennett began her excavations at Buseirah, Bartlett had concluded from a re-examination of the written sources 'that whatever the strength of the early settlers of Edom, it is most unlikely that there was any national unity in Edom before the mid-ninth century BC' (Bartlett, 1972, 26). The results of Bennett's excavations at Buseirah seem to confirm Bartlett's conclusions. Recently Weippert re-examined the pottery collected by Glueck at forty Iron Age sites and conducted a small survey of his own with the following results:

Glueck's use of the term 'Early Iron I/II', therefore, in most cases can only mean that he had collected Iron Age pottery at a particular site. All the material up to now indicates that the main period of settlement in Edom must have been in Early Iron II, especially during the ninth to the seventh centuries. After this, a decline may be noted. Before the ninth century, the settlement of the land was gradual, first of all in the north. I know of six cities from the area between Wadi el-Ḥasa and approximately et-Tafileh which have Early Iron Age I pottery; from the south, however, only one site (Weippert, forthcoming).

There are no known LB sites south of Wadi el-Hesa.

The conquest of the central and northern Transjordan; the defeat of Sihon and Og (Num. 21.21–35; 32; Deut. 2.8–3.17). Both the Egyptian records and archaeological remains testify to the existence of cities and towns in northern and central Transjordan during LB, although these become increasingly scarce as one moves from north to south. The only Egyptian mention of towns south of Pella and Bostra are the questionable references to three Moabite towns, including Dibon, from the reign of Ramesses II (see above, §2). Mittmann's 1963–6 surface survey of the area between the Yarmuk and the Jabbok yielded fourteen LB sites. An LB–Iron I cemetery was discovered at Tell es-Saʿidiyeh (Pritchard, 1964–6), and the LB temple at Tell deir ʿAlla has already been noted. LB sites between the Jabbok and Wadi el-Hesa are extremely scarce, but they are not absent altogether. For example, a rather impressive LB building has been discovered at Amman (G. R. H. Wright; Fritz, 1971). Here again it appears that the surge in sedentary occupation began during Iron I rather than before the end of LB as Glueck believed.

Regarding the cities mentioned in Numbers 21 and 33 which can be located with some confidence, Ashtaroth and Edrei were situated in northern Transjordan and the former is referred to in Egyptian texts from as early as the reign of Tuthmosis III (1504–1450 BCE; *ANET*, 242). Medeba, Heshbon, Dibon, and Aroer were much further south where the evidence for sedentary population during LB is scarce. An LB tomb has been discovered at Medeba (Harding). Excavations at Heshbon have produced some sherds and a possible wall from the twelfth–eleventh centuries BCE, but the earliest clearly recognizable building phase began with the seventh century (Horn). The earliest occupational phase at Dibon was dated by the excavators 'to about the middle of the ninth century BC' (Tushingham,

93). Aroer was a small EB fortress situated on the edge of the gorge of Wadi el-Mojib (the Arnon) which apparently was restored and reused during the Iron Age (Olávarri).

The invasion of the central hill country (Josh. 1–9; see also Judg. 1.22–6). The Middle Bronze Age city at Jericho (Tell es-Sulṭân) was destroyed during the mid-sixteenth century BCE, possibly in connection with the expulsion of the Hyksos from Egypt. A few scanty remains from the mid-fourteenth century were found on the site, but no building remains. The next period for which the site yielded occupational remains is Iron II (Kenyon; Franken, 1965). The situation at Ai (et-Tell) is similar, except that the occupational gap extends from the end of the Early Bronze Age to the beginning of Iron I (from about 2000–1200 BCE). Moreover, the Iron I settlement apparently was no more than a small unfortified village (Marquet-Krause, Callaway). Occasional artifactual remains suggest some occupation at Gibeon (el-Jîb) during the Bronze Age, but the only indication of specifically LB occupation is the reuse at that time of seven MB tombs (Pritchard, 1963). Gibeon was an important city during the Iron Age, however, with the first phase of its fortifications beginning sometime during the twelfth century BCE (Pritchard, 'Excavations at el-Jib').

This archaeological evidence from Jericho, Ai, and Gibeon conflicts with the narratives in Joshua 1–9, regardless of whether one places the conquest during LB or at the beginning of Iron I. To be sure, the absence of occupational remains at a site for a particular period does not necessarily mean that the site was completely unoccupied during that period. Yet the narratives in Joshua 1–9, at least as they stand now, clearly presuppose that the three cities in question were more than simply occupied at the time of the conquest; they are depicted as flourishing and fortified (Josh. 2.15; 7.5; 10.2). It is difficult to believe that this was the case with Jericho, Ai, and Gibeon during LB and/or the beginning of Iron I and that their fortifications and all other structures disappeared without leaving archaeological traces.

The situation is quite different at Bethel (Beitin), where the remains of fortifications from the Middle and Late Bronze Ages as well as much cruder structures from Iron I have been discovered. The LB city ended in destruction, and the Iron I city appears to have been destroyed several times (Kelso). It is tempting to associate one or the other of these destructions with the taking of Bethel by 'the house of Joseph' described in Judges 1.22–6. Caution is in order at this point, however, since the passage does not necessarily imply that the Josephites actually destroyed the city.

The conquest of the southern cities (Josh. 10; see also Josh. 15.13–19; Judg. 1.4–15). The LB–Iron I periods at Jerusalem are not yet very well known, and archaeology sheds no light on the Adoni-zedek/Adoni-bezek episode or the claim in Judges 1.8 that the men of Judah fought against Jerusalem and took it. One season of excavations at Jarmuth has produced two sherds which possibly, but not certainly, are to be attributed to LB, and no pottery from early Iron I (Ben-Tor). Of the other six cities which Joshua is said to have conquered in the Shephelah and the southern hill country only Lachish, Hebron, and Debir can be located with some confidence and have been excavated. We have already identified Lachish (Tell el-Duweir) as one of the LB cities which was destroyed at the end of that age. Albright dated its destruction during Merneptah's reign, largely on the basis of a hieratic bowl inscription discovered there (Albright, 1937). But a Ramesses III scarab (ca. 1206–1175 BCE) was found at the site also, which led Tufnell to date the destruction during the first decades of the twelfth century BCE. In any case, Philistine pottery found in a nearby cave and certain tomb finds suggest continued activity at the site on into Iron I (Dothan). The excavations at Hebron (Jebel er-Rumeide), which were halted prematurely and have not been fully published, apparently produced little or nothing in the way of occupational remains between the Middle Bronze Age and late in Iron I (Hammond). Soundings at Debir (Khirbet Rabud) produced evidence which suggests that it was a relatively large and fortified city during LB and that its occupation continued into Iron I. But there is nothing to suggest any major disturbance at that time (Kochavi).

The defeat of the kings of the north (Josh. 11.1–15). A surface survey with occasional soundings conducted by Aharoni revealed a chain of LB cities in upper Galilee. South of this chain, where the terrain is more mountainous, there was little or no evidence of sedentary occupation until villages began to emerge at the beginning of Iron I (thirteenth–twelfth BCE in Aharoni's judgment). The villages seem to have emerged alongside the LB cities which themselves apparently made the transition into Iron I without major disturbances. The situation turned out to be quite different at Hazor. The huge LB city at Hazor (stratum XIII) ended in destruction and was superseded after a short break by a very poor settlement of what appears to have been little more than squatters (Strata XII–XI; Yadin). The pottery of Hazor XII corresponds roughly to that of the Iron I villages identified by Aharoni; but this does not justify Yadin's insistence that the destruction of Hazor XIII preceded entirely the emergence of the villages. Moreover, given the slight gap between Hazor XIII and XII, one need not and probably should not assume that it was the squatters of Hazor XII who destroyed Hazor XIII.

In summary, it may be said that the archaeological evidence confirms what can be deduced from the written texts; namely that the end of LB and the beginning of Iron I was a period of socio-political turbulence and change in Palestine. Otherwise no clear pattern is discernible in the presently available archaeological remains from the LB and Early Iron I periods which can be identified as artifactual data reflecting a specifically Israelite occupation of the land.

§4. POSSIBLE APPROACHES TO HISTORICAL RECONSTRUCTION

Y. **Aharoni**, *Land of the Bible*, 1967, 174–253; idem, 'New Aspects of the Israelite Occupation in the North', *Near Eastern Archaeology*, 1970, 254–67; idem, 'The Settlement of Canaan', *WHJP* I/3, 1971, 94–128; W. F. **Albright**, 'Archaeology and the Date of the Hebrew Conquest of Palestine', *BASOR* LVIII, 1935, 10–18; idem, 'Further Light on the History of Israel from Lachish and Megiddo', *BASOR* LXVIII, 1937, 22–6; idem, 'The Israelite Conquest of Canaan in the Light of Archaeology', *BASOR* LXXIV, 1939, 11–23; idem, 'Note to Engberg, "Historical Analysis of Archaeological Evidence: Megiddo and the Song of Deborah"', *BASOR* LXXVIII, 1940, 7–9; idem, 'Review of Lamon and Shipton, *Megiddo I* and Shipton, *Notes on the Megiddo Pottery*', *AJA* XLIV, 1940, 546–50; A. **Alt**, *Die Landnahme der Israeliten in Palästina. Territorialgeschichtliche Studien*, Leipzig: Reformationsprogramm der Universität, 1925 = his *KS* I, 1953, 89–125 = 'The Settlement of the Israelites in Palestine', *Essays*, 1966, 133–69; idem, 'Erwägungen über die Landnahme der Israeliten in Palästina', *PJB* XXXV, 1939, 8–63 = *KS* I, 126–75; idem, 'Josua', *BZAW* LXVI, 1936, 13–29 = *KS* I, 176–92; R. **Amiran**, *Ancient Pottery of the Holy Land*, Jerusalem/New Brunswick: Massada Press/Rutgers University Press 1969; C. F. **Burney**, *Israel's Settlement in Canaan*, London: Oxford University Press 1918; J. A. **Callaway**, 'New Evidence on the Conquest of 'Ai', *JBL* LXXXVII, 1968, 312–20; J. **Dus**, 'Das Sesshaftwerden der nachmaligen Israeliten im Lande Kanaan', *CV* VI, 1963, 263–75; idem, 'Mose oder Josua? (Zum Problem des Stifters der israelitischen Religion)', *AOr* XXXIX, 1971, 16–45 = 'Moses or Joshua? (On the Problem of the Founder of

Israelite Religion)', *RR* II, 1975, 26–41; O. **Eissfeldt**, 'Palestine in the Time of the Nineteenth Dynasty: (*a*) The Exodus and Wandering', *CAH* II/2, 307–30; idem, 'The Hebrew Kingdoms', *CAH* II/2, 537–605; idem, 'Die Eroberung Palästinas durch Altisrael', *WO* II 5–6, 1955, 158–71 = his *KS* III, 1966, 367–83; H. J. **Franken**, 'Palestine in the Time of the Nineteenth Dynasty: (*b*) Archaeological Evidence', *CAH* II/2, 331–37; N. K. **Gottwald**, 'Were the Early Israelites Pastoral Nomads?', *Rhetorical Criticism* (see ch. II§1D), 1974, 223–55; idem, 'Domain Assumptions and Societal Models in the Study of Pre-monarchical Israel', *SVT* XXVIII, 1975, 89–100; E. G. **Grant** and G. E. **Wright**, *Ain Shems Excavations* (*Palestine*) V, Haverford: Haverford College, 1939; B. **Halpern**, 'Gibeon: Israelite Diplomacy in the Conquest Era', *CBQ* XXXVII, 1975, 303–16; Y. **Kaufmann**, *The Biblical Account of the Conquest of Palestine*, Jerusalem: Magnes Press 1953; idem, 'Traditions Concerning Early Israelite History in Canaan', *SH* VIII, 1961, 303–34; K. A. **Kitchen**, *Ancient Orient and Old Testament*, 1966; D. **Livingston**, 'Location of Biblical Bethel and Ai Reconsidered', *WTJ* XXXIII, 1970–1, 20–41; idem, 'Traditional Site of Bethel Questioned', *WTJ* XXXIV, 1971–2, 39–50; F. **Maass**, 'Hazor und das Problem der Landnahme', *Von Ugarit nach Qumran*, 1958, 105–17; A. **Malamat**, 'The Danite Migration and the Pan-Israelite Exodus-Conquest: A Biblical Narrative Pattern', *Bib* LI 1970, 1–16; idem, 'Syrien-Palästina in der zweiten Hälfte des 2. Jahrtausends', *FWG* III/2, 1966, 177–221; idem, 'Origins and Formative Period', *The History of the Jewish People*, ed. H. H. Ben-Sasson, 1976, 1–87; idem, 'Conquest of Canaan: Israelite Conduct of War according to the Biblical Tradition', *EJY*, 1975/6, 166–82; B. **Mazar**, 'The Exodus and the Conquest', *WHJP* I/III, 1971, 69–93; T. J. **Meek**, *Hebrew Origins*, New York: Harper & Row, 1936, ³1960; G. E. **Mendenhall**, 'The Hebrew Conquest of Palestine', *BA* XXV, 1962, 66–87 = *BAR* III, 1970, 100–26; idem, *The Tenth Generation*, 1973; S. **Mowinckel**, '"Rahelstämme" und "Leastämme"', *Von Ugarit nach Qumran*, 1958, 129–50; M. **Noth**, *Das System der zwölf Stämme Israels*, BWANT IV/1, 1930; idem, 'Grundsätzliches zur geschichtlichen Deutung archäologischer Befunde auf dem Boden Palästinas', *PJB* XXXIV, 1938, 7–22 = his *Aufsätze*, 1971, 3–16; idem, 'Der Beitrag der Archäologie zur Geschichte Israels', *SVT* VII, 1960, 262–82 = his *Aufsätze* I, 34–51; L. B. **Paton**, 'Israel's Conquest of Canaan', *JBL* XXXII, 1913, 1–53; A. F. **Rainey**, 'Bethel Is Still Beitîn', *WTJ* XXXIII, 1970–1, 175–88; H. H. **Rowley**, *From Joseph to Joshua*, 1950; R. **Schmid**, 'Meerwunder- und Landnahme-Traditionen', *TZ* XXI, 1965, 260–8; J. A. **Soggin**, 'La conquista israelitica della Palestina nei Sec. XIII e XII e le scoperte archeologiche', *Protestantesimo* XVII, 1962, 193–208 = 'Archaeological Discoveries and the Israelite Conquest of Palestine in the Thirteenth and Twelfth Centuries', *OT Studies*, 1975, 11–30; R. **de Vaux**, 'A Comprehensive View of the Settlement of the Israelites in Canaan', *Perspective* XII/1–2, 1971, 23–33; Bruce K. **Waltke**, 'Palestinian Artifactual Evidence Supporting the Early Date of the Exodus', *BS* CXXIX, 1972, 33–47; M. **Weippert**, *The Settlement of the Israelite Tribes*,

1971; Leon T. **Wood**, 'The Date of the Exodus', *New Perspectives on the Old Testament*, ed. J. B. Payne, Waco: Word Books 1970, 66–87; G. E. **Wright**, 'Epic of Conquest', *BA* III, 1940, 25–40; idem, 'The Literary and Historical Problem of Joshua 10 and Judges 1', *JNES* V, 1946, 105–14; idem, *Biblical Archaeology*, 1957, ²1962; Y. **Yadin**, *Military and Archaeological Aspects of the Conquest of Canaan in the Book of Joshua*, New York: Jewish Education Committee Press nd; S. **Yeivin**, *The Israelite Conquest of Canaan*, UNHAII 17, 1971.

The preceding review of the sources of information pertaining to Israel's occupation of the land of Canaan reveals them to be varied and extremely complex. Any attempt to evaluate these sources with regard to their historical implications necessarily involves a significant degree of subjective judgment. It is not surprising, therefore, that scholars often have reached quite different conclusions regarding the process by which Israel gained possession of the land. It will not be possible to review individually the various reconstructions of the conquest/settlement which have been proposed, simply because there are so many of them. It will be useful to identify the main approaches which have emerged during the past scholarly discussion. These approaches are not mutually exclusive in every case, and the more comprehensive historical reconstructions which have been proposed generally combine elements of more than one.

A.   *Pan-Israelite exodus and invasion*

One possible approach, of course, and the one traditionally taken by Jewish and Christian commentators until modern times, is to accept as historically accurate the view of the conquest presented by the compilers and redactors of the hexateuch/Deuteronomistic history. According to this view, the twelve Israelite tribes escaped from Egypt in a single body, wandered in the wilderness for forty years, and then undertook a series of military actions within a span of five years which resulted in their conquest of central and northern Transjordan and virtually all the territory west of the Jordan. This view was accepted as essentially accurate by *Ewald, who attempted (in 1843–55) the first comprehensive reconstruction of Israel's history based on a systematic source-critical analysis of the biblical materials; and it continues to claim adherents, primarily among conservative scholars.

Those who follow this approach have found various ways of explaining and harmonizing the apparent inconsistencies within the biblical account. For example, in reference to the apparent inconsistency between Numbers 21.1–3 and Judges 1.17 regarding the destruction and (re)naming of Hormah, it can be claimed that Hormah was destroyed during Moses' career, rebuilt, and then destroyed again after Joshua's death. Another possibility is to hypothesize a time lapse between verses 2 and 3 of Numbers 21, during which Moses and then eventually Joshua died. In other words, Numbers 21.3 and Judges 1.17 are to be seen as parallel reports of the same event. In regard to the fact that Judges 1 and the narratives which follow reflect a situation in which individual tribes and tribal groups are struggling with only limited success to gain a foothold in the land, it is usually argued that Joshua had in fact conquered the whole land in that his decisive victories 'broke the back' of the Canaanites, but that it remained for the individual tribes to complete the conquest by clearing from their respective territorial allotments remaining enclaves of indigenous peoples. Largely under the influence of Kaufmann, Albright, and Wright, this explanation of the relationship between the conquest claims in Joshua 1–12 and the situation reflected in Judges 1 has gained wide currency among scholars who do not necessarily presuppose a simple pan-Israelite conquest (see especially Wright, 1946).

The matter of assigning dates to the exodus and conquest presents an especially difficult problem for those who see these as sequential events experienced by all Israel. Josephus connected the exodus and conquest with the expulsion of the Hyksos, a view which was generally accepted until modern times. As observed above, however, calculations based on the chronological notations scattered throughout Genesis–II Kings would seem to require that the dates of the exodus and conquest be lowered to the beginning and the middle of the fifteenth century BCE respectively – i.e., later than the expulsion of the Hyksos and during the time of the Eighteenth Dynasty. If there was any direct connection between the Hebrew conquest and the 'Apiru disturbances of the Amarna letters, as a few scholars still hold, then the date of the conquest would need to be lowered still further to the end of the fifteenth or the beginning of the fourteenth centuries BCE. Finally, the references to Pithom and Raamses in Exodus 1.11 would seem to preclude any exodus date before the thirteenth century – i.e., the time of the Nineteenth Egyptian Dynasty at which time Ramesses became a popular throne name. Present-day conservative scholars are divided on the matter. Some prefer to date the exodus and conquest during the fifteenth century and explain away the references to Pithom and Raamses in one way or another (see Wood). Others prefer a thirteenth-century date, which means discounting or reinterpreting the chronological data provided in Genesis–II Kings (see Kitchen, 57–75).

B.   *Independent migrations and settlement by separate tribal groups*

Rapid strides in literary-critical research during the last quarter of the nineteenth century called attention to the inherent diversity within the biblical traditions regarding Israel's origins and the extent to which the concept of a single pan-Israelite conquest has been superimposed upon these traditions by late compilers and redactors. Judges 1 came to be understood as a contrasting and considerably more modest account of how the territory west of the Jordan was won, rather than a description of secondary struggles which supposedly occurred in the aftermath of the fantastic victories of Joshua 1–12. Also it was observed that the older traditions embedded in Numbers–Joshua, when carefully analysed, seem unaware of an initial pan-Israelite conquest. Accordingly, there emerged among critical scholars even before the turn of the century the opinion that the Israelite occupation of Palestine probably occurred as the result of independent migrations and conquests by individual tribes and tribal groups which entered the land over an extended period of time. Only later, according to this view, when these various groups were combined to form the nation Israel, were their individual conquest traditions also combined and telescoped within the careers of Moses and Joshua. Not all or even most of the tribes would have participated in the Egyptian experience, and those who did may have departed from Egypt in more than one exodus.

There has been less agreement among those who follow this approach as to how the different stages of the Israelite conquest and settlement are to be identified and reconstructed. How many waves or stages of tribal settlement were there? Which tribes or tribal groupings entered the land at each stage and from which directions? Which tribe(s) participated in the Egyptian experience, and with which was Moses originally associated? What about Joshua in this regard, and the worship of Yahweh? Paton and Rowley provided excellent summaries of the various reconstructions which had been proposed by 1912 and 1948 respectively, along with reconstructions of their own. Since that time one notices an increasing tendency among those who presume more than one wave of Israelite conquest/settlement to associate these waves primarily with the thirteenth century BCE (see, e.g., *de Vaux, Mazar, and Aharoni, 1967, in contrast to Yeivin). There are at least three reasons for this: Present-day commentators are less inclined than their predecessors to view the patriarchs as essentially personifications of ancient tribes (see above, ch. II §2B–C). The matter of the relationship (if any) between the *'Apiru* and the Hebrews seems less clear now than it did at an earlier stage of research (see above, §2). In addition, Albright's interpretation of the archaeological evidence which presumes a thirteenth-century conquest has been widely accepted (see below).

A related issue encountered by those who follow this approach has to do with the self-identity and religious unity which seem to have characterized the Israelite tribes. If these tribes were of various origins and entered the land at different times and under different circumstances, how did they come to think of themselves as 'Israelites' in contrast to the other peoples of the land; and how did they come to worship the same god, Yahweh? One possibility, suggested by Wellhausen and widely accepted by earlier critical scholars, is that the Israelite tribes came into contact with each other and developed mutual bonds at Kadesh-barnea, from which they staged their various entries into Canaan. Another possibility which gained wide acceptance in connection with the amphictyonic hypothesis is that these tribes developed their sense of common identity after entering the land and establishing there a tribal confederacy. Joshua 24 often is seen as reminiscent of the ancient ceremony by which this confederacy was either established or expanded to include non-Yahwistic tribes. A third possibility is that the concept of 'all Israel' composed of a given number of Yahwistic tribes emerged with the establishment of the monarchy by Saul and David. To be sure, Merneptah's stela testifies to the existence of a people known as 'Israel' already on the scene in Palestine during the thirteenth century BCE. But the Israel of Merneptah's day may have consisted of only one or a few of the tribes who later would consider themselves Israelites. In any case, those who view the Israelite occupation of Palestine in terms of independent migrations and conquests by separate tribal groups must presume that both the name 'Israel' and the worship of Yahweh were extended to some of the tribes secondarily.

A third issue has to do with the means by which the tribes gained possession of the land. It is agreed by those who follow this approach that, at least at first, some of the tribes apparently settled peaceably among the indigenous Canaanite population. But there are also the biblical claims of military conquest to be taken into account. Was there a forced military entry into the land at all? The positions of Alt and Albright summarized below represent opposite poles of opinion on the matter.

C.   *Gradual penetration in search of pasturage*

According to Alt, whose groundbreaking study, 'Die Landnahme der Israeliten in Palästina', appeared in 1925, the Israelite occupation of Palestine began with gradual and generally peaceful movements of individual tribes and clans into the thinly populated hill country. These were nomadic or semi-nomadic tribes with small herds of cattle, and they came in search of summer pasturage for their cattle rather than with the intention of settling permanently. Each year they penetrated further and further into the land, however, and over a period of time began to settle down and take up agriculture. One may suppose that there were occasional contacts between these Israelite tribes and the Canaanite cities all along, and perhaps occasional clashes. But the contacts would have been limited at first and relations generally peaceful, since the tribes neither posed a serious military threat nor encroached upon the better agricultural lands of the plains. Actually Israel's military conquests belonged for the most part to a second stage of occupation, according to Alt, which in his opinion was just beginning at the end of the period of the judges and did not reach fruition until the reigns of David and Solomon. By that time the tribes had gained a firm footing in the hill country, consolidated their strength, and were in a position to expand into the more arable lands of the plains which previously had been dominated by the Canaanite cities.

Alt was able to determine already from the Egyptian sources that the Canaanite city-states were stronger and less widely scattered in the plains – a fact which was to be confirmed archaeologically – and observed that the more thinly populated mountainous regions would have offered the best opportunity for the Israelite tribes to settle down and turn gradually from their semi-nomadic life style to an agricultural economy. He observed further that the mountainous regions were divided into three territorial divisions: firstly, by a chain of city-states which extended from Acco across the Jezreel Valley to Beth-shan, dividing the Galilean hill country from the central hill country, and secondly, by non-Israelite enclaves which extended from the coastal plain into the mountains at approximately Jerusalem, dividing the north central from the south central hill country (see §1B above). It is precisely in these three mountainous areas, Alt pointed out, that the earlier traditions in Joshua, Judges, and I Samuel all depict the Israelite tribes struggling to gain a foot-hold.

Alt's conclusions were developed further by Noth, who combined them with the amphictyonic hypothesis (see below, ch. V §2A) and sought to distinguish two phases of tribal settlement prior to the military expansion from the hill country into the plains. Noth con-cluded from an analysis of the tribal listings and various other bits of information gleaned from the Old Testament that the Leah and concubine tribes were already settled west of the Jordan before the arrival of Joseph and Benjamin, and that an amphictyony composed of the six Leah tribes already was in operation. Shechem served as the central shrine of this early amphictyony; and Reuben, Simeon, and Levi were independent land-holding tribes settled in the north central hill country. Later these three Leah tribes were displaced by the arrival of Joseph and Benjamin. Also the amphictyony was ex-panded into a twelve-tribe league which included the concubine tribes, Joseph, and Benjamin. Joshua 24, according to Noth, recalls the historical occasion when the amphictyony was expanded to include the non-Leah tribes. Moreover, since in his opinion it was the Joseph group which introduced Yahwism into the amphictyony, this was for the other tribes indeed a moment of putting away the gods of the land in favour of Yahweh. Clearly Noth's reconstruction of the phases of tribal settlement depends heavily upon the amphic-tyonic model, as well as upon his assumption that these ancient leagues normally were composed of either six or twelve tribes. But the relevance of the amphictyonic model for understanding Israel's early history is being challenged at the moment, and whatever the outcome it is doubtful that Noth's treatment will escape unscathed (see below, ch. V §2B).

A more basic objection often raised to the Alt–Noth approach is that it disregards altogether the biblical claim that a sweeping Israelite conquest *preceded* the settlement of the individual tribes in their respective territories. Alt and his followers have not considered this a telling objection, since they consider the claim to be largely Deuteronomistic fiction. They also question the historical reliability of the pre-Deuteronomistic traditions combined and intertwined in Joshua 1–12, emphasizing instead the aetiological and cultic charac-teristics of these materials. As for the accusation that their approach ignores the archaeological evidence for an early (pre-Judges) con-quest of Canaan, they respond correctly that this evidence is itself ambivalent, and if anything confirms their view that the conquest narratives are largely folk stories without any recoverable historical basis (particularly the archaeological evidence from Jericho, Ai, and Gibeon; see Weippert, 128–44).

Perhaps the most serious problem with the Alt–Noth approach is that it depends so heavily upon what may turn out to be a romantic and misguided understanding of the role of nomadism in the political affairs of the ancient Near East. Specifically, Alt's treatment of the 'Landnahme' reflects the widespread view that throughout history the desert has been a constant source of nomads who spilled over into the surrounding fertile areas from time to time, temporarily disrupted the village and city life which they found there, but eventually were absorbed themselves into the sedentary population. Recently this view has encountered serious opposition (see above, ch. II §1D; and E below).

D.   *Forced entry: artifactual evidence and military feasibility*

It was only during the second quarter of the present century that the results of archaeological excavations in Palestine began to enter significantly into the discussion. In 1926 Watzinger revised the dating of the Jericho stratigraphy which he and Sellin had established during their 1907–9 excavations and concluded that Canaanite Jericho was destroyed no later than 1600 BCE. This meant that the city would have been in ruins already when the Israelites appeared on the scene, even if one favours the earliest conceivable date for the conquest. Garstang was among the many who found Watzinger's conclusions unacceptable, and in order to clarify the matter made soundings at Ai and Hazor during 1928 and more extensive excavations at Jericho during 1930–6. Citing new evidence recovered during these investigations, Garstang argued that all three cities flourished until ca. 1400 BCE, at which time they were destroyed or at least ceased to be occupied. He considered 1400 BCE an acceptable date for the Israelite conquest, especially in view of the '*Apiru* disturbances mentioned in the Amarna correspondence. Garstang's interpretation of his archaeological evidence was challenged by other specialists from the beginning, however, especially by Vincent and Albright; and later excavations at all three sites were to prove his interpretations largely incorrect (see above, §3).

Albright viewed the Israelite occupation as having occurred in several stages or waves, one of the earliest of these waves (perhaps that of the house of Joseph) possibly to be associated with the '*Apiru* disturbances of the Amarna period. But the main thrust of the occupation, in his opinion, the exodus-conquest led by Moses and

Joshua, involved primarily the Leah tribes and occurred during the second half of the thirteenth century BCE. A thirteenth-century date for the exodus was suggested in the first place, of course, by the Exodus 1.11 reference to Pithom and Raamses. Depending upon data available in the mid-1930s, Albright contended that the archaeological evidence requires a corresponding thirteenth-century date for the conquest and confirms its military character. The evidence which he cited may be summarized as follows: (1) Glueck's explorations in Transjordan seemed to indicate that there was no sedentary population to speak of in the territories of ancient Edom and Moab before the thirteenth century BCE. Apparently, then, there would have been no kingdoms of Edom and Moab before that time to refuse the Israelites passage through their respective lands. (2) Albright's own excavations at Bethel and Tell Beit Mirsim (which he believed to be biblical Debir) and Starkey's excavations at Lachish had revealed that all three cities were destroyed violently at the end of the Late Bronze Age. More specifically, Albright was convinced that the destruction of LB Lachish could be dated during or soon after Merneptah's fourth year (i.e., during the last decades of the thirteenth century); and it seemed reasonable to him that all three destructions should be attributed to the Israelite invasion led by Joshua. (3) Albright isolated an interim Iron I phase at Tell Beit Mirsim which separated the LB destruction from a second Iron I phase, the latter containing Philistine pottery. This stratigraphical pattern corresponds exactly, Albright observed, to the historical sequence suggested in the Bible – i.e., Israelite conquest of certain Canaanite cities including Debir, Israelite settlement in conquered Palestine, arrival of the Philistines and their domination of the Israelite villages.

As it became increasingly apparent from later excavations at other sites that Bethel, Tell Beit Mirsim, and Lachish are representative of a fairly large number of cities which were destroyed at the end of the Late Bronze Age, Albright and especially some of his less cautious followers tended to speak in terms of a wave of destructions of LB cities attributable to Israel. Correspondingly, there has been a tendency to assume that the Iron I settlements which emerged on the LB destruction ruins, along with the newly established settlements which sprang up throughout the central hill country and lower Galilee, were by and large villages of the Israelite conquerors (see e.g., Wright, 1962, 70). Albright isolated a particular ceramic form, the so-called 'collared-rim' jar, which generally occurred in connection with the earliest Iron I phases of these villages. Although he expressed some caution about the matter (*BASOR*, 1970, 7–9), he was inclined to see this as a 'type fossil' characteristic specifically of the Israelite settlers:

> As it happens, this collared store-jar is a 'type-fossil' of great importance for Israelite chronology in the time of the Judges and the United Monarchy, since it is found all over the hill-country proper in the twelfth and early eleventh century, but went out of fashion between ca. 1050 and ca. 1020 BC (*AJA*, 1940, 548).

The results of the excavations at Hazor (Tell el-Kedah) during the years 1955–8 fit Albright's hypothesis especially well. The Bible states specifically that Joshua burned Hazor, and there is equally clear archaeological evidence that LB Hazor (Stratum XIII) was destroyed by burning during roughly the thirteenth century. Then, after a short occupational gap, there emerged on the ruins of LB Hazor a very poor Iron I settlement (Stratum XII) whose inhabitants used 'collared-rim' jars. Nevertheless, it must be said that the most Albright and those who follow his approach have been able to demonstrate is that a certain amount of the available artifactual data is susceptible to interpretation in terms of a thirteenth-century Israelite invasion. Hazor notwithstanding, there is as yet not a single shred of artifactual evidence which actually requires such an interpretation (see de Vaux, 1970). On the contrary, as observed above (see §3), there are some serious problems with Albright's approach in general and the proposed thirteenth-century date in particular.

Some of these problems derive from, or have become more acute as the result of, fairly recent developments in archaeological research. For example, it has become apparent only during the past decade that, contrary to Glueck's conclusions, the surge of sedentary occupation in the territories of ancient Edom and Moab occurred somewhat later than the thirteenth century. Recently also Arad, Heshbon, Hormah (i.e., the candidate sites for Hormah) and now apparently Jarmuth have taken their place alongside Jericho, Ai, and Gibeon as cities which the Bible associates with the period of the conquest but which offer little or no archaeological evidence of having been occupied during the thirteenth century.

Albright offered explanations for the negative archaeological findings (i.e., *vis-à-vis* his hypothesis) at the latter three sites. But these explanations neither correspond to the most natural interpretations of the artifactual evidence nor satisfy the historical implications of the biblical accounts. At first Albright was inclined to associate the destruction of Jericho with one of the pre-thirteenth-century waves of Israelite settlement, possibly that of the house of Joseph. In his later writings he associated its destruction with the main thirteenth-century invasion and explained that the physical remains of this late LB phase of the city's history have been eroded away. Regarding Joshua 10.2, which suggests that Gibeon was a major city at the time of the conquest, Albright explained that this is a scribal gloss introduced by one who 'was no doubt influenced by the impressive situation of the site and its relative importance in his own time' (1963, 30). Actually, according to Albright, Gibeon was but a small settlement at the time of the conquest, which explained for him the virtual absence of LB remains. The biblical and archaeological data relative to Bethel and Ai were problematic for Albright's treatment of the conquest for opposite reasons. The archaeological evidence testifies to a destruction at Bethel during the thirteenth century; but the Bible neither associates the city's conquest with Joshua's invasion nor states that it was physically destroyed (see Judg. 1.22–6). The Bible does unequivocally credit Joshua with the conquest of Ai and emphasizes that he burned the city to the ground (Josh. 7–8); but the archaeological evidence proves that Ai was already a desolate ruin long before the thirteenth century. Albright's solution was to reverse the force of the biblical evidence by insisting that Joshua 7–8 and Judges 1.22–6 are both historically misleading accounts in their present form, but that they both hark back to a single historical event; namely, Joshua's conquest of LB Bethel.

Albright's treatment of the conquest depended heavily upon his findings at Tell Beit Mirsim, which he believed to be the site of biblical Debir conquered by Joshua (Othniel). It now seems certain that Khirbet Rabud is the site of Debir, leaving the ancient identity of Tell Beit Mirsim unknown. Actually the Iron I remains at Tell Beit Mirsim were rather meagre in any case, consisting of a few structures but primarily of grain pits. Albright's division of these scanty Iron I remains into phases depended almost entirely upon the stylistic characteristics of sherds which had fallen into the pits after the latter were no longer in use. Thus the earliest Iron I phase was represented by a few pits which contained early Iron I pottery but no sherds of Philistine ware. Obviously this is not very strong evidence for projecting a phase of the city's history. A somewhat stronger case can be made for the stratigraphical pattern – LB destruction, Iron I without Philistine ware, Iron I with Philistine ware – at a few other sites. But it is noticeable that this pattern belongs primarily to the Philistine coast (Jaffa, Ashdod, Tel Mor) and the Shephelah (possibly Beth-shemesh and Gezer; Grant and Wright,

10, 60; Dever, in §3 above, II, 50). That being the case, it is more likely that the pattern is due to pre-Philistine raids by the Sea Peoples (Malamat, 1971, 29) and to Egyptian activity (e.g., Merneptah) than to an Israelite invasion.

Regarding the 'collared-rim' jars, the most that can be said is that this is a ceramic form characteristic of the early Iron I age in Palestine. It represents a continuous development from LB forms (Amiran, 232), and has been found at sites throughout central Palestine (including Bethel, Tell el-Ful, Tell en-Naṣbeh, Ai, Shiloh, Beth-shemesh, Beth-zur, Tell Beit-Mirsim, Shechem, Megiddo, Afula, Hazor) and Galilee (Aharoni, 1970, 263). Thus it is gratuitous to assign this form to newcomers at the end of LB or, even if it could be demonstrated beyond question on other grounds that there was an Israelite invasion at that time, to associate the form specifically with the Israelite invaders to the exclusion of other groups who may have entered central Palestine and Galilee at roughly the same time and in similar circumstances (Hittites, Hivites, Jebusites, etc.).

Recently Waltke has attempted to demonstrate that the artifactual data actually favours an early fourteenth-century date for the Israelite conquest. There is at least some evidence that Jericho was still occupied at that time, and he proposes that it was Hazor XV rather than Hazor XIII which Joshua destroyed. Ai remains a problem for Waltke. But he gets around this by insisting with Livingston that both Bethel and Ai have been mislocated by modern topographers (see, however, Rainey's response to Livingston). Callaway, on the other hand, thinks that the artifactual data call for a twelfth-century BCE Israelite invasion. Hivites and other such groups were responsible for the earliest Iron I settlements in central Palestine, in his view, and it was these earliest Iron I settlements rather than LB cities which the Israelites destroyed. Callaway's proposal has the advantage that most of the cities which the Bible associates with the conquest have yielded artifactual evidence of having been occupied during Iron I (although Jericho remains a problem). Its chief disadvantage is the absence of any distinctive cultural break or co-ordinated wave of destructions within the early Iron I phases of these cities which could be associated with the Israelite invasion. Callaway attempts to get around this by suggesting that the conquest was a more complex affair than Albright supposed; indeed, that it was a process which may have lasted a half century or more.

The emerging picture of the conquest that I see in the archaeological evidence is one of minor scale raids on small villages like the Phase I settlement at Ai, but mainly it is a picture of political integration with the Iron I inhabitants of the land, such as those at Gibeon (Callaway, 319).

But while Callaway's view of the conquest may be essentially correct, it is not entirely accurate for him to suggest that this view emerges from the archaeological evidence. Were he dependent upon the archaeological evidence alone, he would be unaware of an Israelite conquest of any sort during the twelfth century. A more accurate statement would be that (1) if one presupposes an Israelite invasion which occurred at a time when such cities as Arad, Heshbon, Jericho, Ai, and Gibeon were occupied, then this invasion cannot have occurred before the Iron I age, since it was only then that these cities were resettled after occupational gaps extending in some cases as far back as the Early Bronze Age (Arad and Ai). Moreover (2) if one places the conquest during Iron I, then we must modify radically the view that it was a sweeping military invasion, since the archaeological traces which one would expect such an invasion to have left behind (co-ordinated destruction remains, cultural break, introduction of new artifactual traditions) simply do not occur within Iron I.

What of the military feasibility of the biblical account of the Israelite conquest? Is it reasonable to suppose that the Israelites, emerging from a period of wandering in the wilderness, would have been able to overpower the Canaanite city-states? This was no problem for the Deuteronomistic compiler(s) of the book of Joshua, of course, since it was in keeping with Deuteronomistic theology to emphasize God's miraculous deliverance of the promised land into Israel's hands in spite of overwhelming odds. But it is a legitimate question from the perspective of modern historiography and commentators have attempted to answer it in various ways. Some have seen a carefully planned and executed military strategy reflected in the sequence of events related in Joshua 1–11 (see most recently Halpern). Suggestions have been made also regarding particular military qualities and skills possessed by the Israelites, and attention given to their extensive use of subterfuge and cunning at the time of the conquest (for example, Yadin).

Malamat recently has undertaken an investigation of the military aspects of the conquest traditions, utilizing what he calls a 'typological approach' to these materials (1970, 1976). Emphasizing that the canonical account of the conquest is not to be taken at face value, he insists that it is nevertheless typologically useful to the historian in that its underlying themes and motifs reflect accurately both the general outlines and the largely military character of the

Israelite occupation of Canaan. Actually the Israelite tribes invaded and gained an upper hand only in the mountainous regions of central Palestine at first, according to Malamat, and expanded into the lowlands in later stages, induced by rapid growth in population. This historical invasion and occupation is remembered in the conquest traditions; but the details became obscured and telescoped in the memory of later generations, and eventually there emerged the received canonical account which is strongly influenced by theological reflection.

The Canaanite city-states were impoverished at the end of LB by Egyptian exploitation, Malamat observes, and also torn apart by Egypt's 'divide and rule' policy and their own ethnic heterogeneity. Thus the rulers of these city-states were unable to present a unified front to the Israelites, who for their part were 'kindled by religious and national zeal' (1976, 57). Malamat finds numerous indications in the biblical narratives, on the other hand, that the Israelites engaged in methods of warfare which worked to their advantage and tended to neutralize the strengths of the Canaanites. It would appear, he observes, that the Israelites engaged in extensive intelligence and espionage activities, such as sending out spies on reconnaissance missions prior to military operations (Num. 13; Josh. 2; 7.1–3; Judg. 18.2–10). Malamat finds indications that the Israelites gave careful attention to logistical matters. For example, they crossed the Jordan and invaded western Palestine at a time of the year when crops were ready for harvest (Josh. 3.15), thus providing themselves with an ample food supply during the crucial initial phase of the conquest. Gilgal was an ideal choice for a base camp during this phase, since it assured contact with the Israelite rear in Transjordan. Also, Malamat observes, the Israelites apparently depended heavily upon indirect modes of warfare. Instead of frontal attacks on the fortified cities, they generally found indirect means of penetration (Judg. 1.22–6) or enticed the defenders away from the protection of the cities' walls (Josh. 8). Finally, Malamat observes that the Israelites engaged in psychological warfare and surprise tactics. He suggests that the daily marches around Jericho may have been a psychological device, for example, intended to lower the enemy's guard. The lightning night march from Gilgal to Gibeon (Josh. 10.9) would have been in anticipation of a surprise attack at dawn.

The point is perhaps well taken that the idea of a tribal conquest of central Palestine at the end of LB should not be dismissed simply on the grounds that such a conquest would have been militarily impossible, or even unlikely. One should not presume, on the other hand, and Malamat makes no such claim, that the military feasibility of such a conquest confirms the historicity of the biblical claim that the Israelite occupation of Palestine occurred in that fashion. Obviously not all historians share Malamat's confidence that the biblical account is even typologically correct. It is precisely the underlying (or overriding) themes and motifs of the received canonical account which may be largely the product of late theological reflection.

E. The conquest as internal revolt

In a provocative paper published in 1962, Mendenhall contended that the Israelite 'conquest' of Canaan was less a matter of invasion from the outside than a socio-political upheaval from within. There was an exodus from Egypt which served as a catalyst for the upheaval, in Mendenhall's opinion, and the revolution which resulted probably began in the kingdoms of Sihon and Og before spreading westward across the Jordan. There was, however, no major population movement or displacement and thus no conquest as such. In his words,

... there was no real conquest of Palestine in the sense that has usually been understood; what happened instead may be termed, from the point of view of the secular historian interested only in socio-political processes, a peasant's revolt against the network of interlocking Canaanite city-states (1962, 107).

The end result was an overthrow of the Canaanite overlords and the emergence of a tribal confederacy known as 'Israel'.

For the most part, in Mendenhall's opinion, the emergent tribes of the confederacy had their roots in social units which existed previously in Palestine. The 'slave labour captives' who escaped from Egypt and initiated the revolution would have been a heterogeneous lot also, and statistically accounted for but a small part of the resulting tribal union. It was Yahwism, however, the covenant religion of the exodus group, which became the unifying bond of the confederacy; and Mendenhall interpreted Joshua 24 as reminiscent of an early moment when the emergent tribes were 'called upon to forsake their inherited tribal religion for the worship of Yahweh' (1962, 117). Eventually the descendants of all the tribes identified with the historical remembrances of the exodus group.

Obviously Mendenhall's thesis discounts the biblical claim that the Israelite tribes were an ethnic unit which 'came up out of Egypt'.

Also it challenges the view widely held among modern scholars that these tribes were nomads or semi-nomads who entered Palestine from the desert fringe. Actually the biblical traditions depict Israel's ancestors as pastoralists rather than nomads, Mendenhall contended, and 'the pastoralist was a villager who specialized in animal husbandry, primarily because there was not enough tillable land to support the entire population of a village' (1962, 102 f.). Mendenhall conceded that there were true nomads during the Bronze Age, some of which presumably would have turned to sedentary life. But these nomads were statistically and historically negligible, in his opinion, and there is no reason to suppose that they had anything to do with Israel's origins. A better clue for understanding the emergence of Israel, in Mendenhall's view, is the biblical designation 'Hebrew'. 'Israel', 'Hebrew', and ''*Apiru*' are virtually synonymous terms for him, and the latter seems to be used in the ancient Near Eastern texts to refer to individuals or groups which stood outside the acknowledged social system of a land for one reason or another and thus could not claim the legal rights and protection which the community normally granted (see §2 above). Early Israel would have been truly 'Hebrew'/'*Apiru*, therefore, in that it emerged from an open rebellion against the existing social system.

Gottwald and Dus have accepted Mendenhall's thesis and expanded it. Gottwald argues even more strongly against the idea that the desert was a breeding ground and source of waves of nomads which spilled over into the agricultural zones from time to time (see also ch. II §1D), and sees Israel's tribalization as a more politically conscious power-play than does Mendenhall.

> In my assessment we should view Israelite tribalism as a form chosen by people who consciously rejected Canaanite centralization of power and deliberately aimed to defend their own uncentralized system against the effort of Canaanite society to crush their movement. Israel's tribalism was an autonomous project which tried to roll back the zone of political centralization in Canaan, to claim territories and peoples for an egalitarian mode of agricultural and pastoral life (1975, 9).

Dus emphasizes Joshua's role as the great revolutionary leader, to the extent of claiming 'that the biblical figures of Moses as religious founder and Joshua as his successor in reality go back to the single figure of Joshua as religious founder and social revolutionary' (1975, 39).

Mendenhall's thesis points in new directions which need to be explored. Obviously, even if Israel did invade and conquer Palestine from without rather than emerging from within, indigenous peoples and perhaps whole tribes were eventually absorbed in her ranks, and the process by which this occurred needs to be dealt with more adequately than historians have done in the past. Also in their future discussions biblical historians will need to be more cautious to avoid oversimplifying the role of nomadism in the socio-political history of the ancient Near East. But Mendenhall's thesis has its own problems as well, which become especially obvious at the hands of Gottwald and Dus: (1) Its presumption that '*Apiru*, 'Hebrew', and 'Israelite' were virtually synonymous terms is, at the very least, probably an oversimplification (see §2 of this chapter and Weippert, 63–102). (2) The 'peasants' revolt' model seems to be a modern construct superimposed upon the biblical traditions, and certainly is no more convincing than the 'intruding nomad' model which it is intended to replace. (3) The theory that Israel emerged from a Palestinian peasants' revolt finds no basis in the biblical materials, whether one considers the oldest discernible strata of the conquest tradition or the final canonical account. On the contrary, the idea seems to have been deeply ingrained throughout Israel's memory that the ancestors were tent dwellers who entered Palestine from elsewhere and that they were conscious of not being one with the people of the land. There is not the slightest hint in the biblical traditions regarding the revolution which supposedly brought Israel into existence. Surely one would expect to find some allusion to it in the book of Judges if such a revolution had in fact occurred.

§5. THE OCCUPATION OF THE LAND

In the light of the preceding survey of the written sources and archaeological evidence relevant to the Israelite occupation of Canaan and the review of approaches which leading scholars have taken in their attempts at historical reconstruction, perhaps the one thing which can be said with confidence is that the process by which Israel gained possession of the land remains unclear. The present writer suspects that the general features of this process were essentially as follows.

1. The oldest strata of the conquest traditions and the narratives of the book of Judges associate the tribes of Israel primarily with the mountainous regions of northern, central, and southern Palestine with enclaves in Transjordan. This was the core of their settlement, and only after the establishment of the monarchy was Israelite

domination extended throughout the lowlands of Palestine and central and northern Transjordan. The tribes which were settled in these mountainous regions and eventually came to regard themselves as 'Israelite' were of various origins and gained possession of their respective territories under different circumstances. Some of these tribes may have had pre-settlement ethnic and/or historical ties. This was not true of all of them. In fact, the tribalization process itself may have occurred largely after the settlement and in accordance with the topography of Palestine. The sense of kinship and mutual loyalty which these tribes came to share also emerged gradually after the settlement, due to such factors as geographical proximity, similar life styles elicited by the physical features of the mountainous regions, shared sanctuaries, and the necessity of combined warfare from time to time in the face of common enemies. Yahwism seems to have been associated primarily with warfare during the pre-monarchical period and will also have been a significant ingredient in the emerging sense of inter-tribal kinship and loyalty.

In short, the actual process by which Israel gained possession of the land was probably radically different from the process suggested by the final canonical version of the conquest and settlement found in Numbers–Joshua. Instead of a pan-Israelite invasion and conquest after which the individual tribes entered their respective territories and tended to go their own separate ways, it was rather a matter of the pan-Israelite consciousness gradually emerging in Palestine among tribal groups which had their own individual origins and still were only loosely associated with each other at the time of the establishment of the monarchy. The concept of twelve clearly defined Israelite tribes during the pre-monarchical period also is an oversimplification by Israel's historians, although it already appears in the Yahwistic source. The configuration of tribal divisions and loyalties seems to have been far more complex than this concept allows. Moreover, the name Israel seems to have applied at first not to an alignment of tribes settled throughout Palestine, but to a more localized tribal group situated in the north-central hill country. The patriarchal narratives regarding Jacob (= Israel) focus on this area, and the tribes settled here (Ephraim and Manasseh) were the nucleus of the kingdom of 'Israel' after the division of the monarchy.

2. Since the tribes had their own individual origins and entered Palestine under different circumstances – indeed, since the tribalization itself occurred to some degree after settlement in the land – it is not possible to assign a specific date to the Israelite occupation.

Population elements already settled in the mountainous regions of Palestine (during the Bronze Age) eventually contributed to the constituency of Israel. In addition to the few scattered cities – e.g., Shechem, Bethel, Jerusalem, Hebron, Debir – there were also other inhabitants of these regions during the Bronze Age which probably were not closely associated with the cities. Papyrus Anastasi I, the satirical letter of an Egyptian official, is instructive at this point. It says of the pass near Megiddo:

> The narrow valley is dangerous with Bedouin (*Shasu*), hidden under the bushes. Some of them are four or five cubits from their noses to the heel, and fierce of face. Their hearts are not mild, and they do not listen to wheedling (*ANET*, 477).

For the most part, however, the settlement of the people who emerged as Israel is probably to be associated with the Iron I period of Palestine's history (about 1200–1000 BCE). Merneptah's stela indicates that a group known as 'Israel' was on the scene in Palestine on the eve of this period (i.e., about 1230 BCE); the mountainous regions where the tribes gained their initial foothold experienced a surge in village settlements at the beginning of the period, which suggests an influx of population; and among the villages which were either founded at that time, or reoccupied after occupational gaps which had lasted throughout LB, were a significant number of those which figure in the conquest and Judges narratives.

Semi-nomadic transhumance and gradual sedentarization may have been a contributing factor to this population influx and surge of village life in the mountainous regions during early Iron I. But the role of nomadism in the socio-political history of the ancient Near East is unclear, and in any case was not the only or even the major factor. The political instability of the Syro-Palestinian city-states at the end of LB, combined with and intensified by the movements of the Sea Peoples and Aramaeans, created population pressure upon the mountainous regions from the agriculturally based lowlands of Palestine as well. Also the increased use of iron tools and plaster-lined cisterns rendered it more feasible to clear the forests which covered the Palestinian mountains during ancient times and to establish settlements at places where there was no permanent water supply. Neither the artifactual evidence nor the biblical conquest traditions, when examined critically, suggest that the city destructions which occurred in Palestine and throughout the Levant at the end of LB should be attributed to a westward invasion from Transjordan. To the extent that these destructions were attributable to a common cause, one should think rather in terms of the Sea Peoples.

3. Only occasional glimpses of the early histories of the individual tribes can be attained from the biblical materials. There were essentially three zones of settlement which correspond to the topography of the Palestinian mountains (see Map 3).

(a) *The Galilean mountains.* According to the tribal allotments described in Joshua 19.10–39, Asher, Zebulun, Issachar, and Naphtali were settled along the western, southern, and eastern fringes of the Galilean mountains and among the Canaanite cities in the adjacent lowlands. Asher's allotment is depicted as extending as far as the Mediterranean Sea (see also Judg. 5.17b), and it is noteworthy that the tribal sayings in Genesis 49.13 and Deuteronomy 33.18f. associate Zebulun and Issachar with the sea as well. Possibly these tribes were composed largely of population elements which originally were settled along the sea coast and were forced inland under pressure of the Sea Peoples. Indeed, one or more of these tribes may have been Sea Peoples. Clearly something of this sort occurred in the case of Dan. The Danites were unable to maintain their position along the coastal plains due to Philistine pressure, whereupon either the whole tribe or a large portion of it migrated to the upper reaches of the Jordan. But how did Dan come to be associated with the coastal regions initially? The biblical account, which has all of the tribes invading Palestine from Transjordan, naturally presumes that the Danites had attempted to enter the coastal plain from the central hill country. But when it is recognized that the concept of a pan-Israelite invasion from the Transjordan is ideal, then the possibility arises that the biblical Danites were a branch of the Danuna who, with the Philistines, are mentioned among the Sea Peoples in the inscription of Ramesses III. The account of the battle by the waters of Merom in Joshua 11 may recall an incident which occurred in connection with the settlement of Naphtali. But verses 10–15 of the account are to be seen as primarily, if not entirely, secondary redactional expansion. Certainly it is gratuitous to attribute the destruction of Hazor XIII to Israel on the basis of verses 10f.

(b) *The north-central hill country and the Transjordan.* Little can be said regarding the origin of the tribe of Manasseh, or the circumstances under which it came to occupy the northernmost parts of the central hill country. There are no conquest or settlement traditions pertaining to this area; and it is no doubt significant that Manasseh goes unmentioned in the song of Deborah. In the case of Ephraim and Benjamin, on the other hand, tribalization seems clearly to have been a post-settlement development. That is, 'Ephraim' emerged as the tribal designation for the clans settled in the region of Mount Ephraim, and 'Benjamin' (which means 'sons of the south' or 'southerners') referred to certain clans settled further south. The Benjaminite clans may have been regarded as a southern branch of the tribe of Ephraim at one stage. The narrative complex in Joshua 1–9 presumes an invasion from Transjordan into the Benjaminite area, which could have some historical basis. But if there was such an invasion, it probably had nothing to do with Jericho and Ai. Both the literary character of the accounts of the conquest of these two cities and the archaeological evidence from Tell es-Sultan and et-Tell strongly suggest that we have to do in both cases with folk aetiologies. The account of the taking of Bethel in Judges 1.22–6 seems to have a stronger claim to historical authenticity. But there is no way to date the incident, and it is unclear whether Bethel was destroyed at the time, so it cannot be determined which of the strata of Beitin represents the beginning of 'Josephite' occupation.

Machir, Jair, and Nobah were probably originally tribes west of the Jordan which migrated to northern Gilead and Bashan. The Song of Deborah seems to locate Machir west of the Jordan, and all three of these groups are subsumed under Manasseh in the twelve-tribe scheme. There may have been some Ephraimite expansion into Gilead as well, depending upon how one interprets Judges 12.1–6 and II Samuel 18.6. Gad and Reuben seem to have been originally Transjordan tribes on the other hand, who probably ranged with their cattle through the eastern Arabah and the territory between the Jabbok and the Arnon. The reference in Joshua 15.6 = 18.17 to 'the stone of Bohan the son of Reuben' may indicate that Reubenites once ranged west of the Jordan as well. The Mesha Inscription states that 'the men of Gad had dwelt in the land of Ataroth always' (line 10; Ataroth = present-day 'Attarus, approximately eight miles NNW of Dhiban), but makes no mention of Reuben.

(c) The southern hill country and Negeb. Judah proper consisted of clans settled in the hill country between approximately Jerusalem and Hebron. The tribal name 'Judah' may have been derived from the geographical area in which these clans had settled (i.e., Mount Judah) in the same way that the tribal name 'Ephraim' was derived

from Mount Ephraim. The twelve-tribe scheme subsumes under Judah a number of other tribal groups which settled the hill country from approximately Hebron southward into the adjacent parts of the Negeb – i.e., the Calebites, Othnielites, Kenizzites, Kenites, Jerahmeelites, and Simeonites. The biblical genealogies recognize that at least the first three of these southern tribal groups had close ties with Edom. That is, Caleb and Othniel are both associated genealogically with Kenaz, who in turn is included in the Edomite genealogy of Genesis 36. There is no reason to doubt the essential historicity of the biblical traditions regarding the Calebite/Othnielite conquest of Hebron/Debir. But the context in which these traditions have been placed by the biblical redactors is misleading. The purpose of the traditions seems to have been to explain how the Calebites and Othnielites gained possession of the exceedingly fruitful region of Hebron, and the assumption seems to have been that they entered this region from the south. The campaign described in Joshua 10.29–43 is also authentic but out of place contextually. It probably derives from the reign of Saul or later. The tradition regarding the destruction of Hormah seems to be a folk aetiology, similar to the aetiological explanation for the ruins of Jericho and Ai. It is unclear why Simeon alone among the southern tribes is attributed autonomous tribal status in the twelve-tribe system and depicted as a partner of Judah in Judges 1. Genesis 34 is not adequate basis to postulate that Simeon earlier was settled in the vicinity of Shechem.

V

THE PERIOD OF THE JUDGES AND
THE RISE OF THE MONARCHY

§1. SOURCES

G. **Fohrer**, *Introduction to the OT*, 1968; J. **Gray**, *I and II Kings*, OTL, ²1970;
E. **Jenni**, 'Zwei Jahrzehnte Forschung an den Büchern Josua bis Könige',
TR NF XXVII, 1961, 1–32, 97–146; M. **Noth**, *Überlieferungsgeschichtliche
Studien*, 1957.

The sources for our understanding of the history of the period of the
judges and the rise of the monarchy are to be found almost exclusively within the books of Judges and Samuel. Isolated items of
supplementary information on the period may be gleaned from other
biblical books, particularly Numbers and Joshua, and archaeological
work has helped to fill in the background, perhaps especially of the
culture of those, like the Philistines, with whom the Israelite tribes
came into ever closer contact. But it is on the books of Judges and
Samuel that we must really rely for both the framework and the
detail of Israel's history at this point. The literary analysis of these
books, to determine their origin and development, is, therefore, of
crucial importance.

Judges and Samuel form part of the Deuteronomistic historical
work. This must in turn be taken to imply that it is most unlikely
that the pentateuchal sources should be traced into these books; for,
even if modifications of Noth's description of the Deuteronomistic
historical work are necessary, it remains true that his recognition of
the fundamental character of the work, that it is an original exposition of the history of the period which it covers, is incompatible with
the notion that the work of the Deuteronomist consisted simply of
editing an already existing extended presentation of the history. This
is in addition to the fact that within this corpus it is only very
occasionally, as for example at the beginning of Joshua and in I

Samuel 7–12, that it is possible to accommodate the material to a theory of the continuation into these books of the pentateuchal sources. Generally, it is clear not only that the character of the contents of the Deuteronomistic history is so different from that of the tetrateuch that the independence of the former over against the latter must be upheld, but also that once the various sections have been isolated and the secondary supplements have been removed from the basic tradition, there are no significant variants left to support such a source theory (Jenni, 104–9; Fohrer, 211).

Whether we are to think in terms of a single author and a single work, composed in Palestine during the exile (Noth), or of an earlier pre-exilic work which was then edited during the exilic period (Gray, 6–9), or, in a more complex way, of the separate editing by various Deuteronomistic hands of Judges, Samuel, and Kings (Fohrer, 192–5), the final work is the result of a long history in which the author or authors have brought together material from various sources of varying age and reliability. 'Sources' here should be understood as a neutral designation, not necessarily implying written accounts, since it is clear that the material with which the Deuteronomist worked had a long history in which it was gradually shaped and modified in the course of oral transmission. To a greater or lesser extent such oral transmission has affected all the traditional material which has been preserved, and it is, therefore, more accurate to think in terms of tradition and complexes of tradition in discussing the origin of the material. However, at least in the final stages the material has been edited as literature, and the first step in tracing the history of the growth of Judges and Samuel must be a literary one: it is that of distinguishing between the work of the later editors and the traditions which they have incorporated.

A. Judges

A. G. **Auld**, 'Judges I and History: A Reconsideration', *VT* XXV, 1975, 261–85; W. **Beyerlin**, 'Gattung und Herkunft des Rahmens im Richterbuch', *Tradition und Situation* (see ch. IV §1Aiii), 1963, 1–29; R. C. **Boling**, *Judges*, AB 6a, 1975; G. **Fohrer**, *Introduction to the OT*, 1968; M. **Noth**, *Überlieferungsgeschichtliche Studien*, 1957; idem, 'Das Amt des "Richters Israels"', *Festschrift für Alfred Bertholet*, Tübingen: J. C. B. Mohr, 1950, 404–17 = his *GS* II, 1969, 71–85; W. **Richter**, *Die Bearbeitungen des 'Retterbuches' in der deuteronomischen Epoche*, BBB 21, 1964; idem, 'Die Überlieferungen um Jephtah, Ri 10, 17–12, 6', *Bib* XLVII, 1966, 485–556; K.-D. **Schunck**, 'Die Richter Israels und ihr Amt', *SVT* XV, 1966, 252–62; R. **Smend**,

'Das Gesetz und die Völker: Ein Beitrag zur deuteronomistischen Redaktionsgeschichte', *Probleme biblischer Theologie*, 1971, 494–509.

Judges 1.1–2.5 contains in part some early material on the settlement of the land by the Israelite tribes, but this section has come late into its present position (see Auld). The story of the period of the judges begins in 2.6, which follows directly on Joshua 23, and continues beyond the book of Judges to I Samuel 12, where Samuel's speech marks the end of that era and the beginning of the period of the monarchy (Noth, 1957, 5). Within these chapters the book of Judges presents a variety of materials of different age and origin. It is dominated by accounts of exploits by deliverers who arose at particular times to rescue Israel from oppression. But besides these there are two blocks of material which stand apart. In the first place, there are the five concluding chapters of the book, chs. 17–21. These contain a tradition of the migration of the tribe of Dan, which is properly a settlement tradition (chs. 17–18), and an account of an inter-tribal war in chs. 19–21 which, as we shall later see, probably originated in the area of Ephraim and Benjamin. In both cases, however, we have traditions which fall out of the chronological pattern which the Deuteronomist has otherwise established for the period of the judges, and which, therefore, whatever may be their time and place of origin, must be taken as later additions to the Deuteronomistic edition of the book.

The second block of material does belong very much to the chronological pattern laid down in the book, but, nevertheless, is clearly distinct from the stories of the deliverers. This material comprises the notices of the so-called minor judges in Judges 10.1–5; 12.7–15. With one exception, we have no accounts of heroic exploits attached to the names of these judges. What we have is a tightly bound list of six men, giving the impression of being a formal record which only occasionally departs from a fixed scheme, which is as sparing as possible in the information which it gives. The one exception is with the judge Jephthah, of whom there is a lengthy account the insertion of which has in fact broken this originally closed list. Apart from this case the only information given about the judges who appear in the list is: the name of the judge, his home, the number of years he spent as a judge, and his place of burial. With three of them some other legendary details about numerous posterity have also been attached.

While this list forms an integral part of the Deuteronomistic book of Judges, it is also clear that it has been incorporated by the Deuteronomistic editor as a complete whole, which, as shown by its starkly distinct literary character, had an origin different from that of the accounts of the deliverers which the book otherwise chiefly contains. There is a fixed literary scheme used to introduce and describe each judge. Some minor variations in the scheme may be discerned, which have come about in part at least because of the incorporation of the list within the context of the accounts of the deliverers; but the scheme has certain constant features (Schunck): each judge is connected with his predecessor by the words 'after him'; of each judge it is said that 'he judged Israel for . . .'. This list constitutes one of the major sources used by the Deuteronomist for his portrayal of the period of the judges.

The other major source used by the Deuteronomist described the heroic exploits of several leaders who delivered Israel from foreign oppression. These were Othniel, Ehud, Shamgar, Deborah/Barak, Gideon (Abimelech), Jephthah, and Samson. For three reasons it is widely agreed that the individual accounts of the deeds of these deliverers have been secondarily brought together by the use of linking or framework passages. In the first place, the vocabulary and style of the framework is quite noticeably different from that of the stories themselves; secondly, the framework supplies a chronological system which has no bearing on the actual content of the stories; and, thirdly, the framework supplies a religious interpretation of history, setting the events recorded within the context of Israel's relationship with Yahweh, which is not a feature of the stories themselves. On the other hand, however, there is no such general agreement on the question of whether this framework derives from a single hand or if it is the result of several stages of editing from different hands. The possibility that it was the Deuteronomist as a single editor who was responsible for all the editorial passages linking the separate stories (Noth, 1957, 47f.) appears now to be rather too simple in view of the differences in language and theology which may be discerned within the various framework passages (Beyerlin; Richter, 1964).

It has been shown especially by Richter that several stages in the editing of the deliverer stories must be distinguished. The final stage, which was responsible for the incorporation of the material within the larger context of the Deuteronomistic historical work, and which is therefore to be understood as the work of the Deuteronomist, is to be found mainly in Judges 2.11–19; 10.6–16. This can be demonstrated on the grounds of both language and thought. It is in these passages that linguistic forms which appear elsewhere in the larger work are to be found (Richter, 1964, 75–81), and it is also in these

passages that it is possible to discern a clear development in
theological understanding, as well as a desire to provide an introduction to accounts which already existed (ibid., 74). For this
Deuteronomistic editor, God's deliverance of Israel follows only on
repentance for the sin which has brought punishment in the form of
defeat by enemies (10.16), and is not simply an immediate divine
reaction to Israel's cry for help and relief from oppression; repentance for sin and return to Yahweh are an essential preliminary to
divine help. Also for the Deuteronomist God is with the deliverer
and with Israel throughout the lifetime of that deliverer (2.18f.),
and not only for the limited period of the actual relief of Israel from
oppression. This distinctive characteristic is closely linked with the
third point which marks the Deuteronomist's work, which is that for
the Deuteronomist 'deliverer' and 'judge' are identical (2.16). The
Deuteronomist used accounts of deliverers together with the list of
judges in Judges 10.1–5; 12.7–15 in order to produce a comprehensive picture of the period of the judges, and in so doing he not only
identified the judge and the deliverer but also gave the deliverer an
office which lasted for his lifetime, on the analogy of the judges as
they were already presented to him in the list. This distorted the
function of the deliverer, but it yielded a uniform picture of the
period with which the Deuteronomist was dealing; and this unifor-
mity was strengthened through the occasional addition to the stories
of the deliverers of formulae which properly belong to the list of the
judges (see 3.10, 11; 4.1b; Richter, 1964, 61. See also Judg. 15.20;
16.31).

One further important modification which the Deuteronomist
made to the material which lay before him was that he fitted the
stories within a chronological framework. An old chronology was
already given him in the list of judges, specifying the precise number
of years for which each judge functioned. This the Deuteronomist
supplemented with the addition of the numbers of years for which
Israel was oppressed by enemies, or for which the deliverers 'judged'
Israel, or for which the land of Israel had rest after its deliverance
(e.g. 3.30; 4.3). The basis on which the Deuteronomist decided on
these numbers of years was apparently the requirement that the total
for the period of the judges, added to that of the wilderness wandering and the early monarchy up until the time of the foundation of
the temple, should come to 480 years (see I Kings 6.1). However,
because the Deuteronomist's precise method of reckoning is far from
clear, and because it is possible that some chronological notices in
the book of Judges may have been introduced after the

Deuteronomist's work was finished, it is exceedingly difficult to accommodate the precise figures we are given in the book of Judges to the overall scheme (see the discussions in Noth, 1957, 18–27; Richter, 1964, 132–4; *de Vaux, 689–92; Boling, 23). Yet, because these chronological notices clearly belong within the context of an understanding of the period of the judges as one which lasted for a certain number of years, which in turn point to a wider literary context within which the book of Judges is being included, it is inevitable that these notices, apart from those which form part of the list of judges in Judges 10.1–5; 12.7–15, should be taken as Deuteronomistic.

Distinct from this Deuteronomistic contribution to the book of Judges there is an earlier stage of editing which, while taking up older traditions and providing a framework for them, represents a reworking which is independent of the editing of traditions outside the book of Judges. There is little in the way of linguistic contact or similarity in thought and theology between this framework and Deuteronomistic editing outside the book, while much of the peculiarly Deuteronomistic language and theology either does not appear in this framework or is incompatible with what it expresses (Richter, 1964, 65–8). This pre-Deuteronomistic stage of editing deals with deliverers only, not with deliverers understood as judges; and in its view the deliverer was sent by Yahweh for a specific purpose and for a limited period, and was not understood to occupy a lifelong office. It is to be found, for example, in 3.12, 14, 15a, 30, and consists of the following elements: Israel sinned against Yahweh; Yahweh delivered them into the hand of an enemy; Israel cried to Yahweh; Yahweh raised up a deliverer; the enemy was subdued before Israel; the land of Israel had rest. This is a general scheme which appears fairly consistently. While it is for sin that Israel is punished by being delivered up to an enemy, the nature of the sin is not specified, and Israel's cry to Yahweh for deliverance is the result of enemy oppression and is not related to repentance or confession of sin.

Four problems in particular stand out in connection with the traditions taken up by this framework. These relate to the place of the traditions dealing with Othniel (3.7–11), Shamgar (3.31), Jephthah (10.17–12.6), and Samson (13–16). The Samson traditions do not exhibit any of the formulae belonging to this pre-Deuteronomistic framework. In 15.20 and 16.31 Samson is said to have 'judged' Israel for twenty years, but these are Deuteronomistic additions which serve to bring Samson into the series of deliverer-judges and also to fit him into the chronological scheme of the Deuteronomistic historical work. It must, therefore, be assumed that the Samson traditions had their own separate history, apart from the rest of the deliverer stories, before they were brought into their present place by the Deuteronomist.

In the case of Jephthah there is very little which may be claimed as belonging to the framework; in fact, only in 11.33b is there to be found a part of the framework scheme: the notice that the enemy was subdued before Israel. For this reason it has been argued that the Jephthah tradition had its own history before being incorporated into its present place by the Deuteronomist, who introduced it in 10.6–16 (Richter, 1964, 13–23; 1966). Yet part of this framework does appear in 11.33, and it therefore remains possible that the tradition of Jephthah stood along with the traditions of the earlier deliverers in the collection which was given this framework (*de Vaux, 688f.; Fohrer, 212f.), and that parts of the framework have been suppressed by the later Deuteronomist as a result of his incorporation of the Jephthah tradition within the list of judges (10.1–5; 12.7–15).

In 3.31 there is a brief notice to the effect that Shamgar delivered Israel through defeating six hundred Philistines. Since the verse shows none of the formulae of the framework and breaks the connection between 3.30 and 4.1, which do belong to this framework, it is clear that 3.31 is a fairly late addition, at any rate later than the stage of editing which introduced the framework (Richter, 1964, 6, 65, 92–5; *de Vaux, 822–4).

With Othniel the problem is quite different (see Richter, 1964, 52f., 63, 68–72). In 3.7–11 there is very little if anything which can be claimed as old tradition. Whereas it is usual that the framework should consist of formulae incorporating fairly extensive old tradition, 3.7–11 appears to be composed exclusively of these formulae, apart perhaps from the names of the oppressing enemy and of the deliverer. Moreover, while this section uses formulae otherwise found in the framework, it also contains much that is not found there but is to be found in the Deuteronomistic passages. This would indicate that 3.7–11 belongs to a stage of editing coming between the framework and the Deuteronomistic editing. It has all the appearances of having been composed as a typical example of the way in which God worked through the deliverers on Israel's behalf. It presupposes the existence of the framework on the basis of which it works, and has the intention of making perfectly clear the pattern of history and of God's activity in history as this is to be exemplified in the following stories of the deliverers. It was composed as an introduction to the edited collection of stories of Israel's deliverance from her enemies.

Behind the framework which brought the traditions of early Israel into the context of a history of Israel's sin and deliverance by Yahweh, there stands the earliest collection of deliverer stories. This collection included narratives dealing with Ehud, Deborah-Barak, Gideon, Abimelech (though not a deliverer), and probably also Jephthah. This appears to have been the first collection, and it has two characteristics: in the first place, the action of the stories is related to all Israel; it is not individual tribes which are oppressed and delivered, but all Israel together. Secondly, although the events are not yet presented within a pattern of the sin and deliverance of Israel, it is still the case that the first collection of deliverer stories showed these events as ones in which it was Yahweh acting through the temporary leader to save Israel. The wars were wars of Yahweh in which it was the life of Israel which was at stake, and in which Yahweh was the real war leader at work to deliver his people.

This was edited, as described, first through the addition of a framework which saw Israel's need for deliverance as a consequence of sin, and, secondly, through the addition of 3.7–11 in which a typical example of the way in which Yahweh worked on Israel's behalf was provided as an introduction to the stories of the deliverers which were to follow. The result was a collection of narratives, now closely bound together, relating Israel's experience in the period between the settlement of the land and the rise of the monarchy. It may be true that the 'period of the judges' as such is the later creation of the Deuteronomist (Noth, 1957, 47–50), but well before this stage of the editing of the traditions there already existed an understanding and a description of this time as a clearly defined period of Israel's history in which Israel was guided and saved by Yahweh through deliverers. The peculiar contribution of the Deuteronomist, apart from his introduction of the Samson stories, which had until then been handed down separately, was his general introductions in 2.11–19; 10.6–16 and his joining of the collection of stories about deliverers with another and quite different collection: the list of judges. Of the latter no heroic tales were recorded; they were known only as men who had judged Israel. The one exception to this was Jephthah, for not only did he occupy a place in the list of judges, but there also existed a tradition of his deliverance of Israel from the Ammonites as part of the collection of deliverer stories. It was probably this which persuaded the Deuteronomist to see judge and deliverer as identical and to bring the two literary sources together (Noth, 1969). The result was a complete transformation of the picture of the deliverer. He was no longer the temporary ruler raised up by Yahweh to deal with a specific situation, but was now a judge who delivered Israel and in the course of his lifetime's office ensured that sin would not recur to bring about further oppression.

The Deuteronomist made a second, equally significant, contribution: this lay in the incorporation of the narrative of the pre-monarchic period into the larger literary context of a history of Israel until the exile. For various reasons, this wider interest of the Deuteronomist is clear. Until then the editing of the accounts had been carried out within the context only of the accounts themselves; nothing in the framework or in 3.7–11 points to an involvement of the editor in any larger concern. With the Deuteronomist, however, the chronological details inserted in the narrative, together with the new idea of a steady increase in Israel's sin from one generation to the next (see 2.19), point clearly to a context which extends beyond the period of the judges. The language of this edition confirms this and identifies the editor with the author of the Deuteronomistic presentation of Israel's history from Deuteronomy–II Kings.

In post-Deuteronomistic times this closed presentation was broken not only by occasional additions and expansions, but also by the addition of Judges 1.1–2.5 or 1.1–2.9 (see Smend, 506–9), which interrupted the connection with the book of Joshua, and also by the addition of Judges 17–21, which disturbed the sequence of deliverers of whom, for the Deuteronomist, Samuel was the final representative. The Deuteronomistic passage in Judges 10.10–16 refers to the Ammonites, thus serving as an introduction to the following account of Jephthah; it also refers, however, to the Philistines, and in this the Deuteronomist probably intended to introduce not only the stories of Samson but also the figure of Samuel who also, in the Deuteronomist's view, functioned as Israel's leader in war with this same enemy.

B. Samuel

H. J. **Boecker**, *Die Beurteilung der Anfänge des Königtums in den deuteronomistischen Abschnitten des I. Samuelbuches*, WMANT 31, 1969; R. E. **Clements**, 'The Deuteronomistic Interpretation of the Founding of the Monarchy in I Sam. VIII', *VT* XXIV, 1974, 398–410; O. **Eissfeldt**, *The OT: An Introduction*, 1965; J. H. **Grønbaek**, *Die Geschichte vom Aufstieg Davids (1 Sam. 15–2. Sam. 5). Tradition und Komposition*, AThD 10, 1971; E. **Jenni**, 'Zwei Jahrzehnte Forschung an den Büchern Josua bis Könige', *TR* NF XXVII,

1961, 1–32, 97–146; F. **Langlamet**, 'Les récits de l'institution de la royauté (I Sam., VII–XII). De Wellhausen aux travaux récents', *RB* LXXVII, 1970, 161–200; D. J. **McCarthy**, 'The Inauguration of Monarchy in Israel', *Int* XXVII, 1973, 401–12; I. **Mendelsohn**, 'Samuel's Denunciation of Kingship in the Light of the Akkadian Documents from Ugarit', *BASOR* CXLIII, 1956, 17–22; M. **Noth**, *Überlieferungsgeschichtliche Studien*, 1957; A. N. **Radjawane**, 'Das deuteronomistische Geschichtswerk. Ein Forschungsbericht', *TR* NF XXXVIII, 1973–4, 177–216; A. D. **Ritterspach**, *The Samuel Traditions. An Analysis of the Anti-Monarchical Source* (Dissertation, Berkeley 1967); L. **Rost**, *Die Überlieferung von der Thronnachfolge Davids*, BWANT III/6, 1926 = his *Das kleine Credo*, 1965, 119–253; A. **Weiser**, *Introduction to the Old Testament*, London/New York 1961; idem, *Samuel. Seine geschichtliche Aufgabe und religiöse Bedeutung*, FRLANT 81, 1962.

As with the book of Judges so with the books of Samuel, attempts to trace the continuation of documents beyond the pentateuch have not been successful (see Jenni, 107 f.; Radjawane, 195–200). The material does not yield consistent sources. Instead, as with the book of Judges, we are led to think in terms of traditions which have been taken up and edited by the Deuteronomist as part of his presentation of the history of Israel. Again, as with the book of Judges, we must reckon also in the books of Samuel with a more or less extensive editing of traditions before they were used by the Deuteronomist. It is in the determination of the precise contribution of the Deuteronomist to these traditions that a major problem lies.

The account of the death of Saul in I Samuel 31 marks the limit of our present concern with the books of Samuel; but even within this first book there is much which need not be discussed in detail at this point, since our concern is with Saul alone. I Samuel 1–3 is a self-contained unit dealing with the birth and youth of Samuel and justifying his succession to Eli at Shiloh (see Ritterspach, 133–9). It is a secondary enrichment of the original Samuel tradition and derives from prophetic circles; it has no connection with the following section (I Sam. 4–6). The latter is concerned with the history of the ark and does not refer to Samuel. It finds its continuation in II Samuel 6, and together with this chapter forms a complete entity. Since it is clearly interested in exalting the significance of the ark at Jerusalem, it is probably best seen as having originated in priestly circles, grouped around the ark in Jerusalem, in the time of David or Solomon (see Rost, 122–59). It too, therefore, has no particular relevance at this point.

For the history of Saul we are in fact dependent on two blocks of material: the first in I Samuel 7–15, and the second in I Samuel 16–II Samuel 5. The latter section, however, is much less concerned with Saul than it is with David, and indeed apparently is basically concerned with legitimizing David's accession to the throne by showing that Yahweh chose David as Saul's successor (see Grønbaek, 261–78). Its interest in relating the history of Saul is, therefore, very much a secondary one. However, the analysis of this section belongs to the history of David rather than to that of Saul, and in the present context only incidental reference will be made to it.

The most important part of I Samuel in this context is chs. 7–15, relating the rise of Saul, his military victories and his rejection by Samuel. Traditionally, these chapters have been divided into a pro-monarchic source (see Langlamet), of which the former, in 9.1–10.16; 11; 13–14, has been taken as early and historically reliable, the latter, in 7.1–8.22; 10.17–27; 12; 15, as late and historically unreliable. More recently, Noth (54–63) has to some extent reaffirmed that position, in that much of what was identified as the anti-monarchic source has been assigned by him to Deuteronomistic authorship, based on and 'correcting' the older traditions. Although this approach has been subjected to considerable criticism, one suggested alternative to it – the identification in these chapters of J, E (and L) as the continuation of pentateuchal sources (Eissfeldt, 268–71) – is, as already indicated, a most unlikely solution to the problems of these chapters. On the other hand, a serious challenge to Noth's view has taken the form of an attempt to distinguish the Deuteronomistic contribution to these chapters from an earlier prophetic stage of editing to which much of Noth's Deuteronomistic material has been assigned (see Weiser, 1961, 161–3, 166–8; 1962). Yet, it must be doubted that this view has had more than marginal effect on Noth's presentation. Both in general structure (see McCarthy) and in detail the Deuteronomistic contribution to these chapters has been a weighty one. In 7.15–17 the Deuteronomist has taken up an old tradition of Samuel as 'judge', in the manner of the judges of the list in Judges 10.1–5; 12.7–15, and has supplemented this in the earlier part of that same chapter with his own composition relating how Samuel delivered Israel from the threat of the Philistines. In this way Samuel is presented as the last in the succession of the judge-deliverers, as the Deuteronomist understood the pre-monarchic leaders of Israel, whose place was then taken by Saul. In ch. 8 he has taken up what is probably older material, dealing in the first place with the failure of Samuel's sons to uphold justice (8.1–3), and secondly, in 8.10–22, reflecting either conditions in the

Canaanite city-state system (so Mendelsohn) or conditions in Israel itself under Solomon (see Clements, 403–6), but intended in any case to indicate clearly the great disadvantages which the monarchy brings with it. This material has been used by the Deuteronomist, relying on the royal law of Deuteronomy 17, in order to bring to expression a tension considered basic to the monarchic institution: kingship is introduced in order to ensure continuity and stability in the administration of justice, but in itself it may become the cause of injustice through the unjust burdens which it will inevitably lay on the people (see Boecker, 27–30).

I Samuel 8 finds its Deuteronomistic continuation in 10.17–27, which in its reference to the physical stature of Saul in verse 23 clearly incorporates the old conclusion of the folktale in 9.1–10.16, in which Saul's physical appearance was a major factor in his being made leader of Israel (see 9.2). However, the Deuteronomist has modified this conclusion in order to emphasize the role of Yahweh in the election of the king.

The Deuteronomist's final contribution is in ch. 12, which is a totally Deuteronomistic composition (Noth, 5, 10, 47; Boecker, 63f.), marking the transition from the period of the judges to that of the monarchy. As well as that, the chapter also provides the resolution to the theological problem which the rise of the monarchy posed, and which the Deuteronomist has brought into the open through his arrangement of the material of I Samuel 8–12 into an alternation of sections favourable to the monarchy with sections critical of the monarchy. The issue – that of the real source of leadership and deliverance for Israel, whether Yahweh or the king – is resolved by the description in I Samuel 12 of the integration of the monarchic institution into the covenant relationship between Yahweh and Israel, so that the king, while anointed and therefore approved by Yahweh, must still, like the rest of Israel, be subject to the covenant law. The Deuteronomist's attitude, therefore, is not anti-monarchical as such; indeed, in so far as he sets the people's request for a king within the context of the corruption of justice (I Sam. 8.1–3) and describes the king as chosen and instituted by Yahweh (I Sam. 10.17–27), it is clear that he recognizes its benefits. It is a theological problem which the Deuteronomist sees concerning the proper place of the monarchy in Israel as the covenant people of Yahweh, and this he sets out to illustrate and to resolve. Finally, in I Samuel 13.1, the Deuteronomist has introduced Saul, using the formula he was to use from then on in introducing Israel's kings.

For pre-Deuteronomistic material we are then left with 9.1–10.16

(23); 11; 13.2–15.35. Within these chapters two accounts may be distinguished which are parallel to the extent that both have to do with Saul's election as king over Israel. The one is formed by 11.1–15, which recounts Saul's popular election as king on the basis of his victory over the Ammonites. The other, in 9.1–10.16 (23); 13.2–14.52, recounts Saul's nomination by Samuel as Israel's leader, his acclamation by the people as their king, and his military successes. The last section incorporates, in 13.7b–15, an account of the rejection of Saul by Samuel (to which ch. 15 provides a variant). This whole account, through the emphasis which it places on Samuel and his role not only in the anointing of the king but also in his rejection, has clearly been shaped in prophetic circles which have edited and brought together a number of formerly independent traditions.

It was the Deuteronomist who brought together the two parallel accounts through the insertion of 10.26f. and 11.12–14. These introduce the idea of opposition to Saul and so make possible the harmonization of two originally quite independent accounts of Saul's election by presenting the one as confirmation of the other, a confirmation made necessary by the (groundless) initial opposition to Saul.

It is apparent, therefore, that the Deuteronomist is responsible for a major part of the present form of the Saul tradition. Not only has he brought together older independent accounts but he has set these within the theological context of an attempt to show the true place of the monarchy in Israel. No sources as such can be discerned here. It is independent traditions which the Deuteronomist has used and supplemented. The idea of an anti-monarchic source is quite inappropriate, as is also the idea that the Deuteronomist himself was anti-monarchic. He used material in ch. 8 which is critical of the monarchy, but which is of uncertain provenance; but in setting the people's request for a king in the context of the need to ensure justice in Israel he clearly did not disapprove of the institution in principle. Rather, he saw it as an institution which had the potential for either good or evil, and was concerned to show how it could be compatible with the notion of Israel as the people of Yahweh.

§2.   APPROACHES TO THE PROBLEMS OF HISTORICAL RECONSTRUCTION

A. **Alt**, 'Israel, politische Geschichte', *RGG*² III, 1929, 438f.; idem, *Die Staatenbildung der Israeliten in Palästina*, Leipzig: Reformationsprogramm der

Universität, 1930 = his *KS* II, 1953, 1–65 = 'The Formation of the Israelite State in Palestine', *Essays*, 1966, 171–237; idem, 'Das Königtum in den Reichen Israel und Juda', *VT* I, 1951, 2–22 = his *KS* II, 116–34 = 'The Monarchy in the Kingdoms of Israel and Judah', *Essays*, 1966, 239–59; G. W. **Anderson**, 'Israel: Amphictyony; 'AM; KAHAL; 'EDAH', *Translating and Understanding the Old Testament: Essays in honor of H. G. May*, ed. H. T. Frank and W. L. Reed, Nashville: Abingdon Press 1970, 135–51; W. **Beyerlin**, 'Das Königscharisma bei Saul', *ZAW* LXXIII, 1961, 186–201; G. **Buccellati**, *Cities and Nations of Ancient Syria: An Essay on Political Institutions with Special Reference to the Israelite Kingdoms*, StSem 26, 1967; G. **Fohrer**, 'Altes Testament – "Amphiktyonie" und "Bund"?', *TLZ* XCI, 1966, 801–16, 893–904 = his *Studien*, 1969, 84–119; J. **Hoftijzer**, 'Enige Opmerkingen rond het israëlitischen 12-Stammensystem', *NTT* XIV, 1959/60, 241–63; W. H. **Irwin**, 'Le sanctuaire central israélite avant l'établissement de la monarchie', *RB* LXXII, 1965, 161–84; O. **Kaiser**, 'Stammesgeschichtliche Hintergründe der Josephsgeschichte', *VT* X, 1960, 1–15; H.-J. **Kraus**, *Die prophetische Verkündigung des Rechts in Israel*, TS 51, 1957; idem, *Gottesdienst in Israel: Grundriss einer Geschichte des alttestamentlichen Gottesdienstes²*, München: Chr. Kaiser 1962 = *Worship in Israel*, Oxford/Richmond: Basil Blackwell/John Knox Press 1966; A. D. H. **Mayes**, *Israel in the Period of the Judges*, SBT II/29, 1974; J. **Muilenburg**, 'The "Office" of the Prophet in Ancient Israel', *The Bible in Modern Scholarship*, 1965, 74–97; E. W. **Nicholson**, *Deuteronomy and Tradition*, Oxford/Philadelphia: Basil Blackwell/Fortress Press 1967; M. **Noth**, *Das System der zwölf Stämme Israels*, BWANT IV/1, 1930; idem, *History of Pentateuchal Traditions*, 1972; idem, 'Überlieferungsgeschichtliches zur zweiten Hälfte des Josuabuches', *Alttestamentliche Studien Friedrich Nötscher zum 60. Geburtstag gewidmet*, BBB 1, 1950, 152–67; idem, 'Das Amt des "Richters Israels"', (see §1A) in his *GS* II, 1969, 71–85; H. M. **Orlinsky**, 'The Tribal System of Israel and Related Groups in the Period of the Judges', *Studies and Essays in Honor of A. A. Neuman*, ed. M. Ben-Horin, B. D. Weinryb, S. Zeitlin, Leiden/Philadelphia: E. J. Brill/Dropsie College 1962, 375–87; J. **van der Ploeg**, 'Les chefs du peuple d'Israël et leurs titres', *RB* LVII, 1950, 40–61; R. **Rendtorff**, 'Reflections on the Early History of Prophecy in Israel', *History and Hermeneutic*, JTC 4, 1967, 14–34; E. A. **Speiser**, 'Background and Function of the Biblical Nāśī', *CBQ* XXV, 1963, 111–17 = his *Oriental and Biblical Studies*, ed. J. J. Finkelstein and Moshe Greenberg, Philadelphia: University of Pennsylvania Press 1967, 113–23; E. **Täubler**, *Biblische Studien. Die Epoche der Richter*, Tübingen: J. C. B. Mohr, 1958; A. **Weiser**, *Die Psalmen*, ATD 14–15, ⁵1959 = *The Psalms*, OTL, 1962.

A.   The theory of a twelve-tribe Israelite amphictyony

A number of major problems immediately confront the historian dealing with this period. The oldest collection of stories relating to the deliverers, on the one hand, and the list of judges, on the other, set their activities within the context of 'Israel'. Since, however, it is quite clear that in no case did Israel as defined in the various tribal lists act as a unit in these events, we must ask what the Israel of the deliverer stories is, and what its relation is to those tribes specifically mentioned in the context of the events described; if it was Israel that the Moabites oppressed (Judg. 3.13), though only Benjamin and Ephraim appear to have been involved in any action against Eglon the king of Moab, was there some institutional framework within which Benjamin and Ephraim acted as representatives of Israel, and if so how is this Israel to be defined? Similarly, how is one to define the Israel within which the judges of Judges 10.1–5; 12.7–15 performed their functions? This question of an adequate definition of Israel becomes even more urgent in the context of the rise of the monarchy, for once the nature of the monarchy has been determined (a further problem in itself), the relationship between the monarchic state and the Israel of the pre-monarchic period must be explained. Unless this question is resolved then the description of the historical processes which constitute the transition from pre-monarchic to monarchic Israel will be inadequate.

In fairly recent study of the period two names are predominant: Alt and Noth. Moreover, it was in the same year, 1930, that the publication of their inquiries laid a foundation which has been the basis for further research which still proceeds. Although Alt (1929) and others even earlier (see Noth, 1930, 47) had already pointed to Greek and Italian tribal systems, organized as sacral unions around a common sanctuary, as an analogy by which the structure of Israel in the pre-monarchic period might be elucidated, it was Noth who worked out this analogy in all its detail and expounded it in a most convincing manner. This study was supplemented by Alt's 1930 presentation on the rise of the Israelite monarchy which, in a similarly convincing manner, showed the monarchy in Israel as a novel institution which was yet decisively influenced by the forms of leadership which had existed in Israel in pre-monarchic times.

The evidence for the existence in Israel during the period of the judges of an organization similar to the Greek and Italian sacral unions, or amphictyonies, is derived in the first instance from the tribal lists of the Old Testament. For in common with Old

Testament records relating to non-Israelite peoples (see Gen. 22.20–4; 25.2, 13–16; 36.10–14, 20–8), so with Israel itself there is a remarkable consistency in the appearance of the number twelve, or multiples of it, in the total tribal membership of the people. Israel was a community of twelve tribes descended from the twelve sons of Jacob. Sometimes, as in Genesis 29–30, the lists are of the sons of Jacob; at other times, as in Numbers 26, the lists are of the tribes of Israel rather than the sons of Jacob. But the number twelve of the total is retained. There are other, and important, variations between the lists, however. The main discrepancy is that some of them include Levi while others do not. In fact, the lists may be divided into two categories on the basis of this variation, Genesis 49 being the basic form of that group of lists which includes Levi, and Numbers 26 the basic form of that group where Levi does not appear. The importance of this variation lies in the fact that it helps establish the relative ages of these lists, that which includes Levi being most probably older than the other. The reason for this is that it is easier to explain how Levi should have been secondarily omitted from the list than to explain its subsequent inclusion. Levi in Genesis 49 is one among the others, on an equal footing with his brothers; it may, therefore, be assumed that, as in the tradition of Genesis 34, so here, the existence of a 'secular' tribe of Levi is presupposed. Otherwise, however, Levi is a priestly tribe separate from its fellow tribes and having no possession of land. This is the Levi which is historically known to us, and it is this peculiar status of the tribe which is reflected in its omission from the tribal list of Numbers 26. Levi as a secular tribe, on the other hand, belongs to early conditions of which we have no accurate historical knowledge. So the enumeration of Israelite tribes represented by Genesis 49 is assumed to be older than that given in Numbers 26 (Noth, 1930, 24–8).

Both lists, however, reflect conditions of the pre-monarchic period. This is concluded from Numbers 26. This is a census list, and besides referring to each individual tribe it also mentions the various families included within each tribe. Among the families several, such as Shechem, Tirzah, and Hepher, bear names which correspond to the names of Canaanite city-states, indicating that the city-states in question were considered the property of the individual Israelite tribes. However, the city-states mentioned lay in the mountain territory of Palestine, not in the plains, and this indicates that at the time of origin of the list the Israelite tribes were in possession of the mountain area but had not yet conquered the plains. Since in the time of David the plain of Esdraelon and the coastal plain were absorbed into the Israelite state, the list must then belong to an earlier time, and the same must be the case with Genesis 49, since this list is older than that of Numbers 26.

The institutional framework within which the lists originated and which they reflect is not described for us by the Old Testament, and it is in order to provide such a framework that Noth has used extra-biblical analogies. The chief analogy is provided by the Greek amphictyony centred upon the two sanctuaries of Apollo at Delphi and Demeter at Pylae. Not only is it of this amphictyony that we are best informed, but its tribal as opposed to a city-state organization is an indication of its antiquity. From the information available on this sacral union it may be concluded that the amphictyony was a loose organization of twelve members, each of which was responsible for one month in the year for the maintenance of the central sanctuary, the amphictyony's focal point. Among other amphictyonic regulations there was the obligation laid on each member to send a representative to the central sanctuary where matters of concern to the whole organization were regularly discussed. However, while the central sanctuary was the focal point of the group, and the place of periodic festivals when the members of the amphictyony would gather there, it was not for the purpose of looking after the sanctuary that the amphictyony was founded. Rather, it was apparently to act as a uniting influence on an already existing alliance that the central sanctuary was adopted (further information in Noth, 1930, 46–56; *de Vaux, 697–700).

By using this analogy Noth concluded that the disparate items of information which the Old Testament provides on the period of the judges can be fitted together into a pattern which allows a coherent reconstruction of the history of Israel before the rise of the monarchy. 'Israel' is the amphictyonic organization of the twelve tribes mentioned in the tribal lists. To the extent that the basic lists of each group, Genesis 49 and Numbers 26, do not conform, so the composition of amphictyonic Israel varied. Genesis 49 reflects Israel at the beginning of the period of the judges, while Numbers 26 reflects a later stage when its composition had slightly changed.

The Israelite amphictyony was founded when all the member tribes had entered the land. In this connection Joshua 24 is supremely important, for this chapter records the conclusion of the process of settlement in which the 'house of Joseph', as the last group to settle under the leadership of Joshua, introduced to the worship of Yahweh to tribes already living in Palestine, and thereby established Yahweh as the God of the amphictyony.

Joshua 24, the 'foundation charter' (Kraus, 1966, 136) of the Israelite amphictyony, is set at the sanctuary of Shechem. It may be assumed, therefore, that this became the central sanctuary of the amphictyony. Each tribe would have been responsible for its main-tenance for a month in the year, and it would have served as the focal point of the life of the amphictyony. In that connection it would have been the meeting-place for tribal representatives, and also for gatherings of larger groups on regular festival occasions of the tribes. Numbers 1.5–15 gives a list of the tribal representatives, each of whom bore the title *nāśī'*. While they may have been respons-ible for the organization of the amphictyony, it was in the regular festivals that its character as a sacral union came to expression. Here again Joshua 24 is enlightening, for it not only records the founda-tion of the amphictyony but also reflects the form by which the tribes worshipped Yahweh in their regular festivals. It was a covenant form of worship, in which the tribes affirmed their acceptance of the conditions of the covenant proclaimed to them as the law of Yahweh. One of Israel's most important cult objects was the ark which would in fact have been the real central sanctuary (Noth, 1930, 95–108). This was the visible representation of the presence of Yahweh. Since the ark is found at Gilgal, Bethel, and at Shiloh, it must be assumed that the amphictyonic central sanctuary was moved accordingly.

Within the context of this analogy several other features of the Old Testament record gain significance. In Judges 19–21 there is an account of how men from the city of Gibeah committed an offence. The tribe of Benjamin, in whose territory the city lay, was called on to punish those responsible, but refused to do so. As a result, the remaining tribes of Israel went to battle with Benjamin and decimated the tribe. As a parallel to this in the Greek context we find that the city of Amphissa committed a cultic offence which merited punishment. The amphictyonic member concerned, how-ever, refused to carry out the punishment. This resulted in the Amphissa war of 339 BCE which led to the exclusion of that member from the amphictyony. The event related in Judges 19–21, which is directly parallel to this, is likewise an amphictyonic war caused by breach of amphictyonic law.

Besides this direct parallel, there are other Old Testament records which are understood against an amphictyonic background even though Greek amphictyonic history offers nothing comparable. This is the case with the list of minor judges in Judges 10.1–5; 12.7–15. Theirs is held to have been an amphictyonic office of such central significance that events would have been dated by reference to the name and the year of office of the judge (Noth, 1969, 75). Although the precise functions of the judge are not clear it is suggested (Noth, 1950, 163) that he may have been involved in deciding territorial disputes between tribes.

The amphictyonic organization of the Israelite tribes, however ideal a form it may have been to express Israel's true nature, was yet inadequate to meet the constant threat to the life of the tribes which was posed by the Philistines. So the monarchic state came into existence. Much of our present understanding of the background of the rise of Saul depends on Alt who, while emphasizing the importance of the specifically Israelite background in the form which the monarchy was to assume, argued that it was not in fact a natural development in .Israel (Alt, 1966, 183–5; *Herrmann, 131 f.). Rather, it was a foreign institution which Israel was forced to adopt by the external pressure which the Philistines exerted. In fact, two things form the background to Saul's monarchy: the threat of the Philistines and the older political pattern within Israel itself. In the latter connection it is charismatic leadership which played a decisive role in the rise of the monarchy. Saul rose to power, like the old deliverers, on the basis of his charisma which manifested itself on the occasion of his deliverance of the city of Jabesh-gilead from the Ammonites (I Sam. 11). The one significant thing which distinguished Saul from earlier leaders, which changed him from a deliverer into a king, was popular acclamation. It was through Yahweh's designation that he became *nāgīd*; he became *melek*, king, by popular decision (Alt, 1966, 185). The factor which caused this break in the pattern of traditional leadership was the 'chronic evil' of Philistine domination which the type of temporary leadership exercised by the earlier charismatics could not deal with.

This background was determinative for two distinctive characteristics of Saul's monarchy. On the one hand, it was a national monarchy, and, on the other hand, it was non-dynastic. The kingship was in effect permanent leadership in war, with little or no function in peacetime. But it was also personal leadership, being founded on the charismatic qualities which Saul had displayed. Saul's son Ishbosheth did not appear as leader in battle and, since it was precisely in that way that kingship at this stage functioned in Israel, he cannot then have been king in succession to Saul. This also means that Saul's kingship was national rather than territorial; since its form was that of military leadership it was exercised over people in national terms rather than over a particular geographical area. It was left to David to round out the territorial unity of the kingdom through incorporating non-Israelite areas into the state.

B.   Critique of the amphictyonic theory

This view of Israel in the period of the judges and the early monarchy has found wide following with very little modification (see, e.g., *Bright, 158–66, 179–86). Not only this, but it has also formed the basis of various other developments not immediately concerned with the period in question. So, the context of the amphictyony is held to have been decisive in the development of the traditions of the pentateuch generally (see Noth, 1972, 42–5), while amphictyonic Israel as a covenant people has been taken as the source of the traditions which now find expression in Deuteronomy (see Nicholson, 48–57). The psalms and the prophets too have been linked with the amphictyony; for, on the one hand, the covenant festival has been taken as the setting within which the psalms were used (Weiser), and, on the other, the prophets have been seen as successors of an amphictyonic official who in the covenant cult proclaimed the law to the people (see Kraus, 1957; Muilenburg). As far as the monarchy is concerned, Alt himself applied the distinction between dynastic and non-dynastic or charismatic kingship to the post-Solomonic period, seeing the kings of the northern state of Israel as successors to the charismatic form of kingship initiated by Saul, while Judah continued to be governed by the 'house of David' (Alt, 1966, 241–59).

In recent years a growing volume of studies devoted to the period of the judges and the rise of the monarchy has led to a position in which some re-assessment of the reconstructions of Alt and Noth is necessary.

Etymologically, the word 'amphictyony' points to an organization in which people were settled around a focal point (Buccellati, 114; *de Vaux, 703 f.). So the primary characteristic of the amphictyony is the central sanctuary, the relationship between the members and the sanctuary being the essential factor. On the other hand, the main evidence drawn from the Old Testament for the existence of a parallel institution in Israel consists of the lists of twelve tribes. The use as primary evidence in the Israelite context of what in the extrabiblical context is a secondary characteristic of the amphictyony – the number of its members – constitutes a major weakness in the case for the existence of an Israelite amphictyony. This is all the more serious in view of the fact that there did exist in Greece and Italy amphictyonies whose membership was seven, eleven, or twenty-three (see Anderson, 143; Orlinsky, 376). Moreover, even disregarding this basic point, there are serious questions to be raised in relation to Noth's use of what he accepted as his primary evidence, the Old Testament tribal lists.

The distinction between those lists which include Levi and those which do not is a valid one. However, of the latter category it is clear that Numbers 26 is not the basic form (Hoftijzer, 259f.; *de Vaux, 726f.; Mayes, 16–34), for it is only within the context of the late priestly writing that the order of tribes mentioned here finds its explanation. P in Numbers 1.20–43; 2.3–31; 26, is describing the layout of the Israelite military camp in four companies, each company consisting of three tribes. In order to do this P has used an older list, now to be found in Numbers 1.5–15, and has slightly modified it in order to ensure that Judah, the tribe which he favoured, should appear as the first of the group of three tribes in the company to which it was to belong. This means that there no longer exists a basis for dating this group of lists to the pre-monarchic period, for Numbers 26, which Noth relied on, is a late priestly adaptation.

Secondly, Noth's idea that Genesis 49 represents an older type of list than those of the other group is also doubtful. It depends on the assertion that Levi is a 'secular' tribe in Genesis 49.5–7; but that this is so is far from clear. All we may certainly say of Levi here is that it is a landless tribe (it is this status which Genesis 49 is concerned to explain); but otherwise the landless tribe of Levi is known to us only as a priestly tribe or as one in the process of becoming a priestly tribe (see Mayes, 24–7). Anyway, it may well be that there is no chronological relationship between these lists. They have different interests: the ones which include Levi are genealogical lists, those without Levi are concerned with the independent tribes (see *de Vaux, 718–23). The view that they have a chronological relationship itself depends on the presupposition that they have some kind of institutional background – the very thing which the lists themselves are supposed to prove.

The only other point which can link these lists, in this case Genesis 49, with the pre-monarchic period is the appearance of Joseph in that list, for Joseph is understood to be the original entity which later split into Ephraim and Manasseh (see *Noth, 58–63). However, there are strong indications that, on the contrary, Joseph is a secondary designation, presupposing the existence of Ephraim and Manasseh, and so also the stabilization of tribal movements and relationships which were not completed before the end of the period of the judges (see Täubler, 176–8; Kaiser, 7–12; *de Vaux, 642–53; Mayes, 28–30). The earliest and original use appears to have been 'house of Joseph', which came into existence in the monarchic period as a collective designation for a northern group, parallel to the designation 'house of Judah'. If this is the case, then the background of these lists appears to be the monarchic period rather than that of the judges. In any case, the lists of both groups must be later than the time of the Song of Deborah in Judges 5, for here neither Joseph nor Manasseh have yet appeared; and this Song, as we shall later indicate, commemorates an event which took place towards the end of the period of the judges.

In the Greek and Italian amphictyonies there were not always twelve members, so the number twelve of the Israelite tribes, which Noth found to have its best explanation against the background of an Israelite amphictyony, does not then necessarily point to any such organization. Moreover, to give it an amphictyonic significance in fact is to ignore the way in which the number twelve actually is used, both within and outside the Old Testament. It is used to express totality; in Greece and Rome it is frequently found in this sense in literary and cultic contexts. It has similar cultic usage in Israel (I Kings 7.44; 10.20; 19.19), and the lists of twelve sons of Jacob or twelve Israelite tribes find their best parallel within the Old Testament itself in such passages as Genesis 22.20–4; 25.12–16; 36.10–43, where in each the totality of the people finds its expression through its description as descended from the twelve sons of one man. It is a concern with completeness, a theoretical or literary concern, not a practical one, which is expressed in the use of the number twelve (*de Vaux, 702 f.).

The primary Old Testament evidence for the existence of an Israelite amphictyony is, therefore, quite unreliable. The evidence that is in fact required, that which would show the existence of a central sanctuary, is not given by the Old Testament. Following Noth's description of the assumed Israelite central sanctuary it was characterized by three factors: it was acknowledged and visited by all the tribes or their representatives; the festival of covenant renewal was celebrated there; and it was the place where the ark was kept (see Irwin). Of these three characteristics the most important is clearly that a sanctuary should be acknowledged as central by the members of the supposed amphictyony. This would be indicated by regular visits to the sanctuary by the tribes on festival occasions, by its use as the meeting-place for representatives of the tribes, and by its maintenance by these tribes on a regular basis. But none of the sanctuaries proposed fulfil these criteria (see Mayes, 34–55). There is no evidence of common festivals of this nature. It is not even clear that the tribes had representatives as such; manifestly early usages of the word *nāśī*, which is supposed to have been their title, such as Genesis 34.2; Exodus 22.28, give no specially *tribal* significance to the term (see Speiser, van der Ploeg). Finally, there is nothing to indicate that any sanctuary was maintained by a number of tribes rather than by the particular tribe in whose territory it lay.

The indications are, therefore, that the theory that pre-monarchic Israel had an amphictyonic structure, attractive as it is as an analogy by which to shed light on a particularly obscure period of Israel's history, must be given up. The Greek and Italian amphictyonies belong to the Indo-European rather than to the Semitic world (see Fohrer, 92 f.). In addition, they appeared in the middle of or late in the first millennium BCE, rather than in the second half of the second millennium, to which the period of the judges belongs. So not only does the Old Testament provide no support, but the cultural and chronological separation of Israel from the Greek and Italian amphictyonies argues against the use of the analogy of the amphictyony to understand Israel in the pre-monarchic period.

Alt's views of the nature of the monarchy of Saul have not been subject to criticism of the same severity; yet even here some points have been made to make re-consideration necessary. Firstly, while Alt was concerned to explain Saul's kingship in terms of the pre-monarchic forms of leadership in Israel, Beyerlin (187–90) has insisted that there were some essential differences between Saul and his predecessors which mark Saul off as a quite new phenomenon. This has been said with reference to what is taken as the very basis of Saul's leadership, his charisma, which is understood by Beyerlin to have been of a type different from that of the pre-monarchic leaders. It is described in 'prophetic' terms (I Sam. 10.9–13), which is taken to represent an accommodation of a wholly new phenomenon – charisma deriving from anointing – to Israelite conceptual forms. Saul's royal charisma is a Canaanite form, since the rite of anointing was borrowed from Canaan (Beyerlin, 192–4) and adapted to the Israelite context.

It is probably the case that Beyerlin's view does not take adequate account of the influence of the prophetic context within which many of the Saul stories were handed on, but his further contention that Saul's kingship, whether or not this was 'charismatic' and based on his having been anointed, was dynastic is certainly correct. If one is to find any true successors to the pre-monarchic forms of leadership they are to be found among the prophets as much as among the kings, since it is in prophetic circles that the distinctive concerns of pre-monarchic leadership are to be found (see Rendtorff). Saul was quite different from his predecessors not only in that his own position as leader was a permanent one, but also in that he founded a dynasty (see Buccellati, 127, 195–200). There was no such thing as non-dynastic monarchy. Saul was succeeded by his son Ishbosheth who became king over a substantial area and ruled, moreover, from a capital which had not been his father's. It was as a royal prince that he was put on the throne by Abner, and he evidently enjoyed sufficient support from Israelites generally. Such differences as may have existed between Saul and Ishbosheth derive not from the fact that Ishbosheth was not recognized as king (so *Bright[2], 191 n. 31), but simply from the fact that it was not Ishbosheth but Saul who founded the dynasty. The later kings of the northern kingdom must also be seen as dynastic kings (see Buccellati, 200–8). Kingship means dynastic kingship; so the election of Saul has important elements of discontinuity from the leadership of his predecessors. This does not alter the well-established point that Saul's kingdom was a national rather than a territorial one, and that his rule was effective mainly only in war. This latter feature, however, is attributable to the rudimentary stage of development of the monarchy rather than to any inherent character which it had under Saul.

§3. THE PERIOD OF THE JUDGES

Y. **Aharoni**, 'New Aspects of the Israelite Occupation in the North', *Near Eastern Archaeology*, 1970, 254–67; W. F. **Albright**, 'Further Light on the History of Israel from Lachish and Megiddo', *BASOR* LXVIII, 1937, 22–6; idem, *From the Stone Age to Christianity*, [2]1957; idem, *Yahweh and the Gods of Canaan*, 1968; A. **Alt**, 'Megiddo im Übergang vom kanaanäischen zum israelitischen Zeitalter', *ZAW* LXII, 1944, 67–85 = his *KS* I, 1953, 256–73; idem, 'The Settlement of the Israelites in Palestine' (see ch. IV §4), *Essays*, 1966, 135–69; C. F. **Burney**, *The Book of Judges*, [2]1930; O. **Eissfeldt**, 'Der geschichtliche Hintergrund der Erzählung von Gibeas Schandtat (Richter 19–21)', *Festschrift Georg Beer*, ed. A. Weiser, Stuttgart: W. Kohlhammer 1935, 19–40 = his *KS* II, 1963, 64–80; A. **Globe**, 'The Literary Structure and Unity of the Song of Deborah', *JBL* XCIII, 1974, 493–512; O. **Grether**, 'Die Bezeichnung "Richter" für die charismatischen Helden der vorstaatlichen Zeit', *ZAW* LVII, 1939, 110–21; H. **Haag**, 'Gideon–Jerubbaal–Abimelek', *ZAW* LXXIX, 1967, 305–14; F. F. **Hvidberg**, *Weeping and Laughter in the Old Testament*, Copenhagen: Nyt Nordisk Forlag 1962; G. H. **Jones**, '"Holy War" or "Yahweh War"?', *VT* XXV,

1975, 642–58; E. **Kutsch**, 'Gideons Berufung und Altarbau', *TLZ* LXXXI, 1956, 75–84; B. **Lindars**, 'Gideon and Kingship', *JTS* XVI, 1965, 315–26; J. L. **McKenzie**, *The World of the Judges*, Englewood Cliffs/London: Prentice Hall/G. Chapman 1966; A. **Malamat**, 'The War of Gideon and Midian. A Military Approach', *PEQ* LXXXV, 1953, 61–5; idem, 'Cushan Rishathaim and the Decline of the Near East around 1200 BC', *JNES* XIII, 1954, 231–42; idem, 'The Period of the Judges', *WHJP* I/3, 1971, 129–63; A. D. H. **Mayes**, *Israel in the Period of the Judges*, SBT II/29, 1974; S. **Mowinckel**, '"Rahelstämme" und "Leastämme"', *Von Ugarit nach Qumran*, 1958, 129–50; H.-P. **Müller**, 'Der Aufbau des Deboraliedes', *VT* XVI, 1966, 446–59; M. **Noth**, *Die israelitischen Personennamen im Rahmen der gemeinsemitischen Namengebung*, BWANT III/10, 1928; idem, *Das System der zwölf Stämme Israels*, BWANT IV/1, 1930; G. **von Rad**, *Der heilige Krieg im alten Israel*, ATANT 20, 1951; W. **Richter**, 'Zu den "Richtern Israels"', *ZAW* LXXVII, 1965, 40–72; idem, *Traditionsgeschichtliche Untersuchungen zum Richterbuch*, BBB 18, 1963, ²1966; K.-D. **Schunck**, *Benjamin: Untersuchungen zur Entstehung und Geschichte eines israelitischen Stammes*, BZAW 86, 1963; idem, 'Die Richter Israels und ihr Amt', *SVT* XV, 1966, 252–62; A. **van Selms**, 'Judge Shamgar', *VT* XIV, 1964, 294–309; R. **Smend**, *Jahwekrieg und Stämmebund: Erwägungen zur ältesten Geschichte Israels*, FRLANT 84, 1963 = *Yahweh War and Tribal Confederation*, Nashville: Abingdon Press 1970; J. A. **Soggin**, *Das Königtum in Israel*, BZAW 104, 1967; F. **Stolz**, *Jahwes und Israels Kriege: Kriegstheorien und Kriegserfahrungen im Glauben des alten Israel*, ATANT 60, 1972; M. **Weippert**, '"Heiliger Krieg" in Israel und Assyrien', *ZAW* LXXXIV, 1972, 460–93; A. **Weiser**, 'Das Deboralied', *ZAW* LXXI, 1959, 67–97; G. E. **Wright**, 'Shechem', *AOTS*, 1967, 355–70.

Our earlier discussion of the literary sources which are devoted to the period of the judges indicated that there existed a pre-Deuteronomistic collection of stories of deliverers, including Ehud, Deborah-Barak, Gideon (Abimelech), and Jephthah. Independently of it there also existed a list of judges, now included in Judges 10.1–5; 12.7–15, stories of Samson, an account of the migration of the tribe of Dan, and the story of the outrage at Gibeah. Apart from the last two stories, which are post-Deuteronomistic additions to the book, these separate items were brought together by the Deuteronomist.

The narratives from pre-Deuteronomistic times set the events related within the context of Israel. The deliverers saved Israel from oppression and it was Israel which the judges judged. The identification of this Israel is certainly important for the history of the narratives if not for the history of the period of which they tell. We have seen that an amphictyonic Israel, which might have served as a basis for understanding the use of Israel in the book of Judges, is of doubtful historicity.

It is clear that whatever Israel may precisely mean in the narratives of the deliverers it is to a secondary stage in the transmission of the stories that we owe an involvement of Israel. Only once, in the case of the battle against Sisera related in Judges 5, do we find more than two tribes originally involved. Strictly local actions, and so also locally famous leaders, have secondarily been set in a much wider context. There is in fact much in favour of the view that the editing which first brought the traditions together and introduced Israel took place in the northern kingdom of Israel, and that the Israel in the first instance reflected is exactly that northern state. In the first place, it is just the area of the northern kingdom within which the events took place. Judah is brought into the picture only at a very late stage in the addition of the story of Othniel, a member of a Judaean clan (*de Vaux, 306–8), and does not figure in the original deliverer traditions. Secondly, it is against the background of prophetic groups in the northern kingdom that it is best to see the first collection of the stories of the deliverers being handed down and interpreted. Not only are such circles responsible for the description of the events as occasions of Israel's sinning against Yahweh and of Yahweh's deliverance of Israel, but also the idea that the deliverers were raised up by Yahweh and acted under the influence of the spirit of Yahweh fits best within such a prophetic context (Stolz, 131, 175, 202). In other words, it is not just a question of northern prophetic circles standing in line of succession to the pre-monarchic leaders; but it is also a matter of these groups having transmitted and edited the stories of these pre-monarchic leaders. The editing introduced the setting of sin and deliverance and also turned the occasional, spontaneous leaders of tribal groups into leaders of Israel who acted under the inspiration of the spirit of Yahweh, just as did these prophets themselves. All of this is what is to be expected of intensely nationalistic, religious circles, closely involved in Israel's wars, which is what these prophetic groups were (see *Bright, 241–6; *Herrmann, 209–13). This means among other things that the term 'charismatic', applied especially by Alt to Israel's pre-monarchic leaders, may well be misleading. That these men acted under the spirit of Yahweh is a prophetic idea; the pre-prophetic traditions show them to have been leaders of varying types who came to the fore in different ways to deal with different types of situations.

At the earliest stage the collection of deliverer stories falls apart into independent traditions of local leaders temporarily entrusted with military command in order to meet a threat to tribal life and freedom. What these traditions then reveal is not so much a history of Israel in the period of the judges as an insight into the nature of tribal life in this period. The fact that the events were local ones, of uncertain chronological relationship, makes very hazardous a reconstruction of a pattern of history in the period in which, for example, one can claim that the decline of Moab as a result of Ehud's victory allowed the rise and expansion of Ammon in the context of a struggle for control over a limited area of Transjordan (Malamat, 1971, 152–4). We are presented, rather, in the book of Judges with a series of vignettes in which attention is sharply focused on particular aspects of inter-tribal relations and relations between Israelite tribes and non-Israelites in the period after settlement, while the overall historical context is something which may be reconstructed only in the broadest outline.

The first event recorded, Othniel's victory over Cushan-rishathaim (Judg. 3.7–11), presents particular problems. As already indicated, it was composed as an introduction to the already existing collection of deliverer stories and has close connections with the Deuteronomistic stage of editing. Othniel was of the Judaean clan of the Kenizzites, and the intention in this record is apparently not only to introduce the deliverers by giving a typical example of Yahweh's activity in Israel, but also to provide a deliverer for Judah (McKenzie, 8f., 121 f.; *de Vaux, 807). Any historical basis that there may be to the account will be found only in an investigation of the names of Othniel and his opponent Cushan-rishathaim, 'king of Mesopotamia'. Various identifications of the latter have been proposed (see Malamat, 1954, 231 f.), mainly involving the supposition that the name is corrupt and consequent speculation on its original form. Othniel, however, is otherwise known from Joshua 15.16–19; Judges 1.12–15. These references indicate that if there is any historical foundation to the present story it belongs in the context of the settlement of Judaean clans in the land rather than in the context of events in the period of the judges (*de Vaux, 684).

Judges 3.12–30 contains the first of the early collection of deliverer stories, that of Ehud the Benjaminite who initiated the war which led to Israel's relief from Moabite oppression. The Moabites had evidently banded together with Ammonites and Amalekites on this occasion, but the extent and severity of their oppression is difficult to determine. They apparently occupied the city of Jericho, if this is the place to which 'city of palms' (3.13) refers; at any rate, 3.18f. (see also 3.28), in that it says nothing of Ehud's having crossed the Jordan river between presenting tribute to Eglon the king of Moab and arriving at Gilgal, presupposes a strong foreign presence west of

Jordan. Yet it was only the mid-Palestinian area, specifically
Benjamin and Ephraim, which was affected and which was involved
in the expulsion of the Moabites from the land. What is significant
here also is that Benjamin appears as an independent tribe strong
enough to initiate the revolt and lead the combined forces of
Ephraim and Benjamin against Moab. This would hardly have been
possible after the event recorded in Judges 19–21, and would
indicate that Ehud's revolt is at least earlier than this. Further, there
is no reference to Gad in the story; this tribe, which does not yet
appear in the Song of Deborah in Judges 5 either, came to occupy
the territory just north of Moab, as II Samuel 24.5 and the Moabite
Stone indicate (*de Vaux, 809–11), and would have been in Moab's
direct line of advance had it occupied this territory during the Ehud
revolt. The indications are, therefore, that the position of the story as
first of the series accurately reflects its reference to an event which
took place early in the period of the judges.

Judges 3.31 is a late addition breaking the connection between
3.30 and 4.1. Again here, if anything historical is to be reconstructed
it will be through the name 'Shamgar the son of Anath'. Whether
this means that Shamgar came from Beth-anath (Noth, 1928, 123 n.
1; Albright, 1957, 283), or rather indicates his Canaanite origin,
being named after the Canaanite goddess Anath (see van Selms,
301–3), the reason for his inclusion here is the reference to him in the
Song of Deborah in Judges 5.6 beside Jael. Jael is credited in the
Song with a decisive role in the defeat of Sisera, and so also Shamgar
is understood to have been involved in a similar exploit. This understanding is erroneous, however, for Shamgar is not an Israelite
name; it is unlikely that he was an Israelite leader, and Judges 5.6
does not necessarily presuppose what 3.31 attributes to him. The
most that can certainly be said is that Shamgar was a Canaanite
chieftain of some significance who ruled over part of Canaan in the
days before the battle against Sisera (see Alt's rather speculative
elaboration of this; 1953, 256–73).

In Judges 4 and 5 there are two descriptions, one in prose and the
other in verse, which ostensibly refer to the same event: Israel's
victory over Sisera. The serious differences between the two accounts, especially in relation to the participants in the battle, are not
open to any harmonization such as the idea that different stages of
the same battle are being described (Malamat, 1971, 137–40).
Judges 4 and 5 represent different types of literature which have
been transmitted by different routes; so a valid contrast of the two is
possible only after each has been adequately treated from the point

of view of its origin and growth (see Richter, 1966, 32–46, 61; Mayes, 87–98). In Judges 4 the closest we get to the event of the defeat of Sisera is in verses 17–22 where his death at the hands of Jael is described. In earlier parts of the chapter, especially verses 1–11, a complex situation has arisen as a result of the confusion of the Sisera tradition with a tradition of a quite separate event. The latter is Israel's defeat of Jabin who reigned in Hazor, which is described in Josh 11.1–15. This is a settlement tradition of the Galilean tribes, and the reason for its confusion with the Sisera tradition is apparently that both traditions were handed down at the same place – the sanctuary on Mount Tabor – and the tribes involved in the defeat of Jabin also participated in the battle against Sisera. The two traditions have been amalgamated by making Jabin king of Canaan and Sisera his army commander.

The unity of the Song of Deborah in Judges 5 has been emphasized (Globe), yet it is clear that it too has been elaborated, though in a way rather different from what has happened in Judges 4. In the song its elaboration has gone step by step with the different settings within which the song was in the course of time transmitted (see Richter, 1966, 65–9; Müller; Stolz, 105–13; Mayes, 89–92). In its introduction (5.2–11) and conclusion (5.31) the description of a theophany and the summons to praise Yahweh give the song the style of a psalm, and point to its use as a psalm of praise in the Jerusalem temple (see Ps. 68). In the kernel of the song, verses 12–30, the language is different and the focus of interest has changed. The psalm style is missing and the concern is less with praising Yahweh than with the battle itself and the part played in it by the individual tribes. This kernel represents the earliest part of the song. Apart from verse 18, the kernel is a unity; that verse is an addition which, as in 4.1–11, has introduced an allusion to the Jabin tradition of Joshua 11. The verse has a different form from the others, and in the reference to 'the heights of (*měrōmê*) the field' there may well be an allusion to the 'waters of Merom' where Joshua 11.5 places the defeat of Jabin (see *de Vaux, 791 f.).

The Song of Deborah has been given a cultic setting in a festival of covenant renewal (see Weiser). Such a setting is certainly what it eventually attained, but is not appropriate to the kernel of the song. So it is most unlikely that verses 14–17 should be understood to refer to those tribes which participated in and those which absented themselves from a cultic festival; only the secondary psalmodic additions to the song in its introduction and conclusion can support that view. In fact, verses 14–17 refer to the participants and non-participants in the battle itself. They are most important not only for indicating a wide alliance of six tribes which did in fact take part ('Naphtali' should probably be substituted for the second occurrence of 'Issachar' in verse 15; see Mowinckel, 137 n. 15), but also for the very fact that the poet deemed absence from the battle on the part of four named tribes as worthy of censure. For the first time we have here quite explicitly presupposed an idea of a united people of considerable extent.

The significance of the event in this respect means that its date is of some considerable importance. Unfortunately, however, this date is quite uncertain; proposals range from the late thirteenth century (Aharoni) to the second half of the eleventh century (Alt, 1953, 256–73; Mayes, 93–9). Of one point we may be certain: the argument that a date may be arrived at on the basis of a correlation of literary and archaeological data is quite fallacious. It is this attempted correlation which has led to the widespread view that the battle took place ca. 1125 BCE (Albright, 1937; *Bright, 172), for it is thought that Judges 5.19 presupposes that Megiddo was unoccupied at the time of the battle and a gap in occupation at that site has been fixed to the period between 1150 and 1075 BCE. However, quite apart from the fact that there is dispute even on the question of when Megiddo was unoccupied, it is clear that Judges 5.19 says nothing about the question of the occupation of the site.

On general grounds the battle is probably dated considerably later than this, towards the end of the period of the judges. Its likely cause – the appearance of Israelite tribes in the plains of Palestine as a threat to non-Israelite domination of the area – points to a time considerably later than the settlement, when the tribes felt strongly enough established to venture into the plains from their primary settlement areas in the mountains. Furthermore, an Israelite victory in the plain of Esdraelon which was the result of this battle would not have long remained uncontested, since it left one of the strategically and economically most important parts of Palestine in Israelite control. Yet the first event which can be identified as a repercussion to this Israelite victory is the battle between Israel and the Philistines at Aphek, which took place towards the end of the eleventh century (see *Noth, 165). The connection of these two battles perhaps finds more support in the very name Sisera, which belongs to those Sea People elements of whom the Philistines formed a part (Albright, 1968, 218; Alt, 1953, 266f.; though see also *de Vaux, 792). If it was a coalition led by a Philistine, or one related to them, whom the Israelites under Barak defeated, a counter-attack such as that which took place at Aphek, as described in I Samuel 4, would have been inevitable.

The threat of domination by the Midianites was the occasion of the rise of Gideon, of whom considerable information is given in Judges 6–8. Unfortunately, however, this is not a straightforward account, which makes very uncertain the use of it to reconstruct in detail the military tactics of Gideon (Malamat, 1953; see Richter, 1966, 200f.). Even the introduction to the account, in 6.1–6, is ambiguous as to whether Israelite tribes were under constant domination by the Midianites for a period, or whether this oppression took the form only of seasonal raids by the Midianites on Israelite crops and herds. Probably the latter is the case for the original tradition, which has later been seen in terms of a period of constant domination. If so, then the reference to a Midianite encampment in the plain of Jezreel (6.33) is scarcely original, a point which is also supported by the lack of any reference to the tribe of Issachar which would have been directly affected by such a deep incursion into Israelite territory.

The main story of Gideon is in 6.33–8.3. An alternative conclusion to it has been later added in 8.4–21; but this, which presents many parallels to the preceding section, has in fact nothing to do with the main account, and tells only of an act of blood revenge carried out by Gideon for an attack on his family. Gideon's success in repulsing the Midianites involved (6.34f.) in the first instance the clan of the Abiezrites, then all Manasseh together with Asher, Zebulun, and Naphtali. Subsequently, in the routing of the enemy, the Ephraimites too were called out (7.24). That the battle in fact involved so many may legitimately be doubted. Not only does the second reference to Naphtali, Asher, and Manasseh in 7.23 not harmonize with 6.35, but the constant emphasis of the tradition on the Abiezrite origin of Gideon, together with Gideon's question to the Ephraimites in 8.2, indicate that this was historically a local action initiated by Gideon leading a band of his own clan of Abiezrites, in which Ephraimites became involved at a later stage. If, as is not unlikely, this tradition was transmitted at Tabor, its subsequent elaboration to include reference to those other tribes on which Tabor bordered would not be unexpected.

At the beginning of the Gideon story there are two separate traditions: the first, in 6.11–24, is in the literary form of a call narrative (see Kutsch; Richter, 1966, 112–55), which records that Gideon, who came from Ophrah, was summoned to deliver Israel from the Midianites. The second, in 6.25–32, is more complicated in that here

the reason is given for Gideon's being given a second name –
Jerubbaal. Gideon was given this second name because of his destruction of an altar of Baal set up at Ophrah. The background of
this is far from clear (see Richter, 1966, 157–68; Haag), but since
Jerubbaal is a name more appropriate to a worshipper of Baal than
to an Israelite, it is likely that the traditions of two quite distinct
individuals, one Canaanite and the other Israelite, have been secondarily fused, perhaps simply because they were both famous leaders
from the same city of Ophrah.

It was a son of Jerubbaal, Abimelech, who became king of
Shechem. Although claimed as part of Israelite tradition, it is probable that this should be seen as an episode in the Canaanite history
of the city. There is no record of Israel's having conquered Shechem;
Abimelech's father was apparently Canaanite; the style of
Abimelech's kingship is certainly Canaanite, bearing a close resemb-
lance to the pattern of Labaya's rule over Shechem in the Amarna
period (see Malamat, 1971, 142; *de Vaux, 800–2). It was a city-
state form of kingship quite unrelated to the form of Israelite monarchy as it eventually emerged under Saul (see Soggin, 23–5;
Lindars). This was not so much an abortive attempt at kingship
within Israel as the final act in the Canaanite royal history of
Shechem. The detail of Abimelech's end is obscure; apparently in
the course of crushing a revolt against him he destroyed Shechem,
and then in a further attack on the city of Thebez, which had
perhaps been involved in the revolt or to which Abimelech was
trying to extend his influence, Abimelech himself was killed.
Archaeological investigation dates a destruction of Shechem to the
twelfth century, after which it was not again fully occupied until the
Solomonic period (Wright, 365f.). It is reasonable to connect this
destruction with the Abimelech episode, after which, it may be assumed, the ruined site passed in time into Israelite control. As an
episode of Canaanite rather than Israelite history of the city it is,
however, difficult to integrate it into the course of history generally
in the period of the judges. Its main importance lies in the fact that it
well illustrates the active life of non-Israelite communities in the
midst of territory which the Israelite tribes were attempting to settle.

It is the secondary identification of Jerubbaal with Gideon which
brought this episode into Israelite history and which indeed also is
probably responsible for those features of the Gideon tradition which
apparently assign him royal status (e.g., Judg. 8.18; see Malamat,
1971, 148). That Gideon himself ever was offered the position of
king, as recounted in 8.22–8, is unlikely. The story of the offer,

including as it does the construction of an ephod after which 'all Israel played the harlot' (8.27), has links with the earlier tradition of the destruction of the altar of Baal in 6.25–32, in that both are concerned with Canaanite practice in Israel, and the latter tradition belongs with the figure of Jerubbaal rather than that of Gideon. The authentic Gideon tradition presents him as a temporary local deliverer. The kingship features of the Gideon–Jerubbaal–Abimelech tradition derive from the Canaanite origin of the Jerubbaal–Abimelech tradition which has secondarily been grafted into Israelite traditional history. Israel was not yet ready for the monarchy.

The period of Abimelech may be fixed archaeologically to the end of the twelfth century, if the correlation with the destruction of Shechem is correct. This, however, does not help in the dating of Gideon. He has no original connection with Jerubbaal; and, if our analysis above is correct, so that the reference to Manasseh, Asher, Zebulun, and Naphtali in the Gideon tradition belongs to a secondary stage in the history of its development, then Gideon cannot be dated either in relation to the defeat of Sisera recorded in the Song of Deborah, where there is no reference to Manasseh, which does not seem yet to have emerged as a tribe. All that is clear is that the elaboration of the Gideon tradition presupposes conditions in which such a wide alliance of tribes could have been expected to participate, conditions which the defeat of Sisera brought about; the Gideon episode itself, however, may have been even earlier than this.

The final narrative of the old collection of stories of deliverers concerned Jephthah. To the tradition of his victory over the Ammonites there is appended, firstly, a story of a custom of lamenting the death of his daughter (Judg. 11.30f., 34–40). This, rather than showing that human sacrifice could be practised in Israel at one time (*Bright, 174), is more likely an Israelite historicization of an old cult-myth deriving from an obsolete rite of Canaanite origin attaching to Jephthah's home town (see Hvidberg, 103f.). Secondly, in 11.12–28, there is an extensive account of Jephthah's negotiations with the Ammonites which, however, is appropriate to negotiations rather with the Moabites. The whole section is probably inspired by Numbers 20–1, with which there are verbal contacts, and perhaps originated out of confusion over the two cities of Aroer, the one situated on the edge of the Arnon, the other – original to the Ammonite story in 11.33 – being located near the Ammonite city of Rabbah. It is, at any rate, most unlikely that 11.12–28 indicates the existence of a victory of Jephthah over the Moabites rather than or in addition to that over the Ammonites (Burney, 299–302).

The account of Jephthah's victory over Ammon is contained in 11.1–11, 32 f. It was an event of local significance involving Ammon and Gilead only. Apart from the victory, which indeed was not a final one since it is the Ammonites who constitute a threat once more in the time of Saul, the story is important in two respects. In the first place, it had a sequel which puts it into a pattern of events already well established for the period of the judges. Judges 12.1–6 relates how the Ephraimites, apparently insulted through not having been summoned to participate in the battle with Ammon, declared war on Jephthah and the Gileadites. As on the occasion of Ehud's battle with Moab and Gideon's with Amalek, so here it is Ephraim which claims leadership among the tribes.

Secondly, it is perhaps possible to discern within the Jephthah tradition a tendency towards institutionalizing the temporary type of leadership exercised by the earlier leaders (see Malamat, 1971, 158). Jephthah declined the offer of position as *qāṣīn* or war commander, but accepted the position of *rō'sh*, or head. The contrast between the two may imply a permanence in the latter which is lacking in the former. Moreover, it should not be overlooked that Jephthah is also unique in appearing not only as a deliverer in war but also as one of the judges of the list in Judges 10.1–5; 12.7–15. It is perhaps precisely the latter position which Jephthah was offered by the elders of Gilead which persuaded him to take on first the task of disposing of the Ammonite threat.

Through his introduction in Judges 10.6–16 the Deuteronomist was able to incorporate the formerly independent Samson tradition. That this tradition should have formed no part of the pre-Deuteronomistic collection of deliverer stories is not surprising; Samson is no deliverer from the Philistines. He is an individual champion around whom an elaborate saga gradually developed (see *Herrmann, 120). No certain historical conlusions can be drawn from the story. The raids which he carried out on the Philistines presuppose a time when the tribe of Dan to which he belonged had not yet migrated to its final place of settlement in the north (Judg. 17–18).

Although in many respects out of keeping with other traditions in the book of Judges, the Samson stories have been fittingly introduced by the Deuteronomist at this point, since they bring to prominence that non-Israelite part of the population of the land the conflict with whom was to bring about such dramatic changes within Israel. The

Deuteronomistic account in fact led straight on from Samson to Samuel and the events surrounding the introduction of the monarchy; but this direct connection was later broken through the introduction of two narratives: the first, a settlement tradition of the tribe of Dan (Judg. 17–18), to which reference has already been made; and the second, the story of the outrage at Gibeah (Judg. 19–21). This latter story involves no external oppressor, but it has a strong affinity with earlier traditions in the book of Judges in that it vividly illustrates those internal tensions in the mid-Palestinian area which had already appeared in connection especially with Gideon. The narrative, which describes the revenge taken on Benjamin for an outrageous crime committed by the inhabitants of the Benjaminite city of Gibeah, has been interpreted as an 'amphictyonic' war, with a direct parallel in Greek history (see Noth, 1930, 100–8; Smend, 33–5). However, this is an improbable interpretation quite apart from the question of an Israelite amphictyony (see the detailed treatment of the story in Mayes, 42–6, 79–83). Just as with other traditions of the period, so here a local event has been later set within the context of an action on the part of all the tribes of Israel. Judges 19–21 originally concerned a conflict between Benjamin and Ephraim only. The true nature of the conflict is difficult to determine, especially since accounts of crimes of a sexual nature occasionally in the Old Testament conceal events of a quite different nature (see Gen. 9.20–7; 35.22; 49.3f.; and Eissfeldt). Other references in the book of Judges (8.1–3; 12.1–6) indicate a claim of Ephraim to pre-eminence in mid-Palestine; Judges 3.15–30 indicates a close connection between Ephraim and Benjamin; Genesis 35.16–18 recounts the birth of Benjamin in the land of Palestine; the name Benjamin – 'sons of the south' – seems to classify it as a group inferior to and dependent on a larger entity to the north. It is possible, therefore, that behind Judges 19–21 there lies an attempt on the part of Benjamin to assert its own superiority or perhaps to win its independence from the larger group of Ephraim within which it originated (see *de Vaux, 640–2). Whatever the case, the attempt was a failure (see Schunck, 1963, 57–79); Benjamin was decimated, and only later, under the Benjaminite Saul, was its independent status within Israel assured.

The wars of the period of the judges have been described as 'holy wars' (von Rad), and their leaders have been designated 'charismatic'. On the accuracy of the latter point we have already seen that there is considerable room for doubt, but on the former too there is perhaps place for revision. In the first place, no uniform pattern can be established for the conduct of these wars in the early period; secondly, the idea of divine participation in war was general in the ancient orient (*Herrmann, 119; Weippert), and if Israelite wars are to be distinguished from these they should perhaps better be called wars of Yahweh. The notion of Yahweh as leader in war, both offensive and defensive wars, was general among the Israelite tribes in the period of the judges; but it was only at a later time that anything like a theory of how such wars should be carried out was formulated (Stolz, 163, 203–5; Jones).

Besides provision for leadership in battle, some administrative structures must have existed for the ordinary regulation of the life of the tribes in the period of the judges, if not collectively at least individually. The type of leadership exercised by men such as Ehud and Gideon suited the various crises which attended Israel's early life in the land. But for the daily regulation of its life, its judicial, commercial, and economic administration, other structures would have been required. Of these we have little or no certain information; but it is perhaps within this more general context of government that the 'judges' named in Judges 10.1–5; 12.7–15 are to be placed.

Judges 10.1–5; 12.7–15 originally formed a single list; it is presently broken by the Jephthah tradition, inserted at that point in the list where Jephthah is named as one of the judges. The origin and background of the list are obscure, nor indeed is it clear if it is complete; it has been broken once by the Jephthah tradition, so it is possible that other individuals too occupied the same position as those now mentioned in the list. However, two things may be regarded as probable (see Richter, 1965): all those mentioned in the list belonged to northern tribes, and so it is probable that, as with the original collection of stories of deliverers, the list came originally from a northern context (Bethlehem where Ibzan came from is probably Bethlehem in Zebulun, see Josh. 19.15, and *de Vaux, 757). Secondly, since the best analogy to the way in which the judges are described as succeeding one another is to be found in the royal annals recording the succession of the kings of Israel, it may be that the list was in fact formed on analogy to these royal annals with the purpose of describing how pre-monarchic Israel was governed. If this is so, then for the period of the judges itself the list falls apart into independent notices of various individuals who at different times, or perhaps contemporaneously, in different places 'judged'. The Israel which the list describes them as having judged is the monarchic state of Israel in the context of which the list originated, which then tells us nothing of the actual sphere of activity of these men. Where in fact they did function cannot be exactly described, but there is little reason for going outside the confines of the clan or tribe to which each of the judges belonged.

This conclusion is supported by a further consideration. It is said of a number of individuals outside the list of judges that they 'judged Israel'. As we earlier noted, however, the activity of the Deuteronomist must be seen here, for this editor, as Judges 2.18 indicates, has identified the functions of judge and deliverer. Yet in spite of this, it remains probable that outside the list of judges there is one individual – Samuel – who should be seen in its terms (see Mayes, 59–61). The literary forms by which the activity of Samuel is introduced and described in I Samuel 7.15; 25.1 are almost identical with the forms used for the judges of the list (see Schunck, 1966), and the further details which the Samuel tradition provides conform well with this status. In particular, following I Samuel 7.16, Samuel used to go 'on a circuit year by year to Bethel, Gilgal and Mizpah; and he judged Israel in all these places'. The explicit reference to these places, rather than simply a general reference to Israel, indicates the presence of old Samuel tradition at this point; and if this information is then reliable, it is clear that Samuel's activity as judge was limited to his home territory in mid-Palestine where all these places were situated. Probably the case was the same with the judges mentioned in the list. They, too, with the exception of Tola who though from the tribe of Issachar lived, and probably also judged, in Ephraim, judged within the territory occupied by their respective tribes.

A more difficult problem, however, concerns the meaning of the verb 'judge' when applied to the activities of these men. Although by far the majority of occurrences of the verb show a distinctly legal significance for the term (see Grether), there are a few cases in the Old Testament where the more general sense of 'rule' suits best (see Amos 2.3; Dan. 9.12); while outside the Old Testament this wider sense is well established (see Richter, 1965, 57–70). An instructive parallel has been drawn with the office of the Carthaginian *suffetes* (a term depending on the same root as the Hebrew verb translated 'judge'), which was an office of government in use when there was no hereditary monarchy (see *Herrmann, 124 n. 1). In spite of the general inadequacy of the Old Testament evidence on the question, it may then be assumed that the judges mentioned in the list, and including Samuel, should not be seen strictly within the legal context, but should be treated as rulers of a more general kind within their respective areas. This was not a military but a civil and administrative office to which they were appointed. It would indeed have included the administration of justice, but its responsibilities were wider, covering the whole area of government. The later compilers of the list of these judges were then not totally distorting the historical conditions when they modelled the list on the royal annals. Where they did introduce distortion was in making these local rulers the leaders of a single pre-monarchic Israel.

To the extent that it is impossible to establish either a relative or an absolute chronology for the events which tradition places in the period of the judges, it is also impossible to write a history of Israel in the period of the judges. At best it is possible to provide a picture of the type of life led by the tribes, their wars with the peoples of the land which they were attempting to settle (Deborah and Barak), with the Transjordanian nations of Moab and Ammon (Ehud and Jephthah), with raiding Midianites from the east (Gideon), and with the Philistines (Samson). It was a time too of inter-tribal dispute (Ephraim and Benjamin) and of rivalry for pre-eminence (Ephraim and Gideon, Ephraim and Jephthah). It was especially a time of division among the tribes, resulting not only from their former independence, as semi-nomads, but particularly from the fact that they were separated by foreign city-states which they had been unable to conquer (see Alt, 1966, 167). Judges 1.27–33, 34–6 list two lines of such city-states which divided the south from mid-Palestine, and the latter from Galilee. It may have been primarily with the purpose of destroying the latter line of city-states as an effective barrier that the battle with Sisera took place towards the end of the period of the judges. It was not until later still, however, that it was possible also to remove those obstacles which prevented the southern tribes from coming together with their fellow Israelites.

§4. THE REIGN OF SAUL

Y. **Aharoni**, *Land of the Bible*, 1967; A. **Alt**, 'The Settlement of the Israelites in Palestine' (see ch. IV §4), *Essays*, 1966, 135–69; idem, 'The Formation of the Israelite State in Palestine' (see §2), *Essays*, 171–237; B. C. **Birch**, 'The Development of the Tradition on the Anointing of Saul in I Sam. 9.1–10.16', *JBL* XC, 1971, 55–68; J. **Blenkinsopp**, 'Did Saul Make Gibeon His Capital?', *VT* XXIV, 1974, 1–7; idem, 'The Quest of the Historical Saul', *No Famine in the Land* (Festschrift John L. McKenzie), ed. J. W. Flanagan and A. W. Robinson, Missoula: Scholars Press, 1975, 75–99; H.

Cazelles, 'Déborah (Judg. V 14), Amaleq et Mâkîr', *VT* XXIV, 1974, 235–8; S. R. **Driver**, *Notes on the Hebrew Text and the Topography of the Books of Samuel*, London: Oxford University Press ²1913; O. **Eissfeldt**, 'The Hebrew Kingdom', *CAH* II/2, 1975, 570–80; C. E. **Hauer**, 'The Shape of Saulide Strategy', *CBQ* XXXI, 1969, 153–67; H. W. **Hertzberg**, *I & II Samuel*, OTL, 1964; F. **Langlamet**, 'Les récits de l'institution de la royauté (I Sam., VII–XII): De Wellhausen aux travaux récents', *RB* LXXVII, 1970, 161–200; G. C. **Macholz**, *Untersuchungen zur Geschichte der Samuel-Überlieferungen* (Dissertation, Heidelberg 1966); A. **Malamat**, 'The Egyptian Decline in Canaan and the Sea Peoples', *WHJP* I/3, 1971, 23–38; A. D. H. **Mayes**, *Israel in the Period of the Judges*, SBT II/29, 1974; F. **Mildenberger**, *Die vordeuteronomistische Saul-David-Überlieferung* (Dissertation, Tübingen 1962); J. M. **Miller**, 'Saul's Rise to Power: Some Observations Concerning I Sam. 9.1–10.16; 10.26–11.15 and 13.2–14.46', *CBQ* XXXVI, 1974, 157–74; idem, 'Geba/Gibeah of Benjamin', *VT* XXV, 1975, 145–66; G. **von Rad**, 'Zwei Überlieferungen von König Saul', *GS* II, 1973, 199–211; K.-D. **Schunck**, *Benjamin*, BZAW 86, 1963; H. J. **Stoebe**, 'Zur Topographie und Überlieferung der Schlacht von Mikmas, I. Sam. 13 und 14', *TZ* XXI, 1965, 269–80; G. **Wallis**, *Geschichte und Überlieferung: Gedanken über alttestamentliche Darstellungen der Frühgeschichte Israels und der Anfänge seines Königtums*, AT II/13, 1968; H. **Wildberger**, 'Samuel und die Entstehung des israelitischen Königtums', *TZ* XIII, 1957, 442–69; G. E. **Wright**, 'Fresh Evidence for the Philistine Story', *BA* XXIX, 1966, 70–86.

The Philistines represented a constant threat to the Israelites, endangering their security and thwarting their hopes of territorial expansion. Defeated by Ramesses III, and expelled from Egypt at the beginning of the twelfth century, they had managed to establish themselves in Palestine, mainly along the coast and in the plain of Esdraelon (see Malamat, 1971, 29–32). Their expansion during the twelfth century meant their virtual encirclement of Israelite territory (see Wright, 75–8).

Yet it was not simply Philistine desire to dominate the Israelite area of settlement which led to the disastrous battle between Israel and the Philistines at Aphek towards the end of the eleventh century. Rather, this confrontation resulted from Israelite attempts to expand from their primary bases in the mountain areas into the plains of Palestine. The record of the first Israelite attempt in this direction is in Judges 5. Their defeat of Sisera on that occasion, and their consequent control of the important trade route and strategic area which the plain of Esdraelon formed, inevitably called forth a swift reaction. The result of this reaction, the battle at Aphek, was a major defeat for Israel. In spite of an attempt to retrieve the situation through bringing the ark of God from Shiloh, Israel was again defeated, and the land was now generally under Philistine control. This situation forms the general background to the rise of Saul.

Two pre-Deuteronomistic traditions concerned with the rise of Saul are to be found in I Samuel 9.1–10.16 (23) and 11.1–15. The former has its continuation in 13.2–14.52 where the commissioning of Saul by Samuel (see 10.8) finds its purpose and fulfilment (see 13.4, 8–15). The Deuteronomist combined 9.1–10.16 (23); 13.2–14.52 with 11.1–15 through introducing the idea of initial opposition to Saul's election (10.27; 11.12–14), which provided the opportunity of presenting the originally separate account of Saul's election in 11.1–15 as confirmation of his elevation to the kingship, the opposition having been shown to be groundless.

The context within which the traditions were formed has had an important influence on their development. This is particularly true of 9.1–10.16 (23); 13.2–14.52, for this cycle, with its emphasis on the prophet and his effective role in the anointing and rejecting of the king, has clearly been transmitted within prophetic circles (see Mildenberger, 34–7, 49–58). It is not until considerably later, in the time of the northern kingdom, that an emphasis on the role of the prophet in this context appears historically; and to this time should be assigned those parts of the cycle which cast Samuel in this role. In effect, prophetic editing is responsible for the transformation of an old folktale in 9.1–10.16 (for which, see Birch) into an account of Samuel's anointing of Saul as king, the connection of this with an old story of Saul's victory over the Philistines (13.2–4; cf. Miller, 1974, 160f.), so that the latter now appeared as the task for which Saul was specifically elected. Chapters 13 and 15 were incorporated in the same process to demonstrate how Saul was rejected as king by the prophet.

The old folktale in 9.1–10.16 told how Saul as a young man went in search of his father's asses and was highly honoured by a seer. The story emphasized his physical attributes which were later to commend him to the people as their king. Its purposes was not to describe how Saul was actually anointed king, but to illustrate how from his earliest days Saul was destined for great things. Its timeless character, the anonymity of the seer and the city where he lived, the fairy-tale character of the theme of a search for asses and the finding of a kingdom, show that this is a popular folktale which originated in the time of Saul, in circles favourably disposed towards him, and which is intended to augment the popular esteem in which he was held.

It has long been recognized that I Samuel 11, which recounts

Saul's victory over the Ammonites, offers the most reliable source for
our reconstruction of the event of Saul's elevation to the kingship
(see Alt, 1966, 183–6). Attempts have indeed been made to divorce
the event related here from the election of Saul to be king (see
Langlamet, 196–9; Wildberger, 466–9; Macholz, 152–6), primarily
because it is clear that Samuel does not originally belong in I
Samuel 11 (the reference to him in v. 7 being a clear addition, and
vv. 12–14 being Deuteronomistic), and yet it is felt that Samuel was
in fact intimately involved in the election of Israel's first king. However, these attempts are quite clearly unsuccessful. No satisfactory
explanation of I Samuel 11.15 as a late addition can be given; the
description here of Saul's being made king forms the natural and
expected climax to the rest of the story. Moreover, the fact that the
verse describes the elevation of Saul as something carried out quite
spontaneously by the people, and not by Samuel, gives it an indisputable aura of authenticity. The present prominence of Samuel in
the tradition of the event of Saul's election must be seen as resulting
from the history of the tradition, in the course of which the prophetic
circles which transmitted the tradition have emphasized the prophetic role in king-making.

Saul arose as the leader of a contingent of Israelites, perhaps
drawn only from his native tribe of Benjamin, in order to relieve the
city of Jabesh-gilead of the threat posed by the Ammonites. His
success was such that the people, again perhaps only Benjaminites or
Benjaminites together with the people of Jabesh-gilead, crowned
him as their king at Gilgal (see *Herrmann, 133f.). Saul, therefore,
stands firmly in line with pre-monarchic forms of Israelite leadership. A particular crisis called forth a leader who repulsed the
enemy. On this occasion, however, the temporary leadership with
which Saul was entrusted did not come to an end with the resolution
of the conflict which had called it forth. Saul was made king. This
was a new departure for Israel, for there was no tradition of kingship
among the tribes. With Abimelech, as we have seen, we are in a
Canaanite context. The Old Testament tradition of Saul's election
as king quite credibly puts the event within the general context of
continuing oppression by the Philistines, which had begun with the
defeat of Israel at Aphek (I Sam. 4); it was precisely in order to deal
with this continuing threat that Saul's leadership was made permanent.

The Philistines do not seem to have occupied Israelite territory;
rather, their intention was simply to weaken Israel and to prevent
their expansion into the plains (see von Rad, 1973, 204). So they

deprived the Israelites of the means of manufacturing weapons (I Sam. 13.19–22) and exacted tribute through sending out raiding parties (I Sam. 13.16–18; see Alt, 1966, 182). At any rate, their control of the land was not complete to the extent that Saul could not be elected king at Gilgal. Yet their control was oppressive enough to be what stands behind the new institution of the monarchy in Israel.

Saul established his capital at Gibeah, though it is possible that at some stage he changed this to the city of Gibeon (see Schunck, 1963, 132 f.; Blenkinsopp, 1974). Excavations at Tell el-Ful, frequently identified as the site of Gibeah, reveal it as a fortress rather than a capital (*Bright, 186) and thus indicate the lack of any developed monarchical institution at this early stage. (For a view that denies the association of Tell el-Ful and Gibeah, see Miller, 1975.) Saul's monarchy was founded in a situation of military necessity, and this determined its nature and function. It was for leadership in war, and so a complex monarchic structure was unnecessary (however, see Aharoni, 255–7). If I Samuel 16.15 f., 22.6–28 give the impression that Saul did in fact have a royal court, it should be remembered that these verses form part of the story of the rise of David, which has its focus on David rather than on Saul, and in which there may well be an unconscious projection into the time of Saul of the conditions of David's reign (see Mildenberger, 177 f.). Yet, some rudimentary forms of administration would have been essential; within the Saul stories themselves there is some indication of the first moves towards the creation of a professional standing army loyal to the king alone (I Sam. 13.2; 14.52), which would have demanded the existence of some form of taxation system for its support (see Eissfeldt, 574 f.). In general, however, there is no evidence of Saul's having introduced much change into the internal structure of the tribal organization. The stage of development had not yet been reached and the stage of unity had not yet been achieved on which an elaborate state bureaucracy and a splendid royal court could have been erected. Saul's monarchy was a military one; it was created to deal with the Philistines, and its emphasis lay on the army over which Saul's cousin Abner was placed as commander.

Yet for all its rudimentary form, Saul's military kingdom achieved some remarkable successes. A summary of his victories is given in I Samuel 14.47 f., according to which he defeated Moab, Ammon, Edom, the kings of Zobah, the Philistines, and the Amalekites. More detailed traditions deal with his victories over Ammon (I Sam. 11), the Philistines (I Sam. 13–14), and the Amalekites (I Sam. 15); but there is nothing further on Edom, Moab, and the kings of Zobah. The reason for this is difficult to see, but since victories over Edom and Moab would have been too significant to be neglected by a detailed tradition, the possibility must be reckoned with that in fact here too events from the time of David are put back into the reign of Saul (see Stoebe, 270 f.). Even if this is so, such victories as may be accepted for the time of Saul remain significant. Apart from his initial defeat of the Ammonites, it is possible that a single strategic plan lies behind all his moves (see Hauer), for with the expulsion of the Philistines from the centre of the land (I Sam. 13–14), the defeat of the Amalekites in the south (I Sam. 15) and what may be under- stood as an abortive attempt to secure the north (I Sam. 29–31), there appears the pattern of an attempt to establish a clear area of indisputable Israelite territory covering the whole of the western highlands.

I Samuel 13–14 contains an old tradition which has had a rather complex history. Apart from its prophetic editing, especially in 13.7b–15, it seems that two old traditions, one describing a victory of Saul and the other a victory of Jonathan, have been fused. At the very beginning of the account, in 13.3 and 13.4, where both Saul and Jonathan are credited with the victory over the Philistines, this fusion is clear. A similar confusion in the chapters of Gibeah and Geba is probably to be connected with this; and in fact it is not improbable that the action of Saul is to be located at Gibeah, with which he is otherwise connected, and that of Jonathan at Geba (see Stoebe, 277–80; for a view that identifies Geba and Gibeah with present-day Jeba', see Miller, 1975). This would indicate that behind the present tradition there lies the record of not one major event, but of at least two events in which successful actions against the Philistines were carried through.

The importance of these military undertakings should not be exaggerated (see *Noth, 173; *Bright, 184; von Rad, 1973, 204f.). The Philistine menace was by no means finally eliminated. The decisive battle was still to come. Here we have the report of preliminary skirmishes in which Philistine garrisons and patrols were defeated by surprise tactics. Yet although the Philistines were far from being a spent force, they were at least for the moment expelled from Israelite territory, so that the humiliating situation which resulted from the earlier defeat of Israel at Aphek was temporarily lifted. Furthermore, an exceedingly important advantage which this victory conferred was that the way now lay open, apparently for the first time, between the mid-Palestinian and the Judaean tribes (see

Mayes, 102 f.). Just as the earlier victory of Israelite tribes over
Sisera was connected with the final destruction of the dividing power
of the series of Canaanite city-states separating mid-Palestine from
Galilee, so now the expulsion of the Philistines from the southern
part of the mid-Palestinian mountain territory removed the main
support of the southern series of Canaanite city-states, referred to in
Judges 1.34 f., which had until then separated Judah from the north.

The way was then open for Saul's expedition against the
Amalekites in the south (though see Wallis, 99–105, for the view that
the Amalekites whom Saul opposed were a settled group in the
territory of Ephraim itself; for the presence of Amalekites in the
north, see also Cazelles). These Amalekites were apparently a group
of nomadic tribes in the south with whom the southern Israelite
tribes were more or less constantly in a state of warfare. The account
of Saul's victory over them in I Samuel 15 has, like many other
traditions, been subjected to prophetic editing (see Mildenberger,
13–15). An original popular saga, probably transmitted at Gilgal
(see Hertzberg, 123 f.), told how Saul was commissioned to destroy
the Amalekites and how he brought Agag their king back to the
sanctuary; this has been edited to explain Saul's own eventual
disgrace and inglorious end. His failure to comply with the commission to destroy the Amalekites utterly is interpreted as disobedience
unworthy of the chosen of Yahweh, which brought about his rejection by Samuel. The in many respects sympathetic portrayal of Saul
in this account, which contrasts so starkly with his harsh treatment
by Samuel, is the result of this adaptation of the story.

The Philistine threat, however, continued to dominate the scene.
For the final and decisive battle they gathered their forces at Aphek
(I Samuel 29.1), the scene of their earlier victory over Israel. From
here they marched into the plain of Esdraelon, so not only splitting
the Israelite forces between those of mid-Palestine and those of
Galilee, but also choosing a site for battle where their chariot forces
could be fully and effectively used. It is strange that Saul should
have allowed himself to be drawn into battle in such circumstances;
but possibly he realized that whatever the conditions of this particular battle the plain of Esdraelon would have to be in Israelite
control for full communication to be possible between mid-Palestine
and Galilee. The outcome of the battle was a disaster (I Sam. 31):
Israel was routed; Saul's sons were killed; and Saul himself, badly
wounded, fell on his own sword. This time the Philistines occupied
the land, apparently including Galilee and Transjordan. Saul's career, which began with his deliverance of the inhabitants of Jabesh-

gilead, came to an end with their deliverance of the body of Saul, and those of his sons, from the desecration of the Philistines.

The length of Saul's reign is uncertain. The expression 'two years' in I Samuel 13.1 is given in an unusual Hebrew form (Driver, 97; though see *Noth, 176f.), and so is often thought to be corrupt. The events which are ascribed to his reign do not, however, demand a longer time; two years is quite acceptable, especially if Saul's victory over the Philistines (I Sam. 13–14) took place at the beginning of his reign, for the later Philistine victory over Israel when Saul lost his life belongs best within the context of a Philistine reaction to their earlier defeat (but see Eissfeldt, 575, for arguments for a longer reign).

The precise extent of Saul's kingdom also is unknown. II Samuel 2.9 refers to Gilead, Asher, Jezreel, Ephraim, and Benjamin as the territory over which Saul's son Ishbosheth was made king by Abner, and this has been taken to represent the extent of Saul's kingdom also (see Alt, 1966, 191 n. 47, 216). However, there is evidence that Saul enjoyed at least considerable influence in Judah (see Eissfeldt, 576; Schunck, 1963, 124–6): he passed through Judah to fight the Amalekites; David, a Judaean, feared for his own and his parents' safety in Judah (I Sam. 22.3f.; 27.1). Yet, rather than that it should be concluded that Judah formed part of the kingdom, it seems more likely that the extent of Saul's influence was quite fluid and variable (see Wallis, 63). The kernel of the kingdom was undoubtedly formed by Ephraim, Benjamin, and Gilead; other tribes, or parts of them, both in Galilee and in Judah, would also, though perhaps only for longer or shorter periods, have associated themselves with this nucleus.

The defeat of Saul and the disastrous outcome of Israel's first steps in kingship are perhaps mainly but certainly not wholly to be explained as the result of Israel's defeat by the Philistines. This was a first venture in kingship, and it brought with it intolerable pressures and tensions with which Saul was unable to cope. In the first place, the central government which a monarchic institution involved sharply conflicted with the old traditional independence of the tribes. Secondly, the very nature of the kingship of Saul, as a national rather than a territorial institution, inevitably meant that Saul would be preoccupied with internal security as much as external threat; it is in this context that his persecution of the Gibeonites, echoed in II Samuel 21.1–6, belongs. As long as national purity, rather than territorial unity, was to determine the nature of the kingdom (see Alt, 1966, 161), this type of internal dissension would inevitably weaken it. Thirdly, although by nature the monarchy was dynastic, Saul had come to the throne as the first member of a dynasty, and so would have felt his position, and that of his son as his successor, as very much dependent on his own personality and ability (see I Sam. 20.31; 22.7f.). The rise in power and popularity of David was therefore all the more a burden to him. How David first came to Saul's notice is now unknown – the story of David's slaying of Goliath in I Samuel 17 (which, however, probably represents the secondary ascription to David of a victory which belonged to another, see *Herrmann, 138f.) introduces David as previously unknown to Saul, in spite of I Samuel 16.14–23 – but it was because of his military prowess that a fateful jealousy of David was aroused in Saul whose persecution of David would have caused further internal weakness in the kingdom. I Samuel 24 and 26, which tell of this persecution, show such formal similarity that they may be two versions of one event. Since they are stories about David rather than about Saul (see von Rad, 1973, 200–3), it may be difficult to derive historical information about Saul from them; yet, together with I Samuel 22.6–19 which describes the lengths to which Saul was prepared to go in order to isolate David, they reflect that attitude of Saul towards David which eventually forced David to flee to Israel's national enemy, the Philistines, for safety. Fourthly, the tradition in I Samuel 13 and 15 describes a serious breach between Samuel and Saul. What we are to make of this historically is difficult to say; that the stories reflect a conflict resulting from a general lack of definition of the function of the king particularly in relation to the sacral sphere (see *Noth, 175; *Bright, 187) is not very likely. Both of these traditions of the rejection of Saul by Samuel originated in later prophetic circles, and have the purpose of upholding prophetic rights in relation to the king. In fact, the historical role of Samuel has been considerably exaggerated in the tradition. I Samuel 7.15–17 is probably correct in showing him as a judge in the style of the judges of Judges 10.1–5; 12.7–15. But the Deuteronomist, in conformity with his view of the identity of judge and deliverer, has ascribed a deliverer story to Samuel also (I Samuel 7.5–14), so that Samuel now appears as the predecessor of the king in all his functions.

Nevertheless, it is probably true that at this early stage the functions of the king were ill-defined and that considerable unrest did result from this. The independence of the tribes belonged not only to their pre-settlement days; right through the period of the judges there is no indication of an intense desire to unite to form a single nation. Their unity was forced on them by outside pressure; and although they had characteristics in common – in particular, common worship of Yahweh, a common history of semi-nomadic origins and also a common problem in coping with opposition to their settlement of the land – it would only have been gradually, under the tactful guidance of a recognized leader, that this unity would have come to full expression. The monarchy is not so much an alien institution in Israel as a new but also inevitable step in the progression towards that unity. This first step was apparently a failure; and if the general nature of the history of the period is to be seen in terms of a struggle between Philistines and Israelites to fill the power vacuum left in Palestine by the Egyptians, then it is the Philistines who emerge, at this stage, as the victors.

VI

THE DAVIDIC–SOLOMONIC KINGDOM

§1. THE BIBLICAL SOURCE MATERIAL

With the foundation of a united kingdom under David, the history of Israel leaves the realm of pre-history, of cultic and popular tradition and enters the arena of history proper. The kingdom under David and Solomon constitutes a datum point from which the investigation of Israel's history can be safely begun.

When we look at the biblical sources for the study of this period, we soon realize, however, that they are not 'history' in our sense of the word. We are dealing, in effect, with that particular form of Israelite history which may be called 'prophetic history' or 'theocratic history' or with some other, semantically similar, definition. This type of history can hardly be considered as 'A record or account, usually written in chronological order, of past events, especially those concerning a particular nation, people, field of knowledge or activity, etc.' (Funk and Wagnall, *Standard College Dictionary*). Such is neither the content of this material nor its aim. Still, there can be hardly any doubt that the age of David and Solomon gave a major impulse to Israelite historiography, inasmuch as it brought into being political, economic, and sociological factors which are usually the presuppositions for any kind of historiography. Ancient traditions were thus collected and edited and related to contemporary events (i.e., the pentateuchal source 'J', commonly considered an apologetical work aimed at the legitimation of the new kingdom and monarchy). Various texts illustrating the origins and development of the monarchy were apparently edited and written down.

Biblical sources for this period appear primarily in the books of I and II Samuel and I Kings and in the more or less parallel accounts in the books of Chronicles. The former works belong to the so-called

Deuteronomistic history whose presuppositions, aims and methods
have been discussed above in ch. IV (see pp. 217–21). The latter source
will be considered in some detail in later chapters (see pp. 439, 491 f.).

In I and II Samuel, the following texts are usually considered as
the basic source materials: (1) the narratives about the rise of David
(I Sam. 16–II Sam. 5 + 8); (2) the ark narratives (I Sam. 4–6 and II
Sam. 6); and (3) the narrative of the Davidic succession (II Sam. 9–
20 + I Kings 1–2, to which probably II Sam. 21.1–14 and II Sam.
24 should be attached). When we consider that II Samuel 7 is the
final product of Deuteronomistic reworking of ancient materials
which probably belonged, in origin, to the narrative of the Davidic
succession, this classification accounts for the greater part of the
second half of I Samuel and the whole of II Samuel (except for the
appendices in II Sam. 21.15–22; 22–3) and of I Kings 1–2. There
are but few traces of Deuteronomistic redactional reworking in these
materials. The clearest examples of Deuteronomistic editorial
activity are I Samuel 16.1–13 and II Samuel 7. None the less, the
editorial work of the Deuteronomist is quite clear in the general
structure of the overall narrative about David: 'David under the
blessing – David under the curse' (see the work by Carlson in the
following bibliography). This similar structure of blessing and curse
also appears in the stories of Saul and Solomon and perhaps also in
those of other kings. Such a scheme is obviously fictitious; it is therefore quite probable that the original chronological sequence of
events has not been maintained but has been sacrificed to this
scheme. This is particularly clear in the narrative of David's conquests (II Sam. 5 and 8), as we shall see. The scarcity of thoroughly
Deuteronomistic texts in the traditions about David, therefore,
should not deceive the reader about the amount of Deuteronomistic
influence which has gone into the shaping of this material. In the
traditions on Solomon's reign (I Kings 3–11), the editorial activity of
the Deuteronomist is far more obvious.

A.   The narratives about the rise of David

A. **Alt**, 'The Formation of the Israelite State in Palestine' (see ch. V §2),
Essays, 1966, 171–237; H. J. **Boecker**, *Die Beurteilung der Anfänge des
Königtums in den deuteronomistischen Abschnitten des I. Samuelbuches*, WMANT
31, 1969; R. A. **Carlson**, *David, The Chosen King: A Traditio-Historical
Approach to the Second Book of Samuel*, Stockholm: Almqvist & Wiksell 1964;
J. H. **Grønbaek**, *Die Geschichte vom Aufstieg Davids (1. Sam. 15–2. Sam. 5):
Tradition und Komposition*, AThD 10, 1971; H.-U. **Nübel**, *Davids Aufstieg in*

der frühen israelitischen Geschichtsschreibung Dissertation, Bonn 1959); F. **Mildenberger**, *Die vordeuteronomistische Saul-David-Überlieferung* (Dissertation, Tübingen 1962); R. **Rendtorff**, 'Beobachtungen zur altisraelitischen Geschichtsschreibung anhand der Geschichte vom Aufstieg Davids', *Probleme Biblischer Theologie*, 1971, 428–39; A. **Weiser**, 'Die Legitimation des Königs David', *VT* XVI, 1966, 325–54.

The narratives on the rise of David to power contain a considerable number of texts in duplicate or in contradiction. Three stories report how David first rose to prominence and came to the royal court of Saul (I Sam. 16.1–13; 16.14–23; 17). The first of these narratives, which contains the story of Samuel's anointing of David at Bethlehem in preference to the other seven sons of Jesse, is, as has been noted, the product of Deuteronomistic writing and has hardly any connection with ancient tradition. It can therefore be left out of any attempt to portray the rise of David. The second story sees David appointed as armour-bearer to king Saul whose depressions are relieved by the lyre playing of his youthful recruit. In the third account, David begins his career as a fighter by answering the challenge of the warrior Goliath, a Philistine giant from Gath. According to I Samuel 17.55–8, Saul is totally unacquainted with David. True enough, the Greek translation (LXX[B]) does not contain this and other sections of the narrative. In addition, II Samuel 21.19 reports Goliath as having been killed by an otherwise unknown Elhanan, although the parallel text in I Chronicles 20.5 attributes to Elhanan the killing of a brother of Goliath. It seems therefore that I Samuel 17 attributes to David the mighty feat of this unknown Elhanan. Still, the contradiction between I Samuel 16 and 17 is noteworthy from a redactional point of view.

Parallels appear in I Samuel 18.7; 21.11 and 29.5, where the song in David's honour sung by the people is quoted three times; in 25.1 and 28.3 where Samuel's death is reported twice; in chs. 24 and 26 where two narratives report stories about how David spared Saul's life in a cave. Twice David is shown making contact with the Philistines (21.10–15; 27.1–7). In I Samuel 31, Saul commits suicide by throwing himself on his own sword after his armour-bearer had refused to kill him, but in II Samuel 1, Saul is reported to have been killed at his request by an Amalekite.

The entire narrative of David's rise thus gives a rather fragmentary impression, as if its single components had arisen independently from each other and had then been collected haphazard. However, as has been made reasonably certain by Weiser, there is a red thread

running through the narratives by which the heterogeneous components are bound together, namely, the aim of legitimizing David's
accession to the throne over all Israel replacing the dynasty of Saul.
A pro-Davidic redactor seems therefore to have collected what
materials he considered adequate to back up his thesis. The results
are that David succeeds Saul for many reasons: (1) because of divine
designation (a point carried to the extreme by the Deuteronomist in
I Sam. 16.1–13); (2) through dynastic succession: having married
Saul's daughter, David was a survivor of Saul's family; (3) through
military gallantry; and (4) because he was appointed by the people,
first in Judah and later in Israel. There can hardly be any doubt that
in the mind of the redactor the first reason was of paramount importance. The narrative stresses not so much David's virtues and Saul's
alleged or real vices as God's election: God's elect is to become king,
replacing the former elect of God, from whom the blessing had been
withdrawn.

In any case, the redactor of the narratives about David's rise to
power shows quite clearly that his aims were theological and
apologetic rather than historiographical. Nevertheless, materials
relevant for the historian can be gathered from the narratives: e.g.,
that David was a Judahite who entered the service of the king while
still quite young; that he became through gallantry and valour, but
also through great cunning, a military leader under Saul; that he
soon fell into disgrace, either because of the pathological jealousy of
the king or else because Saul realized David's budding ambitions for
the throne; that he was compelled to flee from the royal court; that
he enlisted a small but very efficient personal army; that he joined
the Philistines, although he never took up arms against his brethren
in the north; that at Saul's death he became king first of Judah, then
of Israel; that the Philistines did not initially object to their vassal
becoming king over Judah; and that he succeeded in subduing the
greater part of Palestine, Syria, and Transjordan. Also, what the
narratives tell us about the surviving son of Saul, Ishbaal, who
reigned as king over Israel for some two years, seems trustworthy.
The theological outlook of the source and its obvious pro-Davidic
bias do not bar a considerable amount of objectivity. The heroism
and military capacities of Saul are fully acknowledged, although the
king is presented as mentally ill during his last days ('. . . an evil
spirit from Yahweh tormented him', I Sam. 16.14 and elsewhere).
Nor does this bias make the editor blind towards the many moral
and political ambiguities of David.

B. The ark narratives

A. **Bentzen**, 'The Cultic Use of the Story of the Ark in Samuel', *JBL* LXVII, 1948, 37–53; A. F. **Campbell**, *The Ark Narrative (1 Sam 4–6; 2 Sam. 6): A Form-Critical and Traditio-Historical Study*, SBLDS 16, 1975; D. **Daube**, *The Exodus Pattern in the Bible*, London: Faber and Faber 1963, 73–88; J. **Maier**, *Das altisraelitische Ladeheiligtum*, BZAW 93, 1965; J. R. **Porter**, 'The Interpretation of 2 Samuel VI and Psalm CXXXII', *JTS* NS V, 1954, 161–73; H. **Timm**, 'Die Ladeerzählung (1. Sam. 4–6; 2. Sam. 6) und das Kerygma des deuteronomistischen Geschichtswerks', *EvTh* XXIX, 1966, 509–26; J. T. **Willis**, 'An Anti-Elide Narrative Tradition from a Prophetic Circle at the Ramah Sanctuary', *JBL* XC, 1971, 288–308.

The narratives about the ark belonged originally to the traditions circulating around the temple in Jerusalem founded by Solomon, whose most sacred cultic object was the ark of the covenant. The narratives report the loss of the ark to the Philistines some time before the reign of Saul, its subsequent surrender by its captors, and finally David's transference of the ark, in festive procession, to Jerusalem.

The original form of the ark traditions no doubt had its setting in the priestly circles of Jerusalem. Most scholars have understood the ark narrative as the *hieros logos* of the Jerusalem sanctuary (for a survey of the scholarly discussions, see Campbell, 1–54). The function and intention of the original ark stories however were more than a sanctuary legend. The intention of the ark narrative

was not merely to justify and legitimate the new sanctuary of the ark in Jerusalem, nor merely to justify and legitimate the new royal regime of David in Jerusalem. Encompassing these and going beyond them, it draws a caesura through Israel's history with Yahweh, a caesura which marks the old epoch with rejection and Yahweh's departure, and the new epoch with election and Yahweh's return (Campbell, 252).

The placement, utilization, and redaction of the ark traditions by the Deuteronomist stress the newness of the Davidic era and at the same time the continuity of that era with previous history and religion (so Timm).

If the ark were utilized in an annual or periodical festival procession in Jerusalem, as has been assumed by many scholars (see Bentzen and Porter), this may have influenced the manner in which not only the Davidic procession but the entire transference of the ark to Jerusalem is described in II Samuel 6. This would make more difficult any attempt to reconstruct historically the events associated with David's introduction of the ark into Jerusalem, a fact which there is no reason to doubt.

C.   The narrative of the Davidic succession

W. **Brueggemann**, 'David and His Theologian', *CBQ* XXX, 1968, 156–81; idem, 'The Trusted Creature', *CBQ* XXXI, 1969, 484–98; idem, 'On Trust and Freedom. A Study of Faith in the Succession Narrative', *Int* XXVI, 1972, 3–19; L. **Delekat**, 'Tendenz und Theologie der David–Salomo-Erzählung', *Das ferne und nahe Wort*, 1967, 26–36; J. W. **Flanagan**, 'Court History or Succession Document? A Study of 2 Samuel 9–20 and 1 Kings 1–2', *JBL* XCI, 1972, 172–81; D. M. **Gunn**, 'David and the Gift of the Kingdom (2 Sam. 2–4, 9–20, 1 Kgs. 1–2)', *Semeia* III, 1975, 14–45; idem, 'Traditional Composition in the "Succession Narrative"', *VT* XXVI, 1976, 214–29; H.-J. **Hermisson**, 'Weisheit und Geschichte', *Probleme biblischer Theologie*, 1971, 136–54; É. **Lipiński**, *Le poème royal du Psaume LXXXIX 1–5, 20–38*, Paris: Gabalda & Cie 1967, 83–6; G. **von Rad**, 'The Beginnings of Historical Writing in Ancient Israel' (see ch. I §1), *The Problem of the Hexateuch*, 1966, 166–204; L. **Rost**, *Die Überlieferung von der Thronnachfolge Davids*, BWANT III/6, 1926 = his *Das kleine Credo*, 1965, 119–253; R. N. **Whybray**, *The Succession Narrative: A Study of II Sam. 9–20 and I Kings 1 and 2*, SBT II/9, 1968; E. **Würthwein**, *Die Erzählung von der Thronfolge Davids – theologische oder politische Geschichtsschreibung?*, TS 115, 1974.

The narrative of the Davidic succession aims at explaining why Solomon and not Adonijah, the rightful heir to the throne in a dynastic succession, became king after David. The narrative was first isolated from its context by Rost and was hailed by *Meyer (II/2, 281–6) as 'real historiography' unequalled by any other people in the Near East or the West before the fifth century BCE, a view shared by von Rad. The narrative has frequently been related to and/or compared with the so-called Yahwistic History (so Brueggemann and von Rad). Now that some decades have elasped since Rost's study, the appreciation of this text has become more sober and realistic. Delekat has argued against the assumed pro-Solomonic tendency of the work and Würthwein has recently argued that the work is the product of the extensive redaction of an originally much shorter work with a decidedly anti-monarchic tone. Nevertheless, the work appears to be rich in materials of high value to the historian. In form, the narrative of the succession is an historical novel, with certain elements that are apparently reflections of its connection with wisdom circles (so Whybray and Hermisson; Würthwein revives the old theory of the work's association with the deposed priest Abiathar). The connection of the work with wisdom interests and circles is suggested by a number of factors, and the impossibility of considering it more than a historical novel appears from the following elements: (1) the presence of anecdotal episodes such as David's encounter with Bathsheba (II Sam. 11.21) and the account of Absalom's death and his father's mourning (II Sam. 18.9–19.8a); (2) the psychological appreciations such as the case of Amnon's complex feelings towards his half-sister Tamar before and after he had raped her (II Sam. 13.1–17); (3) scenes and dialogues not witnessed by anyone since they took place in the bedroom but are none the less described in great detail (II Sam. 13.1–17; I Kings 1.15–31); and (4) the emphasis on the active presence of the hidden but all-knowing, all-judging, and all-rewarding God (II Sam. 11.27b; 12.7–12; 17.14, etc.) These elements make it quite impossible to consider the narrative as a historical record. Although extremely well written and rich in perspectives which without difficulty appear 'modern', it remains a novel. Its oldest parts certainly go back to the time of Solomon.

D. The Solomonic traditions

J. **Liver**, 'The Book of the Acts of Solomon', *Bib* XLVIII, 1967, 75–101; B. **Porten**, 'The Structure and Theme of the Solomon Narrative', *HUCA* XXXVIII, 1967, 93–128.

So far as Solomon is concerned, the sources are contained in the epilogue to the succession story which we have just discussed. I Kings 11.41 mentions a 'book of the acts of Solomon' which is probably to be understood as the royal chronicles (but see Liver). It is impossible to know whether anything, and if so how much and where, has been preserved in the text of Kings and Chronicles from this 'book' or chronicle. Possibly the lists of districts and of the governors ruling over them (I Kings 4.7–19) could be an extract from it, and the same is true about short notices appearing here and there in the narratives: (1) the list of other officials similar to those appearing in the narratives about David (I Kings 4.1–6); (2) the note about forced labour (I Kings 5.13; contrast the Deuteronomistic text in I Kings 9.15–22); and (3) references to Solomon's commercial enterprises (I Kings 10.11f., 22, 28f.). Possibly these texts were composed on the bases of abstracts from the book of the acts of Solomon, but nothing more precise can be said. In the Solomonic traditions, Deuteronomistic historiography is more obvious and not so limited to general editing as in the case of the Davidic traditions. In the Solomonic materials, entire sections and blocks of material are reworked, for example, in Solomon's prayer in

I Kings 8.12–53, although this redactional reworking in this passage may have made use of an original composition found in the book of the acts of Solomon. The text abounds, finally, in several small anecdotal notes and narratives which cannot be related to any special work.

E.   The traditions in Chronicles

R. L. **Braun**, 'Solomonic Apologetic in Chronicles', *JBL* XCII, 1973, 503–16; G. **Goldingay**, 'The Chronicler as a Theologian', *BTB* V, 1975, 99–126; R. **Moses**, *Untersuchungen zur Theologie des chronistischen Geschichtswerkes*, Freiburg: Herder 1973; J. D. **Newsome**, 'Toward a New Understanding of the Chronicler and his Purposes', *JBL* XCIV, 1975, 201–17; P. **Welten**, *Geschichte und Geschichtsdarstellung in den Chronikbüchern*, WMANT 42, 1973; T. **Willi**, *Die Chronik als Auslegung: Untersuchungen zur literarischen Gestaltung der historischen Überlieferung Israels*, FRLANT 106, 1972.

Turning to the books of Chronicles, the picture we obtain is wholly different from that found in I–II Samuel and I Kings. Where there are elements and traditions relevant to the historian, they rarely differ from the parallel texts in I–II Samuel and I Kings. For example, II Samuel 24, when compared with I Chronicles 21, shows how the Chronicler altered the tradition; in the former Yahweh incites David to take a census of Israel whereas in the latter it is Satan, who is already presented with demonic features. In actuality, most of the traditions on David and Solomon in Chronicles deal with the building of the temple. In the case of David, Chronicles presents David as making full preparation for the temple's construction and for the organization of worship in the temple. Also in the Solomonic traditions, a relevant topic for the Chronicler is the temple liturgy and the people in charge of it. These texts on the temple and worship have most often been seen as a reflection of the second temple rebuilt after the Babylonian exile rather than as reflective of the temple of Solomon. The Chronicler diligently suppresses all pejorative elements which the books of Samuel and Kings lavishly relate about David and Solomon. The two kings tend thus to become national heroes out of a school book without any consideration about the importance such elements may have had for the comprehension of successive events. For instance, if we possessed only the Chronicler's history it would be totally impossible to understand why the north (Israel) set forth certain conditions after the death of Solomon and eventually seceded from the personal union (see §3B below) since it tells us nothing about David's policy of administrative centralization and Solomon's taxation system. The present writer would therefore exclude the Chronicles from the relevant sources for the reconstruction of the history of the Davidic–Solomonic kingdom, although they contain some important sections bearing on the later history of the separate states of Israel and Judah.

§2. THE ARCHAEOLOGICAL EVIDENCE

Y. **Aharoni**, 'Arad, Its Inscriptions and Temple', *BA* XXXI, 1968, 2–32; idem, 'The Stratification of Israelite Megiddo', *JNES* XXXI, 1972, 302–11; idem, 'The Horned Altar of Beer-Sheba', *BA* XXXVII, 1974, 2–6; idem, 'The Building Activities of David and Solomon', *IEJ* XXIV, 1974, 13–16; W. G. **Dever**, ed., *Gezer* I–II, Jerusalem: Hebrew Union College 1970, 1974; N. **Glueck**, 'Further Explorations in the Negev', *BASOR* CLXXIX, 1965, 6–29; idem, 'Ezion-Geber', *BA* XXVIII, 1965, 70–87; K. M. **Kenyon**, 'Megiddo, Hazor, Samaria and Chronology', *BIA* IV, 1964, 143–56; idem, *Jerusalem: Excavating 3000 Years of History*, London/New York: Thames and Hudson/McGraw-Hill 1967; idem, *Royal Cities of the Old Testament*, London/New York: Barrie & Jenkins/Schocken 1971; idem, *Digging Up Jerusalem*, 1974; B. **Mazar**, 'Jerusalem in the Biblical Period', *Jerusalem Revealed*, ed. Y. Yadin, Jerusalem: Israel Exploration Society 1975, 1–8; J. B. **Pritchard**, 'The Megiddo Stables: A Reassessment', *Near Eastern Archaeology*, 1970, 268–76; B. **Rothenberg**, 'Ancient Copper Industries in the Western Arabah', *PEQ* XCIV, 1962, 5–71; idem, *Timna: Valley of the Biblical Copper Mines*, London: Thames and Hudson 1972 = *Were These King Solomon's Mines? Excavations in the Timna Valley*, New York: Stein and Day 1972; D. **Ussishkin**, 'King Solomon's Palace and Building 1723 in Megiddo', *IEJ* XVI, 1966, 174–86; G. E. **Wright**, *Biblical Archaeology*, 1957, ²1962; Y. **Yadin**, 'Solomon's City Wall and Gate at Gezer', *IEJ* VIII, 1958, 80–6; idem, 'New Light on Solomon's Megiddo', *BA* XXIII, 1960, 62–8; idem, 'Megiddo of the Kings of Israel', *BA* XXXIII, 1970, 66–96; idem, *Hazor: The Head of All Those Kingdoms*, 1972; idem, 'A Note on the Stratigraphy of Israelite Megiddo', *JNES* XXXII, 1973, 330; idem, *Hazor: The Rediscovery of a Great Citadel of the Bible*, London–Jerusalem/New York: Weidenfeld and Nicolson/Random House 1975.

Archaeological evidence for the Davidic and Solomonic period is fragmentary and, on the whole, disappointingly scarce. Only a limited number of sites have been adequately excavated and the materials obtained are differently interpreted by the competent archaeological scholars.

For Jerusalem, the statement of Wright is still true even after fifteen years of extensive excavations during the 1960s and 1970s: '*Not a single discovery has been made in Jerusalem which can be dated with any certainty to the time of David and Solomon*' (127). The expedition led by Kenyon (1961–7) which worked primarily on Mount Ophel, the site of the old city of Jerusalem, associated a major 'filling' discovered with the biblical *millō*' mentioned in II Samuel 5.9; I Kings 9.24; 11.27, and attributed this to David's building activity in Jerusalem (Kenyon, 1967, 49–53; 1974, 99–106). This 'filling' was a notable enhancement to the existing Canaanite terrace system. Traces of the Solomonic walls may be found under the Herodian walls on which the present-day Haram esh-Sharif is built. Nothing however has been found of the many public and private buildings which the two kings are recorded as having constructed.

Excavations at the site of ancient Megiddo (*Tell el-Mutesellin*) have yielded, in strata IVB–VA, the remains of the north-eastern gateway and an elaborate system of casemate city walls of the type found at other sites from the same period. In addition, two palaces, a northern and southern, were found, the latter having possessed a covered entrance. These structures are connected with the time of Solomon, when the town became the capital city of one of the newly created districts (I Kings 4.12). Archaeologists such as Yadin and Aharoni disagree over whether the walls and the city gates are to be connected or not. Aharoni attributes the palaces (archaeologically designated 6000 and 1723) to David. The gate is a very complex structure: pedestrians ascended to it by a stairway, carts by a rampart; at an outer gate one had to turn left some ninety degrees to reach the gate proper. The main gate was constructed with four successive gateways, each with its own door and guard room. Similar gates have been found in Palestine at other sites: Beth-Shemesh (*Tell er-Rumeileh*), *Tell Beit Mirsim* (identified by some scholars as biblical Debir), Hazor (*Tell el-Qedah*), Gezer (*Tell Jazer*), and recently at Dan (*Tell el-Qāḍī*) and Beersheba (*Tell es-Saba'*). The 'blueprint' for such a gate appears in Ezekiel 40.5–16. The gates and palaces are clearly of Syrian origin.

Some structures unearthed at Megiddo were interpreted by the original excavators as stables for some 450 horses, and were immediately associated with the notice supplied by I Kings 9.15–19, where Megiddo is indicated as one of Solomon's chariot cities. Further investigations by Yadin at Megiddo, undertaken in the 1960s, have proved that these structures belong to a period some one to two centuries later, perhaps to the time of Ahab. Recently, Pritchard has cast serious doubt on the assumption that this complex was in reality stables. Yadin's work and his new relative chronology for Megiddo have been questioned recently by Aharoni, but on the whole they seem trustworthy.

I Kings 9.15 notes that Solomon built not only Megiddo but Hazor and Gezer as well. Excavations at Gezer, first by Macalister (1902–5, 1907–9) and in the late 1960s and early 1970s by a consortium of institutions (see Dever), have unearthed remains from the Solomonic period similar to those at Megiddo. (Macalister had interpreted part of the Solomonic gate and casemate wall as a 'Maccabaean Castle'.) Yadin's work at Hazor has again unearthed remains which are both monumental and Solomonic (1975, 187–99).

Recent excavations conducted at Dan (by Biran) and at Beersheba (by Aharoni) have unearthed impressive and similar city gates which have been dated to the tenth or ninth century BCE by the excavators. These gates differ from the 'Solomonic Gates', possessing only two rather than four guard rooms. Aharoni (*IEJ*, 1974) assigns this phase at both sites to the building activity of David. He argues that the building activity of Solomon, noted in I Kings 9.15–19, concentrated on cities located at strategic points on the main routes passing through Palestine and approaching Jerusalem. The absence of any reference to Solomonic construction in border cities, of which Dan and Beersheba were the classical border points, leads Aharoni to conclude that David had already fortified these sites as part of his border defence system.

Aharoni has argued that during the monarchic period royal border sanctuaries were established and maintained at strategic points and played significant administrative and religious roles. At Tel Arad, he discovered a temple from the monarchic period perhaps destroyed in the seventh century. At Beersheba, no temple but an impressive four-horned altar was unearthed, the stones from the altar having been used in a rebuilding phase from the late eighth century. Whether such royal border sanctuaries existed, and whether or not the evidence uncovered by Aharoni should be so interpreted and whether such sanctuaries, if they existed, as well as the existing archaeological evidence, can be related back to David and Solomon, are still theoretical and debatable issues.

A site in the extreme south of Palestine, *Tell el-Khaleifeh*, some 500 metres from the north shore of the Gulf of Aqaba, half-way between Aqaba and Eilat, was identified in the 1930s by Glueck with biblical Ezion-geber. I Kings 9.26 notes that 'King Solomon built a fleet of ships at Ezion-geber, which is near Eloth on the shore of the Red

Sea, in the land of Edom'. Such identification was quite reasonable at the time, as Aqaba has a plenteous supply of fresh water, good soil, and could have provided anchorage for ships. In addition, the *tell* was the only site in the area known at the time. A building discovered at the site was termed a smelter, since its construction showed regular holes in its walls which could have served as flues through which the strong winds from the north would have been funnelled into the smelting room. On the basis of such an archaeological interpretation, the site was identified with Solomon's shipping activities and with the supposed copper-smelting activities associated with the theory of 'King Solomon's Mines'. As early as 1935 Glueck had found what he called copper slag heaps and seven mining or smelter camps in the Arabah and had attributed the mining and smelting activity in this area to Solomonic times. He argued that the mining operation in this area was one of the sources of David's and Solomon's wealth and of the bronze used for furnishings for the temple (but see I Chron. 18.8 and I Kings 7.46) as well as the cause of later Judaean–Edomite struggles. It became fashionable to speak of the area in terms of Solomon's 'Pittsburgh of Palestine'. Subsequent investigations have proved Glueck's dating and interpretation of the *Tell el-Khaleifeh* materials to be incorrect, as Glueck himself later acknowledged. The building appears to have been a citadel with a storehouse and rooms for a granary. The holes in the walls seemed to be where wooden beams were employed to help hold the structure together and to support the roof (see Glueck, 1965). Meanwhile further exploration of the region has located harbour installations, surrounded by a casemate wall, farther to the southwest in the bay of *ǧazīrat al far'un* (the Island of Pharaoh), a site already known as the Egyptian copper harbour. This may have been the harbour site taken over and used by Solomon. There is further evidence that the mines of Timna (the so-called 'Pillars of Solomon') were not in use during the Davidic–Solomonic period (the tenth century BCE), having ceased operation after the twelfth century (see Rothenberg).

§3. THE REIGN OF DAVID

A. *David's rise to power over Judah and Israel*

A. **Alt**, 'The Formation of the Israelite State in Palestine' (see ch. V §2), *Essays*, 1966, 171–237; G. **Buccellati**, 'Da Saul a David', *BeO* I, 1959, 99–128; idem, *Cities and Nations of Ancient Syria: An Essay on Political Institutions* *with Special Reference to the Israelite Kingdoms*, StSem 26, 1967, 195–238; H. **Cazelles**, 'David's Monarchy and the Gibeonite Claim', *PEQ* LXXXVII, 1955, 165–75; K. **Elliger**, 'Noch einmal Beeroth', *Mélanges bibliques rédigés en l'honneur de André Robert*, Paris: Bloud & Gay 1957, 82–94; E. H. **Maly**, *The World of David and Solomon*, Englewood-Cliffs: Prentice-Hall 1966, 35–48; L. **Schmidt**, *Menschlicher Erfolg und Jahwes Initiative: Studien zu Tradition, Interpretation und Historie in Überlieferungen von Gideon, Saul und David*, WMANT 38, 1970, 120–88; J. A. **Soggin**, 'Il regno di 'Ešba'al, figlio di Saul', *RSO* XL, 1965, 89–106 = 'The Reign of 'Ešba'al, Son of Saul', in his *OT Studies*, 1975, 31–49; idem, *Das Königtum in Israel: Ursprünge, Spannungen, Entwicklung*, BZAW 104, 1967, 58–76 (with additional bibliography); H. J. **Stoebe**, 'David und Mikal. Überlegungen zur Jugendgeschichte Davids', *Von Ugarit nach Qumran*, 1958, 224–43.

The aftermath of what has correctly been called 'the débâcle at Gilboa' (*Bright, 190) left Israel and the whole of Palestine in a chaotic condition. Israel was divided between the south, that is Judah, which was not yet organically united with the north and was politically autonomous, and Israel proper, that is the north, which had been deprived of its king and his immediate successors in the dynastic line. The Israelite army had been severely battered and was probably incapable of any immediate further campaigning. In both sections of the country, however, two major personalities were trying, each on his own account, to restore the monarchical institution. In the north, there was Abner, an uncle of the deceased king Saul (I Sam. 14.50f.) and the commander-in-chief of the army which placed him in a position of enormous power. After the death of Saul and his sons, he was the only centre around which the Israelites could rally.

In the south, the former general of Saul, David, was trying to obtain kingship in Judah for himself. David was a southerner born in Bethlehem to a Judaean father of typical tribal background. David had become Saul's armour-bearer, as the story has it, because of his ability to soothe the king's melancholy by playing the lyre. Thanks to his military exploits, he had risen rapidly to the highest echelons in Saul's army. The last days of David at the court of Saul had been marked by an increasing hostility on the part of Saul, a hostility attributed by the biblical text to the progressive folly of the king but probably also due to his suspicions as to the true intentions of David. The young general felt himself in danger, in spite of his friendship with Saul's son Jonathan, and abandoned his master. After fleeing from Saul's service, David organized, in the southern hills of Judah, a private army, rallying around himself some four hundred outlaws, fugitives, and malcontents: 'Everyone who was in distress, and everyone who was in debt, and everyone who was discontented, gathered to him' (I Sam. 22.2). With these men, he led an adventurous life, not refraining from brigandish enterprises such as the protection-racket operation narrated in I Samuel 25.2–43. During this period he married twice; his marriage to Saul's daughter Michal has to be set at a later time (see Stoebe). Hunted by Saul, David felt it necessary to accept Philistine overlordship (I Sam. 27.1–7), so that, technically speaking, he found himself at the time of the battle of Gilboa on the side of Saul's enemies, although David did not participate in the fighting (I Sam. 29). It is difficult to ascertain whether David joined the Philistines out of sheer desperation, having exhausted all other means of self-preservation, or whether his alliance was part of his astute tactics. The statement that, in the choice of means for his own career, David 'evidently had few inhibitions' (*Noth, 181) seems neither untrue nor ungenerous. At the same time, however, David took pains to establish cordial relations with Judah and the other groups of the south. According to I Samuel 30.26–31, he offered part of the spoil he had made in his personal campaigns to the elders of the groups with whom he had contacts. Such actions and attitudes have won for David the charge of double dealing. One should therefore not wonder that the Philistines did not want to have him on the battlefield when they engaged the Israelites; probably they never trusted completely their mercenary vassal. Be that as it may, David was elsewhere during the battle of Gilboa, a fact which obviously helped him considerably in his later dealings with the north.

Another matter which caused unrest was the fact that the Canaanite city-states still divided the tribes: the south from the centre and the centre from the north. These cities were especially strong in the plains where Israel had been unable to settle (see Judg. 1.27–36). The attitudes of these city-states towards the conflict between Israel and the Philistines are not explicitly stated by the sources; but the fact that the Philistines were able to attack Israel on the heights of Gilboa and later to hang the corpses of Saul and his sons on the walls of Bethshan (I Sam. 31.10) suggests that although they may have appeared somewhat neutral, they were benevolent towards the Philistines, if not altogether allied with them.

After the death of Saul, the Philistines were the only power to be reckoned with: they had neutralized the north of Israel and held in their overlordship the most brilliant of Saul's former generals. Their victory must have seemed complete. It is against this background that one must understand the attempt of Abner to restore the kingship in the north and the crowning of David in the south.

The sources for the period immediately following the death of Saul and up to David's assumption of kingship over Israel and Judah are found in I Samuel 1–4 and belong to the general narrative of David's rise. There seems no reason to question their general reliability and the substantial accuracy of their chronological sequence.

The sources inform us that after the death of Saul, David 'went up' to Hebron, the capital of Judah, on the southern plateau, after consulting the divine oracle (I Sam. 2.1–3). In Hebron, he was anointed king by 'the men of Judah' (I Sam. 2.4a), evidently the representative body of this tribe, gathered in an assembly, 'over the house of Judah', probably a confederation of southern tribes. Presumably, the Philistines made no objects to this new status of their vassal, as David's kingship in Judah perfected the rupture between north and south. Over Judah alone, David is reported to have reigned seven and a half years (II Sam. 2.11; 5.5).

Meanwhile Abner in the north seems to have been busy collecting the scattered remains of Saul's army, trying to reorganize public life in all its aspects. Wisely, he moved his capital city to Transjordan, to Mahanaim, probably located at today's *Tell ḥaǧǧiāǧ* or the nearby *Tulūl ed-dāhab*, near the river Jabbok. Mahanaim offered a secure position out of reach of the Philistines, but it also meant that the political centre of the country was separated from its religious and historical centre, which remained in the central highland. But his task, already quite difficult for objective reasons, was made even more difficult by the plans of David to assume kingship also over the north. To such plans, the king had quite discreetly alluded in a letter to the inhabitants of Jabesh-gilead who had rescued the bodies of Saul and his sons, giving them an honourable burial (II Sam. 2.6f.). After praising them for their gallantry and piety, his message concluded with the ambiguous words: 'Now therefore let your hands be strong, and be valiant; for Saul your lord is dead, and the house of Judah has anointed me king over them.' He was no doubt suggesting to the inhabitants of the north that they might do something similar. This must have made Abner realize the precariousness of every attempt to seize power, unless kingship was restored also in the north, thus ruling out David and his ambitions.

Abner selected and supported a son of Saul, 'an ineffectual weakling' (*Bright, 192), apparently the next in line in the dynastic succession. Over such a person, Abner could easily serve as master (II Sam. 2.8–11). He had him crowned king of Israel in Mahanaim. Saul's son is called Ishbosheth in II Samuel, a name meaning 'man of shame'. This is no doubt a polemical renaming in order to delete editorially the reference to the god Baal, since I Chronicles 8.33 and 9.39 have recorded his true name, Ish-baal, which means 'follower of Baal' or, probably better, 'Baal lives'. Everything points to the fact that Ish-baal was but Abner's puppet. Power, and therefore the rule, belonged to Abner while the presence of the prince gave him all the marks of legitimacy he needed. At the same time, this presence on the throne of a successor to Saul made any legitimate claim on the side of David difficult.

Relations between the two kingdoms were often unfriendly. The sources speak of at least one war between them, although the battle seems to have produced no decisive results (II Sam. 2.12–17).

The territories over which Ish-baal reigned are listed in II Sam. 2.9 and, except for the unclear 'šûrî (Ashurites), the description fits perfectly into what we know from Judges 1.27–33. The territory was limited to the central plateau. The reign of Ish-baal is said to have lasted two years (II Sam. 2.10b), a figure which most scholars dismiss as unreliable. The present writer attempted in 1965 to fit this figure into the period parallel to that of the last two years of David's reign over Judah. For some five years, Abner must have tried to reorganize the north, resolving after this period to restore the monarchy. During this interregnum, Abner must have functioned as king in everything but name. His move to place Ish-baal on the throne after five years was certainly an attempt to curtail the ambitions of David. At any rate, Ish-baal was placed on the throne by Abner (II Sam. 2.9). It may have been that Abner had had his eyes on the throne for himself and only made Ish-baal king when this proved impossible.

The reign of Ish-baal was short-lived. According to the sources, his fall was caused by two, not mutually exclusive, factors. In the first place, Ish-baal broke with Abner whom he reproached, not without cause, for seeking his own succession to the throne of Saul (II Sam. 3.7–11, restoring the text according to the LXX). Abner is reported to have taken over one of Saul's concubines, and since a dead king's harem was passed along to his successor, this act could only be interpreted as a sign of his aim to seize power (see II Sam. 16.21 f.; I Kings 2.13–25). This rupture gave Abner the pretext for betraying his master by starting direct negotiations with David. Abner was trying to ensure himself a safe and prominent position under the command of the man who was certain to emerge the victor over the inept Ish-baal. Abner is then said to have discussed the transference of the throne to David with the elders of Israel and the whole house of Benjamin (II Sam. 3.17–19). Abner's plans came

to an abrupt end when Joab, David's commander-in-chief, killed
Abner in Hebron because of a private blood feud (II Sam. 3.20–30),
and no doubt because of Joab's jealousy of Abner and fear of losing
his own position. Secondly, Ish-baal, deprived of his general and
apparently of much of his support among the people, was killed by
two members of his own guard who seem to have had a feud with
him over some wrong Saul had done (II Sam. 4.1–8). Probably, the
murderers of Ish-baal were motivated by a desire to avenge some
action which Saul had taken against the Canaanite enclaves still
remaining within Israelite territory. The men were from Beeroth,
which is noted in Joshua 9 (see v. 17) as one of the cities of Canaan
entering into a treaty with the Israelites. According to II Samuel 21,
Gibeon, another of these cities, possessed a desire for revenge against
Saul since he 'had sought to slay them in his zeal for the people of
Israel and Judah' (II Sam. 21.2) (see Cazelles). The act of the men
from Beeroth was thus more an exercise of vendetta against the
house of Saul than an act committed purely for personal advantage
or political reasons.

The way was now open for David to appear before the assembly of
the northern tribes. They convened at Hebron, stipulated a covenant with David, and anointed him king over Israel (II Sam. 5.1–5).
The total length of David's reign over Israel and Judah is indicated
as forty years, seven and a half years over Judah at Hebron and
thirty-three years over Israel and Judah at Jerusalem. Forty years is
a round figure, appearing also for Solomon, and identical with some
figures appearing in the Deuteronomistic framework of the book of
Judges. It is therefore generally considered artificial, standing for a
relatively long period, exceeding one generation.

The pattern of David's ascent to rulership over the south and the
north alike is perfectly in accord with what we have called (1967)
the 'democratic' element in ancient Israelite kingship. The 'people'
represented by their 'elders' 'anoint' the king, after his divine designation has been manifested by certain 'charismatic' features, duly
checked by the assembly (this is the case with Saul, I Sam. 11) or by
direct divine designation (see II Sam. 2.1; 3.9, 18; 5.2; 6.21; I Sam.
25.30) where direct or indirect references are made to one and the
same or to several oracles which may have been considered as
equivalent to charismatic designation. It has been made clear, however, by the recent work of Schmidt, that the reports about these
divine oracles are hardly primary in the sources. David became king,
therefore, on the ground of his political and military success and not
through divine designation. Later editors of the tradition considered
this divine designation a fundamental element in the crowning of

kings, probably rightly so, and tried wherever possible to supply this element or to substitute for it something equivalent. They did not see the effectual change which had taken place in the young Israelite monarchy, or if they did, they tried to cover it up with fictitious forms of 'charisma'.

While the Philistines had viewed with favour, or, at worst, with indifference, David's assumption of the crown over Judah, his reign over Israel and Judah at the same time 'could no longer be a matter of indifference' (*Noth, 187) to them. They seem to have attacked almost immediately from the south-west (II Sam. 5.17–21), through the Valley of Rephaim (today's *Baqʻa* where the railway line leaves modern Jerusalem). David routed them in a counter-attack from the south. A second attempt by the Philistines fared no better (II Sam. 5.23–5). So the kingdom was safe at last from its first and most immediate major foe. The Philistines were forced to recognize David's supremacy. It is even suggested by some scholars that the Cherethites and Pelethites mentioned in II Samuel 8.18 and 15.18, and the Gittites of the latter text, were in reality Philistine mercenaries that served in David's personal, regular army. If this is true, the Philistines seem to have taken their defeat at the hands of David not very tragically and to have kept a positive attitude towards their former vassal.

B.   The Davidic empire

Y. **Aharoni**, *The Land of the Bible*, 1967; A. **Alt**, 'The Formation of the Israelite State in Palestine' (see ch. V §2), *Essays*, 1966, 171–237; idem, 'Das Grossreich Davids', *TLZ* LXXV, 1950, 213–20 = his *KS* II, 66–77; idem, 'The Monarchy in the Kingdoms of Israel and Judah' (see ch. V §2), *Essays*, 239–59; idem, *Der Stadtstaat Samaria*, *BVSAWL* CI/5, 1954 = his *KS* III, 1959, 258–302; G. **Buccellati**, *Cities and Nations of Ancient Syria*, StSem 26, 1967, 137–93; K. M. **Kenyon**, *Digging Up Jerusalem*, 1974; A. **Malamat**, 'The Kingdom of David and Solomon in its Contact with Egypt and Aram Naharaim', *BA* XXI, 1958, 96–102 = BAR II, 1964, 89–98; idem, 'Aspects of the Foreign Policies of David and Solomon', *JNES* XXII, 1963, 1–17; E. **Maly**, *The World of David and Solomon*, 1966, 49–94; D. B. **Redford**, 'Studies in Relations between Palestine and Egypt during the First Millennium BC: II. The Twenty-second Dynasty', *JAOS* XCIII, 1973, 3–17; J. **Simons**, *The Geographical and Topographical Texts of the Old Testament*, Leiden: E. J. Brill 1959; J. A. **Soggin**, *Das Königtum in Israel*, *BZAW* 104, 1967, 58–76; H. J. **Stoebe**, 'Die Einnahme Jerusalems und der Sinnor', *ZDPV* LXXIII, 1957, 73–99; idem, *Das Erste Buch Samuelis*, KAT VIII/1, 1973.

If a summary characterization of the Davidic kingdom should be attempted, we may use the expression 'imperialist expansion' without any pejorative meaning or undertone. The Davidic kingdom was born out of the distress of a lost war. It grew rapidly through conquest and soon became a highly artificial entity which included in its final form peoples from different origins and traditions. It could maintain itself only by continuous expansion. Some of this expansion may have been justified in order to protect the kingdom; the Philistine wars were certainly a case in point, but the remaining campaigns resulted more from the dynamics inherent in the very essence of the Davidic kingdom than from real need.

II Samuel 5.6 reports the capture of Jerusalem by 'the king and his men', which can only mean David's private army, although I Chronicles 11.4 renders tendentiously with 'David and all Israel'. It is unclear whether this conquest preceded or followed the Philistine campaigns: in favour of the latter are *Noth (187–90) and *Bright (195). If this be the case, then the capture of Jerusalem would have been one of David's main steps taken to consolidate his power from within, after the king had become free from external danger. How David's men gained entrance into the city is not clear either. The text in II Samuel is incomplete and the exact meaning of the term *ṣinnôr* (II Sam 5.8; missing from the Chronicles parallel) is unknown. The term is usually translated 'water conduit' or 'water shaft', a meaning the word has in modern Hebrew. Probably Joab and a small commando force succeeded in entering the town through the water shaft which was built as a tunnel within the Ophel hill and which can still be used by pedestrians even today, although not without some danger.

In Jerusalem, well known as an ancient Canaanite city-state already mentioned in the Execration Texts and in the letters from el-Amarna, David located his capital city and here he brought the ark for which he set up a special tent (II Sam. 6). The new capital had good defences against all enemies, made favourable by the fact that it was approachable only from the north. David seems to have used the fortifications of the Canaanite city, although II Samuel 5.9 makes reference to the fact that he 'built the city round about from the Millo inward' (Kenyon, 1974, 100). In addition to its fortified position, the new capital was historically and topographically independent of the traditional tribal allotments and could thus belong fully to the crown, i.e., the central government. Located midway between Israel to the north and Judah to the south, the city offered a strategic political location and of course had not been involved in the recent struggles between Davidic Judah and Saulide Israel.

David first vanquished, as we have seen, his former overlords, the Philistines, and reduced them to the role of a small border state, more or less dependent upon Jerusalem. According to II Samuel 5 and 8 and I Chronicles 18, David campaigned against the Moabites (II Sam. 8.2), against the Aramaeans (Syrians) of Zobah (II Sam. 8.3; see II Sam. 10.6) and of Damascus (II Sam. 8.5–8). The Aramaean state of Hamath submitted spontaneously to David's overlordship (II Sam. 8.9f.). II Samuel 10–12, with parallels in I Chronicles 19–20, reports that David subdued the Ammonites as well as the Aramaeans of Beth-rehob, Maacah, and Tob. The well known, but legendary, episode of David, Bathsheba, Uriah the Hittite, and Nathan has its setting within the context of the Ammonite war. Some time during his reign, David must have succeeded in including within his kingdom the Canaanite city-states in the plains which Israel had previously been unable to occupy (see Judg. 1.21–33). According to Judges 1.28, these cities came into Israelite control when 'Israel grew strong', an expression which not only fits the time of David but also is unfitting to any time earlier than David. In the census taken by David, reported in II Samuel 24, and in the list of the administrative districts set up by Solomon, the Canaanite city-states appear fully integrated into the empire.

According to II Samuel 3.3, David, while still in Hebron, had married a daughter of the king of Geshur. From this, we can deduce that this small Aramaean state was allied with David even during his first years of kingship. II Samuel 13.37–9 and 14.23, 32 provide evidence of the fact that these cordial relations continued for a long time. A covenant between equal partners was established with David by Hiram of Tyre (II Sam. 5.11; I Chron. 14.1). Our texts place this agreement at the beginning of the Davidic rule, but in view of the fact that this treaty was in operation chiefly under Solomon, and further, that Hiram seems to have been considerably younger than David, one might doubt the accuracy of the chronology here. According to the Phoenician King List of Menander of Ephesus, quoted by Josephus (*Contra Apionem*, I 18), Hiram would have reigned from about 970/69 until 936 or 926 BCE, which would have made him a contemporary more of Solomon than David. The friendly relationships between David and Solomon and Hiram of Tyre were due to the complementary rather than competitive economies of Israel and Phoenicia and thus to common trading and military interests.

It is noteworthy that Egypt, although in theory the overlord of Palestine and southern Syria, did not intervene during these years but left David completely free to conquer and to organize his empire. Relations between Egypt and the Davidic kingdom seem, further, to have been rather cordial, and this cordiality improved, as we shall see, under Solomon. The Egyptian attitude towards Israel need not be explained as due to Egypt's decline and decadence, and therefore to its impotence, as is often done. That someone should finally conquer the Philistines and the Transjordanian tribal communities, imposing law and order on two particularly unruly areas, would have eliminated raids into Egypt and thus could only have pleased the Egyptians. At the same time, David's cordial relations with Phoenicia would have contributed to good relations with Egypt. 'Extending the hand of friendship to the Phoenicians was in David's own interests, but in so doing he was also respecting an Egyptian sphere of influence of hallowed antiquity' (Redford, 5).

Thus the kingdom under David, in its final phase, included the following territories: (1) the traditional tribal allotments of Judah and Israel; (2) the former city-states of Jerusalem and of the plains; (3) the kingdoms of Moab, Edom, and Ammon (roughly corresponding to the modern Hashemite Kingdom of Jordan) whose political independence had been theoretically maintained, although parts of their population had been decimated or set to forced labour; and (4) the Aramaean city-states roughly corresponding to today's Syria and eastern Lebanon. The kingdom of Geshur was an old ally of David and covenant relations had been established with Tyre. The latter proved long-lasting, as they continued with the kingdom of Israel, after the disruption of the Davidic–Solomonic empire, throughout most of the ninth century. The village of Ziklag seems to have enjoyed a special status, having been given to David by his Philistine overlord. I Samuel 27.6 states that 'Achish gave him Ziklag; therefore Ziklag has belonged to the kings of Judah to this day'.

There can hardly be any doubt that the whole realm had become an extremely complicated political structure (*Noth, 204), being no longer merely an Israelite state but a typical Near Eastern empire. Several different institutions not always, strictly speaking, compatible among themselves were intertwined. There was sovereignty by popular consent through assemblies, the traditional Israelite form of government; sovereignty by right of conquest in the case of Jerusalem and the Canaanite city-states; and the overlordship over Transjordan and the Aramaean states. The whole picture seems not substantially different from what we find in Assyria and Babylon during the first half of the first millennium BCE including many negative aspects such as the possibility that the peripheral regions might rebel against the central government and recover their freedom at its expense. Something like this happened during the last years of Solomon (I Kings 11.14–28).

The first critically founded analysis of the Davidic–Solomonic kingdom from the constitutional point of view goes back, as so many historical and juridical studies of Old Testament subjects, to Albrecht Alt. It was he who first introduced the concept of 'personal union' to define the essential relationship between Israel and Judah during the days of David and Solomon. Alt's points of departure are obvious and are therefore non-controversial matters of fact. First, David was offered kingship and anointed initially by the 'men of Judah' (II Sam. 2.4) and later by 'all the elders of Israel' (II Sam. 5.1–5). Secondly, the successor of Solomon, Rehoboam, had to travel to Shechem, probably considered the traditional capital of the north because of its religious traditions, in order to be crowned by the popular assembly which had convened there (I Kings 12.1–15). This is generally admitted (also by Buccellati) as a sign of a considerable degree of independence and national self-consciousness on the part of the north. Thirdly, during the reign of David, we know about two attempts on the part of the north to secede (II Sam. 15–18; 20). The secession was eventually carried out one generation later when Rehoboam failed to comply with the requests of the assembly. All this points to an originally rather loose union of two different political and administrative entities, a union obtained through the person of the king. This is what Alt called the 'personal union'.

Alt was also the first to stress the special status of the towns of Jerusalem and Ziklag, both of which belonged in a special way to the royal house and thus allegedly retained their former status of city-state. This unique position was founded, in the case of Jerusalem, on David's conquest of the city with his own special troops, and, in the case of the latter, on the gift of the town to him by the Philistines.

A third emphasis in Alt's analysis of the Davidic kingdom was the increasing frequency with which David made use of his own army in place of the popular, national force under the command of Joab. As we have seen, David's personal army had initially gathered around him during his days in the wilderness as a hunted fugitive from Saul. The size and use of this personal army seem to have been extended with the passage of time.

Alt's picture of the situation takes full account of the complexity which existed, from a constitutional point of view, within the kingdom of David. During the past few decades his views have been considered an adequate description of the facts and the legal issues involved. Recently, Alt's analysis has been challenged by Buccellati in what can be considered the most important study on the subject since Alt. Buccellati denies that one can speak of a 'personal union' between the two (or perhaps the three, if we consider the autonomy of Benjamin; see II Sam. 3.19) parts of greater Israel. Further, he argues that there is hardly any conclusive evidence that Jerusalem and Ziklag enjoyed a special status as royal city-states. According to Buccellati, our texts provide no real evidence to support the idea that Jerusalem retained a special status, and in the Old Testament one never sees the Judaean monarch referred to as 'king of Jerusalem'. In the case of Ziklag, Buccellati concludes that I Samuel 27.5 f. means that Ziklag was simply not returned to the Philistines and therefore remained within Judah at later times.

In discussing these differences between Alt and Buccellati, we shall begin with the question of the two cities. First of all, it must be noted that Ziklag was of a completely marginal importance within Israelite history and might therefore be ignored without anybody noticing it; but the exact opposite is obviously true about Jerusalem. This explains why the sources inform us about the latter town but are almost completely silent about the former.

The difficulty with Ziklag lies in two objective facts. One is the semantic ambiguity of I Samuel 27.5 f. and the other is the topographical uncertainty about the town's location. For the first of these, it must be sufficient here to note that none of the commentaries (which, by the way, are not referred to by Buccellati) interpret I Samuel 27.5 f. otherwise than as evidence for the fact that Ziklag belonged not so much to the kingdom of Judah as such as to the royal house (see most recently the commentary by H. J. Stoebe). For the latter problem, the uncertainty of the site has led to two tentative identifications: *Tell el-Khuweilifeh*, some fifteen kilometres NNE of Beer-sheba, and *Tell eš-Sariʿah*, some fifteen kilometres NNW of Beer-sheba. In the first case, the village appears never to have been a part of Philistine territory proper but belonged to it during certain periods of great expansion. If this be the site of Ziklag, then it must be assumed that during the last phase of Philistine expansion the town was allotted to David as perhaps a handy way for the Philistines to shorten their over-extended borders. In this case, there would obviously have been no question of returning the town. In the case of *Tell eš-Sariʿah*, the village and its territory were a typical border area which could change hands easily with the movement of the frontier eastward or westward. Also in this case, it seems difficult to imagine how Ziklag could have been returned to the Philistines, whose borders after the establishment of the Davidic kingdom never extended further eastward than the borders of the original Philistine city-states. Where Buccellati is certainly correct is when he argues that there is no evidence whatsoever that the village was ever a city-state whose hereditary sovereign David might have become. It seems therefore proper to maintain the thesis that Ziklag was governed, as a fief, directly by the house of David. It retained this status later when the original overlord, the Philistine Achish and his successors, lost their prerogatives over David. As to having been a city-state, whose sovereigns David and his successors would have become, all evidence is lacking and furthermore it seems rather improbable.

The situation of Jerusalem is much more complex. Buccellati is obviously right in stressing that there is no evidence to support the thesis that Jerusalem retained the status of a sovereign city-state, first within the Davidic–Solomonic kingdom, and later, within Judah. This evidence lacking, it is difficult to see how David and his successors could have employed the title 'king of Jerusalem', as it appears in the el-Amarna letters but nowhere in the Old Testament. Therefore the absence of such a title for the house of David is nothing more than what we would expect. On the other hand, no pre-exilic text ever speaks, as is well known, of Judah in such a way as to include the capital city. The texts always have Judah and Jerusalem, as two separate entities. In light of these factors, some modification of the thesis of Alt seems necessary.

This special way of referring to Judah and Jerusalem can be explained only by assuming some kind of autonomy for the capital city towards the tribes within whose territory it was situated. This status may tentatively be indicated by suggesting a status similar to the Federal District or Federal Capital in so many American republics (USA, Mexico, Brazil, Argentina, etc.) and in Australia. In other words, the territory of the former city-state of Jerusalem seems to have become some kind of federal district, administered directly by the crown and not subject either to the traditional tribal structures of Israel or to the Canaanite city-state system. The same situation seems to have prevailed two centuries later in the north with regard to Samaria, with the only difference being that Samaria was founded *ex novo* by Omri and had not been a former city-state (I Kings 16.23 f.).

As for the concept of personal union, Buccellati concedes that there is substantial evidence in favour of the concept but that very often other elements point the other way and favour rather the thesis of a strongly centralized state. We think that the solution may be found in admitting the existence of two sets of contrasting elements: one centripetal, emanating from the palace, with the strong trend to eliminate, or at least to curtail, local autonomies in favour of the central, royal government; the other, centrifugal, emanated from the traditional organs of local government, had strong 'democratic' tendencies, and was quite ready to accept the united kingdom concept so long as it gave peace and prosperity, law and order. Its sustainers were, however, equally willing to reject the concept of the combined states as soon as it showed trends to overrule local government and to introduce forms of taxation, of levies, and of *corvées*, which were considered oppressive and alien and therefore iniquitous. For such contrasts between central and local government there are many examples all over history, and one can point, for example, to the history of the English-speaking peoples, from the Middle Ages to the American Civil War.

C. *Civil and military administration under David*

J. **Begrich**, 'Sōfēr und Mazkīr: Ein Beitrag zur inneren Geschichte des davidisch–salomonischen Grossreiches und des Königreiches Juda', *ZAW* LVIII, 1940–1, 1–29 = his *Gesammelte Studien zum Alten Testament*, ed. W. Zimmerli, TB 21, 1964, 67–98; A. **Cody**, 'Le titre égyptien et le nom propre du scribe de David', *RB* LXXII, 1965, 381–93; T. N. D. **Mettinger**, *Solomonic State Officials: A Study of the Civil Government Officials of the Israelite Monarchy*, CBOTS 5, 1971; B. D. **Redford**, 'Studies in Relations between Palestine and Egypt during the First Millennium BC: I. The Taxation System of Solomon', *Studies on the Ancient Palestinian World* (Festschrift F. V. Winnett), ed. J. W. Wevers and D. B. Redford, TSTS 2, 1972, 141–56; R. **de Vaux**, 'Titres et fonctionnaires égyptiens à la cour de David et de Salomon', *RB* XLVIII, 1939, 395–405 = his *Bible et Orient*, 1967, 189–201; G. J. **Wenham**, 'Were David's Sons Priests?', *ZAW* LXXXVII, 1975, 79–82.

Two texts supply us with information about the administration of the kingdom under David. These are II Samuel 8.15–18 (I Chron. 18.14–17) and II Samuel 20.23–6. The latter text is assumed to reflect the administrative situation at a later time than the first text, since it mentions the superintendent of forced labour. In addition to these two texts, there is a third one reflecting the situation at the time of Solomon found in I Kings 4.1–4. These texts contain a list of officials of the empire and are generally considered accurate except for II Samuel 8.17 (I Chron. 18.16), where the reading 'and Zadok, and Abiathar, son of Ahimelech, son of Ahitub' is generally preferred to the reading in the Hebrew text where Ahitub is given as the father of Zadok. Elsewhere, Zadok occurs in all texts without patronymic and therefore without a known father (except in I Chron. 6.8 and elsewhere in Chronicles). The name Ahitub is attested as Abiathar's grandfather (I Sam. 22.20) so one may safely correct the Hebrew text.

The following officials appear in the lists:

Joab: commander-in-chief of the people's levies (II Sam. 8.16; 20.4).

Jehoshaphat: mazkîr (II Sam. 8.17; 20.25).

Zadok and Abiathar: priests (II Sam. 8.16; 20.24).

Seraiah: sôfēr (II Sam. 8.17; 20.25). The name appears as *šᵉya'* (K) or *šᵉwā* (Q) in 20.25, as *šawšā'* in I Chronicles 18.16, while I Kings 4.3 has *šîšā'*. It seems quite probable that we have here nothing but variant readings of the same word and many scholars think that the name originated from the corruption of an Egyptian title, later misunderstood as a proper name: *šš š'.t* or *sḫ š'.t* (*sš* = 'scribe', *š'.t* = 'letter').

Benaiah: commander-in-chief of the king's personal army (II Sam. 8.18; 20.23).

Sons of David: priests (II Sam. 8.18, missing in II Sam. 20.23–6). I Chronicles 18.17 contains a phrase which can mean either 'the sons of David were the chief officials in the service of the king' or 'the eldest sons of David were in the service of the king'. The problem in the Chronicler's reading seems to rest on the Chronicler's view of the legitimate priesthood. According to him, no person of non-levitical descent was allowed to become priest and therefore the sons of David could not have been priests. Since we know nothing about any priestly activity of any of David's sons, different translations and emendations have been proposed. Some are quite ancient: the LXX has *aularchai* = 'stewards', Symmachus has *scholazontes* = 'scholars (of the law)', the Targum has *rabrābîn* = 'teachers (of the law)'. Among modern scholars, 'administrators', 'counsellors', or even 'soothsayers' have been proposed (for a number of proposals, see Wenham). There can be no doubt, however, that the Hebrew word *kōhēn* means 'priest' and nothing else. The text further has the verb *hāyû*, 'were', which may suggest that this sort of an appointment was something unusual, belonging to the past.

Adoram: superintendent of forced labour (only in II Sam. 20.24).
Ira: David's priest (only in II Sam. 20.25). We do not know, nor
  can we ascertain, what this charge meant.
Ahishar: superintendent of the royal palace (only in I Kings 4.6).

The two offices indicated by the words *sôfēr* and *mazkîr* are currently rendered by 'secretary' and 'recorder'. The former would have
been the secretary to the king in charge of his official correspondence. The latter is better rendered 'herald', a function which some
authors see as similar to the speaker in the parliaments of Anglo-
Saxon tradition.

Practically all the officers in these lists had no known parallels in
the court of Saul and certainly none within the older tribal structures. Such a bureaucratic structure was necessary in the administration of such a complex and far-flung empire as that of David. The
officials were 'servants (i.e. ministers) of the kings', members of the
royal entourage, and basically at the service of and subordinate to
the king and the court and to no other entity. The presence of
religious leaders as members of the royal cabinet illustrates how the
figure of the king dominated the affairs of state, religious and otherwise.

Several hypotheses have been proposed to explain the origin of
this rather elaborate system of administration. It certainly was no
organic development out of tribal systems of administration, although
some of its roots were already present in the reign of Saul and were
of course inherent in the needs of any royal administrative system.
The Canaanite city-state and Egyptian royal administrative systems
have been considered the most likely areas for Davidic borrowing.
About the organization of the former at the end of the second millennium we know practically nothing. This explains why scholars have
sought to find the strong influence of Egyptian governmental organization on the Davidic–Solomonic bureaucratic structure. The strongest case for Egyptian parallels are to be found in the offices of
'secretary' and 'herald' (the *sôfēr* and *mazkîr*) where, as we saw,
Egyptian words may be hidden behind the names. Recently,
Redford has challenged the attempt to find Egyptian inspiration in
the Israelite system. In addition to his conclusion that genuine parallels do not exist, he argues that 'the ad hoc nature of the requirements of his [David's] kingdom would have dictated the choice of a
local example. Every Canaanite court would have contained such
officers, not in mimicry of Egyptian ways, but in fulfilment of the
ordinary, day-to-day needs of the administration' (143 f.). None the

less, since Egyptian influence had been so dominant in Phoenicia and Canaan, Egyptian influence may be seen even if at second-hand and adapted to local conditions. Redford's conclusion that 'the biblical lists are the product of secondary tabulations of names that the compiler culled from the scattered literary sources available to him, and in no way reflect a genuine document from the time of the United Monarchy' (143 n. 6) cannot be accepted.

### D.	Political tensions within the Davidic kingdom

R. A. **Carlson**, *David, the Chosen King: A Traditio-Historical Approach to the Second Book of Samuel*, Stockholm: Almqvist & Wiksell 1964, 131–259; H. **Cazelles**, 'David's Monarchy and the Gibeonite Claim (II Sam. XXI, 1–14)', *PEQ* LXXXVII, 1955, 165–75; A. S. **Kapelrud**, 'König David und die Söhne des Saul', *ZAW* LXVII, 1955, 198–205; idem, 'King and Fertility. A Discussion of II Sam. 21.1–14', *Interpretationes ad Vetus Testamentum pertinentes Sigmundo Mowinckel septuagenario missae*, Oslo: Land og Kirke 1955, 113–22; E. **Maly**, *The World of David and Solomon*, 1966, 95–111; K.-D. **Schunck**, *Benjamin: Untersuchungen zur Entstehung und Geschichte eines israelitischen Stammes*, BZAW 86, 1963, 139–53.

In the political field, David and his reign brought forth a long period of peace (almost two generations) after the early war-filled years. Together with peace came prosperity. The 'narrative of the Davidic succession' informs us, however, about palace intrigues and popular rebellions which stand as a contrast to the picture of general peace, although one must admit that these events probably did not touch the greater part of the population, at least not in the south.

The succession narrative places the story of the David and Bathsheba affair within the context of the campaign against Ammon. The story concludes with the king being rebuked by Nathan the prophet and having to yield to public opinion. The image of the king in the story is of a monarch who was still unable to ignore or to overrule public opinion, but who was forced to accept it and to act accordingly. The monarchy is still largely dependent upon the consent of the governed. Unfortunately, we cannot ascertain if we are dealing here with historically trustworthy information, that is, with a realistic description of what used to happen during David's reign, or simply with a popular glorification of the 'good old times' when kings were dependent upon public opinion, listened to rebukes, and could be brought to repentance by godly men. The legendary and fabulous elements in the story make this last interpretation the most probable.

Another element of tension presented in the Davidic traditions is the rebellion of the northern tribes who were, according to the sources, discontented with what they considered an unfair administration of justice (II Sam. 15.1–6), and probably also, although the sources do not mention it, with a system of taxation and forced labour introduced by the central government. We know little about the taxation and labour policies of David; the only hint that it existed comes from II Samuel 20.24 where, as we have noted, a 'superintendent of forced labour' is mentioned. The same person, Adoram, appears also under Solomon in the same capacity. The comparison with Solomon makes it almost certain that the public works ordered by David (see II Sam. 5.11 and other texts) were executed in greater part by forced labour.

The first rebellion of the north was headed by Absalom, the new crown prince after the death of his half-brother Amnon, whom he had killed after Amnon raped his sister (II Sam. 13; for lists of David's sons, see II Sam. 3.2–5 and 5.13–16). The rebellion of Absalom, who had himself crowned king, like David his father, in Hebron (II Sam. 15.7–12), brought the kingdom to the verge of collapse and was squelched only with great difficulty through the use of the private, mercenary army of the king (II Sam. 15–19). Absalom was killed as he tried to flee the scene of battle after his Israelite supporters had been defeated in the forest of Ephraim in Transjordan.

A second but less significant rebellion broke out among the Benjaminites, who are considered by some authors to be a third force between Israel and Judah (see Schunck). This rebellion was again joined by a great part of the north, under the battle-cry:

> We have nothing to share with David,
> Nothing in common with the son of Jesse!
> Every man to his own tent, O Israel (II Sam. 20.1).

The same cry appears a generation later in the assembly of the northern tribes which refused to accept Rehoboam as king. Here an additional line was added to the chant: 'Look after your own house, O David' (I Kings 12.16). This seems to have been the battle-cry of those elements in the north who refused to yield their local autonomy and rights to the central government.

It is impossible to determine if David's harsh treatment of the house of Saul (see II Sam. 21.1–14) was a source of strong irritation to Saul's old tribe of Benjamin. David's participation in the Gibeonite execution of members of the house of Saul, carried out apparently as both a vendetta and a fertility rite, certainly eliminated the possibility of any reassertion of the old monarchic family and thus the leadership of the Benjaminites (see Cazelles and Kapelrud).

There seems to be no good reason to doubt the existence of a historical kernel in the narrative of these two rebellions. They demonstrate that among the Israelite population the ideal of a United Kingdom encompassing the whole of Israel and Judah and ruled over by David rested on rather feeble foundations.

The evidence points further to the fact that, if we leave ideals to the side, the north felt, and not without reason, subjugated by the south, a factor about which we will say more when we come to Solomon. It appears that it was David's mercenary army which was able to prevail over the popular troops of the north, thanks to its greater efficiency and ruthlessness.

E.   *Religious developments under David*

G. W. **Ahlström**, *Psalm 89: Eine Liturgie aus dem Ritual des leidenden Königs*, Lund: CWK Gleerup 1959; idem, 'Der Prophet Nathan und der Tempelbau', *VT* XI, 1961, 113–27; J. **Gray**, *The Legacy of Canaan: The Ras Shamra Texts and Their Relevance to the Old Testament*, SVT 5, ²1965, 152–217; M. **Noth**, 'David und Israel in 2. Samuel 7', *Mélanges bibliques rédigés en l'honneur de André Robert*, Paris: Bloud and Gay 1957, 122–30 = his *GS* I, ²1960, 334–45 = 'David and Israel in II Samuel VII', in his *Laws in the Pentateuch* 1966, 250–9; J. A. **Soggin**, 'Der offiziell geförderte Synkretismus in Israel während des 10. Jahrhunderts', *ZAW* LXXVIII, 1966, 179–204; idem, 'Der Beitrag des Königtums zur altisraelitischen Religion', *SVT* XXIII, 1972, 9–26; G. **Widengren**, *Sakrales Königtum im Alten Testament und im Judentum*, Stuttgart: W. Kohlhammer 1955.

There is some evidence that with David a fully new religious policy was begun which in previous studies we have called 'state syncretism'. The obvious difficulties in establishing and elaborating such a theory lie in the fact that we know so little about the official Israelite religion before prophetic and Deuteronomistic times. However, if we may accept certain elements provided for us by the sources, it is possible to argue that something new happened in this area under David and was brought to perfection under Solomon.

Where different ethnic and religious groups live together, it is quite common, and therefore normal, for spontaneous interaction to occur between them. This can eventually lead to a more or less complete amalgamation of the two, especially if language, custom, and background are not greatly different. This would have happened under normal circumstances between Israel and the Canaanites if existing comparative models are valid. However, something quite different seems to have happened under David. This blending appears to have been fostered by the central government as a matter of policy, especially in the religious field where the differences were the greatest. Even these differences between Israelite and Canaanite religions are not easily discovered and this hinders any attempt to provide a detailed analysis of religious developments under David. Our sources are the products of later reworking and editing, so that the original elements, more often than not, cannot be isolated with any exactitude. The religion presented in the Old Testament texts is certainly not identical with religion as practised in ancient Israel.

On one element of difference between Israelite and Canaanite religion the sources tend to agree: Israel's faith was not, as were the religions of Canaan, anchored in the cyclical movements of nature and therefore in the overriding concern for fertility of flock and field (see Gray). Thus it seems impossible that the king in Israel would have had the same cultic functions as those assumed for the monarch in the cult of the dying-rising Baal in Canaanite religion (but see Ahlström, 1959, and Widengren). The crass and probably intentional misunderstanding or misrepresentation of Canaanite ritual in its forms and its aims (see, e.g., I Kings 18 and the prophets) shows a complete lack of sympathy and empathy.

With the rather loose composition of the Davidic kingdom, it is understandable that the crown should try by all means available to overcome every possible source of division. Religion was certainly the main uniting or dividing factor between Israel and its neighbours both within and without Canaan. Against this background, one must see an attempt carried out by the central government to create something like a national religion which would bind together all subjects of the realm. This religion had to be syncretistic, incorporating many alien elements into the cult of Yahweh, the God of the victor. This form of syncretism must therefore be sharply distinguished from any spontaneous form of syncretism.

One of the first steps of David in this direction was to fetch the ark and to bring it to his newly acquired 'federal' capital where he placed it in a special tent-sanctuary (II Sam. 6). The implications of this act seem not to have met with opposition; perhaps they were not fully understood by the tribal groups. In reality, the removal of the ark to Jerusalem placed the old shrine under the direct patronage of the king. (Remember that under David, the priests Abiathar and Zadok were government officials.)

The next and obvious step would have been the construction of a temple for the ark according to the general pattern in the ancient Near East. These were, as the sources have it, David's plans. He was able to secure the building site (II Sam. 24; I Chron. 21) and nothing seemed to oppose his undertaking. According to II Samuel 7.1–3, even Nathan the prophet hailed the project. But shortly thereafter, 'that same night', as the text has it (II Sam. 7.4), the same Nathan is said to have suddenly opposed the project. Here, we cannot enter into a discussion of the complex literary problems of II Samuel 7, a matter which would not be overly relevant to our subject. Suffice it to state that Nathan, after having been an enthusiastic supporter of the project, suddenly changed his mind and appealed to a divine command received in a vision (II Sam. 7.4–7). That all this should have happened because of the unworthiness of the king is stated in I Chronicles 22.7–10 and 28.3–8. The king was unclean because of the blood he had shed in war. This might have been the official, face-saving motivation of the sudden prohibition. But, as we argued in 1966, there seems to have been much more involved. Nathan must suddenly have realized what the implications of this new course were and forbidden the king to build a temple. In exchange, he gave David God's promise that his dynasty ('his house') would last and rule forever. This certainly meant that the prophet endorsed David's dynastic ambitions. The king was thus victorious, in a way; he did not get all he wanted but he received a very important prophetic and divine sanction. The prophet was theoretically victorious, having asserted his point and won the first round; but it was a victory without a future. Solomon built all he wanted and acted in the cult as he pleased, without asking anybody for permission.

§4. THE REIGN OF SOLOMON

E. W. **Heaton**, *Solomon's New Men: The Emergence of Ancient Israel as a National State*, London: Thames and Hudson 1974; J. A. **Soggin**, *Das Königtum in Israel*, BZAW 104, 1967, 77–89.

A. *Solomon's accession to the throne*

K. **Galling**, *Die israelitische Staatsverfassung in ihrer vorderorientalischen Umwelt*, AOr 28/3–4, 1929; C. E. **Hauer**, Jr., 'Who Was Zadok?', *JBL* LXXXII,

1963, 89–94; E. I. J. **Rosenthal**, 'Some Aspects of the Hebrew Monarchy', *JJS* IX, 1958, 1–18.

The adventurous rise of David to kingship made it possible for later hagiographers to introduce the motive of divine designation through prophetic choice and oracle into the narrative of his rise to power. The manner in which Solomon ascended the throne made any such pretence impossible. The conclusion of the succession narrative (I Kings 1–2) gives us a rather realistic report of what actually happened before Solomon was crowned and everything points to a palace intrigue.

We hear that David was growing old and that his strength and virility were fading. The problem of the succession to the throne was therefore entering the perspective of all those active at the court for some time before the king's death. Legally speaking, after the deaths of Amnon and Absalom, the prince next in line to the succession was Adonijah (see II Sam. 3.4; apparently Chileab had died as a youngster). That the succession was to take place according to dynastic criteria was probably taken for granted after Nathan's oracle of dynastic promise (see II Sam. 7). There seems to have been a tacit agreement between all parties involved not to convene any sort of popular assembly and to let everything follow a strictly dynastic course. After David's strong-armed tactics against the north, one could never be sure of what decisions an assembly would take (an example of what could have happened we have in I Kings 12, where it did happen!). It is not unexpected, therefore, that Adonijah, the first in the dynastic line, tried to secure the succession for himself, perhaps as co-regent with his father (I Kings 1.5–8). Adonijah may have had probable cause for worry about his succession, considering the fact that David had promised Bathsheba, at least according to her, that Solomon would succeed to the throne (I Kings 1.13–17).

Adonijah succeeded in winning over to his plans the former commander of the popular military levy, Joab, and one of the two priests, Abiathar. Against him, more important and powerful elements rallied: Bathsheba, the mother of Solomon and David's favourite wife, and the prophet Nathan (I Kings 1.11–14). Later, Zadok, the other priest, and Benaiah, the commander of the king's personal professional army, joined the plot (I Kings 1.28–38). Nathan and Bathsheba succeeded in persuading David to appoint Solomon as successor-designate. On the basis of this major strength, Solomon succeeded in ascending the throne with almost no struggle and in a few subsequent moves was able to have most of his antagonists eliminated or exiled: Joab and Adonijah were put to death; Abiathar the priest was banished to Anathoth (I Kings 2.13–35).

The division of the court leaders in their support of the two contenders might suggest a conflict between the 'old' and the 'new' orders in Israel. Joab and Abiathar had connections with the older Israelite military and religious institutions. Benaiah, reflecting the new military innovations of David, and Zadok, if his background could be placed in the pre-Israelite cult of Jerusalem (see Hauer), were more clearly the instruments of the new orders established by David. Not too much, however, should be made of this split in the royal officialdom: both groups seemed to have accepted the new dynastic orders and differed only over who should benefit from these and, at any rate, the impetus for Solomon's accession originated with Nathan and Bathsheba. Galling has suggested that perhaps Adonijah was backed by the tribal groups of Judah and that Solomon was supported by the city of Jerusalem (18).

Solomon ascended the throne independent of both the traditional, charismatic-democratic designation through the people and the institutional-dynastic criterion of legitimacy which has always been the accepted procedural pattern in hereditary monarchies. Solomon's kingship, viewed from any angle, seems therefore to have lacked all claims to legitimacy. Still, acquiescence in his accession may have been the lesser evil since it preserved law and order. Had the tribal assemblies or Adonijah fought for their prerogatives, the situation could have become not very different from what it had been after the death of Saul. With the threat of internal anarchy or civil war, there was also the danger that the highly complex, sophisticated, and, to many, profitable structure of the empire might have collapsed. Vested interests and general prosperity may have overridden political tradition and conviction.

B.   The development of royal ideology

M. **Görg**, *Gott-König-Reden in Israel und Ägypten*, BWANT VI/5, 1975; S. **Herrmann**, 'Die Königsnovelle in Ägypten und in Israel', *WZUL* III, 1953–4, 51–62; E. **Kutsch**, 'Die Dynastie von Gottes Gnaden', *ZTK* LVIII, 1961, 137–53; J. B. **Pritchard**, *Gibeon, Where the Sun Stood Still*, Princeton: Princeton University Press 1962; R. N. **Whybray**, 'The Political Novel in Egypt and Israel', in his *The Succession Narrative: A Study of II Sam. 9–20 and I Kings 1 and 2*, SBT II/9, 1968, 96–116.

Most of the biblical texts aim at presenting Solomon as the prototype of the pious and wise king, although it is not difficult to detect other, less edifying elements whose influences have been preserved. The sources must be used with caution, since they have been thoroughly edited by the Deuteronomistic historian, and also because they frequently show an interest in things irrelevant politically and economically. Just as was the case with the traditions about David, those about Solomon have been organized around the blessing-curse scheme: 'Solomon under the blessing – Solomon under the curse.' This scheme means that the order of events has probably been radically rearranged, so that the present chronological frame can be used only with great caution.

The first acts of King Solomon led to the consolidation of his power, that is, the elimination of Adonijah and all other persons who had challenged him. The first official deed following the assumption of power seems to have been, according to the sources, a pilgrimage to the 'High Place' of Gibeon (I Kings 3.4–15), whose location was almost certainly on or near the *tell* excavated in the proximity of today's *el-jib* (see Pritchard). We do not know if the sanctuary there had become an Israelite cult site or if it was still a non-Israelite place of worship. According to I Chronicles 21.29 and II Chronicles 1.3, 5, the tabernacle and the altar used in the desert were located there, which would seem to favour the assumption that the place had become Israelite. These texts, as most commentaries show, aim at justifying David's and Solomon's worship outside Jerusalem by showing that Gibeon was already thoroughly Israelite and, in any case, the temple had not yet been built (see the earlier Deuteronomistic comment in I Kings 3.2). This apologetic character makes it doubtful whether the information about the tabernacle and altar is historically trustworthy. We must leave it at that, for lack of historical information.

According to the Kings text, Solomon slept at the Gibeonite sanctuary where Yahweh appeared to him in a dream, granting him the fulfilment of one wish he might desire. The king asked for 'an understanding heart to govern (*špt*) thy people, that I may discern between good and evil' (I Kings 3.9). This story seeks to give divine endorsement to the popular traditions that made King Solomon a wise man. This wisdom of Solomon is authenticated by another independent tradition in I Kings 4.29–34, which attributes to him 3,000 proverbs and 1,005 songs on botanical and zoological subjects. The Gibeon story, however, seeks to do more than merely explain Solomon's wisdom. It provides Solomon's kingship with divine approval which, as we have seen, was so conspicuously lacking. This is expressed even in the formula of the divine request: 'Ask what I shall give you' (I Kings 3.5) which echoes the terminology of Psalm 2.8: 'Ask of me, and I will make the nations your heritage.' In both passages, the verbs *š'l* and *ntn* are used. At Gibeon, the king thus obtained a divine legitimation for things which had already happened. Again, this is a new element in Israelite history but it is an element that appears frequently in the ancient Near East, where the newly crowned monarchs obtain favourable *omina* from the godhead and even an usurper might be able to prove that he was sovereign by the grace of God! The clearest examples of this phenomenon are known from Egyptian culture (see Herrmann, Görg, and Kutsch).

In other words, Solomon tried to keep the shell of ancient institutions, where things look much as they did before, but at the same time Solomon made substantial changes in institutional content. This is confirmed by what is usually called God's second appearance to Solomon (I Kings 9.1–9) which is explicitly connected with the appearance at Gibeon and refers back also to the dynastic promise to David in II Samuel 7. The passage in its present form stems from the Deuteronomist, who uses it to proclaim his message to the exiles, but it seems to go back to an ancient traditional ritual through which the kingship was periodically renewed. Such a periodic renewal could have taken the place of appointment by charismatic gifts. From a charismatic kingship acknowledged by popular consent through assemblies, Israel now had a kingship, 'by the grace of God', in which God had become the guarantor of secular institutions. Such a pattern of kingship was not substantially different from that found in other states in the ancient Near East.

C.   *Solomon and the Jerusalem temple*

Y. **Aharoni**, 'Arad: Its Inscriptions and Temple', *BA* XXXI, 1968, 2–32; idem, 'The Israelite Sanctuary at Arad', in *New Directions*, 1969, 28–44; A. **Alt**, 'Verbreitung und Herkunft des syrischen Tempeltypus', *PJB* XXXV, 1939, 83–99 = his *KS* II, 1953, 100–15; T. A. **Busink**, *Der Tempel von Jerusalem*, I, *Der Tempel Salomos*, Leiden: E. J. Brill 1970; W. G. **Dever**, 'The MB IIC Stratification in the Northwest Gate Area at Shechem', *BASOR* CCXVI, 1974, 31–53; A. **Kuschke**, 'Der Tempel Salomos und der "syrische Tempeltypus"', *Das ferne und nahe Wort* 1967, 124–32; J. C. **de Moor**, *The Seasonal Pattern in the Ugaritic Myth of Ba'lu*, AOAT 16, 1971; A. **Parrot**, *Le Temple de Jérusalem*, Neuchâtel: Delachaux & Niestlé 1954 = *The Temple of Jerusalem*, London: SCM Press 1957; D. **Ussishkin**, 'Building IV in Hamath and the Temples of Solomon and Tell Tayanat', *IEJ* XVI, 1966, 104–10; G. R. H. **Wright**, 'Pre-Israelite Temples in the Land of Canaan', *PEQ* CIII, 1971, 17–32; Y. **Yadin**, *Hazor: The Rediscovery of a Great Citadel of the Bible*, 1975, 79–120.

As we noted when discussing the reign of David (see above, §3E), one of the unsolved problems in the earliest phase of the Israelite kingdom was the relationship of the king to the cult and his position within it. There seem to have been strong trends, especially in prophetic circles (note the subsequent hostility which the prophets often showed towards the monarchy), to deny to the king any pre-eminent position in the nation's worship. This limitation of the king's prerogatives was perhaps in keeping with the general and earliest Israelite cultic tradition but contrasts sharply with the practice of the Canaanite city-states and the ancient Near Eastern empires in general. The example of Nathan, who first approved and then vetoed the building of the temple by David, is a case in point. Two other texts, I Samuel 13.5–14 (pre-Deuteronomistic, belonging to the intermediate traditions on the introduction of kingship into Israel) and I Samuel 15.12–15 (Deuteronomistic or related material, but echoing motives found in the prophecy of the eighth and seventh centuries) use these problems in order to explain the rupture between Samuel and Saul. David seems not to have been able to alter conditions as radically as Solomon. Solomon built the Jerusalem temple without asking any questions, and he did so accepting many Canaanite theological elements. The temple was constructed with the aid of and craftsmen from Phoenicia (I Kings 5.1–12, 18; 7.13f.). The tripartite structure – vestibule, temple proper, and holy of holies – follows an architectural tradition known from the ruins of temples excavated in Syria (see Alt, Kuschke, and Ussishkin) and at Shechem (see Dever) and Hazor (see Yadin) in Palestine. The dates on which work was begun and completed (I Kings 6.1, 37f.; 8.2) further suggest Canaanite influence. The consecration took place at almost the same time that the temple for Baal was finished and inaugurated in the mythological texts from Ugarit, that is, just before the beginning of the autumn rainy season (see de Moor). The construction of the temple, begun in Solomon's fourth year and completed in his eleventh year, had become the responsibility of the king. What the Israelites as a whole were able to supply was only unskilled labour. If Aharoni is correct in his interpretation of the temple excavated at Arad, then Solomon probably constructed temple(s) outside Jerusalem as well, which, of course, go unnoticed in the biblical text.

The royal supervision over and participation in the Jerusalem cult are illustrated by several actions of Solomon in addition to the construction of the temple. Shortly after his accession, Solomon banished the priest Abiathar who had supported his foe Adonijah, although he represented the traditional priestly line and had been a close friend and supporter of David (I Kings 2.26). Zadok, a man who made his appearance only after the conquest of Jerusalem by David and who has frequently been associated with the city's pre-Israelite cult, was appointed in his place (I Kings 2.35). Solomon offered 'burnt offerings and peace offerings' after his vision at Gibeon (I Kings 3.15), while in I Kings 8.14–66 he performs functions that cannot be considered anything but priestly: he blesses the people, stays before the altar, and pronounces a great prayer of intercession (see also I Kings 9.25). Although I Kings 8 has been radically reworked by the Deuteronomist, there is no reason to doubt the facts reported. These are elements which tradition tells us were forbidden to Saul and David, and which, in the case of the former, are said to have caused the rupture between him and Samuel. The process, however, of royal participation in and supervision of the cult was initiated by David when he brought the ark to Jerusalem and prepared a tent sanctuary for it (see II Sam. 6). The temple in origin was intended for the ark, but it became almost immediately a national sanctuary, attached to the royal palace, a spiritual centre for the empire.

What is strange is that our sources report no resistance to the actions of Solomon by traditionally minded circles in Israel. Was there none, or has it simply been ignored by the sources? There are some clues that such resistance took place: the whole of I Kings 11 is full of reports about foes of Solomon, and this presence of foes is related by the sources to his religious policies. The text in this chapter is primarily Deuteronomistic and was composed to exemplify 'Solomon under the curse'. This scheme, however, should not blind us to the fact that the Deuteronomist may have been drawing on ancient traditions, traditions which served him well in preaching to the exiles. Thus the episodes concentrated here may have well extended over his entire reign. On the other hand, if we look at the criticism voiced by the assembly of the north to Rehoboam in I Kings 12.4–11, we find strong, although rather vague words directed against Solomon's policies. Much later, in Ezekiel 43.6–9, we find a criticism of Solomon, without his name being mentioned, because he built the temple and the palace 'threshold to threshold' and 'door-post beside doorpost' (see Ezek. 43.8). The author of the Ezekiel passage seems quite familiar with the whole matter and is caustic in his criticism of the Judaean kings. There must have been notable opposition against the newly acquired, cultic prerogatives of the king, although the sources report about it only indirectly. Strangely enough, this new position of the king became completely accepted in Judah, even, centuries later, among such conservative groups as the Deuteronomic and Deuteronomistic circles, by whom, as is well known, high praise is bestowed to all kings who exercised what may be called a *jus reformandi* in cultic matters, while kings who did not act in this field are condemned. Anyhow, the opposition may not have been very heavy if it soon ceased or was altogether reduced.

In this way Solomon continued the official religious syncretism which had begun with David. The temple was dedicated to Yahweh, the God of Israel, but it was a Canaanite temple, where all the inhabitants of the region could have felt at home. Behind its official functions, the reality could hardly be concealed that the temple served the national cult more than it did the former Lord of Israel.

D. *Solomon and the state cult*

K.-H. **Bernhardt**, *Das Problem der altorientalischen Königsideologie im Alten Testament*, SVT 8, 1961; R. J. **Clifford**, *The Cosmic Mountain in Canaan and the Old Testament*, HSM 4, 1972; H. **Donner**, 'Adoption oder Legitimation? Erwägungen zur Adoption im Alten Testament auf dem Hintergrund der altorientalischen Rechte', *OA* VIII, 1969, 87–119; I. **Engnell**, *Studies in Divine Kingship in the Ancient Near East*, Uppsala: Almsqvist & Wiksells 1943; 2nd ed., Oxford: Basil Blackwell 1967; J. **de Fraine**, *L'aspect religieux de la royauté israélite. L'institution monarchique dans l'Ancien Testament et dans les textes mésopotamiens*, AnBib 3, 1954; S. H. **Hooke**, ed., *Myth and Ritual: Essays on the Myth and Ritual of the Hebrews in Relation to the Culture Pattern of the Ancient East*, London: Oxford University Press 1933; idem, *The Labyrinth: Further Studies in the Relation between Myth and Ritual in the Ancient World*, London: Oxford University Press 1935; idem, *Myth, Ritual, and Kingship: Essays on the Theory and Practice of Kingship in the Ancient Near East and in Israel*, London: Oxford University Press 1958; A. R. **Johnson**, *Sacral Kingship in Ancient Israel*, Cardiff: University of Wales Press 1955, [2]1967; M. **Metzger**, 'Himmlische und irdische Wohnstatt Jahwes', *UF* II, 1970, 139–58; M. **Noth**, 'Gott, König, Volk im Alten Testament (Eine methodologische Auseinandersetzung mit einer gegenwärtigen Forschungsrichtung)', *ZTK* XLVII, 1950, 157–91 = his *GS* I, 1957, 188–229 = 'God, King and Nation in the Old Testament', in his *Laws in the Pentateuch*, 1966, 145–78; J. J. M. **Roberts**, 'The Davidic Origin of the Zion Tradition', *JBL* XCII, 1973, 329–44; K. **Seybold**, *Das davidische Königtum im Zeugnis der Propheten*, FRLANT 107, 1972; J. A. **Soggin**, 'Der Beitrag des Königtums zur altisraelitischen Religion', *SVT* XXIII, 1972, 9–26.

Some elements of the syncretistic state cult during Solomonic times, in as much as they are relevant to the history of Israel, may be tentatively noted.

The role of the king in public worship has been commented on
briefly in the preceding section. During the early years of the monarchy there was apparently no question of such a role for the king,
and the little that can be gathered from the sources points to the fact
that Israelite tradition was opposed to any privileged status of the
king in the cult. One could therefore question even the existence of a
state cult. Under David, the circles which held this position
succeeded in keeping the king under control, although one gets the
impression they were fighting a rearguard action. At any rate, the
king seems to have generally stayed out of the cult (but see II Sam. 6
and David's role in the ark procession), in the sense that no special
position was accorded him. Under Solomon, the king began acting
as a priest and this might provide the reason why there is almost no
evidence of the existence of a high priest in pre-exilic times. The
evidence of hostility towards the monarchy, which is easy to gather,
especially from prophetic circles, may be partially explained as
polemics against this usurpation of priestly prerogatives by the king.

The relation of the king to the God of Israel quickly came to be
considered a special one, different from that of all other members of
the people. This special relationship was expressed by the concept of
adoption or legitimation by the godhead, a concept which appears
to have been inherited from the ideology of the Canaanite city-state
(see Ps. 2.7; II Sam. 7.14; Isa. 9.6f.). The attributes of the monarch
in these passages, which are often interpreted in an eschatological
sense, seem to have been those of the ordinary king. While most
scholars speak about adoption, the thesis of legitimation has many
elements in its favour, the major one being that the juridical institution of adoption is absent from the whole of the Old Testament (so
Donner). Such a concept of kingship was almost certainly taken over
from the kingship theory of the Canaanite city-states. In the Ugaritic
texts, for example, king Krt is described as a 'son of El' (*CTA*
16.10f.) and Krt's son Ysb is described as one who sucks the breasts
of the goddess Anat (*CTA* 15. II.25–7). In the latter passage, the
question is one of the foster parenthood of the goddess rather than of
adoption or legitimation proper. At Ugarit, the king *was* the
legitimate son of his parents *and* the foster son of the deity. Conced-
ing the figurative character of these concepts in both the Ugaritic
and biblical texts, they may be considered either equivalents or
variants of the same motif. In the Old Testament, the king is the 'son
of God' as in the Ugaritic texts. This explains why Psalm 45.7 can
address the king as 'God' (*elohim*). In spite of the ingenious efforts of
commentators to avoid such a translation, primarily due to the

uniqueness of the expression in the Old Testament, this remains the best expression, and was already so translated by the LXX and Vulgate, although the latter relates the reference in the verse to the deity. Along this same line, we have two further isolated but significant texts in II Samuel 21.17 and Lamentations 4.20. In the former, David is addressed by his 'men': 'You shall no more go out with us to battle, lest you quench the lamp of Israel.' Lamentations 4.20, which speaks about the exiled king, reads: 'The breath of our nostrils, Yahweh's anointed, was taken in their pits; he of whom we said, "Under his shadow shall we live among the nations."' A similar evaluation of the monarchy follows from the charges brought against Naboth, namely that 'he cursed God and the king' (I Kings 21.11–14), a charge the more remarkable since there is no law in the Old Testament in which God and king are mentioned as almost equal partners. A similar equivalence is also found in Psalm 2.2c, a style which some scholars consider inauthentic. In Psalm 18.39, Yahweh himself girds the king for battle, whereas in II Samuel 23.1 (read however *hēqîm ʿal*) Elyon raises the king far above all other men.

While the entire Old Testament, and especially the prophets, Deuteronomy, and the Deuteronomistic historian, combat the fertility and life ideology of Canaan, there remain many important traces of such ideology within the Old Testament in connection with the person of the king, although probably from a time later than Solomon. Some passages should be noted in this regard:

He [the king] asked life of thee [God];
    thou gavest it to him – length of days for ever and ever. (Ps. 21.4)
May he [the king] be like the rain that falls on the mown grass,
    like showers that water the earth (Ps. 72.6).
Long may he [the king] live . . .
May there be abundance of grain in the land;
    on the tops of the mountains may it wave;
May its fruit be like Lebanon;
    And may men blossom forth from the cities
    like the grass of the field! (Ps. 72.5a, 16)

The evidence is therefore sufficient, although somewhat meagre, that in Israel the king was, in certain circles, connected with fertility, and this puts the court and the royal ideology on a similar level. Such ideas are in opposition to what we ordinarily consider typical of Old Testament thought. At Ugarit, the king was also closely associated with fertility, and during the monarch's illness nature withered away (*CTA* 16. 10–23).

The importance and interpretation of this sacral character of the king, his special relationship to Yahweh, and his role in the well-being of the community have been topics of heated debate in Old Testament studies. On the one hand, some scholars understand the Israelite king and the state cult to be reflective of a general cultic pattern which was spread over the entire Near East. In the cult, the king played the role of the deity, undergoing humiliation and exaltation rituals which played out the death and resurrection of nature and deity. Such a view is reflected in the works edited by S. H. Hooke (though less so in the third volume) and in the writings of some Swedish scholars, especially Ivan Engnell. On the other hand, the sacral character of the king has been minimized by other scholars who stress the non-royal elements in Israelite religion (de Fraine, Noth, and Bernhardt). A more moderate position is reflected in the work of Johnson.

The construction of the temple in Jerusalem and the importance and role of the royal-state cult produced a strong emphasis on the sacred character of Zion. Royal ideology and Zion theology were intertwined and mutually supportive (see Pss. 78.68–72; 89.19–29, 35–7; 132). Zion was understood as the chosen dwelling of God, the elect place, the cosmic mountain, and as inviolably protected by Yahweh (see Pss. 46, 48, 76 and the Zion-theology of the prophet Isaiah in the eighth century; on this see Metzger, Clifford, and Roberts).

The origin and development of the royal and Zion ideologies certainly go back to Solomonic times, although they seem to have been further elaborated in Judah after the break-up of the Davidic–Solomonic state.

E. *International affairs under Solomon*

F. C. **Fensham**, 'The Treaty between the Israelites and Tyrians', *SVT* XVII, 1969, 71–87; P. **Garelli**, 'Nouveau coup d'œil sur Muṣur', *Hommages à André Dupont-Sommer*, Paris: Adrien-Maisonneuve 1971, 37–48; S. H. **Horn**, 'Who Was Solomon's Egyptian Father in Law?', *BR* XII, 1967, 3–7; K. A. **Kitchen**, *The Third Intermediate Period in Egypt (1100–650 BC)*, Warminster: Aris & Phillipps 1973, 280–3; B. **Maisler** (Mazar), 'Two Hebrew Ostraca from Tell Qasîle', *JNES* X, 1951, 265–7; B. **Mazar**, 'The Aramaean Empire and its Relations with Israel', *BA* XXV, 1962, 97–120 = *BAR* II, 1964, 127–51; M. **Noth**, *Könige* I, BKAT IX/1, 1968; J. B. **Pritchard**, ed., *Solomon and Sheba*, London/New York: Phaidon/Praeger 1974; D. B. **Redford**, 'Studies in Relations between Palestine and Egypt during the First Millennium BC: II. The Twenty-second Dynasty', *JAOS*

XCIII, 1973, 3–17; H. **Tadmor**, 'Assyria and the West: The Ninth Century and Its Aftermath', *Unity and Diversity*, 1975, 36–48.

In beginning our description of the kingdom under David, we argued that one of its main characteristics was that of 'imperialistic expansion'. Only a dynamic form of government connected with this special feature could keep the empire from falling apart. Did Solomon succeed in pursuing the aims connected with this special feature?

All appearances are certainly against Solomon. There is no information in the sources about conquests or re-conquests he might have made. At the same time, the sources refer to numerous international relations and far-flung diplomatic connections under Solomon, so that he may have obtained results similar to those secured by David through military force. Solomon is reported to have engaged in seafaring trade. Working with Hiram, king of Tyre, Solomon constructed a fleet of ships at Ezion-geber and these were manned by competent Phoenician sailors and Israelite crews (I Kings 9.26f.). Where these ships traded cannot be determined, although reference is made to Ophir (I Kings 9.28; 10.11). It is noted that Solomon's fleet made three-year voyages (I Kings 10.22) returning with gold, silver, ivory, almug wood, precious stones, apes, and peacocks (I Kings 9.28; 10.11f., 22). Ophir cannot be located, though reference to the place has been found on Hebrew ostraca in Palestine (see Maisler). One would assume that Solomon's sea-trading activities were with ports along the Red Sea, that is, with the coastlines along Africa and the Arabian peninsula. The visit of the Queen of Sheba (I Kings 10.1–13), about which so many legends have developed (see Pritchard), which has been widely interpreted as a trade mission, would point to his participation in trade with South Arabia. Solomon's trading in horses and chariots is also noted in the biblical text (I Kings 10.28f.). The horses are said to have come from Egypt and Kue (a province in Cilicia) and the chariots from Egypt. Scholars have assumed that horses were not imported from Egypt and have emended the reading 'Egypt' (*miṣrayim*) to 'Muṣri' and assumed this to have been located in the region of Taurus (see Garelli), but there is little if any evidence for such a locality (see Tadmor, 39, 46f. n. 31). Solomon resold the horses and chariots, exporting them 'to all the kings of the Hittites and the kings of Syria' (I Kings 10.29) which probably refers to the small states of Syria. Thus Solomon functioned as a middleman in the Near Eastern trade. Solomon's power and the strategic location of Palestine gave him control over the trade routes between Egypt and southern Syria, and his friendly relations with Egypt no doubt made him an important figure in the international trade of his day. The Arabian trade in perfumes, spices, and precious stones may also have flowed through Solomon's state (see II Chron. 9.14) and distribution in the Mediterranean world was probably the franchise of the Phoenicians. The Old Testament statements about the wealth which flowed into the Solomonic treasure (I Kings 9.28; 10.25, 27) reflect the biblical tendency to speak of Solomon in gargantuan terms.

The biblical sources present Solomon as a lover of foreign women and of women in general. They state that he possessed 'seven hundred wives and three hundred concubines' (I Kings 11.3). I Kings 11.1 refers to Moabite, Ammonite, Edomite, Sidonian, and Hittite (i.e. Syrian) women; that is, women from states with whom Solomon would have had political and trade relations. Such marriages were part of international and diplomatic relations. Pride of place among Solomon's wives is given to the daughter of Pharaoh, who is mentioned five times in different contexts (I Kings 3.1; 7.8; 9.16, 24; 11.1). The text does not identify the Egyptian Pharaoh whose daughter Solomon married: most probably Siamun (ca. 978–959 BCE), although his successor Psusennes II (ca. 959–945 BCE) has also been considered (see Horn and Kitchen). Whether this unusual marriage should be considered as evidence of the weakness of Egypt in those years is still controversial. However, as we have already seen, many elements point to the friendly attitude of Egypt towards the Davidic–Solomonic state, and this attitude would be an adequate explanation for a marriage alliance among equals (see Redford, 3–5).

The picture of Solomon's international and financial affairs hardly presents us with a portrayal of unalloyed success. He got into trouble with Hiram of Tyre, whom he was unable to pay for the money lent, the services offered, and the materials delivered. Without speaking of state bankruptcy, it must be conceded that something quite similar must have happened to Solomon if he became unable to pay his debts. Something had to be done to meet his obligations and Solomon had to turn over (or perhaps mortgage) some territories of the empire. We hear of twenty towns in Galilee, called by a later gloss 'the land of Cabul' (I Kings 9.10–14), offered to Hiram, but apparently refused, because 'they did not please him' (I Kings 9.12b). II Chronicles 8.2 presents the matter differently: as if Hiram had given Solomon a part of his own lands which were then settled by Israelites. The thesis of I Kings is more probable in our context.

It is not easy to locate these towns, as 'the land of Cabul' is a description given us by the later gloss but it points to the region between Haifa and Acco, that is, the western part of the traditional territory of the tribe of Asher (see Josh. 19.27). Martin Noth, however, considers this notice as untrustworthy and locates the towns in the northern part of eastern Galilee (see Noth's commentary on the passage). So at least one part of the empire seems to have been lost.

Other parts of the empire were soon lost as well. The Aramaean states in Syria which David had brought under his control and where he had placed Israelite garrisons (II Sam. 8.5f.) began to assert their independence. Rezon, a former officer in the service of the king of Zobah, set up a state in Damascus and was 'an adversary to Solomon' (I Kings 11.23–5). Both Damascus and Zobah (according to the LXX text of I Kings 11.25) may have recovered their independence. This would have meant the loss of practically all of eastern Syria. In the south-east of Israel, Edom under Hadad, who had fled to Egypt at the death of David, seems to have rebelled and recovered its freedom (I Kings 11.14–22). All these elements manifest a rather gloomy side to Solomon's international relations and the fact that he succeeded in obtaining Gezer as a dowry for the Egyptian princess he married is one of the few elements in his favour (I Kings 9.16).

F. *Internal affairs under Solomon*

A. **Alt**, 'Israels Gaue unter Salomo', *Alttestamentliche Studien Rudolf Kittel zum 60. Geburtstag dargebracht*, Leipzig: J. C. Hinrichs 1913, 1–19 = his *KS* II 1953, 76–89; idem, 'Die Weisheit Salomos', *TLZ* LXXVI, 1951, 139–44; C. **Kayatz**, *Studien zu Proverbien 1–9*, WMANT 22, 1966; I. **Mendelsohn**, 'State Slavery in Ancient Palestine', *BASOR* LXXXV, 1942, 14–17; idem, *Slavery in the Ancient Near East*, New York/London: Oxford University Press 1949; idem, 'On Corvée Labor in Ancient Canaan and Israel', *BASOR* CLXVII, 1962, 31–5; G. **von Rad**, 'Hiob 38 und die altägyptische Weisheit', *SVT* III, 1955, 293–301 = his *GS* I, 1958, 262–71 = 'Job XXXVIII and Ancient Egyptian Wisdom' in his *Problem of the Hexateuch*, 1966, 281–90; idem, *Theologie des Alten Testaments* I, München: Chr. Kaiser 1957, 56–65 = *Old Testament Theology* I, Edinburgh/New York: Oliver & Boyd/Harper and Brothers 1962, 48–56; A. F. **Rainey**, 'Compulsory Labour Gangs in Ancient Israel', *IEJ* XX, 1970, 191–202; D. B. **Redford**, 'Studies in Relations between Palestine and Egypt during the First Millennium BC: I. The Taxation System of Solomon', *Studies on the Ancient Palestinian World* (see ch. VI §3C), 1972, 141–56; R. B. Y. **Scott**, 'Solomon

and the Beginnings of Wisdom in Israel', *SVT* III, 1955, 262–79; G. E.
Wright, 'The Provinces of Solomon', *EI* VIII, 1967, 58–68.

We have seen that biblical traditions present Solomon as a particularly wise king. This is illustrated by many, mostly anecdotal
stories which testify, if we apply our terminology, rather to his wit,
his cunning, and his smartness than to wisdom proper. The stories
about Solomon, however, illustrate other activities in which the king
was proficient: his construction projects, his administrative measures,
and his commercial enterprises (the latter discussed in the preceding
section). Much that is told about him and these activities is devoted
to personal details often hardly relevant to the historian: power,
enrichment, or even pleasure. Some of his activities, such as his commercial enterprises, may have been an asset to the kingdom since
they produced wealth for the state, but others seem to have been a
heavy liability to the realm and could be upheld only at a high cost.
    From an important source (I Kings 4.7–19), we learn that Israel
(the north) was divided into twelve districts or provinces under the
supervision of twelve officers or governors. These administrative
districts were each responsible for provisions for the upkeep of the
royal household (and the temple?) for one month in the year and
thus comprised a taxation scheme. Redford has drawn a number of
conclusions about Solomon's taxation system on the bases of
Egyptian analogies. (1) The most detailed extant inscription describing such a levy comes from the reign of the Egyptian Pharaoh
Shoshenq I (the biblical Shishak), a younger contemporary of
Solomon. The text stipulates the towns and officials who are responsible for certain provisions and divides these into twelve monthly
sections plus a final section for the five epagomenal days added at
the end of a year of twelve thirty-day months. (2) The list in I Kings
4.7–19, like Shoshenq's list, places emphasis on the officials and not
on the districts, so that it may be 'dangerous and misleading to
interpret the system as an arrangement of provinces. . . . If we had a
document from the United Monarchy similar in intent to the stela of
Shoshenq, we should probably find that it was a group of officials
and towns that was listed by month, and that it was by inference
that we extracted the underlying framework of districts' (154, n. 79).
(3) The description of the needed provisions of Solomon for a single
day (I Kings 4.22f.) may have, according to Redford, been stipulations for a monthly requirement and perhaps for the use of the
Jerusalem temple. (4) Solomon, like the Egyptians, employed the

levy to provide supplies with which to stock his garrison posts (I
Kings 4.28). (5) 'It is highly likely that Solomon was consciously
using this common Egyptian means of taxation for supplying the
organs of a central government with sustenance. Whether he was
directly inspired by contemporary Egyptian practice, or whether he
derived it indirectly through the practice of the former Egyptian
empire in Canaan, is a moot question' (155 f.).

Taxes so levied seem not to have been sufficient, so other forms of
income had to be found. I Kings 4.6; 5.13; 11.28 speak explicitly
about forced (*corvée*) labour: 'Out of all Israel' according to I Kings
5.13; 'all the forced labour of the house of Joseph', according to I
Kings 11.28. It seems, therefore, that, as in the case of the levy, only
Israel (or at best mostly Israel) or the north was subject to this kind
of service. This form of the information, which agrees with the complaints voiced to the new king by the assembly of the north after the
death of Solomon (I Kings 12), seems much more reliable than I
Kings 9.20–2 (II Chron. 8.7–9) according to which only the
Canaanites, not the Israelites, were subjected to slave labour. The
text of I Kings 9.20–2 is lacking in the LXX and thus poses some
problems also from a critical point of view. It has been suggested
that two types of serfdom were involved. One form was a periodical, and therefore part-time, that is a *corvée* levy (Hebrew: *mas* or
sebel), to which every inhabitant of the nation was subjected. It
served for the completion of certain public works and was a form of
taxation in kind, i.e., personal labour. The other was 'state slavery'
proper (Hebrew: *mas ʿōbēd*) to which only the Canaanites were subjected (see Rainey for the discussion of the matter). Another possibility could be that only Canaanites were enrolled into servitude
while Israelites were involved in other kinds of service (compulsory
levies into the army, labour, etc.; *Noth, 211). The dubious sense of
the expressions used and the textual contradictions do not allow for
any final explanation. In any case, the sources and the subsequent
reactions to the system show quite clearly that Israel, and not Judah
(*contra* *Albright, 56), was subjected to services it considered a
grievous infringement of its liberties.

The sources at our disposal inform us of numerous building
activities carried out by Solomon. After the completion of the temple
and palace complex, I Kings 9.15–19 lists some Canaanite towns
which were rebuilt: Hazor, Megiddo, Gezer, Beth-horon, Baalath,
and Tamar as well as 'store-cities', 'cities for his chariots', 'cities for
his horsemen', and other unspecified localities (on some of these sites,
see the discussion of the archaeological evidence, §2 above). Also, the

walls of Jerusalem were repaired. The fact that many Canaanite cities were rebuilt and garrisoned with horses and chariots is probably a sign that they were granted, or retained, an autonomy within the kingdom, thus adding to the complexity of the constitutional situation of the empire. As long as the empire lasted, the Canaanite city-states with their highly specialized fighting units could be kept under control and used for the common good. But as soon as the empire broke apart, the Canaanites seem to have been able to recover a notable part of their independence, and, having control over the greater part of military and economic resources in the north, could exercise great power in the kingdom of Israel.

The taxation and labour policies of Solomon produced widespread discontent in the north that smouldered under the ashes but soon burst into political flame. Jeroboam, superintendent of the forced labour of the house of Joseph, was designated as king over the ten tribes of Israel by a prophet Ahijah (I Kings 11.26–40). Whether this version of the history be accurate or not, it does suggest a general unrest with Solomon's policies. I Kings 11.40 notes that Solomon sought to kill Jeroboam, who took asylum in Egypt until the death of Solomon. As long as Solomon lived, he was able to keep such unrest under control but with his death matters took a different turn.

Finally, a brief comment should be made concerning what has been called 'the Solomonic enlightenment'. According to this thesis, the reign of Solomon was a time when art and learning, wisdom and sophistication, humanism and historical concerns developed in an unparalleled fashion, partially dependent upon foreign influence and the internationalism of the time (von Rad, 1957; *Herrmann, 181 f.). The Yahwistic historian supposedly collected traditions, edited them, and produced a comprehensive history extending from the creation of the world until the settlement in Palestine (on the Yahwistic history, see above, §1C). The narrative concerning the Davidic succession, it has been argued, was produced during this period (see above, §1C of this chapter). References to Solomonic wisdom have been taken to mean that during this period much of Israel's proverbial wisdom came into being (as an advocate of this thesis, see Kayatz; for an opposing view, see Scott). The songs and sayings on botanical and zoological subjects attributed to Solomon (I Kings 4.32f.) have been compared to the encyclopedic lists (*onomastica*) known from other Near Eastern cultures (Alt, 1951; von Rad, 1955). Most of these matters are still subjects of scholarly debate. The least that can be said is that the age of Solomon was a time of wealth (at least among the upper classes), a time when Israel was first fully open to foreign influences through official channels, a time when building and cultural concerns were at a peak, a time when national self-consciousness must have been significant, and a time when education among court circles was not only possible but perhaps a necessity.

VII

THE SEPARATE STATES OF
ISRAEL AND JUDAH

§1. THE COLLAPSE OF THE
DAVIDIC–SOLOMONIC EMPIRE
AND THE DISSOLUTION OF THE PERSONAL UNION
BETWEEN ISRAEL AND JUDAH

M. **Aberbach** and L. **Smolar**, 'Aaron, Jeroboam and the Golden Calves', *JBL* LXXXVI, 1967, 129–40; idem, 'Jeroboam's Rise to Power', *JBL* LXXXVIII, 1969, 69–72; G. W. **Ahlström**, 'Solomon, The Chosen One', *HiRel* VIII, 1968, 94–110; A. **Alt**, 'Festungen und Levitenorte im Lande Juda', *KS* II 1953, 306–15; idem, 'The Monarchy in the Kingdoms of Israel and Judah' (see ch. V §2), in his *Essays*, 1966, 239–59; G. **Beyer**, 'Das Festungssystem Rehabeams', *ZDPV* LIV, 1931, 113–34; S. R. **Bin-Nun**, 'Formulas from Royal Records of Israel and of Judah', *VT* XVIII, 1968, 414–32; G. **Buccellati**, *Cities and Nations of Ancient Syria: An Essay on Political Institutions with Special Reference to the Israelite Kingdoms*, StSem 26, 1967; J. **Conrad**, *Die junge Generation im Alten Testament*, Berlin: Evangelische Verlagsanstalt 1970; J. **Debus**, *Die Sünde Jeroboams: Studien zur Darstellung Jeroboams und der Geschichte des Nordreichs in der deuteronomistischen Geschichtsschreibung*, FRLANT 93, 1967; H. **Donner**, *Herrschergestalten in Israel*, VW 103, 1970, 46–54; idem, '"Hier sind deine Götter, Israel!"', *Wort und Geschichte* (Festschrift Karl Elliger), AOAT 18, 1973, 45–50; O. **Eissfeldt**, 'Israelitisch-philistäische Grenzverschiebungen von David bis auf die Assyrerzeit', *ZDPV* LXVI, 1943, 115–28 = his *KS* II, 1963, 453–63; idem, 'Lade und Stierbild', *ZAW* LVIII, 1940/41, 190–215 = his *KS* II, 1963, 282–305; D. G. **Evans**, 'Rehoboam's Advisers at Shechem, and Political Institutions in Israel and Sumer', *JNES* XXV, 1966, 273–9; D. W. **Gooding**, 'The Septuagint's Rival Versions of Jeroboam's Rise to Power', *VT* XVII, 1967, 173–89; J. H. **Grønbaek**, 'Benjamin und Juda', *VT* XV, 1965, 421–36; S. **Herrmann**, 'Operationen Pharao Schoschenks I. im östlichen Ephraim', *ZDPV* LXXX, 1964, 55–79; A. **Jepsen**, *Die Quellen des Königsbuches*, Halle: Max Niemeyer, 1953, ²1956; K. A. **Kitchen**,

The Third Intermediate Period in Egypt (1100–650 BC), 1973; R. W. **Klein**, 'Jeroboam's Rise to Power', *JBL* LXXXIX, 1970, 217f.; J. **Liver**, 'The Wars of Mesha, King of Moab', *PEQ* XCIX, 1967, 14–31; A. **Malamat**, 'Kingship and Council in Israel and Sumer: A Parallel', *JNES* XXII, 1963, 247–53; idem, 'Origins of Statecraft in the Israelite Monarchy', *BA* XXVIII, 1965, 34–65; B. **Mazar**, 'The Campaign of Pharaoh Shishak to Palestine', *SVT* IV, 1957, 57–66; J. M. **Miller**, 'The Fall of the House of Ahab', *VT* XVII, 1967, 307–24; idem, 'The Moabite Stone as a Memorial Stela', *PEQ* CVI, 1974, 9–18; M. **Noth**, 'Die Schoschenkliste', *ZDPV* LXI, 1938, 277–304 = his *Aufsätze* II, 1971, 73–93; idem, 'Israelitische Stämme zwischen Ammon und Moab', *ZAW* LX, 1944, 11–57 = his *Aufsätze* I, 391–433; idem, *Überlieferungsgeschichtliche Studien*, 1957, I. **Plein**, 'Erwägungen zur Überlieferung von I. Reg. 11, 26–14, 20', *ZAW* LXXVIII, 1966, 8–24; D. B. **Redford**, 'Studies in Relations between Palestine and Egypt during the First Millennium B.C.: II. The Twenty-second Dynasty', *JAOS* XCIII, 1973, 3–17; H. **Seebass**, 'Zur Königserhebung Jerobeams I', *VT* XVII, 1967, 325–33; T. C. G. **Thornton**, 'Charismatic Kingship in Israel and Judah', *JTS* XIV, 1963, 1–11; M. **Weippert**, 'Gott und Stier', *ZDPV* LXXVII, 1961, 93–117.

Opinions vary regarding both the source materials for the events immediately following Solomon's death and the role which the Deuteronomistic historian played in their composition. Noth (1957, 79–80) postulated the existence of a prophetic narrative which had as its theme 'Jeroboam and the Prophet Ahijah of Shiloh' (I Kings 11.29 aβ b–31, 36ab–37; 12.1–20, 26–31; 14.1–18). This supposed narrative, which Noth believed the Deuteronomistic historian incorporated into his presentation and supplemented with materials of different origins, began with the report of Jeroboam's designation by the prophet Ahijah of Shiloh during Solomon's lifetime and included the promise that the former would gain sovereign rule over ten of Israel's tribes. There followed, as a fulfilment of this, an account of the break-up of the personal union between Judah and Israel. The narrative described how Jeroboam, having become king of northern Israel, soon departed from the right way by setting up the golden calves in Bethel and Dan and so received a prophetic threat from Yahweh, announcing the death of his son who had fallen ill, his own downfall, and that of his house. The closest form-critical parallels to this narrative are found in the legends about the prophets Elijah (I Kings 17–19; 21; II Kings 1), Elisha (I Kings 19.19–21; II Kings 2.1–8, 15; 13.14–21) and Isaiah (II Kings 18.13–20.19 = Isa. 36–9). Misgivings concerning Noth's analysis arise especially with regard to I Kings 12.1–19, which consists of a report showing absolutely no interest in Ahijah of Shiloh and only a marginal interest in Jeroboam. More likely then, I Kings 12.1–19 is an independent, short historical work having as its theme the dissolution of the personal union (see Plein). Its major emphasis is on the historical problem expressed in its final sentence: 'So Israel has rebelled against the house of David to this day.' The materials most comparable to this section, from a form-critical perspective, are such historical works as the narrative of the Davidic succession (compare I Kings 12.15 with II Sam. 17.14!). The narrative in I Kings 12.1–19 is linked with what precedes in that it provides a report of the fulfilment of the promise designating Jeroboam as king. That is, the report is used to support the scheme 'prophecy and fulfilment' which appears as an historical and theological device throughout the Deuteronomistic work (compare v. 15b with v. 20). I Kings 12.25–31 consists of extracts adapted by the Deuteronomist from the annals of the kings of Israel. Thus only in I Kings 11.29–40 and 14.1–18 does one find prophetic narratives about Jeroboam and Ahijah of Shiloh. The interrelationship of these two prophetic narratives is not entirely clear, and their original form can scarcely be reconstructed, since they too have been revised considerably by the Deuteronomist.

In summary, the following literary sources are available for reconstructing the period immediately after the death of Solomon: (1) an historical work about the dissolution of the personal union between Judah and Israel (I Kings 12.1–19); (2) individual prophetic legends revised by the Deuteronomist (I Kings 11.29–40; 12.21–4; 14.1–18); and (3) extracts from the annals of the kings of Israel and Judah (I Kings 12.25–31; 14.21–31).

The accession of the crown prince Rehoboam took place in Jerusalem and Judah without any apparent difficulty. The south favoured the dynastic idea and regarded the succession of David's grandson as legitimate, if not a foregone conclusion. Israel in the north, however, was by no means prepared to accept the dynastic kingship of David's family without further ado (see already II Sam. 20). This unwillingness of the north to acquiesce passively in the continuation of the personal union through the family of David was explained by Alt as a reflection of the more 'charismatic' ideal of leadership held by the Israelites (Alt, 'Monarchy'). Alt felt that the old charismatic type of leadership which had prevailed in the period of the judges remained the ideal among the Israelites and tended to counteract any dynastic sentiment, whereas among the Judaeans the concept of dynastic succession was readily adopted. Alt's assessment of early Israelite and Judaean kingship has however been called into question by scholars who tend to see a greater similarity between kingship in the two states than did Alt (see Thornton; Ahlström; and Buccellati, 195–212). The current tendency away from the 'amphicty-onic hypothesis' and the closely related view that the judges were charismatic figures (see above, ch. V) tends to undercut the impor-tance of the charismatic ideal in the north although this does not completely repudiate Alt's charismatic explanation or what Soggin has called Israel's democratic tendencies (see above, pp. 355f.). The fact remains that, in addition to the failure to establish a lasting dynasty in the northern kingdom, there was a noticeable pattern of prophetically supported assassinations in Israel (see Miller, 1967) which probably can best be explained by some form of charismatic hypothesis.

As a minimum, Israel in the north expected that the successor to David's throne would present himself before the representatives of the northern tribes in order to receive from them their own par-ticular acclamation and to renew the personal union. Rehoboam appears to have understood this clearly, for he journeyed to Shechem, an ancient northern religious centre (see Josh. 24 and elsewhere) in order to obtain there the kingship. The representa-tives of the tribes of Israel, however, were determined to make this as difficult as possible for him. We do not know whether they were prepared to renew the personal union at all or whether they had decided already in advance against acknowledging the son of Solomon. At any rate, they presented Rehoboam with their objec-tions, made their acclamation of him dependent upon the fulfilment of certain conditions, and demanded that he agree to submit to election. Their main objection was to the harsh service of forced labour which Solomon had imposed upon Israel (I Kings 5.13–18; 9.15–22; 11.26). The fiscal requirements which Solomon's division of his kingdom into districts brought with it (I Kings 4.7–19) may have played a part also, particularly because the burdens of these require-ments apparently were not imposed upon the Judaean south. Even David's rule over Israel had in his last years become despotic. Condi-tions would scarcely have been any different under Solomon, and were probably even worse. Now the northern tribes took advantage of their opportunity to make their political will count.

Rehoboam asked for and was given three days to consider the request. During this time he convened his crown council, which was not a unified body and represented polarized opinions. It consisted both of old councillors who had grown grey in Solomon's service and of young men whom Rehoboam presumably had appointed himself.

This juxtaposition is hardly to be understood in terms of a 'bicameral system' (so Malamat, 1963). Rather, it was simply a repetition of the same 'tragedy in council' which earlier had brought about Absalom's downfall (II Sam. 17) and now was aggravated by the generation gap. The old councillors advised Rehoboam to meet the demands of the representatives. Certainly in the back of their minds they must have considered the possibility of tightening the reins again once the acclamation had taken place. The young men advised him not to allow himself to be drawn into negotiations but to carry out a policy of strength from the outset. Behind this was the fateful political error of judgment which supposed that the question was entirely a matter involving Rehoboam's authority and prestige. Perhaps the young councillors were primarily from Jerusalem and did not recognize that Rehoboam's authority in the north could not be taken for granted and that his prestige there would have to be built up carefully. It was Rehoboam's folly and misfortune – and at the same time Yahweh's guidance, according to I Kings 12.15 – that he followed the advice of his contemporaries. The elders of Israel presented him with his marching orders and withdrew for all time from David's dynasty: 'What portion do we have in David? No inheritance in the son of Jesse! To your tents, Israel! Look to your own house, David' (I Kings 12.16; cf. II Sam. 20.1). Rehoboam made the situation worse with a final offer to negotiate which he entrusted to Adoniram, of all persons, who was his minister of forced labour. The old man was stoned to death and Rehoboam fled to Jerusalem.

The outcome of these events cannot be described properly with the usual term, 'Division of the Kingdom'. Actually it involved not the division of an inherently unified national structure but the non-renewal of a personal union between Judah and Israel and the restoration and solidification of the duality of south and north which this personal union had temporarily overcome but had not dissolved. This was not fully appreciated, or conceded, in Jerusalem and Judah, where the people preferred to speak of 'secession' (Isa. 7.17). The hope for a reunification always remained alive in the south. Later, following the downfall of the northern kingdom in 722 BCE, there were those who expected the reunion to occur at the time of the future messianic king (Isa. 8.23–9.6; Jer. 23.5f.; Ezek. 37.15–22 and elsewhere).

Israel, on the other hand, did not strive for a restoration of unity but rather rejoiced in her freedom. The charismatic ideal was given real political value and Yahweh was accorded a free hand, as it

were, to bring a *homo novus* to the throne as he once had done with
Saul. The identity of the person who would occupy the throne
presented no difficulties. The right man had been available for a
long time in the person of Jeroboam the Ephraimite, who had served
as territorial officer under Solomon in charge of the forced labour of
the 'house of Joseph' (I Kings 11.28). Yahweh, according to I Kings
11.29–40, had already designated Jeroboam king over Israel during
Solomon's lifetime. This might be a projection of later events back to
an earlier time (as in the case of Samuel's anointing of David as king
in I Sam. 16). At any rate, Jeroboam had been forced to flee to
Egypt for reasons which are not entirely clear and had been granted
political asylum by Pharaoh Shoshenq I (the biblical Shishak) of the
Twenty-second Libyan Dynasty. He returned after Solomon's death
– whether before or after the events at Shechem is uncertain, and the
LXX and MT texts differ (see Aberbach–Smolar, Gooding, and
Klein) – and was made king over Israel by acclamation of the
representatives of the northern tribes (I Kings 12.20).

   Thus the core area of the empire which David had erected fell
apart soon after Solomon's death. It was now only a matter of time
before the foreign territories which had not yet rebelled under
Solomon would regain their independence also. In the case of the
Ammonite state and the Philistine cities this probably took place
relatively soon, although the precise date is not known. Moab may
have remained a vassal of the northern kingdom until the middle of
the ninth century (see II Kings 3.5 and the Mesha inscription) when
Edom also separated from Judah (II Kings 8.20). There is a possibility, however, that Israel lost control of Moab, including part or all
of the territory north of the Arnon, during the period of fraternal
warfare which followed Solomon's death. This may be reflected in
the fact that the Mesha inscription credits Omri with 'humbling
Moab' and with dwelling in the land of Madeba 'during his days
and half the days of his son' (see Noth, *Aufsätze* I, 419–22; Liver;
Miller, 1974). In any case, the dissolution of the personal union was
likewise a time of rebirth for the system of small independent states
in Palestine and central Syria as it had existed before David's day.

A.   *Jeroboam I* (927–907 BCE)

The question which immediately confronted the new king of Israel
was where he should reside. Saul's old capital, Gibeah (*Tell el-Ful*),
could not be considered because of its geographical proximity to
Judah. According to I Kings 12.25, Jeroboam enlarged the towns of

Shechem (*Tell Balāṭa*) and Penuel (*Tilāl edh-Dhahab* in the valley of the Jabbok) in order to live there, and also, according to I Kings 14.17, Tirzah (*Tell el-Fārʿa*). This strange plurality of capitals has been explained in terms of a consecutive sequence, with the king fleeing into the region east of the Jordan in 922 BCE before Shoshenq I and returning to the west after the latter's departure, though not to Shechem. It is also conceivable, however, that Jeroboam exercised his royal office during the first years of his reign by travelling about in his land and thus made use of these capitals simultaneously – as the German emperors used their palaces during the Middle Ages.

Of greater importance by far were questions of a cult-political nature. Jeroboam had good reason to be apprehensive about the dangers which might arise from the pilgrimages to Solomon's temple where the ark of Yahweh rested. One could not preclude the possibility that the pilgrims might become consciously or unconsciously, as a result of their visits to Jerusalem, instruments of pro-Davidic propaganda and so undermine the stability of the kingdom of Israel from within. Thus Jeroboam proposed to create in the north substitutes for the Jerusalem shrine. Accordingly, he erected two national shrines on the territory of the northern kingdom in imitation of the Davidic national temple (I Kings 12.26–9), locating one in Bethel (*Bētīn*), a site which lay on the road to Jerusalem and which had been considered sacred since remote antiquity, the other in Dan (*Tell el-Qāḍī*), on Israel's northern border. There he set up golden bull images, certainly not as cult objects but – remotely comparable to the ark of Yahweh – as animal-shaped pedestals for Yahweh, who was thought to be standing on them invisibly. Probably it was not Jeroboam's intention that popular piety should be reminded by these 'golden calves' of the bull symbols of Canaanite fertility deities and soon begin to venerate these pedestals as if they were gods (cf. already I Kings 12.28 and Ex. 32.4) unless by specifically choosing bull images he wanted to build a religious-political bridge between the Israelite and Canaanite elements of his kingdom and so to make a contribution to the solution of the problem of the Canaanites (*Herrmann, 195). Dan in all likelihood never did achieve great importance; but Bethel experienced a glorious ascendancy and flourished until and even subsequent to the end of the kingdom of Israel (Amos 7.10–13; II Kings 17.24–28 and elsewhere). Furthermore, apparently with the intention of supporting Yahwism, Jeroboam enlarged the country's hilltop shrines, which probably were already strongly Canaanized, and placed in them priests taken from the people. However, this was in violation of the priestly privileges of the tribe of Levi (I Kings 12.31; 13.33). Jeroboam certainly did not dream that he would be remembered by later generations as the king who more than any other exemplified apostasy from Yahweh. He owes this reputation to the Deuteronomist, who reproved him and all his successors for the establishment and maintenance of the two national shrines (the 'sin of Jeroboam'), because they did not accord with the Deuteronomic demand for the centralization of the cultus (see Debus). Jeroboam could not have known anything about this Deuteronomic law on centralization, of course, since it came into being only centuries later. The Deuteronomist incorrectly presumed it to be genuinely Mosaic. Since Jerusalem came to be regarded as the sole legitimate shrine in the Deuteronomic sense from Josiah (622 BCE) on, Jeroboam's cultic policies must be seen in the final analysis as having miscarried. Jerusalem, in opposition to which he had built his national shrines, was ultimately victorious.

B.   Rehoboam (926–910 BCE)

In the southern kingdom the continuity of the dynastic monarchy precluded any radical changes in political life. To be sure, some adjustments to the new political realities were necessary in Judah also; but Jerusalem remained the capital city even though, following the dissolution of the personal union, its location was no longer an advantageous one. Too much capital had been invested in Jerusalem for anyone to be able to or to want to give it up. After a temporary breather, Rehoboam heated up the civil war between Judah and Israel, one of his main purposes probably being to clear the approaches to his capital city (I Kings 12.21–4; 14.30).

The decline of the power of the Judaean south is most evidently reflected in Rehoboam's programme of constructing fortifications. According to II Chron. 11.5–10 – a very ancient list (against Alt, 'Festungen') – he surrounded the Judaean heartland with a string of fortresses. The line of fortifications ran from Jerusalem southward along the mountain ridge, south of Hebron it curved towards the west, and then moved northward through the Shephelah to Aijalon where it finally turned back to Jerusalem. The sixteen stations in this system are scarcely ever more than five kilometres apart. It is noteworthy that the coastal plain and the Beersheba plain lay outside of the ring of fortresses, which suggests that they no longer belonged to the territory of the southern kingdom. Judah consequently had no direct access to the Mediterranean Sea, or even to the old trade and military road which ran along the coastal plain connecting the

African continent with Asia. From the standpoint of its geographical lines of communication, the southern kingdom was isolated, allowing it a situation of historical calm. This state of affairs was certainly favourable to its conservatism and stubborn adherence to the Davidic monarchy.

The Palestine campaign of Pharaoh Shoshenq I in 922 BCE disturbed this relative quiet only temporarily. In the list of conquered towns, which at Shoshenq's direction was placed on one of the walls of the great temple of Amun in Karnak, Judaean cities are completely missing (but see Kitchen, 293–300, 432–47). This accords with I Kings 14.25–8, where we read that Rehoboam gathered together his temple and palace treasures in order to purchase his domain's independence. Shoshenq reached the plain of Megiddo in the north, even sent troops into the region east of the Jordan, and so must have caused severe distress to the kingdom of Israel. Unfortunately our sources tell us nothing about the reactions of Jeroboam I to this, unless his change of capitals belongs in this context. To be sure, this campaign was nothing more than a demonstration of strength which was designed to show that Egypt once again was on the rise after a long lull. Shoshenq was not in a position seriously and permanently to revive the old Egyptian domination of Palestine.

§2. THE KINGDOM OF JUDAH FROM REHOBOAM TO AZARIAH/UZZIAH

W. F. **Albright**, 'The Judicial Reform of Jehoshaphat', *Alexander Marx Jubilee·Volume*, New York: Jewish Publication Society 1950, 61–82; A. **Alt**, 'Bemerkungen zu einigen judäischen Ortslisten des Alten Testaments', *BBLA* LXVIII, 1951, 193–210 = his *KS* II, 1953, 289–305; G. **Fohrer**, 'Der Vertrag zwischen König und Volk in Israel', *ZAW* LXXI, 1959, 1–22 = his *Studien*, 115, 1969, 330–51; M. **Haran**, 'Observations on the Historical Background of Amos 1.2–2.6', *IEJ* XVIII, 1968, 201–12; C. C. **McCown** and J. C. **Wampler**, *Tell en-Nasbeh: Excavated under the Direction of the Late W. F. Badè* I–II, New Haven: American Schools of Oriental Research, 1947; E. W. **Nicholson**, 'The Meaning of the Expression '*m h'rṣ* in the Old Testament', *JSS* X, 1965, 59–66; W. **Rudolph**, 'Die Einheitlichkeit der Erzählung vom Sturz der Atalja (2 Kön 11)', *Festschrift für Alfred Bertholet*, Tübingen: J. C. B. Mohr 1950, 473–8; J. A. **Soggin**, 'Der judäische '*Am – Ha'ares* und das Königtum in Juda: Ein Beitrag zum Studium der deuteronomistischen Geschichtsschreibung', *VT* XIII, 1963, 187–95; T. **Willi**, *Die Chronik als Auslegung: Untersuchungen zur literarischen Gestaltung der historischen Überlieferung Israels*, FRLANT 106, 1972; E. **Würthwein**, *Der 'amm hā'ārez im Alten Testament*, BWANT IV/17, 1936.

The sources at our disposal for reconstructing the century and a half of history of the southern kingdom to the beginning of the Assyrian period (745 BCE) are almost entirely limited to those excerpts from the annals of the kings of Judah which have been preserved in the books of Kings (I Kings 15.1–II Kings 15.7) and edited by the Deuteronomist. A different type of historical material is available only in so far as the events between 845 and 839 BCE are concerned, namely two short historical works on Jehu's revolt in the northern kingdom (II Kings 9.1–10.27) and the downfall of Athaliah in Judah (II Kings 11). The historical reports provided by the Chronicler as a rule are to be viewed with caution. Their origin is unclear, and in many instances they represent merely an exegetical treatment of materials in the books of Kings (so-called tertiary history writing: see Willi).

The fraternal war between Judah and Israel was concerned to no minor degree with the question of the position of the boundary across the central hill country between these two kingdoms. The kings of Judah must have been anxious to push the boundary as far to the north as possible in order to clear the approaches to their endangered capital city of Jerusalem. Neither Rehoboam nor his son Abijah (910–908 BCE) were very successful in this regard. The decisive resolution was reached only under Asa (908–868 BCE) (I Kings 15.16–22). At first the advantage went to Israel. Baasha (906–883 BCE) gained secure control of the town of Ramah (*er-Rām*) only about nine kilometres north of Jerusalem, began to fortify it, and thus dominated both the main north–south road along the watershed of the mountains and the old access roads leading up to Jerusalem from the coastal plain. Asa extricated himself from this trouble by a clever political move. He made diplomatic contact with Ben-hadad of Aram-Damascus, and persuaded him by means of expensive gifts to break his pact with Israel and to invade her northernmost regions. When the Aramaeans threatened Abel-beth Maacah (*Ābil el-Qamḥ*), Ijon (*Tell Dibbīn* in *Merǧ ʿAyyun*), Dan (*Tell el-Qāḍī*) and the territory of Naphtali, Baasha was forced to withdraw his troops from the south and abandon Ramah. Asa immediately pushed forward and seized Ramah. Instead of completing the fortification of the city, however, he advanced Judah's border four additional kilometres northward to Mizpah (*Tell en-Naṣbe*). Using the building material which Baasha had left behind in Ramah he constructed both Mizpah on the main road and Geba (*Ǧebaʿ*) over against Michmash (*Muḥmās*) as border fortresses against the kingdom of Israel. The excavations at *Tell en-Naṣbe* have supplemented these particulars in so far as they have shown that Mizpah must originally have been a bastion of the northern kingdom against Judah, and that Asa simply took it over and reoriented it towards the north by means of certain makeshift alterations (see McCown and Wampler). Henceforth the boundary across the mountains between the two kingdoms remained basically unchanged. The Davidides apparently did not incorporate the conquered territory into Judah but added it instead to the city state of Jerusalem (II Kings 23.5; so Alt). They thus avoided having to obtain the consent of the tribe of Benjamin, whose territory henceforth was divided in two and whose larger portions from now on belonged to the south. This development was later projected back into the traditions concerning the dissolution of the personal union. In I Kings 12.23 Benjamin is included in the southern kingdom (also in 12.20 in the LXX, and perhaps also in 11.31, where the meaning of the number ten, however, is disputed). In the Jordan Valley no border changes occurred. Jericho was and remained Israelite (I Kings 16.34). But in the hill country Judah could show a slight gain in its holdings, perhaps even before Asa, for Aijalon (*Yālō*), which under Solomon belonged to one of the districts of the northern kingdom (I Kings 4.9) appears to have become a link in Rehoboam's chain of fortresses (II Chron. 11.10).

The war hatchet remained buried for a long time under Asa's successors. The offer to make peace was certainly initiated by the kings of the Omride dynasty of the northern kingdom who held sway between 878 and 845 BCE. The Omrides were confronted with grave foreign and international problems and were vitally interested in getting rid of the burdens of the strife with their Judaean neighbours. I Kings 22.44 seems to place the termination of the warfare between the two kingdoms in the time of Jehoshaphat of Judah (868–847 BCE), although this passage may be referring to an earlier peace which Jehoshaphat simply left intact. The existing balance of power soon resulted in drawing the Judaean kings out of their isolation, so that Judah fell into the wake of the energetic rulers of the north to such a degree that one is tempted to speak of a veiled vassal relationship of Judah to Israel. Judah furnished Israel with military forces against the Aramaeans of Damascus (I Kings 22.2–4; II Kings 8.28; 9.14) and against the Moabites (II Kings 3.4–8). Finally, the two royal houses even became related by marriage when Jehoshaphat's son, Jehoram, married a daughter or sister of Ahab of Israel named Athaliah (II Kings 8.18, 16). This was a political marriage intended to solidify the new friendship between north and south.

Only little is known about the foreign and internal political conditions of the southern kingdom under Jehoshaphat (868–847 BCE),

Jehoram (847–845 BCE) and Ahaziah (845 BCE), for the Chronicler's detailed report on Jehoshaphat (II Chron. 17.1–21.1) can scarcely be taken into consideration as a historical source. Edom in Jehoshaphat's day was still subject to Judah (I Kings 22.47). It was only under Jehoram that the final secession by the Edomites and the re-establishment of their kingdom took place (II Kings 8.20–22). According to I Kings 22.48f., Jehoshaphat attempted to revive the trade monopoly of his ancestor Solomon on the Red Sea. This attempt, however, failed. Profitable journeys to the legendary gold country of Ophir were out of the question because the ships proved to be unseaworthy while still in the port of Ezion-geber. Perhaps Jehoshaphat's shipbuilding was limited to a makeshift renovation of Solomon's old and now rotted merchant ships. He moreover declined an offer of participation made by the Israelite king Ahaziah. Apparently he was concerned to maintain some independence from the northern kingdom, at least economically.

Finally the political and familial intertwining of the Davidides with the kings of the Omride dynasty moved to its tragic climax. When the last Omride, Joram, was wounded in the battles with the Aramaeans around Ramoth-Gilead (*Tell er-Rāmīt*) and then went to Jezreel to recover his health, the revolt of the army officer Jehu began, bringing about the end of the rule of the Omrides (II Kings 9–10). Jehu arrived in Jezreel and slew Joram. Ahaziah of Judah, who as Joram's ally and cousin was also staying in Jezreel, tried hurriedly to flee to Jerusalem but was overtaken and killed on the height of Ibleam (*Ḥirbet Belʿame*). Thus the Davidic throne became vacant and the regular process of succession should have taken place. Instead, Jerusalem went through a macabre Omride sequel. When news of Ahaziah's death arrived, the queen-mother Athaliah took the reigns of government into her own hands. The short history work in II Kings 11 reports on these events. In order to secure her own autocratic rule, Athaliah immediately proceeded to exterminate all the living male members of the Davidic dynasty and thereby to interrupt violently the Davidic succession which was the constitutive element of the Judaean monarchy. Athaliah's actions could indeed have meant the end of David's dynasty had not Princess Jehosheba succeeded in stealing away the little prince Joash, son of Ahaziah, and thus saving him from his grandmother's madness. At first he was hidden, not yet a year old, in the bedchamber of his nurse and later in the temple of Yahweh where he grew up under the care of the priest Jehoiada. It was possible to keep his existence hidden from Athaliah for six years. This shows that the queen-mother's *coup d'état* had not gained any sympathies in the circles of the priesthood of the Jerusalem temple. One can no longer determine what governmental and cult-political measures Athaliah carried out during her reign as absolute monarch. One should not exclude the possibility that, as a member of the house of Omri, she not only practised the cult of the Tyrian Baal herself but also encouraged its acceptance in Jerusalem and Judah. The fact that it was the priest Jehoiada who headed the counter-revolution and that the oath of the revolutionaries was sworn in Yahweh's temple might favour this conclusion. But this assumption is not at all necessary, especially since the tradition is silent about any religious motives which might have brought about Athaliah's eventual downfall. What are emphasized all the more clearly are political motives.

Neither the Jerusalem priesthood nor the Judaean rural nobility could accept the existing interruption of the Davidic succession as permanent. These conservative circles must have been vitally interested in restoring the old order of things. It is now widely recognized that 'the people of the land' (*'am hā'āreṣ*; see II Kings 11.14, 18–20; 14.21; 21.24) were the landowners of Judah who appear to have been politically conservative and strong supporters of the Davidic dynasty (see Würthwein, Nicholson, and below pp. 456–8). It was this Judaean rural nobility which Jehoiada mobilized when the time was ripe and the little prince was old enough to be presented as the successor to the throne. After careful preparations and with the support of the mercenary troops, Joash was acclaimed king and anointed in the temple on a sabbath. This marked the end of Athaliah's rule. She appeared in the temple, crying 'Treason! Treason!', but was immediately arrested by army officers and shortly afterwards was put to death in the forecourt of the palace. A solemn ceremony of covenant-making followed in the temple (II Kings 11.17): 'And Jehoiada made a covenant between Yahweh and the king and people that they should be Yahweh's people, also between the king and the people.' This verse reports a new beginning after the interruption of the Davidic succession. It is not to be seen as an interpretation by the Deuteronomist reflecting the standpoint of the ideal unity of God, king, and people against the worship of Baal (so *Herrmann, 224f.). The king stepped between Yahweh and the people, who were the old covenant partners, because kingship had become discredited by the Athaliah affair and required a new consecration. It seems that the special covenant of Yahweh with the house of David (II Sam. 7) is considered here to be a special instance of Yahweh's covenant with his chosen people. This would represent an

advanced stage in the theology of the covenant, a stage made understandable by the deep and continued commitment to the Davidic
dynasty. In the course of the re-establishment of orderly conditions,
the temple of the Tyrian Baal, standing not far from Yahweh's
temple, was levelled. Perhaps it had been no more than a private
chapel for Athaliah. The Judaean rural nobility was now in control
of the situation and the Jerusalem circles which had supported
Athaliah's rule kept to their houses and remained quiet (II Kings
11.20b–21). This was the end of the Omride interlude in Judah
(845–840 BCE).

Once again little is known of the period which followed. The nature
of the reports allows one to infer that the Deuteronomist, in addition
to the royal annals, also had access to a sort of temple chronicle.
Joash (840–801 BCE), who had begun to reign at the age of seven,
must have required at the outset a regent and councillor. One
could well imagine Jehoiada the priest in this role. This is precisely
what the Chronicler has done (II Chron. 24.2 f., 15, 22). Later on
Joash devoted himself to urgently needed repair work on Solomon's
temple in Jerusalem (II Kings 12.4–16). In order to prevent the
priests from lining their pockets with the temple receipts (the 'collection money'), Jehoiada invented the collection box. From time to
time it was emptied by royal officials under the direction of the chief
of the civil service (*sōphēr*), and its contents were turned over to the
overseers of the battalions of construction workers. From this there
developed a permanent institution (the audit of temple accounts)
about which we are informed only because two hundred years later
under king Josiah it was still in effect (II Kings 22.3–7). Under
Joash there also occurred a strange incident involving foreign affairs
(II Kings 12.17 f.). The Aramaean king, Hazael of Damascus,
invaded Palestine and captured, perhaps as an ally of the Philistines,
the city of Gath. Joash was able to turn away an Aramaean attack on
Jerusalem by paying off Hazael from his temple and palace treasures. We hear nothing about this in the annals of the northern
kingdom.

After ruling for forty years Joash fell victim to a palace revolt and
was slain by two of his own servants (II Kings 12.21 f.). The Davidic
succession, however, was not endangered thereby. The crown prince
Amaziah (801–773 BCE) ascended the throne and had the murderers
of his father executed (II Kings 14.5 f.). Later he gained a victory
over the Edomites in the otherwise unknown 'Valley of Salt' (II
Kings 14.7). He captured the city of Sela ('Rock') and renamed it
Joktheel. Some have taken this to refer to the Edomite capital of

Petra, but this is unlikely for various, especially strategic, reasons (see Haran, 207–12). The success of the campaign against the Edomites was scarcely more than transitory, since there are no reports of a restoration of Judaean authority over Edom. The reported battle of Beth-shemesh (*er-Rumēle* near *'En Šems*) against Joash of Israel, the grandson of Jehu, is also very curious. The Judaeans were defeated; Amaziah was actually captured, but then brought to Jerusalem, where the Israelites contented themselves with destroying a part of the city's walls and plundering the temple and palace treasures (II Kings 14.8–14). In the end Amaziah, like his father, fell victim to a court conspiracy (II Kings 14.19–21). He was able, however, to flee to Lachish (*Tell ed-Duwēr*) but was slain there by the conspirators. The Judaean rural nobility then placed his sixteen-year-old son on the throne.

The name of this successor has been transmitted in two forms. It is given as Azaria(hu) in II Kings 14.21; 15.1, 6, 7, 8 and Uzzia(hu) in II Kings 15.13, 30, 32, 34; Hos. 1.1; Amos 1.1; Isa. 1.1; 6.1 and elsewhere. He ruled from 773 to ca. 736 (BCE) and was a contemporary of Jeroboam II of Israel, during whose reign the northern kingdom experienced a late resurgence. This seems to have had its effects upon Judah, for there, too, peace and prosperity prevailed. Azariah regained for Judah the harbour city of Elath on the Gulf of 'Aqabā (II Kings 14.22). The Chronicler's reports cannot be checked historically, although Azariah is there said to have battled successfully against Philistines, Arabs, Meunites, and Ammonites (II Chron. 26.6–15). In his internal affairs he is said also to have carried out the construction of fortifications in Jerusalem, the rearming of the standing army, the advancement of agriculture, and the colonization of unproductive areas. Towards the end of his life Azariah was afflicted with leprosy and had to be isolated. Jotham, the crown prince, took charge of the affairs of government (II Kings 15.5). No one can tell whether the Chronicler's note (II Chron. 26.23) to the effect that Azariah was not buried in the Davidic family tomb is dependable. It is conceivable that the Chronicler, in view of his strict understanding of the law, could not imagine that an unclean leper might have been interred in the family grave of the dynasty of David.

§3. THE KINGDOM OF ISRAEL FROM JEROBOAM I TO JEROBOAM II

Y. **Aharoni** and R. **Amiran**, 'A New Scheme for the Sub-Division of the Iron Age in Palestine', *IEJ* VIII, 1958, 171–84; A. **Alt**, 'Das Gottesurteil

auf der Karmel', *Festschrift Georg Beer*, Stuttgart: W. Kohlhammer 1935, 1–
18 = his *KS* II, 1953, 135–49; idem, *Der Stadtstaat Samaria*, BVSAWL
101/5, 1954 = his *KS* III, 1959, 258–302; F. I. **Andersen**, 'The Socio-
Juridical Background of the Naboth Incident', *JBL* LXXXV, 1966, 46–57;
M. C. **Astour**, '841 BC: The First Assyrian Invasion of Israel', *JAOS* XCI,
1971, 383–9; K. **Baltzer**, 'Naboths Weinberg (I. Kön. 21). Der Konflikt
zwischen israelitischem und kanaanäischem Bodenrecht', *WD* NF VIII,
1965, 73–8; J. W. **Crowfoot** et al., *Samaria-Sebaste* I–III, London: Palestine
Exploration Fund, 1938–1957; H. **Donner**, 'Adadnirari III. und die
Vasallen des Westens', *Archäologie und Altes Testament* (Festschrift Kurt
Galling), ed. A. Kuschke and E. Kutsch, Tübingen: J. C. B. Mohr 1970,
49–59; idem, *Herrschergestalten in Israel*, VW 103, 1970, 55–73; O. **Eissfeldt**,
Der Gott Karmel, SAB 1, 1953; idem, 'Der Zugang nach Hamath', *OA* X,
1971, 269–76 = his *KS* V, 1973, 205–11; M. **Elat**, 'The Campaigns of
Shalmaneser III against Aram and Israel', *IEJ* XXV, 1975, 25–35; G.
Fohrer, *Elia*, ATANT 53, 1957, ²1968; F. S. **Frick**, 'The Rechabites
Reconsidered', *JBL* XC, 1971, 279–87; K. **Galling**, 'Der Gott Karmel und
die Ächtung der fremden Götter', *Geschichte und Altes Testament* (Festschrift
Albrecht Alt), BHT 16, 1953, 105–26; H. L. **Ginsberg**, 'The Omrid–
Davidid Alliance and its Consequences', *Fourth World Congress of Jewish
Studies* I, Jerusalem: World Union of Jewish Studies, 1967, 91–3; W. W.
Hallo, 'From Qarqar to Carchemish: Assyria and Israel in the Light of
New Discoveries', *BA* XXIII, 1960, 33–61 = *BAR* II, 1964, 152–90; M.
Haran, 'The Rise and Decline of the Empire of Jeroboam ben Joash', *VT*
XVII, 1967, 266–97; idem, 'Observations on the Historical Background of
Am 1.2–2.6', *IEJ* XVIII, 1968, 202–12; J. B. **Hennessy**, 'Excavations at
Samaria-Sebaste 1968', *Levant* II, 1970, 1–21; A. **Jepsen**, *Nabi. Soziologische
Studien zur alttestamentlichen Literatur und Religionsgeschichte*, München: C. H.
Beck 1934; idem, 'Israel und Damaskus', *AfO* XIV, 1941/44, 153–72; idem,
'Ahabs Busse. Ein kleiner Beitrag zur Methode literarhistorischer
Einordnung', *Archäologie und Altes Testament* (see above under Donner),
1970, 145–55; H. J. **Katzenstein**, 'Who Were the Parents of Athaliah?',
IEJ V, 1955, 194–7; K. **Kenyon**, 'Megiddo, Hazor, Samaria and
Chronology', *BIA* IV, 1964, 143–56; E. **Lipiński**, 'Le Ben-hadad II de la
Bible et l'histoire', *Fifth World Congress of Jewish Studies* I, Jerusalem: World
Union of Jewish Studies, 1969, 157–73; J. **Liver**, 'The Wars of Mesha,
King of Moab', *PEQ* XCIX, 1967, 14–31; B. **Mazar**, 'The Aramean
Empire and its Relations with Israel', *BA* XXV, 1962, 97–120 = *BAR* II,
1964, 127–51; P. K. **McCarter**, ' "Yaw, Son of Omri": A Philological Note
on Israelite Chronology', *BASOR* CCXVI, 1974, 5–8; A. R. **Millard** and
H. **Tadmor**, 'Adad-Nirari III in Syria: Another Stele Fragment and the
Dates of his Campaigns', *Iraq* XXXV, 1973, 57–64; J. M. **Miller**, 'The Elisha
Cycle and the Accounts of the Omride Wars', *JBL* LXXXV, 1966, 441–54;
idem, 'The Fall of the House of Ahab', *VT* XVII, 1967, 307–24; idem, 'The
Rest of the Acts of Jehoahaz (I Kings 20; 22.1–38)', *ZAW* LXXX, 1968, 337–
42; idem, 'So Tibni Died (I Kings XVI 22)', *VT* XVIII, 1968, 392–4; idem,

'The Moabite Stone as a Memorial Stela', *PEQ* CVI, 1974, 9–18; B. D. **Napier**, 'The Omrides of Jezreel', *VT* IX, 1959, 366–78; B. **Oded**, 'The Campaigns of Adad-Nirari III into Syria and Palestine', *Studies in the History of the Jewish People and the Land of Israel* II, ed. B. Oded et al., Haifa: University of Haifa 1972, 25–36 (Hebrew with English summary); S. **Page**, 'A Stela of Adad-nirari III and Nergal-ereš from Tell al Rimah', *Iraq* XXX, 1968, 139–53; W. L. **Reed** and F. V. **Winnett**, 'A Fragment of an Early Moabite Inscription from Kerak', *BASOR* CLXXII, 1963, 1–9; G. A. **Reisner** et al., *Harvard Excavations at Samaria 1908–1910* I–II, Cambridge: Harvard University Press 1924; H. H. **Rowley**, 'Elijah on Mount Carmel', *BJRL* XLIII, 1960–1, 190–219 = his *Men of God*, 1963, 37–65; H.-C. **Schmitt**, *Elisa: Traditionsgeschichtliche Untersuchungen zur vorklassischen nordisraelitischen Prophetie*, Gütersloh: Gerd Mohn 1972; O. H. **Steck**, *Überlieferung und Zeitgeschichte in den Elia-Erzählungen*, WMANT 26, 1968; H. **Tadmor**, 'Assyria and the West: The Ninth Century and its Aftermath', *Unity and Diversity*, 1975, 36–48; R. **de Vaux**, 'Tirzah', *AOTS*, 1967, 371–83; P. **Welten**, 'Naboths Weinberg (I. Kön 21)', *EvTh* XXXIII, 1973, 18–32; C. F. **Whitley**, 'The Deuteronomic Presentation of the House of Omri', *VT* II, 1952, 137–52.

The source material for the history of the northern kingdom of Israel between Jeroboam I and the onset of the Assyrian period (745 BCE) is far richer and more diversified than it is for Judah in the same time span. Within the Deuteronomistic History one can differentiate: (1) excerpts from the annals of the kings of Israel (I Kings 15.25–II Kings 14.29); (2) prophetic legends about the appearances of the prophet Elijah, which in part, as a circle of legends, already existed in a unified pre-Deuteronomistic form (I Kings 17.1–19.18; 21; II Kings 1.2–17); (3) prophetic legends about the appearances of the prophet Elisha, also probably collected and recorded in pre-Deuteronomistic form (I Kings 19.19–21; II Kings 2.1–25; 3.4–8.15; 13.14–21); (4) two historical narratives concerning the wars with the Aramaeans probably originating in prophetic circles (I Kings 20.1–43; 22.1–38); (5) the history of the revolt of the army officer, Jehu (II Kings 9.1–10.27). Furthermore, from here on one must take the inscriptions of the kings of the Neo-Assyrian empire into account. Finally, for the period of the reign of Jeroboam II one must also mention the literary legacy of the prophet Amos who, though he came from Judah, made his public appearance in Israel.

From every point of view the Israelite north had incomparably greater difficulties than the Judaean south. The territory of Israel was more diverse than that of the kingdom of Judah and its geographical lines of communication were much more open. The state reached the maritime plain and the Mediterranean Sea in the region of Mount Carmel. Its location at the intersection of major roads running north and south and east and west had the effect of constantly requiring Israel to defend its borders on all sides – to the south of Carmel against the Philistines, north of Carmel against the Phoenicians, in Upper Galilee and in northern Transjordan against the Aramaeans and in southern Transjordan against the Moabites. Israel stood in the path of history. It scarcely ever remained uninvolved in the major political happenings which took place on the Syrian–Palestinian land-bridge and in the ancient Orient. This is all the more reason why it needed a uniform, continuous, and strong leadership. But the charismatic ideal of kingship, tied as it was to designation and acclamation, gave Israel's monarchical institution an unstable and insecure quality which was always threatened from within. This was symptomatic of the historical openness and turbulence of the kingdom. Israel again and again, until its downfall in 722 BCE, was not only threatened from without but was also afflicted from within with revolts and usurpations.

Efforts to solidify the monarchy institutionally in the sense of a dynastic cohesiveness were by no means lacking. After the death of Jeroboam I, his son Nadab (907–906 BCE) ascended the throne (I Kings 15.25–32). His candidacy for the throne may perhaps have been arranged for even during Jeroboam's lifetime, for the latter must have known the dangers which the charismatic ideal of kingship carried with it for the stability of the kingdom. Nadab went into battle against the Philistines, whose political intentions are unclear to us but who in any case had long since regained their independence. It is possible that Nadab was hoping to gain the acclamation of the army after proving himself militarily and thus to re-establish a military kingdom such as Saul's had been. This, however, did not happen. In the army camp at Gibbethon (*Tell el-Melāt*), about five kilometres south-west of Gezer, Baasha from Issachar, who presumably had been designated, rose up in rebellion, slew Nadab, and exterminated all male members of the family of Jeroboam I.

Little is known about the reign of Baasha (906–883 BCE) (I Kings 15.33–16.7) beyond what has already been indicated above. His son Elah (883–882 BCE) succeeded him, which represents a second attempt to establish a dynasty in the northern kingdom. But this effort was even more hopeless than in Nadab's case (I Kings 16.8–14), for while the army was once more in the field against the Philistines, this successor to the throne failed to prove himself militarily. He remained in his capital city, Tirzah, and was slain there during a drinking bout by Zimri, the commander of the royal chariot corps and perhaps a Canaanite. This Zimri is credited with a reign of only seven days (I Kings 16.15–20). Obviously, the army at Gibbethon could not simply accept this palace revolt and usurpation. The units of the army proclaimed as king Omri, who was their commanding general. He immediately abandoned the war against the Philistines in order to move against Tirzah. Zimri, shut up in the city and without any hope, burned the palace over himself and died in the flames. According to the MT, Zimri is said to have reigned for seven days during the twenty-seventh year of Asa king of Judah, although Omri is said to have become king in the thirty-first year of Asa (I Kings 16.15, 23). This would suggest that four years passed before Omri (878–871 BCE) was finally able to begin his reign. During this time he slowly, and apparently without any fighting, gained the upper hand over a rival candidate by the name of Tibni (I Kings 16.21f.). Then began a long break in the continuous revolts and usurpations which previously had kept Israel in suspense. This dynasty and its successor reigned over the northern kingdom for a total of about 130 years. The transition from one of these dynasties to the other again was marked by a revolt of first magnitude which proceeded in classical fashion with both designation and acclamation (II Kings 9–10).

A. The dynasty of Omri (878–845 BCE)

The difficult foreign and internal political problems which confronted the northern kingdom in the first half of the ninth century required a high degree of political ability and wisdom of the kings from the house of Omri. The Omrides were not found wanting in these qualities, least of all Omri himself and his son Ahab (871–852 BCE). They belong to the most gifted and energetic rulers who ever occupied Israel's throne. If many of their solutions, especially those in the area of internal affairs, did not prove to be durable in the long run, this is largely to be accounted for by the fact that it was difficult to assess the ever-changing conditions of the political situation. It is not hard in retrospect to enumerate against the Omrides the various reasons for their failures, but in doing so one also should appreciate their achievements.

The Aramaean kingdom of Damascus constituted the chief foreign threat to Israel. Under Solomon it had established its independence and since then had grown steadily in power and influence. Unfortunately, it is just at this point that our sources for the period become rather uncommunicative. We do not know for sure whether there were military conflicts in Omri and Ahab's time between Aram and Israel. The historical narratives in I Kings 20 and 22 (Ahab against Ben-hadad of Damascus) are perhaps of a later date. The kings involved in these narratives were at first certainly anonymous and were identified as Ahab and Jehoshaphat only secondarily. This was also true of the Elisha narrative in II Kings 6.8–7.20 which probably came to be associated with Joram's reign secondarily. According to II Kings 8.28f. we find Joram (851–845 BCE) in battle against Hazael of Damascus at Ramoth (*Tell er-Rāmīt*) in northern Transjordan. This war can hardly have broken out upon Israel all at once. Moreover, the Aramaean threat was by no means the only foreign problem at the time of the Omrides. On the distant horizon, the colossus of the Neo-Assyrian empire rose up in the ninth century and began to reach into the territory of the Syrian–Palestinian land-bridge. At this time, however, Israel was not immediately and directly affected by this development. The Old Testament tradition is therefore silent about this early expansion of the Assyrians.

Certain details about the Assyrian expansion may be learned from the inscriptions of the Assyrian Great Kings, especially those of Asshurnasirpal II (884–859 BCE) and Shalmaneser III (859–824 BCE). In these inscriptions, the latter king claims to have undertaken six military campaigns into Syria–Palestine, in his sixth, tenth, eleventh, fourteenth, eighteenth, and twenty-first years. These campaigns are noted in the Black Obelisk, the Monolith, and the Bull inscriptions (see *AR* I, 200–23, 236–41; *ANET*, 278–80). In 853 BCE, Shalmaneser encountered an anti-Assyrian coalition in Syria under the leadership of Damascus and found himself opposed by this coalition's combined fighting forces at Qarqar (*Ḥirbet Qerqūr*) on the lower Orontes. The participants in the battle, which ended in a draw, included, according to Shalmaneser's monolithic inscription, twelve kings from northern and central Syria, among them Hadadezer of Damascus, Irḫuleni of Hamath, and Ahab of Israel, the latter with a contingent of 2,000 chariots and 10,000 soldiers (the numbers are probably exaggerated). Shalmaneser claims to have fought this same alliance on three subsequent occasions in 849, 848, and 845 BCE (see Elat). We do not know whether this solidarity between Israel and Damascus represented a temporary interruption of the tensions and hostilities or whether Ahab was actually successful in establishing a friendly relationship between the two countries, although the latter seems likely.

In the area of internal affairs the Omrides found it above all necessary to turn to the old problem of the relationship between Israelites and Canaanites, a problem which David's incorporation of Canaanite territory into the structure of the kingdom of Israel had not resolved but only postponed. It needs to be clearly understood that the northern kingdom in this respect also was forced to assume a more difficult part of the legacy of the Davidic–Solomonic personal union than did the southern kingdom. Right through the centre of its territory ran a barrier made up of the northern Canaanite cities. In the west lay the areas, chiefly settled by Canaanites, which previously had belonged to the third and fourth Solomonic districts (see I Kings 4.10f.). Moreover, in the tribal territory of Manasseh, Israelite and Canaanite towns had coexisted since ancient times. There were two possible solutions to the Canaanite problem which in the northern kingdom was particularly acute: (1) One might try to integrate the Canaanite and Israelite populations as much as possible, to efface their differences – including their religious differences – and so to encourage the already existing movement towards integration. This would entail the risk of not being able to anticipate what reactions and forces might be let loose, for there was absolutely no assurance that Israelites and Canaanites would be capable of completely merging with one another. (2) The possibility of separating both parts of the population in the sense of a clear and possibly legally established dualism also existed. This solution, too, was not without its dangers, for it involved an action which would counteract the historical trend towards fusion already in effect for a long time. If the Omrides did not wish to relinquish all internal political activity, they would have to be prepared in any case to take risks. Solomon had already moved in the direction of the second possibility, for he had placed Israelite tribal districts and Canaanite city districts side by side, giving them equal rights but probably treating them independently of one another. The Omrides chose to travel this road unswervingly all the way and decided in favour of a radically dualistic solution of the Canaanite problem. It must be noted, it is true, that this understanding of the situation represents the result of a historical reconstruction (see Alt, *Der Stadtstaat Samaria*), but then a historian cannot really forgo reconstructions if he does not wish to be satisfied with an enumeration of disconnected items. No reconstruction has thus far been proposed which combines the reports transmitted to us into a more adequate general picture.

According to I Kings 16.24, Omri purchased from a private citizen named Shemer, for two talents of silver, an extensive piece of property located on a hill in the north-western part of the central

Palestinian mountains and began to build a city there to which he gave the name *Šomᵉrōn* (= Samaria, today *Sebaṣṭye*). He made Samaria his capital and during the sixth year of his reign transferred his residence there from Tirzah. The excavations in Tirzah and especially in Samaria have fully confirmed and given vivid colour to these statements. On the basis of I Kings 16.24, the excavators at Samaria assigned the first building phase to Omri. However, the pottery from this earliest phase has its closest parallels in remains from tenth-century levels at other sites (especially Hazor X). This apparent discrepancy has been explained as the result of misleading recording procedures by the excavators (see Kenyon). An alternative interpretation suggests that there was a tenth-century pre-Omride settlement at Samaria which Omri's builders razed to the ground (see Aharoni and Amiran). Both Omri and Ahab invested tremendous economic resources in this new royal undertaking and from literally nothing produced in the course of a few years a respectable capital city. The excavations give eloquent testimony to this, even though the literary sources prefer to remain silent. I Kings 22.39 does make mention of an 'ivory house' belonging to Ahab (for the time of Jeroboam II see Amos 3.15), i.e., a palatial structure with ivory decorations of the type which were actually brought to light during the excavations (in their themes they showed strong dependence upon Egypt but were of local manufacture). A temple was also soon established (I Kings 16.32; II Kings 10.18–27), not however for Yahweh but for Baal. For reasons which will be discussed later nothing of this temple has been preserved.

The founding of Samaria raises the question concerning the political goal which motivated the Omrides. It is completely unlikely that the new capital was nothing but the result of Omri's restlessness or of Ahab's delight in building enterprises. When considering the details of our sources, which are not very informative, one is struck by the following: (1) Omri apparently purchased the land for the city from a Canaanite according to Canaanite legal principles (similar transactions in real estate are reported in Gen. 23; 33.19; II Sam. 24.18–25). Within the area in which Israelite law relating to landed property was valid, according to which Yahweh was the owner of all the land and soil, such a procedure would have been totally impossible. Samaria now became the personal possession of Omri and his family. (2) Omri or Ahab accorded the city a special legal status which set it clearly apart from Israel and which was still respected by Jehu in connection with his revolt (II Kings 10). It would appear, in other words, that Samaria was not incorporated

into the structure of the northern kingdom. (3) The city, under
Ahab, received an aura of sanctity, however, not by the establish-
ment of a Yahweh shrine but by the building of a Baal temple (I
Kings 16.32). (4) From Omri's time at the earliest and from Ahab's
at the latest, the Omrides possessed a second capital, namely Jezreel
(*Zerʿīn*), taken probably from Baasha's family property (I Kings 21;
II Kings 9–10).

All these indications lead one to conclude that the Omrides were
inspired, in establishing their new capital, by the example of the
conditions in the southern kingdom of Judah. The parallel with
Jerusalem in its special relationship to Judah is obvious. Samaria
was planned from the outset as an independent city-state in which
the Omrides would govern according to the Canaanite model, as
city rulers, like the Davidides in Jerusalem. Beyond that, the coexis-
tence, which has no analogy, of two capitals in the territory of the
northern kingdom and the absence of any cult of Yahweh in
Samaria point to still another conclusion, namely, that Samaria was
to constitute the centre of the Canaanite part of the population and
Jezreel the capital of the Israelite part. If this is correct, then the
founding and enlargement of Samaria represented a well-planned
step in national policy intended to provide a consistent dualistic
solution of the Canaanite problem: in Samaria the kings from the
house of Omri were kings over the Canaanite portion of the kingdom
and in Jezreel they were kings of Israel. They acted according to the
principle: for the Canaanites a Canaanite and for the Israelites an
Israelite. The constitutional concept underlying all this was that of
the 'personal union', such as had been practised in an exemplary
fashion over a century by the Davidides in Jerusalem and Judah.

The problems associated with this dualistic solution were bound to
become evident in its religious-political effects, which were not long
in coming. According to I Kings 16.31 Ahab married – on the basis
of good relations which Omri perhaps already had established with
the Phoenician coastal area – the Phoenician princess Jezebel, the
daughter of the city-king of Tyre, Ittobaal (so corrected according to
Menander of Ephesus in Flavius Josephus, *Antiquities*, VIII 324). It
is possible that Israel by this Tyrian marriage was able to record a
modest territorial gain, for the region of Mount Carmel, which apparently had temporarily fallen to Tyre, was recovered by Israel
(I Kings 18). The consequences for the kingdom's religious policies
were more serious. According to I Kings 16.31–33 Ahab had a
temple built for 'the Baal', probably the city god of Tyre, Melqart.
This state of affairs might at first remind one of Solomon, who had

had small shrines built to the east of Jerusalem for the foreign wives in his harem (I Kings 11.7f.). In this case the Baal temple in Samaria would have no other significance than that of a place where Jezebel and the Tyrian members of her court might practise the religion of their homeland. Still one wonders whether a private chapel on the territory of Samaria, which was a Canaanite city-state anyhow, would have provoked the storm which the Baal temple did. The conclusion suggested instead is that the Baal temple was another link in the chain of measures which the Omrides took in carrying out their internal policies. What Ahab intended was to give to the Canaanite metropolis of his kingdom an aura of sanctity akin to that acquired by Jerusalem when the ark of Yahweh was transferred to it under David (II Sam. 6) and also to that possessed by the two Israelite state-shrines of Bethel and Dan since Jeroboam I set up the two golden calves there (I Kings 12.26–33). The Baal temple in Samaria thus represented the state shrine for the Canaanite population of the northern kingdom of Israel.

The religious policies of the Omrides soon precipitated a counter-action from the Israelite side in the northern kingdom. It arose in support of Yahweh's claim to exclusiveness and fought for this claim with a degree of rigour hitherto unknown. This is by no means self-explanatory, for the mere existence of the Baal cult in Samaria would scarcely have brought about a conflict between Yahweh and the Baal of Tyre or a sharpening of the ancient struggle of Yahweh with the Baal generally. Samaria was – assuming that our historical reconstruction of conditions is correct – a Canaanite reservation, a state within the state. Its cultic constitution could not possibly have affected Yahweh's claim to exclusiveness in Israel (against *Noth, 242). Israel's reaction could scarcely have been directed against the existence of the Baal cult in Samaria. At most it would have been directed against the royal family, which had become compromised by its protection of that cult. It is also unlikely that the central government would have sought to force the cult of the Baal of Tyre upon the Israelites living out in the country. Notice is often taken of Jezebel, the king's consort, in this connection while Ahab is relieved of any responsibility, he supposedly having adhered to the Yahweh faith but simply having failed to show enough energy in seriously resisting Jezebel's cult propaganda (so *Kittel, and others). This view, however, does not fit into the basic characteristics of the religious policies of the Omrides. Whoever reaches such a conclusion underestimates the king's dualistic posture and overestimates Jezebel's influence, which may very well have carried some weight

VII.§3A] *The kingdom of Israel from Jeroboam I to Jeroboam II*   405

in individual instances but was scarcely great enough to frustrate the important political principle of the separation of Canaan and Israel. If this is so, then developments must have occurred which the kings could not have anticipated. Either the Canaanite world from its centre in Samaria set political and religious forces in motion out into the country and so advanced indirectly against the religion of Yahweh – e.g., by means of the officials in the governmental agencies, who were probably all Canaanites or at least predominantly so – or Israelites might have rebelled in principle against the pro-Canaanite policies of the dynasty and provoked a struggle, not between Yahweh and the Baal of Tyre, but between Yahweh and what one might call the 'duo-theistic' posture of the kings. Both of these seem to have happened, and the central figure of Israelite resistance was the great solitary individual, the prophet Elijah from Tishbe in the region east of the Jordan. To be sure, the Elijah legends do not permit a direct retracing of the course of this 'Phoenician crisis' in Israelite religion because, as prophetic legends, they are interested in the person of the prophet and not primarily in the developments and conditions which led to his appearance. Yet this much is evident: the latent Canaanization of Israelite religion, which had been at work since the conquest of the land, entered into its acute phase during the days of the Omrides. Otherwise, this contest over Yahweh's claim to exclusiveness, which had been going on for years, would not have been able to achieve the full degree of intensity it did at this time. To be able to produce a figure like Elijah, Israel must have felt itself under attack at the very core of its being. The chronic threat of a slow blending of Yahweh and Baal suddenly had to enter the full light of Israel's consciousness if it was to be opposed effectively. This is what happened in Ahab's time, because the religious policies of the Omrides were everywhere strengthening the backbone of the Canaanite world and were thus indirectly endangering the religious heritage of the tribes of Israel.

It is easier to obtain a picture of the general character of the Phoenician crisis than of the events in which it manifested itself. Ahab, who was confined by his dualistic policy to certain limits, seems inwardly to have actually stood on the side of the Canaanite world. In the building of Samaria and in the introduction of the Tyrian Baal he demonstrated a notable degree of personal initiative while, at the same time, his attitude towards the Israelite portion of his kingdom seems to have been one of toleration. One can point, in this connection, to the story of Naboth's vineyard or orchard (I Kings 21). Perhaps it should be mentioned that the Elijah and

Elisha legends are not necessarily to be taken as historically valid in every detail. The story of Naboth's vineyard in I Kings 21 is particularly open to question, since there are noticeable differences in detail between it and the brief reference to the Naboth affair in II Kings 9. I Kings 21 is primarily a short story or small novella placed in an historical context (see Miller, 1967; Baltzer; Welten). The Elijah–Naboth story reveals that Ahab had lost all appreciation for the inalienability of inherited property which Yahweh had bestowed. Nevertheless he resigned himself, though very reluctantly, to the rejection of his purchase offer by Naboth the Jezreelite and it remained finally for Jezebel to obtain the desired property as an addition to the crown estates by flagrantly violating the law and custom of Israel. In any case, one should not overlook the fact that Ahab did make an effort to respect the religion and law of Israel. The Elijah legend of the judgment of God on Mount Carmel (I Kings 18) shows that Ahab could act as king of Israel completely true to the Israelite spirit. Moreover, he gave to his two sons Ahaziah and Joram names which contained the name of Yahweh. Nor did anything change in this regard under his successors. The Elijah legend about the salvation oracle of the Canaanite Baal-Zebub (or Zebul ?) in II Kings 1 should not be evaluated in a cult-political sense; it illumines only the king's personal attitude. According to II Kings 3.2, during Joram's reign, a display of pro-Israelite tendencies seems even to have manifested itself in the religious policies of the kings, although the factual content of the report remains unclear. We may certainly assume that Jezebel as queen encouraged the strengthening of the Canaanite world. As queen-mother she probably exerted a certain influence in the governmental affairs of her sons, Ahaziah and Joram. This does not mean that she engaged in open cultic propaganda. The disruption which the Canaanites initiated in the political and religious equilibrium did not occur as an attack on the existing order in the Israelite part of the kingdom but as an indirect strengthening of the Canaanite world out in the country by means of Canaanite officials. This development inevitably came to a standstill because of the rise of Israelite counter-forces. One can understand why it was that the Canaanites for their part attempted to mount a defence. Jezebel may well have contributed to this. This is where the 'four hundred and fifty prophets who eat from Jezebel's table' (I Kings 18.19) fit in, as does also the spotlighting of the measures which under Jezebel's protection were taken against Israel, such as the persecution of the prophets of Yahweh and the destruction of Yahweh altars (I Kings 18.4, 10, 13;

19.1, 10, 14). How completely these tensions reached even to the very circles surrounding the king himself is shown by the fact that Obadiah, who was minister of the palace and the royal estates, joined the side of those who remained faithful to Yahweh (I Kings 18.3). Our tradition mentions that the attitude of the people was one of indecision – Elijah accused them of 'limping with two different opinions' (I Kings 18.21) – and that they slowly began to succumb to an ongoing process of Canaanization. The degree to which the Phoenician crisis thus undermined Israel's religious legacy cannot be determined fully from the reports in the Old Testament.

One thing, in any case, soon became clear. A change in conditions in favour of the Israelite part of the kingdom could only be achieved if the groups which maintained resistance against the strengthening of the Canaanite world were to shift the struggle from the religious to the political plane. The dualistic national policy of the Omrides had to be brought to an end. But that could only happen if the dynasty itself were eliminated and if the city-state of Samaria were liquidated as the centre and protector of the Canaanite world. This undertaking was attended to by an officer of the Israelite army named Jehu with a thoroughness which left nothing to be desired. Behind him stood the circles in Israel which remained faithful to Yahweh, the most prominent being Elisha and his fellow prophets.

A few notices taken from the royal annals of the kings of Israel need to be added. Of Ahab it is reported that he devoted himself to enlarging and fortifying Israelite cities (I Kings 22.39). During his reign Jericho was rebuilt and resettled. It had lain deserted and had been regarded as accursed since the days of the conquest of the land (I Kings 16.34). One of the Elisha legends (II Kings 2.19–22) provides information about the earliest colonists. Not long after Ahab's death Moab regained its political independence (II Kings 1.1 and the Elisha legend in II Kings 3.4–20). We are informed more accurately about this in the inscription, which came to light in 1868 in east-Jordanian *Dībān*, of the Moabite king Mesha (*KAI* 181, *ANET*, 320f.). A fragmentary three-line inscription left by the same king and found in 1960 in el-Kerak does not add anything of significance (see Reed and Winnett). The large Mesha inscription reveals, to begin with, that Dibon, the king's home-city, had fallen into Moabite hands some time earlier. The attack by Moab on the territory north of the Arnon (*Wādi Sēl el-Mōǧib*) had therefore already begun before the time of the Omrides. Although Moab's vassal-relationship to Israel continued in principle under Omri and his son, Mesha after Ahab's death succeeded in throwing off these bonds once and for all. His inscription was presumably set up after Joram's end, for it not only looks back upon these events but also declares (line 7) that Israel 'has been destroyed for all time' (an allusion to Jehu's revolt?). Beyond regaining political independence, Mesha was also able to enlarge Moab's territorial holdings considerably by a major campaign (note the parallel with the so-called holy wars of Israel). In the end Mesha's territory included all of the plateau north of the Arnon up to a theoretical line running eastward from the northern end of the Dead Sea. Many topographical details of the inscription remain unclarified. Still it is possible to locate with certainty several of the towns which previously had belonged to Gad but which Mesha captured and fortified, such as Madeba, Baal Meon (*Ma'īn*), Ataroth (*'Aṭṭārūs*), Qaryatēn (*Ḫirbet el-Qurēye*, west of Madeba, the biblical Qiryataim), Nebo (*Ḫirbet el-Muḫayyiṭ*), Yaḥaṣ (*Ḫirbet Iskander* in the *Wādi el Wāle*), and others. In a word, Mesha's activities constituted a territorial expansion which reveals that the Omrides were not able to play a totally successful role, either politically or militarily, in the area east of the Jordan.

B.   The dynasty of Jehu (845–747 BCE)

The revolt of Jehu, which brought Omri's house to its end, took place in ancient, classical, specifically northern Israelite style. It was no court rebellion, as in Zimri's case, but proceeded on the basis of a regular charismatic summons such as Saul had once received. Behind the historical work in II Kings 9–10 lies the conception that Yahweh had himself recognized the distress of his people in the Phoenician crisis and had decided to remove the dynasty of the Omrides as a failure and to raise a new man to the throne.

This new man was the army officer, Jehu ben Nimshi. He was, according to the biblical traditions, stationed in Ramoth in northern Transjordan, where the armed forces of Israel were locked in stationary combat with the Aramaeans of Damascus. A pause in the fighting had set in. Joram the Omride had been wounded shortly before and had gone to Jezreel to recover his health. One day there appeared in Ramoth a member of one of the guilds of ecstatic prophets, serving as an emissary of the prophet Elisha. He took Jehu aside, designated him in Yahweh's name and anointed him king over Israel. Jehu's fellow officers asked him, not without noticeable excitement, what this 'mad fellow' (Hebrew: *hammᵉ šuggaʿ*) had wanted of him. After hesitating diplomatically for a while Jehu told them. The officers took their garments, spread them out on the steps, and shouted, 'Jehu is king' (II Kings 9.13). Thus the army officer had become *de iure* king of Israel by designation and acclamation. But he was not yet king *de facto*, for Joram the Omride was still alive and in residence in Jezreel, the capital of the Israelite part of the northern kingdom. Jehu, therefore, had to capture Jezreel and exterminate, as his charismatic predecessors had done, the male members of the preceding dynasty. He swore the officers of Israel's armed forces to strictest silence, mounted his chariot, and drove hurriedly with a small troop of loyal followers through the Jordan depression, the plain of Bethshan, up the valley of the *Nahr Ğālūd* to Jezreel. The watchman on the tower saw a cloud of dust from afar, which continued to come closer and promised nothing good. After receiving his report Joram sent out messengers who, however, immediately joined the conspirators. The author of this historical work has brilliantly described these dramatic events by using the artistic device of *teichoscopy* (wall viewing). Soon there could be no further doubt in Jezreel: 'The driving is like the driving of Jehu the son of Nimshi; for he drives as though he is furious!' (II Kings 9.20). In this threatening situation Joram decided to ride out towards the obstinate army officer in order to make him see reason. The meeting took place on the property of Naboth the Jezreelite which had once played a role in the controversy between Ahab and Elijah (I Kings 21). Joram called out to Jehu, 'Are you coming with peaceful intensions, Jehu?' He answered, 'What peaceful intentions can there be as long as the harlotry and the countless sorceries of your mother Jezebel continue?' (II Kings 9.22). Joram realized that nothing could now be saved and turned to flight. Jehu, however, shot him in the heart from behind so that he collapsed bleeding in his chariot. The unfortunate king Ahaziah of Judah, who was accompanying Joram, fled in the direction of Jerusalem. However, he did not get far, for he was shot near Ibleam (*Ḫirbet Belʿame* near *Ğenīn*) and succumbed from his wounds soon afterwards in Megiddo. Jehu's motive in murdering the Judaean king is unclear. Perhaps it was merely a case of revolutionary zeal. At any rate, the situation of the southern kingdom must have been wretched at that time since Jehu did not find it necessary to curb his actions out of political considerations. After eliminating the two kings Jehu entered Jezreel as victor. The queen-mother, Jezebel, made one last effort to gain recognition for the authority of the house of Omri. She stepped painted and adorned, that is, with regal dignity, to the presentation window of the palace and called down into the court, 'Is it well with Zimri, murderer of his master?' (II Kings 9.31). This comparison must have embittered

Jehu, particularly because it did not apply and because it revealed that the Tyrian queen had no conception of the character of Israel's charismatic kingship. Jehu needed no more than a signal and a shout to prompt two eunuchs to throw Jezebel out of the window. Jehu, thereupon, entered the palace and celebrated the completion of his *coup d'état* with a banquet.

The problem of the second Omride capital, the Canaanite city-state of Samaria, was, however, still unsolved. Jehu clearly recognized, very much in keeping with the dualistic conception of his predecessors, that, though he had attained royal rank in Israel, he had not automatically become the city-king of Samaria. He respected the special constitutional status of Samaria and began a diplomatic exchange of letters with the city aristocracy of Samaria. The author of the historical work has provided us with authentic extracts from these letters (II Kings 10.1–7). In the first one Jehu challenged the city elders to place an Omride prince at their head as king and to defend the city. This frightened the aristocrats to their very bones and they hurried to assure Jehu of their submissiveness. Jehu then wrote a second letter stating that he was prepared to accept their capitulation on the condition that 'the heads of your royal house' (II Kings 10.6 according to numerous manuscripts, the Syriac Peshitta and the Vulgate) be sent to him in Jezreel. This was a devious diplomatic formulation which left Jehu's real intention ambiguously unclear. For the Hebrew word *rō'š* means literally 'head' and in a figurative sense 'chief, master'. It thus remained open whether he meant the senior members of the Omride family or the heads of all the male members of the royal house. The upper classes of Samaria in any case took the demand literally and this is the way it was undoubtedly intended. Seventy male Omrides were killed, their heads cut off and transported in baskets to Jezreel. There Jehu had them piled up on the outside of one of the gates and on the following morning went before the horrified people and said, 'You are not guilty! I have conspired, it is true, against my master and have slain him. But who has struck down all of these?' (II Kings 10.9).

Jehu thereupon set out for Samaria. On the way he met forty-two Judaean princes, had them killed and thrown into a cistern. This was mass murder, the motives for which are just as dark as those for the murder of king Ahaziah. Continuing on his way he met Jehonadab ben Rechab, the head of the sect of the Rechabites who were fanatically loyal to Yahweh. He took him up into his chariot. The traditional interpretation of the Rechabites sees them as a subgroup of the Kenites which had taken land but had persistently and deliberately remained on a nomadic level of life and had practised a strict abstinence from agriculture (see Jer. 35) in order to protest against Israel's entanglement with the life-style of agriculture and the accompanying infiltration of Canaanite ideas into the religion of Yahweh. Recently, this interpretation of the Rechabites and their espousal of the 'nomadic ideal' have been called into question (see Frick). This alternative portrayal, while continuing to consider them as radical supporters of Yahwism, sees them as 'a guild of craftsmen, probably . . . a guild of metal-workers involved in the making of chariots and other weaponry' (Frick, 285) whose life-style was determined as much by occupational as by theological considerations.

At any rate, Jehu thus was fraternizing with extreme groups of Yahweh adherents and was identifying his political intentions with the endeavours of those groups in Israel whose banners proclaimed their commitment to keeping pure the religion of Yahweh. The bloody overthrow thereby acquired in the eyes of Jehu, a portion of his contemporaries, and of the writer of the history a religious basis and legitimation (II Kings 10.28–31).

After arriving in Samaria Jehu exterminated everyone still left of the Omride dynasty. Thereupon he arranged for a great festival to offer sacrifices to the Baal of Samaria and invited to it the Canaanite cultic community from the city and the countryside. He pretended to foster the Baal cult even more intensively than the Omrides had done. He thus created the impression that he intended in every way to follow in the footsteps of the Omrides in Samaria and that he wanted to receive from the Baal his consecration as city-king of Samaria even as he had been consecrated by Yahweh as king of Israel. But it was all a trick. The ones who were involved should have noticed this finally when they were given special festival garments from the wardrobe and thus had to leave their weapons outside. It is, of course, also possible that this was customary. Jehu would otherwise not have been completely successful. The events now moved on to a climax. Officiating as a priest, Jehu had barely prepared the burnt offering for Baal when, at a signal from him, mercenary soldiers forced their way in, slaughtered every living soul, and carried out a dreadful bloodbath. They desecrated the temple of Baal and threw the corpses of the slain into the inner sanctuary. The building was torn down, the temple furnishings were demolished and burned. Not satisfied with this much, Jehu had latrine holes dug all over the sacred precinct. Samaria was thus deprived of everything that hitherto had constituted its own special character, its aura of

sanctity and a large part of its population. Jehu replaced the dualistic internal policies of the Omrides with a homogeneous structure
and order and so brought the Phoenician crisis of Israel's religion to
a conclusion.

The above reconstruction of Jehu's *coup d'état* has drawn strongly
upon the traditions of II Kings 9–10. This material deliberately
stresses the strong Yahwistic undercurrent in and the prophetic pre-
cipitation of Jehu's actions. Were his actions so clearly religiously
determined? One certainly must take into account Jehu's origins –
he was a military commander – as well as his own personal ambitions. Recently, Astour has suggested that Jehu's revolt should be
understood within the context of international events which he
reconstructs along new lines. Three conclusions of his are noteworthy. (1) The reference to Shalman in Hosea 10.14 is understood
as a reference to Shalmaneser III's defeat of the Israelites in
Transjordan in 841 BCE. (2) In one of Shalmaneser's inscriptions, the
king is said to have 'marched as far as the mountains of Ba'li-ra'si
which is a promontory' in his eighteenth year. Astour identifies this
with Mount Carmel and envisages a march across Israel after the
Assyrian's Transjordanian victory. (3) Jehu led his revolt to put
down the anti-Assyrian factions in Israel in order to placate the
Assyrians.

Jehu's revolt and the convulsion of the state's structure which it
caused brought the northern kingdom of Israel to the edge of the
abyss. The Israel of Jehu's dynasty was, at least during its first half
century, a hard-pressed, powerless, and threatened Israel. Jehu himself neither wished nor was he in a position to continue the foreign
policy of the Omrides. The friendly relations with the Phoenician
coastal cities were discontinued, for these relations, of course, had
brought the Baal of Tyre into the country. However, war did not
break out, for the seafaring Phoenicians, with their preoccupation
with trade, were hardly interested in that. The fraternal relationship
with Judah, understandably, also came to an end. Any leadership of
the Israelite north over the Judaean south was from here on completely out of the question. Neither did Jehu participate in anti-
Assyrian activities. He kept from being drawn into the constant
quarrels between Assyria and the Aramaeans of Damascus but,
instead, hurried to enter upon a course which was friendly to the
Assyrians. During the Syrian campaign of Shalmaneser III (841
BCE) Jehu brought tribute to the Great King. On Shalmaneser's
black obelisk he is seen lying on his stomach before his sovereign,
behind him are his servants with gifts, and above the scene there is

the inscription, *Ya-ú-a mār Ḫu-um-ri-i* ('Jehu, the son of Omri'; *ANET*, 280). This genealogically inaccurate name shows that the Assyrians simply retained the appellation under which an Israelite king had first entered Assyria's field of vision. (Recently, however, McCarter has argued that Shalmaneser's black obelisk does not refer to Jehu but to Joram. Consequently, he places the overthrow of the Omride dynasty in 839 BCE.)

Jehu's renunciation of all foreign political activity, however, made it possible for the northern kingdom to become an easy prey for the Aramaean kingdom of Damascus which was rapidly gaining strength. At about the same time as Jehu's revolt, a usurper, by name Hazael, had ascended the throne in Damascus (II Kings 8.7–15). A basalt stela of Shalmaneser refers to Hazael as 'a son of a nobody' (*ANET*, 280). The Elisha tradition is able to report that he was designated by the prophet Elisha himself. In the Elijah tradition too, Elijah and Hazael are found side by side (I Kings 19.15–17).

At first, however, Jehu had peace and quiet for a few years while Hazael's forces were tied down in fighting against Assyria. In 841 and 838 BCE, the Assyrians harassed the city but could not conquer it and had to be satisfied with plundering and devastating the country-side. After 838 BCE, Hazael's hands were freed so that he was then able to turn against Israel and increase the might of the Aramaean kingdom. The effects of this assault were catastrophic for the nor-thern kingdom. In Israel's consciousness Hazael was remembered for a long time as a particularly dangerous and dreaded foe (II Kings 8.11 f.; Amos 1.3–5; Isa. 9.11 f.). His attack for obvious reasons was first directed against the area east of the Jordan. The northern king-dom lost almost all of its territory there (II Kings 10.32 f., though the report that the loss extended to Aroer on the Arnon is possibly exaggerated, since it would appear from the Mesha inscription that a considerable portion of the territory north of the Arnon had been lost already to Moab). Soon afterwards Hazael also appeared in the Philistine coastal plain (II Kings 12.17 f.); no one was in a position to deny him access to the region. The northern kingdom's losses in men and equipment must have been considerable, for under Jehu's son, Jehoahaz (818–802 BCE), there remained of Israel's army only 10,000 footmen, 50 horsemen, and 10 chariots (II Kings 13.7). Still, the fortunes of war did on occasion favour Israel. II Kings 13.4 f., 24 f., report successes by kings Jehoahaz and Joash against the Aramaeans. These successes may have been connected with the change from Hazael to his successor, Ben-hadad II. It was noted earlier that the events narrated in I Kings 20 and 22 probably belong to a later context than Ahab's reign. The indications point to the reign either of Jehoahaz (so Miller, 'House of Ahab') or of Joash (so Jepsen, 1944, and Whitley) and to one of these kings as the opponent of Ben-hadad who would be the son of Hazael rather than his predecessor.

Not until the reign of Jeroboam II (787–747 BCE) did Israel once again enjoy a belated prosperity. The basis for this was the decline of the power of the Aramaean kingdom of Damascus, a decline which was precipitated by the reviving expansionist policy of the Assyrian kingdom. In the last decade of the ninth century Adad-Nirari III (809–782 BCE) marched westward no fewer than four times (805, 804, 802, 796 BCE; see *ANET*, 281 f.). During one of these campaigns (probably in 802 BCE) he besieged Damascus and forced the Aramaean king to submit and to pay tribute. Three inscriptions report on this. One of them, found at *Tell er-Rimāḥ* in 1967, contains the oldest Assyrian reference to Samaria and the name of king Joash (802–787 BCE): *ma-da-tu šá Ya-'a-su Sa-me-ri-na-a-a*, 'the tribute of Joash of Samaria' (see Page). He also received the tribute of the princes of Tyre and Sidon. This event would scarcely have immediately ended the war between the Aramaeans and Israel. But even so, the Aramaeans from now on were again forced to take Assyria into consideration and were tied down politically as well as militarily. For this reason, Jeroboam II was able to accomplish more than just temporary military successes. He succeeded, rather, in restoring the territorial borders of the northern kingdom almost to their former lines (II Kings 14.25). The tremendous expansion of his territory (from the Dead Sea to *Lᵉbō Ḥamāt*, probably the northern exit of the *Biqāᶜ* between the Lebanon and the Antilebanon) corresponds, however, more to the ideal of the Davidic empire than to political reality. In any case, the time of Jeroboam II was a period of peace and tranquillity in external as well as internal affairs. Territorial gains must have been in the area east of the Jordan (Amos 6.13; the conquest of Karnaim, *Tell ᶜAštara* near *Šeḫ Saᶜd*). Within the country were found affluence and economic prosperity. To be sure, wealth and prestige were concentrated in the large cities, especially Samaria, and promoted an unfortunate social cleavage of the population into rich and poor, masters and slaves, owners of large estates and landless farmers. The lustre of the reign of Jeroboam II covered over the social inequities within the country only imperfectly. They were only too clearly visible and became, in the prophetic message of Amos, the theme of a whole section of his proclamation.

§4. THE BEGINNING OF THE ASSYRIAN PERIOD OF THE HISTORY OF ISRAEL AND JUDAH

E. **Forrer**, *Die Provinzeinteilung des assyrischen Reiches*, Leipzig: J. C. Hinrichs 1920; K. A. **Kitchen**, *The Third Intermediate Period in Egypt (1100–650 BC)*, 1973; B. **Oded**, 'The Phoenician Cities and the Assyrian Empire in the Time of Tiglath-pileser III', *ZDPV* XC, 1974, 38–49; D. B. **Redford**, 'Studies in Relations between Palestine and Egypt during the First Millennium BC: II. The Twenty-second Dynasty', *JAOS* XCIII, 1973, 3–17; W. **von Soden**, *Der Aufstieg des Assyrerreiches als geschichtliches Problem*, AO 37, 1/2, 1937; idem, *Herrscher im Alten Orient* (V 54, Berlin: Springer 1954); H. **Tadmor**, 'Assyria and the West: The Ninth Century and Its Aftermath', *Unity and Diversity*, 1975, 36–48.

Around 1200 BCE, the turmoil created by the sea peoples had destroyed the system of the balance of power which had been built up during the second half of the second millennium between the great powers and had either eliminated the great powers, as in the case of the Hittites of Asia Minor, or pushed them back to their home areas and condemned them to unimportance, as in the case of Egypt and Mesopotamia. It was only in this way that the history of Israel and of the Aramaean states of Syria was able to take the course which has previously been described. However, the river basin powers did not remain for all time in a condition of weakness. They recovered and began once again to be active and to take control of the affairs of the entire Near East, including the Syrian–Palestinian land-bridge. The formation of a territorially large, imperial political structure, however, did not this time, as had been the case around the middle of the second millennium, emanate from Egypt. There the Twenty-first Theban Dynasty (1085–950 BCE) had been founded by Herihor in a time of severe internal disorders following the end of the period of the Ramessides. The kings of this dynasty cultivated an unusual governmental ideal, one which Egypt had hitherto not known, namely the idea of the 'theocracy' of the Theban god Amun in which the offices of high priest and king were united in a 'personal union'. In the strict theocratic sense of the word, Amun was regarded as the ruler of Egypt. The priest-kings considered themselves as his administrators. The separation of civil, religious, and military authority no longer prevailed. In theory, such a separation had never actually existed in Egypt. Under the cover of this theocratic conception the process of internal dissolution continued. The petty principalities of Lower Egypt, largely independent, came more and more under the influence of Libyan mercenary commanders. Finally the Libyan general Shoshenq I set up from Bubastis a kingdom which was at first confined to Lower Egypt but which under his leadership and that of his successors Osorkon I and Takelotis I gained increasing strength. Shoshenq I was the first Pharaoh of the so-called Bubastide period (Twenty-second–Twenty-third Dynasties, 950–730 BCE). He succeeded in uniting Egypt under one sceptre. The theory of the theocracy of Thebes was, to be sure, not called into question. The Bubastides ruled Upper Egypt through the medium of secundogeniture, that is, they installed princes of their own royal house as priest-kings in Thebes. The Bubastides, however, were able to bring the process of disintegration only to a temporary halt. In the Delta especially, minor princes rose up and finally the Libyan Pharaohs also lost control of Ethiopia. There an independent state developed with its centre at Napata on the fourth cataract of the Nile. The native, but culturally strongly Egyptianized rulers of this kingdom soon began to reach into Egypt. With them there began the Ethiopian period (Twenty-fifth Dynasty, 751–656 BCE). The first of the Ethiopian rulers known to us succeeded in subjugating the region of Thebes without any noticeable use of force. The last of the Bubastides were unable to put up any resistance against him. Even in Lower Egypt their rule was only a nominal one. Nevertheless, in 730 BCE an anti-Ethiopian coalition developed among the minor princes of Lower Egypt. But the venture failed and King Pi (whose name was formerly read as Pianchi), son of Kashta, was able in a counter-attack to subjugate temporarily all parts of the land of Egypt. After his return to Napata, Lower Egypt broke up anew into a multiplicity of minor kingdoms, among them the ephemeral Twenty-fourth Dynasty of Tefnachte of Sais and of his son Bokchoris. This interim condition came to a temporary end in 715 BCE when Pi's son and successor, Shabaka (716–701 BCE), brought all of Egypt into final subjection to Ethiopia.

The new ordering of the conditions of the Near East emanated from Mesopotamia, though not from the old cultural centre of Babylonia, but from the Assyrians on the upper Tigris. The rise of the Neo-Assyrian kingdom to its eventual position as dominant power in the ancient Orient did not happen suddenly but proceeded step by step. The outcome was an empire of a completely new type, an incomparable power structure which determined the destinies of the Near East for almost half a millennium. In several campaigns which took him beyond the Assyrian homeland, Tiglath-pileser I (1112–1074 BCE) had already made the first move by intervening in the system of Aramaean national states which was coming into being in Upper Mesopotamia and Northern Syria. Lasting success, however, was not to be his because a clear political and military conception was missing for the time being, and therefore strongly established structures expressing Assyrian supremacy in the subjugated territories did not emerge.

However, from Adad-Nirari II (909–889 BCE) onwards the kings were no longer interested in a temporary acquisition of extensive territories but in a firm annexation of the conquered areas to the Assyrian state. This presupposed a strong central government with the king, as the delegated agent of the national god Asshur, standing at the head of a boundless host of civilian and military officials who were accountable to him. It also required, as an inescapable precondition for an imperialistic foreign policy, the formation of and attention to an effective standing army with chariot divisions and, for the first time, with cavalry. The Great King's troops were not strangers to any kind of soldierly cruelty. Whenever they met resistance they left behind dead communities and burned out countrysides.

The Assyrian military units remained for centuries the terror of the entire ancient Orient (see Isa. 5.26–29). What was new in its policy of expansion was that from Adad-Nirari II onwards Assyria did not leave the conquered areas – at first chiefly in Upper Mesopotamia – to themselves but incorporated them as provinces under Assyrian governors into the empire. The foundations were thus laid for the classical Assyrian provincial system which the rulers of the following centuries refined step by step. Among the kings of the ensuing period who increased the lustre of the Neo-Assyrian empire one needs to mention especially Asshurnasirpal II (883–859 BCE). He constructed, with a tremendous expenditure of effort, a new capital, Kalaḫ (*Nimrūd*), an Assyrian Babylon. His conquests were considerable, but he did not succeed at this time in any systematic extension of the Assyrian provincial structure to the areas outside Mesopotamia. Instead he continued in a grand manner to build up a ring of vassal countries around the Assyrian homeland. The princes of the territories with which he came in contact on his campaigns were forced to make regular payments of tribute and often to provide auxiliary troops as well. The political freedom of the vassal princes was restricted, to be sure, only as long as Assyria was strong enough to keep the reins firmly in hand. Whenever this was not the case, the vassals would quietly recover their independence and engage quite frequently in joint anti-Assyrian ventures which, in turn, would force the Assyrian king to undertake new campaigns.

The ring of vassal states was and remained for a while a source of insecurity for the Neo-Assyrian empire. Shalmaneser III (858–824 BCE) continued the internal and foreign policies of his father without any appreciable change. He, however, for the first time invaded those areas of central Syria which Assyrian expansion had hitherto left almost untouched. His chief antagonist there was the Aramaean kingdom of Damascus with which he carried on long and constantly changing wars. In 853 BCE, in the battle of Qarqar on the Orontes, he fought a coalition of Syrian minor princes who were led by Damascus and Hamath and in which Ahab of Israel also participated. To the north, he encountered the kingdom of Urartu which was expanding energetically under Sardur I and which, in the following period, developed into one of Assyria's main adversaries and not infrequently made common cause against Assyria with the rulers of northern and central Syria.

Under Adad-Nirari III (809–782 BCE) the ring of vassal states was extended. In the meantime, however, the earlier friendly relationship to neighbouring Babylonia had been shattered, thus raising a problem with which the Assyrian rulers were never quite able to cope. Babylonia was and remained an uncertain element in the Neo-Assyrian empire, particularly because it was never integrated into the Assyrian provincial system. In the rugged warriors from the north there lived a reverence for neighbouring Babylonia as the mother of their culture and morality, their language, writing, and religion. They simply could not apply to Babylonia the same standards which they applied to any of the other border regions. The Assyrian rulers acknowledged the Babylonian kingdom and assured their control over it either by according it vassal status or by ascending the Babylonian throne themselves ('personal union') or by appointing viceroys of Assyrian blood according to the principle of secundogeniture. In every instance Babylonia was accorded a special status and remained for Assyria an object of respectful admiration or bitter hatred.

This was the state of affairs when Tiglath-pileser III (745–727 BCE) ascended the Assyrian throne. After the start made by his predecessors, it was his lot to lead the Neo-Assyrian empire to the pinnacle of power and to bring it to its completion in concept and system if not in territory. On the basis of a central administrative reform, wherein the great provinces were sacrificed in favour of smaller administrative districts, he devised a new kind of imperialistic foreign policy, the effectiveness of which cannot be emphasized strongly enough. It was no longer a matter of tying the neighbouring smaller states to Assyria in the form of a more or less loose vassal relationship, but rather of occupying them once and for all. He developed a system of destroying step by step the political independence of these petty states for the purpose of incorporating them into the provincial structure of the Assyrian empire. The stages in this system may be described as follows.

First stage: The first level of Assyrian domination was based on the establishment of a vassal relationship by a demonstration of Assyrian military might. The vassal was subjected to a binding commitment to a regular, usually annual, payment of tribute and to the furnishing of auxiliary troops. Up to this point there is almost no difference between Tiglath-pileser's procedures and those of his predecessors. Right at the outset of his reign he was able to take over a considerable number of petty states which found themselves on this first stage of vassalage.

Second stage: When an anti-Assyrian conspiracy was proved or suspected, there followed immediate military intervention, the removal of the disloyal vassal, and the appointment of a new prince, loyal to Assyria and, when possible, taken from the native royal house. Furthermore, not infrequently there were drastic territorial reductions. Areas severed from the territory were either transformed into Assyrian provinces or turned over as fiefs to vassals who were loyal to Assyria. Finally, there was the deportation of portions of the upper class to distant parts of the empire. Naturally, at this stage the political and military pressure on the dependent vassal state rose appreciably. The obligations in regard to tribute were raised and foreign policy of the vassal state was kept under control.

Third stage: At the slightest sign of any effort directed against Assyria there was renewed military intervention, removal of the vassal, liquidation of the political independence of the region in question, and the establishment of an Assyrian province with an Assyrian governor and the necessary staff of officials. In this connection there occurred a deportation of the native upper class and the introduction of a foreign one in its place. The latter measure had the purpose of depriving the indigenous population of its leadership and of thus rendering it politically ineffective. Moreover, Assyria hoped that the mixed population, which had thus been brought into being, would be more governable.

It is obvious that Tiglath-pileser III and his successors could not adhere to this system in every instance. Particular configurations required exceptions to the rule and a sufficient elasticity in Assyria's foreign policy. When in 743 BCE, for example, an anti-Assyrian coalition of the north Syrian petty states of Arpad, Milid, Gurgum, and Kummuḫ under the leadership of Sardur III of Urartu had to be suppressed, Tiglath-pileser III did not intervene, contrary to his usual practice, in the dynastic affairs of the vassals but was satisfied with territorial reductions. The reasons for this are not known. A by-passing of one of the stages of vassalage could also occur (e.g., Damascus from the first to the third stage in 732 BCE).

The progress of the expansion of the Neo-Assyrian empire over nearly the entire Near East cannot be described here in detail. In any case, that was the result, and it was a result which also decisively shaped the destinies of the Syrian–Palestinian land-bridge. To be sure, porous and leaky spots remained in this immense imperial structure, especially on its borders. The special position of Babylonia has already been mentioned. The old, wealthy ports and commercial cities on the Phoenician coast were never converted into provinces as long as the Assyrian empire existed. They retained their relative political independence at the first stage of vassalage, probably above all because the Assyrians did not want to endanger their extensive commercial connections but wanted to use them themselves. In the south, too, Assyria allowed a number of semi-independent states to exist, even though rebellions broke out there again and again and forced the Assyrian troops to intervene. These included Judah, the city-states of the Philistine pentapolis (with the exception of Ashdod which temporarily became a province), and the border states of Ammon, Moab, and Edom east of the Jordan. They were all viewed as buffer states against Egypt, for Assyria tried to avoid all direct contact between its empire and Egypt. In the days of Tiglath-pileser III and of his immediate successors these tactics represented prudent self-limitation in view of the growing might of the Twenty-fifth Ethiopian Dynasty. But when this began to wane, Esarhaddon (680–669 BCE) considered the time right for a conquest of Egypt (during two campaigns in 673 and 671 BCE) in order thereby to place the territorial capstone on the edifice of the huge Assyrian empire. Yet, this incomparable consummation of Assyrian imperial might already carried within itself the seed of its own decay and constituted the turning-point in the drama of Assyrian history. Assyria had now reached the limits of its possibilities, not at the time of its first impetuous expansion but following a century of debilitating effort to preserve and secure the internal and external stability of the empire. The conquest of Egypt was like a euphoria which immediately preceded the decline. The last great Assyrian ruler, Asshurbanipal (669–627 BCE) was forced to take bitter account of that decline during his long reign. He represented a type of king on the Assyrian throne who was different from his predecessors. He was an educated person with an appreciation for literature and science, for the cultivation of the arts and for those things which make life pleasant. His library with thousands of cuneiform tablets, which the excavators of Nineveh recovered, has rightly achieved world fame. This does not mean that Asshurbanipal was unwarlike. On the contrary, he fought ceaselessly, and this was necessary because the empire was forced more and more to go onto the defensive. An empire, however, which is no longer on the offensive has basically ceased to exist, even when its external stability can still be maintained for a while. Asshurbanipal was unable to prevent Egypt from regaining its independence in 655 BCE under Psammetichus I, the founder of the Twenty-sixth Saite Dynasty. Between 652 and 648 BCE, there raged the unfortunate civil war with Shamash-shum-ukin, the viceroy of Babylonia. Asshurbanipal remained in control of the situation, it is true, but the empire emerged from the conflict greatly weakened. Moreover, there was continuous fighting on the borders against unruly vassals and the nomads of the Syrian–Arabian desert. With Asshurbanipal the Assyrian era in the Near East came to its end. When he died in 627 BCE it was only a question of a few years before newly developing powers were to complete the ruin of the Assyrian world empire.

§5. THE SYRO-EPHRAIMITE WAR AND THE END OF THE KINGDOM OF ISRAEL

A. **Alt**, 'Hosea 5, 8–6, 6. Ein Krieg und seine Folgen in prophetischer Beleuchtung', *NKZ* XXX, 1919, 537–68 = his *KS* II, 1953, 163–87; idem, 'Das System der assyrischen Provinzen auf dem Boden des Reiches Israel', *ZDPV* LII, 1929, 220–42 = his *KS* II, 188–205; idem, 'Tiglathpilesers III. erster Feldzug nach Palästina', *KS* II, 150–62; J. **Begrich**, 'Der syrisch-ephraimitische Krieg und seine weltpolitischen Zusammenhänge', *ZDMG* LXXXIII, 1929, 213–37 = his *Gesammelte Studien zum Alten Testament*, ed. W. Zimmerli, TB 21, 1964, 99–120; R. **Borger**, 'Das Ende des ägyptischen Feldherrn Sib'e = Sô'', *JNES* XIX, 1960, 49–53; H. **Donner**, *Israel unter den Völkern: Die Stellung der klassischen Propheten des 8. Jahrhunderts v. Chr. zur Aussenpolitik der Könige von Israel und Juda*, SVT 11, 1964; idem, 'Der Feind aus dem Norden: Topographische und archäologische Erwägungen zu Jes. 10, 27b–34', *ZDPV* LXXXIV, 1968, 46–54; O. **Eissfeldt**, '"Juda" und "Judäa" als Bezeichnungen nordsyrischer Bereiche', *FF* XXVIII, 1964,

20–25 = his *KS* IV, 1968, 121–31; H. **Goedicke**, 'The End of "So, King of Egypt"', *BASOR* CLXXI, 1963, 64–6; L. D. **Levine**, 'Two Neo-Assyrian Stelae from Iran', *Art and Archaeology, Occasional Paper XXIII*, Toronto: Royal Ontario Museum 1972, 11–24, 64–81; idem, 'Menahem and Tiglath-Pileser: A New Synchronism', *BASOR* CCVI, 1972, 40–2; N. **Na'aman**, 'Sennacherib's "Letter to God" on His Campaign to Judah', *BASOR* CCXIV, 1974, 25–39; B. **Oded**, 'The Historical Background of the Syro-Ephraimite War Reconsidered', *CBQ* XXXIV, 1972, 153–65; R. **Sayed**, 'Tefnakht ou Horus *SI3* – (*IB*)', *VT* XX, 1970, 116–18; R. B. Y. **Scott**, 'Isaiah', *IB* V, 245f.; H. **Tadmor**, 'Azriyau of Yaudi', *SH* VIII, 1961, 232–71; idem, 'The Campaigns of Sargon II of Assur: A Chronological-Historical Study', *JCS* XII, 1958, 22–40, 77–100; E. **Vogt**, 'Samaria a. 722 et 720 ab Assyriis capta', *Biblica* XXXIX, 1958, 535–41; idem, 'Die Texte Tiglath-Pilesers III. über die Eroberung Palästinas', *Biblica* XLV, 1964, 348–54; M. **Weippert**, 'Menahem von Israel und seine Zeitgenossen in einer Steleninschrift des assyrischen Königs Tiglathpileser III aus dem Iran', *ZDPV* LXXXIX, 1973, 26–53; D. J. **Wiseman**, 'Two Historical Inscriptions from Nimrud', *Iraq* XIII, 1951, 21–6.

The situation as far as the sources for the time span between 747 and 722 BCE are concerned is not unfavourable, even though it is not as good as a historian would wish. We have no contemporary historical presentations of the main events of this period, the Syro-Ephraimitic War and the conquest of Samaria by the Assyrians, but are forced to rely on Deuteronomistic excerpts from the royal annals and on the inscriptions of the Neo-Assyrian Great Kings. The reports these provide do, however, back up, interpret, and complement one another. Another body of source material needs to be included, although sufficient consideration is not usually given to it, namely, the oracles of the prophets Isaiah, Hosea, and Micah in so far as they belong to this period. The reason they have been underestimated is easily understood, for prophetic oracles represent historical sources of a peculiar type. As a rule they require interpretation before they can be used as historical evidence.

For the period of somewhat more than a decade before the outbreak of the Syro-Ephraimitic War – except for short passages in the texts of Tiglath-pileser III – the only materials at our disposal are the Deuteronomistic excerpts from the annals of the kings of Israel and Judah (II Kings 15.8–26). Nor do the Old Testament sources exactly flow copiously for the decade which followed the war up to the conquest of Samaria. They consist of II Kings 17.1–6; 18.9–12; the Deuteronomistic tract in II Kings 17.7–41; with appropriate caution, the prophetic oracles in Isa. 9.8–10.4; 5.25–30; 28.1–6; Hos.

7.8–12; 9.11–14; 11.1–7; 12.1; Micah 1.2–16 and, finally, reports in the inscriptions of Shalmaneser V (727–722 BCE) and Sargon II (721–705 BCE).

Our knowledge of the Syro-Ephraimitic War itself is based on three different groups of literary sources: (*a*) Deuteronomistic excerpts from the annals of the kings of Israel and Judah. They do not provide connected accounts but are distributed among the passages which pertain to the different kings of the northern and southern kingdoms (II Kings 15.29f.; 15.37; 16.5–9); (*b*) prophetic oracles, in their present context not in chronological order (Isa. 7.1–17; 8.1–15; 10.27b–34; 17.1–11; Hos. 5.1f.; 5.8–6.6; 8.7–10); and (*c*) brief reports about the end of the war and its results in the annals and minor inscriptions of Tiglath-pileser III (see *AR* I, 269–96 and *ANET*, 282–4).

It is worth observing that the chronology of the Judaean kings during this particular period of time is extremely uncertain. There are various reasons for this; among these are the illness of Uzziah and the resulting co-regency of Jotham (II Kings 15.1–7) and also the contradictory notices about the year of the death of Ahaz and the accession of Hezekiah (II Kings 16.19f.; 18.1). The details need not be enlarged upon.

After the death of Jeroboam II (747 BCE) the dynasty which Jehu had founded drew inexorably to a close in the northern kingdom of Israel. First of all, Jeroboam's son Zechariah ascended the throne. After a reign of six months he was eliminated by a usurper named Shallum. The latter, in turn, died at the hands of a man who proved to be the strongest figure during the disturbances, Menahem (747–738 BCE) from Tirzah (*Tell el Fār'a*). In the course of his reign the northern kingdom returned to a condition of relative quiet (II Kings 15.8–22). However, it was the lull before the storm. This was the time when the Neo-Assyrian empire under Tiglath-pileser III developed into a power factor of hitherto unknown proportions. The states in the southern part of the Palestinian–Syrian land-bridge were bound soon to feel its effects. In the first years of his reign Tiglath-pileser was occupied in the east and north of his empire. But as early as 738 BCE he intervened for the first time in central Syria in a major way. He succeeded in conquering the Aramaean state of Hamath, which only a century earlier had been one of the main opponents of Shalmaneser III at Qarqar on the Orontes, and incorporated it for the most part into his provincial system. This success had considerable effect on the neighbouring petty states, which discovered overnight that they were close neighbours of the Assyrian colossus and were now thrown into a panic. A whole series of states in Asia Minor and northern Syria, the coastal cities of Byblos and Tyre, and the majority of the central Syrian kingdoms hurried to make contributions to the Great King and to assure him of their submission. They thereby established or renewed the first stage of vassalage. According to the annals of Tiglath-pileser III they also included *Me-ni-ḫi-im-me Sa-me-ri-na-a-a* (= Menahem of Samaria) and *Ra-ḫi-a-nu Ša-imērišu-a-a* (Raṣyān of Aram–Damascus; incorrectly vocalized in the Old Testament as Reṣīn, II Kings 15.37; 16.5f.; Isa. 7.1–8). A recently published stela of Tiglath-pileser, possibly from western Iran, also provides a reference to the receipt of tribute from Menahem along with other kings (see Levine, Weippert). Both states, Damascus and Israel, brought about through their submission a renewal of the first stage of vassalage in which, at least theoretically, they had remained since the days of Shalmaneser III. Menahem may also have been guided by a secondary aim of seeking to strengthen his unstable kingdom with the help of the authority of the Assyrian overlord. In order to raise the amount of the contribution he invented the poll-tax (II Kings 15.19f.) and distributed the required sum, 1,000 talents of silver, among the landowners who were obligated to military service, so that each was liable for 50 shekels. There were, therefore, approximately 60,000 such landowners in the northern kingdom of that day.

The southern kingdom of Judah appears for the time being to have remained untouched by these events. To be sure, there has been a dispute since the beginning of our century about whether a certain *Az-ri-ya-a-u Ya-u-da-a-a*, who it was assumed was mentioned in Tiglath-pileser's annals as an ally of Hamath, might be identical with Azariah/Uzziah of Judah or not. Recently, Naʿaman has shown conclusively that the fragment presumably mentioning Azriau king of Yaudi actually belongs to the time of Sennacherib and refers not to Azariah but to Hezekiah. In Tiglath-pileser's annals there are two references to an Azariah (in line 123 as Az-ri-a-[u] and in line 131 as Az-ri-ja-a-ú) but neither of these make any reference to his country. Thus the Azriau of Tiglath-pileser's annals and Azariah of the Bible should be regarded as two different individuals. Azriau's country cannot, at the present, be determined. The other areas named in the text of the annals generally lie in northern and central Syria. It is therefore likely that Azriau was from a petty state in northern or central Syria of which otherwise nothing is known. One cannot exclude the possibility that his country was the north Syrian state of Ya'udi-Sam'al from which two Phoenician (*KAI* 24–5, ca. 825

BCE) and eight Aramaic inscriptions (*KAI* 214–21, ca. 750 – ca. 730 BCE) were discovered at Sindjerli. A king named Azriau, however, is not attested there.

In the following four years Syria and Palestine enjoyed peace, for Tiglath-pileser was once again tied down militarily in the north and south of his domain. However, for the year 734 BCE the Assyrian eponym list (*ANET*, 272) records a campaign *a-na Pi-liš-ta*, 'to Philistia'. More detailed information about this campaign is contained in the inscription ND 400 from Nineveh (see Wiseman). It is unfortunately so fragmentary that its restoration and interpretation are difficult undertakings. None the less, one can perceive that the military action of the Great King was especially directed – though the reasons for it are not known – against the Philistine city of Gaza whose king, Ḫanūnu, fled to Egypt and abandoned his city without a struggle when the Assyrians approached. In Israel, following the short reign of Pekahiah (spring 737–736 BCE), a usurper named Pekah (spring 735–732 BCE) had come to power. Some have considered it possible that Tiglath-pileser may already in 734 BCE have detached Israel's coastal zone and incorporated it as the province Dū'ru into the Assyrian provincial system, perhaps in order to secure the Palestinian maritime region as a passageway to Philistia. But one cannot exclude the possibility that the province Dū'ru was established later, following the Syro-Ephraimite War. In any event, Tiglath-pileser drew from his drive against Gaza certain noteworthy military and political achievements and established in the city of *Naḥal Muṣur* on the *Wādi el-ʿArīš* a remote military strong point which may have been intended to serve him at some possible future date as a springboard to Egypt. Tiglath-pileser's actions in southern Palestine were different in other respects from his usual practice. He pardoned the fugitive city-ruler of Gaza after his fairly early return from Egypt and reinstated him in his privileges, i.e., he decided to forgo placing Gaza on the second stage of vassalage. His political purpose is readily seen since a country in the second stage of vassalage, separated from the Assyrian provincial territory by a ring of vassal states in the first stage, would have been difficult to control effectively.

All these events occurred in the immediate vicinity of the southern kingdom of Judah. They demonstrated to the Davidides for the first time at close range how Assyrians dealt with any opposition they encountered. The effects of such visual education quickly materialized. When in the late spring or summer of 734 BCE Raṣyān of Damascus and Pekah of Israel attempted to draw the Davidide Ahaz into an anti-Assyrian coalition, the latter met this demand with stubborn opposition. This led to the Syro-Ephraimite War during which the course was set for the future political development of both Palestinian states.

However well-known the main events of the war might be, the reconstruction of the details which help to complete the total picture and to deepen our understanding of it is difficult. Since the fundamental discussion by Begrich (1929) almost all studies up to the present suffer both from overestimating the 'international inter-relationships' of the Syro-Ephraimite War and from underestimating the value of the prophetic traditions as historical sources. With respect to the latter point, it must of course be admitted that difficulties in interpretation force one to formulate hypotheses and that it is possible, therefore, to hold differing views. Should one succeed, however, in determining at least the relative chronology of the oracles of Isaiah and of Hosea and in relating them to the course of events which is known from other sources (see Donner, 1964), then an unusually high degree of probability can be attained.

First of all the main outlines. Raṣyān of Aram-Damascus and Pekah of Israel, who were both in the first stage of vassalage as it had been re-established in 738 BCE, deemed the time right, for reasons unknown, to unite in an anti-Assyrian coalition and to throw off their Assyrian shackles. They took pains to enlarge their not very extensive political and military base of action and attempted, apparently by diplomatic means at first, to persuade Ahaz of Judah to take part in the undertaking they were planning. The Davidide, however, not only saw no grounds for getting himself and Judah involved in an anti-Assyrian adventure, but from the outset and for good reason also regarded the allies' chances of success as unfavourable. Raṣyān and Pekah, however, believed that under no circumstances could they do without Judah as a partner in the coalition. So when Ahaz rejected their offer, they decided on a highly irregular action. They collected troops on the territory of the northern kingdom of Israel and prepared to advance with their armed might against Jerusalem, not for the purpose of carrying the war into all of Judah but in order to depose the obstinate Davidide and to place a pliant Aramaean named Ben-Ṭāb'ēl on the Judaean throne. The military forces of Judah were undoubtedly to be spared as much as possible, since they would be urgently needed later on against Assyria. Because of this Ahaz now found himself in serious trouble, for he could foresee that Jerusalem would not be able to withstand a siege by the two attackers for any length of time. In this situation he decided – against the urgent advice of the prophet Isaiah – to conjure up those spirits from which Judah was never able to free itself. He sent a contribution to no less a person than the Assyrian Great King himself and requested his aid against Raṣyān and Pekah. This step was similar to the one which Asa of Judah had taken in his day in order to get rid of the pressure exerted by Baasha (I Kings 15.16–22). In so doing Ahaz moved voluntarily to the first stage of vassalage. Tiglath-pileser immediately took advantage of the chance to nip in the bud a coalition directed against him. He advanced with his armies from the north against the allies and forced military action upon them long before they expected it. Raṣyān and Pekah were obliged to remove their troops at once from Jerusalem in order to hurl them against the Assyrians. But this obviously was not of much use, for the Assyrian armies were in the long run irresistible. Even so, Raṣyān was able to maintain himself for a while in Damascus. Finally, the city was taken by storm in 732 BCE and Tiglath-pileser decided to render this dangerous opponent harmless then and there. He passed over the second stage of vassalage and turned Aram-Damascus into an Assyrian province. He also made short shrift of Pekah, who was the weaker partner in the coalition. Tiglath-pileser probably appeared in Israel as early as 733 BCE, annexed Galilee and the area east of the Jordan and established both regions as the Assyrian provinces Magidū (= Megiddo) and Gal'azu (= Gilead). Pekah was restricted to the rump state of Ephraim, i.e., to the mountain country of Ephraim and of Samaria. Tiglath-pileser deported the urban upper class of the conquered territories to Assyria. The native rural population remained and received, in keeping with Assyrian practice, a new foreign upper class. Tiglath-pileser had no need to intervene in the dynastic relationships of the northern kingdom, for soon after his defeat Pekah fell victim to a conspiracy arising from the ranks of the pro-Assyrian party in Samaria. The head of the conspiracy, a man named Hoshea, was confirmed by Tiglath-pileser as a dependent vassal king of the rump state of Ephraim. The northern kingdom thereby entered the second stage of vassalage in its relationship to Assyria.

So much for the events in general. There is, however, no agreement about how they happened in detail or how they are to be distributed over the available time period. There can, of course, be no doubt regarding the date of the end of the Syro-Ephraimite War, for it coincides with the final defeat of Damascus in 732 BCE. Its beginnings, however, are shrouded in obscurity. They can scarcely have begun earlier than Pekah's accession to the throne, i.e., earlier than 735 BCE (734 BCE according to Begrich); yet they must be placed before the Assyrian siege of Damascus in 733 BCE. Now Tiglath-pileser's campaign against Gaza in the spring or summer of 734 BCE occurred in the middle of this designated period of time. Begrich resolves the chronological difficulty thus created by placing the onset of the Syro-Ephraimite War shortly before the Philistine campaign, i.e., at least before June/July 735 BCE, and by explaining the Philistine campaign as the start of the Assyrian punitive expedition against the participants in the anti-Assyrian coalition. According to Begrich, the coalition must have included the Philistine coastal cities along with Damascus and Israel, and perhaps also the border states east of the Jordan, with Egypt undoubtedly in the background. Tiglath-pileser wanted by his surprise campaign into the coastal plain in 734 BCE to prevent any intervention by the Egyptians which, if it came at all, could be expected to come from that direction. According to this reconstruction, the flight of Ḫanūnu of Gaza and the apparently uncontested surrender of his city was strategy on the part of the coalition, intended to mobilize Egyptian military aid in the moment of greatest threat. Thus the campaign against Damascus in 733 BCE would have originated from the Philistine coastal plain where the Assyrian army spent the winter of 734/733 BCE.

There are some problems, however, with this reconstruction. The Assyrian records, especially inscription ND 400 which was not discovered until 1950, contain no indication whatever that the Philistine campaign of 734 BCE had anything to do with the anti-Assyrian coalition which brought about the Syro-Ephraimite War. Nor is anything said about Egypt's participation. Begrich's opinion that Ahaz could have turned to Egypt for help during the war does not hold, especially if Egypt had been a partner in the anti-Assyrian coalition, as Begrich suggests. A more likely explanation for Ahaz's failure to turn to Egypt for help is the fact that intervention by Egypt against Israel and Damascus would have, in all probability, turned the Judaean countryside into a field of battle. Furthermore, such an intervention would have prematurely attracted Assyria's attention southward because of the possible jeopardy to her interests. Obviously, this would not have served Ahaz's purpose since his only concern was to bring about the departure of the coalition's forces from Jerusalem.

Another problem with Begrich's solution is that the Assyrian reinstatement of Ḫanūnu of Gaza would have been a strange action if only recently he had sought to obtain Egyptian military aid. Also, the time from Pekah's accession to the throne in 735 BCE at the earliest until the Philistine campaign in June/July of 734 BCE is too short a time span to allow for all the events involved: the negotiations which produced the coalition between Damascus and Israel, the first diplomatic contacts of the coalition with Judah, the actual advance of the Syro-Ephraimite troops against Jerusalem, and finally the Assyrian advance. In addition, it is quite unlikely that the Syro-Ephraimite War would have coincided with the Assyrian campaign in Philistia in 734 BCE. One can scarcely believe that the coalition would have taken action at a time when the Assyrians were already in the area. This would have been a political and strategic blunder that would certainly have attracted the attention of the Assyrians in the coastal plain.

For these reasons the only period left for the Syro-Ephraimite War is the period after 734 BCE. The sudden appearance of the Assyrians in the Palestinian coastal plain (possibly even connected with some loss of territory) may have strengthened the anti-Assyrian mood of the royal court in Samaria so that the negotiators from Damascus found willing ears for their plans. The events of the Syro-Ephraimite War thus occurred during the time period between spring/summer 734 BCE and spring/summer 733 BCE, a whole year into which it is possible to fit satisfactorily the prophetic traditions of Isaiah and Hosea.

There is no reason to date, with Begrich, the Philistine campaign of Tiglath-pileser to the end of the spring of 734 BCE. The Assyrian army's mobility which the entire Near East had come to dread and the undoubtedly only short delay occasioned by the advance through Phoenicia and Israel make it appear likely, rather, that the Great King arrived in the Palestinian coastal plain in April/May 734 BCE at the latest. This and the time immediately following is the period in which there ocurred both the negotiations between Damascus and Israel about a coalition and the first diplomatic contacts with Judah. One cannot, of course, exclude the possibility that these negotiations might have started earlier. Presumably they would then have been interrupted during the Philistine campaign. This provides the context for Isaiah 17.1–11, a saying in which the prophet sees the projected anti-Assyrian venture as condemned to catastrophic failure. Soon the allies reached the decision to use force in displacing the Davidic dynasty and to compel Judah to join the coalition. The Aramaeans dispatched military contingents into the territory of the northern kingdom of Israel for the purpose of advancing against Jerusalem in concert with Israelite units (Isa. 7.1–

16). This concentration of troops could, however, only take place after the departure of the Assyrians from the coastal plain, for it must have been clear to the allies that any military operations while the Assyrians were still present in Palestine would challenge Assyria's interests at an inopportune time. The whole point was to compel Judah to participate in the coalition without having to take, if possible, any immediate military risks. Isaiah 7.1–16 is to be dated, accordingly, to an earlier or later period in the months of May to July 734 BCE. Ahaz was at that time awaiting the impending attack of the allies and was also probably already considering calling on Assyria for help. The latter involved going against the advice of Isaiah, who regarded it not only as a shameful lack of faith in Yahweh but also apparently believed that the attack by Aram and Israel would not take place. Isaiah 7.4: 'Fear not and may your heart not be faint because of these two stumps of smouldering firebrands, despite the burning anger of Raṣyān and of the Aramaeans and of the son of Remaliah!' Similarly also Isaiah 7.16: 'For before the lad learns to reject the evil and to choose the good, the land before whose two kings you are in terror will be deserted.' Had the Assyrian punitive expedition begun soon after the conversation between prophet and king as reported in Isaiah 7.1–16, then two things would be incomprehensible. (1) Ahaz would already have sent Tiglath-pileser his call for help in 734 BCE. Why, then, did the Great King wait until 733 BCE before doing anything? This is not what one would have expected of him nor would it have been wise. (2) In view of the clearly recognizable signs of threatening danger, could the prophet Isaiah be expected not only to minimize the military ventures of the allies (Isa. 7.4) but also specifically to count on a longer duration of the tensions (Isa. 7.16)? One can scarcely believe him capable of that, for he was a man of unusually clear political judgment and of great far-sightedness. For these reasons it is necessary to assume that the march of Raṣyān and Pekah against Jerusalem occurred only shortly before the intervention of the Assyrians, in other words, in 733 BCE. This time differential is also indicated by another, though uncertain and disputed, observation. In Isaiah 7.14–16, the birth of a child is announced to whom the name Immanuel (= With us is God) is to be given. To all appearances the name is a sign that Yahweh would be with Judah and that there was no reason for despair in the presence of the danger. This child whose birth is imminent might have been a son of Isaiah. Now in Isaiah 8.1–4 another son of the prophet is mentioned who receives the name 'Speed to the booty, Rob soon' (*Mahēr šālāl ḥāš baz*). This too still occurs against the background of the Syro-Ephraimite War. Unless one assumes that both children are born to different mothers, then it must be conceded that the birth of 'Speed to the booty, Rob soon' could at the earliest only have occurred 10 or 11 months after the birth of Immanuel, that is between March and May 733 BCE. However that may be, one should consider the possibility that the plans of the allies did not get under way in the early summer of 734 BCE. Reasons for this are not indicated anywhere, but several possibilities come to mind which might explain a delay. The year was no longer just beginning. If Jerusalem could not be taken in a surprise attack it would be necessary to prepare for a fairly long siege. Perhaps the military means were not sufficient for this or perhaps the season was too far gone and there was thus reason to be apprehensive about an inconclusive ending to the enterprise because the soldiers would want to get home to their fields. It needs also to be kept in mind that the coalition had come into being rapidly if not actually precipitously. Perhaps political or strategic differences of opinion consequently developed between the allies regarding their concerted actions. The details can no longer be cleared up. In any case, the plan was taken up again in the spring of 733 BCE and immediately put into effect. Isaiah 10.27b–34 reports the advance against Jerusalem of an invading army. Commentators have generally related this invasion to the movement of Assyrians against Jerusalem during the days of Hezekiah. However, and this is still a disputed point, this text may refer to the movement of the Syro-Ephraimite troops against Jerusalem and thus belong to the context under discussion (see Scott and Donner, 1964, 30–8; 1968). The allies did not advance against Jerusalem by way of the main road along the watershed of the mountains, as one might have expected, but on a considerably more difficult side-road to the east. The purpose of this arduous march was to go round the Judaean border fortress of Mizpah (*Tell en Naṣbe*) and thus to reach the main road to Jerusalem south of the fortress. Isaiah in this dangerous situation does not anticipate any longer that an attack will not occur (as earlier in Isa. 7.4) but he does expect a miraculous intervention by Yahweh on behalf of Ahaz. From this one can conclude that the policy of union with Assyria, so sharply condemned by Isaiah, had not yet gone into effect. If this is so, then Ahaz seems to have hesitated up to the last moment to dispatch the embassy to Tiglath-pileser. It was only when he saw no other alternative that he decided to adopt this plan of action. The following passages presuppose this situation: Isa. 8.5–8; 8.9f. (?); 8.11–15; Hos. 5.8f. A week can scarcely have passed before the Assyrian military units began their march. When the news of the advance reached the allies they had to withdraw their fighting forces from Jerusalem. The Judaeans pursued and conquered a part of Ephraim's territory (Hos. 5.10). Within the interval of perhaps only a few weeks, between May and June of 733 BCE, the collapse of the coalition occurred. Tiglath-pileser advanced against Damascus and Israel. Whereas he was held down at Damascus until 732 BCE by Raṣyān's defensive strength, his efforts against Israel immediately had the desired result. The territories of Galilee and Gilead were cut off, transformed into Assyrian provinces, and thus the northern kingdom of Israel was restricted to the rump state of Ephraim in the second stage of vassalage. This outcome is presupposed in Hosea 5.1 f.; 5.11; 8.7–10; 5.12–14; 5.15–6.6.

After the conquest of Damascus in 732 BCE, the situation in the Syro-Palestinian system of petty states remained unchanged for a time. The interventions by Tiglath-pileser III in the structure and territorial order of Palestine and central Syria, as a consequence of the Syro-Ephraimite War, had a lasting and paralysing effect on the vassals and their aspirations for emancipation. The quiet after the storm had set in. This was also true of Judah and the rump state of Ephraim, both of which remained in a vassal relationship with Assyria and made no attempt to restore the earlier situation. This is how things remained at first. Even after the death of Tiglath-pileser III and the accession to the throne of his successor, Shalmaneser V, the satellite relationship of both countries continued without trouble. Neither Ahaz nor Hoshea succumbed to the temptation to take political advantage of the crisis situation brought on in the Assyrian empire by the death of Tiglath-pileser.

In the year 724 BCE, however, Hoshea of Ephraim decided that the time had come to renounce his allegiance to Assyria. He discontinued the annual tribute payments to Shalmaneser V and began to establish diplomatic contact with Egypt, always relatively Assyria's most important opponent (II Kings 17.4). Egypt at this time was characterized by the rising power of the Twenty-fifth Ethiopian Dynasty, even though the Ethiopians had not yet succeeded in bringing all of Egypt under their rule. In the Nile Delta there were several relatively independent petty kingdoms, among them the so-called Twenty-fourth Dynasty of Tefnachte of Sais and his son Bokchoris. It is no longer possible to identify the Pharaoh with whom Hoshea conducted his negotiations. Most likely it was not with the Ethiopians, who were geographically at a considerable distance, but with one or more of the kings in the Delta. According to

II Kings 17.4 it was 'Sō', king of Egypt'. It was thought by nearly all scholars until 1960 that the name 'Sō'' (vocalized possible as Sewe) could be identified with the name of an Egyptian commander-in-chief who is mentioned often in the inscriptions of Sargon II as *Sib'-e-(e) tar-ta-nu Mu-ṣu-ri*, 'Sib'u (or Sib'e), general of Egypt'. But this equation had to be abandoned when Borger proved that the syllabic reading of the cuneiform sign SIPA as *sib* did not exist at this particular time. For this reason one must read ideographically, '$Rē'ē^{c-(e)}$' = the genitive of $Rē'û$ ('shepherd'), as the personal name of a man who is otherwise unknown. The name Sō' remains unexplained, unless it is to be regarded as an inaccurate rendering of the Egyptian appellation *nj-św.t⟩nšw.t⟩nšw*, 'king'. The so-called 'Horus name' of Tefnachte of Sais (*šj3-3b*) can scarcely be taken into consideration (see Sayed) for Pharaohs were never called by their Horus names outside Egypt.

In any case, Hoshea's action was a grave political mistake. It is hard to understand what might have motivated Hoshea to attempt a rebellion in 724 BCE of all times. The situation in the Neo-Assyrian empire was stable. There was not the slightest sign of any internal or external political crisis. Hoshea must have realized that he would have to deal with Assyria's entire and undivided might. Furthermore, he did not have behind him a unified Egypt which might have served as a counter balance to Assyria. One cannot tell whether and in what number other south Palestinian states participated in the conspiracy. They also would not have represented a sufficient increase in military strength to promise success to the venture. Hoshea did not have the slightest chance. It is conceivable that the anti-Assyrian party in the court at Samaria forced his hand, threatened to overthrow him, and thus compelled him to shift to an anti-Assyrian course.

What had to come, came without delay. Shalmaneser V did not hesitate to suppress with violence the movement directed against him. He succeeded in ways not known to us in capturing king Hoshea himself. Samaria was able to hold out for about two more years against the Assyrian siege. It was not until the late summer or early autumn of 722 BCE – shortly before the death of Shalmaneser V and the beginning of the reign of Sargon II – that the city succumbed to the Assyrian onslaught. Sargon II later boasted a number of times in his inscriptions of having conquered Samaria (see *ANET*, 284f.), but it is to be taken as certain that the city had already fallen under Shalmaneser. The area of the rump state of Ephraim was made into the Assyrian province of Samerīna, the fourth and last province on the territory of the kingdom of Israel. Here we find the origin of the use of the name 'Samaria' as a designation for a region. The upper class was deported to Babylonia and Media (II Kings 17.6) and, following Assyrian practice, a new upper class was brought in from Babylonia and perhaps also from Syria (II Kings 17.24). As time went on the newcomers mingled with the native population. In their religious policies the Assyrians relaxed the reins. The new upper class brought along their gods (II Kings 17.29–31), while the Israelite farmers continued to worship Yahweh. To be sure, the priesthoods of the national shrines at Bethel and Dan had been exiled. When a lion plague broke out the cause for it was thought to be the neglect of the cult of the god of the land. Sargon II thereupon allowed a deported priest of Yahweh to return to Bethel (II Kings 17.25–8) who resumed and carried on the Yahweh cult. Later on groups of foreign colonists came into the land on two different occasions, the first under Esarhaddon (Ezra 4.2; Isa. 7.8b) and the second under Asshurbanipal (Ezra 4.10). This changed the make-up of the population even more.

Thus the last remnant of the northern kingdom of Israel ceased to exist. This kingdom, which earlier had been one of the centres of political power play on the Syrian–Palestinian land-bridge, now dropped out for a long time as an influential factor. The prophet Micah from Moresheth-Gath recognized with remarkable discernment that this development would not be without consequences for the neighbouring southern kingdom of Judah. He lamented over the downfall of Samaria:

> Therefore will I lament and wail, will go barefoot and naked,
> Will raise a lamentation like the jackals and mourning cries like the ostriches,
> For its wound is incurable, for it reaches all the way to Judah; it knocks on the gate of my people, as far as Jerusalem (Micah 1.8f.).

VIII

JUDAH AND THE EXILE

§1. GENERAL BACKGROUND AND SOURCES

A. *The general background*

Y. **Aharoni**, *Land of the Bible*, 1967; W. F. **Albright**, *From the Stone Age to Christianity*, 1940, 240–55; K. S. **Freedy** and D. B. **Redford**, 'The Dates in Ezekiel in Relation to Biblical, Babylonian and Egyptian Sources', *JAOS* XC, 1970, 462–85; W. W. **Hallo**, 'From Qarqar to Carchemish: Assyria and Israel in the Light of New Discoveries', *BA* XXIII, 1960, 34–61 = *BAR* II, 1964, 152–88; B. **Oded**, 'Observations on Methods of Assyrian Rule in Transjordania after the Palestinian Campaign of Tiglath-Pileser III', *JNES* XXIX, 1970,177–86; H. W. F. **Saggs**, *The Greatness that was Babylon*, London/New York: Sidgwick and Jackson/Hawthorn 1962, 111–53; 238–68; J. A. **Wilson**, *The Culture of Ancient Egypt*, Chicago: University of Chicago Press 1951.

The chapter 'Judah and the Exile' covers a period of less than two hundred years (720–538 BCE). In terms of ancient history, it is a relatively short historical span; but it was a period filled with consequential historical events and significant developments both on the international scene and in Jewish history. Before we review and examine the detailed events according to their subject matter and chronology, let us first outline the general background of the period under discussion and present the important factors which shaped the period and played a decisive role in the fate of the countries of the Fertile Crescent.

First and foremost, the Assyrian empire must be noted. This empire, which began to play a decisive role on the historical stage of the ancient Near East in the ninth century, consolidated its power and expanded its domination until it reached its climax in the days of Asshurbanipal (669–627 BCE; see Hallo). The powerful military machine which the Assyrians had constructed and the efficiency of the imperial administrative organization which they had created enabled them to conquer lands, to overwhelm national states, and to organize these into Assyrian provinces. They deported peoples to distant places, constructed new cities and restored old ones, populating them both with Assyrians and people from conquered countries. They developed an international transportation network, erected fortified outposts in strategic places, and stationed military garrisons throughout the entire empire both to crush any attempted revolts and to guard the borders of the empire from invasion (see Oded). Those national states and city-states which did not become provinces – and their number was small – were forced to recognize Assyrian authority. Their kings became vassals to Assyria. These subjected states bore the burden of Assyrian domination, a burden expressed in the payment of taxes and tribute and in the expenditure of production and labour.

The Judaean state was one of the few kingdoms in the Syro-Palestinian area which averted the catastrophe that overcame so many nations and countries during the eighth century, especially during the reigns of the Assyrian kings Tiglath-pileser III (745–727 BCE) and Sargon II (722–705 BCE). The liquidation of Aram-Damascus (732 BCE) and Samaria (722 BCE) as independent states created a fundamental change in the political situation of the entire area. Both of these, Damascus and Samaria, were powerful centres which had dominated political affairs in Syria and Israel. On the one hand, they constituted a major obstacle to the expansion of Assyrian power and, on the other hand, they had also been centres of agitation against the Assyrian empire. When these two cities were transformed into Assyrian provinces, the possibility of setting up a significant political-military coalition of states in Syria–Palestine against the spread of the Assyrian empire was eliminated.

The end of the kingdom of Israel and the destruction of Samaria, its capital, involved certain consequences for Judah. On the one hand, Judah was rid of a sister-state which had been a rival and competitor and with whom she had many conflicts because of border disputes and the struggle for hegemony in the area. Thus the fall of the northern kingdom encouraged Judaean kings to revive national and political hopes of reuniting the whole area of Israel under the rule of the house of David as it had been in the days of David and Solomon. On the other hand, Assyrian conquest of the northern kingdom brought the border of the Assyrian empire nearer to the gates of Judah (Aharoni, 327–35). The Assyrian province of Samerina became the northern neighbour of Judah, and thus any attempt of the Judaean kings to expand their territory to the north would have meant immediate conflict with the might of Assyria. Moreover, the Assyrian system of mass deportations worked both ways: the introduction of Assyrian importees into Israel produced a significant ethnic composition in the population. The Israelite population which was related to Judah through historical, national, and religious ties dwindled and the Assyrians had replenished the population of the province which they had established on the ruins of Israel with people from various countries (see II Kings 17.24 and the royal inscriptions of Sargon II, *ANET*, 284).

Parallel to the development and expansion of the Assyrian movement to the west, new powers were awakening during the last third of the eighth century. These powers grew in strength during the seventh century and eventually decided the fate of many peoples and states – including the kingdom of Judah at the beginning of the sixth century. In the north, the Chaldeans under Nebuchadrezzar II ascended to power and brought to an end the Assyrian empire as well as the kingdom of Judah (Saggs, 1962, 140–53). To the south, Egypt began to revive near the end of the eighth century and again became a power with increased involvement in the Syro-Palestinian area. One of the clearest expressions of Egypt's recovery and her renewed strength on the international political scene was the re-newal of her military expeditions to Palestine and Syria, through which she sought to regain hegemony over all the intervening territory between Egypt and Mesopotamia. The Egyptian aim was first of all to remove the Assyrian threat from their borders and, in the long run, to restore Egyptian rule over 'Canaan' as in former times (Freedy and Redford).

The location of the states in the Syro-Palestinian region between Mesopotamia and Egypt, of which Judah was one, meant that they were caught up in the cauldron of the struggle for hegemony over Syria and Palestine, at first between Assyria and Egypt and later between Egypt and Chaldean Babylonia. Finally, it is important to note a widespread phenomenon characteristic of the time. This was the resurgence throughout the ancient Near East of nationalistic movements which found expression in a revival of the spiritual-religious life within national frameworks (Albright, 240–4). In Egypt, this phenomenon found expression in the Twenty-fifth and Twenty-sixth Dynasties after a long period of political and cultural lethargy which had commenced in the eleventh century. During the Twenty-fifth Dynasty and even more so during the Twenty-sixth, we can discern a reorganization of government, and together with that, a renovation of the material and spiritual culture as it finds expression in architecture, sculpture, and literature (Wilson, 294–6).

In Babylon, this phenomenon was manifest in the rise of the Chaldean or Neo-Babylonian dynasty, to which Nebuchadrezzar II belonged. At that time, but especially during the period of Nabonidus (555–539 BCE), the ancient literary works of the third millennium were rediscovered and recopied (Albright, 242).

Even in Assyria itself, there was a reawakening and a flourishing of cultural interests. During Asshurbanipal's reign there arose a movement to revive the religious and cultural traditions of Assyria. As a result, Asshurbanipal established an enormous library at Nineveh, his capital, a library partially recovered centuries later by archaeologists (Albright, 242).

A national-cultural renaissance also took place among the Phoenicians where authors collected the ancient mythological literature as well as the historical Phoenician documents. These works have not survived in either their original or collected form, but fragmentary evidence of their existence and echoes of their content are known from later Greek and Hellenistic writers (Albright, 242–4). This revival of national cultural treasures and the tendency to return to the traditions of the fathers – which developed primarily as a reaction against Assyrian subjugation – also took place during this period in the kingdom of Judah, bginning in the days of Hezekiah at the end of the eighth century (see Prov. 25.1) and reaching its apogee in the reign of Josiah at the end of the seventh century.

B.   The source material

Y. **Aharoni**, 'Hebrew Ostraca from Tel Arad', *IEJ* XVI, 1966, 1–7; idem, *Arad Inscriptions*, Jerusalem: Bialik Institute and Israel Exploration Society 1975 (Hebrew); M. **Broshi**, 'The Expansion of Jerusalem in the Reigns of Hezekiah and Manasseh', *IEJ* XXIV, 1974, 21–6; F. M. **Cross**, 'A Reconstruction of the Judean Restoration', *JBL* XCIV, 1975, 4–18 = *Int* XXIX, 1975, 187–203; N. K. **Gottwald**, *All the Kingdoms of the Earth: Israelite Prophecy and International Relations in the Ancient Near East*, New York: Harper & Row 1964; J. M. **Myers**, *I and II Chronicles*, AB 12–13, 1965; J. M. **Newsome**, Jr., 'Toward a New Understanding of the Chronicler and His Purpose', *JBL* XCIV, 1975, 201–17; W. **Rudolph**, *Chronikbücher*, HAT I/21, 1955; E. **Stern**, 'Israel at the Close of the Period of the Monarchy: An Archaeological Survey', *BA* XXXVIII, 1975, 26–54; H. **Torczyner** (Tur-Sinai), *Lachish I: The Lachish Letters*, London: Oxford University Press 1938; D. J. **Wiseman**, *Chronicles of the Chaldean Kings (625–556 BC) in the British Museum*, London: British Museum 1956.

The study of this period is primarily based upon four sources: the biblical literature, the epigraphical material, the results of archaeological excavations, and the references to Judah in Greek and Hellenistic literature.

As regards the people of Israel, the Bible is the primary and in many cases the only source for the people's history. Most of the biblical information about the eighth to the sixth centuries BCE is found in the concluding chapters of the books of II Kings and II Chronicles. The book of Kings is part of the Deuteronomistic history written to explain the tragic chain of events which befell the people, a chain of events understood as the result of continuing sin which ultimately brought the climactic punishment in the days of Zedekiah: the end of the state, the destruction of Jerusalem and the temple, and the subsequent exile (II Kings 17.7–23). The book of Chronicles was compiled in the Persian Period and is based on various sources (Rudolph, X–XIII; Myers, XLI–XC) and perhaps went through various editions (see Cross and Newsome). The Chronicler describes the history of Israel from a different view from that of the book of Kings, and the book should therefore not be considered as merely 'additions' ('*Paralipomena*' in Greek and Latin) to the book of Kings, but as a completely new post-exilic work. For example, Abijah's sermon on Mount Zemaraim (II Chron. 13) is really a literary expression of the political and religious ideology of the Chronicler. In this sermon his main articles of faith are presented: (1) the Davidic kingdom's rule over all Israel is eternal and exclusive; there is thus no other legitimate kingdom for Israel; (2) the Israelite northern kingdom is the work of slaves and scoundrels; and (3) the temple in Jerusalem is the only place for the worship of God. The Chronicler chose and explained the details and events in accordance with his creed. Unlike the book of Kings, which tells of the kingdom of Israel and the kingdom of Judah, the Chronicler concentrates only on the kingdom of Judah, and deliberately ignores the northern kingdom, mentioning it only rarely and then only in cases when it is essential and serves his purpose.

Beside the two historiographic books of Kings and Chronicles, important evidence for the period can be found in many chapters of the classical prophetical books of Isaiah, Jeremiah, and Ezekiel (see Gottwald). The historical details in the books of the prophets are described from a prophetic point of view and as part of the prophets' activities. The books of Kings and Chronicles draw much information from the prophetic literature. Most of the description of Sennacherib's campaign in the Bible is of prophetic origin (II Kings

18.17–19.19; II Chron. 32.9–32, and especially v. 32). In the books of Jeremiah, Ezekiel, and Second Isaiah, we find much information concerning the last years of the kingdom of Judah and the events that befell Judah and the exiles after the destruction of Jerusalem. At the same time, it should be noted that since the books of the prophets are not and were not intended to be historiographic works, the historical background of the prophecies is in many cases not clear, and their interpretation is a matter of dispute among the commentators.

Hebrew epigraphic material sheds light on this period. Of special importance are the letters unearthed at Lachish and Arad and numerous seal impressions and ostraca (inscribed potsherds) found at various places in Judah. Although scholars are not in agreement as to the interpretation of some of the Hebrew inscriptions and their exact function, meaning, and date, the epigraphic materials have provided primary and indispensable details pertaining to paleography and the Hebrew language. The Hebrew inscriptions also supply historical details on the political, military, social, and economic situation in the kingdom of Judah, as well as contributing to the study of religion and royal administration.

The most important inscriptions from outside Judah are the royal inscriptions of the Assyrian kings and the Neo-Babylonian Chronicles. The royal inscriptions of Assyrian kings, especially the annals, describe Assyrian campaigns to the west – to Syria–Palestine and Egypt – and they thus contribute greatly to the understanding of the international historical background of the events that took place in Judah. The Assyrian description of Sennacherib's expedition to Judah during the reign of Hezekiah adds many details to the biblical story and makes especially clear Hezekiah's political position and military strength in Palestine on the eve of Sennacherib's campaign. At the same time, the Assyrian and Neo-Babylonian sources make it possible for us to compare what is related in the Bible with non-biblical information. The Akkadian documents gain additional importance by providing us with synchronisms with whose help we can arrive at some absolute dates for events and kings in Judah. Thanks to the annals of Sennacherib we know that the Assyrian march against Hezekiah took place in the year 701 BCE, and thanks to the Babylonian Chronicles (Wiseman) we know that in the year 597 BCE, which was the seventh year of Nebuchadrezzar, Jerusalem surrendered and Jehoiachin was taken into exile. In Egypt, the kingdom which played an important role during the last days of Judah, no inscriptional material exists which deals directly with Judah. The archaeological excavations in the great tells in Judah, like Lachish, Tell Mor, Beer Sheba, Arad, Ein Gedi, and others, cast light on the material culture of the state during the Iron II period and can be used to supplement the information obtained from written sources (see Stern). Archaeological surveys reveal that in the eighth century and especially in the seventh century, many settlements were established in Judah – in the Judaean Hills, the Negev, the Judaean Desert, and along the Dead Sea. During this period the city of Jerusalem, Judah's capital, expanded to the west and northwest (Broshi; Stern, 35 f.).

The historian attempting to reconstruct the course of events which befell Judah and her neighbours can also be aided by some of the Greek and Hellenistic literature which contains valuable information on Phoenicia, Egypt, and Mesopotamia. Portions of this literature related to the history of Judah have been incorporated into the writings of Josephus Flavius.

§2. THE KINGDOM OF JUDAH DURING THE REIGN OF HEZEKIAH

Y. **Aharoni**, *Land of the Bible*, 1967; idem, 'The Israelite Sanctury at Arad', *New Directions*, 1969, 28–44; idem, 'The Horned Altar of Beer-Sheba', *BA* XXXVII, 1974, 2–6; J. A. **Brinkman**, 'Merodach-Baladan II', *Studies Presented to A. L. Oppenheim*, Chicago: Oriental Institute 1964, 6–53; B. S. **Childs**, *Isaiah and the Assyrian Crisis*, SBT II/3, 1967; J. **Gray**, *I and II Kings*, OTL, 1964, ²1970; S. H. **Horn**, 'Did Sennacherib Campaign Once or Twice Against Hezekiah?', *AUSS* IV, 1966, 1–28; K. A. **Kitchen**, *The Third Intermediate Period in Egypt (1100–650 BC)*, 1973, 154–72; idem, 'Late-Egyptian Chronology and the Hebrew Monarchy', *JANES* V, 1973 (Festschrift Theodor Gaster), 225–33; B. **Mazar**, 'The Campaign of Sennacherib in Judaea', *EI* II, 1953, 170–5 (Hebrew); F. L. **Moriarty**, 'The Chronicler's Account of Hezekiah's Reform', *CBQ* XXVII, 1965, 399–406; N. **Na'aman**, 'Sennacherib's "Letter to God" on his Campaign to Judah', *BASOR* CCXIV, 1974, 25–39; E. W. **Nicholson**, 'The Centralisation of the Cult in Deuteronomy', *VT* XIII, 1963, 380–9; H. H. **Rowley**, 'Hezekiah's Reform and Rebellion', *BJRL* XLIV, 1962, 395–431 = his *Men of God*, 1963, 98–132; H. **Tadmor**, 'Philistia under Assyrian Rule', *BA* XXIX, 1966, 86–102; M. **Weinfeld**, 'Cult Centralization in Israel in the Light of a Neo-Babylonian Analogy', *JNES* XXIII, 1964, 202–12; Y. **Yadin**, 'Beer-sheba: The High Place Destroyed by King Josiah', *BASOR* CCXXII, 1976, 5–18.

The period of Hezekiah's rule (715/4–687/6 BCE) was characterized by three events which are succinctly described in II Kings 18.4–8.

(1) the cultic reform, (2) the wars with the Philistines, and (3) the revolt against Assyria.

A. The cultic reform of Hezekiah

The book of Kings (II Kings 18), in describing Hezekiah's rule, emphasizes the purification of the cult from pagan practices: the removal of the high places (*bamoth*), the destruction of the sacred pillars (*masseboth*), the cutting down of the Asherah, and the breaking of the bronze serpent (see Num. 21.6–9), whereas II Chronicles 29–31 stresses the revival of the national cult and the restoration of divine worship as it had existed during the period of David and Solomon. Ahaz, Hezekiah's predecessor, had closed the gates of the house of God (II Chron. 28.24) whereas Hezekiah opened them (II Chron. 29.3).

What was the purpose of Hezekiah's reform? The Bible gives a personal religious reason for the reform. The reform resulted from the personal desire of the king who was a righteous man (II Kings 18.3–6; II Chron. 31.20f.). It is also possible to assume that the exhortations of Isaiah and Micah concerning the moral and religious sins of the nation (Isa. 1.5; Micah 1.2–9; 3.1–3, 9–11; 6.1–8, etc.) had their influence on the king and people and aided in precipitating the reform. However, it is necessary to note the political purposes of this cultic reform (Weinfeld). This will not only aid us in understanding Hezekiah's policy but will also provide a perspective from which to view the question of the historicity of his cultic reform.

Two biblical passages give expression to some of the political undercurrents of the cultic reform. In the first, II Kings 18.22, the Assyrian Rabshakeh in demanding the surrender of the city says to the citizens of Jerusalem: 'But if you say to me, "We rely on the Lord our God," is it not he whose high places and altars Hezekiah has removed, saying to Judah and to Jerusalem, "You shall worship before this altar in Jerusalem."' The passage makes explicit reference to the suppression of worship at the high places in Jerusalem and in the provincial towns of Judah, as in Beer-Sheba and Arad (Aharoni, 1974, 6; 1971; Yadin); and notes the concentration of holy worship in the temple of Jerusalem. The cessation of worship at the high places, which had been customary, and the consequent elevation of the Jerusalem temple as the only place for the worship of God were intended to strengthen the ties between the people of Judah and the house of David which reigned in Jerusalem, the capital. The temple in Jerusalem was also the royal sanctuary (see Amos 7.10–

13). It was built by the founders of the Davidic dynasty and its worship was organized and conducted by the kings (see I Chron. 26.30–2). This implies that one of the aims of Hezekiah's cultic reform, with its emphasis on the concentration of the cult in the Jerusalem temple, was to increase the king's authority by consolidating and strengthening the ties which existed between the royal court, the Jerusalem temple, and the provincial towns (Weinfeld, 206f.).

The second passage, II Chronicles 30.1, notes that 'Hezekiah sent to all Israel and Judah, and wrote letters also to Ephraim and Manasseh, that they should come to the house of the Lord at Jerusalem, to keep the passover to the Lord the God of Israel'. This invitation to celebrate the passover in Jerusalem was addressed to the remnants of Israel living outside the kingdom of Judah. The purpose of this invitation was to deepen the recognition of national unity for the whole of the children of Israel. This act was a preparatory stage for political and territorial claims involving the entire area where believers in the Israelite cult could be found and thus for the political unity of the area previously ruled over by the house of David, that is, Israel and Judah. The removal of the pagan cultic places and practices was expressive of a national renaissance which came as a reaction against the political humiliation by foreign powers (see above p. 438). The political aims of the cultic reform which was connected with the temple and pilgrimage to Jerusalem are expressed in a fascinating manner in Solomon's actions on the one hand, and in Jeroboam's on the other hand (I Kings 12.25–33). Under Hezekiah, this move to restore the kingdom of David over the entire area of Israel encountered an imperial power, since the territory of the former kingdom of Israel had become an Assyrian province partially populated by people from various countries which had been conquered by Assyria (II Kings 17.24). This part of the population, of course, had no ethnic, national, or religious associations with the people of Judah. But at the same time there were some factors, after the fall of Samaria, which gave new life to the old ambitions of the Judaean rulers to restore the kingdom of David and Solomon. After the fall of Samaria, when there was no king in Israel, it was easy for the Judaean monarchs to present themselves to the Israelite 'survivors' as legitimate heirs to the northern state and as the ones who would free the country from foreign oppression. The Israelite residents of the former kingdom of Israel who had not been exiled no doubt did not approve of the penetration and settlement of non-Israelite elements in the promised land. These remnants of the state of Israel were of course too weak to restore the Israelite kingdom. Thus it was only logical to expect that they would turn to their brothers in Judah who had remained independent. Hezekiah understood that, in order to regain authority over the entire land, he would have to bring over to his cause the Israelite population in the north and foster in them the idea of political and national unity.

The passover holiday, celebrated by enormous crowds, could be expected to feed the feeling of national unity because the holiday was connected with historical memories of release and freedom. The fact that Hezekiah chose to celebrate the passover in the second month of the year, and not in the first month as was customary in Judah (II Chron. 30.13), indicates that he acquiesced in the pattern prevalent in the north, where the holiday was celebrated about one month later than in the south because of agricultural conditions. In addition, the naming of his heir to the throne, Manasseh, after the name of one of the most respected tribes of the northern kingdom, a tribe which was settled on both sides of the Jordan River, can be seen as a political act embodying the hope of reuniting all the tribes of Israel under the reign of the Davidic dynasty.

Finally, one should recognize that Hezekiah's cultic reform was a movement combining religion and nationalism and also a territorial and political project whose aim was to prepare the road for the incorporation of the former area of the kingdom of Israel under the reign of the house of David (Nicholson, 383–9). But Hezekiah's actions towards the northern territory were only one part of a broader plan to restore the kingdom of David and Solomon with its old borders. Another part of this plan can be found in Hezekiah's wars against the Philistines.

B. The war against the Philistines

II Kings 18.8 notes that 'he (Hezekiah) smote the Philistines as far as Gaza and the borders thereof, from watchtower to fortified city'. This text implies that Hezekiah not only restored to Judah the regions which had been lost to the Philistines during the reign of his father Ahaz (II Chron. 28.18) but also that he penetrated deeply into Philistia and reached Gaza, the southernmost Philistine city-state. This activity of Hezekiah against Philistia receives no mention in the parallel and detailed account of his reign in II Chronicles 29–31, but echoes of this activity in Philistia do occur in three other texts. (1) I Chronicles 4.34–43 describes the expansion of the Simeonites southward into Philistine territory during the days of Hezekiah.

They journeyed to the entrance of Gedor, to the east side of the valley, to seek pasture for their flocks, where they found rich, good pasture, and the land was very broad, quiet, and peaceful; for the former inhabitants then belonged to Ham. These (the sons of Simeon), registered by name, came in the days of Hezekiah, king of Judah, and destroyed their tents ... (I Chron. 4.39–41).

The LXX here reads Gerar for Gedor and this reading is to be preferred. Gerar was located on the crossroads between Gaza and Beer-Sheba. II Kings 18.8, which mentions not only the Philistines but Gaza's borders, should thus be associated with the conquest of this area noted in I Chronicles 4.39–41. (2) In the annals of Sennacherib, describing Sennacherib's campaign in Palestine, it is noted that 'the officials, the politicians, and the people of Ekron had thrown Padi, their king, into fetters ... and had handed him over to Hezekiah, the Jew' (*ANET*, 287). The surrender of the king of Ekron to Hezekiah and the fact that afterwards no other king was enthroned in Ekron provide a hint of the influence, and maybe even the control, which Hezekiah had in Ekron. (3) In Sennacherib's 'Letter to God' on his campaign to Judah there is mention of 'a royal (city) of the Philistines, which H(ezek)iah had captured and strengthened for himself' (Na'aman, 27).

Hezekiah seems to have made use of three factors which prepared for the successful Judaean expansion into Philistia. (1) The Assyrian campaigns against Philistia from 734 BCE on and especially the campaign of Sargon II against Ashdod in 712 BCE (*ANET*, 286; Tadmor) had weakened the Philistine cities and enabled Judah, who was not hurt by the Assyrian campaigns, to regain the territory taken from her by the Philistines during the days of Ahaz. (2) Hezekiah supported local dissident circles in Ekron and Ashkelon, thus undermining the royal governments in those cities while strengthening his own influence in Philistia. (3) Hezekiah's support of Ashkelon against the other cities of Philistia, especially against Ashdod and Gaza, aided Hezekiah in annexing Philistine territories belonging to Ashdod and Gaza.

Hezekiah's open rebellion against Assyria which culminated in 701 BCE was the result of his plan to reconstitute the kingdom of David and Solomon and to establish his hegemony over the land of all Israel. Thus Hezekiah, on one hand, took action against countries which were subordinate and loyal to Assyria, including Edom (I Chron. 4.42 f.), and, on the other hand, disrupted the territorial and administrative structures authorized by the Assyrians during the eighth century. In addition, the revolt against Assyria was a result of the natural ambition of the Judaean king and his people to rid themselves of foreign rule and reach complete national independence.

We can sum up by stating that the biblical testimony concerning Hezekiah's cultic reform is authentic, since centralization of the cult fits well with Hezekiah's successive political activities, whose aims were to strengthen the Davidic dynasty in Jerusalem and to restore the ancient borders of the Davidic kingdom (Rowley, 128–32; Weinfeld, 204–12; Moriarty, 399–406).

C. Hezekiah's rebellion and Sennacherib's campaign against Judah

After a long period of Judaean loyalty to Assyria, Hezekiah dared to revolt openly in 701 BCE. Hezekiah assumed that he had a better chance to succeed than to fail. At the time of Sennacherib's enthronement (705 BCE) and during his first years of rule circumstances developed which appeared very promising to Hezekiah (Na'aman, 33–5). (1) Sargon died on the battlefield in 705 BCE and his death was accompanied by an inner disquietude in Assyria. Both these factors encouraged other states to attempt to throw off the burden of Assyria. (2) The recovery of Egypt and its developing strength under the reign of the Twenty-fifth Nubian Dynasty aroused in Hezekiah, as in other kings, the hope of ridding himself of Assyrian dominance with the help of Egypt (see II Kings 18.21; Isa. 18; 30.2; 31.1). Egypt had watched with increasing fear as the Assyrians had taken control over the coastal cities all the way to the 'town of the brook of Egypt' (*El-Arish*) and thus would spare no efforts to evoke agitation against the Assyrian empire to prevent any possible invasion of her homeland. (3) As soon as Sargon II had died, the Chaldean Merodach-baladan returned to Babylon, supported by the Elamite king and Arab tribes. This action could be expected to occupy the Assyrian army in the east, thus increasing the chances of Judaean success in the west in its revolt against Assyria. The visit of Merodach-baladan's messengers to Jerusalem (II Kings 20.12) no doubt had a political-military purpose. Although the II Kings account places this visit after Sennacherib's invasion, the Babylon mission probably preceded the Assyrian campaign (Gray, 700–3; Brinkman, 31–3). (4) The rebellion against Assyria by Luli, king of Tyre and Sidon, the strongest ruler in Phoenicia, must have greatly encouraged Hezekiah. The Sidonian kingdom controlled the main highway between Syria and Israel and Hezekiah probably saw this control as a major obstacle to the Assyrian army in case the Assyrian king should move on a punitive expedition against Judah. It is reasonable to assume that Hezekiah had co-ordinated his activities with Luli before beginning his open revolt against Assyria. (5) Hezekiah's strong position in Philistia, especially in Ekron, and the mutual understanding which existed between him and Sidqa, the king of Ashkelon who ruled over the northern Shephelah (Jaffa and its environs), created another obstacle to any expedition by the Assyrians into the land of Judah.

The carefully thought out policy of Hezekiah is discernible not only in his patient waiting for the opportune moment to rebel against Assyria and in the extensive diplomatic manoeuvres which created an association of allies far and near, but also in his efforts to fortify Judah itself against the inevitable struggle against the Assyrians. In a major engineering feat, Hezekiah devised the means for transferring the water from the spring of Gihon, located outside the Jerusalem walls, through an underground tunnel to the pool of Siloam located within the city walls (II Kings 20.20; Isa. 22.9–11; II Chron. 32.30). Monumental evidence for the digging of Hezekiah's tunnel has been preserved in the 'Siloam Inscription' (*ANET*, 321). Furthermore, Hezekiah strengthened the walls of Jerusalem and fortified numerous Judaean cities (II Chron. 32.5; Isa. 22.9–11). He reorganized the army, prepared military weapons (II Chron. 32.5 f.), and it seems also that he brought mercenary troops (*urbu*) into Jerusalem. The reorganization of the army was no doubt associated with the census carried out by Hezekiah in southern Judah (I Chron. 4). He built store cities or warehouses for agricultural supplies (II Chron. 32.28f.). There is also the possibility that Hezekiah restructured the royal administrative system. Evidence for this political reorganization may be seen in the transference of the office of 'the royal steward' from Shebnah to Eliakim (Isa. 22; II Kings 18.18) and also in the royal seal impressions which contain the inscription 'to the king' (*lmlk*) followed by one of four place names: Hebron, Ziph, Socho, and *mmšt*. According to some scholars, these seal impressions reflect the division of the kingdom into four administrative districts, with each district possessing a royal administrative centre or store city for the collection of taxes (Aharoni, 1967, 340–6, and see below, p. 464f.).

As Hezekiah could have expected, an Assyrian punitive campaign was not long in coming. In 701 BCE, the third year of Sennacherib's reign (see II Kings 18.13), the Assyrian monarch left for the land of 'Hatti' for a military campaign against the centres of revolt in

Phoenicia, Philistia, and Judah. A wealth of information on and evidence for this undertaking is given in the Bible (II Kings 18.13–19.37; Isa. 36f.; II Chron. 32.1–23; Isa. 1.5–9, 10.28–32; Micah 1.9–14), in external sources (Sennacherib's Annals, Herodotus, Josephus), and in archaeological remains from excavated sites. In spite of all the difficulties which arise from the biblical sources and the problems involved in correlating the biblical with the Assyrian texts (*Bright, 296–308; Gray, 672–96), it is none the less possible to outline the general nature and route of the campaign. (1) First stage: Sennacherib penetrated to the Phoenician sea-coast from the north and concentrated his army against Luli, the king of Sidon. Luli escaped from Tyre to Cyprus. Sennacherib placed Ethbaal on the throne in Sidon in place of Luli, probably also making him ruler of Tyre. Sennacherib received, in the city of *ushu*, the tribute of various kings who demonstrated their loyalty to Assyria, among whom were Mitinti of Ashdod and the Transjordanian rulers. (2) Second stage: Sennacherib pushed his campaign to the south and conquered several cities in northern Philistia (Jaffa, Beth Dagon, Azur, and Banai-Barqa) which were part of the kingdom of Ashkelon. Sennacherib reported that he took captive Sidqa the king of Ashkelon and enthroned Sharuludari in his place. (3) Third stage: The Assyrian ruler next concentrated his efforts against the Philistine city of Ekron. Sennacherib reports that the people of Ekron who had turned over their king, Padi, to Hezekiah appealed to the Egyptian Pharaoh for help. The Assyrian battle against Ekron and the Egyptian forces under the leadership of 'Tirhakah king of Cush' (II Kings 19.9) took place near the city of Eltekeh. For years, scholars debated the authenticity of II Kings 19.9 since it was thought that Tirhakah was still a small lad in 701 BCE. However, recent study and new inscriptions demonstrate that Tirhakah was certainly old enough to have commanded the Egyptian troops in Palestine in 701 BCE (see Kitchen). The Egyptian army was defeated, Ekron captured, and the Philistine rebels who had deposed their monarch were executed. Sennacherib concluded his description of this phase of his exploits by noting that 'I made Padi, their king, come from Jerusalem and set him as their lord on the throne, imposing upon him the tribute due to me as overlord' (*ANET*, 288). (4) Fourth stage: Sennacherib next turned his attention to Hezekiah. The Assyrian army subdued numerous cities in Judah and Jerusalem was besieged (II Kings 18.13–19.37; II Chron. 32.9f.; Micah 1.10–15; Isa. 10.28–32). Sennacherib described the action against Judah in the following manner:

As to Hezekiah, the Jew, (*Hazaqiaú Iaúdaai*), he did not submit to my yoke, I laid siege to 46 of his strong cities, walled forts, and to the countless small villages in their vicinity, and conquered them by means of well-stamped earth-ramps, and battering-rams brought thus near to the walls combined with the attack by foot soldiers, using mines, breeches as well as sapper work. I drove out of them 200,150 people, young and old, male and female, horses, mules, donkeys, camels, big and small cattle beyond counting and considered them booty. Himself I made a prisoner in Jerusalem, his royal residence, like a bird in a cage. I surrounded him with earthwork in order to molest those who were leaving his city's gate. His towns which I had plundered, I took away from his country and gave them to Mitinti, king of Ashdod, Padi, king of Ekron, and Sillibel, king of Gaza. Thus I reduced his country, but I still increased the tribute and the *katru*-presents due to me as his overlord which I imposed upon him beyond the former tribute, to be delivered annually (*ANET*, 288).

This paragraph is parallel to the story of II Kings 18.13–16, which notes that Sennacherib conquered the fortified cities of Judah and that Hezekiah surrendered and sent tribute to the Assyrian king who had set up his headquarters at Lachish (II Kings 18.17; II Chron. 32.9; and see Micah 1.13–15). The capture of Lachish is known from an Assyrian relief which depicts Sennacherib's conquest of the city *Lakisu* and his receipt of booty (*ANEP*, nos. 371–4).

The main problem of interpretation, and this is if we can avoid other ones (see Rowley and Childs), is created because of the discrepancy between the biblical account and the Assyrian description of the final outcome of the campaign. According to Sennacherib, the campaign ended with an absolute Assyrian victory. According to the biblical traditions, Hezekiah, after he had paid tribute, heard that the Egyptian Tirhakah was advancing from Egypt to fight against the Assyrian army headquartered in Lachish. This information encouraged Hezekiah so that he did not surrender and refused to open the gates of Jerusalem to Rabshakeh, Sennacherib's emissary. Isaiah is said to have twice addressed the people and mockingly attacked Rabshakeh's words (Isa. 37; II Kings 19). Isaiah is shown promising the people:

Therefore thus says the Lord concerning the king of Assyria: He shall not come into this city, or shoot an arrow there, or come before it with a shield, or cast up a siege mound against it. By the way that he came, by the same shall he return, and he shall not come into this city, says the Lord. For I will defend this city to save it, for my own sake and for the sake of my servant David (Isa. 37.33–5).

According to the biblical story, Sennacherib's army was

decimated by a miracle before the gates of Jerusalem as the prophet had predicted: 'And that night the angel of the Lord went forth, and slew a hundred and eighty-five thousand in the camp of the Assyrians . . .' (II Kings 19.35).

In the research on Sennacherib's campaign against Judah, two main theories have been formulated about its outcome. According to the first, the biblical account and the Assyrian description speak about one campaign only, which took place in 701 BCE, but a campaign which had two stages (Mazar, Rowley). The first stage which is described in II Kings 18.13–16 and in Sennacherib's annals ended with Hezekiah's surrender. The second stage which ended in an Assyrian defeat is narrated in the biblical account but not, as one would expect, in the Assyrian royal inscriptions. The payment of tribute to Sennacherib by Hezekiah is described in the Assyrian annals as follows:

> Hezekiah himself, whom the terror-inspiring splendour of my lordship had overwhelmed and whose irregular and elite troops which he had brought into Jerusalem, his royal residence, in order to strengthen it, had deserted him, did send me, later, to Nineveh, my lordly city, together with 30 talents of gold, 800 talents of silver, precious stones, antimony, large cuts of red stone, couches inlaid with ivory, *nimedu*-chairs inlaid with ivory, elephant-hides, ebony-wood, boxwood, and all kinds of valuable treasures, his own daughters, concubines, male and female musicians. In order to deliver the tribute and to do obeisance as a slave he sent his personal messenger (*ANET*, 288).

The fact that Sennacherib says that Hezekiah sent his tribute to Nineveh suggests that Sennacherib did not remain in Judah to receive the tribute but was obliged to return, hurriedly, to Assyria.

A second theory concludes that the biblical materials combine the accounts of two chronologically separated invasions of Judah by Sennacherib. The first, in 701 BCE, ended with Hezekiah's surrender. This invasion is described in II Kings 18.13–16 and in the Assyrian annals. The second invasion occurred ten or even fifteen years later and concluded with an Assyrian defeat, a defeat which is echoed in the Bible. However, an editor combined the account of the second invasion with that of the 701 BCE campaign to produce the present form of the biblical texts. Scholars (*Bright, 296–308; Horn) find traces of this second invasion in the history of Herodotus, who is followed by Josephus, which describes a sudden defeat of Sennacherib – 'the king of the Arabs and the Assyrians' – in Pelusium at the gates of Egypt (Herodotus, II 141; Josephus, *Ant.* X 18–20).

Both of these theories have evidence for and against them, and 'each suffered from an inability to do full justice to all the material' (Childs, 118). The fact is that Jerusalem, unlike cities such as Sidon, Ekron, Ashkelon, and others, was spared in spite of the mighty power of the Assyrian empire. Furthermore, Hezekiah, in spite of his role as a central figure in the organization of the revolt which precipitated the Assyrian invasion, continued to rule while other kings who participated in the conspiracy lost their thrones. Thus, one can hardly be surprised that an unexpected result was interpreted by the people, who were no doubt influenced by Isaiah's prophecies, as a divine and miraculous deliverance. Isaiah himself opposed the policy of Judaean kings who attempted to rid themselves of Assyrian oppression through reliance on military power, especially Egypt (Isa. 20; 28; 30.15). The prophet saw in Assyria a messenger whom God had sent to punish the people for their sins (Isa. 1.10–20; 2.6–21; 5.26–30 and compare Micah 1.2–9). The purpose of the punishment was to purify the people (Isa. 1.24–6) for a peaceful future, but this was not to happen before God had also punished Assyria for its arrogance and pride (Isa. 10.7–19; 14.24–7). Within the prophet's view of a universal future plan, a special role was to be played by the house of David and Jerusalem (Isa. 9.1–6; 11). Thus, Isaiah's strong belief in the eternity of the house of David and in the sacredness of Zion against any earthly power (Isa. 14.32) awakened and pushed the prophet to encourage the king and the people during the Assyrian siege (see Isa. 37.33–5).

Thus Jerusalem was delivered but Judah was decimated. Archaeological excavations have unearthed destruction levels from the remains of important Judaean cities (Arad, Beer-sheba, Lachish; cf. Micah 1.10–15; Isa. 1.7–9) which are quite likely the result of Sennacherib's campaign. Philistine cities received territory previously held by Judah. Sennacherib increased the tribute required from Judah. Thus, one can sum up by saying that in the historical growth and expansion of the Assyrian empire there was no chance of any combination of powers to halt the spread of the Assyrians. Thus Judah was forced, throughout the remainder of the reign of Hezekiah and during the rule of Manasseh and Amon, to confine itself to its borders and to carry the burdens of Assyrian domination while awaiting a new international coalition that could bring about the collapse of the Assyrian power.

§3. THE REIGNS OF MANASSEH AND AMON

A. **Alt**, 'The Monarchy in Israel and Judah' (see ch. V §2), in his *Essays*, 1966, 239–59; E. **Auerbach**, *Wüste und Gelobtes Land II*, Berlin: Schocken Verlag 1936; idem, ' 'Am-ha'ares', *Proceedings of the First World Congress of Jewish Studies*, Jerusalem: World Union of Jewish Studies 1952, 362–6 (Hebrew); M. **Broshi**, 'The Expansion of Jerusalem in the Reigns of Hezekiah and Manasseh', *IEJ* XXIV, 1974, 21–6; H. **Cazelles**, 'Sophonie, Jérémie, et les Scythes en Palestine', *RB* LXXIV, 1967, 24–44; M. **Cogan**, *Imperialism and Religion: Assyria, Judah and Israel in the Eighth and Seventh Centuries BCE*, SBLMS 19, 1974; S. **Daiches**, 'The Meaning of ''Am-haaretz' in the Old Testament', *JTS* XXX, 1929, 245–9; E. L. **Ehrlich**, 'Der Aufenthalt des Königs Manasse in Babylon', *TZ* XXI, 1965, 281–6; K. **Galling**, 'Die israelitische Staatsverfassung in ihrer vorderorientalischen Umwelt', *AO* XXVIII, 1929, 5–64; R. **Gordis**, 'Sectional Rivalry in the Kingdom of Judah', *JQR* NS, XXV, 1934/5, 237–59; A. **Malamat**, 'The Historical Background of the Assassination of Amon King of Judah', *IEJ* III, 1953, 26–9; J. **McKay**, *Religion in Judah Under the Assyrians 732–609 BC*, SBT II/26, 1973; E. W. **Nicholson**, 'The Meaning of the Expression '' *'Am-ha'ares'* in the Old Testament', *JSS* X, 1965, 59–66; E. **Nielsen**, 'Political Conditions and Cultural Developments in Israel and Judah During the Reign of Manasseh', *Fourth World Congress of Jewish Studies* I, Jerusalem: World Union of Jewish Studies 1967, 103–6; M. **Smith**, *Palestinian Parties and Politics that Shaped the Old Testament*, New York: Columbia University Press 1971; J. A. **Soggin**, 'Der judäische 'am-ha'ares und das Königtum in Juda', *VT* XIII, 1963, 187–95; M. **Sulzberger**, *'Am-ha-aretz, the Ancient Hebrew Parliament*, Philadelphia: Julius H. Greenstone 1909; S. **Talmon**, 'The Judean 'am ha'ares in Historical Perspective', *Fourth World Congress of Jewish Studies* I, 1967, 71–6; R. **de Vaux**, 'Les sens de l'expression "peuple du pays" dans l'Ancien Testament et le rôle politique du peuple en Israël', *RA* LVIII, 1964, 167–72; M. **Weinfeld**, 'Cult Centralization in Israel in the light of a Neo-Babylonian Analogy', *JNES* XXIII, 1964, 202–12; idem, 'The Worship of Molech and the Queen of Heaven and its Background', *UF* IV, 1972, 133–54.

Manasseh, the son of Hezekiah, ruled over Judah for the lengthy period of fifty-five years, and they were stormy years on the international political scene. The biblical description of his reign in the books of Kings and Chronicles (II Kings 21.1–18; II Chron. 33.1–20) concentrates primarily on the cultic and religious aspects of his reign and ignores the other internal and international factors connected with Manasseh. The central concerns of the biblical materials are the social and religious 'sins of Manasseh' (so also in Zeph. 1.4–6; 3.1–4). Manasseh, according to biblical historiography, cancelled his father's reforms, 'for Manasseh built again the high places' (II Kings

21.3). He is accused of introducing the cults of Baal and Astarte as well as the worship of the host of heaven into the sanctuary of Jerusalem, the latter perhaps under the influence of Assyrian religion (see Jer. 8.2; Zeph. 1.5). Manasseh 'made his son pass through the fire' (II Kings 21.6), a form of worship whose exact meaning and origin are not clear (see Weinfeld, 1972) although it is known that it was practised in a place called 'Tophet' in the valley of Ben-Hinnom (II Kings 23.10). The Israelites were forbidden to worship in this cult (Lev. 20.2) and its practice was opposed by the zealous loyalists (Jer. 32.35). Manasseh allowed the practice of magic and divination which was also forbidden (Lev. 20.6). His sins were considered by the authors of King and Chronicles as the worst in ancient Israel and as the ultimate cause of the destruction of the temple (II Kings 21.9–14; 24.3f.; cf. Jer. 15.4).

It seems that the idea of the severity of the 'sins of Manasseh' originated in the fact that he not only legitimized the cult of foreign gods as the official cult (as had Jezebel and Ahab) but also that he introduced these cults into the temple of Yahweh (II Kings 21.4–8). Thus, he seems to have intended the creation of a genuine syncretism of Yahwistic and pagan cults. While Ahab's sins were explained by the influence of Jezebel, the biblical historians saw in Manasseh's personality the reason for his evil behaviour.

Some scholars explain 'Manasseh's sins' in terms of his submission to the Assyrians. Just as Hezekiah's purification of the temple cult is to be seen as the expression of a nationalistic revival movement, so also Manasseh's deviation from the national cult is seen as the result of Assyrian oppression (Weinfeld, 1964; *Bright, 311). At the same time it is plausible to assume that the sequence of Hezekiah's reform followed by Manasseh's cultic activity and subsequently Josiah's reform reflect an internal domestic struggle which occurred in Judah (see II Kings 21.16; 24.4) between those advocating a pure Israelite cult – which included an experiment in the centralization of Yahweh worship in the Jerusalem temple – with a contrasting movement which inclined towards an adjustment to Gentile customs (see Smith, 15–56). The latter was also inclined towards reconciliation with the Assyrian oppression including all its cultic aspects, perhaps finally seeking to create out of the entire population of the country a society characterized by its syncretistic culture. Such a society already had its beginnings in the amalgamation of diverse cultures following the fall of Samaria (II Kings 17). If this view is correct, then the first group would have included the prophets from the circles of Isaiah, Zephaniah, and Jeremiah (Jer. 7.18; Zeph. 1.8) together with the priests of the Jerusalem temple (Nielsen, 105). The second group would probably have included the members of the royal court, most of the leaders and princes, the priests of Baal and Astarte, and other Judaean circles which had close contact with the foreign population of the country and with the Assyrian administration (see Zeph. 1.8f.). It is mainly because of these latter groups that the reign of Manasseh became a period of syncretism and international interchange (so Nielsen) and was not due to any Assyrian policy or practice of imposing their religion upon subjected peoples (see Cogan and McKay). The internal struggle of these two Judaean groups was a bloody one (II Kings 21.16; 24.4).

II Chronicles 33.11–16 gives a rather strange bit of information about Manasseh. This passage reports his being taken to Babylon with hooks and bound in fetters by the commander of the army of the Assyrian king, his repentance and return to Jerusalem, his subsequent fortification of the western side of Jerusalem (see Broshi), and his strengthening of the army in all the fortified cities of Judah. Since these details are found only in II Chronicles and go totally unnoted in the book of II Kings, some scholars would deny the authenticity of this information and dismiss it by claiming that the author of Chronicles created a story with no historical basis in order to explain how it was possible for such a great sinner as Manasseh to have ruled for such a long time (for bibliography and discussion see Ehrlich). According to this opinion, the stories about Amon (II Chron. 33.22) and Josiah (II Kings 23.12) show that Manasseh actually did not repent and did nothing to counteract the worship of foreign gods (Jer. 15.4). The fact that Babylon is mentioned (instead of Nineveh or Calah) suggests that the story is an historical *midrash* based on Isaiah's words in II Kings 20.18. Moreover, the non-biblical documents provide no hints of a rebellion against Esarhaddon or Asshurbanipal which involved Manasseh. On the contrary, Judah, together with Ammon and Moab, is mentioned as one who faithfully paid tribute to Assyria. Manasseh himself appears in the Assyrian annals as a faithful subject to Assyria. Esarhaddon (680–669 BCE) enumerates Manasseh (*Me-na-si-i*) together with '22 kings of Hatti, the seashore and the islands; all these I sent out and made them transport under terrible difficulties, to Nineveh, the town where I exercise my rulership, as building material for my palace: big logs, long beams and thin boards from cedar and pine trees, products of the Sirara and Lebanon mountains' (*ANET*, 291). Manasseh also appears in inscriptions of Asshurbanipal (668–627 BCE) describing his campaign to Egypt in 667 BCE:

I called up my mighty armed forces which Ashur and Ishtar have entrusted to me and took the shortest road to Egypt and Nubia. During my march 22 kings from the seashore, the islands and the mainland ... [including] Manasseh, king of Judah ... servants who belong to me, brought heavy gifts to me and kissed my feet. I made these kings accompany my army over the land – as well as over the sea-route with their armed forces and their ships (*ANET*, 294).

There is here clear evidence that Manasseh, as a vassal king, was obliged to collect taxes and also to provide some military forces to the Assyrian campaign. Judah's enslavement during the days of Manasseh is further borne out by the stationing in Lachish of a Philistine garrison under Assyrian control (*ABL* 218). In addition, the reigns of Esarhaddon and Asshurbanipal were the climactic apogee of Assyrian domination. The capture of the Egyptian city of No-Amon (Thebes) by Asshurbanipal left a strong impression on nations such as Judah (Nahum 3.8–10) and such an accomplishment would have offered Manasseh no encouragement to rebel.

Nevertheless, in spite of all these reasons which cast doubt on the historicity of the story of Manasseh's rebellion reported in II Chronicles 33.11–16, it is difficult to assume that the author of Chronicles created a totally imaginary episode with no historical kernel. Thus there are scholars who try to associate Manasseh's rebellion with one of those which did take place in his day, such as the rebellion in 677 BCE of Abdimilkutte king of Sidon during the reign of Esarhaddon (*ANET*, 291), the rebellion of Baal king of Tyre in 668/7 BCE against Asshurbanipal (*ANET*, 295f.), the war of Psammetichus I (664–610 BCE) who, with the help of Gyges king of Lydia, rebelled against Assyria in 655, or the rebellion of Shamash-shum-ukin against Asshurbanipal during the years 652–648 BCE (see Ehrlich).

The reference to Manasseh's being carried to Babylon might give support to the theory that there was some connection between Manasseh's exile and the rebellion by Shamash-shum-ukin, since Babylon first came under Asshurbanipal's direct control in 648 BCE after he suppressed the revolt led by his own brother. In addition, the lenient treatment, amnesty one might say, which Asshurbanipal displayed towards the king of Tyre, the Egyptian ruler Necho I, and Psammetichus I would parallel the type of treatment reportedly given Manasseh. Asshurbanipal's reconciliation with and lenient treatment of the rulers in the west can be explained by the dangers which Assyria faced in the east from Babylon, Elam, and the Arabic tribes. As additional evidence for the authenticity of the story, scholars have pointed to the reference concerning an importation of foreigners into Samaria by Esarhaddon and Asshurbanipal (Ezra 4.2, 10). These importations may have been preceded by military action in Israel by these two Assyrian rulers. Even if we accept this interpretation of Manasseh's revolt, his exile to Babylon, and his restoration as authentic information, it is still difficult to know whether the fortification of Jerusalem and Judaean cities was carried out by Manasseh (II Chron. 33.14) after his return from Babylon as the biblical historian reports or whether these activities took place as preparations for a rebellion like those projects of Hezekiah before Sennacherib's campaign.

Amon, Manasseh's son, ruled over the country for only a short time because he was assassinated after two years: 'The servants of Amon conspired against him and killed the king in his house' (II Kings 21.23; II Chron. 33.24). The biblical narrative does not explain the reason for the assassination nor disclose the ideological, political, or religious background of the conspirators. Thus there are several opinions concerning the matter. One possibility is that Amon, of whom it is said in both Kings and Chronicles that he continued in the sinful ways of his father Manasseh (II Kings 21.20–2; II Chron. 33.22f.), was murdered by factions who were faithful to the tradition of Israel and in favour of Hezekiah's reform. In this view, Amon's murder has a religious and cultic background (*Kittel, II, 378f.; Nielsen, 105f.). A second possibility is that the murder reflects an anti-Assyrian political act, probably instigated by Egypt and carried out by factions opposed to Assyrian rule. Scholars holding this opinion thought that the international political situation, i.e., the decline of the Assyrian empire, the growing strength of the Chaldeans, and the renewed rise of Egypt, make the time ripe for a rebellion against Assyria (Auerbach, 159; Malamat; Cazelles, 27f., 42f.).

At any rate, Amon's assassination was not followed by the establishment of a new dynasty in Judah. This phenomenon of stability within a dynastic succession was typical of Judah in contrast to Israel, where assassinations on several occasions led to the overthrow of dynasties. The text reports the following about Amon's murder and the enthronement of Josiah: 'The people of the land slew all those who had conspired against King Amon, and the people of the land made Josiah his son king in his stead' (II Kings 21.24). The expression 'people of the land' ('*am ha'areṣ*) is a problematic one and there are many interpretations concerning its meaning (see Talmon). The difficulty in explaining the term '*am ha'areṣ* lies in the fact that the biblical verses in which it occurs do not permit a precise definition of the concept. The expression appears by itself, unaccompanied by any comment as to the political, social, or religious nature of the body which is referred to as '*am ha'areṣ*. There is no stand taken nor evaluation made by the biblical authors concerning this body. Moreover, the verses in the Bible in which the concept appears pertain to different periods, from the time of the patriarchs (Gen. 23.12f.) up to Daniel (Dan 9.6). In most cases the term refers to Israelites, but in some cases also to non-Israelites (e.g. Gen. 23.12f.; Ezra 3.3; Neh. 9.30).

It is not surprising that the term was interpreted by researchers in different and opposing ways. If we limit ourselves mainly to the cases from the period of the monarchy (most of these are mentioned in II Kings, Jeremiah, Ezekiel, and II Chronicles), we find that the concept is connected with the history of the kingdom of Judah and is not mentioned in connection with the kingdom of Israel. In a few verses, '*am ha'areṣ* is mentioned with or next to other important figures – king, *nasi, śar*, and priest (Jer. 1.18; 37.2; Ezek. 7.27; 22.29). Jeremiah charges the '*am ha'areṣ* with not freeing slaves (34.9) and Ezekiel presents the '*am ha'areṣ* as a body which robs and persecutes the poor. '*Am ha'areṣ* appears as a body with judicial authority (Jer. 36; II Kings 21.9) and military strength (II Kings 25.19). On the basis of these verses, some scholars have concluded that we have here a body which represents a privileged social and political class or an aristocratic institution of landowners which was active on the legal and military level and which had political influence. In time of crisis, it had the power to determine the fate of the dynasty (Daiches and Gordis). There are some who view this privileged body as a kind of national council which represented the people before the king. This 'democratic' institution would, thus, have developed out of the ancient institution of the elders, the body which was made up of the heads of the clans (Sulzberger, especially 72–8; Auerbach, 362–6).

Another interpretation, which has variations, views the concept '*am ha'areṣ* as a collective name for the simple people. This is the 'proletariat' – robbed, exploited, driven off the land and without rights – as opposed to the nobility. This opinion is based on verses such as Exodus 5.5 and II Kings 24.14. The above-mentioned references in Ezekiel 7.27 and Jeremiah 1.18 are interpreted in this approach as showing the '*am ha'areṣ* in opposition to the authorities and not as a parallel body (Galling, 32–4). Another opinion holds that the concept should be interpreted as referring collectively to the free citizens and property-owners who have both obligations and privileges (de Vaux). Alt theorized that '*am ha'areṣ* refers to the population of the provincial towns of Judah, especially the farmers, as opposed to and as distinguished from the residents of Jerusalem. Alt found a distinction between the men of Judah and the residents of Jerusalem as two separate political and social bodies in such passages as II Kings 23.2 and Isaiah 5.3. Whenever the citizens of Jerusalem would plot against the house of David, the 'people of Judah' (= '*am Jehudah*), also called '*am ha'areṣ*, would pour into Jerusalem, kill the conspirators and forcibly enthrone a descendant of David to whom the throne belonged by virtue of heredity. In Alt's opinion, the story of the enthroning of Joash, which ends with the words: 'And all the people of the land rejoiced and the city was quiet' (II Kings 11.20), reflects the political contrast between Jerusalem and the land of Judah (Alt, 251–4). Alt's opinion is fraught with difficulties, as there is no real evidence that Judah and Jerusalem constituted two distinct political units which were united in a 'personal union' by the house of David, nor for any real differences between the population of Judah and the residents of Jerusalem (but see above, pp. 353–6, 393).

Soggin holds that the term '*am ha'areṣ* refers to a large group in the population which worshipped God in the spirit of the prophets. This body represented those who were faithful to the Yahwistic tradition in Judah and had no special class or social associations. Because of the many meanings which can be given the term '*am ha'areṣ* and the varied and inconsistent use of the concept in the Bible itself Nicholson reaches the conclusion that the concept has no set, precise definition (Nicholson, 66). It can be said for sure, however, that 'the people of the land' was a political-social element which was loyal to the house of David. This element in the society was the main factor behind the phenomenon of hereditary succession in Judah (Talmon). If indeed the murder of Amon had an anti-Assyrian political background, the counter-revolution which was carried out by the '*am ha'areṣ* against the conspirators placated the Assyrians, who carried out no acts of reprisal against Jerusalem.

§4. JOSIAH AND THE DEUTERONOMIC REFORMATION

P. R. **Ackroyd**, *Exile and Restoration: A Study of Hebrew Thought of the Sixth Century BC*, OTL, 1968; Y. **Aharoni**, *The Land of the Bible*, 1967; idem, 'Arad: Its Inscriptions and Temple', *BA* XXXI, 1968, 2–32; idem, 'Trial Excavation in the "Solar Shrine" at Lachish', *IEJ* XVIII, 1968, 157–69;

idem, 'The Israelite Sanctuary at Arad', *New Directions*, 1969, 28–44; idem, 'The Horned Altar of Beer-Sheba', *BA* XXXVII, 1974, 2–6; idem, *Arad Inscriptions*, Jerusalem: Bialik Institute/Israel Exploration Society, 1975 (Hebrew); A. **Alt**, 'Judas Gaue unter Josia', *PJB* XXI, 1925, 100–16 = his *KS* II, 1953, 276–88; N. **Avigad**, 'Excavations in the Jewish Quarter of the Old City of Jerusalem 1971 (Third Preliminary Report)', *IEJ* XXII, 1972, 193–200; H. **Cazelles**, 'Soponie, Jérémie, et les Scythes en Palestine', *RB* LXXIV, 1967, 24–44; W. E. **Claburn**, 'The Fiscal Basis of Josiah's Reform', *JBL* XCII, 1973, 11–22; F. M. **Cross** and D. N. **Freedman**, 'Josiah's Revolt against Assyria', *JNES* XII, 1953, 56–8; F. M. **Cross**, 'Epigraphic Notes on Hebrew Documents of the Eighth–Sixth Centuries BC', *BASOR* CLXV, 1962, 34–46; idem, 'Judean Stamps', *EI* IX, 1969, 20–7; H. L. **Ginsberg**, 'Judah and the Transjordan States from 734–582 BC', *Alexander Marx Jubilee Volume*, 1950, 347–68; K. A. **Kitchen**, *The Third Intermediate Period in Egypt (1100–650 BC)*, 1973; M. **Kochavi**, *Judea, Samaria and the Golan*, Jerusalem: Carta 1972; H. D. **Lance**, 'The Royal Stamps and the Kingdom of Josiah', *HTR* LXIV, 1971, 315–32; A. **Lemaire**, 'MMŠT – Amwas, vers la solution d'une enigme de l'épigraphie Hébraïque', *RB* XCII, 1975, 15–23; M. **van Loon**, 'Review of *Die Skythen in Südrussland* by J. A. H. Potratz', *JNES* XXIX, 1970, 66–72; A. **Malamat**, 'Josiah's Bid for Armageddon', *JANES* V, 1973, 267–78; B. **Mazar** et al., *En-Gedi: The First and Second Seasons of Excavation 1961–1962*, AES 5, 1966; G. E. **Mendenhall**, 'Covenant Forms in Israelite Tradition', *BA* XVII, 1954, 50–76 = *BAR* III, 1970, 25–53; J. M. **Miller**, 'The Korahites in Southern Judah', *CBQ* XXXII, 1970, 58–68; J. **Naveh**, 'A Hebrew Letter from the Seventh Century BC', *IEJ* X, 1960, 129–39; XII, 1962, 27–32, 89–99; E. W. **Nicholson**, 'The Centralisation of the Cult in Deuteronomy', *VT* XIII, 1963, 380–9; idem, *Deuteronomy and Tradition: Literary and Historical Problems in the Book of Deuteronomy*, Oxford/Philadelphia: Basil Blackwell/Fortress Press 1967; E. **Nielsen**, 'Political Conditions and Cultural Developments in Israel and Judah During the Reign of Manasseh', *Fourth World Congress of Jewish Studies* I, Jerusalem: World Union of Jewish Studies 1967, 103–6; H. W. F. **Saggs**, *The Greatness that was Babylon*, London/New York: Sidgwick and Jackson/Hawthorn, 1962; H. **Tadmor**, 'Philistia under Assyrian Rule', *BA* XXIX, 1966, 86–102; A. D. **Tushingham**, 'A Royal Israelite Seal (?) and the Royal Jar Handle Stamps', *BASOR* CC, 1970, 71–8; CCI, 1971, 23–35; R. P. **Vaggione**, 'Over All Asia? The Extent of the Scythian Domination in Herodotus', *JBL* XCII, 1973, 523–30; M. **Weinfeld**, 'Cult Centralization in Israel in the Light of a Neo-Babylonian Analogy', *JNES* XXIII, 1964, 202–12; idem, 'The Awakening of National Consciousness in Israel in the Seventh-Century BC', *'Oz le-David, Biblical Essays in Honor of D. Ben-Gurion*, Jerusalem: Kiryath Sepher, 1964, 396–420 (Hebrew); idem, 'Deuteronomy – the Present State of Inquiry', *JBL* LXXXVI, 1967, 249–62; idem, *Deuteronomy and the Deuteronomic School*, London: Oxford University Press 1972; P. **Welten**, *Die Königs-Stempel: Ein Beitrag zur Militärpolitik Judas* *unter Hiskia und Josia*, ADPV 4, 1969; D. J. **Wiseman**, *Chronicles of Chaldean Kings (626–556 BC)*, 1956.

Josiah was placed on the throne while still a young lad of eight years (640/39 BCE). The narratives about him in II Kings 22–3 and II Chronicles 34–5 are concentrated around his cultic activity and the discovery of 'the book of the law' in the temple. In dealing with Josiah's reform, one must distinguish between the purification of the cult and its centralization in Jerusalem. The purification of the cult refers to the destruction of the pagan foreign cults which the biblical tradition states had been introduced into Israel in Solomon's days (II Kings 23.13), were expanded during the time of Ahaz, and reached their climax in the reign of Manasseh (II Kings 23.12). Josiah's actions in purifying the cult were not limited to Judah but extended to Bethel (II Kings 23.4, 15) and the 'cities of Samaria' (II Kings 23.8, 19; II Chron. 34.6). According to II Kings, Josiah's reforming activity took place in his eighteenth year (623/2 BCE) after 'the book of the law' was discovered in the temple by Hilkiah the priest (II Kings 22.3–20). On the other hand, the account in II Chronicles places the purification of the cult from its pagan elements in the twelfth year of Josiah (629/8 BCE) while the 'book of the law given by Moses' (II Chron. 34.14) was found six years later in the eighteenth year and after the temple was repaired. According to II Chronicles, the influence of the book was limited to the renewal of the covenant between the people and God 'to keep his commandments and his testimonies and his statutes' (II Chron. 34.31). This of course differs radically from the account in II Kings which explains the purification of the cult against the background of the discovery of the law book.

Actually, Josiah was not the first to attempt a purification of the cult of its pagan elements. Several Judaean kings did the same but about them it was said: 'However, the high places were not taken away' (i.e. I Kings 15.14; II Kings 12.3). The worship of Yahweh, the God of Israel, at the high places (*bamoth*) was rooted in the life of the people and these earlier kings had not dared eliminate this aspect of their religious life (Weinfeld, 1964, 202–4; Nielsen, 106). Elijah did not hesitate to construct an altar on Mount Carmel and even complained that those who tore down God's altars were abandoning the tradition of Israel (I Kings 19.10, 14). Cultic places from the period of the Judaean monarchy have been excavated at Arad and Beer-Sheba (Aharoni, 1971 and 1974). Hezekiah was the first king to attempt making an end of these Yahwistic high places and to begin the centralization of the cult in Jerusalem. Josiah followed Hezekiah's ways, in order to unify the cult completely (Weinfeld, 1964, 211). Such unification meant the destruction of the high places in towns and cities outside Jerusalem and the limitation of worship to the Jerusalem temple. Any other place was unqualified for divine worship.

Josiah's activities undertaken in his centralization of the cult are noted in II Kings 23.8, 15, 19 and were given special symbolic significance in his destruction of the high place in Bethel which had been erected by Jeroboam, the son of Nebat, the first northern monarch (II Kings 23.15). According to Aharoni, archaeological evidence for the destruction of temples outside Jerusalem during the reign of Josiah has been unearthed at Arad (Aharoni, 'Arad', 26f.). Josiah brought to Jerusalem the priests who had served in the Judaean high places (II Kings 23.8; cf. Deut. 18.6f.; see Miller). It may be assumed that the destruction of the *bamoth* was opposed by certain circles which did not consider such worship at the high places to be sinful. Some of this objection finds echoes in Jeremiah 11.3; 44.17–19. The existence of a Yahwistic temple at Elephantine in Egypt (see below, ch. IX §3D) as well as a post-exilic Jewish temple (not Edomite) at Lachish (Aharoni, 'Trial Excavation') proves that the idea of the centralization of the cult was not accepted by everyone. Jeremiah's prophecies suggest that the reform was supported by the prophets as well as the priests of the Jerusalem temple (Jer. 11.6, 13; 22.15f.; see II Chron. 35.25). It was perhaps no accident that the book of the law was found by Hilkiah the priest and that, according to Kings, the discovery of the book helped motivate the reform.

What was the 'book of the law' or the 'book of the covenant' which was discovered in the temple? This question has produced an enormous amount of literature since the problem is so interwoven with the difficult and complicated issue of the literary sources of the pentateuch (for bibliography see Weinfeld, 1967). Here we shall limit ourselves to some of the historical aspects of the issue. Since the beginning of the nineteenth century, biblical scholars have generally agreed with de Wette that the book found in the temple during Josiah's reign was Deuteronomy or rather an old form of that book. Furthermore, it has been assumed that the book was composed during Josiah's days and related anachronistically to Moses. These opinions are based on some important connections between the 'book of the law' found in the temple, the reform of Josiah, and our present book of Deuteronomy which is also called the book of the law (Deut. 31.24, 26; 29.21). (1) The command to centralize the cult in the one

place chosen by God is only found in the book of Deuteronomy
(12.5). Josiah's reform abolished the worship of the *bamoth* and
required a centralization of the cult in one place – Jerusalem.
(2) The book found in the temple included curses and threats (II
Kings 22.16; II Chron. 34.24) and only in the book of Deuteronomy
do we find collected together curses which God will visit upon the
people if they fail to keep the covenant. Among the Deuteronomic
curses, we find the threat of exile and destruction (Deut. 28.36f., 63–
65). (3) Josiah sent a delegation to Huldah the prophetess (II Kings
22.11–20) according to the law of Deuteronomy 18.15. (4) Both in
Kings and Chronicles, the passages which discuss the book that was
found, and its association with Josiah's activity to centralize the cult,
and the celebration of the passover in Jerusalem appear together (II
Kings 23; II Chron. 34–5). A similar juxtaposition between centralization and passover is again found in Deuteronomy (16.5–8)
according to which the passover is to be celebrated at 'the place
which the Lord thy God shall choose'.

In spite of these and other reasons, there are those who have
doubts about the theory that the book of Deuteronomy was composed in Josiah's days and that Josiah's reform actually dealt with
the centralization of the cult. Such doubts have been raised by
scholars who claim that an emphasis on the centralization of the cult
first occurred during the period of the exile and restoration. On the
other hand, there are scholars who claim that the idea of cultic
centralization and the book of Deuteronomy are much earlier than
the time of Josiah (see II Chron. 17.9). (See the discussions and
bibliography in Nicholson, 1963 and 1967; Weinfeld, 1967.)

Similarly, scholars are divided as to the 'school' from which the
book of Deuteronomy, unique in its homiletic and rhetorical style
and phraseology, originated (see Weinfeld, 1972). Was the
Deuteronomic author one of the Levites, among whose duties was
the teaching of the law (see II Chron. 17.9; Neh. 8). Or was he one
of the prophets who struggled against idolatry and worship on the
high places and whose preaching had much in common with the
book of Deuteronomy in phraseology (especially the book of
Jeremiah)? Or perhaps the Deuteronomic author was one of the
court scribes, who dealt with literary and written documents and
were familiar with the structure of covenants (see the discussion and
bibliography in Weinfeld, 1972).

Indeed, the whole question is very complicated and here we can
only note the assumptions we accept. (1) The book of Deuteronomy

does demand the centralization of the cult in one place, but the idea itself was not invented in Josiah's time as the previous discussion of Hezekiah illustrates. Thus Josiah's reform need not necessarily be closely associated with the discovery of the book of the law. According to Chronicles, the book was found in the temple after the reform was already under way. (2) The book designated 'the book of the covenant' (II Kings 23.2) was obviously some form of the book of Deuteronomy, though whether in its present or an earlier form is uncertain (see II Chron. 17.9 for reference to a 'book of the law of God' at the time of Jehoshaphat). The book of Deuteronomy has the style of a covenant in a form found in Near Eastern international treaties (Mendenhall; Weinfeld, 1972, 59–81). Usually these treaties included three elements: (*a*) a historical introduction intended to justify the covenant (cf. Deut. 1–11); (*b*) the conditions of the treaty (see Deut. 12–26); and (*c*) curses which were to come upon the participant who did not observe the treaty stipulations (cf. Deut. 27–8). Thus the name 'book of the covenant' is an appropriate description of the book of Deuteronomy. (3) One can suggest that the book was hidden in the temple during the days of Manasseh and Amon, that is, at the height of the Assyrian oppression and the religious-cultic syncretism, and then discovered when Josiah's reform took place. (4) The strong impression which the book had on Josiah can be explained by the fact that only in the book of Deuteronomy do Israelite legal traditions speak about the institution of kingship and its responsibilities (see Deut. 17.18). In the rebuking words of Huldah the prophetess (II Kings 22.15–17), one can hear an echo of the words of Deuteronomy 28.36 concerning the destiny of the king and nation.

Either the reform was the result of the discovery of the book of the law, as in II Kings, or else the discovery of the book followed the reform, as in Chronicles. With either alternative, one cannot neglect the political aspects of Josiah's reform any more than was the case with Hezekiah. The centralization of the cult in Jerusalem must be viewed in connection with the desire to strengthen the relations between the residents of the provincial cities and the central government in Jerusalem. In addition, Josiah's reform extended beyond the borders of Judah into areas which belonged to the former kingdom of northern Israel (II Kings 23.4; II Chron. 34.6–7). These areas were part of Assyrian provinces where exiled people from other countries had been settled (II Kings 17.24; Ezra 4.9). Josiah's attempt to halt Pharaoh Necho at Megiddo shows that Josiah had extended his rule over the north towards Galilee (II Chron. 34.6f.;

see Cross and Freedman). Whether the fortress of Megiddo II was held by Josiah or by the Egyptians is a controversial issue (Aharoni, 1967, 349; Malamat).

Josiah also succeeded in enlarging his kingdom to the west, to the sea-coast, in the area of Philistia, as is evident from the archaeological discoveries at *Mesad Hashavyahu* (*Yabneh-Yam*) which included Hebrew inscriptions (Naveh, 1960, and Cross, 1962, 42–6). Surveys along the western shore of the Dead Sea (see Bar-Adon, in Kochavi, 93 f.) together with the excavations at Ein Gedi (see Mazar, 16) provide evidence of extensive settlement and the construction of fortifications in this area during the eighth–seventh century.

In the south, the fortress at Arad was strengthened and additional fortifications erected to defend the southern border (Aharoni, 'Arad', 30–2). One of the Arad inscriptions (ibid., 13 f.) refers to the Kittim which probably points to the existence of a Greek mercenary force in Josiah's service. Similarly, the presence of eastern Greek pottery at Mesad Hashavyahu probably also indicates Greek mercenaries in Josiah's service (Tadmor, 102). Excavations in old Jerusalem show that the city expanded towards the west and north-west in the later period of the monarchy (Avigad, 200) probably during the days of Josiah. In addition, Josiah's marriage to Zebidah from a family in Rumah in Galilee (II Kings 23.36) and to Hamutal from a family in Libnah (II Kings 23.31) located on the Philistine border are evidence of the enlarged extent of Judah during Josiah's reign. It is plausible that Josiah had to reorganize the kingdom's administration and needed funds to carry out his policy, whose main aims were to solidify his rule over Judah from the capital of Jerusalem, to strengthen his country by fortifying cities and enlarging the army, and to widen the boundaries of his kingdom especially to the north. In the opinion of Claburn, Josiah's reform, which mainly involved the centralization of the cult, constituted a fiscal reorganization of his kingdom. He derives this from verses in the book of Deuteronomy (such as Deut. 12.3–6; 14.24–6) which obligated the people to bring offerings and tithes to the temple in Jerusalem. Through the centralization of the cult, according to Claburn, Josiah could collect taxes from the population of the provincial towns and supervise the Levites in Judah who were made to come to Jerusalem.

Scholars have sought to use the so-called *lmlk* seal-impressions in order to understand Josiah's administrative reorganization as well as the boundaries of his kingdom. In Judah proper, hundreds of royal seal-impressions on jar-handles have been found. The impressions are of two types: (1) a four-winged scarab and (2) a two-winged solar disc. On the upper part of the stamps is written *lmlk* ('of/to the king') and the lower part has one of the following four names, Hebron, Ziph, Socho, and *mmšt*. The first three are known place-names whereas *mmšt* is unknown. Various suggestions seeking to identify *mmšt* have been made (see Lemaire). It seems most likely that the word refers to one of the cities which served as an administrative centre in the kingdom of Judah.

Since the stamps have nearly all been found somewhere within the borders of Judah, it is reasonable to assume that their presence at *Tell en-Naṣbeh* (Mizpah) in the north, Gezer and *Tell el-Ereini* in the west, Beer-Sheba and Arad in the south, and Ein Gedi, Qumran and Jericho in the east suggest that all of these places were within the borders of the kingdom of Josiah.

There is a tendency on the part of some scholars to connect the group of the four-winged type with the era of Hezekiah or shortly thereafter (Aharoni, 1967, 340f.; Welten) and the two-winged type with the era of Josiah (Cross, 1969, 20–2; Lance, 329). In Tushingham's opinion, both types belong to Josiah's time; the four-winged type was formerly the symbol of the northern kingdom of Israel and was brought into use in Judah by Josiah alongside the two-winged Judaic stamp as a symbolic action of Josiah towards the restoration of the Davidic kingdom (Tushingham, 1970, 71–8; 1971, 24f.).

The function of these stamps is also in dispute; various opinions have been expressed (Welten, 118–42). According to Aharoni, the jars bearing the royal stamps were made to contain a standard official measure. The four cities were four main administrative centres and store-cities for storing tribute in kind (Aharoni, 1967, 346). In Welten's opinion, the jars with *lmlk* stamps were part of a royal network supplying the fortresses and strongholds. The four cities were royal estates which were responsible for supplying food (wine and oil) to the fortresses (Welten, 142–74).

It seems that the stamps give us information concerning the area of the kingdom of Judah in Josiah's reign, during which time it included Gezer and Jericho; this fits in to some degree with what is said in II Kings 23.8: 'from Geba to Beer-Sheba'. With regard to the more northerly areas, no *lmlk* stamps have been found there, possibly because Josiah did not manage to organize the new areas – which were far from Jerusalem – according to the model in use in the kingdom of Judah itself (so Tushingham, 1971).

All attempts, however, to reconstruct the boundaries of Josiah's kingdom beyond the borders of Judah proper and vicinity are speculations, being dependent upon sources which are ambiguous. Alt, for example, is of the opinion that the source of the town lists in the book of Joshua, pertaining to both the southern and northern tribes (as Josh. 15.21–62; 19.2–7) is an administrative document from Josiah's reign. The lists of towns in Joshua 13 and Numbers 32.3, 34–8 relate to Josiah's territory in Transjordan. Ginsberg is of the opinion that from the oracle against the Ammonites in Jeremiah 49 and from Isaiah 9.1–7 we may conclude that Josiah ruled over the Gilead. In his opinion, Josiah, in restoring the ancient empire of king David, brought not only practically all of the former territories of Judah and Israel under his direct rule but also the three Transjordan states (minus some territories) under his suzerainty (Ginsberg, 355–63). Malamat tends to exclude Galilee from Josiah's rule, and states that Josiah 'extended his rule over territories which coincided, more or less, with the former Assyrian province of *Samerina* (II Kings 23.15, 19, in contrast to II Chron. 34.6f., 33)' (Malamat, 271).

What was the background to the national revival and what were the political conditions which enabled Josiah to enlarge his kingdom even into those areas which were under Assyrian sovereignty? The Assyrian empire which reached its zenith during the time of Manasseh was shaken and collapsed in a relatively short time as a result, on the one hand, of internal crises and, on the other hand, of extensive pressure from the outside. The turmoil in Assyria which followed Asshurbanipal's death in 627 BCE weakened the authority of the central government and simultaneously awakened nationalistic movements in the subjected states. In the east, Nabopolasar, the Chaldean founder of the Neo-Babylonian empire, took advantage of the instability in the Assyrian royal court and asserted the independence of Babylon in 626 BCE. He was supported by Media and the two powers together sought to destroy the Assyrian empire in a series of military campaigns which are reported in the Babylonian Chronicles (see Wiseman). On the western border of the empire, in Egypt, Psammetichus I (664–610 BCE), the leader of the Egyptian national revival movement, had already asserted the independence of Egypt in 655/4 BCE (see Kitchen, 399–408). Psammetichus not only brought an end to Assyrian sovereignty in Egypt but also planned campaigns into Palestine in order to restore long-lost Egyptian control over the area (see Herodotus, II 157 on the conquest of Azotus [= Ashdod] by Psammetichus I).

Another factor that upset the balance of the Assyrian empire came from the north (see Jer. 1.14). The Akkadian sources mention invasions of tribes with such names as Gimirraya and Ashkuzaya (see Gen. 10.4; Ezek. 38.6; Jer. 51.27; Saggs, 124, 129f.; van Loon). These tribes seem to have come from the regions around the Caspian and Black Seas and they penetrated forcefully into Mesopotamia, Asia Minor, Syria, and perhaps Palestine (see Cazelles and Vaggione). The Babylonian Chronicles mention the Umman-Manda as a power supporting Babylon and Media in their wars against Assyria (see Wiseman). Besides these northern tribes, Arabian tribes also penetrated the borders of the fertile crescent from the desert, destroying vast areas such as the Transjordanian region in Palestine (Oded, 185f., and bibliography there, n. 61).

The events associated with Josiah's reign in Judah can thus be easily understood in light of the gradual disintegration of the Assyrian empire. Josiah's cultic reform, which was accomplished gradually, in three stages (II Chron. 34.3–8), reflects the international political situation (Aharoni, 1972, 349; Cross and Freedman) and was an expression of the nationalistic and spiritual revival attendant upon the overthrow of Assyrian dominance. The king's invitation to all the people of Israel to celebrate passover in Jerusalem (II Chron. 35) was significant, since this festival recalled the memories of freedom from Egyptian slavery and the covenant with Yahweh. Furthermore, Josiah renewed the covenant between God and the nation (II Kings 23.3). The book of Deuteronomy, 'the book of the covenant', is permeated with nationalistic ideology. Several features in this ideology are noteworthy. The people are Yahweh's people (Deut. 27.9); they are the chosen people out of all nations (Deut. 7.6; 14.2, etc.). The book requires the destruction (*ḥerem*) of all the nations of Canaan (Deut. 2.34; 7.2, 16) and the isolation of Israel in order to preserve the national and religious uniqueness of the people (Deut. 7.6–11). In addition to these features, Deuteronomy encourages the cultivation of the individual's identification with the larger public, national solidarity, and his support of social equality (see Deut. 17.10). The book well reflects the patriotic attitude and the national excitement which flourished among the people during Josiah's days (Weinfeld, 'Awakening'; Ackroyd, 68 and bibliography there).

The collapse of the Assyrian empire, echoed in the vision of the prophet Nahum, created an opportune time for Josiah to fill the vacuum which was created in Israel. The process of restoring the kingdom of the house of David, however, was halted before it reached completion, halted by strong powers interested in the

Assyrian legacy in Syria and Israel. II Kings 23.29 and II Chronicles 35.20 refer to Pharaoh Necho's military expedition to Carchemish on the Euphrates (609 BCE). As the Egyptian forces passed through the valley of Megiddo, Josiah attacked Necho and was killed (see Malamat).

Because of Josiah's activities and the high hopes held out for him by the people we may understand, on the one hand, the book of Kings' evaluation of Josiah: 'before him there was no king like him . . . nor did any like him arise after him' (II Kings 23.25), and on the other hand, why his death was considered a great catastrophe for the nation: 'all Judah and Jerusalem held mourning rites for Josiah . . . and the singers have spoken of Josiah in their laments to this day and have made this a rule in Israel . . .' (II Chron. 35.24f.). The Babylonian Chronicles make it clear that the Egyptian king marched to the Euphrates on his way to Haran in support of Assur-uballit, the Assyrian ruler, who was struggling against Nabopolasar and his allies (Wiseman, 19; also Josephus, *Ant.* V 1). Thus the political situation clearly demonstrates that Egypt and Babylon fought for the right of inheritance to the Assyrian empire. Already in 616 BCE, the Egyptians had moved to the aid of Assyria (Wiseman, 55), not in an effort to salvage the Assyrian hegemony but, on the one hand, to regain control of Syria and Palestine. The activities of Psammetichus I in Philistia and Phoenicia demonstrate Egypt's ambition in the buffer regions between Egypt and Mesopotamia. Josiah clearly understood the political consequences for his kingdom should the Egyptians be victorious over Babylon. It is possible, that Josiah believed that by offering resistance to Pharaoh Necho II he would be demonstrating a pro-Babylonian policy (see Cross and Freedman). In exchange, he probably expected that distant Babylon would recognize his hegemony over Israel after the fall of Assyria and the defeat of Egypt. Josiah's failure and death at Megiddo placed Judah at the mercy of the Egyptians. With this altered political situation in Palestine should be associated the information about Pharaoh Necho's capture of Gaza (Kadytis) reported by Herodotus in his *History* (II 159) and Jeremiah (47.1), and probably the destruction of the fortress of Mesad Hashavyahu (Naveh, 1962, 98f.).

After the encounter with Josiah at Megiddo, Necho hurried on to Carchemish, unconcerned for the moment with the modest life of Judah. The people of the land (the *'am ha'areṣ*) enthroned Jehoahaz (= Shallum, see I Chron. 3.15), the son of Josiah, as the new king of Judah (II Kings 23.30; II Chron. 36.1). But Jehoahaz ruled for only three months. Pharaoh Necho, on his return from Carchemish by way of Riblah, deposed Jehoahaz and enthroned Eliakim, another son of Josiah, changing his name to Jehoiakim. Jehoahaz was carried to Egypt where he died (II Kings 23.31–4; II Chron. 36.3–4; Jer. 22.10–12; Ezek. 19.1–4).

§5.   THE LAST DAYS OF JUDAH AND THE DESTRUCTION OF JERUSALEM (609–586 BCE)

Y. **Aharoni**, 'Excavations at Ramat Rahel', *BA* XXIV, 1961, 98–118; idem, 'Arad: Its Inscriptions and Temple', *BA* XXXI, 1968, 2–32; W. F. **Albright**, 'The Seal of Eliakim and the Latest Preëxilic History of Judah', *JBL* LI, 1932, 77–106; M. **David**, 'The Manumission of Slaves under Zedekiah', *OS* V, 1948, 63–79; K. S. **Freedy** and D. B. **Redford**, 'The Dates in Ezekiel in Relation to Biblical, Babylonian and Egyptian Sources', *JAOS* XC, 1970, 462–85; S. B. **Frost**, 'The Death of Josiah: A Conspiracy of Silence', *JBL* LXXXVII, 1968, 369–82; H. L. **Ginsberg**, 'Judah and the Transjordan States from 734 to 582 BC', *Alexander Marx Jubilee Volume*, 1950, 347–68; M. **Greenberg**, 'Ezekiel 17 and the Policy of Psammetichus II', *JBL* LXXVI, 1957, 304–9; S. H. **Horn**, 'Where and When was the Aramaic Saqqara Papyrus Written?', *AUSS* VI, 1968, 29–45; K. **Kenyon**, *Archaeology in the Holy Land*, London/New York: Ernest Benn/Frederick A. Praeger 1960, ³1970; E. **Kutsch**, 'Das Jahr der Katastrophe: 587 v. Chr.', *Biblica* LV, 1974, 520–45; G. **Larsson**, 'When did the Babylonian Captivity Begin?', *JTS* XVIII, 1967, 417–23; A. **Malamat**, 'The Last Kings of Judah and the Fall of Jerusalem', *IEJ* XVIII, 1968, 137–56; idem, 'The Twilight of Judah: in the Egyptian–Babylonian Maelstrom', *SVT* XXVIII, 1975, 123–45; S. **Moscati**, *L'epigrafia Ebraica antica*, BibOr 15, 1951; J. M. **Myers**, 'Edom and Judah in the Sixth–Fifth Centuries BC', *Near Eastern Studies*, 1971, 377–92; E. **Stern**, 'Israel at the Close of the Period of the Monarchy: An Archaeological Survey', *BA* XXXVIII, 1975, 26–54; H. **Tadmor**, 'Chronology of the Last Kings of Judah', *JNES* XV, 1956, 226–30; E. R. **Thiele**, *The Mysterious Numbers of the Hebrew Kings: A Reconstruction of the Chronology of the Kingdoms of Israel and Judah*, Grand Rapids/Exeter: Wm. B. Eerdmans/The Paternoster Press ²1965; M. **Tsevat**, 'The Neo-Assyrian and Neo-Babylonian Vassal Oaths and the Prophet Ezekiel', *JBL* LXXVIII, 1959, 199–204; S. S. **Weinberg**, 'Post Exilic Palestine: An Archaeological Report', *IASHP* IV, 1971, 78–97; D. J. **Wiseman**, *Chronicles of the Chaldean Kings (625–556 BC)*, 1956.

The death of Josiah and the exile of Jehoahaz, whom the Judaeans preferred to his elder brother, shocked the people of Judah. Jeremiah 22.10–12 and II Chronicles 35.25 give expression to their sentiment. Jehoiakim (Eliakim) was hated by most of his people both because of his pro-Egyptian policy and because of his tyrannical rule and the heavy financial burdens which he placed on his subjects in contrast to the rule of his father (II Kings 23.35; Jer. 22.13–19; and see Aharoni, 1961, 118). Prophets who complained about the activities of the king, his ministers, and the priests were persecuted and some sentenced to death (Jer. 26; II Kings 24.2–4). In the view of the prophets and in comparison with Josiah's cultic reform, the reign of Jehoiakim witnessed a religious decline.

The struggle between Egypt and Babylon for hegemony in Syro-Palestine continued for some time. After 609 BCE, the Egyptians ruled over Palestine and Syria. The battleground between Egypt and Babylon was located along the Euphrates River (see II Kings 24.7). Jehoiakim faithfully carried the Egyptian burden (II Kings 23.35; II Chron. 36.3) and it appears that Judah's borders reverted to those under Manasseh and Amon. The decisive shift in the power balance took place in 605 BCE. In that year, Nebuchadrezzar defeated the Egyptian army at Carchemish (Wiseman, 66–8; Jer. 46.2; Josephus, *Ant.* X 84–6; see Freedy and Redford, 465). This decisive battle led to the dominance of Chaldean Babylon over Syro-Palestine (II Kings 24.1; Jer. 25.1–14; 36.29; cf. Dan 1.1 f.). The tremendous impression which the Chaldean army made on the people of Syro-Palestine finds expression in Habakkuk 1.5–10.

Judah's submission to Babylon occurred in one of the years 605–601 BCE, during which time Nebuchadrezzar made campaigns to the land of 'Hatti' (Syro-Palestine) and received tribute from the local kings. Ashkelon, which refused to surrender to the Chaldeans, was conquered (604 BCE) and her king taken into captivity (Wiseman, 68f.; see Jer. 36.9). When Jehoiakim chose to rebel against Babylon (c. 600 BCE), three years after submitting to Nebuchadrezzar (II Kings 24.1), he did so because of the failure of the Babylonian invasion of Egypt and in hopes of receiving significant support from Egypt (see Herodotus, II 159 and Freedy and Redford, 475 n. 57; Malamat, 1975, 131 f.). An Aramaic letter discovered in Saqqarah in Egypt which addresses the Pharaoh as 'the master of the kings' and requests the Pharaoh to hurry and send help against the approaching Chaldean army was probably written at this time by Adon, a ruler from Philistia or Phoenicia (Malamat, 1974, 128f.; Horn; Freedy and Redford, 477f.).

In response to the rebellion of Jehoiakim, Nebuchadrezzar sent Chaldean units which were already in the area as well as battalions from the subject states of Moab, Ammon, and Edom against Judah (II Kings 24.2). The biblical information on this action is probably related to the notice in the Arad inscriptions which speak of Edomite movements into the Judaean Negeb (Aharoni, 1968, 17f.; Myers, 390–2). Nebuchadrezzar, in the seventh year of his reign (598/7 BCE), marched on a punitive campaign against Judah. The Babylonian Chronicles reports this action as follows:

Year 7, month Kislimu: The king of Akkad moved his army into Hatti land, laid siege to the city of Judah (*al ia-a-ḫu-du*) and the king took the city on the second day of the month Addaru. He appointed in it a king to his liking, took heavy booty from it and brought it into Babylon (*ANET*, 564).

Thus Jerusalem fell into Babylonian hands on March 15/16, 597 BCE.

The Babylonian inscription reports neither the name of the Judaean king who was defeated nor the name of the new ruler installed in his place by Nebuchadrezzar. There is no agreement in the Bible at this point (cf. II Kings 24.6–12 with II Chron. 36.6–10; Dan. 1.1f.; see Larsson; Albright, 90f.). The most reasonable possibility is that Jehoiakim died (or was killed, see II Kings 24.6; Jer. 22.19; 36.30) during the siege and was succeeded by his son Jehoiachin (597 BCE), who preferred to surrender to Nebuchadrezzar rather than continue resistance, and thus to save Judah and Jerusalem from total destruction (II Kings 24.12; II Chron. 36.10; Ezek. 17.12). This act of Jehoiachin, taken on his own initiative, may explain the reason for his special treatment in exile. Along with Jehoiachin, members of the royal family, nobles, land-owners, military leaders, elders of the people, artisans, priests, and prophets were exiled, among whom was the prophet Ezekiel (II Kings 24.14–16; Jer. 24.1; 27.20; 24.1f.; 52.28; Ezek. 1.1–3). The exact total number of the deportees is not known since the biblical sources are in contradiction at this point (II Kings 24.14, 16; Jer. 52.28; see Malamat, 1975, 133f.). This exile was a severe blow to Judah because it removed from the land the upper crust of Judaean society or, according to Jeremiah, 'the basket of good figs' (Jer. 24).

Many of the people of Judah apparently did not accept the new king Zedekiah (Mattaniah) and it seems that they continued to consider Jehoiachin as the legal king of Judah, waiting and hoping for his return (Jer. 28). Jeremiah spoke against this forlorn hope because he accepted Zedekiah's reign as a fact and saw it as part of the plan of God (Jer. 27; Albright, 92f.).

Zedekiah saw himself as the legitimate king in all matters, since he was of the legitimate house of David. Zedekiah inherited a 'lowly kingdom' (Ezek. 17.14 and see Jer. 13.19), a small weak state, weak militarily and economically, and a state torn by internal divisive parties. Zedekiah himself was not the right king at the right time. He lacked the character which could have halted the national decline before the end – the destruction of the country, the capital, and the temple. He was a weak ruler with a character which lacked self-confidence and was given to hesitation and straddling the fence. He was inclined to listen to Jeremiah's advice concerning rebellion against Babylon (Jer. 27) but he feared his pro-Egyptian ministers and was dragged by them into open revolt against Babylon (Jer. 38.5).

During his first years, Zedekiah kept his oath of allegiance to the Babylonian king (II Chron. 36.13; Ezek. 17.12–14) but after four years, in 594/3 BCE, he, together with other rulers, took part in a conspiracy against Babylon (Jer. 27–8) with the encouragement of the Egyptian king Psammetichus II (Greenberg; Freedy and Redford, 470–6). For unknown reasons this revolt did not materialize, and Zedekiah humbly submitted himself before the Babylonian king (Jer. 29.3; 51.59). Open rebellion broke out in 589/8 BCE. It appears that Zedekiah was encouraged by Pharaoh Hophra, the son of Psammetichus II (Ezek. 17.15; 29). The Lachish letters make it clear that Judah acted in close association with Egypt, since military commanders were sent there, as reported in Lachish Ostracon III: 'It was reported to your servant that the commander of the host, Coniah son of Elnathan, has come down in order to go to Egypt' (*ANET*, 322). Even Tyre joined in Zedekiah's rebellion against Babylon, according to Josephus, who refers to Nebuchadrezzar's siege of Tyre at the time of his siege of Jerusalem (*Contra Apionem*, I 21). The king of Ammon may have joined with the conspirators (see Ezek. 21.24f. and Ginsberg, 365f.). Nebuchadrezzar was, at the time, at the peak of his power and a coalition of two or three kings could not oust the rule of Babylon from Phoenicia and Judah.

Furthermore, Zedekiah's chances of success in his revolt were poor because of the domestic situation in Judah. The people were divided in their attitudes towards Babylon and Egypt. The army officers who were inclined to adventurism and who made their career by war, together with prophets – whom Jeremiah called 'false prophets' (Jer. 28–9) – agitated for revolt, basing their case upon dependence on Egypt. These prophets implanted in the people the confidence that the God of Israel would not desert his people nor allow the destruction of the temple (Jer. 5.12; 14.13). In order to solidify the Judaean population around the king, to strengthen the idea of national brotherhood, and to increase the defending forces, a covenant was made between the king and people and all Hebrew slaves were released (Jer. 34.8–10). This enthusiasm for national brotherhood was short-lived and the former slave owners quickly re-enslaved their former subjects (Jer. 34.11–16; see David).

Jeremiah protested against the social and religious evils among the people and declared the Judaean residents to be 'bad figs' as contrasted with the 'good figs' which had gone into exile (Jer. 24.1–10). He prophesied that the people of Judah would die and that the land and the capital would be destroyed by an 'enemy from the north' (Jer. 1.13–15; 4.5–8; 6.1–8, 22–6; 34.17–22). According to the prophet, the people's fate was already sealed as a result of their religious sins and social abuses, in light of which God would have no pity on his people and his temple (Jer. 7; 21; 26.7–11). The same religious and social situation is reflected in the prophecies of Ezekiel (Ezek. 8–9). According to God's plan, Babylon was to rule over all the nations for 'seventy' years (Jer. 25.12; 27.6). Thus the prophet Jeremiah proclaimed that the people remaining in Judah, as well as those already exiled, should be loyal to Babylon, since any rebellion against Babylon was doomed to failure in advance and was contrary to the will of God (Jer. 21.8f.; 29.1–9; 38.2–4). A similar view of Babylon as the nation to be used by God for the punishment of his people, as well as the idea that God would later save his people and subsequently punish Babylon, also appear in the prophecies of Habakkuk.

When the rebellion broke out, it did not take long for Nebuchadrezzar to react against Zedekiah's breach of trust (II Kings 25.1; II Chron. 36.13; Ezek. 17.16; see Tsevat). At the beginning of 588 BCE, the Babylonian army began the siege of Jerusalem which lasted until August, 587 BCE or August, 586 BCE (II Kings 25; Jer. 21.3–7; 39; 52.4f.; Ezek. 24.1f.). Egypt under Pharaoh Apries (= Hophra) did support Judah militarily (Jer. 37.5–11 and see Ezek. 17; 29–32; Lam. 4.17) but her military operation in 588–587 BCE was unable to save Judah (Jer. 37.6–10; Ezek. 30.20–6; 31.10–13; Freedy and Redford, 470f., 481).

During the siege of Jerusalem, the Babylonian battalions spread out over the country, capturing and destroying Judaean cities (Jer. 34.7; 44.2; Lam. 2.2–5). The tension and distress of the time are reflected in the Lachish ostraca. The commander of one of the Judaean fortresses wrote to the army officer in Lachish: 'And let (my lord) know that we are watching for the signals of Lachish, according to all the indications which my lord has given, for we cannot see Azekah' (Ostracon IV; *ANET*, 322). Possibly this letter reflects the

situation in which Azekah was captured by the Chaldeans and its
signals were no longer seen (see Jer. 34.7). The despair which overcame many of the people during the war led to their flight to neighbouring countries (Jer. 40.11) and to the leaders' accusation against
Jeremiah – 'Let this man be put to death' (Jer. 38.4 and compare
Lachish Ostracon IV, *ANET*, 322). When he tried to go to the land
of Benjamin to see some property he had bought, Jeremiah was
suspected of desertion and betrayal and was imprisoned (Jer. 37.12–
21; 38.28; 39.14).

In Hezekiah's days, the fortified cities of Judah had been captured
and Jerusalem placed under siege, but at that time, Judah was ruled
by a king who knew how to plan carefully, to think first and then
act, and a king who knew how to rule over his ministers and subjects. At that time, the people were united by the king, and
Rabshakeh's propaganda did not discourage them. The prophet
Isaiah on that occasion supported the king and inspired trust in
divine salvation. The situation in the days of Zedekiah was
absolutely the opposite. Zedekiah feared both his ministers and his
people (Jer. 38.14). He himself had ambivalent feelings about the
revolt. Jeremiah advised the people to leave the battlefield and to
surrender to the Babylonians (Jer. 21.8–10) and he also predicted
catastrophe upon the king, the nation, and Jerusalem. As a result,
some of the people surrendered to the Chaldeans.

Zedekiah did not escape from Jerusalem during the siege for fear
of the Jews who had already moved into the Babylonian camp (Jer.
38.14). Many refugees from the outlying regions did seek safety in
Jerusalem, and the situation in the capital city deteriorated and
became almost unbearable because of starvation (Jer. 37.21; 52.6,
24–7; II Kings 25.3, 18–21). The city fell to the Babylonians in the
summer of 587 (*Bright, 329; Kutsch, 520) or in the summer of 586
BCE (Malamat, 1974, 145; Thiele, 169; Tadmor).

It is impossible to date precisely the fall of the city of Jerusalem
and the events in the closing years of the Judaean monarchy because
of the uncertainty as to which chronological system was used in
Judah to reckon the regnal year: the one employing the month of
Nisan (March/April) as the beginning of the year or the one in
which the month of Tishri (September/October) was the beginning
of the year. It is also uncertain whether the years were reckoned by
post-dating or ante-dating (see Freedy and Redford, 464–70;
Malamat, 1975, 123f.). The uncertainty concerning the exact date
on which Jerusalem fell stems also from discrepancies in the dates of
the siege as given according to the reigns of Zedekiah, Jehoiachin,

and Nebuchadrezzar (for discussions see Malamat, 1968, and bibliography there).

With the breach of the city walls (Jer. 39.2; 52.6f.), Zedekiah, together with the nobles of Jerusalem, escaped from the city and fled towards Transjordan, probably hoping to find shelter with Baalis, the king of Ammon (II Kings 25; Jer. 52.7). Zedekiah was captured in the area of Jericho and was taken to Riblah in Syria where the Babylonian headquarters were located. Here his sons were slaughtered in front of him and his eyes blinded. Zedekiah was then taken captive to Babylon. Nebuzaradan, the commander of the Babylonian guard, systematically destroyed Jerusalem and burned the temple (II Kings 25.8–10; Jer. 52.12–14; Ezek. 33.21 and compare Neh. 2.13f.). The pain and sorrow which the people suffered as a result of the destruction of Jerusalem are vividly expressed in the book of Lamentations and in Psalm 137. The day of the destruction (the ninth of Ab) became a day of fasting and mourning for Israel for all generations (Zech. 7.3–7). The archaeological finds show clearly that many Judaean cities and important centres were destroyed in the Babylonian campaign. Among these were Lachish, Tell Zakariya (Azekah), Eglon, Tell Beth Mirsim, Tell el-Ful, Beth Zur, Ramat Rachel, Beth-Shemesh, Bethel, Arad, Ein Gedi, and others (cf. Jer. 34.7; 44.2; Albright, 103–6; Weinberg, 80; Kenyon, 291; Stern, 35). Judah's defeat was used by the Edomites as an occasion for invading the southern areas of Judah (Ezek. 25.12–14; 35; Obad. 10–14; Mal. 1.3–5; Lam. 4.21f.; Ps. 137.7; see Myers).

In addition to the destruction of the capital city, the temple, and the land, many Jews were exiled. II Kings 25.11 reports: 'The rest of the people who were left in the city and the deserters who had deserted to the king of Babylon, together with the rest of the multitude, Nebuzaradan the captain of the guard carried into exile' (see Jer. 52.29f.). The Babylonians employed a system of mass deportation, well known from the Assyrian period. There were two differences, however, between the Babylonian and Assyrian practices. (1) The Babylonians did not settle new populations in the areas depleted by exile; the Babylonian deportation was in one direction only. Therefore, Judaean cities remained in their destroyed state until they were rebuilt by those returning from exile in the restoration period. (2) The Babylonians preferred to appoint a local governor rather than a Babylonian to govern the population not carried into exile (II Kings 25.12; Jer. 39.9f.). Gedaliah, the son of Ahikam, who came from a noble family (see II Kings 22.12; Jer. 26.24), was appointed governor to rule over the survivors, 'the poor of the land'

(II Kings 25.12; Jer. 40; 41; 52.16). Gedaliah was also in charge of Jeremiah after the latter's release from his prison 'in the court of the guard' (Jer. 39.14, but cf. Jer. 40.1–6). A clay seal-impression discovered in Lachish with the legend 'Belonging to Gedaliah who is over the household' (Moscati, 61) probably refers to this Gedaliah, the son of Ahikam. If so, as most scholars agree, then Gedaliah had probably already served in a high position under Zedekiah. He was no doubt appointed by the Babylonians as their governor because he was known for his pro-Babylonian stance (see Jer. 26.24).

§6. JUDAH DURING THE EXILIC PERIOD
(586–538 BCE)

P. R. **Ackroyd**, *Exile and Restoration*, 1968; Y. **Aharoni**, *The Land of the Bible*, 1967; W. F. **Albright**, 'The Seal of Eliakim and the Latest Preëxilic History of Judah', *JBL* LI, 1932, 77–106; idem, *From the Stone Age to Christianity*, 1940; idem, *The Archaeology of Palestine*, 1949; A. **Alt**, 'Die Rolle Samarias bei der Entstehung des Judentums', *Festschrift Otto Procksch*, Leipzig: A. Deichert and J. C. Hinrichs, 1934, 5–28 = his *KS* II 1953, 316–37; H. L. **Ginsberg**, 'Judah and the Transjordan States from 734 to 582 BC', *Alexander Marx Jubilee Volume*, 1950, 347–68; E. **Janssen**, *Juda in der Exilszeit: Ein Beitrag zur Frage der Entstehung des Judentums*, FRLANT 69, 1956; K. **Kenyon**, *Archaeology in the Holy Land*, 1960, ³1970; J. M. **Myers**, 'Edom and Judah in the Sixth–Fifth Centuries BC', in *Near Eastern Studies*, 1971, 377–92; R. **Sack**, *Amēl-Marduk, 562–560 BC: A Study Based on Cuneiform, Old Testament, Greek, Latin and Rabbinical Sources*, AOAT 4, 1972; S. S. **Weinberg**, 'Post Exilic Palestine, An Archaeological Report', *IASHP* IV, 1971, 78–97.

Gedaliah settled in Mizpah (*Tell en-Naṣbeh*) in the land of Benjamin and invited the survivors who had not been exiled, some of whom had apparently hidden in caves or found shelter in the deserts of Judah (see Ezek. 33.21–7), to settle in the cities of Judah and Benjamin (II Kings 25.22–6; Jer. 40.10; cf. Ezek. 33.21–7). The exact status of Gedaliah's position is not certain. It is not known whether he was appointed by the Babylonians as governor over Judah and Benjamin with help and supervision by Babylonian troops (Jer. 40.10; 41.3) or whether Judah and Benjamin had been added to the province of Samaria with Gedaliah then having been appointed to represent only Jewish matters. In the latter case, he would have functioned in a position subordinate to the governor of Samaria (Alt, 328f.). At any rate, Gedaliah, after only a short period of rule, was murdered by Ishmael, the son of Nethaniah, a member

of the royal Davidic family (Jer. 41.1 f.), perhaps under the provocation of Baalis, the Ammonite king (Ginsberg, 366f.). Ishmael, however, did not get the sympathy and support of the Jewish population
and was forced to take refuge in Transjordan. Citizens of Benjamin
and Judah, fearing the reprisal of the Babylonians, fled to Egypt (II
Kings 25.26). Those who escaped to Egypt carried Jeremiah with
them in spite of the prophet's attempt to dissuade them from fleeing
and his efforts to persuade them to remain in Judah (Jer. 42–3).

What was the situation in Judah after the destruction of
Jerusalem? From a political point of view, the kingdom of Judah had
ceased to exist and the country had become an integral part of the
Neo-Babylonian empire. There is no record of how the Babylonians
organized the governed Judah. Alt is of the opinion that the
Babylonians did not make Judah into a separate province but rather
annexed its territory, including the area southward to Beth-Zur and
Hebron, to the jurisdiction of the province of Samaria, while the
western strip of Judah in the plain was annexed to Ashdod. It is
possible that Gedaliah was from the beginning subordinate to the
governor of Samaria. Only in the Persian period, in Nehemiah's
time, did Judah, to Beth-Zur in the south, become a province of its
own (so Alt). Edomites had invaded the southern part of Judah even
in the period of the last kings of Judah. With the destruction of
Jerusalem' and later, the flow of Edomites and Arabian tribes to the
southern area of Judah increased and this region was called
Idumaea (Ginsberg, 363f., 367f.; Myers, 390–2; Aharoni, 354–6).
Unfortunately, there is no clear information concerning the population of Judah during the period under discussion and it is hard to
know the extent of the devastation in the towns, the precise size of
the deportations, and what kind of Judaean community continued to
live in Judah during the exilic period.

According to some biblical texts, the Babylonians burned and
looted the temple and systematically destroyed Jerusalem (II Kings
25.9f.; II Chron. 36.18f.; Jer. 52.13f., 17–23; Lam. 1.4; 5.18). The
cities of Judah were destroyed (Jer. 34.7; 44.2; Ezek. 33.24; Lam.
2.2–5). The deportation was total (II Kings 25.11; II Chron. 36;
Jer. 52.15). In Judah only 'the poorest of the land', whom the
Babylonian conqueror had left 'to be vinedressers and husbandmen',
remained (II Kings 25.12; Jer. 39.10; 52.16). Part of the population
of Judah which did not go into exile joined Gedaliah, who made his
abode in Mizpah, north of Jerusalem (II Kings 25.23; Jer. 40.7–12).
After Gedaliah's murder, a portion of the people left Judah and went
to Egypt: 'and all the people, both small and great, and the captains

of the forces, arose, and came to Egypt; for they were afraid of the Chaldeans' (II Kings 25.26; see also Jer. 41.16; 43.7).

The picture of destruction and devastation of Judah as portrayed in the above sources fits – in the opinion of Albright, Kenyon, and others – the archaeological finds in Judah. These scholars point to the destruction of many settlements in Judah (see above p. 475). Albright is of the opinion that we may speak of 'a complete devastation of Judah' (Albright, 1932, 104; 1940, 264–8; 1949, 141–3). Other archaeologists also hold that the Judaean cities were destroyed, urban culture declined, and the population that remained lived in small, poor communities (Kenyon, 296; Weinberg, 84, 96). Albright estimates the population remaining in Judah as less than 20,000 people (*Albright, 87, 110f., n. 180).

However, a quite different picture of the situation of Judah and of the Jews remaining there may be drawn, based on a different interpretation of the above mentioned sources and on additional texts (Janssen, 39–42; Ackroyd, 20–31). While it is true that some cities in Judah, such as Jerusalem, Lachish, and many strongholds were destroyed, not all the cities were abandoned. Moreover, some of the settlements which had been destroyed were resettled by those who had not gone into exile and also by those who had at first run away from the Chaldeans to the countries of Transjordan and the Judaean Desert (see Ezek. 33.27) and later returned to their settlements (Jer. 40.10–12). From Ezekiel 33.24 we may assume that even in the destroyed cities life did not entirely cease. While it is true that the Chaldeans deported residents, the deportation was not total but was limited to the leaders and members of the free professions. The numbers quoted in the biblical sources of those exiled in the deportations of the years, 597, 587/6, and 582 BCE attest the limited scope of these deportations (II Kings 24.14, 16; 25.19; Jer. 52.28–30). Those who remained in the country, 'of the poor of the people, that had nothing' (Jer. 39.10) were given land that had belonged to those exiled and to the royal estates (Janssen, 49–54).

In this light, Jer. 41.5 is of interest:

> There came certain men from Shechem, from Shiloh, and from Samaria, even fourscore men, having their beards shaven and their clothes rent, and having cut themselves, with meal-offerings and frankincense in their hand to bring them to the house of the Lord.

This passage raises the question of whether the Chaldeans really completely destroyed the temple and whether the cult fully came to an end. The verse may suggest the restoration – albeit on a modest scale – of the temple, or at least the continuation of cultic worship in the Jerusalem temple. In the opinion of Janssen, the book of Lamentations attests the great catastrophe that befell the men of Jerusalem and Judah with the destruction of the temple and Jerusalem and the deportation (1.4; 2.2), but at the same time the book demonstrates that Jerusalem and Judah were not emptied of their inhabitants (Janssen, 39).

What the exact situation was in the land of Judah during the period of Chaldean rule will remain a matter of debate until new, unambiguous data are discovered. What can be said with a high degree of probability is as follows: (1) The year 587/6 BCE marks a turning point in the history of Israel. The burning of the temple, the destruction of the city of Jerusalem, and the end of the Davidic dynasty's rule surely brought about fundamental changes in the people's thinking, which had been nourished on the belief in the eternity of the house of David and in the invulnerability of the temple in Jerusalem (see II Sam. 7; Jer. 7.14; and above pp. 370–5).

(2) The political and religious institutions which took form in Israel after the destruction of the first temple were different from those known in Judah before 587/6 BCE. (3) We may certainly speak of a catastrophe which befell Judah and her people in the first quarter of the sixth century BCE, but it is difficult to assume that there was a deportation of the majority of the Jewish population or a total destruction of the Judaean communities. The leadership, the holders of state and religious offices, families of high standing, the wealthy and the professionals went into exile, but a large part of the population of the provincial towns of Judah and its villages remained. (4) There is no clear, explicit information concerning the situation of this population, but it seems that in the absence of civilian and military leadership and the destruction of the strongholds on the one hand, and the persecution and strict control by the Babylonians on the other (Lam. 5), the Jewish population which remained in the country was in a state of depression, lack of confidence, economic poverty, and political and national inactivity. This is the situation reflected in the book of Lamentations. (5) On the question of whether various religious opposition arose between them and those who returned from the diaspora, it is not possible to give a clear answer and the matter is in dispute (Janssen, 50–4); one's view depends on the interpretation of the prophecies of Second Isaiah (mainly ch. 65), Haggai, and Zechariah.

The dearth of information about the Jewish community which remained in Judah is not an accident, since the centre of gravity in

the events which influenced the nation's historical development
moved from Judah to the diaspora.

§7. EXILE AND DIASPORA

P. R. **Ackroyd**, *Exile and Restoration*, 1968; W. F. **Albright**, 'The Seal of
Eliakim and the Latest Preëxilic History of Judah', *JBL* LI, 1932, 77–106;
idem, 'King Joiachin in Exile', *BA* V, 1942, 49–55 = *BAR* I, 1961, 106–12;
idem, *Archaeology and the Religion of Israel*, Baltimore: John Hopkins Press
³1953; idem, 'An Ostracon from Calah and the North-Israelite Diaspora',
BASOR CXLIX, 1958, 33–6; N. **Avigad**, 'Seals of Exile', *IEJ* XV, 1965,
222–30; M. D. **Coogan**, 'Life in the Diaspora: Jews at Nippur in the Fifth
Century BC', *BA* XXXVII, 1974, 6–12; idem, *West Semitic Personal Names
in the Marušu Documents*, HSM 7, 1976; K. S. **Freedy** and D. B. **Redford**,
'The Dates in Ezekiel in Relation to Biblical, Babylonian and Egyptian
Sources', *JAOS* XC, 1970, 462–85; M. **Greenberg**, 'Ezekiel 17 and the
Policy of Psammetichus II', *JBL* LXXVI, 1957, 304–9; Y. **Kaufmann**,
The Babylonian Captivity and Deutero-Isaiah, New York: Union of American
Hebrew Congregations 1970; B. **Maisler**, 'The Israelite Exiles at Gozan',
BIES XV, 1949–1950, 83–5 (Hebrew); A. **Malamat**, 'Exile, Assyrian', *EJ*
VI, 1034–6; M. **Noth**, *Überlieferungsgeschichtliche Studien*, 1957; B. **Porten**,
Archives from Elephantine: The Life of An Ancient Jewish Military Colony, Los
Angeles/London: University of California Press/Cambridge University
Press 1968; idem, 'Exile, Babylonian', *EJ* VI, 1971, 1036–41; D. W.
Thomas, 'The Sixth Century BC: A Creative Epoch in the History of
Israel', *JSS* VI, 1961, 33–46; E. F. **Weidner**, 'Jojachin, König von Juda, in
babylonischen Keilschrifttexten', *Mélanges Syriens offerts à M. René Dussaud,
II*, Paris: Paul Geuthner 1939, 923–35; M. **Weinfeld**, 'The Awakening of
National Consciousness in Israel in the Seventh Century BC', *'Oz le-David,
Biblical Essays in Honour of D. Ben-Gurion*, 1964, 396–420 (Hebrew); idem,
'Josiah', *EJ* X, 1971, 288–93; C. F. **Whitley**, *The Exilic Age*,
London/Philadelphia: Longmans, Green & Co/Westminster Press 1957; J.
M. **Wilkie**, 'Nabonidus and the Later Jewish Exiles', *JTS* NS II, 1951, 36–
44; J. **Zablocka**, 'Landarbeiter im Reich der Sargoniden', *RAI* XVIII,
1972, 209–15.

A. Mesopotamia

The largest Jewish diaspora was centred in Mesopotamia. This exile
was created as a result of several deportations which occurred under
the Assyrians and Babylonians. Tiglath-pileser III had exiled
Israelites from Galilee and the eastern Transjordan in 733–732 BCE
(II Kings 15.29; I Chron. 5.6–26; *ANET*, 283). According to Sargon

II's inscriptions, he deported 27,290 (or 27,280) from the land of Samaria; according to the Bible, these Samarian exiles were scattered in various places in Mesopotamia and Media (II Kings 17.6, 18). Sennacherib claimed to have exiled or displaced 200,150 people from Judah (*ANET*, 288). All of this means that even before Nebuchadrezzar there was in Mesopotamia an Israelite exile which is known in the Jewish tradition as the 'Ten Lost Tribes'. Information concerning these exiles is very scant and occasional and mostly based only on assumptions (Maisler; Albright, 1958; Malamat).

In Nebuchadrezzar's days, the size of the Mesopotamian diaspora was greatly enlarged with the deportations in the reigns of Jehoiachin and Zedekiah and a subsequent exile in 582 BCE (Jer. 52.30; see Josephus, *Ant.* X 79). The Babylonians carried away to their capital the main political, social, economic, and religious leaders and left behind in Judah only the 'poor people of the land'. Actually, the main centre of the people of Israel between the fall of Jerusalem and the return under Cyrus, that is, from 586–538 BCE, was located in Babylonia and was concentrated around the exiled royal family. II Kings 25.27 (see Jer. 52.31–4) reports that the exiled Jehoiachin, in the thirty-seventh year of his exile (561/60 BCE), was freed from prison by Evil-merodach (= Amel-Marduk) king of Babylon in the first year of his reign. In Babylonian inscriptions unearthed in the royal palace in Babylon, Jehoiachin is mentioned by his title 'the king of Judah' (*ANET*, 308; Freedy and Redford, 463) and it is noted that he and his five sons were allocated food rations from the royal storehouse (*ANET*, 308). These facts suggest that Jehoiachin had the status of a king-in-exile and that he was imprisoned in comfortable conditions (Albright, 1961). These special conditions granted by Nebuchadrezzar to Jehoiachin may have been due to either Jehoiachin's voluntary surrender to the Chaldeans or because Nebuchadrezzar intended to keep him as an exiled king in order to keep pressure on Zedekiah, ruling in Jerusalem. Should Zedekiah cause trouble, Nebuchadrezzar could have planned to use Jehoiachin against Zedekiah, for example, by returning him to and reinstating him as king in Jerusalem (Albright, 1961, 111).

In the exile itself, Jehoiachin was considered the leader of the Jewish community. The years were reckoned by the Jews according to his exile (Ezek. 1.2; 33.21; 40.1). In various places in Judah (Beth-Shemesh, Tell Beth Mirsim, Ramat Rachel), seal impressions were discovered inscribed: 'Belonging to Eliakim steward of Yaukin'. According to Albright, the Eliakim spoken of on these impressions held a position as the administrator of the crown property of

Jehoiachin (Albright, 1932, 1961; but see below, p. 520). Thus, according to this theory, Jehoiachin's property was not transferred to Zedekiah and Jehoiachin was viewed, at least by some of the people, as the legal king of Judah, while Zedekiah was considered an imposition forced upon Judah by the Babylonian king (see Jer. 28). Jehoiachin's sons, Shealtiel and Shesh-bazzar, just as Zerubbabel the son of Shealtiel, played important roles in Jewish life both in the exile and in the restoration. Shesh-bazzar is called 'the prince of Judah' (Ezra 1.8; 5.14) and Zerubbabel, according to Ezra 2.2, was the leader of those who returned to Judah and was appointed governor of Judah (Hag. 1.1). The literature of the period indicates that the Jewish hopes for redemption were connected with the house of David and the growth of the shoot sprung from the stock of Jesse who would sit on the throne in a renewed Jerusalem (Jer. 23.5f.; Ezek. 37.24; Isa. 11.1; Hag. 2.23; Zech. 4.6–9; 6.9–15).

The number of Jews exiled in the Mesopotamian diaspora is unknown. The places where the exiles lived and something about them can be determined from several biblical references and from various inscriptions from Mesopotamia. II Kings 17.6 and 18.11 mention the names Halah (*ḫallaḫu*), the Habor river, Gozan (*Gūzāna*), and the cities of the Medes (*Madaja*) (cf. I Chron. 5.26). Both the Assyrians and the Babylonians were accustomed to settling exiles in places which had been destroyed and rebuilt, in areas which were to be developed agriculturally, and also in administrative centres like Calah, Nineveh, Babylon, Gozan, and Nippur (Weidner and Zablocka). Psalm 137 mentions the 'rivers of Babylon' as a place where Jewish exiles were settled. Thus it can be assumed that large concentrations of Israelites and Jews were located near the water canals (*naháru* in Akkadian) which ran from the Euphrates and also on the tributaries of the Euphrates like the Habor river. A large Jewish centre was located in southern Babylonia at a place called Tel-abib on the river Chebar (Ezek. 1.3; 3.15). This river canal passed through the large commercial city of Nippur. Light has been shed on the life of this Jewish population in Nippur by a collection of Akkadian documents from the fifth century BCE which were discovered in Nippur and are referred to as the documents of the Murashû family (see Coogan and also below, p. 496). Several names in these texts can be identified as Jewish, such as Yahunatan, Tobyaw, Banayaw, and Zabadyaw. Other places in which Jews were settled are mentioned in Ezra 2.59 and Nehemiah 7.61. The element 'tel' (mound) found in some of the place names where Jews were settled may indicate that the exiles were settled in places which were destroyed and then were rebuilt (Porten, *EJ*, 1038). This also suggests that some of the exiles were engaged in agriculture, which is in agreement with what is said in Jeremiah 29.5–7:

> Build houses and live in them; plant gardens and eat their produce. Take wives and have sons and daughters; take wives for your sons, and give your daughters in marriage, that they may bear sons and daughters; multiply there, and do not decrease. But seek the welfare of the city where I have sent you into exile, and pray to the Lord on its behalf, for in its welfare you will find your welfare.

One may assume, at least at the beginning, that the exiles received land from the royal authorities and became land tenants of the king, as was the case with other nations (see Rabshakeh's words in II Kings 18.32). Later, the Jews also dealt in commerce as is clear from the Murashû documents. Obviously, the craftsmen were occupied on royal projects, especially in the big cities, and were paid from the royal treasure (Weidner). Some of the exiles whose occupation was cultic service, that is, priests, levites, singers, and temple servants (*nethinim*), retained their status as cultic officials even in the diaspora and were inclined to congregate in certain places such as the settlement of Casiphia (Ezra 8.15–20).

There is no clear and explicit evidence that the Mesopotamian exiles lived under conditions of suppression or were subjected to religious persecution at any time during the years 586–538 BCE, not even in the reign of Nabonidus (but see Wilkie). One gets the impression that they had a certain internal autonomy and that they enjoyed the freedom to manage their community life (Ezek. 33.30–3). The leader of the Jews in the Babylonian diaspora was a descendant of the house of David (see above) who was aided in conducting community affairs by the 'elders of the diaspora', the 'elders of the people' or the 'elders of Israel' (Jer. 29.1; Ezek. 8.1; 14.1; 20.1). They were organized according to families (Ezra 2; Neh. 7) and they preserved their genealogical records (Ezra 2.59; Neh. 7.61; Esth. 2). The exiles had the benefit of personal freedom. They were allowed to live according to the customs of their fathers and were allowed to buy property (Jer. 29.5) and even slaves (Ezra 2.65). One can deduce something of the economic situation of a part of the exiles from Ezra 1.6; 2.68f., which reports that the exilic Jews sent expensive presents to Jerusalem. There were exiled Jews who served in the imperial administration of Assyria and Babylon (Malamat, 1035; *ABL* 633). Some of the exiles were incorporated into military and mercenary units in accordance with the customary practice of both Assyrians and Babylonians, who used prisoners from captured countries in the imperial battalions (ND 2443; *ABL* 1009).

In spite of the integration of the exiles into the general economical and social life, they succeeded in preserving their ethnic and national uniqueness. The national religious identity survived because of the celebration of such traditional customs as sabbath observance (see Isa. 56.2–4; 58.13; Ezek. 44–6) and circumcision and because of the activity of prophets like Jeremiah, Ezekiel, and the so-called Second Isaiah or Deutero-Isaiah (Isa. 40–55). The prophets preached the idea that the tragedies which befell the people – the destruction of the temple and Jerusalem, the destruction of the land of Judah, the loss of political independence, and the exile – were not a result of the triumph of the Babylonian over the Israelite religion. Rather, everything stemmed from the will of the God of Israel, the one and only God on earth. The prophets therefore emphasized the absurdity of the cult of the idols, for they are wood and stone, made by man, and are not able to bring salvation (Jer. 1.16; 2.13; 8.19; Ezek. 20.32; Isa. 44; 46). The prophets encouraged the people's belief in the God of Israel and cultivated among the exiles a hope in future redemption and salvation (i.e. Jer. 23.7f.). Ezekiel, who was taken into exile with Jehoiachin (597 BCE) and began his prophetic career in the fifth year of Jehoiachin's exile (593 BCE), illustrates this prophetic activity. His prophecies concentrated on two subjects: (1) the destruction of the temple and Jerusalem and the subsequent exile are proclaimed as God's punishment and as the means for discovering divine judgment and justice (Ezek. 4.13–17; 5.7–17; 6; 7, etc.); and (2) the hope of redemption and restoration is expounded in terms of the return to the rebuilt and reorganized land by both Israelites and Judaeans as a united people, the renewal of the covenant between God and people, the revival of the cult in the temple in Jerusalem, and the recovery of the kingdom of the house of David (Ezek. 11.17–20; 16.59–63; 20.41–4; 34.23–31; 37.40–8). Second Isaiah, whose prophecies were delivered against the background of Babylon's decline, stimulated the hopes of the exiles for a speedy delivery by deepening and emphasizing the concept of God as ruler over the cosmos who controls the whole course of history (Isa. 44; 46) and by pointing to Cyrus as Yahweh's emissary who would accomplish the divine plan for Israel and the nations (Isa. 41.1–7; 45.1–7). Jeremiah raised the people's hopes that they would be redeemed – which meant the return of the exiles to Judah, the rebuilding of the land, and the restoration of the Davidic kingdom (Jer. 30.3, 9; 32.6–15; 33.6–9).

Without doubt, the prophetic activity in the diaspora and particularly the prophetic explanations and reinterpretation of the difficult national and ideological issues raised by the massive national calamity (Jer. 44.15–19; Ezek. 20.32; 18.2, 25; 33.10; 37.11; Isa. 63.19; Lam. 5.7) saved the people from complete despair (Ps. 74.9–11; Lam. 5.9) and prevented the total absorption and assimilation of the exiles which would have led to the loss of national identity and religious uniqueness (as was the case with the Edomites, Moabites, and Ammonites).

There is no clear, explicit information concerning the form that the worship of God took in the Babylonian diaspora in the years 586–538 BCE. Nor is there any record of a temple to God in Babylonia (unlike Egypt), any intention to erect one, or the existence of sacrificial worship (but see Ackroyd, 34). For the prevalent opinion that in this period we find the beginning of synagogue worship, there is also no real proof (see the discussions in Ackroyd, 32–8; Weinfeld, *EJ*, 292).

Biblical historiography – the Deuteronomistic and Priestly works – developed and crystallized during the exilic age, in the diaspora and perhaps also in Judah (see Noth, 1957, 97). The masterpiece of biblical historiography is the composition or Deuteronomistic re-editing of the books of Kings. Within the centre of the Deuteronomistic ideology stands the conception of the eternal election of the 'house of David and the city of Jerusalem (Weinfeld, 1964, 398–408). Lamentations, psalms, prophecies, and historiographic works are clear expression of the 'creative epoch in the history of Israel' in the sixth century BCE (Thomas; Ackroyd, 7–12, 62–102).

The fact that the Jews were living in the midst of a foreign population and dealing in agriculture, commerce, crafts, and administration naturally led to Babylonian, Aramaic, and Persian cultural influence. Perhaps the most outstanding influence upon the Jews was the Aramaic language. The Babylonian Jewish community adopted Aramaic as the spoken language and used the square Aramaic script for writing the letters of the alphabet, thus giving up the older tradition of Hebrew writing. The Babylonian influence can be seen in proper names like Shesh-bazzar, Zerubbabel, Belshazzar, and others, which are clearly Babylonian names used by the leaders of the Jewish community. Even the Babylonian names for the months (Tishri, Heshvan, etc.) were employed by the Jews in place of the old Canaanite-Hebrew month names used in Palestine. Nevertheless, these influences were only exterior ones and, as a whole, the tendency was to differ from the foreign surroundings in matters of

national tradition and faith and to avoid any pagan cult and practices.

The characteristics of the Jewish relationship to alien culture are
graphically demonstrated in a seal with a two-line inscription which
reads: 'Belonging to Yehoyishma daughter of Šawaš-sar-uṣuz.' The
father's name reflects the assimilation to Babylonian life. The daughter's name – Yehoyishma – meaning 'Yahu will hear' not only illustrates the continuing belief in the national God, Yahweh, but also
reflects the yearning which found expression in the hope of redemption and return (Avigad, 228–30, and see Ps. 137).

B. Egypt

The Egyptian diaspora becomes noticeable in the Persian period,
that is, after the last quarter of the sixth century. Although it is clear
that the Jewish diaspora in Egypt was earlier than the Persian conquest of that country, no real evidence exists which can elucidate the
circumstances under which this diaspora originated. In Isaiah 11.11
there is mention of Jews in 'Egypt, Pathros, and Nubia'. The prophet
Jeremiah addressed the Jews who 'dwelt in the land of Egypt, at
Migdol, at Tahpanhes (Daphnae), at Memphis, and in the land of
Pathros' (Jer. 44.1). The prophet's speech comes from the time after
the destruction of the temple (Jer. 44.10). Migdol, Tahpanhes, and
Noph were located in Lower Egypt, and from Jeremiah 46.14 it is
clear that these were fortified border stations whose purpose was to
check any Chaldean advance from the north. Some of the Jews
settled in these towns were Judaean refugees who had escaped to
Egypt out of fear of the Babylonians (see Jer. 42; 43.7). These Jews
were welcomed by the Egyptians, who settled them in border fortresses perhaps in the position of a mercenary army. In the same
fashion, Jeremiah refers to Pathros located in the land of Cush, one
of the names of Upper Egypt. In this area, the most famous settlement was Elephantine (see Isa. 49.12: 'Sinim' – Syene – Aswan?).
Clear evidence demonstrates the existence of a Judaean military
colony at Elephantine during the Persian period. The Jewish group
settled there was called 'the Jewish Army' and their function was to
protect the southern border of Egypt (Porten, 28–42). When this
Jewish settlement in Egypt began is unknown. There are those who
claim that, since the Jews had a temple to Yahweh in Elephantine
where they worshipped God with burnt offerings, sacrifices, and
incense, they must have immigrated to Egypt before the time of

Josiah's reform, since during his reign the dominant idea was the prohibition of Yahweh worship outside Jerusalem (see Isa. 19.18; for discussion see Porten, 8–13). One of the Elephantine documents notes that the temple there was built before Egypt was conquered by Persia in 525 BCE (*ANET*, 492). Some scholars argue that the most suitable time for such a Jewish immigration to Egypt was during the reign of Manasseh (Porten, 8–13). According to Asshurbanipal's inscriptions, it is clear Manasseh sent troops from Judah with the Assyrian king on his campaign to Egypt (*ANET*, 294). According to this assumption, part of the Jewish contingent was settled by the Assyrian army in Egyptian fortresses. Additional evidence for the existence of Jewish soldiers in Egypt before the Persian period is found in the *Letter of Aristeas* (paragraph 13) which refers to Jews sent as mercenary soldiers to aid the Egyptian king Psammetichus in his war against the king of the Ethiopians. It is difficult to decide whether Psammetichus I (664–610/9 BCE) or Psammetichus II (594/3–588 BCE) is meant (see Greenberg, 307; compare Porten, 8–13).

The information in the Elephantine documents (see below, ch. IX §3D) and the existence of a Yahweh temple (*agora*) there indicate quite clearly two factors concerning the situation and character of the Egyptian diaspora. (1) The Egyptian Jews possessed internal autonomy and were allowed to live according to the customs of their fathers. (2) They worshipped YHW, that is Yahweh, the God of Israel, and observed the sabbath and national festivals like passover (Porten, 103–50). On the other hand, in contrast to the Babylonian Jews but like the Samaritan Jews, the Jews at Elephantine recognized neither the prohibition against building a temple to Yahweh in a foreign land nor Jerusalem as the sole place for the worship of Yahweh. The Aramaic documents from Elephantine show that the Jewish community there was influenced by pagan religion (see Jer. 44.17–28). According to some scholars the fact that Elephantine Jews took judicial oaths by foreign gods and that epistolary salutations invoked many deities such as Eshem-Beth-El and Anath-Beth-El, Nebo, Sati, Anathyahu, and others indicates the syncretistic character of the religion of the Elephantine Jews (see Ezek. 23.13; Jer. 5.7; 12.16; see the discussion in Albright, 1953, 168–75; Porten 151–86). Thus one can understand Jeremiah's different attitudes towards the Babylonian diaspora Jews on the one hand (Jer. 29.5), and towards the Egyptian Jews on the other hand (Ackroyd, 55 f.). The negative attitude of Jeremiah towards the Judaean community in Egypt is explicitly expressed in Jeremiah 42.17: 'So shall it be with all the men that set their faces to go into Egypt to sojourn there; they shall die by the sword, by the famine, and by the pestilence' (see also Jer. 44.14, 24–30; 42.9–22).

In light of what has been said, it is perhaps not by accident that the declaration of Cyrus, the Persian king (Ezra 1.2–4; cf. 6.3–5), which proclaimed the restoration of the Jewish community and cult in Palestine awakened a great nationalistic enthusiasm among certain circles of Mesopotamia's Jewish diaspora, as is evident in Second Isaiah, and yet we hear nothing about any return to Zion by the Jewish diaspora of Egypt when that country was conquered by the Persian king, Cambyses, in 525 BCE.

IX

THE PERSIAN PERIOD

§1. LITERARY SOURCES AND ARCHAEOLOGICAL REMAINS

The literary sources upon which one must depend in reconstructing the life of the Jewish community within the great empire of the Persians may be divided into Jewish and non-Jewish sources. The Jewish sources in turn may be subdivided into biblical and non-biblical materials.

A. Biblical Jewish sources

W. F. **Albright**, 'The Date and Personality of the Chronicler', *JBL* XL, 1921, 104–24; W. T. **In der Smitten**, *Esra: Quellen, Überlieferung und Geschichte*, SSN 15, 1973; S. **Japhet**, 'The Supposed Common Authorship of Chronicles and Ezra–Nehemiah Investigated Anew', *VT* XVIII, 1968, 330–71; O. **Kaiser**, *Introduction to the Old Testament*, Oxford/Minneapolis: Basil Blackwell/Augsburg Publishing House 1975; U. **Kellermann**, *Nehemia: Quellen, Überlieferung und Geschichte*, BZAW 102, 1967; R. **Klein**, 'Old Readings in I Esdras: The List of Returnees from Babylon (Ezra 2 = Nehemiah 7)', *HTR* LXII, 1969, 99–107; E. **Meyer**, *Die Entstehung des Judenthums*, Halle: Max Niemeyer 1896; idem, *Julius Wellhausen und meine Schrift Die Entstehung des Judenthums: Eine Erwiderung*, Halle: Max Niemeyer 1897; S. **Mowinckel**, *Studien zu dem Buche Ezra–Nehemia* I: *Die nachchronische Redaktion des Buches. Die Listen*; II: *Die Nehemia-Denkschrift*; III: *Die Ezrageschichte und das Gesetz Moses*, SNVAO II. NS 3, 5, 7, 1964–1965; M. **Noth**, *Überlieferungsgeschichtliche Studien*, 1957, 110–80; K.-F. **Pohlmann**, *Studien zum dritten Esra: Ein Beitrag zur Frage nach des Gestalt und der Theologie des ursprünglichen Schlusses des chronistischen Geschichtswerkes*, FRLANT 104, 1970; G. **von Rad**, 'Die Nehemia-Denkschrift', *ZAW* LXXVI, 1964, 176–87 = his *GS* I, ³1965, 297–310; W. **Rudolph**, *Esra und Nehemia*, HAT I/20, 1949; C. C. **Torrey**, *Ezra Studies*, Chicago: University of Chicago Press

1910; idem, *The Chronicler's History of Israel*, New Haven/London: Yale University Press/Oxford University Press 1954.

The most important and extensive biblical sources for this period are the Ezra and Nehemiah traditions which now comprise a portion of the Chronicler's History. An assessment of the value of these traditions is to some extent dependent upon one's assessment of the Chronicler as a historical source. Was the Chronicler, that is, the person or persons responsible for the final form of the material in I–II Chronicles – Ezra–Nehemiah, primarily an editor who compiled and arranged his sources and materials or was he an author who wrote, using few if any major sources, producing out of his imagination great stretches of 'historical' description? Answers to this question range from the traditional view, espoused by Albright, that Ezra was the chronicler and was thus frequently reporting first-hand information, to that of Torrey, who argued that there was no major deportation nor return from exile and that the figure of Ezra was a pure fabrication of the Chronicler. (For further discussion of the Chronicler's work as a historical source, see above, ch. VI §1E and ch. VIII §1B.)

Whatever one's view of the date and character of the Chronicler's history, important and valuable sources are to be found in the books of Ezra and Nehemiah. The Ezra narrative (Ezra 7–10; Neh. 8–10) is an important source, the value of which, however, has been reduced by the redactional reworking carried out by the Chronicler. The Greek text of I Esdras is important in evaluating the extent and content of the original Ezra narrative. This document, which parallels II Chronicles 35.1 to Ezra 10 plus Nehemiah 7.73–8.12, is now given far greater importance in Ezra studies than was previously the case (see most recently, Mowinckel, I, 1–28 and Pohlmann). I Esdras demonstrates that the Ezra narrative was originally a separate work and that the memoirs of Ezra (Ezra 7.12–9.15) were independent of the narrative. The Chronicler's activity associated these two sources and made of them one single work, though not without leaving remarkable traces of redactional reworking.

The Ezra narrative describing the activities of Ezra is now joined with chapters 1–6 of the book of Ezra. These chapters are simply the continuation of II Chronicles. This fact is demonstrated by three circumstances. (1) The opening verses of Ezra are found, in a mutilated version, at the end of II Chronicles. (2) In the editorial parts of the two works, the style is the same. (3) The editor's interest in Chronicles and Ezra 1–6 is concentrated on the temple, statistics, and genealogies. It is evident that Chronicles and Ezra 1–6 once comprised a continuous single work.

Ezra 1–6 presents material on the history of the Jews from the first regnal year of Cyrus until the departure of Ezra for Jerusalem. In these chapters we find some Aramaic documents which will be discussed below. In Ezra 2.1–67 (70) there is a list of returning exiles which recurs in Nehemiah 7.6–73a. The date and authenticity of this list has been much discussed but modern critics have not been able to refute Meyer's opinion that the list actually is what it pretends to be: an enumeration of the people who returned from Babylonia with Zerubbabel and Joshua (Meyer, 1896, 190). It seems possible to assign a date for the composition of this list to the period 539/8–515 BCE (Rudolph, 17). This list of returning exiles provides us with the possibility of calculating the size of the Jewish population in the province of Judah.

Ezra 1–6 also contains a notice about the temple vessels given back by Cyrus (Ezra 1.9–11a), obviously based on an official list, although in its present form perhaps not totally reliable (Meyer, 1896, 72).

Besides these sources, that is, the Aramaic documents and the lists, the author of Ezra 1–6, to be identified as we have said with the Chronicler, did not possess any other sources than the writings of the prophets Haggai and Zechariah. For the rest of his narrative, he relied on free combination of known facts (Noth, 145). Even so, he fills a gap. Above all else, he provides us with authentic sources.

Within the book of Nehemiah, the so-called 'Memoirs of Nehemiah' are a primary source for the political and partly also for the religious history of the Jewish community. These are detailed and reliable, though of course biased, because things are seen exclusively from the author's point of view. The memoirs were apparently addressed to God (see Neh. 4.4f.; 5.19; 6.14; 13.29, 31). They have been compared by Mowinckel and von Rad with ancient Near Eastern inscriptional materials, some of which were written primarily for the divine reader. The memoirs of Nehemiah also have many similarities to the psalms of lament, especially the so-called psalms of the accused (see Kellermann, 84–8). As in these psalms, Nehemiah presents his case in the first person, appeals to God for remembrance, makes reference to his enemies, and prays for their punishment.

The memoirs of Nehemiah originally existed as an independent work. They have been joined to the book of Ezra in such a way that after Nehemiah 1.1–7.73a, Nehemiah 8–10 has been interpolated from the Ezra narrative. This is a widely recognized scholarly assumption. The section Nehemiah 7.73b + chapters 8–10 obviously continue the story of Ezra 7–10. The various opinions concerning the original position of Nehemiah 7.73b need not occupy us (see the standard commentaries). The reason for the interpolation of material from the Ezra narrative is obvious: the redactor wanted to associate Ezra and Nehemiah with one another in a common activity.

The real continuation of Nehemiah 7.73a is therefore found in Nehemiah 11.1 following. The list in Nehemiah 11.3–19, 21–4 provides an invaluable enumeration of the families living in Jerusalem, but possibly does not belong to the memoirs of Nehemiah. Nehemiah 11.20, 25–35 provides a description of the territory of Judah, including Benjamin, and concludes with a single notice about the levites. Nehemiah 12 provides a further list of priests and 12.27–43 contains a narrative of the dedication of the walls of Jerusalem. Nehemiah 12.44–13.3 describes the willingness of priests and community to observe the law. Nehemiah 13.4–31 provides an account of Nehemiah's activity during his second stay in Jerusalem. Nehemiah 13.28f. relates how Nehemiah dealt with a member of the high priest's family because of his marrying a foreign woman.

Thus in Nehemiah 11–13, the memoirs of Nehemiah have been interspersed with various lists and notices by the redactor. It is not necessary to give a complete survey of how literary criticism looks upon the problem of what originally belonged to the memoirs, as opinions differ. The survey already given may be sufficient. What is important for source analysis is the fact that editorial activity in the greater part of the memoirs has left the text untouched. This circumstance gives the memoirs their great historical value.

Other biblical materials besides Ezra and Nehemiah are valuable sources for Jewish life during the Persian period. Second-Isaiah (Isa. 40–55) introduces us to the heated atmosphere of messianic expectations among the Jews immediately before the downfall of the Neo-Babylonian kingdom and the triumph of Cyrus. The books of Haggai and Zechariah are primary sources for the history of the period immediately following the return. Trito-Isaiah (Isa. 56–66) and Malachi are valuable for our understanding of some of the internal conditions in the Jewish community, but they are unfortunately not easy to locate within a specific historical context.

The book of Esther purports to be a narrative about events which took place at the Persian court during the days of king Ahasuerus

(Xerxes), but it is primarily a piece of propaganda on behalf of the feast of Purim and without much historical value.

It can be demonstrated without difficulty that Esther is not a factual account, but a historical romance. Ahasuerus, the Greek Xerxes I, reigned from 486–465/4 BC. He had neither a wife called Vashti nor one called Esther. She was in fact called Hutaosa, or in Greek Atossa. In the seventh year (cf. 2.16) Xerxes had other things on his mind than choosing a new wife: the battle of Salamis fell in the year 480. Finally Mordecai, who according to 2.6 was deported together with Jeconiah or Jehoiachin under Nebuchadnezzar (597 BC), would now be about 120 years old and his cousin an ageing matron rather than an attractive girl (Kaiser, 201).

B.   *Non-biblical Jewish sources*

A. E. **Cowley**, *Aramaic Papyri of the Fifth Century BC*, London: Oxford University Press 1923; F. M. **Cross**, 'Papyri of the Fourth Century BC from Dâliyeh: A Preliminary Report on Their Discovery and Significance', *New Directions*, 1969, 45–69; idem, 'A Reconstruction of the Judaean Restoration', *JBL* XCIV, 1975, 4–18 [= *Int* XXIX, 1975, 187–203]; W. **Honroth** et al., 'Bericht über die Ausgrabungen auf Elephantine in den Jahren 1906–1908', *ZÄS* XLVI, 1909–10, 14–61; E. G. **Kraeling**, *The Brooklyn Museum Aramaic Papyri: New Documents of the Fifth Century BC from the Jewish Colony at Elephantine*, New Haven/London: Yale University Press/Oxford University Press 1953; P. W. and N. **Lapp**, *Discoveries in Wadi ed-Daliyeh*, AASOR 41, 1976; R. **Marcus**, 'Josephus on the Samaritan Schism', *Josephus VI*, LCL, 1937, 498–511; E. **Meyer**, *Der Papyrusfund von Elephantine*, Leipzig: J. C. Hinrichs 1911, ²1912; E. **Sachau**, *Aramäische Papyrus und Ostraka aus einer jüdischen Militär-Kolonie zu Elephantine*, Leipzig: J. C. Hinrichs 1911; A. H. **Sayce** and A. E. **Cowley**, *Aramaic Papyri Discovered at Assuan*, London: Alexander Moring 1906; Z. **Shunnar**, 'Ein neuer aramäischer Papyrus aus Elephantine', *Geschichte Mittelasiens im Altertum*, ed. F. Altheim und R. Stiehl, Berlin: Walter de Gruyter 1970, 111–18; C. G. **Tuland**, 'Josephus, *Antiquities*. Book XI. Correction or Confirmation of Biblical Post-Exilic Records', *AUSS* IV, 1966, 176–92.

Among the non-biblical Jewish sources related to the history of the Jewish community during the Persian period are Josephus and the papyri from Elephantine and Samaria. Book XI of Josephus' *Antiquities* relates the history of the Jews from the time of Cyrus, the first Persian ruler, to the time of Darius III, the last Achaemenian ruler. Josephus' account is based on I Esdras, the Greek version of the book of Esther, and some unidentified Jewish extra-biblical traditions. At times Josephus elaborates and at other times simplifies the biblical material. He places both Ezra and Nehemiah in the reign of King Xerxes, although reporting the death of Ezra before the beginning of the activity of Nehemiah. The description of the work of Nehemiah in *Antiquities* differs considerably from that found in the biblical text, for example, on the time required for the reconstruction of the walls. It is difficult to assess the full value of Josephus as a source for this period (for a rather conservative discussion, see Tuland). At times he supplies details of information not found elsewhere and some of these will be noted in our reconstruction of the history.

The Elephantine papyri are Aramaic documents from the fifth century BCE discovered in Egypt at Elephantine Island opposite Assuan. The first acquired collection of these writings was purchased in 1893 but not published until 1953 (see Kraeling). A second collection of texts was acquired from dealers and published by Sayce and Cowley in 1906. A third lot was recovered in excavations carried out by the Berlin Museum and was published in 1911 by Sachau. Recently an additional papyrus text from Elephantine has been published (see Shunnar). Many of these texts are legal documents and others are letters.

The Elephantine documents reflect the life of a Jewish military colony living on Elephantine Island (called Yeb) during the Persian period. They offer us a glimpse of Jewish life under rather unusual conditions during the fifth century and present us with facets of both religious and legal conditions prevailing in this colony. From an historical perspective, the papyri provide us with some synchronisms for the latter half of the fifth century. The texts testify to the strong Persian linguistic influence in the Aramaic of this period. A full discussion of the discovery of the texts, the archaeological excavations at Elephantine, and the contents of the texts are provided by Kraeling.

The Samaria papyri were discovered in 1962 in a cave of Wadi Daliyeh about fourteen kilometres north of ancient Jericho. The documents were first located and offered for sale by the Ta'âmireh Bedouin, known for their role in discovering the Qumran scrolls. Subsequent excavation at the site were carried out by the American Schools of Oriental Research (see Lapp). The papyri, which have not yet been published, are legal documents dated to the middle third of the fourth century. Discovered in the caves were numerous skeletons and it has been surmised that the owners of these legal documents carried them there at the time of the destruction of Samaria in the days of Alexander the Great. These documents inform us about the family of Sanballat. On the basis of these texts and evidence drawn from the Bible and Josephus, Cross has postulated the existence of three different Sanballats: Sanballat I, born ca. 485, Sanballat II, born ca. 435, and Sanballat III, born ca. 385 (Cross, 1975, 17).

C.   Non-Jewish sources

W. **Baumgartner**, 'Das Aramäische im Buche Daniel', *ZAW* XLV, 1927, 81–133; E. J. **Bickermann**, 'The Edict of Cyrus in Ezra 1', *JBL* LXV, 1946, 249–75; G. **Cardascia**, *Les Archives des Murašū: Une famille d'hommes d'affaires babyloniens à l'époque perse (455–403 av. J.-C.)*, Paris: Imprimerie nationale 1951; A. T. **Clay**, *Business Documents of Murashū Sons of Nippur Dated in the Reign of Darius II (424–404 BC)*, BEUP 10, 1904; idem, *Business Documents of Murashū Sons of Nippur Dated in the Reign of Darius II*, UMBS II/1, 1912; M. D. **Coogan**, 'Life in the Diaspora: Jews at Nippur in the Fifth Century BC', *BA* XXXVII, 1974, 6–12; idem, *West Semitic Personal Names in the Murašû Documents*, HSM 7, 1976; G. R. **Driver**, *Aramaic Documents of the Fifth Century BC*, London: Oxford University Press 1954, abridged and revised ed. 1957; K. **Galling**, *Studien zur Geschichte Israels im persischen Zeitalter*, Tübingen: J. C. B. Mohr 1964, 61–88; P. **Grelot**, *Documents Araméens d'Egypt*, LAPO 5, 1972; H. V. **Hilprecht** and A. T. **Clay**, *Business Documents of Murashū Sons of Nippur Dated in the Reign of Artaxerxes I. (464–424 BC)*, BEUP 9, 1898; W. T. **In der Smitten**, 'Historische Probleme zum Kyrosedikt und zum Jerusalemer Tempelbau von 515', *Persica* VI, 1974, 167–78; A. S. **Kapelrud**, *The Question of Authorship in the Ezra-Narrative, A Lexical Investigation*, SNVAO 1944 1, 1944; O. **Krückmann**, *Neubabylonische Rechts- und Verwaltungstexte*, Leipzig: J. C. Hinrichs 1933; E. **Meyer**, *Die Entstehung des Judenthums*, 1896; F. **Rosenthal**, *A Grammar of Biblical Aramaic*, PLONS 5, 1961; H. H. **Rowley**, *The Aramaic of the Old Testament: A Grammatical and Lexical Study of its Relations with Other Early Aramaic Dialects*, London: Oxford University Press 1929; idem, 'Nehemiah's Mission and its Background', *BJRL* XXXVII, 1954–5, 528–61 = his *Men of God: Studies in Old Testament History and Prophecy*, 1963, 211–45; W. **Rudolph**, *Esra und Nehemia*, HAT I/20, 1949; H. H. **Schaeder**, *Iranische Beiträge I*, SKGG VI/5, 1930, 197–296; S. **Smith**, *Babylonian Historical Texts Relating to the Capture and Downfall of Babylon*, London: Methuen 1924; R. **de Vaux**, 'Les décrets de Cyrus et de Darius sur la reconstruction du Temple', *RB* XLVI, 1937, 29–57 = his *Bible et Orient*, 1967, 83–113 = 'The Decrees of Cyrus and Darius on the Rebuilding of the Temple', in his *The Bible and the Ancient Near East*, London/Garden City: Darton, Longman & Todd/Doubleday 1971, 63–96.

A number of non-Jewish texts are valuable sources for reconstructing Jewish life and history during this period. Cuneiform historical texts from the time of Nabonidus and Cyrus depict the religious policies of the last Neo-Babylonian king, the discontent of the Marduk priesthood with the rule of Nabonidus, and provide insight into the religious policies of Cyrus (see Smith and *ANET*, 311–16, 560–3). The Cyrus Cylinder is a primary source of great importance and the most significant of these historical cuneiform texts. It has been called the *magna carta* of freedom and tolerance. It is, at any rate, a most remarkable document demonstrating the principles guiding Persian policy under Cyrus and his successors. It provides us with the background of Cyrus' permission to the Jews to return to their home in Palestine and his handing over to them of the temple vessels carried away by the Babylonian king.

In addition to the Elephantine texts, discussed above, additional Aramaic papyri and leather documents inform us about the way in which the huge Achaemenian empire functioned, from the top to the bottom. The most important of these Aramaic documents come from Egypt and allow us to glimpse the administrative functions of that portion of the Persian empire during the last years of the fifth century BCE (see Driver and Grelot). These documents, like the Elephantine papyri, demonstrate the extent of Persian linguistic influence upon the Aramaic of the empire.

Some cuneiform documents from Babylonia provide information about the conditions under which the Jews of the Babylon diaspora lived. The most important of these are the so-called Murashū Texts unearthed in the 1893 excavations of the University of Pennsylvania at the site of ancient Nippur. These were published by Hilprecht, Clay, and Krückmann. Some of these clay tablets were also additionally inscribed with Aramaic inscriptions written in ink. The texts are business documents of the Murashū firm, but among the names of the business transactors are some that are clearly Jewish, suggesting that many of the exiles had become well integrated into the economic life of the Persian empire (see Cardascia and Coogan).

Of special importance for reconstructing the history of Jewish life during this period are the Aramaic documents from Persian chancelleries preserved in the book of Ezra (Ezra 6.2–5; 7.12–26). These are the decree of Cyrus concerning the return from exile and the rebuilding of the Jerusalem temple and the rescript of Artaxerxes concerning Ezra's return to and work in Jerusalem.

The authenticity of these texts, partly or totally, has been disputed, but Eduard Meyer demonstrated that they were genuine (Meyer, 8–71). After him, their authenticity was generally accepted, especially in the case of the rescript of Artaxerxes concerning Ezra's

mission. Some scholars have been, however, of the opinion that the
type of Aramaic found in these documents was from a date later
than that claimed. Especially important was the argument that the
Aramaic of the Ezra documents was later than the Aramaic of the
Elephantine papyri (Baumgartner; Rowley, 1939, 156, and see
Rowley, 1963, 214-19 for the diversity of scholarly opinion). However, it has been convincingly shown that this view is definitely
wrong (Schaeder, 228-54). Schaeder demonstrated that phenomena
in the Aramaic documents which had been taken as signs of later
development were due to an adaptation of an archaic stage of a
written language to the stage of a spoken language. Also, when new
forms appear they may not be caused by historical development but
by the fact that they reflect a living language. The prevalent opinion
has been well expressed by a leading authority who says:

> The Aramaic of the Bible . . . has preserved the Official Aramaic charac-
> ter. This is what makes it nearly uniform in linguistic appearance. It also
> makes it largely identical with the language used in other official Aramaic
> texts (Rosenthal, 6).

The usual name of this 'Official Aramaic' is 'Imperial Aramaic',
and this name is preferable because it was the administrative language of the Persian chancelleries in the Achaemenian empire.

It is understandable that the rescript of Artaxerxes (Ezra 7.12–26)
has been looked upon with suspicion. It has not without reason been
argued that the document is possessed of such a specific Jewish
colour that it can hardly be genuine. As a specific term, the name of
Yahweh as 'the God of heaven' cannot, at any rate, be invoked as
indicative of inauthenticity, since this expression was used by the
Jews in other official documents, e.g. in the letter from the
Elephantine colony to the Persian governor Bagohi (*AP* 30.2; Bigwai
is a wrong vocalization since the name is a hypocoristicon; see
Schaeder, 265). Undoubtedly there are Jewish expressions in the
rescript. These are due to the obvious fact that the rescript was based
on a memorandum presented to the Great King by Ezra and his
friends. It stands to reason that the king and his counsellors were
moved to their favourable response because of some Jewish petition.
Meyer, who has fully understood the background of the rescript, has
suggested that there may also have been a religious motive behind it
and not only political considerations on the side of Artaxerxes
(Meyer, 63–5). The king could have been inspired by respect for the
God of the Jews (see Ezra 8.22). The Jewish worship of the God of
heaven may have appeared to the Persians as of the same kind as

their own worship of Ahura Mazdā, their God of heaven. While this suggestion may be true, the main motives, however, were undoubtedly political. The mere policy of tolerance by the Persians is not sufficient to explain the extremely benevolent attitude of the government towards the Jews. One must take into consideration the political and military reasons. Egypt was unreliable and it was necessary to possess safe lines of communication with the Persian garrisons in that country. Palestine with the province of Judah was of primary importance from that point of view. History shows that the Jews really were loyal subjects and for that reason of great use to the Persian Great King.

In spite of the convincing arguments in favour of the authenticity of the rescript, a very energetic attempt to prove its fictitious character has been undertaken. Its language was examined and it was maintained that 'the rescript, at any rate in its present shape, cannot be genuine' (Kapelrud, 42). A detailed refutation of the linguistic analysis undertaken by Kapelrud is out of place here. Suffice it to say that a statistical method is used with the aim of ascertaining whether a word belonging to the vocabulary of the rescript is found in other parts of the Old Testament with a comparison of corresponding Hebrew words. But from the point of method, it would have been both more correct and profitable to extend the comparison to other examples of Imperial Aramaic instead of to Hebrew terms. For example, Kapelrud notes that *niḵsā*, 'riches, goods', is used in Ezra 7.26 and 6.8 'but not elsewhere in the Aramaic sections'. Actually, it is one of the most common terms in the Aramaic papyri and is used as an ideogram in Pahlavi. Had this method been used, Kapelrud would have noted the close agreement between the style of the rescript and that of the Persian chancelleries, not the least in the use of Babylonian and Persian loan-words.

To sum up: the arguments against the authenticity of the rescript in Ezra 7.12–26 do not carry conviction.

The authenticity of the decree of Cyrus (Ezra 6.2–5) has also been questioned (see Galling, 61–88). This edict, given already in the first regnal year of Cyrus (538 BCE), not only contains details concerning the measurement of the new temple to be built but also permits the Jews to carry back their looted temple vessels. It has been thought strange that Cyrus gives regulations concerning the measurement of the Jewish temple and also takes the responsibility for its costs. But it has been observed that Cyrus wanted to control the expenses by giving strict orders as to how the government's money was to be spent. That the expenses were paid and the temple vessels brought back was in keeping with the general Persian policy, the principles of which were laid down in the Cyrus Cylinder. There is no reason to doubt the authenticity of the decree (so also Bickermann).

One detail deserves mention. According to Ezra 6.1 f. search was made and the document ultimately found in Media in the fortress of Ecbatana (Hagmatāna). Important documents were thus preserved in a fortress. This was a tradition which continued for many centuries, for in the Sassanian period, documents were still kept in the so-called *diz i nipišt*, 'the fortress of the archives'. Such a detail adds to the reliability of the story as to how the document was found.

There are, however, some signs that this document in its present text is incomplete and in some details should be reconstructed (see Rudolph, 54). But the substance is correct.

If the authenticity of these documents is acknowledged, it stands to reason that their historical value is basic for our reconstruction of the history. Our reconstruction of the history must be based to a large extent upon these documents, that is, for the period from the return to the time of Ezra. They provide us with knowledge of the relations between the Persian government and the province of Judah and with the Jewish people in general.

D. *Archaeological remains*

Y. **Aharoni**, 'Beth-haccherem', *AOTS*, 1967, 171–84; N. **Avigad**, *Bullae and Seals from a Post-Exilic Judean Archive*, QMIA 4, 1976; M. **Avi-Yonah**, 'The Walls of Nehemiah – A Minimalist View', *IEJ* IV, 1954, 239–48; D. **Barag**, 'The Effects of the Tennes Rebellion on Palestine', *BASOR* CLXXXIII, 1966, 6–12; M. **Buttenwieser**, *The Psalms: Chronologically Treated with a New Translation*, Chicago: University of Chicago Press 1938; T. K. **Cheyne**, *The Origin and Religious Contents of the Psalter*, London: Kegan Paul, Trench, Trübner 1891; F. M. **Cross**, 'A Reconstruction of the Judean Reconstruction', *JBL* XCIV, 1975, 4–18 [= *Int* XXIX, 1975, 187–203]; K. **Galling**, 'Denkmäler zur Geschichte Syriens und Palästinas unter der Herrschaft der Perser', *PJB* XXXIV, 1938, 59–79; H. **Gelzer**, *Sextus Julius Africanus und die byzantinische Chronographie* I, Leipzig: B. G. Teubner 1885; R. **Grafman**, 'Nehemiah's "Broad Wall"', *IEJ* XXIV, 1974, 50f.; B. **Kanael**, 'Ancient Jewish Coins and their Historical Importance', *BA* XXVI, 1963, 38–62; K. **Kenyon**, *Digging up Jerusalem*, 1974; A. T. **Olmstead**, *History of the Persian Empire*, Chicago/London: University of Chicago Press/Cambridge University Press 1948; L. Y. **Rahmani**, 'Silver Coins of the Fourth Century BC from Tel Gamma', *IEJ* XXI, 1971, 158–60; M. **Smith**, *Palestinian Parties and Politics that Shaped the Old Testament*, New York: Columbia University Press 1971; E. **Stern**, 'Eretz–Israel in the Persian period', *Qadmoniot* II, 1969, 110–

24 (Hebrew); idem, 'A Burial of the Persian period near Hebron', *IEJ* XXI, 1971, 25–30; idem, *The Material Culture of the Land of the Bible in the Persian period, 538–332 BCE*, Jerusalem: Bialik Institute/Israel Exploration Society 1973 (Hebrew); M. **Stern**, *Greek and Latin Authors on Jews and Judaism*, I: *From Herodotus to Plutarch*, Jerusalem: Israel Academy of Sciences and Humanities 1974.

Over fifty Palestinian sites have yielded archaeological remains from the Persian period. E. Stern has collected and discussed all of the relevant evidence from these sites which was available at the time of his dissertation (1968).

Several Palestinian sites show destruction levels during this period and recently this fact has been combined with a few incidental references by ancient authors to a deportation of Jews by the Persians so as to produce a theory of a major calamity which befell the Jewish community in the mid-fourth century. Josephus quotes Hecataeus of Abdera to the effect that 'many myriads of our race had already been deported to Babylon by the Persians' (*Contra Apionem* I 194; see M. Stern, 42 f.). Eusebius in his *Chronicon* (ed. Schöne, II 112) refers to Artaxerxes III Ochus' banishment of Jews to Hyrcania on the shores of the Caspian Sea. Gelzer has attempted to trace this reference back to Justus of Tiberias via Julius Africanus (I, 118). Orosius (*Adversos paganos* III 7.6) repeats the material in Eusebius. Syncellus (ed. Dindorf, I 486. 10–14) supplies similar information but adds that Jews were deported to Babylon and associates this deportation with Ochus' campaign to Egypt. Solinus (*Collectanea*, ed. Mommsen[2], 35.4) states that Jericho was destroyed by Artaxerxes. Earlier scholars, utilizing these references from ancient sources, sometimes spoke of 'the third of Israel's great captivities' (Cheyne, 53) and interpreted various biblical passages, especially certain psalms, in light of this supposed calamity (so Buttenweiser, 555–658).

Evidence of destruction at several sites (Hazor, Megiddo, Athlit, Lachish, and Jericho) has been combined with Diodorus' report of the Phoenician rebellion led by Tennes the king of Sidon in 351/0 BCE (XVI 40–6) to conclude that 'rebellion was more serious than suggested by the description of Diodorus and that Phoenicia and Palestine had not recovered by the time of Alexander's invasion' (Barag, 12). The archaeological evidence plus the reinterpretation of Diodorus' report when combined with the ancient references to a Jewish deportation has made it possible to speak of the 'suffering and chaos of the mid-fourth century BC, when Judah joined in the

Phoenician rebellion, harshly put down by Artaxerxes III and his general, Bagoas' (Cross, 12).

Further evidence supplied by Josephus has been associated with Artaxerxes III. In *Ant.* XI 297–301, Josephus reports that Johanan and his brother Jeshua were in competition for the office of high priest with the latter having been promised the position by Bagoses, the general of Artaxerxes (there is some textual evidence that makes this Artaxerxes, Artaxerxes II Mnemon, 404–358 BCE). Johanan slew Jeshua within the temple. As a result of this event, Bagoses defiled the temple (entered the sacred precincts), imposed a fee upon each Jewish sacrifice, and made the Jews suffer seven years for the death of Jeshua. The association of this passage with Artaxerxes III has led to statements about 'the capture of Jerusalem by Artaxerxes III (Ochus) probably in the 350s' and that 'both Jerusalem and Jericho were taken and punished by Artaxerxes III' (Smith, 185, 60).

The views of Barag, Cross, and Smith suggest that the Jewish community was involved in a major military action against the Persians. The crux of the issue depends upon whether the ancient references and the archaeological evidence support such a view. With regard to the references in ancient sources, a number of factors argue against any major Jewish involvement in anti-Persian revolts. (1) Diodorus nowhere makes reference to any Jewish participation in the revolt at the time of Tennes nor during Ochus' subsequent invasion of Egypt. (2) Eusebius' statements on Artaxerxes III date his accession in 365/4 BCE, several years too soon. This casts some doubt on the reliability of his traditions. (3) It must be assumed that Josephus was totally unaware of this major calamity which befell the Jewish community, or else he deliberately chose to suppress the evidence, but no compelling reason can be offered for such suppression. (4) Josephus' reference to the defilement of the temple by Bagoses is best understood with reference to the Persian governor of the same name near the end of the fifth century who is known from the Elephantine papyri (so Olmstead, 398). (5) Hecataeus' reference to Persian deportation of Jews to Babylon is probably the result of his confusion of Persians and Babylonians, the former being the better known in his day. (6) It is entirely possible that some Jews were settled in Hyrcania by the Persians during the fourth century. They may have been mercenaries or supporters of either the Phoenicians or the Egyptians during their wars with the Persians, but none of the ancient sources suggest any major participation in rebellion by the province of Judah.

With regard to the archaeological evidence, here too there is little that would suggest any major Persian action against Judah. The destroyed sites noted by Barag, with the exception of Jericho, all lay outside the boundaries of the Persian province of Judah. The destruction of various Palestinian sites during the fifth–fourth centuries has been explained by Stern in the following manner and without resorting to any assumed Judaean rebellion against Persia. (1) Many towns in Benjamite territory were destroyed during the first quarter of the fifth century which Stern sees as the result of some minor war between powers in the Palestinian area. (2) During the first quarter of the fourth century, extensive destruction took place along the coast, in the Shephelah, and the Negeb. Stern associates this with Egyptian efforts to regain independence from Persia beginning after the turn of the century. The discovery of an inscription of Neferites I (399–393 BCE) at Gezer and of inscriptions of Achoris (393–380 BCE) at Acco and Sidon confirm extensive Egyptian activity in the area. (3) A final phase of destruction extended throughout the last half of the fourth century. Stern associates these with events ranging from the Sidonian revolt in 351 BCE to the wars of the Diadochi.

The evidence of Persian garrisons and warehouse complexes have been discovered at Tell Jemme south of Gaza and a tomb of a Persian further south on the Wādi Ghazze (see Galling, 79; *Noth, 318). These date from the fifth–fourth centuries and indicate the intensive Persian efforts to protect and police this area bordering on the ever troublesome Egyptian frontier.

In her excavations in Jerusalem, Kenyon unearthed a wall from the Persian period which suggests that Nehemiah's fortification of the city did not follow the old wall lines of the period of the monarchy on the eastern ridge. Instead, Nehemiah's wall was considerably higher up the slope and thus the extent of the city was less on the eastern side than previously during the period of the monarchy (Kenyon, 172–87). Evidence suggests also that Nehemiah's Jerusalem was located solely on the eastern ridge and did not include the western ridge (see Avi-Yonah and Grafman).

Coins and seal impressions inscribed with *Yehud* testify to the existence of Judah as a Persian province and the coins, strongly influenced by Greek coinage, show that the small province possessed its own coinage (see Galling, 75–7; Kanael, 40–2). Some epigraphic material mentions not only the name of the province but also that of the governor. From this material, we now possess the names of four previously unknown governors of Judah during the Persian period (see Aharoni, 173–6; Avigad; and Rahmani). Utilizing paleogra-

phical considerations, Avigad dates three of these governors to the
period between Zerubbabel and Nehemiah: Elnathan (late sixth
century), Yeho'ezer and Aḥzai (early fifth century). The fourth
governor Yeḥezqiyah, known from coins found at Beth-zur and Tell
Jemme, is probably to be dated very late in the Persian period (on
the entire question, see Avigad, especially 26–36).

§2. PROBLEMS IN RECONSTRUCTING JEWISH HISTORY IN THE PERSIAN PERIOD

A.   The chronological order of Ezra and Nehemiah

J. **Bright**, 'The Date of Ezra's Mission to Jerusalem', *Yehezkel Kaufmann
Jubilee Volume*, ed. M. Haran, Jerusalem: Magnes Press 1960, 70–87; H.
Cazelles, 'La mission d'Esdras', *VT* IV, 1954, 113–40; F. M. **Cross**,
'Papyri of the Fourth Century BC from Dâliyeh: A Preliminary Report on
Their Discovery and Significance', *New Directions*, 1969, 45–69; idem, 'A
Reconstruction of the Judean Restoration', *JBL* XCIV, 1975, 4–18 [= *Int*
XXIX, 1975, 187–203]; J. A. **Emerton**, 'Did Ezra Go to Jerusalem in 428
BC?', *JTS* XVII, 1966, 1–19; A. **van Hoonacker**, 'Néhémie et Esdras,
une nouvelle hypothèse sur la chronologie de l'époque de la restauration',
Le Muséon IX, 1890, 151–84, 317–51, 389–401 = idem, Louvain:
Imprimerie Istas 1890; idem, *Une communauté Judéo-Araméene à Éléphantine, en
Égypte, aux VIᵉ et Vᵉ siècles av. J-C*, London: H. Milford 1915; idem, 'La
succession chronologique Néhémie–Esdras', *RB* XXXII, 1923, 481–94;
XXXIII, 1924, 33–64; U. **Kellermann**, 'Erwägungen zum Problem der
Esradatierung', *ZAW* LXXX, 1968, 55–87; W. H. **Kosters**, *Die
Wiederherstellung Israels in der persischen Periode*, Heidelberg: J. Hörning 1895;
M. **Noth**, *Die israelitischen Personennamen im Rahmen der gemeinsemitischen
Namengebung*, BWANT III/10, 1928; H. H. **Rowley**, 'The Chronological
Order of Ezra and Nehemiah', *Ignace Goldziher Memorial Volume I*, ed. S.
Löwinger and J. Somogyi, Budapest: Globus 1948, 117–49 = his *The
Servant of the Lord*, 1965, 135–68; idem, 'Nehemiah's Mission and its
Background', *BJRL* XXXVII, 1954–5, 528–61 = his *Men of God*, 1963,
211–45; W. **Rudolph**, *Esra und Nehemia*, HAT I/20, 1949.

The question of the chronological order of Ezra and Nehemiah is
one of the most controversial and vexing problems in Old Testament
research. It is extremely difficult to solve in a satisfactory way.

According to the arrangement of the books of Ezra and Nehemiah
it appears that Ezra preceded Nehemiah, for Ezra 7.8 says that Ezra
arrived in Jerusalem in the fifth month of the seventh year of King

Artaxerxes, whereas Nehemiah, according to Nehemiah 1.1–3 and
2.1, left the royal court of Artaxerxes in the latter's twentieth year. If
this Artaxerxes is the first ruler with this name (Persian: Artaxšassa),
Ezra would have arrived in Jerusalem in 458 BCE and Nehemiah in
445 BCE.

That Nehemiah was active in the reign of Artaxerxes I is demonstrated by various facts and accepted by a vast majority of scholars
(see Rowley). A close examination of the relationship between Ezra
and Nehemiah, however, has revealed a number of points which
have cast doubt on the 'traditional' chronological order. Several
scholars, first and foremost van Hoonacker in a series of publications,
have argued that only Nehemiah belonged to the reign of Artaxerxes
I, whereas the Artaxerxes under whom Ezra lived actually was
Artaxerxes II. An increasing number of scholars have accepted this
view (see Rowley, 1965, 139–41), supported by a number of considerations.

1. Nehemiah rebuilt the walls of Jerusalem (Neh. 7). It was his
special task to carry out this work. Ezra, however, found the walls
already built when he arrived in Jerusalem (Ezra 9.9). How would
that have been possible if Ezra preceded Nehemiah? That Judah
and Jerusalem are said to possess a wall (*gader*; Ezra 9.9) does not
contradict the meaning of the term 'wall' in the case of *gader*, for how
could Judah possess a protective wall if Jerusalem did not (*contra*
Rudolph, 88, and Cross, 1975, 14 n. 60)?

2. Ezra and Nehemiah in reality never appear together in the text,
although the editor has tried to associate them. In Nehemiah 8.9, for
example, in a chapter which was later added to the memoirs of
Nehemiah (as we noted earlier), Nehemiah plays only an insignificant role on the occasion of the reading of the law brought by Ezra.
'He is a mere passenger in the story, and his name could be omitted
without the slightest loss to the story' (Rowley, 1963, 233).
Undoubtedly, Nehemiah has been secondarily introduced into the
episode by the editor. The verb in the verse is given in the singular
form and it is significant that in the parallel passage in I Esdras 9.49
his name is missing, an important fact, as I Esdras reflects a more
original text. The speaker, therefore, is Ezra alone (Rudolph, 148).
Inversely, it is probable that Ezra's name has been added alongside
Nehemiah's in Nehemiah 12.26 (Rowley, 1963, 232 n. 4). If we
assume that the name of Nehemiah instead of Ezra has been added
to the text, the conclusion would be the same (Rudolph, 195).

These references may suffice to demonstrate the rather clumsy
manner in which the editor artificially tried to associate Nehemiah

and Ezra in a work of cooperation as contemporaries. Many scholars, however, have tried to reconstruct the work of Ezra and Nehemiah so that the careers of the two men overlap (Kosters; *Bright, 402f.; already Rudolph, 71). This is sometimes done by assuming that 'the seventh year' in Ezra 7.7f. should read 'the thirty-seventh year' (see Bright and, for a refutation, see Emerton). The editorial character of the references which associate the two and the lack of any textual support for reading 'thirty-seventh year' make it impossible to assume that they were jointly engaged in activity in Jerusalem. This opinion cannot be refuted by appealing to the assumption that since their fields of activity were different there would be no reason for them to appear together since their activities overlapped (see Rowley, 1965, 165). Thus we must conclude that Ezra and Nehemiah exercised their activity in Jerusalem independently of one another. The general conclusion that they were active at different times is confirmed by I Esdras, where the section corresponding to Nehemiah 7.73b–8.12 is placed immediately after Ezra 10 (= I Esdras 9.37–55).

3. When Nehemiah reviewed the census of the families that returned with Zerubbabel, this action, performed in conjunction with his endeavour to strengthen the defence of Jerusalem, is undertaken without any mention of the considerable number of people said to have returned with Ezra (cf. Neh. 7.5–73 with Ezra 8.1–14). The natural impression is that Nehemiah is completely ignorant of those who returned with Ezra (Rowley, 1965, 165) who with their families numbered about 5,000 people.

4. Nehemiah was contemporary with the high priest Eliashib (Neh. 3.1) whereas Ezra lived in the time of Jehohanan ben Eliashib (Ezra 10.6) who, however, was the grandson, not the son, of Eliashib (Neh. 12.11, reading Johanan [= Jehohanan] not Jonathan, in accordance with 12.22!). The genealogy of Johanan would go back to Joshua, the contemporary of Zerubbabel, about 520 BCE. Joshua (Jeshua) was succeeded by Joiakim, who was followed by Eliashib who was still active in 445 BCE. He again was succeeded by Joiada whose successor was Johanan, followed by Jaddua (Neh. 12.10f., 22). For Johanan, we possess a reliable date from an Elephantine papyrus (*AP* 30) which informs us that he was active in the years 410–407 BCE.

The fact that, between Joshua and Eliashib, only one name appears, that of Joiakim, creates some problems. It has therefore been assumed that the name of one high priest is missing in the genealogy (*Kittel, III, 649). To this question we shall have occasion to return.

The fact that Ezra was contemporary with Johanan would be a strong argument in favour of placing his activity some decades later than those of Nehemiah. Such being the state of the problems it cannot be denied that there is much to support the opinion, in recent years skilfully and energetically defended by Rowley, that Ezra lived and worked in Jerusalem during the reign of Artaxerxes II (404–359 BCE).

Recently, however, this position has been challenged by Cross. He has offered a proposal to overcome the chronological difficulties associated with the genealogy of high priests and presented this in a highly persuasive manner. His argument leads to the conclusion that the 'traditional' chronological order of Ezra and Nehemiah should be accepted. Assuming a haplography, Cross reconstructs the end of the high priestly genealogy so that it is comprised of Johanan, Jaddua, Johanan, Jaddua (Cross, 1975, 5–6). Finding in the Samaria papyri irrefutable evidence of 'papponymy' (i.e. the practice of naming a son after his grandfather) among the descendants of Sanballat (= Sinuballit), he posited the same practice in the family of high priests in Jerusalem. This postulate he thinks is confirmed by his reconstructed list.

From here, he proceeds a step further. Without the additional Johanan and Jaddua, the recorded genealogy would give eight generations for a period of about 275 years from Jozadak the father of Jeshua (who aided in the rebuilding of the temple) to Simon. That would give each generation nearly thirty-five years, an extremely high figure he thinks. In the list of high priests in the sixth and fifth centuries, from Jozadak to Johanan, the genealogy covers a period of 150 years. Only six priests are mentioned for five generations. Cross considers the figure of 150 years for five generations to be at least five years per generation too high. For that reason, he assumes 'that at least one generation, two high priests' names, has dropped out of the list through a haplography owing to the repetition produced by papponymy' (Cross, 1975, 10). As the centre of the difficulties he posits the high priest Eliashib.

As brother of Yōyaqīm [Joiakim], in the third generation of the Return, he should have been born about 545 BC. This would make him one hundred or more, when he built the wall of Jerusalem with Nehemiah, and about seventy-five when he begot Yōyada' [Joaiada]. The key to the solution, however, is in the juxtaposition of the priests Yōhanan [Johanan] son of 'Elyašīb [Eliashib] and Yōyada' son of 'Elyašīb. We must reckon with two high priests named 'Elyašīb, and given papponymy, two priests named Yōhanan (Cross, 1975, 10).

Cross then reconstructs the following list of the twelve generations of high priests from Jozadak to Simon, with priests in brackets being 'restored' by him to provide the original line:

1. Jozadak before 587
   father of
2. Jeshua b. ca. 570
   father of
3. Joiakim b. ca. 545
   [brother of]
[3. Eliashib I b. ca. 545]
   [father of]
[4. Johanan I b. ca. 520]
   [father of]
5. Eliashib II b. ca. 495
   father of
6. Joiada I b. ca. 470
   father of

7. Johanan II b. ca. 445
   (*AP* 30.18)
   father of
8. Jaddua II b. ca. 420
   father of
[9. Johanan III b. ca. 395]
   [father of]
[10. Jaddua III b. ca. 370]
   [father of]
11. Onias I b. ca. 345
   [= Johanan IV]
   father of
12. Simon I b. ca. 320

In this way, Cross assumes that Johanan I was the contemporary of Ezra and was followed by Eliashib II, who was contemporary with Nehemiah and grandfather of Johanan II, who is the high priest mentioned in *AP* 30. 'Evidently, one pair fell out of the list by haplography. This reconstruction solves all chronological problems' (Cross, 1975, 10).

We must now examine this attractive reconstruction to ascertain whether it is free from problems.

1. The reconstruction is based exclusively on the hypothesis that papponymy was prevalent among the high priests of Jerusalem from the sixth to the fourth century. In order to demonstrate this papponymy, Cross is forced to assume no less than two haplographies in the test – without any textual support whatsoever. This is surely a weak point.

2. Even if we accept the hypothesis of these two haplographies, the assumed papponymy is not irreproachable. The *reconstructed* papponymy starts with the *reconstructed* (3) Eliashib I and the *reconstructed* (4) Johanan I who are followed by the historically authentic (5) Eliashib II and (6) Joiada I, followed by (7) Johanan II and (8) Jaddua II. The high priests 5–8 do not in reality constitute a real papponymy for after (5) Eliashib II, the name of Eliashib disappears and Eliashib II is not followed like the *reconstructed* Eliashib I by one son Johanan but by (6) Joiada I, who is followed by (7) Johanan II. He is followed by (8) Jaddua I to be followed by the *reconstructed*

(9) Johanan III who is followed by the *reconstructed* (10) Jaddua III, followed by the authentic (11) Onias. The list is concluded by a deviation from the supposed papponymy, namely (12) Simon.

Granted that Joiada and Jaddua on the one hand and Johanan and Onias on the other hand are the same names, the supposed papponymy would concern (3) Eliashib + (4) Johanan, both *reconstructed* names, then the authentic (5) Eliashib + the authentic (6) + (7) + (8), followed by the *reconstructed* (9) + (10) + the authentic (11). Of a supposed list of 12 names (in reality 13 names!), 9 names would be illustrations of papponymy. We have already observed, however, that the name of Eliashib disappears from the list with Eliashib II. After him the supposed papponymy has changed character in so far as we do not find a sequence Eliashib + Johanan but Joiada + Johanan.

Moreover, Joiada and Jaddua are *not* identical names, for Jaddua is a hypocoristicon of the qaṭṭul-type (Noth), whereas Joiada is a complete theophoric name. And although Onias undoubtedly is the Greek form of Ḥonai, this name again is a hypocoristicon, whereas Johanan is a complete theophoric name. These facts are not denied by Cross, but he looks upon the complete and hypocoristic names as identical (Cross, 1975, 6 n. 12). Otherwise, he could not appeal to them as illustrations of papponymy. When the list ends with Simon, the principle of papponymy is broken. Such is the case also with (6) Joiada.

The authentic or attested names which we find in our texts are: Jozadak, Jeshua, Joiakim, Eliashib, Joiada, Johanan, Jaddua, Onias, and Simon. In this list, only Joiada, Johanan, Jaddua, and Onias show a tendency towards papponymy – that is, granted that we accept the hypocoristica as identical with the complete names.

3. His argument that every generation could not comprise thirty years which would give five years too many (Cross, 1975, 10) is excellent from a purely mathematical point of view and provides a very neat and schematic chronological sequence, being based as it is on an average figure of twenty-five years. From an historical point of view, however, such an argument is highly questionable. Cross's point of departure in establishing twenty-five years as a generation period is the youthful marriages attested for the members of the Davidic dynasty – which of course may not have been the same for the high priestly family. The sixth century was a very dark and difficult period and it would not be astonishing at all if during prevailing conditions not *every* priest both married and begot sons at an early stage of his life. Conditions were not normal. This objection has, of

course, its limits, but nevertheless some weight should perhaps be attached to it.

4. Really decisive against Cross's thesis, however, is another fact. We have noted that Cross says that the centre of difficulties is Eliashib who, according to him, would have been '100 and more, when he built the wall of Jerusalem with Nehemiah' (Cross, 1975, 10). This is calculated by Cross's assumption that Eliashib was the *brother* of the high priest Joiakim whom he supposes to have been born about 545 BCE (he could actually have been born about 535 BCE!). This is definitely wrong. According to Nehemiah 12.10, Joiakim was the *father* of Eliashib, for it explicitly says there $w^e y \bar{o}$-$y \bar{a} q \bar{\imath} m \ h \bar{o} l \bar{\imath} d \ '$et *'elyāšib̲*, 'and Yōyaqīm [Joiakim] begot 'Elyašib [Eliashib]'. If Joiakim was born about 535 BCE, Eliashib could have been born about 500 BCE or some years earlier. That would give him in 445 BCE an age of fifty-five to sixty years. Such an age could not possibly have been an obstacle to his participation in the work on the walls. Furthermore, the reference to his 'work' on the walls (Neh. 3.1) may refer to work that was partly symbolic. As high priest, he must have been rather fully occupied with the temple service. With this mistake and miscalculation, Cross' reconstruction loses still more of its reliability.

To sum up: persuasive and attractive as Cross' hypothesis is, it is nevertheless based on so many uncertainties and reconstructions, as well as one fundamental mistake, that chronology cannot be based on it. It is not able to turn the scales in favour of the 'traditional' chronological order of Ezra and Nehemiah.

This does not mean that the problem is in any way finally settled. The chronological order is still an open question. But, until new material is presented, the evidence would suggest that Nehemiah preceded Ezra; the former being active in the reign of Artaxerxes I, the latter in the reign of Artaxerxes II. This provisional solution has been widely accepted and in our exposition of the history of the period, it will be taken for granted.

B.   *The administrative relationship of Judah and Samaria*

A. **Alt**, 'Die Rolle Samarias bei der Entstehung des Judentums', *Festschrift Otto Procksch zum 60. Geburtstag*, Leipzig: A. Deichert und J. C. Hinrichs 1934, 5–28 = his *KS* II, 1953, 316–37; K. **Galling**, *Studien zur Geschichte Israels im persischen Zeitalter*, 1964; E. **Meyer**, *Die Entstehung des Judenthums*, 1896; W. **Rudolph**, *Esra und Nehemia*, HAT I/20, 1949; M. **Smith**, *Palestinian Parties and Politics*, 1971.

The administrative position of Judah in its relation to Samaria has been frequently discussed. The problem is to some extent connected with the hostile attitude of Samaria towards the restoration of Judah. The difference in administrative status between Samaria and Judah has been noted in scholarly discussions. After the fall of the kingdom of Israel, Samaria was transformed into an Assyrian province. The Neo-Babylonian kings did not change this position. Judah on the other hand did not receive a special status as a province; instead, it was ruled by a governor appointed by the Neo-Babylonian government, a *peḥâ* (although this title is never used of Gedaliah). It has therefore been argued that the governor of the province of Samaria felt entitled to interfere in the affairs of Judah and Jerusalem. Such being the case, there inevitably arose hostilities between Samaria and the reorganized community of Judah with its centre in Jerusalem. This state of affairs, it has been argued, lasted until Nehemiah was appointed *peḥâ* of Judah (so Alt).

This opinion, to some degree, links up with that of Meyer, who thought that, quite apart from religious dissension, it must have been a disappointment to Samaria to see a new Jewish community emerge in the territory Samaria had looked upon as an object of possible expansion (Meyer, 125).

There is a kernel of truth in Alt's argument, but he has probably overstated his case. The thesis that Judah was some kind of southern annex of Samaria cannot be supported from the relevant passages in the biblical texts, although it is accepted in some quarters (Galling, 92 n. 3). Actually Ezra 2.63 mentions the governor of Judah, called a *tiršātā*, a Persian title probably meaning 'Excellency' (old Iranian: *trašta*, reverendus). This title is here given either to Sheshbazzar or Zerubbabel (Rudolph, 25; *contra* Galling, 91). The other title for governor, *peḥâ* (Akkadian *paḫātu*), is given to Zerubbabel (Hag. 1.1 and elsewhere). Later this title is used of Nehemiah (Neh. 12.26) and is also used in speaking of the earlier governors (*paḫôṯ*) who had been active before him (Neh. 5.15). The Persian title *tiršātā* is also used of Nehemiah (Neh. 7.65 and elsewhere). Accordingly, there had been Persian governors of Judah from the time of Sheshbazzar and Zerubbabel to that of Nehemiah. This is what we would expect when Judah is called a *meḏīnāh*, a territory of jurisdiction (Ezra 2.1; Neh. 1.3; 7.6; 11.3). The term *meḏīnāh* is a term found in Imperial Aramaic and was used in the Persian chancelleries to designate a small or a large province. The term *peḥâ* was also a term in Imperial Aramaic, designating a governor, either of a great satrap or of a small province. Accordingly, there is no doubt that Judah from the beginning of the Persian period was given the status of a province by the Persian government, and Alt's opinion seems improbable in view of these facts which were not taken into account by him (see Smith, 193–201, for a critique of Alt).

C.   The Samaritan schism and the construction of the Samaritan temple

R. J. **Coggins**, *Samaritans and Jews: The Origins of Samaritanism Reconsidered*, Oxford/Atlanta: Basil Blackwell/John Knox Press 1975; F. M. **Cross**, 'Papyri of the Fourth Century BC from Dâliyeh', *New Directions*, 1969, 45–69; idem, 'A Reconstruction of the Judean Restoration', *JBL* XCIV, 1975, 4–18 [= *Int* XXIX, 1975, 187–203]; J. **Macdonald**, *The Samaritan Chronicle No. II (or: Sepher Ha-Yamim) From Joshua to Nebuchadnezzar*, BZAW 107, 1969; E. **Meyer**, *Die Entstehung des Judenthums*, 1896, H. H. **Rowley**, 'Sanballat and the Samaritan Temple', *BJRL* XXXVIII, 1955–6, 166–98 = his *Men of God*, 1963, 246–76; idem, 'The Samaritan Schism in Legend and History', *Israel's Prophetic Heritage*, ed. B. W. Anderson and W. Harrelson, New York/London: Harper & Brothers/SCM Press 1962, 208–22; M. **Smith**, *Palestinian Parties and Politics*, 1971, 148–92; G. **Widengren**, 'Israelite–Jewish Religion', *HR* I, 1969, 225–317.

In the last centuries BCE, relations between Judaeans and the citizens of Samaria were often strained and frequently found expression in open hostility. These antagonistic relations were later embodied in the so-called Jewish–Samaritan schism. According to the later Samaritans, the roots of this schism went back to the time of Eli (Macdonald, 113–18; Coggins, 120f.). According to later Jewish tradition, the real separation occurred in the eighth century, when the destroyed city of Samaria was resettled by foreigners imported into Palestine by the Assyrians (II Kings 17), which led to a mixed population and a syncretistic religion. Recent investigations of the Jewish–Samaritan relations by Rowley, Smith, Cross, and Coggins have tended to interpret the breach between the Judaeans and Samaritans as a gradual development rather than the product of any one particular event. Coggins summarizes this view in the following manner:

All the evidence suggests that the decisive formative period for Samaritanism was the epoch from the third century BC to the beginning of the Christian era; and that it emerged from the matrix of Judaism during this time, with some measure of communication continuing well into the Christian era between Samaritans and various Jewish groups. The characteristic Samaritan emphases were conservative – an anxiety to retain the

old faith rather than to launch out into new and uncharted areas, and in
one sense this has been the strength and the weakness of Samaritanism ever
since. There is no evidence that any one decisive event played a special part
in widening the breach between Jews and Samaritans. What is clear is that
differences concerning the priesthood and the true sanctuary were among
those that did most to ensure that reconciliation was unlikely (164).

Hostility between Jerusalem and Samaria was certainly a factor
during the Persian period. This antagonism must be considered as
probably brought about more by political than by religious causes,
especially if we accept the view of Meyer that Samaria looked with
dissatisfaction upon the establishment of Judah as a special province.
In this regard, the hostility would have represented a continuation of
the north–south antagonism reflected throughout the history of Israel
and Judah. This does not mean that religious causes were negligible.
There is no doubt that, both politically and religiously, an ancient
conflict from the period of the disruption of the Solomonic kingdom
was renewed and an old contrast between Israel and Judah brought
to life again. In the long run, exactly as in older times, the religious
motives got the upper hand and were at last the dominant factor.
The exclusiveness of the Jews in Judah with the hard measures
brought about by Nehemiah and Ezra caused a sharpening of the
hostile attitude. Meyer has rightly emphasized the fact that these
measures created Judaism. Samaria, however, for the most part
continued at an earlier stage of religious development: more
traditional, conservative, clinging to the old customs of popular
religion, and certainly open to syncretistic influences. As Nehemiah
and Ezra saw the situation, they thought the way of exclusiveness the
only possibility for the Jews to survive as a nation with a national
religion (Widengren, 306f.).

Samaritan tradition associated the antagonism between Jews and
Samaritans during the Persian period primarily with the figure of
Ezra. It is surely significant that Samaritan tradition does not associate the breach in relations with the name of Nehemiah, but
mentions Ezra in extremely bitter words.

This would suggest that Ezra played a larger part in bringing it about
than did Nehemiah. This is to be understood. For while the particularism of
Nehemiah was largely of political inspiration, Ezra's was religiously based
(Rowley, 1963, 271).

This again would presuppose that Ezra carried out his reforms
later than the time of Nehemiah.

In light of the Judaean exclusivism fostered by Nehemiah and

Ezra, the behaviour of Nehemiah's energetic adversary Sanballat
was a model for later generations of his descendants. The fact that
the family of the Sanballatids were able to remain in office as governors in Samaria testifies to their great political capacity. There was a
remarkable continuity in Samaria, in contrast to Jerusalem where
the Jews Nehemiah and Ezra were succeeded by the Persian Bagohi.

The extreme Judaean exclusivism, it should be noted, found its
strongest expression while the radical separatists Nehemiah and Ezra
were on the scene. At other times, the Jewish community may have
been far more conciliatory towards the citizens of the province of
Samaria and other 'foreigners' as well. (This thesis has been given
radical formulation by Smith, who sees much of Jewish history as
reflective of assimilationist and exclusivistic party struggles in Jerusalem.) During Nehemiah's absence from Jerusalem, the high priest
Eliashib prepared a chamber in the temple for Tobiah the Ammonite
(Neh. 13.4–9). Even the Sanballatids undoubtedly from time to time
succeeded in infiltrating the official circles in Jerusalem. Nehemiah
reports as follows on such an alliance between the family of Sanballat
and the high priestly family in Jerusalem: 'One of the sons of Jehoiada,
the son of Eliashib the high priest, was the son-in-law of Sanballat the
Horonite; therefore I chased him from me' (Neh. 13.28). Josephus (*Ant.*
XI 302 f.) reports a story about the marriage of Manasseh, the brother of
the Jerusalem high priest, to Nicaso, the daughter of one Sanballat,
governor of Samaria. In discussing the controversy over Manasseh's
marriage, Josephus reports that 'many priests and Israelites were
involved in such marriages' (*Ant.* XI 312). The authenticity of this
narrative has been frequently questioned (see Rowley, 1963, 249–58)
since it is beset with various difficulties and is suspiciously reminiscent of the account in Nehemiah 13.28. To give a considered opinion on the historicity of this case seems next to impossible, although
Cross is willing 'to reckon with the possibility of repeated intermar-
riage between the aristocracy of Samaria and the theocratic family
of Jerusalem', and assumes that Nicaso was the daughter of
Sanballat III who died in 332 BCE (Cross, 1969, 63; 1975, 5f.).

The hostility between Jerusalem and Samaria eventually led to
the building of the Samaritan temple on Mount Gerizim. Here
again, the Samaritans showed themselves true heirs to ancient
Israelite tradition by choosing Shechem-Gerizim as the site for construction. The date of the construction of this temple probably falls
outside the Persian period, since the Persians obviously favoured the
temple of Jerusalem over Samaritan cult-places. The Persian policy
would hardly have looked approvingly upon the building of another

temple in Samaritan territory (*Noth, 354 f.). This fact may be the grain of truth reflected in the legendary narrative about the building of the Samaritan temple in the early days of Alexander's conquest, as reported by Josephus (*Ant.* XI 306–47).

D.   The identity of Ezra's law-book

U. **Kellermann**, 'Erwägungen zum Esragesetz', *ZAW* LXXX, 1968, 373–85; F. K. **Kienitz**, *Die politische Geschichte Ägyptens vom 7. bis zum 4. Jahrhundert vor der Zeitwende*, Berlin: Akademie-Verlag 1953; S. **Mowinckel**, *Studien zu dem Buche Ezra–Nehemia, III: Die Ezrageschichte und das Gesetz Moses*, SNVAO II. NS 7, 1965, 124–41; M. **Noth**, *History of Pentateuchal Traditions*, 1972, 8–19; H. H. **Rowley**, *The Growth of the Old Testament*, London/New York: Hutchinson's University Library/Harper Torchbooks 1950/1963; W. **Spiegelberg**, *Die sogenannte demotische Chronik*, Leipzig: J. C. Hinrichs 1915.

According to the edict of Artaxerxes, Ezra returned to Jerusalem as 'the scribe of the law of the God of heaven' (Ezra 7.12) with the task of making inquiries about Judah and Jerusalem according to the law of his God which was in his hand (Ezra 7.14). The identity of this law which Ezra brought with him from Babylonia has been a much discussed problem. Four proposed identifications of the law have tended to dominate discussions.

1. The hypothesis that the law was practically identical with the pentateuch was advocated by Wellhausen and has been accepted by a host of scholars (see Kellermann, 374–6). This thesis is primarily based on two arguments. First of all, the reformation of Ezra seems to have relied upon legislation found in Exodus and Deuteronomy (cf. Neh. 10.31; 13.1–3 with Ex. 34.16 and Deut. 7.2–5; and Neh. 10.32 with Deut. 15.2), that is, upon laws that were not found in the so-called 'priestly source' of the pentateuch. Secondly, it has been argued that the pentateuch must have been in final form before the Samaritan schism took place and, if the schism is related to the time of Ezra, then the pentateuch must have existed in practically finished form by that time. However, neither of these two arguments is sufficient to support the view that Ezra's law-book was the pentateuch, which may not have reached its final form until the Hellenistic period.

2. Attempts have been made to identify Ezra's law-book with the Priestly Code of the pentateuch. This was first proposed in 1887 by A. Kuenen and strongly defended by E. Meyer (see Kellermann,

376f.). This view has been opposed by Noth, who argued that 'P' was no law at all, but a narrative. According to him, all the regulations and legal requirements attributed to the Priestly Code originally had nothing whatsoever to do with the P narrative (Noth, 8). Over against this view, Rowley argued that P was first promulgated by Ezra and that P, like Ezra's reforms, attempted to regulate cultic ritual (Rowley, 34). The relationship of Ezra's law-book to P, and some association seems certain, remains a problem, not least of all because of the different views concerning P itself.

3. The Deuteronomic code as Ezra's law-book was proposed in 1670 by Spinoza and has found some defenders (see Kellermann, 378f.). And finally, (4) some interpreters simply suggest that Ezra's law-book was a collection of laws which are now found in the pentateuch but which cannot be explicitly equated with any penteteuchal source or legal collection (see Kellermann, 377f.).

The interest of the Persian court in Jewish law is not without parallel. The so-called Demotic Chronicle, a papyrus of miscellaneous contents and from a time long after Darius, contains a demotic account of Darius' order to the satrap over Egypt, commanding that the wisest men of the country set in writing the complete law of Egypt (see Spiegelberg). This codified law was introduced as the provincial law of Egypt and an Aramaic copy of the code was delivered to the Persian authorities (Kienitz, 61). If similar procedures were followed in the case of Ezra's law-book, then Artaxerxes and the Persian court may have played a significant role in the formation of Ezra's law-book – decreed to be the provincial law of Judah – and may have possessed a copy in the Persian archives.

§3. THE JEWISH COMMUNITY UNDER
THE PERSIANS

A. *The return and the reconstruction of the temple*

P. R. **Ackroyd**, *Exile and Restoration: A Study of Hebrew Thought of the Sixth Century BC*, 1968, 138–217; idem, 'The Temple Vessels – A Continuity Theme', *SVT* XXIII, 1972, 166–81; F. I. **Andersen**, 'Who Built the Second Temple?', *ABR* VI, 1958, 1–35; G. C. **Cameron**, *History of Early Iran*, Chicago: University of Chicago Press 1936; idem, 'Ancient Persia', *The Idea of History in the Ancient Near East*, ed. R. C. Dentan, AOS 38, 1955, 77–97; S. A. **Cook**, 'The Age of Zerubbabel', *Studies in Old Testament Prophecy*, ed. H. H. Rowley, Edinburgh: T. & T. Clark, 1950, 19–36; C. J.

Gadd, 'The Harran Inscriptions of Nabonidus', *AS* VIII, 1958, 35–92; K. **Galling**, *Studien zur Geschichte Israels im persischen Zeitalter*, 1964; A. **Gelston**, 'The Foundations of the Second Temple', *VT* XVI, 1966, 232–5; J. **Lewy**, 'The Late Assyro–Babylonian Cult of the Moon and its Culmination at the Time of Nabonidus', *HUCA* XIX, 1945/46, 405–89; E. **Meyer**, *Die Entstehung des Judenthums*, 1896; R. **Meyer**, *Das Gebet des Nabonid*, SSAWL 107/3, 1962; J. M. **Myers**, *The World of the Restoration*, Englewood Cliffs: Prentice-Hall 1968; H. S. **Nyberg**, 'From a Theocratic Imperialism to an Imperium', *Iran through the Ages*, ed. A. Aadahl, Stockholm: Norstedt 1972, 11–19; A. F. **Rainey**, 'The Satrapy "Beyond the River"', *AJBA* I, 1969, 51–78; L. **Rost**, 'Erwägungen zum Kyroserlass', *Verbannung und Heimkehr: Beiträge zur Geschichte und Theologie Israels im 6. and 5. Jahrhundert v. Chr.* (Festschrift Wilhelm Rudolph), ed. A. Kuschke, Tübingen: J. C. B. Mohr 1961, 301–7; S. **Smith**, *Isaiah Chapters XL–LV: Literary Criticism and History*, London: Oxford University Press 1944; G. **Widengren**, *The King and the Tree of Life in Ancient Near Eastern Religion*, UUA 1951: 4, 1951; idem, 'La légende royale de l'Iran antique', *Hommages à George Dumézil*, Collection Latomus 45, Bruxelles: Berchom 1960, 225–37; idem, 'The Persians', *Peoples of OT Times*, 1973, 312–57; H. **Wohl**, 'A Note on the Fall of Babylon', *JANES* I/2, 1969, 28–38.

The meteoric rise of the Persians to dominance over the Near East during the third quarter of the sixth century created new conditions for the Jews which made possible a reconstitution of the Jewish community in Judah. The founder of the Persian Empire was Cyrus (*Kuruš*). His mother, Mandane, was the daughter of the Median king, Astyages, and his father was Cambyses I, the Persian king of Anshan. Herodotus and Ctesias provide stories about Cyrus' birth, exposure, and remarkable deliverance which reflect the traditional royal birth legend among Iranian peoples (Widengren, 1960) and, like the birth stories of Sargon (*ANET*, 119) and Moses (Ex. 2), lack any historical value. Cyrus was able to unite the Persian tribes under his sceptre while preserving friendly relations with Nabonidus (Nabūna'id) the Babylonian ruler (556–539 BCE) who was suspicious of Media and its imperial aspirations. Cyrus revolted against his Median overlord and grandfather and with the aid of the Median general Harpagus was able to capture and loot the Median capital at Ecbatana (Agamatana). The Nabonidus Chronicle reports the event as follows, assigning it apparently to the sixth year of the Babylonian king (550 BCE):

> King Ishtumegu [Astyages] called up his troops and marched against Cyrus, king of Anshan, in order to meet him in battle. The army of Ishtumegu revolted against him and in fetters they delivered him to Cyrus.

Cyrus marched against the country Agamatana; the royal residence he seized; silver, gold, other valuables . . . of the country Agamatana he took as booty and brought them to Anshan (*ANET*, 305).

The leadership over the Median territories then passed into the hands of Cyrus, and Media was turned into the first satrapy of the Persian empire.

Cyrus turned his attention westward and moved against the former enemy of the Medes, the Lydian kingdom, now ruled by Croesus. On his campaign, he conquered Armenia, Cappadocia, and Cilicia and organized them into satrapies. After an initial, inconclusive battle, Cyrus attacked Croesus just before winter set in but after Croesus had dismissed his provincial levies. The city of Sardis was taken after fourteen days in 547 BCE and Croesus was killed, according to the Nabonidus Chronicle (II. 17; *ANET*, 306). The Greek cities in Asia Minor were subdued, only Miletus surrendered voluntarily; the Lycians were conquered as well as the Greek islands off the coast. The area was then organized into the satrapy of Ionia.

In the east, Cyrus secured the whole of the Iranian plateau and extended his control into north-west India, into what was the later satrapy of Gandara. This eastward movement brought under his control the military resources of Iran (in its geographical sense) and provided him with an overpowering cavalry force.

The Babylonian empire was disintegrating internally. Nabonidus possessed many internal enemies and Cyrus not a few secret supporters even within Babylon itself. The most dangerous of Nabonidus' internal enemies were the members of the Marduk priesthood. They opposed the enigmatic Nabonidus because of his predilection for Sin, the moon-god of Harran, and because of his neglect of the Marduk cult of the national god of Babylon. Both Nabonidus and his mother, apparently a priestess in the Sin cult (see Lewy) who lived to an age of 104, were strong devotees of the god Sin (see the inscriptions in *ANET*, 560–3). Being of northern Mesopotamian origin, Nabonidus was something of an outsider in Babylon. For several years, the Nabonidus Chronicle monotonously reports the king's apparent disregard for the official Babylonian cult: 'The king did not come to Babylon for the ceremony of the month Nisanu; the god Nebo did not come to Babylon, the god Bel did not go out of Esagila in procession, the festival of the New Year was omitted' (*ANET*, 306). For ten years, Nabonidus resided at the oasis in Tema in north-west Arabia, having gone there, he said, because of the impiety and lawlessness of his subjects. During these years, he did not enter

Babylon. Since his third year, his son Belshazzar (Bēl-šar-usur) had
practically reigned as co-regent over Babylonia. That Nabonidus
should have been considered by some of his subjects as, at best,
eccentric, at worst, demented, is not surprising. Among the scrolls
from Qumran, a Jewish text 'reports' Nabonidus' mental derange-
ment and his cure by a Jewish exorcist (see R. Meyer).

During these last years of the reign of the enigmatic Nabonidus,
when the Neo-Babylonian kingdom was showing fatal signs of decay,
many of the Jews in Babylon were among the internal enemies of the
king and the secret supporters of the Achaemenian Cyrus. The prophet, 'Deutero-Isaiah' (Isa. 40–55), extolled Cyrus in his poetical
oracles, calling him the chosen and anointed (*messiah*) of Yahweh. 'I
[Yahweh] stirred up one from the north, and he has come, from the
rising of the sun, and he shall call on my name; he shall trample on
rulers as on mortar, as the potter treads clay' (Isa. 41.25).

> Thus says Yahweh to his anointed, to Cyrus,
>   whose right hand I have grasped,
> to subdue nations before him
>   and ungird the loins of kings,
> to open doors before him
>   that gates may not be closed . . . (Isa. 45.1).

This meant that Cyrus, at least in some Jewish circles, was looked
upon as the Messiah, the promised king and saviour of the people. It
can hardly be doubted that these prophecies were the expression not
only of Jewish expectations, but also of Jewish propaganda (see
Smith). These underground activities must to some degree have
helped undermine the position of Nabonidus.

The inner dissolution of the kingdom, economic problems, and
strategic moves by the Persian army (see Wohl) led to an easy
conquest of Babylon. After a decisive victory at Opis in July 539,
Cyrus' troops took Babylon in early October and Cyrus himself
entered the city on October 29, being greeted with enthusiasm by the
population of the capital. In Babylon, Cyrus declared himself 'king
of the world, great king, legitimate king, king of Babylon, king of
Sumer and Akkad, king of the four rims of the earth, son of
Cambyses, great king, king of Anshan, grandson of Cyrus, great
king, king of Anshan, descendant of Teispes, great king, king of
Anshan, of a family which always exercised kingship: whose rule Bel
and Nebo love, whom they want as king to please their hearts'
(*ANET*, 316). The Cyrus Cylinder, from which this passage comes,
describes Cyrus as a worshipper of Marduk who had led the inhab-

itants of Babylon to love him. Such a document and such claims
were obviously intended to make an enormous propaganda impact
(see Cameron, 1955, 81–6).

Cyrus introduced a new policy towards the subjugated peoples.
The cult images which had been carried to Babylon in conjunction
with the deportation of conquered nations were collected, together
with the most prominent of the worshippers of these foreign deities.
The Cyrus Cylinder reports the action in the following terms:

> As far as Ashur and Susa, Agade, Eshnunna, the towns Zamban, Me-
> Turnu, Der as well as the region of the Gutians, I returned to these cities on
> the other side of the Tigris, the sanctuaries of which had been ruins for a
> long time, the images which used to live therein and established for them
> permanent sanctuaries. I also gathered all their former inhabitants and
> returned their habitations (*ANET*, 316).

This action was not without precedent, for it belonged to the royal
ideology of Mesopotamia as a traditional motif to care for what we
could call 'the ingathering of the dispersed'. Esarhaddon, for
example, in his inscriptions tells us that he acted in accordance with
this pattern (Widengren, 1973, 318). The fact that the return to
Palestine was one of the leading themes in the oracles of Deutero-
Isaiah shows that his expectations were based on contemporary,
current hopes.

Nevertheless we may say that Cyrus introduced a new era into
Near Eastern political and religious thought, for this motif in the
royal ideology was made by him into a leading principle in his whole
policy in a manner altogether different from that guiding the policy
of the great oriental kingdoms. For that reason, the development has
been said to have gone 'from a theocratic Imperialism to an
Imperium' (Nyberg).

In this universal empire, every nation possessed its proper place.
The Great King, as far as possible, allowed the peoples to preserve
their traditional customs and institutions, but under the leadership of
Persians and Medes. In conformity with his policy proclaimed in the
Cyrus Cylinder, Cyrus sent back to Palestine those Jews who wanted
to go. The Jews, of course, are not mentioned in the Cyrus Cylinder.
In spite of many attempts to disprove the initial return under Cyrus
(see Galling; *Herrmann, 299–301; *Noth, 306–10), there are no
reasons to doubt its historicity. Cyrus wrote an edict in which he not
only ordered the rebuilding of the temple (Ezra 6.1–5) but also gave
permission to the returning Jews to bring back the temple vessels
that the Babylonian king had taken from Jerusalem and deposited in

the temple of Babylon (Ezra 1.7f.). In this edict, moreover, Cyrus gave directions for the cult and promised that the costs would be paid from the royal treasury. The document is found in Ezra 6.3–5 but does not mention the vessels. Of them, on the other hand, we possess a list in Ezra 1.9f., the total reliability of which is dubious (on the theological importance of these vessels to the Chronicler, see Ackroyd, 1972). He dispatched the Jewish prince Sheshbazzar (Shash-apal-uṣur), who was almost certainly not a member of the Davidic dynasty (in spite of efforts to identify him with Shenazzar, the son of Jehoiachin, mentioned in I Chron. 3.18; see *Albright, 86; *Bright, 362). Sheshbazzar was to be governor in Judah and to take charge of the temple vessels. There is no reason to doubt that the vessels really were handed over to Sheshbazzar (*contra* Galling, 1964, 79, 88).

The leading figure among the returning exiles was Zerubbabel (Zērbābili) (Ezra 2.2). In spite of his common Babylonian name, he was a member of the Davidic family, son of Shealtiel, son of Jehoiachin (Ezra 3.2; I Chron. 3.17). The fact that both Sheshbazzar and Zerubbabel had Babylonian names shows a certain degree of assimilation to Babylonian conditions. Political considerations in this regard were perhaps influential among persons of prominence.

Sheshbazzar was the governor (*peḥâ*) of Judah and in accordance with Cyrus' orders laid the foundations of the temple (Ezra 5.14–16; see Gelston and Andersen). The conditions in the country, however, were difficult, both the capital and the countryside being wasted and ruined. A comparatively large number, about 50,000, had returned from exile and the upkeep of all these people created difficulties. Whether all these people returned under Cyrus or later is impossible to ascertain (Meyer, 94–6). It is possible that a considerable number returned in 521/20 BCE.

The rebuilding of the temple was interrupted and Sheshbazzar disappears from history. Then the situation suddenly changed. Cambyses (530–522 BCE), Cyrus' son, had moved to expand the empire in the west and invaded Egypt. The aged Pharaoh, Amasis, had been succeeded by his son Psammetichus III, and although Egypt had the support of Greece as well as Greek mercenaries, Cambyses quickly overcame the Egyptians and conquered Memphis in 525 BCE. The Persian ruler thus became the ruler of the eastern Mediterranean where he was now in possession of the Egyptian, Phoenician, and Ionian fleets. On his return from Egypt in 522 BCE, Cambyses learned of an insurrection at home, but he died in Syria before he was able to deal with matters. Before leaving Persia to attack Egypt, Cambyses had had his brother Bardiya killed in order to prevent any insurrection. The insurrection in 522 BCE was led by a usurper – 'the false Smerdis' – who claimed to be Bardiya, whose death was a secret known only to a few. In reality, he was a Median Magian, Gaumāta. With the death of Cambyses and the uprising of Gaumāta, general chaos ensued throughout the Persian empire. The Achaemenian Darius, who belonged to a non-reigning branch of the family and was spearbearer (*arshtibara*) to Cambyses, led a counter-movement against Gaumāta and on September 29, 522 BCE succeeded in capturing the latter's stronghold and killed him. Darius was proclaimed king. But rebellions tore at the fabric of the empire: in Babylonia, Media, Armenia, Sardis, Egypt, and elsewhere.

The reports of this internal dissension in the empire created rather wild expectations among the Jews in Jerusalem. They were now waiting for the decisive turn of events which would bring the kingdom of God through the Anointed of Yahweh, the Messiah, this time, however, a Davidic prince. Their hopes were concentrated on Zerubbabel, who was at this time the appointed governor of Judah (Hag. 1.1). Together with the high priest, Joshua, he was the leading figure in the Jewish community. The prophets Haggai and Zechariah came forth in Jerusalem in the years 520 and 519 BCE, exhorting their compatriots to resume work on the temple which would be linked with the restoration of the royal house. The future glory is described by Zechariah in glowing terms (Zech. 8). Zerubbabel was in the centre of the messianic hopes, but it should be observed that Zechariah assigns a leading role also to the high priest Joshua (Zech. 3). Nevertheless, Zech. 6.11–13 (in the original form of the text) glorifies Zerubbabel as the branch of David's house, an ancient messianic designation (Widengren, 1951, 52f.).

These messianic prophecies, from the moment when they were proclaimed, had no foundation in real life. Darius I was able to crush the numerous revolts, restore order, and still the unrest. Only two satrapies were not yet subdued at the end of 521 BCE: Asia Minor and Egypt.

The messianic fervour in Judah does not seem to have stirred up any great political unrest. We hear nothing of any measures taken against the province of Judah. We do not know whether Zerubbabel continued in office or was removed as being a dangerous figure from the government's point of view. The effect of the enthusiasm called forth by the prophecies was, however, that the rebuilding of the temple was finished in spite of new difficulties of a special nature.

Tattenai, the satrap of the large province of Ebir-Nāri ('Beyond the River' or 'Trans-Euphrates'), of which Palestine was an administrative unit, was suspicious of the undertaking (Ezra 5). He inquired of the Jews as to who had given them permission to rebuild the temple. Upon receiving their answer that it was Cyrus, Tattenai reported to Darius, asking for instructions. An investigation carried out by the Persian government led to the discovery of the Cyrus edict in the archives of Ecbatana. In conformity with the policy of his predecessor, Darius ordered that the work should be continued and put the necessary resources at the disposal of the Jews. The cult, moreover, was to be paid for. The authentic documents are now found in Ezra 6.3–5 and 6.6–12. Tattenai received strict orders not to interfere in the work. The temple was accordingly finished and dedicated in the year 516/5 BCE (Ezra 6.15–18).

After this date there is a long silence in our records. From Nehemiah 5.15 we may conclude that Zerubbabel was succeeded by other governors, but whether Jews or Persians we do not know. The province (*m^e dīnāh*) itself was small. It can hardly have comprised more than 2,500 to 3,000 square kilometres. The province was divided into nine districts (*pelek*) under the command of an official called *śar* (Neh. 3.14). The district in turn was subdivided into half-districts commanded by an administrative officer also called *śar* (Neh. 3.9). This administrative system eliminated the importance of the old clans and families as local units. The borders of the province in the north probably went along a line between Mizpah and Gibeon to the river Jordan north of Jericho. In the south, the boundary ran along a line between Beth-zur and Hebron (E. Meyer, 105 f., 166 f.).

The capital itself was still a great city, but it was not densely enough populated to be secure against attacks from neighbouring peoples. The population of Jerusalem at the time has been calculated at about 10,000 (E. Meyer, 185).

When the interests of the Persian government were not directly involved, the province was a self-governing body. It was the task of the governor to pass judgments and collect taxes in order to have the sums handed over to the royal treasury. In other affairs, the governor collaborated with the assembly representing the population. This assembly was composed exclusively of Jews, the sons of the exiles, as they are called (Ezra 10.7). Foreigners living in the country did not belong to this body known as the *qāhāl* (Ezra 10.12, 14). In this assembly, we meet as designations of the leading figures various terms: the noblemen (*ḥōrīm*), the old men (*z^e qēnīm*), the chiefs (*śārīm*), the magnates (*'addīrīm*), and the heads of the families (*rōšē hā'ăḇoṯ*). These designations, however, overlap and seem to signify the same category: the one hundred and fifty chiefs of the families who made up a separate body above the assembly of the people. This was an executive body, exercising jurisdiction under the governor and probably in some collaboration with him. It was the predecessor of the later sanhedrin. In pre-exilic times, the same constitutional organization was in effect except that now the Persian governor was a substitute for the king (E. Meyer, 132–5).

The governor had no Persian troops under his command. For the defence of Jerusalem, he had to rely on the clans and families, among whom the full citizens, the *'am hā-'āreṣ*, composed the fully equipped ban. The clans and their chiefs were called up to defend the people in critical situations (Neh. 4.13f.).

To sum up the administrative situation: there was one territorial organization comprised of districts and another organization comprised only of Jewish inhabitants. In this latter organization every family was included and was registered in the official lists which were strictly controlled (E. Meyer, 135–41).

B.   From Zerubbabel to Nehemiah

Y. **Aharoni**, *Land of the Bible*, 1967; J. **Morgenstern**, 'Jerusalem – 485 BC', *HUCA* XXVII, 1956, 101–79; XXVIII, 1957, 15–47; XXXI, 1960, 1–29; idem, 'The Dates of Ezra and Nehemiah', *JSS* VII, 1962, 1–11; J. M. **Myers**, *The World of the Restoration*, Englewood Cliffs: Prentice-Hall 1968, 82–102; H. H. **Rowley**, *The Growth of the Old Testament*, 1950/63; G. E. **Wright**, *Shechem*, 1965.

Darius I (522–486 BCE) appeared in Palestine in the winter of 519–518 BCE on his expedition to Egypt to regulate matters there after the revolt. An Egyptian, Udjahorresne, who had earlier taken refuge with Darius, had preceded him to prepare for his visit. It is interesting to note that Zerubbabel disappeared from the scene early in 519 BCE after being warned by the prophet Zechariah: 'This is the word of Yahweh to Zerubbabel: Not by might, nor by power, but by my Spirit says the Lord of hosts' (Zech. 4.6). There is no evidence that Darius visited Judah on his way to Egypt or that the disappearance of Zerubbabel is to be associated with his passage through the area. Most probably, he followed the main road along the coast that passed near Gaza. The province of Judah, though small and somewhat distant from the main line of communications was, nevertheless, of great importance as protection to the flank of an advancing Persian army, whether marching down to Egypt or returning from this satrapy. Unmistakable traces of Persian garrisons have been found south of Gaza (see above, §1D). While it is true that these date from the fifth century, strategic conditions would have been the same in the time of Darius. It is quite understandable that the Persian government was interested in having a reliable province of Judah (*Noth, 316–18). This military and political interest – as well as the general Persian policy – explains their benevolent attitude towards the Jews.

In Egypt, Darius acted in accordance with the general policy of his predecessors, respecting the Egyptians' national and religious customs. He assumed the full titles of the Egyptian monarchy and acted as an indigenous Egyptian ruler. Before leaving Egypt, Darius completed an old construction project begun by Pharaoh Necho – the digging of a canal through Suez that provided a link between the Mediterranean Sea and the Indian Ocean.

It was under Darius that close contact and eventual conflict with the Greek mainland occurred – a factor that meant that hereafter Persian and Greek politics were to be dominated by concern with each other. Sometime before 513 BCE, Darius sought to bring the area west of the Hellespont and along the western shore of the Black Sea under his control. Action was taken against the Saka people (Scythians) living in what today would be southern Russia, the Greek colonies along the western and northern shores of the Black Sea, and Thracia and Macedonia were forced to recognize Persian supremacy. The Persian empire was now a neighbour of Hellas.

Just after the turn of the century, Darius was confronted with a major revolt by the Ionians under the leadership of the Miletians. The revolt was supported by the Athenian navy. After the revolt of the Ionian cities had been mercilessly suppressed, Darius decided to invade Greece proper, but the Greeks won a significant victory over Persian forces at Marathon (490 BCE). This victory boosted the fighting morale of the Greeks and demonstrated that the heavily-armed Greek foot soldiers were a match for the Persian cavalry provided the battleground was chosen to the disadvantage of Persian manoeuvrability. Darius intensified his desire to conquer Greece and military preparations were begun for another expedition which involved increased taxation. At the time of his death, Darius was confronted by a major revolt in Egypt precipitated by administrative corruption and taxation burdens. It remained for Xerxes (Xšāyarša), the son and successor of Darius, to suppress the Egyptian revolt.

From the early days of Darius and throughout the reign of Xerxes (486–465 BCE), practically nothing is known of the life of the Jewish community in Judah. After the temple had been rebuilt, the next logical task would have been the rebuilding of the city walls, thus reconstructing the fortifications of the capital. The subsequent efforts to rebuild the city walls before the time of Nehemiah are noted in Ezra 4.7–23 in a text which the Chronicler has chronologically misplaced by setting it within the context of efforts to get the temple rebuilt, although the events belong to a later period (see Ezra 4.7). The Chronicler probably incorporated this document at this point to illustrate the local Palestinian hostility to efforts at reconstruction of Jerusalem. In its present form, Ezra 4 suggests two bases for the difficulties involved in this reconstruction work. First of all, Zerubbabel, Joshua, and the chiefs of the families are shown declining the offer of their adversaries to aid in the reconstruction of the temple (Ezra 4.1–3). Ezra 4.3, which contains the refusal of the Jewish leaders, does not state the reason for their refusal, but a reference to II Kings 17.25–8 would be sufficient to show that the northern Israelites and the inhabitants of Samaria were suspicious from a Judaean religious point of view. Probably, however, political reasons were at least as decisive as the religious causes. Samaria had inherited the political ambitions and traditions of the kingdom of Israel. Samaria thus wanted to include Judah in its own sphere of influence and perhaps ultimately to annex it. Thus, one must see, as a second .cause of the hostile relations over the reconstruction of Jerusalem, the political ambitions of Samaria. A reconstructed temple and a refortified city would have posed a threat to these political ambitions. The province of Judah, being the southern kingdom, with all its might tried to defend itself against these aspirations.

Ezra 4.6 contains an enigmatic reference to an accusation made against Judah and Jerusalem at the beginning of the reign of Ahasuerus (Xerxes). The text tells us nothing about the provocation or background for such an official accusation, nor does it discuss the outcome of and consequences of this accusation. In a number of articles, Morgenstern has argued that a major catastrophe befell the Jewish community in the year of the ascension of the Persian throne by Xerxes. Morgenstern summarizes his theory in the following manner:

With the approval, and even with the encouragement and token support, of the Persian royal administration, the land was overrun by a coalition of ruthless enemies, the nations immediately adjacent to it, the Edomites, Moabites, Ammonites, and Philistines, and with some measure of participa-

tion by the Syrians and Sidonians. The Judaean community, totally
unprepared for actual warfare, could offer no effective resistance. It was
conquered completely and speedily. Jerusalem was besieged and captured.
Its walls were breached and its gates burned [Pss. 79.1–4; 137.7; Isa. 64.9 f.;
Ezek. 25.3; Lam. 2.5–9]. The city itself was depopulated and laid in ruins.
The temple too was burned and destroyed [Pss. 74.3–8; 79.16; Isa. 63.18;
64.10; Ezek. 25.3; Lam. 1.10; 2.6 f., 20b; 5.18]. A large section of the people
were massacred. Another, apparently equally large section were carried off
as captives and sold as slaves in the slave-markets of Tyre, Sidon, and Gaza,
and thus came to be scattered throughout the vast Mediterranean world
[Joel 4.2b–8; Neh. 5.8; Isa. 60.4, 8–22]. The Jewish community of Judaea
which survived this catastrophe was only a tiny, insignificant, pitifully
helpless fragment of what it had been previously (1962, 1).

Morgenstern's theory has found little acceptance, although
Aharoni (358) adopts it and points, like Wright (164), to the
archaeological evidence of major disturbance at sites like Shechem,
Bethel, Gibeon, and Tel el-ful during the fifth century. There may
certainly have been disturbances in Palestine during the first half of
the fifth century, for example, during Egyptian periods of revolt in
486–483 BCE and 459 BCE. However, Morgenstern's theory cannot be
accepted for two reasons: (1) it is a hypothesis built on the basis of
certain texts which are explainable on other grounds, and (2) it
requires one to assume that the second temple was destroyed and a
third one erected by Ezra; two major events for which there is no
explicit reference made in scripture (but see Ezra 2.27; 9.9, which
Morgenstern claims 'attests positively to the fact that Ezra did build
or rebuild the Temple' [1962, 3]).

Much of Xerxes' reign was spent in his struggles with Greece. The
Persian navy was defeated in the strait of Salamis (September 22,
480 BCE); the Persian army was humiliated at Plataea (479 BCE) and
forced to retreat to Asia. The Greeks sought to carry the conflict into
Asia; they landed troops in Asia Minor, and defeated part of the
Persian fleet and an army corps of levies at Mycale. Xerxes was
forced to put down a major revolt in Babylonia which was finally
suppressed in forcible fashion and Babylonia made a part of a special
satrapy along with Assyria. The aged Xerxes was murdered by his
chiliarch Artabanus in 465 BCE.

Artaxerxes (465–424 BCE), a younger son of Xerxes, succeeded his
father after a period of political confusion. During his reign, we hear
of new initiatives being taken by the Jewish community in
Jerusalem. In the Aramaic document found in Ezra 4.11–16, it is
related that the Jews were rebuilding the walls of Jerusalem. When

such activity was undertaken cannot be determined, but at any rate must be dated some time after 465 BCE. Various administrative officials (Ezra 4.7f.) sent a letter to Artaxerxes concerning this building activity of the Jews. In denouncing the work in Jerusalem, the letter refers to the city's record of constant rebellion (Ezra 4.15) and warns that 'if this city is rebuilt and the walls finished, they will not pay tribute, custom, or toll, and the royal revenue will be impaired' (Ezra 4.13). The arguments in the accusatory letter seem to have convinced the Persian ruler who issued a response decreeing that the work should cease (Ezra 4.17–22) and noting that official search had disclosed 'that this city from of old has arisen against kings, and that rebellion and sedition have been made in it' (Ezra 4.19). The opponents of the reconstruction of the city, supported by the royal decree, halted the work 'by force and power' (Ezra 4.23). It is significant that associated with this denunciation of the Jerusalem community we find representatives of the foreign, non-Israelite population settled in the cities of Samaria and throughout the province Beyond the River (Ezra 4.9f.).

The inner conditions of the Jewish community at this time can be known to some extent from the prophetic book of Malachi, to be dated before 460 BCE (so Rowley, 123, and Myers, 96–103). From these prophecies, we learn what an important place the temple cultus and the question of worthy offerings occupied in the Jewish religion of this period. A remarkable development had taken place in the prophetical attitude which now concerned itself with the temple and its cultus. Malachi 1.8 demonstrates that governors still existed in Judah (*contra* *Albright, 88), a circumstance confirmed also by Nehemiah 5.15.

C. *Nehemiah and the refortification of Jerusalem*

W. F. **Albright**, 'Dedan', *Geschichte und Altes Testament*, BHT 16, 1953, 1–12; A. **Alt**, 'Judas Nachbarn zur Zeit Nehemias', *PJB* XXVII, 1931, 66–74 = his *KS* II, 1953, 338–45; F. M. **Cross**, 'A Reconstruction of the Judean Restoration', *JBL* XCIV, 1975, 4–18 [= *Int* XXIX, 1975, 187–203]; W. J. **Dumbrell**, 'The Tell el-Maskhuṭa Bowls and the "Kingdom" of Qedar in the Persian Period', *BASOR* CCIII, 1971, 33–44; U. **Kellermann**, *Nehemia: Quellen, Überlieferung und Geschichte*, BZAW 102, 1967; G. M. **Landes**, 'Ammon', *IDB* I, 108–14; B. **Mazar**, 'The Tobiads', *IEJ* VII, 1957, 137–45, 229–38; J. M. **Myers**, *The World of the Restoration*, 1968, 103–30; A. T. **Olmstead**, *History of the Persian Empire*, 1948; I. **Rabinowitz**, 'Aramaic Inscriptions of the Fifth Century BCE from a North-Arab Shrine in Egypt', *JNES* XV, 1956, 1–9; H. H. **Rowley**, 'Nehemiah's Mission and its Background', *BJRL* XXXVII, 1954–5, 528–61 = his *Men of God*, 1963, 211–45; W. **Rudolph**, *Esra und Nehemia*, HAT I/20, 1949; M. **Smith**, *Palestinian Parties and Politics*, 1971, 126–47.

In 445 BCE, the twentieth year of Artaxerxes, conditions in Jerusalem were still the same: the city remain unfortified, the walls were in ruins and the gates burned. Nehemiah, a Jew living in Susa where he was a cup-bearer at the royal court (Neh. 1.11), learned about this state of affairs from some of his compatriots coming from Judah (Neh. 1.3). Olmstead has suggested that Hanani and the certain men out of Judah (Neh. 1.2) may have come to Susa to present an appeal to the Persian court on behalf of Jerusalem, having to use indirect channels because of the opposition to Judah in the administrative system of the satrap Beyond the River (314).

Nehemiah's position was a high one (see Herodotus, III 34) but the Hebrew expression would not seem to indicate that he was the chief of cup-bearers, not *the* cup-bearer. His position, however, afforded him the opportunity of intimate contact with the king and Nehemiah knew how to take advantage of such an opportunity.

On the occasion of a royal banquet when the queen was also present – that she is mentioned probably shows that Nehemiah was in favour with her – Nehemiah was asked by the king why he had such a sad look. Nehemiah described to Artaxerxes the situation in Jerusalem and asked for royal permission to return to Jerusalem and rebuild the walls. He also asked to have the necessary timber handed over to him from the royal park over which Asaph – probably a Jew – had supervision. Artaxerxes granted him his request and provided him with both a letter to the governors through whose territories he had to pass and an escort of cavalry (Neh. 2.1–10).

It is striking that Nehemiah in his memoirs does not mention that he was appointed governor of Judah on this occasion. With diplomatic skill, Nehemiah had put the whole affair to Artaxerxes on a very personal level: he wanted, he told the king, to rebuild the city where the tombs of his ancestors were situated. This was an *argumentum ad hominem* that had its desired effect. Nehemiah perhaps followed this course because of the suspicions against Jerusalem which had earlier caused the cessation of all repairs on the capital's defences. Such being the case, Nehemiah was presumably not appointed governor initially, but was given a special royal commission, and only later appointed governor (see Neh. 5.14; Rudolph, 107).

The cooperative attitude of the Persian monarch should not be understood as a purely magnanimous act. For the Persian government political motives may have been the decisive factor. The early years of Artaxerxes had been filled with political problems. In Bactria, his brother Hystaspes had led a short-lived revolt immediately after Artaxerxes' enthronement. More difficult problems, and in the vicinity of Palestine, had broken out in Egypt. There, Inarus, who may have been a son of Pharaoh Psammetichus III, led a major nationalistic revolt. In 460 BCE, he had appealed to and received help from Athens, now under the leadership of Pericles. The Persian satrap in Egypt was killed in battle and Memphis taken by the rebels in 459 BCE. The Persians were able to squelch the revolt and the combined Athenian and Egyptian manoeuvre ended in defeat in 455 BCE. The experience however must have demonstrated how valuable it would be to the Persians to have a loyal province and reliable governor in the territory bordering on Egypt. In addition, Megabyzus, the satrap of the province Beyond the River, had rebelled in 448 BCE and, although he was quickly reconciled to the Persian king, two expeditionary forces had been unable to subdue him.

Arriving in Jerusalem, Nehemiah undertook a night-time reconnaissance tour, inspecting the city walls to ascertain the situation (Neh. 2.11–16). He had to act with caution for, when passing through Samaria, he had learned of the hostile attitude of Sanballat, the governor of that province, and of Tobiah of Ammon, possibly his second in command in the area (Neh. 2.10). (It has been suggested by Albright, who is followed by Landes (113) and Cross (7 n. 21 and 17), that the phrase 'Tobiah the servant, the Ammonite' in Nehemiah 2.10 should be read 'Tobiah and Abd the Ammonite', the latter being identified with 'Abd a governor of Dedan who is known from an inscription from El-'Ulā (Dedan). This suggestion, however, has no support either in the text or any version. Even in Jerusalem, these two were dangerous enemies, so far as Nehemiah was concerned, because they had succeeded in infiltrating Jerusalem circles, among whom they had kinsmen (Neh. 6.17f.; 13.4, 28).

As soon as possible, Nehemiah summoned the leading personalities of the capital and, telling them of the king's decision, exhorted them to begin the work of rebuilding the walls, an undertaking in which their national honour was involved (Neh. 2.17f.). The assembly, including the 150 chiefs of the families to whom were added the priests and officials, promised to tackle the task.

The opponents of the reconstruction of Jerusalem's fortifications are given as Sanballat the governor of Samaria, Tobiah the Ammonite, Geshem the Arab, and the Ashdodites (Neh. 2.19; 4.7; the latter are omitted in the LXX text). Tobiah may have been the governor of Ammon in Transjordan (see Mazar). Geshem the Arab was probably the king of the Arab kingdom of Qedar. A recently discovered inscription of his son Qain confirms his *floruit* in the latter half of the fifth century BCE (see Rabinowitz and Dumbrell). The Ashdodites would appear to refer to the citizens of the old Philistine state to the west. Sanballat of Samaria was obviously the ringleader of the opposition. Nehemiah 4.7 pictures the Jerusalem community surrounded by opponents – to the north, Sanballat, to the east, Tobiah, to the south, the Arabs, and to the west, the Ashdodites (on Jerusalem's neighbours at this time, see Alt and Kellermann, 166–73).

Upon hearing reports of the rebuilding activity, Sanballat, Tobiah, and Geshem sent a desultory message but Nehemiah answered that they had no share in Jerusalem (Neh. 2.19f.). Did he by his answer intentionally return the exclamation of the ten tribes: 'What share have we in David?' (I Kings 12.16). With his sharp reply, Nehemiah at any rate once for all had drawn a line of demarcation between Judah and her neighbours, thus pursuing the same policy as Zerubbabel and his collaborators (see Ezra 4.3).

Nehemiah organized the reconstruction work by allotting the whole circuit of the capital in sections, assigning these to the clans as well as to the districts, concentrating his efforts on the most dangerous parts of the northern wall (Neh. 3). Sanballat and the others, however, when the walls were finished to half of their height, planned to attack Jerusalem in order to halt the undertaking. Nehemiah on the other hand acted with characteristic vigour and skill. He called into service the ban of Judah, composed of the men of the clans capable of bearing arms. He placed them behind the walls in the open spaces, armed with swords and spears, in that way protecting the most vulnerable parts of the city (Neh. 4.13). These measures deterred the opponents from an open attack, but after this menace Nehemiah divided the inhabitants into two divisions: one half working on the walls, the other half posted as guards (Neh 4.16, 21). He also ordered all the people of the countryside to pass the night in Jerusalem (Neh. 4.22) and he and his men slept with their work clothes on (Neh. 4.23). Thanks to this combined system of defence and work, the repair of the walls was completed in fifty-two days – an astonishing achievement (Neh. 6.15; Josephus however reports, *Ant.* XI 179, that the repairs to the wall took two years and four months and were completed in 437 BCE).

Nehemiah's opponents devised several schemes against him, hoping that they might seize him or that fear would dissuade him or that

he could be discredited before his Jewish compatriots (Neh. 6). Sanballat and Tobiah tried, on several occasions, to arrange a private
meeting with Nehemiah, no doubt with plans to put him out of the
way (Neh. 6.1–4). Nehemiah was accused of plotting revolt and of
laying plans for his own prophetic designation as king (Neh. 6.5–9).
Nehemiah denied such charges (Neh. 6.8) and there is no reason to
think that Nehemiah assumed any messianic pretensions or that he
was himself a member of the Davidic family (*contra* Kellermann,
179–91). On another occasion, his enemies sought to get Nehemiah
to take refuge in the temple with tales of a plot to assassinate him
(Neh. 6.10–14). Nehemiah saw through the plot and recognized it as
an effort to get him to 'sin, so they could give me an evil name, in
order to taunt me' (Neh. 6.13). It has been argued that Nehemiah's
reference here to his 'sin' of entering the temple was based on the
fact that, as a royal Persian official with close contact with the royal
family (see Neh. 2.6), Nehemiah was a eunuch and eunuchs were
forbidden admission to the temple (Deut. 23.1; Lev. 21.17–23; see
*Albright, 90f.). However, when Herodotus discussed the cup-
bearer's position, he had nothing to say on this point.

Even after the completion of the walls, all dangers were not overcome. The city-gates had to be carefully guarded and a reliable
regular watch organized to prevent any surprise attack (Neh. 7.1–3).
Nehemiah divided the people with one tenth selected by lot to be
settled in Jerusalem and the other nine tenths to live in the towns of
the countryside (Neh. 11.1 f.). These measures carried through, there
followed a solemn dedication of the walls (Neh. 12.27–43).

Nehemiah not only occupied himself with the defence of
Jerusalem but also sought to reform the internal affairs of the
population. Even before the walls were finished he took measures
against the plundering of the proletarians and small farmers who
were in debt because of their inability to pay their taxes (Neh. 5.1–
5). In the people's assembly, he accused the chiefs of usury and –
pointing to the examples set by himself and his brothers – forced
them to give up their active debts (Neh. 5.6–13). By taking an oath
from the chiefs, he obligated them to keep their promise. No doubt
the poor by working on the walls were prevented from earning their
living, and this had aggravated their economic situation. This fact
was, of course, not mentioned by Nehemiah. As governor, Nehemiah
possessed the right to tax the people for a food allowance for himself
and his administrative staff. Nehemiah, apparently a man of wealth,
refused to impose this additional burden upon the already oppressed
population (Neh. 5.14–19).

In 433 BCE, Nehemiah was recalled to Susa (Neh. 13.6). When he returned, intolerable practices, in the eyes of Nehemiah, had been accepted in the community. He discovered that Eliashib the priest had prepared a chamber in the temple for his old enemy Tobiah. Since Tobiah, being an Ammonite, was of foreign extraction (see Neh. 13.1; Deut. 23.3–5), Nehemiah made an end to this and had the chamber purified (Neh. 13.4–9). He also saw that the levites received their portion of the offerings (Neh. 13.10–14) and reacted against the transgression of the sabbath commandment, taking strong measures to abolish such abuses (Neh. 13.15–22).

From the social point of view, the measure most interfering in the life of the community was Nehemiah's intervention in the so-called mixed marriages, a practice also implying religious consequences. Although his policy encountered resistance and demanded some strong-armed tactics, Nehemiah succeeded in abolishing such marriages (Neh. 13.23–9).

We do not know how long Nehemiah served as governor of Judah, but presumably his office ended in the last years of Artaxerxes' reign, about 430 BCE. His work had been chiefly of a political, social, and military nature (*Noth, 329f.) but it also had very important religious implications. Undoubtedly, he was one of the great figures of Jewish history. The measures he took, often in rather tyrannical fashion (see Smith, 141–4), paved the way for the further development of Judaism. He was a typical representative of the exclusiveness of Jewish religion as it had taken shape in the exile. He consolidated Judaism and adapted it to an existence within a world empire.

D.   *The Jewish colony at Elephantine*

A. **Cowley**, *Aramaic Papyri of the Fifth Century BC*, London: Oxford University Press, 1923; P. **Grelot**, 'Etudes sur le "Papyrus Pascal" d'Éléphantine', *VT* IV, 1954, 349–84; idem, 'Le Papyrus Pascal d'Éléphantine et le problème du Pentateuque', *VT* V, 1955, 250–65; idem, 'Le Papyrus Pascal d'Éléphantine: Essai de Restauration', *VT* XVII, 1967, 201–7; E. G. **Kraeling**, *The Brooklyn Museum Aramaic Papyri*, 1953; E. **Meyer**, *Der Papyrusfund von Elephantine*, ²1912; B. **Porten**, *Archives from Elephantine: The Life of an Ancient Jewish Military Colony*, 1968; A. **Vincent**, *La religion des judéo-araméens d'Éléphantine*, Paris: P. Geuthner 1937.

During the Persian period, Jewish religion was still in a transitional stage. This is demonstrated by the evidence of the Elephantine papyri which reflect the religious life of a Jewish military garrison stationed in Egypt but under Persian control. The oldest of these documents dates from 495 BCE, but the colony must be at least a century older (Kraeling, 41–8, and see above, ch. VIII, §7B). There is direct evidence in one of the documents to the fact that the Jews at Elephantine were employed as mercenaries before the time of Cambyses (*AP* 30. 13–14). The number of the colony was not very large, for we hear only of a *degel*, a company of 100 men (Old Persian: *drafša* = banner). These Jewish mercenaries possessed a temple where they worshipped Yāhū, a form of the name Yahweh. Apparently they seemed to have been uninfluenced by the spirit of Deuteronomy with its emphasis on the centralization of the cult in one place. Actually, their religion shows clear signs of syncretism, for along with Yāhū they also worshipped Bethel, Harambethel, Ašambethel, and Anat. This polytheistic attitude, and especially the worship of the goddess Anat, hints at a worship of north Israelite origin. On the other hand, one cannot deny that, for the greater part, the mercenaries must have come from Judah.

From the year 419 BCE, there is a papyrus regulating the celebration of the festival of unleavened bread (Maṣṣoth) as ordered by a certain Hananiah. What is remarkable is that Hananiah says in his letter that the Great King (Darius II) had written to Arsham, his satrap in Egypt, giving orders for the strict regulation of this festival. The order probably stipulated that the Jews were to be left to celebrate the Massoth in conformity with their established custom (*AP* 21; see Grelot). Contrary to what has been assumed, however, the passover was most probably not mentioned in the letter (but see Grelot, 1967).

During the absence of the satrap Arsham, the Jewish temple (*'egōrā*) was sacked and destroyed because of the hostility of the Egyptian priests of the god Khnum. The reason for their hostility may to some extent have been religious, since the Jews offered rams as burnt offerings, and the ram was the symbolic animal of Khnum. The chief reason, however, must have been political: the Jews were in the service of Persia and were thus an arm of the foreign oppressor (Kraeling, 102–4). The Jews were loyal to the Persian crown and could therefore be used by the satrap against the Egyptians when they rebelled, as they actually did repeatedly. That the local Persian governor Vidrang on one occasion acted in concert with the Egyptians (*AP* 27) was due to a case of bribery – to judge from the Jewish accusations in the letter. In a petition, probably sent to Arsham, the Jews pointed out that while the Egyptians had rebelled, they had remained loyal. They then requested the rebuilding of the destroyed temple or altar (the word is destroyed in the papyrus; *AP* 27. 1–2, 24).

As this letter of request obviously had no effect, the Jews sent another letter in the year 410 BCE to Bagohi (Bagoas), the Persian governor of Judah, asking him to order the rebuilding of their temple (*AP* 30 and 31). Letters were also sent to Johanan and his colleagues, the priests in Jerusalem (*AP* 30. 18–19). From the letter to Bagohi, it is clear that a Persian was now governor in Jerusalem and that it is to be taken for granted that this governor was entitled to exercise authority concerning conditions of a Jewish garrison in Egypt. This first petition, sent in 410 BCE, was left unanswered and was thereafter repeated in 407 BCE in a letter to Bagohi.

Another petition had been sent to Delaiah and Shelemiah, the sons of Sanballat, the governor of Samaria and the old enemy of Nehemiah. That these two sons lived in Jerusalem is highly improbable (Cowley, 118; otherwise, Kraeling, 108).

A memorandum was sent by Bagohi and Delaiah jointly (*AP* 32). In this message, instruction is given to Arsham concerning 'the altar-house (*beth maḏbᵉḥā*) of the God of heaven' 'to rebuild it in its place'. The Jews 'may offer the meal-offering and incense upon that altar as was formerly done' (*AP* 32. 3–4, 8–11). Accordingly they were allowed to offer *minḥāh* (meal-offering) and *lᵉḇōnāh* (incense), but not the *'ōlāh*, the burnt-offering, for which they also had asked. Various explanations of this restriction have been offered, but no satisfactory solution has been presented.

The cult of Yahu was thus resumed. For how long we do not know since the colony disappears shortly after 400 BCE. Artaxerxes II was still recognized as sovereign at Elephantine in 402/1 BCE, as demonstrated in the Brooklyn papyrus 12 (Kraeling, 268–80). Later, however, the Egyptian revolt which had started in 405 BCE got the upper hand. The Persian garrisons were conquered, and with them their Jewish mercenaries. The colony itself, however, continued to exist under the new rulers, the Egyptian Pharaohs, as is shown in the Brooklyn papyrus 13 (Kraeling, 283–90).

The beginning of Artaxerxes II's reign was a time of great internal dissension within the empire. The Great King was confronted not only with the Egyptian revolt but also by the attempt to take over the throne by his brother Cyrus the Younger who was supported by his famous 'Ten Thousand' Greek mercenaries. During these troubles, the Jews in Palestine seemed to have remained loyal to Artaxerxes II. A few notices found in late and not very reliable authors and some archaeological evidence, difficult to place in any historical context, can hardly be invoked as testifying to Jewish revolts against the Persian government (see above, §1D). On the contrary, Josephus (*Ant.* XI 317–20) stresses the loyalty of the Jewish community to the Persians even down to Darius III after Alexander the Great had begun his siege of Tyre.

E.   The activity of Ezra

A. **Alt**, 'Zur Geschichte der Grenze zwischen Judäa und Samaria', *PJB* XXXI, 1935, 94–111 = his *KS* II, 1953, 346–62; D. K. **Andrews**, 'Yahweh the God of the Heavens', *The Seed of Wisdom* (Festschrift T. J. Meek), ed. W. S. McCullough, Toronto: University of Toronto Press 1964, 45–57; H. **Cazelles**, 'La mission d'Esdras', *VT* IV, 1954, 113–40; F. M. **Cross**, 'A Reconstruction of the Judean Restoration', *JBL* XCIV, 1975, 4–18 = *Int* XXIX, 1975, 187–203; K. **Galling**, *Studien zur Geschichte Israels im persischen Zeitalter*, 1964; K. **Koch**, 'Ezra and the Origins of Judaism', *JSS* XIX, 1974, 173–97; H. H. **Schaeder**, *Esra der Schreiber*, BHT 5, 1930; M. **Smith**, *Palestinian Parties and Politics*, 1971.

Before the events that produced the fall of the Persian empire, we find Ezra active in Jerusalem, probably in 398/7 BCE. If the arguments presented above in the discussion on the chronological order of Ezra and Nehemiah are correct (see above, §2A), then Ezra was commissioned by the Great King, Artaxerxes II. Ezra was both a priest (*kāhnā*) and a secretary or scribe (*sāfrā*). The first office was Jewish, the second Persian. From all the information we have it is evident that he held a high position in the Persian chancellery. Schaeder (39–59) argued that Ezra was a secretary of state for Jewish affairs, but that he occupied such a position is highly uncertain (Galling, 166f.).

Ezra was a special commissioner appointed by the Persian government with the task of regulating some internal affairs in the province of Judah. With Egypt in full revolt, it was more urgent than ever that the Persian government should be sure of peace and order in Judah. How Ezra's position was related to that of the local Persian governor, still Bagoas (Bagohi), remains unknown. Since his name does not appear in the memoirs of Ezra, it would seem there was no clash between the two men.

Ezra's commission was strictly defined in the royal edict given him (Ezra 7.12–26). (1) Any of the people, priests, or levites in the kingdom who wished to return to Jerusalem were allowed to accompany Ezra. According to Ezra 8.1–14, about five thousand people returned with him, which amounted to a considerable increase in the Jewish population in the province. (2) Ezra was ordered to investigate conditions in Judah and Jerusalem in accordance with 'the law of your God, which is in your hand', i.e., a religious code for the Jews. (3) Considerable funds from the royal treasury to be used for the temple cult were to be conveyed to Jerusalem. (4) Ezra was granted permission to carry with him money raised by the Jews in exile as well as vessels for the temple services. (5) Ezra was granted the authority to appoint magistrates and judges. The edict of the king decreed that the treasurers in the province should make funds and supplies available to Ezra.

'The law of the God of heaven' (Ezra 7.12, 21), according to which the cultic regulations had to be carried through, cannot be identified. The description of Yahweh as 'the God of heaven' possibly had its origin in the diplomatic terminology of the Persian administration (Andrews, 52), although such expressions as Baal Shamēm and *'elōhē haššāmayīm* (I Kings 8.27) should be noted. The law carried back to Jerusalem cannot be identified with the Priestly Code – though affinities are found. The idea that it can be identified with the whole pentateuch (*Albright, 54) or the 'pentateuch in penultimate form' (Cross, 16) is an impossible hypothesis.

Ezra succeeded in consolidating the community and carrying through his cultic reform. The law was read, according to Nehemiah 8, on the first day of the seventh month (Rosh Hashshanah) which was then followed by the observance of the feast of tabernacles (Sukkot), although there is, interestingly enough, no reference to the day of atonement (Yom Kippur). This is no evidence that Ezra exercised authority to carry out cultic–legal reform other than in the province of Judah; certainly his authority did not extend to the province of Samaria (so Alt, 355–8, who is followed by Cazelles, 131; see Smith 193–201) nor include all of the satrapy of Beyond the River (so Koch, 193–5).

Ezra's ambition was also to undertake a purge of foreign, non-Jewish elements from the community. In his policy of excluding foreign marriages – which can be interpreted as implicit in his commission – Ezra went further than Nehemiah. In spite of some opposition, he succeeded in dissolving mixed marriages (Ezra 10). Such measures had both religious and political consequences, since they sharpened the division between the Jews and their neighbours and perhaps helped pave the way for a final break between Jerusalem and Samaria.

F.   *Jerusalem and Samaria*

R. J. **Bull**, 'An Archaeological Context for Understanding John 4.20', *BA* XXXVIII, 1975, 54–9; J. D. **Purvis**, *The Samaritan Pentateuch and the Origin of the Samaritan Sect*, HSM 2, 1968; for additional bibliography, see §2C above.

The hostility between Jerusalem and Samaria ultimately led to an open breach, although the date and details of this breach are unknown. The Samaritans, however, recognize the pentateuch as holy scripture. The Massoretic text of the Jewish pentateuch does not differ from the Samaritan pentateuch except in details. A more or less fixed canonical text was accordingly shared by the Jews and Samaritans at a date when a definite breach had not yet occurred. A crucial point in dating the breach would be therefore to ascertain at what date the pentateuch was accepted as a canonical writing, for then we would have at least a *terminus post quem*. Unfortunately, we are not able to say more than this date falls some time after the fourth century. Purvis has recently argued that the Samaritan pentateuch represents a textual development which had its origin in the first century BCE. According to him, the Massoretic and Samaritan pentateuchal texts are merely variations of a commonly shared Palestinian text. If this be the case, then the question of the origin of the Samaritan pentateuch would suggest a very late date for the final breach between Jews and Samaritans.

We have noted earlier (see above, §2C) that the relationship between Jerusalem and Samaria had become very strained by the time the Samaritans constructed their own temple on Mount Gerizim, faithful to their old traditions. The existence of the rival temple on Mount Gerizim would have made a final break between the two communities inevitable. In all likelihood, the construction of the Samaritan temple is to be placed outside the Persian period. This would certainly be the case if the Hellenistic Age altar excavated or Tell er-Ras on Mount Gerizim was part of the Samaritan temple (see Bull).

Here we can say no more than that the measures taken by Ezra aggravated the relations between Jews and Samaritans, for Ezra, as we noted earlier, left a bad memory in Samaritan records. Some time in the middle of the fourth century, the situation must have become so hostile that an eventual breach became inevitable. But, it is to be assumed that there was a gradual deterioration and no dramatic rupture. The temple on Mount Gerizim gave symbolic expression to this developing hostility.

G. Summary

The Persian period was the time when Judaism was consolidated and found its new way of living, a way of living adapted to an existence within a universal empire, without political independence but preserving itself as a self-governing religious community, separated from other peoples and religions by means of a rigid exclusiveness. This exclusiveness, however, possessed a social and cultic character. It did not exclude an open-mindedness in the field of ideas and the languages in which these ideas were expressed. In this period, Persian influence already made itself felt, chiefly in the linguistic field. By degrees, however, a vast influx of Iranian ideas is found and this influence presumably started in this period.

Nehemiah and Ezra, the creators of the post-exilic Jewish community in Palestine, are two of the greatest figures in Jewish history.

X

THE HELLENISTIC AND MACCABAEAN PERIODS

§1. LITERARY SOURCES AND ARCHAEOLOGICAL EVIDENCE

A. Literary sources

(i)   The book of Daniel

W. **Baumgartner**, 'Ein Vierteljahrhundert Danielforschung', *TR* XI, 1939, 59–83; 125–44; 201–28; M. A. **Beek**, *Das Danielbuch. Sein historischer Hintergrund und seine literarische Entwicklung*, Leiden: Ginsberg 1935; A. **Bentzen**, *Daniel*, HAT I/19, 1937, ²1952; E. **Bickermann**, *Der Gott der Makkabäer: Untersuchungen über Sinn und Ursprung der makkabäischen Erhebung*, Berlin: Schocken Verlag, 1937; J. G. **Bunge**, *Untersuchungen zum Zweiten Makkabäerbuch* (Dissertation, Bonn 1971); R. H. **Charles**, *A Critical and Exegetical Commentary on the Book of Daniel*, London: Oxford University Press 1929; M. **Delcor**, *Le livre de Daniel*, Paris: Lecoffre, J. Gabalda and Cie. 1971; O. **Eissfeldt**, *The OT: An Introduction*, 1965, 512–29; G. **Fohrer**, *Introduction to the OT*, 1968, 471–9; H. L. **Ginsberg**, *Studies in Daniel*, TSJTS 14, 1948; J. **Goettsberger**, *Das Buch Daniel*, HSAT VIII/2, 1928; E. W. **Heaton**, *The Book of Daniel*, London: SCM Press 1956; M. **Hengel**, *Judaism and Hellenism*, 1974; A. **Jepsen**, 'Bemerkungen zum Danielbuch', *VT* XI, 1961, 386–91; J. C. H. **Lebram**, 'Apokalyptik und Hellenismus im Buche Daniel. Bemerkungen und Gedanken zu Martin Hengels Buch über "Judentum und Hellenismus"', *VT* XX, 1970, 503–24; idem, 'Perspektiven der gegenwärtigen Danielforschung', *JSJ* V, 1974, 1–33; A. **Mertens**, *Das Buch Daniel im Lichte der Texte vom Toten Meer*, SBM 12, 1971; J. A. **Montgomery**, *A Critical and Exegetical Commentary on the Book of Daniel*, ICC, 1927; F. **Nötscher**, *Das Buch Daniel*, HSDU 3, 1958; P. **Oschwald**, *Le Livre de Daniel*, Neuchâtel–Paris: Delachaux et Niestle 1957; O. **Plöger**, *Das Buch Daniel*, KAT 18, 1965; N. W. **Porteous**, *Daniel, A Commentary*,

OTL, 1965; H. **Sahlin**, 'Antiochus IV. Epiphanes und Judas Mackabäus. Einige Gesichtspunkte zum Verständnisse des Danielbuches', *ST* XXIII, 1969, 41–68; J. M. **Schmidt**, *Die spätjüdische Apokalyptik: Die Geschichte ihrer Erforschung von den Anfängen bis zu den Textfunden von Qumran*, Neukirchen-Vluyn: Neukirchener Verlag, 1969, 35–63; V. **Tcherikover**, *Hellenistic Civilization and the Jews*, Philadelphia/Jerusalem: Jewish Publication Society of America/Magnes Press 1959.

The biblical book of Daniel is not the unified work of a single author but a collected work in which materials of diverse sorts and from different historical periods have been reworked (see Eissfeldt; Fohrer; Hengel, I, 176, speaks of 'a whole cycle, probably backed by a school'). The unknown compiler or redactor was, as Porphyrius already recognized, very likely a contemporary of Antiochus IV Epiphanes. Since the book mentions neither Epiphanes' military campaign into Asia (begun in 165 BCE) nor the rededication of the temple (December, 164 BCE), the year 165 BCE is fixed as the *terminus ad quem* for the work's final redaction (against Porphyrius, see Jerome on Dan. 11.44, who incorrectly associated Dan. 11.44 with the eastern campaign). The year 167 BCE serves as a *terminus a quo* since the 'little help' of Dan. 11.34 must be seen as an allusion to the first success of the Maccabaean uprising.

The book is an important source for the Hellenistic period and particularly for the reign of Antiochus IV. The following chapters especially include valuable historical material: (*a*) Chapter 7 (the dream of the four empires): references are made to the Babylonian, Median, Persian, and Greco-Hellenistic kingdoms. The 'ten horns' (Dan. 7.7) refer to the Ptolemaic-Seleucid kings of the latter kingdom and the 'little horn' (Dan. 7.8) refers to Antiochus IV Epiphanes. (*b*) Chapter 8 (the vision of the battle between the ram and the he-goat): the ram (= the Median–Persian kingdom) is defeated by the he-goat (= Alexander the Great) who in turn 'at the height of his strength' (Dan. 8.8) has to give place to the 'four horns' (= the Diadochi). The last in the series is again the 'little horn' (Dan. 8.9), who is, of course, Antiochus IV. (*c*) Chapter 11: After a brief review of the last Persian kings, Alexander the Great, and the Diadochi (to a certain extent heavily disguised and identified only with some difficulty), the various conflicts between the Ptolemies and Seleucids are depicted (Dan. 11.1–20). There follows a detailed summary of the reign of Antiochus IV (Dan. 11.21–45) which corresponds fairly closely to the essentials of historical fact. Only with Daniel 11.40 ff. does the book depart from the realm of historical reality in its prediction of a third (and successful) Egyptian military campaign of Antiochus IV (see Bickermann, 173; Plöger, 166f.).

The exact order of events, and in particular the question of the two Egyptian campaigns of Antiochus IV, is a matter of dispute (on the different views below, §2C). Bickermann (144, 169–73) has advanced the position that the presentation of the book of Daniel 'regarding the *order* of the events can be accepted without qualifications'. He associated Daniel 11.28 with the events of the year 169 BCE (the plundering of the temple), 11.29–30 with those of the year 168 BCE (the second Egyptian campaign, Antiochus' humiliation by the Romans, and the expedition of Apollonius against Jerusalem), and 11.31 with the events of 167 BCE (the desecration of the temple). Bunge (462–4) has recently challenged this interpretation. He does not associate Daniel 11.31 with the final desecration of the temple but, like Daniel 11.30, with the actions of Apollonius in Jerusalem. A decision on this matter depends upon how one determines the chronological relationship between the punitive action of Apollonius and the desecration of the temple in December in 167 BCE (see below, §2C).

(ii)   First and Second Maccabees

F.-M. **Abel**, *Les livres des Maccabées*, Paris: Éditions du Cerf 1948, ²1951; F.-M. **Abel** and J. **Starcky**, *Les livres des Maccabées*, Paris: Éditions du Cerf ³1961; J. R. **Bartlett**, *The First and Second Books of the Maccabees*, London: Cambridge University Press 1973; E. **Bickermann**, 'Ein jüdischer Festbrief vom Jahre 124 v. Chr. (2 Makk. 1, 1–9)', *ZNW* XXXII, 1933, 233–54; idem, *Der Gott der Makkabäer*, 1937; J. G. **Bunge**, *Untersuchungen zum Zweiten Makkabäerbuch* (Dissertation, Bonn 1971); idem, 'Zur Geschichte und Chronologie des Untergangs der Oniaden und des Aufstiegs der Hasmonäer', *JSJ* VI, 1975, 1–46; J. C. **Dancy**, *A Commentary on I Maccabees*, Oxford: Basil Blackwell 1954; O. **Eissfeldt**, *The OT: An Introduction*, 1965; R. **Hanhart**, 'Zur Zeitrechnung des I und II Makkabäerbuches', *Untersuchungen zur israelitisch-jüdischen Chronologie*, ed. A. Jepsen and R. Hanhart, BZAW 88, 1964, 49–96; M. **Hengel**, *Judaism and Hellenism*, 1974; W. **Kolbe**, *Beiträge zur syrischen und jüdischen Geschichte*, BWANT II/10, 1926; R. **Laqueur**, *Kritische Untersuchungen zum Zweiten Makkabäerbuch*, Strassburg: Trübner 1904; E. **Meyer**, *Ursprung und Anfänge des Christentums, II: Die Entwicklung des Judentums und Jesus von Nazaret*, Berlin: J. G. Cotta 1921; A. **Momigliano**, 'The Second Book of Maccabees', *CP* LXX, 1975, 81–91; O. **Mørkholm**, *Antiochus IV of Syria*, CMD 8, 1966; G. O. **Neuhaus**, 'Quellen im 1. Makkabäerbuch? Eine Entgegnung auf die Analyse von K.-D. Schunck', *JSJ* V, 1974, 162–75; B. **Niese**, 'Kritik der beiden Makkabäerbücher. Nebst Beiträgen zur

Geschichte der makkabäischen Erhebung', *Hermes* XXXV, 1900, 268–307, 453–527 = idem, Berlin: Weidmann 1900; A. J. **Sachs** and D. J. **Wiseman**, 'A Babylonian King List of the Hellenistic Period', *Iraq* XVI, 1954, 202–11; J. **Schaumberger**, 'Die neue Seleukidenliste BM 35603 und die makkabäische Chronologie', *Bib* XXXVI, 1955, 423–35; K.-D. **Schunck**, *Die Quellen des I. und II. Makkabäerbuches*, Halle: Max Niemeyer 1954; V. **Tcherikover**, *Hellenistic Civilization and the Jews*, 1959; H. **Willrich**, *Urkundenfälschung in der hellenistisch-jüdischen Literatur*, FRLANT 38, 1924; S. **Zeitlin** and S. S. **Tedesche**, *The First Book of Maccabees*, New York: Harper and Brothers 1950; idem, *The Second Book of Maccabees*, New York: Harper and Brothers 1954.

The first book of Maccabees describes the history of the Maccabaean revolt from the enthronement of Antiochus IV Epiphanes (175 BCE) to the death of Simon (135/34 BCE), and thus deals with a time span of forty years. Numerous letters and documents are incorporated into its description of the historical events. The authenticity and historical value of these letters and documents are today, generally speaking, no longer in dispute (but see Willrich).

The question of the sources for I Maccabees has been examined in detail by Schunck, who has attempted to prove that the author of the book made use of various literary traditions. Schunck categorizes these traditions in the following manner: (1) for the time of Judas, a so-called life of Judas and an independent Mattathias tradition (52–74); (2) for the time of Jonathan and Simon, the so-called high priestly annals from the archives of the Jerusalem temple (65 f., 74–8; see already Bickermann, 1937, 145); (3) in addition to these two Jewish sources, the author is believed to have made use of a Gentile source, the so-called Seleucid Chronicle (36–51). Schunck's source theory is not generally accepted (see Hengel I, 96 f. and, more recently, Neuhaus).

A consensus has now developed with respect to the chronology of the two books of Maccabees, although this problem was controversial for a long time. With the publication of the king lists of the Seleucids (see Sachs–Wiseman and Schaumberger), it was apparent that I Maccabees employs two different calendars. One of these was a Seleucid–Babylonian calendar which began in the spring of 311 BCE and was used for religious and cultic dates. The second calendar follows a Seleucid–Macedonian system, which began in the autumn of 312 BCE and was used for certain events in political history (see Hanhart, 56, 80–2; Mørkholm, 160 f.; *Schürer, 18; Bunge, however, interprets the material differently, see 1971, 335–85; 1975, 17).

The unknown author of I Maccabees lived in Palestine and was in

closest sympathy with the supporters of the Maccabaean movement
and their goals. 'It is possible to say that I Maccabees presents a
semi-official account of the rise of the Hasmonaeans' (Bickermann,
1937, 145). The question, often asked, as to whether the author was
a Sadducee or a Pharisee, cannot be answered with any certainty
when it is asked in these terms. During the author's day, a strongly
established party system scarcely existed. The time of the composition is to be placed around 100 BCE. The *terminus post quem* is the
death of Hyrcanus I (104 BCE) which is presupposed in I Macc.
16.23f.

The second book of Maccabees deals with the events from about
180 to 161 BCE, that is to say, with a time span of approximately
twenty years, although the period before the beginning of the reign of
Antiochus IV (175 BCE) is discussed only very briefly. The book is
divided into two very unequal parts, namely, two letters (II Macc.
1.1–2.18) and the history proper (II Macc. 2.19–15.39). The first
letter (II Macc. 1.1–10a) contains a request from the Jews of
Jerusalem to the Jews of Egypt to celebrate the feast of tabernacles in
the year 124 BCE. The second letter (II Macc. 1.10b–2.18) is a
'festival letter' from the Jews, their council (*gerousia*), and Judas to
Aristobulus, the teacher of King Ptolemy VI Philometor, and to the
Egyptian Jews. After a brief transition (II Macc. 2.19–32), there
follows the description proper of the events associated with the attempted robbery of the temple by Heliodorus under Seleucus IV,
the persecution under Antiochus IV, the rebellion under Judas
Maccabaeus, the purification of the temple, the two campaigns by
Lysias and the campaign by Nicanor (II Macc. 3–15).

The chief source of II Maccabees is the history work, now lost, of
Jason of Cyrene, who wrote a history in five books of the
Maccabaean revolt from its beginnings to Judas' victory over
Nicanor. The author of II Maccabees, as he himself states (II Macc.
2.23), has summarized Jason's history and condensed it into one
book. His work is, therefore, an abridgment of Jason's history.
Whether and to what degree Jason had already made use of written
sources is a matter of dispute (see Niese, *Hermes*, 304; Tcherikover,
385f.; Meyer, 457f.; Bickermann, 1937, 34, 150; Schunck, 84–7,
116–26). Agreeing with Schunck, Bunge (324–9) now assumes that
the following served as sources for Jason's work: (1) the so-called
Judas source which served as the basic document and provided the
framework for II Maccabees (as well as for I Maccabees);
(2) reports taken from Hellenistic historians; according to Bunge, it
is less likely that the so-called Seleucid Chronicle, which Schunck

had identified as a source of I Maccabees and which he considered to have been a source for II Maccabees as well, was actually also available to Jason; (3) documents of the Syrian kings sent to the Jews which Jason may have examined in the temple archives in Jerusalem; and (4) the parts 'which have given to II Maccabees its reputation as a work evoking compassion', i.e., the martyr legends and other legendary pieces.

The relationship of the two introductory letters to the following abridgment of Jason's work is problematic. Especially questioned is the authenticity of the second letter and whether it originally belonged to the abridgment (see Kolbe, 118–22; Laqueur, 63–71; Schunck, 96–109; for an opposing view, see Niese, *Hermes* 276–92, 290). Recently, Bunge (1971, 155–63) has argued for the unity of both letters and the abridgment and worked out the following components in II Maccabees: (1) 1.10b–2.18, a fictitious 'festival letter' which the abridger composed by using a genuine letter from the year 164 BCE as well as material taken from Jason's work; (2) chapters 3–15, to the above letter, an abridgment of Jason's work was attached as an historical 'appendix'; and (3) 1.1–10a, a 'covering letter' for the entire work.

With respect to the question of the date of II Maccabees, important arguments have been presented against a late date (Bickermann, 1933, 234; Schunck, 125; Eissfeldt, 579–81). If one begins with the assumption that both introductory letters originally belonged to the work of the abridger, then the date given in the first letter (1.10a; 188 Seleucid–Babylonian calendar = 124 BCE) must provide the date of the entire work (see Meyer, 455; Abel, XLIII; Bunge, 195–202). Nothing is known about the author of the book. However, he probably lived in Palestine and may have come 'from circles which stood close to the Pharisees' and 'which were loyally devoted to the temple but tended to reject and be in opposition to the ruling house of the Hasmonaeans' (Bunge, 615).

(*iii*)   *Josephus*

H. **Bloch**, *Die Quellen des Flavius Josephus in seiner Archäologie*, Leipzig: Teubner 1879; J. v. **Destinon**, *Die Quellen des Flavius Josephus*, Kiel: Schmidt & Klaunig 1882; M. **Hengel**, *Judaism and Hellenism*, 1974; G. **Hölscher**, *Die Quellen des Josephus für die Zeit vom Exil bis zum Jüdischen Kriege*, Leipzig: Teubner 1904; R. **Laqueur**, *Der jüdische Historiker Flavius Josephus*, Giessen: Münchow 1920; B. **Niese**, 'Zur Chronologie des Josephus', *Hermes* XXVIII, 1893, 194–229; M. **Stern**, *Greek and Latin Authors on Jews and Judaism*,

I: From Herodotus to Plutarch, 1974; H. **Schreckenberg**, *Bibliographie zu Flavius Josephus*, Leiden: E. J. Brill 1968; H. St J. **Thackeray**, *Josephus: The Man and the Historian*, 1929; B. Z. **Wacholder**, *Nicolaus of Damascus*, UCPH 75, 1962.

Among the works of Josephus, who was born 37/38 CE, the following books of his *Antiquities* are especially important for the Hellenistic period: XI (from Cyrus to Alexander the Great), XII (from Alexander the Great to the death of Judas Maccabaeus), XIII (from Jonathan to the death of Salome Alexandra), and the beginning of book XIV (from the death of Alexandra to the conquest of Jerusalem by Pompey). In his *Jewish War*, book I covers the period from Antiochus Epiphanes to the death of Herod.

Josephus employed numerous Jewish and non-Jewish sources in the sections noted above. The most important were the following: (1) For the time between 440 and 175 BCE: various legends about Alexander the Great, a novel about the Tobiads (preserved only in his *Antiquities* XII 160–236 and possibly derived from a family chronicle of the Tobiads from the second century BCE; see Hengel I, 88, 268–72), and an extract from the Letter of Aristeas (*Ant*. XII 11–118). (2) For the period between 175 and 134 BCE: The chief source used was I Maccabees although it is not clear whether Josephus was familiar with the last chapters of the book. He also depends on the Greek writer Polybius for the period down to 146 BCE and, for the description of the plundering of the temple by Antiochus IV in *Contra Apionem* II 84, on Apollodorus of Athens (see Stern, no. 34; mediated to him by Nicolaus of Damascus or Strabo ?), Castor of Rhodes (see Stern, no. 77), Timagenes (see Stern, no. 80, from Strabo ?), Strabo, and Nicolaus of Damascus. (3) For the period between 134 and 37 BCE: his most important authorities for the period after Simon's death are Nicolaus of Damascus (see Stern, nos. 83–93) and Strabo (see Stern, nos. 98–108) whose historical works are lost and known only through citations. Both are frequently mentioned. For Nicolaus of Damascus see *Antiquities* XIII 250 f. (on Hyrcanus I), XIII 345–7 (on Alexander Jannaeus), XIV 8 f. (on Hyrcanus II and Antipater), and XIV 66–8 (on the capture of Jerusalem). For Strabo, see *Antiquities* XIII 284–7 (on Hyrcanus I), XIII 319 (on Aristobulus I), XIII 345–7 (on Alexander Jannaeus), XIV 34–6 (on Aristobulus II), and XIV 66–8 (on the capture of Jerusalem). Timagenes of Alexandria is also cited but Josephus probably knew him only through Strabo's *Historica Hypomnemata* (see Stern, nos. 80–82).

(*iv*)   *Greek and Roman authors*

M. **Hengel**, *Judaism and Hellenism*, 1974; M. **Stern**, *Greek and Latin Authors on Jews and Judaism*, I, 1974; B. Z. **Wacholder**, *Nicolaus of Damascus*, UCPH 75, 1962; idem, *Eupolemus: A Study of Judaeo-Greek Literature*, Cincinnati/Jerusalem: Hebrew Union College – Jewish Institute of Religion 1974.

A number of Greek and Roman authors provide source material for the reconstruction of this period of Jewish history. Only the most important authors can be discussed here and are treated in alphabetic order.

1. Appian. This author described himself as 'Appian of Alexandria, who attained the highest position in my native city and appeared as advocate at Rome before the emperors, after which they considered me worthy to be made their procurator'. Appian, about the middle of the second century CE, wrote a *Roman History* in which he surveyed the history of various nations up to the time of their conquest by Rome. Not all of his twenty-four book history has been preserved, but book XI (*Syriaca*) on the Syrian wars are among those extant (see *Schürer, 65).

2. Curtius Rufus. Practically nothing is known of this author although he is generally dated to the first century BCE. In his work *De Gestis Alexandri Magni*, he reports the burning of the governor of Samaria, Andromachos, and the city's punishment by Alexander (IV, 8(34).9–11; see Stern, no. 197).

3. Diodorus. This Sicilian native of the first century CE wrote a universal history in forty books entitled *Bibliotheca Historica*. This work contains numerous reports on the history and religion of the Jews. Books I–V, XI–XX and fragments of the remaining books have been preserved. Especially important is the fragment from book XXXIV on Antiochus IV's entry into the Jerusalem temple (see Stern, nos. 55–66, especially no. 63, *Schürer, 64).

4. Eupolemus. This Jewish historian is generally dated to the second century BCE and may be identified with the negotiator whom Judas Maccabaeus sent to Rome in 161 BCE (see I Macc. 8.17 and II Macc. 4.11). He composed a work 'On the Kings of Judaea'. The fragments which have been preserved cover the period from Moses to the destruction of the first temple. His work may, however, have covered the history from the time of Adam to his own day. His work is important because his description of the Davidic kingdom clearly reflects 'the political situation of the Maccabean struggle and the

beginning of Jewish expansion in Palestine' (Hengel, I, 93; see also Wacholder, 1974, 138f.; on Eupolemus, see Hengel, I, 92–5 and Wacholder, 1974).

5. Jason of Cyrene. This author has been discussed above in conjunction with the analysis of II Maccabees. Here one may be content with a statement of Hengel (I, 98):

> If Jason was in all probability a Jew of the Diaspora – the attempt which has often been made to identify him with Jason son of Eleazar, the second delegate to Rome mentioned in I Macc. 8.17, remains an undemonstrable hypothesis – his work nevertheless points to a very close connection with Palestine, despite its completely Hellenistic form; perhaps it even arose there.

(On Jason, see Hengel, I, 95–9.)

6. Nicolaus of Damascus. A historian and prolific writer, Nicolaus was born in Damascus about 64 BCE and after serving in various capacities entered the service of King Herod about 14 BCE where he served as counsellor and close friend. Among his important works were his *Historiae*, comprising one hundred and forty-four books which apparently covered the ancient history of the eastern monarchies and extended down to the time of the author. Josephus made greater use of Nicolaus than any other writer for the post-biblical period. (On Nicolaus, see Wacholder, 1962; *Schürer, 28–32; Stern, nos. 83–97.)

7. Polybius of Megalopolis. This distinguished Achaean, who resided in Rome for some time about the middle of the second century BCE, wrote a world history in forty books which extended from about 220/19 to 146/45 BCE. Only parts of his work survive. His history was an important source for Josephus (see the citations in *Ant.* XII 135f., 358 and *Contra Apionem* II 84). Stern (113) writes: 'It seems that either direct or, more probably, indirect use of Polybius coloured the account of non-Jewish history included in the latter part of the twelfth book and the first part of the thirteenth book of *Antiquitates*.' (On Polybius, see Stern, nos. 31–3; *Schürer, 63f.).

8. Strabo of Amaseia. A native of Pontus, Strabo lived from about 64/3 BCE until around 21 CE. He composed a major history in forty-three books but his work survives only in fragments. Those that survive are primarily the ones quoted by Josephus. The latter first quotes Strabo in discussing the plundering of the temple of Jerusalem by Antiochus Epiphanes. Josephus' final reference to Strabo concerns the execution of Antigonus by Antony in 37 BCE. (On Strabo, see Schürer, 64f.; Stern, nos. 98–124).

(v)   Papyri

F. M. **Cross**, 'The Discovery of the Samaria Papyri', *BA* XXVI, 1963,
110–21 = *BAR* III, 1970, 227–39; idem, 'Papyri of the Fourth Century BC
from Dâliyeh: A Preliminary Report on Their Discovery and Significance',
New Directions, 1969, 45–69; P. W. and N. **Lapp**, *Discoveries in Wadi ed-
Daliyeh*, AASOR 41, 1976.

Two collections of papyri are of importance for this period. One
group, discovered only recently (1962–3), comes from a cave just
north of Jericho (Mugharet Abū Sinjeh in Wadi Daliyeh) and
belongs to the fourth century BCE. The papyri, discovered along with
about two hundred skeletons, are legal or administrative documents,
and although they all seem to predate the time of Alexander the
Great, Cross has suggested that these documents found their way
into the cave in conjunction with the events surrounding the destruction of Samaria early in the Hellenistic period.

   The so-called Zenon papyri are of great importance for the history
of Palestine in the third century BCE. Zenon was an official of the
'finance minister' Apollonios under Ptolemy II Philadelphos (284–
246 BCE) and undertook a trip to the province of 'Syria and
Phoenicia' which lasted from the end of 260 to the beginning of 258
BCE. Zenon's archives were discovered in 1915 at Fayyum in Egypt
and contain several hundred documents, letters, treaties, bills and so
on. The papyri, which are important for the history of the Jews and
of Palestine, can be found in V. Tcherikover and A. Fuks, *Corpus
Papyrorum Judaicarum* I, Cambridge: Harvard University Press 1957.
These papyri and their importance will be further discussed in §4 of
this chapter.

(vi)   Megillat Taanit

H. **Lichtenstein**, 'Die Fastenrolle: Eine Untersuchung zur jüdisch-
hellenistischen Geschichte', *HUCA* VIII/IX, 1931/32, 257–351; S. **Zeitlin**,
'Megillat Taanit as a Source for Jewish Chronology and History in the
Hellenistic and Roman Periods', *JQR* IX, 1918/19, 71–102; X, 1919/20,
49–80, 237–89.

The *Megillat Taanit* (Scroll of Fasts), written in Aramaic, contains a
list of the thirty-six days on which one was not permitted to fast
because of the joyful events in Jewish history which had occurred on
these days during the period of the second temple. To be sure, the
date of its composition is relatively late (end of the first century/

beginning of the second century CE), but it transmits many historically significant accounts. Such a calendar of days as this work notes
is apparently already assumed in Judith 8.6 (see *Schürer, 114f.).

B.   *Archaeological evidence*

Numerous sites in Palestine provide artifactual evidence which assists
in the reconstruction of historical life during this period. The sites
which are discussed in this section are organized alphabetically according to place names. The coins are discussed below under the
entry on Jerusalem as well as in section 2/A of this chapter.

(i)   *Acco/Ptolemais*

Y. H. **Landau**, 'A Greek Inscription from Acre', *IEJ* XI, 1961, 118–26; J.
Schwartz, 'Note complémentaire (à propos d'une inscription grecque de
St Jean d'Acre)', *IEJ* XII, 1962, 135f.

Acco, the most significant port city in the north of Palestine, surrendered without resistance to Alexander the Great and, after his death,
came under Ptolemaic rule. Following the battle at Paneion, the
Seleucids took control of the city. An attempt by Alexander
Jannaeus to capture the town did not succeed. The Hellenistic city is
located under the present Acco and, with the exception of a few
accidental finds, has not been excavated. The most important find –
besides the remains of the Hellenistic city wall and a small
Hellenistic temple from the second half of the second century BCE – is
a religious inscription which mentions Antiochus VII Sidetes and is
probably to be dated between 130 and the spring of 129 BCE, when
Antiochus VII died. The dedicator of the inscription was 'chief
secretary of the forces' and at the same time governor of the coastal
district of Acco (possibly during the absence of the king while on his
campaign against the Parthians).

(ii)   *Alexandreion*

F.-M. **Abel**, 'Exploration de la Vallée du Jourdain, IX: De l'ouady Far'a a
Faṣa'il. – L'Alexandreion', *RB* XXII, 1913, 227–34; W. J. **Moulton**, 'A
Visit to Qarn Sarṭabeh', *BASOR* LXII, 1936, 14–18; O. **Plöger**, 'Die
makkabäischen Burgen', *ZDPV* LXXI, 1955, 141–72; N. **Schmidt**,
'Alexandrium', *JBL* XXIX, 1910, 77–83.

A fortress on Mount Sartaba = Qarn Sarṭaba, south-east of Nablus,
overlooking the Jordan valley) was built by Alexander Jannaeus or

Salome Alexandra. The Hebrew name is Shelomey (*šlwmy*), a shortened form of the Hebrew name of Queen Shelomziyyon (*šlwmṣywn*) Alexandra. Aristobulus II surrendered the fortress to Pompey when the latter was on his way to Jerusalem (*Ant.* XIV 49–52; *War* I 134–7). Among other things, remains of a wall from Hasmonaean times have been preserved.

(*iii*)   '*Araq el-Emîr*

M. J. B. **Brett**, 'The Qasr el-'Abd: A Proposed Reconstruction', *BASOR* CLXXI, 1963, 39–45; D. K. **Hill**, 'The Animal Fountain of 'Arâq el-Emîr', *BASOR* CLXXI, 1963, 45–55; P. W. **Lapp**, 'Soundings at 'Arâq el-Emîr (Jordan)', *BASOR* CLXV, 1962, 16–34; idem, 'The 1961 Excavations at 'Arâq el-Emîr', *ADAJ* VI/VII, 1962, 80–9; idem, 'The Second and Third Campaigns at 'Arâq el-Emîr', *BASOR* CLXXI, 1963, 8–39; idem, 'The 1962 Excavation at 'Arâq el-Emîr', *ADAJ* X, 1965, 37–42.

This site of imposing ruins in Transjordan lies about 17 kilometres west of Amman and about 29 kilometres east of Jericho. On the basis of Lapp's excavations, it is probably to be identified with the fortress of Hyrcanus the Tobiad in Ammanitis from the second half of the second century BCE (see *Ant.* XII 230–4 where it is mentioned under the name 'Tyros', presumably derived from the Hebrew *ṣwr*, and perhaps preserved in the name Wadi eṣ-Ṣir). The most important structure at the site is the so-called Qasr el-'Abd ('slave castle') which was probably never completed. The building was rectangular (about 37 by 19 metres), possessed a basilica-like inner room and four tower-like chambers in the corners, stood on a platform, and was surrounded by a reservoir. Four figures from an imposing lion frieze were still found in their original position on the outer wall. Also discovered was a relief of a feline beast of prey which probably belonged to a fountain. The excavations confirmed an earlier conjecture that the installation represented a temple, possibly a rival of the Jerusalem temple (comparable to the sanctuaries at Elephantine and Leontopolis in Egypt and on Mount Gerizim). The 'Tobiad' inscription discovered in a cave nearby (see *CIJ* II, 105 no. 868) could be related, despite its archaic character, to Hyrcanus, the builder of the temple installation. 'Tobias' may have been the Jewish name of Hyrcanus.

(*iv*)   *Ashdod*

M. **Dothan**, 'The Ancient Harbour of Ashdod', *CNI* XI, 1969, 16–19; idem, 'Ashdod: Preliminary Report on the Excavations in Seasons

1962/1963', *IEJ* XIV, 1964, 79–95; M. **Dothan** and D. N. **Freedman**, *Ashdod I: The First Season of Excavations 1962*, AES 7, 1967; idem, *Ashdod II–III: The Second and Third Seasons of Excavations 1963 and 1965, Soundings in 1967*, AES 9–10, 1971; idem, 'Ashdod – Seven Seasons of Excavation', *Qadmoniot* V, 1972, 2–13 (Hebrew).

Ashdod (its Hellenistic name was Azotus) was captured by Alexander the Great and set on fire during the time of Jonathan (I Macc. 10.84) and John Hyrcanus (I Macc. 16.10). The city probably remained in Hasmonaean hands from its conquest by John Hyrcanus to the beginning of Roman rule. The excavations have disclosed four periods of settlement during the Hellenistic period as well as destructions in level IV A (conquest by Jonathan ?) and III A (conquest by John Hyrcanus ?). In the vicinity of the new harbour (Tell Mor/Murra), a Hellenistic installation was discovered which was used in the extraction of dye from purple shellfish (*murex*).

(v)   *Beth-Shan*

M. **Avi-Yonah**, 'Scythopolis', *IEJ* XII, 1962, 123–34; A. **Rowe**, *The Topography and History of Beth-Shan*, Philadelphia: University Museum 1930.

In Ptolemaic times, this city was resettled under the name of Scythopolis ('city of the Scythians'). It did not receive city status until the reign of Antiochus IV, when it was given the dynastic name of Nysa. In 108/07 BCE the city came under Hasmonaean control during the reign of John Hyrcanus I and was fortified by Alexander Jannaeus. Among the scanty pre-Roman finds is a marble head of Dionysus, leading one to infer the existence of a Hellenistic temple at the site dedicated to this deity.

(vi)   *Beth-Zur*

P. W. and N. **Lapp**, 'Comparative Study of a Hellenistic Pottery Group from Beth-Zur', *BASOR* CLI, 1958, 16–27; O. R. **Sellers**, *The Citadel of Beth-Zur*, Philadelphia: University Museum 1933; O. R. **Sellers** et al., *The 1957 Excavation at Beth-Zur*, AASOR 38, 1968.

Beth-Zur was a fortress on the border between Judaea and Idumaea. The city played a most important role in the Maccabaean struggles and was finally brought under uninterrupted Hasmonaean control during the time of Simon (I Macc. 11.65f.; 14.7). The excavations of 1931 and 1957 uncovered remains of the Maccabaean fortifications together with huge cisterns hewn from bed-rock. Three building phases can be differentiated in the fortress which are probably to be assigned to the Persian or Ptolemaic period and to the respective reconstructions carried out under Judas Maccabaeus (about 165–163 BCE) and Bacchides (about 161 BCE).

(vii)   'Ein Gedi

B. **Mazar** et al., 'En-Gedi: Archaeological Excavations 1961–1962', *BIES* XXVII, 1963, 1–133 (Hebrew) = idem, *En-Gedi: The First and Second Seasons of Excavations*, AES 5, 1966; B. **Mazar** and I. **Dunayevsky**, 'En-Gedi: Third Season of Excavations. Preliminary Report', *IEJ* XIV, 1964, 121–30; idem, 'En-Gedi: Fourth and Fifth Seasons of Excavations. Preliminary Report', *IEJ* XVII, 1967, 133–43.

The remains of a fortress from Hasmonaean times have been discovered in stratum II at this site. It was probably destroyed during the Parthian invasion and the war between Herod and the last of the Hasmonaeans. In addition, coins from the time of Alexander Jannaeus have been recovered.

(viii)   Gezer/Gazara

W. G. **Dever**, 'Gezer – A City Coming to Life', *Qadmoniot* III, 1970, 57–62 (Hebrew); idem, 'Further Excavations at Gezer', *BA* XXXIV, 1971, 94–132; W. G. **Dever** et al., *Gezer I: Preliminary Report of the 1964–66 Seasons*, Jerusalem: Hebrew Union College Biblical and Archaeological School in Jerusalem 1970; idem, *Gezer II: Report on the 1967–70 Seasons in Fields I and II*, (Jerusalem: Hebrew Union College/Nelson Glueck School of Biblical Archaeology 1974; R. A. S. **Macalister**, *The Excavation of Gezer 1902–1905 and 1907–1909* I–III, London: John Murray 1912.

This site was one of the most important localities in Hasmonaean times. Conquered by Simon in 142 BCE, the city was placed under the command of his son John Hyrcanus (I Macc. 13.43–8) after the Gentile population had been expelled. The semi-circular bastions inside the towers of the 'outer wall' come from this time, as does the reconstruction of the old Solomonic gate. A graffito, probably written by a Greek prisoner of war, suggests that there was resistance against the Maccabaean garrison: '(says) Pampras: may fire follow up Simon's palace!' After the conclusion of the rule of the Hasmonaeans, Gezer was probably abandoned. Bilingual boundary-stones from the first century BCE show that the locality belonged to the landholdings of a Greek named Alkios.

(ix)   *Ḥefzibah*

Y. H. **Landau**, 'A Greek Inscription Found Near Hefzibah', *IEJ* XVI, 1966, 54–70.

From the vicinity of Ḥefzibah in Galilee comes a stele with inscriptions elucidating the various phases of the Fifth Syrian War which Antiochus III began in 202/201 BCE and which ended decisively for the Seleucids with the victory at Paneion. The stele contains several Greek inscriptions including letters and memoranda of Antiochus III and his general Ptolemaios. Also included is an inscription warning about the security of the area after the victory over the Ptolemaic kingdom.

(x)   *Hyrcania*

O. **Plöger**, 'Die makkabäischen Burgen', *ZDPV* LXXI, 1955, 141–72; G. R. H. **Wright**, 'The Archaeological Remains at el Mird in the Wilderness of Judaea', *Biblica* XLII, 1961, 1–21.

A Maccabaean fortress was located on this site, about 15 kilometres south-east of Jerusalem in the Judaean mountains (Kirbet el-Mird), having been constructed by John Hyrcanus or Alexander Jannaeus. Excavations in 1960 uncovered, among other things, remains of buildings and an aqueduct from Hasmonaean times.

(xi)   *Jaffa/Joppa*

J. **Kaplan**, 'Tel Aviv – Yafo', *IEJ* XXIV, 1974, 137 f.; A. **Kindler**, 'The Jaffa Hoard of Alexander Jannaeus', *IEJ* IV, 1954, 170–85; B. **Lifshitz**, 'Beiträge zur palästinischen Epigraphik', *ZDPV* LXXVIII, 1962, 64–88.

First conquered by Jonathan (I Macc. 10.75 f.), this city came under continued Maccabaean occupation in Simon's day (I Macc. 12.33 f.) and long remained a centre of conflict between the Seleucids and Maccabaeans. Excavations have revealed parts of its fortifications in Hasmonaean times. Recently, during building operations, a grave from the time of Alexander Jannaeus was discovered. From the pre-Maccabaean period comes an inscription in honour of Ptolemy IV Philopator from the time when he and his sister Arsinoe visited the province of 'Syria and Phoenicia' following the Ptolemaic victory over the Seleucids at Raphia (217 BCE).

(*xii*)   *Jericho*

E. **Netzer**, 'The Hasmonean and Herodian Palaces at Jericho', *Qadmoniot* VII, 1974, 27–36 (Hebrew); idem, 'The Hasmonean and Herodian Winter Palaces at Jericho', *IEJ* XXV, 1975, 89–100; Y. **Tsafrir**, 'Jericho in the Period of the Second Temple', *Qadmoniot* VII, 1974, 24–6 (Hebrew).

The most recent excavations at Jericho have unearthed the remains of a Hasmonaean palace at the mouth of Wadi Kelt. A main building, about 65 by 50 metres, and a swimming pool have been excavated as well as a smaller building, apparently surrounded by columns, located south of the swimming pool and which may have served as a pavilion. The exact date of the palace's construction has not been determined. In any case, coins discovered at the site are almost entirely from Hasmonaean times. In all likelihood, the palace was still in use at the beginning of Herod's rule and the swimming pool may have been the site of the dramatic assassination of Aristobulus III, who was the young high priest and brother of Mariamne (*Ant.* XV 50–55). Later Herod built a new palace on the foundations of the older Hasmonaean palace.

(*xiii*)   *Jerusalem*

(*a*) R. **Amiran**, 'The First and Second Walls of Jerusalem Reconsidered in the Light of the New Wall', *IEJ* XXI, 1971, 166f.; M. **Avi-Yonah**, 'The Third and Second Walls of Jerusalem', *IEJ* XVIII, 1968, 98–125; idem, 'The Newly-Found Wall of Jerusalem and its Topographical Significance', *IEJ* XXI, 1971, 168f.; idem, 'Jerusalem of the Second Temple Period', *Jerusalem Revealed: Archaeology in the Holy City 1968–1974*, ed. Y. Yadin, Jerusalem: Israel Exploration Society 1975, 9–13 (see *Qadmoniot* I, 1968, 19–27 [Hebrew]); idem, 'Excavations in Jerusalem – Review and Evaluation', *Jerusalem Revealed*, 21–4 (see *Qadmoniot* V, 1972, 70–3 [Hebrew]); D. **Bahat** and M. **Broshi**, 'Excavations in the Armenian Garden', *Jerusalem Revealed*, 55f. (see *Qadmoniot* V, 1972, 102f. [Hebrew]).

(*b*) R. **Amiran** and A. **Eitan**, 'Excavations in the Courtyard of the Citadel, Jerusalem, 1968–1969 (Preliminary Report)', *IEJ* XX, 1970, 9–17; idem, 'Excavations in the Jerusalem Citadel', *Jerusalem Revealed*, 52–4; N. **Avigad**, 'Excavations in the Jewish Quarter of the Old City of Jerusalem, 1969/70 Preliminary Report', *IEJ* XX, 1970, 1–8, 129–40; XXII, 1972, 193–200; idem, 'Excavations in the Jewish Quarter of the Old City, 1969–1971', *Jerusalem Revealed*, 41–51 (see *Qadmoniot* V, 1972, 91–101 [Hebrew]); Y. **Tsafrir**, 'The Location of the Seleucid Akra in Jerusalem', *Jerusalem Revealed*, 85–6 (see *Qadmoniot* V, 1972, 125–6 [Hebrew]).

(c) N. **Avigad**, 'Aramaic Inscriptions in the Tomb of Jason', *IEJ* XVII, 1967, 101–11; idem, 'The Architecture of Jerusalem in the Second Temple Period', *Jerusalem Revealed*, 14–20 (see *Qadmoniot* I, 1968, 28–36 [Hebrew]); P. **Benoit**, 'L' Inscription grecque du tombeau de Jason', *IEJ* XVII, 1967, 112f.; L. Y. **Rahmani**, 'Jason's Tomb', *IEJ* XVII, 1967, 61–100.

(d) V. **Tzaferis**, 'A Hasmonean Fort in Jerusalem', *Qadmoniot* III, 1970, 95–7 (Hebrew).

(e) D. **Jeselsohn**, 'A New Coin Type with Hebrew Inscription', *IEJ* XXIV, 1974, 77f.; A. **Kindler**, 'Silver Coins Bearing the Name of Judea from the Early Hellenistic Period', *IEJ* XXIV, 1974, 73–6.

(a) Hasmonaean Jerusalem extended over the old Israelite city of David on Mount Ophel as well as over the so-called upper city on the western hill. The course of the so-called 'first wall' (*War* V 142–5) which ran around Mount Zion, along the Hinnom Valley to the Kidron Valley and to the east side of the temple is now identified with certainty. Remains of this wall have been found, especially in the citadel (there also the remains of a tower), to the south of the west side of the later palace of Herod and on the eastern hill (there, too, the remains of a Hasmonaean tower). To the north, the upper city was connected with the temple mount (at the location of the so-called Wilson's Arch). Still in dispute is the exact course and the date of the so-called 'second wall' (*War* V 146) running northwards from the citadel by way of the Damascus Gate to the fortress Antonia at the north-west corner of the temple. This wall is usually dated to Hasmonaean times as well, although Avi-Yonah favours a later date (chiefly because the oldest remains beneath the Damascus Gate come from Herodian times).

(b) During recent excavations in the Jewish Quarter on the western hill of the city, remains of a Hasmonaean building have been found on top of the old Israelite city wall. Beside it were discovered the foundations of a rectangular building, possibly a fortification. The most important artifact among the individual finds is a relief with two horns of plenty and a pomegranate in the centre, i.e. a symbol otherwise known only from Hasmonaean coins. It is conceivable that this relief came from the Hasmonaean palace. Avi-Yonah wants to assign a column base and an Ionic capital which were also found in the Jewish Quarter to a temple (for the Olympian Zeus?) planned by Antiochus IV. Also in dispute is the location of the Syrian Acra. Josephus (*Ant.* XII 252) located the Acra in the lower city, i.e. on Jerusalem's south-eastern hill, the old city of David. Contrary to this statement, most investigators suspect that the Acra was located in the upper city, in other words, in the area of the Jewish Quarter, although convincing archaeological proof is still lacking. Recently, Tsafrir has defended the accuracy of Josephus' statement. He would like to locate the Acra at the famous 'seam' north of the south-eastern corner of the temple mount where Herodian and Hellenistic (?) wall construction meet.

(*c*) Among the numerous tombs which have been discovered inside as well as outside of Jerusalem, a number certainly come from Hasmonaean times. Only the most important can be noted here.

The tomb of Bene Hezir is the oldest tomb installation in the Kidron Valley. It comes from the beginning of the first century BCE and was hewn from the rock in a severe, almost classic Dorian style. A Hebrew inscription reads: 'This is the tomb and monument of Eleazar, Hania, Joezer, Judah, Simeon (and) Johanan, sons of Joseph son of Obed; Joseph and Eleazar, sons of Hania, priests of the Bene Hezir.'

The Jason tomb in the western section of the city of Jerusalem also comes from the first century BCE, a date verified by the coins discovered there; the oldest belong to the time of Alexander Jannaeus. The façade is divided in half by a single column with door openings on both sides. The roof is crowned by a pyramid. On the inside are found various graffiti, among them three ships which allow one to infer the occupation of the main owner. The excavator surmises that Jason 'in some way (was) connected with the naval exploits of the coast of Palestine in the years 100–64 BCE' (Rahmani, 97). A single tomb-chamber for the skeletons of the whole family shows the absence of any influence of Pharisaic piety with its belief in an individual resurrection. Instead it provides a picture of a 'wealthy Sadducee family living in the late Hasmonaean period' (Rahmani, 97). Various inscriptions containing laments in Aramaic and Greek mention the name 'Jason'. The Aramaic inscription is possibly 'the oldest inscription written in a Jewish cursive script found so far' (Avigad, 1967, 108).

(*d*) A tower from the period between the end of the second century and the beginning of the first century BCE has been excavated at Givat Shaul near Jerusalem. The tower probably belonged to a series of fortifications or watch-towers which were erected by Alexander Jannaeus along the main traffic routes.

(*e*) From the environs of Jerusalem come a few coins which are to be dated to the beginning of the Ptolemaic period. They carry the portrait of Ptolemy I as well as the picture of an eagle (standing on a lightning bolt?) and, in the old Hebrew script, the inscription *yhdh*.

Their similarity to the Persian *yhd*-coins indicates that the Ptolemaic kings took over the Persian system of government without change. The old Hebrew inscription demonstrates the local character of the coins since all Ptolemaic coins otherwise contain Greek inscriptions.

(xiv)   Lachish

Y. **Aharoni**, 'Trial Excavation in the "Solar Shrine" at Lachish: Preliminary Report', *IEJ* XVIII, 1968, 157–69; idem, 'Excavations in the "Solar Shrine" at Lachish', *Qadmoniot* II, 1969, 131–4 (Hebrew); Y. **Aharoni** et al., *Investigations at Lachish: The Sanctuary and the Residency (Lachish V)*, Tel Aviv: Gateway Publishers 1975; O. **Tufnell** et al., *Lachish III*, London: Oxford University Press 1953.

A temple (solar shrine) which was found on the tell at Lachish and a structure with pillars about 40 metres away are now dated to the Hellenistic period. 'In view of the new data the possibility cannot be ignored that the Lachish temple was built by Jews and that it is a traditional Israelite shrine, exactly as was the earlier Arad temple' (Aharoni, 1968, 161).

(xv)   Machaerus

O. **Plöger**, 'Die makkabäischen Burgen', *ZDPV* LXXI, 1955, 141–72; A. **Strobel**, 'Machärus. Geschichte und Ende einer Festung im Lichte archäologisch-topographischer Beobachtungen', *Bibel und Qumran* (Festschrift H. Bardtke), ed. S. Wagner, Berlin: Evangelische Haupt-Bibelgesellschaft 1968, 198–225.

Machaerus was a fortress in Transjordan about 8–10 kilometres east of the Dead Sea, probably built by Alexander Jannaeus as a fortification against the Nabataeans (*War* VII 164).

(xvi)   Maresha/Marisa

F.-M. **Abel**, 'Tombeaux récemment découverts à Marisa', *RB* XXXIV, 1925, 267–75; F. J. **Bliss** and R. A. S. **Macalister**, *Excavations in Palestine during the Years 1898–1900*, London: Palestine Exploration Fund, 1902; J. P. **Peters** and H. **Thiersch**, *Painted Tombs in the Necropolis of Marissa (Marêshah)*, London: Palestine Exploration Fund 1905.

In Hellenistic times, Marisa served as an administrative centre on the Jewish–Idumaean border. Its population consisted in the main of Idumaeans and of Sidonian colonists. The city was conquered about 110 BCE by John Hyrcanus, when Idumaea was absorbed into the territory of the Jewish state. Under Pompey it was again freed and soon afterwards was destroyed by the Parthians. The excavations at the site have revealed a Hellenistic city laid out according to a hippodamic plan as well as painted tombs, containing inscriptions and graffiti, in use from the end of the third century on. One of the tombs was the family tomb of a certain Apollophanes who served for thirty-three years as the head of the Sidonian community in Marisa. Among the graffiti found was an erotic poem in which a courtesan ridicules her lover. An inscription from pre-Hasmonaean times for Ptolemy IV Philopator (similar to the inscriptions from Jaffa) has also been found at the site.

(*xvii*)   *Qumran*

R. **de Vaux**, 'Fouille au Khirbet Qumrân. Rapport préliminaire', *RB* LX, 1953, 83–106; idem, 'Fouilles au Khirbet Qumrân. Rapport préliminaire sur la deuxième campagne', *RB* LXI, 1954, 206–36; idem, 'Fouilles de Khirbet Qumrân. Rapport préliminaire sur les 3^c, 4^c et 5^c campagnes', *RB* LXIII, 1956, 533–77; idem, 'Fouilles de Feshkha', *RB* LXVI, 1959, 225–55; idem, *L'Archéologique et les manuscrits de la Mer Morte*, London: Oxford University Press 1961; idem, *Archaeology and the Dead Sea Scrolls*, London: Oxford University Press 1973.

Qumran was a settlement on the north-western shore of the Dead Sea. The exact beginnings of the settlement have not been clarified with any precision, but they probably go back to the time of John Hyrcanus I. From this period (phase IA), only a few remains which were incorporated in the following phase were recovered. The major construction at the site occurred under Alexander Jannaeus (phase IB), during whose reign Qumran experienced its most developed stage. This date accords with the coins found there which in the majority of cases come from the time of Alexander Jannaeus. This first settlement phase came to an end during the early years of the reign of Herod and was probably destroyed by an earthquake. During its second settlement phase, from the death of Herod to its destruction by the Romans in the first Jewish war, the old ground-plan of the installation remained basically unchanged.

(*xviii*)   *Samaria*

J. W. **Crowfoot** et al., *Samaria–Sebaste* I–III, London: Palestine Exploration Fund 1938–1957; J. B. **Hennessy**, 'Excavations at Samaria-Sebaste, 1968', *Levant* II, 1970, 1–21; G. A. **Reisner** et al., *Harvard Excavations at Samaria, 1908–1910*, Cambridge: Harvard University Press 1924.

Samaria was conquered by Alexander the Great in 332 BCE and transformed soon afterwards into a military colony. For the most part, the local inhabitants migrated to Shechem. In 107 BCE, John Hyrcanus conquered the city and forcibly Judaized the inhabitants. The most important remains from the Hellenistic period are a round tower within the Israelite wall (possibly from the time of the city's new foundation under Perdiccas between 323 and 321 BCE) and the remains of a fortification.

(xix)   Shechem

R. J. **Bull**, 'The Excavation of Tell er-Ras on Mount Gerizim', *BA* XXXI, 1968, 58–72; idem, 'An Archaeological Context for Understanding John 4.20', *BA* XXXVIII, 1975, 54–9; R. J. **Bull** and G. E. **Wright**, 'Newly Discovered Temples on Mount Gerizim in Jordan', *HTR* LVIII, 1965, 234–7; R. J. **Bull** and E. F. **Campbell**, 'The Sixth Campaign at Balâṭah (Shechem)', *BASOR* CXC, 1968, 2–41; E. F. **Campbell** et al., 'The Eighth Campaign at Balâṭah (Shechem)', *BASOR* CCIV, 1971, 2–17; E. F. **Campbell** and G. E. **Wright**, 'Excavations at Shechem, 1956–1969', *Qadmoniot* III, 1970, 126–33 (Hebrew); N. R. **Lapp**, 'Pottery from some Hellenistic Loci at Balâṭah (Shechem)', *BASOR* CLXXV, 1964, 14–26; G. E. **Wright**, 'The First Campaign at Tell Balâṭah (Shechem)', *BASOR* CXLIV, 1956, 9–20; idem, 'The Second Campaign at Tell Balâṭah (Shechem)', *BASOR* CXLVIII, 1957, 11–28; G. E. **Wright** and L. E. **Toombs**, 'The Third Campaign at Balâṭah (Shechem)', *BASOR* CLXI, 1961, 11–54; G. E. **Wright**, 'The Samaritans at Shechem', *HTR* LV, 1962, 357–66; idem, 'The Fourth Campaign at Balâṭah (Shechem)', *BASOR* CLXIX, 1963, 1–60; G. E. **Wright** et al., 'The Fifth Campaign at Balâṭah (Shechem)', *BASOR* CLXXX, 1965, 7–41; G. E. **Wright**, *Shechem*, 1965.

Shechem was the centre of the Samaritans after the conquest of Samaria by Alexander the Great. The new inhabitants made use of the old fortifications and rebuilt them. On Mount Gerizim, the remains of the Samaritan shrine were found underneath the remains of a Hadrianic temple. The point in time when the city was destroyed by the Hasmonaeans is uncertain. Since the latest coins come from about 110 BCE, it is assumed that John Hyrcanus did not finally destroy the city during his first campaign against Shechem (128 BCE) but did so in 107 BCE at the time of the destruction of Samaria. Among the finds from Shechem was an important collection of coins from the second century BCE containing coins from Ptolemy I to Ptolemy V.

§2. SOME IMPORTANT PROBLEMS OF THE PERIOD

A.   The coins of the Hasmonaean period

A. **Ben-David**, 'When Did the Maccabees Begin to Strike Their First Coins?' *PEQ* CXXIV, 1972, 93–103; R. S. **Hanson**, 'Toward a Chronology of the Hasmonean Coins', *BASOR* CCXVI, 1974, 21–3; B. **Kanael**, 'The Beginning of Maccabean Coinage', *IEJ* I, 1950/51, 170–5; idem, 'The Greek Letters and Monograms on the Coins of Jehohanan the High Priest', *IEJ* II, 1952, 190–4; idem, 'Ancient Jewish Coins and Their Historical Importance', *BA* XXVI, 1963, 38–62; idem, 'Altjüdische Münzen', *JNGG* XVII, 1967, 159–298; A. **Kindler**, 'Rare and Unpublished Hasmonean Coins', *IEJ* II, 1952, 188f.; idem, 'Addendum to the Dated Coins of Alexander Janneus', *IEJ* XVIII, 1968, 188–91; Y. **Meshorer**, *Jewish Coins of the Second Temple Period*, Tel Aviv: Am Hassefer 1967; idem, 'The Beginning of the Hasmonean Coinage', *IEJ* XXIV, 1974, 59–61; J. **Naveh**, 'Dated Coins of Alexander Janneus', *IEJ* XVIII, 1968, 20–5.

The identity of the first Hasmonaean to begin striking coins is one of the chief problems in the study of early Jewish numismatics. I Maccabees 15.6, it is true, specifically notes that Antiochus VII Sidetes (138–129 BCE) accorded to the high priest Simon the right to strike coins, but today it is widely recognized that the shekel coins which were previously ascribed to him all belong to the period of the first war against Rome (66–70 CE). Jewish coins from the period before the Roman conquest of Judaea by Pompey (63 BCE) exist which bear the Jewish names Jehohanan, Jehudah, and Jehonathan (or the shortened form Jonathan) but the datings of these coins are uncertain. The question of the association of these coins with the Jewish rulers from Hyrcanus I (135/4–104 BCE) to Hyrcanus II (63–40 BCE) is still open. Since the association of the Jehonathan coins with Alexander Jannaeus is assured on the basis of bilingual coins which also mention his Greek name (see Naveh), only the Jehohanan and Jehudah coins are in dispute. Earlier scholars sought to assign all of these to Hyrcanus I and Aristobulus I (104–103 BCE) since Josephus provides the Hebrew names Jehohanan and Jehudah respectively for these two rulers. However, for some time it has been recognized that most of the Jehohanan coins were first struck by Hyrcanus II (Kanael, 1952; 1967, 167; Kindler, 1952). This view presumes that Hyrcanus II – the grandson – had the same Hebrew name as Hyrcanus I – the grandfather. Meshorer has gone a step further and has ascribed all of the Jehohanan coins to Hyrcanus II

(1967, 46–52; 1974) and has attributed the few Jehudah coins not to the weak Aristobulus I who ruled for only a single year but to Aristobulus II (67–63 BCE) who was very active politically (1967, 53–5). If Meshorer's interpretation, which is supported with weighty arguments but which has not yet been universally accepted, should be correct, then the beginning of Hasmonaean coinage does not date to Hyrcanus I but to Alexander Jannaeus (103–76 BCE) at the earliest. On the basis of Meshorer's interpretation of the Hasmonaean coinage, the following distribution may be made.

1. *Alexander Jannaeus* (Jehonathan): Most of the Hasmonaean coins which have been found (about four-fifths) come from the time of this ruler. The four different inscriptions which appear on these coins may be arranged in the following relative chronology (Kanael, 1967, 167–71; Meshorer, 1967, 56–9): (a) *Jehonathan the High Priest and the Congregation (ḥbr) of the Jews* (in Hebrew); (b) *Jehonathan the King* (in Hebrew)/*King Alexander* (in Greek); (c) *Jonathan* (!) *the High Priest and the Congregation of the Jews* (in Hebrew); and (d) *King Alexander* (in Aramaic)/*King Alexander* (in Greek). More than 90% of the royal coins bearing the inscription referred to under (b) were struck over with the inscription referred to under (c). For these coins, the spelling 'Jonathan' (instead of 'Jehonathan') is characteristic. The restriking of these coins is generally believed to relate to the conflict between Alexander Jannaeus and the Pharisees. The Aramaic–Greek royal coins (d) which Naveh deciphered bear a date of either the twentieth or the twenty-fifth year of the reign of Jannaeus (see also Kindler, 1968) and accordingly are to be associated with the end of his reign.

2. *John Hyrcanus II* (Jehohanan): Here two different types may be distinguished: (a) *Jehohanan the High Priest and the Congregation of the Jews* and (b) *Jehohanan the High Priest, the Head of the Congregation of the Jews*. The coins referred to under (b) are to be dated to the last years of the reign of Hyrcanus (from 47 BCE on?). The Greek letters, *alpha* and *pi*, or monograms, which appear on many of the coins, are interpreted as referring to Queen Alexander or to Antipater (Kanael, 1952 and 1963).

3. *Aristobulus II* (Jehudah): The Jehudah coins are very rare. They represent – as is true of almost all of the coins of Hyrcanus and a few coins of Jannaeus – the standard type of Hasmonaean coinage with the inscription: *Jehudah the High Priest and the Congregation of the Jews*.

The most important symbol on the coins of Hasmonaean kings is the double horn of plenty (cornucopiae) with a pomegranate between the two horns. On the Hebrew–Greek coins of Alexander

Jannaeus which bear the title of king, a star and an anchor are also found partially surrounded by a circle and a flower (lily).

B.   The causes of the religious persecution

E. **Bickermann**, *Der Gott der Makkabäer: Untersuchungen über Sinn und Ursprung der makkabäischen Erhebung*, 1937; J. G. **Bunge**, *Untersuchungen zum zweiten Makkabäerbuch* (Dissertation, Bonn 1971); M. **Hengel**, *Judaism and Hellenism*, 1974; M. **Stern**, 'Review of M. Hengel's *Judentum und Hellenismus*', *KS* XLVI, 1970, 94a–99b (Hebrew); V. **Tcherikover**, *Hellenistic Civilization and the Jews*, 1959. See also the bibliography for §5.

The evaluation of the character of Antiochus IV Epiphanes (175–164 BCE) and of the reasons which led to the escalation of events in December 167 BCE is extremely controversial. Already, in antiquity, the opinion of non-Jewish writers who regarded the king as a supporter of culture and a fighter against the superstitious barbarism of the Jews stood in sharp contrast to the Jewish view of history which saw in Antiochus the personification of evil and absolute *hubris* (see Dan. 7.25). The question of who took the initiative which precipitated the course of events has been an especially debated issue. Was it king Antiochus or the Jews who made the primary move? In other words, was the escalation of events primarily an inner-Jewish development or was it a political measure initiated by the Syrians?

The thesis of a local, internal Jewish struggle, in which the Syrian king became an actor without precise knowledge of the rules of the game, was first advocated by Bickermann. He surmises: 'Since the persecution was territorially limited, it can readily be taken for granted that it was instigated by the local authority' (126) and finds this indicated, for example, in II Maccabees which brands Menelaus as the 'originator of the whole calamity' (see II Macc. 13.4). Bickermann summarizes his enquiry thus (p. 133):

Like the unspoiled nature worshippers of Greek theory 'the sons of the Akra', Menelaus and his followers, thus worshipped the celestial god of the ancestors without temple and statues under the open skies at the altar which stood on Mount Zion, free from the yoke of the law and, in mutual toleration, at one with the pagans. What could have been more human, more natural, than that they wanted to force this toleration upon their co-religionists who were still deluded? *That was the persecution of Epiphanes.*

A counter-thesis has been proposed by Tcherikover. Against Bickermann, Tcherikover represents the view that the religious edicts of Antiochus are to be understood as the king's reaction to a rebellion which was already under way and which was carried out by the Hasideans against the measures taken by the *mysarch* Apollonius. The construction of the Acra, the transformation of Jerusalem into a *polis*, and the attendant opening of the temple to the pagan citizens of this *polis* were, in the eyes of those devout and loyal to the Torah (the Hasideans), blows directed at the very roots of Jewish existence.

The Jewish faith was faced, not *after* Antiochus' decree, but *before* it, with the alternative of renouncing its existence or of fighting for its life. . . . It was not the revolt which came as a response to the persecution, but the persecution which came as a response to the revolt (Tcherikover, 196, 191).

In his book, *Judaism and Hellenism*, Hengel has taken up Bickermann's thesis again and, in carrying it further, has deepened and concretized it. Hengel assigns the

greatest probability to Bickermann's view that the impulse to the most extreme escala-tion of events in Judea came from the extreme Hellenists in Jerusalem itself. . . . Thus Menelaus and the Tobiads who supported him appear as the authors of the edict of persecution (I, 287, 289).

In his review of Hengel's work, Stern views such pointed opinions as really turning Bickermann's theses upside down. He especially disputes the one-sided emphasis on the internal Jewish interpretation of the events according to which Antiochus was 'no more than a tool in the hands of the Hellenists' (97a). Stern formulates the following ironic statement in protest against this view:

I would not be surprised if an investigator would arise who would go further on the road which Hengel has taken and would voice the thought that Menelaus and his group were the real embodiments of universal mono-theism and the true heirs of the prophets over against their opponents who were subservient to the letter of the Torah within the provincial borders of little Judaea (99a).

Bunge has recently continued the discussion of the causes of the persecution of Antiochus Epiphanes and given it a better factual grounding. Bunge (469–79) calls attention to the importance which until now has been neglected, of the international events for an understanding of Antiochus' action. He emphasizes the connection between the events which occurred during Antiochus' Egyptian campaign and events which occurred in Jerusalem. He surmises that the erection of the 'Abomination of Desolation' was related to 'a kind of total "seizure of power"' by the Hellenists in Jerusalem on the occasion of an invitation to a 'victory' demonstration and celebration for the king whom the Romans had humiliated. On 25 Kislev (= 15 December) 167 BCE, a sacrifice is thought to have been offered in honour of Epiphanes, thereby introducing the royal cult into Jerusalem. 'This sacrifice in honour of the king does not seem to have been the result of an initiative taken by the enthusiastic Hellenists of Jerusalem but to have been demanded by the royal emissary' (477). The refusal of numerous Jews to carry out the sacrifice is thought to have led the king to institute his infamous measures.

Even though the exact course of events has not been clarified in all its details and will very likely remain controversial (see *Schürer, 153, end of n. 37), it is perhaps possible to agree with Bunge in his conclusions: 'Thus it is possible for us to support both Bickermann . . . and Tcherikover. For action and reaction of both the Syrian and Jewish sides affected each other reciprocally' (478).

C.   *Jason's rebellion and the Egyptian campaigns of Antiochus IV*

See the bibliography in B above and §5 below.

Scholars disagree over the exact chronology of the events which immediately preceded the religious persecution of Antiochus. Particularly problematic are the precise placement in time of Jason's rebellion and, in connection with this, the visit (or visits) of Antiochus IV to Jerusalem.

The course of events is described in great detail but, in part, also with very real contradictions in I Maccabees 1.20–3; II Maccabees 5.1–26; *War* I 31–3; *Ant.* XII 239–50; Dan. 11.28–31. On the basis of the contradictory reports in the sources, it is possible to draw two different conclusions.

1. Several scholars (see Tcherikover, 186; Hengel, II, 186 n. 146) start with the observation that Antiochus visited Jerusalem twice, once near the end of 169 BCE on his return from his first Egyptian campaign and, a second time, in the summer of 168 BCE on his return from his second Egyptian campaign which the Romans halted so humiliatingly. The king, it is thought, had correspondingly also plundered the temple twice, namely, in 169 and 168 BCE. The reports in I Maccabees 1.22 and II Maccabees 5.11–23 should thus be related to two separate events. The main support for this view is provided by Daniel 11.28–31, where two actions by Antiochus following his two campaigns are clearly differentiated. Josephus,

similarly, notes specifically that Antiochus twice afflicted Jerusalem with a large army (*Ant.* XII 246–50).

2. Other scholars hold the view that, though Antiochus did undertake actions against Jerusalem after both campaigns, he personally participated in such action only after the first campaign. Already Bickermann (167f.) had disputed the report in *War* I 31–3 which claimed that Antiochus, whom the Tobiads had asked for help, had come to Jerusalem in 168 BCE after the second Egyptian campaign. Bickermann characterized this source as 'Seleucid'. According to the chronology held by scholars defending a single visit of Antiochus to Jerusalem, the two reports in I Maccabees 1.22 and II Maccabees 5.11–23 are concerned with the same event, namely a single plundering of the temple by Antiochus in the autumn of 169 BCE. In connection with the second Egyptian campaign by Antiochus, only Apollonius would have visited Jerusalem, at which time he demolished the walls of the city, built the Acra, and presumably defiled the temple. Exactly when Apollonius' action took place is still, to be sure, in dispute. The majority of scholars postulate a date in the year 167 BCE (thus in fairly close connection with the events of December 167 BCE). Bunge, on the other hand, dates Apollonius' attack on Jerusalem as early as July 168 BCE, i.e. immediately following Antiochus' rebuff by the Romans (464–8, 624).

The above-mentioned view of the events is represented in most recent times by *Schürer (152 n. 37) and Bunge (461–3) and is the basis for the description of the events given below. This view begins with the assumption (contrary to Tcherikover, 186) that Daniel 11.28–31 cannot be drawn upon to support two visits to Jerusalem by Antiochus, since nothing is said there about a personal intervention by the king himself. Finally, no real value should be attached to the reports in *Ant.* XII 246–50 because Josephus, in his attempt to combine two different sources, has completely jumbled both the chronology and the course of events (Bickermann, 163; *Schürer, 152 n. 34; Bunge, 542f.).

Opinions differ, accordingly, regarding the date of Jason's rebellion. Those scholars who surmise that there were two visits by Antiochus to Jerusalem place the rebellion between the two visits and date it to 168 BCE, seeing the rebellion as the direct cause for the king's second intervention (Tcherikover, 186f.; Hengel, I 280f.). Bickermann (167), it is true, dates the rebellion to 168 BCE but declares against a personal intervention by the king. Others, by contrast, place the rebellion earlier, in the year 169 BCE, and correlate it with the visit by Antiochus to Jerusalem in the autumn of

169 BCE and the associated plundering of the temple (*Schürer, 150f. and n. 32; Bunge, 537–46; 623). The events of the year 168 BCE, in this view of things, would have had nothing to do with Jason's rebellion in Jerusalem, but would instead have been connected exclusively with the retreat from Egypt forced upon Antiochus. On this point, also, the description provided below follows the opinion of Schürer and Bunge.

D.   *The chronology of I Maccabees 4.26–35 and II Maccabees 11.1–15*

J. R. **Bartlett**, *The First and Second Books of the Maccabees*, 1973; J. B. **Bunge**, *Untersuchungen zum zweiten Makkabäerbuch* (Dissertation, Bonn 1971); R. **Hanhart**, 'Zur Zeitrechnung des I und II Makkabäerbuches', *Untersuchungen zur israelitisch-jüdischen Chronologie*, ed. A. Jepsen and R. Hanhart, BZAW 88, 1964, 49–96; W. **Kolbe**, *Beiträge zur syrischen und jüdischen Geschichte*, BWANT II/10, 1926; O. **Mørkholm**, *Antiochus IV of Syria*, CMD 8, 1966; B. **Niese**, 'Kritik der beiden Makkabäerbücher. Nebst Beiträgen zur Geschichte der makkabäischen Erhebung', *Hermes* XXXV, 1900, 268–307; 453–527 = idem, Berlin: Weidmann 1900. See also the bibliography in §5.

The events associated with the first campaign of the Syrian general Lysias and with the purification of the temple by Judas Maccabaeus are described in the two books of Maccabees in totally different chronological order (see also *Ant.* XII, 313–15). In I Maccabees we find the following scheme of events: the first campaign of Lysias follows directly upon Judas' victory over Gorgias and Nicanor, then follows the occupation of Jerusalem and the purification of the temple, then the death of Antiochus IV and the accession of his son, and finally, the second campaign of Lysias in the company of the king who is still a minor. In II Maccabees the following is the sequence of events: Judas defeats Gorgias and Nicanor, Antiochus dies, Jerusalem is seized and the temple purified, the young son Antiochus V Eupator succeeds his father, then occurs the first campaign by Lysias which ended with a conclusion of peace (in proof, four letters are cited in II Macc. 11.16–38 which are not noted in I Maccabees), and finally we have the second campaign with Eupator. As already noted by Niese (469–76; 60f.), the chief differences between these two accounts are the divergent datings of the death of Antiochus IV Epiphanes and of Lysias' first campaign, which are practically interchanged in the two accounts.

In recent research, which does not follow the course of events provided by either of the two reports in every detail, three questions are especially in dispute.

1. The first of these issues concerns the date of the first campaign of Lysias. According to the majority of scholars, this already occurred in the autumn of 165 BCE or very soon after Judas' victory over Nicanor and Gorgias. On this point, the chronology of II Maccabees would be wrong (see Hanhart, 82f.; *Schürer, 161f.). The letter of Lysias (II Macc. 11.16–21) is to be dated to a time immediately following Lysias' first campaign. The connection of this letter with that campaign is not disputed even by those who follow a different chronology.

Bunge champions another thesis which on the whole follows II Maccabees more and involves a lowering of the chronology (401–36). According to Bunge, Lysias' first campaign is possibly to be dated to the summer of 164 BCE and the letter correspondingly later (October 164 BCE).

The doubts which Kolbe (79–81) expressed in his day regarding the historicity of the first campaign by Lysias have recently been revived by Mørkholm (152–4). This attempt to demonstrate the non-historical character of this campaign, however, has not stood up to scholarly scrutiny (see *Schürer, 160 n. 59; Bunge, 416).

2. A second issue concerns the conquest of Jerusalem and the repurification of the temple. A date for the death of Antiochus IV in the autumn of 164 BCE (shortly before the repurification of the temple) and 25 Kislev in the Seleucid year 148 (= 14 December 164 BCE) as the occasion for the Hanukkah festival have been widely accepted and are firmly established. However, Bunge has challenged this and proposed a theory in which he goes against all previous scholarship (402–49). He suggests that we are dealing fundamentally with two different festivals, namely, the first dealing with the purification of the temple and the reconsecration of the altar which occurred (as indicated by II Maccabees) immediately after the victory over Gorgias and Nicanor in December 165 BCE and the second concerned with a joyful festival on the occasion of the death of Epiphanes in December 164 BCE. I Maccabees would then have synchronized these two festivals which were originally separate and distinct.

3. A particularly difficult problem concerns the authorship and date of the third of the four letters which are transmitted in II Maccabees 11.16–33. That letter is directed by the Syrian king to the Jews and brings about a decisive shift in Seleucid policies (II Macc. 11.27–33). According to II Maccabees 11.33, it was written

on the fifteenth of the month Xanthicus in the Seleucid year 148 (=
March 164 BCE) after the death of Antiochus IV, in other words by
Antiochus V who was still a minor. Since the death of Antiochus IV
has, however, been clearly dated incorrectly in II Maccabees the
letter must have come from Antiochus IV, who did not die until the
end of 164 BCE. This is the usual view in recent scholarship (Bartlett,
307; *Schürer, 162, who, it is true, has in mind a date at the beginning of 164 BCE because of the precise agreement of this date with
the letter of the Roman envoys in I Maccabees 11.34–8). Bunge
(432 f.), on the other hand, is forced to date the letter precisely a
year later, in March 163 BCE, because of his generally later chronological starting-point. He remains within the framework of the
relative chronology of II Maccabees inasmuch as the letter must
necessarily come from Antiochus V. Bunge's explanation, that Jason
of Cyrene in order to avoid any confusion changed the date of the
third letter from 149 (Seleucid–Macedonian year) to 148 (Seleucid–
Babylonian year) appears really quite forced (432).

   On all three of these points, the presentation below follows the
'traditional' chronology and not that of Bunge.

§3. THE BEGINNING OF THE HELLENISTIC PERIOD IN PALESTINE (331–301 BCE)

F.-M. **Abel**, 'Alexandre le Grand en Syrie et en Palestine', *RB* XLIII, 1934,
528–45; XLIV, 1935, 42–61; D. **Auscher**, 'Les relations entre la Grèce et la
Palestine avant la conquête d'Alexandrie', *VT* XVII, 1967, 8–30; R. J. **Bull**
and G. E. **Wright**, 'Newly Discovered Temples on Mount Gerizim in Jordan',
HTR LVIII, 1965, 234–7; F. M. **Cross**, 'Papyri of the Fourth Century BC
from Dâliyeh: A Preliminary Report on Their Discovery and Significance',
New Directions, 1969, 45–69; A. **Kindler**, 'Silver Coins Bearing the Name of
Judea from the Early Hellenistic Period', *IEJ* XXIV, 1974, 73–6; L. Y.
Rahmani, 'Silver Coins of the Fourth Century BC from Tel Gamma', *IEJ*
XXI, 1971, 158–60; M. **Smith**, *Palestinian Parties and Politics That Shaped the
Old Testament*, 1971; M. **Stern**, *Greek and Latin Authors on Jews and Judaism I*,
1974; V. **Tcherikover**, *Hellenistic Civilization and the Jews*, 1959; G. E. **Wright**,
'The Samaritans at Shechem', *HTR* LV, 1962, 357–66. See also the biblio-
graphy in §4.

The decisive battle of Issus (333 BCE) opened a new chapter
in the history of the Near East. Within two years, Alexander

the Great, by conquering Tyre and Gaza, pushing forward to Egypt, and returning once again through Palestine on his way to the conquest of Mesopotamia, had brought the entire Near East under Greek control. The cities and countries of the Near East had been influenced by Hellenistic civilization and culture before Alexander the Great (see Auscher), but now began, because of almost unlimited economic opportunities, a period of unrestricted expansion of Hellenistic influence.

In the autonomous Persian province of *Jahud* (Judah), this political change of authority did not bring about any decisive shifts at first. Despite Josephus' report (*Ant.* XI 336–9) and the popularity of this legend in later Judaism (see R. Marcus, *Josephus* VI, LCL, 512–32), it is scarcely likely that Alexander visited Jerusalem and interfered directly in the conditions there. Presumably, he was satisfied to receive the recognition of Greek overlordship by the high priest in his role as the representative of the people (*Ant.* XI 329–32) and left untouched, in all other respects, the organizational structure of Judah with the high priest and the 'council of elders' at the head of the state. The Samaritans fared differently. They submitted initially even before Judah (*Ant.* XI 321) and, according to Josephus (*Ant.* XI 322–4), were granted permission by Alexander to construct a temple on Mount Gerizim (see Bull and Wright). The Samaritans however rebelled against Andromachus, the governor Alexander had appointed, and were punished by having their city changed into a (Macedonian) military colony – a fate which was not allotted to Jerusalem until the time of the Seleucids and, again at a later time, under the Romans. Aramaic papyri and skeletons discovered in a cave in Wadi Dâliyeh seem to reflect the grim fate which befell the Samaritans (see Cross and above, pp. 494f., 548).

After Alexander died in Babylon in 323 BCE, at the high point of his military success, there began a power struggle among his generals over his legacy. Palestine, which had been fought over from antiquity by the two great cultural centres of Syria with Mesopotamia to the north and Egypt to the south, now found itself again in the centre of rival interests. At first, the satrap of Egypt, Ptolemy, occupied Coele-Syria in 320 BCE in order to bring it under Egyptian control. In doing so, he placed himself completely within the tradition of the Pharaohs who also had taken pains to gain possession of the Phoenician coastal cities and thus to control the most important commercial routes in the area. From this time until the decisive battle of Ipsus, Coele-Syria changed masters several times. In 315 BCE, Antigonus Monophthalmos, Alexander's most powerful governor, conquered Syria and Palestine but lost them again to Ptolemy in 312 BCE. Soon afterwards, however, Ptolemy pulled back and Syria–Phoenicia fell again, without a fight, to Antigonus and his son Demetrius Poliorketes. This was repeated again in 302 BCE. Ptolemy conquered Coele-Syria a third time and once again withdrew immediately. For this reason, he did not participate in the decisive battle between the Macedonian generals Seleucus and Lysimachus (who in the meantime had assumed the title of king) and Antigonus at Ipsus in 301 BCE. As a result of this battle, four successor (*diadochi*) monarchies emerged. Still, Ptolemy was able to enforce his claims to Coele-Syria against his one-time comrade-in-arms, Seleucus (I) who was the founder of the Seleucid dynasty. Ptolemy acquired permanent control of Syria–Palestine and the area thus came under the rule of the Ptolemaic kingdom, where it remained for approximately a century.

During this fluctuating history of Palestine between 320 and 301 BCE, Jerusalem was directly drawn into the course of events. Two rival parties probably came into existence in the face of the unclear political situation, with one group sympathizing with Ptolemy and another with Antigonus (see Smith, 148–92 for background). A report in Josephus, derived from Hecataeus of Abdera, mentions a Jewish high priest named Hezekiah – he was probably not a high priest who was in office but a member of the 'high-priestly oligarchy' (Stern, 40f.) – who after Ptolemy's retreat from Palestine in 312–11 BCE accompanied the latter together with his followers to Egypt. He probably left the area because he had good reason to fear that he would be accused by Antigonus of pro-Ptolemaic sympathies (*Contra Apionem* I 186–9 = Stern, no. 12). Coins from this period have been discovered with the inscription *Yeḥezqyo/ah ha-peḥah* but it is not certain that the reference on these coins is to the same Hezekiah (see Kindler, 76; Rahmani).

Another report by Josephus, which is drawn from the historian Agatharchides of Cnidus, even notes a conquest of Jerusalem by Ptolemy on the sabbath – a military move which was to be made also by the Seleucids at the beginning of the Maccabaean revolt – and the deportation of numerous Jews to Egypt (*Ant.* XII 5–6 = *Contra Apionem* I 209–11 = Stern, no. 30 a/b). Appian (*Syr.* 50) also mentions the destruction of Jerusalem by Ptolemy. The dating of these events is, to be sure, in dispute but there is much in favour of associating them with the third conquest of Coele-Syria by Ptolemy in 302 BCE (see Tcherikover, 55–9; Stern, 108). Those who voluntarily emigrated to Egypt and those whom Ptolemy deported became the core of the Jewish-Hellenistic diaspora which later flourished in Egypt, especially in Alexandria.

§4. PALESTINE UNDER PTOLEMAIC RULE
(301–200 BCE)

F.-M. **Abel**, *Histoire de la Palestine depuis la Conquête d'Alexandre jusqu'à l'Invasion arabe* I–II, EB, 1952; Y. **Baer**, *Israel Among the Nations*, Jerusalem: Bialik Institute 1955 (Hebrew); H. **Bengtson**, *Griechische Geschichte von den Anfängen bis in die römische Kaiserzeit*, HAW III/4, 1950, ⁴1969; E. R. **Bevan**, *A History of Egypt under the Ptolemaic Dynasty*, London: Methuen 1927; E. **Bickermann**, *From Ezra to the Last of the Maccabees: Foundations of Post-Biblical Judaism*, New York: Schocken Books 1962; A. **Bouché-Leclercq**, *Histoire des Lagides* I–IV, Paris: Leroux 1903–7; P. M. **Fraser**, *Ptolemaic Alexandria* I–III, London: Oxford University Press 1972; M. **Hengel**, *Judaism and Hellenism*, 1974; idem, *Juden, Griechen und Barbaren*, SBS 76, 1976; J. **Klausner**, *History of the Second Temple* I–V, Jerusalem: Ahiasaf 1949, ⁶1963 (Hebrew); J. **Maier**, *Das Judentum*, München: Kindler 1973, 159–223; B. **Mazar**, 'The Tobiads', *IEJ* VII, 1957, 137–45; 229–38; S. **Mittmann**, 'Zenon im Ostjordanland', *Archäologie und Altes Testament* (see ch. VII §3), 1970, 199–210; W. O. E. **Oesterley**, *The Jews and Judaism During the Greek Period*, London: SPCK 1941; O. **Plöger**, 'Hyrkan im Ostjordanland', *ZDPV* LXXI, 1955, 70–81; M. **Rostovtzeff**, *The Social and Economic History of the Hellenistic World* I–III, London: Oxford University Press 1941; D. S. **Russell**, *The Jews from Alexander to Herod*, London: Oxford University Press 1967; A. **Schalit**, ed., *The Hellenistic Age*, WHJP I/6; A. **Schlatter**, *Geschichte Israels von Alexander dem Grossen bis Hadrian*, Stuttgart: Calver Verlag 1900, ³1925; M. **Stern**, 'Notes on the Story of Joseph the Tobiad (Josephus, *Ant.* XII, 154ff.)', *Tarbiz* XXXII, 1962, 35–47 (Hebrew); idem, 'The Period of the Second Temple', in *Ben-Sasson, 185–303; W. W. **Tarn**, *Hellenistic Civilization*, London: E. Arnold 1927, ³1952; H.-J. **Thissen**, *Studien zum Raphiadekret*, BKP 23, 1966; V. **Tscherikower** (Tcherikover), 'Palestine Under the Ptolemies (A Contribution to the Study of the Zenon Papyri)', *Mizraim* IV–V, 1937, 9–90; idem, *Hellenistic Civilization and the Jews*, 1959; S. **Zeitlin**, *The Rise and Fall of the Judaean State* I, Philadelphia: Jewish Publication Society of America 1962; H. **Zucker**, *Studien zur jüdischen Selbstverwaltung im Altertum*, Berlin: Schocken Verlag 1936.

By 286 BCE, at the latest, the Ptolemaic kingdom was in effective control over the whole province of 'Syria and Phoenicia', as it was officially designated. The Ptolemaic kingdom, in contrast to the Seleucid kingdom, was an internally unified, tightly centralized governmental organism. At the head of the state stood the king who was all-powerful and was endowed with divine honours. The land belonged to him as his personal possession. 'Thus under the first Ptolemies the oriental idea of the divinely sanctioned omnipotence of the king was put into effect, with Greek logic, down to the final consequence' (Hengel, I, 18f.). The country's monopolistic economy, in which the native population served only as objects of exploitation (see Bengtson, 444), was completely directed to securing and increasing the king's power. The real administrator of the kingdom, along with the king, was the *dioikētēs* ('the minister of finance and economic affairs') whose prototype we meet under Ptolemy II in the Zenon papyri in the person of Apollonius.

The newly won province of 'Syria and Phoenicia' was considered, like the Egyptian mother-country and the other provinces, to be the property of the king and was incorporated into the ingenious Ptolemaic system of taxes and leases. There is some disagreement, however, about whether all areas and provinces were equally affected by this administrative system or whether especially the Jewish *ethnos* (nation) was accorded an autonomous or semi-autonomous status. While the very limited existence of source material does not permit a definitive decision on the matter, none the less much speaks against assuming that Judah enjoyed any extensive autonomy (see Hengel, I 24, against Zucker, 32, and Tcherikover, 59).

After the first generation of the Diadochi had passed on (Ptolemy I died in 283 BCE and Seleucus I in 281 BCE), Egypt was ruled by the energetic Ptolemy II Philadelphus (283–246 BCE). He was able in the First Syrian War against Antiochus I (274–271 BCE) to maintain his Syrian and Phoenicia possessions and, together with his *dioikētēs* Apollonius, to accelerate the process of systematically opening up Syria–Palestine economically. The journey of a certain Zenon, known from the Zenon papyri, provides insight into this economic activity. The journey was undertaken in the year 259–258 BCE at the direction of Apollonius and apparently took Zenon through all of Palestine, to the military colony of the Jewish 'local prince' Tobias (was he a descendant of the Tobiah mentioned in Neh. 6.17–19; 13.4–9?) in Transjordan, and to a large wine-growing estate which Apollonius owned in Beth-Anath in Galilee. Probably the main objectives of this journey were the inspection and improvement of the financial administration and the betterment of economic relations between the Egyptian mother-country and its northern province. On the Jewish side, it seems especially to have been the family of Tobias which took advantage of the new economic opportunities, for the Zenon papyri preserve two letters of Tobias to

Apollonius in which Tobias makes references to gifts for the king and for Apollonius himself (*CPJ* I, nos. 4f.). The pro-Ptolemaic tendencies of the Tobiad family, dating from this period and based on common commercial interests, were for a long time an important factor in Jewish politics and were even maintained in one branch of the family after Palestine came under Seleucid control.

After Ptolemy II had victoriously held his own against a Seleucid–Macedonian coalition in the Second Syrian War (260–253 BCE), the Third Syrian War (246–241 BCE) occurred under his successor Ptolemy III Euergetes (246–221 BCE). In general, this war also turned out successfully for the Ptolemaic king, but in Jerusalem there appears to have been resistance against Ptolemaic rule. Josephus reports, although his chronology of the events is in the wrong order (see Tcherikover, 130f.; Stern, 1962), that Onias II who was then high priest, refused to pay the regular tribute to Ptolemy. Josephus traces this refusal back to the 'filthy character' and greed of the high priest (*Ant.* XII 158f.). This, however, was scarcely the real reason. Presumably Onias II took his action in anticipation of a Seleucid conquest of Palestine. The Egyptian king, in any case, took the discontinuance of the payment of tribute as indicative of open rebellion against Ptolemaic overlordship and threatened at once to turn Jerusalem into a *kleruchia*, i.e. to settle military colonists there and thus bring the limited self-government to an end.

In the context of this dangerous situation, the family of the Tobiads, which had originally been at home in the area east of the Jordan, began its steep political ascent. Joseph, the son of Tobias and nephew of the high priest Onias II, had already moved to Jerusalem and established a residence there. Joseph now made himself the spokesman for the opposition to the high priest and demanded of the latter that he abandon his anti-Ptolemaic politics and reconcile himself to the king. Onias was forced to submit to this opposition which apparently had strong support among the people. This meant that Onias was forced to surrender practically all political leadership. He remained, nominally, as high priest but could not prevent the transfer to Joseph of the office of *prostasia*, i.e. the office of political representative of the people before the king (*Ant.* XII 160–66). Joseph then borrowed money 'from his friends in Samaria' (!) for a personal visit to the king in Alexandria. There he obtained, by outbidding his competitors and by promising to double the amount of taxes, the office of 'general leaseholder of taxes' for all of Syria and Palestine. In addition, he was assigned a contingent of 2,000 soldiers to assist him in his duties (*Ant.* XII 167–80). According to Josephus (*Ant.* XII 186), he held this office for twenty-two years, probably from about 240 to about 218 BCE. His favour with the Ptolemies lasted until the Fourth Syrian War when, with the anticipated successes of Antiochus III, his loyalty to the Ptolemaic kingdom began to wane.

Joseph understood how to apply radically the instrumentalities of power at his disposal in exploiting the people financially. He captured Ashkelon and Scythopolis, which had refused to pay their (increased) taxes, and had the most prominent, and probably also the richest, citizens of both cities executed and their wealth confiscated (*Ant.* XII 180–83). In this manner, he not only collected the taxes promised the Ptolemaic king but also 'made great profits from farming the taxes' which he used 'to make permanent the power he now had, thinking it prudent to preserve the source and foundation of his present good fortune by means of the wealth which he had himself acquired' (*Ant.* XII 184). Behind this description there hides, more likely, a practitioner of power politics concerned more with his own interests rather than a representative of the 'young and ambitious people who struggled to break through the narrowness of their homeland and to make more room for the new spirit which was gradually making itself felt even in Jerusalem' (Hengel, I, 56). It may be that backward Jerusalem 'gained economic and political significance' from Joseph's policies (Hengel I, 28) but these advances probably only benefited the small and powerful upper class and certainly not the great masses of the poorer inhabitants. It is very unlikely that Joseph 'was able to protect his people against excessive exploitation' (Hengel I, 28 on the basis of *Ant.* XII 224, a passage which he himself later correctly characterizes as tendentious because of the pro-Hellenistic ideology of the so-called Tobiad novel; see Hengel, I, 269f.). There is nothing to indicate that he extracted double taxes only from non-Jewish cities such as Ashkelon and Scythopolis and that he spared his Jewish co-religionists. We must, on the contrary, begin with the assumption that the policies of the Tobiads played an important role in sharpening the social differences in Palestine and thus also in giving rise to apocalyptic tendencies and revolutionary movements.

After the death of Ptolemy III, there occurred, in the years 221–217 BCE, the Fourth Syrian War between his successor Ptolemy IV Philopater (221–204 BCE) and Antiochus III, 'the Great' (223–187 BCE) who was able to lead the Seleucid kingdom to new glory. Antiochus III was able to occupy a large part of Coele-Syria but was defeated in the battle at Raphia in southern Palestine (217 BCE). He was forced to retreat from Coele-Syria. The victorious Ptolemaic king took a trip through the province which he had recaptured and reorganized its administration. On this occasion, he probably also visited Jerusalem (see the report in III Macc. 1.8–2.24 which, to be sure, is legendary).

The struggle for the province 'Syria–Phoenicia' now reached its critical stage. The weakness of the Ptolemaic kingdom which was becoming more and more apparent finally led to a split in the family of the Tobiads, who were for all practical purposes the rulers of Judaea. The Tobiad novel of which Josephus made use reports that Joseph sent his youngest son Hyrcanus to Egypt for the celebration of the birth of the crown prince (about 210 BCE?). The latter took advantage of the opportunity – in accordance with family tradition – to buy the favour of the king with rich monetary gifts (*Ant.* XII 196–202). Perhaps hê even succeeded in having the office of *prostasia* transferred from his father to himself, or at least in having it promised to him (Tcherikover, 135f.). This decision by the king may have been facilitated by Joseph's more or less hidden pro-Seleucid inclinations during the Fourth Syrian War. In any case, this is the best explanation of the enmity which developed between Hyrcanus and Joseph and his remaining sons. The latter moved and fought against Hyrcanus on his return, though without success (*Ant.* XII 221f.). Hyrcanus, however, was not able to assume his office and was compelled to retreat to the family property at 'Arâq el-Emîr in Transjordan. There he maintained himself against his family as a loyal adherent of the Ptolemaic kingdom even at the time when Palestine had finally become Seleucid. It was only under Antiochus IV Epiphanes that his power collapsed leading him to commit suicide (169–168 BCE?; *Ant.* XII 236).

Following his defeat at Raphia, Antiochus III had concentrated his attention on the eastern portion of his kingdom. He expanded through all of Asia to India and established a system of vassal states. He assumed the title of 'Great King' and came to an agreement in a secret treaty with Philip V of Macedonia over the partition of the Ptolemaic kingdom after the death of Ptolemy IV and his sister-wife Arsinoe (204 BCE). In 201 BCE, he again invaded Syria–Palestine and conquered the entire province in a very short time. A temporary success by the Ptolemaic army commander Scopas did not produce any reversal of the situation. Scopas was decisively defeated in 200 BCE at Paneion near the sources of the river Jordan and was unable to save the province for his king, Ptolemy V Epiphanes, still a minor.

§5. PALESTINE UNDER SELEUCID DOMINATION
(200–135 BCE)

F.-M. **Abel**, 'Topographie des campagnes machabéennes', *RB* XXXII, 1923, 495–521; XXXIII, 1924, 201–17, 371–87; XXXIV, 1925, 194–216; XXXV, 1926, 206–22, 510–33; idem, 'Le fête de Hanoucca', *RB* LIII, 1946, 538–46; E. **Abishar**, *The Wars of Judas Maccabaeus*, Tel Aviv: Masada 1955 (Hebrew); Y. **Baer**, 'The Persecution of Monotheistic Religion by Antiochos Epiphanes', *Zion* XXXIII, 1968, 101–24 (Hebrew); E. R. **Bevan**, *The House of Seleucus* I–II, London: E. Arnold 1902; idem, *A History of Egypt Under the Ptolemaic Dynasty*, 1927; E. **Bickermann**, 'La charte séleucide de Jérusalem', *REJ* C, 1935, 4–35; idem, *Der Gott der Makkabäer*, 1937; idem, *Institutions des Séleucides*, BAH 26, 1938; A. **Bouché-Leclercq**, *Histoire des Séleucides (323–64 avant J.C.)*. I–II, Paris: Leroux 1913–14; A. **Büchler**, *Die Tobiaden und die Oniaden im II. Makkabäerbuche und in der verwandten jüdisch-hellenistischen Litteratur*, JITLW 6, 1898–9; J. G. **Bunge**, 'Zur Geschichte und Chronologie des Untergangs der Oniaden und des Aufstiegs der Hasmonäer', *JSJ* VI, 1975, 1–46; H. E. **Del Medico**, 'Le cadre historique de fêtes des Hanukkah et de Purim', *VT* XV, 1965, 238–70; T. **Fischer**, *Untersuchungen zum Partherkrieg Antiochos' VII im Rahmen der Seleukidengeschichte* (Dissertation, München/Tübingen 1970); idem, 'Zu den Beziehungen zwischen Rom und den Juden im 2. Jahrhundert v. Chr.', *ZAW* LXXXVI, 1974, 90–3; A. **Giovanni** and H. **Müller**, 'Die Beziehungen zwischen Rom und den Juden im 2. Jh. v. Chr.', *MH* XXVIII, 1971, 156–71; M. D. **Herr**, 'Hanukkah', *EJ* VII, 1280–8; T. **Liebmann-Frankfort**, 'Rome et la conflit judéo-syrien (164–161 avant notre ère)', *AC* XXXVIII, 1969, 101–20; J. **Maier**, *Die Texte vom Toten Meer* I–II, München: Ernst Reinhardt 1960; E. **Meyer**, *Ursprung und Anfänge des Christentums* II, 1921; A. **Momigliano**, *Alien Wisdom: The Limits of Hellenization*, Cambridge: Cambridge University Press 1975, 74–96; O. **Mørkholm**, *Antiochos IV of Syria*, CMD 8, 1966; H. H. **Schmitt**, *Untersuchungen zur Geschichte Antiochos' des Grossen und seiner Zeit*, HES 6, 1964; H. **Stegemann**, *Die Entstehung der Qumrangemeinde* (Dissertation, Bonn 1971); S. **Stein**, 'The Liturgy of Hanukkah and the First Two Books of the Maccabees', *JJS* V, 1954, 100–6, 148–55; M. **Stern**, 'The Death of Onias III (II Macc. 4.30–8)', *Zion* XXV, 1960, 1–16 (Hebrew); idem, *The Documents on the History of the Hasmonaean Revolt*, Tel Aviv: Hakibbutz Hameuchad 1965 (Hebrew); G. **Vermes**, *The Dead Sea Scrolls in English*, Harmondsworth/Baltimore: Penguin Books, 1962; W. **Wirgin**, 'Judah Maccabee's Embassy to Rome and the Jewish-Roman Treaty', *PEQ* CI, 1969, 15–20. See also the bibliographies in §§3 and 4.

With the victory of Antiochus III at Paneion, Ptolemaic sovereignty over Palestine, which had lasted for almost exactly one hundred years, had come to an end. Palestine now fell to the Seleucids and remained, to a greater or lesser degree, within the sphere of Seleucid influence until its conquest by the Romans in 62 BCE.

Antiochus required about two years after the battle of Paneion to bring Syria–Phoenicia completely under his control, which he succeeded in doing in 198 BCE. His fundamentally positive relationship towards the populace, the majority of which was inclined to be pro-Seleucid, is demonstrated in the inscription discovered at Ḥefzibah near Beth-shan/Scythopolis (see above, §1Bv, ix) and in his letter to his general Ptolemaios (*Ant.* XII 138–44). The letter grants numerous privileges in addition to the right to live according to the 'ancestral laws'. In practice, this right meant the recognition of the Torah as the 'national law' and thus the granting of internal autonomy. The entire population of Jerusalem was exempted from taxes for three years and also given a one-third reduction from all future tribute. The *Gerousia* and temple personnel were granted complete exemption from taxation and, finally, generous financial aid was provided for the rebuilding of Jerusalem and the temple. To be sure, there were still adherents to the Ptolemaic kingdom in Jerusalem. This is probably what the obscure allusion in Daniel 11.14 refers to, with its mention of 'men of violence' who rise against the king of the south. One may also include here the comment by Jerome in his commentary on Daniel 11.14 that the 'adherents of the Ptolemaic party' went into exile in Egypt (PL XXV, 562). Nevertheless, the majority of the population and the politically influential circles must have been pro-Seleucid, even though their reasons may have been very different in character and have included solid economic expectations as well as religious hopes and messianic expectations.

A further decree, which probably followed closely upon the granting of the privileges just mentioned, strengthened the pro-Seleucid and conservative faction in Jerusalem (*Ant.* XII 145f.). In this decree, non-Jews were forbidden to enter the temple court and, moreover, all importation and even the rearing of ritually impure animals were prohibited. This second regulation may have been aimed – at least indirectly – at the economic power and the connections of the Tobiads, since naturally all commerce with non-Jewish merchants was thereby made more difficult.

A.   Oniads and Tobiads

Simon II, the son of Onias II, was high priest at the time of the Syrian conquest of Palestine. At a relatively early point, he had joined the Seleucid side and was confirmed in his judgment when

Antiochus III was victorious at Paneion. The pro-Jewish decrees of the Syrian king are, to a large extent, to be attributed to Simon's skilful policies, which are extolled in Sirach 50 and which later gained him the epithet 'the righteous'.

The powerful family of the Tobiads increasingly became the crucial enemies of the high priest. Although he was initially an active adherent of the Ptolemaic dynasty and had stood in close economic relationship with 'Ptolemaic high finance' (Hengel I, 270), Joseph, the head of the family, had changed sides at the right time and had gone over to the Seleucids. Still the high priest was probably able to solidify his power by adroit political tactics and, because of the internal strife within Joseph's family, may have even regained the office of *prostasia* and thus have been the chief representative of the Jewish people before the Seleucid administration.

After Simon II's death, shortly after the final conquest of Palestine by Antiochus III, an open power struggle broke out between the high priest and the Tobiads. The successor to Simon II was Onias III who, however, was apparently not able to assert himself in the political, economic, and religious tangles as well as had his father. He seems to have quickly broken with his brother Jason/Yeshua, who was more strongly inclined towards Hellenism. Also, Onias III does not seem to have been a match for the influence of the pro-Seleucid sons of Joseph at the Seleucid court (see Hengel, I, 272).

An important factor influencing the state of affairs in Jerusalem was a change in the foreign constellation of power. Rome, which was then becoming a major international power, had defeated Philip V of Macedonia in the Second Macedonian War and had proclaimed the 'freedom of all Hellenes' at the Isthmian games of 196 BCE. Under the pressure of these events, Antiochus III and the young Ptolemy V Epiphanes made peace and Antiochus gave his daughter Cleopatra (I) to Ptolemy in marriage in 194–193 BCE (Dan. 11.17; *Ant.* XII 154). Nevertheless, Antiochus, only a short time later, was lured into mounting an expedition to Greece. To this the Romans responded with a landing in that country. Antiochus was forced to flee and to leave the way to Asia open to the Romans. In the decisive battle of Magnesia, at the end of 190 BCE, Antiochus' army was defeated and Antiochus was subsequently forced, in the Peace of Apamea (188 BCE), to relinquish his European possessions and the Seleucid holdings in Asia Minor and, in addition, to pay high reparation costs. This (first) constriction of the Seleucid kingdom and its limitation to its Syrian, Mesopotamian, and western Iranian territories not only brought to an end Antiochus' far-reaching plans but also initiated the disintegration of the Seleucid state. The kingdom's financial condition was left in desperate straits. The new and unscrupulous means for the acquisition of money adopted by Antiochus III found its first victim in the king himself, who was killed while plundering the temple of Bel in Susa. Under his son and successor, the weak Seleucus IV Philopator (187–175 BCE), new pro-Ptolemaic tendencies began to appear in Jerusalem and obviously gained the support of the high priest Onias III. The tax burden which was certainly noticeable also in Jerusalem, the disappointment of the hopes which had been associated with the change in rule and, not least of all, the internal power struggle with the Tobiads may have played a role in the reassertion of his pro-Ptolemaic sentiment.

The most important evidence for this increasingly critical turn of events is the so-called Heliodorus affair. According to the report in II Maccabees 3.4–40 (see Dan. 11.20), a certain Simon, the head of the temple administration and a follower of the Tobiads, laid claim to the additional office of administrator of the city market (*agoranomia*). When Onias refused to combine the two important offices in one person, Simon entered into a conspiracy with the Seleucid governor, Apollonius, against the high priest and accused Onias of hoarding untold riches in the temple treasury. Apollonius informed the king who – in view of the kingdom's chronic financial distress – sent his treasurer, Heliodorus, to Jerusalem with instructions to confiscate a part of the money. Onias defended himself before Heliodorus. The money on deposit, he said, consisted of money 'belonging to widows and orphans, and also some money of Hyrcanus, son of Tobias' (II Macc. 3.10f.). Without doubt, this was an allusion to assets of Hyrcanus the Tobiad, who was loyal to the Ptolemaic king and who now resided in Transjordan. Heliodorus appears, for unknown reasons, not to have confiscated the money. Legend has painted a highly-coloured picture of a marvellous deliverance (II Macc. 3.22–40). Simon, however, slandered the high priest before the king and accused him of having, in all probability, pro-Ptolemaic inclinations. Onias attempted, after conditions approaching civil war developed in Jerusalem (see II Macc. 4.3), to save the situation by making a personal appearance at the court in Antioch. This attempt, however, was frustrated by political events, for Seleucus IV was murdered by Heliodorus and his brother, returning from Rome, took over the government as Antiochus IV Epiphanes.

The Tobiads took advantage of the disorders attendant upon the change of rulers and seized power in Jerusalem. They promised the new king that they would raise the annual tribute to 360 talents of silver and make a one-time payment of 80 talents if he would appoint Jason, the brother of Onias, as high priest. Antiochus, whose position was still not totally consolidated, assented to the petition. For Antiochus, the bestowal of offices for financial considerations was developed as a normal procedure. In the view of circles in Jerusalem who were loyal to the Torah – this means in all likelihood the majority of the population – the appointment of Jason during the lifetime of a high priest who was legitimately in office represented a forcible governmental intervention into the autonomy of the Jewish city-state.

B.   The 'Hellenistic reform'

With Jason, not only had a representative of the Tobiads come to power but also – and the two are related – one of the leaders of the so-called Hellenistic reform party. The main goal of the reform, which beyond doubt initially had its origin among the ruling classes in Jerusalem and was not supported by the majority of the (largely poor) population, was a constitutional reform which would move Jerusalem towards the status of a Hellenistic *polis* (city). As a logical consequence, Jason thus offered to pay another 150 talents for the permission 'to establish by his authority a gymnasium and a body of youth (*ephebeion*) for it, and to enrol the men of Jerusalem as citizens of Antioch' (or as Antiochenes) (II Macc. 4.9).

This transformation of Jerusalem into the new polis of 'Antiochia', which Antiochus IV approved, abrogated the Torah as the city's constitution and meant the suspension of the 'edict' promulgated by Antiochus III which basically had only been an endorsement of the old rights of the Jewish community which had existed since Persian times. The citizen lists and the admission to the gymnasium which were controlled by Jason and his followers made it possible to choose the future citizens and members of the gymnasium according to the notions of the Hellenists. The poorer people of the city and, particularly, of the country were thus in practice deprived of their rights. Of course, this transformation of Jerusalem into a *polis* according to the Hellenistic model did not take place all at once but in several phases. The beginning would have been the organization of a corporation similar to that of the 'Antiochians in Ptolemais' (Bickermann, 1937, 62). None the less, the change was no less revolutionary. It basically represented a complete departure from

the traditional concept of the Jewish temple-state and thus 'an attempt to do away with the result of five hundred years of Jewish and
Israelite history' (Hengel, I, 73).

Although the reform by Jason and his followers was only a constitutional reform and was in no way synonymous with the abandonment of the Torah as a religious norm, this distinction would hardly
have been understood, much less accepted, by a pious Jew. In the
eyes of the people who were loyal to the law, it would not have been
a case of reform but of apostasy from the 'law of the fathers'. This in
any case is the way the development was viewed by the author of I
Maccabees:

> In those days lawless men came forth from Israel, and misled many,
> saying, 'Let us go and make a covenant with the Gentiles round about us,
> for since we separated from them many evils have come upon us.' This
> proposal pleased them. . . . So they built a gymnasium in Jerusalem accord-
> ing to Gentile custom, and removed the marks of circumcision and aban-
> doned the holy covenant. They joined with the Gentiles and sold them-
> selves to do evil (I Macc. 1.11–15).

According to II Maccabees 4.12–15, the gymnasium was erected
near the temple, 'right under the citadel', and even the priests
preferred to participate in the athletic contests rather than perform
the service at the altar. These contests, in accordance with Greek
custom, were carried out naked, and for this reason many young
men went so far as to undergo operations to remove the marks of
circumcision (see also *Ant.* XII 241). This must have increased the
indignation of the population which remained loyal to the law as
much as the fact that even in Jerusalem this sports activity could
hardly be separated from the cult of Heracles and Hermes, who were
the patron deities of the gymnasium (Bickermann, 1937, 64). The
episode of the pagan athletic contests at Tyre is characteristic. The
'Antiochians of Jerusalem' sent a delegation to them with a gift for
Heracles. The bearers of the gift when they arrived, however, could
not make up their minds to present the offerings to Heracles but –
contrary to their instructions – asked diplomatically that the money
be used for the construction of triremes (war vessels) (II Macc. 4.18–
20).

Events became even more critical when, about three years after
Jason's appointment, another change took place in the high priestly
office. Jason sent Menelaus, the brother of Simon the temple official
mentioned earlier, to Antioch to deliver the tribute money. Menelaus, who was an extreme Hellenist and probably even more loyally

devoted to the Seleucid dynasty than Jason, took advantage of the opportunity and bought the high priestly office for himself by offering a higher bid for the post (II Macc. 4.23–5). Behind this second and even more portentous change in authority stood once again the party of the Tobiads who succeeded, by overthrowing the moderate Jason, in removing the Oniads once and for all. Thereby not only was the internal succession in the high priestly office broken – Jason as an Oniad still belonged to the family of the Zadokites – but with Menelaus, for the first time, a non-Zadokite came to power as high priest. Jason was forced to leave Jerusalem and flee to the region east of the Jordan, probably taking refuge with Hyrcanus, who was friendly towards the Ptolemaic king (II Macc. 4.26).

This radical move by the Tobiads must have embittered to the utmost those pious Jews who were loyal to tradition. When Menelaus, because of the high tribute payments, openly embezzled part of the temple treasures, a revolt broke out in Jerusalem during which his brother and second-in-command, Lysimachus, was killed (II Macc. 4.39–42). Menelaus in the meantime was staying in Antioch and bribed – in order to solidify his power in Jerusalem – a royal official to murder the deposed high priest Onias III (II Macc. 4.32–4). In both instances, Menelaus stayed out of trouble. Because of the murder of Onias, Antiochus IV ordered the execution of the guilty official but Menelaus, who was the instigator of the deed, remained unmolested. When the Jerusalem *gerousia*, because of the events in Jerusalem, sent three envoys to Antioch to present accusations against Menelaus to the king, Menelaus opportunely resorted to bribery and the king had the three envoys promptly executed.

International events again became of decisive importance for further developments. The weak government of the guardians of Ptolemy VI Philometor, who was still a minor, provided Antiochus IV with the desired opportunity to intervene in Egypt at the end of 170 BCE (the Sixth Syrian War). With his victory at Pelusium, Antiochus gained control of all Egypt except for Alexandria, following a favourable treaty with Ptolemy which allowed Antiochus to assume the crown of both Lower and Upper Egypt. The king's departure from Egypt may have been the result of events in Jerusalem. There the deposed high priest Jason, on the basis of a rumour that the king had died, had attacked Jerusalem with more than a thousand men and had forced Menelaus to take refuge in the citadel. According to Josephus (*War* I 31–3; *Ant.* XII 239–41), this revolt was primarily a struggle for power between the pro-Ptolemaic Oniads and the pro-Seleucid Tobiads. Jason, who was probably

supported by the majority of the population which was loyal to the
law and which may have been, once again, expecting the fulfilment
of its religious hopes from this political change of affairs, drove the
Seleucids from the city and thereby provoked the king's intervention. Even before the arrival of Antiochus IV in Jerusalem, Jason
was forced to leave the city, fleeing towards Egypt through the
regions controlled by the Ammonites and Nabataeans (II Macc.
5.5–9). Even the Transjordanian tribes had gone over to the
Seleucids, and Hyrcanus committed suicide.

Antiochus IV conquered Jerusalem in the autumn of 169 BCE,
took dreadful revenge on the residents, and plundered the temple (II
Macc. 5.11–16). How close the 'solid basis of a mutual money interest' (Bickermann, 1937, 67) was between the king and the high priest
Menelaus, who had been reappointed, is shown by the fact that
Menelaus personally assisted in the plundering (II Macc. 5.15). The
narrative in I Maccabees 1.21–8 (see Dan. 11.28; *Contra Apionem* II
83) which apparently refers to this event shows tremendous rage
over the king's greed for money:

He arrogantly entered the sanctuary and took the golden incense altar,
the lampstand for the light, and all its utensils. He took also the table for
the bread of the Presence, the cups for drink offerings, the bowls, the golden
censers, the curtain, the crowns, and the gold decoration on the front of the
temple; he stripped it [the gold] all off.

Upon his departure from Jerusalem, Antiochus left behind, in
addition to the hated high priest Menelaus, two *epistates* (governors),
one in Jerusalem (Philip) and one on Mount Gerizim (Andronicus)
along with occupation troops (II Macc. 5.22f.).

In the spring of 168 BCE, Antiochus was forced a second time to go to
Egypt where Ptolemy VI had come to an agreement with his brother
and sister, Ptolemy VIII and Cleopatra II, who were co-regents to the
young king. Antiochus reached Alexandria but there, at Eleusis, his
expansionist policies came to a sudden halt. In June, 168 BCE, the
Romans had decisively defeated the last Macedonian king at Pydna
and had gained a free hand against the Seleucids. The Roman emissary
in Egypt, Popillius Laenas, delivered to Antiochus in a humiliating
fashion the senate's ultimatum that he terminate the war and depart
from Egypt at once. As had happened to Antiochus III in his day in the
north, now Antiochus IV in the south of his kingdom was thus
prevented from realizing his political plans by Roman might and in a
decisive manner. The escalation of events which now followed in
Jerusalem and eventually led to a religious persecution appears to be

immediately connected with the frustration of the king's Egyptian plans (see Dan. 11.29f.).

Very probably, Antiochus himself did not visit Jerusalem on his way out of Egypt, but attempted to bring order to the Phoenician coastal cities, which had also become restless. The *mysarch* Apollonius was sent to Jerusalem at the beginning of 167 (or summer of 168 BCE?). Apollonius captured the city by treachery on the sabbath, carried out a bloodbath among the inhabitants, tore down the walls of the city, and above all constructed in the City of David (south of the temple mount (?); on this see above §1B xiiib) a stronghold known as the Acra (I Macc. 1.29–33; II Macc. 5.24–6; *Ant.* XII 251f.). He stationed in the fortress a non-Jewish garrison, 'godless people, lawless men' (I Macc. 1.34; see Dan. 11.39). The Acra, which 'became a great snare' (I Macc. 1.35), was the strong-point and centre of the Hellenistic presence in Jerusalem for a long time. The city itself became a kind of *klerouchia* (military colony; see Tcherikover, 1961, 189; Bickermann, 1937, 73, 80) with a mixed Gentile–Jewish populace: 'Because of them, the residents of Jerusalem fled; she became a dwelling of strangers' (I Macc. 1.38). Menelaus was, to be sure, still high priest, but the real authority in the *polis* of Jerusalem lay, for all practical purposes, in the hands of non-Jews, especially the *epistates* Philip. It is certain that the temple became the common property of all the citizens of the *polis*, including the non-Jews.

Though any further developments were thus basically already prejudiced, the decrees of the king which were sent, it would seem, soon after the action carried out by Apollonius (I Macc. 1.41–51; II Macc. 6.1f.) signified the last and decisive phase in the efforts at Hellenization. The order, which initially was directed to the entire Seleucid kingdom – 'that all should be one people and that each should give up his special religious customs' (I Macc. 1.41f.) – was then followed by a special edict for Jerusalem and Judaea:

to follow customs strange to the land, to forbid burnt offerings in the sanctuary, to profane sabbath and feasts, to defile the sanctuary and the priests, to build altars and sacred precincts and shrines for idols, to sacrifice swine and unclean animals, and to leave their sons uncircumcised. They were to make themselves abominable by everything unclean and profane, so that they should forget the law and change all the ordinances. 'And whoever does not obey the command of the king shall die' (I Macc. 1.44–50).

Inspectors were appointed everywhere who made certain that the pagan sacrifices were offered, if necessary with force. Whoever circumcised his children or gave obedience to the Torah and secretly observed the sabbath was punished by death. The Seleucid measures reached their climax on 6 December 167 BCE with the erection of a pagan altar on top of the great altar of sacrifice – the abomination of desolation (Dan. 11.31; 12.11) – and with the dedication of the Jerusalem temple to Zeus Olympios (= Ba'al Šamem). It was at this time, at the latest, that the daily (*tamid*) offering (Dan. 11.31) was discontinued and probably on 15 December that the first offerings in honour of the king were presented.

C.   *The Maccabaean rebellion*

(i)   *The beginnings under Mattathias and Judas*

The measures carried out by the king against the Torah and the Jewish cult had – consciously or unconsciously – struck Judaism's vital nerve. One should, for this reason, not overemphasize such passages as I Maccabees 1.52 and 2.16 which refer to the 'many people' who willingly obeyed the Seleucid officials (see Hengel, I, 289f.). All told, it must have been only a relatively small minority of 'Hellenists' who were confronted by the majority of the (common) people still loyal to the Torah. The narrative, which is certainly legendary, of the martyrdom of the aged Eleazar and the mother and her seven sons (II Macc. 6.18–7.42; IV Macc. 5–18) probably mirrors in its nucleus the people's initially passive resistance.

Passive resistance changed into open rebellion when the priest Mattathias from the village of Modein intervened together with his five sons (Judas, Jonathan, Simon, John, and Eleazar). According to the account in I Maccabees 2.1–26, which is, it is true, tendentious but still essentially historical, Mattathias refused to obey the order to offer sacrifice. He then killed a Jew, who was willing to offer sacrifice, as well as the royal official and destroyed the altar:

> Even if all the nations that live under the rule of the king obey him, and have chosen to do his commandments, departing each one from the religion of his fathers, yet I and my sons and my brothers will live by the covenant of our fathers (I Macc. 2.19f.).

Mattathias retreated to the impenetrable mountains and began organized guerrilla warfare (I Macc. 2.27–30, 43–8). From the start it was Mattathias' son Judas who appears to have played the most prominent role and, in the description of the origin of the movement in II Maccabees, Judas is the only one mentioned (II Macc. 5.27). It was he who later acquired the epithet 'Maccabi' ('the hammer') for which the whole dynasty was named. Soon devout persons loyal to the Torah (the Hasideans), who had initially fled into the inaccessible desert areas, joined the family of the Maccabees (I Macc. 2.42). After one group of such devout persons, to whom the sanctity of the sabbath was more important than the defence of their lives, had been attacked on the sabbath by Syrian troops and had been massacred without putting up any resistance (I Macc. 2.29–38), even these circles recognized the necessity of active resistance (I Macc. 2.31–41).

Not long after the onset of the rebellion, probably in the year 166 BCE, Mattathias, the head of the family, installed his son Judas as the commander-in-chief in the conflict with the Syrians. Shortly thereafter the old man died (I Macc. 2.66–70). Judas, by avoiding open battles and through the use of surprise attacks, was able to gain a whole series of victories. First of all, he defeated a Syrian army under Apollonius (I Macc. 3.10–12; *Ant.* XII 287) at which time Apollonius himself was killed. Shortly thereafter, at Beth-horon, he administered a devastating defeat to a second Syrian army under a commander named Seron (I Macc. 3.13–26; *Ant.* XII 289). A third defeat was suffered by the Syrian army at Emmaus under its commanders Nicanor and Gorgias. Judas demonstrated that he was able to play off the various units of the huge Syrian army against each other. While Gorgias sought to mount a surprise attack with his cavalry forces against the Jewish camp, Judas unexpectedly attacked the main army and put it to flight (I Macc. 3.38–4.25; II Macc. 8.9–29; *Ant.* XII 305–12).

Meanwhile, in Syria, Antiochus IV had left (in 165 BCE) on a campaign against the Parthians (according to I Macc. 3.31, in order to enrich his state treasury) and had left Lysias behind as viceroy and educator of the minor Antiochus V. Still in the same year, Lysias intervened personally in the Jewish conflict and marched from the south through Idumaea against Judah (I Macc. 4.29). The two armies met in the vicinity of Beth-zur, south of Jerusalem, and Lysias was defeated completely (on this see the narratives in I Macc. 4.34f. and II Macc. 11.10–12). This report, however, is questioned by Bunge (416–25) who, in accordance with his different chronology (see above, pp. 566–8), has put forward the thesis that this alleged Judaean victory was actually a defeat of which the Syrians took no advantage only because Lysias was forced to withdraw following the sudden death of Antiochus IV.

Following Judas' brilliant victory, Lysias seems, initially on his own authority, to have inaugurated a revision of Seleucid policies.

According to the letter preserved in II Maccabees 11.16–21, he promised to champion the affairs of the Jews before the king and held out the prospect of further negotiations. Only slightly later, probably at the beginning of 164 BCE, there followed a letter from Antiochus IV himself to the Jewish people (II Macc. 11.27–33). II Maccabees also reports the receipt of a letter from the Romans at the same time (II Macc. 11.34–8). Whether this letter from the Roman emissaries to the Jews is genuine is disputed (see Liebmann-Frankfort and Bunge, 392–5, 421 f.). If it is genuine, the letter would be the first evidence of contact between Romans and Jews and should be placed chronologically between Lysias' letter and that of the king. In his letter, Antiochus specifically allowed the Jews 'permission to enjoy their own food and laws' and, at the same time, extended amnesty to all rebels who returned to their home towns within fourteen days. Thus, after about three years both the prohibitions against obeying the Torah and the *polis* constitution which had been forced upon the people were rescinded. Judas proceeded to conquer Jerusalem (with the exception of the Acra), to purify the temple and to reinstate the temple cult on 25 Chislev of the Seleucid year 148 (= 14 December 164 BCE). This festival of temple dedication lives on in contemporary Judaism as the festival of Hanukkah (I Macc. 4.36–59; II Macc. 10.5–8; *Ant.* XII 316–27).

Despite the king's concessions and the reconquest of Jerusalem, peace however had not been achieved by any means. The Maccabaean movement had in the meantime developed its own dynamics which went beyond the immediate goals that had been originally pursued. Judas now began to consolidate his rule. He fortified the temple mount as well as the important fortress of Beth-zur and undertook military campaigns into the areas adjacent to Judaea (I Macc. 4.60–5.8). After receiving an appeal for help from Jewish communities in Galilee and Transjordan, Judas moved into Transjordan and Simon, his brother, invaded Galilee in order to aid their co-religionists in distress. Both were victorious in numerous battles and for safety brought the Jewish population of these predominantly pagan regions to Judaea (I Macc. 5.54). During the absence of the two brothers, two of their deputies, Joseph and Azariah, undertook military action against the coastal city of Jabneh/Jamnia, but this undertaking miscarried and they were beaten back by the Syrian commander Gorgias (I Macc. 5.55–62). Upon his return, Judas moved once more to the south, captured Hebron, and destroyed the altars and statues of the pagan gods in Ashdod/Azotus (I Macc. 5.65–8).

During all these events, the Seleucid court in Antioch had held back initially – chiefly because a change in power occurred in the meanwhile and conditions were not yet sufficiently stabilized. Towards the end of 164 BCE, Antiochus IV had died in the course of his Persian ventures and authority in the kingdom was now exercised, for all practical purposes, by Lysias. Contrary to the stated will of the deceased king, Lysias had made himself the nation's regent and the guardian of the minor Antiochus V Eupator (I Macc. 6.1–17). When Judas prepared to capture the Acra (I Macc. 6.18–27), Lysias was forced to intervene and undertook his second campaign to Judaea accompanied by Eupator. Initially, the Syrian army again besieged Beth-zur. At Beth-Zechariah, south of Bethlehem, battle was joined and the Seleucids gained their first great victory over the Maccabaeans (I Macc. 6.28–47). Because it lacked sufficient food supplies on account of the sabbatical year, Beth-zur was forced to capitulate and Lysias began the siege of Jerusalem (I Macc. 6.48–54). Here, too, capitulation was imminent when Lysias and Eupator were forced to withdraw suddenly because of a rebellion by Philip, whom Antiochus IV had originally appointed as regent over his kingdom. Thus at the end of 163 BCE a peace settlement was unexpectedly negotiated to the advantage of the Jews (I Macc. 6.55–9). Eupator permitted them explicitly 'to live by their laws as they did before' (I Macc. 6.59) and officially returned to them the temple which Judas had previously captured at the end of 164 BCE. The letter in II Maccabees 11.22–6 which discusses these concessions to the Jews is placed in the wrong order and cannot, like the following letter, be from Antiochus IV since his death is presupposed in it.

With this peace of 163 BCE, at the latest, the power of the extreme Hellenists in Jerusalem was decisively weakened if not actually broken. Menelaus was deposed and executed by the Syrians as 'the cause of all misfortunes' (II Macc. 13.3–8; *Ant.* XII 385). The moderate Hellenist, Alcimus, again a Zadokite, became his successor and was initially even recognized by the Hasideans (I Macc. 7.12–14). It is uncertain whether or not this took place while Eupator was still alive (I Macc. 7.5–20; II Macc. 14.3–14; *Ant.* XII 385). According to Josephus (*Ant.* XII 387 against *War* I 33), the legitimate high priest Onias IV, the son of the murdered Onias III, fled to Egypt following the appointment of Alcimus and erected there the schismatic sanctuary of Leontopolis. Bunge (1971, 561–6; 1975, 9–11), surmises that the flight took place after the installation of Menelaus, the first of the non-Oniads, as high priest, about 173 BCE. The erection of the temple of Leontopolis by Onias IV is to be dated, according to Bunge (567–72), to the time of the desecration of the Jerusalem sanctuary between 168 and 165 BCE.

In the meantime, Judas and his followers, for whom more was at stake than the installation of a legitimate high priest, did not abandon their resistance. When Alcimus, soon after his accession, ordered the execution of sixty members of the Hasidean party (I Macc. 7.16), open conflict broke out between the Maccabaeans and the new high priest. Alcimus was forced to flee from Jerusalem and accused Judas before the king (II Macc. 14.7–10).

In Antioch, Demetrius I Soter, a son of Seleucus IV Philopator, had come to power (162 BCE) and had his cousin Antiochus V and Lysias murdered. Demetrius sent the general Nicanor with an army to Judaea in order to reinstate Alcimus in his office. On 13 Adar 161 (or 160 BCE?) a decisive battle occurred at Adasa. The Syrian army was defeated and destroyed. Nicanor was killed in the battle and from that time forth, the 'day of Nicanor' was festively observed every year in commemoration of the event (II Macc. 15.36).

Probably even before Nicanor's campaign (against the chronology in I Macc. 8; see Bunge, 1971, 660 n. 59a), Judas had sent a delegation to Rome in order 'to establish friendship and alliance' with the Romans (I Macc. 8.17). Since the Romans were doubtlessly interested in strengthening their influence in Syria–Palestine, a treaty of friendship resulted in which the Romans pledged that 'if war comes first to the nation of the Jews, the Romans shall willingly act as their allies' though with the restriction 'as the occasion may indicate to them' (I Macc. 8.27). At the same time, the Romans sent a letter to Demetrius and threatened him: 'If now they (the Jews) appeal again for help against you, we will defend their rights and fight you on sea and on land' (I Macc. 8.32). Whether and when Demetrius received this warning is not known. Demetrius undoubtedly, even without an explicit threat, had reason to fear an intervention by the Romans, who did not recognize him as king until the autumn of 160 BCE. Accordingly, Demetrius hastened to bring about a *fait accompli* in Judaea. For this reason, he sent an army under Bacchides into Judaea, probably immediately after the failure of Nicanor's campaign. In the autumn of 161 BCE (April 160 BCE according to Bunge), this army administered a defeat to the Jewish forces under Judas in the vicinity of Jerusalem. Judas lost his life in the battle and was buried in Modein (I Macc. 9.1–22). With this, the Hellenistic party in Jerusalem had once gained an interim victory. Alcimus was reinstated as high priest and was able, with Bacchides' help, to suppress all resistance for a time: 'After the death of Judas, the lawless emerged in all parts of Israel; all the doers of injustice appeared' (I Macc. 9.23).

(*ii*) *Jonathan* (161–142 BCE)

Soon after the death of Judas, the scattered insurgents succeeded in reassembling and in reorganizing their armed resistance under Jonathan, a brother of the deceased Judas. Their first undertaking was directed against an Arabian tribe in Transjordan which had attacked and killed Jonathan's brother John (I Macc. 9.35–42). On his return from this successful campaign, Bacchides sought to engage Jonathan, who saved himself by fleeing (I Macc. 9.43–9).

Bacchides consolidated the newly won Syrian supremacy in the land by fortifying numerous cities in Galilee and Judaea (I Macc. 9.50–3). Alcimus, who was once again firmly in the saddle in Jerusalem, ordered, in May 160 BCE (May 159 BCE according to Bunge), that the wall of the inner court of the sanctuary be torn down, probably in order to make it possible for non-Jews to gain access to the temple. The stroke which he suffered apparently shortly thereafter was interpreted by the pious as God's intervention (I Macc. 9.54–6). According to Josephus (*Ant.* XX 237), a seven-year 'vacancy in office' began in the office of the high priest which did not end until Jonathan took over the position in 152 BCE. It is possible that Josephus simply inferred all this from the silence of his sources regarding any new high priest to succeed Alcimus. It is certain, however, that his contradictory statement in *Ant.* XII 414 is inaccurate. He says there that Judas had become high priest after the death of Alcimus, but Judas died, according to the chronology of I Maccabees, before Alcimus.

After the death of Alcimus, Bacchides withdrew from the land and did not return until 158 BCE (I Macc. 9.57). His return was at the invitation of the 'apostates', i.e. the party of the Hellenists in Jerusalem (I Macc. 9.58), who asked for help apparently because the power of the Maccabaeans had noticeably increased. How justified the fears of the Hellenists were soon became evident. Bacchides was defeated by Jonathan, who vented his anger on those 'who had counselled him to come into the country' (I Macc. 9.69). Bacchides made peace with Jonathan, swearing that 'he would not try to harm him as long as he lived' (I Macc. 9.71). Prisoners were returned to Jonathan and Bacchides departed from Judaea, never to return (I Macc. 9.72). Jonathan settled in Michmash, north of Jerusalem, and 'began to judge the people and destroyed the ungodly out of Israel' (I Macc. 9.73). This reference allows one to conclude that Jonathan, despite all progress, was still not in a position to take over authority personally in Jerusalem.

I Maccabees is completely silent about the events of the next five years, for its account does not resume until the year 153–152 BCE. In Syria, internal struggles for the throne came to dominate political concerns. Various pretenders to the Seleucid throne found that the Maccabaeans in Judaea had gained sufficient strength to be a power which they had to take seriously. The first usurper was Alexander Balas who, as the alleged son of Antiochus IV, laid claim to the throne with the support both of the kings who were allied against Demetrius and of the Roman senate. Balas landed in Ptolemais/Acco and both he and Demetrius sought to secure the support of Jonathan. Jonathan soon decided in favour of Alexander Balas, but in the meantime accepted from Demetrius the latter's permission to return to Jerusalem and his release of the hostages held in the Acra (I Macc. 10.4–9). Furthermore, he was able to refortify the city and the temple mount unhindered, and apparently succeeded in getting the Syrian garrisons removed from all their strongholds with the exception of Beth-zur (I Macc. 10.10–14). Alexander Balas soon afterwards offered even more concessions than Demetrius and appointed Jonathan 'the king's friend' and high priest of the Jewish nation (I Macc. 10.15–20). During the feast of tabernacles in the year 153 (152?) BCE, Jonathan was installed as high priest and became officially, and with the approval of the Seleucid court, head of the Jewish nation (I Macc. 10.21). To be sure, in the eyes of the pious devotees to the law, he probably had no more legitimate right to the office than the bitterly opposed Menelaus and certainly less right than the Zadokite Alcimus who, in the beginning, had been acknowledged by the Hasideans as well.

One should not, therefore, exclude the possibility that Jonathan was the 'wicked priest' of the devout of Qumran who had separated themselves from the official cult. This is the view especially of Vermes (61–8; see further *Schürer, 188 n. 42, and Maier II, 139–41). The 'teacher of righteousness' in the Qumran texts, who was the antagonist of the wicked priest, was, according to Stegemann (95–252), a Jerusalem high priest whom Jonathan had driven out of office. Bunge goes a step further and wants to see in the 'teacher of righteousness' the legitimate high priest who reigned during the alleged seven-year 'vacancy of office' between Alcimus and the assumption of the high priestly office by Jonathan (1975, 27–39). Thus, Bunge must make the 'teacher of righteousness' a Hellenist and this position, as well as the archaeological findings (see above,

§1B xvii), does not make his construction very plausible.

One last and – if it is actually historical – completely desperate attempt by Demetrius to gain Jonathan's favour was ignored by Jonathan as he realistically assessed the balance of power (I Macc. 10.22–47). Alexander gained the upper hand against Demetrius (I Macc. 10.48–50). In connection with Alexander's marriage to Cleopatra, a daughter of Ptolemy VI Philometor, Jonathan was rewarded with the office of military and civil govenor (*strategos* and *meridarches*) of Coele-Syria (*Ant.* XIII 80–5; I Macc. 10.51–66). I Macc. 10.61 notes that groups from Judaea sought to accuse Jonathan before Alexander, but the ruler paid them no heed. These were probably representatives of the Hellenists. According to Bunge (1975, 38f.) these opponents of Jonathan would have been followers of the Qumran 'teacher of righteousness' whom Jonathan had expelled from office. Bunge's view, however, does not accord very well with the observation that they, as Bunge correctly surmises, were probably representatives of the Hellenized (!) priestly nobility and are specifically called 'lawless' in the text.

Under Alexander, Jonathan's claims, which extended beyond the borders of Judaea, were for the first time acknowledged and sanctioned by the Syrians. When, in the year 148–147 (147–146 BCE?), Demetrius II, a son of Demetrius I, laid claim to the throne, Jonathan fought 'loyally' against Apollonius, the governor of Coele-Syria, who had joined Demetrius. Jonathan defeated Apollonius, conquered Jaffa/Joppa, burned Ashdod and its Dagon temple, and accepted the homage of the inhabitants of Askalon (I Macc. 10.67–86). In gratitude, Alexander gave him the city of Ekron (I Macc. 10.87–9). For all practical purposes, Jonathan now controlled an important part of the maritime plain.

Jonathan had thus become so powerful that he was not only able to survive without trouble a change of administration in Syria but also was successful in obtaining further concessions in the struggle for power. Ptolemy VI withdrew his favour as well as his daughter Cleopatra from Alexander Balas and sided with Demetrius II. Alexander was defeated, forced to flee to Arabia, and was murdered there (I Macc. 11.1–17). Jonathan felt strong enough to besiege the Acra in Jerusalem after Demetrius II's accession (145 BCE) and thus to strive for full sovereignty (I Macc. 11.18–22). When Demetrius summoned Jonathan to Ptolemais/Acco, the latter gave orders to continue the siege of the Jerusalem citadel and submitted to the king's will only after Demetrius had made extensive concessions to him. He confirmed Jonathan in all the offices he held and moreover carried out Jonathan's desire to consolidate the three Samaritan districts of Aphairema, Lydda, and Ramathaim with Judaea. In addition, he secured an exemption from taxation for this enlarged Jewish domain (I Macc. 11.23–37; *Ant.* XIII 120–8). Jonathan thus achieved under Demetrius II what had appeared to be altogether too utopian under Demetrius I.

Another new struggle for the Syrian throne broke out and involved Demetrius II and Trypho, a former general of Alexander Balas, who wanted to place Alexander's son, Antiochus (VI), on the throne (I Macc. 11.39f.; *Ant.* XIII 131–44; Diodorus XXXIII 4a; Appian, *Syr.* 68/357). Jonathan made skilful use of the occasion to demand control of the Acra in Jerusalem, which represented a final vestige of Syrian influence in the city. Demetrius, who was in dire straits because of an insurrection among the inhabitants of Antioch, promised to grant Jonathan his wish if the latter would only come to his aid with an army. Jonathan moved against Antioch and rescued the king from his precarious situation (I Macc. 11.41–51). When Demetrius, however, refused to honour his promise, Jonathan entered into preliminary negotiations with Trypho and Antiochus VI, who not only confirmed all his privileges but also appointed Jonathan's brother Simon as commander of the coastal region from the Ladder of Tyre to the border of Egypt (I Macc. 11.52–9). Thereupon, the brothers began, in part even with Syrian help, to enlarge their domain. Jonathan captured Askalon and Gaza and at Hazor defeated the army of Demetrius, who in the meantime had been driven from Antioch. Simon took control of the fortress of Beth-Zur which, next to the Acra, was the most important stronghold of Syrian power in Judaea (I Macc. 11.60–74; *Megillat Taanit, HUCA* VIII/IX, 281–2).

Jonathan did not hesitate to make contact with other and significant powers outside the area. He sought to secure the support of Rome and to establish relations with Sparta, which had increased in power after the defeat of the Achaean League (146 BCE). An embassy was sent to Rome 'to renew the former friendship and alliance with them' (I Macc. 12.3) and a letter to the Spartans (I Macc. 12.5–23) in which Jonathan referred to earlier contacts between Sparta and the high priest Onias (I?).

After an unsuccessful campaign against Demetrius which took Jonathan all the way to Damascus (I Macc. 12.24–32), he further fortified Jerusalem and attempted, by constructing a wall, to cut off the Acra from the rest of the city (I Macc. 12.35–8; *Ant.* XIII 179– 86). Trypho, who apparently had developed an ambition to take the

Seleucid throne for himself, followed the events in Jerusalem with growing distrust. He met Jonathan in Beth-shan/Scythopolis, later lured him without his army to Acco/Ptolemais, and there had him imprisoned (I Macc. 12.39–48). When Trypho prepared to come to Jerusalem to imprison Simon, Jonathan's brother, the popular assembly elected Simon as Jonathan's successor and commissioned him to continue the conflict (I Macc. 13.1–9; *Ant.* XIII 191–202). Simon added to Jerusalem's fortifications and took possession once and for all of the coastal city of Jaffa/Joppa. Trypho was forced to break off his campaign against Judaea, had Jonathan killed at the beginning of 142 BCE, and returned to Syria (I Macc. 13.10–30; *Ant.* XIII 203–12).

(iii)   *Simon* (142–135/34 BCE)

No later than the time of Jonathan's murder, Simon established contact again with Demetrius II who, more than ever, was dependent upon the support of the Maccabaeans. Trypho, in the meanwhile, had the young Antiochus murdered and took the title of king for himself. Demetrius marked the new change in alignment with an amnesty decree, a grant of total and permanent exemption from taxation, and an acknowledgment of the political *status quo*, i.e. for all practical purposes a recognition of Judaea's sovereignty (I Macc. 13.31–42; *Ant.* XIII 213–22). For the author of I Maccabees, 142 BCE was the year in which 'the yoke of the Gentiles was removed from Israel' (I Macc. 13.41) and marked the decisive break in the history of the Maccabaean rebellion. This new feeling of freedom found expression in the fact that the Jews began their own era and dated their documents and contracts according to the years of Simon's administration (I Macc. 13.41f.).

Simon consistently increased his power, captured the strategically important Gezer/Gazara, expelled the pagan residents, and placed a Jewish garrison in the city under the command of his son John (I Macc. 13.43–8). Shortly afterwards, he succeeded in capturing the Acra in Jerusalem, the last of the Syrian bastions in Judaea. At the beginning of June 141 BCE, he entered the Acra 'with praise and palm branches, and with harps and cymbals and stringed instruments, and with hymns and songs, because a great enemy had been crushed and removed from Israel' (I Macc. 13.51). The hymn in I Maccabees 14.4–15 celebrates Simon and his success in almost messianic tones as the saviour of the nation and prince of peace. The confirmation and high point of this development was the decision of the Jerusalem popular assembly of the year 140 BCE to legitimize the Maccabaean family formally and to grant Simon as hereditary honours the offices of prince (*ethnarch, naśi*), of high priest (*archiereus*), and of commander (*strategos*) (I Macc. 14.25–49). The restriction 'until a trustworthy prophet should arise' (I Macc. 14.41) seems to point to a compromise between the dynastic ambitions of the Maccabaeans and the eschatological expectations of the 'devout' (Maier, 204).

In his foreign relations, Simon appears to have safeguarded his sovereignty by renewing relations with Sparta (I Macc. 14.20–3) and Rome. He sent an embassy to Rome (I Macc. 14.24) which secured a confirmation of the treaty of friendship. At the same time, the Romans sent letters to Ptolemy VIII (Euergetes II) and numerous other kings in which they were called upon to hand over to Simon the fugitive adherents of the party of the Hellenists (I Macc. 15.15–21). The precise circumstances surrounding this letter are problematic (see *Schürer, 194–7). *Ant.* XIV 145–8 contains a decree which Josephus assigned to the time of Hyrcanus II but which may belong to the time of Simon. Stern (1961, 6) has however attempted to date this letter to the beginning of the reign of Hyrcanus I.

In the meantime, Demetrius II had undertaken a campaign against Persia and was taken prisoner by Mithridates I in the year 139 BCE (I Macc. 14.1–3; *Ant.* XIII 184–6; Appian, *Syr* 67/356). His brother and successor Antiochus VII Sidetes at first renewed all of Simon's privileges and, in addition, granted him the right to mint his own coinage (I Macc. 15.1–9). However, after he had forced Trypho to flee (I Macc. 15.10–14, 25–31, 37–41) and gained a free hand within the country, Antiochus disavowed his promises. He demanded the return of the cities of Jaffa/Joppa, Gezer/Gazara, and the Acra in Jerusalem. In addition, he demanded taxes from all the cities and places lying outside Judaea proper or, in their stead, one thousand talents of silver (I Macc. 15.25–31). When Simon was prepared to pay only one hundred talents for Joppa and Gazara, Antiochus appointed a general named Cendebeus as commander of the coastal district with orders to imperil Judaea. Simon sent his sons Judas and John into battle against Cendebeus. They defeated him decisively and burned Ashdod, the second time such a fate had befallen the city within a matter of years (I Macc. 16.1–10; *Ant.* XIII 225–7).

Though Simon had scarcely any reason to fear serious danger to his rule from the outside, he was the first Maccabaean to fall victim to an intrigue from within. His son-in-law Ptolemy, who was governor of Jericho, sought to gain control of the government and had Simon and his sons Mattathias and Judas treacherously murdered at the beginning of 135 (134?) BCE during a banquet in the fortress of Dok near Jericho (I Macc. 16.11–22; *Ant.* XIII 228).

§6. THE HASMONAEAN DYNASTY

A. *John Hyrcanus I* (135/34–104 BCE)

L. **Finkelstein**, *The Pharisees: The Sociological Background of their Faith*, Philadelphia: Jewish Publication Society of America 1938, ³1946; T. **Fischer**, 'Johannes Hyrkan I. auf Tetradrachmen Antiochos' VII.?' *ZDPV* XCI, 1975, 191–6; R. **Marcus**, 'The Pharisees in the Light of Modern Scholarship', *JR* XXXII, 1952, 153–64; A. **Michel** and J. **Le Moyne**, 'Pharisiens', *DBS* VII, 1966, 1022–115; M. **Stern**, 'The Relations Between Judea and Rome During the Rule of John Hyrkanus', *Zion* XXVI, 1961, 1–22 (Hebrew); S. **Zeitlin**, 'Johanan the High Priest's Abrogations and Decrees', *Studies and Essays in Honor of A. A. Neuman* (see ch. V §2), 1962, 569–79.

Simon's son John Hyrcanus became his successor. He had been governor of Gazara and was the sole survivor of Ptolemy's attack on his father-in-law's family. It appears that Ptolemy's attack may possibly have been inspired by the Seleucid ruler Antiochus VII. Hyrcanus was able to gain the upper hand over Ptolemy, but found himself, probably already in his first year which was a sabbath-year, facing an invasion of Judaea by Antiochus VII. Judaea was laid waste and Hyrcanus was besieged in Jerusalem (*Ant.* XIII 236). Jerusalem was cut off completely from the outside world and starvation set in. Food became so scarce that Hyrcanus – according to the report by Josephus – expelled all the disabled from the city. The Syrians, however, refused to allow them passage through the siege lines which ringed the city and Hyrcanus was finally forced to re-admit them. This occurred at the time of the Feast of Tabernacles during which Antiochus not only granted an armistice but also 'sent a magnificent sacrifice, consisting of bulls with gilded horns and cups of gold and silver filled with all kinds of spices' (*Ant.* XIII 242f.). Hyrcanus finally had to capitulate and sue for peace. Antiochus demanded the surrender of all weapons, taxes for Joppa and all the cities lying outside of Judaea, and hostages as well as the sum of five hundred talents of silver. In addition, the 'crowns' of the city walls were ordered pulled down (*Ant.* XIII 245–8). In comparison with the actions of Antiochus IV, the conditions laid down by Antiochus VII were mild. None the less, they formally re-established Syrian overlordship. Hyrcanus was soon afterwards forced to render military service to the king when the latter began a campaign against the Parthians in 130–129 BCE (*Ant.* XIII 249).

The military fiasco of the Parthian campaign and the death of Antiochus VII (129 BCE) weakened the Seleucid state so decidedly that the Syrian demonstration of strength in Judaea was nothing more than a short interlude. Antiochus' successor was Demetrius II, who had been released from Parthian captivity shortly before this and thus now began his second reign. Demetrius immediately found himself embroiled in internal struggles and had to defend himself against a pretender to the throne (Alexander Zabinas). The latter was supported by Ptolemy VII Physcon of Egypt. At Damascus, Demetrius was defeated by Alexander and was shortly thereafter murdered (125 BCE). Antiochus' son, Antiochus VIII Gryphos, succeeded his father and successfully repelled the usurper Alexander. However, in 113 BCE, he was set aside by his cousin and stepbrother Antiochus IX Cyzicenus. From 111 BCE, the two were forced to divide the rule (*Ant.* XIII 267–72).

Because of these internal Syrian struggles for the throne, Judaea became, for all practical purposes, an independent state and John Hyrcanus a sovereign ruler. Immediately after the death of Antiochus VII, Hyrcanus undertook his first campaign of conquest, the beginning of a persistent enlargement of his state's borders and his influence. In the east, he captured Medaba, in the north Shechem and Mount Gerizim, and in the south Adora and Marisa, and forced circumcision upon the Edomites (*Ant.* XIII 255–8). He also appears to have been the first Maccabaean to employ hired pagan mercenaries to strengthen his military forces. His plundering of the grave of David to obtain the means for such a policy probably did not make the best impression upon his Judaean subjects (*Ant.* XIII 249). In the eyes of many of the 'devout' this must have awakened unhappy memories of the rule of the Hellenists whom the people hoped had now been overcome. On his second campaign of conquest, he took advantage of the quarrels between the two step-brothers, Antiochus VIII and Antiochus IX, and marched against Samaria (*Ant.* XIII 275–81). A twofold intervention by Antiochus IX Cyzicenus and his generals Callimandrus and Epicrates on behalf of Samaria provided the city no help. Hyrcanus captured Samaria (about 108–107 BCE) and 'not being content with that alone, he effaced it entirely and left it to be swept away by the mountain-torrents, for he dug beneath it until it fell into the beds of the torrents . . .' (*Ant.* XIII 281). Since, shortly before, he had by treason gained control of Beth-shan/Scythopolis, he had now pushed his territorial control to the borders of Galilee.

Like his predecessors, Hyrcanus took pains to maintain good relations with Rome. At least two decisions of the Roman senate regarding Judaea belong in his reign (*Ant.* XIII 259–66; XIV 247–55). The concrete reasons for these two initiatives in foreign affairs were probably disputes over the two fortresses Jaffa/Joppa and Gezer/Gazara, whose control had been in question since the time of Antiochus VII Sidetes. The exact dating of the two documents is, certainly, controversial (see *Schürer, 204–6; Stern, 1961, 7–22; Fischer, 64–77; Giovanni and Müller, 156–60) but there is good reason for placing the first near the beginning of Hyrcanus' reign (under Demetrius II, about 128–125 BCE?) and the second, which Josephus has certainly placed in the wrong chronological order, towards the end of his rule (under Antiochus IX?). In both documents, the treaty of friendship with the Romans is renewed and in the second 'Antiochus, the son of Antiochus' (= Antiochus IX?) is ordered to turn over all fortresses and, in particular, to withdraw his garrison from Joppa (*Ant.* XIV 249f.).

Internally, during Hyrcanus' reign, there occurred a decisive turn of events. As it progressively consolidated its rule, the Maccabaean/Hasmonaean family had moved further and further from the original goals of the Maccabaean movement. Developments were almost of necessity headed in the direction of a conflict between the ruling family and the 'devout'. When the party of the Pharisees, which had emerged from the circle of the devout and had originally been quite friendly to the Maccabaeans, demanded of Hyrcanus that he resign from the high priestly office and confine himself to his powers as head of state, an open breach occurred. The Pharisees had probably opposed Hyrcanus because of his tyrannical demeanour after the fashion of a Hellenistic potentate (*Ant.* XIII 288–98; b. Kiddushin 66a, although here mistakenly associated with Alexander Jannaeus rather than Hyrcanus I). With logical consistency, Hyrcanus turned to the old state-supporting party of the Sadducees, the wealthy priestly nobility, who because of their economic interests were more prepared to make religious compromises, a capacity which they had already demonstrated under the Hellenists prior to the Maccabaean uprising. Even later rabbinic literature, which mentions a number of Hyrcanus' anti-Pharisaic measures (see M. Maaser Sheni 5.15; Sotah 9.10) is still aware of this reversal in internal policies under Hyrcanus.

At his death, Hyrcanus left behind a state which, in addition to the Jewish heartland, included the most important cities of the coastal plain in the west, Samaria in the north, parts of Transjordan in the east, and Idumaea in the south. Not by chance does Josephus, therefore, praise him as the ideal image of a ruler with charismatic-messianic traits to whom God had granted 'three of the greatest privileges: the rule of the nation, the office of high priest, and the gift of prophecy' (*Ant.* XIII 299f.; *War* I 68f.).

B.   *Aristobulus I* (104–103 BCE)

The eldest son and successor of Hyrcanus, Aristobulus I, remained at the head of the government for only about one year. In an internal power struggle against both his mother, whom Hyrcanus had designated as regent, and his brothers, he succeeded in gaining the upper hand and was the first Hasmonaean officially to assume the title of king (*Ant.* XIII 301; *War* I 70; differently Strabo, *Geographica* XVI 2.40 = Stern, 1974, no. 115). In this shift towards a more Hellenistic form of government, Aristobulus completed a development which had begun long before and had become manifest under his father Hyrcanus. It was not by chance that Aristobulus, like his brothers, had a Greek name in addition to his Hebrew name (Jehudah) and that he is explicitly called a 'Philhellene' (friend of the Greek) by Josephus (*Ant.* XIII 318). Whether he minted coins is in dispute, as is also the case with his father. None of the coins which have been ascribed to him by many scholars carries his Greek name or his royal title.

During his brief reign, the most important event in foreign affairs was the conquest and forcible conversion to Judaism of extensive parts of Ituraea in the north (*Ant.* XIII 318; Timagenes = Stern, 1974, no. 81; Strabo = Stern, no. 100) although it is still unclear what precise area is meant. It is highly probable that the somewhat unclear report which Josephus has preserved does not actually refer to the heartland of the Ituraeans in Lebanon but to the northern part of Galilee. This is suggested by the fact that Hyrcanus had moved northward only as far as Samaria and Beth-shan/Scythopolis, and that the conquest of Galilee is otherwise not reported.

C.   *Alexander Jannaeus* (103–76 BCE)

Y. **Efron**, 'Shimon ben Shetah and King Yannai', *In Memory of Gedaliahu Alon: Essays in Jewish History and Philology*, Tel Aviv: Hakibbutz Hameuchad 1970, 69–132 (Hebrew); B. **Kanael**, 'Notes on Alexander

Jannaeus' Campaigns in the Coastal Region', *Tarbiz* XXIV, 1954/5, 9–15 (Hebrew); L. I. **Levine**, 'The Hasmonean Conquest of Strato's Tower', *IEJ* XXIV, 1974, 62–9; B. Z. **Luria**, *King Yannai*, Jerusalem: Kiryat Sepher 1960 (Hebrew); idem, *From Yannai to Herod*, Jerusalem: Kiryat Sepher 1973–4 (Hebrew); C. **Rabin**, 'Alexander Jannaeus and the Pharisees', *JJS* VII, 1956, 3–11; U. **Rappaport**, 'La Judée et Rome pendant le règne d'Alexandre Jannée', *REJ* CXXVII, 1968, 329–45; A. **Schalit**, 'Alexander Yannai's Conquests in Moab', *EI* I, 1951, 104–21 (Hebrew) = 'Die Eroberungen des Alexander Jannäus in Moab', *Theokrateia* I, Leiden: E. J. Brill 1969, 3–50; M. **Stern**, 'The Political Background of the Wars of Alexander Jannai', *Tarbiz* XXXIII, 1963/4, 325–36 (Hebrew).

With Alexander Jannaeus, the third son of John Hyrcanus ascended the throne. Together with his brothers, he had spent the brief reign of Aristobulus in prison. He married his sister-in-law, Salome Alexandra, who was Aristobulus' widow.

The reign of Alexander, whose characterization in Jewish history fluctuated as that of scarcely any other Hasmonaean, was marked by numerous wars without and by conflicts reaching the point of civil war with the Pharisees within. At the very outset of his reign, Alexander marched against Acco/Ptolemais and was defeated in the battle of Asophon (or Asaphon) by the Egyptian king Ptolemy Lathyros. At the time, the Egyptian king was ruling over Cyprus and was appealed to for help by the inhabitants of Acco (*Ant.* XIII 334f. and Levine). An intervention by Cleopatra, Ptolemy's mother, who regarded her own son as too powerful, saved Alexander from Ptolemy but did not remove the Egyptian threat (*Ant.* XIII 348–51). Cleopatra, before whom the Jewish territory practically lay wide open, seems to have seriously considered annexation of this area but, according to Josephus' account (*Ant.* XIII 352–4), was deterred from this plan only by the intervention of her Jewish general Ananias. A peace treaty was subsequently concluded in Scythopolis between Alexander and Cleopatra in which Alexander was given a free hand for his further activities (*Ant.* XIII 355). In the east, Alexander conquered Gadara, south-east of the Sea of Galilee, and the fortress Amathus. In the west, he took the coastal cities of Raphia and Anthedon as well as Gaza, which had for years been independent (96 BCE; *Ant.* XIII 356–64). A second campaign took him into the regions east of the Jordan against the Moabites and Gileadites, at which time the fortress Amathus was destroyed once and for all. He then plotted to start a war against the Nabataean king Obodas, but this turned out less successfully. Near

Gadara, Alexander was caught in an ambush and only escaped with great difficulty to Jerusalem (*Ant.* XIII 374f.).

Within the country, the conflict with the 'devout' which had been smouldering since the days of Hyrcanus reached its climax. The Pharisaic party, which had become an important force in the nation, was no longer disposed to tolerate the 'Hellenistic tyranny' of the Hasmonaean prince. (It is no accident that Alexander was the first Hasmonaean who, for certain, minted his own coinage bearing his title of king.) Josephus reports that the people, presumably incited by the Pharisees, threw lemons at the king while he was officiating as high priest during the feast of tabernacles. Significantly, the reason given for this outburst was that the king 'was descended from captives and was unfit to hold office and to sacrifice' (*Ant.* XIII 372f.; *War* I 88; see M. Sukkah 4.9; b. Yoma 26b; j. Sukkah IV 8 folio 54 d). This was of course a reference to the fact that Alexander's grandmother had apparently been held captive during the days of Antiochus Epiphanes and could have undergone sexual abuse (see Lev. 21.14 and *Ant.* XIII 292). Alexander took revenge against this popular sentiment and, according to Josephus, had his mercenaries massacre six thousand Jews (*Ant.* XIII 372f.). The story preserved in the rabbinic literature about the dispute between Jannaeus and Simeon ben Shetach (Bereshit Rabba 91.3; j. Berakhoth VII 2 folio 11b; b. Berakhoth 48a) also points, despite its legendary traits, to a fundamental conflict between the king and the Pharisees. When Alexander was forced to flee from the Nabataean king Obedas, open rebellion finally broke out and resulted in a civil war lasting for six years during which 'no fewer than fifty thousand Jews' lost their lives (*Ant.* XIII 376). The Pharisees even appealed for help to Demetrius III Eukairos, a son of Antiochus VIII Gryphos. In 88 BCE, he defeated Alexander's mercenary army near Shechem and with Jewish support! Alexander was forced to flee, but a fairly large number of Jews came over to his side after this defeat and Demetrius retreated. The remaining insurrectionists were exterminated and 800 of them, according to the report of Josephus (*Ant.* XIII 377–83), were crucified, their wives and children being slaughtered before their eyes. This reign of terror, which earned Alexander the title 'lion of wrath' in the Qumran literature (4QpNah I 5f. on Nah. 2.12f.), caused many domestic political enemies to leave the land for the remainder of his reign (*Ant.* XIII 383).

The domestic tranquillity which his radical actions had achieved was utilized by Alexander for new foreign activities. His main opponent – after the decline of the Seleucid kingdom and the conquest of Syria by the Armenian king Tigranes in 83 BCE – was the Nabataean king Aretas, whose power had greatly increased and who, at the onset, inflicted Alexander with defeat. This, however, did not prevent him from undertaking new campaigns in Transjordan. In three years (about 83–80 BCE), Alexander conquered the cities of Pella, Dium, and Gerasa in Gileaditis and Gaulana, Seleucia, and Gamala in Gaulanitis (*Ant.* XIII 393f.; *War* I 104f.). With these, his last conquests, Alexander Jannaeus was once again able to extend the area of Jewish control to a considerable degree, especially eastward. When he died three years later after a prolonged illness (Josephus says 'because of drunkenness') during the siege of the fortress Ragaba (near Gerasa), the constantly growing Hasmonaean state had reached its hitherto greatest extent (*Ant.* XIII 395–8).

D.   *Salome Alexandra* (76–67 BCE)

The reign of Alexander's widow and successor, Salome Alexandra, was a time of internal as well as external tranquillity. On his deathbed, Alexander is said to have instructed her to make peace with the Pharisees and 'not take any action, while you are on the throne, without their consent' (*Ant.* XIII 403). This complete reversal in domestic policy, which produced an agreement with the Pharisees, was indeed the most important characteristic of her reign. She appointed her son, Hyrcanus, a member of the Pharisaic party, to be high priest. She appears also to have reorganized the *gerousia*, the old council representing the nobility and priests, so as to favour the Pharisees. The Pharisees thereby became the real power in the country:

> And so, while she had the title of sovereign, the Pharisees had the power. For example, they recalled exiles, and freed prisoners, and, in a word, in no way differed from absolute rulers (*Ant.* XIII 409).

When the Pharisees finally began to take revenge on the supporters of Alexander Jannaeus who had advised him to murder the insurrectionists, open resistance broke out among the nobility. A delegation of Sadducees, which included Alexandra's younger son Aristobulus, was able to obtain a suspension of the Pharisaic excesses and thus, initially at least, an avoidance of armed conflict between the two rival parties (*Ant.* XIII 410–16). Alexandra, nevertheless, was not able to prevent Aristobulus, shortly before her death, from occupying, with Sadducean help, the most important fortresses and from thus gaining an important advantage in the inevitable power struggle with his brother Hyrcanus (*Ant.* XIII 417).

In the area of foreign affairs, Alexandra's reign progressed without any special occurrences – except for an unsuccessful campaign by Aristobulus against Damascus (*Ant.* XIII 418; *War* I 115f.). The danger of an invasion by Tigranes of Armenia, which threatened for a time, proved unfounded when Lucullus defeated Tigranes in 69 BCE and the Romans began preparation for an intervention in the affairs of Palestine (*Ant.* XIII 419–21).

E.   *Aristobulus II* (67–63 BCE)

F.-M. **Abel**, 'Le siège de Jérusalem par Pompée', *RB* LIV, 1947, 243–55; E. **Bammel**, 'Die Neuordnung des Pompeius und das römisch-jüdische Bündnis', *ZDPV* LXXV, 1959, 76–82.

As expected, immediately following the death of Salome Alexandra, civil war broke out between her two sons, Aristobulus II and Hyrcanus II. Hyrcanus was defeated at the battle of Jericho and relinquished his claims to the royal and high priestly offices in favour of Aristobulus (*Ant.* XIV 4–7; *War* I 120–2). This, however, did not signal the cessation of the internal struggle for power. Antipater, the Idumaean and father of the later king Herod, had brought the south under his control while functioning as governor of Idumaea. Antipater now intervened on Hyrcanus' side in the fraternal strife at the Hasmonaean court. He persuaded Hyrcanus to flee to the Nabataean king, Aretas, in Petra and to request Aretas' support against his brother. Upon Hyrcanus' assurance that he would return several cities which Alexander Jannaeus had taken from the Nabataeans, Aretas moved against Aristobulus and defeated him. Aristobulus fled to Jerusalem and was placed under siege on the temple mount by Aretas and Hyrcanus (*Ant.* XIV 8–21; *War* I 123–6).

In the meantime, however, the initiative in the power struggle between the different parties in Jerusalem no longer lay exclusively with those directly involved. The Romans, who gained entrance into the Qumran literature as the 'Kittim' (see 1QpHab and 4QpNah), had, under Pompey, pushed ahead to the vicinity of the borders of the Jewish state. They skilfully took advantage, for their own purposes of course, of the internal conflict between the two Hasmonaean brothers. Pompey sent the later governor Scaurus to Judaea. He received the rival groups, who were attempting to outbid each other with money, and finally decided for Aristobulus. Aretas and Hyrcanus were forced to retreat and were subsequently defeated by Aristobulus' pursuing forces (*Ant.* XIV 29–33; *War* I 127–30).

In the year 64 BCE, Pompey sealed the fate of the Seleucid kingdom once and for all and in the spring of 63 BCE set out from Antioch(?) for Damascus. There no fewer than three Jewish delegations sought to gain his favour. In addition to Aristobulus and Hyrcanus, representatives of the 'devout' appeared before Pompey. The latter aspired to a restoration of the old theocracy (*Ant.* XIV 41–5). Pompey, whose immediate intent was to move against the Nabataeans, did not decide in favour of any of the contending parties but admonished all to remain quiet until he should find opportunity to put Judaean affairs in order. When Aristobulus, however, did not observe this arrangement, Pompey changed his plans and moved on to Jerusalem by way of Pella and Jericho. There he took Aristobulus prisoner and besieged the city. Finally, the followers of Hyrcanus opened the gates and permitted Pompey's emissary Piso to take possession of the city and the royal palace, while the supporters of the imprisoned Aristobulus entrenched themselves on the temple mount. Late in the autumn of 63 BCE, Pompey captured the temple mount, attacking from the north, and thus brought Jerusalem completely under Roman control (*Ant.* XIV 61–76; *War* I 145–51).

Pompey redrew the borders of the Jewish state by withdrawing from Jewish jurisdiction all the coastal cities and all non-Jewish cities in Transjordan as well as Scythopolis and Samaria, placing these directly under Scaurus, the first governor of the new Roman province of Syria. He set Hyrcanus over the remainder of the state as high priest, but without the title of king, and moreover made him tributary to the Romans (*Ant.* XIV 73f.; *War* I 153f.). He took Aristobulus, his two daughters and two sons, Alexander and Antigonus, with him to Rome (Alexander escaped on the way) and made them march in his triumphal procession. Thus after less than one hundred years, the independence of the Jewish nation, achieved with great difficulty by the Maccabaeans against the Seleucids, had fallen victim to that great power, Rome.

XI

THE ROMAN ERA

At the beginning of the Roman period, the Jewish people were consciously or unconsciously looking for identity in a world which offered them thought categories and life-styles repugnant to their own genius. At the end they had succumbed outwardly to the pressure of alien peoples and alien ideas, but retained unseen those qualities which enabled them to survive their apparent destruction.

The stresses and contradictions of the age are embodied in the historian Josephus, who is the paramount source for the period, even at times the paramount personality. This is true in particular of his *Jewish War*, of which only I 1–119 fall outside the period, and to a lesser degree in the *Antiquities*, whose Books XIV–XX cover the period exactly, except that Josephus concluded Book XX at 66 CE and refers the reader to the *War* for events from this time onwards. The *War* seems to be mainly accurate in what it asserts and to imply inaccuracy only by its omissions. This fact is illustrated by the *Life* which Josephus published with the *Antiquities*. The *Life* is not a true autobiography but a rebuttal of criticism of his conduct in Galilee as narrated in the *War*. Its evidence is noted where relevant. The *War* is indispensable for the whole period; it may be supplemented or modified by the *Antiquities* for 67 BCE to 66 CE, but is virtually the only source worthy of the term for 66–74 CE, especially as Josephus writes about this period from direct observation as a participant. Motives for distortion or falsification are evident; some such suspected blemishes are noticed below, but they are the blemishes typical of a primary source. Josephus' use of many written sources remains unproved. Use of oral sources was no doubt manifold, and included Jewish deserters as well as Romans. It is hard to know in which category to place himself.

It is then probably wrong to argue for the use of other sources in the *War*, with the exception of Nicolaus of Damascus (64 BCE to beginning of first century CE), who appears in that book indeed only as a courtier of Herod, but some parallel passages in the *Antiquities* suggest that Nicolaus' work was used as a source in the *War*'s account of Herod. In the *Antiquities*, Nicolaus is praised as a historian and Josephus seems certainly to have used him in this work for material on Herod, revealing his now more open hostility to the king and on several occasions his critical though respectful appraisal of Nicolaus. In the *Antiquities*, Josephus writes to recommend Judaism not only to Romans but also to the entire Hellenistic world; he is therefore able freely to contrast Jewish ways with those of Herod. When he condemns him it is probably from his own judgment: the material obtained from Nicolaus could be used as easily in reproach as in adulation of Herod.

Josephus appeals also to Strabo several times in *Antiquities*, XIV and once in XV. He appeals to the evidence of the Roman historian Livy on one occasion (*Ant.* XIV 68).

Philo of Alexandria becomes a primary source in his *Legatio ad Caium* for material concerning Agrippa I and the affair of Caius' statue. His *In Flaccum* is not directly relevant for Judaea. The character of Tacitus as a historian of Judaism is noted later in the text.

§1. FROM ALEXANDRA TO POMPEY (67–57 BCE)

F.-M. **Abel**, 'Le siège de Jérusalem par Pompée', *RB* LIV, 1947, 243–55; E. **Bammel**, 'Die Neuordnung des Pompeius und das römisch-jüdische Bündnis', *ZDPV* LXXV, 1959, 76–82; idem, 'The Organization of Palestine by Gabinius', *JJS* XII, 1961, 159–62; H. **Bietenhard**, 'Die Dekapolis von Pompeius bis Traian: Ein Kapitel aus der neutestamentlichen Zeitgeschichte', *ZDPV* LXXIX, 1963, 24–58; A. H. M. **Jones**, *The Cities of the Eastern Roman Provinces*, London: Oxford University Press 1937, ²1971; B. **Kanael**, 'The Partition of Judea by Gabinius', *IEJ* VII, 1957, 98–106; A. D. **Momigliano**, 'Ricerche sull organizzazione della Giudea sotto il dominio romano (63 a.C.–70 d.C.)', *ASNP* III, 1934, 183–221, 347–96 = Amsterdam: A. M. Hakkert 1967; S. T. **Parker**, 'The Decapolis Reviewed', *JBL* XCIV, 1975, 437–41; A. **Schalit**, *König Herodes: Der Mann und sein Werk*, SJ 4, 1969, 1–36; E. M. **Smallwood**, 'Gabinius' Organisation of Palestine', *JJS* XVIII, 1967, 89–92; S. **Zeitlin**, *The Rise and Fall of the Judaean State* I, Philadelphia: Jewish Publication Society of America, 1962, 317–63.

In the Hasmonaean period, a Jewish patriotic movement against Hellenistic influences so far succumbed to them that it embarked on adventures typical of a Hellenistic people. The high priesthood was usurped and turned into kingship, a queen ruled because she was the widow of such a high priest, and on her death her sons were rivals for this largely secularized office. The elder Hyrcanus II (high priest 67 BCE) was the legitimate heir to the position and his temperament seems to have fitted him for the older religious duties rather than for the new political scene in which he found himself. It was a scene where his younger brother Aristobulus II, possessed of charm and energy, moved with a brash confidence as typical of the times as it was unjustified by events (*Ant.* XIV 4–7; *War* I 117–22). The reluctant Hyrcanus was a centre for the rival activity of men representing four nationalities – Idumaea, Nabataea, Rome and Parthia – though himself willing enough to remain in lay obscurity. The first two entered the stage almost simultaneously: Antipater the Idumaean called upon Aretas III of Nabataea to assist Hyrcanus (*Ant.* XIV 8–20; *War* I 123–6). Antipater's father (also called Antipater) had been a local commander (*strategos*) under Alexander Jannaeus, a title inherited by the son, who evidently wished to maintain and extend his power by supporting a feeble figurehead rather than lose it to the energetic Aristobulus. Hyrcanus thus gained an able ally by his very weakness, but he had to promise to restore to Aretas twelve towns which his father Alexander had taken. Aretas seems to have been a veteran warrior who had at some time rather fleetingly possessed parts of Syria, and by occasional activity outside his own ill-defined borders had staked his claim to be considered yet another petty Hellenistic prince (see *Schürer, 578f.). He received Hyrcanus at Petra and made a successful attack on Aristobulus who retreated with a few supporters to the temple mount in Jerusalem.

Rome now made its entry. The territory where its famous representative Pompey had been waiting in the wings of the Judaean stage is, along with Judaea itself, in reality no subordinate scene; Cilicia, Syria (destined to include Judaea and to be united in one province with Cilicia), and Egypt, with the contiguous parts of the Mediterranean Sea, provided the stage for the events which decided the fate not only of Judaea but also of the Roman Republic. Cn. Pompeius Magnus was more than the rival of Julius Caesar; he was an excellent general and possessed political qualities which have led many both contemporary and later judges to believe that if he rather than Caesar had been victorious in their final struggle he might have found a way to preserve rather than to make obsolete the constitution of the republic. His work in the east included much which was the sheer restoration of order. He had defeated the pirates of the

Eastern Mediterranean and, assisted by able lieutenants, reduced Mithridates of Pontus to the loss of power which led to his suicide in the following year (69 BCE). In the years 64–63 BCE, Pompey restored order in Syria which after the departure of Tigranes was overrun by brigands. His lieutenants Gabinius and Scaurus had in 64 BCE favoured Aristobulus, but in 63 BCE Pompey received deputations at Damascus and decided in favour of Hyrcanus (*Ant.* XIV 41–6; *War* I 128–31). The occasion presents an opportunity to consider the various factions involved. Antipater appeared as ambassador for Hyrcanus when the final decision was made, while a certain Nicodemus appeared for Aristobulus, who made enemies by accusing Gabinius and Scaurus of corruption and by his entourage of flashy young men. The 'nation' (*ethnos*) significantly enough pleaded against Aristobulus and Hyrcanus (*Ant.* XIV 41). If we may trust Josephus, this conservative group objected to being governed by a king rather than by priests and complained that both brothers, though descendants of priests, were trying to enslave the nation to an alien form of rule. Such a view was deeply entrenched in the Jewish people and found its expression both in quietism and in nationalist zeal. Not for nothing does Josephus call its protagonists 'the nation'.

Aristobulus showed no disposition to accept the overlordship of Pompey and marched with an army into Judaea. This was his undoing; Pompey was about to set out for Nabataea and warned Aristobulus, though courteously, to 'keep quiet', fearing that he would rouse the country and hinder Pompey's return. Although Josephus says this is what Aristobulus did (*Ant.* XIV 47), his exact reaction on Pompey's departure is not entirely clear, except that he took refuge in Alexandrium (*Qarn Sartabeh*), a hill fortress apparently built by the Maccabees on a commanding and strategic height which towers above the Jordan valley at its junction with the Wadi Fariya, and commanded an important crossroads. He might have been more successful if he could have remained there, though no doubt it was not an easy fortress to supply. When Pompey appeared at Coreae, opposite the fortress, Aristobulus agreed to leave but then repented of his submission and took refuge in Jerusalem (*Ant.* XIV 48–53; *War* I 133–7). This was to exchange one fortress for another, although Jerusalem was never easy to protect on its northern side, and it was here that the Roman army broke into it. Before being forced to lay siege to the city, Pompey had hopes of a peaceful surrender, since Aristobulus once more repented of his resistance, but on this occasion it was his supporters who would not follow him. There seems no need for Niese's conjecture that these were 'rebels' (*stasiōtōn*) rather than 'soldiers' (*stratiōtōn*) (*Ant.* XIV 56). The activity of Aristobulus was fiercely patriotic but in a narrow and limited sense: he was a Hasmonaean who inherited the pugnacity and persistence of his father Alexander Jannaeus, but his concept of the nation seems typically Hellenistic in that it was sharply concentrated upon his own person and fortunes. Either he or some unknown adviser influenced his policy in different and apparently inconsistent directions, one of which was to play the part of a guerrilla warrior such as fell to the lot of other leaders and ambitious men of the period who for the time being were not strong enough to engage in open warfare. In this role he made use of the lofty and impressive Alexandrium, one of a number of such places which were destined to play their part in Judaea's subsequent history. Those who refused to yield to Pompey were no doubt of the stuff of which zealots were made, whether it is appropriate to call them by this name or not. Their nationalism had its roots in the keen religious exclusiveness of the early Maccabees and especially their Hasidic supporters; at the far end of the spectrum, among the heroic pacifists, were the priests who would not abandon their duties even when the temple was overrun, and were cut down as they were performing them (*Ant.* XIV 64–8; *War* I 150f.).

Pompey's own behaviour was not outrageous, except in one particular; he entered the Holy of Holies with 'not a few others' and saw there the furniture which it was proper only for the high priest to view. Josephus does not seem anxious to dwell on this incident and goes on to commend Pompey for not taking any of the temple treasure and for restoring worship there (*Ant.* XIV 71–3; *War* I 152f.). Pompey's settlement of the east, ratified under the Lex Manilia and carried out in most of its details by his able lieutenant Gabinius, was a decisive event for the countries concerned, if only for the obvious reason that henceforth Rome took her place in the long line of foreign conquerors to whom they, among them Judaea, had been tributary. The Hellenistic empires both of Ptolemies and Seleucids had made them accustomed but not acquiescent to such overlordship. Their own rebel leaders had in rather less than a century from John Hyrcanus I onwards assumed the guise and latterly the open title and manners of Hellenistic princes. The miracle was the survival of any genuine patriotic feeling which could distinguish itself from Hellenism. Certainly the Roman settlement did nothing to encourage the Jewish nation to maintain its own pride and peculiar ethos; Bithynia and Cilicia were enlarged and two more territories, Crete and Syria, including Judaea, were added to the Roman empire. This policy was continuous with that of the protection of local inhabitants from piracy which had from the beginning been one of Pompey's main tasks. The Hasmonaeans lost the coastal strip from Gaza to Carmel, Samaria, and above all the cities of the Decapolis which were returned to their inhabitants. These cities thus became city-states with treaties binding them to Rome (*Ant.* XIV 74–6; *War* I 155–7). Although the Hasmonaeans retained, along with Judaea, Idumaea, Peraea, and Galilee, the last-named was too near southern Syria and the Decapolis for the inhabitants to be controlled effectively from Jerusalem, in either a political or religious sense. Galilee continued to be known for its bandits and for its religious eccentrics, and it is significant that some of the places named in the gospel of Mark as scenes of the early activity of Jesus were southern Syria (the districts of Tyre and Sidon) and the Decapolis alongside his native Galilee.

Although the Pompeian settlement gave an undoubted impetus to Hellenistic civilization and the idea of the city-state, the choice of local ruler was sometimes careless and often looked like cynical disregard for any interest other than that of Rome. This may be true of the recognition of Hyrcanus, which however extended to his high priesthood and not to kingship (*Ant.* XIV 73; *War* I 153). Leaving Syria – which meant at this time a territory from the Euphrates to Egypt – to the government of Scaurus, with whom he left two legions, Pompey returned to Rome with captive Aristobulus, the latter's two daughters and a younger son Antigonus. Another son, Alexander, escaped and began a campaign for the recovery of his father's coveted land. Gabinius, who arrived in Syria as *legatus* in succession to Scaurus in 57 BCE, found that Alexander had fortified a number of the hill-fortresses, Alexandrium (*Qarn Sartabeh*), Hyrcanium (*Ḥirbert Mird*), and Machaerus (*Mukāwer*) and occupied them with his troops (*Ant.* XIV 83; *War* I 161).

Alexander was able to draw together a significant number of supporters willing to serve with him in somewhat desperate conditions. His vigorous personality probably encouraged that considerable number who were still fired with the ideals of the early Maccabees, however significantly both times and leaders had changed. The star of the Hasmonaeans was in inevitable decline, but another twenty years were to elapse before it was extinguished altogether. For the time being Rome was to have a great deal of trouble from them; Alexander was defeated but took refuge in Alexandrium. A number of his force were encamped in front of the fortress and were again defeated by a Roman army which included the rising Mark Antony and a force under Antipater, besides Jews loyal to Rome (*Ant.* XIV 84–6; *War* I 162–6). Alexandrium, for all its apparent natural strength, was not adequately organized for a long siege or for the accommodation of large numbers. Some realization of these facts and the general hopelessness of resistance to Rome may well have influenced the wife of Aristobulus, Alexander's mother, in her intercession with Gabinius. Alexander had already submitted by a herald's message and offered to hand over the three strongholds when she begged Gabinius to dismantle them so that they should encourage no further warlike adventures (*Ant.* XIV 89f.; *War* I 167f.).

Gabinius' implementation of Pompey's settlement proceeded apace even before the reduction of Alexandrium, in which Mark Antony distinguished himself. The accounts in Josephus in the *Antiquities* and the *War* are not altogether clear or consistent, but the main outline is clear (*Ant.* XIV 90f.; *War* I 169f.). It seems that Hyrcanus was given only the supervision of the temple and its worship, and that the city of Jerusalem as a political entity was entrusted to an aristocratic group. It is not clear whether this was in addition to one of the five divisions of the country, one of which was centred on Jerusalem. The other centres were Jericho, Sepphoris in Galilee, Amathus and 'Gadara'.

The political concept underlying this division of the country demands for its understanding in part a solution of the geographical problems; which cities were regarded as the best centres from the Roman point of view – were they the strongest or those most easily accessible? Jericho and Sepphoris for reasons both of status and position were obvious choices. Amathus, east of the Jordan, is also intelligible for its position not far south of the site which was to be chosen by Herod Antipas for his modern secular capital, and may have been already provided with baths and other Roman amenities. 'Gadara' cannot be the Greek city of the Decapolis (*Schürer, 268 n. 5) and Gazara, on the site of the ancient Gezer, has been a strong candidate among scholars. Kanael plausibly suggests Adora (west-south-west of Hebron) which would give a centre further south such as seems to be required.

§2. THE REVOLT OF ARISTOBULUS AND THE RISE
OF HEROD (56–37 BCE)

T. **Corbishley**, 'The Chronology of the Reign of Herod the Great', *JTS* XXXVI, 1935, 22–32; N. C. **Debevoise**, *A Political History of Parthia*,

Chicago: University of Chicago Press 1938; W. E. **Filmer**, 'The Chronology of the Reign of Herod the Great', *JTS* NS XVII, 1966, 283–98; A. H. M. **Jones**, *The Herods of Judaea*, London: Oxford University Press 1938, ²1967, 1–48; Y. **Meshorer**, *Jewish Coins of the Second Temple Period*, Tel Aviv: Am Hassefer 1967; G. F. **Moore**, *Judaism in the First Centuries of the Christian Era* I, Cambridge: Harvard University Press 1927; J. **Neusner**, *The Rabbinic Traditions about the Pharisees before 70*, I–III, Leiden: E. J. Brill 1971; A. **Schalit**, *König Herodes*, SJ 4, 1969, 53–97; S. **Zeitlin**, *The Rise and Fall of the Judaean State* I, 1962, 364–411.

In 56 BCE the Hasmonaeans once more demonstrated their tenacity and pugnacity; indeed the escape that year from prison in Rome of Aristobulus and his second son Antigonus (*Ant.* XIV 92; *War* I 171) demonstrates also the existence of factors at which we can only guess. There were many influential men in Rome who were willing to help such claimants if they espied a possible advantage to themselves, and we need not doubt that the two warriors owed their escape to intrigue in Rome rather than to skill and daring alone. Aristobulus attempted the same kind of adventure which his elder son Alexander had recently failed to bring to a conclusion. He too was defeated and sent back to Rome (*Ant.* XIV 92–7; *War* I 171–4). His ability to rally any army to his side and Alexander's later efforts just immediately after this abortive adventure, when Gabinius was absent in Egypt (*Ant.* XIV 98–102; *War* I 176–8), again demonstrate the continuing loyalty to the Hasmonaeans of a considerable number of the people. Aristobulus used the fortress of Machaerus as a refuge when driven back over the Jordan, illustrating again the indispensable part which these strongholds played in popular resistance to Rome.

At this point Josephus records the return of Gabinius to Rome (remarking that his authorities for the period now closing, Nicolaus and Strabo, do not contradict one another in any particular) and introduces M. Licinius Crassus, the new proconsul over Syria (*Ant.* XIV 104; *War* I 179). Something like nemesis attended Crassus in the east: without the scruples of Pompey, he plundered the Jerusalem temple of all its wealth and in 53 BCE he invaded Parthia, whose influence on the history of Judaea was as yet indirect. On this occasion, by inflicting a severe defeat which included the death of Crassus at Carrhae, the Parthians, vicarious avengers, cast before them the long shadow they were destined to throw over the complicated history of Judaea (*Ant.* XIV 105f., 119; *War* I 179). C. Cassius Longinus, the quaestor of Crassus, thus held power in Syria, resisting the Parthians and maintaining order in the years 53–51 BCE. Josephus, in describing the situation, gives the impression that Cassius' main object was to stay the Parthian advance and that for this he had to make sure of the subjugation of Judaea. Cassius fell upon Tarichaeae, a city on the western shore of the Sea of Galilee, took it, and enslaved thirty thousand men. Since, in addition, Cassius put to death Peitholaus who had 'succeeded to the [leader-ship of] the rebellious activity of Aristobulus' we must suppose that the men of Tarichaeae were actual or potential rebels (*Ant.* XIV 119–22; *War* I 180). The incident illustrates the complexity of the popular resistance. This Peitholaus and Malichus, a relative or friend of Hyrcanus, had been the leaders of Jewish forces serving under Gabinius in his campaign against Alexander. Their hostility to the latter was internecine, for at heart they were anti-Roman patriots. The activity of Peitholaus seems to have been clandestine, for Cassius was persuaded to kill him by Antipater, whose fortunes at this moment took a decidedly upward turn. At this point, Josephus formally introduces Antipater as having married Cypros of Arabia (i.e. Nabataea) and having by her four sons, Phasael, Herod, Joseph, and Pheroras, and a daughter Salome (*Ant.* XIV 121; *War* I 181). Josephus knows well that Antipater has been met before but perhaps he wishes to draw attention to his formidable family, who are now to take more and more of the prominent parts on the stage of Judaean history, a stage becoming increasingly the most important scene for the declining history of the Roman republic, and for the war of the two main factions, the Caesars and the republicans, and from 49 to 46 BCE that of Caesar and Pompey.

Antipater increased his influence by rendering Caesar consider-able service. Caesar's defiance of the republic and his virtual seizure of Rome in 49 BCE was facilitated by the flight of Pompey, but the influence of the latter and of his subordinates in the east was of paramount importance, and Caesar knew that he must gain the mastery in this area, including the corn-supplying country of Egypt. His immediate move was to release the imprisoned Aristobulus and give him two legions with which to oppose Pompey's supporters in Syria (*Ant.* XIV 123; *War* I 183). The friends of Pompey who remained in Rome were equal to the crisis: Aristobulus was poisoned. A further disastrous blow was struck at the Hasmonaean family at this time; Aristobulus' elder son Alexander, presumably a prisoner since his failure against Gabinius, was beheaded at Antioch on Pompey's orders by the latter's father-in-law, Metellus Scipio (*Ant.* XIV 124f.; *War* I 184f.). Those patriots who supported the

Hasmonaeans now had only one man on whom they could pin their
hopes; this was Antigonus, the younger son of Aristobulus. It was
ironic that, perhaps inevitably, he lost the support of Caesar, which
in effect decided both his fate and the grim course of events which
followed.

Caesar's campaign in Egypt, begun by his landing there in 48 BCE
after his victory at Pharsalus, did not at first go well. Pompey had
indeed been decisively beaten; and was murdered when he landed in
Egypt in September of that year. Caesar's initial lack of success was
due in part to inability to establish contact with the forces brought to
his aid by Mithridates of Pergamum in the spring of 47 BCE, for they
were hindered by the Jews in and near Pelusium. Antipater, seizing
the opportunity to render Caesar a service, reversed the situation
with considerable help from Hyrcanus. Pelusium was captured and
the local Jewish population compelled to assist Antipater with his
force of 3,000 Jews; Hyrcanus even persuaded the Egyptian Jews to
go over to Caesar (*Ant.* XIV 127–36; *War* I 187–92). In 47 BCE the
victorious Caesar came to Syria and made a settlement which was
popular ever afterwards with the Jewish nation as a whole but which
was a bitter disappointment to Antigonus. Hyrcanus was confirmed
as high priest and even given back the title of ethnarch of which he
had been deprived by Gabinius. Most significantly, Antipater was
given the authority of procurator of Judaea, which at this time
meant something much closer to steward or representative (*Ant.*
XIV 137–40; *War* I 193f.); there was as yet no imperial authority
from whom he might derive that great power over a province which
from Claudius onwards is associated with the word. Indeed the title
reflects personal responsibility to Caesar.

In *Antiquities* XIV 190–216, Josephus has compiled a fragmentary
collection of decrees and letters to cities concerning privileges to
Jews, first from Caesar and then others dating from a month after his
assassination, the last being a decree addressed to the Ephesians
under the proconsulship of Brutus about 43 BCE. Josephus concludes the collection by remarking that further decrees existed 'in
favour of Hyrcanus and our nation'. The difficulties of arranging
these chronologically, and especially of identifying the original decree of Caesar of the year 47 BCE (if indeed it is represented here), are
discussed by *Schürer, 273 n. 23. But the collection is certainly
evidence for that beneficence towards Jews which occasioned the
grief which Jewish crowds demonstrated at his burial in Rome (see
Suetonius, *Julius Caesar* 84.5).

Caesar now disappears from the Judaean stage, occupied with successful campaigns in other parts of the Roman empire against the Pompeians but destined to be removed altogether from the world stage by assassination in 44 BCE.

Antipater was now for a short time virtually master of Judaea; Phasael he appointed governor of Jerusalem and Herod to the administration of Galilee (*Ant.* XIV 158; *War* I 203). Herod's energetic suppression of rebel groups led by Hezekiah, the first effective native resister whom we meet in this region, is remarkable less for its success than for the opposition which it aroused in Jerusalem among the Sanhedrin. The death of Hezekiah and a large number of his followers was regarded by them as murder by Herod and they tried to make Hyrcanus bring Herod to book for it. Sextus Caesar, legate in Syria, wrote to defend Herod, who was able to escape his armed guard and to fly to Damascus, Antipater and Phasael dissuading him from marching on Jerusalem (*Ant.* XIV 159f., 168–84; *War* I 204–15). In 46 BCE the Pompeians enjoyed a temporary success; Q. Caecilius Bassus acted as ruler of Syria after bringing about the assassination of S. Caesar; but Caesar sent L. Statius Murcus to replace his relative and he besieged Bassus in Apamea with the help of Q. Marcius Crispus, governor of Bithynia. After Caesar's assassination in 44 BCE, Cassius, who had been named as governor of Syria by the master whom he had assisted in murdering, returned to the province and won over both the official Roman governors and the legion which had supported Bassus. Cassius went on to levy high taxes for the cause of the conspirators; once more Antipater changed sides, pursuing his policy of supporting whichever Roman seemed most likely to establish himself, and undertook the task of collecting the taxes, dividing the task among Phasael, Herod, and Malichus, a concession presumably to Hyrcanus which is hard to understand, for Malichus was as ill-disposed to Antipater as Cassius was to him (*Ant.* XIV 268–76; *War* I 216–22). We may guess that it was not only the comparative slowness with which he gathered his share of the taxes but more open hostility (at which Josephus hints rather obscurely; *Ant.* XIV 273) which occasioned Cassius' enmity; Malichus probably inherited from his erstwhile colleague Peitholaus the leadership of popular revolt, and may have shared some of the religious scruples natural in a supporter of Hyrcanus. His position among Jews was in that case strong and explains the hostility between him and Antipater the Idumaean as well as Antipater's softness towards him, while the suspicions of Cassius are equally natural. Whatever the true ambitions of Malichus, he was a ruthless and cunning man: he procured the death of Antipater by poison and was himself subsequently murdered on the seashore near Tyre at the behest of Herod (*Ant.* XIV 277–93; *War* I 225–35).

These last fateful events occurred in 43 BCE when Cassius was planning to leave Syria. He left in the following year, and the province immediately showed its weakness after the oppression which it had recently suffered, for it became the prey of different ambitious local rulers (*Ant.* XIV 294–9; *War* I 236–40). Marion of Tyre seized some Galilaean territory in spite of the efforts of Herod, who was more successful in thwarting the attempt of Antigonus to obtain, with the help of Marion and of Mennaeus, a bandit-like ruler of Chalcis, the throne which he so persistently regarded as his right. Herod's success against Antigonus was welcomed in Jerusalem by Hyrcanus, with whom Herod was now united by being betrothed to Mariamme (who was to be his second wife), a Hasmonaean indeed since she was the granddaughter of Hyrcanus through her mother Alexandra, his daughter, and his great-niece through her father Alexander, Aristobulus II's son (*Ant.* XIV 300).

A new turn was given to events in Syria in 42 BCE by the battle of Philippi in Macedonia, where the remnants of the Pompeians, including Cassius, were defeated by Octavian and Antony, the latter receiving Asia as his sphere of rule. While he was in Bithynia he received a deputation from a number of Jews to complain about Herod and Phasael. Josephus describes these men by a phrase which ordinarily means 'those in office' (*Ant.* XIV 302; *War* I 242). It is perhaps a mistake to describe them as the nobility or as Jewish aristocrats, which assimilates them to Hellenistic politics. More likely, they were members of the 'sanhedrins' which had been set up by Gabinius and had an undisputed right in Roman law to speak on behalf of the people. Herod appeared at the same hearing and relied not only on Antony's old friendship with Antipater but also on money to ensure a decision in his favour. Hyrcanus, who came to a later similar meeting at Antioch, was as successful in procuring the action of Antony to restore the territory taken by Marion and to emancipate Jews enslaved by Cassius (*Ant.* XIV 303–5; *War* I 242). That Antony was moved by private motives rather than by justice is hardly in doubt; the deputation to Bithynia did not obtain a hearing and that to Antioch and a subsequent deputation to Tyre were put to death (*Ant.* XIV 324–9; *War* I 243–7). The persistence of these men, representing the nation rather than its more warlike and am- bitious members, is a remarkable tribute to their courage and the extent of their sufferings. The only further result was that Antony made Phasael and Herod tetrarchs, Hyrcanus retaining his title as ethnarch (*Ant.* XIV 326; *War* I 244).

In 40 BCE the dalliance of Antony with Cleopatra VII of Egypt and his preoccupation later with affairs in Italy, together with anti-Caesarean intrigue, gave an unexpected chance to the surviving Hasmonaean Antigonus. The intrigue was of a desperate and dangerous kind. Q. Labienus had been sent by Cassius to solicit the help of the Parthians before Philippi. After that battle Labienus had to remain in Parthia, but in 41 BCE he obtained Parthian help with which to oppose Antony, and the Parthian armies overran most of the territory in the Near East. The Parthian ruler, Pacorus, son of king Orodes, marched down the Phoenician coast and sent a detachment to Jerusalem, while the satrap Barzapharnes took the inland road southwards. Antigonus had collected some supporters and entered Jerusalem, where he was fighting a recurrent battle with Herod and Phasael. When Pacorus' representative arrived he persuaded Phasael and Hyrcanus to come to the camp of Barzapharnes. It is not clear why Phasael, though warned by Herod, walked into this trap. When Herod heard that both had been made prisoners he escaped with his family and settled them in the hill-fortress of Masada, on the western shore of the Dead Sea, under the direction of his brother Joseph. The Parthians behaved as though they knew well enough that they were the real masters; Antigonus indeed was set up as king, and enjoyed for the moment the satisfaction of dealing with Phasael, who committed suicide, and Hyrcanus whose ears were cut off to prevent him permanently from being high priest (*Ant.* XIV 327–69; *War* I 248–73).

If it was obvious to everyone that Antigonus reigned as a puppet of the Parthians, it was obvious also to Herod that any hope of reversing his ill-fortune depended as certainly on obtaining the favour of Rome, which he energetically set about securing. Though not without difficulty, he made the journey thither and was entirely successful in obtaining the support of Antony, who saw the advantages of appointing Herod king of Judaea rather than following the usual Roman practice of supporting the local legitimate ruler (*Ant.* XIV 370–80; *War* I 274–81). Josephus makes a remarkable list of motives influencing Antony: pity, reflections on the mutability of fortune even for great ones, his old friendship with Antipater, both the money promised now and that delivered in the past, but above all the conviction that Antigonus was an enemy of Rome, in Josephus' phrase 'a rebel'. Octavian concurring for a list of reasons no less impressive and less mixed, Herod's position was ratified by a ceremonial decree of the senate (*Ant.* XIV 381–5; *War* I 282–5). He left as soon as possible and landed at Ptolemais in 39 BCE.

Antigonus was still reigning in Jerusalem, after paying heavy tribute to the legate appointed by Antony, P. Ventidius Bassus, who defeated the Parthians, Labienus being taken and killed. Herod apparently had no difficulty in raising an army 'both of foreigners and of fellow-countrymen' and appears to have made quickly an impression of one who, enjoying Roman support, was most likely to succeed. Unhindered by the local Roman commanders, he began by subduing Galilee and then turned south to set free his family from their virtual prison in Masada, taking Joppa on the way. Nevertheless his forces were not sufficient to conquer Antigonus nor to take Jerusalem (*Ant.* XIV 394–405; *War* I 290–6).

Ventidius had left for a further campaign against renewed Parthian attack; the forces he left in Palestine under his assistant Silo were not enough to strengthen Herod's for a siege, and for a time there seemed a chance for Antigonus to win over the Romans by bribery. Even Ventidius' second victory over the Parthians, in which Pacorus was killed, was not immediately decisive for Judaea since it was not until Herod, finding it necessary also to quell renewed risings in Galilee, appealed directly to Antony so that larger forces were sent under the command of C. Sosius, Antony's new governor of Syria. These larger forces defeated those of Antigonus in a battle at Isana, twenty miles north of Jerusalem, and the stage was set for the siege of the city. It lasted five months and, in spite of the extreme bravery of the defenders, Antigonus was forced to surrender to Sosius. Herod demanded his death and Antony found it impossible to refuse, recognizing the danger of a Hasmonaean remaining alive even if, like his father, as a prisoner who adorned a triumph in Rome. This was not the fate of Antigonus, who was beheaded at Antioch (*Ant.* XIV 406–91; *War* I 297–357). Thus perished the last of the Hasmonaeans to rule, a man of vigour and courage who commanded much popular support at a time when the odds against him were always too great; the Jewish inscriptions on his coins exhibited the name of Mattathias and the title of high priest, though in Greek he appears as king (see Meshorer, 60–3, 124–6). This was not distinctive, but the table of the shewbread and a small representation (accompanying the word king in Greek) of the menorah are motifs eloquent either of some piety or of a desire to court patriotic feeling. There is no doubt that this was forthcoming in large measure and that many, for whom the by now legendary Mattathias of his ancestry took his place among the heroes of the nation, willingly gave their lives for a patriotic cause with which they could identify, that of a Hellenistic prince whose claim to the high priesthood might be technically weak but was made with pride. Nor was he lacking either in charm or ability. Herod's success was due less to superior ability than to the might of Rome. He inspired fear rather than popularity; but he had enormous persistence, friends in high places and above all the ruthlessness which makes or breaks a man determined to attain the highest position.

The extreme kind of Jewish patriotism demanded obedience to the law of God regardless of the consequences, and attributed national disaster to divine punishment, seeing no virtue in a heroic war which because of the nation's sin could not be holy. Such uncompromising piety is so rare that an historical instance of it at the beginning of Herod's reign deserves record. Two sages are reported by Josephus to have advised the people to submit to Herod and it appears that their ground was belief that he brought a just punishment on them (*Ant.* XV 3). Josephus calls them Pollion and Samaias, and creates a problem by calling the former a Pharisee and the latter his disciple, for in the previous book he records that Samaias prophesied dire punishment on the people who would not themselves punish and restrain Herod when on trial for the murder of the Galilaean rebels in 48 BCE (*Ant.* XIV 172–4); thus Samaias, fulfilling the role of prophet both by foretelling and by denunciation in the name of the Lord, is the more prominent. They are usually identified with the fourth pair in the *zugoth* in the opening passages of the tractate *Aboth*, Shemaiah and Abtalion, and when cited almost always appear together. Neusner thinks that the pair probably had their place in the original list of pairs used in a modified form at the beginning of the tractate and were followed by Shammai and Hillel in that order (see 1971). One is tempted to wonder whether Josephus has not preserved an ancient tradition about Shammai from the many which have been obliterated by the Yohanan b. Zakkai and Hillelite tradition; Samaias seems as near to Shammai as to Shemaiah and all three name forms may belong originally to the same person. Moore (I, 313) thinks Josephus' 'Samaias' to be Shammai but not Abtalion's colleague Shemaiah.

§3. THE REIGN OF HEROD (37–4 BCE)

G. **Allon**, 'The Attitude of the Pharisees to the Roman Government and the House of Herod', *SH* VII, 1961, 53–78; M. **Avi-Yonah**,

'Archaeological Sources', *CRINT* I/1, 1974, 46–61; T. D. **Barnes**, 'The Date of Herod's Death', *JTS* NS XIX, 1968, 204–9; P. **Benoit**, 'L'Antonia d'Hérode le Grand et le Forum Oriental d'Aelia Capitolina', *HTR* LXIV, 1971, 135–67; V. **Corbo**, 'L'Herodion de Gebal Fureidis', *LASBF* XIII, 1962/3, 219–77; XVII, 1967, 65–121; J. W. **Crowfoot** et al., *Samaria-Sebaste I. The Buildings at Samaria*, London: Palestine Exploration Fund, 1942, 31–5, 39–41, 123–9; C. T. **Fritsch**, 'Herod the Great and the Qumran Community', *JBL* LXXIV, 1955, 173–81; idem (ed.), *Studies in the History of Caesarea Maritima*, SBASOR 21, 1975; G. **Harder**, 'Herodes-Burgen und Herodes-Städte im Jordangraben', *ZDPV* LXXVIII, 1962, 49–63; J. **Jeremias**, *Jerusalem in the Time of Jesus: An Investigation into the Economic and Social Conditions during the New Testament Period*, London/Philadelphia: SCM Press/Fortress Press 1969; A. H. M. **Jones**, *The Herods of Judaea*, ²1967, 39–155; J. L. **Kelso**, *Excavations at NT Jericho and Khirbet en-Nitla*, AASOR 29–30, 1955; K. M. **Kenyon**, *Digging up Jerusalem*, 1974; L. I. **Levine**, *Roman Caesarea: An Archaeological–Topographical Study*, QMIA 2, 1975: idem, *Caesarea under Roman Rule*, SJLA 7, 1975; J. **Meyshan**, 'The Symbols on the Coinage of Herod the Great and their Meanings', *PEQ* XCI, 1959, 109–21; J. **Murphy-O'Connor**, 'The Essenes and their History', *RB* LXXXI, 1974, 215–44; J. **Neusner**, *The Rabbinic Traditions about the Pharisees before 70*, I–III, 1971; idem, *From Politics to Piety: The Emergence of Pharisaic Judaism*, Englewood Cliffs: Prentice-Hall 1973; S. **Perowne**, *The Life and Times of Herod the Great*, London/Nashville: Hodder & Stoughton/Abingdon 1956/9; J. B. **Pritchard**, *The Excavation at Herodian Jericho, 1951*, AASOR 32–3, 1958; G. A. **Reisner** et al., *Harvard Excavations at Samaria*, 1908–10 I, Cambridge: Harvard University Press 1924, 170–80; S. **Sandmel**, *Herod: Profile of a Tyrant*, Philadelphia: J. B. Lippincott 1967; A. **Schalit**, *König Herodes*, SJ 4, 1969; M. **Stern**, *Greek and Latin Authors on Jews and Judaism I: From Herodotus to Plutarch*, 1974; idem, 'The Reign of Herod and the Herodian Dynasty', *CRINT* I/1, 1974, 216–308; R. **de Vaux**, *Archaeology and the Dead Sea Scrolls*, 1973; B. Z. **Wacholder**, *Nicolaus of Damascus*, UCPH 75, 1962; G. R. H. **Wright**, 'The Archaeological Remains at El Mird in the Wilderness of Judaea', *Biblica* XLII, 1961, 1–21; Y. **Yadin**, *Masada: Herod's Fortress and the Zealots' Last Stand*, London/New York: Weidenfeld and Nicolson/Random House 1966; idem, ed., *Jerusalem Revealed: Archaeology in the Holy City 1968–1974*, 1975.

A.   Herod: his family and court

Herod reigned as Rome's representative and for about six years that meant Antony's representative, a fact which restricted not only his foreign policy but even the extent of his kingdom. Cleopatra VII of Egypt dreamed of restoration by fascination of Antony of those territories lost by the Ptolemies a century and a half before; she asked him for Judaea and Arabia. Antony gave her 'the cities within the river Eleutherus' – presumably the mainly Greek cities on the coastal strip from the Eleutherus to Egypt. Herod was also obliged to cede to her and then lease back from her the fertile land of Jericho and its district (*Ant.* XV 88–96; *War* I 360–2). Cleopatra had other opportunities for intrigue against Herod; she had as an ally the latter's mother-in-law Alexandra, who wished to advance the claims of her handsome son Aristobulus III (by Alexander son of Aristobulus II), brother of Mariamme whom Herod had married just before the siege of Jerusalem. Alexandra by her championship of her son made a desperate attempt to implement the claims of the Hasmonaeans to the high priesthood (*Ant.* XV 23f.), for Herod, though he had brought back the aged Hyrcanus from his exile in Babylonia, had appointed an obscure priest from there named Hananel (*Ant.* XV 18–22; apparently the Hanamael of the Mishnah, Parah 3.5, though there called 'the Egyptian'; see Schalit, 693–5). The effort by the two women failed; Herod had Aristobulus drowned in a bath in Jericho shortly after appointing him high priest (*Ant.* XV 42–56). Through the influence of Cleopatra, Herod had to appear before Antony to answer for this murder, but he bought his acquittal and returned to Jerusalem (*Ant.* XV 62–79). In 32 BCE, when hostilities broke out between Octavian and Antony, the latter directed Herod to make war on the Nabataeans as a punishment for their recent failure to pay tribute to Cleopatra, who however sent forces to assist them against Herod. At first the campaign was unsuccessful and in 31 BCE an earthquake killed so many in the country that Herod attempted to make peace with the Arabs. He failed, but then, rallying his army by a speech recorded (or invented) by Josephus or his source, gained a decisive victory (*Ant.* XV 108–60; *War* I 364–85).

September of the same year provided a climax to the bewildering series of changes in Herod's fortunes; this was the battle of Actium in which Antony was defeated by Octavian and which ended the period when Herod's security lay in the favour of an old friend as callous and as brutal as himself.

Josephus gives two accounts of the grim incident which prefaced Herod's self-presentation to Octavian: the death of the octogenarian Hyrcanus. According to the first account (*Ant.* XV 165–73), the death was an inevitable retribution for consenting to a plot of Alexandra to obtain refuge for them both with the Nabataean king Malchus while Herod was away and for awaiting his downfall at the hands of the new Caesar as a signal for their own restoration to power (which Josephus says, significantly, would have had popular support). The other account (*Ant.* XV 174–8), not from Herodian circles, makes Herod the author of a feeble plot to make Hyrcanus look a conspirator and then execute him. There is no doubt that the aged Hyrcanus was an obvious and tempting figurehead for the many who obstinately favoured even now the Hasmonaeans' claims; it seems to be the universal verdict that it was out of character, whether true or not, for him to plot against anyone. Hyrcanus' temperament was such as to make him unfit for the many changing situations and misfortunes which were thrust upon him and never of his own choosing (for Josephus' characterization of him, see *Ant.* XV 179–82).

Herod's elaborate dispositions of his family during his visit to Octavian proved unnecessary but are instructive: his brother Pheroras was left in charge of the whole family, but this was divided into Herod's own and that of his wife Mariamme; his mother Cypros and his sister and their dependants were left at Masada, Mariamme and her mother Alexandra in Alexandrium under the protection of a steward Joseph and a certain Soaemus (*Ant.* XIV 183–6). Herod then went to meet Octavian in Rhodes, where he presented himself openly as one who had backed the wrong side but was clearly able and willing to become the faithful supporter of the new master of the Roman world. Octavian saw the truth and clarity of the situation: Herod needed and would be obedient to Rome, whomever that might mean (*Ant.* XV 187–93; *War* I 387–92). In 30 BCE, the new Caesar was received with great pomp at Ptolemais when on his way to Egypt in a campaign which ended with the suicide of Herod's old friend Antony as well as of his enemy Cleopatra. Octavian restored to him the Jericho region together with the cities Gadara, Hippos, Samaria, Gaza, Anthedon, Joppa and Strato's Tower (*Ant.* XV 194–201; *War* I 394–7).

Herod was now secure on his hearth. The fierce jealousy he felt for Mariamme became the occasion through his mother Cypros and his sister Salome of her tragic death. Soaemus had been charged with the macabre task (like Herod's uncle Joseph before him; *Ant.* XV 65) of putting her to death in the event of circumstances by which Herod might lose her to become the wife of another (*Ant.* XV 186). Like Joseph he revealed Herod's order, and Mariamme enraged Herod on his return with her coldness. Fanned by the two women, the quarrel became a palace plot in which Soaemus was executed for revealing his orders and Mariamme shortly afterwards on the suspicion of infidelity thus aroused (*Ant.* XV 202–39). This was in 29 BCE, and in the following year Alexandra also was executed, being betrayed by the two commanders of the Herodian fortresses in Jerusalem when she approached them for support against Herod (*Ant.* XV 247–52). Perhaps a year later Herod executed two sons of Babas, distantly related to the Hasmonaeans, and Costobar, an Idumaean, who had hidden them, and who was betrayed by his wife Salome, Herod's sister (*Ant.* XV 252, 261–6). Thus were obliterated all the remaining male Hasmonaeans, leaving of the family only the daughter of Antigonus the last king of the line, whom Herod's eldest son (by Doris the Idumaean) Antipater had married.

The court of Herod was never at peace with itself. He had ten wives during his kingship, not always one at a time (*Ant.* XVII 19–22; *War* I 562–3); the most famous was the second Mariamme, daughter of the high priest Simeon, son of Boethus of Alexandria; she was the mother of his son Herod. Also important were the Samaritan Malthace, mother of Antipas and Archelaus, and Cleopatra of Jerusalem, mother of Philip. But it was the two elder sons among the children of Mariamme I, Alexander and Aristobulus, who were to be the causes – most probably innocent – of the tragic and terrible events within Herod's family. In 23 BCE, they were sent to Rome for their education and resided in the house of C. Asinius Pollio, probably chosen less for his political loyalties than for his scholarship, for he was almost certainly the distinguished Roman historian of that name (*Ant.* XV 342f.). Though an old friend of Julius Caesar and Antony, Pollio did not hide his convinced republican principles. Herod brought his sons home in 17 BCE and married Alexander to Glaphyra daughter of Archelaus, king of Cappadocia, a man of culture, and Aristobulus to his cousin Berenice, daughter of Salome (*Ant.* XVI 11). The two young men with the Hasmonaean names thus reintroduced the element of the old royal house into the court and aroused the jealousy of Antipater. He was supported by the formidable Salome and Pheroras, tetrarch of Peraea, Herod's only surviving brother. This clique was successful in poisoning Herod's mind against the two brothers to the advantage of Antipater, who accompanied the influential M. Vipsanius Agrippa to Rome in 13 BCE (*Ant.* XVI 78–86; *War* I 445–51). During this time his two half-brothers were accused of plotting against Herod, who referred the matter to Augustus. The latter heard evidence at Aquileia and effected a reconciliation between the father and his sons (*Ant.* XVI 87–126; *War* I 452–4); but back in Jerusalem Herod publicly declared Antipater to be his heir and Alexander and Aristobulus next in line (*Ant.* XVI 130–5; *War* 457–66). Pheroras and Herod remained at enmity, largely due to Herod's irritation with his brother for his excessive devotion to his slave-girl wife (*Ant.* XVI 194–200). The family trouble was not over; some eunuchs now made a confession that Alexander had schemed to seize power when Herod died. The latter's anger was fed by further accusations, including a plot by both brothers to kill him. Archelaus of Cappadocia came to Jerusalem and for a time succeeded in patching up the rift, but others at court, such as Eurycles of Sparta, fomented the trouble. Finally Augustus, once more appealed to, recommended a court of 150 assessors, including Saturninus the governor of Syria, to sit at Berytus. A majority found both brothers guilty and they were strangled at Sebaste and buried at Alexandrium, 300 military men who protested on their behalf being killed by the mob at Caesarea, Herod's new city peopled largely by those known to be loyal and under obligation to him (*Ant.* XVI 229–70, 300–34, 356–404; *War* I 488–551).

Antipater endeavoured to confirm his now strong position by obtaining Augustus' approval, and went again to Rome; but while he was there Pheroras died and enquiries which Herod made in his household revealed a Pheroras–Antipater conspiracy which involved also Mariamme II whom Herod therefore had evidently now rejected (*Ant.* XVII 51–77; *War* I 552–5, 567–73, 578–600). Her son Herod, who had been put next in line to Antipater, was struck from the king's will, and Simeon, son of the Alexandrian Boethus, deposed from the high priesthood (*Ant.* XVII 78; *War* I 599f.). Antipater, returning from Rome, only heard of the events when already as far on his journey as Cilicia. He decided to continue but was made prisoner by a commission of enquiry which included Varus, now governor of Syria, and Nicolaus. Herod reported the events to Augustus and at the same time plots made by Antipater in Rome came to light. Herod, now seventy, made a new will bequeathing his kingdom to Antipas son of Malthace. When Augustus empowered Herod to do as he decided Antipater was executed and buried at Hyrcania (*Ant.* XVII 79–145, 187; *War*, 601–43, 663f.). Herod now made a yet further will and died (probably 4 BCE) and was buried at Herodium (*Ant.* XVII 188–99; *War* I 664–73).

It is appropriate to tell the story of family and court plots which led to so many tragic deaths and were ended only by the death of the king himself, since they echo in a measure the stories of more ancient kings of Judaea, not least David, the extent of whose kingdom Herod enjoyed; but it is necessary to expand and to balance this otherwise one-sided picture. The court was less typical of an ancient king than of an eastern Hellenistic monarch. It seems hardly correct to speak of

a harem but the times when Herod's ten wives wielded effective
influence in some cases overlapped and eunuchs were among the
king's servants. A Greek named Ptolemy acted as a kind of prime
minister and Nicolaus of Damascus, a distinguished author, was the
most important of a number of literary men at court (on Nicolaus,
see Wacholder). Herod encouraged him to write history, not least
because he devoted much time to a description of Herod's life and
times, a work widely used by Josephus. Herod wrote his own
memoirs in Greek (*Ant.* XV 174) and it was to the Hellenic culture
that numerous teachers, athletes, musicians, and actors belonged. It
is difficult now to define what at this time and in this area was
designated by 'Hellene' or 'Hellenic', since it included sometimes
those who were Semitic by race but had adopted Greek culture.
That it also sometimes meant Greek by race seems to be suggested
for example by Nicolaus' report that one of the reasons for the unrest
on Herod's death was constituted by the over 10,000 Hellenes whom
he had employed (see Stern, 254).

B. Herod as king of Judaea

In the years 23–20 BCE Augustus (the title had been adopted by
Octavian in January 27 BCE) was in the east making dispositions of
boundary and government; he added to Herod's domains parts of
Trachonitis, Batanaea, and Hauran, Herod's task being the familiar
one of suppressing banditry in these regions, which had been
encouraged rather than prevented by a local chief Zenodorus (*Ant.*
XV 343–8; *War* I 398–400). The latter died in 20 BCE and Herod
then received his territory of Ulatha and Panias, and thus his kingdom reached its maximum extent (*Ant.* XV 360). The king of
Judaea had become an integral part of the organization of the
Roman Empire and was probably 'ally and friend of the Roman
people' (*socius et amicus populi Romani*), a status which gave him
absolute power within his own territory but placed restriction on
him in that he could not wage war or make alliances without approval (*Ant.* XVII 246; see *Schürer, 316 n. 104). He had to supply
auxiliary troops when required and protect the boundaries of the
empire, which were coincident with his own. That he minted only
copper coins suggested to Schürer an officially limited right of coinage and indicated that Herod was not one of the most privileged
client kings (see *Schürer, 317). On the other hand, Herod's power
was very considerable and extended to his right to demand extradi-
tion from neighbouring states of criminal fugitives, and to such

privileges as naming his own successor, though the latter had to meet with the approval of Augustus.

Herod's personal unpopularity is indicated by the frequency of plots against him and the sympathy with which they were received. He had his own centres of support, but among earnestly religious men he was wholly unwelcome, even with those for whom on grounds of rational convictions he was regarded as tolerable. Their main fear arose from his innovations in customs. The attitude of Pollion and Samaias, who through their being the leaders of a group of disciples were more significant than the occasional incidents recorded of them would suggest, was not favourable to Herod, as appears at first sight, but was founded on a bitter hatred; for they regarded him as a divine scourge for a disobedient people (*Ant.* XV 4). Nevertheless Herod respected this group and those Essenes who refused to take the oath of allegiance to him and imposed fines on them instead of the death penalty. The account of the Pharisaic refusal to swear allegiance is told in connection with the two leaders in *Antiquities* XV 370–2. The roughly parallel account in XVII 41–5 gives the number of 'non-jurors' as 6,000; it is told in the context of the story of the opposition of Pheroras and his wife, and is worded so curiously that it betrays, not only by its anti-Pharisaic motif, an imperfect fit with the surrounding material; it probably comes therefore from Nicolaus. Jeremias is surely right in thinking this is the same story from two different sources, although Schürer argued that they are distinct (see Jeremias, 263 n. 56; *Schürer, 314 n. 94; on Herod's relations with the Pharisees, see Allon, and Jeremias, 228–32). In this incident as in others Herod manifested the secular tyrant's characteristic respect for men whose opposition and rebukes proceeded from disinterested piety and from that complete absence of narrow political ambition which arises from enjoying social influence. This temper is illustrated by the story of Menahem the Essene, who prophesied Herod's coming eventually to the kingship and who treated the king with familiarity and to a sermon when the prophecy was fulfilled (*Ant.* XV 373–9); but it is doubtful indeed whether Herod showed special favour to the Essenes indiscriminately, for their influence depended on receiving no favour. It is a violent *tour de force* to attempt to identify these Essenes with the Herodians of Mark 3.6; 12.13; Matthew 22.16, and to erect a theory which explains the absence from Qumran of the sectarians from 31 BCE to about 6 CE by supposing that Herod's favour protected them from persecution and enabled them to live at large or in a group elsewhere. The retirement of the sectarians, who seem to have gone to Qumran in the reign of John Hyrcanus I, was due to their religious need to separate themselves from a corrupt Israel and not just to escape the attentions of a pagan monarch (for the problems of Essene–Qumran history, see Murphy-O'Connor). The case founded on archaeological evidence for abandonment because of destruction by the earthquake in 31 BCE may well be correct (see de Vaux, 20–4). No doubt the eagerness of those nationalists who afterwards went under the name of Zealots was sharpened by the reign of Herod, but the more purely religious and pietist sect of Qumran needed no stimulus from the sons of Herod to send them back to the wilderness.

Herod's attitude to the temple in Jerusalem illustrates well the apparently contradictory mind of the secular ruler to religious matters. He appears to have used the temple area as a place for a popular assembly on at least one occasion (*Ant.* XVI 132–5); although Herod's speech begins almost by chance, he does dismiss the *ekklesia* at the end. It is his decision to rebuild the temple which marks out his purpose and motive: his wish to make it the most distinguished of all his achievements and an everlasting memorial of him could easily be represented as the main redeeming feature in a life compounded of cruelty and generosity, warm affection and cold selfish calculation. Josephus remarks with admirable prophetic insight that it was in fact Herod's most distinguished achievement; but he does not for a moment suggest that it was a work of Jewish piety (*Ant.* XV 380). In truth Herod was too rough to be a rough diamond. The Jerusalem temple was the greatest of those building works by which Herod acquired fame and support from the people to which he donated them. It was begun apparently in 20 BCE and completed, if the tradition of John 2.20 is correct, in 26 CE; but in *Antiquities* XX 219, Josephus says it was completed in the procuratorship of Albinus (62–64 CE) (see *Schürer, 292, 308). In Greek cities the temple might be erected more to add to the reputation of the city than of its god, but in Jerusalem such motives would be suspect, and special scruples had to be observed to avoid giving offence to the pious. Herod was careful to avoid offence and took pains to dispel it when it threatened to develop; but he made a surprising blunder in erecting over what Josephus calls the Great Gate of the temple 'a very costly decoration in the form of a large golden eagle' (*Ant.* XVII 151). Shortly before Herod's death, when he had reached the age of seventy, a bold and heroic gesture was made at the instigation of two men, Judas and Matthias, whom Josephus describes in laudatory terms, saying that they were experts in their traditional laws, but does not call them Pharisees. Since he

does call them *sophistai* and says that they had a large daily following
of pupils, they were probably scribes, as Jeremias assumes. Some of
their pupils sought to earn immortal reputation by cutting down the
offensive eagle; and according to the *War* account both they and
their two mentors were burned alive by the enraged Herod, who
seems already to have been suffering acutely in his terminal illness
(*Ant.* XVII 149–67; *War* I 648–55).

The advisory council used by Herod can hardly have been continuous either in membership or in character with any Jewish
Sanhedrin (*Ant.* XV 173). It was more like a Hellenistic king's privy
council peopled by 'Hellenes' and conducted in the Greek language.
Occasionally popular assemblies were called together to hear news
or intentions, even in order to demand some violent action, such as
the stoning of the supporters of Alexander and Aristobulus (*Ant.*
XVI 392–4; *War* I 550f.); no doubt with the factitious 'spontaneity'
with which the twentieth century has made some countries familiar.
The crowds on this latter occasion came from Caesarea; with Sebaste
it provides the clearest example of new towns founded by Herod and
peopled with his veterans or with Jews and others from abroad
whom he had settled and housed, and who were therefore likely to
feel more politic gratitude than moral indignation towards him.

The country over which Herod reigned was divided into meridar-
chies – Idumaea, Judaea, Samaria, Galilee, and Peraea – and these
were ruled by reliable men, usually relatives. Greek cities, for all
Herod's Hellenization, did not like his tyrannical style of rule and
Gadara, a centre of Hellenic culture of some fame, complained of his
overbearing rule to Agrippa while the latter was in the east in 22–21
BCE. The spokesmen were sent on to Herod (*Ant.* XV 351, 354).
Their lack of success did not prevent the same city asking for annex-
ation to Syria in 20 BCE, a plea finally successful after Herod's death
(*Ant.* XVII 320).

Herod had his own army, of varied ingredients, partly mercenaries especially from Galatia and Thrace; and as time went on he
was able to recruit from his new cities as well as from non-Jewish
settlers in old military colonies (*Ant.* XVII 198). Jews were
recruited, but selectively, a large number of them being immigrants
from Babylonia (see Schalit, 167–83). As the history of Antipater
and his half-brothers Alexander and Aristobulus shows, officers had
a considerable influence upon affairs but were not strong enough to
withstand the opposition of Herod himself.

The famous Rabbi Hillel or his immediate ancestors came from
Babylonia about this time. The traditions tell us nothing solid about

his life, but several facts emerge from a study of them and of the period from Herod to the destruction of the temple. One is that during this period Hillel achieved through great perseverance an advance from poverty and obscurity to a dominant position as an halakhic interpreter, although he is never mentioned by Josephus (see Neusner, I 212–302). Other facts are that all references to Pharisees in Josephus suggest that, while a religious brotherhood, they constituted also a political party during the period of which he writes, but after 70 CE emerged as a quietist sect exhibiting the same legalistic preoccupations as they show in the gospels (see Neusner, *From Politics to Piety*). From Jamnia onwards Hillel becomes the authority *par excellence* and is the name impressed on a vast number of accepted decisions. From this far from abundant evidence it may be fair to infer that Hillel became a superlatively revered figure after his death when his own policy of quietism, during his lifetime against the stream, proved to be the means of saving Judaism from the wreck of Judaea.

Such a kingdom needed much money for its own local expenses, in addition to the heavy taxes which were regularly paid to Rome. Some came from Herod's own estates, enlarged by those of his political enemies as they fell victims to his success (*Ant.* XV 5), and enlarged by business interests abroad such as the copper mines of Cyprus, half whose revenue was a gift from Augustus, the other half under Herod's administration (*Ant.* XVI 128); but a great deal came from the taxes paid by Herod's subjects (see *Ant.* XVII 205, 308; *War* II 85 f.). Thus was perpetuated the cruel burden which Judaea and so many countries had been accustomed to endure, usually with resignation when placed upon them by their own sovereign rulers, with indignation or fierce resentment when imposed by Ptolemies, Seleucids, Romans – or an Idumaean. In the game of life the peasant may cheat but cannot win. As always and everywhere, so for Judaea at this time there was a flaw even in the long desired peace which the Roman empire, exhausted by the struggles which changed the republic into a principate, brought to so many lands which it had itself impoverished and subdued. The prosperity which the long peace from 31 to 4 BCE brought to Judaea enabled more land to be cultivated with less interruption, so increasing a prosperity which could the more easily and the more heavily be taxed, as could the profits of merchants and artisans. The resentment was contained while Herod lived but flared up when he died. He was able to contain it largely by the constant presence of his army in his own client kingdom; for his forces were not required to assist the

Roman army in the east to the extent which might have been expected at the beginning of his reign. The sense of relief which came in 31 BCE after the battle of Actium blossomed into something like a sense of security after 20 BCE when Augustus made an agreement with Parthia and stabilized the eastern frontier. Herod assisted Aelius Gallus, prefect of Egypt, in his unsuccessful expedition into southern Arabia in 25–24 BCE, and Agrippa in the Black Sea area in 14 BCE, but his resources were not strained; his relations with the Romans were rather enhanced by these minor operations (*Ant.* XV 317; XVI 16–62).

C. *Herod and Rome*

Herod was fortunate in enjoying for almost all his reign the favour and friendship of Augustus himself; they exchanged gifts of money (the balance was in favour of the princeps), and met frequently; and Herod did honour to his chief by the naming of his great towns Sebaste (*Ant.* XV 292, 296–8; *War* I 403) (to replace the nearby ancient Samaria) which is the Greek feminine form of Augustus, and Caesarea on the site of Strato's Tower (*Ant.* XV 331–41; *War* I 408–14). This latter, which contained many great buildings, included both a temple in honour of Augustus and annual games held in honour of the princeps (*Ant.* XVI 136–8; *War* I 415). Suetonius in *Augustus* 60 remarks that each of the allied kings who enjoyed the friendship of Augustus founded a city called Caesarea in his own territory. Herod's Caesarea was destined to become the administrative capital of the province when government by prefect or procurator began in 6 CE, a destiny assisted by its magnificence and superb harbour. Suetonius goes on to suggest a cosy picture of Augustus receiving client kings at all times, in Rome or in the provinces, and describes the relations between them as resembling the devotion of family dependants. At times Herod's attitude was not unlike this picture of a client king, but the attitude was politic and necessary and did not proceed from pure affection.

In ruthlessness and ability Herod was the equal of his patron; he was his subordinate from circumstance. That he was a man able to hold his own in the company of the great in the Roman empire is illustrated by his long friendship with the Roman general M. Vipsanius Agrippa, Augustus' famous right-hand man, a man of culture and practical ability. Agrippa was entrusted with wide powers and was busy solving problems in the east, residing at Mytilene in Lesbos in 23–21 BCE when he received – and rejected – the deputation from

Gadara (*Ant.* XV 350–8). This was but one of the marks of favour which he showed to Herod, who successfully pressed him to visit Judaea in 15 BCE (*Ant.* XVI 12–15). On this occasion he was shown by Herod all the buildings in Sebaste and Caesarea, and significantly the fortress mini-townships of Alexandrium, Herodium, and Hyrcania. The people of Jerusalem received him in festive garb and with what Josephus calls *euphemiais*. Stern says he received 'an enthusiastic welcome' (*CRINT*, 242) from the king and the Jewish masses, but what Liddell and Scott encourage us to call acclamations may have been more polite than sincere and the translation 'fair words' may not be amiss. There need be no suggestion of reserve about the warm feelings which Herod himself entertained for his powerful friend. He accompanied him on a journey through Paphlagonia, greater Phrygia, Ephesus and Samos in 14 BCE and pleaded successfully on behalf of the people of Chios and Ilium besides securing privileges for Jews in Ionia (*Ant.* XVI 16–62). The name Agrippa was perpetuated in that given to the city that was formerly Anthedon, and especially in Herod's family.

The statesman and historian C. Asinius Pollio, host in Rome to Herod's ill-fated sons, had been a supporter of Herod since 40 BCE, being consul when the king of Judaea was crowned in Rome (*Ant.* XV 343). Herod was on close terms also with C. Petronius, prefect of Egypt (24–21 BCE; *Ant.* XV 307) and with Titius, legate of Syria between Agrippa and Saturninus (*Ant.* XVI 270; the dates are uncertain, but Agrippa probably relinquished his second period as legate in 13 BCE and Saturninus became legate in 10 or 9 BCE).

Herod is called 'the Great' usually to distinguish him from the minor Herods who followed him (so Josephus, *Ant.* XVIII 130); but if the title may mean one whose actions in many spheres were (without judgment as to their morality) habitually on the grand scale, he richly deserves the title. It is as a Hellenistic ruler that he deserves it rather than as a patriotic king of Judaea, and we may think of him as a despot ruling a relatively small territory with a mixed population representative of the Roman empire, and in which Jews, while providing the numerical majority, contributed an important element to rather than determined the entire character of the state. As a Hellenistic prince, Herod gave more than a normal share of money and energy towards the glory of the Roman empire. He made grants to Greek cities for various purposes, as was the fashion, but the extent and range of his bounty were enormous. The Greek cities included such famous giants of the past as Athens and Sparta, and he supported the Olympic Games. Among other cities, he assisted

generously the towns of Lycia, Pamphylia, and Cilicia besides the
Phoenician and Syrian coastal cities nearer home. Buildings which
owed their existence or repair to him included the temple of Pythian
Apollo at Rhodes, the basilica of Chios, buildings in Augustus' new
city of Nicopolis which celebrated the victory of Actium, baths at
Ascalon, a gymnasium at Ptolemais, temples and markets at Tyre
and Berytus, a theatre at Sidon, as at Damascus, where Herod also
provided a gymnasium. Laodicea owed him an aqueduct, Antioch
the marble paving of its city thoroughfare (*Ant.* XVI 18f., 146–9;
War I 422–8; see also *Ant.* XV 311). In Judaea, besides Caesarea
and the other buildings already mentioned, Herod built Phasaelis
(*Ḥirbet Fasayil*) in memory of his brother Phasael in the valley of
Jericho, Antipatris (*Rās el-ʿAin*), and the fortress of Machaerus. His
enhancement and strengthening of Masada – destined to provide the
final refuge for the last and most desperate rebels from among his
own subjects or their descendants – has become one of the most
spectacular revelations of archaeology in Palestine of our own time.
Herodian Jerusalem was no doubt his greatest monument; not only
the temple but the towers of Hippicus, Phasael, and Mariamme, and
the Antonia fortress; a theatre and an amphitheatre were important
instances of his work – and of offences to strict Jews among his
people (*Ant.* XV 380–425; see Kenyon and Yadin, 1975).

The non-Roman nations who were of the most importance to
Herod were naturally those nearest his kingdom – Parthia and
Nabataea. The threat of the Parthians lay always in the background,
although it receded somewhat after 20 BCE, but its power to disturb
is illustrated by a charge against Alexander, extracted from a victim
of Herod's suspicion under torture; no doubt untrue, it is important
for the light it throws on the circumstances: Alexander was said to
wish to flee to Rome to lay information against Herod that the latter
was conspiring with the Parthian king against Rome (*Ant.* XVI
253). A more plausible accusation was that against Pheroras, when
Herod was angry with him for refusing to marry his daughter, that
he planned to escape to the Parthians (*War* I 486).

The Nabataeans had been Herod's enemies even before his kingship and the relations between them during his reign were usually
bad. Most serious was the support given by the Nabataeans to the
revolt in Trachonitis in 12 BCE by the regent Syllaeus, acting for the
king Obodas, who kept out of politics, for which his dull intellect did
not fit him. In the complicated situation which developed, Herod
gave the impression of exceeding his authority as a subject prince
and had to send Nicolaus to Rome to state his case. The envoy was

able to use successfully the situation created by the death of Obodas
and the accession of Aretas IV who was confirmed as king, Syllaeus
being found guilty of conspiring to murder Herod and finally
executed in the year in which Herod died (*Ant.* XVI 130, 271–99,
335–55; *War* I 574–7).

Herod's death tested the wisdom and success or otherwise of his
government. It turned out that the settlement he had made for
Judaea was no settlement: disturbances broke out in such measure
that direct Roman rule had to be imposed.

§4. HEROD'S IMMEDIATE SUCCESSORS

M. **Avi-Yonah**, 'The Foundation of Tiberias', *IEJ* I, 1951, 160–9; M.
Black, 'Judas of Galilee and Josephus' "Fourth Philosophy"', *Josephus-
Studien: Untersuchungen zu Josephus, dem antiken Judentum und dem Neuen
Testament* (Festschrift Otto Michel), ed. Otto Betz et al., Göttingen:
Vandenhoeck & Ruprecht 1974, 45–54; F. F. **Bruce**, 'Herod Antipas,
Tetrarch of Galilee and Peraea', *ALUOS* V, 1963–5, 6–23; H. W. **Hoeh-
ner**, *Herod Antipas*, SNTSMS 17, 1972; A. H. M. **Jones**, *The Herods of
Judaea*, ²1967, 156–83; J. S. **Kennard**, 'Judas of Galilee and his Clan', *JQR*
XXXVI, 1945/6, 281–6; S. **Perowne**, *The Later Herods*, 1956/8; A. **Segal**,
'Herodium', *IEJ* XXIII, 1973, 27–9; E. M. **Smallwood**, 'High Priests and
Politics in Roman Palestine', *JTS* NS XIII, 1962, 14–34.

Archelaus supervised the burial of his father's body in Herodium,
which Herod had selected as his resting-place (*Ant.* XVII 199; *War* I
673; see Segal), and took up his position as his heir. When faced with
demands from the people he made a number of promises to rule
better than Herod which he was neither able nor willing to carry out
(*Ant.* XVII 200–5; *War* II 1–3). Actual revolt developed out of a
popular demand to punish those advisers of Herod who had urged
the savage execution of Judas and Matthias and their followers (*Ant.*
XVII 214; *War* II 5–7). Archelaus succeeded in quelling the rising
for the time being and made the journey to Rome necessary to
submit the provisions of Herod's will to the princeps (*Ant.* XVII
215–20; *War* II 8–13). Such a journey is reflected in Luke 19.11–27
and was commonplace enough to be familiar to Jesus, whether he
actually composed the story as we now have it or not. Certainly
Archelaus hoped to receive a kingdom and to return; and others
came to Rome to say clearly that they were 'not willing to have this
man to reign over us'. Factions from the court formed the con-
testants in the wordy trial of strength, Nicolaus supporting Archelaus,

and Antipater son of Salome opposing him with support of Antipas, to whom other relatives rallied less out of affection for the latter than through detestation of Archelaus (*Ant.* XVII 224–47; *War* II 20–36). They wanted above all their freedom but recognized that this was impossible except in the modified form of freedom from the house of Herod, but under Roman government (*Ant.* XVII 299–314; *War* II 80–91). Augustus did not decide at once and waited long enough to receive serious news from Judaea (*Ant.* XVII 248–50; *War* II 37f.). He had sent a procurator, Sabinus, to supervise the implementation of the financial elements of Herod's will; this officer was so harsh in his methods that the troubles which Archelaus had scarcely suppressed by a ruthless use of troops against unarmed crowds quickly broke out again. Sabinus was forced to call upon Varus, the legate of Syria, for support (*Ant.* XVII 221–3, 250–70; *War* II 16–19, 39–55). The ensuing massacre of hastily gathered and brave but uncoordinated Jewish soldiers was decisive, and sufficiently explains the relative quietness of Judaea when Roman government was in fact imposed about ten years later. The war of Varus was terrible enough to dissuade many, defeating the efforts of three disunited popular leaders (*Ant.* XVII 285–98; *War* II 66–79). One of these was Judas of Sepphoris, son of the Hezekiah whom Herod had killed in 48 BCE: another a shepherd named Athronges and a third slave named Simon (*Ant.* XVII 271–85; *War* II 56–65). All used royal titles, the last being the only one named by Tacitus in the *Histories* (5.9) in the course of an account which unconsciously but vividly demonstrates his almost total lack of sympathy, of appreciation of patriotism, or even the faintest understanding of the peculiar characteristics of the Jewish people. The nonsense with which he introduces his account of the Jewish revolt, purporting to be ancient history, was shared widely in antiquity, but his ignorance – or studied neglect – of the very existence of the Septuagint is not the only sign of a contempt which his studies and clipped style so well expresses – and deserves.

Augustus did not wait for the result of the fighting before making his decision, which authenticated the dispositions of Herod's last will. Antipas thus became tetrarch of Galilee, which he retained until 39 CE, Philip tetrarch of the remoter areas of Batanaea, Trachonitis, Auranitis, Gaulanitis, Panias and probably Ituraea, which he retained until his death in 34 CE, and Archelaus received Judaea, the princeps' sole concession to strong dissent from both court and people being to give him the title of ethnarch rather than king (*Ant.* XVII 317–24; *War* II 93–101). Varus had suppressed the revolt with great cruelty, among other atrocities crucifying about two thousand. Archelaus had still to extinguish its embers, and it is not clear how he finally succeeded. He appears, however, to have aped his father in cruelty without enjoying his ability.

As ruler of Judaea, Archelaus inherited the custom of appointing the high priest; Matthias having been deposed in 4 BCE (being held partially responsible for the eagle affair; *Ant.* XVII 164) and succeeded by his brother-in-law Joazar, the latter in his turn was now deposed as having been on the side of the rebels (which was no doubt true, though he had not been actively engaged in the rebellion) in favour of his brother Eleazar (*Ant.* XVII 339). This last was deposed in about a year in favour of Jesus son of Sie, for which no reason is given (*Ant.* XVII 341). It may be conjectured that these rapid changes were due to bribery, although the reappointment of Joazar (if it is indeed the same person) at the time of the census seems to have been intelligible policy (*Ant.* XVIII 3). The people endured the tyranny and cruelty of Archelaus until 6 CE, when the prominent men of the Jews and Samaritans accused him to Caesar, who banished him to Vienne in Gallia Narbonensis (*Ant.* XVII 342–4; *War* II 111).

Herod Antipas (the Herod of the gospels) had married a daughter of Aretas IV, part of a joint effort to make peace by the Nabataean king and Herod the Great (*Ant.* XVIII 109). The marriage and the good relations between the countries were shattered by Antipas' love for Herodias, daughter of Aristobulus IV, half-brother of Antipas and already married to another half-brother, Herod Philip. Antipas' taking her in marriage away from Philip was the action which according to the gospels was rebuked by John the Baptist and thus occasioned his execution (*Ant.* XVIII 110–12). Less notorious are the somewhat later frontier skirmishes which the renewed enmity between Judaea and Nabataea provoked and in which Antipas suffered defeat. Tiberius (emperor from 14 BCE), being appealed to, ordered L. Vitellius (legate of Syria from 35 CE) to make a punitive expedition against the Nabataeans (*Ant.* XVIII 113–20). Antipas seems to have regained high status, for when Parthia again became active he played host – on a bridge over the Euphrates – to king Artabanus and Vitellius for a meeting at which an agreement was reached (*Ant.* XVIII 101–5). Antipas thus played a part in the history of the Roman empire; in a small way he resembled his father also as a Hellenistic prince (inscriptions show his active relations with Athens and Cos) and as a builder (see Hoehner, 106 n. 3 and *Schürer, 341 n. 1); he restored Sepphoris (*Saffuriyah*) and rebuilt Beth ha-Ramtah (*Tell er-Rameh*) which received the name of Livias, changed later to Julias(*Ant.* XVIII 26f.). Antipas took advantage of the warm if very humid climate of the area around the Sea of Galilee to build himself a secular capital at the southern end of the lake; the site embraced hot springs so that the new city could have baths, which helped it to become a *polis* of the Graeco-Roman world; and as such it flourished, though for a time the site was taboo for strict Jews owing to the proximity of a burial-ground. It was named Tiberias after the emperor, and its importance was so great that it became in due course a centre for orthodox Jews also, housing R. Meir the pupil of Aqiba and forerunner of Judah ha-Nasi, compiler of the Mishnah (*Ant.* XVIII 36–8; *War* II 168).

Philip (son of Herod by Cleopatra of Jerusalem) was remarkable among Herodians for his popularity and benevolence as a ruler. His reign being peaceful, there is less to report of him; but he too was a builder, and a straightforward supporter of the Roman empire (*Ant.* XVIII 28; *War* II 168). He rebuilt ancient Paneas (*Banias*), giving it the name of Caesarea. During his reign it was suitably distinguished from the Roman provincial capital on the coast by the addition of Philippi and under the double name it became famous as the place where Simon Peter, most prominent of the disciples, ventured the title of Messiah for Jesus who, according to the oldest tradition, rejected it (Mark 8.27–33), an incident drastically altered into acceptance as revelation in the late gospel of Matthew (16.13–20) and predominant in Christian tradition ever since. Philip married Salome, the daughter of Herodias by her first husband Herod Philip (son of Mariamme II; *Ant.* XVIII 139). She goes down in history as the girl whose dance before Antipas secured the boon for Herodias of the execution of John the Baptist, according to the gospels of Mark and Matthew (Mark 6.14–29; Matt. 14.1–12). Philip died childless in 34 CE and his kingdom was allotted to Agrippa after a few years of being annexed for administrative purposes to Syria (*Ant.* XVIII 106–8, 237; *War* II 181).

§5. JUDAEA AS A ROMAN PROVINCE (6–66 CE)

A. Judaea under Roman governors (6–41 CE)

S. A. **Appelbaum**, 'The Zealots: The Case for Revaluation', *JRS* LXI, 1971, 155–70; G. **Aulén**, *Jesus in Contemporary Historical Research*, Philadelphia/London: Fortress Press/SPCK 1976; J. **Blinzler**, 'Die Niedermetzelung von Galiläern durch Pilatus', *NT* II, 1957, 24–9; S. G. F. **Brandon**,

Jesus and the Zealots: A Study of the Political Factor in Primitive Christianity, Manchester/New York: The University Press/Charles Scribner's Sons 1967; W. R. **Farmer**, *Maccabees, Zealots, and Josephus*, New York: Columbia University Press 1956; A. **Frova**, 'L'iscrizione di Ponzio Pilato a Cesarea', *RIL* XCV, 1961, 419–34; M. **Hengel**, *Die Zeloten: Untersuchungen zur jüdischen Freiheitsbewegung in der Zeit von Herodes I bis 70 n. Chr.*, AGSU 1, 1961; idem, 'Zeloten und Sikarier: Zur Frage nach der Einheit und Vielfalt der jüdischen Befreiungsbewegung 6–74 n. Chr.', *Josephus-Studien* (Festschrift Otto Michel) (see §4 above), 1974, 175–96; A. H. M. **Jones**, 'Procurators and Prefects', *Studies in Roman Government and Law*, Oxford: Basil Blackwell 1960, 115–25; J. **Klausner**, *Jesus of Nazareth: His Life, Times and Teaching*, London/New York: Macmillan 1925; C. H. **Kraeling**, *John the Baptist*, New York: Charles Scribner's Sons 1951; E. **Lohse**, 'Die römischen Statthalter in Jerusalem', *ZDPV* LXXIV, 1958, 69–78; D. M. **Rhoads**, *Israel in Revolution 6–74 CE: A Political History Based on the Writings of Josephus*, Philadelphia: Fortress Press 1976; A. **Schweitzer**, *The Quest of the Historical Jesus: A Critical Study of its Progress from Reimarus to Wrede*, London/New York: A. & C. Black/Macmillan 1910/50; A. N. **Sherwin-White**, *Roman Society and Roman Law in the New Testament*, London: Oxford University Press 1963; E. M. **Smallwood**, 'The Date of the Dismissal of Pontius Pilate from Judaea', *JJS* V, 1954, 12–21; M. **Smith**, 'Zealots and Sicarii: Their Origins and Relation', *HTR* LXIV, 1971, 1–19; J. **Vardaman**, 'A New Inscription Which Mentions Pilate as "Prefect"', *JBL* LXXXI, 1962, 70f.; G. **Vermes**, *Jesus the Jew: A Historian's Reading of the Gospels*, London/New York: Collins/Macmillan 1973; W. **Wink**, *John the Baptist in the Gospel Tradition*, SNTSMS 7, 1968; P. **Winter**, *On the Trial of Jesus*, SJ 1, 1961, 2 1975; S. **Zeitlin**, 'Who Were the Galileans?', *JQR* LXIV, 1973/4, 189–203.

Josephus explains fully the manner in which the country of Judaea was taken over for direct Roman rule when Archelaus was banished (*Ant.* XVIII 1–3). Augustus sent a well-qualified man, (P. Sulpicius) Quirinius, as *legatus iuridicus*, i.e. governor with full civil powers, and *assessor* of property (for taxation) in Syria to which Judaea now became an addition (*prostheke*). With him was sent Coponius as governor of the Jews with absolute authority over Judaea. Josephus explains that Quirinius also came into Judaea to assess them and to 'dispose of' Archelaus' money. In the *War* (II 117) he says that, Archelaus' territory being enrolled as a province (*eparchia*), Coponius was sent with life and death powers as a *procurator* by Caesar. It seems clear from these two passages that the form of Roman rule over Judaea evolved through circumstances: the first governor was the emperor's agent or steward and, when the office assumed necessarily a more military character, the governor was called a *praefectus*.

The census for the purpose of taxation, apparently supervised by Coponius in Judaea under the general direction of Quirinius, was important for the intense nationalist–religious passion which it aroused in Judas the Gaulonite, who recruited followers in Galilee and helped further to earn for the term 'Galilean' the implication of 'bandit' (*Ant.* XVIII 2–10, 23–5; *War* II 118). This Judas is perhaps to be identified with the Judas who attempted a rising at the death of Herod in 4 BCE. According to Acts 5.37, on this second occasion he lost his life and his followers were scattered.

Far too much has been made of the mention by Luke 2.1–5 of this census under Quirinius by scholars whose motivation was to show that the evangelist was as good a historian as, or better than, Josephus. Luke indeed places this census in direct connection with the birth of Jesus, but he does so in the early parts of his gospel which would now be regarded with equanimity by most New Testament scholars as legendary; though it remains a most intriguing question why Luke made this connection, it is no part of the historian's task to reconcile his narrative with Josephus. It is clear that Schürer is right to emphasize that the census of 6 CE was occasioned by the special circumstances surrounding the collapse of Archelaus' rule and is not to be explained by reference to Roman practice elsewhere (*Schürer, 399–427). He deals with five issues raised if the account in Luke is treated as fact: history does not otherwise record a general imperial census in the time of Augustus; Joseph would not have been obliged to go to Bethlehem and Mary would not have been obliged to accompany him; a Roman census could not have been carried out in Palestine during the time of king Herod, since this would have infringed his authority; Josephus knows nothing of a Roman census in Palestine in the reign of Herod; and Quirinius was not governor of Syria in Herod's lifetime. Some of these points meet the ingenious theories which have sought to find a time when Quirinius might have carried out a census, invested with special powers, during the legateship of another, e.g. Sentius Saturninus, in about 9 BCE; others are fatal to an interpretation of Luke's language which would hold that Quirinius carried out more than one census. Every such theory suffers from some fatal flaw and the historian has no duty to reconcile the gospel with Josephus' account, in itself perfectly clear.

The form of this account in the *Antiquities* mentions support for Judas from a Pharisee named Saddok (*Ant.* XVIII 4), illustrating that the school still acted as a political party with many different shades of opinion and was not yet the quietist sect it became perforce after 70 CE. The question whether Judas' followers are the *sicarii* whom Josephus describes later is an idle one: the enduring motif is not that of nomenclature but of resistance, passive or, as in this case, fiercely militant. That all such movements carry a hysteric fringe venting frustration in murder of neutrals as well as opponents is illustrated not only in the pages of Josephus but in our own newspapers. Suppression of the rising was aided by the persuasions of Joazar, evidently reappointed after his deposition by Archelaus (*Ant.* XVIII 3). It is hard to understand why Quirinius afterwards deposed him again in favour of Ananus, the Annas of the New Testament, thus putting in power a family who except in 15–16 and 37–41 provided the high priest until 62 CE (*Ant.* XVIII 26).

Virtually nothing is known of M. Ambibulus or Annius Rufus, the next two procurators (*Ant.* XVIII 31 f.). The emperor Tiberius succeeded during the latter's term of office (in 14 CE) and appointed Valerius Gratus as *praefectus*. His conduct was apparently irresponsible, since he deposed Ananus and three other high priests in quick succession before appointing Caiaphas, who is well known from the gospels (*Ant.* XVIII 33–6). If this was due to his cupidity we may guess that the same tendency, encouraged by the arrogance and cruelty of Cn. Calpurnius Piso, legate of Syria, caused him to inflict more than usually oppressive taxes on Judaea, since Tacitus (*Ann.* 2.42) reports that in 17 CE Syria and Judaea sought relief from Tiberius, although he does not relate the result.

It is unlikely that Pontius Pilatus, who succeeded Gratus in 26 CE, was sent to relieve the Jews of a burdensome prefect (*Ant.* XVIII 35). No man has received more consistent whitewashing from those who would be his natural detractors than this rapacious and relentlessly cruel governor. The gospels have inspired more than one interpretation of his career which represents him as an honest and conscientious proconsular type of servant of an uncomprehending but well-intentioned empire; such an account is based on the gospels but owes little to Josephus, who makes clear that Pilate deliberately provoked the Jews. Indeed – although the evidence is slim – it has been plausibly argued that Pilate owed his appointment to the anti-Semitic Sejanus, the ambitious Roman whose private influence on the emperor had immense consequences for the latter as for the empire at large (see Brandon, 69).

Pilate began his rule by bringing the legionary standards (*signa*) from Caesarea to winter quarters in Jerusalem and was astonished at the strength of the religious conviction which compelled so many to offer their lives rather than submit to his action (*Ant.* XVIII 55–9;

War II 169–74). Philo also tells the story in his *Legatio ad Caium* (299–305), no doubt influenced by the point he must make in his speech but certainly representing Tiberius as having been favourable, Pilate deliberately hostile to the people. A further incident arose from his appropriation of temple funds for the construction of an aqueduct which would certainly have benefited Jerusalem (*Ant.* XVIII 60–2; *War* II 175–7). This time Pilate anticipated the crowd's non-violent opposition and caused death and wounds among them from clubs which soldiers, mingling with the throng, had concealed under their clothes (see also Luke 13.1 and Blinzler). The character of a ruthless developer of the province without regard to religious scruple of its subjects emerges, and may be enhanced by the knowledge that he was more of a builder than Josephus describes. We know from the inscribed stone discovered at Caesarea that he built a Tiberieum, which was perhaps connected with the imperial cult (see Frova and Vardaman), but he may have embarked on a useful series of public buildings. The streak of cruelty, on which Josephus' description seems to insist, remains.

Modern historians, unlike Old Testament writers, have generally regarded moral questions as of importance only when these affect the course of the political history which is their main concern. Even Josephus recorded of his own time more of politics and warfare; but he was sharply aware of moral and religious currents. One of his passages which reflects the miscellaneous interest of a writer so steeped in the Old Testament belongs to the prefecture of Pilate. It is a short account of John the Baptist whom (according to *Ant.* XVIII 116–19) Antipas put to death at Machaerus because of his growing popularity. Josephus relates nothing of any rebuke by John for Antipas' unlawful marriage, but links the two matters very indirectly: the divorce of Aretas' daughter led to war and Antipas' defeat, which many Jews thought a divine vengeance for the king's treatment of John, which is recorded after the defeat. There are other passages in the so-called Slavonic text of the *War* which appear to incorporate traditions about John; but they reveal obvious confusion and errors, contributing nothing solid to history (see Josephus, LCL, III, 644–8). Such material has inevitably suffered manuscript changes in different Christian eras.

Josephus (*Ant.* XVIII 63f.) has a passage about Jesus of which there is an expanded version in the Slavonic text of the *War* (see LCL, III, 648–50). This latter owes much to later material and is largely interpolated; but the *Antiquities* passage appears to have suffered fewer changes, and several reasonable reconstructions of the original text have been suggested. There seems to be a fair consensus that Josephus wrote of Jesus perhaps that he was regarded by some as the Messiah, certainly that he attracted a large following, was condemned to death on the indictment of important Jews, and crucified by Pilate, but that his followers, the Christians, persisted. Some such account Josephus may well have written; it has been embellished for Christian readers as though expanded by the kind of kerygmatic summary which seems to have formed the basis of early Christian preaching (see *Schürer, 428–41).

Jesus of Nazareth was plainly a very controversial figure; material in ancient authors suffers manipulation by Christians, rabbinic traditions are suppressed for one reason by Jews, for another by Christians (see Klausner). The gospels themselves provide the fullest and most instructive examples of fervent embellishment of and interpolation into historical material; yet they are indispensable to the historian, who has so little other material about Jesus at his disposal. Indeed it may still be possible, in spite of, perhaps in part because of the very thorough and radical critical work of the last century and a half, to reconstruct not indeed the life of Jesus but a significant silhouette of his enigmatic personality and of his achievement, thrown by the light of contemporary history on to a screen already busy with characters in full colour (see Schweitzer and Aulén for various attempts at a historical reconstruction of his ministry).

Jesus was probably born in or near Nazareth, an undistinguished village of Galilee near Sepphoris; the connection with Bethlehem in Judaea and that with the census of Quirinius may be dismissed as later attempts to dramatize the birth of the Messiah. Nothing firm can be said of him until he was about thirty, when he abandoned his work (probably as a builder-carpenter; but see Vermes, 21 f.) for a mission to his own people, a mission begun by an inaugural vision at his baptism by John. He seems to have belonged for a time (perhaps like his small inner circle of disciples) to the rough and unorganized national reform and renaissance movement led by John, but the two men may not have met otherwise than at the baptism, and were in any case far apart in temperament.

To present the shape of the career of Jesus is a matter of forming the most probable hypothesis to cover those facts which can be reasonably entertained after radical synoptic criticism. It seems then that Jesus believed himself entrusted by God with the reformation of his people for the task of converting the world; that he believed it necessary to win back those who lived among Gentiles in the north in his own Galilee, in southern Syria, in the Decapolis, and in the

territory of Philip. He ranged widely over these areas from a headquarters at Capernaum on the north side of the Lake of Galilee, and
to his own surprise found himself accepted by Gentiles as well as by
penitent Jews. His morality was traditional but his intellectual grasp
of its basis was original and unconventional. More articulate than
other Galilean religious figures, he had an extraordinary gift both for
the poetic expression of his interpretation of his nation's wisdom and
for facing men and women with their own crises. Supremely in
history his impact challenged both humble individuals and well-
established authority, the latter disturbed both by his abandonment
(necessary for his mission) of the laws of uncleanness and by his
apparent willingness to associate with Rome and its agents.

To represent such a popular leader as a dangerous rebel or even
sincerely to believe that he was, was the inevitable reaction of authority. Equally inevitable in the climate of the time was the popular
hope that he might prove to be at least the successful messianic
rescuer. Jesus himself forswore and repudiated any such claim, but
his radical reappraisal of God's will for his people constituted an
inevitable challenge to local scribes, and finally to the authorities in
Jerusalem, consisting of the high priest's family and the Sanhedrin.
To the Pharisees he was closer, and he admired their tenacity and
loyalty; but he rejected the high value they placed on their own
version of the Torah (their *halakah*) and came to regard it as obscur-
ing rather than implementing its essence. The evangelists have
represented what was an opposed religious outlook as almost total
hostility and thereby obscured the characteristically Jewish – perhaps rather Galilean – genius of their subject. Jesus' challenge crystallized sharply (and laid him disastrously open to misunderstanding) when at the end of a short ministry whose duration cannot now
be determined he led his reluctant disciples to Jerusalem, dominated
for a time the temple precincts which, like many others, he used as a
forum, and exacerbated both the jealousy and the equally intelligible fears of the Jewish authorities.

In the year of this climax to his mission the passover, always an
anxious time for the prefect with Jerusalem swollen by crowds cele-
brating this festival of national deliverance, provided an almost
automatic trigger for the arrest, interrogation and deliverance by
the Sanhedrin to the prefect of this leader of a band of men from
Galilee, famous for its fostering of bandits. Pilate was scarcely notable
for his sympathy towards Jewish religious personalities but was
unable to find a charge suitable for this prisoner. However, his position *vis-à-vis* the emperor was already dangerous, and he therefore

obliged both the high priest and his party by ordering Jesus' cruci-fixion as 'the king of the Jews'. The fickle mob concurred, perhaps precisely because this was the claim which their hero had refused to make. Thus Jesus, crucified between two no doubt genuine bandits, passed from Judaean history. That he does not belong to it alone, but to the world, is only one claim for him which millions would make but is not a matter for the historian.

In 36 CE L. Vitellius, legate of Syria, intervened to dismiss Pilate to face charges arising from complaints by Samaritans (*Ant.* XVIII 85–9). Pilate therefore returned to Rome, but his eventual fate is unknown. Legends have obscured the man and hindered the task of judging his character and policy. His certain hostility to the Jews may be the explanation of the attitude attributed to him in the gospels; unable to find a sound charge against Jesus, he nevertheless had him crucified to curry favour with the leading high priestly faction in Jerusalem. If he ordered the 'title' advertising the con-demned man as king of the Jews, as the gospels relate, this may have been due to inability to resist the temptation to wreak one further insult upon the Jews whom he did not cease to hate when he sought their favour. It is possible that the fall of Sejanus in 31 CE left him in a bad position in relation to Tiberius (*Ant.* XVIII 180–3), who reversed the policy of Sejanus towards Jews in the empire. According to Josephus, Pilate escaped a summons to appear before the emperor by the latter's timely death (*Ant.* XVIII 89). This occurred in 37 CE, which seems to be the end of Pilate's prefecture; a duration of ten years from 26 may well represent, as Smallwood suggests (1954), Josephus' round number. It is not clear whether the two next gover-nors of Judaea, Marcellus, 36–7 CE, and Marullus, 37–41 CE, were the same person; nothing is known about them and they probably illustrate the type of underling sent by an emperor to govern the province for him without understanding the difficulty of the task (*Ant.* XVIII 89, 237).

For a time, towards the end of Tiberius' reign, relations with Rome were, on the dismissal of Pilate, much better (*Ant.* XVIII 90–5). Vitellius restored to the people the custody of the high priest's robes, though they remained under Roman supervision in a stone house; it is not clear whether this was part of the fortress Antonia where they had formerly been housed. Whatever the exact arrange-ment, it appears to have gained the popular approval. Further, Vitellius remitted some taxes and, near the time when Tiberius died, agreed at the request of the prominent citizens not to bring troops with standards through Judaea.

We have already seen that Antipas was in sufficient favour to act as a kind of mediator between Vitellius and the Parthian Artabanus. However, the favour in which Agrippa, his brother-in-law, stood with the new emperor Caius was Antipas' undoing; Agrippa was given the territory of Philip (since his death, attached to Syria) and the title of king. Antipas went to Rome to plead for the same privileged title but fell victim to charges brought there against him by Agrippa's freedman Fortunatus and was banished to Gaul (*Ant.* XVIII 224–56).

B.   The reign of Agrippa I (41–44 CE)

M. **Avi-Yonah**, 'The Third and Second Walls of Jerusalem', *IEJ* XVIII, 1968, 98–125; J. P. V. D. **Balsdon**, 'The Chronology of Gaius' Dealings with the Jews', *JRS* XXIV, 1934, 13–24; idem, *The Emperor Gaius (Caligula)*, London: Oxford University Press 1934; P. W. **Barnett**, 'Under Tiberius All Was Quiet', *NTS* XXI, 1974/5, 564–71; K. M. **Kenyon**, *Digging up Jerusalem*, 1974; Y. **Meshorer**, *Jewish Coins of the Second Temple Period*, 1967, 78–80, 138–41; J. **Meyshan**, 'The Coinage of Agrippa the First', *IEJ* IV, 1954, 186–200; E. M. **Smallwood**, 'The Chronology of Gaius' Attempt to Desecrate the Temple', *Latomus* XVI, 1957, 3–17; idem, ed., *Philonis Alexandrini Legatio ad Gaium*, Leiden: E. J. Brill 1961, ²1970; J. W. **Swain**, 'Gamaliel's Speech and Caligula's Statue', *HTR* XXXVII, 1944, 341–9.

The government of Judaea after the departure of Pilate and the death of Tiberius is obscure. The vague statement of Tacitus in *Annals* 6.32 cannot establish that Vitellius included the governorship of the province among his specific tasks, and Josephus tells us nothing of the career of Marullus. Officially the province was restored to a Herodian, Agrippa I, son of Aristobulus IV, Herod's second son by Mariamme I, executed with his brother Alexander in 7 BCE. His sister was Herodias.

The circumstances by which this man, bearing the glamour of a Hasmonaean by his descent and of a Roman by his name, obtained his kingship, were more typical of Herodians than Hasmonaeans. He had been sent to Rome for his education at the age of six and grew up close to the imperial family, being a close friend of Drusus, son of Tiberius (*Ant.* XVIII 143–6). On Drusus' death in 23 CE Agrippa, who had formed expensive tastes and fallen into debt, felt compelled to leave Rome. In Idumaea he contemplated suicide but was given an administrative post in the new town of Tiberias by Antipas his brother-in-law (*Ant.* XVIII 147–50). Neither this nor any other arrangement lasted, and Agrippa reversed his direction to escape this time from Palestine to Rome, having raised a loan through the credit of his wife Cypros, 200,000 drachmae coming from Alexander the brother of Philo (*Ant.* XVIII 151–60). He became the close friend of Caius Caligula and was unwise enough to express to him his wish that Caius might soon displace Tiberius on the throne. The emperor heard of the remark and imprisoned Agrippa for six months, but soon after his accession Caius released him and gave him the former territory of Philip as a kingdom. In 39 CE he received also the tetrarchy of Antipas and in 41 CE Judaea and Samaria (*Ant.* XVIII 161–70, 185–90, 237–56).

The year 41 CE saw a threat to the temple which might have brought the war of 66 CE twenty-five years earlier. Tacitus (*Hist.* 5.9) after his laconic summary, *sub Tiberio quies* ('under Tiberius all was quiet'), briefly says that when ordered by Caius to place an effigy of himself in the temple the Jews chose rather to take up arms, a rising halted only by Caesar's death. In fact the people once more showed willingness to die rather than to fight, in order to prevent the sacrilege. Both Josephus and Philo (in his *Legatio ad Caium*) tell the story at length. The variations and attempts to reconcile them have been documented by Smallwood, who summarizes the situation in the Introduction to her excellent edition of the *Legatio*. Philo lived nearer the time and his account does not contain the fairy-story element found in Josephus.

In the spring of 40 CE, Caius decided to punish the Jews for their destruction of a Greek altar in Jamnia by turning the temple at Jerusalem into a centre of the imperial cult (*Leg.* 200–3; *Ant.* XVIII 261). He instructed P. Petronius, legate of Syria (39–41/42 CE), to make a statue of the emperor and take it when it was ready to Jerusalem, and to take with him two legions (*Ant.* XVIII 262; cf. *War* II 186). Although Petronius wisely chose distant Sidon as the place for the statue's construction and received a number of Jews in Antioch to report to them the proposed action of the Caesar, he was obliged to move to Ptolemais with the legions, impressed by the representatives' assurance that they would rather die than consent to the proposal (*Leg.* 207–23; *Ant.* XVIII 263–71). Petronius was concerned also by the neglect of the grain harvest, which was the result of the populace's preoccupation with the mass demonstrations to which he was subjected, even at Tiberias in the province itself (*Ant.* XVIII 272–86).

Petronius' conduct of this affair was as near exemplary as a Roman could contrive. Using every device appropriate to the slow-

ing up of the operation he warned Caius of the danger of an insurrection (*Leg.* 243–53; *Ant.* XVIII 287 f.). Caius replied ordering the
statue to be put up as soon as possible, though not writing with the
anger which he felt. Petronius delayed still further and meanwhile
Agrippa arrived in Italy for Caius' imperial ovation, ignorant of
what had been going on in the province. Caius told his friend of the
situation and shocked him so much that Agrippa was taken suddenly
ill. When he recovered a little he wrote Caius a letter begging him
not to carry out his threat, and this plea from a friend succeeded
where no official advice could (*Leg.* 261–338; *Ant.* XVIII 289–301).
According to Philo, Caius countermanded the order with the condition that Jews were not to hinder Gentiles when operating the imperial cult outside Jerusalem (*Leg.* 334–6). According to Josephus,
Caius ordered that if the statue had been placed in position by the
time the letter reached Petronius it was to remain (*Ant.* XVIII 301).
Philo's version is preferred on the ground that in the *Legatio* he is
inclined to make Caius' actions more rather than less heinous.
Josephus may well have been influenced in his version by a religious
conviction which he shows in several other places; he relates the
angry letter which Caius sent to Petronius, hinting that he should do
well to commit suicide (*Ant.* XVIII 302 f.), a fate which Petronius
escaped through news of Caius' death arriving before the letter (*Ant.*
XVIII 304), and Josephus concludes that Petronius was rewarded by
divine protection just as Caius was punished through the hand of the
assassin for his presumption in promoting his own worship instead of
that of God (*Ant.* XVIII 305–9). This interpretation of providential
action is parallel to his understanding of the fall of Antipas; and the
intention to let the statue remain if it had got as far as its place in
Jerusalem maintains as it were the emperor's guilt even though his
design was not carried out. It is curious that there is no record in all
this of a protest by the high priest. The appendix to the story in
Philo's account, that Caius had a splendid statue made in Rome,
intending to take it for erection in Jerusalem without telling the Jews
in advance, but did not live to carry out the plan, is of a piece with
the mad egoism and cruelty which led to his assassination, but there
is no means of knowing whether it is true or not (*Leg.* 337).

Agrippa proved a most acceptable ruler. M. Sotah 7.8 relates that
when he read the *sedarim* for the feast of tabernacles he wept on
reaching the admonition in Deuteronomy 17.15 forbidding an alien
ruler, but the crowd cried out assuring him he was their brother. He
has a good reputation in Josephus and the Talmud, both bearing
witness to his care for the law, which he scrupulously observed (*Ant.*

XIX 294, 331; XX 139; M. Bikkurim 3.1–9). Agrippa undertook a
building project to strengthen the defences of Jerusalem and began
the construction of a wall to the north of the city which Josephus
says would have made the city too strong for any human force (*Ant.*
XIX 326f.). However Marsus, the governor of Syria, protested and
prevented the completion of the wall and the refortification of the
city. The exact location of this north or 'third' wall (*War* V 147) is a
matter of archaeological debate (see Avi-Yonah and Kenyon).
Buildings, statues, and coins testify to his equal familiarity with just
those elements of pagan culture which were abhorrent to a pious
Jew (*Ant.* XIX 335–7, 343, 357; see Meshorer and Meyshan). It
may well be the external quality of his Judaism which accounts for
his apparent hostility to the tiny incipient church in Jerusalem
which led to the martyrdom of James son of Zebedee and the imprisonment of Peter (Acts 12.1–19). This was probably motivated
more by his desire to please the Jewish aristocracy than by any
conviction about Jesus and his followers; for there is no reason to
doubt the statements in Acts that the small but growing band was
popular with the people, giving no cause to be otherwise. Apart from
this unnecessary act of tyranny, his conduct may be said to consist
with a wise desire to keep the peace in a country of mixed culture, a
task which he performed with less ostentation and more success than
his grandfather. The accounts of his death in Acts (12.23) and in
Josephus (*Ant.* XIX 343–52), while not exactly the same, share some
curious elements which unite them. It is enough to say that it was
unpleasant and sudden and, though explicable as due to natural
causes, occurred soon after an adulatory crowd at the games at
Caesarea had acclaimed him as a god.

C.   *Judaea under Roman procurators* (44–66 CE)

M. **Aberbach**, 'The Conflicting Accounts of Josephus and Tacitus
Concerning Cumanus and Felix's Terms of Office', *JQR* XL, 1949, 1–14;
M. **Borg**, 'The Currency of the Term "Zealot"', *JTS* NS XXII, 1971,
504–12; S. G. F. **Brandon**, *Jesus and the Zealots*, 1967; idem, 'The Death of
James the Just: A New Interpretation', *Studies in Mysticism and Religion
Presented to Gershom Scholem*, ed. E. E. Urbach et al., Jerusalem: Magnes
Press, 1967, 57–69; J. **Goldin**, 'The Period of the Talmud (135 BCE–1035
CE)', *The Jews: Their History, Culture, and Religion*, ed. L. Finkelstein, New
York: Harper & Brothers 1949, ³1960, 115–215; M. **Hengel**, *Die Zeloten*,
AGSU 1, 1961; idem, 'Zeloten und Sikarier: Zur Frage nach der Einheit
und Vielfalt der jüdischen Befreiungsbewegung 6–74 n. Chr.', *Josephus-
Studien* (Festschrift Otto Michel), (see §4 above), 1974, 175–96; P. **Kingdon**,

'The Origins of the Zealots', *NTS* XIX, 1972, 74–81; Y. **Meshorer**, *Jewish Coins of the Second Temple Period*, 1967, 81–7, 141–53; idem, 'A New Type of Coins of Agrippa II', *IEJ* XXI, 1971, 164f.; D. M. **Rhoads**, *Israel in Revolution: 6–74 CE*, 1976; E. M. **Smallwood**, 'Some Comments on Tacitus, Annals xii 54', *Latomus* XVIII, 1959, 560–7; idem, 'High Priests and Politics in Roman Palestine', *JTS* NS XIII, 1962, 14–34; M. **Smith**, 'Zealots and Sicarii: Their Origins and Relation', *HTR* LXIV, 1971, 1–19; E. G. **Turner**, 'Tiberius Iulius Alexander', *JRS* XLIV, 1954, 54–64; S. **Zeitlin**, 'Zealots and Sicarii', *JBL* LXXXI, 1962, 395–8.

Claudius, who succeeded Caius in 41 CE, on the death of Agrippa placed Judaea under direct Roman rule and governed through procurators; the first was Cuspius Fadus (44–46 CE; *Ant.* XIX 363, *War* II 220). The right to make appointment to the office of high priest was awarded by Claudius to Herod of Chalcis at the latter's request (*Ant.* XX 15–16), Agrippa's son Agrippa II being too young to inherit either this privilege or his father's kingdom, although he received the honour in 48 CE on the death of Herod. In the meantime he was educated at the Roman court (*Ant.* XIX 354, 360–2). Fadus is in the *War* credited with not disturbing the country's customs (*War* II 220), but he did propose to regain custody of the high priest's robes and was dissuaded only when a deputation to the emperor brought back a letter from him upholding their objection and saying he had been influenced by the young Agrippa's support for their appeal (*Ant.* XX 6–14).

Fadus was energetic in putting down banditry in the country, but such activity was not always as benign as it seemed. Many Jews would have rejected Josephus' favourable verdict of Fadus in the *War* in the light of his ruthless suppression of Theudas and his followers related in the *Antiquities* (XX 97–9). Theudas called himself a prophet, which may be a dim sign of religious as well as nationalist patriotism. He is one of a list of popular leaders (Theudas appearing badly out of chronological order) mentioned in a speech attributed to Gamaliel in Acts 5.36f. and including also the followers of Jesus in Jerusalem at the time of the speech. The other person mentioned in the Acts list is Judas 'the Galilean', whose sons Jacob and Simon were crucified, according to Josephus, by the next procurator Tiberius Julius Alexander (46–48 CE), a son of the Jewish alabarch of the same name at Alexandria and so a nephew of Philo (*Ant.* XX 100–2). It is remarkable that a renegade Jew rising high enough to govern a province should go down in history as the executioner of Jewish patriots. Goldin in Finkelstein's volumes on the Jews remarks very well of this period that 'the *Weltanschauung*, the universe of discourse of the region with which the procurators and the Roman garrisons in this instance were charged, was entirely beyond their comprehension' (Goldin, 135), but this cannot apply to the Jewish Alexander.

Ventidius Cumanus, procurator 48–52 CE, showed the disability Goldin describes, although he was twice put in a difficult position by the ignorant rashness of serving soldiers (*Ant.* XX 103; *War* II 223). The first occurred at the passover of 49 CE when a soldier from the fortress Antonia and stationed in the outskirts of the temple precinct made an indecent gesture to the crowd, causing a riot which resulted according to Josephus in the death of about 20,000 people (*Ant.* XX 105–12; *War* II 224–7). Such an incident illustrates the fact that the first Jewish revolt did not really begin in 66 CE but rather at the death of Herod the Great, with periods of uneasy quiet between outbursts. A further incident was the looting of villages near Jerusalem by Roman soldiers as punishment for an attack on an imperial slave. In the course of this a soldier tore up a copy of the Torah before the people, and Cumanus had to concede to the mass deputation which demanded revenge, the execution of this soldier (*Ant.* XX 113–17; *War* II 228–31). Such incidents show that feeling was running very high and is illustrative of that nervousness in an occupying army which is produced by and in its turn produces more tension in the local population and turns unrest into a running guerrilla war between army and inhabitants. That there were organized guerrilla resisters is proved by the next incident recorded of the rule of Cumanus: some Galilean Jews were murdered on their way to a festival by Samaritans (whose tendency to harass Jews in this manner is illustrated by Luke 9.51–6). Cumanus refused justice to the aggrieved Jews, having been bribed by the Samaritans, and this blindness brought something like a full war against Samaria at the hands of an armed band led by Eleazar son of Dinaeus and Alexander (the latter mentioned only in the *War*). Pleas from Jerusalem Jews after military action by Cumanus restrained the rebels, but Josephus adds that from then the whole of Judaea was infested with gangs of bandits. This is in effect testimony to the activity, as badly organized as it was ever to be, of groups of zealots (*Ant.* XX 118–28; *War* II 232–40).

Cumanus' career came to an end when all the parties concerned were judged with very rough justice by Ummidius Quadratus, legate of Syria; while many were punished, Cumanus was sent into exile by Claudius before whom he had to appear (*Ant.* 129–33; *War* II 241–

6). His successor was Felix, brother of the influential freedman Pallas, a choice requested by Jonathan (high priest briefly in 37 CE). Goldin includes Felix in his list of those, headed by Pilate, for whom 'the country was no more than a gold mine to be exploited for private benefit' (135), a verdict mild compared with Tacitus' estimate of his character (*Ann.* 12.54). Judaea's fate in receiving Felix was the more miserable in that his cupidity was practised on a nation already at breaking point. *Schürer judges with some moderation towards Felix's predecessors when he says that 'under Felix rebellion became permanent' (460).

Felix had some success: he captured (by treachery) and sent to Rome Eleazar, who had ravaged the country for twenty years and crucified a large number of other 'bandits'; but his very success had sinister consequences, in that it drove the already desperate militants into clandestine action even in Jerusalem, starting the appalling phenomenon of the *sicarii*, who mingled with crowds, concealing beneath their clothes short daggers; their terrorism fed by success with these weapons turned inevitably into destruction not only of enemies but of those who wished to remain non-belligerent, including the high priest Jonathan, whom Felix bribed some of them to murder (*Ant.* XX 137–44, 160–6; *War* II 247, 253–60). A clear sign of the hysteria now seizing the people was the rise of a number of religious fanatics, who Josephus says, in comparison with the *sicarii*, had 'cleaner hands but wickeder intentions'. The fanatics pathetically looked to direct divine intervention for succour and freedom, and led people into the wilderness to await this intervention (*Ant.* XX 167f.).

One of these leaders was an Egyptian for whom Paul was mistaken when arrested in Jerusalem (Acts 21.38) after an active and devoted career as a Christian missionary (*Ant.* XX 169–72; *War* II 261–3). It is impossible to say accurately when Paul experienced the remarkable conversion which he himself never describes but to which he firmly witnesses, and which in Acts is told in the form of a kind of theophany in the Hellenistic-Jewish manner. This experience convinced him that the Jesus whose followers he had hitherto persecuted was calling him to his service. Paul drew firmly the conclusion that Jesus must be alive and, since he had been crucified, enormous consequences followed. He had been raised by God, therefore he was the Messiah whom Paul along with some other contemporary Pharisees expected to come to establish his kingdom. The totally unexpected phenomenon of a crucified Messiah demanded a bold explanation: that he was the sacrificial means of atonement provided by God for all those who would accept him and call him Lord. All such, and these would include even Gentiles, must await the consummation of the general resurrection now evidently inaugurated, and it was the duty of all who acknowledge these truths to tell as many as possible of all nations of the coming judgment by the Messiah and the graciously offered opportunity of salvation.

Such a message involved too much rethinking and was too bold a claim for the average Jew, however moderate and liberal, and for the fanatic it meant the necessity of ruthless opposition to Paul's plans. It is small wonder therefore that he needed protective custody when in about 58 or 59 CE he returned to Jerusalem, after about twenty years as a Christian; and he was fortunate that in those troubled times he escaped murder at Jewish hands by rescue at those of Romans.

The duration of Felix's procuratorship is not certain; it appears to be 52–60 CE, but it may be argued that he must have been recalled, to be saved from disgrace by the intervention of Pallas, by 55 CE when Pallas fell from favour. This makes it necessary to reject the implied date for the taking over of the governorship by his successor Festus in 60 CE. We ought not to press the 'two years' of Acts 24.27, for we do not know whether this refers to the time which elapsed between Felix's last dealings with Paul and the arrival of Festus or to the whole of Felix's procuratorship. Probably it is best to assume that, though less powerful after 55 CE, Pallas was still able effectively to plead for Felix in 58 CE (see *Schürer, 465 n. 42, for a discussion of the chronological problems).

Some comfort can be derived both from the rescue of Paul and from the eventual recall of Felix for those who in the face of many facts like to believe in the ultimate benignity of Roman government. Acts plots the date of Paul's appearance before Felix with some accuracy. Felix had in 53 or 54 CE married Drusilla, sister of Agrippa II, and already a widow at a tender age (*Ant.* XX 141–3). She is mentioned in Acts 24.24. A little later Paul appears before Festus, who invites Agrippa II to attend a hearing, which he does with his other sister Berenice who at that time was living – as she did for a short period – with her brother. It is plausible guess, or perhaps historical, that according to Acts 24.25 Paul spoke before Felix and Drusilla suitably enough of 'righteousness and self-control and of the coming judgment' and that Felix took fright at this preaching. It is altogether in character that Felix should 'expect money to be given him by Paul'. Paul was probably still held prisoner in Caesarea when a dispute arose there between the Syrian and Jewish inhabitants, the latter claiming priority as the nationality appropriate to the Herodian foundation (*Ant.* XX 173–8; *War* II 266–70). Street fighting had not been quelled in 60 CE when Felix was recalled to Rome, where he was undeservedly acquitted. Moreover, Nero cancelled the Jewish *isopoliteia* in Caesarea which had granted the Jews civil rights (*Ant.* XX 183f.).

Nero had been emperor since 54 CE. In 60 CE he sent Festus to Judaea (*Ant.* XX 182; *War* II 271). This governor seems to have been well-intentioned, but he was unable to stop the banditry now in full flood (*Ant.* XX 185–8). Having inherited Paul as a prisoner, he entertained Agrippa II and Berenice to a hearing of him and then sent him to Rome. Agrippa II, who had been educated at Rome and was in favour with Claudius, seems also to have enjoyed that of Nero. Claudius had given him (in about 50 CE) the kingdom of his uncle Herod of Chalcis, together with the right, which he frequently exercised, of appointing the high priest (*Ant.* XX 104; *War* II 223). He took up residence in Palestine late, and was in 53 CE given the territory of Philip's former tetrarchy, Abila, and some land in Lebanon instead of the kingdom of Chalcis where he may never have resided (*Ant.* XX 138; *War* II 247). Nero added to all this the cities of Tiberias and Tarichaeae and Julias, each with neighbouring villages (*Ant.* XX 159; *War* II 252). Paul's challenge to him at the hearing before Festus according to Acts 26.27: 'I know you believe', was founded on the king's known carefulness, like that of his father, towards Judaism, but he was even more firmly identified with the Roman side, his coins bearing the image of reigning emperors (see Meshorer). He represents a phenomenon inevitable at those times – a king of the Jews who acted on behalf of Rome and was probably right in his conviction that to be a loyal province of the Roman empire was a *sine qua non* condition for survival as a state.

Festus had to deal with yet another fanatical leader seeking inspiration in the wilderness (*Ant.* XX 188; *War* II 271). He did so with severity, but when he died in office in 60 CE the flood of opposition was stronger than ever. There was virtual anarchy for two years after Festus' death, during which the high priest Ananus, although he served for only three months, was able to pursue policies of a private hatred (*Ant.* XX 197–9, 203). It is significant that he secured the death of James the brother of Jesus, reflecting the active part played by his father of the same name in the death of Jesus; and that his murder was strongly resented by moderate Jews in Jerusalem by whom James was much revered (*Ant.* XX 200–2).

The last two procurators immediately before the war, Albinus

(62–64 CE) and Gessius Florus (64–66 CE) can hardly be said to have governed (*Ant.* XX 197, 204–15, 252–8; *War* II 272–9). Agrippa did something to help his fellow-countrymen, seeking to alleviate the unemployment caused by the completion of the temple at this time by setting the labourers to pave the city with white stone (*Ant.* XX 219–22) but the procurators contributed to anarchy by dealing with the *sicarii*, by allowing theft and corruption, and behaving as though they were bandit chiefs. Josephus makes the only difference between them that Albinus plundered individuals under a cloak of governing but Florus plundered whole cities and villages, the actual bandits paying him off like regular gangsters (*War* II 277–9).

Josephus devotes much space to details of the increasing disorder under Florus; his account is a well-documented defence of the pacific efforts of moderates in the face of wild but deliberate provocation by the procurator (*War* II 280–335). These representatives of the people secured the intervention of C. Cestius Gallus, the governor of Syria, whose envoy, the tribune Neapolitanus, met Agrippa at Jamnia on his way home from Alexandria, and the two did what they could to prevent open rebellion (*War* II 336–44). Josephus here inserts a speech by Agrippa which expounds the futility of war with Rome, half-conceals a hint that Jews of the diaspora, especially in Babylonia, might also rebel (though in vain), and meets directly their hope for divine intervention by icy logic: observance of the law involves the sabbath, which gives the enemy an overwhelming advantage; transgression of it forfeits divine aid (*War* II 345–404).

§6. THE FIRST JEWISH REVOLT (66–74 CE)

Y. **Baer**, 'Jerusalem in the Times of the Great Revolt', *Zion* XXXVI, 1971, 127–90 (Hebrew); S. G. F. **Brandon**, *The Fall of Jerusalem and the Christian Church*, London: SPCK 1951, ²1957; A. **Büchler**, 'On the Provisioning of Jerusalem in the Year 69–70 CE', in his *Studies in Jewish History*, ed. I. Brodie and J. Rabbinowitz, London: Oxford University Press 1956, 98–125; G. R. **Driver**, *The Judaean Scrolls*, Oxford: Basil Blackwell 1965; W. **Eck**, 'Die Eroberung von Masada und eine neue Inschrift des L. Flavius Silva Nonius Bassus', *ZNW* LX, 1969, 282–9; idem, *Senatoren von Vespasian bis Hadrian*, München: C. H. Beck 1970, 93–111; P. **Kingdon**, 'Who Were the Zealots and Their Leaders in AD 66?', *NTS* XVII, 1970, 68–72; Y. **Meshorer**, *Jewish Coins of the Second Temple Period*, 1967, 88–91, 154–8; J. **Neusner**, *From Politics to Piety*, 1973; D. M. **Rhoads**, *Israel in Revolution: 6–74 CE*, 1976; I. A. **Richmond**, 'The Roman Siegeworks of Masada, Israel', *JRS* LII, 1962, 142–55; C. **Roth**, 'An Ordinance Against Images in Jerusalem, AD 66', *HTR* XLIX, 1957, 169–77; idem, 'The Zealots in the

War of 66–73', *JSS* IV, 1959, 332–55; idem, 'The Debate on the Loyal Sacrifices, AD 66', *HTR* LII, 1960, 93–7; idem, 'The Historical Implications of the Jewish Coinage of the First Revolt', *IEJ* XII, 1962, 33–46; idem, 'The Pharisees in the Jewish Revolution of 66–73', *JSS* VII, 1962, 63–80; idem, 'The Constitution of the Jewish Republic of 66–70', *JSS* IX, 1964, 295–319; S. G. **Sowers**, 'The Circumstances and Recollection of the Pella Flight', *TZ* XXVI, 1970, 305–20; R. **de Vaux**, 'The Judaean Scrolls: 2. Essenes or Zealots', *NTS* XII, 1966, 89–104; Y. **Yadin**, 'The Excavation of Masada – 1963/4. Preliminary Report', *IEJ* XV, 1965, 1–120; idem, *Masada: Herod's Fortress and the Zealots' Last Stand*, 1966; S. **Zeitlin**, 'The Sicarii and Masada', *JQR* LVII, 1967, 251–70.

Agrippa was but momentarily successful: he could persuade the people to submit to Rome in general but not to Florus; he therefore retired to his own kingdom (*War* II 405–7). About this time (66 CE) some zealots captured Masada by a trick, and began their occupation which lasted until 74 CE (*War* II 408). This was also the year in which Eleazar, son of the high priest Ananus and captain of the temple guard, persuaded the temple ministers to accept no gift or sacrifice belonging to an alien (*War* II 409). It appears that this meant the cessation of sacrifices on behalf of Rome and Caesar; no sacrifices were to be accepted from or on behalf of aliens (see Roth, 1960). Tantamount to a declaration of war, the measure provoked at once a meeting of moderates – the peace party – including high priestly circles and Pharisees. They decided to appeal to the insurgents, and the arguments which according to Josephus they used are interesting: they urged the propriety of what they claimed to be an old tradition that no man had ever been debarred from sacrifice, and they pointed out that the sanctuary had been adorned at foreign expense (*War* II 410–17). It seems that this is rather more than an argument made up by Josephus, for he says that the advocates of peace produced well-informed priests as witnesses to testify that their ancestors had always accepted offerings from aliens. Encouraged by Florus, to whom they reported, the peace party occupied the Upper City, the higher of the two hills west of the Tyropoeon valley, the Lower City with the temple and the Acra or fortress being in rebel hands (*War* II 418–22). There followed the first of the senseless and tragic internecine struggles among the inhabitants of Jerusalem (and indeed of Judaea) which augured the certain failure of the revolt (*War* II 423–32). The divisions do not seem to have followed the old lines of the days of the Maccabees, when an opponent of revolt was probably a 'Hellenist'; it is true that the Zealots were true spiritual descendants of the Maccabees, but their opponents were not

Hellenists and accepted the Roman rule less because of their eagerness for modern culture than because they acknowledged the inevitability of that rule. Their culture, though influenced by Hellenism, was Jewish and they wished it to remain so; but the pressure of weighty facts was turning many religious patriots, especially Pharisees, into quietists (see Neusner). When they became militant, it was for the time being, and in order to assert their conviction that submission to Rome was necessary. We may wonder whether to admire more the heroism and courage of zealots or the wisdom (which itself demanded courage) of the moderates, but we should not ignore the fact that these latter were for the most part men of some means or at least enjoyed some security. They clearly had a stake in the maintenance of the *status quo*. What is certain is that heroism and bravery on many sides were marred by acts of savage cruelty towards fellow-countrymen which it is hard to understand or to excuse.

Menahem, a son of the original 'zealot' Judas, emerged in this crisis. He went to Masada and brought back arms stored there by Herod, returning 'like a veritable king to Jerusalem'. With a few men whom he armed with these he was successful in turning out the Roman cohorts from the upper palace, whither they had gone from the Antonia; some escaped into the towers of Hippicus, Phasael, and Mariamme, but those who were too slow were butchered by Menahem. In this situation the moderates fared ill; Ananias (son of Nebedaeus and high priest 48–59 CE) had already suffered the loss of his house and Agrippa and Berenice that of their palaces. Ananus was found in hiding and murdered along with his brother Hezekiah (*War* II 433–47). Menahem did not live to enjoy his success, for he was opposed by Eleazar and perished along with many of his followers. Among those who escaped was another Eleazar, son of Yair, also descended from Judas; he made his way to Masada, where he was to achieve fame as the desperate leader of the last stand in the war (*War* II 448–56).

The uprising in Jerusalem was reflected strongly elsewhere; where there was a Jewish colony sometimes the Jews took the initiative, suggesting a feeling of revolt against non-Jewish culture in general, but in Caesarea at least the Syrian population massacred the Jews (*War* II 457–65). There was similar slaughter in Scythopolis and this set off a series of such events in other cities, not only in the Decapolis but also in Ascalon and Ptolemais (*War* II 466–86). A wave of anti-Semitism also engulfed Alexandria, where trouble between the Greek and Jewish sections of the population was endemic (*War* II

487–98). Josephus makes this seem the last straw, but in reality (as he is aware) it was the evidently universal involvement of Jews in uprisings which moved C. Cestius Gallus, legate of Syria from about 63 to 66 CE, to advance on Judaea. He attacked Zebulun, Ptolemais, and Caesarea and was welcomed in Sepphoris. For the moment the rebellion seemed to have subsided in Galilee and Cestius moved on to Jerusalem. Here he was unexpectedly repulsed by a furious on-slaught on a sabbath day, and though his fortunes seemed to change and he was in sight apparently of victory, he did not press his advan-tage but withdrew, Jewish forces pursuing the Romans as far as Antipatris. The legion involved in this defeat was the twelfth, henceforth in disgrace (*War* II 499–555).

Jewish success naturally did nothing for the cause of the moder-ates, some of whom left the city (*War* II 556); others saw that there was now no alternative to resistance, perhaps persuaded by per-vasive hostility to their race, another pogrom occurring at this junc-ture in Damascus (*War* II 559–61). The inhabitants of Jerusalem now therefore chose their commanders: to be in charge of the city they appointed Joseph son of Gorion and Ananus son of Ananus, who had been high priest briefly in 62 CE and had then secured the death of James the brother of Jesus; his choice probably indicates a mood of acceptance of diehard aristocrats, although Eleazar soon recovered his ascendancy over the people. Others are of lesser note, except the historian Josephus, to whom all Galilee was assigned along with Gamala (*War* II 562–8). Extensive parts of the sub-sequent section of his history are devoted to favourable accounts of his conduct; he writes with the same wily skill as appears often in his behaviour; sometimes he acts (as at the outset) as an enthusiastic patriot sensibly training those under him to meet Roman might with Roman methods; at other times he acts as if convinced that Rome was divinely destined to victory owing to the past sins and present wicked folly of the Jewish people.

The details of Josephus' adventures in Galilee are uncertain (*War* II 569–84). According to the *War* he had as subordinate John of Gischala, who fortified his native town under Josephus' supervision (though it is doubtful if the latter contributed anything practical to the plan), but won Josephus' persistent hatred by cornering supplies of oil and making a large profit by selling to Jews in Syria (*War* II 585–94). In the *Life*, John appears in a much more favourable light; he tried to restrain elation in Gischala at the outbreak of revolt, but extremists destroyed the city. John regained possession of it and rebuilt it more strongly than before (*Life* 43–5, 70–6). Josephus is probably right in thinking that John was unscrupulous and that he planned to supplant Josephus himself as leader in Galilee. He is also probably correct in his report that John spread a rumour that Josephus planned to betray the country to the Romans, but here he is less justified in his indignation (*War* II 594).

There follow tales of various tricks and subterfuges; robbers foiled by Josephus denounced him as a traitor, again a case of a pot calling black a kettle which was not altogether white (*War* II 595–631). He escaped death several times by devices in which the will to survival appears prominently. If he can hardly be blamed for these, nor for escaping assassination by John, his ruses against dissidents in Tiberias and his subsequent looting of that city and of Sepphoris are among actions which reveal a streak of cruelty which his candour does nothing to commend (*War* II 632–46).

In the *Life*, Josephus is even more candid; he relates how he went over to a policy of paying the robbers but hesitated to implement this policy to the full (*Life* 126–31). When John sent a request to Jerusalem for the removal of Josephus, the latter outwitted the four sent to supersede him, asserted his position as general and prepared to fight the Roman forces (*Life* 189–335).

The first year saw also the rise of Simon son of Gioras, who began by ravaging Idumaea, using Masada as a base, although Ananus and his assistant were able to deter him from coming to Jerusalem (*War* II 652–4).

Cestius appears to have died early in 67 CE (Tacitus hints that he may have committed suicide; *Hist.* 5.10) and Nero sent T. Flavius Vespasianus to take his place. Vespasian, who made his name as a commander in the invasion of Britain under Claudius (43–44 CE), had held various offices with distinction. Before his arrival the rebels made a determined attack on the town of Ascalon, a Greek city since the conquest of Alexander, but suffered a severe defeat (*War* III 2–28). Agrippa met Vespasian at Antioch and they marched at once to Ptolemais, where they met a deputation from Sepphoris, whose submission enabled Vespasian to garrison that town. He thus easily gained a most important base in Galilee (*War* III 29–34). His son Titus had been summoned from Alexandria with the fifteenth legion; he duly arrived in Ptolemais so that their combined forces included the fifth, tenth, and fifteenth legions as well as auxiliaries from the third and twenty-second (*War* III 8, 64–70). This large force required time for full organization. During this time Josephus successfully defended the strongly fortified town of Jotapata, fourteen Roman miles from Ptolemais and overlooking Sepphoris from a mountain seven miles to the north. During the siege he stole away to Tiberias, whence he wrote to Jerusalem proposing submission to the Romans. It shows one of his strange changes of mood that he reports that on returning to Jotapata he was able to put new heart into the defenders. The town fell only after a protracted siege described in much ghastly detail and which includes at the end an account of his own escape from death: left with one other as the last two of a suicide pact group, he eloquently persuaded his companion of the logical impropriety of completing the bargain (*War* III 110–306, 316–91). He thus fell prisoner to Vespasian, who treated him well and whom he astonished by asking for a hearing in which he prophesied that Vespasian would be emperor, and claimed to have come as a divine messenger. Vespasian's suspicion of a hoax was changed into wonder by enquiry which revealed that Josephus had correctly prophesied the events and times connected with the fall of Jotapata (*War* III 392–408).

It is possible that Josephus was led by genuine religious conviction concerning himself as merely part of the portents now beginning to multiply; or he may have engineered the whole episode and partly or wholly deceived himself about his own motives. He was capable of either or a mixture of both. In his subsequent writing Vespasian and Titus are his heroes, but he does not lose his religious convictions nor his admiration for the people to whom he was less than completely loyal. It is to his credit that he gives a full account of the distress and feelings of hatred towards himself which the news of Jotapata's fall caused in Jerusalem (*War* III 438–42).

Vespasian and Titus continued their gradual, costly and grisly conquests. Operating from Caesarea, Vespasian captured Joppa and by September 67 CE had put down rebellion in Agrippa's territory, including Tiberias and Tarichaeae (*War* III 409–502). With the surrender of the latter all remaining Galileans gave in except Gischala and a garrison on Mount Tabor. They were supported by Gamala on the east side of the lake. This town was besieged and here Agrippa was slightly wounded; the defenders had some success, necessitating a restoration of morale in his forces by Vespasian, who secured the capture of Mount Tabor. When Gamala fell at last its inhabitants were cruelly treated, but Gischala under John still held out until John and some followers fled to Jerusalem. With the consequent fall of Gischala all Galilee was by the end of 67 CE again in Roman hands (*War* IV 1–120).

John appears to have thought that Jerusalem was the one place possible to defend, and on his arrival tried to persuade the people that it would never fall (*War* IV 121–7). Some may have believed him, but despair was already beginning in 68 CE to grip the citizens; this increased the intensity of factious divisions in the city which the circumstances make almost incredible (*War* IV 128–61). It is doubtful if by this time any reasonable terms could have been expected for a surrender, and this prevailing sense must have further increased the strife, so that a veritable miniature civil war raged within the city (*War* IV 193–223). Ananus seems to have been energetic in discharging his office, and he was probably right to counsel peace in spite of the severe terms to be expected (*War* IV 162–92). But Josephus is not justified in dismissing all the zealots as criminals, bloodthirsty and pitiless as they were. His own record was more respectable but did not really invite scrutiny. It must be admitted that the zealots now behaved with some fierce cruelty: they called in Idumaeans for support and in a resultant blood-bath several of the conservative leaders fell, including Ananus and Jesus son of Gamaliel (high priest 63–64 CE) (*War* IV 224–344). When the Idumaeans left, the zealots continued the same reign of terror (*War* IV 345–65).

*Schürer (498) thinks that it may have been about this time that the Christian church in Jerusalem migrated to Pella, warned by an oracle to leave 'before the war began'; on this interpretation the 'war' would be confined to the siege of Jerusalem, and the difficulties of making their way to Pella may have been considerable. Moreover Eusebius, who related this event in his *Ecclesiastical History* 3.5.3–4, has greatly condensed his chronology in the passage (if this is the correct understanding). On the other hand James, the leader of the church, seems to have been in Jerusalem until his death in 62 CE, and the conquests so far of Vespasian may have produced enough tranquillity for such a migration before the storm burst upon Jerusalem (see Brandon and Sowers on the problem).

For the time being the Romans made no move and insurgents grew bolder still in all Judaea, including Masada, which they used as a base for raids on the neighbourhood (*War* IV 366–77, 398–409). In the Decapolis, Gadara, fearing the consequences of Jewish success, sent to Vespasian with an offer of surrender. The Jewish population fled on his approach but many were massacred; the slaughter was terrible and dead bodies were carried down the Jordan even as far as the Dead Sea (*War* IV 413–37).

On the eve of decisive action against Jerusalem Vespasian was delayed, in June 68 CE, by the arrival of the news of the death of Nero. Once more Roman politics played an important part in the fate of Judaea. Vespasian sent his son to do homage to Galba but

tidings of the latter's assassination met Titus at Corinth. He returned
to Caesarea, but no immediate action followed (*War* IV 491–502).
The troubles of Jerusalem continued to be those which her own
people inflicted on her; for this year saw the rise of Simon son of
Gioras as a freelance guerrilla who used his ravages of the countryside to train an army to advance upon Jerusalem. The zealots attacked him in vain and he defeated the Idumaeans by a trick. His
wife having been stolen from him by his Jerusalem opponents, he
appeared before the city and demanded her return, strengthening
his plea with acts of atrocity against those on whom he could lay his
hands. Successful, he fell to further acts of brigandage (*War* IV 503–
44). Josephus estimates that for the Jews within the city John inside
was worse than Simon outside, and both worse than the Romans. It
was not long before some opponents of John brought in Simon who
became master of the city (*War* IV 556–82).

Vespasian still remained inactive in Caesarea, but in 69 CE
resolved to go to Rome in what proved to be a successful bid for the
throne. Before he left he made sure that all Judaea was quiet, except
Jerusalem, Herodium, Machaerus, and Masada; and he organized
support for his own cause in Egypt, where he had eager assistance
from Tiberius Alexander, the former procurator over Judaea and
since about 64 CE prefect of Egypt (*War* IV 585–606, 616–21). It was
also at this time that Vespasian, in the judgment of Josephus, felt
that he was beginning to succeed, and saw that his prisoner's prophecy was on the way to vindication; and for this reason he set him
free (*War* IV 622–9). Hence Josephus became an observer of the rest
of the grim campaign from the Roman side and took some part in it
as a would-be negotiator.

Vespasian left Titus in charge of the Roman forces for the reduction of Jerusalem, with the assistance of Alexander as *praefectus
praetorio*, the equivalent of chief staff officer and therefore often effectively the commander of the whole force and always chief adviser to
Titus himself (*War* IV 658–63). The eve of the siege saw the city's
defenders in absurd and tragic division; the zealots were themselves
split into factions and over against them Simon pursued his own ends
(*War* V 1–38). These groups carried on active warfare among themselves so that Tacitus' reference (*Hist.* 5.12) is a masterpiece of ab-
breviation:

> Three leaders, as many armies. Simon had fortified the furthest and
> longest part of the walls, John the middle city, Eleazar the temple. Num-
> bers and weapons were the strength of John and Simon, position that of

Eleazar; but there were battles, ambush and arson against one another, and a great store of corn was burnt.

Titus' first attack was unsuccessful and it even produced some measure of unity among the defenders, but after further successes they were again divided (*War* V 39–135, 248–57). Josephus claims to have made several attempts and two major speeches to convince the people of the uselessness of their defence, striking the note of divine retribution for past sins, and especially for not submitting to Rome, which was divinely destined to rule. He supports his argument with historical references, interesting chiefly for their sometimes extravagant inaccuracy, strange in so well-read an author but reflecting in some degree the contemporary Hellenistic-Jewish tradition of the times, along with an interesting inability to appreciate the lengths of time involved in the history upon which he draws (*War* V 114, 261, 361–420, 541–7; VI 96–110).

The siege continued through different military stages which Josephus describes in detail; at first the battle was for the northern walls, but attacks here were ineffective until Titus decided to build a $4\frac{1}{2}$-mile siege wall right round the city (*War* V 258–90, 299–347, 424–59, 499–511). By this time the state of the besieged had become that of endurance of horrors and atrocities as terrible as any in history. Internecine murders were part of everyday life. Simon owed his position in the city to Matthias (called here by Josephus 'son of Boethus' but probably identical with Matthias, son of Theophilus [*Ant.* XX 223] and high priest between 64 and 66 CE). This very man who had secured his invitation Simon now brutally murdered after forcing him to witness the death of three of his sons (*War* V 527–32). In the end famine assisted suicidal divisions and was decisive in weakening the defenders (*War* V 424–45; VI 193–213). The Antonia was captured and laid flat; the wall still dividing the attackers from the temple was scaled by the use of platforms, and the gates on the north were fired (*War* VI 23–95, 129–52, 220–8). Titus is reported to have ordered the fire to be put out since he feared for the temple. He then initiated among his staff a debate on the propriety of burning the temple, during which the fire took hold. Even then Titus is credited with trying to stop it but being unable to restrain his soldiers (*War* VI 236–66). The temple was thus destroyed by fire, an event which from the point of view of Judaism exceeded in importance anything else reported by Josephus. The Upper City was not long in falling after the capture of the temple area and Lower City. What was left was systematically destroyed.

The year was 70 CE and the month Elul (August/September) (*War* VI 354f., 363f., 392–408).

Titus left the tenth legion to garrison what had been Jerusalem, and dismissed the twelfth to the Armenian–Cappadocian border; the fifth and fifteenth were to accompany him to Egypt whence they eventually departed to Moesia and Pannonia. For the present Titus returned to Caesarea, whence he proceeded to Caesarea Philippi for games in which some prisoners were compelled to fight to the death in gladiatorial shows (*War* VII 17–36). Visits to other cities for similar barbarities ended in Alexandria where he discharged the legions and reserved prisoners, including Simon and John, for the Roman triumph which took place the following year (71 CE), a double triumph with that of Vespasian. The execution of Simon formed part of it, as did also the procession of booty which included the Menorah and other temple furniture, made famous by the carving on the inner side of the Arch of Titus (*War* VII 116–62).

To Lucilius Bassus, governor of Judaea, was left the task of capturing the fortresses still holding out. He reduced Herodium and Machaerus (the latter with some difficulty) but Masada was set for a siege destined to surpass that of Jerusalem in the reputation which excavation in our time has given it (*War* VII 163–215). Bassus having died, the task of attacking it fell to his successor Flavius Silva and the tenth legion. Its defenders were zealots, no doubt many of them refugees from Jerusalem, supplementing the original force which had held it since 66 CE. There were present, presumably since 68 CE, some of the sectarians from Qumran which had been destroyed by Vespasian in his campaign of that year. It matters little whether these were zealots or Essenes (see Driver and de Vaux) since they were now united by a common desperate situation and many of them by as desperate a religious belief that they were about to take part in the final war of the age in which God himself would intervene on their behalf. This had been the expectation of some of the defenders of Jerusalem, but what appears to have united the defenders of Masada far more were the sentiments expressed by their leader, Eleazar, son of Yair and a descendant of the famous Judas the Galilaean. Again Josephus describes in detail the course of the siege and the measures taken by the Romans to make a breach in the defences of a fort well strengthened by nature and human ingenuity (*War* VII 252–406). His description has now been substantially confirmed by excavation (see Yadin). When defeat was seen to be inevitable, the inhabitants were persuaded to commit mass suicide rather than endure slavery at the hands of the Romans, and the only survivors were two women and five children. It has been thought for centuries, following Josephus, that the date of the final fall of Masada must be April 73 CE, but two newly-discovered inscriptions show that Silva cannot have become governor of Judaea until 73 CE (see Eck). Thus the earliest date for the fall is 74 CE, and this must be the year which completes with tragic finality a sad period of Jewish history.

§7. JUDAISM AFTER THE DESTRUCTION OF THE TEMPLE

S. W. **Baron**, *A Social and Religious History of the Jews* II: *Ancient Times*, II, New York: Columbia University Press, 1952, 89–122, 368–77; M. **Douglas**, *Purity and Danger*, London/New York: Routledge & Kegan Paul/Praeger 1966; J. **Neusner**, *A History of the Jews in Babylonia*, I–V, SPB 9, 11–12, 14–15, 1965–70; idem, *Development of a Legend: Studies on the Traditions Concerning Yohanan ben Zakkai*, SPB 16, 1970; idem, *A Life of Yohanan ben Zakkai*, SPB 6, ²1970; idem, *Eliezer ben Hyrcanus: The Tradition and the Man*, I–II SJLA 3–4, 1973; idem, *From Politics to Piety*, 1973; idem, *The Idea of Purity in Ancient Judaism: The Haskell Lectures, 1972–1973*, SJLA 1, 1973; idem, *A History of the Mishnaic Laws of Purities*, I–, SJLA 6, 1974–; idem, *First-Century Judaism in Crisis: Yohanan ben Zakkai and the Renaissance of Torah*, Nashville: Abingdon Press 1975; Y. **Yadin**, *The Finds from the Bar Kokhba Period in the Cave of Letters*, Jerusalem: Israel Exploration Society 1963; idem, *Bar-Kokhba: The Rediscovery of the Legendary Hero of the Last Jewish Revolt Against Imperial Rome*, London/New York: Weidenfeld & Nicolson/Random House 1971.

The history of the Jews in the period between the destruction of the second temple in 70 CE and the outbreak of the Bar-Kokhba War in 132 CE is to be divided into two parts, political and social, and religious. In the writer's opinion, one cannot improve upon the discussion of political and social history by Salo W. Baron. We therefore shall concentrate on the history of Judaism. This decision, furthermore, is justified by the nature of our sources. They do not make possible the description of the history of the period. We simply do not know, in a more or less coherent and continuous way, precisely what happened from year to year or decade to decade. It is important to specify the difference in extant sources pertinent to the period before us and those which preceded it.

Since Josephus provides extensive foundations for the study of the history of the Jews and of Judaism, the period before 70 CE is treated in narrative style. We are able to tell a fairly continuous story.

Indeed, the main outlines of that story commonly consist of a paraphrase of Josephus. After 70 CE we have no such source; no continuous or narrative history is possible. Instead, we have religious
documents of various kinds; we can never be entirely certain whom
these documents represent, all the more so to whom they spoke. Our
own concerns naturally lead to stress upon the two groups in
Palestinian Jewry between 70 and 132 CE who are seen by contemporaries as 'spiritual' ancestors, the Christians, whether or not still
identified with the larger Jewish group, and the rabbis. Apocalyptic
writings, preserved under Christian auspices, hardly yield considerable information on what was happening in the country. While
Talmudic and related sources contain many stories about authorities
assumed to have lived between 70 and 132 CE, none of these stories
can be shown to have been composed during the period of which
they speak. The laws of Mishnah-Tosefta assigned to these same
authorities, to be sure, probably do derive, in some instances even in
their exact wording, from this period. But they do not address themselves to those subjects normally regarded as important in the writing of history, for example, political, social, economic, and other
practical matters. Accordingly, it is not possible to supply the continuous narrative of historical events, even those of primarily religious
interest, for the period under discussion, in a way parallel to the
narrative which pertains to the Hasmonaean and early Roman periods.

Yet there is the firmly established fact of history, the Bar-Kokhba
War, from which many other historical facts flow naturally. We
know that between 132 and 135, a second major war of rebellion
against Roman rule was fought and lost. Accordingly, a great many
people thought that such a war should be fought. It follows that they
believed it was the time to rebel, and we may from that fact infer
that something in their conception of the world led them to risk
everything in such a war. Exactly what they thought made such a
war, if not promising, at least necessary, of course is difficult to say.
Speculation on that fact cannot be tested against the writings of the
leaders of the war, diaries or memoranda of people who fought in, or
opposed, it, reports of the course of the war from apologists, of one
side or the other, let alone reporters or other objective onlookers, and
memoirs of the war produced by those who survived. All we have are
a few references, of later provenance and obviously polemical purpose, as well as the trivial detritus uncovered by Yadin. One fact is
suggestive, again a fact of history.

Between the destruction of the temple in 70 CE and the outbreak of the second rebellion in 132 CE, three generations, sixty-two years, had gone by; it may be that people expected the legendary interval of seventy years between the destruction of the first temple and the return to Zion to be reproduced. Bar-Kokhba's war may have represented an effort to prepare for the restoration of the temple by extirpating gentile, pagan rule over the Holy Land. But this is only a surmise. A more reliable surmise is that the same motives which produced the first war produced the second, and these in some measure included the view of the Zealots and others amply described by Josephus. They assuredly thought they fought an eschatological and messianic fight. Rabbinic stories about the period of Bar-Kokhba similarly exhibit messianic motives. All of this is at best reasonable speculation. If people fought a war, they probably thought they had good reason, and the stated reasons being unavailable, we can at best surmise that continuing traits of the religious and cultural life of the country, persistent expectations and enduring yearnings, may explain that fact.

Accordingly, we may suppose that in the background of the sources we do have are two facts, first, a profound sense of disorientation because of the loss of the temple, second, confusion about how it was to be restored. As to these facts, we need speculate very little, since sources produced in this period, e.g., II Baruch and II Esdras, are explicit that the destruction of the temple produced a profound sense of mourning joined to a deep yearning for restoration. To be sure, we cannot demonstrate that these sentiments were widely held, but the fact of history – the war six decades later – suggests that there was a chronic cause of war, and, given the motivations for fighting the first one, we may suppose that the second one in some measure came in consequence of those sentiments available to us in writings of just a few people of the day.

I refer to the result of the destruction of the temple as disorientation to state the problem in the broadest possible terms. The full weight and meaning of the temple's destruction and the cessation of the cult, the devastation of the Holy City and the devastation of the priesthood – these should not be reduced to terms which, if not trivial, also do not comprehend the matter's full implications. It is not merely that one form of rite was lost and had to be replaced by another, or that one set of religious leaders supplanted another.

What kind of issue faced the Jews after the destruction of the temple? It was, I contend, a fundamentally religious issue, not a matter of government or politics. For historians of the Jews it is a common axiom that the destruction of Jerusalem and its temple in

70 CE marked a decisive political turning-point. For example, current rhetoric uses the year 70 CE as the date for the end of 'Jewish self-government'. Precisely what is meant by that rhetorical flourish is difficult to determine. If one means the end of Jewish independent government in Palestine, then that came to an end with the procurators, and, one might say, even with the advent of Herod. So the importance of the date must be located elsewhere. The Jews continued to govern themselves, much as they had in procuratorial times, though through different institutions, long after 70 CE. Patriarchal government finally ended at the start of the fifth century – a matter of Byzantine policy – but by that time large numbers of Jews had already left the land, and their institutions of self-government persisted in the countries of their dispersion.

The significant event was the destruction of the temple. Still, long before 70 CE the temple had been rejected by some Jewish groups. Its sanctity had been arrogated by others. And for large numbers of ordinary Jews outside of Palestine, as well as substantial numbers within, the temple was a remote and, if holy, unimportant place. For them, piety was fully expressed through synagogue worship. In a very real sense, therefore, for the Christian Jews, who were indifferent to the temple cult, for the Jews at Qumran, who rejected the temple, for the Jews of Leontopolis, in Egypt, who had their own temple, but especially for the masses of Jews of the diaspora who never saw the temple to begin with, but served God through synagogue worship alone, the year 70 CE cannot be said to have marked an important change.

The Jews of the diaspora accommodated themselves to their distance from the temple by 'spiritualizing' and 'moralizing' the cult, as did Philo. To be sure, Philo was appropriately horrified at the thought of the temple's desecration by Caligula, but I doubt that his religious life would have been greatly affected had the temple been destroyed in his lifetime. For the large Babylonian Jewish community, we have not much evidence that the situation was any different. They were evidently angered by the Romans' destruction of the temple, so that Josephus had to address them with an account of events exculpating Rome from guilt for the disaster. But Babylonian Jewry did absolutely nothing before 70 CE to support the Palestinians, and, thereafter, are not heard from. The Babylonian and Mesopotamian Jews' great war against Rome, in Trajan's time, was the result not of the temple's destruction, but, in my opinion, of Trajan's evident plan to rearrange the international trade routes to their disadvantage. Nor do we hear of any support from the diaspora for Bar-Kokhba, so apparently no one was ready to help him re-establish the temple in a new Jerusalem. At any rate, the political importance of the events of 70 CE cannot be taken for granted. It was significant primarily for the religious life of various Palestinian Jewish groups, not to mention the ordinary folk who had made pilgrimages to Jerusalem and could do so no more.

We shall rapidly examine four responses to the destruction of Jerusalem, the end of the temple, and the cessation of the cult. The four responses are of, first, the apocalyptic writers represented in the visions of II Ezra; second, the Dead Sea community; third, the Christian church; and finally, the Pharisaic sect. When the apocalyptic visionaries looked backward upon the ruins, they saw a tragic vision. So they emphasized future supernatural redemption, which they believed was soon to come. The Qumranians had met the issues of 70 CE long before in a manner essentially similar to that of the Christians. Both groups tended to abandon the temple and its cult and to replace them by means of the new community on the one hand, and the service or pious rites of the new community, on the other. The Pharisees come somewhere between the first and the second and third groups. They saw the destruction as a calamity, like the apocalyptists, but they also sought the means, in both social forms and religious expression, to provide a new way of atonement and a new form of divine service, to constitute a new, interim temple, like the Dead Sea sect and the Christians.

The apocalypse of Ezra is representative of the apocalyptic state of mind. The compiler of the Ezra apocalypse (II Esdras 3–14), who lived at the end of the first century, looked forward to a day of judgment, when the Messiah would destroy Rome and God would govern the world. But he had to ask, how can the suffering of Israel be reconciled with divine justice? To Israel, God's will had been revealed. But God had not removed the inclination to do evil, so men could not carry out God's will:

> For we and our fathers have passed our lives in ways that bring death . . . But what is man, that thou art angry with him, or what is a corruptible race, that thou art so bitter against it? . . . (II Esdras 8.31, 34).

Ezra was told that God's ways are inscrutable (4.10f.), but when he repeated the question 'Why has Israel been given over to the gentiles as a reproach?' he was given the answer characteristic of this literature – that a new age was dawning which would shed light on such perplexities. The pseudepigraphic Ezra thus regarded the catastrophe as the fruit of sin, more specifically, the result of man's natural incapacity to do the will of God. He prayed for forgiveness and found hope in the coming transformation of the age and the promise of a new day, when man's heart would be as able, as his mind even then was willing, to do the will of God.

For the Dead Sea community, the destruction of the temple cult took place long before 70 CE. That is why we consider that group, even though it did not survive the war. By rejecting the temple and its cult, the Qumran group had had to confront a world without Jerusalem even while the city was still standing. The spiritual situation of Yavneh, the community formed by the Pharisaic rabbis after the destruction of the temple in 70 CE, and that of Qumran, are strikingly comparable. Just as the rabbis had to construct, at least for the time being, a Judaism without the temple cult, so did the Qumran sectarians have to construct a Judaism without the temple cult. The difference, of course, is that the rabbis merely witnessed the destruction of the city by others, while the Qumran sectarians did not lose the temple, but rejected it at the outset.

The founders of the community were temple priests, who saw themselves as continuators of the true priestly line, that is, the sons of Zadok. For them the old temple was, as it were, destroyed in the times of the Maccabees. Its cult was defiled, not by the Romans, but by the rise of a high priest from a family other than theirs. They further rejected the calendar followed in Jerusalem. They therefore set out to create a new temple, until God would come and, through the Messiah in the line of Aaron, would establish the temple once again. The Qumran community believed that the presence of God had left Jerusalem and had come to the Dead Sea. The *community* now constituted the new temple, just as some elements in early Christianity saw the new temple in the body of Christ, in the church, the Christian community. In some measure, this represents a 'spiritualization' of the old temple, and the temple worship was affected through the community's study and fulfilment of the Torah. Thus the Qumranians represent a middle point between reverence for the old temple and its cult, in the here and now, and complete indifference to the temple and cult in favour of the Christians' utter spiritualization of both, represented, for example, in the Letter to the Hebrews.

Because of their faith in the crucified and risen Christ, Christians experienced the end of the old cult and the old temple before it actually took place, much like the Qumran sectarians. They had to work out the meaning of the sacrifice of Jesus on the cross, and whether the essays on that central problem were done before or after

70 CE is of no consequence. The issue of August 70 CE confronted Qumranians and Christians for other than narrowly historical reasons; for both, the events of that month took place in other than military and political modes. But the effects were much the same. The Christians, therefore, resemble the Qumranians in having had to face the end of the cult before it actually took place, but they were like the Pharisees in also having to confront the actual destruction of the temple, here and now.

Like the Qumranians, the Christian Jews criticized the Jerusalem temple and its cult. Both groups in common believed that the last days had begun. Both believed that God had come to dwell with them, as he had once dwelt in the temple. The sacrifices of the temple were replaced, therefore, by the sacrifice of a blameless life and by other spiritual deeds. But the Christians differ on one important point. To them, the final sacrifice had already taken place; the perfect priest had offered up the perfect holocaust, his own body. So, for the Christians, Christ on the cross completed the old sanctity and inaugurated the new. This belief took shape in different ways. For Paul, in I Corinthians 3.16f., the church is the new temple, Christ is the foundation of the 'spiritual' building. Ephesians 2.18–22 has Christ as the cornerstone of the new building, the company of Christians constituting the temple.

Perhaps the single most coherent statement of the Christian view of cult comes in Hebrews. Whether or not Hebrews is representative of many Christians or comes as early as 70 CE is not our concern. What is striking is that the letter explores the great issues of 70 CE, the issues of cult, temple, sacrifice, priesthood, atonement, and redemption. Its author takes for granted that the church is the temple, that Jesus is the builder of the temple, and that he is also the perfect priest and the final and unblemished sacrifice. It is Jesus who is that most perfect sacrifice, who has entered the true, heavenly sanctuary and now represents his people before God: 'By his death he has consecrated the new covenant together with the heavenly sanctuary itself.' Therefore, no further sacrifice – his or others' – is needed.

We know very little about the Pharisees before the time of Herod. During Maccabaean days, according to Josephus, our sole reliable evidence, they appear as a political party, competing with the Sadducees, another party, for control of the court and government. Afterwards, they all but fade out of Josephus' narrative. But the later rabbinical literature fills the gap – with what degree of reliability I do not here wish to say – and tells a great many stories about

Pharisaic masters from Shammai and Hillel to the destruction. It also ascribes numerous sayings, particularly on matters of law, both to the masters and to the Houses of Shammai and of Hillel. These circles of disciples seem to have flourished in the first century, down to 70 CE and beyond.

The legal materials attributed by later rabbis to the Pharisees before 70 CE are thematically congruent with the stories and sayings about Pharisees in the New Testament Gospels, and I take them to be accurate in substance, if not in detail, as representations of the main *issues* of Pharisaic law. After 70 CE, the masters of Yavneh seem to have included a predominant element of Pharisees, and these rabbis assuredly regarded themselves as the continuators of Pharisaism. Yoḥanan ben Zakkai, who first stood at the head of the Yavnean circle, was later on said to have been a disciple of Hillel. More credibly, Gamaliel II, who succeeded Yoḥanan as head of the Yavnean institution, is regarded as the grandson of Gamaliel, a Pharisee in the council of the temple who is mentioned in Acts 5.34 in connection with the trial of Paul. In all, therefore, we may regard the Yavnean rabbis as successors (if not in all details continuators) of the Pharisees before 70 CE, and treat the two as a single continuous sect of Judaism.

What was the dominant trait of Pharisaism before 70 CE? It was, as depicted both in the rabbinic traditions about the Pharisees and in the gospels, concern for certain matters of rite, in particular, eating one's meals in a state of ritual purity as if one were a temple priest, and carefully giving the required tithes and offerings due to the priesthood. The gospels' agenda on Pharisaism also added tithing, fasting, sabbath observance, vows and oaths, and the like, but the main point was keeping the ritual purity laws outside the temple, where the priests had to observe ritual purity when they carried out the requirements of the cult. To be sure, the gospels also include a fair amount of hostile polemic, some of it rather extreme, but these intra-Judaic matters are not our concern. All that can be learnt from the accusations, for instance, that the Pharisees were a brood of vipers, morally blind, sinners, and unfaithful, is one fact: Christian Jews and Pharisaic Jews were at odds.

The Pharisees, therefore, were those Jews who believed that one must keep the purity laws outside the temple. Other Jews, following the plain sense of Leviticus, supposed that purity laws were to be kept only in the temple, where the priests had to enter a state of ritual purity in order to carry out the requirements of the cult, such as animal sacrifice. They also had to eat their temple food in a state of ritual purity, but lay people did not. To be sure, everyone who went to the temple had to be ritually pure, but outside the temple the laws of ritual purity were not observed, for it was not required that non-cultic activities be conducted in a state of levitical cleanness.

But the Pharisees held, to the contrary, that even outside the temple, in one's own home, one had to follow the laws of ritual purity in the only circumstance in which they might apply, namely, at the table. They therefore held that secular food, that is, ordinary, everyday meals, must be eaten in a state of ritual purity *as if one were a temple priest*. The Pharisees thus arrogated to themselves – and to all Jews equally – the status of the temple priests and did the things which priests must do on account of that status. The table of every Jew in his home was seen to be like the table of the Lord in the Jerusalem temple. The commandment, 'You shall be a kingdom of priests and a holy people' (Ex. 19.6), was taken literally. The whole country was holy. The table of every man possessed the same order of sanctity as the table of the cult. But, at this time, only the Pharisees held such a viewpoint, and eating unconsecrated food as if one were a temple priest at the Lord's table was thus one major signification that a Jew was a Pharisee, a sectarian.

We see, therefore, that the Dead Sea Sect, the Christian Jews, and the Pharisees all stressed the eating of ritual meals. But while the Qumranians and the Christians tended to oppose sacrifice as such, and to prefer to achieve forgiveness of sin through ritual baths and communion meals, the Pharisees before 70 CE continued to revere the temple and its cult, and afterwards they drew up the laws which would govern the temple when it should be restored. In the meantime, they held that (b. Berakhot 55a), 'As long as the temple stood, the altar atoned for Israel. But now a man's table atones for him.'

The response of the Pharisees to the destruction of the temple is known to us only from rabbinic materials, which underwent revisions over many centuries. A story about Yohanan ben Zakkai and his disciple, Joshua ben Hananiah, gives us in a few words the main outline of the established Pharisaic–rabbinic view of the destruction:

Once, as Rabban Yoḥanan ben Zakkai was coming forth from Jerusalem, Rabbi Joshua followed after him and beheld the temple in ruins.
'Woe unto us,' Rabbi Joshua cried, 'that this, the place where the iniquities of Israel were atoned for, is laid waste!'
'My son,' Rabban Yoḥanan said to him, 'be not grieved. We have another atonement as effective as this. And what is it? It is acts of loving-

kindness, as it is said, *For I desire mercy and not sacrifice* [Hos. 6.6] (*Aboth de Rabbi Nathan, ch. 4*).

How shall we relate the arcane rules about ritual purity to the public calamity faced by the heirs of the Pharisees at Yavneh? What connection between the ritual purity of the 'kingdom of priests' and the atonement of sins in the temple?

To Yohanan ben Zakkai, preserving the temple was not an end in itself. He taught that there was another means of reconciliation between God and Israel, so that the temple and its cult were not decisive. What really counted in the life of the Jewish people? Torah, piety. For the zealots and messianists of the day, the answer was power, politics, the right to live under one's own rulers.

What was the will of God? It was doing deeds of lovingkindness: 'I desire mercy, not sacrifice' (Hos. 6.6) meant to Yohanan, 'We have a means of atonement as effective as the temple, and it is doing deeds of lovingkindness.' Just as willingly as men would contribute bricks and mortar for the rebuilding of a sanctuary, so they ought to contribute renunciation, self-sacrifice, love, for the building of a sacred community. Earlier, Pharisaism had held that the temple should be everywhere, even in the home and hearth. Now Yohanan taught that sacrifice greater than the temple's must characterize the life of the community. If one were to do something for God in a time when the temple was no more, the offering must be the gift of selfless compassion. The holy altar must be the streets and market-places of the world, as, formerly, the purity of the temple had to be observed in the streets and market-places of Jerusalem. The earlier history of the Pharisaic sect thus had laid the groundwork for Yohanan ben Zakkai's response to Joshua ben Hananiah. It was a natural conclusion for one nurtured in a movement based upon the priesthood of all Israel.

The Pharisees determined to elevate the life of the people, even at home and in the streets, to what the Torah had commanded: *You shall be a kingdom of priests and a holy people*. A kingdom in which everyone was a priest, a people all of whom were holy – a community which would live as if it were always in the temple sanctuary of Jerusalem. Therefore, the purity laws, so complicated and inconvenient, were extended to the life of every Jew in his own home. The temple altar in Jerusalem would be replicated at the table of all Israel. To be sure, only a small minority of the Jewish people, to begin with, obeyed the law as taught by the Pharisaic party. Therefore, the group had to reconsider the importance of political life,

through which the law might everywhere be effected. The party
which had abandoned politics for piety now had to recover access to
the instruments of power for the sake of piety. It was the way towards realization of what was essentially not a political aspiration.

For the history of Judaism, the sole significant force to emerge
from the catastrophe of 70 CE was the Pharisees. As we noted, that is
not to suggest their influence from 70 to 135 CE was considerable. It
almost certainly was negligible, because the very fact of the war of
132–5 CE suggests that others, not Pharisees, held predominance in
the life of the Jewish people. Whatever we may think of the Pharisaic
and larger rabbinic movement of this period, we cannot suppose it
bore primary responsibility for the eschatological and messianic
aspirations which seem to have produced the new war. The question
before us is, How did the Pharisaic stress on the 'priesthood of all
Israel', on constituting the temple in the everyday life of the people,
develop in response to the task of the new age? For our present
purpose, we shall take a single instance of the appropriation and
revision of the temple's symbolic structure to exemplify a much
larger phenomenon. That instance is the matter of 'leprosy'. Scripture held that a leper was unclean and therefore prohibited from
entering the temple. Now, as we shall see, leprosy was given a social
interpretation and assigned a place in the moral life of the community.

Leprosy is said to be caused by slander or pride. The connection
with slander is based upon the case of Miriam, the connection with
pride on that of Uzziah:

> [Take heed in an attack of leprosy to be very careful to do according to all
> that the levitical priests shall direct you . . .] Remember what God did to
> Miriam' (Deut. 24.9).
> What has one thing to do with the other?
> But it teaches that she was punished only on account of gossip.
> And is it not an argument *a fortiori*? If this happened to Miriam, who did
> not speak in such a way in Moses' presence, one who speaks ill of his fellow
> in his very presence, how much the more so!
> R. Simeon b. Eleazar says, 'Also leprosy comes on account of arrogance,
> for so we find concerning Uzziah, about whom Scripture says: "But when
> he was strong, he grew proud, to his destruction. For he was false to the
> Lord his God and entered the temple of the Lord to burn incense on the
> altar of incense. But Azariah the priest went in after him, with eighty priests
> of the Lord who were men of valour; and they withstood King Uzziah and
> said to him, 'It is not for you, Uzziah, to burn incense to the Lord, but for
> the priests the sons of Aaron, who are consecrated, to burn incense. Go out
> of the sanctuary, for you have done wrong, and it will bring you no honour

from the Lord God.' Then when he became angry with the priests, leprosy
broke out on his forehead . . ."' (II Chron. 26.16–19).
  (Sifra Mesora' Parashah 5.9 [Tos. Neg. 6.7; Sifré Deut. 275])

  The rabbinic view that leprosy is caused by gossip or slander ('evil
speech') depends upon the interpretation of Miriam's behaviour. In
Numbers 12.1–15, Miriam and Aaron are guilty of criticizing Moses
because of his wife and saying that they are capable of prophecy just
as much as he: 'Has the Lord indeed spoken only through Moses?
Has he not spoken through us also?' So Moses' authority is called
into question, and the divine response is to declare Moses' prophecy
of a higher order than theirs. Then Miriam is turned into a leper.
The issue of 'gossip' therefore is hardly obvious. To the rabbinic
eisegetes, the rebellion against Moses is of no consequence, the
criticism of his marriage is central. Then this criticism is interpreted
as slander, *lashon hara'*, and the rest follows.

  Simeon b. Eleazar has a better case, for II Chronicles 26.16–21
says clearly that Uzziah was made a leper because of his intervening
in the cult, and he did so because of pride. Both views of the origin of
leprosy take for granted the established notion that the punishment
of impurity signifies the commission of an antecedent crime; and the
punishment will exactly fit the crime. Later on this latter idea will
generate efforts to show *why* the punishment is fitting to the crime.
Then all the other biblical references to leprosy will be tied to
specific sins. In the first stage, towards the middle of the second
century, of rabbinic thought on the subject, the attempt to spell out
this correspondence produces only Judah b. Ilai's and Eliezer b. R.
Yose's explanations for the association of croup with the mouth. The
innovation of earlier rabbinic Judaism is the view of impurity –
leprosy – not as a metaphor for sin in general, but as a sign that a
specific sin has been committed. This then will generate the effort to
show the reasonable relationship between a particular form of punishment, on the one side, and a specific sin on the other, an approach
to be richly elaborated later on.

  This mode of thought is part of a larger rabbinic view that suffering comes primarily in consequence of human failings. 'Measure for
measure' characterizes divine justice. The employment of purity
laws in this connection therefore constitutes part of the rabbinic
accounting for and justification of the fate of the Jewish people after
the destruction of the second temple, and in particular, the disaster
of the Bar-Kokhba War. Just as the people were told by the rabbis
that they had sinned *but* could achieve regeneration through atonement and good behaviour, so in the specific and very ordinary

instances of disease or early death one might try to show that a particular sin lay at the origin of the suffering. The purity rules provide an explanation for individual suffering because the impurity – leprosy, menstruation – afflicts the private person. So through their interpretation of the purity laws, the generalized allegation of the rabbis after 70 CE that Israel suffered on account of sin, after 135 CE is made precise and concrete in the life of the private person. The emphasis on the individual and his personal impurity is consistent with the stress of the priestly prophet, Ezekiel, that the individual bears the burden of his own guilt. The person who sins will die, but his family will not. Ezekiel's view of purity is part of the larger priestly ideology; but the stress on the individual – in connection with either sin or uncleanness – seems to have been at first Ezekiel's peculiar contribution, for priestly law commonly views sacrifices as collective. Ezekiel introduces his notion of individual retribution as a novelty, given him by revelation and contradicting the common opinion.

I think this broader theological task provides the context in which to understand the sayings before us. If the rabbis of the second century occur most commonly, it is because after the disaster of the Bar-Kokhba War the problem of theodicy and the application of the peculiarly rabbinic solution proved most pressing for ordinary folk, who suffered in the general *débâcle* far more severely than was the case after 70 CE. But the general outlines of their answer, linking suffering to sin, had of course been well-established for many generations.

The rabbinic theodicy of individual suffering occurs within a still larger conception, beginning with Pharisaism before 70 CE and carried forward by rabbinic Judaism afterwards. The Pharisees before 70 CE extended the temple's sanctity to the affairs of ordinary folk, requiring that people eat their meals in a state of purity appropriate for the sanctuary and preserve their food from impurity originally pertinent only to the cult and priesthood. After 70 CE the rabbinical continuators of Pharisaism treated sacrifice itself as something to be done in everyday life, comparing deeds of lovingkindness to the sacrifices by which sins were atoned for. So it was an established trait of Pharisaism and later rabbinism to apply cultic symbols to extra-cultic, communal matters, and thus to regard the temple's sanctity as extending to the streets of the villages. This was done after 70 CE by assigning ethical equivalents to temple rites, on the one side, and by comparing study of Torah to the act of sacrifice and the rabbi to the temple priest, on the other. It is in this context that the interpretation of the purity rules was undertaken. By locating ethical lapses as the cause of impurity, beginning with the view that leprosy is a sign that one is guilty of having gossiped or been arrogant, the second-century rabbis simply carried forward the established trait of rabbinism and its antecedent Pharisaism. Just as earlier, cultic purity was extended to the home, and, later on, study of Torah was substituted for cultic sacrifice and deeds of lovingkindness for sin-offering, so it now was natural to take over the purity rules and to endow them with ethical, therefore with everyday, communal significance, instead of leaving them wholly within the cult. It was a continuation of an earlier tendency to ethicize, spiritualize, and moralize the cult by treating the holy people – the *community* of Israel – as equivalent to the holy sanctuary. This tendency to be sure had already been present in a vague and general way in the biblical treatment of purity as a metaphor for righteousness and impurity for sin. But it was now greatly elaborated and extended to the minutiae of daily life, as was normal for rabbinism in many other ways.

What is noteworthy therefore is the extensive rabbinic use of the symbols of impurity in connection with social ills. Sermons against gossiping or selfishness may readily be constructed without inclusion of the claim that it is the leper in particular who has gossiped or acted selfishly. The cultic metaphor, 'unclean', and its specification in terms of leprosy or bodily discharges seem curiously inappropriate or unnatural to the specific social vices against which the rabbis inveighed. *They are used by the rabbis because the community of Israel now is regarded as the temple.* What kept people out of the sanctuary in olden times therefore is going even now to exclude them from the life of the community. The thrust of the rabbis' sermons is to remove from the community people guilty of gossiping or arrogance and the like; this very act of removal is offered by them as the *explanation* for their relating gossiping to leprosy, as we observed.

The rabbis' larger tendency to preserve, but to take over within the rabbinical system, the symbols of the temple is herein illustrated. Just as the rabbi is the new priest, study of Torah is the new cult, deeds of lovingkindness the new sacrifice, so the community formed on the basis of the rabbinic Torah is going to be protected from social uncleanness just as the old temple was protected from cultic uncleanness. This accounts not only for the preservation, but for the considerable elaboration and extension, of the cultic symbols of uncleanness. These usages after 70 CE were no more pertinent to, or part of the ordinary life of, the Jewish community in the land of Israel than they were before that time to Alexandrian Jewry. Two motives lie behind the rabbinic tendency to claim that impurity signifies antecedent sin: first, to extend the generalized theodicy to the specific situation of ordinary folk, and second, to exploit the temple's imagery for the rabbinic community. The second motive in general sets the context for what is done in a concrete way in the first.

Fully to appreciate the meaning of the destruction of the temple, we turn finally to the major anthropological statement on the subject of purity on which we have centred our attention. Professor Mary Douglas, studying pollution and uncleanness, produces results of consequence to the much larger issue of the temple and its place in the imagination of society. She shows what is at issue and allows us to interpret the full weight and significance of the temple – and its destruction – in the structure of being created by Israelite faith. She states, 'The more deeply we go . . . the more obvious it becomes that we are studying symbolic systems . . .' (34). This constitutes the main result of the inquiry before us. Ideas of purity and impurity were inseparable from, and expressive of, the larger conceptions of reality of the communities that held them. Because of that fact, the ideas adduced to explain or interpret purity are going to carry implications for the larger system of which they are a part. And that fact is admirably explained within Douglas's larger theory:

Now is the time to identify pollution. Granted that all spiritual powers are part of the social system. They express it and provide institutions for manipulating it. This means that the power in the universe is ultimately hitched to society, since so many changes of fortune are set off by persons in one kind of social position or another. But there are other dangers to be reckoned with, which persons may set off knowingly or unknowingly, which are not part of the psyche and which are not to be bought or learned by initiation and training. These are pollution powers which inhere in the structure of ideas itself and which punish a symbolic breaking of that which should be joined or joining of that which should be separate. It follows from this that pollution is a type of danger which is not likely to occur except where the lines of structure, cosmic or social, are clearly defined (113).

The full weight and meaning of the loss of the temple of Jerusalem cannot be more forcefully stated.

APPENDIX

CHRONOLOGY OF THE ISRAELITE AND JUDAEAN KINGS

W. F. **Albright**, 'The Chronology of the Divided Monarchy of Israel', *BASOR* C, 1945, 16–22; idem, 'Prolegomenon' to the reissue of C. F. Burney's *The Book of Judges with Introduction and Notes* and *Notes on the Hebrew Text of the Books of Kings*, New York: KTAV 1970, 1–38; K. T. **Andersen**, 'Die Chronologie der Könige von Israel und Juda', *ST* XXIII, 1969, 67–112; J. **Begrich**, *Die Chronologie der Könige von Israel und Juda*, Tübingen: J. C. B. Mohr 1929; D. J. A. **Clines**, 'The Evidence for an Autumnal New Year in Pre-exilic Israel Reconsidered', *JBL* XCIII, 1974, 22–40; J. **Finegan**, *Handbook of Biblical Chronology*, Princeton: Princeton University Press 1964; D. N. **Freedman**, 'The Chronology of Israel and the Ancient Near East', *The Bible and the Ancient Near East*, 1961, 203–14; A. **Jepsen**, 'Ein neuer Fixpunkt für die Chronologie der israelitischen Könige?', *VT* XX, 1970, 359–61; A. **Jepsen** and R. **Hanhart**, *Untersuchungen zur israelitisch-jüdischen Chronologie*, *BZAW* 88, 1964; A. **Kamphausen**, *Die Chronologie der hebräischen Könige*, Bonn: Max Cohen & Sohn 1883; F. X. **Kugler**, *Von Moses bis Paulus*, Münster: Aschendorffsche Verlagsbuchhandlung 1922, ch. III; E. **Kutsch**, 'Das Jahr der Katastrophe: 587 v. Chr.', *Bib* LV, 1974, 520–43; J. **Lewy**, *Die Chronologie der Könige von Israel und Juda*, Giessen: Alfred Töpelmann 1927; A. **Malamat**, 'The Last Kings of Judah and the Fall of Jerusalem', *IEJ* XVIII, 1968, 137–56; idem, 'The Twilight of Judah: in the Egyptian–Babylonian Maelstrom', *SVT* XXVIII, 1974, 123–45; J. M. **Miller**, 'Another Look at the Chronology of the Early Divided Monarchy', *JBL* LXXXVI, 1967, 276–88; S. **Mowinckel**, 'Die Chronologie der israelitischen und judäischen Könige', *AcOr* X, 1932, 161–277; R. A. **Parker** and W. H. **Dubberstein**, *Babylonian Chronology, 626 BC–AD 75*, Providence: Brown University Press, 1956; V. **Pavlovsky** and E. **Vogt**, 'Die Jahre der Könige von Juda und Israel', XLV, 1964, 321–47; R. **Rühl**, 'Chronologie der Könige von Israel und Juda', *DZGW* XII, 1894–5, 44–76; C. **Schedl**, 'Textkritische Bemerkungen zu den Synchronismen der Könige von Israel und Juda', *VT* XII, 1962, 88–119; J. D. **Shenkel**, *Chronology and Recensional Development in the Greek Text of Kings*, HSM 1, 1968; H. **Tadmor**, 'Chronology of the Last Kings of Judah', *JNES* XV, 1956, 226–30; S. **Talmon**, 'Divergences in Calendar-Reckoning in Ephraim and

Judah', *VT* VIII, 1958, 48–74; E. R. **Thiele**, 'The Chronology of the Kings of Judah and Israel', *JNES* III, 1944, 137–86; idem, *The Mysterious Numbers of the Hebrew Kings: A Reconstruction of the Chronology of the Kingdoms of Israel and Judah*, 1965; idem, 'Coregencies and Overlapping Reigns Among the Hebrew Kings', *JBL* XCIII, 1974, 174–200; M. **Vogelstein**, *Biblical Chronology: I. The Chronology of Hezekiah and His Successors*, Cincinnati: Hebrew Union College 1944; J. **Wellhausen**, 'Die Zeitrechnung des Buchs der Könige seit der Theilung des Reichs', *JDT* XX, 1874, 607–40; W. R. **Wifall**, Jr., 'The Chronology of the Divided Monarchy of Israel', *ZAW* 80, 1968, 319–37.

Saul, David, and Solomon belong to the early and mid-tenth century BCE, but cannot be dated more specifically than that. The forty-year regnal periods ascribed to David and Solomon should not be taken as exact reckonings. I Samuel 13.1, which states that Saul ruled over Israel two years, is considered by many commentators to be a faulty text.

The books of Kings provide for the rulers of the separate states of Israel and Judah (1) a series of synchronistic reckonings which locate the beginning of each king's reign in relation to that of the contemporary ruler of the other kingdom and (2) a reckoning of the length of each king's reign (I Kings 14.20f.; 15.1, 9, 25, 33, etc.). This basic chronological framework is augmented by other chronological notations scattered here and there in I–II Kings, II Chronicles, Isaiah and Jeremiah (I Kings 14.25; II Kings 25.1, 3, 8; II Chron. 16.1; Isa. 36.1; Jer. 32.1, etc.). Moreover, certain events of the last years of Judah are dated by these notations in terms of the regnal years of Nebuchadrezzar and Amel-Marduk (II Kings 24.12; 25.8; Jer. 32.1; 52.12, 28–30). The Mesopotamian rulers, on the other hand, occasionally refer to the Israelite and Judaean kings in their royal records, which is extremely useful to biblical historians since the reigns of the Mesopotamian kings can be assigned absolute dates in terms of the Julian calendar.

In spite of this abundance of relative chronological data supplied by the Old Testament and occasional fixed points afforded by the Mesopotamian records, establishing precise dates for the rulers of Israel and Judah has turned out to be extremely problematic for several reasons. (1) There are a number of textual variations for the biblical chronological data. (2) The biblical figures do not seem to be entirely consistent, either internally or in relation to the chronological fixed points provided by the Mesopotamian texts. For example, it is difficult to correlate the synchronistic reckonings with the reckonings of the lengths of the reigns, and in any case the biblical figures seem to presume longer periods of rule for the Israelite and Judaean kings than is allowed by the Mesopotamian records. (3) It is unknown what sort of calendar (New Year in the autumn or New Year in the spring) or reckoning system (ante-dating, whereby the year in which a king ascended the throne was counted as his first year, or post-dating, whereby the length of a king's reign was calculated from his first New Year) is presupposed by the biblical figures, and even uncertain whether the same calendar and/or reckoning system is presupposed throughout. (4) The nature of the source(s) from which the biblical writers derived their chronological information, the extent to which these writers introduced secondary calculations of their own, and whether the biblical figures have been modified during the process of transmission in order to conform to idealistic and/or schematic views of history remain unclear. At least some secondary calculation and modification seems certainly to have been involved.

It is not surprising, then, that a number of competing chronological systems for the Israelite and Judaean kings have been advanced. German scholars in recent years, including Donner in ch. VII above, have generally followed the system worked out by Begrich in 1929 and revised by Jepsen in 1964. *Herrmann, however, in his *History of Israel in Old Testament Times*, has opted for Andersen's dates. The Begrich–Jepsen system presumes that a shift in the calendar (from a year beginning in the autumn to one beginning in the spring) and reckoning system (from ante-dating to post-dating) occurred when Israel and Judah became Assyrian vassals. Andersen's system presumes the autumn New Year and the ante-dating system until the reign of Manasseh. Works in English generally follow either the system worked out by Thiele, first advanced in 1944, or the one advanced by Albright in 1945. Thiele places much confidence in the detailed accuracy of the biblical figures, particularly those of the Massoretic tradition, explaining the apparent discrepancies in terms of different calendars used by the two kingdoms, several coregencies, and also changes in reckoning procedures from time to time; he thereby achieves precise dates for each king of Israel and Judah. Albright was less confident that the biblical figures as they stand now are so accurate as to allow precision dating, took the liberty of making some minor revisions in them in order to remove the apparent discrepancies, and emphasized that the resulting dates were to be considered only tentative. In 1970 ('Prolegomenon', 33–6) he cited three developments which had occurred since 1945 calling for modification of his system: (1) Albright affirmed the results of Shenkel's investigation of the recensional development of the Greek texts of the books of Kings, which emphasizes the relative authenticity of the chronological data supplied by the Lucianic recension of the LXX *vis-à-vis* that preserved in the Massoretic tradition. (2) Albright agreed that the Adad-nirari stela calls for a synchronism between Adad-nirari and Joash in 802 BCE and accepted, at least in part, Miller's chronology for the early separate kingdoms which favours the Lucianic synchronisms and allows for Joash's accession to the throne in 802. (3) Albright acknowledged that the first surrender of Jerusalem (= the end of Jehoiachin's reign) is to be fixed with the Nebuchadrezzar chronicle on 16 March 597 BCE.

The various chronological systems produced by the scholars discussed above can be compared in the following chart.

Kings: *Judah(italic)* Israel (roman)	*Begrich– Jepsen*	*Andersen*	*Thiele*	*Albright*	*Miller*
Rehoboam	926–910	932/31–916/15	931/30–913	922–915	925/23–908/7
Jeroboam	927–907	932/31–911/10	931/30–910/09	922–901	925/23–905/3
Abijah	910–908	916/15–914/13	913–911/10	915–913	908/7–906/4
Asa	908–868	914/13–874/73	911/10–870/69	913–873	906/4–876/74
Nadab	907–906	911/10–910/09	910/09–909/8	901–900	905/3–904/2
Baasha	906–883	910/09–887/86	909/8–886/85	900–877	904/2–887/85
Elah	883–882	887/86–886/85	886/85–885/84	877–876	887/85–886/84
Zimri	882	886/85	885/84	876	886/84
Omri	882–871*	886/85–875/74*	885/84–874/73*	876–869*	886/84–875/73*
Jehoshaphat	868–847	874/73–850/49	873/72–848*	873–849	876/74–852/50
Ahab	871–852	875/74–854/53	874/73–853	869–850	875/73–853/51
Ahaziah	852–851	854/53–853/52	853–852	850–849	853/51–851/49
Jehoram	847–845	850/49–843/42	853–841*R	849–842	852/50–844/42
Jehoram	851–845	853/52–842/41	852–841	849–842	851/49–844/42
Ahaziah	845	843/42–842/41	841	842	844/42
Jehu	845–818	842/41–815/14	841–814/13	842–815	844/42–
Athaliah	845–840	842/41–837/36	841–835	842–837	844/42–
Jehoash	840–801	836/35–797/96	835–796R	837–800	
Jehoahaz	818–802	815/14–799/98	814/13–798R	815–801	
Joash	802–787	799/98–784/83	798–782/81	801–786	

Amaziah	801–773	797/96–769/68	796–767	800–783
Jeroboam II	787–747	784/83–753/52	793/92–753*	786–746
Azariah/Uzziah	787–736*	769/68–741/40	792/1–740/39*	783–742
Zechariah	747	753/52–752/51	753–752	746–745
Shallum	747	752/51–751/50	752	745
Menahem	747–738	751/50–742/41	752–742/41	745–738
Jotham	756–741*	741/40–734/33	750–732/31*	750–735*
Pekahiah	737–736 CR	742/41–741/40	742/41–740/39	738–737
Pekah	735–732	741/40–730/29	752–732/31*	737–732
Jehoahaz I	741–725	734/33–715/14	735–716/15*	735–715
Hoshea	731–723	730/29–722/21	732/31–723/22	732–724
Hezekiah	725–697 CR	715/14–697/96	716/15–687/86	715–687
Manasseh	696–642	697/96–642/41 CR	697/96–643/42*	687–642
Amon	641–640	642/41–640/39	643/42–641/40	642–640
Josiah	639–609	640/39–609/8	641/40–609	640–609
Jehoahaz II	609	609/8	609	609
Jehoiachim	608–598	609/8–598/97	609–598	609–598
Jehoiachin	598	598/97	598	598
Zedekiah	597–587	598/97–587/86	597–586	598–587

*A coregency is presumed at this point; except in the case of Omri whose dates include a period of rival rulership with Tibni, and in the case of Azariah/Uzziah where the Begrich–Jepsen system presumes that Amaziah was deposed before his death.

R   A change in the reckoning system is presumed at this point.

CR   A change in calendar and reckoning system is presumed at this point.

INDEX OF NAMES AND SUBJECTS

INDEX OF AUTHORS

INDEX OF BIBLICAL PASSAGES

OLD TESTAMENT

NEW TESTAMENT

728

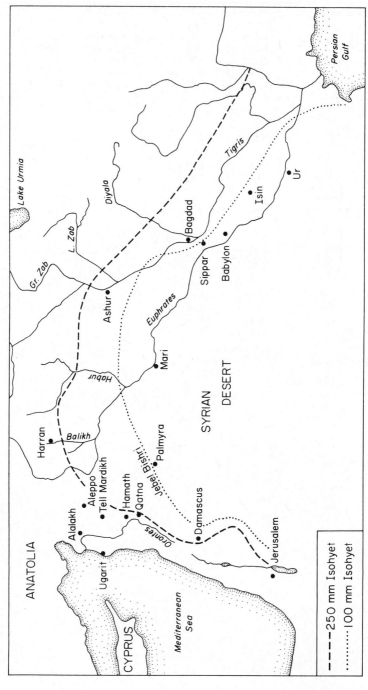

1. The 'Fertile Crescent', showing zone suitable for pastoralism (100–250 mm. annual rainfall)

- - - 250 mm Isohyet
········· 100 mm Isohyet

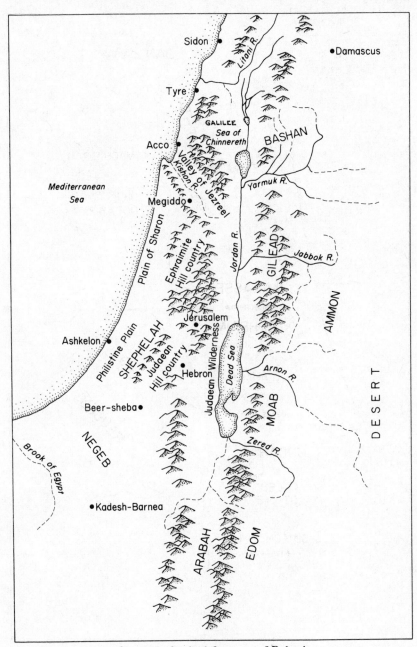

2. General physical features of Palestine

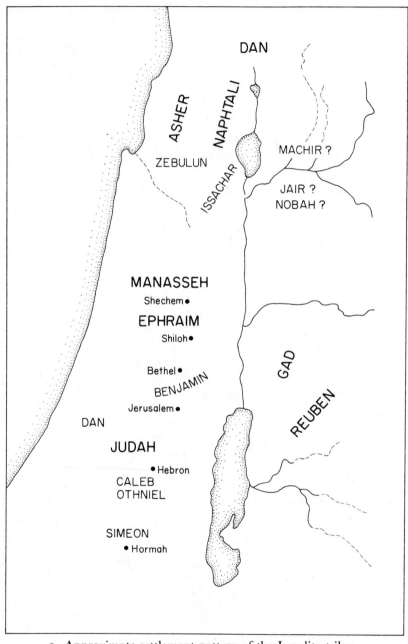

3. Approximate settlement pattern of the Israelite tribes

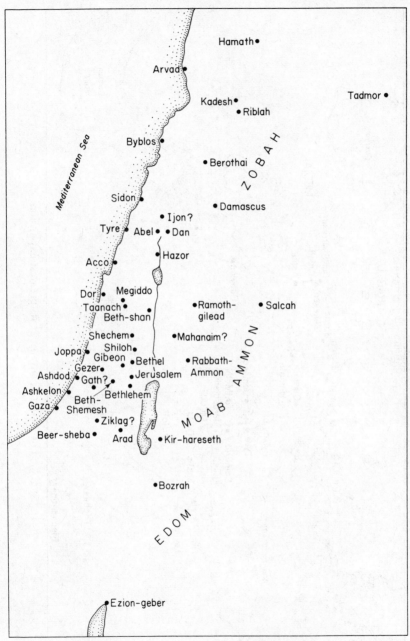

4. Syro-Palestine at the time of David and Solomon

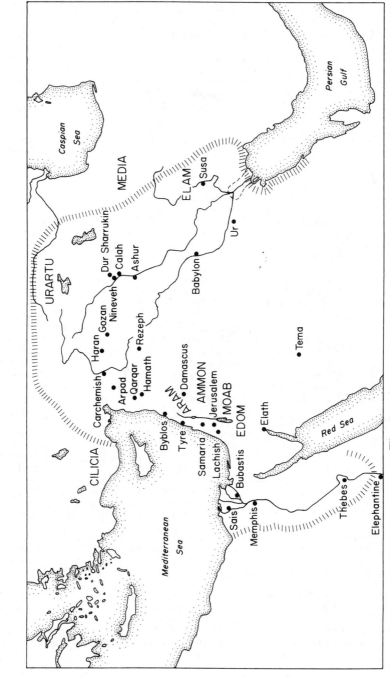

5. The Assyrian empire at its greatest expansion

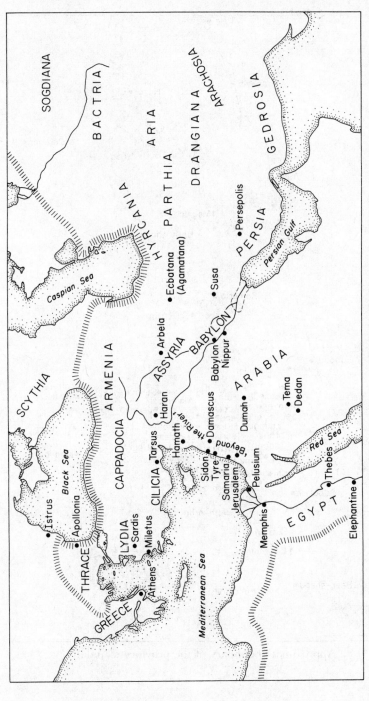

6. The Persian empire at its greatest expansion

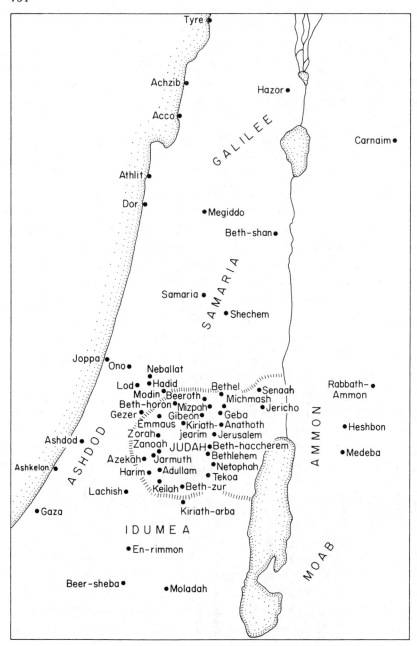

7. Approximate boundary of the province of Judah

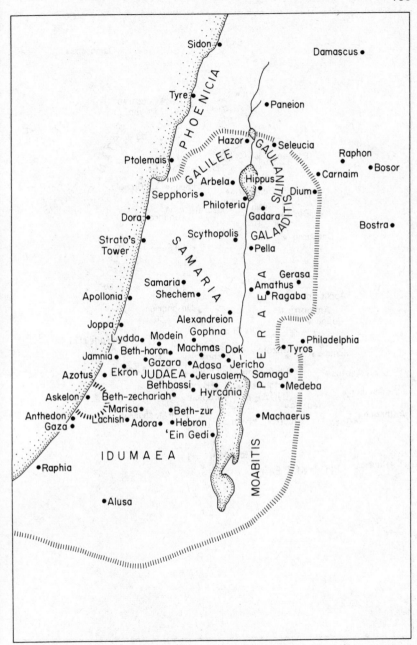

8. Palestine during the Hellenistic period, showing maximum extent
of the Hasmonaean kingdom

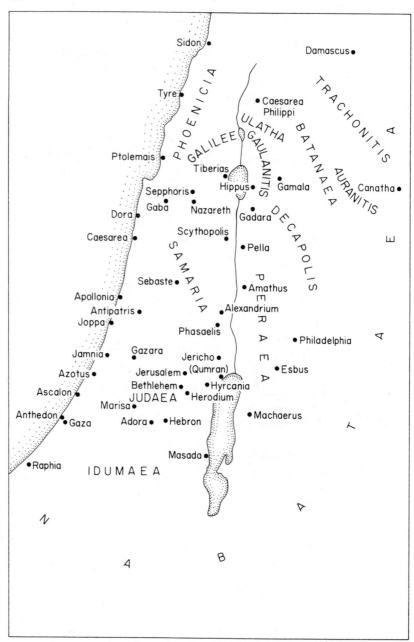

9. Palestine during the time of Herod and his successors